(2) Equity value-to-book ratio $= 1 + \dfrac{ROE_1 - r_e}{(1 + r_e)} + \dfrac{(ROE_2 - r_e)(1 + gbve_1)}{(1 + r_e)^2}$

$$+ \dfrac{(ROE_3 - r_e)(1 + gbve_1)(1 + gbve_2)}{(1 + r_e)^3} + \ldots$$

where ROE_t = return on beginning book equity for year t

$gbve_t$ = growth in book equity from year t-1 to year t or $\dfrac{BVE_t - BVE_{t-1}}{BVE_{t-1}}$

r_e = cost of equity capital

Asset Valuation

(1) Asset value $= BVA_0 + \dfrac{NOPAT_1 - WACC \cdot BVA_0}{(1 + WACC)} + \dfrac{NOPAT_2 - WACC \cdot BVA_1}{(1 + WACC)^2} + \ldots$

where BVA_t = book value of assets at the end of year t

$NOPAT_t$ = net operating profit after tax for year t

$WACC$ = weighted-average cost of debt and equity capital

(2) Asset value-to-book ratio $= 1 + \dfrac{ROA_1 - WACC}{(1 + WACC)} + \dfrac{(ROA_2 - WACC)(1 + gbva_1)}{(1 + WACC)^2}$

$$+ \dfrac{(ROA_2 - WACC)(1 + gbva_1)(1 + gbva_2)}{(1 + WACC)^3} + \ldots$$

where ROA_t = ratio of $NOPAT$ in year t to beginning-of-year operating assets

$gbva_t$ = growth in book assets from year t-1 to year t or $\dfrac{BVA_t - BVA_{t-1}}{BVA_{t-1}}$

$WACC$ = weighted-average cost of debt and equity capital

Business Analysis & Valuation

Using Financial Statements

Second Edition   Text & Cases

Krishna G. Palepu, PhD

Ross Graham Walker Professor of Business Administration
Harvard University

Paul M. Healy, PhD, ACA

MBA Class of 1949 Professor of Business Administration
Harvard University

Victor L. Bernard, PhD, CPA

Late Price Waterhouse Professor of Accounting
University of Michigan

South-Western College Publishing
Thomson Learning

Australia • Canada • Denmark • Japan • Mexico • New Zealand • Philippines
Puerto Rico • Singapore • South Africa • Spain • United Kingdom • United States

Business Analysis and Valuation: Using Financial Statements, by Palepu, Healy, Bernard

Acquisitions Editor: Rochelle Kronzek

Developmental Editor: Ken Martin

Marketing Manager: Dan Silverburg

Production Editor: Marci Dechter

Manufacturing Coordinator: Doug Wilke

Internal Design: Michael H. Stratton

Production House: Julia Chitwood, Bay Island Books

Compositor: John Richards

Printer: R. R. Donnelley - Crawfordsville

Printed in the United States of America

2 3 4 5 02 01 00

For more information contact South-Western College Publishing, 5101 Madison Road, Cincinnati, Ohio, 45227, or find us on the Internet at http://www.swcollege.com.

For permission to use material from this text or product, contact us by
• telephone: **1-800-730-2214**
• fax: **1-800-730-2215**
• web: **http://www.thomsonrights.com**

Library of Congress Cataloging-in-Publication Data
Palepu, Krishna G., 1954-
    Business analysis and valuation : using financial statements : text
& cases / Krishna G. Palepu, Paul M. Healy, Victor L. Bernard.—2nd ed.
        p.   cm
Includes bibliographical references and index.
    ISBN 0-324-01565-8 (alk. paper) — ISBN 0-324-02002-3 (pbk. : alk. paper)
    1. Business enterprises—Valuation.   2. Financial statements.
3. Business enterprises—Valuation—Case studies.   I. Title: Business
analysis and valuation   II. Healy, Paul M.   III. Bernard, Victor L.
(Victor Lewis), 1952- .   IV. Title
HF5681.V3P3 2000
658.15—dc21   99-058727

This book is printed on acid-free paper.

preface

Financial statements are the basis for a wide range of business analysis. Managers use them to monitor and judge their firms' performance relative to competitors, to communicate with external investors, to help judge what financial policies they should pursue, and to evaluate potential new businesses to acquire as part of their investment strategy. Securities analysts use financial statements to rate and value companies they recommend to clients. Bankers use them in deciding whether to extend a loan to a client and to determine the loan's terms. Investment bankers use them as a basis for valuing and analyzing prospective buyouts, mergers, and acquisitions. And consultants use them as a basis for competitive analysis for their clients. Not surprisingly, therefore, we find that there is a strong demand among business students for a course that provides a framework for using financial statement data in a variety of business analysis and valuation contexts. The purpose of this book is to provide such a framework for business students and practitioners.

The first edition of this book has been successful well beyond our original expectations. The book has been used in Accounting and Finance departments in business schools in the U.S. and around the world.

CHANGES FROM THE FIRST EDITION

Many of our colleagues who used the first edition provided us with valuable feedback. Based on this feedback, we made the following changes:

- We expanded the coverage of accounting issues in the text. There are now five new chapters that provide analytical approaches to evaluating a firm's accounting choices and estimates with respect to assets, liabilities, entities, revenues, and expenses. The materials in these chapters cover a variety of accounting transactions.
- We expanded and revised extensively the chapters on valuation in order to make the material more accessible, and also to reflect the growing body of accounting research in this area.
- We included a discussion of corporate strategy in the strategy analysis chapter. In the previous edition, we focused only on industry analysis and the competitive positioning of a company in a single industry. The new material helps students analyze multibusiness organizations as well.

- We used a variety of company situations to help illustrate the concepts. In the previous edition, we used one company example throughout the book.
- We included fifteen new cases in this edition. However, we also retained several popular cases from the previous edition because they have proved to be very effective for many instructors.
- To facilitate the selection of cases, we paired each chapter with a case that we think is best suited to illustrate the concepts in that chapter. However, to retain some flexibility for instructors, we also included a set of multipurpose cases at the end of the book.
- To supplement the cases, we added conceptual questions and problems at the end of each chapter. These questions can be used in class discussions or for after-class assignments.

KEY FEATURES

This book differs from other texts in business and financial analysis in a number of important ways. We introduce and develop a framework for business analysis and valuation using financial statement data. We then show how this framework can be applied to a variety of decision contexts.

Framework for Analysis

We begin the book with a discussion of the role of accounting information and intermediaries in the economy, and how financial analysis can create value in well-functioning markets. We identify four key components of effective financial statement analysis:

- Business Strategy Analysis
- Accounting Analysis
- Financial Analysis
- Prospective Analysis

The first of the components, business strategy analysis, involves developing an understanding of the business and competitive strategy of the firm being analyzed. Incorporating business strategy into financial statement analysis is one of the distinctive features of this book. Traditionally, this step has been ignored by other financial statement analysis books. However, we believe that it is critical to begin financial statement analysis with a company's strategy because it provides an important foundation for the subsequent analysis. The strategy analysis section discusses contemporary tools for analyzing a company's industry, its competitive position and sustainability within an industry, and the company's corporate strategy.

Accounting analysis involves examining how accounting rules and conventions represent the firm's business economics and strategy in its financial statements, and, if necessary, developing adjusted accounting measures of performance. In the accounting analysis section, we do not emphasize accounting rules. Instead, we develop general approaches to analyzing assets, liabilities, entities, revenues, and expenses. We believe that such an approach enables students to effectively evaluate a company's accounting choices and accrual estimates, even if students have only a basic knowledge of accounting rules and standards.

Financial analysis involves analyzing financial ratio and cash flow measures of operating, financing, and investing performance of a company, relative either to key competitors or historical performance. Our distinctive approach focuses on using financial analysis to evaluate the effectiveness of a company's strategy and to make sound financial forecasts.

Finally, under prospective analysis we show how to develop forecasted financial statements and how to use these to make estimates of a firm's value. Our discussion of valuation includes traditional discounted cash flow models as well as techniques that link value directly to accounting numbers. In discussing accounting-based valuation models, we integrate the latest academic research with traditional approaches, such as earnings and book value multiples that are widely used in practice.

While we cover all four components of business analysis and valuation in the book, we recognize that the extent of their use depends on the user's decision context. For example, bankers are likely to use business strategy analysis, accounting analysis, financial analysis, and the forecasting portion of prospective analysis. They are less likely to be interested in formally valuing a prospective client.

Application of the Framework to Decision Contexts

The next section of the book shows how our business analysis and valuation framework can be applied to a variety of decision contexts, including:

- Securities Analysis
- Credit Analysis
- Corporate Financing Policies Analysis
- Merger and Acquisition Analysis
- Management Communications Analysis

For each of these topics we present an overview chapter to provide a foundation for the class discussions. Where possible we discuss relevant institutional details and the results of academic research that are useful in applying the analysis concepts developed earlier in the book. For example, the chapter on credit analysis shows how banks and rating agencies use financial statement data to develop analysis for lending decisions and to rate public debt issues. This chapter also discusses academic research on how to analyze whether a company is financially distressed.

CASE APPROACH

We have found that teaching a course in business analysis and valuation is significantly enhanced, both for teachers and students, by using cases as a pedagogical tool. Students want to develop "hands-on" experience in business analysis and valuation so that they can apply the concepts in decision contexts similar to those they will encounter in the business world. Cases are a natural way to achieve this objective by presenting practical issues that might otherwise be ignored in a traditional classroom exercise. Our cases all present business analysis and valuation issues in a specific decision context, and we find that this makes the material more interesting and exciting for students.

To provide both guidance and flexibility in the choice of cases, we include one case at the end of each chapter, especially chosen for applying the concepts in that chapter. The multipurpose cases at the end of the book can be used with more than one chapter.

USING THE BOOK

We designed the book so that it is flexible for courses in financial statement analysis for a variety of student audiences–MBA students, Masters in Accounting students, executive program participants, and undergraduates. Depending upon the audience, the instructor can vary the manner in which the conceptual materials in the chapters, end-of-chapter questions, and case examples are used.

Prerequisites

To get the most out of the book, students should have completed basic courses in financial accounting, finance, and either business strategy or business economics. The text provides a concise overview of some of these topics, primarily as background for preparing the cases. But it would probably be difficult for students with no prior knowledge in these fields to use the chapters as stand-alone coverage of them. We have integrated only a small amount of business strategy into each case, and do not include any cases that focus exclusively on business strategy analysis.

The extent of accounting knowledge required for the cases varies considerably. Some require only a basic understanding of accounting issues, whereas others require a more detailed knowledge at the level of a typical intermediate financial accounting course. However, we have found it possible to teach even these more complex cases to students without a strong accounting background by providing additional reading on the topic. For some cases, the Teaching Manual includes a primer on the relevant accounting issue, which instructors can hand out to help students prepare the case.

How to Use the Text and Case Materials

The materials can be used in a variety of ways. If the book is used for students with prior working experience or for executives, the instructor can use almost a pure case approach, adding relevant lecture sections as needed. However, when teaching students with little work experience, a lecture class can be presented first, followed by an appropriate case. It is also possible to use the book primarily for a lecture course and include some of the cases as in-class illustrations of the concepts discussed in the book.

Alternatively, lectures can be used as a follow-up to cases to more clearly lay out the conceptual issues raised in the case discussions. This may be appropriate when the book is used in undergraduate capstone courses. In such a context, cases can be used in course projects that can be assigned to student teams.

We have designed the cases so that they can be taught at a variety of levels. For students that need more structure to work through a case, the Teaching Manual includes a set of detailed questions that the instructor can hand out before class. For students who need less structure, there are recommended questions at the end of each case.

ACKNOWLEDGMENTS

We gratefully acknowledge the contributions of colleagues who co-authored several cases in this book: James Chang and Tarun Khanna (Korea Stock Exchange 1998); James Chang (Sensormatic Electronics Corporation—1995); Amy Hutton (America Online, The Upjohn Company: The Upjohn-Pharmacia Merger); and Kenneth Merchant (Kansas City Zephyrs Baseball Club). We also wish to thank Sarayu Srinivisan for research assistance for several cases; Chris Allen for assistance with data on financial ratios for U.S. companies; and the Division of Research at the Harvard Business School for assistance in developing materials for this book.

We especially thank the following colleagues who gave us feedback as we wrote this edition: Steven Balsam (Temple University), Jan Barton (Emory University), Ilia Dichev (University of Michigan), David Guenther (University of Colorado), Eric Hirst (University of Texas—Austin), Ronald King (Washington University), Robert Lin (California State University—Hayward), Philip Little (Western Carolina University), Phil Regier (Arizona State University), and Gary Taylor (University of Alabama).

We are also very grateful to Laurie McKinzey and Deborah Marlino for their help and assistance throughout this project, and to Ken Martin, Marci Dechter, and Julia Chitwood for their patient editorial and production help.

We would like to thank our parents and families for their strong support and encouragement throughout this project.

authors

Krishna G. Palepu is the Ross Graham Walker Professor of Business Administration and the Chair of the Accounting and Control Department at the Harvard Business School. During the past fifteen years, Professor Palepu's research has focused on the effectiveness of firms' merger and acquisition strategies, corporate financing choices, and investor communication processes. Currently Professor Palepu is working on the development of capital market institutions in emerging markets of Asia and Latin America. He lectures and consults with companies worldwide on these issues, and he is on the boards of Vision Compass Inc., Global Trust Bank, and Chrysalis Capital. Professor Palepu is winner of the American Accounting Association's Notable Contributions to Accounting Literature Award (in 1999) and the Wildman Award (in 1997).

Paul Healy is the MBA Class of 1949 Professor of Business Administration at the Harvard Business School. Professor Healy's research has focused on corporate disclosure policies and their impact on the cost of capital, the effectiveness of mergers and acquisitions, earnings management, and management compensation. He has previously worked at the MIT Sloan School of Management, ICI Ltd., and Arthur Young in New Zealand. Professor Healy has won the Notable Contributions to Accounting Literature Award (in 1990 and 1999) and the Wildman Award (in 1997) for contributions to practice.

Vic Bernard, who passed away November 14, 1995, was a CPA and held a PhD from the University of Illinois. He was the Price Waterhouse Professor of Accounting and Director of the Paton Accounting Center at the University of Michigan and Director of Research for the American Accounting Association. His research examined issues in financial reporting, financial statement analysis, and financial economics. He received the Notable Contributions to Accounting Literature Award in 1991, 1993, and 1999, the Outstanding Accounting Educator Award in 1997, and the Wildman Award in 1997.

contents

Part 3   Business Analysis and Valuation Applications

13   Equity Security Analysis   13-1

14   Credit Analysis and Distress Prediction   14-1

15   Mergers and Acquisitions   15-1

16   Corporate Financing Policies   16-1

p a r t 1

Framework

1

A Framework for Business Analysis and Valuation Using Financial Statements

The purpose of this chapter is to outline a comprehensive framework for financial statement analysis. Because financial statements provide the most widely available data on public corporations' economic activities, investors and other stakeholders rely on financial reports to assess the plans and performance of firms and corporate managers.

A variety of questions can be addressed by business analysis using financial statements, as shown in the following examples:

- A security analyst may be interested in asking: "How well is the firm I am following performing? Did the firm meet my performance expectations? If not, why not? What is the value of the firm's stock given my assessment of the firm's current and future performance?"
- A loan officer may need to ask: "What is the credit risk involved in lending a certain amount of money to this firm? How well is the firm managing its liquidity and solvency? What is the firm's business risk? What is the additional risk created by the firm's financing and dividend policies?"
- A management consultant might ask: "What is the structure of the industry in which the firm is operating? What are the strategies pursued by various players in the industry? What is the relative performance of different firms in the industry?"
- A corporate manager may ask: "Is my firm properly valued by investors? Is our investor communication program adequate to facilitate this process?"
- A corporate manager could ask: "Is this firm a potential takeover target? How much value can be added if we acquire this firm? How can we finance the acquisition?"
- An independent auditor would want to ask: "Are the accounting policies and accrual estimates in this company's financial statements consistent with my understanding of this business and its recent performance? Do these financial reports communicate the current status and significant risks of the business?"

Financial statement analysis is a valuable activity when managers have complete information on a firm's strategies and a variety of institutional factors make it unlikely that they fully disclose this information. In this setting, outside analysts attempt to create "inside information" from analyzing financial statement data, thereby gaining valuable insights about the firm's current performance and future prospects.

To understand the contribution that financial statement analysis can make, it is important to understand the role of financial reporting in the functioning of capital markets and the institutional forces that shape financial statements. Therefore, we present first a brief description of these forces; then we discuss the steps that an analyst must perform to extract information from financial statements and provide valuable forecasts.

THE ROLE OF FINANCIAL REPORTING IN CAPITAL MARKETS

A critical challenge for any economy is the allocation of savings to investment opportunities. Economies that do this well can exploit new business ideas to spur innovation and create jobs and wealth at a rapid pace. In contrast, economies that manage this process poorly dissipate their wealth and fail to support business opportunities.

In the twentieth century, we have seen two distinct models for channeling savings into business investments. Communist and socialist market economies have used central planning and government agencies to pool national savings and to direct investments in business enterprises. The failure of this model is evident from the fact that most of these economies have abandoned it in favor of the second model—the market model. In almost all countries in the world today, capital markets play an important role in channeling financial resources from savers to business enterprises that need capital.

Figure 1-1 provides a schematic representation of how capital markets typically work. Savings in any economy are widely distributed among households. There are usually many new entrepreneurs and existing companies that would like to attract these savings to fund their business ideas. While both savers and entrepreneurs would like to do business with each other, matching savings to business investment opportunities is complicated for at least two reasons. First, entrepreneurs typically have better information than savers on the value of business investment opportunities. Second, communication by entrepreneurs to investors is not completely credible because investors know entrepreneurs have an incentive to inflate the value of their ideas.

Figure 1-1 Capital Markets

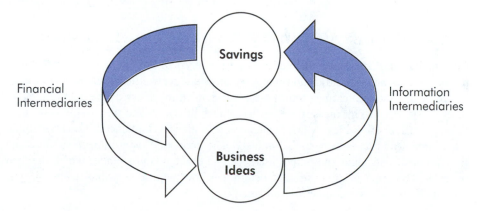

These information and incentive problems lead to what economists call the "lemons" problem, which can potentially break down the functioning of the capital market.[1] It works like this. Consider a situation where half the business ideas are "good" and the other half are "bad." If investors cannot distinguish between the two types of business ideas, entrepreneurs with "bad" ideas will try to claim that their ideas are as valuable as the "good" ideas. Realizing this possibility, investors value both good and bad ideas at an average level. Unfortunately, this penalizes good ideas, and entrepreneurs with good ideas find the terms on which they can get financing to be unattractive. As these entrepreneurs leave the capital market, the proportion of bad ideas in the market increases. Over time, bad ideas "crowd out" good ideas, and investors lose confidence in this market.

The emergence of intermediaries can prevent such a market breakdown. Intermediaries are like a car mechanic who provides an independent certification of a used car's quality to help a buyer and seller agree on a price. There are two types of intermediaries in the capital markets. Financial intermediaries, such as venture capital firms, banks, mutual funds, and insurance companies, focus on aggregating funds from individual investors and analyzing different investment alternatives to make investment decisions. Information intermediaries, such as auditors, financial analysts, bond-rating agencies, and the financial press, focus on providing information to investors (and to financial intermediaries who represent them) on the quality of various business investment opportunities. Both these types of intermediaries add value by helping investors distinguish "good" investment opportunities from the "bad" ones.

Financial reporting plays a critical role in the functioning of both the information intermediaries and financial intermediaries. Information intermediaries add value by either enhancing the credibility of financial reports (as auditors do), or by analyzing the information in the financial statements (as analysts and the rating agencies do). Financial intermediaries rely on the information in the financial statements, and supplement this information with other sources of information, to analyze investment opportunities. In the following section, we discuss key aspects of the financial reporting system design that enable it to play effectively this vital role in the functioning of the capital markets.

FROM BUSINESS ACTIVITIES TO FINANCIAL STATEMENTS

Corporate managers are responsible for acquiring physical and financial resources from the firm's environment and using them to create value for the firm's investors. Value is created when the firm earns a return on its investment in excess of the cost of capital. Managers formulate business strategies to achieve this goal, and they implement them through business activities. A firm's business activities are influenced by its economic environment and its own business strategy. The economic environment includes the firm's industry, its input and output markets, and the regulations under which the firm operates. The firm's business strategy determines how the firm positions itself in its environment to achieve a competitive advantage.

As shown in Figure 1-2, a firm's financial statements summarize the economic consequences of its business activities. The firm's business activities in any time period are too numerous to be reported individually to outsiders. Further, some of the activities undertaken by the firm are proprietary in nature, and disclosing these activities in detail could be a detriment to the firm's competitive position. The firm's accounting system provides a mechanism through which business activities are selected, measured, and aggregated into financial statement data.

Intermediaries using financial statement data to do business analysis have to be aware that financial reports are influenced both by the firm's business activities and by its

Figure 1-2 From Business Activities to Financial Statements

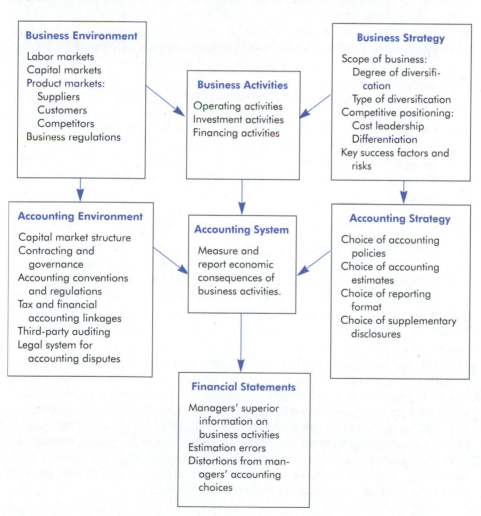

accounting system. A key aspect of financial statement analysis, therefore, involves understanding the influence of the accounting system on the quality of the financial statement data being used in the analysis. The institutional features of accounting systems discussed below determine the extent of that influence.

Accounting System Feature 1: Accrual Accounting

One of the fundamental features of corporate financial reports is that they are prepared using accrual rather than cash accounting. Unlike cash accounting, accrual accounting distinguishes between the recording of costs and benefits associated with economic activities and the actual payment and receipt of cash. Net income is the primary periodic performance index under accrual accounting. To compute net income, the effects of economic transactions are recorded on the basis of *expected,* not necessarily *actual,* cash receipts and payments. Expected cash receipts from the delivery of products or services are recognized as revenues, and expected cash outflows associated with these revenues are recognized as expenses.

The need for accrual accounting arises from investors' demand for financial reports on a periodic basis. Because firms undertake economic transactions on a continual basis, the arbitrary closing of accounting books at the end of a reporting period leads to a fundamental measurement problem. Since cash accounting does not report the full economic consequence of the transactions undertaken in a given period, accrual accounting is designed to provide more complete information on a firm's periodic performance.

Accounting System Feature 2: Accounting Standards and Auditing

The use of accrual accounting lies at the center of many important complexities in corporate financial reporting. Because accrual accounting deals with *expectations* of future cash consequences of current events, it is subjective and relies on a variety of assumptions. Who should be charged with the primary responsibility of making these assumptions? A firm's managers are entrusted with the task of making the appropriate estimates and assumptions to prepare the financial statements because they have intimate knowledge of their firm's business.

The accounting discretion granted to managers is potentially valuable because it allows them to reflect inside information in reported financial statements. However, since investors view profits as a measure of managers' performance, managers have incentives to use their accounting discretion to distort reported profits by making biased assumptions. Further, the use of accounting numbers in contracts between the firm and outsiders provides another motivation for management manipulation of accounting numbers. Income management distorts financial accounting data, making them less valuable to external users of financial statements. Therefore, the delegation of financial reporting decisions to corporate managers has both costs and benefits.

A number of accounting conventions have evolved to ensure that managers use their accounting flexibility to summarize their knowledge of the firm's business activities, and not to disguise reality for self-serving purposes. For example, the measurability and conservatism conventions are accounting responses to concerns about distortions from managers' potentially optimistic bias. Both these conventions attempt to limit managers' optimistic bias by imposing their own pessimistic bias.

Accounting standards (Generally Accepted Accounting Principles), promulgated by the Financial Accounting Standards Board (FASB) and similar standard-setting bodies in other countries, also limit potential distortions that managers can introduce into reported numbers. Uniform accounting standards attempt to reduce managers' ability to record similar economic transactions in dissimilar ways, either over time or across firms.

Increased uniformity from accounting standards, however, comes at the expense of reduced flexibility for managers to reflect genuine business differences in their firm's financial statements. Rigid accounting standards work best for economic transactions whose accounting treatment is not predicated on managers' proprietary information. However, when there is significant business judgment involved in assessing a transaction's economic consequences, rigid standards which prevent managers from using their superior business knowledge would be dysfunctional. Further, if accounting standards are too rigid, they may induce managers to expend economic resources to restructure business transactions to achieve a desired accounting result.

Auditing, broadly defined as a verification of the integrity of the reported financial statements by someone other than the preparer, ensures that managers use accounting rules and conventions consistently over time, and that their accounting estimates are reasonable. Therefore, auditing improves the quality of accounting data.

Third-party auditing may also reduce the quality of financial reporting because it constrains the kind of accounting rules and conventions that evolve over time. For example, the FASB considers the views of auditors in the standard-setting process. Auditors are likely to argue against accounting standards producing numbers that are difficult to audit, even if the proposed rules produce relevant information for investors.

The legal environment in which accounting disputes between managers, auditors, and investors are adjudicated can also have a significant effect on the quality of reported numbers. The threat of lawsuits and resulting penalties have the beneficial effect of improving the accuracy of disclosure. However, the potential for a significant legal liability might also discourage managers and auditors from supporting accounting proposals requiring risky forecasts, such as forward-looking disclosures.

Accounting System Feature 3: Managers' Reporting Strategy

Because the mechanisms that limit managers' ability to distort accounting data add noise, it is not optimal to use accounting regulation to eliminate managerial flexibility completely. Therefore, real-world accounting systems leave considerable room for managers to influence financial statement data. A firm's reporting strategy, that is, the manner in which managers use their accounting discretion, has an important influence on the firm's financial statements.

Corporate managers can choose accounting and disclosure policies that make it more or less difficult for external users of financial reports to understand the true economic picture of their businesses. Accounting rules often provide a broad set of alternatives from which managers can choose. Further, managers are entrusted with making a range of estimates in implementing these accounting policies. Accounting regulations usually prescribe *minimum* disclosure requirements, but they do not restrict managers from *voluntarily* providing additional disclosures.

A superior disclosure strategy will enable managers to communicate the underlying business reality to outside investors. One important constraint on a firm's disclosure strategy is the competitive dynamics in product markets. Disclosure of proprietary information about business strategies and their expected economic consequences may hurt the firm's competitive position. Subject to this constraint, managers can use financial statements to provide information useful to investors in assessing their firm's true economic performance.

Managers can also use financial reporting strategies to manipulate investors' perceptions. Using the discretion granted to them, managers can make it difficult for investors to identify poor performance on a timely basis. For example, managers can choose accounting policies and estimates to provide an optimistic assessment of the firm's true performance. They can also make it costly for investors to understand the true performance by controlling the extent of information that is disclosed voluntarily.

The extent to which financial statements are informative about the underlying business reality varies across firms—and across time for a given firm. This variation in accounting quality provides both an important opportunity and a challenge in doing business analysis. The process through which analysts can separate noise from information in financial statements, and gain valuable business insights from financial statement analysis, is discussed next.

FROM FINANCIAL STATEMENTS TO BUSINESS ANALYSIS

Because managers' insider knowledge is a source both of value and distortion in accounting data, it is difficult for outside users of financial statements to separate true information from distortion and noise. Not being able to undo accounting distortions completely, investors "discount" a firm's reported accounting performance. In doing so, they make a probabilistic assessment of the extent to which a firm's reported numbers reflect economic reality. As a result, investors can have only an imprecise assessment of an individual firm's performance. Financial and information intermediaries can add value by improving investors' understanding of a firm's current performance and its future prospects.

Effective financial statement analysis is valuable because it attempts to get at managers' inside information from public financial statement data. Because intermediaries do not have direct or complete access to this information, they rely on their knowledge of the firm's industry and its competitive strategies to interpret financial statements. Successful intermediaries have at least as good an understanding of the industry economics as do the firm's managers, and a reasonably good understanding of the firm's competitive strategy. Although outside analysts have an information disadvantage relative to the firm's managers, they are more objective in evaluating the economic consequences of the firm's investment and operating decisions. Figure 1-3 provides a schematic overview of how business intermediaries use financial statements to accomplish four key steps: (1) business strategy analysis, (2) accounting analysis, (3) financial analysis, and (4) prospective analysis.

Figure 1-3 Analysis Using Financial Statements

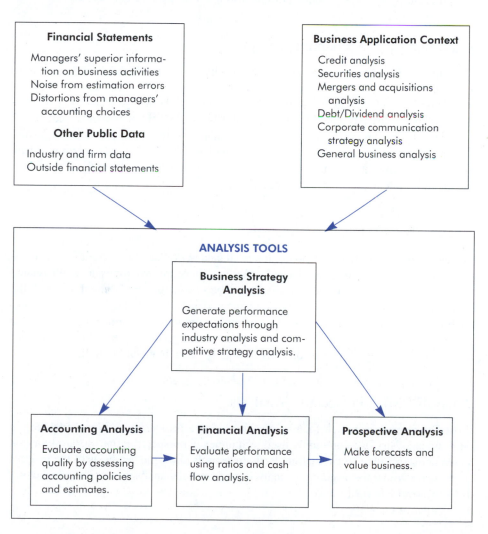

Analysis Step 1: Business Strategy Analysis

The purpose of business strategy analysis is to identify key profit drivers and business risks, and to assess the company's profit potential at a qualitative level. Business strategy analysis involves analyzing a firm's industry and its strategy to create a sustainable competitive advantage. This qualitative analysis is an essential first step because it enables the analyst to frame the subsequent accounting and financial analysis better. For example, identifying the key success factors and key business risks allows the identification of key accounting policies. Assessment of a firm's competitive strategy facilitates evaluating whether current profitability is sustainable. Finally, business analysis enables the analyst to make sound assumptions in forecasting a firm's future performance.

Analysis Step 2: Accounting Analysis

The purpose of accounting analysis is to evaluate the degree to which a firm's accounting captures the underlying business reality. By identifying places where there is accounting flexibility, and by evaluating the appropriateness of the firm's accounting policies and estimates, analysts can assess the degree of distortion in a firm's accounting numbers. Another important step in accounting analysis is to "undo" any accounting distortions by recasting a firm's accounting numbers to create unbiased accounting data. Sound accounting analysis improves the reliability of conclusions from financial analysis, the next step in financial statement analysis.

Analysis Step 3: Financial Analysis

The goal of financial analysis is to use financial data to evaluate the current and past performance of a firm and to assess its sustainability. There are two important skills related to financial analysis. First, the analysis should be systematic and efficient. Second, the analysis should allow the analyst to use financial data to explore business issues. Ratio analysis and cash flow analysis are the two most commonly used financial tools. Ratio analysis focuses on evaluating a firm's product market performance and financial policies; cash flow analysis focuses on a firm's liquidity and financial flexibility.

Analysis Step 4: Prospective Analysis

Prospective analysis, which focuses on forecasting a firm's future, is the final step in business analysis. Two commonly used techniques in prospective analysis are financial statement forecasting and valuation. Both these tools allow the synthesis of the insights from business analysis, accounting analysis, and financial analysis in order to make predictions about a firm's future.

While the value of a firm is a function of its future cash flow performance, it is also possible to assess a firm's value based on the firm's current book value of equity, and its future return on equity (ROE) and growth. Strategy analysis, accounting analysis, and financial analysis, the first three steps in the framework discussed here, provide an excellent foundation for estimating a firm's intrinsic value. Strategy analysis, in addition to enabling sound accounting and financial analysis, also helps in assessing potential changes in a firm's competitive advantage and their implications for the firm's future ROE and growth. Accounting analysis provides an unbiased estimate of a firm's current book value and ROE. Financial analysis allows you to gain an in-depth understanding of what drives the firm's current ROE.

The predictions from a sound business analysis are useful to a variety of parties and can be applied in various contexts. The exact nature of the analysis will depend on the context. The contexts that we will examine include securities analysis, credit evaluation, mergers and acquisitions, evaluation of debt and dividend policies, and assessing corporate communication strategies. The four analytical steps described above are useful in each of these contexts. Appropriate use of these tools, however, requires a familiarity with the economic theories and institutional factors relevant to the context.

SUMMARY

Financial statements provide the most widely available data on public corporations' economic activities; investors and other stakeholders rely on them to assess the plans and performance of firms and corporate managers. Accrual accounting data in financial statements are noisy, and unsophisticated investors can assess firms' performance only imprecisely. Financial analysts who understand managers' disclosure strategies have an opportunity to create inside information from public data, and they play a valuable role in enabling outside parties to evaluate a firm's current and prospective performance.

This chapter has outlined the framework for business analysis with financial statements, using the four key steps: business strategy analysis, accounting analysis, financial analysis, and prospective analysis. The remaining chapters in this book describe these steps in greater detail and discuss how they can be used in a variety of business contexts.

DISCUSSION QUESTIONS

1. John, who has just completed his first finance course, is unsure whether he should take a course in business analysis and valuation using financial statements, since he believes that financial analysis adds little value, given the efficiency of capital markets. Explain to John when financial analysis can add value, even if capital markets are efficient.
2. Accounting statements rarely report financial performance without error. List three types of errors that can arise in financial reporting.

3. Joe Smith argues that "learning how to do business analysis and valuation using financial statements is not very useful, unless you are interested in becoming a financial analyst." Comment.
4. Four steps for business analysis are discussed in the chapter (strategy analysis, accounting analysis, financial analysis, and prospective analysis). As a financial analyst, explain why each of these steps is a critical part of your job, and how they relate to one another.

NOTE

1. G. Akerolf, "The Market for 'Lemons': Quality Uncertainty and the Market Mechanism," *Quarterly Journal of Economics* (August 1970): 488–500.

In July 1998 Hong In-Kie, Chairman and CEO of the Korea Stock Exchange, was pondering on how best to attract a significant amount of long-term capital into the Korean stock market. Mr. Hong, a graduate of Harvard Business School AMP 85, avid mountain climber, church leader, and accomplished tenor, was aware that there were stiff challenges ahead. At the pinnacle of a successful career as a bureaucrat and as ex-president of a large conglomerate in one of the world's most dynamic economies, he had a unique birds-eye view of Korean society and the economy.

During the past 30 years, the Korean economy had grown at 8.6 percent annually. At the end of 1996, South Korea became the eleventh largest economy in the world and a member of the Organization for Economic Cooperation and Development (OECD). Used to hosannas as a worldwide leader in areas as diverse as shipbuilding, construction, semiconductors, and automobiles, Korea found itself in the unenviable position of having practically depleted its foreign exchange reserves by November of 1997, and having had to seek assistance from the International Monetary Fund (IMF). As a result of the economic crisis, the Korea Composite Stock Price Index (KOSPI) closed at 376.31 by the end of 1997, down 42.2 percent from the closing index of 651.22 in 1996 (see Exhibit 1 for selected economic data).

Mr. Hong described the current situation as follows: "It is like a movie unfolding every day, and we are all watching and on stage at the same time. Events are occurring so fast that the headlines in the evening version of the paper and the morning version of the same paper are often substantially different." Mr. Hong was convinced that finding a way to spur the development of the stock market was a crucial part of the change needed to shepherd Korea out of its current economic predicament.

KOREAN ECONOMIC SYSTEM

Prior to the 1997 economic crisis, the Korean economy was viewed by many, both inside and outside the country, as a dramatic success story. While there were many facets to the export-oriented economic strategy of Korea, two features stood out: a bank-centered financial system that financed the rapid industrial growth, and the chaebol system that created globally competitive enterprises.

Professors James Jinho Chang (The Wharton School), Tarun Khanna, and Krishna Palepu prepared this case as the basis for class discussion rather than to illustrate either effective or ineffective handling of an administrative situation. Copyright © 1998 by the President and Fellows of Harvard College. Harvard Business School case 9-199-033.

Note: All references in this case to the country of Korea mean South Korea.

Bank-Centered Financial System

Unlike the U.S. and the U.K. economies' reliance on the stock market, the Korean economy relied heavily on the banking system for channeling savings to industrial investments. In this respect, Korea followed the example of Germany and Japan in the development of its financial system. Many commentators, both in Korea and abroad, believed that the bank-centered financial system facilitated long-term investments, largely due to the close relationships between industrial enterprises and financiers. Because stock market investors typically had no long-term relationship with the firms that they invested in, the U.S.-style stock market system was alleged to lead to "myopic management."

Even though Korean banks operated in the private sector, the national government had significant influence on the banking industry. Through ownership and the appointment of bank directors, the Korean government could influence banks' lending decisions to further its economic development plans. For example, in the 1970s government policies favored the development of heavy industries, such as construction, machinery, and shipbuilding. The government encouraged companies to expand business in these industries and provided favorable capital related to that expansion through banks.

Business Groups

The Korean economy was dominated by multibusiness organizations known as chaebols. The largest chaebols, such as Samsung, Daewoo, Hyundai, LG, and the SK Group, operated in a wide variety of industries such as construction, shipbuilding, automobiles, consumer electronics, computing, telecommunication, and financial services. The 30 largest chaebols accounted for 51.8 percent of the total industrial output of Korea in 1996. The top four chaebols, Hyundai, Samsung, LG, and Daewoo, accounted for 31.2 percent of the total industrial output of Korea in 1996.

Historically, government policy favored the growth of chaebols. These policies included granting industrial licenses, distributing foreign borrowings, and providing favored access to bank financing.[1] The promotion of chaebols was seen by the Korean government as a way to create domestic industry that could compete in global markets. Indeed, Korean chaebols played a very critical role in the export-led growth of the Korean economy. By 1996 the top seven trading companies of chaebols accounted for 47.7 percent of Korea's total exports.[2]

The chaebol organizational structure conferred several advantages in the early growth stage of the Korean economy by enabling entrepreneurs to overcome the problem of underdeveloped product, labor, and financial markets. At this stage, many of the institutions

1. In the early 1970s, the interest rate on foreign borrowing was 5–6 percent, whereas the interest rate on domestic bank debt was 25–30 percent. The interest rate for nonbank borrowing was higher than that from banks. The privilege of using foreign borrowing and bank loans significantly contributed to the accumulation of the chaebols' wealth.

2. The top seven trading companies are Hyundai, Samsung, LG, Daewoo, SK, Ssangyong, and Hyosung.

that underpin the functioning of advanced markets were either missing or underdeveloped in Korea.

In advanced markets, intermediary institutions and legal structures address potential information and incentive problems. These institutions permit individual entrepreneurs to raise capital, access management talent, and earn customer acceptance, and they require all parties to play by the same rules. Entrepreneurs and investors can be sure of the stable legal environment in advanced markets to protect property rights, giving entrepreneurs the confidence that they will reap the fruits of their entrepreneurial activity. In this context found in advanced markets, it is less likely that the entrepreneur will benefit significantly by being associated with a large corporate entity. Hence, the costs of business diversification are likely to exceed any potential benefits.

In an emerging market like Korea, in contrast, there were a variety of market failures, caused by information and incentive problems. For example, the financial markets were characterized by a lack of adequate disclosure and weak corporate governance and control. Intermediaries such as financial analysts, mutual funds, investment bankers, venture capitalists, and the financial press were either absent or not fully evolved. Finally, securities regulations were generally weak, and their enforcement was uncertain. Similar problems abounded in product markets and labor markets, once again because of the absence of intermediaries.

The absence of intermediary institutions made it costly for individual entrepreneurs to acquire necessary inputs like finance, technology, and management talent. Market and legal imperfections also made it costly to establish quality brand images in product markets, and to establish contractual relationships with joint venture partners. As a result, an enterprise could often be more profitably pursued as part of a large diversified business group, a chaebol, which acted as an intermediary between individual entrepreneurs and imperfect markets.

Affiliates of chaebols also enjoyed preferential access to financing from domestic banks because of their strong connections with bankers and government officials. In addition, established companies in a chaebol often provided cross-guarantees on loans to new affiliates, making it easier for new ventures to raise financing from domestic and foreign lenders.

Korean chaebols such as Samsung and Daewoo were also able to use their size and scope to invest in world-class brand names. These brand names enabled new companies promoted by these leading chaebols, even in unrelated fields, to gain instant credibility in export markets and with technology partners.

Chaebols were the preferred employers for students graduating from prestigious Korean universities. Because of their size and scope, chaebols could offer job security in an economy with no safety nets. Further, chaebols such as Samsung and the SK Group made extensive investment in the training and development of their employees, in effect creating their own "business schools." Due to their size, they could hire professors from top business schools around the world to lead their in-house training programs. Because Korea did not have many world-class business schools, the in-house "business schools" of chaebols were in a unique position to develop management talent.

As a result of the above advantages, chaebols were uniquely positioned to launch new ventures in the Korean economy. Chaebols relied extensively on domestic and foreign debt to finance their rapid growth. Reliance on domestic debt arose as a result of the bank-centered nature of the financial system. Further, with a view to keep the control of Korean businesses in Korean hands, government policy restricted foreign direct investment in Korean chaebols. While foreign investors could invest through the stock market, banks and other financial institutions were a more significant channel through which foreign money was invested in Korean companies.[3]

One of the key characteristics of a chaebol is family ownership and cross-holding. In 1995 the average family ownership in the top 30 chaebols was 10.6 percent and the average ownership through cross-holding equity ownership among member firms was 32.8 percent. Cross-holdings increased the founder family's control on large business groups.[4] Traditionally, the voting rights of institutional investors, such as securities firms and insurance companies, were limited by the law and minority shareholders were not active.[5] As a result, the founder or founder's family could effectively control the business group with relatively small direct ownership, and family members took top management positions.[6]

By 1996, prior to the economic crisis, the median debt-to-equity ratio of the top 30 Korean chaebols stood at 420 percent (see Exhibit 2). While each company in a chaebol borrowed money independently, bankers often demanded and received cross-guarantees from the other firms in the chaebol. Since Korean financial accounting rules did not require the disclosure of these cross-guarantees, it was difficult for outsiders to assess the true debt commitments of a given Korean company.

The "IMF Crisis"

The Korean economic crisis in 1997 was part of a broader Asian financial crisis that first started in Thailand, when the baht weakened as foreign investors lost confidence in the Thai economy. Amid the Asian currency crisis, foreign financial institutions, concerned about potential financial distress for Korean firms, started calling in their loans rapidly. Foreign portfolio investors also began to sell their investments and repatriate the sales proceeds for fear of the depreciation of the Korean won.[7]

....

3. *The details of the institutional investor market in Korea can be found in "The growing financial market importance of institutional investors: the case of Korea," by Yu-Kyung Kim,* OECD Proceedings: Institutional Investors in the New Financial Landscape, *1998.*

4. *Suppose that a family owns 20 percent of Company A and manages it, and Company A has a controlling ownership of Companies B and C, which in turn own 20 percent each of Company A. Through these cross-holdings, the founder's family can effectively own 60 percent of Company A, and control B and C as well.*

5. *Under these regulations, institutional investors were restricted to so called "shadow voting," which essentially meant that they voted with the management. After the recent crisis, this practice was abolished.*

6. *In 1995, among the top 30 chaebols, only one, KIA Motors, had a CEO who was not related to the founder's family.*

7. *1997 Fact Book published by Korea Stock Exchange.*

The outflow of foreign portfolio investment funds continued for four consecutive months, from August to November, bringing Korea close to depleting its foreign exchange reserves. On November 21 the Korean government requested the IMF's assistance to avoid a potential default on its obligations. After frenzied negotiations, the IMF agreed to provide Korea with U.S.$55 billion or more in a bailout package. Exhibit 3 shows the chronology of events surrounding the crisis; the rapid change in the value of Korean won during 1997 and 1998 is shown in Exhibit 4.

The Search for Causes

Many observers, both inside and outside Korea, were stunned by the rapid change of investor sentiment. The darling of foreign investors and economists until then, Korea found itself in the middle of an economic crisis that threatened to wipe out the fruits of hard work of a whole generation. As a sense of gloom enveloped the country, a heated debate focused on the search for the root causes of the crisis.

The nexus of the banking system and the chaebols, once viewed as the means to rapid economic growth, came under increased attack. Influential policy makers, including those at the IMF, believed that the chaebols, with their close connections to politicians and government officials, could get loans without much resistance from banks. As a result, the vaunted "relationship financing" model, meant to facilitate long-term investments, was now viewed more as facilitating "crony capitalism." A consensus began to emerge that, with easy access to financing, a lack of supervision by banks, and the government's emphasis on job creation, chaebols focused excessively on growth and expansion and ignored profitability.

On December 19, 1997, in the middle of the serious economic crisis, Kim Dae-Jung won the election as president of South Korea. Soon after entering office, President Kim noted that big business groups, together with government officials in power in the past, must take responsibility for having brought the economy to near collapse. He proclaimed that it was the collusion between the government and business, the government's control of finance, and widespread corruption that had battered the economy. Kim said, "Unless chaebols implement reform, they would face the recall of existing debts or the suspension of fresh credit. Only profitable enterprises and exporting companies will be regarded as 'patriotic' firms eligible for government supports."[8]

The IMF Program

As a condition for IMF bailout loans, receiving countries must adhere to the economic programs prescribed by the IMF. Michel Camdessus, IMF managing director, stated: "The program comprises strengthened fiscal and monetary policies, far-reaching financial reforms and further liberalization of trade and capital flows, as well as improvement

Korea Stock Exchange 1998

....

8. Lee Chang-sup, "Kim rules out new currency crisis, Korea Times, September 28, 1998.

in the structure and governance of Korean corporations." The IMF's program for Korea was heavily influenced by the conclusion that it was time for Korea to significantly restructure its financial and industrial sectors (see Exhibit 5 for details of the IMF-supported program of economic reform).

Some Koreans were positive about the IMF program because they felt that it could serve as an opportunity to sharpen Korea's international competitiveness, even though it was to be carried out by the force of outsiders. There were, however, others who expressed concern that the rapid changes proposed under the program were not only unrealistic but could lead to significant layoffs and social instability. In fact, the common reference to the economic crisis as the "IMF crisis" reflected the ambivalence in the Korean reaction to both the causes and the remedies being debated.

ECONOMIC RESTRUCTURING [9]

To implement the IMF program and to restore international confidence in Korea, the newly elected government of President Kim Dae-Jung began to pursue aggressively financial sector reforms and a total restructuring of chaebols. To this end, the Financial Supervisory Commission (FSC) was established on April 1, 1998, under the Prime Minister's jurisdiction to supervise all financial institutions including banks, securities firms, and insurance companies. The restructuring process of the financial industry and the corporate sector was administered by the FSC. The FSC pursued a strategy of sequential restructuring, beginning with banks and accelerating corporate sector restructuring through bank reform.

Bank Restructuring

The FSC requested twelve banks that fell short of the 8 percent capital adequacy ratio (as of December 1997) set by the Bank for International Settlement (BIS) to submit rehabilitation plans. Bank appraisal committees and accounting firms assessed the size of nonperforming loans through asset due diligence reviews and made full provision and write-offs based on the actual size of nonperforming loans. Based on this review, the FSC conditionally approved the bailout of seven banks and ordered the closure of five nonviable banks. Conditionally approved banks were asked to submit implementation plans which included changes in management, cost reductions, and recapitalization plans such as mergers, joint ventures, or rights issues.

The five banks which were classified as nonviable were to be acquired by healthy banks. To protect acquiring banks from spilled-over problem loans, several measures were taken: only good assets would be sold with a six-month put option; government

----

9. *This section is based on reports published by the Ministry of Finance and Economy (MOFE) and the Financial Supervisory Commission (FSC) in Korea.*

would inject fresh capital to enhance the acquiring bank's capital adequacy to pre-acquisition level; the acquiring bank's bad assets would be purchased by Korea Asset Management Corporation, funded by public resources; and deposit guarantees would be honored until the completion of all restructuring in order to prevent any bank runs.

One example of bank restructuring was a merger between Commercial Bank of Korea and the Hanil Bank. On July 31, 1998, following the guidelines of the FSC, the two banks announced a one-to-one merger. The newly merged bank proposed that in order for it to succeed, the following actions would be taken: (1) an accountable management system through drastic management improvement; (2) early resolution of nonperforming loans through injection from public resources; and (3) capital injection from international investors.[10]

A key issue in the normalization of the Korean financial sector was to develop a plan to clear nonperforming loans. At the end of March 1998, the nonperforming loans of financial institutions were estimated to be about 120 trillion won, which is about 23.3 percent of Korean financial institutions' entire credit portfolio. The Korean government estimated that the total market value of the nonperforming loans would be equal to 50 percent of their book value. The realized losses borne by financial institutions were therefore estimated to be approximately 60 trillion won.

To finance these losses, the Korean government planned to raise 50 trillion won through government bonds. From this amount, 41 trillion won would be used to purchase nonperforming loans and to recapitalize the affected financial institutions; the remaining nine trillion won would be reserved for the potential new demand for increased deposit protection. The government expected financial institutions to issue new equity worth twenty trillion won, which accounted for as much as one-third of total current capitalization in the Korean stock market.

Corporate Restructuring

In the short term, the Korean government's focus with respect to corporate restructuring was to shut down nonviable enterprises, and to improve the financial condition of the rest. In the long term, the objective was to improve the management and governance of the corporate sector in general, and of the chaebols in particular. To achieve these objectives, the FSC delineated five principles of corporate restructuring: (1) improving the financial structure, (2) eliminating the practice of mutual guarantees of loans among affiliated firms, (3) focusing on "core" business sectors, (4) increasing transparency, and (5) improving corporate governance (e.g., increasing major shareholders' and management's accountability).

In order to direct the restructuring process, the FSC classified all Korean companies into three categories. Companies classified as "viable" would receive full support from

---

10. *Joint press conference upon announcement of merger between the Commercial Bank of Korea and the Hanil Bank.*

financial institutions; those that were classified as "subject to exit" would be sold off or shut down on a timely basis; and those that were classified as "subject to restructuring" would benefit from proactive support toward restructuring from financial institutions. In June 1998, 55 corporations, which represented 17 percent of the total number of corporations subject to the assessment, were classified as nonviable and ordered to exit. Of these 55 corporations, twenty were affiliated companies of the top five chaebols (Hyundai, Samsung, LG, Daewoo, and SK), and 32 were affiliates of the top 6 to 64 business groups.

One of the senior officials at FSC stated: "To reduce excessive reliance on debt financing, the government set a target for reducing Korean companies' debt to equity (D/E) ratio from the current level of approximately 500 percent to a level of 200 percent by the end of 1999. To meet this requirement, Korean companies had to raise more equity or sell off some of their assets."

Korean chaebols were directed by the FSC to formulate restructuring plans with a view to identifying core businesses on which they would focus, and to close down or divest the rest. To improve transparency and governance of individual companies in a chaebol, new guidelines curtailed the role of the central corporate office, and prohibited cross-guarantees. The top five chaebols were cajoled into the so-called "Big Deal" swaps of business units in order to boost national competitiveness by cutting out some domestic competition. To expedite the pace of corporate restructuring, government submitted the legislative articles, such as allowing tax benefits to restructuring, simplifying the mergers and acquisitions process, and permitting corporate spin-offs/carve-outs, to the coming session of the National Assembly.

Attracting Foreign Capital

Recognizing the importance of foreign capital for the successful restructuring of Korean banks and chaebols, President Kim Dae-Jung proclaimed his intention to make South Korea a haven for foreign investors. Foreign investors were essential in several ways. First, since all major Korean companies were looking to sell assets and raise new capital, the only viable buyers were foreigner investors. Second, foreign investors brought with them world-class management and governance practices to Korea.

To attract foreign capital, the government proposed several new policies. Under the new policy, foreign firms were allowed to freely establish mutual funds in Korea. At the same time, restrictions on foreign investors were also reduced. Earlier, foreign investors needed the approval of the board of directors of a company to buy more than ten percent of its outstanding shares. On May 25, 1998, under the new rules, the ten percent limit was completely abolished. The government also granted special privileges to domestic companies that attracted foreign investment or sold their assets to foreigners.

While these moves were somewhat effective in increasing foreign investors' interest in Korea, several hurdles remained. Deals for foreign direct investment could not be consummated because of widespread disagreement in valuation estimates of Korean sellers and foreign buyers. These valuation difficulties were exacerbated by the poor quality of accounting information. Further, foreign buyers were uncertain about the ease with which they could lay off employees. Despite the recent agreement between government, industry, and labor unions to cooperate in the restructuring process, the possibility of widespread lay-offs, especially by foreign owners, could be received with hostility.

The popular sentiment towards foreign direct investment was also ambiguous. On the one hand, the Korean government undertook a process of educating Koreans that attracting international investors was critical to economic rebuilding. On the other hand, there was a popular feeling against foreign investment, partly due to the 40-year Japanese rule of the country that ended in 1945. As a result, while many American franchises such as McDonald's and KFC have prospered in Korea, symbolic gestures against foreign investment abounded. When Microsoft attempted to buy a Korean word processing software company in financial distress, there was a fund-raising campaign to save the company and keep it in Korean hands. Even though the amount of foreign investment involved in this deal was only about U.S.$20 million, it was symbolic.

Foreign investors were also wary of the risks involved in investing in Korean companies through the stock market. Even in advanced capital markets, investing in stocks involves taking additional risks relative to investment in bonds or bank deposits. Unlike debt holders, shareholders are not promised a fixed payoff. Finally, when insiders have a controlling stake, they can take actions that are potentially harmful to the minority shareholders. In advanced markets, these potential risks faced by public shareholders are mitigated through a variety of mechanisms such as credible financial reporting, minority shareholder protection laws, the threat of hostile takeovers, scrutiny by an aggressive analyst community, and the supervision of management by an independent board of directors.

In Korea as of early 1998, many of these institutional mechanisms that protect shareholders and reduce their risks were either absent, underdeveloped, or poorly enforced. Relative to international standards, accounting rules and disclosure regulations were lax; there was a widespread belief that external auditors were either unwilling or unable to exercise independence; it was rare for shareholders to sue corporate managers or auditors successfully; boards were viewed as being too close to corporate managers; there was no effective threat of a hostile takeover or a proxy fight to replace a company's management; and the financial analysts themselves often worked for brokerage houses owned by large chaebols. The net result of these institutional voids was a perception among investors, both domestic and foreign, that investing in Korean stocks was very risky.

DEVELOPING THE CAPITAL MARKETS

As Chairman and CEO of the Korea Stock Exchange, Hong In-Kie was committed to leading the development of the Korean capital markets to a truly world-class level. He believed that the long-term prosperity of Korea depended critically on the success of this initiative.

Traditionally, the stock market played a relatively small role in the Korean financial system. The first significant boost to the Korean stock market came in 1976 when the Securities and Exchange Law underwent extensive revision. The main objective of the amendment was to ensure more effective supervision of the securities industry and to reinforce investor protection.

Throughout the latter half of the 1970s, the Korean securities market experienced an unprecedented rush of public offerings. The number of listed corporations, which stood at only 66 in 1972, jumped to 356 by the end of 1978. At the end of 1997, the number of listed companies was 776. During the period from 1972 to 1997, the traded value of listed stocks jumped more than two thousandfold from 71 billion won to 162.3 trillion won and the total market capitalization increased from 246 billion won to 71 trillion won (see Exhibit 6 and Exhibit 7).

Even though the absolute amount of both the traded value of stocks and market capitalization has increased over time, the relative magnitude of market capitalization to GDP declined in recent years. In 1994 and 1995, the market value to GDP ratio was greater than 40 percent, but it declined to 30 percent in 1996 and to 17 percent in 1997 (see Exhibit 8). The significance of equity as a source of financing also decreased over the last decade: The proportion of financing from the stock market relative to all sources of external financing declined from 23 percent in 1989 to 7.87 percent in 1997 (see Exhibit 9 and Exhibit 10).

The KOSPI composite index (100 as of January 4, 1980) rose from 532 on January 1, 1988, to 1007 on April 1, 1989. Many small investors were counting capital gains in excess of 100 percent in a little over a year. However, this 1988–89 upturn in the Korea Stock Exchange was not sustainable. The composite index has since dived and climbed like a roller coaster. On August 21, 1992, the composite index bottomed out at 460. Many small investors became seriously disillusioned with the stock market in 1992, blaming the government for their losses. Indeed, for political reasons the government had repeatedly intervened to prop up share prices by infusing large inflows of cash from various stabilization funds. Hardly anyone approached the market from a long-term perspective of focusing on the fundamental financial soundness of the company, managerial acumen, or on dividend performance.[11]

Recent Developments

After Mr. Hong became the CEO of the stock exchange in 1993, he initiated several efforts to modernize it. In 1996 the stock exchange moved to a new skyscraper with a fully computerized trading floor and a strict computerized surveillance system to monitor trading activity. Under Mr. Hong's leadership, the Korea Stock Exchange introduced derivative products for the first time—KOSPI 200 stock index futures contracts in May 1996, and KOSPI 200 stock index option contracts in July 1997. While Mr. Hong was proud of these innovations, and the investments in improving the physical infrastructure

11. James M. West, "Korea Stock Exchange," Korea Herald, August 30, 1998.

of the exchange, he was aware that the exchange would not become truly world-class without significantly more support of *institutional* infrastructure. Mr. Hong noted with satisfaction some recent developments in this direction.

Recognizing the fact that lack of transparency was one of the weaknesses that contributed to the current crisis, the Korean government proposed major changes in accounting rules. New regulations required the 30 largest conglomerates to prepare certified financial statements which would cover all the affiliated companies on a combined basis beginning in the 1999 fiscal year. The objective of this requirement was to improve the transparency of large conglomerates. There was also a move to make a fundamental change in Korean Generally Accepted Accounting Principles by adopting the more stringent International Accounting Standards.

There was also a change in the process through which accounting standards were set. Earlier, the Korea Securities and Exchange Commissions (KSEC) used to set accounting standards. When a new accounting standard was proposed, the KSEC would form a temporary board to review that standard. Board members included auditors, accounting professors, and government officials. Starting in April 1998, the KSEC became a part of the Financial Supervisory Board, and the FSC took over the supervision of accounting standard setting.

To improve shareholder rights, the Korean government took a number of steps. For example, in April 1998, to improve minority sharcholders' rights, the current requirement of 1 percent ownership to bring suits against management was eased to 0.05 percent; the requirement of 1 percent ownership to request the dismissal of a director or an auditor for an illegal act was relaxed to 0.5 percent; the minimum share-ownership required to examine corporate books was reduced from 3 percent to 1 percent.

New regulations also attempted to ease restrictions that had previously made hostile takeovers of Korean companies very difficult. Earlier, a company or an individual could not acquire more than 25 percent of the outstanding shares of another company unless an open tender offer to purchase more than 50 percent of the outstanding shares was made. However, in February 1998, this provision was abolished. Also, restrictions on institutional investors' voting rights were eliminated.

Public shareholders were also becoming more vocal in demanding management accountability. In May 1998, for the first time, foreign shareholders were beginning to have a voice in the management of Korean companies. The New York-based hedge fund Tiger Management, with the coalition of other foreign funds, staged a successful revolt at SK Telecom, the country's leading cellular phone operator. These outsider shareholders forced the phone company to stop subsidizing its sister companies in the SK Group. SK Telecom, for instance, backed a $50 million loan to its sibling SK Securities, which recently suffered heavy losses in derivatives trading. To guard against such maneuvers in the future, minority shareholders demanded—and got—three outside directors on the board of SK Telecom and an independent auditor.[12,13]

12. Louis Kraar, "Korea's comeback ... Don't expect a miracle," Forbes, May 25, 1998, p.120.

13. Starting in 1999, all Korea Stock Exchange listed firms are required to have at least 25 percent of their board members be outside directors.

Management accountability was also being championed by nongovernmental organizations such as The People's Solidarity for Participatory Democracy (PSPD). The organization was founded in September, 1994, and headed by Professor Chang Ha-sung at Korea University. In July 1998 PSPD successfully won a legal judgment against the management of the Korea First Bank for failure to exercise due diligence in its lending to a failed company, Hanbo Steel. The court order required four former top managers of Korea First Bank to pay about U.S.$30 million with their personal wealth to the bank (not to the plaintiffs) to make up for the losses caused by their negligence. The Korean press hailed it as the first case where plaintiffs won in a suit against management based on the failure to perform due diligence.

Future Challenges

Mr. Hong was convinced that a lot of progress had been made in the past few months. There was evidence that foreign investors were beginning to come back. Korea was also winning praise from the IMF for following closely its prescriptions. However, he was also aware that much more needed to be done.

Although the new accounting regulations were aimed at improving the quality of information available to investors to monitor corporate managers, there was much skepticism about the rules that had been mandated. The editor of a major Korean newspaper commented, "It's fine for the government and the international investors to demand transparency. However, it's important to realize that the different facets of Korean society are closely tied together—the government, business, and the banks. The entire system will have to be made transparent, not just a part of it."

Mr. Hong also noted that without effective auditing, financial reports were unlikely to be viewed by investors as reliable. One of the senior partners at a Big Five accounting firm in the United States echoed this sentiment: "Foreign investors know that the quality of audits in Korea is suspect; they will not be satisfied unless the financial statements of their Korean companies are signed by reputable international accounting firms."

The recent victory of minority shareholders represented the coming of major changes in Korean financial markets. However, this development was viewed with mixed feelings by several observers. Given the average Korean citizen's lack of sophistication about financial markets, there was a concern that minority shareholder rights would be pushed forward without adequate attention paid to minority shareholder responsibilities. Would the prospect of shareholder lawsuits and second-guessing management decisions by courts hamper the restructuring process?

There was also a debate in Korea and other emerging markets on the appropriate speed of opening capital markets to foreign investors, given the experience of the past few months. One of the major concerns was the instability of the stock market due to speculative hot money. There was a concern that rapid outflow would significantly damage not only the stock market but also the foreign exchange rate. In order to prevent this, many emerging countries imposed regulations on foreign investment and intervened in their stock markets.

Mr. Hong believed that full liberalization of the stock market was the fundamental solution. He stated, "Government regulations, as in the case of Malaysia, or government interventions in the stock market, as in the case of Hong Kong, do not guarantee the long-term development of a stock market. While in the rest of the world the acronym PKO may stand for Peace Keeping Operation, the same term in Asian securities markets is known as Price Keeping Operation, a derogatory term for intervention by the government. As the underlying philosophy of the government is based on democracy and a market economy, stock market participants must not rely on government to implement artificial market-boosting measures. In the short term, the stock market may have difficulty in breaking out of the doldrums, but as the market finds itself free from any sort of intervention, it will grow into a more independent, transparent, predictable, accountable, and self-sustaining market. Korea is following closely the IMF prescription toward a fully open market. The earlier we can get to the open market, the better." However, he wondered whether Korea had the institutional infrastructure necessary to support an open stock market.

As he pondered over these issues, Mr. Hong knew that the stakes were high. A senior editor of one of Korea's leading newspapers summed up the situation: "The newly elected President asked for a year to resolve matters. It has been six months already. If things don't improve, Korean people may not remain patient much longer." Due to the efforts made by government and business, there was a sign of increase in the foreign investment in Korean stocks (see Exhibit 11). However, the level has not met Mr. Hong's expectation. Mr. Hong wondered which of several possible directions the Korean stock market should pursue to attract foreign investment.

QUESTIONS

1. What are the merits and demerits of a stock versus a bank system of financing?
2. To prevent another bad loan problem in the future, what changes should be made in South Korean banks?
3. Is it a good idea for South Korea to rely more on the stock market as a source of corporate finance? Is it a good idea from the perspective of the chaebols?
4. How long do you think it will take South Korea to develop a vibrant stock market? What are the impediments? Are the changes contemplated adequate for the development of a vibrant stock market? What other steps would you recommend?

Korea Stock Exchange 1998

EXHIBIT 1
Selected Economic Indicators for South Korea

	1995	1996	1997	1998 (estimate)
Korea Composite Stock Price Index (year-end)	882.94	651.22	376.31	
Real GDP growth (percent change)	8.8	5.5	−0.4	−4.0 to −5.5
Consumer prices (percent change)	7.4	4.8	7.7	10.0
Central government balance (% of GDP)	3.0	2.4	−0.9	−2.4
External debt (billion US$)	82.6	90.5	91.8	89.7

Source: International Monetary Fund.

EXHIBIT 2

Top 30 Chaebols,[a] 1996 Financial Data

(amounts in billion won)	Assets	Owners' Equity	Debt-to-Equity	Return on Equity
1 Hyundai	52,821	9,842	437%	5.69%
2 Samsung	50,705	13,809	267%	1.71%
3 LG	37,068	8,302	346%	5.64%
4 Daewoo	34,197	7,817	337%	5.90%
5 Sunkyung	22,743	4,703	384%	12.73%
6 Ssangyong	15,802	3,102	409%	−1.90%
7 Hanjin	13,907	2,118	557%	−10.49%
8 Kia	14,121	2,289	517%	−4.70%
9 Hanwha	10,592	1,244	751%	−11.01%
10 Lotte	7,753	2,654	192%	5.34%
11 Kumho	7,399	1,281	478%	−0.58%
12 Halla	6,627	306	2066%	12.89%
13 Dong-Ah	6,289	1,383	355%	4.64%
14 Doosan	6,369	808	688%	−23.33%
15 Daelim	5,849	1,118	423%	6.35%
16 Hansol	4,214	1,075	292%	1.10%
17 Hyosung	4,131	879	370%	7.16%
18 Dongkuk Steel	3,698	1,161	219%	4.75%
19 Jinro	3,826	99	3765%	−169.06%
20 Kolon	3,840	919	318%	4.80%
21 Kohap	3,653	529	591%	7.34%
22 Dongbu	3,423	946	262%	3.00%
23 Tongyang	2,631	646	307%	0.05%
24 Haitai	3,398	448	658%	5.89%
25 New Core	2,796	211	1225%	15.99%
26 Anam	2,638	456	479%	10.22%
27 Hanil	2,599	384	577%	−40.00%
28 Keopyung	2,296	513	348%	−0.04%
29 Miwon	2,233	432	417%	−7.42%
30 Shinho	2,139	362	491%	−2.93%
Mean	11,325	2,328	617%	−5.01%
Median	5,032	1,011	420%	3.82%

a. Excluding financial and insurance industries

Source: Korea Fair Trade Commissions.

Korea Stock Exchange 1998

EXHIBIT 3

Chronological Highlights of the Korean Economic Crisis

Date	Events
August 20, 1997	The IMF approves a US$4 billion stand-by credit for Thailand, and releases a disbursement of US$1.6 billion.
October 8, 1997	The IMF announces support for Indonesia's intention to seek support from the IMF and other multilateral institutions.
November 21, 1997	The IMF welcomes Korea's request for IMF assistance.
December 4, 1997	The IMF approves a US$21 billion stand-by credit for Korea, and releases a disbursement of US$5.6 billion.
December 11, 1997	Korean government increases the foreigners' stock ownership ceiling from 26% to 50% (which later changed to 100%).
December 12, 1997	Korean government allows foreigners to invest in short-term financial instruments in domestic market.
December 31, 1997	The Korea Composite Stock Price Index closes the year at 376.31, down 42.2% from the closing index of 651.22 in 1996. Total market capitalization is reduced to about 71 trillion won.
April 1, 1998	Financial Supervisory Commission (FSC) is established to supervise all financial institutions, including banks, securities firms, and insurance companies.
April 9, 1998	The Foreign Exchange Equalization Bonds of US$4 billion are issued successfully and the Korean government shifts its focus from escaping the currency crisis to financial and corporate sector restructuring.
May 25, 1998	The ceiling on foreigners' stock investment is abolished, fully liberalizing the Korean stock market to foreign investors.
June 10, 1998	President Kim Dae-Jung delivers address at the U.S. Chamber of Commerce in Washington, D.C. He promises that Korea will become one of the best countries for international investors to freely and safely do business. Foreign Investment Promotion Act is designed to make Korea hospitable to foreign investors by providing financial concessions and administrative support.
June 18, 1998	The Financial Supervisory Committee (FSC) classified 55 corporations as financially nonviable and ordered them to liquidate.
June 29, 1998	Financial Supervisory Committee (FSC) orders 5 banks to shut down their operation and merge with other banks. FSC requests 7 banks, classified as conditional approval, to submit restructuring implementation plans.
July 24, 1998	Minority shareholders win, for the first time in history, against bank management for their failure to exercise due diligence.
July 31, 1998	Two conditionally approved banks, the Commercial Bank of Korea and the Hanil Bank, announce one-to-one merger.

EXHIBIT 4
Bilateral U.S. Dollar–Korean Won Exchange Rate

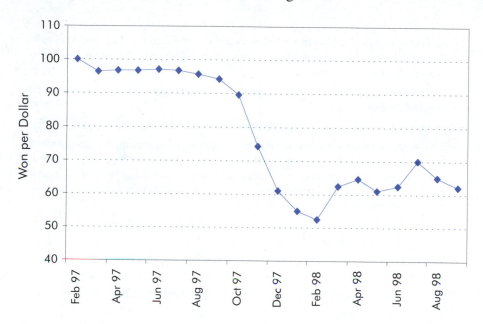

Source: Bank of Korea.

Korea Stock Exchange 1998

Korea Stock Exchange 1998

EXHIBIT 5
IMF-Supported Program of Economic Reform for South Korea

....

Financial sector restructuring

Comprehensive financial sector restructuring that introduced a clear and firm exit policy for financial institutions, strong market and supervisory discipline, and independence for the central bank.

Abolishment of regulations prohibiting a foreigner from becoming a director of a commercial bank.

Requirement that all merchant banks meet their capital adequacy ratios.

Transparency and corporate sector restructuring

Efforts to dismantle the nontransparent and inefficient ties among the government, banks, and businesses, including measures to upgrade accounting, auditing, and disclosure standards. Requirement that corporate financial statements be published every half year, on a consolidated basis, and certified by external auditors according to the international accounting standards.

Submission of legislation fully liberalizing hostile takeovers of Korean corporations by domestic companies and foreigners.

Amendment of the Bankruptcy Law to accelerate the corporate bankruptcy procedure.

Phase-out of the system of cross-guarantees within conglomerates.

Foreign investment

Full liberalization measures to open up the Korean money, bond, and equity markets to capital inflows, and to liberalize foreign direct investment.

Permission for foreign banks' securities companies to establish subsidiaries in Korea.

Labor market reform

Amendment of layoff-related laws which facilitate the redeployment of labor.

Increase in the government's financial support for the unemployed.

Expansion in the number of companies whose employees are eligible for unemployment insurance, and raising the minimum unemployment subsidy.

Trade policy

Trade liberalization measures, including setting a timetable in line with WTO commitments to eliminate trade-related subsidies and the import diversification program, as well as streamlining and improving transparency of import certification procedures.

....

Source: Adapted from reports published by Financial Supervisory Commissions.

EXHIBIT 6
Ten-year history of Korea Composite Stock Price Index (KOSPI)

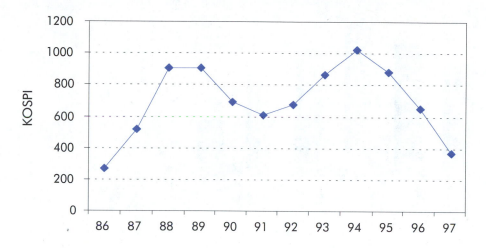

Source: Fact Book published by Korea Stock Exchange.

Korea Stock Exchange 1998

EXHIBIT 7
Stock Trading Value

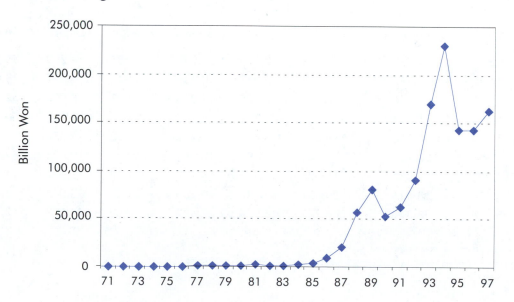

Source: Fact Book published by Korea Stock Exchange.

EXHIBIT 8
Market Value to GDP Ratios

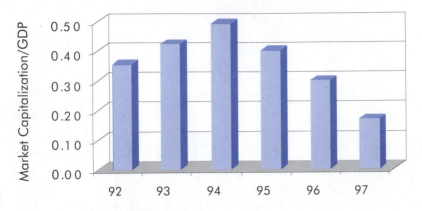

Source: Fact Book published by Korea Stock Exchange.

EXHIBIT 9
Financing of Korean Corporations (in billion won)

	Through Financial Institutions		Through Capital Markets					
	Bank	Non-Bank	CP	Stock	Bonds	Foreign[a]	Others[b]	Total
1989	5,698	7,963	5,131	8,310	4,932	−185	4,292	36,140
1990	7,995	11,477	1,902	5,987	10,931	3,247	6,517	48,056
1991	11,487	12,686	−2,211	5,555	14,065	2,501	8,002	52,085
1992	8,313	11,599	4,183	7,177	6,616	2,527	9,737	50,152
1993	8,440	11,718	9,017	8,619	9,218	−1,298	9,857	55,571
1994	18,367	20,981	4,405	13,198	13,568	4,037	10,423	84,978
1995	14,991	16,884	16,096	14,445	14,958	5,568	11,656	94,597
1996	18,571	18,424	20,691	13,342	20,265	12,063	13,542	116,899
1997	15,116	28,399	4,773	8,974	27,422	7,162	22,127	113,973

a. Foreign implies funds borrowed from overseas capital markets.

b. Others include letters of credit, loans from government, reserve for retirement allowances, etc.

Source: Bank of Korea.

EXHIBIT 10
Financing of Korean Corporations (in percent)

	Through Financial Institutions	Through Bond/CP Markets	Through Stock Markets	Foreign	Others	Total
1989	37.80%	27.84%	22.99%	–0.51%	11.87%	100.00%
1990	40.52%	26.70%	12.46%	6.76%	13.56%	100.00%
1991	46.41%	22.76%	10.66%	4.80%	15.36%	100.00%
1992	39.70%	21.53%	14.31%	5.04%	19.42%	100.00%
1993	36.27%	32.81%	15.51%	–2.34%	17.74%	100.00%
1994	46.30%	21.15%	15.53%	4.75%	12.27%	100.00%
1995	33.69%	32.83%	15.27%	5.89%	12.32%	100.00%
1996	31.65%	35.04%	11.41%	10.32%	11.58%	100.00%
1997	38.18%	28.25%	7.87%	6.28%	19.41%	100.00%

Source: Bank of Korea.

Korea Stock Exchange 1998

EXHIBIT 11
Foreign Investment in Korean Stock

Source: Korea Stock Exchange.

part 2

Business Analysis and Valuation Tools

Strategy Analysis

Strategy analysis is an important starting point for the analysis of financial statements. Strategy analysis allows the analyst to probe the economics of the firm at a qualitative level so that the subsequent accounting and financial analysis is grounded in business reality. Strategy analysis also allows the identification of the firm's profit drivers and key risks. This, in turn, enables the analyst to assess the sustainability of the firm's current performance and make realistic forecasts of future performance.

A firm's value is determined by its ability to earn a return on its capital in excess of the cost of capital. What determines whether or not a firm is able to accomplish this goal? While a firm's cost of capital is determined by the capital markets, its profit potential is determined by its own strategic choices: (1) the choice of an industry or a set of industries in which the firm operates (industry choice), (2) the manner in which the firm intends to compete with other firms in its chosen industry or industries (competitive positioning), and (3) the way in which the firm expects to create and exploit synergies across the range of businesses in which it operates (corporate strategy). Strategy analysis, therefore, involves industry analysis, competitive strategy analysis, and corporate strategy analysis.[1] In this chapter, we will briefly discuss these three steps and use the personal computer industry and Amazon.com, respectively, to illustrate the application of the steps.

INDUSTRY ANALYSIS

In analyzing a firm's profit potential, an analyst has to first assess the profit potential of each of the industries in which the firm is competing, because the profitability of various industries differs systematically and predictably over time. For example, the ratio of earnings before interest and taxes to the book value of assets for all U.S. companies between 1981 and 1997 was 8.8 percent. However, the average returns varied widely across specific industries: for the bakery products industry, the profitability ratio was 43 percentage points greater than the population average, and 23 percentage points less than the population average for the silver ore mining industry.[2] What causes these profitability differences?

There is a vast body of research in industrial organization on the influence of industry structure on profitability.[3] Relying on this research, strategy literature suggests that the average profitability of an industry is influenced by the "five forces" shown in Figure 2-1.[4] According to this framework, the intensity of competition determines the potential for creating abnormal profits by the firms in an industry. Whether or not the potential profits are kept by the industry is determined by the relative bargaining power of the

Figure 2-1 Industry Structure and Profitability

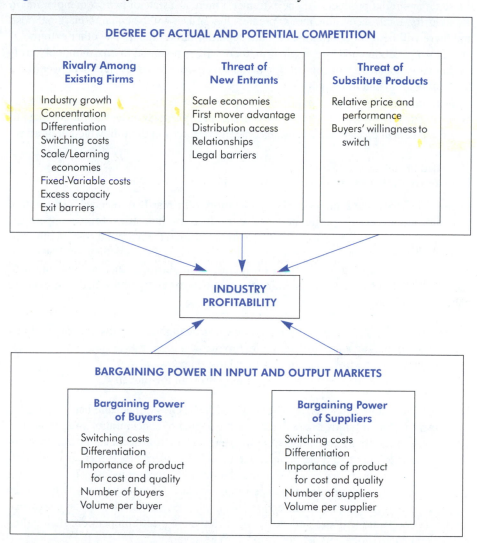

firms in the industry and their customers and suppliers. We will discuss each of these industry profit drivers in more detail below.

DEGREE OF ACTUAL AND POTENTIAL COMPETITION

At the most basic level, the profits in an industry are a function of the maximum price that customers are willing to pay for the industry's product or service. One of the key determinants of the price is the degree to which there is competition among suppliers of the same or similar products. At one extreme, if there is a state of perfect competition in the industry, micro-economic theory predicts that prices will be equal to marginal cost, and there will be few opportunities to earn supernormal profits. At the other extreme, if the industry is dominated by a single firm, there will be potential to earn monopoly profits. In reality, the degree of competition in most industries is somewhere in between perfect competition and monopoly.

There are three potential sources of competition in an industry: (1) rivalry between existing firms, (2) threat of entry of new firms, and (3) threat of substitute products or services. We will discuss each of these competitive forces in the following paragraphs.

Competitive Force 1: Rivalry Among Existing Firms

In most industries, the average level of profitability is primarily influenced by the nature of rivalry among existing firms in the industry. In some industries, firms compete aggressively, pushing prices close to (and sometimes below) the marginal cost. In other industries, firms do not compete aggressively on price. Instead, they find ways to coordinate their pricing, or compete on nonprice dimensions, such as innovation or brand image. Several factors determine the intensity of competition between existing players in an industry:

INDUSTRY GROWTH RATE.   If an industry is growing very rapidly, incumbent firms need not grab market share from each other to grow. In contrast, in stagnant industries, the only way existing firms can grow is by taking share away from the other players. In this situation, one can expect price wars among firms in the industry.

CONCENTRATION AND BALANCE OF COMPETITORS.   The number of firms in an industry and their relative sizes determine the degree of concentration in an industry.[5] The degree of concentration influences the extent to which firms in an industry can coordinate their pricing and other competitive moves. For example, if there is one dominant firm in an industry (such as IBM in the mainframe computer industry in the 1970s), it can set and enforce the rules of competition. Similarly, if there are only two or three equal-sized players (such as Coke and Pepsi in the U.S. soft-drink industry), they can implicitly cooperate with each other to avoid destructive price competition. If an industry is fragmented, price competition is likely to be severe.

DEGREE OF DIFFERENTIATION AND SWITCHING COSTS.   The extent to which firms in an industry can avoid head-on competition depends on the extent to which they can differentiate their products and services. If the products in an industry are very similar, customers are ready to switch from one competitor to another purely on the basis of price. Switching costs also determine customers' propensity to move from one product to another. When switching costs are low, there is a greater incentive for firms in an industry to engage in price competition.

SCALE/LEARNING ECONOMIES AND THE RATIO OF FIXED TO VARIABLE COSTS.   If there is a steep learning curve or there are other types of scale economies in an industry, size becomes an important factor for firms in the industry. In such situations, there are incentives to engage in aggressive competition for market share. Similarly, if the ratio of fixed to variable costs is high, firms have an incentive to reduce prices to utilize installed capacity. The airline industry, where price wars are quite common, is an example of this type of situation.

EXCESS CAPACITY AND EXIT BARRIERS.   If capacity in an industry is larger than customer demand, there is a strong incentive for firms to cut prices to fill capacity. The problem of excess capacity is likely to be exacerbated if there are significant barriers for firms to exit the industry. Exit barriers are high when the assets are specialized, or if there are regulations which make exit costly.

Competitive Force 2: Threat of New Entrants

The potential for earning abnormal profits will attract new entrants to an industry. The very threat of new firms entering an industry potentially constrains the pricing of existing firms within it. Therefore, the ease with which new firms can enter an industry is a key determinant of its profitability. Several factors determine the height of barriers to entry in an industry:

ECONOMIES OF SCALE.   When there are large economies of scale, new entrants face the choice of having either to invest in a large capacity which might not be utilized right away, or to enter with less than the optimum capacity. Either way, new entrants will at least initially suffer from a cost disadvantage in competing with existing firms. Economies of scale might arise from large investments in research and development (the pharmaceutical or jet engine industries), in brand advertising (soft-drink industry), or in physical plant and equipment (telecommunications industry).

FIRST MOVER ADVANTAGE.   Early entrants in an industry may deter future entrants if there are first mover advantages. For example, first movers might be able to set industry standards, or enter into exclusive arrangements with suppliers of cheap raw materials. They may also acquire scarce government licenses to operate in regulated industries. Finally, if there are learning economies, early firms will have an absolute cost advantage over new entrants. First mover advantages are also likely to be large when there are significant switching costs for customers once they start using existing products. For example, switching costs faced by the users of Microsoft's DOS operating system make it difficult for software companies to market a new operating system.

ACCESS TO CHANNELS OF DISTRIBUTION AND RELATIONSHIPS.   Limited capacity in the existing distribution channels and high costs of developing new channels can act as powerful barriers to entry. For example, a new entrant into the domestic auto industry in the U.S. is likely to face formidable barriers because of the difficulty of developing a dealer network. Similarly, new consumer goods manufacturers find it difficult to obtain supermarket shelf space for their products. Existing relationships between firms and customers in an industry also make it difficult for new firms to enter an industry. Industry examples of this include auditing, investment banking, and advertising.

LEGAL BARRIERS.   There are many industries in which legal barriers, such as patents and copyrights in research-intensive industries, limit entry. Similarly, licensing regulations limit entry into taxi services, medical services, broadcasting, and telecommunications industries.

Competitive Force 3: Threat of Substitute Products

The third dimension of competition in an industry is the threat of substitute products or services. Relevant substitutes are not necessarily those that have the same form as the existing products, but those that perform the same function. For example, airlines and car rental services might be substitutes for each other when it comes to travel over short distances. Similarly, plastic bottles and metal cans substitute for each other as packaging in the beverage industry. In some cases, threat of substitution comes not from customers' switching to another product but from utilizing technologies that allow them to do without, or use less of, the existing products. For example, energy-conserving technologies allow customers to reduce their consumption of electricity and fossil fuels.

   The threat of substitutes depends on the relative price and performance of the competing products or services, and on customers' willingness to substitute. Customers' perception of whether two products are substitutes depends to some extent on whether they perform the same function for a similar price. If two products perform an identical function, then it would be difficult for them to differ from each other in price. However, customers' willingness to switch is often the critical factor in making this competitive dynamic work. For example, even when tap water and bottled water serve the same function, many customers may be unwilling to substitute the former for the latter, enabling bottlers to charge a price premium. Similarly, designer label clothing commands a price premium even if it is not superior in terms of basic functionality, because customers place a value on the image offered by designer labels.

RELATIVE BARGAINING POWER
IN INPUT AND OUTPUT MARKETS

While the degree of competition in an industry determines whether or not there is *potential* to earn abnormal profits, the *actual profits* are influenced by the industry's bargaining power with its suppliers and customers. On the input side, firms enter into transactions with suppliers of labor, raw materials and components, and finances. On the output side, firms either sell directly to the final customers, or enter into contracts with intermediaries in the distribution chain. In all these transactions, the relative economic power of the two sides is important to the overall profitability of the industry firms.

Competitive Force 4: Bargaining Power of Buyers

Two factors determine the power of buyers: price sensitivity and relative bargaining power. Price sensitivity determines the extent to which buyers care to bargain on price; relative bargaining power determines the extent to which they will succeed in forcing the price down.[6]

PRICE SENSITIVITY.   Buyers are more price sensitive when the product is undifferentiated and there are few switching costs. The sensitivity of buyers to price also depends on the importance of the product to their own cost structure. When the product represents a large fraction of the buyers' cost (for example, the packaging material for soft-drink producers), the buyer is likely to expend the resources necessary to shop for a lower cost alternative. In contrast, if the product is a small fraction of the buyers' cost (for example, windshield wipers for automobile manufacturers), it may not pay to expend resources to search for lower-cost alternatives. Further, the importance of the product to the buyers' product quality also determines whether or not price becomes the most important determinant of the buying decision.

RELATIVE BARGAINING POWER.   Even if buyers are price sensitive, they may not be able to achieve low prices unless they have a strong bargaining position. Relative bargaining power in a transaction depends, ultimately, on the cost to each party of not doing business with the other party. The buyers' bargaining power is determined by the number of buyers relative to the number of suppliers, volume of purchases by a single buyer, number of alternative products available to the buyer, buyers' costs of switching from one product to another, and the threat of backward integration by the buyers. For example, in the automobile industry, car manufacturers have considerable power over component manufacturers because auto companies are large buyers, with several alternative suppliers to choose from, and switching costs are relatively low. In contrast, in the personal computer industry, computer makers have low bargaining power relative to the operating system software producers because of high switching costs.

Competitive Force 5: Bargaining Power of Suppliers

The analysis of the relative power of suppliers is a mirror image of the analysis of the buyer's power in an industry. Suppliers are powerful when there are only a few companies and there are few substitutes available to their customers. For example, in the soft-drink industry, Coke and Pepsi are very powerful relative to the bottlers. In contrast, metal can suppliers to the soft drink industry are not very powerful because of intense competition among can producers and the threat of substitution of cans by plastic bottles. Suppliers also have a lot of power over buyers when the suppliers' product or service is critical to buyers' business. For example, airline pilots have a strong bargaining power in the airline industry. Suppliers also tend to be powerful when they pose a credible threat of forward integration. For example, IBM is powerful relative to mainframe computer leasing companies because of IBM's unique position as a mainframe supplier, and its own presence in the computer leasing business.

APPLYING INDUSTRY ANALYSIS: THE PERSONAL COMPUTER INDUSTRY

Let us consider the above concepts of industry analysis in the context of the personal computer (PC) industry.[7] The industry began in 1981 when IBM announced its PC with Intel's microprocessor and Microsoft's DOS operating system. In 1997 the U.S. had an installed base of 100 million personal computers. The shipments in 1997 alone totaled 30 million units, up 21 percent from 1996. Despite this spectacular growth, however, the industry in 1998 was characterized by low profitability. Even the largest companies in the industry, such as IBM, Compaq, Dell, and Apple, reported poor performance in the early 1990s and were forced to undergo internal restructuring. What accounted for this low profitability? What was the computer industry's future profit potential?

COMPETITION IN THE PERSONAL COMPUTER INDUSTRY.   The competition was very intense for a number of reasons:
- The industry was fragmented, with many firms producing virtually identical products. Even though the computer market became more concentrated in the 1990s, with the top five vendors controlling close to 60 percent of the market, competition was intense, leading to routine price cuts on a monthly basis.
- Component costs accounted for more than 60 percent of total hardware costs of a personal computer, and volume purchases of components reduced these costs. Therefore, there was intense competition for market share among competing manufacturers.
- Products produced by different firms in the industry were virtually identical, and there were few opportunities to differentiate the products. While brand name and service were dimensions that customers valued in the early years of the industry, they became less important as PC buyers became more informed about the technology.
- Switching costs across different brands of personal computers were relatively low because a vast majority of the personal computers used Intel microprocessors and Microsoft Windows operating systems.

- Access to distribution was not a significant barrier, as demonstrated by Dell Computers, which distributed its computers by direct mail through the 1980s and introduced Internet-based sales in the mid-1990s. The advent of computer superstores like CompUSA also mitigated this constraint, since these stores were willing to carry several brands.
- Since virtually all the components needed to produce a personal computer were available for purchase, there were very few barriers to entering the industry. In fact, Michael Dell started Dell Computer Company in the early 1980s by assembling PCs in his University of Texas dormitory room.
- Apple's Macintosh computers offered competition as a substitute product. Workstations produced by Sun and other vendors were also potential substitutes at the higher end of the personal computer market.

THE POWER OF SUPPLIERS AND BUYERS.   Suppliers and buyers had significant power over firms in the industry for these reasons:

- Key hardware and software components for personal computers were controlled by firms with virtual monopoly. Intel dominated the microprocessor production for the personal computer industry, and Microsoft controlled the operating system market with its DOS and Windows operating systems.
- Buyers gained more power during the ten years from 1983 to 1993. Corporate buyers, who represented a significant portion of the customer base, were highly price sensitive since the expenditure on PCs represented a significant cost to their operations. Further, as they became knowledgeable about personal computer technology, customers were less influenced by brand name in their purchase decision. Buyers increasingly viewed PCs as commodities, and used price as the most important consideration in their buying decision.

As a result of the intense rivalry and low barriers to entry in the personal computer industry, there was severe price competition among different manufacturers. Further, there was tremendous pressure on firms to spend large sums of money to introduce new products rapidly, maintain high quality, and provide excellent customer support. Both these factors led to a low profit potential in the industry. The power of suppliers and buyers reduced the profit potential further. Thus, while the personal computer industry represented a technologically dynamic industry, its profit potential was poor.

There were few indications of change in the basic structure of the personal computer industry, and there was little likelihood of viable competition emerging to challenge the domination of Microsoft and Intel in the input markets. Attempts by industry leaders like IBM to create alternative proprietary technologies have not succeeded. As a result, the profitability of the PC industry may not improve significantly any time in the near future.

LIMITATIONS OF INDUSTRY ANALYSIS.   A potential limitation of the industry analysis framework discussed in this chapter is the assumption that industries have clear boundaries. In reality, it is often not easy to clearly demarcate industry boundaries. For example, in analyzing Dell's industry, should one focus on the IBM-compatible personal computer industry or the personal computer industry as a whole? Should one include workstations in the industry definition? Should one consider only the domestic manufacturers of personal computers, or also manufacturers abroad? Inappropriate industry definition will result in incomplete analysis and inaccurate forecasts.

COMPETITIVE STRATEGY ANALYSIS

The profitability of a firm is influenced not only by its industry structure but also by the strategic choices it makes in positioning itself in the industry. While there are many ways to characterize a firm's business strategy, as Figure 2-2 shows, there are two generic competitive strategies: (1) cost leadership and (2) differentiation.[8] Both these strategies can potentially allow a firm to build a sustainable competitive advantage.

Figure 2-2 Strategies for Creating Competitive Advantage

Cost Leadership

Supply same product or service at a lower cost.

Economies of scale and scope
Efficient production
Simpler product designs
Lower input costs
Low-cost distribution
Little research and development or brand advertising
Tight cost control system

Differentiation

Supply a unique product or service at a cost lower than the price premium customers will pay.

Superior product quality
Superior product variety
Superior customer service
More flexible delivery
Investment in brand image
Investment in research and development
Control system focus on creativity and innovation

Competitive Advantage

- Match between firm's core competencies and key success factors to execute strategy
- Match between firm's value chain and activities required to execute strategy
- Sustainability of competitive advantage

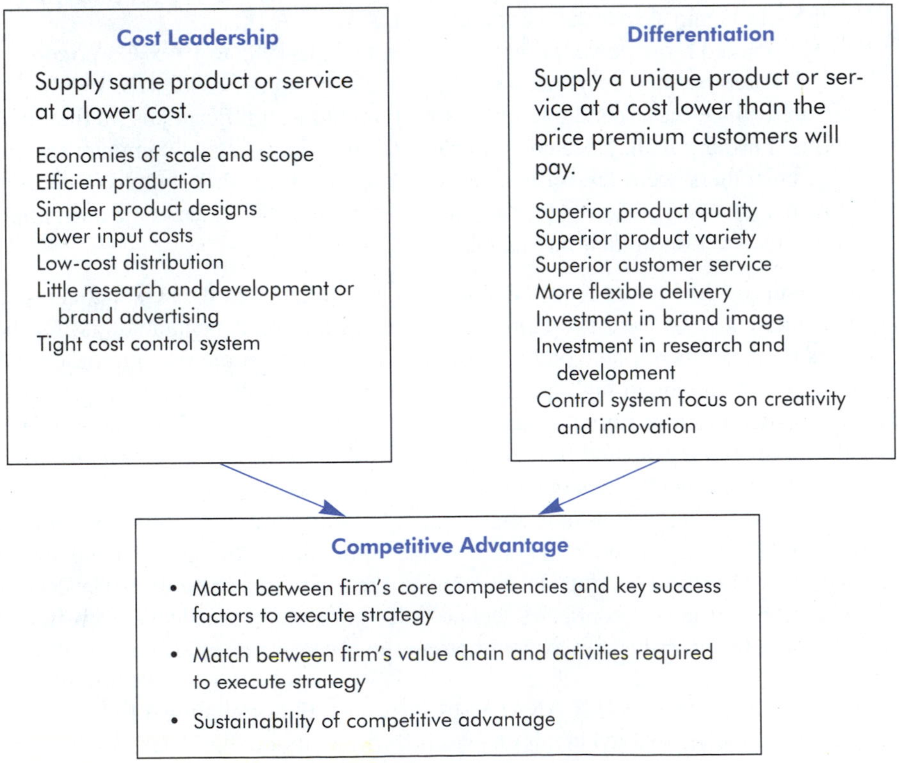

Strategy researchers have traditionally viewed cost leadership and differentiation as mutually exclusive strategies. Firms that straddle the two strategies are considered to be "stuck in the middle" and are expected to earn low profitability.[9] These firms run the risk of not being able to attract price conscious customers because their costs are too high; they are also unable to provide adequate differentiation to attract premium price customers.[10]

SOURCES OF COMPETITIVE ADVANTAGE

Cost leadership enables a firm to supply the same product or service offered by its competitors at a lower cost. Differentiation strategy involves providing a product or service that is distinct in some important respect valued by the customer. For example, in retailing, Nordstrom has succeeded on the basis of differentiation by emphasizing exceptionally high customer service. In contrast, Filene's Basement Stores is a discount retailer competing purely on a low-cost basis.

Competitive Strategy 1: Cost Leadership

Cost leadership is often the clearest way to achieve competitive advantage. In industries where the basic product or service is a commodity, cost leadership might be the only way to achieve superior performance. There are many ways to achieve cost leadership, including economies of scale and scope, economies of learning, efficient production, simpler product design, lower input costs, and efficient organizational processes. If a firm can achieve cost leadership, then it will be able to earn above-average profitability by merely charging the same price as its rivals. Conversely, a cost leader can force its competitors to cut prices and accept lower returns, or to exit the industry.

Firms that achieve cost leadership focus on tight cost controls. They make investments in efficient scale plants, focus on product designs that reduce manufacturing costs, minimize overhead costs, make little investment in risky research and development, and avoid serving marginal customers. They have organizational structures and control systems that focus on cost control.

Competitive Strategy 2: Differentiation

A firm following the differentiation strategy seeks to be unique in its industry along some dimension that is highly valued by customers. For differentiation to be successful, the firm has to accomplish three things. First, it needs to identify one or more attributes of a product or service that customers value. Second, it has to position itself to meet the chosen customer need in a unique manner. Finally, the firm has to achieve differentiation at a cost that is lower than the price the customer is willing to pay for the differentiated product or service.

Drivers of differentiation include providing superior intrinsic value via product quality, product variety, bundled services, or delivery timing. Differentiation can also be achieved by investing in signals of value, such as brand image, product appearance, or reputation. Differentiated strategies require investments in research and development, engineering skills, and marketing capabilities. The organizational structures and control systems in firms with differentiation strategies need to foster creativity and innovation.

While successful firms choose between cost leadership and differentiation, they cannot completely ignore the dimension on which they are not primarily competing. Firms that target differentiation still need to focus on costs, so that the differentiation can be achieved at an acceptable cost. Similarly, cost leaders cannot compete unless they achieve at least a minimum level on key dimensions on which competitors might differentiate, such as quality and service.

ACHIEVING AND SUSTAINING COMPETITIVE ADVANTAGE

The choice of competitive strategy does not automatically lead to the achievement of competitive advantage. To achieve competitive advantage, the firm has to have the capabilities needed to implement and sustain the chosen strategy. Both cost leadership and differentiation strategy require that the firm make the necessary commitments to acquire the core competencies needed, and structure its value chain in an appropriate way. Core competencies are the economic assets that the firm possesses, whereas the value chain is the set of activities that the firm performs to convert inputs into outputs. The uniqueness of a firm's core competencies and its value chain and the extent to which it is difficult for competitors to imitate them determines the sustainability of a firm's competitive advantage.[11]

To evaluate whether or not a firm is likely to achieve its intended competitive advantage, the analyst should ask the following questions:

- What are the key success factors and risks associated with the firm's chosen competitive strategy?
- Does the firm currently have the resources and capabilities to deal with the key success factors and risks?
- Has the firm made irreversible commitments to bridge the gap between its current capabilities and the requirements to achieve its competitive advantage?
- Has the firm structured its activities (such as research and development, design, manufacturing, marketing and distribution, and support activities) in a way that is consistent with its competitive strategy?
- Is the company's competitive advantage sustainable? Are there any barriers that make imitation of the firm's strategy difficult?
- Are there any potential changes in the firm's industry structure (such as new technologies, foreign competition, changes in regulation, changes in customer requirements) that might dissipate the firm's competitive advantage? Is the company flexible enough to address these changes?

APPLYING COMPETITIVE STRATEGY ANALYSIS

Let us consider the concepts of competitive strategy analysis in the context of Dell Computer Corporation. In 1998 Round Rock, Texas-based Dell Computer was the fourth largest computer maker, behind IBM, Hewlett-Packard, and Compaq. The company, founded by Michael Dell in his University of Texas dorm room, started selling "IBM clone" personal computers in 1984. From the beginning, Dell sold its machines directly to end users, rather than through retail outlets, at a significantly lower price than its competitors.

After rapid growth and some management hiccups, Dell firmly established itself in the personal computer industry by following a low cost strategy. By 1998 Dell achieved $18 billion in revenues and $1.5 billion in net income. Dell's growth rates over the previous three years were extraordinary: 51 percent growth in revenues, and 78 percent growth in net income. Dell's stellar performance made it one of the most profitable personal computer makers in a highly competitive industry. How did Dell achieve such performance?

Dell's superior performance was based on a low-cost competitive strategy that consisted of the following key elements:

- *Direct selling*. Dell sold most of its computers directly to its customers, thus saving on retail markups. As computer users become sophisticated, and as computers become standardized on the Windows-Intel platform, the value of distribution through retailers declines. Dell was the first company to capitalize on this trend. In 1996 Dell began selling computers through its Internet web site. By 1999 the company was generating several million dollars of sales per day through the Internet.
- *Made-to-order manufacturing*. Dell developed a system of flexible manufacturing that allowed the company to assemble and ship computers very quickly, usually within five days of receiving an order. This allowed the company to avoid large inventories of parts and assembled computers. Low inventories allowed Dell to save working capital costs; it also reduced costly write-offs of obsolete inventories, a significant risk in the fast-changing computer industry.
- *Third-party service*. Dell used two low-cost approaches to after-sales service: telephone-based service and third-party maintenance service. Dell had several hundred technical support representatives accessible to the customers by phone any time of the day. Using a comprehensive electronic maintenance system, the service representatives could diagnose and help the customer to resolve problems in the vast majority of cases. In the rare case where on-site maintenance was required, Dell used third-party maintenance contracts with office equipment companies such as Xerox. Through this service strategy, Dell was able to avoid investing in an expensive field service network without compromising on service quality.
- *Low accounts receivable*. Dell was able to reduce its accounts receivable days to an industry minimum by encouraging its customers to pay by credit card at the time of the purchase, or through electronic payment immediately after the purchase.

- *Focused investment in R&D.* Dell recognized that most of the basic innovations in the personal computer industry were led by the component suppliers and software producers. For example, Intel and Microsoft, two key suppliers, invested billions of dollars in developing new generation processors and software, respectively. Dell's innovations were primarily in creating a low-cost, high-velocity organization that can respond quickly to these changes. By focusing its R&D innovations, Dell was able to minimize these costs and get high return on its investments.

As a result of the above strategy, Dell achieved a significant cost advantage over its competitors in the personal computer industry. This advantage resulted in a consistent pattern of rapid growth, increasing market share, and very high profitability in an industry that is characterized by rapid technological changes, significant supplier and buyer power, and intense competition. Further, because the strategy involved activities that are highly interrelated and involved continuous organizational innovations, Dell's business model was difficult to replicate, making Dell's competitive advantage sustainable. In fact, Dell's success inspired several of its competitors, including Compaq and IBM, to attempt to replicate parts of its strategy. However, no competitor to date has been able to replicate Dell's business model. The extraordinarily high earnings and book value multiples at which Dell's stock has been trading in recent years is evidence that investors are betting that Dell's competitive advantage and its superior profit performance is likely to be sustained for the foreseeable future.

CORPORATE STRATEGY ANALYSIS

So far in this chapter, we have focused on the strategies at the individual business level. While some companies focus on only one business, many companies operate in multiple businesses. For example, the average number of business segments operated by the top 500 U.S. companies in 1992 is eleven industries.[12] In recent years, there has been an attempt by U.S. companies to reduce the diversity of their operations and focus on a relatively few "core" businesses. However, multibusiness organizations continue to dominate the economic activity in most countries in the world.

When analyzing a multibusiness organization, an analyst has to not only evaluate the industries and strategies of the individual business units but also the economic consequences—either positive or negative—of managing all the different businesses under one corporate umbrella. For example, General Electric has been very successful in creating significant value by managing a highly diversified set of businesses ranging from aircraft engines to light bulbs, but Sears has not been very successful in managing retailing together with financial services.

Sources of Value Creation at the Corporate Level

Economists and strategy researchers have identified several factors that influence an organization's ability to create value through a broad corporate scope. Economic theory suggests that the optimal activity scope of a firm depends on the relative transaction cost of performing a set of activities inside the firm versus using the market mechanism.[13] Transaction cost economics implies that the multiproduct firm is an efficient choice of organizational form when coordination among independent, focused firms is costly due to market transaction costs.

Transaction costs can arise out of several sources. They may arise if the production process involves specialized assets, such as human capital skills, proprietary technology, or other organizational know-how that is not easily available in the marketplace. Transaction costs also may arise from market imperfections such as information and incentive problems. If buyers and sellers cannot solve these problems through standard mechanisms such as enforceable contracts, it will be costly to conduct transactions through market mechanisms.

For example, as discussed in Chapter 1, public capital markets may not work well when there are significant information and incentive problems, making it difficult for entrepreneurs to raise capital from investors. Similarly, if buyers cannot ascertain the quality of products being sold because of lack of information, or cannot enforce warranties because of poor legal infrastructure, entrepreneurs will find it difficult to break into new markets. Finally, if employers cannot assess the quality of applicants for new positions, they will have to rely more on internal promotions, rather than external recruiting, to fill higher positions in an organization. Emerging economies often suffer from these types of transaction costs because of poorly developed intermediation infrastructure.[14] Even in many advanced economies, examples of high transaction costs can be found. For example, in many countries other than the U.S., the venture capital industry is not highly developed, making it costly for new businesses in high technology industries to attract financing. Even in the U.S., transaction costs may vary across economic sectors. For example, until recently electronic commerce was hampered by consumer concerns regarding the security of credit card information sent over the Internet.

Transactions inside an organization may be less costly than market-based transactions for several reasons. First, communication costs inside an organization are reduced because confidentiality can be protected and credibility can be assured through internal mechanisms. Second, the headquarters office can play a critical role in reducing costs of enforcing agreements between organizational subunits. Third, organizational subunits can share valuable nontradable assets (such as organizational skills, systems, and processes) or nondivisible assets (such as brand names, distribution channels, and reputation).

There are also forces that increase transaction costs inside organizations. Top management of an organization may lack the specialized information and skills necessary to manage businesses across several different industries. This lack of expertise reduces the possibility of realizing economies of scope in reality, even when there is potential for such economies. This problem can be remedied by creating a decentralized organization, hiring specialist managers to run each business unit, and providing them with proper incentives. However, decentralization will also potentially decrease goal congruence among subunit managers, making it difficult to realize economies of scope.

Whether or not a multibusiness organization creates more value than a comparable collection of focused firms is, therefore, context dependent.[15] Analysts should ask the following questions to assess whether or not an organization's corporate strategy has the potential to create value:

- Are there significant imperfections in the product, labor, or financial markets in the industries (or countries) in which a company is operating? Is it likely that transaction costs in these markets are higher than the costs of similar activities inside a well managed organization?
- Does the organization have special resources such as brand names, proprietary know-how, access to scarce distribution channels, and special organizational processes that have the potential to create economies of scope?
- Is there a good fit between the company's specialized resources and the portfolio of businesses in which the company is operating?
- Does the company allocate decision rights between the headquarters office and the business units optimally to realize all the potential economies of scope?
- Does the company have internal measurement, information, and incentive systems to reduce agency costs and increase coordination across business units?

Empirical evidence suggests that creating value through a multibusiness corporate strategy is hard in practice. Several researchers have documented that diversified U.S. companies trade at a discount in the stock market relative to a comparable portfolio of focused companies.[16] Studies also show that acquisitions of one company by another, especially when the two are in unrelated businesses, often fail to create value for the acquiring companies.[17] Finally, there is considerable evidence that value is created when multibusiness companies increase corporate focus through divisional spinoffs and asset sales.[18]

There are several potential explanations for the above diversification discount. First, managers' decisions to diversify and expand are frequently driven by a desire to maximize the size of their organization rather than to maximize shareholder value. Second, diversified companies suffer from agency problems leading to suboptimal investment decisions and poor operating performance. Third, capital markets find it difficult to monitor and value multibusiness organizations because of inadequate disclosure about the performance of individual business segments.

In summary, while companies can theoretically create value through innovative corporate strategies, there are many ways in which this potential fails to get realized in practice. Therefore, it pays to be skeptical when evaluating companies' corporate strategies.

Applying Corporate Strategy Analysis

Let us apply the concepts of corporate strategy analysis to Amazon.com, a pioneer in electronic commerce. Amazon started operations as an online bookseller in 1995 and went public in 1997 with a market capitalization of $561 million dollars. The company grew rapidly and began to pose a serious threat to the dominance of leading traditional booksellers like Barnes & Noble. Investors rewarded Amazon by increasing its market capitalization to a remarkable $36 billion dollars by April 1999.

Flush with his success in online book-selling, Jeff Bezos, the founder and chief executive officer of Amazon, moved the company into many other areas of electronic commerce. Amazon claimed that its brand, its loyal customer base, and its ability to execute electronic commerce were valuable assets that can be exploited in a number of other online business areas. Beginning in 1998, through a series of acquisitions, Amazon expanded into online selling of CDs, videos, gifts, pharmaceutical drugs, pet supplies, and groceries. In April 1999, Amazon announced plans to diversify into the online auction business by acquiring LiveBid.com. Bezos explained, "We are not a book company. We're not a music company. We're not a video company. We're not an auctions company. We're a customer company."[19]

Amazon's rapid expansion attracted controversy among the investment community. Some analysts argued that Amazon could create value through its broad corporate focus because of the following reasons:

- Amazon has established a valuable brand name on the Internet. Given that electronic commerce is a relatively new phenomenon, customers are likely to rely on well known brands to reduce the risk of a bad shopping experience. Amazon's expansion strategy is sensible because it exploits this valuable resource.
- Amazon has been able to acquire critical expertise in flawless execution of electronic retailing. This is a general competency that can be exploited in many areas of electronic retailing.
- Amazon has been able to create a tremendous amount of loyalty among its customers through superior marketing and execution. As a result, a very high proportion of Amazon's sales comes from repeat purchases by its customers. Amazon's strategy exploits this valuable customer base.

There were also some skeptics who believed that Amazon was expanding too rapidly, and that its diversification beyond book retailing was likely to fail. These skeptics questioned the value of Amazon's brand name. They argued that traditional retailers, such as Barnes & Noble, Wal-Mart, and CVS, who are boosting their online efforts, also have valuable brand names, execution capabilities, and customer loyalty. Therefore, these companies are likely to offer formidable competition to Amazon's individual business lines. Amazon's critics also pointed out that expanding rapidly into so many different areas is likely to confuse customers, dilute Amazon's brand value, and increase the chance of poor execution. Commenting on the fact that Amazon is losing money in all of its businesses while it is expanding rapidly, *Barron's* business weekly stated, "Increasingly, Amazon's strategy is looking like the dim-bulb businessman who loses money on every sale but tries to make it up by making more sales."[20]

Investor concerns about Amazon's corporate strategy began to affect its share price, which dropped from a high of $221 dollars in April 1999 to $118 dollars by the end of May 1999. Still, at a total market capitalization of about $19 billion dollars, many investors are betting that Amazon's corporate strategy is likely to yield rich dividends in the future.

SUMMARY

Strategy analysis is an important starting point for the analysis of financial statements because it allows the analyst to probe the economics of the firm at a qualitative level. Strategy analysis also allows the identification of the firm's profit drivers and key risks, enabling the analyst to assess the sustainability of the firm's performance and make realistic forecasts of future performance.

Whether or not a firm is able to earn a return on its capital in excess of its cost of capital is determined by its own strategic choices: (1) the choice of an industry or a set of industries in which the firm operates (industry choice), (2) the manner in which the firm intends to compete with other firms in its chosen industry or industries (competitive positioning), and (3) the way in which the firm expects to create and exploit synergies across the range of businesses in which it operates (corporate strategy). Strategy analysis involves analyzing all three choices.

Industry analysis consists of identifying the economic factors which drive the industry profitability. In general, an industry's average profit potential is influenced by the degree of rivalry among existing competitors, the ease with which new firms can enter the industry, the availability of substitute products, the power of buyers, and the power of suppliers. To perform industry analysis, the analyst has to assess the current strength of each of these forces in an industry and make forecasts of any likely future changes.

Competitive strategy analysis involves identifying the basis on which the firm intends to compete in its industry. In general, there are two potential strategies that could provide a firm with a competitive advantage: cost leadership and differentiation. Cost leadership involves offering the same product or service that other firms offer at a lower cost. Differentiation involves satisfying a chosen dimension of customer need better than the competition, at an incremental cost that is less than the price premium that customers are willing to pay. To perform strategy analysis, the analyst has to identify the firm's intended strategy, assess whether or not the firm possesses the competencies required to execute the strategy, and recognize the key risks that the firm has to guard against. The analyst also has to evaluate the sustainability of the firm's strategy.

Corporate strategy analysis involves examining whether a company is able to create value by being in multiple businesses at the same time. A well-crafted corporate strategy reduces costs or increases revenues from running several businesses in one firm relative to operating the same businesses independently and transacting with each other in the marketplace. These cost savings or revenue increases come from specialized resources that the firm has to exploit synergies across these businesses. For these resources to be valuable, they must be nontradable, not easily imitated by competition, and nondivisible. Even when a firm has such resources, it can create value through a multibusiness organization only when it is managed so that the information and agency costs inside the organization are smaller than the market transaction costs.

The insights gained from strategy analysis can be useful in performing the remainder of the financial statement analysis. In accounting analysis, the analyst can examine whether a firm's accounting policies and estimates are consistent with its stated strategy. For example, a firm's choice of functional currency in accounting for its international operations should be consistent with the level of integration between domestic and international operations that the business strategy calls for. Similarly, a firm that mainly sells housing to low-income customers should have higher bad debts expenses.

Strategy analysis is also useful in guiding financial analysis. For example, in a cross-sectional analysis the analyst should expect firms with cost leadership strategy to have lower gross margins and higher asset turnover than firms that follow differentiated strategies. In a time series analysis, the analyst should closely monitor any increases in expense ratios and asset turnover ratios for low-cost firms, and any decreases in investments critical to differentiation for firms that follow differentiation strategy.

Business strategy analysis also helps in prospective analysis and valuation. First, it allows the analyst to assess whether, and for how long, differences between the firm's performance and its industry (or industries) performance are likely to persist. Second, strategy analysis facilitates forecasting investment outlays the firm has to make to maintain its competitive advantage.

DISCUSSION QUESTIONS

1. Judith, an accounting major, states, "Strategy analysis seems to be an unnecessary detour in doing financial statement analysis. Why can't we just get straight to the accounting issues?" Explain to Judith why she might be wrong?
2. What are the critical drivers of industry profitability?
3. One of the fastest growing industries in the last twenty years is the memory chip industry, which supplies memory chips for personal computers and other electronic devices. Yet the average profitability for this industry has been very low. Using the industry analysis framework, list all the potential factors that might explain this apparent contradiction.

4. Rate the pharmaceutical and lumber industries as high, medium, or low on the following dimensions of industry structure:

	Pharmaceutical Industry	Lumber Industry
Rivalry		
Threat of new entrants		
Threat of substitute products		
Bargaining power of buyers		
Bargaining power of suppliers		

Given your ratings, which industry would you expect to earn the highest returns?

5. Joe Smith argues, "Your analysis of the five forces that affect industry profitability is incomplete. For example, in the banking industry, I can think of at least three other factors that are also important; namely, government regulation, demographic trends, and cultural factors." His classmate Jane Brown disagrees and says, "These three factors are important only to the extent that they influence one of the five forces." Explain how, if at all, the three factors discussed by Joe affect the five forces in the banking industry.

6. Coca-Cola and Pepsi are both very profitable soft drinks. Inputs for these products include sugar, bottles/cans, and soft drink syrup. Coca-Cola and Pepsi produce the syrup themselves and purchase the other inputs. They then enter into exclusive contracts with independent bottlers to produce their products. Use the five forces framework and your knowledge of the soft drink industry to explain how Coca-Cola and Pepsi are able to retain most of the profits in this industry.

7. In the early 1980s, United, Delta, and American Airlines each started frequent flier programs as a way to differentiate themselves in response to excess capacity in the industry. Many industry analysts, however, believe that this move had only mixed success. Use the competitive advantage concepts to explain why.

8. What are the ways that a firm can use to create barriers to entry to deter competition in its business? What factors determine whether these barriers are likely to be enduring?

9. Explain why you agree or disagree with each of the following statements:
   a. It's better to be a differentiator than a cost leader, since you can then charge premium prices.
   b. It's more profitable to be in a high technology than a low technology industry.
   c. The reason why industries with large investments have high barriers to entry is because it is costly to raise capital.

10. There are very few companies that are able to be both cost leaders and differentiators. Why? Can you think of a company that has been successful at both?

11. Many consultants are advising diversified companies in emerging markets, such as India, Korea, Mexico, and Turkey, to adopt corporate strategies proven to be of val-

ue in advanced economies, like the U.S. and the U.K. What are the pros and cons of this advice?

NOTES

1. The discussion presented here is intended to provide a basic background in strategy analysis. For a more complete discussion of the strategy concepts, see, for example, *Contemporary Strategy Analysis* by Robert M. Grant (Cambridge, MA: Blackwell Publishers, 1991); *Economics of Strategy* by David Besanko, David Dranove, and Mark Shanley (New York: John Wiley & Sons, 1996); *Strategy and the Business Landscape* by Pankaj Ghemawat (Reading, MA: Addison Wesley Longman, 1999); and *Corporate Strategy: Resources and the Scope of the Firm* by David J. Collis and Cynthia Montgomery (Burr Ridge, IL: Irwin/McGraw-Hill, 1997).

2. These data are taken from "Do Competitors Perform Better When They Pursue Different Strategies?" by Anita M. McGahan (Boston: Harvard Business School, working paper, May 12, 1999).

3. For a summary of this research, see *Industrial Market Structure and Economic Performance*, second edition, by F. M. Scherer (Chicago: Rand McNally College Publishing Co., 1980).

4. See *Competitive Strategy* by Michael E. Porter (New York: The Free Press, 1980).

5. The four-firm concentration ratio is a commonly used measure of industry concentration; it refers to the market share of the four largest firms in an industry.

6. While the discussion here uses the buyer to connote industrial buyers, the same concepts also apply to buyers of consumer products. Throughout this chapter, we use the terms buyers and customers interchangeably.

7. The data on Dell and the personal computer (PC) industry discussed here and elsewhere in this chapter is drawn from "Dell Computer Corporation" by Das Narayandas and V. Kasturi Rangan (Boston: Harvard Business School Publishing Division, 9-596-058) and "Dell Online" by V. Kasturi Rangan and Marie Bell (Boston: Harvard Business School Publishing Division, 9-598-116).

8. For a more detailed discussion of these two sources of competitive advantage, see Michael E. Porter, *Competitive Advantage: Creating and Sustaining Superior Performance* (New York: The Free Press, 1985).

9. Ibid.

10. In recent years, one of the strategic challenges faced by corporations is having to deal with competitors who achieve differentiation with low cost. For example, Japanese auto manufacturers have successfully demonstrated that there is no necessary trade-off between quality and cost. Similarly, in recent years several highly successful retailers like Wal-Mart and Home Depot have been able to combine high quality, high service, and low prices. These examples suggest that combining low cost and differentiation strategies is possible when a firm introduces a significant technical or business innovation. However, such cost advantage and differentiation will be sustainable only if there are significant barriers to imitation by competitors.

11. See *Competing for the Future* by Gary Hammel and C. K. Prahalad (Boston: Harvard Business School Press, 1994) for a more detailed discussion of the concept of core competencies and their critical role in corporate strategy.

12. Cynthia Montgomery, "Corporate Diversification," *Journal of Economic Perspectives*, Summer 1994.

13. The following works are seminal to the transaction cost economics: "The Nature of the Firm" by Ronald Coase, *Economica* 4, 1937: 386–405; "Markets and Hierarchies: Analysis and Antitrust Implications" by Oliver Williamson (New York: The Free Press, 1975); "Toward an Economic Theory of the Multi-product Firm" by David Teece, J*ournal of Economic Behavior and Organization* 3, 1982: 39–63.

14. For a more complete discussion of these issues, see "Building Institutional Infrastructure in Emerging Markets" by Krishna Palepu and Tarun Khanna, *Brown Journal of World Affairs*, Winter/Spring 1998, and "Why Focused Strategies May Be Wrong for Emerging Markets," by Tarun Khanna and Krishna Palepu, *Harvard Business Review*, July/August, 1997.

15. For an empirical study which illustrates this point, see "Is Group Affiliation Profitable in Emerging Markets? An Analysis of Diversified Indian Business Groups," by Tarun Khanna and Krishna Palepu, *Journal of Finance*, forthcoming.

16. See "Tobin's q, diversification, and firm performance" by Larry Lang and Rene Stulz, *Journal of Political Economy* 102: 1248–1280, and "Diversification's Effect on Firm Value" by Phillip Berger and Eli Ofek, *Journal of Financial Economics* 37: 39–65.

17. See "Which Takeovers are Profitable: Strategic or Financial?" by Paul Healy, Krishna Palepu, and Richard Ruback, *Sloan Management Review,* 1996.

18. See "Effects of Recontracting on Shareholder Wealth: The Case of Voluntary Spinoffs" by Katherine Schipper and Abbie Smith, *Journal of Financial Economics* 12: 437–467; "Asset Sales, Firm Performance, and the Agency Costs of Managerial Discretion" by L. Lang, A. Poulsen, and R. Stulz, *Journal of Financial Economics* 37: 3–37.

19. "eBay vs. Amazon.com," *Business Week,* May 31, 1999.

20. "Amazon.Bomb" by Jacqueline Doherty, *Barron's*, May 31, 1999.

*W*hen it comes to technology companies, the stock market's current
mania, it's hard to top America Online, Inc. Technology stocks are hot, up about
50 percent on average this year, but AOL is positively scalding, up about 135 percent. In fact, AOL's stock has soared more than 2,000 percent from its initial public
offering, in 1992. The Vienna-based company has 35 times the customers and 20
times the revenue it had five years ago. It's the nation's biggest on-line company
and is building a recognized brand.

But look closely and you see that AOL is as much about accounting technology
as it is about computer technology. So make sure you understand the numbers before rushing out to buy AOL, which is valued at about $4 billion.

The above report written by Allan Sloan appeared on October 24, 1995, in *Newsweek*'s business section.[1]

COMPANY BACKGROUND

Founded in Vienna, VA, America Online, Inc. (AOL) was a leader in the development of
a new mass medium that encompassed online services, the Internet, multimedia, and other interactive technologies. Through its America Online service the company offered
members a broad range of features including real-time talk, electronic mail, electronic
magazines and newspapers, online classes and shopping, and Internet access. In addition
to its online service, AOL's business had expanded during 1995 to include access software for the Internet, production and distribution of original content, interactive marketing and transactions capabilities, and networks to support the transmission of data.

AOL generated revenues principally from consumers through membership fees, as
well as from content providers and merchandisers through advertising, commissions on
merchandise sales and other transactions, and from other businesses through the sale of
network and production services. Through continued investment in the growth of its existing online service, the pursuit of related business opportunities, its ability to provide

....

This case was prepared by Professors Krishna Palepu and Amy Hutton as the basis for class discussion rather than to
illustrate either effective or ineffective handling of an administrative situation. Copyright © 1996 by the President and
Fellows of Harvard College. Harvard Business School case 9-196-130.

1. "Look Beyond the High-Tech Accounting To Measure America Online's Market Risk," Allan Sloan, Newsweek, October 24, 1995.

a full range of interactive services, and its technological flexibility, the company positioned itself to lead the development of the evolving mass medium for interactive services.

Stephen Case and James Kimsey founded America Online's predecessor, Quantum Computer Services, in 1985. Quantum offered its Q-Link service for Commodore computers. In 1989, the service was extended to Apple computers. The company changed its name to America Online in 1991 and went public in 1992. That same year, AOL licensed its on-line technology to Apple for use in eWorld and NewtonMail services for which AOL continues to receive a usage-based royalty. In 1993, the company expanded its market with a Windows version of its software and began developing a version for palmtop computer. In 1994, AOL's subscription base surpassed those of CompuServe and Prodigy, two rival online service providers, making AOL the number one consumer online service in the United States. By the end of October 1995, AOL had a subscriber base of more than four million members.

AOL's Products

The broad range of features offered by the America Online service was designed to meet the varied needs of its four million members. A key feature of the online service was the ease with which members with related interests could communicate through real-time conferences, e-mail, and bulletin boards. Members used the interactive communications facilities to share information and ideas, exchange advice, and socialize. It was America Online's goal to continue developing and adding new sources of information and content in support of these member activities. The range of features offered by America Online included the following:

- *Online Community*. In addition to its e-mail service, AOL promoted real-time online communications by scheduling conferences and discussions on specific topics, offering interactive areas that served as "meeting rooms" for members to participate in lively interactive discussions with other members, and providing public bulletin boards on which members could share information and opinions on subjects of general or specialized interest.
- *Computing*. AOL provided its members access to tens of thousands of public domain and "shareware" software programs, to online help from 300 hardware and software developers, and to online computer shopping and online computer magazines such as *MacWorld*, *PC World,* and *Computer Life.*
- *Education and References*. AOL's online educational services allowed adults and children to learn without leaving their homes. AOL contracted with professional instructors to teach real-time interactive classes in subjects of both general academic interest and adult education (such as creative writing and gourmet cooking). Regular tutoring sessions were offered in English, biology, and math. Education and reference services included the Library of Congress, College Board, CNN, Smithsonian, *Consumer Reports*, and *Compton's Encyclopedia.*

- *News and Personal Finance.* AOL offered a broad range of information services, including domestic and international news, weather, sports, stock market prices, and personalized portfolio tracking. Members could search news wires for stories of interest, access mutual fund information through Fidelity Online and Morningstar, and execute brokered trades online through PC Financial Network. Subscribers had access to over 70 newspapers, periodicals, and wire services, including *The New York Times, Chicago Tribune, San Jose Mercury News, Time, Scientific American, Investors Business Daily,* and Reuters.
- *Travel and Shopping.* AOL members also had access to travel and shopping reference materials and transaction services. Subscribers could send customized greeting cards through Hallmark Corporation, send flowers through 1-800-Flowers, shop for CDs and tapes online at Tower Records, book vacation packages with Preview Vacations, and access account data and travel information and services with American ExpressNet. Additionally, AOL had introduced its own interactive shopping service, 2Market, which featured goods and services from numerous catalogs and retailers.
- *Entertainment and Children's Programming.* AOL provided various clubs and forums for games and sports, multi-player games, and other related content for both adults and children. Specialized content was provided by such organizations as MusicSpace, the Games Channel, Disney Adventures, Comedy Clubs, Nintendo Power Source, Kids Only, Hollywood Online, Warner-Reprise Records, American Association for Retired Persons, MTV, Cooking Club, Environment Club, and Baby Boomers' Forum.

Customer Acquisition and Retention

AOL's biggest expenditure was the cost of attracting new subscribers. AOL aggressively marketed its online service using both independent marketing efforts, such as direct mail packets with AOL software disks and television and print advertising featuring a toll-free telephone number for ordering the AOL software, as well as co-marketing efforts with computer magazine publishers and personal computer hardware and software producers. These companies bundled the AOL software with their computer products, facilitating easy trial use by their customers. With the AOL software in hand, the customer needed only a personal computer, a telephone line, and a computer modem to gain access to AOL's online service. Accompanying each program disk was a unique registration number and password that could be used to generate a new AOL account. Customers could activate their accounts by providing AOL with their credit card account number. The first ten hours of access by this new account were free, after which AOL automatically billed the customer's credit card account the standard monthly rate until the customer canceled the AOL account.

These types of promotions were expensive, costing more than $40 per new subscriber in 1994. Thus, to retain these new subscribers and increase customer loyalty and satisfaction, AOL invested in specialized retention programs including regularly scheduled online events and conferences, online promotions of upcoming events and new features, and the regular addition of new content, services, and software programs. AOL's goal was to maximize customer subscription life.

Critical to customer retention and usage rates was the content available on AOL. To build and create unique content America Online participated in numerous joint ventures. During 1995 its alliances grew to include American Express, ABC, Reuters, Shoppers Express, Business Week, Fidelity, Vanguard, and the National Education Association. Also important to AOL were the newest stars of cyberspace, special-interest sites created by entrepreneurs such as Tom and David Gardner, who created Motley Fool and Follywood, two of the most popular sites offered on America Online. These hot special-interest sites kept customers on line, running up metered time and revenues. Traditionally, AOL had kept 80 percent or more of the revenues generated by these sites and had demanded exclusive contracts with the entrepreneurs creating them. However, content providers now had the option of setting up sites on the Internet World Wide Web. While they could not yet collect fees from Web browsers, this new distribution channel was changing the balance of power between AOL and its content providers.[2]

Compared to its competitors, AOL's rate structure was the easiest for consumers to understand and anticipate. A monthly fee of $9.95 provided access to all of America Online's services for up to five hours each month. Each additional hour was $2.95 and no additional downloading fees were charged. CompuServe and Prodigy offered the same standard pricing but charged additional fees for premium services and downloading. Microsoft Network (MSN), the newest entrant into the online services industry, offered a standard monthly plan of up to three hours for $4.95, with each additional hour costing $2.50. Content providers on MSN also applied charges to customers based on usage rates. The additional fees charged by AOL's competitors made it more difficult for their customers to anticipate their monthly spending.

Strategy for Future Growth

Through a tapestry of alliances and subsidiaries AOL's goal was to establish a central and defining leadership position in the worldwide market for interactive services. Toward this end, AOL had signed new strategic partnerships with American Express, Business Week Online, and NTN Communications; shipped the 2Market CD-ROM shopping service with an online connection; and completed its acquisitions of Internet software developers BookLink Technologies, Inc., NaviSoft, Inc., and Internet backbone developer Advanced Network & Services (ANS). These deals, along with AOL's growing membership base, its enhanced look and feel, and its ability to program content to appeal to users, uniquely positioned America Online to lead the development of the new interactive services industry. In implementing its strategy, AOL pursued a number of initiatives:

2. "On-Line Stars Hear Siren Calls to Free Agency," Steven Lohr, New York Times, November 25, 1995.

- *Invest in Growth of Existing Service.* America Online planned to continue to invest in the rapid growth of its existing online service. AOL believed it could attract and retain new members by expanding the range of content and services it offers, continuing to improve the engaging multimedia context of its service and building a sense of community online. At the same time, by offering access to a large, growing, and demographically attractive audience, together with software tools and services to develop content and programming for that audience, AOL believed it would continue to appeal to content and service providers.
- *Exploit New Business Opportunities.* AOL intended to leverage its technology, management skills, and content packaging skills to identify and exploit new business opportunities, such as electronic commerce, entry into international markets, and the "consumerization" of the Internet with its highly graphical interface software and its World Wide Web browser, which used high-speed compression technology to improve access speed and graphic display performance.
- *Provide a Full Range of Interactive Services.* Through acquisitions and internal development, AOL had assembled content development, distribution capabilities, access software, and its own communications network to become a full service, vertically integrated provider of interactive services. As a result, AOL believed it was well positioned to influence the evolution of the interactive services market.
- *Maintain Technological Flexibility.* AOL recognized the need to provide its services over a diverse set of platforms. Its software worked on different types of personal computers and operating systems (including Macintosh, Windows 3.xx and Windows 95) and supported a variety of different media, including online services, the Internet, and CD-ROM. AOL intended to adapt its products and services as new technologies become available.

While AOL currently generated revenues largely from membership fees, AOL's management believed that these initiatives would allow the company to increase the proportion of its revenues generated from other sources, such as advertising fees, commissions on merchandise sales to consumers, and revenues from the sale of production and network services to other enterprises.

INDUSTRY COMPETITION AND OUTLOOK

The online consumer services industry represented $1.1 billion in revenues in 1994 and was expected to grow by 30 percent to $1.4 billion in 1995. Eleven million customers subscribed to commercial online services worldwide and this number was expected to explode in the next five years. Industry leaders America Online, CompuServe, and Prodigy served about 8.5 million of the existing subscribers (4.0 million, 2.8 million, and 1.6 million, respectively). This oligopoly had very successfully acted as middlemen between thousands of content providers and millions of customers. They were the publishers, closely controlling the product and paying content providers, the writers, only modest royalties. However, with the advent of the Internet World Wide Web and the entrance of Microsoft Network, content providers now had alternative distribution channels which offered greater control over their products and potentially higher revenues.

Forbes discussed this topic in its August 28, 1995 issue:

> *Until recently the only way to reach cyberspace browsers was through one of the big three on-line services, America Online, CompuServe and Prodigy. That oligopoly is set to fade fast, and it's not just Microsoft that threatens. It's the whole Internet, the pulsating, undisciplined and rapidly expanding network of World Wide Web computers that contain public data bases.[3]*

While the big three acted as publishers, Microsoft had decided to act more like a bookstore, one in which every author (content provider) was his/her own publisher. Customers of MSN paid $4.95 per month for up to three hours (each additional hour was $2.50). Then, each content provider charged whatever it wanted for its material, so much per hour, per page, or per picture. Microsoft kept a 30 percent commission out of the provider's fee and passed along the rest to the content provider. In addition to offering content providers a larger share of the revenues, MSN also offered content providers greater control over their own products. In contrast to the standardized screen displays and icons of the big three, MSN permitted content providers to use any font and format they wished. Thus, while Microsoft still acted as a middleman, it played a very limited and passive role in determining content and fees charged for that content.

Beyond Microsoft lurked the vast potential of the Internet World Wide Web, where the middleman's role was shrunk still further. On the Internet, everyone with a computer was his/her own publisher. Customers would sign up for an Internet on-ramp service, of the sort offered by PST, Netcom, or MCI. Once on the net, the subscriber used browsing software like Netscape or Spyglass to roam the world's databases. While it remained difficult for self-publishers on the Internet to collect fees from browsers who read their pages, that was expected to change quickly as banks, Microsoft, and other intermediaries worked on systems to provide on-line currency.

Many content providers were beginning to take advantage of these alternative distribution channels. For example, *Wired* magazine, unwilling to settle for just 20 percent of the revenues from subscribers spending time on its pages on AOL, created HotWired on the Internet. Andrew Anker, chief technologist at *Wired*, believed that HotWired would soon be more lucrative than the America Online venture and he noted that on the Internet his firm had greater control of its own product. General Electric's NBC decided to switch from AOL to Microsoft Network. "While we had many users visiting us on America Online, we weren't making much revenue," explained Martin Yudkovitz, a senior vice-president at NBC.[4]

With the migration of proprietary services and content to Web sites, the unique offerings of the big three services were declining. However, the online services were still bet-

---

3. *"Who Needs the Middleman?," Nikhil Hutheesing,* Forbes, *August 28, 1995.*

4. *Ibid.*

ter for interactive communications with full-fledged message boards and live chat. The Web, on the other hand, was mainly a publication environment for reading. The question remained, what would be the role of online service providers in the future? Would they become just another Internet access provider with their own look and browsers or could they continue to offer something unique to users?

Some analysts were projecting that the U.S. online services market would grow 30–35 percent annually through the year 2000, and that the Internet market would grow even faster. These analysts expected America Online to retain about a 20 percent market share.[5] On the other hand, Forrester Research of Cambridge, Mass., predicted that the big three, America Online, CompuServe, and Prodigy, would continue to add subscribers only through 1997. After that, Forrester predicted, it would be all downhill for the big three.[6]

AOL'S RECENT PERFORMANCE

For the fourth quarter ended June 30, 1995, America Online announced that its earnings were $0.16, excluding $0.01 merger expenses and $0.02 amortization of goodwill. This was a significant improvement over 1994's fourth-quarter earnings, $0.02, and above analysts' estimate, $0.14. Service revenues surged to $139 million, versus analysts' estimate of $132 million, and total revenues rose to $152 million versus $40.4 in the fourth quarter of 1994. For the fiscal year ended June 30, 1995, AOL reported a loss of $33.6 million on revenues of $394 million compared with a profit of $2.5 million on revenues of $116 million a year earlier. New charges recorded for the first time in 1995 included $50.3 million for acquired R&D, $1.7 million amortization of goodwill, and $2.2 million in merger expenses. (See Exhibit 3, America Online's 1995 Abridged Annual Report.)

New subscriber momentum continued to be strong, increasing 233 percent year-over-year and adding 691,000 new net subscribers during the fourth quarter. All major metrics used by analysts to evaluate AOL's franchise and gauge the "health" of its rapidly growing subscriber base also improved during the quarter: projected retention rates rose to 41 months from 39 months; paid usage grew to 2.93 hours from 2.73, and projected lifetime revenues per subscriber increased to $714 from $667. (See Exhibit 2 for the history of America Online's User Metrics.) However, analysts were projecting lower gross margins in the future as subscribers continued to transition to higher-speed access and as AOL introduced a heavy-usage pricing plan in response to Microsoft's lower per-hour pricing.

On November 8, 1995, America Online announced its results for the first quarter of fiscal 1996 ended September 30, 1995. Even though revenues rose to $197.9 million from $56 million a year earlier, America Online reported a loss of $10.3 million com-

5. *"America Online, Inc. — Company Report,"* A. Pooley, *The Chicago Corporation, April 18, 1995.*

6. *Op. cit.,* Forbes, *August 28, 1995.*

pared with a profit of $1.5 million a year earlier. America Online took a $16.9 million charge to reflect research and development taking place at Ubique, a company it acquired on September 21, 1995, as well as to pay off other recently acquired assets. It took another charge of $1.7 million for amortization of goodwill. These charges were partially offset by AOL's decision to increase the period over which it amortized subscriber acquisition costs. Effective July 1, 1995, these costs would be amortized over 24 months rather than 12–18 months. The effect of the change in accounting estimates for the three months ended September 30, 1995, was to decrease the reported loss by $1.95 million. AOL also announced that it added 711,000 subscribers in the first quarter of 1996, bringing its total subscriber base to four million.[7]

America Online's stock price had been on the move since the company's initial public offering (IPO) in March 1992. The stock price appreciated from the IPO price of $2.90 to $7.31, $14.63, and $28.00 at calendar year end 1992, 1993, and 1994, respectively. At its current price of $81.63 (dated November 8, 1995), the company's market value was around $4.0 billion. (See Exhibit 1 for the stock price history of America Online, its equity beta, and additional market-based data.)

THE CONTROVERSY SURROUNDING AOL

America Online's stock was one of the most controversial of this period. Some analysts promoted the stock's potential for price appreciation, while others recommended selling the shares short to profit from a decline in price. Bulls saw America Online as part of a revolution in communication, like cellular phones and cable television in the early days. They considered AOL's graphical interface software, its high-speed Web browser, and Mr. Case's marketing genius (subscribership had quadrupled to over four million in a little over a year) to be major competitive advantages. Bears, on the other hand, anticipating new entrants competing in the online services industry and a migration of subscribers to the Internet, questioned whether AOL would continue to experience high growth in its subscriber base or be able to retain existing subscribers.

Shortsellers had sold around seven million America Online shares, betting that the stock's price would not go up forever. Shortsellers pointed to the recent hedging activities by Apple Computer to lock in profits on its 5.7 percent stake as an indication that AOL's stock was overvalued. Adding fuel to the shortsellers' fire, corporate insiders at AOL had sold some of their shareholdings. Between March 9 and March 15 of 1995, seventeen insiders sold approximately 200,000 shares, including the company founders, President Steven Case (25,000 shares for $2.1 million) and Chairman James Kimsey (40,000 shares for $3.3 million).[8]

....

7. "America Online Posts $10.3 Million Loss But Says Revenue Rose 250% in Quarter," *The Washington Post, Nov. 8, 1995.*

8. *As of August 15, 1995 all executive officers and directors as a group continued to own 3,729,547 shares, Steven Case owned 1,036,790 shares and James Kimsey owned 679,616 shares.*

Adding to the controversy, some analysts labeled AOL's accounting "aggressive." AOL amortized its software development costs over five years, a long time in the fast-changing, uncertain online services industry, and AOL capitalized subscriber acquisition costs when its number one competitor, CompuServe, did not. Furthermore, effective July 1, 1995, AOL extended the amortization period for its subscriber acquisition costs from about 15 months to 24 months. Given the uncertainties surrounding AOL's subscriber retention rates and revenue growth as competition emerged in the young industry, analysts questioned the wisdom of AOL's accounting decisions. The big risk AOL faced was that eventually customers could switch on-line services as frequently as they now move among long-distance carriers.

While America Online expensed the free trial expenses (i.e., those charges incurred from the ten free hours given away in the initial month), it capitalized the marketing costs associated with acquiring a customer including direct mail, advertising, start-up kits, and bundling costs. As indicated in its annual report, prior to July 1, 1995, the capitalization had occurred on two schedules depending on the acquisition method. Costs for subscribers acquired through direct marketing programs were amortized over a 12-month period. Costs for subscribers acquired through co-marketing efforts with personal computer producers and magazine publishers were amortized over an 18-month period, as these bundling campaigns had historically shown a longer response time. However, effective July 1, 1995, AOL increased the period over which it amortized subscriber acquisition costs to 24 months for both acquisition methods.

Defending AOL's accounting choices, Lennert Leader, the Chief Financial Officer of America Online, Inc., said that the company was following standard accounting procedures in matching the timing of expenses with the period over which the revenues would be received. He argued that the company's marketing and software development expenses produced customer accounts that last a long time. Thus, he said, it was appropriate to write off the costs over a period of years, even though AOL had spent the cash.[9]

However, some analysts raised red flags about AOL's accounting choices. As noted in the October 24, 1995 *Newsweek* article:

> *One of AOL's hidden assets is the brilliant accounting decision it made to treat its marketing and research and development costs as capital items rather than expenses. . . .*
>
> *AOL charges R&D expenses over a five-year period, a very long time in the on-line biz. In July, AOL began charging off marketing expenses over two years, up from about 15 months.*
>
> *Why change to 24 months from 15? Leader said it's because the average life of an AOL account has climbed to 41 months from 25 months in 1992. How many AOL customers have been around for 41 months? Almost none, as Leader concedes. That's understandable, considering that AOL has added virtually all its*

9. *Op. cit.*, Newsweek, October 24, 1995.

America Online

customers in the past 36 months. Leader says the 41-month average live number comes from projections. Of course, it will take years to find out if he's right. . . .[10]

Analysts were also concerned about AOL's cash flow situation and the signal sent by the timing of its latest equity offering. The *Newsweek* article continued:

Accounting is terribly important to AOL. The better the numbers look, the more Wall Street loves it and the easier AOL can sell new shares to raise cash to pay its bills. . . . On October 10 [AOL] raised about $100 million by selling new shares. AOL sold the stock even though its shares had fallen to $58.37 from about $72 in September, when the sale plans were announced. Most companies would have delayed the offering, waiting for the price to snap back. AOL didn't, prompting cynics to think the company really needed the money. . . .

Some analysts believed that AOL issued shares when its stock price was low because the company needed the cash immediately. Others argued that AOL was building a war chest needed because deep-pocketed rivals such as Microsoft were about to start an online price war and because increasingly information providers were going directly to the Internet, rather than using middlemen such as AOL. Some analysts interpreted CompuServe's recent adoption of more aggressive accounting techniques as a sign that it too was readying for war. Beginning the first quarter of fiscal 1996, CompuServe would capitalize direct response advertising costs associated with customer acquisition activity.[11]

While AOL's stock price rebounded to $81.63 by November 8, 1995, there were many questions concerning AOL's future. How would the demand for AOL's services be affected by the entry of Microsoft Network and the growth of Internet? Would AOL's accounting choices stand the test of time? What if AOL's subscription growth rates slowed or subscriber renewal rates fell? Did AOL have the financial flexibility to face these competitive pressures and accounting risks?

QUESTIONS

1. Prior to 1995, why was America Online (AOL) so successful in the commercial online industry relative to its competitors, CompuServe and Prodigy?
2. As of 1995, what are the key changes taking place in the commercial online industry? How are they likely to affect AOL's future prospects?
3. Was AOL's policy to capitalize subscriber acquisition costs justified prior to 1995? Given the changes (Question 2), do you think AOL should change its accounting policy as of 1995? Is the company's response consistent with your view?
4. What would be the effect on AOL's 1995 balance sheet if all the capitalized subscriber acquisition costs were written off? If AOL expensed all the subscriber acquisition costs incurred in fiscal 1995 during the same year, what would be the effect on its income statement?
5. AOL's book value as of June 30, 1995, was $217,944 million. Assuming that the only change in the book value is due to the new shares, compute AOL's market to book ratio as of November 8, 1995. Based on your analysis, do you think this ratio is realistic?

10. *Op. cit., Newsweek, October 24, 1995.*

11. *Op. cit., Newsweek, October 24, 1995.*

EXHIBIT 1

Stock Price History for America Online, Inc.

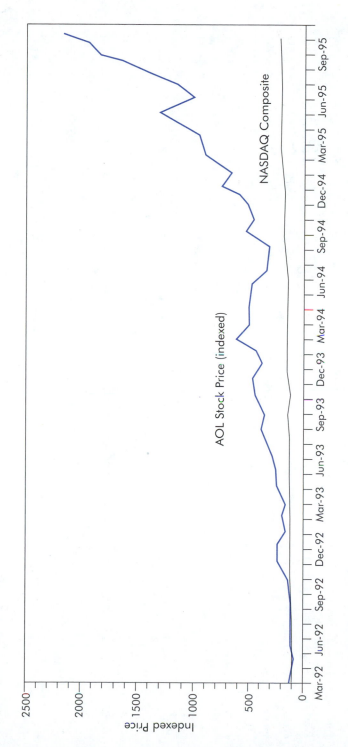

Additional market-based data:

America Online's equity beta	1.4
Moody's AAA corporate debt in November 1995 (%)	7.02
Treasury bills rate in November 1995 (%)	5.35
Government 30-year treasury rates in November 1995 (%)	6.26

Sources: Datastream International, Standard and Poor's Compustat, and the *Wall Street Journal.*

America Online

America Online

EXHIBIT 2
America Online, Inc. User Metrics to June 30, 1995

	Dec-93	Mar-94	Jun-94	Sep-94	Dec-94	Mar-95	Jun-95
Paid usage (hours)	1.85	2	2.1	2.27	2.46	2.73	2.93
Projected average months' retention	30	32	32+	34	36	39	41
Projected average lifetime revenue	$443	$496	$496	$551	$612	$667	$714
Internet usage (% time)		1%	3%	4%	5%	6%	9%

Source: Alex Brown & Sons, Inc., August 24, 1995.

EXHIBIT 3

America Online 1995 Abridged Annual Report

REPORT OF INDEPENDENT AUDITORS

Board of Directors and Stockholders
America Online, Inc.

We have audited the accompanying consolidated balance sheets of America Online, Inc., as of June 30, 1995 and 1994, and the related consolidated statements of operations, changes in stockholders' equity and cash flows for each of the three years in the period ended June 30, 1995. These financial statements are the responsibility of the Company's management. Our responsibility is to express an opinion on these financial statements based on our audits.

We conducted our audits in accordance with generally accepted auditing standards. Those standards require that we plan and perform the audit to obtain reasonable assurance about whether the financial statements are free of material misstatement. An audit includes examining, on a test basis, evidence supporting the amounts and disclosures in the financial statements. An audit also includes assessing the accounting principles used and significant estimates made by management, as well as evaluating the overall financial statement presentation. We believe that our audits provide a reasonable basis for our opinion.

In our opinion, the financial statements referred to above present fairly, in all material respects, the consolidated financial position of America Online, Inc. at June 30, 1995 and 1994, and the consolidated results of their operations and their cash flows for each of the three years in the period ended June 30, 1995, in conformity with generally accepted accounting principles.

As discussed in Note 9 to the consolidated financial statements, in fiscal 1994 the Company changed its method of accounting for income taxes. As discussed in Note 2 to the consolidated financial statements, in fiscal 1995 the Company changed its method of accounting for short-term investments in certain debt and equity securities.

Ernst & Young LLP

Vienna, Virginia
August 25, 1995

America Online

SELECTED CONSOLIDATED FINANCIAL AND OTHER DATA
(In Thousands, Except Per Share Data)

America Online

			Year Ended June 30,		
	1995	1994	1993	1992	1991
Statements of Operations Data:					
Online service revenues	$358,498	$100,993	$38,462	$26,226	$19,515
Other revenues	35,792	14,729	13,522	12,527	10,646
Total Revenues	394,290	115,722	51,984	38,753	30,161
Income (loss) from operations	(19,294)	4,608	1,925	3,685	1,341
Income (loss) before extraordinary items	(33,647)	2,550	399	2,344	1,100
Net income (loss) [1]	(33,647)	2,550	1,532	3,768	1,761
Income (loss) per common share:					
Income (loss) before extraordinary item	$ (0.99)	$ 0.07	$ 0.01	$ 0.10	$ 0.06
Net income (loss)	$ (0.99)	$ 0.07	$ 0.05	$ 0.17	$ 0.09
Weighted average shares outstanding	33,986	34,208	29,286	22,828	19,304

			As of June 30,		
	1995	1994	1993	1992	1991
Balance Sheet Data:					
Working capital (deficiency)	$ (456)	$47,890	$10,498	$12,363	$ (966)
Total assets	406,464	154,584	39,279	31,144	11,534
Total debt	21,810	9,302	2,959	2,672	1,865
Stockholders' equity (deficiency)	217,944	98,297	23,785	21,611	(8,623)
Other data (at fiscal year end):					
Subscribers	3,005	903	303	182	131

(1) Net loss in the fiscal year ended June 30, 1995, includes charges of $50.3 million for acquired research and development and $2.2 million for merger expenses. See Note 3 of the Notes to Consolidated Financial Statements.

MANAGEMENT'S DISCUSSION AND ANALYSIS OF FINANCIAL CONDITIONS AND RESULTS OF OPERATIONS

Overview

The Company has experienced a significant increase in revenues over the past three fiscal years. The higher revenues have been principally produced by increases in the Company's subscriber base resulting from growth of the online services market, the introduction of a Windows version of America Online in the middle of fiscal 1993, which greatly increased the available market for the Company's service, as well as the expansion of its services and content. Additionally, revenues have increased as the average monthly revenue per subscriber has risen steadily during the past three years, primarily as a result of an increase in the average monthly paid hours of use per subscriber.

The Company's online service revenues are generated primarily from subscribers paying a monthly member's fee and hourly charges based on usage in excess of the number of hours of usage provided as part of the monthly fee. Through December 31, 1994, the Company's standard monthly membership fee, which includes five hours of service, was $9.95, with a $3.50 hourly fee for usage in excess of five hours per month. Effective January 1, 1995, the hourly fee for usage in excess of five hours per month decreased from $3.50 to $2.95, while the monthly membership fee remained unchanged at $9.95.

The Company's other revenues are generated primarily from providing new media and interactive marketing services, data network services, and multimedia and CD-ROM production services. Additionally, the Company generates revenues related to online transactions and advertising, as well as development and licensing fees.

In fiscal 1995 the Company acquired RCC, NaviSoft, BookLink, ANS, WAIS, Medior and Global Network Navigator, Inc. Additionally, in August 1995, the Company entered into an agreement to acquire Ubique. For additional information relating to these acquisitions, refer to Notes 3 and 13 of the Notes to Consolidated Financial Statements.

The online services market is highly competitive. The Company believes that existing competitors, which include, among others, CompuServe, Prodigy and MSN, are likely to enhance their service offerings. In addition, new competitors have announced plans to enter the online services market, resulting in greater competition for the Company. The competitive environment could require new pricing programs and increased spending on marketing, content procurement and product development; limit the Company's opportunities to enter into and/or renew agreements with content providers and distribution partners; limit the Company's ability to grow its subscriber base; and result in increased attrition in the Company's subscriber base. Any of the foregoing events could result in an increase in costs as a percentage of revenues, and may have a material adverse effect on the Company's financial condition and operating results.

During September 1995, the Company modified the components of subscriber acquisition costs deferred and will be expensing certain subscriber acquisition cost as incurred, effective July 1, 1995. All costs capitalized before this change will continue to be amortized. The effect of this change for the year ended June 30, 1995 (including the amortization of amounts capitalized as of June 30, 1994) would have been to increase marketing costs by approximately $8 million. This change will have a greater impact on the Company's marketing costs in fiscal 1996, as the Company expects to significantly increase subscriber acquisition activity, including those subscriber acquisition expenditures which the Company will be expensing as incurred.

In addition, effective July 1, 1995, the Company changed the period over which it amortizes subscriber acquisition cost from twelve and eighteen months to twenty-four months. Based on the Company's historical average customer life experience, the change in amortization period is being made to more appropriately match subscriber acquisition costs with associated online service revenues. The effect of this change in accounting estimate for the year ended June 30, 1995 would have been to

America Online

decrease the amount of the amortization of subscriber acquisition costs by approximately $27 million. While this change will thereby positively impact operating margins, the Company expects that any such positive impact will be partially offset by increased investments in marketing and other business activities during fiscal 1996 and the decision, effective July 1, 1995, to expense certain subscriber acquisition costs as incurred.

Results of Operations

Fiscal 1995 Compared to Fiscal 1994

Online Service Revenues. For fiscal 1995, online service revenues increased from $100,993,000 to $358,498,000, or 255%, over fiscal 1994. This increase was primarily attributable to a 289% increase in revenues from IBM-compatible subscribers and a 196% increase in revenues from Macintosh subscribers as a result of a 273% increase in the number of IBM-compatible subscribers and a 143% increase in the number of Macintosh subscribers. The percentage increase in online service revenues in fiscal 1995 was greater than the percentage increase in subscribers principally due to an increase in the average monthly online service revenue per subscriber, which increased from $15.00 in fiscal 1994 to $17.10 in fiscal 1995.

Other Revenues. Other revenues, consisting principally of new media and interactive marketing services, data network services, multimedia and CD-ROM production services, and development and licensing fees, increased from $14,729,000 in fiscal 1994 to $35,792,000 in fiscal 1995. This increase was primarily attributable to data network revenues and multimedia and CD-ROM production service revenues from companies acquired during fiscal 1995.

Cost of Revenues. Cost of revenues includes network-related costs, consisting primarily of data and voice communication costs, costs associated with operating the data center and providing customer support, royalties paid to information and service providers and other expenses related to marketing and production services. For fiscal 1995, cost of revenues increased from $69,043,000 to $229,724,000, or 233%, over fiscal 1994, and

decreased as a percentage of total revenues from 59.7% to 58.3%.

The increase in cost of revenues was primarily attributable to an increase in data communication costs, customer support costs and royalties paid to information and service providers. Data communication costs increased primarily as a result of the larger customer base and more usage by customers. Customer support costs, which include personnel and telephone costs associated with providing customer support, were higher as a result of the larger customer base and a large number of new subscriber registrations. Royalties paid to information and service providers increased as a result of a larger customer base and more usage and the Company's addition of more service content to broaden the appeal of the America Online service.

The decrease in cost of revenues as a percentage of total revenues is primarily attributable to a decrease in expenses related to marketing services and personnel related costs as a percentage of total revenues, partially offset by an increase in data communication costs as a percentage of total revenues, primarily resulting from an increase in higher baud speed usage at a higher variable rate as well as lower hourly pricing for online service revenue which became effective January 1, 1995.

Marketing. Marketing expenses include the costs to acquire and retain subscribers and other general marketing expenses. Subscriber acquisition costs are deferred and charged to operations over a twelve or eighteen month period, using the straight-line method, beginning the month after such costs are incurred. For additional information regarding the accounting for deferred subscriber acquisition costs, refer to Note 2 of the Notes to Consolidated Financial Statements. For fiscal 1995, marketing expenses increased from $23,548,000 to $77,064,000, or 227%, over fiscal 1994, and decreased as a percentage of total revenues from 20.3% to 19.5%. The increase in marketing expenses was primarily due to an increase in the number and size of marketing programs to expand the Company's subscriber base. The decrease in marketing expenses as a percentage of total revenues is primarily attributable to a decrease as a percentage of total revenues in personnel related costs.

Product Development. Product development costs include research and development expenses, other product development costs and the amortization of software costs. For fiscal 1995, product development expenses increased from $4,961,000 to $12,842,000, or 159%, over fiscal 1994, and decreased as a percentage of total revenues from 4.3% to 3.3%. The increase in product development costs was primarily attributable to an increase in personnel costs related to an increase in the number of technical employees. The decrease in product development costs as a percentage of total revenues was principally a result of the substantial growth in revenues, which more than offset the additional product development costs. Product development costs, before capitalization and amortization, increased by 126% in fiscal 1995.

General and Administrative. Fiscal 1995 general and administrative costs increased from $13,562,000 to $41,966,000, or 209%, over fiscal 1994, and decreased as a percentage of total revenues from 11.7% to 10.6%. The increase in general and administrative expenses was principally attributable to higher office and personnel expenses related to an increase in the number of employees. The decrease in general and administrative costs as a percentage of total revenues was a result of the substantial growth in revenues, which more than offset the additional general and administrative costs, combined with the semi-variable nature of many of the general and administrative costs.

Acquired Research and Development. Acquired research and development costs, totaling $50,335,000, relate to in-process research and development purchased pursuant to the Company's acquisition of two early-stage Internet technology companies, BookLink and NaviSoft. The purchased research and development relating to the BookLink and NaviSoft acquisitions was the foundation of the development of the Company's Internet related products.

Amortization of Goodwill. Amortization of goodwill relates to the Company's acquisition of ANS, which resulted in approximately $44 million in goodwill. The goodwill related to the ANS acquisition is being amortized on a straight-line basis over a ten-year period.

Other Income. Other income consists primarily of investment and rental income net of interest expense. For fiscal 1995, other income increased from $1,774,000 to $3,023,000. This increase was primarily attributable to an increase in interest income generated by higher levels of cash available for investment, partially offset by a decrease in rental income and an increase in interest expense.

Merger Expenses. Non-recurring merger expenses totaling $2,207,000 were recognized in fiscal 1995 in connection with the mergers of the Company with RCC, WAIS and Medior.

Provisions for Income Taxes. The provision for income taxes was $3,832,000 and $15,169,000 in fiscal year 1994 and fiscal 1995, respectively. For additional information regarding income taxes, refer to Note 9 of the Notes to Consolidated Financial Statements.

Net Loss. The net loss in fiscal 1995 totaled $33,647,000. The net loss in fiscal 1995 included charges of $50,335,000 for acquired research and development and $2,207,000 for merger expenses.

Liquidity and Capital Resources

The Company has financed its operations through cash generated from operations, sale of its common stock and funding by third parties for certain product development activities. Net cash provided by operating activities was $2,205,000, $1,884,000 and $15,891,000 for fiscal 1993, fiscal 1994 and fiscal 1995, respectively. Included in operating activities were expenditures for deferred subscriber acquisition costs of $10,685,000, $37,424,000 and $111,761,000 in fiscal 1993, fiscal 1994 and fiscal 1995, respectively. Net cash used in investing activities was $8,915,000, $41,870,000 and $85,725,000 in fiscal 1993, fiscal 1994 and fiscal 1995, respectively. Investing activities included $20,523,000 in fiscal 1995 related to business acquisitions, substantially all of which were related to the acquisition of ANS.

In December 1993 the Company completed a public stock offering of 4,000,000 shares of common stock which generated net cash proceeds of approximately $62.7 million.

In April 1995 the company entered into a joint venture with Bertelsmann to offer interactive online services in Europe. In connection with the agreement, the Company received approximately $54 million through the sale of approximately 5% of its common stock to Bertelsmann.

The Company leases the majority of its equipment under noncancelable operating leases, and as part of its network portfolio strategy is building AOLnet, its data communications network. The buildout of this network requires a substantial investment in telecommunication equipment, which the Company plans to finance principally though leasing. In addition, the Company has guaranteed minimum commitments under certain data and voice communication agreements. The Company's future lease commitments and guaranteed minimums are discussed in Note 6 of the Notes to Consolidated Financial Statements.

The Company uses its working capital to finance ongoing operations and to fund marketing and content programs and the development of its products and services. The Company plans to continue to invest aggressively in acquisition marketing and content programs to expand its subscriber base, as well as in computing and support infrastructure. Additionally, the Company expects to use a portion of its cash for the acquisition and subsequent funding of technologies, products or businesses complementary to the Company's current business. Apart from its agreement to acquire Ubique, as discussed below, the Company has no agreements or understandings to acquire any businesses. The Company anticipates that available cash and cash provided by operating activities will be sufficient to fund its operations for the next fiscal year.

Various legal proceedings have arisen against the Company in the ordinary course of business. In the opinion of management, these proceedings will not have a material effect on the financial position of the Company.

The Company believes that inflation has not had a material effect on its results of operations.

On August 23, 1995, the Company entered into a stock purchase agreement to purchase Ubique, an Israeli company. The Company has agreed to pay approximately $15 million ($1.5 million in cash and $13.5 million in common stock) in the transaction, which is to be accounted for as a purchase. Subject to the results of an in-process valuation, a substantial portion of the purchase price may be allocated to in-process research and development and charged to the Company's operations in the first quarter of fiscal 1996.

CONSOLIDATED STATEMENTS OF OPERATIONS
(Amounts in Thousands, Except Per Share Data)

	Year ended June 30,		
	1995	1994	1993
Revenues:			
Online service revenues	$358,498	$100,993	$ 38,462
Other revenues	35,792	14,729	13,522
Total revenues	394,290	115,722	51,984
Costs and expenses:			
Cost of revenues	229,724	69,043	28,820
Marketing	77,064	23,548	9,745
Product development	12,842	4,961	2,913
General and administrative	41,966	13,562	8,581
Acquired research and development	50,335	—	—
Amortization of goodwill	1,653	—	—
Total costs and expenses	413,584	111,114	50,059
Income (loss) from operations	(19,294)	4,608	1,925
Other income, net	3,023	1,774	371
Merger expenses	(2,207)	—	—
Income (loss) before provision for income taxes and extraordinary item	(18,478)	6,382	2,296
Provision for income taxes	(15,169)	(3,832)	(1,897)
Income (loss) before extraordinary item	(33,647)	2,550	399
Extraordinary item—tax benefit arising from net operating loss carryforward	—	—	1,133
Net income (loss)	$ (33,647)	$ 2,550	$ 1,532
Earnings (loss) per share:			
Income (loss) before extraordinary item	$ (0.99)	$ 0.07	$ 0.01
Net income (loss)	$ (0.99)	$ 0.07	$ 0.05
Weighted average shares outstanding	33,986	34,208	29,286

See accompanying notes.

America Online

CONSOLIDATED STATEMENTS OF CASH FLOWS
(Amounts in Thousands)

	Year ended June 30,		
	1995	1994	1993
Cash flows from operating activities:			
Net income (loss)	$ (33,647)	$ 2,550	$ 1,532
Adjustments to reconcile net income to net cash provided by operating activities:			
Depreciation and amortization	11,136	2,965	1,957
Amortization of subscriber acquisition costs	60,924	17,922	7,038
Loss/(Gain) on sale of property and equipment	37	5	(39)
Charge for acquired research and development	50,335	—	—
Changes in assets and liabilities:			
Trade accounts receivable	(14,373)	(4,266)	(936)
Other receivables	(9,057)	(681)	(966)
Prepaid expenses and other current assets	(19,641)	(2,867)	(1,494)
Deferred subscriber acquisition costs	(111,761)	(37,424)	(10,685)
Other assets	(8,432)	(2,519)	(89)
Trade accounts payable	60,824	10,204	2,119
Accrued personnel costs	1,846	367	336
Other accrued expenses and liabilities	5,703	9,526	1,492
Deferred revenue	7,190	2,322	1,381
Deferred income taxes	14,763	3,832	759
Deferred rent	44	(52)	(200)
Total adjustments	49,538	(666)	673
Net cash provided by operating activities	15,891	1,884	2,205
Cash flows from investing activities:			
Short-term investments	5,380	(18,947)	(5,105)
Purchase of property and equipment	(57,751)	(17,886)	(2,041)
Product development costs	(13,011)	(5,132)	(1,831)
Sale of property and equipment	180	95	62
Purchase costs of acquired businesses	(20,523)	—	—
Net cash used in investing activities	(85,725)	(41,870)	(8,915)
Cash flows from financing activities:			
Proceeds from issuance of common stock, net	61,253	67,372	609
Principal and accrued interest payments on line of credit and long-term debt	(3,298)	(7,716)	(6,924)
Proceeds from line of credit and issuance of long-term debt	13,741	14,200	7,181
Tax benefit from stock option exercises	—	—	6
Principal payments under capital lease obligations	(375)	(142)	(112)

CONSOLIDATED STATEMENT OF CASH FLOWS (continued)

	Year ended June 30,		
	1995	1994	1993
Net cash provided by financing activities	71,321	73,714	760
Net increase (decrease) in cash and cash equivalents	1,487	33,728	(5,950)
Cash and cash equivalents at beginning of period	43,891	10,163	16,113
Cash and cash equivalents at end of period	$ 45,378	$ 43,891	$ 10,163
Supplemental cash flow information			
Cash paid during the period for:			
Interest	1,067	575	193
Income taxes	—	—	15

See accompanying notes.

CONSOLIDATED BALANCE SHEETS
(Amounts in Thousands, Except Per Share Data)

	June 30,	
	1995	1994
ASSETS		
Current assets:		
Cash and cash equivalents	$ 45,378	$ 43,891
Short-term investments	18,672	24,052
Trade accounts receivable	32,176	8,547
Other receivables	11,103	2,036
Prepaid expenses and other current assets	25,527	5,753
Total current assets	132,856	84,279
Property and equipment at cost, net	70,466	20,306
Other assets:		
Product development costs, net	18,914	7,912
Deferred subscriber acquisition costs, net	77,229	26,392
License rights, net	5,537	53
Other assets	11,479	2,800
Deferred income taxes	35,627	12,842
Goodwill, net	54,356	—
	$406,464	$154,584

(continued)

America Online

CONSOLIDATED BALANCE SHEETS (continued)

America Online

	June 30, 1995	June 30, 1994
LIABILITIES AND STOCKHOLDERS' EQUITY		
Current liabilities:		
Trade accounts payable	$ 84,639	$ 15,642
Accrued personnel costs	2,829	896
Other accrued expenses and liabilities	23,509	13,076
Deferred revenue	20,021	4,488
Line of credit	484	1,690
Current portion of long-term debt and capital lease obligations	1,830	597
Total current liabilities	133,312	36,389
Long-term liabilities:		
Notes payable	17,369	5,836
Capital lease obligations	2,127	1,179
Deferred income taxes	35,627	12,842
Deferred rent	85	41
Total liabilities	188,520	56,287
Stockholders' equity:		
Preferred stock, $.01 par value; 5,000,000 shares authorized, none issued	—	—
Common stock, $.01 par value; 100,000,000 shares authorized, 37,554,849 and 30,771,212 shares issued and outstanding at June 30, 1995 and 1994, respectively	375	308
Additional paid-in capital	251,539	98,836
Accumulated deficit	(33,970)	(847)
Total stockholders' equity	217,944	98,297
	$406,464	$154,584

See accompanying notes.

NOTES TO CONSOLIDATED FINANCIAL STATEMENTS

1. Organization

America Online, Inc. ("the Company") was incorporated in the State of Delaware in May 1985. The Company, based in Vienna, Virginia, is a leading provider of online services, offering its subscribers a wide variety of services, including e-mail, online conferences, entertainment, software, computing support, interactive magazines and newspapers, and online classes, as well as easy and affordable access to services of the Internet. In addition, the Company is a provider of data network services, new media and interactive marketing services, and multimedia and CD-ROM production services.

2. Summary of Significant Accounting Policies

Principles of Consolidation – The consolidated financial statements include the accounts of the Company and its subsidiaries. All significant intercompany accounts and transactions have been eliminated. Investments in affiliates owned twenty percent or more and corporate joint ventures are accounted for under the equity method. Other securities in companies owned less than twenty percent are accounted for under the cost method.

Business Combinations – Business combinations which have been accounted for under the purchase method of accounting include the results of operations of the acquired business from the date of acquisition. Net assets of the companies acquired are recorded at their fair value to the Company at the date of acquisition.

Other business combinations have been accounted for under the pooling of interests method of accounting. In such cases, the assets, liabilities, and stockholders' equity of the acquired entities were combined with the Company's respective accounts at recorded values. Prior period financial statements have been restated to give effect to the merger unless the effect of the business combination is not material to the financial statements of the Company.

Revenue and cost recognition – Online service revenue is recognized over the period services are provided. Other revenue, consisting principally of marketing, data network and multimedia production services, as well as development and royalty revenues, are recognized as services are rendered. Deferred revenue consists principally of third-party development funding not yet recognized and monthly subscription fees billed in advance.

Property and equipment – Property and equipment are depreciated or amortized using the straight-line method over the estimated useful life of the asset, which ranges from 5 to 40 years, or over the life of the lease.

Property and equipment under capital leases are stated at the lower of the present value of minimum lease payments at the beginning of the lease term or fair value at inception of the lease.

Deferred subscriber acquisition costs – Subscriber acquisition costs are deferred and charged to operations over a twelve or eighteen month period (straight-line method) beginning the month after such costs are incurred. These costs, which relate directly to subscriber solicitations, principally include printing, production and shipping of starter kits and the costs of obtaining qualified prospects by various targeted direct marketing programs (i.e., direct marketing response cards, mailing lists) and from third parties, and are recorded separately from ordinary operating expenses. No indirect costs are included in subscriber acquisition costs. To date, all subscriber acquisition costs have been incurred for the solicitation of specific identifiable prospects. Costs incurred for other than those targeted at specific identifiable prospects for the Company's services, and general marketing, are expensed as incurred.

The Company's services are sold on a monthly subscription basis. Subscriber acquisition costs incurred to obtain new subscribers are recoverable from revenues generated by such subscribers within a short period of time after such costs are incurred.

America Online

Effective July 1, 1992, the Company changed, from twelve months to eighteen months, the period over which it amortizes the costs of deferred subscriber acquisition costs relating to marketing activities in which the Company's starter kit is bundled and distributed by a third-party marketing company. The change in accounting estimate was made to more accurately match revenues and expenses. Based on the Company's experience and the distribution channels used in such marketing activities, there is a greater time lag between the time the Company incurs the cost for the starter kits and the time the starter kits begin to generate new customers than with direct marketing activities. Also, the period over which new subscribers (and related revenues) are generated is longer than that experienced with the use of traditional independent, direct marketing activities. The effect of this change in accounting estimate for the year ended June 30, 1993 was to increase income before extraordinary item and net income by $264,000 ($.01 per share).

In the first quarter of fiscal 1995 the Company adopted the provisions of Statement of Position ("SOP") 93-7, "Reporting on Advertising Costs," which provides guidance on financial reporting on advertising costs. The adoption of SOP 93-7 had no effect on the Company's financial position or results of operations.

Product development costs – The Company capitalizes cost incurred for the production of computer software used in the sale of its services. Costs capitalized include direct labor and related overhead for software produced by the Company and the costs of software purchased from third parties. All costs in the software development process which are classified as research and development are expensed as incurred until technological feasibility has been established. Once technological feasibility has been established, such costs are capitalized until the software is commercially available. To the extent the Company retains the rights to software development funded by third parties, such costs are capitalized in accordance with the Company's normal accounting policies. Amortization is provided on a product-by-product basis, using the greater of the straight-line method or current year revenue as a

percent of total revenue estimates for the related software product not to exceed five years, commencing the month after the date of product release.

Product development costs consist of the following:

	Year ended June 30,	
	1995	1994
	(in thousands)	
Balance, beginning of year	$ 7,912	$3,915
Cost capitalized	13,011	5,132
Cost amortized	(2,009)	(1,135)
Balance, end of year	$18,914	$7,912

The accumulated amortization of product development costs related to the production of computer software totaled $7,894,000, and $5,885,000 at June 30, 1995 and 1994, respectively.

Included in product development costs are research and development costs totaling $3,856,000, $2,126,000, and $1,130,000 and other product development costs totaling $6,977,000, $1,050,000 and $579,000 in the years ended June 30, 1995, 1994 and 1993, respectively.

License rights – The cost of acquired license rights is amortized using the straight-line method over the term of the agreement for such license rights, ranging from one to three years.

Goodwill – Goodwill consists of the excess of cost over the fair value of net assets acquired and certain other intangible assets relating to purchase transactions. Goodwilll and intangible assets are amortized over periods ranging from 5–10 years.

Operating lease costs – Rent expense for operating leases is recognized on a straight-line basis over the lease term. The difference between rent expense incurred and rental payments is charged or credited to deferred rent.

Cash, cash equivalents and short-term investments – The Company considers all highly liquid investments with an original maturity of three months or less to be cash equivalents. In fiscal 1995, the Company adopted Statement of Financial

Accounting Standards No. 115 ("SFAS 115"), "Accounting for Certain Investments in Debt and Equity Securities." The adoption was not material to the Company's financial position or results of operations. The Company has classified all debt and equity securities as available-for-sale. Available-for-sale securities are carried at fair value, with unrealized gains and losses reported as a separate component of stockholders' equity. Realized gains and losses and declines in value judged to be other-than-temporary on available-for-sale securities are included in other income. Available-for-sale securities at June 30, 1995, consisted of U.S. Treasury Bills and other obligations of U.S. Government agencies totaling $7,579,000 and U.S. corporate debt obligations totaling $11,093,000. At June 20, 1995, the estimated fair value of these securities approximated cost.

Net income (loss) per common share – Net income (loss) per share is calculated by dividing income (loss) before extraordinary item and net income (loss) by the weighted average number of common and, when dilutive, common equivalent shares outstanding during the period.

Reclassification – Certain amounts in prior years' consolidated financial statements have been reclassified to conform to the current year presentation.

3. Business Combination

Pooling Transactions

On August 19, 1994, Redgate Communications Corporation ("RCC") was merged with and into a subsidiary of the Company. The Company exchanged 1,789,300 shares of common stock for all of the outstanding common and preferred stock and warrants of RCC. Additionally, 401,148 shares of the Company's common stock were reserved for outstanding stock options issued by RCC and assumed by the Company. The merger was accounted for under the pooling of interests method of accounting, and accordingly, the accompanying consolidated financial statements have been restated for all periods prior to the acquisition to include the financial position, results of operations and cash flows of RCC. Effective August 1994, RCC's fiscal year-end has been changed from December 31 to June 30 to conform to the Company's fiscal year-end.

Revenues and net earnings (loss) for the individual entities are as follows:

	Three months ended September 30, 1994 (unaudited)	Year ended June 30, 1994	Year ended June 30, 1993
	(in thousands)		
Total revenues:			
AOL	$50,783	$104,410	$40,019
RCC	3,813	11,312	11,965
Less intercompany sales	(173)	—	—
	$54,423	$115,722	$51,984
Net income (loss):			
AOL	$ 3,018	$ 6,210	$ 4,210
RCC	(42)	(3,660)	(2,678)
Merger expenses	(1,710)	—	—
	$ 1,266	$ 2,550	$ 1,532

America Online

In connection with the merger of the Company and RCC, merger expenses of $1,710,000 were recognized during 1995.

During fiscal 1995, Medior, Inc. and Wide Area Information Servers, Inc. were merged into subsidiaries of the Company. The Company issued 1,082,019 shares of its common stock in the transactions. The transactions were accounted for under the pooling of interests method of accounting. Prior year financial statements have not been restated for the transactions because the effect would not be material to the operations of the Company.

Purchase Transactions

During fiscal 1995, the Company acquired NaviSoft, Inc. ("NaviSoft"), BookLink Technologies, Inc. ("BookLink"), Advanced Network & Services, Inc. ("ANS") and Global Network Navigator, Inc., in transactions accounted for under the purchase method of accounting. The Company paid a total of $97,669,000, of which $75,697,000 was in stock and $21,972,000 was in cash for the acquisitions. Of the aggregate purchase price, approximately $50,335,000 was allocated to in-process research and development and $55,314,000 was allocated to goodwill and other intangible assets.

The following unaudited pro forma information relating to the BookLink and ANS acquisitions is not necessarily an indication of the combined results that would have occurred had the acquisitions taken place at the beginning of the period, nor is necessarily an indication of the results that may occur in the future. Pro forma information for NaviSoft and Global Network Navigator, Inc. is immaterial to the operations of the consolidated entity. The amount of the aggregate purchase price allocated to in-process research and development for both the NaviSoft and BookLink acquisitions has been excluded from the pro forma information as it is a non-recurring item.

| | Year ended June 30, | |
	1995	1994
	(in thousands except per share data)	
Revenues	$410,147	$135,785
Income (loss) from operations	23,117	(5,465)
Pro forma income (loss)	11,205	(4,694)
Pro forma income (loss) per share	$ 0.25	$ (0.16)

4. Property and Equipment

Property and equipment consist of the following:

| | June 30, | |
	1995	1994
	(in thousands)	
Computer equipment	$49,167	$12,418
Furniture and fixtures	4,992	1,398
Buildings	13,800	5,648
Land	6,075	2,052
Building improvements	6,284	1,343
Property under capital leases	8,486	2,686
Leasehold improvements	3,059	306
	91,863	25,851
Less accumulated depreciation and amortization	(21,397)	(5,545)
Net property and equipment	$70,466	$20,306

5. License Rights

License rights consist of the following:

| | June 30, | |
	1995	1994
	(in thousands)	
License rights	$ 7,484	$ 954
Less accumulated amortization	(1,947)	(901)
	$ 5,537	$ 53

6. Commitments and Contingencies

The Company leases equipment under several long-term capital and operating leases. Future minimum payments under capital leases and noncancelable operating leases with initial terms of one year or more consist of the following:

	Capital Leases	Operating Leases
	(in thousands)	
Year ending June 30,		
1996	$1,654	$20,997
1997	1,236	21,264
1998	641	19,450
1999	310	8,711
2000	103	3,511
Thereafter	—	2,636
Total minimum lease payments	3,944	$76,569
Less amount representing interest	(402)	
Present value of net minimum capital lease payments, including current portion of $1,415	$3,542	

The Company's rental expense under operating leases in the years ended June 30, 1995, 1994 and 1993 totaled approximately $10,001,000, $2,889,000, and $2,155,000, respectively.

Communication networks – The Company has guaranteed monthly usage levels of data and voice communications with one of its vendors. The remaining commitments are $113,400,000, $59,000,000, $9,000,000 and $6,750,000 for the years ending June 30, 1996, 1997, 1998 and 1999, respectively. The related expense for the years ended June 30, 1995, 1994 and 1993 was $138,793,000, $40,315,000 and $11,226,000, respectively.

Contingencies – Various legal proceedings have arisen against the Company in the ordinary course of business. In the opinion of management, these proceedings will not have a material effect on the financial position of the Company.

7. Notes Payable

Notes payable at June 30, 1995 totaled approximately $18 million and consist primarily of amounts borrowed to finance the purchases of two office buildings. The notes are collateralized by the respective properties. The notes have a variable interest rate equal to 105 basis points above the 30 day London Interbank Offered Rate and a fixed interest rate of 8.48% per annum at June 30, 1995. Aggregate maturities of notes payable for the years ended June 30, 1996, 1997, 1998, 1999, 2000 and thereafter are $415,000, $429,000, $445,000, $462,000, $480,000 and $15,553,000, respectively.

8. Other Income

The following table summarizes the components of other income:

	Year ended June 30,		
	1995	1994	1993
	(in thousands)		
Interest income	$3,920	$1,646	$572
Interest expense	(1,054)	(575)	(172)
Other	157	703	(29)
	$3,023	$1,774	$371

America Online

America Online

9. Income Taxes

The provision for income taxes is attributable to:

| | Year ended June 30, | | |
	1995	1994	1993
	(in thousands)		
Income before extraordinary item	$15,169	$3,832	$1,897
Tax benefit arising from net operating loss carryforward	—	—	(1,133)
	$15,169	$3,832	$ 764
Current	$ —	$ —	$ 5
Deferred	15,169	3,832	759
	$15,169	$3,832	$ 764

The provision for income taxes differs from the amount computed by applying the statutory federal income tax rate to income before provision for income taxes and extraordinary item. The sources and tax effects of the differences are as follows:

| | Year ended June 30, | | |
	1995	1994	1993
	(in thousands)		
Income tax at the federal statutory rate of 34%	$ (6,283)	$2,170	$ 781
State income tax, net of federal benefit	1,597	403	200
Losses relating to RCC	—	1,259	916
Nondeductible merger expenses	750	—	—
Nondeductible charge for purchased research and development	17,114	—	—
Loss, for which no tax benefit was derived	1,632	—	—
Other	359	—	—
	$15,169	$3,832	$1,897

Deferred income taxes arise because of differences in the treatment of income and expense items for financial reporting and income tax purposes, primarily relating to deferred subscriber acquisition and product development costs.

As of June 30, 1995, the Company has net operating loss carryforwards of approximately $109 million for tax purposes which will be available, subject to certain annual limitations, to offset future taxable income. If not used, these loss carryforwards will expire between 2001 and 2010. To the extent that net operating loss carryforwards, when realized, relate to stock option deductions, the resulting benefits will be credited to stockholders' equity.

The Company's income tax provision was computed on the federal statutory rate and the average state statutory rates, net of the related federal benefit.

Effective July 1, 1993 the Company changed its method of accounting for income taxes from the deferred method to the liability method required by FASB Statement No. 109, "Accounting for Income Taxes." As permitted under the new rules, prior years' financial statements have not been restated.

No increase to net income resulted from the cumulative effect of adopting Statement No. 109 as of July 1, 1993. The deferred tax asset increased by approximately $5,965,000 as a result of the adoption. Similarly, the deferred tax liability, stockholders' equity and the valuation allowance increased by approximately $3,173,000, $759,000 and $2,033,000, respectively.

Deferred income taxes reflect the net tax effects of temporary differences between the carrying amounts of assets and liabilities for financial reporting purposes and the amounts used for income tax purposes. Significant components of the Company's deferred tax liabilities and assets are as follows:

	Year ended June 30,	
	1995	1994
	(in thousands)	
Deferred tax liabilities:		
Capitalized software costs	$ 7,008	$ 2,962
Deferred member acquisi-		
tion costs	28,619	9,880
Net deferred tax liabilities	$35,627	$12,842
Deferred tax assets:		
Net operating loss carry-		
forwards	$39,000	$17,510
Total deferred tax assets	39,000	17,510
Valuation allowance for		
deferred assets	(3,373)	(4,668)
Net deferred tax assets	$35,627	$12,842

13. Subsequent Event

On August 23, 1995, the Company entered into a stock purchase agreement to purchase Ubique, Ltd., an Israeli company. The Company has agreed to pay approximately $15 million ($1.5 million in cash and $13.5 million in common stock) in the transaction, which is to be accounted for under the purchase method of accounting. Subject to the results of an in-process valuation, a substantial portion of the purchase price may be allocated to in-process research and development and charged to the Company's operations in the first quarter of fiscal 1996.

QUARTERLY INFORMATION (unaudited)

	Quarter Ended				
	September 30	December 31	March 31	June 30	Total
Fiscal 1995[a]					
Online service revenues	$50,056	$69,712	$99,814	$138,916	$358,498
Other revenues	6,880	6,683	9,290	12,939	35,792
Total revenues	56,936	76,395	109,104	151,855	394,290
Income (loss) from operations	4,623	(35,258)	233	11,108	(19,294)
Net income (loss)	1,481	(38,730)	(2,587)	6,189	(33,647)
Net income (loss) per share[b]	$ 0.04	$ (0.20)	$ (0.07)	$ 0.13	$ (0.99)
Fiscal 1994					
Online service revenues	$14,299	$20,292	$28,853	$37,549	$100,993
Other revenues	4,780	4,239	2,836	2,874	14,729
Total revenues	19,079	24,531	31,689	40,423	115,722
Income from operations	531	520	1,931	1,626	4,608
Net income	303	70	1,272	905	2,550
Net income per share[b]	$ 0.01	$ —	$ 0.03	$ 0.02	$ 0.07

a. Historical financial information for amounts previously reported in fiscal 1995 has been adjusted to account for pooling of interest transactions.

b. The sum of per-share earnings (loss) does not equal earnings (loss) per share for the year due to equivalent share calculations which are impacted by the Company's loss in 1995 and by fluctuations in the Company's common stock market prices.

3
chapter

The purpose of accounting analysis is to evaluate the degree to which a firm's accounting captures its underlying business reality.[1] By identifying places where there is accounting flexibility, and by evaluating the appropriateness of the firm's accounting policies and estimates, analysts can assess the degree of distortion in a firm's accounting numbers. Another important skill is recasting a firm's accounting numbers using cash flow and footnote information to "undo" any accounting distortions. Sound accounting analysis improves the reliability of conclusions from financial analysis, the next step in financial statement analysis.

THE INSTITUTIONAL FRAMEWORK FOR FINANCIAL REPORTING

There is typically a separation between ownership and management in public corporations. Financial statements serve as the vehicle through which owners keep track of their firms' financial situation. On a periodic basis, firms typically produce three financial reports : (1) an income statement that describes the operating performance during a time period, (2) a balance sheet that states the firm's assets and how they are financed, and (3) a cash flow statement (or in some countries, a funds flow statement) that summarizes the cash flows of the firm. These statements are accompanied by several footnotes and a message and narrative discussion written by the management.

To evaluate effectively the quality of a firm's financial statement data, the analyst needs to first understand the basic features of financial reporting and the institutional framework that governs them, as discussed in the following sections.

Building Blocks of Accrual Accounting

One of the fundamental features of corporate financial reports is that they are prepared using accrual rather than cash accounting. Unlike cash accounting, accrual accounting distinguishes between the recording of costs and benefits associated with economic activities and the actual payment and receipt of cash. Net income is the primary periodic performance index under accrual accounting. To compute net income, the effects of economic transactions are recorded on the basis of *expected,* not necessarily *actual,* cash receipts and payments. Expected cash receipts from the delivery of products or services are recognized as revenues, and expected cash outflows associated with these revenues are recognized as expenses.

While there are many rules and conventions that govern a firm's preparation of financial statements, there are only a few conceptual building blocks that form the foundation of accrual accounting. The principles that define a firm's assets, liabilities, equities, revenues, and expenses are as follows[2]:

- **Assets** are economic resources owned by a firm that (a) are likely to produce future economic benefits and (b) are measurable with a reasonable degree of certainty.
- **Liabilities** are economic obligations of a firm arising from benefits received in the past that are (a) required to be met with a reasonable degree of certainty and (b) at a reasonably well-defined time in the future.
- **Equity** is the difference between a firm's net assets and its liabilities.

The definitions of assets, liabilities, and equity lead to the fundamental relationship that governs a firm's balance sheet:

Assets = Liabilities + Equity

While the balance sheet is a summary at one point in time, the income statement summarizes a firm's revenues and expenses and its gains and losses arising from changes in assets and liabilities in accord with the following definitions:

- **Revenues** are economic resources earned during a time period. Revenue recognition is governed by the realization principle, which proposes that revenues should be recognized when (a) the firm has provided all, or substantially all, the goods or services to be delivered to the customer and (b) the customer has paid cash or is expected to pay cash with a reasonable degree of certainty.
- **Expenses** are economic resources used up in a time period. Expense recognition is governed by the matching and the conservatism principles. Under these principles, expenses are (a) costs directly associated with revenues recognized in the same period, or (b) costs associated with benefits that are consumed in this time period, or (c) resources whose future benefits are not reasonably certain.
- **Profit** is the difference between a firm's revenues and expenses in a time period.[3]

Chapters 4 through 7 discuss the key isues to consider for analyzing accounting policies and estimates reflected in the financial statements. The chapters present each financial statement account type (assets, liabilities, equity, revenues, and expenses) separately to reflect the way that analysts typically approach financial statements. Obviously, however, there are close links between these types of accounts; these are noted where appropriate.

Delegation of Reporting to Management

While the basic definitions of the elements of a firm's financial statements are simple, their application in practice often involves complex judgments. For example, how should revenues be recognized when a firm sells land to customers and also provides customer financing? If revenue is recognized before cash is collected, how should potential defaults be estimated? Are the outlays associated with research and development activities, whose payoffs are uncertain, assets or expenses when incurred? Do frequent flyer reward programs create accounting liabilities for airline companies? If so, when and at what value?

Because corporate managers have intimate knowledge of their firms' businesses, they are entrusted with the primary task of making the appropriate judgments in portraying myriad business transactions using the basic accrual accounting framework. The accounting discretion granted to managers is potentially valuable because it allows them to reflect inside information in reported financial statements. However, since investors view profits as a measure of managers' performance, managers have an incentive to use their accounting discretion to distort reported profits by making biased assumptions. Further, the use of accounting numbers in contracts between the firm and outsiders provides a motivation for management manipulation of accounting numbers.

Earnings management distorts financial accounting data, making them less valuable to external users of financial statements. Therefore, the delegation of financial reporting decisions to managers has both costs and benefits. Accounting rules and auditing are mechanisms designed to reduce the cost and preserve the benefit of delegating financial reporting to corporate managers.

Generally Accepted Accounting Principles

Given that it is difficult for outside investors to determine whether managers have used their accounting flexibility to signal their proprietary information or merely to disguise reality, a number of accounting conventions have evolved to mitigate the problem. Accounting conventions and standards promulgated by the standard-setting bodies limit potential distortions that managers can introduce into reported accounting numbers. In the United States, the Securities and Exchange Commission (SEC) has the legal authority to set accounting standards. The SEC typically relies on private sector accounting bodies to undertake this task. Since 1973 accounting standards in the United States have been set by the Financial Accounting Standards Board (FASB). There are similar private sector or public sector accounting standard-setting bodies in many other countries. In addition, the International Accounting Standards Committee (IASC) has been attempting to set worldwide accounting standards, though IASC's pronouncements are not legally binding as of now.

Uniform accounting standards attempt to reduce managers' ability to record similar economic transactions in dissimilar ways either over time or across firms. Thus they create a uniform accounting language and increase the credibility of financial statements by limiting a firm's ability to distort them. Increased uniformity from accounting standards, however, comes at the expense of reduced flexibility for managers to reflect genuine business differences in a firm's accounting decisions. Rigid accounting standards work best for economic transactions whose accounting treatment is not predicated on managers' proprietary information. However, when there is a significant business judgment involved in assessing a transaction's economic consequences, rigid standards are likely to be dysfunctional, because they prevent managers from using their superior business knowledge. Further, if accounting standards are too rigid, they may induce managers to expend economic resources to restructure business transactions to achieve a desired accounting result.

External Auditing

Broadly defined as a verification of the integrity of the reported financial statements by someone other than the preparer, external auditing ensures that managers use accounting rules and conventions consistently over time, and that their accounting estimates are reasonable. In the U.S., all listed companies are required to have their financial statements audited by an independent public accountant. The standards and procedures to be followed by independent auditors are set by the American Institute of Certified Public Accountants (AICPA). These standards are known as Generally Accepted Auditing Standards (GAAS). While auditors issue an opinion on published financial statements, it is important to remember that the primary responsibility for the statements still rests with corporate managers.

Auditing improves the quality and credibility of accounting data by limiting a firm's ability to distort financial statements to suit its own purposes. However, third-party auditing may also reduce the quality of financial reporting because it constrains the kind of accounting rules and conventions that evolve over time. For example, the FASB considers the views of auditors in the standard-setting process. Auditors are likely to argue against accounting standards that produce numbers which are difficult to audit, even if the proposed rules produce relevant information for investors.

Legal Liability

The legal environment in which accounting disputes between managers, auditors, and investors are adjudicated can also have a significant effect on the quality of reported numbers. The threat of lawsuits and resulting penalties have the beneficial effect of improving the accuracy of disclosure. However, the potential for a significant legal liability might also discourage managers and auditors from supporting accounting proposals requiring risky forecasts, such as forward looking disclosures. This type of concern is often expressed by the auditing community in the U.S.

Limitations of Accounting Analysis

Because the mechanisms that limit managers' ability to distort accounting data themselves add noise, it is not optimal to use accounting regulation to eliminate managerial flexibility completely. Therefore, real-world accounting systems leave considerable room for managers to influence financial statement data. The net result is that information in corporate financial reports is noisy and biased, even in the presence of accounting regulation and external auditing.[4] The objective of accounting analysis is to evaluate the degree to which a firm's accounting captures its underlying business reality and to "undo" any accounting distortions. When potential distortions are large, accounting analysis can add considerable value.[5]

Factors Influencing Accounting Quality

There are three potential sources of noise and bias in accounting data: (1) the noise and bias introduced by rigidity in accounting rules, (2) random forecast errors, and (3) systematic reporting choices made by corporate managers to achieve specific objectives. Each of these factors is discussed below.

ACCOUNTING RULES.   Accounting rules introduce noise and bias because it is often difficult to restrict management discretion without reducing the information content of accounting data. For example, the Statement of Financial Accounting Standards No. 2 issued by the FASB requires firms to expense research outlays when they are incurred. Clearly, some research expenditures have future value while others do not. However, because SFAS No. 2 does not allow firms to distinguish between the two types of expenditures, it leads to a systematic distortion of reported accounting numbers. Broadly speaking, the degree of distortion introduced by accounting standards depends on how well uniform accounting standards capture the nature of a firm's transactions.

FORECAST ERRORS.   Another source of noise in accounting data arises from pure forecast error, because managers cannot predict future consequences of current transactions perfectly. For example, when a firm sells products on credit, accrual accounting requires managers to make a judgment on the probability of collecting payments from customers. If payments are deemed "reasonably certain," the firm treats the transactions as sales, creating accounts receivable on its balance sheet. Managers then make an estimate of the proportion of receivables that will not be collected. Because managers do not have perfect foresight, actual defaults are likely to be different from estimated customer defaults, leading to a forecast error. The extent of errors in managers' accounting forecasts depends on a variety of factors, including the complexity of the business transactions, the predictability of the firm's environment, and unforeseen economy-wide changes.

MANAGERS' ACCOUNTING CHOICES.   Corporate managers also introduce noise and bias into accounting data through their own accounting decisions. Managers have a variety of incentives to exercise their accounting discretion to achieve certain objectives, leading to systematic influences on their firms' reporting[6]:

- *Accounting-based debt covenants.* Managers may make accounting decisions to meet certain contractual obligations in their debt covenants. For example, firms' lending agreements with banks and other debt holders require them to meet covenants related to interest coverage, working capital ratios, and net worth, all defined in terms of accounting numbers. Violation of these constraints may be costly because it allows lenders to demand immediate payment of their loans. Managers of firms close to violating debt covenants have an incentive to select accounting policies and estimates to reduce the probability of covenant violation. The debt covenant motivation for managers' accounting decisions has been analyzed by a number of accounting researchers.[7]

- *Management compensation.* Another motivation for managers' accounting choice comes from the fact that their compensation and job security are often tied to reported profits. For example, many top managers receive bonus compensation if they exceed certain prespecified profit targets. This provides motivation for managers to choose accounting policies and estimates to maximize their expected compensation.[8]

- *Corporate control contests.* In corporate control contests, including hostile takeovers and proxy fights, competing management groups attempt to win over the firm's shareholders. Accounting numbers are used extensively in debating managers' performance in these contests. Therefore, managers may make accounting decisions to influence investor perceptions in corporate control contests.[9]

- *Tax considerations.* Managers may also make reporting choices to trade off between financial reporting and tax considerations. For example, U.S. firms are required to use LIFO inventory accounting for shareholder reporting in order to use it for tax reporting. Under LIFO, when prices are rising, firms report lower profits, thereby reducing tax payments. Some firms may forgo the tax reduction in order to report higher profits in their financial statements.[10]

- *Regulatory considerations.* Since accounting numbers are used by regulators in a variety of contexts, managers of some firms may make accounting decisions to influence regulatory outcomes. Examples of regulatory situations where accounting numbers are used include antitrust actions, import tariffs to protect domestic industries, and tax policies.[11]

- *Capital market considerations.* Managers may make accounting decisions to influence the perceptions of capital markets. When there are information asymmetries between managers and outsiders, this strategy may succeed in influencing investor perceptions, at least temporarily.[12]

- *Stakeholder considerations.* Managers may also make accounting decisions to influence the perception of important stakeholders in the firm. For example, since labor unions can use healthy profits as a basis for demanding wage increases, managers may make accounting decisions to decrease income when they are facing union contract negotiations. In countries like Germany, where labor unions are strong, these considerations appear to play an important role in firms' accounting policy. Other important stakeholders that firms may wish to influence through their financial reports include suppliers and customers.

- *Competitive considerations.* The dynamics of competition in an industry might also influence a firm's reporting choices. For example, a firm's segment disclosure decisions may be influenced by its concern that disaggregated disclosure may help competitors in their business decisions. Similarly, firms may not disclose data on their margins by product line for fear of giving away proprietary information. Finally, firms may discourage new entrants by making income-decreasing accounting choices.

In addition to accounting policy choices and estimates, the level of disclosure is also an important determinant of a firm's accounting quality. Corporate managers can choose disclosure policies that make it more or less costly for external users of financial reports to understand the true economic picture of their businesses. Accounting regulations usually prescribe minimum disclosure requirements, but they do not restrict managers from voluntarily providing additional disclosures. Managers can use various parts of the financial reports, including the Letter to the Shareholders, Management Discussion and Analysis, and footnotes, to describe the company's strategy, its accounting policies, and its current performance. There is wide variation across firms in how managers use their disclosure flexibility.[13]

DOING ACCOUNTING ANALYSIS

In this section we will discuss a series of steps that an analyst can follow to evaluate a firm's accounting quality. In the subsequent five chapters, these concepts are illustrated for the analysis of assets, liabilities and equity, revenues, expenses, and business entity accounting.

Step 1: Identify Key Accounting Policies

As discussed in the chapter on business strategy analysis, a firm's industry characteristics and its own competitive strategy determine its key success factors and risks. One of the goals of financial statement analysis is to evaluate how well these success factors and risks are being managed by the firm. In accounting analysis, therefore, the analyst should identify and evaluate the policies and the estimates the firm uses to measure its critical factors and risks.

For example, one of the key success factors in the leasing business is to make accurate forecasts of residual values of the leased equipment at the end of the lease terms. For a firm in the equipment leasing industry, therefore, one of the most important accounting policies is the way residual values are recorded. Residual values influence the company's reported profits and its asset base. If residual values are overestimated, the firm runs the risk of having to take large write-offs in the future.

Key success factors in the banking industry include interest and credit risk management; in the retail industry, inventory management is a key success factor; and for a manufacturer competing on product quality and innovation, research and development and product defects after the sale are key areas of concern. In each of these cases, the analyst has to identify the accounting measures the firm uses to capture these business constructs, the policies that determine how the measures are implemented, and the key estimates embedded in these policies. For example, the accounting measure a bank uses to capture credit risk is its loan loss reserves, and the accounting measure that captures product quality for a manufacturer is its warranty expenses and reserves.

Step 2: Assess Accounting Flexibility

Not all firms have equal flexibility in choosing their key accounting policies and estimates. Some firms' accounting choice is severely constrained by accounting standards and conventions. For example, even though research and development is a key success factor for biotechnology companies, managers have no accounting discretion in reporting on this activity. Similarly, even though marketing and brand building are key to the success of consumer goods firms, they are required to expense all their marketing outlays. In contrast, managing credit risk is one of the critical success factors for banks, and bank managers have the freedom to estimate expected defaults on their loans. Similarly, software developers have the flexibility to decide at what points in their development cycles the outlays can be capitalized.

If managers have little flexibility in choosing accounting policies and estimates related to their key success factors (as in the case of biotechnology firms), accounting data are likely to be less informative for understanding the firm's economics. In contrast, if managers have considerable flexibility in choosing the policies and estimates (as in the case of software developers), accounting numbers have the potential to be informative, depending upon how managers exercise this flexibility.

Regardless of the degree of accounting flexibility a firm's managers have in measuring their key success factors and risks, they will have some flexibility with respect to several other accounting policies. For example, all firms have to make choices with respect to depreciation policy (straight-line or accelerated methods), inventory accounting policy (LIFO, FIFO, or Average Cost), policy for amortizing goodwill (write-off over forty years or less), and policies regarding the estimation of pension and other post-employment benefits (expected return on plan assets, discount rate for liabilities, and rate of increase in wages and health care costs). Since all these policy choices can have a significant impact on the reported performance of a firm, they offer an opportunity for the firm to manage its reported numbers.

Step 3: Evaluate Accounting Strategy

When managers have accounting flexibility, they can use it either to communicate their firm's economic situation or to hide true performance. Some of the strategy questions one could ask in examining how managers exercise their accounting flexibility include the following:

- How do the firm's accounting policies compare to the norms in the industry? If they are dissimilar, is it because the firm's competitive strategy is unique? For example, consider a firm that reports a lower warranty allowance than the industry average. One explanation is that the firm competes on the basis of high quality and has invested considerable resources to reduce the rate of product failure. An alternative explanation is that the firm is merely understating its warranty liabilities.
- Does management face strong incentives to use accounting discretion for earnings management? For example, is the firm close to violating bond covenants? Or, are the managers having difficulty meeting accounting-based bonus targets? Does management own significant stock? Is the firm in the middle of a proxy fight or union negotiations? Managers may also make accounting decisions to reduce tax payments, or to influence the perceptions of the firm's competitors.
- Has the firm changed any of its policies or estimates? What is the justification? What is the impact of these changes? For example, if warranty expenses decreased, is it because the firm made significant investments to improve quality?
- Have the company's policies and estimates been realistic in the past? For example, firms may overstate their revenues and understate their expenses during the year by manipulating quarterly reports, which are not subject to a full-blown external audit. However, the auditing process at the end of the fiscal year forces such companies to make large fourth-quarter adjustments, providing an opportunity for the analyst to assess the quality of the firm's interim reporting. Similarly, firms that expense acquisition goodwill too slowly will be forced to take a large write-off later. A history of write-offs may be, therefore, a sign of prior earnings management.
- Does the firm structure any significant business transactions so that it can achieve certain accounting objectives? For example, leasing firms can alter lease terms (the length of the lease or the bargain purchase option at the end of the lease term) so that the transactions qualify as sales-type leases for the lessors. Firms may structure a takeover transaction (equity financing rather than debt financing) so that they can use the pooling of interests method rather than the purchase method of accounting. Finally, a firm can alter the way it finances (coupon rate and the terms of conversion for a convertible bond issue) so that its reported earnings per share is not diluted. Such behavior may suggest that the firm's managers are willing to expend economic resources merely to achieve an accounting objective.

Step 4: Evaluate the Quality of Disclosure

Managers can make it more or less easy for an analyst to assess the firm's accounting quality and to use its financial statements to understand business reality. While accounting rules require a certain amount of minimum disclosure, managers have considerable choice in the matter. Disclosure quality, therefore, is an important dimension of a firm's accounting quality.

In assessing a firm's disclosure quality, an analyst could ask the following questions:

- Does the company provide adequate disclosures to assess the firm's business strategy and its economic consequences? For example, some firms use the Letter to the Shareholders in their annual report to clearly lay out the firm's industry conditions, its competitive position, and management's plans for the future. Others use the Letter to puff up the firm's financial performance and gloss over any competitive difficulties the firm might be facing.

- Do the footnotes adequately explain the key accounting policies and assumptions and their logic? For example, if a firm's revenue and expense recognition policies differ from industry norms, the firm can explain its choices in a footnote. Similarly, when there are significant changes in a firm's policies, footnotes can be used to disclose the reasons.

- Does the firm adequately explain its current performance? The Management Discussion and Analysis section of the firm's annual report provides an opportunity to help analysts understand the reasons behind the firm's performance changes. Some firms use this section to link financial performance to business conditions. For example, if profit margins went down in a period, was it because of price competition or because of increases in manufacturing costs? If the selling and general administrative expenses went up, was it because the firm is investing in a differentiation strategy, or because unproductive overhead expenses were creeping up?

- If accounting rules and conventions restrict the firm from measuring its key success factors appropriately, does the firm provide adequate additional disclosure to help outsiders understand how these factors are being managed? For example, if a firm invests in product quality and customer service, accounting rules do not allow the management to capitalize these outlays, even when the future benefits are certain. The firm's Management Discussion and Analysis can be used to highlight how these outlays are being managed and their performance consequences. For example, the firm can disclose physical indexes of defect rates and customer satisfaction so that outsiders can assess the progress being made in these areas and the future cash flow consequences of these actions.

- If a firm is in multiple business segments, what is the quality of segment disclosure? Some firms provide excellent discussion of their performance by product segments and geographic segments. Others lump many different businesses into one broad segment. The level of competition in an industry and management's willingness to share desegregated performance data influence a firm's quality of segment disclosure.

- How forthcoming is the management with respect to bad news? A firm's disclosure quality is most clearly revealed by the way management deals with bad news. Does it adequately explain the reasons for poor performance? Does the company clearly articulate its strategy, if any, to address the company's performance problems?

- How good is the firm's investor relations program? Does the firm provide fact books with detailed data on the firm's business and performance? Is the management accessible to analysts?

Step 5: Identify Potential Red Flags

In addition to the above analysis, a common approach to accounting quality analysis is to look for "red flags" pointing to questionable accounting quality. These indicators suggest that the analyst should examine certain items more closely or gather more information on them. Some common red flags are:

- *Unexplained changes in accounting, especially when performance is poor.* This may suggest that managers are using their accounting discretion to "dress up" their financial statements.[14]

- *Unexplained transactions that boost profits.* For example, firms might undertake balance sheet transactions, such as asset sales or debt for equity swaps, to realize gains in periods when operating performance is poor.[15]

- *Unusual increases in accounts receivable in relation to sales increases.* This may suggest that the company might be relaxing its credit policies or artificially loading up its distribution channels to record revenues during the current period. If credit policies are relaxed unduly, the firm may face receivable write-offs in the subsequent periods as a result of customer defaults. If the firm accelerates shipments to the distribution channels, it may either face product returns or reduced shipments in the subsequent periods.

- *Unusual increases in inventories in relation to sales increases.* If the inventory build-up is due to an increase in finished goods inventory, it could be a sign that the demand for the firm's products is slowing down, suggesting that the firm may be forced to cut prices (and hence earn lower margins) or write down its inventory. A build-up in work-in-progress inventory tends to be good news on average, probably signaling that managers expect an increase in sales. If the build-up is in raw materials, it could suggest manufacturing or procurement inefficiencies, leading to an increase in cost of goods sold (and hence lower margins).[16]

- *An increasing gap between a firm's reported income and its cash flow from operating activities.* While it is legitimate for accrual accounting numbers to differ from cash flows, there is usually a steady relationship between the two if the company's accounting policies remain the same. Therefore, any *change* in the relationship between reported profits and operating cash flows might indicate subtle changes in the firm's accrual estimates. For example, a firm undertaking large construction contracts might use the percentage-of-completion method to record revenues. While earnings and operating cash flows are likely to differ for such a firm, they should bear a steady relationship to each other. Now suppose the firm increases revenues in a period through an aggressive application of the percentage-of-completion method. Then its earnings will go up, but its cash flow remains unaffected. This change in the firm's accounting quality will be manifested by a *change* in the relationship between the firm's earnings and cash flows.

- *An increasing gap between a firm's reported income and its tax income.* Once again, it is quite legitimate for a firm to follow different accounting policies for financial reporting and tax accounting, as long as the tax law allows it.[17] However, the relationship between a firm's book and tax accounting is likely to remain constant over time, unless there are significant changes in tax rules or accounting standards. Thus, an *increasing* gap between a firm's reported income and its tax income may indicate that the firm's financial reporting to shareholders has become more aggressive. As an example, consider that warranty expenses are estimated on an accrual basis for financial reporting, but are recorded on a cash basis for tax reporting. Unless there is a big change in the firm's product quality, these two numbers bear a consistent relationship to each other. Therefore, a change in this relationship can be an indication either that the product quality is changing significantly or that financial reporting estimates are changing.

- *A tendency to use financing mechanisms like research and development partnerships and the sale of receivables with recourse.* While these arrangements may have a sound business logic, they can also provide management with an opportunity to understate the firm's liabilities and/or overstate its assets.[18]

- *Unexpected large asset write-offs.* This may suggest that management is slow to incorporate changing business circumstances into its accounting estimates. Asset write-offs may also be a result of unexpected changes in business circumstances.[19]

- *Large fourth-quarter adjustments.* A firm's annual reports are audited by the external auditors, but its interim financial statements are usually only reviewed. If a firm's management is reluctant to make appropriate accounting estimates (such as provisions for uncollectable receivables) in its interim statements, it could be forced to make adjustments at the end of the year as a result of pressure from its external auditors. A consistent pattern of fourth-quarter adjustments, therefore, may indicate an aggressive management orientation towards interim reporting.[20]

- *Qualified audit opinions or changes in independent auditors that are not well justified.* These may indicate a firm's aggressive attitude or a tendency to "opinion shop."

- *Related-party transactions or transactions between related entities.* These transactions may lack the objectivity of the marketplace, and managers' accounting estimates related to these transactions are likely to be more subjective and potentially self-serving.

While the preceding list provides a number of red flags for potentially poor accounting quality, it is important to do further analysis before reaching final conclusions. Each of the red flags has multiple interpretations; some interpretations are based on sound business reasons, and others indicate questionable accounting. It is, therefore, best to use the red flag analysis as a starting point for further probing, not as an end point in itself.[21]

Step 6: Undo Accounting Distortions

If the accounting analysis suggests that the firm's reported numbers are misleading, analysts should attempt to restate the reported numbers to reduce the distortion to the extent possible. It is, of course, virtually impossible to undo all the distortion using outside information alone. However, some progress can be made in this direction by using the cash flow statement and the financial statement footnotes.

A firm's cash flow statement provides a reconciliation of its performance based on accrual accounting and cash accounting. If the analyst is unsure of the quality of the firm's accrual accounting, the cash flow statement provides an alternative benchmark of its performance. The cash flow statement also provides information on how individual line items in the income statement diverge from the underlying cash flows. For example, if an analyst is concerned that the firm is aggressively capitalizing certain costs that should be expensed, the information in the cash flow statement provides a basis to make the necessary adjustment.

Financial statement footnotes also provide a lot of information that is potentially useful in restating reported accounting numbers. For example, when a firm changes its accounting policies, it provides a footnote indicating the effect of that change if it is material. Similarly, some firms provide information on the details of accrual estimates such as the allowance for bad debts. The tax footnote usually provides information on the differences between a firm's accounting policies for shareholder reporting and tax reporting. Since tax reporting is often more conservative than shareholder reporting, the information in the tax footnote can be used to estimate what the earnings reported to shareholders would be under more conservative policies.

ACCOUNTING ANALYSIS PITFALLS

There are several potential pitfalls in accounting analysis that an analyst should avoid. First, it is important to remember that from an analyst's perspective, conservative accounting is not the same as "good" accounting. Financial analysts are interested in evaluating how well a firm's accounting captures business reality in an unbiased manner, and conservative accounting can be as misleading as aggressive accounting in this respect. Further, conservative accounting often provides managers with opportunities for "income smoothing." Income smoothing may prevent analysts from recognizing poor performance in a timely fashion.

A second potential mistake is to confuse unusual accounting with questionable accounting. While unusual accounting choices might make a firm's performance difficult to compare with other firms' performance, such an accounting choice might be justified if the company's business is unusual. For example, firms that follow differentiated strategies or firms that structure their business in an innovative manner to take advantage of particular market situations may make unusual accounting choices to properly reflect their business. Therefore, it is important to evaluate a company's accounting choices in the context of its business strategy.

Another potential pitfall in accounting analysis arises when an analyst attributes all changes in a firm's accounting policies and accruals to earnings management motives.[22] Accounting changes might be merely reflecting changed business circumstances. For example, as already discussed, a firm that shows unusual increases in its inventory might be preparing for a new product introduction. Similarly, unusual increases in receivables might merely be due to changes in a firm's sales strategy. Unusual decreases in the allowance for uncollectable receivables might be reflecting a firm's changed customer focus. It is therefore important for an analyst to consider all possible explanations for accounting changes and investigate them using the qualitative information available in a firm's financial statements.

VALUE OF ACCOUNTING DATA AND ACCOUNTING ANALYSIS

What is the value of accounting information and accounting analysis? Given the incentives and opportunities for managers to affect their firms' reported accounting numbers, some have argued that accounting data and accounting analysis are not likely to be useful for investors.

Researchers have examined the value of accounting by estimating the return that could be earned by an investor with perfect earnings foresight one year prior to an earnings announcement.[23] The findings show that by buying stocks of firms with increased earnings and selling stocks of firms with decreased earnings each year, a hypothetical investor could earn an average portfolio return of 37.5 percent in the period 1954 to 1996. This is equivalent to 44 percent of the return that could have been earned if the investor had perfect foresight of the stock price itself for one year, and bought stocks with increased prices and sold stocks whose price decreased. Perfect foresight of ROE permits the investor to earn an even higher rate of return, 43 percent, than perfect earnings foresight. This is equivalent to 50 percent of the return that could be earned with perfect stock price foresight.

In contrast, cash flow data appear to be considerably less valuable than earnings or ROE information. Perfect foresight of cash flows from operations would permit the hypothetical investor to earn an average annual return of only 9 percent, equivalent to 11 percent of the return that could be earned with perfect foresight of stock prices.

Overall, this research suggests that the institutional arrangements and conventions created to mitigate potential misuse of accounting by managers are effective in providing assurance to investors. The research indicates that investors do not view earnings management as so pervasive as to make earnings data unreliable.

A number of research studies have examined whether superior accounting analysis is a valuable activity. By and large, this evidence indicates that there are opportunities for superior analysts to earn positive stock returns. Research findings indicate that companies criticized in the financial press for misleading financial reporting subsequently suffered an average stock price drop of 8 percent.[24] Firms where managers appeared to inflate reported earnings prior to an equity issue and subsequently reported poor earnings performance had more negative stock performance after the offer than firms with no apparent earnings management.[25] Finally, firms subject to SEC investigation for earnings management showed an average stock price decline of 9 percent when the earnings management was first announced and continued to have poor stock performance for up to two years.[26]

These findings imply that analysts who are able to identify firms with misleading accounting are able to create value for investors. The findings also indicate that the stock market ultimately sees through earnings management. For all of these cases, earnings management is eventually uncovered and the stock price responds negatively to evidence that firms have inflated prior earnings through misleading accounting.

SUMMARY

In summary, accounting analysis is an important step in the process of analyzing corporate financial reports. The purpose of accounting analysis is to evaluate the degree to which a firm's accounting captures the underlying business reality. Sound accounting analysis improves the reliability of conclusions from financial analysis, the next step in financial statement analysis.

There are six key steps in accounting analysis. The analyst begins by identifying the key accounting policies and estimates, given the firm's industry and its business strategy. The second step is to evaluate the degree of flexibility available to managers, given the accounting rules and conventions. Next, the analyst has to evaluate how managers exercise their accounting flexibility and the likely motivations behind managers' accounting strategy. The fourth step involves assessing the depth and quality of a firm's disclosures. The analyst should next identify any red flags needing further investigation. The final accounting analysis step is to restate accounting numbers to remove any noise and bias introduced by the accounting rules and management decisions.

The subsequent five chapters apply these concepts to the analysis of assets, liabilities and equity, revenues, expenses, and business entity accounting.

DISCUSSION QUESTIONS

1. A finance student states, "I don't understand why anyone pays any attention to accounting earnings numbers, given that a 'clean' number like cash from operations is readily available." Do you agree? Why or why not?
2. Fred argues, "The standards that I like most are the ones that eliminate all management discretion in reporting—that way I get uniform numbers across all companies and don't have to worry about doing accounting analysis." Do you agree? Why or why not?
3. Bill Simon says, "We should get rid of the FASB and SEC, since free market forces will make sure that companies report reliable information." Do you agree? Why or why not?
4. Many firms recognize revenues at the point of shipment. This provides an incentive to accelerate revenues by shipping goods at the end of the quarter. Consider two com-

panies, one of which ships its product evenly throughout the quarter, and the second of which ships all its products in the last two weeks of the quarter. Each company's customers pay thirty days after receiving shipment. How can you distinguish these companies, using accounting ratios?

5. a. If management reports truthfully, what economic events are likely to prompt the following accounting changes?
   - Increase in the estimated life of depreciable assets
   - Decrease in the uncollectibles allowance as a percentage of gross receivables
   - Recognition of revenues at the point of delivery, rather than at the point cash is received
   - Capitalization of a higher proportion of software R&D costs

   b. What features of accounting, if any, would make it costly for dishonest managers to make the same changes without any corresponding economic changes?

6. The conservatism principle arises because of concerns about management's incentives to overstate the firm's performance. Joe Banks argues, "We could get rid of conservatism and make accounting numbers more useful if we delegated financial reporting to independent auditors rather than to corporate managers." Do you agree? Why or why not?

7. A fund manager states, "I refuse to buy any company that makes a voluntary accounting change, since it's certainly the case that its management is trying to hide bad news." Can you think of any alternative interpretation?

NOTES

1. Accounting analysis is sometimes also called quality of earnings analysis. We prefer to use the term accounting analysis, since we are discussing a broader concept than merely a firm's earnings quality.

2. These definitions paraphrase those of the Financial Accounting Standards Board, Statement of Financial Accounting Concepts No. 6, "Elements of Financial Statements" (1985). Our intent is to present the definitions at a conceptual, not technical, level. For more complete discussion of these and related concepts, see the FASB's *Statements of Financial Accounting Concepts*.

3. Strictly speaking, the comprehensive net income of a firm also includes gains and losses from increases and decreases in equity from nonoperating activities or extraordinary items.

4. Thus, although accrual accounting is theoretically superior to cash accounting in measuring a firm's periodic performance, the distortions it introduces can make accounting data less valuable to users. If these distortions are large enough, current cash flows may measure a firm's periodic performance better than accounting profits. The relative usefulness of cash flows and accounting profits in measuring performance, therefore, varies from firm to firm. For empirical evidence on this issue, see "Accounting earnings and cash flows as measures of firm performance: The role of accounting accruals" by Patricia M. Dechow, *Journal of Accounting and Economics* 18, 1994.

5. For example, Abraham Brilloff wrote a series of accounting analyses of public companies in *Barron's* over several years. On average, the stock prices of the analyzed companies changed by about 8 percent on the day these articles were published, indicating the potential value of

performing such analysis. For a more complete discussion of this evidence, see "Brilloff and the Capital Market: Further Evidence" by George Foster, Stanford University, working paper, 1985.

6. For a complete discussion of these motivations, see *Positive Accounting Theory* by Ross L. Watts and Jerold L. Zimmerman (Englewood Cliffs, NJ: Prentice-Hall, 1986).

7. The most convincing evidence supporting the covenant hypothesis is reported in a study of the accounting decisions by firms in financial distress: "Debt-covenant violations and managers' accounting responses," Amy Patricia Sweeney, *Journal of Accounting and Economics* 17, 1994.

8. Studies that examine the bonus hypothesis report evidence supporting the view that managers' accounting decisions are influenced by compensation considerations. See, for example, "The effect of bonus schemes on accounting decisions," Paul M. Healy, *Journal of Accounting and Economics* 12, 1985; R. Holthausen, D. Larcker, and R. Sloan, 1995, "Annual Bonus Schemes and the Manipulation of Earnings," *Journal of Accounting and Economics* 19: 29–74; and Flora Guidry, Andrew Leone, and Steve Rock, 1998, "Earnings-Based Bonus Plans and Earnings Management by Business Unit Managers," *Journal of Accounting and Economics*, forthcoming.

9. "Managerial competition, information costs, and corporate governance: The use of accounting performance measures in proxy contests," Linda DeAngelo, *Journal of Accounting and Economics* 10, 1988.

10. The trade-off between taxes and financial reporting in the context of managers' accounting decisions is discussed in detail in *Taxes and Business Strategy* by Myron Scholes and Mark Wolfson (Englewood Cliffs, NJ: Prentice-Hall, 1992). Many empirical studies have examined firms' LIFO/FIFO choices.

11. Several researchers have documented that firms affected by such situations have a motivation to influence regulators' perceptions through accounting decisions. For example, J. Jones documents that firms seeking import protections make income-decreasing accounting decisions in "Earnings management during import relief investigations," *Journal of Accounting Research* 29, 1991. A number of studies find that banks that are close to minimum capital requirements overstate loan loss provisions, understate loan write-offs, and recognize abnormal realized gains on securities portfolios (see S. Moyer, 1990, "Capital Adequacy Ratio Regulations and Accounting Choices in Commercial Banks," *Journal of Accounting and Economics* 12: 123–154; M. Scholes, G. P. Wilson, and M. Wolfson, 1990, "Tax Planning, Regulatory Capital Planning, and Financial Reporting Strategy for Commercial Banks," *Review of Financial Studies* 3: 625–650; A. Beatty, S. Chamberlain, and J. Magliolo, 1995, "Managing Financial Reports of Commercial Banks: The Influence of Taxes, Regulatory Capital and Earnings," *Journal of Accounting Research* 33, No. 2: 231–261; and J. Collins, D. Shackelford, and J. Wahlen, 1995, "Bank Differences in the Coordination of Regulatory Capital, Earnings and Taxes," *Journal of Accounting Research* 33, No. 2: 263–291). Finally, Petroni finds that financially weak property-casualty insurers that risk regulatory attention understate claim loss reserves: K. R. Petroni, 1992, "Optimistic Reporting in the Property Casualty Insurance Industry," *Journal of Accounting and Economics* 15: 485–508.

12. "The effect of firms' financial disclosure strategies on stock prices," Paul Healy and Krishna Palepu, *Accounting Horizons* 7, 1993. For a summary of the empirical evidence, see P. Healy and J. Wahlen, "Earnings Management," (Harvard Business School, working paper, 1999).

13. Financial analysts pay close attention to managers' disclosure strategies; the Financial Analysts' Federation publishes annually a report evaluating them in U.S. firms. For a discussion of these ratings, see "Cross-sectional Determinants of Analysts' Ratings of Corporate Disclosures" by Mark Lang and Russ Lundholm, *Journal of Accounting Research* 31, Autumn 1993: 246–271.

14. For a detailed analysis of a company that made such changes, see "Anatomy of an Account-

ing Change" by Krishna Palepu in *Accounting & Management: Field Study Perspectives,* edited by William J. Bruns, Jr. and Robert S. Kaplan (Boston: Harvard Business School Press, 1987).

15. An example of this type of behavior is documented by John Hand in his study, "Did Firms Undertake Debt-Equity Swaps for an Accounting Paper Profit or True Financial Gain?," *The Accounting Review* 64, October 1989.

16. For an empirical analysis of inventory build-ups, see "Do Inventory Disclosures Predict Sales and Earnings?" by Victor Bernard and James Noel, *Journal of Accounting, Auditing, and Finance,* Fall 1991.

17. This is true by and large in the United States and in several other countries. However, in some countries, such as Germany and Japan, tax accounting and financial reporting are closely tied together, and this particular red flag is not very meaningful.

18. For research on accounting and economic incentives in the formation of R&D partnerships, see "Motives for Forming Research and Development Financing Organizations" by Anne Beatty, Philip G. Berger, and Joseph Magliolo, *Journal of Accounting & Economics* 19, 1995.

19. For an empirical examination of asset write-offs, see "Write-offs as Accounting Procedures to Manage Perceptions" by John A. Elliott and Wayne H. Shaw, *Journal of Accounting Research,* Supplement, 1988.

20. Richard R. Mendenhall and William D. Nichols report evidence consistent with the hypothesis that managers take advantage of their discretion to postpone reporting bad news until the fourth quarter. See "Bad News and Differential Market Reactions to Announcements of Earlier-Quarter versus Fourth-Quarter Earnings," *Journal of Accounting Research,* Supplement, 1988.

21. This type of analysis is presented in the context of provisions for bad debts by Maureen McNichols and G. Peter Wilson in their study, "Evidence of Earnings Management from the Provisions for Bad Debts," *Journal of Accounting Research,* Supplement, 1988.

22. This point has been made by several accounting researchers. For a summary of research on earnings management, see "Earnings Management" by Katherine Schipper, *Accounting Horizons,* December 1989: 91–102.

23. See James Chang, 1998, "The Decline in Value Relevance of Earnings and Book Values," Unpublished dissertation, Harvard University. Similar evidence is reported by J. Francis and K. Schipper, 1998, "Have Financial Statements Lost Their Relevance?," working paper, University of Chicago; and W. E. Collins, E. Maydew, and I. Weiss, 1997, "Changes in the Value-Relevance of Earnings and Book Value over the Past Forty Years, *Journal of Accounting and Economics* 24: 39–67.

24. See G. Foster, 1979, "Briloff and the Capital Market," *Journal of Accounting Research* 17 (Spring): 262–274.

25. See S. H. Teoh, I. Welch, and T. J. Wong, 1998a, "Earnings Management and the Long-Run Market Performance of Initial Public Offerings," *Journal of Finance* 53, No. 6, December 1998: 1935–1974; S. H. Teoh, I. Welch, and T. J. Wong, 1998b, "Earnings Management and the Post-Issue Underperformance of Seasoned Equity Offerings," *Journal of Financial Economics* 50, No. 1, October 1998: 63–99; and S. H. Teoh, T. J. Wong, and G. Rao, 1998, "Incentives and Opportunities for Earnings Management in Initial Public Offerings," *Review of Accounting Studies*, forthcoming.

26. See Patricia Dechow, Richard G. Sloan, and Amy P. Sweeney, 1996, "Causes and Consequences of Earnings Manipulation: An Analysis of Firms Subject to Enforcement Actions by the SEC," *Contemporary Accounting Research* 13, No. 1: 1–36; and M. D. Beneish, 1997, "Detecting GAAP Violation: Implications for Assessing Earnings Management among Firms with Extreme Financial Performance," *Journal of Accounting and Public Policy* 16: 271–309.

In February 1985, Peter Roberts, the research director of Exeter Group, a small Boston-based investment advisory service specializing in turnaround stocks, was reviewing the 1984 annual report of Harnischfeger Corporation (Exhibit 4). His attention was drawn by the $1.28 per share net profit Harnischfeger reported for 1984. He knew that barely three years earlier the company had faced a severe financial crisis. Harnischfeger had defaulted on its debt and stopped dividend payments after reporting a hefty $7.64 per share net loss in fiscal 1982. The company's poor performance continued in 1983, leading to a net loss of $3.49 per share. Roberts was intrigued by Harnischfeger's rapid turnaround and wondered whether he should recommend purchase of the company's stock (see Exhibit 3 for selected data on Harnischfeger's stock).

COMPANY BUSINESS AND PRODUCTS

Harnischfeger Corporation was a machinery company based in Milwaukee, Wisconsin. The company had originally been started as a partnership in 1884 and was incorporated in Wisconsin in 1910 under the name Pawling and Harnischfeger. Its name was changed to the present one in 1924. The company went public in 1929 and was listed on the New York Stock Exchange.

The company's two major segments were the P&H Heavy Equipment Group, consisting of the Construction Equipment and the Mining and Electrical Equipment divisions, and the Industrial Technologies Group, consisting of the Material Handling Equipment and the Harnischfeger Engineers divisions. The sales mix of the company in 1983 consisted of: Construction Equipment 32 percent; Mining and Electrical Equipment 33 percent, Material Handling Equipment 29 percent, and Harnischfeger Engineers 6 percent.

Harnischfeger was a leading producer of construction equipment. Its products, bearing the widely recognized brand name P&H, included hydraulic cranes and lattice boom cranes. These were used in bridge and highway construction and for cargo and other material handling applications. Harnischfeger had market shares of about 20 percent in hydraulic cranes and about 30 percent in lattice boom cranes. In the 1980s the construction equipment industry in general was experiencing declining margins.

Electric mining shovels and excavators constituted the principal products of the Mining and Electrical Equipment Division of Harnischfeger. The company had a dominant share of the mining machinery market. The company's products were used in coal, copper, and iron mining. A significant part of the division's sales were from the sale of spare parts. Because of its large market share and the lucrative spare parts sales, the division was traditionally very profitable. Most of the company's future mining product sales were expected to occur outside the United States, principally in developing countries.

The Material Handling Equipment Division of Harnischfeger was the fourth largest supplier of automated material handling equipment, with a 9 percent market share. The division's products included overhead cranes, portal cranes, hoists, monorails, and components and parts. The demand for this equipment was expected to grow in the coming years as an increasing number of manufacturing firms emphasized cost reduction programs. Harnischfeger believed that the material handling equipment business would be a major source of its future growth.

Harnischfeger Engineers was an engineering services division engaged in design, custom software development, and project management for factory and distribution automation projects. The division engineered and installed complete automated material handling systems for a wide variety of applications on a fee basis. The company expected such automated storage and retrieval systems to play an increasingly important role in the "factory of the future."

Harnischfeger had a number of subsidiaries, affiliated companies, and licensees in a number of countries. Export and foreign sales constituted more than 50 percent of the total revenues of the company.

FINANCIAL DIFFICULTIES OF 1982

The machinery industry experienced a period of explosive growth during the 1970s. Harnischfeger expanded rapidly during this period, growing from $205 million in revenues in 1973 to $644 million in 1980. To fund this growth, the company relied increasingly on debt financing, and the firm's debt/equity ratio rose from 0.88 in 1973 to 1.26 in 1980. The worldwide recession in the early 1980s caused a significant drop in demand for the company's products starting in 1981 and culminated in a series of events that shook the financial stability of Harnischfeger.

Reduced sales and the high interest payments resulted in poor profit performance leading to a reported loss in 1982 of $77 million. The management of Harnischfeger commented on its financial difficulties:

There is a persistent weakness in the basic industries, both in the United States and overseas, which have been large, traditional markets for P&H products. Energy-related projects, which had been a major source of business of our Construction Equipment Division, have slowed significantly in the last year as a result of lower oil demand and subsequent price decline, not only in the U.S. but throughout the world. Lack of demand for such basic minerals as iron ore, copper and bauxite have decreased worldwide mining activity, causing reduced sales for mining equipment, although coal mining remains relatively strong worldwide. Difficult economic conditions have caused many of our normal customers to cut capital expenditures dramatically, especially in such depressed sectors as the steel industry, which has always been a major source of sales for all P&H products.

The significant operating losses recorded in 1982 and the credit losses experienced by its finance subsidiary caused Harnischfeger to default on certain covenants of its loan agreements. The most restrictive provisions of the company's loan agreements required it to maintain a minimum working capital of $175 million, consolidated net worth of $180 million, and a ratio of current assets to current liabilities of 1.75. On October 31, 1982, the company's working capital (after reclassification of about $115 million long-term debt as a current liability) was $29.3 million, the consolidated net worth was $142.2 million, and the ratio of current assets to current liabilities was 1.12. Harnischfeger Credit Corporation, an unconsolidated finance subsidiary, also defaulted on certain covenants of its loan agreements, largely due to significant credit losses relating to the financing of construction equipment sold to a large distributor. As a result of these covenant violations, the company's long-term debt of $124.3 million became due on demand, the unused portion of the bank revolving credit line of $25.0 million became unavailable, and the unused short-term bank credit lines of $12.0 million were canceled. In addition, the $25.1 million debt of Harnischfeger Credit Corporation also became immediately due. The company was forced to stop paying dividends and began negotiations with its lenders to restructure its debt to permit operations to continue. Price Waterhouse, the company's audit firm, qualified its audit opinion on Harnischfeger's 1982 annual report with respect to the outcome of the company's negotiations with its lenders.

CORPORATE RECOVERY PLAN

Harnischfeger responded to the financial crisis facing the firm by developing a corporate recovery plan. The plan consisted of four elements: (1) changes in the top management, (2) cost reductions to lower the break-even point, (3) reorientation of the company's business, and (4) debt restructuring and recapitalization. The actions taken in each of these four areas are described below.

To deal effectively with the financial crisis, Henry Harnischfeger, then Chairman and Chief Executive Officer of the company, created the position of Chief Operating Officer. After an extensive search, the position was offered in August 1982 to William Goessel, who had considerable experience in the machinery industry. Another addition to the management team was Jeffrey Grade, who joined the company in 1983 as Senior Vice President of Finance and Administration and Chief Financial Officer. Grade's appointment was necessitated by the early retirement of the previous Vice President of Finance in 1982. The engineering, manufacturing, and marketing functions were also restructured to streamline the company's operations (see Exhibits 1 and 2 for additional information on Harnischfeger's current management).

To deal with the short-term liquidity squeeze, the company initiated a number of cost reduction measures. These included (1) reducing the workforce from 6,900 to 3,800; (2) eliminating management bonuses and reducing benefits and freezing wages of salaried and hourly employees; (3) liquidating excess inventories and stretching payments to creditors; and (4) permanent closure of the construction equipment plant at Escanaba, Michigan. These and other related measures improved the company's cash position and helped to reduce the rate of loss during fiscal 1983.

Concurrent with the above cost reduction measures, the new management made some strategic decisions to reorient Harnischfeger's business. First, the company entered into a long-term agreement with Kobe Steel, Ltd., of Japan. Under this agreement, Kobe agreed to supply Harnischfeger's requirements for construction cranes for sale in the United States as Harnischfeger phased out its own manufacture of cranes. This step was expected to significantly reduce the manufacturing costs of Harnischfeger's construction equipment, enabling it to compete effectively in the domestic market. Second, the company decided to emphasize the high technology part of its business by targeting for future growth the material handling equipment and systems business. To facilitate this strategy, the Industrial Technologies Group was created. As part of the reorientation, the company stated that it would develop and acquire new products, technology, and equipment and would expand its abilities to provide computer-integrated solutions to handling, storing, and retrieval in areas hitherto not pursued—industries such as distribution warehousing, food, pharmaceuticals, and aerospace.

While Harnischfeger was implementing its turnaround strategy, it was engaged at the same time in complex and difficult negotiations with its bankers. On January 6, 1984, the company entered into agreements with its lenders to restructure its debt obligations into three-year term loans secured by fixed as well as other assets, with a one-year extension option. This agreement required, among other things, specified minimum levels of cash and unpledged receivables, working capital, and net worth.

The company reported a net loss of $35 million in 1983, down from the $77 million loss the year before. Based on the above developments during the year, in the 1983 annual report the management expressed confidence that the company would return to profitability soon:

> *We approach our second century with optimism, knowing that the negative events of the last three years are behind us, and with a firm belief that positive achievements will be recorded in 1984. By the time the corporation celebrates its 100th birthday on December 1, we are confident it will be operating profitably and attaining new levels of market strength and leadership.*

During 1984 the company reported profits during each of the four quarters, ending the year with a pre-tax operating profit of $5.7 million, and a net income after tax and extraordinary credits of $15 million (see Exhibit 4). It also raised substantial new capital through a public offering of debentures and common stock. Net proceeds from the offering, which totaled $150 million, were used to pay off all of the company's restructured debt. In the 1984 annual report the management commented on the company's performance as follows:

> *1984 was the Corporation's Centennial year and we marked the occasion by rededicating ourselves to excellence through market leadership, customer service and improved operating performance and profitability.*
>
> ⋮
>
> *We look back with pride. We move ahead with confidence and optimism. Our major markets have never been more competitive; however, we will strive to take advantage of any and all opportunities for growth and to attain satisfactory profitability. Collectively, we will do what has to be done to ensure that the future will be rewarding to all who have a part in our success.*

QUESTIONS

1. Identify all the accounting policy changes and accounting estimates that Harnischfeger made during 1984. Estimate, as accurately as possible, the effect of these on the company's 1984 reported profits.
2. What do you think are the motives of Harnischfeger's management in making the changes in its financial reporting policies? Do you think investors will see through these changes?
3. Assess the company's future prospects, given your insights from questions 1 and 2 and the information in the case about the company's turnaround strategy.

EXHIBIT 1

Harnischfeger Corporation Board of Directions in 1984

	Director Since	Current Term	Shares Owned
Edward W. Duffy Chairman of the Board and Chief Executive Officer of United States Gypsum Company, manufacturer of building materials and products used in industrial processes, since 1983; Vice Chairman from 1981 to 1983; President and Chief Operating Officer from 1971 to 1981. Director, American National Bank and Trust Company of Chicago, Walter E. Heller International Corporation, W. W. Grainger, Inc., and UNR Industries, Inc. Age 64.	1981	1985	100
Herbert V. Kohler, Jr. Chairman, Chief Executive Officer, and Director of Kohler Company, manufacturer of plumbing and specialty products, engines, and generators, since 1972; President since 1974. Age 44.	1973	1985	700
Taisuke Mori Executive Vice Chairman and Director of Kobe Steel, Ltd., a Japanese manufacturer of steel and steel products, industrial machinery, construction equipment, aluminum, copper and alloy products, and welding equipment and consumables. Age 63.	1981	1985	None
William W. Goessel President and Chief Operating Officer of the Corporation since 1982. Executive Vice President of Beloit Corporation from 1978 to 1982. Director, Goulds Pumps, Inc. Age 56.	1982	1986	15,000
Henry Harnischfeger Chairman of the Board and Chief Executive Officer of the Corporation since 1970; President from 1959 to 1982. Director, First Wisconsin Corporation and First Wisconsin National Bank of Milwaukee. Age 60.	1945	1986	611,362
Karl F. Nygren Partner in Kirkland & Ellis, attorneys, since 1959. Age 56.	1964	1986	2,000

continued

Harnischfeger Corporation

Harnischfeger Corporation

	Director Since	Current Term	Shares Owned
John P. Gallagher Senior lecturer, Graduate School of Business, University of Chicago. Director, IC Industries, Inc., Stone Container Corporation, UNR Industries, Inc., American National Bank and Trust Company of Chicago, and Walter E. Heller International Corporation. Age 67.	1979	1987	500
Jeffrey T. Grade Senior Vice President/Finance and Administration and Chief Financial Officer of the Corporation since August 1, 1983. Vice President Corporate Finance of IC Industries from 1981 to 1983; Assistant Vice President from 1976 to 1981. Age 40.	1983	1987	3,750
Donald Taylor President, Chief Operating Officer, and Director of Rexnord, Inc., a major manufacturer of industrial components and machinery, since 1978. Director, Johnson Controls, Inc., Marine Corporation, and Marine Bank, N.A. Age 56.	1979	1987	100
Frank A. Lee Director of Foster Wheeler Corporation since 1971; Chairman of the Board from 1981 to 1982; President and Chief Executive Officer from 1978 to 1981. Director, Belco Pollution Control Corporation, International General Industries, Inc., and Banker's Life Insurance Co. Age 59.	1983	1987	None

EXHIBIT 2

Executive Compensation, Harnischfeger Corporation

The following table sets forth all cash compensation paid to each of the Corporation's five most highly compensated executive officers and to all executive officers as a group for services rendered to the Corporation and its subsidiaries during fiscal 1984.

		Cash Compensation
Henry Harnischfeger	Chairman of the Board and Chief Executive Officer	$ 364,004
William W. Goessel	President and Chief Operating Officer	280,000
C. P. Cousland	Senior Vice President and group executive, P&H Heavy Equipment	210,000
Jeffrey T. Grade	Senior Vice President-Finance and Administration and Chief Financial Officer	205,336
Douglas E. Holt	President, Harnischfeger Engineers, Inc.	152,839
All persons who were executive officers during the fiscal year as a group (14 persons)		2,159,066

1985 EXECUTIVE INCENTIVE PLAN

In December 1984, the board of directors established an Executive Incentive Plan for fiscal 1985 which provides an incentive compensation opportunity of 40% of annual salary for 11 senior executive officers only if the Corporation reaches a specific net after-tax profit objective; it provides an additional incentive compensation of up to 40% of annual salary for seven of those officers if the corporation exceeds the objective. The Plan covers the chairman, president, senior vice presidents; president, Harnischfeger Engineers, Inc.; vice president, P&H World Services; vice president; Material Handling Equipment; and secretary. Awards made in fiscal year 1984 are included in the compensation table above.

EXHIBIT 3
Harnischfeger Corporation, Selected Stock Price and Market Data

A. STOCK PRICES

	Harnischfeger's Stock Price			S&P 400 Industrials Index		
	High	Low	Close	High	Low	Close
January 4, 1985	9 1/8	8 6/8	9	186.4	181.8	182.2
January 11, 1985	10 6/8	8 7/8	10 5/8	188.2	182.2	182.8
January 18, 1985	11	10	10 4/8	191.9	186.9	191.3
January 25, 1985	11 2/8	10 1/8	11	199.7	191.3	198.6
February 1, 1985	11 5/8	10 7/8	11 2/8	201.8	198.6	200.0

Harnischfeger's stock beta = 0.95 (Value Line estimate)

B. MARKET DATA

	February 1985
Median P/E ratio of Dow Jones Industrials	10.9
Median P/E ratio of Value Line stocks	11.3
Median P/E ratio of machinery industry (construction and mining equipment)	10.0
Prime rate	10.5%
91-day Treasury bill rate	8.4%
30-year Treasury bond yield	11.4%
Moody's Aaa corporate bond yield	12.0%

EXHIBIT 4
Harnischfeger Corporation 1984 Annual Report (abridged)

TO OUR SHAREHOLDERS

The Corporation recorded gains in each quarter during fiscal 1984, returning to profitability despite the continued depressed demand and intense price competition in the world markets it serves.

For the year ended October 31, net income was $15,176,000 or $1.28 per common share, which included $11,005,000 or 93¢ per share from the cumulative effect of a change in depreciation accounting. In 1983, the Corporation reported a loss of $34,630,000 or $3.49 per share.

Sales for 1984 improved 24% over the preceding year, rising to $398.7 million from $321 million a year ago. New orders totaled $451 million, a $101 million increase over 1983. We entered fiscal 1985 with a backlog of $193 million, which compared to $141 million a year earlier.

ALL DIVISIONS IMPROVED

All product divisions recorded sales and operating improvements during 1984.

Mining equipment was the strongest performer with sales up over 60%, including major orders from Turkey and the People's Republic of China. During the year we began the implementation of the training, engineering and manufacturing license agreement concluded in November, 1983 with the People's Republic of China, which offers the Corporation long-term potential in modernizing and mechanizing this vast and rapidly developing mining market.

Sales of material handling equipment and systems were up 10% for the year and the increasingly stronger bookings recorded during the latter part of the year are continuing into the first quarter of 1985.

Sales on construction equipment products showed some signs of selective improvement. In the fourth quarter, bookings more than doubled from the very depressed levels in the same period a year ago, although the current level is still far below what is needed to achieve acceptable operating results for this product line.

FINANCIAL STABILITY RESTORED

In April, the financial stability of the Corporation was improved through a public offering of 2.15 million shares of common stock, $50 million of 15% notes due April 15, 1994, and $100 million of 12% subordinated debentures due April 15, 2004, with two million common stock purchase warrants.

Net proceeds from the offering totaled $149 million, to which we added an additional $23 million in cash, enabling us to pay off all of our long-term debt. As a result of the refinancing, the Corporation gained permanent long-term capital with minimal annual cash flow requirements to service it. We now have the financial resources and flexibility to pursue new opportunities to grow and diversify.

Furthermore, should we require additional funds, they will be available through a $52 million unsecured three-year revolving credit agreement concluded in June with ten U.S. and Canadian banks. An $80 million product financing capability was also arranged through a major U.S. bank to provide financing to customers purchasing P&H products.

OUTLOOK

Throughout 1985 we believe we will see gradual improvements in most of our U.S. and world markets.

For our mining excavator product line, coal and certain metals mining are expected to show a more favorable long-term outlook in selected foreign requirements and our capability to source equipment from the U.S., Japan or Europe places us in a strong marketing position. In the U.S., we see only a moderate strengthening in machinery requirements for coal, while metals mining will remain weak.

Continuing shipments of the Turkish order throughout 1985 will help to stabilize our plant utilization levels and improve our operating results for this product line.

In our material handling and systems markets, particularly in the U.S., we are experiencing a moderately strong continuation of the improved bookings which we began to see in the third and fourth quarters of last year.

In construction lifting equipment markets, we expect modest overall economic improvement in the U.S., which should help to absorb the large numbers of idle lifting equipment that have been manufacturer, distributor and customer inventories for the last three years. As this overhang on the market is reduced we will see gradual improvement in new sales. Harnischfeger traditionally exports half of its U.S.-produced lifting products. However, as with mining equipment, the continued strength of the U.S. dollar severely restricts our ability to sell U.S.-built products in world markets.

In addition to the strong dollar and economic instability in many foreign nations, overcapacity in worldwide heavy equipment manufacturing remains a serious problem in spite of some exits from the market as well as consolidations within the industry.

The Corporation continues to respond to severe price competition through systematic cost reduction programs and through expanded sourcing of P&H equipment from our European operation and, most importantly, through our 30-year association with our Japanese partner, Kobe Steel, Ltd. P&H engineering and technology have established world standards for quality and performance for construction cranes and mining equipment, which customers can expect from every P&H machine regardless of its source. More than a dozen new models of foreign-sourced P&H construction cranes will be made available for the first time in the U.S. during 1985, broadening our existing product lines and giving competitive pricing to our U.S. distributors and customers.

To improve our future operating results, we restructured our three operating divisions into two groups. All construction and mining related activities are in the new "P&H Heavy Equipment Group." All material handling equipment and systems activities are now merged into the "Industrial Technologies Group." More information on these Groups is reported in their respective sections.

We are pleased to announce that John P. Moran was elected Senior Vice President and Group Executive, Industrial Technologies Group, and John R. Teitgen was elected Secretary and General Counsel.

In September Robert F. Schnoes became a member of our Board of Directors. He is President and Chief Executive Officer of Burgess, Inc. and of Ultrasonic Power Corporation, and a member of the Board of Signode Industries, Inc.

BEGINNING OUR SECOND CENTURY

1984 was the Corporation's Centennial year and we marked the occasion by rededicating ourselves to excellence through market leadership, customer service and improved operating performance and profitability.

Our first century of achievement resulted from the dedicated effort, support and cooperation of our employees, distributors, suppliers, lenders, and shareholders, and we thank all of them.

We look back with pride. We move ahead with confidence and optimism. Our major markets have never been more competitive; however, we will strive to take advantage of any and all opportunities for growth and to attain satisfactory profitability. Collectively, we will do what has to be done to ensure that the future will be rewarding to all who have a part in our success.

Henry Harnischfeger
Chairman of the Board

William W. Goessel
President

January 31, 1985

MANAGEMENT'S DISCUSSION & ANALYSIS

RESULTS OF OPERATIONS

1984 Compared to 1983

Consolidated net sales of $399 million in fiscal 1984 increased $78 million or 24% over 1983. Sales increases were 62% in the Mining and Electrical Equipment Segment, and 10% in the Industrial Technologies Segment. Sales in the Construction Equipment Segment were virtually unchanged reflecting the continued low demand for construction equipment world-wide.

Effective at the beginning of fiscal 1984, net sales include the full sales price of construction and mining equipment purchased from Kobe Steel, Ltd. and sold by the Corporation, in order to reflect more effectively the nature of the Corporation's transactions with Kobe. Such sales aggregated $28.0 million in 1984.

The $4.0 million increase in Other Income reflected a recovery of certain claims and higher license and technical service fees.

Cost of Sales was equal to 79.1% of net sales in 1984 and 81.4% in 1983; which together with the increase in net sales resulted in a $23.9 million increase in gross profit (net sales less cost of sales). Contributing to this increase were improved sales of higher-margin replacement parts in the Mining Equipment and Industrial Technologies Segments and a reduction in excess manufacturing costs through greater utilization of domestic manufacturing capacity and economies in total manufacturing costs including a reduction in pension expense. Reductions of certain LIFO inventories increased gross profit by $2.4 million in 1984 and $15.6 million in 1983.

Product development selling and administrative expenses were reduced, due to the funding of R&D expenses in the Construction Equipment Segment pursuant to the October 1983 Agreement with Kobe Steel, Ltd., to reductions in pension expenses and provision for credit losses, and to the absence of the corporate financial restructuring expenses incurred in 1983.

Net interest expense in 1984 increased $2.9 million due to higher interest rates on the outstanding funded debt and a reduction in interest income.

Equity in Earnings (Loss) of Unconsolidated Companies included 1984 income of $1.2 million of Harnischfeger Credit Corporation, an unconsolidated finance subsidiary, reflecting an income tax benefit of $1.4 million not previously recorded.

The preceding items, together with the cumulative effect of the change in depreciation method described in Financial Note 2, were included in net income of $15.2 million or $1.28 per common share, compared with net loss of $34.6 million or $3.49 per share in 1983.

The sales orders booked and unshipped backlogs of orders of the Corporation's three segments are summarized as follows (in million of dollars):

Orders Booked	1984	1983
Industrial Technologies	$132	$106
Mining and Electrical Equipment	210	135
Construction Equipment	109	109
	$451	$350

Backlogs at October 31		
Industrial Technologies	$ 79	$ 71
Mining and Electrical Equipment	91	50
Construction Equipment	23	20
	$193	$141

1983 Compared to 1982

Consolidated net sales of $321 million in fiscal 1983 were $126 million or 28% below 1982. This decline reflected, for the second consecutive year, the continued low demand in all markets served by the Corporation's products, with exports even more severely depressed due to the strength of the dollar. The largest decline was reported in the Construction Equipment Segment, down 34%; Mining and Electrical Equipment Segment shipments were down 27%, and the Industrial Technologies Segment, 23%.

Cost of Sales was equal to 81.4% of net sales in 1983 and 81.9% in 1982. The resulting gross profit was $60 million in 1983 and $81 million in 1982, a reduction equal to the rate of sales decrease.

The benefits of reduced manufacturing capacity and economies in total manufacturing costs were offset by reduced selling prices in the highly competitive markets. Reductions of certain LIFO inventories increased gross profits by $15.6 million in 1983 and $7.2 million in 1982.

Product development, selling and administrative expenses were reduced as a result of expense reduction measures in response to the lower volume of business and undertaken in connection with the Corporation's corporate recovery program, and reduced provisions for credit losses, which in 1982 included $4.0 million in income support for Harnischfeger Credit Corporation.

Net interest expense was reduced $9.1 million from 1982 to 1983, due primarily to increased interest income from short-term cash investments and an accrual of $4.7 million in interest income on refundable income taxes not previously recorded.

The Credit for Income Taxes included a federal income tax benefit of $5 million, based upon the recent examination of the Corporation's income tax returns and refund claims. No income tax benefits were available for the losses of the U.S. operations in 1983.

The losses from unconsolidated companies recorded in 1983 included $0.5 million in Harnischfeger Credit Corporation; $2.1 million in Cranetex, Inc., a Corporation-owned distributorship in Texas; and $0.8 million in ASEA Industrial Systems Inc., then a 49%-owned joint venture between the Corporation and ASEA AB and now 19%-owned with the investment accounted for on the cost method.

The preceding items were reflected in a net loss of $34.6 million or $3.49 per share.

LIQUIDITY AND FINANCIAL RESOURCES

In April 1984, the Corporation issued in public offerings 2,150,000 shares of Common Stock, $50 million principal amount of 15% Senior Notes due in 1994, and 100,000 Units consisting of $100 million principal amount of 12% Subordinated Debentures due in 2004 and 2,000,000 Common Stock Purchase Warrants.

The net proceeds from the sales of the securities of $149 million were used to prepay substantially all of the outstanding debt of the Corporation and certain of its subsidiaries.

During the year ended October 31, 1984, the consolidated cash balances increased $32 million to a balance of $96 million, with the cash activity summarized as follows (in million of dollars):

Funds provided by operations	$10
Funds returned to the Corporation upon restructuring of the Salaried Employees' Pension Plan	39
Debt repayment less the proceeds of sales of securities	(9)
Plant and equipment additions	(6)
All other changes—net	(2)
	$32

In the third quarter of fiscal 1984 the Corporation entered into a $52 million three-year revolving credit agreement with ten U.S. and Canadian banks. While the Corporation has adequate liquidity to meet its current working capital requirements, the revolver represents another step in the Corporation's program to strengthen its financial position and provide the required financial resources to respond to opportunities as they arise.

CONSOLIDATED STATEMENT OF OPERATIONS

(Dollar amounts in thousands except per share figures)	Year Ended October 31		
	1984	1983	1982
Revenues:			
Net sales	**$398,708**	$321,010	$447,461
Other income, including license and technical service fees	**7,067**	3,111	5,209
	405,775	324,121	452,670
Cost of Sales	**315,216**	261,384	366,297
Operating Income	**90,559**	62,737	86,373
Less:			
Product development, selling and administrative expenses	**72,196**	85,795	113,457
Interest expense—net	**12,625**	9,745	18,873
Provision for plant closing	**—**	—	23,700
Income (Loss) Before Provision (Credit) for Income Taxes, Equity Items and Cumulative Effect of Accounting Change	**5,738**	(32,803)	(69,657)
Provision (Credit) for Income Taxes	**2,425**	(1,400)	(1,600)
Income (Loss) Before Equity Items and Cumulative Effect of Accounting Change	**3,313**	(31,403)	(68,057)
Equity items:			
Equity in earnings (loss) of unconsolidated companies	**993**	(3,397)	(7,891)
Minority interest in (earnings) loss of consolidated subsidiaries	**(135)**	170	(583)
Income (Loss) Before Cumulative Effect of Accounting Change	**4,171**	(34,630)	(76,531)
Cumulative Effect of Change in Depreciation Method	**11,005**	—	—
Net Income (Loss)	**$ 15,176**	$(34,630)	$ (76,531)
Earnings (Loss) per Common and Common Equivalent Share:			
Income (Loss) before cumulative effect of accounting change	**$ .35**	$(3.49)	$(7.64)
Cumulative effect of change in depreciation method	**.93**	—	—
Net income (loss)	**$1.28**	$(3.49)	$(7.64)
Pro forma Amounts Assuming the Changed Depreciation Method Had Been Applied Retroactively:			
Net (loss)		$ (33,918)	$ (76,695)
(Loss) per common share		$(3.42)	$(7.65)

(The accompanying notes are an integral part of the financial statements.)

Harnischfeger Corporation

CONSOLIDATED BALANCE SHEET

	October 31	
(Dollar amounts in thousands except per share figures)	**1984**	1983
Assets		
Current Assets:		
Cash and temporary investments	**$ 96,007**	$ 64,275
Accounts receivable	**87,648**	63,740
Inventories	**144,312**	153,594
Refundable income taxes and related interest	**1,296**	12,585
Other current assets	**5,502**	6,023
Prepaid income taxes	**14,494**	14,232
	349,259	314,449
Investments and Other Assets:		
Investments in and advances to:		
Finance subsidiary, at equity in net assets	**8,849**	6,704
Other companies	**4,445**	2,514
Other assets	**13,959**	6,411
	27,253	15,629
Operating Plants:		
Land and improvements	**9,419**	10,370
Buildings	**59,083**	60,377
Machinery and equipment	**120,949**	122,154
	189,451	192,901
Accumulated depreciation	**(93,259)**	(107,577)
	96,192	85,324
	$472,704	$415,402

(continued)

CONSOLIDATED BALANCE SHEET (continued)

	October 31	
(Dollar amounts in thousands except per share figures)	**1984**	1983
Liabilities and Shareholders' Equity		
Current Liabilities:		
Short-term notes payable to banks by subsidiaries	$ **9,090**	$ 8,155
Long-term debt and capitalized lease obligations payable within one year	**973**	18,265
Trade accounts payable	**37,716**	21,228
Employee compensation and benefits	**15,041**	14,343
Accrued plant closing costs	**2,460**	6,348
Advance payments and progress billings	**20,619**	15,886
Income taxes payable	**1,645**	3,463
Account payable to finance subsidiary	**—**	3,436
Other current liabilities and accruals	**29,673**	32,333
	117,217	123,457
Long-Term Obligations:		
Long-term debt payable to:		
Unaffiliated lenders	**128,550**	139,092
Finance subsidiary	**—**	5,400
Capitalized lease obligations	**7,870**	8,120
	136,420	152,612
Deferred Liabilities and Income Taxes:		
Accrued pension costs	**57,611**	19,098
Other deferred liabilities	**5,299**	7,777
Deferred income taxes	**6,385**	134
	69,295	27,009
Minority Interest	**2,400**	2,405
Shareholders' Equity:		
Preferred stock $100 par value—authorized 250,000 shares:		
Series A $7.00 cumulative convertible preferred shares: authorized, issued and outstanding 117,500 shares in 1984 and 100,000 shares in 1983	**11,750**	10,000
Common stock, $1 par value—authorized 25,000,000 shares: issued and outstanding 12,283,563 shares in 1984 and 10,133,563 shares in 1983	**12,284**	10,134
Capital in excess of par value of shares	**114,333**	88,332
Retained earnings	**19,901**	6,475
Cumulative translation adjustments	**(10,896)**	(5,022)
	147,372	109,919
	$472,704	$415,402

(The accompanying notes are an integral part of the financial statements.)

Harnischfeger Corporation

CONSOLIDATED STATEMENT OF CHANGES IN FINANCIAL POSITION

Harnischfeger Corporation

(Dollar amounts in thousands)	Year Ended October 31,		
	1984	1983	1982
Funds Were Provided by (Applied to):			
Operations:			
Income (loss) before cumulative effect of accounting change	**$ 4,171**	$ (34,630)	$(76,531)
Cumulative effect of change in depreciation method	**11,005**	—	—
Net income (loss)	**15,176**	(34,630)	(76,531)
Add (deduct) items included not affecting funds:			
Depreciation	**8,077**	13,552	15,241
Unremitted (earnings) loss of unconsolidated companies	**(993)**	3,397	7, 891
Deferred pension contributions	**(500)**	4,834	—
Deferred income taxes	**6,583**	(3,178)	1,406
Reduction in accumulated depreciation resulting from change in depreciation method	**(17,205)**	—	—
Other—net	**(2,168)**	(67)	2,034
Decrease in operating working capital (see below)	**7,039**	11,605	72,172
Add (deduct) effects on operating working capital of:			
Conversion of export and factored receivable sales to debt	**—**	23,919	—
Reclassification to deferred liabilities:			
Accrued pension costs	**—**	14,264	—
Other liabilities	**—**	5,510	—
Foreign currency translation adjustments	**(6,009)**	(1,919)	(5,943)
Funds provided by operations	**10,000**	37,287	16,270
Financing, Investment and Other Activities:			
Transactions in debt and capitalized lease obligations —Long-Term debt and capitalized lease obligations:			
Proceeds from sale of 15% Senior Notes and 12% Subordinated Debentures, net of issue costs	**120,530**	—	—
Other increases	**1,474**	—	25,698
Repayments	**(161,500)**	(760)	(9,409)
Restructured debt	**—**	158,058	—
Debt replaced, including conversion of receivable sales of $23,919, and short-term bank notes payable of $9,028	**—**	(158,058)	—
	(39,496)	(760)	16,289
Net increase (repayment) in short-term bank notes payable	**2,107**	(3,982)	(2,016)
Net increase (repayment) in debt and capitalized lease obligations	**(37,389)**	(4,742)	14,273

(continued)

CONSOLIDATED STATEMENT OF CHANGES IN FINANCIAL POSITION (continued)

(Dollar amounts in thousands)	Year Ended October 31,		
	1984	1983	1982
Issuance of:			
Common stock	**21,310**	—	449
Common stock purchase warrants	**6,663**	—	—
Salaried pension assets reversion	**39,307**	—	—
Plant and equipment additions	**(5,546**)	(1,871)	(10,819)
Advances to unconsolidated companies	**(2,882)**	—	—
Other—net	**269**	1,531	848
Funds provided by (applied to) financing, investment and other activities	**21,732**	(5,082)	4,751
Increase in Cash and Temporary Investments Before Cash Dividends	**$ 31,732**	$ 32,205	$21,021
Cash Dividends	**—**	—	(2,369)
Increase in Cash and Temporary Investments	**$ 31,732**	$ 32,205	$ 18,652
Decrease (Increase) in Operating Working Capital (Excluding Cash Items, Debt and Capitalized Lease Obligations):			
Accounts receivable	**$ (23,908)**	$ (5,327)	$ 42,293
Inventories	**9,282**	56,904	26,124
Refundable income taxes and related interest	**11,289**	(2,584)	(6,268)
Other current assets	**259**	10,008	(439)
Trade accounts payable	**16,488**	(1,757)	(3,302)
Employee compensation and benefits	**698**	(15,564)	(3,702)
Accrued plant closing costs	**(3,888)**	(14,148)	20,496
Other current liabilities	**(3,181)**	(15,927)	(3,030)
Decrease in operating working capital	**$ 7,039**	$ 11,605	$ 72,172

(The accompanying notes are an integral part of the financial statements.)

Harnischfeger Corporation

Harnischfeger Corporation

CONSOLIDATED STATEMENT OF SHAREHOLDERS' EQUITY

(Dollar amounts in thousands except per share figures)	Preferred Stock	Common Stock	Capital in Excess of Par Value of Shares	Retained Earnings	Cumulative Translation Adjustments	Total
Balance at October 31, 1981	$10,000	$10,085	$ 87,932	$120,005	$ —	$228,022
Cumulative translation adjustments through October 31, 1981					(1,195)	(1,195)
Issuance of Common Stock:						
10,000 shares to Kobe Steel, Ltd.		10	91			101
38,161 shares under stock purchase and dividend reinvestment plans		39	309			348
Net (loss)				(76,531)		(76,531)
Cash dividends paid on:						
Preferred stock				(350)		(350)
Common stock $.20 per share				(2,019)		(2,019)
Translation adjustments, net of deferred income taxes of $128					(2,928)	(2,928)
Balance at October 31, 1982	10,000	10,134	88,332	41,105	(4,123)	145,448
Net (loss)				(34,630)		(34,630)
Translation adjustments, including deferred income taxes of $33					(899)	(899)
Balance at October 31, 1983	10,000	10,134	88,332	6,475	(5,022)	109,919
Issuance of:						
2,150,000 shares of common stock		2,150	19,160			21,310
2,000,000 common stock purchase warrants			6,663			6,663
17,500 shares of Series A $7.00 cumulative convertible preferred stock in discharge of dividends payable on preferred stock	1,750			(1,750)		—
Net income				15,176		15,176
Translation adjustments, net of deferred income taxes of $300					(5,874)	(5,874)
Other			178			178
Balance at October 31, 1984	$11,750	$12,284	$114,333	$ 19,901	$(10,896)	$147,372

(The accompanying notes are an integral part of the financial statements.)

FINANCIAL NOTES

Note 1
Summary of Significant Accounting Policies:

Consolidation—The consolidated financial statements include the accounts of all majority-owned subsidiaries except a wholly-owned domestic finance subsidiary, a subsidiary organized in 1982 as a temporary successor to a distributor, both of which are accounted for under the equity method, and a wholly-owned Brazilian subsidiary, which is carried at estimated net realizable value due to economic uncertainty. All related significant intercompany balances and transactions have been eliminated in consolidation.

Financial statements of certain consolidated subsidiaries, principally foreign, are included, effective in fiscal year 1984, on the basis of their fiscal years ending September 30; previously, certain of such subsidiaries had fiscal years ending July (See Note 2). Such fiscal periods have been adopted by the subsidiaries in order to provide for a more timely consolidation with the Corporation.

Inventories—The Corporation values its inventories at the lower of cost or market. Cost is determined by the last-in, first-out (LIFO) method for inventories located principally in the United States, and by the first-in, first-out (FIFO) method for inventories of foreign subsidiaries.

Operating Plants, Equipment and Depreciation—Properties are stated at cost. Maintenance and repairs are charged to expense as incurred and expenditures for betterments and renewals are capitalized. Effective in 1981, interest is capitalized for qualifying assets during their acquisition period. Capitalized interest is amortized on the same basis as the related asset. When properties are sold or otherwise disposed of, the cost and accumulated depreciation are removed from the accounts and any gain or loss is included in income.

Depreciation of plants and equipment is provided over the estimated useful lives of the related assets, or over the lease terms of capital leases, using, effective in fiscal year 1984, the straight-line method for financial reporting, and principally accelerated methods for tax reporting purposes. Previously, accelerated methods, where applicable, were also used for financial reporting purposes (See Note 2). For U.S. income tax purposes, depreciation lives are based principally on the Class Life Asset Depreciation Range for additions, other than buildings, in the years 1973 through 1980, and on the Accelerated Cost Recovery System for all additions after 1980.

Discontinued facilities held for sale are carried at the lower of cost less accumulated depreciation or estimated realizable value, which aggregated $4.9 million and $3.6 million at October 31, 1984 and 1983, respectively, and were included in Other Assets in the accompanying Balance Sheet.

Pension Plans—The Corporation has pension plans covering substantially all of its employees. Pension expenses of the principal defined benefit plans consist of current service costs of such plans and amortization of the prior service costs and actuarial gains and losses over periods ranging from 10 to 30 years. The Corporation's policy is to fund at a minimum the amount required under the Employee Retirement Income Security Act of 1974.

Income Taxes—The consolidated tax provision is computed based on income and expenses recorded in the Statement of Operations. Prepaid or deferred taxes are recorded for the difference between such taxes and taxes computed for tax returns. The Corporation and its domestic subsidiaries file a consolidated federal income tax return. The operating results of Harnischfeger GmbH are included in the Corporation's U.S. income tax returns.

Additional taxes are provided on the earnings of foreign subsidiaries which are intended to be remitted to the Corporation. Such taxes are not provided on subsidiaries' unremitted earnings which are intended to be permanently reinvested.

Investment tax credits are accounted for under the flow-through method as a reduction of the income tax provision, if applicable, in the year the related asset is placed in service.

Reporting Format—Certain previously reported items have been conformed to the current year's presentation.

Note 2
Accounting Changes:

Effective November 1, 1983, the Corporation includes in its net sales products purchased from

Kobe Steel, Ltd. and sold by the Corporation, to reflect more effectively the nature of the Corporation's transactions with Kobe. Previously only the gross margin on Kobe-originated equipment was included. During fiscal year 1984 such sales aggregated $28.0 million. Also, effective November 1, 1983, the financial statements of certain foreign subsidiaries are included on the basis of their fiscal years ending September 30 instead of the previous years ending July 31. This change had the effect of increasing net sales by $5.4 million for the year ended October 31, 1984. The impact of these changes on net income was insignificant.

In 1984, the Corporation has computed depreciation expense on plants, machinery and equipment using the straight-line method for financial reporting purposes. Prior to 1984, the Corporation used principally accelerated methods for its U.S. operating plants. The cumulative effect of this change, which was applied retroactively to all assets previously subjected to accelerated depreciation, increased net income for 1984 by $11.0 million or $.93 per common and common equivalent share. The impact of the new method on income for the year 1984 before the cumulative effect was insignificant.

As a result of the review of its depreciation policy, the Corporation, effective November 1, 1983, has changed its estimated depreciation lives on certain U.S. plants, machinery and equipment and residual values on certain machinery and equipment, which increased net income for 1984 by $3.2 million or $.27 per share. No income tax effect was applied to this change.

The changes in accounting for depreciation were made to conform the Corporation's depreciation policy to those used by manufacturers in the Corporation's and similar industries and to provide a more equitable allocation of the cost of plants, machinery and equipment over their useful lives.

Note 3

Cash and Temporary Investments:

Cash and temporary investments consisted of the following (in thousands of dollars):

	October 31,	
	1984	1983
Cash—in demand deposits	**$ 2,155**	$11,910
—in special accounts principally to support letters of credit	**4,516**	—
Temporary investments	**89,336**	52,365
	$96,007	$64,275

Temporary investments consisted of short-term U.S. and Canadian treasury bills, money market funds, time and certificates of deposit, commercial paper and bank repurchase agreements and bankers' acceptances. Temporary investments are stated at cost plus accrued interest, which approximates market value.

Note 4

Long-Term Debt, Bank Credit Lines and Interest Expense:

Outstanding long-term debt payable to unaffiliated lenders was as follows (in thousands of dollars):

	October 31,	
	1984	1983
Parent Company:		
15% Senior Notes due April 15, 1994	**$ 47,700**	$ —
12% Subordinated Debentures, with an effective interest rate of 16.3%; sinking fund redemption payments of $7,500 due annually on April 15 in 1994–2003, and final payment of $25,000 in 2004	**100,000**	—
Term Obligations— Insurance company debt:		
9% Notes	**—**	20,000
9 7/8 Notes	**—**	38,750
8 7/8 Notes	**—**	40,500
Bank debt, at 105% of prime	**—**	25,000
Paper purchase debt, at prime or LIBOR, plus 1¼%	**—**	18,519
9.23% Mortgage Note due monthly to April, 1998	**4,327**	4,481
	152,027	147,250

	October 31,	
	1984	1983
Consolidated Subsidiaries:		
Notes payable to banks in German marks	—	9,889
Contract payable in 1985–1989, in South African rands, with imputed interest rate of 12%	**1,024**	—
Other	**—**	36
	153,051	157,175
Less: Amounts payable within one year	**644**	17,799
Unamortized discounts	**23,857**	284
Long-Term Debt—excluding amounts payable within one year	**$128,550**	$139,092

Note 5

Harnischfeger Credit Corporation and Cranetex, Inc.

Condensed financial information of Harnischfeger Credit Corporation ("Credit"), an unconsolidated wholly-owned finance subsidiary, accounted for under the equity method, was as follows (in thousands of dollars):

Balance Sheet	October 31,	
	1984	1983
Assets:		
Cash and temporary investments	**$ 404**	$19,824
Finance receivables—net	**4,335**	11,412
Factored account note and current account receivable from parent company	**—**	8,836
Other assets	**4,181**	661
	$8,920	$40,733
Liabilities and Shareholder's Equity:		
Debt payable	**$ —**	$32,600
Advances from parent company	**950**	—
Other liabilities	**71**	1,429
	1,021	34,029
Shareholder's equity	**7,899**	6,704
	$8,920	$40,733

Statement of Operations	Year Ended October 31,		
	1984	1983	1982
Revenues	**$1,165**	$2,662	$9,978
Less:			
Operating Expenses	**1,530**	3,386	14,613
Provision (credit) for income taxes	**(1,560)**	(222)	180
Net income (loss)	**$1,195**	$(502)	$(4,815)

Credit's purchases of finance receivables from the Corporation aggregated $1.1 million in 1984, $46.7 million in 1983 and $50.4 million in 1982. In 1982, Credit received income support of $4.0 million from the Corporation.

In 1982, the Corporation organized Cranetex, Inc. to assume certain assets and liabilities transferred by a former distributor of construction equipment, in settlement of the Corporation's and Credit's claims against the distributor and to continue the business on an interim basis until the franchise can be transferred to a new distributor. The Corporation recorded provisions of $2.5 million in 1983 and $2.3 million in 1982 and Credit recorded a provision of $6.7 million in 1982, for credit losses incurred in the financing of equipment sold to the former distributor.

The condensed balance sheet of Cranetex, Inc. was as follows (in thousand of dollars):

	October 31,	
	1984	1983
Assets:		
Cash	**$ 143**	$ 49
Accounts receivables	**566**	428
Inventory	**2,314**	3,464
Property and equipment	**1,547**	1,674
	$4,570	$5,615
Liabilities and Deficit:		
Loans payable	**$4,325**	$6,682
Other liabilities	**338**	620
	4,663	7,302
Shareholder's (deficit), net of accounts and advances payable to parent company	**(93)**	(1,687)
	$4,570	$5,615

The net losses of Cranetex, Inc. of $.2 million in 1984, $2.1 million in 1983 and $1.0 million in 1982 were included in Equity in Earnings (Loss) of Unconsolidated Companies in the Corporation's Statement of Operations.

Note 6

Transactions with Kobe Steel, Ltd. and ASEA Industrial Systems Inc.

Kobe Steel, Ltd. of Japan ("Kobe"), has been a licensee for certain of the Corporation's products since 1955, and has owned certain Harnischfeger Japanese construction equipment patents and technology since 1981. As of October 31, 1984, Kobe held 1,030,000 shares or 8.4% of the Corporation's outstanding Common Stock (See Note 13). Kobe also owns 25% of the capital stock of Harnischfeger of Australia Pty. Ltd., a subsidiary of the Corporation. This ownership appears as the minority interest on the Corporation's balance sheet.

Under agreements expiring in December 1990, Kobe pays technical service fees on P&H mining equipment produced and sold under license from the Corporation, and trademark and marketing fees on sales of construction equipment outside of Japan. Net fee income received from Kobe was $4.3 million in 1984, $3.1 million in 1983, and $3.9 million in 1982; this income is included in Other Income in the accompanying Statement of Operations.

In October 1983, the Corporation entered into a ten-year agreement with Kobe under which Kobe agreed to supply the Corporation's requirements for construction cranes for sale in the United States as it phases out its own manufacture of cranes over the next several years, and to make the Corporation the exclusive distributor of Kobe-built cranes in the United States. The Agreement also involves a joint research and development program for construction equipment under which the Corporation agreed to spend at least $17 million over a three-year period and provided it does so, Kobe agreed to pay this amount to the Corporation. Sales of cranes outside the United States continue under the contract terms described in the preceding paragraph.

The Corporation's sales to Kobe, principally components for mining and construction equipment, excluding the R&D expenses discussed in the preceding paragraph, approximated $5.2 million, $10.5 million and $7.0 million during the three years ended October 31, 1984, 1983 and 1982, respectively. The purchases from Kobe of mining and construction equipment and components amounted to approximately $33.7 million, $15.5 million and $29.9 million during the three years ended October 31, 1984, 1983 and 1982, respectively, most of which were resold to customers (See Note 2).

The Corporation owns 19% of ASEA Industrial Systems Inc. ("AIS"), an electrical equipment company controlled by ASEA AB of Sweden. The Corporation's purchases of electrical components from AIS aggregated $11.2 million in 1984 and $6.1 million in 1983 and its sales to AIS approximated $2.6 million in 1984 and $3.8 million in 1983.

The Corporation believes that its transactions with Kobe and AIS were competitive with alternative sources of supply for each party involved.

Note 7

Inventories

Consolidated inventories consisted of the following (in thousand of dollars):

	October 31,	
	1984	1983
At lower of cost or market (FIFO method):		
Raw materials	**$ 11,003**	$ 11,904
Work in process and purchased parts	**88,279**	72,956
Finished goods	**79,111**	105,923
	178,393	190,783
Allowance to reduce inventories to cost on the LIFO method	**(34,081)**	(37,189)
	$144,312	$153,594

Inventories valued on the LIFO method represented approximately 82% of total inventories at both October 31, 1984 and 1983.

Inventory reductions in 1984, 1983 and 1982 resulted in a liquidation of LIFO inventory quantities carried at lower costs compared with the current cost of their acquisitions. The effect of these liquidations was to increase net income by 2.4 million or $.20

per common share in fiscal 1984, and to reduce the net loss by approximately $15.6 million or $1.54 per share in 1983, and by $6.7 million or $.66 per share in 1982; no income tax effect applied to the adjustment in 1984 and 1983.

Note 8

Accounts Receivable

Accounts receivable were net of allowances for doubtful accounts of $5.9 million and $6.4 million at October 31, 1984 and 1983, respectively.

Note 9

Research and Development Expense

Research and development expense incurred in the development of new products or significant improvements to existing products was $5.1 million in 1984 (net of amounts funded by Kobe Steel, Ltd.) $12.1 million in 1983 and $14.1 million in 1982.

Note 10

Foreign Operations

The net sales, net income (loss) and net assets of subsidiaries located in countries outside the United States and Canada and included in the consolidated financial statements were as follows (in thousands of dollars):

	Year Ended October 31,		
	1984	1983	1982
Net sales	**$78,074**	$45,912	$69,216
Net income (loss) after minority interests	**828**	(1,191)	3,080
Corporation's equity in total net assets	**17,734**	7,716	7,287

Foreign currency transaction losses included in Cost of Sales were $2.7 million in 1984, $1.2 million in 1983 and $1.3 million in 1982.

Note 11

Pension Plans and Other Postretirement Benefits

Pension expense for all plans of the Corporation and its consolidated subsidiaries was $1.9 million in

1984, $6.5million in 1983 and $12.2 million in 1982.

Accumulated plan benefits and plan net assets for the Corporation's U.S. defined benefit plans, at the beginning of the fiscal years 1984 and 1983, with the data for the Salaried Employees' Retirement Plan as in effect on August 1, 1984, were as follows (in thousands of dollars):

	1984	1983
Actuarial present value of accumulated plan benefits:		
Vested	**$52,639**	$108,123
Nonvested	**2,363**	5,227
	$55,002	$113,350
Net assets available for benefits:		
Asset s of the Pension Trusts	**$45,331**	$112,075
Accrued contributions not paid to the Trusts	**16,717**	12,167
	$62,048	$124,242

The Salaried Employees' Retirement Plan, which covers substantially all salaried employees in the U.S., was restructured during 1984 due to overfunding of the Plan. Effective August 1, 1984, the Corporation terminated the existing plan and established a new plan which is substantially identical to the prior plan except for an improvement in the minimum pension benefit. All participants in the prior plan became fully vested upon its termination. All vested benefits earned through August 1, 1984 were covered through the purchase of individual annuities at a cost aggregating $36.7 million. The remaining plan assets, which totaled $39.3 million, reverted to the Corporation in cash upon receipt of regulatory approval of the prior plan termination from the Pension Benefit Guaranty Corporation. For financial reporting purposes, the new plan is considered to be a continuation of the terminated plan. Accordingly, the $39.3 million actuarial gain which resulted from the restructuring is included in Accrued Pension Costs in the accompanying Balance Sheet and is being amortized to income over a ten-year period commencing in 1984. For tax reporting purposes, the asset reversion will be treated as a fiscal 1985 transaction. The initial unfunded actuarial liability of the new plan, computed as of November 1, 1983, of $10.3 million is also included in Accrued Pension Costs.

In 1982 and 1983, the Pension Trusts purchased certain securities with effective yields of 13% and 12%, respectively, and dedicated these assets to the plan benefits of a substantial portion of the retired employees and certain terminated employees with deferred vested rights. These rates, together with 9% for active employees in 1984, 8% in 1983 and 7¼% in 1982, were the assumed rates of return used in determining the annual pension expense and the actuarial present value of accumulated plan benefits for the U.S. plans.

The effect of the changes in the investment return assumption rates for all U.S. plans, together with the 1984 restructuring of the U.S. Salaried Employees' Plan, was to reduce pension expense by approximately $4.0 million in 1984 and $2.0 million in 1983, and the actuarial present value of accumulated plan benefits by approximately $60.0 million in 1984. Pension expense in 1983 was also reduced $2.1 million from the lower level of active employees. Other actuarial gains, including higher than anticipated investment results, more than offset the additional pension costs resulting from plan changes and interest charges on balance sheet accruals in 1984 and 1983.

The Corporation's foreign pension plans do not determine the actuarial value of accumulated benefits or net assets available for retirement benefits as calculated and disclosed above. For those plans, the total of the plans' pension funds and balance sheet accruals approximated the actuarially computed value of vested benefits at both October 31, 1984 and 1983.

The Corporation generally provides certain health care and life insurance benefits for U.S. retired employees. Substantially all of the Corporation's current U.S. employees may become eligible for such benefits upon retirement. Life insurance benefits are provided either through the pension plans or separate group insurance arrangements. The cost of retiree health care and life insurance benefits, other than the benefits provided by the pension plans, is expensed as incurred; such costs approximated $2.6 million in 1984 and $1.7 million in 1983.

Note 12

Income Taxes

Domestic and foreign income (loss) before income tax effects was as follows (in thousands of dollars):

| | Year Ended October 31, | | |
	1984	1983	1982
Domestic	**$1,578**	$(35,412)	$(77,600)
Foreign:			
Harnischfeger GmbH	**432**	(2,159)	(475)
All other	**3,728**	4,768	8,418
	4,160	2,609	7,943
Total income (loss) before income tax effects, equity items and cumulative effect of accounting change	**$5,738**	$(32,803)	$(69,657)

Provision (credit) for income taxes, on income (loss) before income tax effects, equity items and cumulative effect of accounting change, consisted of (in thousands of dollars):

	1984	1983	1982
Currently payable (refundable):			
Federal	**$ —**	$(7,957)	$(9,736)
State	**136**	297	70
Foreign	**2,518**	3,379	5,376
	2,654	(4,281)	(4,290)
Deferred (prepaid):			
Federal	**—**	2,955	2,713
State and foreign	**(229)**	(74)	(23)
	(229)	2,881	2,690
Provision (credit) for income taxes	**$2,425**	$(1,400)	$(1,600)

During 1983 an examination of the Corporation's 1977–1981 federal income tax returns and certain refund claims was completed by the Internal Revenue Service, and as a result, a current credit for federal income taxes of $8.0 million was recorded in 1983, $3.0 million of which was applied to the reduction of prepaid income taxes.

In 1984, tax credits fully offset any federal income tax otherwise applicable to the year's income, and in 1983 and 1982, the relationship of the tax benefit to the pre-tax loss differed substantially from the U.S. statutory tax rate due principally to losses from the domestic operations for which only a partial federal tax benefit was available in 1982. Consequently, an analysis of deferred income taxes and variance from the U.S. statutory rate is not presented.

Unremitted earnings of foreign subsidiaries which have been or are intended to be permanently reinvested were $19.1 million at October 31, 1984. Such earnings, if distributed, would incur income tax expense of substantially less than the U.S. income tax rate as a result of previously paid foreign income taxes, provided that such foreign taxes would become deductible as foreign tax credits. No income tax provision was made in respect of the tax-deferred income of a consolidated subsidiary that has elected to be taxed as a domestic international sales corporation. The Deficit Reduction Act of 1984 provides for such income to become nontaxable effective December 31, 1984.

At October 31, 1984, the Corporation had federal tax operating loss carry-forwards of approximately $70.0 million, expiring in 1998 and 1999, for tax return purposes, and $88.0 million for book purposes. In addition, the Corporation had for tax purposes, foreign tax credit carry-forwards of $3.0 million (expiring in 1985 through 1989), and investment tax credit carry-forwards of $1.0 million (expiring in 1997 through 1999). For book purposes, tax credit carry-forwards approximately $8.0 million. The carry-forward will be available for the reduction of future income tax provisions, the extent and timing of which are not determinable.

Differences in income (loss) before income taxes for financial and tax purposes arise from timing differences between financial and tax reporting and relate to depreciation, consolidating eliminations for inter-company profits in inventories, and provisions, principally, for warranty, pension, compensated absences, product liability and plant closing costs.

REPORT OF INDEPENDENT ACCOUNTANTS

Milwaukee, Wisconsin
November 29, 1984

To the Directors and Shareholders of Harnischfeger Corporation:

In our opinion, the financial statements, which appear on pages 18 to 34 of this report, present fairly the consolidated financial position of Harnischfeger Corporation and its subsidiaries at October 31, 1984 and 1983, and the results of their operations and the changes in their financial position for each of the three years in the period ended October 31, 1984, in conformity with generally accepted accounting principles consistently applied during the period except for the change, with which we concur, in the method of accounting for depreciation expense as described in Note 2 on page 23 of this report. Our examinations of these statements were made in accordance with generally accepted auditing standards and accordingly included such tests of the accounting records and such other auditing procedures as we considered necessary in the circumstances.

Price Waterhouse

Harnischfeger Corporation

Asset Analysis

Assets are resources owned by a firm that are likely to produce future economic benefits and that are measurable with a reasonable degree of certainty. Assets can take a variety of forms, including cash, marketable securities, receivables from customers, inventory, fixed assets, long-term investments in other companies, and intangibles.

The key principles used to identify and value assets are historical cost and conservatism. Under the historical cost principle, assets are valued at their original cost; conservatism requires asset values to be revised downward if fair values are less than cost.

Analysis of assets involves asking whether an outlay should be recorded as an asset in the firm's financial statements, or whether it should be reported as a current expense. This requires analysts to understand who has the rights of ownership to the resource, whether it is expected to generate future benefits, and whether those benefits are measurable with reasonable certainty. Finally, asset analysis involves evaluating the value of the assets reported in the financial statements, requiring an evaluation of amortization, allowances, and write-downs.

In this chapter we discuss the key principles underlying the recording of assets. We also show the challenges in asset reporting and opportunities for analysis.

HISTORICAL COST AND CONSERVATISM

Assets are used to generate future profits for owners. Investors are interested in learning whether the resources they have invested in the firm have been spent wisely. The balance sheet provides a useful starting point for this type of analysis because it provides information on the value of the resources that management acquires or develops. In most countries the assets reported in the balance sheet are valued at historical exchange prices. Historical exchange prices rather than fair values, replacement values, or values in use, are used to record assets because they can typically be more easily verified. From the perspective of investors, this is important because managers have an incentive to present a favorable view of their stewardship of the firm's resources. By requiring that transactions be recorded at historical exchange prices, accounting places a constraint on managers' ability to overstate the value of the assets that they have acquired or developed. Of course, historical cost also limits the information that is available to investors about the potential of the firm's assets, since exchange prices are usually different from fair values or values in use.

The conservatism principle establishes one exception to the use of historical cost values. It requires management to write down to their fair value assets that have been impaired. The lower of cost or market rule for valuing inventory, the estimation of expected receivable losses from uncollectible accounts, and write-downs of operating assets that are not expected to recover their cost are all applications of this concept. Conservatism therefore provides additional assurance for investors that management's estimate of the value of the firm's resources is not overstated. As a result, asset values reported on the balance sheet can be considered a lower bound on the value of future benefits resulting from management's current business strategy.

Adherence to the principles of historical cost and conservatism has been challenged recently. In the U.S., some financial instruments are required to be valued at fair values rather than historical cost. Further, in the U.K., Australia, and several other countries, other classes of tangible and intangible assets are permitted to be valued at fair values.

ASSET REPORTING CHALLENGES

The critical challenge for financial reporting is to determine which types of expenditures qualify as assets. Figure 4-1 shows the major criteria for recognizing an asset. Not surprisingly, these are related to the criteria used for recognizing expenses, discussed in Chapter 7. The key questions for recognizing an asset involve assessing who has ownership of the resources in question, whether those resources are expected to provide future economic benefits, and whether benefits can be measured with reasonable certainty.

Figure 4-1 Criteria for Recognizing Assets and Implementation Challenges

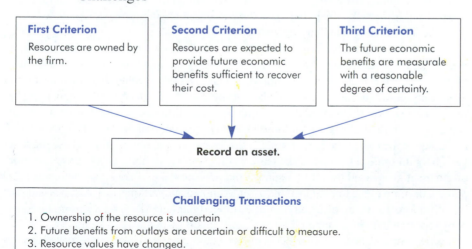

First Criterion	Second Criterion	Third Criterion
Resources are owned by the firm.	Resources are expected to provide future economic benefits sufficient to recover their cost.	The future economic benefits are measurable with a reasonable degree of certainty.

Record an asset.

Challenging Transactions
1. Ownership of the resource is uncertain
2. Future benefits from outlays are uncertain or difficult to measure.
3. Resource values have changed.

As we discuss throughout this chapter, asset recognition creates a number of opportunities for management to exercise financial reporting judgment. These opportunities are particularly prevalent for transactions where ownership of a resource is uncertain. They can also arise when the economic benefits from outlays are uncertain or difficult to quantify, or when resource values have changed. Below we discuss these types of reporting challenges.

Challenge One: Ownership of Resources Is Uncertain

For most resources used by a firm, ownership is relatively straightforward: the firm using the resource owns the asset. However, for some transactions the question of who owns a resource can be subtle. We discuss two examples of transactions that provide interesting challenges for deciding on ownership. The first is for a leased resource. Who is the effective owner of the asset—the lessor or the lessee? The second transaction is for employee training. Who effectively owns the benefits created by a training program—the company providing the training or the employee?

EXAMPLE: LEASED RESOURCES.   On December 31, 1998, American Airlines reported that it leased 42 percent of its fleet of aircraft (273 planes) for lease periods of 10 to 25 years. American Airlines reported that it had annual obligations under these leases in excess of $1 billion for each of the next five years and $13.4 billion thereafter. In its annual report the company noted that "aircraft leases can generally be renewed at rates based on fair market value at the end of the lease term for one to five years. Most aircraft leases have purchase options at or near the end of the lease term at fair market value, but generally not to exceed a stated percentage of the defined lessor's cost of the aircraft or at a predetermined fixed amount." Who was the effective owner of these aircraft? Did American Airlines effectively purchase them using financing provided by the lessor, or were the leases really rental arrangements?

Assessing whether a lease arrangement is equivalent to a purchase or rental is subjective. It depends on whether the lessee has effectively accepted risks of ownership, such as obsolescence and physical deterioration. In an attempt to standardize the reporting of lease transactions, accounting standards have created clear criteria for distinguishing between the two types. Under SFAS 13, a lease transaction is equivalent to an asset purchase if any of the following conditions hold: (1) ownership of the asset is transferred to the lessee at the end of the lease term, (2) the lessee has the option to purchase the asset for a bargain price at the end of the lease term, (3) the lease term is 75 percent or more of the asset's expected useful life, and (4) the present value of the lease payments is 90 percent or more of the fair value of the asset. As noted above, American Airlines had purchase options for many of its aircraft at estimated market prices. In addition, the company reported that the assumed life for aircraft that it owned was 25 years.

Lease contracts that satisfy the criteria for an effective purchase are recorded as capital leases at the present value of the lease payments. This same amount is also shown as a liability, to reflect the financing of the asset purchase. In subsequent periods, the leased equipment is depreciated over the life of the lease, and the lease payments are treated as interest and liability payments. In 1998 American capitalized leases for 187 planes and recorded a lease liability for these aircraft for $1,671 million.

Lease contracts that do not qualify as an effective purchase for accounting purposes are termed operating leases. The lessee then reports rental expense throughout the lease term. American Airlines reported only 86 lease agreements as operating leases in 1998.

Of course, because the criteria for reporting leases are objective, they create opportunities for management to circumvent the spirit of the distinction between capital and operating leases. For example, American Airline's management can write the lease terms in such a way that a transaction satisfies the definition of either an operating lease or a capital lease. In addition, implementing the lease reporting standards requires management to forecast leased planes' useful lives and their fair values. By comparing the company's capital lease liability ($1,671 million) to the payments for all lease obligations from 1999 to 2003, analysts can see that although it had more capital than operating leases, American used operating leases for its most expensive equipment. Was this a conscious operating strategy, or was the company seeking to keep the effective liability to finance its more expensive aircraft off the balance sheet?

EXAMPLE: HUMAN CAPITAL.   Companies spend considerable amounts on professional development and training for their employees. Formal employee training by U.S. firms is estimated to cost anywhere from $30 to $148 billion per year. If one factors in informal, on-the-job training these costs increase by a factor of two to three times.[1]

Training programs range from those that emphasize the enhancement of firm-specific skills that are unlikely to be transferable to other jobs, to training that upgrades an employee's general skills and would be valued by other employers. Firms may be willing to provide general training only if the employee makes a commitment to remain with the company for some period after completing the training. This type of commitment is typical for firms that pay for employees to attend MBA programs.

Firms that spend resources for formal training typically do so in anticipation that they will have long-term benefits for the firm through increased productivity and/or product or service quality. How should these expenditures be recorded? Should they be viewed as an asset and amortized over the employees' expected life with the firm? Or should they be expensed immediately?

Accountants argue that skills created through training are not owned by the firm but by the employee. Thus, employees can leave one firm and take a position with another without the current employer's approval. It is also difficult to calibrate the effect of training on future performance. As a result, accounting standards in the U.S. and elsewhere require that training costs be written off immediately.

Given the accounting treatment of training costs, financial analysis can add value by distinguishing between firms that succeed and those that fail to create value through employee training. This can be critical for firms where human capital is a key resource. Such is the case for professional firms. Training can also create a valuable asset for firms that rely on sales staffs with specialized knowledge of the technical details of their firms' products. Training for these types of firms may be critical to the creation of customer value and to the firms' reputations in their product markets.

Key Analysis Questions

The above discussion implies that when ownership is difficult to define, management sometimes has the opportunity to use judgment to decide whether to record the acquisition of a resource as an asset. In other cases management may not have any judgment because accounting standards do not permit *any* firms to record the acquisition of resources as assets. Both situations create opportunities for financial analysis. The first creates an opportunity to evaluate the assumptions that underlie the method of reporting used by management. The second creates an opportunity to distinguish firms that are likely to retain the benefits of resource outlays, even when ownership is vague, from those that cannot. As a result, the following questions are likely to be useful for analysts:

- What resources for a firm are excluded from its balance sheet because ownership of resulting benefits is uncertain? If these resources are critical to its strategy and value creation, what alternative metrics are available for evaluating how well these resources have been managed? For example, if human capital is a key asset, how much does the firm spend on training? What is the rate of employee turnover? What metrics does the firm use to evaluate the effectiveness of its training programs?
- Does management appear to be deliberately writing contracts to avoid full ownership of key resources? If so, what factors explain this behavior? For example, what types of leasing arrangement does the firm have? Are leases used to manage technology risks that are outside management's control or to report key assets (and liabilities) off the balance sheet?
- If leases are used to avoid reporting key assets and liabilities, what is the effect of recording these items on the financial statements?
- Has the firm changed its method of reporting for resource outlays where there are ownership questions? For example, has it changed its method of amortizing capital lease assets? What factors explain these decisions? Has it changed its business or operating model?

Challenge Two: Economic Benefits Are Uncertain or Are Difficult to Measure

A second challenge in determining whether an outlay qualifies as an asset arises when the future economic benefits attributable to the outlay are difficult to measure or highly uncertain. It is almost always difficult to accurately forecast any future benefits associated with capital outlays because the world is uncertain. A company does not know whether a competitor will offer a new product or service that makes its own obsolete. It does not know whether the products manufactured at a new plant will be the type that customers want to buy. It does not know whether changes in the price of oil make its oil drilling equipment less valuable. When do accountants view these uncertainties and measurement problems to be sufficiently severe that they require outlays with multi-period benefits to be expensed? When can such expenditures be capitalized?

The economic values of most resources are based on estimates of uncertain future economic benefits. For example, receivables values are net of uncollectibles, leased and owned assets have future residual values, and marketing and R&D outlays create brand values. Below we discuss reporting for three types of outlays to illustrate how accountants view uncertainty in recording assets: goodwill, brands, and deferred tax assets.

EXAMPLE: GOODWILL.   On February 9, 1996, Walt Disney Co. acquired Capital Cities/ABC Inc. for $10.1 billion in cash and 155 million shares of Disney valued at $8.8 billion based on the stock price at the date the transaction was announced. Cap Cities owned and operated the ABC Television Network, eight television stations, the ABC Radio Networks and 21 radio stations, and 80 percent of ESPN, Inc., and it provided programming for cable television. It also published daily and weekly newspapers, shopping guides, various specialized and business periodicals, and books. The bulk of these assets were intangible. In 1994, immediately prior to the acquisition, Cap Cities estimated that approximately 85 percent of its $5.3 billion of broadcasting revenues and 70 percent of its $1.1 billion publishing revenues came from the sale of advertising, rather than any tangible product or service.

Disney estimated the fair value of ABC's tangible assets at $4.0 billion ($1.5 billion in cash) and its liabilities at $4.3 billion. How should the acquisition be recorded on Disney's books? Should the difference between the $18.9 billion purchase price and the $0.3 billion of net liabilities be recorded as an intangible asset on Disney's books? If so, what are the benefits Disney expects to realize from the acquisition? Alternatively, should the $19.2 billion difference be written off?

Prior to Disney's offer, the market valued ABC's equity at approximately $9 billion. This implies that Disney paid more than a 100 percent premium for ABC's intangible assets. Here is where the accounting issues become tricky. If the full acquisition price is to be shown as an asset, Disney's management and auditors have to be confident that this outlay is recoverable. But what makes ABC's intangibles worth twice as much to Disney as they were to the company's prior owners? Or did Disney simply overpay for Cap Cities/ABC, implying that it is unlikely to recover the $19 billion in goodwill?

Accountants in most countries now require companies like Disney to record the value of acquired tangible assets and liabilities at their fair values and to show the full $19 billion of goodwill as an asset. The justification for this approach is that there has been an arm's-length transaction between the buyer and seller. There is a presumption that Disney's management has made an acquisition that does not destroy value for its own stockholders, and that it has the best information on the value created as a result of its plans for the new firm. These presumptions underlie the valuation of goodwill, unless there is evidence to the contrary. After the acquisition, Disney is required under U.S. accounting to amortize the goodwill over a maximum of forty years (see Chapter 7).

Two challenges arise from this form of accounting. First, since it is difficult to assess whether the merger is achieving the expected benefits, it is difficult to estimate whether goodwill has become "badwill." This is complicated by management's incentives. If the merger does not work out as planned, management is unlikely to want to own up to making a mistake. Second, the creation of an arbitrary period for amortizing goodwill makes it difficult for firms that make successful acquisitions to distinguish themselves from those that make neutral ones. If both use a forty-year amortization period, the firm that has enhanced shareholder value reports the acquisition in exactly the same manner as the firm that created no new value.

EXAMPLE: BRANDS.   Coca-Cola Inc. reports a book value of equity of $8.4 billion and has a market value of $165 billion. Much of this difference is attributable to the value of Coke's brand. Coke created the brand through years of investment in advertising, promotion, and packaging. Other well-known brands include Marlborough, Nescafe, Kodak, Microsoft, Budweiser, Kellogg's, Gillette, McDonald's, Gucci, Mercedes, and Baccardi. Brand-name products can create value for their owners by (a) permitting lower levels of marketing than the competition, due to high market awareness, (b) creating leverage with distributors and retailers, since customers expect them to carry the brand, and (c) enabling higher prices than the competition, due to higher customer perception of value. Unlike patents or copyrights, brands have no limit in terms of how long they can apply. If they are well managed, they can be enduring assets.

As noted in Chapter 7, the advertising, promotion, and packaging activities that give rise to brands are typically expensed. This convention was adopted because of the difficulty in linking advertising outlays with brand creation. Given the difficulty in valuing brands in the first place, and given the challenge in assessing when and how much advertising enhances brand values and affects only the current period's sales, accountants have traditionally avoided showing brand capital as an asset. In the U.S., even brands that have been acquired are not reported separately and are included as part of intangible assets.

In Australia and the U.K., however, firms have been permitted to report brand assets on their books. The driving force behind this phenomenon has been mergers and acquisitions. Target firms have valued and revalued brands on their books. For example, in 1989, following an increased acquisition interest from General Cinema, Cadbury Schweppes valued brands acquired since 1985. These assets were not amortized but reviewed annually for any diminution in value. In 1997 Cadbury reported brand intangibles on its balance sheet at £1.575 billion, representing one-third of its total assets.

Showing brands on the books as assets provides management with a way of communicating their value to investors. It also signals that managers are aware of the importance of these assets and provides an annual indication of how well they have been managed. Brands that have been managed well are likely to retain their value, whereas mismanaged brands will have to be written down. However, including brands on the balance sheet also raises opportunities for misuse of management judgment. Given the difficulty in estimating brand values, investors are likely to be concerned that management overstates the value of brands and fails to recognize any declines in value on a timely basis. Management may be able to mitigate these concerns by using independent valuation experts to value brand assets and by having auditors sign off on the valuations. However, even these forms of verification are unlikely to completely eliminate investors' concerns.

For firms where brands are not reported as assets (i.e., most firms), the challenge for management is to provide other ways to convince investors of the value of brands. For example, in its 1998 annual report, Coca-Cola provided the following performance data for its key brands in North America:

AVERAGE ANNUAL GROWTH U.S. UNIT CASE VOLUME	GROUP PROFILE		
	Population		305 million
1 Year	Per Capita		377
Coca-Cola USA ▇▇▇▇▇ 6%	High Per Capita	Rome, Georgia, at 821	
Rest of Industry* ▇▇ 3%	Low Per Capita	Quebec, Canada, at 142	
5 Years	**BRAND HIGHLIGHTS** 1998 vs. 1997 Unit Case Sales Growth	Coca-Cola Classic	3%
Coca-Cola USA ▇▇▇▇▇ 6%		Diet Coke	4%
Rest of Industry* ▇ 2%		Sprite	9%
		Also Notable:	
*Rest of industry includes soft drinks only.		Fruitopia	105%
		POWERaDE	33%
		Minute Maid soft drinks	29%
		Nestea	20%
		Barq's	18%

Source: Coca-Cola Annual Report, 1998

Coca-Cola also outlined its initiatives to support its brands. In North America these included sponsorship of NASCAR and the distribution of 50 million Coca-Cola cards offering discounts at more than 10,000 retailers across the United States. In addition, the company announced 1999 plans for extensions of its brands by adding two new POWERaDE flavors (Arctic Shatter and Dark Downburst), a new flavor for Fruitopia (Kiwiberry Ruckus), and the launch of Dasani, a purified water with added minerals. Similar details were provided for Coke's other markets. For example, in Argentina a new marketing campaign was initiated to encourage use of Coke products at meal times. In Asia the company focused on increasing the availability of its products through expanded use of vending machines. In Mexico sponsorship of basketball was used to boost consumption of Sprite. The challenge for investors and financial statement users is to assess whether these marketing initiatives and brand extensions are likely to be successful in creating value for Coca-Cola.

EXAMPLE: DEFERRED TAX ASSETS.   Tax laws in the U.S. and many other countries permit firms with tax operating losses to carry them forward to future periods when they can be offset against positive earnings. These carryforwards potentially provide future economic benefits in the form of reduced future tax obligations. In 1998, for example, Amazon.com, the Internet retailer of books, music, and video products, had generated operating losses of $207 million, equivalent to $73.1 million of future tax savings since its inception. These "tax loss carryforwards" provided potential future economic benefits for Amazon.com. Of course, the carryforwards are only valuable if Amazon.com actually earns future profits. The company reported that these loss carryforwards begin to expire in 2011.

How should financial reports record the operating loss carryforwards for Amazon.com? Should they be reported as an asset in the balance sheet? If so, what is their value given the likelihood that they may never be used if the firm continues to show losses? Under SFAS 109, U.S. firms are required to show a deferred tax asset for the value of operating loss carryforwards, net of a valuation allowance for the portion of the asset that is unlikely to be realized. The FASB stated that deferred tax assets with more than a 50 percent probability of being unrealized should be included in the valuation allowance. This approach is similar to the valuation of accounts or notes receivable. Receivables are shown at their gross value, net of an allowance for bad debts.

Deferred tax assets can also arise if tax reporting realizes income prior to financial reporting. For example, prepaid revenues are often recognized for tax purposes prior to financial reporting recognition. Warranty expenses are accrued for financial reporting purposes but are recognized when an obligation is incurred for tax purposes. As a result of these temporary differences between taxable and reported income, taxes can be paid prior to recognition of earnings in financial statements. The matching principle requires the creation of an accrual to recognize this prepayment. SFAS 109 rules for recording these prepayments are similar to those used to report operating loss carryforwards. A deferred tax asset is created and a valuation allowance is set up to record the portion of the asset that is unlikely to be realized.

Financial reporting for deferred tax assets provides management with an opportunity to exercise judgment in estimating the valuation allowance. The basis for this estimate is management forecasts of whether the firm is likely to earn future profits and, if so, whether they are sufficient to take full advantage of operating loss carryforwards and tax prepayments. Recent research finds little evidence that managers use this judgment to manage earnings.[2]

Amazon.com reported that it has $12.8 million of deferred tax benefits due to temporary differences between tax and financial reporting methods of recognizing income. Combined with its $73.1 million of operating loss carryforwards, this amounted to an $85.9 million gross deferred tax asset. The challenge for financial reporting was to estimate what portion of this asset was actually likely to be realizable. The company had never earned a profit. Since 1996 its operating performance had actually deteriorated, with losses of $6.2 million in 1996, $31.0 million in 1997, and $124.5 million in 1998. Further, as of March 19, 1999, financial analysts did not anticipate the company to report a profit in either 1999 or 2000. Forecasts for these years are for losses of $400 million and $140 million, respectively. On this basis it seemed unlikely that Amazon.com would be able to take advantage of its deferred tax asset anytime soon.[3] Consequently, the company reported that it included the full value of the deferred tax asset in the valuation allowance, leaving a net book value of zero.

Key Analysis Questions

The above discussion illustrates three methods of reporting for outlays whose economic benefits are uncertain or difficult to measure. The first, which requires immediate expensing of the outlays, does not allow for any use of management judgment in financial reporting. This method is commonly used for brand development outlays and for R&D. The second method, which records an asset at the amount of the outlay, provides for management judgment in subsequent periods through amortization or write-downs. Examples include goodwill and fixed assets. The third method requires the expected value of benefits from an outlay to be recorded, requiring considerable management judgment. Examples include receivables and deferred tax assets. These three methods give rise to the following challenges and questions for financial analysts:

- Which assets reported on the balance sheet are most difficult to measure and value? Assets with liquid markets, such as marketable securities, are relatively easy to value, whereas unique or firm-specific assets, such as goodwill and brands, are most challenging. What is the basis for valuing these types of assets? What assumptions have been made for financial reporting? For example, what are the amortization lives of these assets, and what are management's estimates of allowances?

- How do any assumptions or estimates made by management in valuing assets compare with assumptions in prior years? Has there been a change in assumed goodwill lives? Is the current receivable or deferred tax asset allowance as a percentage of the gross asset very different from prior years? What factors might explain any changes? Has the firm made changes to its business strategy or its operating policies? Has there been a change in the outlook for the industry or the economy as a whole?

- How do management's assumptions for valuing assets compare to those made by competitors? Once again, if there are any differences, what are the potential explanations? Do the firms have different business strategies? Do they operate in different geographic regions? Does management have different incentives to manage earnings?

- Does management have a history of over- or underestimating the value of difficult-to-value assets? For example, does it consistently sell these types of assets at a loss or at a gain?

- What key assets are not reported on the balance sheet because of measurement difficulties or uncertainties? These include brands, R&D, and other intangibles. How does the firm appear to be managing these assets? Does management discuss its strategy for preserving, enhancing, and leveraging these assets? What indicators does the firm look at to evaluate how well it has managed these assets?

Challenge Three: Changes in Future Economic Benefits

The final challenge in recording assets is how to reflect changes in their values over time. What types of assets, if any, should be marked up or down to their fair values? Below we discuss this question for changes in values of operating assets, financial instruments, and foreign exchange rate fluctuations.

EXAMPLE: CHANGES IN VALUES OF OPERATING ASSETS.   Changes in operating asset values are reflected in financial statements in a variety of ways. For example, changes in receivable values are reflected in bad debt allowances, changes in the value of loan portfolios are reflected in loss reserves, revisions in asset lives and residual values are reflected in amortization estimates, and declines in inventory and long-term asset values are reflected in write-downs.

Accounting standards in the U.S. do not permit the recognition of any increases in operating asset values beyond their historical cost. However, as noted in Chapter 7, SFAS 121 requires operating assets whose value is impaired to be written down to their market value, below cost. This approach is consistent with the conservatism principle. Of course, the challenge in implementing this standard is that it is often difficult to assess whether an asset has been impaired and, if so, the amount of the loss. As a result, there appears to be considerable management discretion in deciding when to recognize that an asset has been impaired and how much to write it down. Questions can arise as to whether firms delay recording asset impairments or underestimate the effect of impairments. Alternatively, some have questioned whether managers use impairment charges to overzealously write down assets to improve future reported performance.

In some other parts of the world, management is permitted to value assets at their fair values. U.K. and Australian standards, for example, permit managers to revalue fixed assets and intangibles if they have appreciated in value. Thus, in its 1998 annual report, News Corp, the Australian news and media company run by Rupert Murdoch, reported that the intangible asset Publishing Rights, Titles, and Television Licenses was revalued to its fair value. Fair values were estimated by "discounting the expected net inflow of cash arising from their continued use or sale." (See Footnote 1 of News Corp's annual report.) As a result, the firm showed intangible assets that cost A\$7,283 million at a fair value of A\$12,030 million.

By permitting firms to revalue assets, U.K. and Australian standards potentially permit managers to communicate their estimates of the value of the firm's key assets to investors. However, they also provide increased opportunity for asset overstatements.[4]

EXAMPLE: CHANGES IN FINANCIAL INSTRUMENT VALUES.   Many financial assets are traded in a liquid capital market, permitting relatively objective values to be obtained. For debt securities, even though markets may not be very deep or liquid, financial valuation models enable relatively reliable estimates of value to be made. Finance theory posits that firms (or individuals) can typically buy or sell financial instruments in financial markets at the current market price, provided they are perceived to have the same information on the instruments' values as other investors. As a result, since fair values can be obtained at low cost, can be independently verified, and are more relevant to financial statement users than acquisition cost, a good argument can be made for marking assets up or down to market prices.

Of course, if the owner of financial instruments exercises control over the other company, the owner is unlikely to be able to transact at market prices. Attempts to sell the instruments will be interpreted by other investors as indicating that the seller considers it a good time to sell, reducing the price. This suggests that marking such assets to market is less appropriate.

Figure 4-2 summarizes the valuation effects of accounting for changes in values of financial instruments. It shows that the reporting effects depend primarily on the owner's motives.

U.S. accounting rules do not permit instruments to be recorded at their fair values if they are owned for control reasons. Instead, the investment is recorded using either the equity method or the consolidation approach. The equity method is used when a firm owns 20–50 percent of another company's stock and is considered to have partial but not full control of the other company (called an associated company). The investment is then valued at its original cost plus the owner's share of the associated company's accumulated changes in retained earnings since the investment was acquired. For investments in excess of 50 percent, the owner is considered to have full control over the subsidiary company. The acquirer then consolidates the assets of the subsidiary with its own assets. Two methods of consolidation are used. If the subsidiary is purchased in a cash transaction, purchase accounting is used. The assets of the subsidiary are then included in the owner's balance sheet at their fair values at acquisition and subsequently amortized. Any difference between the purchase price and the fair value of net tangible assets is recorded as goodwill and amortized over its useful life up to a maximum of forty years. If the subsidiary is acquired for stock, the pooling of interest method is used to record the acquisition. The assets of the subsidiary are then included in the owner's balance sheet at their original book values. No goodwill is recognized.

If the owner of financial instruments does not exercise control over the other company, accountants are more inclined to value the instruments at their fair market values. For example, if the purpose of ownership is to hedge changes in the fair value of another

Figure 4-2 Valuation of Financial Instruments

Q: What is the motivation for ownership of the financial instruments?

A: Used as a way to exercise some level of control over another company. If so, what is the level of control?

A: Short-term alternative to holding cash.
1. Intend to sell or make available for sale.
   Valuation Method: Fair value
2. Intend to hold to maturity.
   Valuation Method: Cost

A: Used as part of strategy to hedge fair values of assets or liabilities, or to hedge uncertain future cash flows.
Valuation Method: Fair value

A: Own between 20% and 50% of the other company.
Valuation Method: Equity method: Investment shown at initial cost plus share of accumulated changes in associated company's retained earnings.

A: Own more than 50% of the other company.
Valuation Methods:
Purchase accounting: Tangible assets recorded at fair values at acquisition, and then depreciated. Goodwill recorded at difference between purchase price and fair value of net assets, and then amortized.
Pooling: All assets recorded at book values at acquisition. No goodwill.

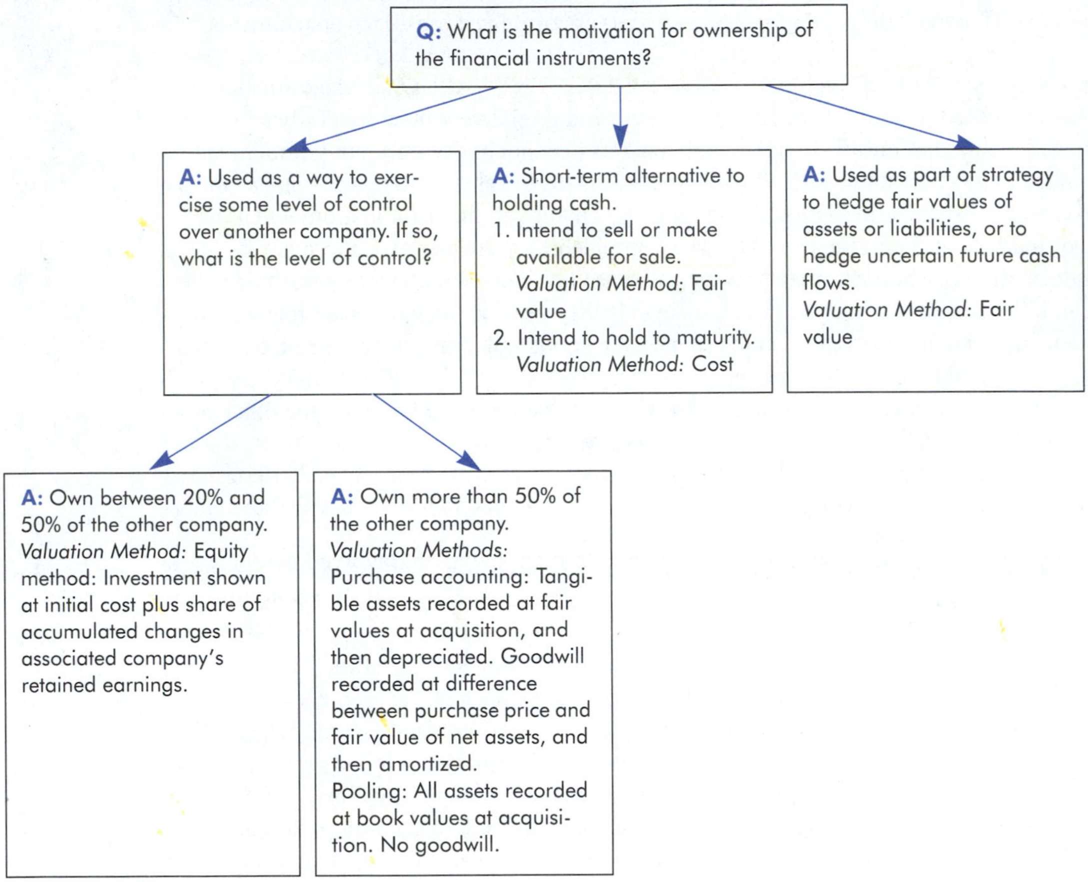

item or to hedge fluctuations in expected future cash inflows or outflows, the instrument is reported at fair value. If a firm holds an instrument as a store of cash and either intends to sell it or has it available for sale, it is reported at fair value. Only if management expects that an instrument will be held to maturity is it reported at historical cost.

EXAMPLE: CHANGES IN VALUES OF FOREIGN SUBSIDIARIES.   Many companies have foreign subsidiaries that subject their assets to exchange rate fluctuations. How are these fluctuations recognized? Are assets of foreign subsidiaries translated into local currency at the historical rates when the assets were acquired? Alternatively, are they translated at current rates?

U.S. rules for reporting foreign currency effects on assets require management to make a decision about the exchange rate risk borne by a new foreign venture at the time it is undertaken. A foreign subsidiary is considered to be largely insulated from the effect of exchange rates if its sales, costs, and sources of financing primarily occur in the local currency rather than in the parent's currency, and there are few transactions between the parent and subsidiary. In this case, the subsidiary's assets and liabilities provide a natural hedge against much of any exchange rate volatility. Only the net asset value is considered to be subject to exchange rate effects. SFAS 52 therefore requires the subsidiary's assets (and liabilities) to be translated at the current rate. The parent will only be subject to the effect of changes in exchange rates on net assets. These effects are reflected in shareholders' equity as a translation adjustment.[5]

Foreign currency risks for the combined firm are considered to be more severe if the subsidiary's sales or costs are incurred in the parent's currency or if there are frequent transactions between the two. SFAS 52 then requires assets and liabilities for the subsidiary to be valued using the monetary/nonmonetary method. Under this approach, monetary assets and liabilities (such as cash, receivables, payables, and financing) are translated at current rates, whereas nonmonetary assets and liabilities (such as inventory, fixed assets, and intangibles) are valued at the historical rate (when the transaction occurred).[6]

Key Analysis Questions

The above discussion indicates that the management judgment involved in reporting the effect of changes in asset values depends on the type of asset, the country in which the firm operates, and the way it manages its businesses. For financial analysts, these factors raise the following questions:

- Do operating assets appear to be impaired? Evidence of impairment could include systemic poor performance and/or write-downs by other firms in the industry. If assets appear to be impaired but are not written down, what is management's justification for not recognizing any impairment?
- Does management appear to have over- or understated prior impairment losses for operating assets, making it difficult to evaluate future performance? Has the firm consistently reported impairment losses, indicating an unwillingness to appreciate the full extent of the impairment? Does management appear to have a viable business model or plan to correct the problems?
- If management revalues operating assets, either up or down, what is the basis for the estimation of the fair value? Is the valuation based on an independent appraisal, or is it a management estimate?
- What are management's reasons for revaluing assets that have increased in value?
- What is management's motive for holding financial instruments? Is that motivation consistent with shareholders' interests? For example, is the firm hedging risks for shareholders' benefits or for the benefit of managers?
- What is the market value of all financial instruments?

> • What are the foreign currency risks the company is exposed to from its foreign operations? What foreign currency gains and losses are reported, either in the income statement or in the equity section of the balance sheet? Does management hedge foreign currency risks? How effective are these hedges?

COMMON MISCONCEPTIONS ABOUT ASSET ACCOUNTING

The above discussion of accounting for assets reveals a number of popular misconceptions about the nature of accounting.

1. If a firm paid for a resource, it must be an asset.

This logic is frequently used to justify showing goodwill as an asset. It gives management the benefit of the doubt in recording the full value of acquisition outlays as an asset, presupposing that management would not have made the outlay if it did not anticipate the prospect of some future benefit.

However, this logic ignores the possibility that well-intended managers can make mistakes or that some managers take actions that are not in the best interests of shareholders. Mergers and acquisitions have frequently been cited as such events. Recent evidence indicates that mergers and acquisitions typically do not create value for acquiring shareholders. The value of the goodwill recorded for these transactions may very well not be an asset, but simply reflect management's overpayment for the target or its overestimate of any merger benefits. Indeed, the negative stock returns for many acquirers at the announcement of an acquisition indicate that investors are skeptical of merger benefits. Accountants, however, do not reflect this skepticism in goodwill values until there is evidence of its impairment.

It is also worth noting that the logic that payment is evidence of an asset is not used consistently in accounting. For example, outlays for research and development are not viewed as assets, even though managers also make outlays for R&D in expectation of generating future benefits. Several justifications for the apparent contradiction in treatment have been offered. One is that there is considerable risk of failure for any single research project. However, a research program is more likely to generate successes. Indeed, it is not obvious which is more risky—a research program or a takeover program. A second justification for the different treatments is that R&D is more difficult to verify than goodwill. However, even this is not clear. After all, for many acquisitions it is not clear exactly what benefits are likely to be generated from the acquisition, making it difficult to verify whether goodwill has been impaired. In contrast, research programs have identifiable output to verify whether outlays generated successful products.

2. **If you can't kick a resource, it really isn't an asset.**

This view is commonly used to justify the rapid write-off or exclusion of intangibles from the balance sheet. It is certainly true that it can be difficult to estimate the economic benefits from some intangibles. As noted above, this is particularly true for goodwill. However, the intangible nature of some assets does not mean that they do not have value. Indeed, for many firms these types of assets are their most valued. For example, Merck's two most valued assets are its research capabilities which permit it to generate new drugs, and its sales force which enables it to sell those drugs to doctors. Yet neither is recorded on Merck's balance sheet.

From the investors' point of view, accountants' reluctance to value intangible assets does not diminish their importance. If they are not included in financial statements, investors have to look to alternative sources of information on these assets.

3. **If you bought a resource, it must be an asset; if you developed it, it must not be.**

This statement is frequently used to justify recording acquired intangible assets, such as R&D and brands, but not recording assets for the cost of internally generated intangibles. The logic for this distinction seems to be that intangible assets that are completed, such as completed R&D and established brands, can be valued more readily than intangible assets that are in development. While this may be true, it permits two firms that own the same types of intangible assets to have very different accounting for their activities. Firms that generate these assets internally show no values for the assets, whereas firms that purchase these assets reflect them on the balance sheet.

The real question for investors in distinguishing between purchased and internally developed assets is whether there is any difference in the certainty of expected future benefits for the two assets. If there is no difference, investors will view both as valuable assets and are interested in assessing their value, how they are managed, and whether they have been impaired during the period. Consequently, if accountants do not choose to recognize internally generated assets, investors will be forced to find alternative sources of information on these assets.

4. **Market values are only relevant if you intend to sell an asset.**

It has been common among accountants to regard fair values of assets as only being relevant if the owner intends to sell them. For example, as discussed above, U.S. rules for valuing marketable securities held as a store for cash require owners to value these assets at their fair values only if they intend to sell them or the instruments are available for sale. If management intends to hold these instruments to maturity, they are valued at their historical cost.

This logic implies that it is possible to avoid incurring an economic loss by simply not selling the asset. An economist would view such an approach as ludicrous. If you own stock in Microsoft and its fair value increases, your own equity increases accordingly. This is true regardless of whether you intend to sell the Microsoft stock. The fair value of the stock reflects the market's best estimate of the resources that would be available if you sold the asset. Your plans to sell or hold are irrelevant to its value. Note that this may not be true for operating assets. A plant's fair value may be less than its value in use. Further, assets with high values in use are precisely the types of assets that firms are likely to retain. Thus, fair values of separable operating assets may not be fully reflected in their values to the firm.

SUMMARY

The recording of assets is primarily determined by the principles of historical cost and conservatism. Under the historical cost principle, resources owned by a firm that are likely to produce reasonably certain future benefits are valued at their cost. However, if an asset's cost exceeds its fair value, the conservatism principle requires that the resource be written down to fair value. The U.S. has been a strong advocate of the historical cost/conservatism approach to valuing assets. However, even in the U.S., adherence to these rules has diminished during the last twenty years as firms have been permitted to revalue marketable securities to fair values. Outside the U.S., some countries permit firms to revalue other types of assets, including intangibles.

The implementation of the principles of historical cost and conservatism can be challenging if:

1. There is uncertainty about the ownership of those resources, as is the case for lease transactions and training outlays.
2. Future benefits associated with resources are highly uncertain and/or difficult to measure, such as for goodwill, R&D, brands, and deferred tax assets.
3. Resource values have changed, as in the case of impaired operating assets, changes in fair values of financial instruments, and changes in exchange rates for valuing foreign subsidiaries.

Corporate managers are likely to have the best information on the ownership risks and uncertainty about future benefits associated with their firms' resources. As a result, they are assigned the primary responsibility for deciding which outlays qualify as assets and which do not, and for assessing whether assets have been impaired. Of course, given managers' incentives to report favorably on their stewardship of owners' investments and accounting requirements that preclude recording some key economic assets (e.g., R&D, brands, human capital), there is ample opportunity for analysts to independently assess how a firm's resources are being managed.

DISCUSSION QUESTIONS

1. An airline operator signs an agreement to lease an aircraft for twenty years. Annual lease obligations, payable at the beginning of the year, are $4.7 million. What are the financial statement effects of this transaction if the lease is recorded as (a) a capital lease or (b) an operating lease? As a corporate manager, what forecasts do you have to make to decide which alternative to use? Which method would you prefer to use to report the lease? Why? As a financial analyst, what questions would you raise with the firm's CFO?

2. The American Society for Training and Development has recently advocated that firms be permitted to report training costs as an asset on their balance sheet. As a corporate manager, how would you respond to this proposal? What are its merits and what concerns would you have?

3. In 1991 AT&T, the largest long-distance telephone operator in the U.S., paid $7.5 billion to acquire NCR, a computer manufacturer. Prior to the acquisition, the book value of NCR's assets was $4.5 billion, and its liabilities were $1.5 billion. Assuming that there was little significant difference between the fair value and the book value of NCR's assets, show the effect of the acquisition on AT&T's balance sheet from using (a) the pooling of interests method and (b) the purchase method.

4. AT&T's managers had a strong preference for recording the acquisition of NCR under the pooling of interests method. Indeed, the offer was actually contingent on approval for pooling. Why do you think AT&T's managers were so concerned about the accounting used for the transaction? As a financial analyst, what questions would you raise with the firm's CFO?

5. What approaches would you use to estimate the value of brands? What assumptions underlie these approaches? As a financial analyst, what would you use to assess whether the brand value of £1.575 billion reported by Cadbury Schweppes in 1997 was a reasonable reflection of the future benefits from these brands? What questions would you raise with the firm's CFO about the firm's brand assets?

6. A firm records bad debt expenses on an accrual basis for financial reporting and on a cash basis for tax reporting. In its 1999 annual report, it reported that the opening and closing balances in Allowance for Uncollectibles (a contra against receivables) were $1,200 million and $1,650 million, respectively, and that customers owing $550 million defaulted during the year. The company's tax rate is 40 percent. How much is the deferred tax asset as a result of this temporary difference between financial and tax reporting? If 30 percent of the asset is deemed to be unrecoverable, how would the transaction be recorded? As a financial analyst, what questions would you raise with the firm's CFO about the firm's deferred tax asset?

7. As the CFO of a company, what indicators would you look at to assess whether your firm's long-term assets were impaired? What approaches could be used, either by management or an independent valuation firm, to assess the dollar value of any asset impairment? As a financial analyst, what indicators would you look at to assess

whether a firm's long-term assets were impaired? What questions would you raise with the firm's CFO about any charges taken for asset impairment?

8. Give two examples of instruments designed to hedge changes in the fair values of assets or liabilities. When would you recommend that a firm hedge against changes in the fair values of its assets or liabilities? Give two examples of instruments designed to hedge uncertain future cash flows. When would you recommend hedging uncertain cash flow obligations or inflows?

NOTES

1. See Lisa M. Lynch, "A Needs Analysis of Training Data," in *Labor Statistics Measurement Issues: Studies in Income and Wealth*, Volume 60 (Chicago: University of Chicago Press, 1998).

2. See G. Miller and D. Skinner, "Determinants of the Valuation Allowance for Deferred Tax Assets Under SFAS No. 109," *The Accounting Review* 73, No. 2, 1998.

3. Despite this poor reported performance, in the 22 months since its initial public offering, the company's stock price increased from $1.70 to in excess of $170, indicating that investors were very optimistic about the company's long-term prospects.

4. P. Easton, P. Eddey, and T. Harris, "An Investigation of Revaluations of Tangible Long-Lived Assets," *Journal of Accounting Research* 31, 1993, examine asset revaluations by Australian firms and find that they are weakly related to lagged returns, suggesting that investors view revaluations as relevant but not very timely disclosures.

5. Owners' equity is therefore translated at historical rates (when equity was invested), and any gain or loss on adjustment is reported as a translation adjustment. All revenues and expenses are translated at the weighted average rate for the year. No exchange rate gains and losses are reflected in the income statement.

6. Under the monetary/nonmonetary approach, owners' equity is again translated at historical rates (when equity was invested). Ongoing revenues and expenses are translated at the weighted average rate for the period, but depreciation is translated at the historical rate. Finally, any exchange gain or loss is included in income.

P*erhaps no company better captures the spirit of the new economy than Boston Chicken Inc., which aims to do for the rotisserie what Colonel Sanders did for the deep fryer. . . . There is nothing particularly new about rotisserie chicken—those birds have been turning succulently in delicatessen windows for generations. But Boston Chicken is not really about poultry—it is about developing a market-winning formula for picking real estate, designing stores, organizing a franchise operation and analyzing data. These are Boston Chicken's innovations—trade secrets that can be every bit as valuable as a new drug or computer chip design. With them, Boston Chicken has not only developed the secret for delivering generous quantities of home-cooking at affordable prices, but also transformed what had been a mom-and-pop business into a new national category— take-out home-cooked food—that potentially can draw business away from both supermarkets and restaurants.*

The Washington Post, July 4, 1994

Boston Chicken was founded in 1989 by Scott Beck to operate and franchise food service stores that sold meals featuring rotisserie-cooked chicken, fresh vegetables, salads, and other side dishes. The firm's concept was to combine fresh, flavorful, and appealing meals associated with traditional home cooking with a high level of convenience and value. Meals cost less than $5 per person, were sold in bright, inviting retail stores, and were available for take-out or for on-site consumption. "Our strategy," Beck noted, "is to be a home meal replacement. Our number one competitor is pizza."[1]

To help operationalize his vision, Beck assembled a management team with considerable prior experience in both the fast-food business and franchising operations. Beck himself became one of the first and largest franchisees for Blockbuster Video while still in his twenties. He later sold his franchises back to the parent company for $120 million. Other top executives included the former president of Kentucky Fried Chicken, and former vice-presidents of Bennigan's, Taco Bell, Red Lobster, Chili's, and Baker's Square.

....

Professor Paul M. Healy prepared this case as the basis for class discussion rather than to illustrate either effective or ineffective handling of an administrative situation. Copyright © 1997 by the President and Fellows of Harvard College. Harvard Business School case 9-198-032.

1. *The Washington Post, July 4, 1994.*

COMPANY STRUCTURE AND GROWTH STRATEGY

By the end of 1994, the Boston Chicken system operated 534 stores, compared to only 34 stores at the end of 1991. This translated to an annual rate of growth of almost 500 percent per year, with a new store being opened on average every two days. As reported in the financial statements presented in Exhibit 1, revenues for this period increased dramatically, from $5.2 million in 1991 to $96.2 million in 1994 and net income rose to $16.2 million (from a loss of $2.6 million). This growth continued throughout 1995; by the third quarter there were more than 750 stores in operation and quarterly sales had reached $38 million (see Exhibit 2 for a summary of quarterly results). The company was voted "America's Favorite Chicken Chain" in a 1995 survey published by *Restaurant and Institutions* magazine.

To provide financing for its rapid growth, Boston Chicken went public in November 1993. The offering, for 1.9 million shares, was highly successful, as the stock price soared from the initial offering price of $10 to a high of $26.50. However, within months of the offer the stock had fallen back to $18. Nonetheless, a second offering for two million shares at $18.50 in August 1994 was oversubscribed. The company responded by increasing the offer to six million shares, raising $105 million of new capital (after issue costs).

Competition in the $200 billion restaurant industry was fierce, and several other companies were quick to take advantage of Boston Chicken's success. For example, in mid-1993 Pepsico's Kentucky Fried Chicken (KFC) introduced "rotisserie-gold" roasted chicken in most of its 5,100 restaurants. Within four months KFC reported that sales of the new chicken had topped $160 million, making KFC the world's largest rotisserie chicken chain. KFC spent $100 million to launch the new product, including a national network advertising campaign. However, some analysts believed that Boston Chicken's biggest challenge would not come from other competitors, but on how well the company met its goals.[2]

In its 1994 Annual Report, Boston Chicken described its main goals as strengthening its area developer organizations, creating communications infrastructure to support area developers, building an organization to continue new market development, and continuing operational improvements to ensure that the retail concept kept pace with changes in consumer tastes.

Area Developer Organizations

The company's franchising strategy was different from that of most other successful franchisers. Instead of selling store franchises to a large number of small franchisees,

---

2. See discussion by Stacy Dutton at Kidder Peabody's equity research department, quoted in Reuters news report, November 9, 1993.

Boston Chicken focused on franchising to large regional developers. It established a network of 22 regional franchises, which targeted the 60 largest U.S. metropolitan markets. Each franchise was expected to have the scale necessary to ensure operational efficiency and marketing clout. The typical franchisee was an independent businessman with 15–20 years of relevant management experience, strong financial resources, and a mandate to open 50 to 100 new stores in the region. This structure was intended to provide the entrepreneurial energy of a franchise operation with the control and economies of scale of company-owned operations.

Under typical franchise agreements, developers paid Boston Chicken a one-time $35,000 per store franchise fee, a $10,000 fee to cover grand opening expenses, and an annual 5 percent royalty on gross revenues. In addition, franchisees contributed 2 percent and 3.75 percent of sales per year, respectively, for national and local advertising campaigns. In 1994 royalties from these agreements amounted to $17.4 million, and initial franchise fees for new stores were $13 million. The company also earned interest income from franchise developers, since it provided a line of credit to assist them in new store development. This source of revenue grew rapidly in 1994 to $11.6 million. Other revenue sources included income from leasing some of its stores to franchise operators, and fees for software services provided to developers.

Area developer financing was provided to qualifying developers to assist them in expanding their operations. Under these arrangements, Boston Chicken provided the developer with a revolving line of credit which became available once at least 75 percent of the developer's equity capital had been spent on developing stores. The agreement provided limits on the amount that the developer could draw over time, primarily as a function of developers' equity capital. Once the drawing period expired, the loan converted to an amortizing four- to five-year term loan, with a variable interest rate set at 1 percent over the Bank of America Illinois "reference rate." Some loans also included a conversion option, permitting Boston Chicken to convert the loan into equity in the developer after two years, usually at a 12–15 percent premium over the equity price at the loan's inception.

Communications Infrastructure

The company invested $8–10 million to build computer software that provided support for its network of stores, and linked headquarters to developer stores. This software used information entered at the checkout counter to advise store managers when to put on another rack of chickens or to heat up another tray of mashed potatoes. It made appropriate adjustments for the day of the week, the season, and customer preferences at a particular store in making its recommendations. The software also provided information on employee work schedules to match daily peaks in customer purchases, automatically reordered food supplies from approved vendors, and updated the store's financial performance on an hourly basis.

Boston Chicken

Boston Chicken

New Market Development

New store site selection was critical to the company's future success. In 1995 it employed more than 180 real estate and construction professionals to ensure that the pace of development was sustained and that site standards were maintained. Given these resources the company was optimistic that it could open at least 325 new stores per year in the foreseeable future.

Operating Improvements

In 1994 the company implemented a number of plans to improve operating efficiency and reduce store-level costs. These included long-term agreements with key suppliers, the introduction of flagship stores, expanded menus, in-store computer feedback from customers, and drive-thru lanes. Long-term agreements with suppliers provided opportunities to lock in prices for key inputs. For example, in October 1994 the firm reached a five-year cost-plus agreement with Hudson Foods to purchase the entire capacity from two Hudson poultry processing plants.

Flagship stores included a retail store and a kitchen facility with enough space and equipment to perform the initial stages of food preparation, such as washing and chopping vegetables, for up to 20 "satellite" stores. Prepared food was then sent to satellite stores, which completed the cooking process and served the products. This concept increased the quality and freshness of the side items, because a flagship had more frequent delivery of fresh ingredients. It also led to greater consistency in food taste, facilitated increased innovation in menu items (since there were fewer production people to train), and utilized facilities more effectively.

In fall 1994 the company added vegetable pot pies, Caesar salad, and cinnamon apples to its menu to satisfy customer demand for more variety in food offerings. Rotisserie-roasted turkey, ham, and meat loaf entrees were added in mid-1995. Stores offering these new products showed double-digit sales gains without any significant new advertising campaign. A new line of deli-type sandwiches featuring turkey, ham, and meat loaf on fresh-baked bread was also added to boost lunch sales. In 1995 the firm invested $20 million in Progressive Bagels (PBCI), a retailer of fresh gourmet bagels. Under this agreement, Boston Chicken provided an eight-year senior secured loan to Progressive Bagels, as well as providing administrative, real estate, and systems support services. Management argued that this investment provided the firm with the opportunity to learn more about the potential of morning service, which could further increase store productivity. By late 1995 this investment was increased to $80 million, and PBCI had grown to 53 stores (from a base of 20 units), with plans to open 200–225 stores in 1996. Finally, in an attempt to increase sales in the traditionally weak fourth quarter, the company began offering whole hams and turkeys for Thanksgiving and Christmas meals. As a result of these expanded product offerings, Boston Chicken decided to change its name to Boston Market.

In 1995 the company began using technology to keep in better touch with store customers. Touch-activated computer terminals were added to some stores, enabling customers to rate the quality of food and service. Blaine Hurst, the former Ernst & Young partner who headed Boston Chicken's computer operations, pointed out, "If I can save half a percentage point on food costs, that's a lot of money. But if I can know almost instantaneously that customers don't like the drink selection and I can have that changed within a week—that's worth a lot more money."

Finally, to improve convenience for customers, the company decided to add drive-thru lanes to its stores. By late 1994, 62 stores in eighteen states had drive-thru windows. In some cases, as much as 30 percent of store sales came from these windows. The company's market research indicates that as many as two-thirds of these customers would not have visited the stores had this convenience not been available. Drive-thrus were planned for a further 65 stores in 1995, and ultimately 70 percent of the stores were expected to be converted to drive-thru.

EXPECTED FUTURE PERFORMANCE

In late 1995, most restaurant analysts were bullish about Boston Chicken's future performance. For example, Michael Moe of Lehman Brothers noted: "Boston Chicken is truly the leader in the home meal replacement market. . . . Dual-income families are searching for an affordable alternative to preparing meals at home. Boston Chicken satisfies this need by preparing food that customers view as high quality, healthy and convenient. This home meal replacement is a hit with value-minded consumers. The bagel industry is another hot area of opportunity for Boston Chicken. Presently the bagel industry is one of the hottest growth areas in America."[3] Moe rated the stock to be a strong buy, and projected that EPS would be $0.63 in 1995, $0.90 in 1996, and would continue to grow by 45 percent per year from 1997 to 2001.

However, not everyone was impressed. Roger Lipton of Lipton Financial Services contended that Boston Chicken's franchisees had actually lost money. Lipton Financial Services is an affiliate of Axiom Capital Management, which had shorted the stock. He estimated that sales at a franchised store had to average $23,000 a week (net of promotional discounts) to cover labor, cost of sales, and other expenses. Actual average weekly sales, Lipton claimed, were only $18,900 per store, implying that franchisees were losing money. Lipton pointed out that "the quality of earnings is very low, since all of Boston Chicken's income comes from fees, royalties, and interest payments from franchisees, most of whom were financed by the franchiser."[4]

Management responded to concerns about the economics of franchisees by reporting that average weekly store sales were $23,388 for the third quarter of 1995, versus

3. Michael Moe, Lehman Brothers, October 25, 1995.

4. Inside Wall Street," Business Week, June 12, 1995.

Boston Chicken

$22,227 for the second quarter, and that EBITDA store margins were running at about 15–16 percent. On December 1, 1995, the stock closed at $33.75, up more than 100 percent over the beginning of the year price (versus a 56 percent increase for the S&P 500).[5] But uncertainty about the company persisted. Short interest positions in the stock were at an all-time high of 10 million shares, more than 20 percent of the shares outstanding and double the short interest position at the beginning of 1995.

QUESTIONS

1. Assess Boston Chicken's business strategy. What are its critical success factors and risks?
2. How is the company reporting on its performance and risks? What are the key assumptions behind these policies? Do you think that its accounting policies reflect the risks?
3. What adjustments, if any, would you make to the firm's accounting policies?
4. What questions would you ask management about the company's performance?
5. How is Boston Chicken performing?
6. What assumptions is the market making about the company's future performance and risks? Do you agree with those assessments?

5. *The equity beta for Boston Chicken was 1.50, and at December 1, 1995, the 30-year U.S. Government Treasuries yielded 6.04%.*

EXHIBIT 1

Boston Chicken, Inc., Abridged 1994 Annual Report, Financial Highlights

| | Fiscal Years Ended | |
| | December 25, | December 26, |
(dollars in thousands, except per share data)	1994	1993
Systemwide store revenue	$383,691	$152,056
Company revenue	96,151	42,530
Net income	16,173	1,647
Net income per share	$0.38	$0.06
Shareholders' equity	$259,815	$94,906
Weighted average number of shares outstanding	42,861	32,667

Boston Chicken

MANAGEMENT'S DISCUSSION AND ANALYSIS

GENERAL

The total number of stores in the Boston Market system increased from 34 at the year ended December 29, 1991, to 534 at the year ended December 25, 1994. This rapid expansion significantly affects the comparability of results of operations from year to year as well as the Company's liquidity and capital resources. The following table sets forth information regarding store development activity for the years indicated.

	Stores at Beginning of Year	Net Stores Opened in Year	Net Stores Transferred in Year[a]	Stores at End of Year
Year Ended December 27, 1992:				
Company-operated	5	15	(1)	19
Financed area developers	0	3	0	3
Non-financed area developers and other	29	31	1	61
Total	34	49	0	83
Year Ended December 26, 1993:				
Company-operated	19	28	(9)	38
Financed area developers	3	66	9	78
Non-financed area developers and other	61	40	0	101
Total	83	134	0	217
Year Ended December 25, 1994:				
Company-operated	38	49	(46)	41
Financed area developers	78	168	68	314
Non-financed area developers and other	101	100	(22)	179
Total	217	317	0	534

[a]*Stores transferred during the year primarily reflect the Company's practice of opening new Company-operating stores to seed development in targeted markets prior to execution of area development agreements relating to such markets. At the time such agreements are executed, the Company typically sells Company-operating stores located in the market to the area developer in that market. Stores transferred also reflect the purchase and/or sale of Boston Market stores in markets with multiple area developers in order to facilitate consolidation of such markets.*

RESULTS OF OPERATIONS

Fiscal Year 1994 Compared to Fiscal Year 1993

Revenue

Total revenue increased $53.7 million (126%) from $42.5 million for 1993 to $96.2 million for 1994. Royalty and franchise-related fees increased $42.5 million (335%) to $55.2 million for 1994, from $12.7 million for 1993. This increase was primarily due to an increase in royalties attributable to the larger base of franchise stores operating systemwide, from 179 stores at December 16, 1993 to 493 stores at December 5, 1994, an increase in franchise fees related to the increase in the number of stores that commenced operation as franchised stores during the year, and higher interest income generated on increased loans made to certain area developers. Additional factors contributing to the increase in revenue from royalty and franchise-related fees include an increase in lease income due to a higher number of store sites which the Company owns and leases to area developers, and recognition of software license and maintenance fees for store-level computer software systems developed by the Company for use by franchisees. No software-related fees were earned in 1993.

Revenue from Company-operated stores increased $11.1 million (37%) from $29.8 million for 1993 to $40.9 million for 1994. This increase was due to a higher average number of Company-operated stores open during the year. The Company had 38 Company-operated stores at December 26, 1993, compared to 41 at December 25, 1994. During 1994, the Company sold 54 Company-operated stores which it had opened to seed new markets.

Cost of Products Sold

Cost of products sold increased $4.6 million (41%) , to $15.9 million for 1994 compared with $11.3 million for 1993. This increase was primarily due to an increase in the number of Company-operated stores open during the periods. Management does not believe that the cost of products sold as a percentage of store revenue at Company-operated stores is indicative of cost of products sold as a percentage of store revenue at franchise stores due to the Company's practice of opening new stores primarily to seed new markets. These newer stores, which constitute the majority of the Company-operated store base, tend to have higher food and paper costs as a result of increased food usage for free tasting, inefficiencies resulting from employee inexperience, and a lack of store-specific operating history to assist in forecasting daily food production needs.

Salaries and Benefits

Salaries and benefits increased $7.2 million (47%), from $15.4 million in 1993 to $22.6 million in 1994. The increase resulted from an increase in the number of employees at the Company's support center necessary to support systemwide expansion and an increase in the number of employees at Company-operated stores due to a higher average number of Company-operated stores open during the year.

General and Administrative

General and administrative expenses increased $14.0 million (101%) to $27.9 million for 1994 from $13.9 million for 1993. The increase is attributable to the development of the Company's support center infrastructure necessary to support systemwide expansion and higher general and administrative expenses at Company-operated stores resulting from a higher average number of Company-operated stores open during the year. Included in general and administrative expenses were depreciation and amortization charges of $6.1 million in 1994 and $2.0 million in 1993. The increase in depreciation and amortization expense is primarily attributable to a substantially higher fixed asset base reflecting the Company's investment in its infrastructure.

Provision for Relocation

In September 1994, the Company consolidated its four Chicago-based support center facilities into a single facility and relocated to Golden, Colorado. The total cost of relocation was $5.1 million.

Other Expense

The Company incurred other expense of $4.2 million in 1994, compared with other expense of $0.3 million in 1993. This increase reflects higher interest expense, primarily attributable to the $130.0 million of convertible subordinated debt and short-term borrowings under its unsecured credit facility, partially offset by higher interest income.

Boston Chicken

Income Taxes

Included in income taxes in 1994 is a $3.5 million benefit reflecting the realization of deferred tax assets attributable to the increased level of operating income, offset by a current provision for income taxes.

Liquidity and Capital Resources

Liquidity

The Company's primary capital requirements are for store development, including providing partial financing for certain of its area developers, purchasing real estate which is then leased to its area developers, and opening Company-operated stores. The remainder of the Company's capital requirements related primarily to investments in corporate infrastructure, including property and equipment and software development, which are necessary to support the increase in the number of stores in operation systemwide. For the year ended December 25, 1994, the Company expended approximately $268.1 million on store development, including financing area developers, purchasing real estate and opening Company-operated stores. The Company also expended approximately $52.3 million on corporate infrastructure, including its new support center facility.

The Company has entered into secured loan agreements with certain of its area developers whereby the area developers may draw on a line of credit, with certain limitations, in order to provide partial funding for expansion of their operations. In connection with certain of these loans, after a specified moratorium period, the Company has the right to convert the loan which typically results in a controlling equity interest in the area developer. As of December 25, 1994, The Company had secured loan commitments aggregating approximately $332.5 million, of which approximately $201.3 million had been advanced. The Company anticipates fully funding its commitments pursuant to its loan agreements with these area developers, and anticipates increasing such loan commitments and entering into additional loan commitments with other area developers in targeted market areas. In connection with entering into new area development agreements, the Company intends to sell Company-operated stores located in any such areas to the respective area developer. The Company is currently negotiating such agreements for a number of metropolitan areas, including Kansas City, Minneapolis, Omaha, New York, and San Francisco/San Jose. The timing of such transactions will have significant effect on the size and timing of the Company's capital requirements.

In 1994, the Company sold 54 Company-operated stores to its area developers in the Philadelphia, Detroit, Denver, Colorado Springs, Phoenix, Tucson, Las Vegas, Albuquerque, Salt Lake City, Southern New Jersey, and Boston metropolitan areas. In addition to opening stores to seed development in new markets and subsequently selling such stores to the new area developer for such market, the Company purchases and resells Boston Market stores in markets with multiple area developers in order to facilitate consolidation of such markets. In connection with these consolidation activities, the Company has issued a total of 1,112,436 shares of common stock pursuant to its shelf registration statement for the acquisition of 32 Boston Market stores and paid cash for 2 Boston Market stores. Of the 34 stores purchased, 26 stores were subsequently sold. The Company believes that all of the shares issued in connection with these consolidation activities have been sold by the recipients pursuant to Rule 145 (d) under the Securities Act of 1933, as amended. The aggregate proceeds from the sale of Company-operated stores to seed new markets and from the sale of stores which were acquired to consolidate markets were approximately $62.3 million. There were no material gains recognized as a result of these sales.

In March 1995, the Company entered into a secured loan agreement providing $20 million of convertible debt financing to Progressive Bagel Concepts, Inc. ("PBCI"). The Company has agreed to increase the amount available to PBCI under the loan agreement subject to PBCI's ability to meet certain conditions.

Capital Resources

For the year ended December 25, 1994, the Company's primary sources of capital included $35.9 million generated from operating activities, $130.0 million from the issuance of 4½% convertible subordinated debentures maturing February 1, 2004 (the "Debentures"), and $125.7 million from the sale of shares of common stock. The Debentures are convertible at any time prior to maturity into shares of the Company's common stock at a conversion rate of $27.969 per share, subject to adjustment under certain conditions. Beginning February 1, 1996, the Debentures may be reduced at the option of the Company, provided that until February 1, 1997, the Debentures cannot be redeemed unless the closing price of the Company's common stock equals or exceeds $39.16 per share for at least 20 out of 30 consecutive trading days. The Debentures are redeemable initially at 103.6% of their principal amount and at declining prices thereafter, plus accrued interest. Interest is payable semi-annually on February 1 and August 1 of each year.

In 1994, the Company entered into a $75.9 million master lease agreement to provide equipment financing for stores owned by certain of its area developers and certain Company-operated stores. The lease bears interest at LIBOR plus an applicable margin and, including renewal terms, expires in December 1998. As of December 25, 1994, the Company had utilized $66.1 million of the facility.

As of December 25, 1994, the Company had $25.3 million available in cash and cash equivalents, $75.0 million available under its unsecured revolving credit facility, and $8.9 million available under its master lease agreement.

The Company anticipates that it and its area developers will have need for additional financing during the 1995 fiscal year. The timing of the Company's capital requirements will be affected by the number of Company-operated and franchise stores opened, operational results of stores, the number of real estate sites purchased by the Company for Company use and for leasing by the Company to franchisees, and the amount and timing of borrowings under the loan agreements between the Company and certain of its existing or future area developers and by PBCI. As the Company's capital requirements increase, the Company will seek additional funds from future public or private offerings of debt or equity securities. There can be no assurance that the Company will be able to raise such capital on satisfactory terms when needed.

Seasonality

Historically, the Company has experienced lower average store revenue in the months of November, December, January, and February as a result of the holiday season and inclement weather. The Company's business in general, as well as the revenue of Company-operated stores, may be affected by a variety of other factors, including, but not limited to, general economic trends, competition, marketing programs, and special or unusual events. Such effects, however, may not be apparent in the Company's operating results during a period of significant expansion.

Boston Chicken

CONSOLIDATED BALANCE SHEETS

	1994	1993
Assets		
Current assets		
Cash	$25,304	$ 4,537
Accounts receivable, net	6,540	2,076
Due from affiliates	6,462	3,126
Notes receivable	16,906	1,512
Inventory — Prepaid expenses & other current assets	2,282	1,843
Deferred income taxes	1,835	
Total current assets	59,329	13,094
Property & equipment, net	163,314	51,331
Notes receivable	185,594	44,204
Deferred financing costs	8,346	358
Other assets	10,399	1,077
Total assets	$426,982	$110,064
Liabilities & Stockholders' Equity		
Current liabilities		
Accounts payable	$15,188	$6,216
Accrued expenses	6,587	1,835
Deferred franchise revenue	5,505	2,255
Total current liabilities	27,280	10,306
Deferred franchise revenue	5,815	3,139
Convertible subordinated debt	130,000	
Other noncurrent liabilities	1,061	1,713
Deferred income taxes	3,011	
Stockholders' Equity		
Common stock	447	347
Additional paid-in capital	252,298	103,662
Retained earnings (deficit)	7,070	(9,103)
	259,815	94,906
Total liabilities and stockholders' equity	$426,982	$110,064

CONSOLIDATED STATEMENTS OF OPERATIONS

	1994	1993	1992
Revenue			
Royalties & franchise-related fees	$55,235	$12,681	$2,627
Company-operated stores	40,916	29,849	5,656
Total revenues	96,151	42,530	8,283
Costs and expenses			
Cost of products sold	15,876	11,287	2,241
Salaries and benefits	22,637	15,437	7,110
General and administrative	27,930	13,879	5,241
Provision for relocation	5,097	—	—
Total costs and expenses	71,540	41,603	14,592
Income (loss) from operations	24,611	927	(6,309)
Other income (expense)			
Interest income (expense), net	(4,235)	(440)	270
Other income, net	74	160	189
Total other income (expense)	(4,161)	(280)	459
Income (loss) before income taxes	20,450	647	(5,850)
Income taxes	4,277	—	—
Net income (loss)	$16,173	$ 647	$(5,850)
Net income (loss) per share common and equivalent share	$0.38	$0.06	$ (0.21)
Number of shares	42,861	32,667	28,495

CONSOLIDATED STATEMENTS OF CASH FLOWS (In thousands)

	Fiscal Years Ended		
	Dec. 25, 1994	Dec. 26, 1993	Dec. 27, 1992
Cash from operating activities			
Net income (loss)	$ 16,173	$ 1,647	$ (5,850)
Adjustments to reconcile income (loss) to net cash provided by (used in) operating activities			
Depreciation and amortization	6,074	1,970	260
Deferred income taxes	4,277		
Vesting of common stock for services rendered			39
Gain on disposal of assets	(368)	(150)	(29)
Changes in assets and liabilities			
Accounts receivable and due from affiliates	(7,800)	(4,343)	(689)
Accounts payable and accrued expenses	13,724	6,247	1,102
Deferred franchise revenue	5,926	3,236	1,223
Other assets and liabilities	(2,088)	(561)	332
Net cash from (used in) operations	35,198	8,046	(3,612)
Cash from investing activities			
Purchase of plant, property & equipment	(163,622)	(49,151)	(8,453)
Proceeds from sale of assets	62,342	6,161	385
Acquisition of other assets	(12,790)	(1,093)	(273)
Issuance of notes receivable	(225,282)	(45,690)	(773)
Repayment of notes receivable	68,498	747	—
Net cash used in investing activities	(270,854)	(89,026)	(9,114)
Cash from financing activities			
Proceeds from issue common stock	125,703	66,150	19,843
Proceeds from convertible subordinate notes	130,000	9,658	
Borrowings under credit facility	96,130	32,275	
Repayments under credit facility	(96,130)	(32,275)	
Payment of capital lease obligation	—	—	(300)
Net cash from financing activities	255,703	75,808	19,543
Net increase (decrease) in cash	20,767	(5,172)	6,817
Cash, beginning of year	4,537	9,709	2,892
Cash, end of year	$ 25,304	$ 4,537	$ 9,709
Supplemental cash flow information			
Interest paid	$ 3,395	$ 226	$ 29
Noncash transactions			
Conversion of convt. subord. notes into common stock	$ —	$ 10,072	$ —
Issuance of common stock for assets	$ 19,931	$ —	$ —

The accompanying notes to the consolidated financial statements are an integral part of these statements.

Boston Chicken

OTHER INFORMATION

	1994	1993	1992	1991
Store Information				
Company operated	41	38	19	5
Finance area developers	314	78	3	0
Nonfinanced area developers	179	101	61	29
Total	534	217	83	34
Systematic store revenue	383.7	152.1	42.7	20.8
Quarterly Data Revenue				
1st quarter	23,449			
2nd quarter	20,360			
3rd quarter	25,186			
4th quarter	27,165			
Net Income				
1st quarter	2,561			
2nd quarter	3,383			
3rd quarter	4,679			
4th quarter	5,550			

Boston Chicken

Boston Chicken

NOTES TO CONSOLIDATED FINANCIAL STATEMENTS

1. Description of Business

Boston Chicken, Inc., and Subsidiary (the "Company") operate and franchise food service stores that specialize in complete meals featuring home style entrees, fresh vegetables, salads, and other side items. At December 26, 1993, there were 217 stores systemwide, consisting of 38 Company-operated stores and 179 franchise stores. At December 25, 1994, there were 534 stores systemwide, consisting of 41 Company-operated stores and 493 franchise stores. In 1992, 1993, and 1994, in connection with its practice of opening new stores to seed development in targeted markets, the Company sold 1, 13, and 54 Company-operated stores, respectively, to new formed area developers or franchisees of the Company. During 1994, in connection with its practice of acquiring stores in markets with multiple area developers in order to facilitate consolidation of such markets, the Company purchased 34 stores and resold 26 of them.

2. Summary of Significant Accounting Policies

Principles of Consolidation

The accompanying consolidated financial statements include the accounts of the Company and its subsidiary. All material intercompany accounts and transactions have been eliminated in consolidation.

Fiscal Year

The Company's fiscal year is the 52/53-week period ending on the last Sunday in December. Fiscal years 1992, 1993, and 1994 each contained 52 weeks, or thirteen four-week periods. The first quarter consists of four periods and each of the remaining three quarters consists of three periods, with the first, second, and third quarters ending 16 weeks, 28 weeks, and 40 weeks, respectively, into the fiscal year.

Cash and Cash Equivalents

Cash and cash equivalents consist of cash on hand and on deposit, and highly liquid instruments purchased with maturities of three months or less.

Inventories

Inventories, which are classified in prepaid expenses and other current assets, are stated at the lower of cost (first-in, first-out) or market and consist of food, paper products, and supplies.

Property and Equipment

Property and equipment is stated at cost, less accumulated depreciation and amortization. The provision for depreciation and amortization has been calculated using the straight-line method. The following represent the useful lives over which the assets are depreciated and amortized:

Buildings and improvements	15–30 years
Leasehold improvements	15 years
Furniture, fixtures, equipment and computer software	6–8 years
Pre-Opening costs	1 year

Property and equipment additions include acquisitions of property and equipment, costs incurred in the development and construction of new stores, major improvements to existing stores, and costs incurred in the development and purchase of computer software. Pre-opening costs consist primarily of salaries and other direct expenses relating to the set-up, initial stocking, training, and general management activities incurred prior to the opening of new stores. Expenditures for maintenance and repairs are charged to expense as incurred. Development costs for franchised stores are expensed when the store opens.

Deferred Financing Costs

Deferred financing costs are amortized over the period of the related financing, which ranges from two to ten years.

Revenue Recognition

Revenue from Company-operated stores is recognized in the period related food and beverage products are sold. Revenue derived from initial franchise fees and area development fees is recognized when the franchise store opens. Royalties are recognized in the same period related franchise store revenue is generated. The components of royalties and franchise-related fees are comprised of the following:

(In thousands of dollars)	Dec. 25, 1994	Dec. 26, 1993	Dec. 27, 1992
Royalties	$17,421	$5,464	$1,491
Initial franchise and area development	13,057	5,230	1,136
Interest income from area developer financing (See Note 8)	11,632	1,130	—
Lease income	5,361	253	—
Software fees	6,480	—	—
Other	1,284	604	—
Total royalties and franchise-related fees	$55,235	$12,681	$2,627

Subject to the provisions of the applicable franchise agreements, the Company is committed and obligated to allow franchisees to utilize the Company's trademarks, copyrights, recipes, operating procedures, and other elements of the Boston Market system in the operation of franchised Boston Market stores.

Per Share Data

Net income (loss) per common share is computed by dividing net income (loss), adjusted in 1993 for interest related to the conversion of 7% convertible subordinated notes (See Note 9), by the weighted average number of common shares and dilutive common stock equivalent shares outstanding during the year.

Common and equivalent share include any common stock, options, and warrants issued within one year prior to the effective date of the Company's initial public offering, with a price below the initial public offering price. These have been included as common stock equivalents outstanding, reduced by the number of shares of common stock which could be purchased with the proceeds form the assumed exercise of the options and warrants, including tax benefits assumed to be realized.

Employee Benefit Plan

The Company has a 401(k) plan for which employee participation is discretionary and to which the Company makes no contribution.

Reclassification

Certain amounts shown in the 1992 and 1993 financial statements have been reclassified to conform with the current presentation.

4. Debt

The Company has entered into a revolving credit agreement on an unsecured basis providing for borrowings of up to $75 million through June 30, 1997. Borrowings under the agreement may be either floating rate loans with interest at the bank's reference rate of eurodollar loans with interest at the eurodollar rate, plus an applicable margin. In addition, a commitment fee of .25% of the average daily unused portion of the loan is required. The agreement contains various covenants including restricting other borrowings, prohibiting cash dividends, and requiring the Company to maintain interest coverage and cash flow ratios and a minimum net worth. As of December 25, 1994, no borrowings were outstanding.

In February, 1994, the Company issued $130 million of 4.5% convertible subordinated debentures maturing February 1, 2004. Interest is payable semi-annually on February 1 and August 1 of each year. The debentures are convertible at any time prior to maturity into share of common stock at a conversion rate of $27.969 per share, subject to adjustment under certain conditions. Beginning February 1, 1996, the debentures may be redeemed at the option of the Company, provided that through February 1, 1997, the debentures cannot be redeemed unless the closing price of the common stock equals or exceeds $39.16 per share for at least 20 out of 30 consecutive trading days. The debentures are redeemable initially at 103.6% of their principal amount and at declining prices thereafter, plus accrued interest.

5. Income Taxes

As of December 25, 1994, the Company has cumulative Federal and state net tax operating loss carryforwards available to reduce future taxable income of approximately $30.5 million which begin to expire in 2003. The Company has recognized the benefit of the loss carryforwards for financial reporting, but not for income tax purposes. Certain ownership changes which have occurred will result in an annual limitation of the Company's utilization of its net operating losses.

At December 28, 1992, the first day of fiscal 1993, the Company adopted SFAS No. 109 "Accounting for Income Taxes" ("SFAS 109"). Upon adoption of SFAS 109 there was no cumulative effect on the Company's financial statements

Boston Chicken

Boston Chicken

because the Company's deferred tax assets exceeded its deferred tax liabilities and a valuation allowance was recorded against the net deferred tax assets due to uncertainty regarding realization of the related tax benefits.

The primary components that comprise the deferred tax assets and liabilities at December 26, 1993, and December 25, 1994, are as follows:

(In thousands of dollars)	Dec. 25, 1994	Dec. 26, 1993
Deferred tax assets:		
Accounts payable and accrued expenses	$ 794	$ 78
Deferred franchise revenue	3,469	1,992
Other noncurrent liabilities	262	623
Net operating losses	11,639	4,844
Other	173	52
Total deferred tax assets	16,337	7,589
Less valuation allowance	—	(3,847)
Net deferred taxes	16,337	3,742
Deferred tax liabilities:		
Due from area developers	—	(814)
Property and equipment	(17,047)	(2,807)
Other assets	(466)	(121)
Total deferred tax liabilities	(17,513)	(3,742)
Net deferred tax liability	$ (1,176)	$ —

The decrease in the valuation allowance from December 26, 1993 to December 25, 1994 was $3,847,000 and the decrease in the valuation allowance from December 27, 1992 to December 26, 1993 was $180,000, which was net of a $446,000 increase related to the tax benefit from the exercise of stock options.

The provision for income taxes for the fiscal year ended December 25, 1994, consists of $4,277,000 of deferred income taxes, which is net of an income tax benefit of $3,102,000 pertaining to the exercise of stock options.

The difference between the Company's 1993 and 1994 actual tax provision and the tax provision by applying the statutory Federal income tax rate is attributable to the following:

(In thousands of dollars)	Fiscal Years Ended	
	Dec. 25, 1994	Dec. 26, 1993
Income tax expense at statutory rate	$6,953	$ 560
State taxes, net of Federal benefit	818	66
Other	26	—
Change in valuation allowance	(3,520)	(626)
Provision for income taxes	$4,277	$ —

6. Marketing and Advertising Funds

The Company administers a National Advertising Fund to which Company-operated stores and franchisees make contributions based on individual franchise agreements (currently 2% of base revenue). Collected amounts are spent primarily on developing marketing and advertising materials for use systemwide. Such amounts are not segregated from the cash resources of the Company, but the National Advertising Fund is accounted for separately and not included in the financial statements of the Company.

The Company maintains Local Advertising Funds that provide comprehensive advertising and sales promotion support for the Boston Market stores in particular markets. Periodic contributions are made by both Company-operated and franchise stores (currently 3% to 3.75% of base revenue). The Company disburses funds and accounts for all transactions related to such Local Advertising Funds. Such amounts are not segregated from the cash resources of the Company, but are accounted for separately and are not included in the financial statements of the Company.

The National Advertising Fund and certain Local Advertising Funds had accumulated deficits at December 26, 1993, and December 25, 1994, which were funded by advances from the Company. Such advances are reflected in Due from affiliates, net.

8. Area Developer Financing

The Company currently offers partial financing to certain area developers for use in expansion of their operations. Only developers which are developing a significant portion of an area of dominant influence ("ADI") or metropolitan area of a major city and which meet all of the Company's requirements are eligible for such financing. Certain of these financing arrangements permit the Company to obtain an equity interest in the developer at a predetermined price after a moratorium (generally two years) on conversion of the loan into equity. The maximum loan amount is generally established to give the Company majority ownership of the developer upon conversion (or option exercise, as described further below) provided the Company exercises its right to participate in any intervening financing of the developer.

Area developer financing generally requires the developer to expend at least 75% of its equity capital toward developing stores prior to drawing on the revolving loan account, with draws permitted during a two- or three-year draw period in a pre-determined amount, generally equal to two to four times the amount of the developer's equity capital. Upon expiration of the draw period, the loan converts to an amortizing term loan payable over four to five years in periodic installments, sometimes with a final balloon payment. Interest is generally set at 1% over the applicable "reference rate" of Bank of America Illinois from time to time and is payable each period. The loan is secured by a pledge of substantially all of the assets of the area developer and any franchisees under its area development agreement and generally by a pledge of equity of the owners of the developer.

(a) Loan Conversion Option

For loans with a conversion option, all or any portion of the loan amount may be converted at the Company's election (at any time after default of the loan or generally after the second anniversary of the loan and generally up to the later of full repayment of the loan or a specified date in the agreement) into equity in the developer at the conversion price set forth in such loan agreement, generally at a 12% to 15% premium over the per equity unit price paid by the developer for the equity investment made concurrently with the execution of the loan agreement or subsequent amendments thereto. To the extent such loan is not fully drawn or has been drawn and repaid, the Company has a corresponding option to acquire at the loan conversion price the amount of additional equity it could have acquired by conversion of the loan, had it been fully drawn.

There can be no assurance the Company will or will not convert any loan amount or exercise its option at such time as it may be permitted to do so and, if it does convert, that such conversion will constitute a majority interest in the area developer. Absent a default under any such agreement, the Company currently cannot exercise these conversion or option rights.

(b) Commitment to Extend Area Developer Financing

The following table summarizes credit commitments for area developer financing, certain of which are conditional upon additional equity contributions being made by area developers:

(In thousands of dollars, except number of area developers)	Dec. 25, 1994	Dec. 26, 1993
Number of area developers receiving financing	13	5
Loan commitments	$332,531	$ 51,041
Unused loans	(131,265)	(7,243)
Loans outstanding (included in Notes Receivable)	$201,266	$ 43,798
Allowance for loan losses	$ —	$ —

The principal maturities on the aforementioned notes receivable are as follows:

(In thousands of dollars)	
1995	$16,288
1996	4,456
1997	13,132
1998	12,132
1999	15,417
Thereafter	139,841
	$201,266

(c) Credit Risk and Allowance for Loan Losses

The allowance for credit losses is maintained at a level that in management's judgment is adequate to provide for estimated possible loan losses. The amount of the allowance is based on management's review of each area developer's financial condition, store performance, store opening schedules, and other factors, as well as prevailing economic conditions. Based upon this review and analysis, no allowance was required as of December 26, 1993 and December 25, 1994.

11. Relocation

In September 1994, the Company consolidated its four Chicago-based support center facilities into a single facility and relocated to Golden, Colorado. The cost of the relocation, including moving personnel and facilities, severance payments, and the write-off of vacated leasehold improvements was $5.1 million.

12. Subsequent Events

In March 1995, the Company entered into a convertible secured loan agreement providing $20 million of financing to Progressive Bagel Concepts, Inc. ("PBCI"). The Company has agreed to provide PBCI additional convertible secured loans subject to PBCI's ability to meet certain conditions.

In March 1995, PBCI entered into stock purchase agreements with the Company to purchase $19.5 million of common stock. The number of shares to be issued will be based upon the market value of the stock two days prior to the closing date. The Company has granted PBCI registration rights and has provided a price guarantee equal to the per share purchase price on any shares sold within a specified number of days of the registration becoming effective.

REPORT OF INDEPENDENT PUBLIC ACCOUNTANTS

To the Board of Directors and Stockholders of Boston Chicken, Inc.:

We have audited the accompanying consolidated balance sheets of Boston Chicken, Inc. (a Delaware corporation) and Subsidiary as of December 25, 1994 and December 26, 1993, and the related consolidated statements of operations, stockholders' equity, and cash flows for the fiscal years ended December 25, 1994, December 26, 1993, and December 27, 1992. These financial statements are the responsibility of the Company's management. Our responsibility is to express an opinion on these financial statements based on our audits.

We conducted our audits in accordance with generally accepted auditing standards. Those standards require that we plan and perform the audit to obtain reasonable assurance about whether the financial statements are free of material misstatements. An audit includes examining, on a test basis, evidence supporting the amounts and disclosures in the financial statements. An audit also includes assessing the accounting principles used and significant estimates made by management, as well as evaluating the overall financial statement presentation. We believe that our audits provide a reasonable basis for our opinion.

In our opinion, the financial statements referred to above present fairly, in all material respects, the financial position of Boston Chicken, Inc. and Subsidiary as of December 25, 1994 and December 26, 1993, and the results of their operations and their cash flows for the fiscal years ended December 25, 1994, December 26, 1993, and December 27, 1992, in conformity with generally accepted accounting principles.

(Arthur Andersen LLP)
Denver, Colorado
January 31, 1995 (except with respect to the matters discussed in Note 12, as to which the date is March 24, 1995)

EXHIBIT 2

Boston Chicken Inc., Summary of 1994–1995 Quarterly Results

	1st Quarter	2nd Quarter	3rd Quarter	4th Quarter
1995				
Revenue ($000)	$40,107	$34,800	$38,671	
Net Income ($000)	7,116	7,420	8,814	
EPS	$0.15	$0.15	$0.17	
1994				
Revenue ($000)	$23,449	$20,360	$25,186	$27,165
Net Income ($000)	2,561[a]	3,383[a]	4,679[a]	5,550
EPS	$0.06	$0.08	$0.11	$0.12

a. Pre-tax provisions for relocation were $4,708,000 in the second quarter of 1994, and $389,000 in the third quarter of 1994.

Boston Chicken

Liability and Equity Analysis

Firms have two broad classes of financial claims on their assets: liabilities and equity. The key distinction between these claims is the extent to which their payoffs can be specified contractually. The firm's obligations under liabilities are specified relatively clearly, whereas equity claims tend to be difficult to specify.

The economic differences between liabilities and equity are reflected in their accounting definitions. Liabilities are defined as economic obligations that arise from benefits received in the past, and for which the amount and timing is known with reasonable certainty. Liabilities include obligations to customers that have paid in advance for products or services; commitments to public and private providers of debt financing; obligations to federal and local governments for taxes; commitments to employees for unpaid wages, pensions, and other retirement benefits; and obligations from court or government fines or environmental cleanup orders.

For accounting purposes, equity financing is defined as the claim on the gap between assets and liabilities. It can therefore be thought of as a residual claim. Equity funds can come from issues of common and preferred stock, from profits that are reinvested, and from any reserves set aside from profits.

It is important for users of financial statements to analyze the nature of the firm's liabilities and its equity in order to assess the financial risks faced by both debt and equity investors. Managers are likely to have the best information about the extent of the firm's future commitments. However, they also have incentives to understate the value of these commitments and the firm's financial risks. Analysis of liabilities involves assessing the extent, nature, and measurability of any obligations the firm has incurred. Equity values are a primary input for the valuation approach discussed in Chapters 10, 11, and 12. It is therefore important that equity values be reliable estimates of stockholders' claims on the firm's assets. However, since equity is defined as a residual, analysis of equity is indirect, through analysis of assets, liabilities, revenues, and expenses. Additional questions about equity focus on classification of items within equity and hybrid securities.

In this chapter we discuss the key principles underlying the recording of liabilities and equity. We also show the challenges in reporting these types of claims and the opportunities for analysis of each.

LIABILITY DEFINITION AND REPORTING CHALLENGES

Under accrual accounting, liabilities can arise in three ways. First, they can arise when a firm has received cash from a customer but has yet to fulfill any of its contractual obligations required for recognizing revenue (see Chapter 6). These types of liabilities are termed deferred or unearned revenues. Second, a liability can arise if a firm has used goods and/or services in the course of its operating cycle or during the current period, but has yet to pay the suppliers of these inputs. These are called payables and accrued liabilities. Finally, a firm incurs a liability when it raises debt capital from banks, financial institutions, and the public. Under this form of financing arrangement, the firm borrows a fixed amount of capital that it commits to repay, with interest, over a fixed period.

As shown in Figure 5-1, under accrual accounting these three types of liabilities are reflected in the financial statements when a firm incurs an obligation to another party for which the amount and timing are measurable with reasonable certainty. Measurement challenges for liabilities arise when there is ambiguity about whether an obligation has really been incurred, whether the obligation can be measured, and when there have been changes in the value of liabilities.

Challenge One: Has an obligation been incurred?

For most liabilities there is little ambiguity about whether the firm has incurred an obligation. For example, when a firm buys supplies on credit, it has incurred an obligation to the supplier. However, for some transactions it is more difficult to decide whether there is any such obligation. Consider a situation where a firm assigns the cash flows from a note receivable to a bank, but where the bank has recourse against the firm should the receivable default. Has the firm effectively sold its receivables, or has it really used the receivables as collateral for a bank loan? If a firm announces a plan to restructure its business

Figure 5-1 Criteria for Recording Liabilities and Implementation Challenges

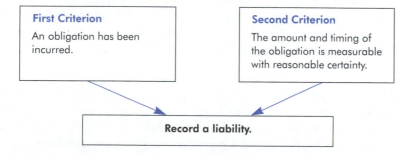

First Criterion

An obligation has been incurred.

Second Criterion

The amount and timing of the obligation is measurable with reasonable certainty.

Record a liability.

Challenging Transactions
1. It is uncertain whether the firm has incurred an obligation.
2. The amount and timing of future obligations is difficult to measure.
3. Liability values have changed.

by laying off employees, has it made a commitment that would justify recording a liability? Similarly, has an airline that uses a frequent flyer program as a marketing device created an obligation to provide future travel to its customers? Finally, has a firm that is subject to a legal suit incurred an obligation? Below we discuss several of these types of transactions and the challenges they provide for financial reporting. Although our discussion of these transactions focuses on whether they create future commitments for the firm, they frequently also raise questions about whether any commitment can be measured.

EXAMPLE: RESTRUCTURING RESERVES.   On October 12, 1994, in response to intense competition from the Australian spice producer Burns, Philp & Co., McCormick & Co. announced plans to lay off 7 percent of its 8,600-person staff, close two spice plants, and sell off a money-losing onion-ring operation. How should this announcement be recorded in McCormick's financial statements? Had McCormick actually made a commitment to expend resources to restructure its business? If so, what were the estimated costs of these actions? Alternatively, had McCormick merely announced a plan to restructure the firm? A plan does not necessarily create an obligation on McCormick's part. It can be modified or abandoned, just as announcements of projected capital outlays for the coming year can be changed.

The question of whether a restructuring announcement creates an economic liability from the firm's standpoint is difficult to resolve. It depends on management's intentions when it announces the plan. It is also worth noting that a successful restructuring not only creates a commitment, but an associated benefit in terms of improved subsequent performance. How are these effects reflected in firms' financial statements?

Current accounting rules on restructuring charges are covered by a number of accounting standards (APB 30 and SFAS 5) as well as SEC rulings. These rules require firms to create a liability when management has a formal restructuring plan. The liability includes estimates for costs of eliminating product lines, relocating plants and workers, new system costs, retraining costs, and severance pay. However, the SEC has argued that the mere announcement of employee terminations is not sufficient grounds for accruing a liability until specific affected employees have been notified. It is also interesting to note that accounting rules do not permit restructuring firms to recognize any future benefits expected from these activities.

These rules leave considerable room for management judgment in reporting for restructuring charges. Indeed, as noted in Chapter 7, the SEC has expressed concern that managers have overstated restructuring charges by making aggressive asset write-downs, called "taking a bath." Future performance is then enhanced both by the effect of any restructuring benefits and by reduced depreciation charges or restructuring credits.

The McCormick restructuring raised concerns among some analysts that the firm had used write-offs to manage future earnings. In its financial statements for the fourth quarter of 1994, McCormick created a $70.5 million liability for the costs of the restructuring. However, in February 1995 it reduced the amount of the charge by $3.9 million, which it added to earnings in the first quarter of 1995. As a result, it reported a 5.7 percent increase in earnings for the quarter, when earnings would otherwise have declined.

Analysts criticized McCormick for failing to mention the restructuring credit in its earnings announcement and only disclosing the fact in later reports to the SEC.

Subsequent disclosures on restructuring activities at McCormick further illustrate the difficulties in assessing whether a restructuring announcement is a commitment, and whether firms have deliberately overestimated the restructuring liability to create a cushion for future years. In 1996 McCormick announced a second restructuring. Most of the costs of the restructuring ($58.1 million) were recognized as a restructuring liability immediately. However, the firm noted that some charges related to costs of moving equipment and personnel from a closed U.S. packaging plant could not be accrued. These charges (for $1.9 million) were eventually recognized in the fourth quarter of 1998. In the third quarter of 1997, McCormick reevaluated its restructuring plans and recorded a restructuring credit of $9.5 million because plans to sell an overseas food brokerage and distribution business were not completed. The 1996 restructuring was concluded in the fourth quarter of 1998, and a further restructuring credit of $3.1 million was reported.

EXAMPLE: FREQUENT FLYER OBLIGATIONS.   Many airlines have frequent flyer programs for their passengers. These programs are designed to enhance customer loyalty by offering bonus award miles every time the passenger flies with the same airline. Passengers who accumulate sufficient award miles can then redeem them for future flights, hotel accommodations, or rental cars. Since their creation in the early 1980s, airline mileage programs have become increasingly popular, prompting some airlines to actually sell award miles to credit card and phone companies to offer their members as promotions.

The challenge for accounting is to assess whether the airlines have incurred a liability for the future travel commitments under the mileage programs. There are several reasons for not viewing the program as creating a commitment. First, the airlines have discretion to modify or even abandon their mileage programs, should they wish to avoid the commitments. For example, in 1987, United Airlines (UAL) made it more difficult for passengers to earn free flights, at least in part in response to growing concerns about the potential liability under the program. The changes reduced the number of double and triple mileage bonuses offered to passengers who flew during certain months or on certain routes. It also required more miles to be earned to qualify for a free ticket to Hawaii, one of the most popular destinations in the program, and to destinations in Asia and the South Pacific. Finally, the company announced that awards would expire within three years of the date of issue.

Airlines can also regulate their commitment under frequent flyer programs by limiting the number of seats available to frequent flyers. In 1997 the number of outstanding frequent flyer miles totaled 3 trillion, compared to only 16.3 billion a decade earlier. Yet the number of available free seats had not expanded at the same rate. Randy Petersen, of the trade magazine *Inside Flyer*, estimated that most airlines made only 7 percent of their seats available for frequent flyer awards on a particular route.

In addition to questions on whether an obligation has been incurred, frequent flyer programs raise questions about the amount of the obligation. For example, what is the cost of frequent flyer obligations? Given normal load factors and the incremental costs of an additional passenger, the opportunity and out-of-pocket costs of frequent flyer awards could be minimal.

Of course, changing the requirements for mileage awards and making it more difficult to collect on awards can be costly—UAL was sued over its plan changes. Further, the recent sale of mileage awards by airlines reduces the likelihood that there can be significant additional reductions in program benefits. As a result of these conflicting views on the economics of the programs, there are legitimate differences in opinion about the nature of airlines' commitments under these programs.

Current accounting rules reflect the uncertainty about the extent of the commitment. They provide no definitive guidance on how to report these obligations, potentially providing an opportunity for management to exercise judgment. In its 1999 annual report, United Airlines noted that approximately 6.1 million frequent flyer awards were outstanding. Based on historical data, the firm estimated that 4.6 million of these awards would ultimately be redeemed. The firm predicted that the remainder would never be redeemed, would be redeemed for nontravel benefits, or would be redeemed on partner carriers. The firm recorded a liability for $195 million for award redemption, reflecting the "additional costs of providing service for what would otherwise be a vacant seat, such as fuel, meal, personnel and ticketing costs" (see UAL 1999 10-K).

EXAMPLE: LITIGATION.   In November 1988, the Public Citizen's Health Research Group requested that the U.S. Food and Drug Administration ban silicone gel implants because a new study by the major manufacturer, Dow Corning Corp., found that the gel causes a type of cancer in laboratory rats. A number of other experts in the field, however, disputed the risks of silicone gel implants, pointing out that the type of cancer found in the rats has never been observed in women with implants. Dow Corning also argued that the implants should be allowed to remain on the market. However, the company subsequently faced a litigation deluge related to the research findings.

How should these legal claims be reflected in Dow Corning's financial statements? Should a liability be recognized for potential costs of fighting the claims? Should a liability be created for the potential cost of any settlement? If so, should the liability be reported on a discounted or undiscounted basis? Or is there no basis for recording any liability? Dow Corning can certainly argue that any estimate of liability could be viewed as an admission of guilt and thereby prejudice its case. However, from the perspective of financial statement users, the uncertainty surrounding the firm's legal status is critical to valuing the firm, and potentially to assessing the performance of its management.

The accounting rules for these types of contingencies are covered in the U.S. by SFAS 5. Under this standard, a firm is required to accrue a loss if it is probable that a liability has been incurred and the amount can be reasonably estimated. The standard argues that if a range of estimates is available, the best estimate within this range should be reported as a liability. If there is no best estimate, the minimum estimate should be reported. The FASB recognized that the most difficult issue that arose in reporting contingencies was for litigation. It resolved that in most cases such events are reflected only in the footnotes.

Between 1988 and 1993, Dow Corning provided no liability for the litigation, although it recognized that monetary damages claimed in the cases might be substantial. In September 1993, the company announced that it had reached an agreement with representatives of the plaintiffs and with other defendants for a settlement of up to $4.75 billion to be paid out over a period of 30 years. As a result, in January 1994, a charge of $640 million (before tax) was taken for the fourth quarter of 1993. A further pretax charge of $221 million for the fourth quarter of 1994 was announced in January 1995. These charges included Dow Corning's best estimate of its potential liability under the agreement and were determined on a present value basis. In the second quarter of 1995, the company changed the method of accounting for the potential losses from the present value basis to an undiscounted basis. On May 15, 1995, it voluntarily filed for protection under Chapter 11 of the U.S. Bankruptcy Code.

Given the delicate nature of litigation, management has a strong incentive to underestimate potential losses. Indeed, this is likely to also be in shareholders' best interests. However, for important litigation cases, such as those for Dow Corning and for cigarette companies, this implies that investors will have to analyze firms' effective litigation risks and costs without much guidance from the firm, leading to potential speculation.

Challenge Two: Can the obligation be measured?

Many liabilities specify the amount and timing of obligations precisely. For example, a twenty-year $100 million bond issue, with an 8 percent coupon payable semi-annually, specifies that the issuer will pay the holders $100 million in twenty years, and will pay out interest of $4 million every six months for the duration of the loan.

However, for some liabilities it is difficult to estimate the amount of the obligation. We saw that this can be an issue for accrued restructuring charges and frequent flyer programs. Other examples include environmental liabilities, pension and retirement benefit liabilities, insurance company loss reserves, and warranties. These examples are discussed below.

EXAMPLE: ENVIRONMENTAL LIABILITIES. In 1980 the Comprehensive Environmental Response, Compensation, and Liability Act (CERCLA) was passed by the U.S. Congress to clean up inactive hazardous waste sites. The legislation authorized the federal government to make those responsible for the improper disposal of hazardous waste at the nation's worst hazardous waste sites (termed Superfund sites) bear the cost of cleanup. In addition, polluters must pay to restore damaged or lost natural resources at Superfund sites. By December 23, 1996, 1,259 current and proposed Superfund sites had been identified. Estimates of the cost of cleanups at known sites ranged from $34 to $75 billion.[1]

There are two challenges in estimating the costs of Superfund cleanups. First, responsibility for the damage and cleanup is uncertain. All parties associated with a site, even those that have contributed only a small amount of low-toxicity waste, are liable for the cost of cleaning it up. Consequently, there are protracted negotiations and legal disputes over the allocation of costs among these parties. Firms involved in these disputes are reluctant to report an estimate of the cost of their share of a Superfund site cleanup, since to do so could affect their negotiations and legal liability. Second, there is considerable uncertainty about the actual costs of cleanup, since prior to a detailed study of the site it is difficult to assess the extent of the damage and the cost of cleanup. Consistent with this concern, research shows that the explanatory power of models to predict the relation between cleanup costs and hazard site characteristics is relatively low.[2]

As a result of the difficulty in estimating the costs of cleanups, it is unclear when a company responsible for waste cleanup should record a liability for its cost. Should it be when the party is suspected of being responsible for hazardous waste? Should it be when it is named as a responsible party for a particular site cleanup? Should it occur when a study has been conducted to estimate the cleanup costs? Or, should it be when a settlement has been reached with other liable parties for the cost of the cleanup?

The difficulties in assessing legal liability for cleanup are illustrated by the case of Hanson Plc, a U.K. building materials firm that was formed from the breakup of the Hanson conglomerate. In 1991 Hanson acquired the U.S. firm Beazer, a homebuilding firm. Prior to its acquisition by Hanson, Beazer had owned and then sold a chemical company, Koppers, which had been prosecuted by the Environmental Protection Agency (EPA) for leaking dangerous chemicals at 119 sites in the U.S. Under U.S. law, Hanson was considered liable for some of the environmental cleanup costs for Koppers' sites. The cleanup costs were initially thought to be in excess of $2 billion. Hanson, however, disputed the cost effectiveness of the cleanup procedures required by the EPA and its share of these costs relative to its own insurers. In its 1996 annual report, Hanson noted that it had set aside £938 million as a liability to cover the cleanup costs. However, in 1997 the company reported that, based on a third-party appraisal, its estimate could be reduced by £430.3 million. The liability was consequently reduced and an exceptional credit recorded in the profit and loss account. In 1998 Hanson agreed to pay further costs of £168 million, and two insurance companies guaranteed to cover any remaining costs to settle the dispute, up to £488 million. After the agreement, £67 million of the estimated liability was no longer required and was recorded as an unusual credit.

Given the challenges in measuring cleanup costs, accounting rules permit firms to delay recording a liability for environmental costs until much of the uncertainty over the cost of cleanup and the firm's responsibility have been resolved. SFAS 5 and Statement of Position 96-1 require that an obligation be reported when the following conditions hold:

1. A firm has been identified as a potentially responsible party.
2. The firm is participating in a remedial feasibility study.
3. A remedial feasibility study has been completed.
4. A decision has been made as to the method of cleanup and an estimate made of the cleanup cost.
5. The firm has been ordered to clean up a site.

Research findings indicate that there is considerable variation in the quality of financial statement disclosures on estimated environmental cleanup liabilities for affected firms. Factors influencing firms' disclosures include regulatory enforcement, management's information on allocation uncertainty, litigation and negotiation concerns, and capital market concerns.[3]

EXAMPLE: PENSION AND OTHER POSTEMPLOYMENT BENEFIT LIABILITIES. Many firms make commitments to employees under defined benefit plans for prespecified pension or retirement benefits at some point in the future. The challenge that arises in reporting on these commitments comes from the difficulty in measuring the benefits provided. For example, consider the September 1996 agreement reached between the Big Three U.S. auto manufacturers and the United Auto Workers union. The agreement provided the following incremental benefits for hourly employees:

a. Basic pension benefits were increased by $4.55 ($1.15) a month for every year worked for new (current) retirees. New retirees are employees who retired after September 1996, and current retirees are those who retired before this date.

b. New retirees who retired prior to age 62 but had 30 years of service received an $80-a-month increase in pension benefits in 1997, a $160-per-month increase in 1998, and a $265-per-month increase thereafter. Current retirees who had retired prior to 62 but had 30 years of service received an $80-a-month increase in pension benefits.

c. Current retirees received two cost-of-living lump sum payments in 1997 and 1998. The amount of the payment depended on the retiree's years of service and inflation rates for those years.

d. Retired employees (new and current) were eligible for up to $1,000 a year in tuition assistance for approved courses through the Retiree Tuition Assistance Plan.

What are the economic obligations that GM, Ford, and Chrysler incurred under this pension plan? To estimate the timing and expected pension benefits for current and past employees, the firms have to forecast the life expectancies of current and past employees, as well as the future working lives with the firm and retirement ages of current employees. The present value of these future commitments, net of pension plan assets, represents the economic obligation under the pension plan. The obligation increases over time to reflect the incremental pension earned with years of service, and interest accruing on the liability. The obligation also changes if the firm retroactively changes the benefits to be paid to employees for past service. Finally, the pension obligation decreases as the firm funds its obligation, as plan assets increase in value, and as the firm pays out benefits to retired employees.

How does accounting reflect this obligation, given the challenge of making actuarial assumptions about employees' working lives and retirement decisions? The current rules, discussed in SFAS 87, recognize most of the above effects, but they require firms to amortize changes in the obligations that arise from retroactive changes in pension benefits (called prior service costs) and from changes in pension asset values over time, rather than recognizing them immediately. As a result, the reported pension liability is likely to be understated. However, current rules also require firms to disclose in the footnotes the full liability, termed the projected benefit obligation, and the fair value of plan assets.[4] For example, in its 1996 annual report, Ford reported the projected benefit obligation for U.S. plans at $28.2 billion, and the fair value of the plan's assets at $30.9 billion. In contrast, GM's projected benefit obligation was reported at $44.5 billion, and its plan assets had fair values of $40.2 billion. Ford thus had surplus assets in its pension plan, whereas GM showed a shortfall for which the company is ultimately liable.

The range of actuarial assumptions, discount rate assumptions, and amortization periods for prior period service costs and gains or losses on plan assets all provide management with an opportunity to exercise discretion in the reporting of pension and postemployment benefit liabilities.[5] In addition, accounting rules for these liabilities do not always reflect the full effect of changes in plan obligations and fair values. Both these factors create opportunities for analysis.

EXAMPLE: INSURANCE LOSS RESERVES.   Insurance companies typically recognize revenues before the amount and timing of claims for the period have been fully resolved. As a result, insurance managers have to estimate the expected costs of unreported claims and reported claims where the claim amount has not been settled. Management bases its estimates on data on reported claims and estimates of the costs of settlement, as well as historical data and experience in estimating unreported losses. For example, in its 1995 financial statements, Travelers Property Casualty Corp. estimated that its gross loss reserve was $13.9 billion. The company also reported details on differences between its estimated losses on a yearly basis and subsequent loss realizations for those years. It estimated loss reserves for 1985 claims at $5.5 billion in 1985. In subsequent years, Travelers management steadily revised this estimate upward. In 1986 the estimate was increased to $5.9 billion, in 1990 to $6.9 billion, and in 1995 to $8.5 billion. A similar pattern of under-reserving arose for each of the years 1986 to 1992. The deficiencies amounted to $2.6 billion, $2.3 billion, $2.0 billion, $1.7 billion, $1.2 billion, $0.7 billion, and $0.3 billion for these years.

The data for Travelers illustrate how difficult it can be to forecast future claims. The data also show that there are potentially significant opportunities for management to make mistakes in forecasting, and to bias its estimates either for regulatory purposes or for stock market valuation purposes.[6] The disclosures of estimates and subsequent revisions of estimates provide analysts with extensive information to evaluate management's reporting for reserves. However, even with these data, it can be challenging to assess whether systematic under- or overestimates arose from poor management forecasting, unforeseen events, or management bias in reporting.

EXAMPLE: WARRANTIES.   Many manufacturers provide implicit or explicit product warranties on their products. How should these be reported in the financial statements?

Should a liability be created when sales are recognized to reflect an estimate of the costs of returns or repairs? Alternatively, should firms wait until returns actually occur before recognizing the financial implications of the warranty commitment?

Accounting rules require that firms that offer warranties establish a liability for probable losses that have been incurred at the financial statement date. Thus, in its 1998 annual report, General Motors reported that it had a $14.6 billion liability for "warranties, dealer and customer allowances, claims and discounts."

Of course, estimating the potential commitment for warranty costs is not an easy task. It should come as no surprise that there are sometimes sizable errors in management's estimates. For example, on December 21, 1994, Intel, the world's largest silicon chip manufacturer, bowed to consumer pressure and agreed to replace millions of Pentium chips that contained a flaw in long-division calculations requiring maximum precision. The recall was the largest in computer history. Intel announced that it would replace all the chips without question, and gave users the option of requesting a replacement chip to fit into their own computers or having the work done by a dealer. Since no prior liability had been created to allow for any such possibility, Intel created a $475 million liability at the end of the fourth quarter. This liability covered replacement costs, replacement material, and inventory write-down related to the division problem. It is interesting to note that Intel still has not created a liability for other possible losses from explicit or implicit warranties on their products.

Key Analysis Questions

Given the role of management judgment in assessing whether a firm has incurred an obligation that can be measured with reasonable certainty, there is ample opportunity for analysts to question whether there are significant liabilities that are not reported on the balance sheet. Specific questions can include the following:

- What potential obligations are not included on the balance sheet? What factors explain these omissions? Does the firm adopt a business strategy that gives rise to off-balance-sheet financing? Does management appear to be using off-balance-sheet financing to improve the balance sheet's appearance? If so, what factors underlie this decision?
- Are any off-balance-sheet liabilities likely to be significant in terms of evaluating the firm's effective leverage and financing risks, either relative to its own historical standard or relative to the norms of other firms in the industry? If so, is it possible to make an estimate of their effect?
- Does the firm report liabilities where the amount and timing of the obligations are based largely on management judgment? If so, what are the key management assumptions?

- If liability values are dependent on management assumptions or forecasts, is management likely to have information about these parameters that is superior to that of analysts? If so, what is management's track record in prior years' forecasts? Has management systematically made optimistic or pessimistic forecasts?
- If liability values are dependent on management assumptions or forecasts, are analysts likely to be as informed on these parameters as management? For example, management is unlikely to have any superior insight about market interest rates. In such cases, are management's estimates consistent with those of experts in the market?

Challenge Three: Changes in the Value of Liabilities

Fixed-rate liabilities are subject to changes in fair values as interest rates change. Rates can change, either because of market-wide fluctuations or because of firm-specific rate fluctuations attributable to changes in the market assessment of risks borne by debt owners. How are such changes in value reflected in the financial statements? Does the firm report liabilities at their historical cost, or mark them up or down to fair values? We examine the reporting for troubled debt to illustrate the issues in reporting for changes in liability values.

EXAMPLE: TROUBLED DEBT.   On January 15, 1996, Muscocho Explorations Ltd., Flanagan McAdam Resources, and McNellen Resources Inc., three Canadian gold mining companies, signed an agreement with their principal secured creditor, Canadian Imperial Bank, to restructure the CA$8.95 million secured debt the three companies owed the bank. Under the agreement, Canadian Imperial received proceeds from the sale of the Magnacon Mill as well as a $500,000 payment for the Magino Mill. The bank agreed to convert its remaining debt to 10 percent of the equity in a new company created by combining Muscocho, Flanagan, and McNellen. The companies'' other major secured creditor, Echo Bay Mines Ltd., also agreed on similar terms to convert the CA$4.46 million owed by Flanagan and McNellen.

What are the economic effects of a debt restructuring? A troubled debt restructuring arises when a firm's assets and cash flow generation decline. Most of this decline in asset values is borne by the shareholders. However, the creditors can also suffer a loss if there is an increase in the likelihood that the firm will be unable to meet debt principal and interest obligations. The creditors then have to decide whether to make concessions to the firm by exchanging their current claims for new claims, or to force the firm into bankruptcy.

How would the above events be reported in the firm's financial statements? Impairments in asset values should have been recorded as asset write-downs, with accompanying disclosures about the reasons for impairment and management's future plans.

Further, under SFAS 107, U.S. firms would continue to show liabilities at their historical cost, but would disclose the fair value of interest-bearing debt instruments in a footnote. It is worth noting that fair value estimates of debt are likely to be imprecise when a firm is in financial distress. This occurs because the debt claim can be converted into equity if the firm defaults. As discussed below, equity claims are more complex to value since they are residual claims on the firm's cash flows, rather than fixed commitments.

How would the troubled debt restructuring itself be recorded? Under SFAS 15, there would be no change in the valuation of the debt until a formal restructuring takes place. If such an agreement provides for the debt to be retired in exchange for assets, as is the case for Muscocho, Flanagan, and McNellen, an extraordinary gain is recognized to reflect the difference between the book value of the debt and the fair value of the assets. This transaction may require the firm to initially revalue the assets involved to their fair values, recording a gain or loss as ordinary income. Alternatively, as discussed in SFAS 118, if the terms of the debt are modified (by changing the interest rate or principal, or by extending the payment dates), no gain is recorded. Instead, the implied interest rate on the modified debt is computed to equate the present value of the modified and original payments. The debt continues to be reported at its book value, and the new interest rate is used to compute the revised interest expense.

The above method of reporting for a troubled debt restructuring indicates that investors potentially have access to relevant information about declines in asset and debt values prior to the actual restructuring. However, management has considerable opportunity to bias this information by delaying reporting losses for asset impairments, or by misestimating the fair values of assets at a debt restructuring.

Key Analysis Questions

As noted above, both debt and equity investors are interested in changes in the fair value of liabilities. Current reporting rules require U.S. firms to report these values and to estimate the consequences of changes in value for restructured debt instruments. However, these rules create opportunities for management to use judgment in reporting these effects. This raises several opportunities for analysts:

- Has the fair value of debt declined? If so, what factors prompted this decline? Have interest rates in the economy increased since the debt was issued at a fixed rate? Or have the firm's assets and future cash flows become riskier, increasing the risk faced by creditors? If the latter, has the firm written down the value of impaired assets?
- Has the fair value of debt increased? If so, is the change due to decreases in interest rates or to a change in the firm's business?
- If debt has become riskier, how reliable are the management estimates of the debt's value?
- If the firm's debt value has increased, does it appear to be in financial difficulty?

COMMON MISCONCEPTIONS
ABOUT LIABILITY ACCOUNTING

The above discussion of accounting for liabilities reveals a number of popular misconceptions about the nature of accounting for liabilities.

1. It's prudent to provide for a rainy day.

Some firms take the approach that it pays to be conservative in financial reporting and to set aside as much as possible for contingencies. This logic is commonly used to justify large loss reserves for insurance companies, for merger expenses, and for restructuring charges. This argument presumes that investors are not able to see through current overestimates and will give the firm credit for its performance when it reverses these charges.

From the standpoint of a financial statement user, it is important to recognize that conservative accounting is not the same as "good" accounting. Financial statement users want to evaluate how well a firm's accounting captures business reality in an unbiased manner, and conservative accounting can be as misleading as aggressive accounting in this respect. Further, conservative accounting often provides managers with opportunities for "income smoothing," which may prevent analysts from recognizing poor performance in a timely fashion. Finally, over time, investors are likely to figure out which firms are conservative and may discount their management's disclosures and communications.

2. Off-balance-sheet financing is preferable to on-balance-sheet financing.

Some managers appear to believe that off-balance-sheet financing is preferable to financing on the balance sheet because unsophisticated financial statement users are then likely to underestimate the firm's true leverage. Once again, this view is predicated on investors being financially naïve. There may be good reasons for using types of debt arrangements that are off-balance-sheet. For example, operating leases tend to reduce the risks of ownership of assets, which may be important for firms that want to be able to quickly upgrade to the latest technology. However, it seems unlikely that investors will continuously be fooled by off-balance-sheet liabilities, particularly given the increased importance of well-trained institutional investors in the market. Further, there is a risk that once they have discovered the firm's attempts to mislead them, investors will be wary of subsequent management reports.

EQUITY DEFINITION AND REPORTING CHALLENGES

As noted earlier, it is difficult to specify the payoffs attributable to stockholders, which in turn makes it difficult to value equity. Accountants therefore treat equity as a residual claim, whose value is defined exclusively by the values assigned to assets and liabilities.

Consequently, the challenges discussed for valuing assets and liabilities also apply to equity valuation. In addition, there are two reporting challenges that are specific to equity: the reporting for hybrid securities, and the allocation of equity values between reserves, capital, and retained earnings.

Challenge One: Hybrid Securities

On August 11, 1998, Helix Hearing Care of America Corp., a Montreal-based hearing aid chain, sold $2 million of convertible debentures. The debentures had a five-year term and a 13 percent coupon rate and were convertible into Helix common shares at CA$1.70. Is this security a debt instrument or an equity claim? This question is further complicated by the fact that the likelihood that the claim will be converted to equity changes over time as Helix's stock price increases and decreases.

Convertible debt is a hybrid security. Typically it commands a lower rate of interest than a straight debenture, since the seller also receives the option to convert the debt into common shares. The value of the conversion right depends on the conversion price, the firm's current stock price, the government bond rate, and the estimated variance of the firm's stock returns. A good case can be made for separating the debt and equity components of a convertible issue, since the value of each can be separately estimated. The value of the debt claim will vary over time with interest rates. The value of the option will vary with the firm's stock price.

However, accounting rules do not recognize any value attached to the conversion right. The convertible debenture is therefore reported as if it were nonconvertible debt (see APB 14). If the debt converts, it can be recorded using either the book value or market value methods. The book value approach records the exchange at the book value of the convertible debt. No gain or loss is recorded on conversion. The market value method values the equity issued at its market value and records any difference between the market value of the equity and the book value of the convertible debt as an ordinary gain or loss.

The accounting rules for hybrid securities are simplifications of the underlying economics. This raises questions about how to compare two firms that use the same effective capital structure, but where one uses hybrid securities and the other does not. Simply looking at the financial statements of the two will not give an accurate reflection of the leverage of each. The firm with the hybrid securities will appear to be more highly leveraged, using book values of debt and equity, because the conversion right is not recorded. Ideally, an analyst would attempt to separate the debt and equity components of hybrid securities to make a more valid comparison of capital structures.

Challenge Two: Classification of Unrealized Gains and Losses

The second challenge for equity valuation relates to how to allocate certain unrealized gains and losses within the equity segment of the balance sheet. Should these items be included in the income statement and then in retained earnings? Alternatively, should they be treated as separate non-operating items that can only go through income when they have been realized?

As discussed in other chapters on accounting, current accounting rules require some unrealized gains and losses to be charged to a reserve rather than going through the income statement. These include gains and losses on

- financial instruments that are available for sale (see Chapter 7),
- financial instruments used to hedge uncertain future cash flows (see Chapter 7), and
- foreign currency translations for foreign operations whose transactions occur in the local currency rather than in the parent's currency (see Chapter 4).

These types of gains and losses are sometimes referred to as "dirty surplus" charges, since they are not recorded in the income statement. A system where all accounting charges are reflected in income is called "clean surplus" accounting. We will see that this concept is important in subsequent chapters, where we discuss earnings-based valuation models.

It is worth noting that changes in equity book values from many of the "dirty surplus" gains and losses are difficult to predict from year to year, since they depend on changes in financial instrument and foreign currency prices, which are themselves difficult to forecast. Consequently, their expected impact in any given year is likely to be zero.

How should analysts and users of financial statements view equity changes that are not reported in income? Conceptually, there is no strong economic justification for treating them differently from gains and losses that are included in the income statement. For example, from an analyst's point of view they are no different from gains and losses on asset sales, realized gains and losses on sales of financial instruments, and unrealized gains and losses on financial instruments intended to be traded, all of which are included in income. The justification for treating all gains and losses comparably is reinforced by the potential concern that management might use reporting judgment to exclude certain types of gains and losses from earnings. Perhaps in response to these concerns, the FASB now requires firms to prepare a statement of comprehensive income, showing all changes in equity, other than capital transactions, in one place (see SFAS 130).

Key Analysis Questions

Analysis of equity values is largely covered in the earlier discussion of asset and liability analysis. The following questions are unique to equity analysis:

- What charges are included in earnings, and what are excluded? How should these charges be viewed?
- Does the firm have hybrid securities? If so, is it worthwhile separating their debt and equity components? How has the conversion value changed since their issue? Is it likely that the debt will be converted, making it closer to equity than debt?

SUMMARY

To recognize a liability, a firm has to have incurred an obligation to provide a future benefit to another entity, and to be able to estimate the value of that obligation with reasonable certainty. Liabilities continue to be recorded at their historical cost on the balance sheet. However, in footnote disclosures, firms are required to report fair value estimates for interest-bearing debt. In future years we may even see balance sheet values based on fair values as accountants become more confident that fair values of liabilities can be estimated reliably.

However, valuation of certain types of liabilities can be challenging if there is uncertainty about

1. whether an obligation has been incurred, as is the case for restructuring reserves, frequent flyer programs, and litigation;
2. the value of the obligation, as in the case of environmental liabilities, warranty reserves, insurance loss reserves, and pensions; and
3. changes in values of liabilities, as in the case of a troubled debt restructuring.

Managers are likely to have the best information about the extent of the firm's liabilities. However, they also have incentives to understate the firm's financial risks, creating opportunities for liability analysis.

The other major claimant on the firm's assets—equity—can be viewed as the residual owner of the firm. Because it represents that portion of the claims on the firm that are most difficult to specify, it cannot be valued as precisely as liabilities. Consequently, financial reporting treats equity as the difference between asset and liability values. The challenges in measuring and reporting for assets and liabilities are therefore also relevant to the valuation of equity. In addition, there are several challenges that are specific to equity reporting, such as the valuation of hybrid securities (e.g., convertible debt) and the classification of certain gains and losses.

DISCUSSION QUESTIONS

1. As discussed in the chapter, the following restructuring events were reported by McCormick:
   a. In October 1994, the company announced plans to lay off 7 percent of its 8,600-person staff, close two spice plants, and sell off a money-losing onion-ring operation. A $70.5 million restructuring liability was created for the costs of the restructuring.
   b. In February 1995, the company reduced the amount of the charge by $3.9 million, which it added to earnings in the first quarter of 1995.
   c. In 1996 McCormick announced a second restructuring. Most of the costs of the restructuring ($58.1 million) were recognized immediately as a restructuring liability. However, the firm noted that some charges related to costs of moving

equipment and personnel from a closed U.S. packaging plant could not be accrued. These charges (for $1.9 million) were eventually recognized in the fourth quarter of 1998.

d. In the third quarter of 1997, McCormick reevaluated its restructuring plans and recorded a restructuring credit of $9.5 million because plans to sell an overseas food brokerage and distribution business were not completed.

e. The 1996 restructuring was concluded in the fourth quarter of 1998 and a further restructuring credit of $3.1 million was reported.

What are the financial statement effects of these events? As a corporate manager, what forecasts do you have to make to record these events? As a financial analyst, what questions would you raise with the firm's CFO about the restructuring events?

2. What are the economic costs and benefits to airlines from frequent flyer programs? What information would you need to measure these costs and benefits? As a financial analyst, what questions would you raise with the firm's CFO about its frequent flyer program?

3. The cigarette industry is subject to litigation for health hazards posed by its products. The industry has been negotiating a settlement of these claims with state and federal governments. As the CFO for Philip Morris, one of the larger firms in the industry, what information would you report to investors in the annual report on the firm's litigation risks? How would you assess whether the firm should record a liability for this risk, and if so, how would you assess the value of this liability? As a financial analyst following Philip Morris, what questions would you raise with the CEO over the firm's litigation liability?

4. As discussed in the chapter, Hanson Plc incurred an environmental liability from its 1991 acquisition of the U.S. firm Beazer. In 1997 the company reported that, based on third party appraisal, its estimate could be reduced by £430.3 million. In 1998 Hanson agreed to pay further costs of £168 million, and two insurance companies guaranteed to cover any remaining costs up to £488 million. After the agreement, £67 million of the estimated liability was no longer required and was recorded as an unusual credit. What are the financial statement effects of these events?

5. Hewlett Packard reported the following information on its U.S. retiree medical plan:

Key Assumptions	1998	1997	1996
Discount rate	6.5%	7.0%	7.5%
Expected return on assets	9.0%	9.0%	9.0%
Current medical cost trend rate	8.65%	9.6%	10.0%
Ultimate medical cost trend rate	5.5%	6.0%	6.0%
Year current medical cost trend rate decreases to ultimate rate	2007	2007	2007
Effect of a 1% increase in the medical cost trend rate (millions):			
Increase in benefit obligation	$116	$101	$90
Increase in annual retiree medical cost	$17	$15	$13

Funding Status (in millions)	1998	1997
Fair value of plan assets	$503	$448
Benefit obligation	(543)	(475)
Plan assets in excess of (less than) benefit obligation	(40)	(27)
Unrecognized net experience (gain) loss	(255)	(268)
Unrecognized prior service cost (benefit) related to plan changes	(144)	(154)
Prepaid (accrued) costs	$(439)	$(449)

What assumption is Hewlett Packard making about medical cost inflation in 2000 and 2010? What is the firm assuming it will earn on plan assets? As a financial analyst, how would you evaluate these assumptions? Are these rates reasonable? In 1998, what is the liability for the medical plan reported on the balance sheet? Is the plan over- or underfunded? What other factors would you consider in evaluating Hewlett Packard's liability and risk under its medical plan?

6. Acceptance Insurance Companies Inc. underwrites and sells specialty property and casualty insurance. The company is the third largest writer of crop insurance products in the United States. In its 1998 10-K report to the SEC, it discloses the following information on the loss reserves created for claims originating in 1990:

Cumulative net liability paid through:	12/31/90
One year later	40.6
Two years later	70.8
Three years later	88.5
Four years later	101.2
Five years later	107.5
Six years later	109.7
Seven years later	111.4
Eight years later	111.8

Net reserves reestimated as of:	
One year later	100.3
Two years later	102.3
Three years later	107.4
Four years later	110.7
Five years later	112.7
Six years later	112.0
Seven years later	112.5
Eight years later	113.4
Net cumulative redundancy (deficiency)	−13.4

What was the initial estimate for loss reserves originating in 1990? How has the firm updated its estimate of this obligation over time? What liability remains for 1990 claims? As a financial analyst, what questions would you have for the CFO on its 1990 liability?

7. At the end of fiscal year 1997, Intel reported that it had set aside a liability of $87.9 million for potential warranty costs. At the end of 1998, Intel increased this estimate to $115.5 million. As a financial analyst, what questions would you ask the firm's CFO about the warranty liability?

8. As discussed in the chapter, Muscocho Explorations Ltd., Flanagan McAdam Resources, and McNellen Resources Inc. signed an agreement in January 1996 with their principal secured creditor, Canadian Imperial Bank, to restructure the CA$8.95 million secured debt the three companies owed the bank. Under the agreement, Canadian Imperial received proceeds from the sale of the Magnacon Mill as well as a $500,000 payment for the Magino Mill. The bank agreed to convert its remaining debt to 10 percent of the equity in a new company created by combining Muscocho, Flanagan, and McNellen. What information would you need to record the effects of this transaction in the books of the new combined firm? What financial statement effects of the transaction can you quantify? As a financial analyst, what questions would you ask management of the new firm about the debt restructuring?

9. As discussed in the chapter, on August 11, 1998, Helix Hearing Care of America Corp. sold $2 million of convertible debentures. The debentures had a five-year term and a 13 percent coupon rate and were convertible into Helix common shares at CA$1.70. If Helix's common stock were valued at $2.50 at conversion, what would be the financial statement effects of conversion under (a) the book value method and (b) the market value method? Which method do you consider best reflects the economics of the conversion? Why?

10. For the first quarter of 1998, Microsoft reported the following reconciliation between net income and comprehensive income:

Three Months Ended September 30 (millions of dollars):	1997	1998
Net income	$663	1,683
Net unrealized investment gains	56	150
Translation adjustments and other	(117)	43
Comprehensive income	602	1,876

What types of events give rise to the adjustments made by Microsoft? As a financial analyst, what questions would you have for the CFO about the comprehensive income statement?

NOTES

1. See Milton Russell and Kimberly L Davis. "Resource Requirements for NPL Sites: Phase II Interim Report," Knoxville, JIEE, September 1995; and U.S. Congress Budget Office, "The Total Costs of Cleaning Up Nonfederal Superfund Sites," Washington, D.C., U.S. GPO, 1994.

2. See Mary E. Barth and Maureen McNichols, 1994, "Estimation and Market Valuation of Environmental Liabilities Relating to Superfund Sites," *Journal of Accounting Research* 32, Supplement.

3. See Mary E. Barth, Maureen F. McNichols, and G. Peter Wilson, 1997, "Factors Influencing Firms' Disclosures about Environmental Liabilities," *Review of Accounting Studies* 2, (1): 35–64.

4. M. Barth, "Relative Measurement Errors Among Alternative Pension Asset and Liability Measures," *The Accounting Review* 66, No. 3, 1991, finds that investors regard these footnote disclosures to be more useful than the liability reported in the financial statements.

5. E. Amir and E. Gordon, "A Firm's Choice of Estimation Parameters: Empirical Evidence from SFAS No. 106," *Journal of Accounting, Auditing & Finance* 11, No. 3, Summer 1996, show that firms with larger postretirement benefit obligations and more leverage tend to make more aggressive estimates of postretirement obligation parameters.

6. Research by K. Petroni, "Optimistic Reporting in the Property Casualty Insurance Industry," *Journal of Accounting and Economics* 15, 1992; K. Petroni, S. Ryan, and J. Wahlen, "Discretionary and Non-discretionary Revisions of Loss Reserves by Property-Casualty Insurers: Differential Implications for Future Profitability, Risk, and Market Value," working paper, Indiana University; and R. Adiel, "Reinsurance and the Management of Regulatory Ratios and Taxes in the Property-Casualty Insurance Industry, *Journal of Accounting and Economics* 22, Nos. 1–3, 1996, shows that financially weak property-casualty insurers that risk regulatory attention understate claim loss reserves and engage in reinsurance transactions.

This Winston-Salem company sells affordable Southern comfort: fully furnished and carpeted mobile homes for as little as $10,000. Robert Sauls, the 59-year-old founder and chairman, was an orphaned boy who never finished high school. Through acquisitions, Sauls has built the retailer into the industry's largest, with annual sales ballooning to about $180 million in four years. The company sells the homes, built primarily by Fleetwood Enterprises and Redman Industries, to rural blue-collar workers in the Southeast. "Our people buy in good times and bad," says Sauls. If he can raise the capital, he foresees a doubling of sales in four to five years. The stock recently sold at 6.5 times estimated 1988 earnings.

Jane Edwards, Director of Research at a small Boston-based investment management firm specializing in growth stocks, noted the above review of Manufactured Homes in the February 15, 1988 issue of *Fortune* magazine's Companies To Watch column. She knew that attractive growth stocks are hard to find and wondered whether Manufactured Homes would be a good addition to her firm's growth stock portfolio. She checked the recent performance of Manufactured Homes' common stock and noted that the stock performed favorably relative to the stock market (see Exhibit 1). Jane Edwards asked her assistant Peter Herman to gather additional information on the company and to write a report analyzing the company's recent financial statements.

COMPANY BACKGROUND AND MARKETING FOCUS

Herman's preliminary research on Manufactured Homes indicated that the company was founded in 1975 with two retail outlets for mobile homes. The company grew rapidly and by March 31, 1987, had a network of 120 retail outlets located in seven southeastern states. Eighty-five percent of the company's retail centers were located in North Carolina, South Carolina, Alabama, Georgia, and Florida, with the remaining sales centers in Virginia and West Virginia. The company went public in 1983 and was listed on the American Stock Exchange in January 1987.

The southeastern U.S. was the country's fastest growing market for mobile homes due to suitable climate, the easy availability of vacant land for mobile-home parks, and

Professor Krishna G. Palepu prepared this case as the basis for class discussion rather than to illustrate either effective or ineffective handling of an administrative situation. Copyright © 1989 by the President and Fellows of Harvard College. Harvard Business School case 9-190-090.

the region's demographics. Potential customers for manufactured homes included individuals seeking a single-family primary residence but lacking the ability to purchase conventional housing, retirees, and those wanting a second home for vacation purposes.

The company targeted individuals in the low income category, which was a segment of the manufactured homes market in the company's seven-state operating area. The company's customers were typically between the ages of 18 and 40, blue-collar workers in manufacturing, service, and agricultural industries, and earned approximately $20,000 per year. Many of them were seeking single-family accommodations for their families and turned to manufactured homes because conventional low-cost housing was becoming increasingly less affordable.

Manufactured homes came in a wide variety of styles, including both single and multi-sectional units. They typically had a living room, a kitchen and dining area, and bedrooms and baths, with a wide variety in the size, number and layout of rooms among the various models. The single-sectional homes ranged in size from 588 to 1008 square feet and retailed at prices between $10,000 and $25,000, with the majority selling below $17,000. The multi-sectional homes were 960–2016 square feet and sold at prices ranging from $17,000 to $40,000. Single-sectional homes represented most of the company's sales. While approximately 30 percent of all unit sales in the industry in 1986 were multi-sectional homes, they represented only about 20 percent of Manufactured Homes' unit volume.

The company believed that its focus on the lower end of the market had two advantages. First, since its customers were seeking to fulfill an essential housing need, sales were less affected by changes in general economic conditions. Second, the company's repossession rates were significantly lower than those of the industry since its customers were likely to work very hard to keep their primary residences even when times were bad.

Assumptions

REVENUES

Most of Manufactured Homes' sales were credit sales where the customer paid a down payment of 5 to 10 percent of the sales price and entered into an installment sales contract with the company to pay the remaining amount over periods ranging from 84 to 180 months. The company generally sold the majority of its retail installment contracts to unrelated financial institutions on a recourse basis. Under this agreement, Manufactured Homes was responsible for payments to the financial institution if the customer failed to make the payments specified in the installment contract.

Liability

While the installment sale interest rate that Manufactured Homes charged its customers was limited by competitive conditions, it was typically higher than market interest rates. Therefore, the financial institutions to whom these contracts were sold on a recourse basis usually paid the company the stated principal amount of the contract and a portion of the differential between the stated interest rate and the market rate. (The remainder of the interest rate differential was retained by the financial institutions as a security against credit losses and was paid to the company in proportion to customer payments received. The reserve required varied up to seven percent of the aggregate amount financed, including principal and interest.) The company therefore had two sources of revenue: the sale of homes (sales revenue), and the interest rate "spread" (finance participation income).

Peter Herman noted that Financial Accounting Board's Statement 77 (FASB-77) governs the accounting treatment for installment sales receivables that are transferred by a company to a third party on a recourse basis. Transfers of receivables that are subject to recourse must be reported as sales if the following three conditions are satisfied:

1. The seller unequivocally surrenders the receivable to the buyer.
2. The seller's remaining obligations to the buyer under the recourse provision must be subject to reasonable estimation on the date of the transfer of the receivable. For this purpose, the seller should be able to estimate:
   (a) The amount of bad debts and related costs of collection and repossession, and
   (b) The amount of prepayments. If the seller cannot make these estimates reasonably well, a transfer of the receivable cannot be reported as a sale.
3. The seller cannot be required to repurchase the receivable from the buyer except in accordance with the recourse provision.

If any of the above conditions is not satisfied, the seller of the receivable must report the proceeds from the transfer as a loan against the receivable.

FINANCIAL PERFORMANCE

Manufactured Homes' revenues increased rapidly in recent years, from $11 million in 1983 to $120 million in 1986. In the company's 1986 annual report, Robert Sauls, the CEO, forecasted the company's growth to continue and expected the 1987 revenues to be $140–$145 million. Herman noted that the company's sales for the first nine months of 1987 exceeded this forecast. The company's latest 10-Q statement reported $148 million revenues for the nine months ended September 30, 1987.

Based on the performance in the first nine months of 1987, the *Value Line Investment Survey* forecasted that Manufactured Homes would achieve $180 million revenues and $6 million net income (or $1.65 per share) in 1987, and $210 million revenues and $7.5 million net income (or $2.00 per share) in 1988. *Value Line* commented on the company's near term prospects as follows:[1]

> We look forward for [per] share net [income] to advance 20% in 1988, despite a difficult selling environment. Industrywide shipments for the company's core Carolina markets were down in the December quarter and are likely to remain soft

1. *Reprinted with permission from* Value Line Investment Survey, *February 26, 1988.*

in the year ahead. We think, however, that Manufactured Homes will nevertheless find growth opportunities. True, the number of retail centers probably won't increase much this year. On the other hand, the rapid expansion of retail centers over the past five years has put in place a large number of dealerships that have plenty of opportunity for increasing volume.

Management is seeking to average 100 units per store as these sales locations mature. At the end of 1986, stores were selling 47 units per year on average, and that figure rose 20% for the first nine months of 1987. Although the market will be very competitive this year, we think the company's special attention to the low-end of the market, to which many large competitors pay less attention, will give Manufactured Homes a solid niche position. Adding in the reduced tax rate, we think full year [per] share net [income] may well reach the $2.00 mark.

Volume buying gives this retailer an edge. Because Manufactured Homes buys in bulk, it can negotiate lower prices from the manufacturers it deals with. And by passing the savings on to customers, the company is able to underprice smaller, "mom and pop" outlets. Furthermore, because of its size, the company is able to more efficiently handle inventory financing and mortgage assistance for its customers.

Before making a final recommendation to Edwards, Herman wanted to take a detailed look at Manufactured Homes' financial statements for the fiscal year 1986 (Exhibit 2) and the interim statements for the first nine months of 1987 (Exhibit 3).

QUESTIONS

1. Identify the accounting policies of Manufactured Homes which have the most significant impact on the company's financial statements. What are the key assumptions behind these policies? Do you think that these assumptions are justified?
2. Evaluate the company's financial and operating performance during 1986 and the first nine months of 1987.
3. Given the company's business strategy, accounting policies, and recent performance, what is your assessment of its current condition and future potential?

EXHIBIT 1

Performance of Manufactured Homes' Common Stock and S&P 500 Stock Index
Relative to Their Levels on January 2, 1987

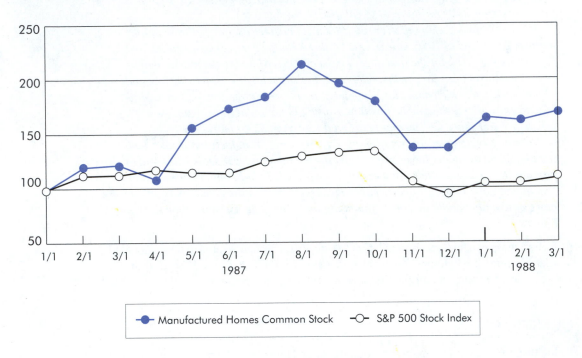

	Manufactured Homes' Stock Price	S&P 500
January 2, 1987	$ 9.000	246.45
March 1, 1988	14.875	267.82
Value Line estimated β	1.05	1.0

EXHIBIT 2

Manufactured Homes, Annual Report for the Year Ended December 31, 1986

Chairman's Letter to Stockholders

The year 1986 was a period of significant accomplishment for your company which served to strengthen our leadership position in the manufactured homes industry. The results achieved were the culmination of a corporate development plan set in motion years ago. For the fourth consecutive year revenues reached record levels, $120 million compared with $80 million in 1985. We are now one of the largest retailers of manufactured, single-family homes in the nation.

As part of our long-term efforts to increase market share, we added 39 retail outlets, bringing the total to 114 at year end. We now have retail outlets in seven states that combined represent approximately 40 percent of the total U.S. market for manufactured homes.

We continue to be primarily a sales and marketing company with manufacturing and retail financing on a limited basis to support the company's growth plan.

We completed a major financing in April 1986 and a second financing in February 1987, both managed by Wertheim Schroder and Company, that totaled $43 million. A portion of the proceeds was used to pay down variable rate debt associated with inventory financing with fixed rate debt and save money in the process. The remainder of the proceeds is to be used for general corporate purposes.

We were pleased at the recognition we received for the growth we have achieved over the last four years as both *Business Week* and *INC. Magazine* included our company in their lists of the fastest growing companies in America. Some describe our growth as explosive. We, however, consider these accomplishments a direct result of a well-structured and carefully executed corporate development plan. Our plans for growth are founded on the basic premise that expansion not exceed our ability to manage our affairs.

From $11 million in revenues in 1983 and a position of near obscurity in the industry, our progress has led us to a position of leadership in the industry.

While we are extremely pleased with our revenue performance, we are also mindful that we must operate profitably. Net earnings per share for 1986 were only 53 cents. The sharp decline in 1986 earnings is directly related to a fourth quarter net loss of $1,347,642. Charges against earnings in the fourth quarter for losses on credit sales and other charges totaling more than three million dollars, coupled with the cost of strengthening your company's position in the marketplace, created a temporary setback in earnings while establishing a basis for a strong 1987.

A strategic plan can only be confirmed as correct when tested by adversity; and last year was something of an acid test for our industry. During 1986, many retailers, in hopes of gaining greater market share, or in some cases hoping for survival, engaged in excessive price cutting. In addition, financial institutions in response to concern over the economy in some geographic areas tightened their policies. We not only dealt with the problems that confronted us but turned some into opportunities.

Over the years management has made it a practice to monitor the various retailers of the manufactured homes in our operating area. First, we wanted to understand our competition; and second, we were looking for acquisition candidates. From a large list of companies, we singled out those that best met our standards of performance. We wanted only those firms with superior management and sales teams. We were able to acquire two of these firms on favorable terms and left management in place.

As a result we succeeded in not only enlarging our market penetration in our traditional states of North Carolina, South Carolina, Georgia, Florida and Alabama, but were able to enter new markets with nine retail outlets in Virginia and West Virginia and six additional outlets in Alabama.

Our independent dealer network continues to grow, and now numbers 26 in five states. The independent dealer program offers important advantages and opportunities. Because of the advantages we bring

Manufactured Homes

to these small dealers, we continue to receive more requests to join our team.

During the last half of 1986 we sacrificed short-term results to increase market share. We attained that share and as expected it cost us dearly. Selling, general and administrative expense increased from an average of $4.5 million in the first and second quarters to $6 million in the third quarter and to $8 million in the fourth quarter.

As we look to 1987, it is with the knowledge that we are working from a solid foundation. Our financial position is strong. Our debt service requirements are manageable without impairing future earnings performance. Our retail network continues to mature, and sales by location will increase.

Our goal in 1987 is to maintain our market share and show a substantial increase in profit margins. Your Board of Directors has shown confidence in our ability to perform by authorizing me to give you a conservative estimate of our 1987 revenues. Our first quarter revenues are expected to be $32 million with earnings per share of 24 cents. If current economic conditions continue, we expect 1987 revenues to be $140-145 million. The expected significant increase in margins should make this a great year.

I am grateful for the confidence and support of our employees, financial institutions, suppliers and customers; and to you, our shareholders, I would like to say a special "Thanks!"

Robert M. Sauls
Chairman of the Board, President
and Chief Executive Officer

Operating Philosophy

We are convinced that a company is no better than the people selected to manage its affairs. Quality of product and service are vital to any successful enterprise; but again without quality managers and line employees, the business will not succeed. Manufactured Homes has consistently sought and employed only the highest quality individuals at every level within the organization.

It is our practice to provide our employees, at all levels with suitable working conditions and remunera-

tion. We ask only that they perform to the highest level of ability and be innovative in terms of how we can best operate our business.

We believe that the results of the past four years speak for themselves in terms of the invaluable contributions made by our management team and employees.

Industry Profile

The manufactured homes industry is fragmented. At this time there are approximately 10,000 manufactured home retailers throughout the nation, most of which fall into the category of "mom and pop" operations. The industry is presently undergoing a period of transition and consolidation. More and more of the smaller firms, lacking volume buying power and adequate capitalization, are disappearing or becoming a part of a larger company like Manufactured Homes.

The industry has always been competitive but has become more so in recent years. The continuing increases in the average price of conventional housing have forced low income families to seek other alternatives. And more and more are turning to manufactured homes, which have much more to offer than an apartment with the added advantage of equal to lower monthly payments.

In the past, the manufactured home industry suffered from consumer misconceptions created in large part by the use of the term "mobile home." While manufactured homes can be transported from place to place, only five percent are ever relocated once in place. In addition, 60 percent of all homes sold are placed on private property.

Furthermore, the features offered in today's homes are equal to that found in conventional housing but at far less cost.

Industry estimates indicate there are 12 million people living in 6 million manufactured homes. Because of the quality and price advantage, this number is expected to increase on a year-to-year basis for the foreseeable future.

As competition for market share increases, companies like Manufactured Homes will benefit if for no other reason than the financial advantages volume buying affords. This is the primary reason so many independent dealers are actively seeking a working relationship with our company. The same can be said of those companies willing to be acquired.

Retail Operations

During 1986 we sold 6,239 new and used homes, a 61 percent increase over the previous year. These sales generated $113 million in revenues or 46 percent above the previous year. With our enlarged retail network in place, we anticipate that sales will again reach record levels in 1987.

The potential market for manufactured homes includes individuals seeking a single-family residence, but lacking the ability to purchase conventional housing. In addition, these homes are sold to retirees and those wanting a second home for vacation purposes. The latter two groups are increasing in great numbers as our population grows older. However, for our company we have concentrated on a single portion of the marketplace, those individuals in the low income category. This market segment is in great numbers in our seven-state operating area as well as other parts of the nation.

Manufactured Homes had its beginning 11 years ago in Winston-Salem, North Carolina. We began with one retail outlet. Our initial growth took place in North Carolina and eventually South Carolina. These two states accounted for 90 percent of sales in 1985. To continue to market only in these two states eventually could have resulted in corporate stagnation. In 1983, the year we became a publicly-held company, we began to formulate what might be best termed as a geographic expansion plan. The real question was, in which states could we operate most effectively and profitably.

Our initial planning went beyond the southeastern states, which remain the largest single regional source of manufactured home sales. We looked at a number of states including Texas which, at the time, was the number one state in manufactured home sales. After careful evaluation, we concluded that our interests and those of our stockholders would best be served in the southeastern portion of the United States. Texas was the most tempting, but it was obvious to management that the reward was not worth the risk; and as time has proven, Texas

has become a graveyard for many manufactured home retail companies.

Like many other retail businesses, presence in the marketplace is critical. After determining to concentrate in the seven states management selected, North Carolina, South Carolina, Georgia, Alabama, Florida, Virginia and West Virginia, we moved aggressively to open new retail outlets and acquire others. In 1983, we had 13 retail outlets; in 1984, the number was 32 and as of March 31, 1987 it's 120.

One of the major keys to success for our company is the insistence that our retail people listen to the customers in terms of interior design and features. When we sense a major trend developing, we go to our suppliers seeking what eventually becomes an entire new line of homes.

We also provide important incentives for our retail managers and sales force. Our base salaries are among the finest in the industry, and we add to that a bonus incentive plan tied directly to margin performance. When times require, we can deal with competitive pricing, but our goal is to maximize sales without sacrificing margins.

Manufacturing

We acquired a manufacturing facility but not as a means of competing with the major manufacturers. In fact, last year we were the largest single retailer of Fleetwood and Redman homes, two of the nation's largest builders of manufactured homes. We acquired the facility to safeguard the company during periods when demand for homes outpaced supply. It also provides the opportunity to manufacture especially designed homes in smaller numbers, thereby eliminating the major commitment that would be required by unaffiliated suppliers.

The firm we acquired was Craftsman Homes, and we continue to manufacture under this brand name. When we acquired the company in 1985, it was producing one home per day. That operation is now producing ten floors per day. Large numbers of our customers have been asking for more entertainment features in the home. With our manufacturing capabilities, we have responded with a home we call the Entertainment Center, and sales have been most rewarding.

Manufactured Homes

We have no immediate need nor intention to enlarge this facility. As it stands, manufacturing can make important contributions, but we can also put this operation on hold without damage to either revenues or earnings.

Financial Considerations

Believing that interest rates will eventually return to the double digit range, we have been successful in replacing our variable rate debt with fixed rate debt. In April 1986, we completed an $18 million private placement of 9% convertible subordinated notes, due 2001. The notes are convertible into common stock at $17.50 per share. The notes were purchased by Prudential Insurance Company of America and Equity-Linked Investors.

In February 1987, we completed a private placement of $25 million of unsecured senior notes in two series. Series A notes, due 1990, were issued in the amount of $15 million at an interest rate of 8.64%. Series B notes, due 1992, were issued in the amount of $10 million at an interest rate of 9.42%. The entire placement was managed by Wertheim Schroder and Co. and purchased by Prudential Insurance Company of America, and we are gratified with the trust they have placed in the future of Manufactured Homes.

There are four key elements that bear on our financial performance related to the sale of homes. These elements are repossessions, recourse financing, loan losses and finance participation.

In almost all cases mortgages executed by the Company are sold to financial institutions. At this moment all of the elements mentioned come into play. The recourse financing provision requires that the Company reassume ownership of the home when the buyer becomes in default of mortgage payments. We knew this when the company was started 11 years ago, and the actions required to deal with this situation are a part of each year's operating plan.

The possibility of repossessions is another reason for selecting the low income segment of the marketplace. Families in this category will make extreme sacrifices to save their homes. We experience one of the lowest repossession rates in the industry. Of the homes returned, we move quickly to renovate and refurbish them and have them resold, normally within 60 to 90 days, at a price equal to or greater than the loan payoff.

We also make provisions for those instances when loan losses do occur. Based on our historical experience, we now maintain a financial reserve equal to 1.7 percent of total net contingent liability for credit sales. Our annual loan loss provisions have consistently exceeded actual losses by more than 20 percent, even though homes which have been sold for four or more years are seldom repossessed. Finance participation is an important source of income for the Company. Simply, funds derived from finance participation is the "spread" between the finance charges included in the mortgage agreement initiated by the Company and those required by the financial institution. A portion of the "spread" is paid in cash to the Company and the remainder over the life of the mortgage contract. The portion retained by the financial institution is accounted for by discounting to present value based on the time period, normally 120 to 180 months, required to actually collect the funds.

Financial Services Subsidiary

Plans for our finance operations, MANH Financial Services Corp., are similar in nature to that for our manufacturing division. The company did not enter this business segment to compete with the financial institutions that have historically provided our mortgage banking requirements. This new entity will be employed primarily to facilitate financing agreements with our banks.

Financial Services does have mortgage lending capabilities that will only be employed at those times when our conventional banking arrangements are unable to act on a timely basis. Again, like our manufacturing operations, management has no intention of expanding Financial Services. As it exists now, it provides the Company with the flexibility required to deal quickly with mortgage finance transactions.

Selected Financial Data

Years Ended December 31,	1986	1985	1984	1983	1982
Operating Results:					
Revenues	$120,264,954	$79,525,988	$36,195,802	$10,986,036	$7,477,966
Earnings (loss) before cumulative effect of change in accounting principle[1]	2,033,425	3,718,325	2,694,529	536,881	(59,570)
Earning (loss) per share	.53	.98	.77	.21	(.03)
Net earnings (loss)	2,033,425	3,213,754	2,694,529	536,881	(59,570)
Net earnings (loss) per share	.53	.85	.77	.21	(.03)
Financial Position at Year-End:					
Total assets	$81,377,803	$50,944,924	$17,660,984	$6,836,087	$5,025,130
Long-term debt	18,609,987	1,082,543	400,000	—	491,280
Stockholders' equity	14,167,119	11,052,759	7,633,005	4,938,654	733,195
Working capital	15,111,883	4,820,912	4,819,203	3,699,184	(147,124)

Quarterly Financial Data (unaudited)

Quarter	First	Second	Third	Fourth	Total
1986[2]:					
Revenues	$23,324,633	$29,724,418	$33,295,241	$33,920,662	$120,264,954
Net earnings (loss)	641,702	1,562,205	1,177,160	(1,347,642)	2,033,425
Net earnings (loss) per share	.17	.40	.30	(.36)	.53
Average shares and equivalents	3,850,277	3,944,518	3,922,406	3,733,968	3,864,161
1985:					
Revenues	$10,965,457	$22,103,134	$24,083,556	$22,373,841	$ 79,525,988
Earnings before cumulative effect of change in accounting principle[1]	741,395	1,312,511	1,112,714	551,705	3,718,325
Earnings per share	.21	.34	.29	.14	.98
Net earnings	236,824	1,312,511	1,112,714	551,705	3,213,754
Net earnings per share	.08	.34	.29	.14	.85
Proforma amounts:					
Net earnings	741,395	1,312,511	1,112,714	551,705	3,718,325
Net earnings per share	.21	.34	.29	.14	.98
Average shares and equivalents	3,488,968	3,820,016	3,870,857	3,838,486	3,802,693

[1]See Note 2 of notes to consolidated financial statements for information regarding a change in accounting principle for finance participation income in 1985.

[2]During the fourth quarter of 1986, the Company provided approximately $3,000,000 for losses on credit sales, primarily due to industry conditions, which are causing unusually high costs relating to the repossession of homes. In addition, the Company incurred abnormal costs in the fourth quarter of approximately $300,000 relating primarily to the write-off of previously recognized finance participation income. The aggregate provision for these items amounted to approximately $3,300,000 in the fourth quarter. The Company cannot determine the extent to which these fourth quarter provisions may be applicable to the first, second and third quarter of 1986.

Manufactured Homes

Common Stock Prices and Dividend Information

The Company's common stock is traded on the American Stock Exchange under the symbol MNH.

| | 1986 | | 1985 | |
	High	Low	High	Low
First	15 3/4	10	8 3/4	4 3/8
Second	16 1/2	12 1/4	13 1/4	8 1/4
Third	15	9 3/4	15 3/8	10 1/2
Fourth	12	8 7/8	14	8 3/4

The Company has never paid a cash dividend and does not intend to for the foreseeable future. The weighted average number of shares outstanding for 1986 was 3,660,048 shares, for 1985 and 1984, 3,488,968 shares, for 1983, 2,588,518 shares and for 1982, 2,100,000 shares. The approximate number of stockholders at March 1987 was 2,000.

MANAGEMENT DISCUSSION AND ANALYSIS

Results of Operations

1986 Versus 1985

The Company's net sales in 1986 were $106,095,667 compared with $68,674,779 in 1985, an increase of $37,420,888 or 54%.

The Company's program of managed sales growth resulted in greater penetration due to:

	1986	1985	Increase
An increase of 44% in the number of company-owned and operated sales centers	92	64	28
A 100% expansion of the MANH Independent Retailer network	22	11	11
A total increase of 52% in sales centers for the year	114	75	39

The total number of new and used homes sold in 1986 was 6,239, a 61% increase over the 3,866 homes sold in 1985. New home sales for both years were 87% of total home sales.

A manufactured home sales center usually experiences a five-year growth and development period. The Manufactured Homes (AMEX Symbol: MNH) sales center should develop a sales production level of at least 100 new homes per year at maturity, although this average annual sales volume can vary widely by geographic location. The Company in 1986 averaged 47 new sales per sales center versus 45 in 1985. The average reflects the rapid expansion of new sales centers. Approximately 47% of the average potential capacity per sales center had been achieved, leaving significant growth potential within the Company's current sales center network without the need for significantly increasing the number of sales centers.

New home sales were 80% single-wides in 1986, as compared with 84% in 1985. This reflects a shift to more double-wides resulting from the acquisition of two subsidiaries. In addition, a number of our customers are able to purchase double-wide homes since interest rates are lower. However, the primary emphasis of MNH's marketing plan continues to be towards the less expensive, single-wide home which fits the economic capability of a significant percentage of potential customers within the MNH market area of the five southeastern states, plus Virginia and West Virginia.

The average MNH selling price of new homes by Company sales centers for 1986 was $17,300 versus $17,400 in 1985. The gross profit margins were unchanged for 1985.

Craftsman Manufactured Homes, Inc., a wholly owned subsidiary of MNH, expanded its production capability from one production line to two. Revenues in 1986 were in excess of $15,746,000 of which $7,489,000 were direct sales to non-affiliated dealers with $8,257,000 being sold to Company sales centers for resale. The Company purchased the manufacturing facility in September 1985. The Craftsman manufacturing subsidiary sold 481 homes directly to dealers not associated with MNH in 1986 as compared with 130 homes in 1985.

Repossessions and Early Pay-offs

Manufactured housing, as an industry, has been significantly impacted by the slow economic growth of the economy coupled with an extended period of low interest rates. These factors are reflected by a year-to-year decrease in 1986 of 15% in manufactured homes sold throughout the Company's market area.

Lower interest rates have resulted in two noticeable shifts within the housing industry: (1) certain owners may select conventional homes over manufactured homes; and (2) an intensive marketing effort by financial institutions for mortgage refinancing has resulted in many home owners refinancing their mortgages at lower interest rates, which for MNH usually means a mortgage prepayment.

The Company's experience relative to prepayments of home mortgages, until 1986, had been minor. However, late in 1986, prepayments became a recognized concern. Prepayment of mortgages caused management to reevaluate certain assumptions resulting in a significant increase in the reserve for

credit losses related to mortgage prepayments in order to address the prospects of mortgage interest rates continuing to remain at present levels of 8½ to 9½ percent.

Repossessions of homes result primarily from customers' inability to meet their mortgage payment commitment. Approximately 70% of all MNH credit sales are with recourse, which means the Company will buy back from the financial institution holding a customer's mortgage those homes repossessed by the mortgage holder which were originally sold by MNH subsidiaries.

The Company's experience related to repossessions has shown very little change during the past ten years. However, during the fourth quarter of 1986, approximately $2,000,000 of repossession expense and interest chargebacks were experienced and charged off. Therefore, a charge to earnings, for both prepayments and repossessions, was made and the reserve for credit losses was increased to $3,000,000 at December 31, 1986.

One of the causes of the $2,000,000 charge was the refusal of some unrelated financial institutions to refinance the repossession that occurred in their portfolio, and a second cause was that the Company had to finance them through MANH Financial Services thereby having an immediate charge in finance participation on the pay-off and not recognizing the finance participation income of the resale.

During the first three quarters of 1986, the provision for credit losses was approximately 1% of net sales. Due to the recent fourth quarter charges, management will increase the provision for losses for 1987 to 1½% of net sales as a precautionary measure against future repossession and early pay-off.

Finance Participation

Finance participation was $12,084,108 in 1986 versus $9,715,558 in 1985, a 24.4% increase. As a percentage of net sales, it was 11.4% in 1986 compared with 14.1% in 1985. Several factors caused the percentage of decrease in realized finance participation: (1) increased cash sales; (2) increased non-recourse sales where no finance participation is received; (3) contributions of manufacturing to the sales volume where no finance participation is received; and (4) a decrease in the interest rate

Manufactured Homes

Manufactured Homes

spread earned by the Company when the sales contracts are sold to financial institutions. The decreased "spread" was the most important factor in 1986 as two major financial institutions changed their "retail rate" and reduced the "spread" received by the Company by 33%.

Finance participation is an important part of the Company's revenue. This source of revenue is monitored closely and alternative sources of financing are considered for customer mortgage funding on an ongoing basis.

Insurance

The Company earns commissions for writing homeowner insurance policies at the time of sale of the home and from renewal premiums. Income from insurance sales was $721,758 in 1986 compared with $413,282 in 1985, a 75% increase.

Selling, General and Administrative

The Company's selling, general and administrative expense (SG&A) has historically ranged around 17% of revenue. This range varies according to the Company's growth pattern and marketing emphasis.

In 1986, the significant factors affecting the Company's SG&A expense, which was 19% of revenue, were that: (1) the Company initiated a second production line at its manufacturing plant; (2) acquired two additional subsidiaries — Piggy Bank Homes of Alabama and Jeff Brown Homes in Virginia and West Virginia, in mid-September 1986; (3) initiated two additional operating subsidiaries — AAA Mobile Homes (formerly part of MNH), and MANH Independent Retailers Corp. (formerly spread among several subsidiaries for operational purposes); (4) opened 13 new company sales centers; added 11 independent dealers to the retail network; and (5) formed MANH Financial Services Corp. as of October 1986. This expansion and realignment of subsidiaries, which occurred mostly during the fourth quarter, were part of an overall marketing strategy to more effectively penetrate the Company's market. The significant increase in sales over 1985 of 54% resulted from staffing an additional 13 company-owned sales centers, with special emphasis on bonus programs to sell aged inventory and homes received in trade for new sales, as well as improving the percentage of homes which were sold with

recourse. This aggressive marketing program was designed to achieve momentum for a strong 1987, but increased SG&A expense significantly at the same time.

Several other cost factors effecting SG&A expense were: (1) An increase in liability insurance rates on policy renewals during 1986 at an annual rate 40% higher than in 1985, or approximately an additional $350,000; and (2) the cost incurred during the year related to the completion of a 15-month standardization of accounting procedures and data processing enhancement program which centralized the Company's management information with on-line capability to each subsidiary. This is a significant step forward in better data management and timely preparation of financial information.

Interest Expense

Interest expense increased $1,543,352 to $3,367,940 in 1986 from $1,824,588 in 1985, or 85%. The increase resulted from a $12,536,000 increase in total inventory and approximately an $8,000,000 increase in total receivables directly related to the expansion of 39 sales centers in 1986.

Income Taxes

The Company's effective income tax rate was 49.8% in 1986 compared to 47.2% in 1985. This increase resulted primarily from the elimination of investment tax credits under the Tax Reform Act of 1986.

Organization

Each of the Company's nine subsidiaries are profit centers. Each subsidiary has its own chief executive officer with total profit and loss responsibility. The Company's long-range plan for growth is by strategic acquisitions, expanding market share, and developing management talent through a newly organized salesperson training program, all to meet the need of providing low-cost housing to the American consumer.

Manufacturing

Craftsman Manufactured Homes, Inc., the MNH manufacturing subsidiary, commenced operations in September 1985. It has grown from virtually a start-up operation to a sales volume in excess of $15,000,000 in 1986. Approximately 57% of the

1,119 homes manufactured were sold to and through Company related sales centers. The balance of the homes were sold to non-related independent retailers. The Craftsman plant operates two production lines with a plant capacity of approximately 3,500 floors (multi-section homes require more than one floor) per year.

Financial Services

MANH Financial Services Corp. was organized on October 14, 1986 to facilitate the marketing of new, repossessed and pre-owned homes. Two major retail financial sources curtailed the purchase of conditional sales contracts which resulted in slow response to contract applications and therefore lost sales. The Company responded with the formation of MANH Financial Services Corp. to operate on a limited basis. The growth of this subsidiary will depend largely on whether or not the unrelated financial institutions continue to service the Company's growth.

1985 Versus 1984

The Company's net sales for 1985 were $68,674,779 compared to $30,480,571 for 1984, an increase of 125%. The majority of this increase was due to the addition of eight retail sales centers during the first quarter and the acquisition of Country Squire Mobile Homes, Inc. on March 22, 1985, with 20 retail sales centers. The Company also opened seven retail sales centers in the second quarter, six in the third quarter, and two in the fourth quarter. Volume increases in sales centers which were in operation at the end of 1984 also occurred while the average sales price per unit remained fairly constant from 1984 to 1985. The Company's purchase of a manufacturing facility on September 4, 1985, contributed approximately 7% of the 1985 sales increase.

Finance participation income for 1985 was $9,715,558 compared to $5,221,279, an increase of 86%. This was less than the percentage increase in sales due to three factors: (1) The election to discount the unreceived portion of finance participation income to its present value; (2) Country Squire earned significantly less finance participation income than the other retail groups, primarily because of non-recourse sales; and, (3) the inclu-sion of manufacturing sales which do not earn finance participation income. Insurance commissions, interest and other revenues increased proportionally in relation to the increase in sales.

Cost of sales as a percentage increased approximately 2% in 1985. This increase was due to the substantial increase in sales to independent retailers which traditionally have lower margins, and a slight decrease in margins at Company-owned sales centers. Selling, general and administrative expenses increased in 1985 as a result of increased sales volume and reflect the increase in number of sales centers and additional personnel to support our continued growth. Provision for losses on credit sales remained relatively constant as a percentage of net sales from 1984 to 1985. Interest rates were generally lower in 1985; however, total interest cost increased significantly due to increased inventories to support the added sales centers.

Liquidity and Capital Resources

The Company, in April 1986, sold $18,000,000 of 9% convertible subordinated notes due May 15, 2001. The proceeds were used primarily to reduce floor plan notes payable and to significantly improve the Company's liquidity. During 1986, the Company purchased Jeff Brown Homes, Inc. with nine sales centers and Piggy Bank Homes of Alabama, Inc. with six sales centers, added 13 Company-owned sales centers, formed a finance company subsidiary with an initial capitalization of $500,000, expanded the principal offices of its wholly-owned subsidiary, Tri-County Homes, Inc., and opened a second production line at its manufacturing facility, using funds generated from the sale of the subordinated notes and from operations.

At December 31, 1986, the Company had available $1,000,000 in a bank line of credit and $8,000,000 in unused floor plan lines of credit. On February 13, 1987, the Company sold $25,000,000 of unsecured senior notes due in 1990 and 1992 bearing interest at a blended rate of 8.95%. The proceeds have been partially used to reduce floor plan notes payable.

Although working capital increased significantly in 1986, operations used working capital of $2,956,041 compared to providing working capital of $2,847,026 in 1985 and $2,599,953 in 1984.

The use of working capital by operations in 1986 was principally due to the interest rate spread applicable to finance participation and significant reductions in deferred income taxes applicable to the provision for credit losses and finance participation income.

The Tax Reform Act of 1986 will benefit the Company through a reduction of the corporate income tax rate. However, beginning January 1, 1987, the Act will require the Company to accelerate the payment of Federal income taxes. However, the Company believes that funds to be generated by operations, combined with credit lines currently available, will be sufficient to satisfy capital needs for current operations.

CONSOLIDATED BALANCE SHEET

December 31,	1986	1985
ASSETS		
Current Assets		
Cash and cash equivalents:		
Cash and temporary investments	$2,486,024	$2,968,837
Contract proceeds receivable from financial institutions (Note 9)	11,496,078	5,189,535
Total cash and cash equivalents	13,982,102	8,158,372
Finance participation receivable – current portion (Note 2)	2,691,497	2,486,001
Deferred finance participation income	(801,511)	(523,038)
Net finance participation receivable	1,889,986	1,962,963
Other receivables (Note 4)	3,746,863	2,057,674
Refundable income taxes (Note 11)	778,971	—
Inventories (Notes 5 and 9)	38,163,712	25, 628,156
Prepaid expenses	538,419	408,124
Deferred income taxes (Note 11)	761,262	436,496
Total current assets	59,861,315	38,651,785
Finance participation receivable – noncurrent portion (Note 2)	16,128,799	10, 269,713
Deferred finance participation income	(3,923,178)	(2,968,629)
Net finance participation receivable	12,205,621	7,301,084
Property, plant and equipment at cost (Notes 6 and 10)	7,504,272	5,467,164
Accumulated depreciation and amortization	(2,410,812)	(1,555,427)
Net property, plant and equipment	5,093,460	3,911,737
Excess of costs over net assets of acquired companies less amortization (Note 3)	2,107,874	973, 860
Other assets	2,109,533	106,458
	$81,377,803	$50,944,924

Manufactured Homes

December 31,	1986	1985
LIABILITIES AND STOCKHOLDERS' EQUITY		
Current Liabilities		
Notes payable	$1,099,971	$ —
Long-term debt – current installments (Note 10)	810,901	1,100,624
Floor plan notes payable (Note 9)	35,207,386	27,468,153
Accounts payable	4,899,250	2,210,560
Income taxes (Note 11)	—	1,828,234
Accrued expenses and other liabilities (Note 8)	2,731,924	1,223,302
Total current liabilities	44,749,432	33,830,873
Long-term debt – noncurrent installments (Note 10)	18,609,987	1,082,543
Reserve for losses on credit sales (Note 7)	3,000,000	1,863,992
Deferred income taxes (Note 11)	851,265	3,114,757
Total liabilities	67,210,684	39,892,165
Stockholders' Equity (Notes 10 and 12)		
Common stock — $.50 par value per share; authorize 10,000,000 shares; issued and outstanding 3,733,968 shares in 1986 and 3,488,968 shares in 1985	1,866,984	1,744,484
Additional paid-in capital	3,508,351	2,549,916
Retained earnings	8,791,784	6,758,359
Total stockholders' equity	14,167,119	11,052,759
Commitments and contingent liabilities (Notes 3 and 13)		
	$81,377,803	$50,944,924

CONSOLIDATED STATEMENTS OF EARNINGS

Years Ended December 31,	1986	1985	1984
Revenues:			
Net sales	$106,095,667	$68,674,779	$30,480,571
Finance participation income	12,084,108	9,715,558	5,221,279
Insurance commissions	721,758	413,282	231,618
Interest	338,447	163,663	123,564
Other	1,024,974	558,706	138,770
Total revenues	120,264,954	79,525,988	36,195,802
Costs and expenses:			
Cost of sales	86,212,901	56,222,412	24,324,851
Selling, general and administrative	22,852,093	13,639,942	5,895,891
Provision for losses on credit sales (Note 7)	3,777,900	793,497	253,004
Interest	3,367,940	1,824,588	570,527
Total costs and expenses	116,210,834	72,480,439	31,044,273
Earnings before income taxes	4,054,120	7,045,549	5,151,529
Income taxes (Note 11)	2,020,695	3,327,224	2,457,000
Earnings before cumulative effect of change in accounting principle (Note 2)	2,033,425	3,718,325	2,694,529
Cumulative effect on prior years of change in accounting principle for finance participation (Notes 2 and 11)	—	(504,571)	—
Net earnings	$2,033,425	$3,213,754	$2,694,529
Earnings per share:			
Before cumulative effect of change in accounting principle	$.53	$.98	$.77
Cumulative effect on prior years of change in accounting principle for finance participation	—	(.13)	—
Net earnings per share — primary	$.53	$.85	$.77
Net earnings per share — fully diluted	$.53	$.84	$.77
Proforma amounts assuming retroactive application of the change in accounting principle (Note 2):			
Net earnings	$2,033,425	$3,718,325	$2,365,334
Net earnings per share — primary	$.53	$.98	$.68

Manufactured Homes

Manufactured Homes

CONSOLIDATED STATEMENTS OF CHANGES IN FINANCIAL POSITION

Year Ended December 31,	1986	1985	1984
Working capital was provided by			
Operations:			
Net earnings	$2,033,425	$3,213,754	$2,694,529
Adjustments for items not requiring (providing) working capital:			
Depreciation and amortization	946,858	556,23 6	210,699
Noncurrent deferred income taxes	(2,197,061)	78,637	1,412,812
Provision for losses on credit sales, net of actual charges	699,343	(217,402)	134,614
Issuance of nonqualified stock options	142,000	206,000	—
Finance participation income	(12,084,108)	(9,715,558)	(5,221,279)
Collections, current and deferred finance participation income portion of finance participation receivable	7,503,502	8,725,359	3,316,397
Other	—	—	52,181
Working capital provided (used) by operations	(2,956,041)	2,847,026	2, 599,953
Proceeds from long-term debt	18,396,000	1,651,822	400,000
Exercise of stock options	938,935	—	—
Decrease in other assets	—	4,024	—
	16,378,894	4,502,872	2,999,953
Working capital was used for			
Net assets, exclusive of working capital of $806,363 in 1985 and deficits in working capital of $1,109,080 in 1986 and $140,604 in 1984, of acquired companies (Note 3)	1,285,935	422,179	1,220,198
Additions to property, plant and equipment	1,917,489	2,756,178	580,259
Current installments and repayment of long-term debt	1,071,308	1,322,806	70,423
Additions to other assets and excess costs	1,813,191	—	9,054
	6,087,923	4,501,163	1,879,934
Increase in working capital	$10,290,971	$ 1,709	$1,120,019
Changes in working capital, by component			
Cash and cash equivalents	$ 5,823,730	$6,136,129	$ 579,418
Finance participation receivable – current portion	(72,977)	1,193,013	569,838
Other receivables	1,689,189	1,715,543	233,696
Refundable income taxes	778,971	—	—
Inventories	12,535,556	17,448,795	5,616,654
Prepaid expenses	130,295	371,403	25,918
Deferred income taxes	324,766	102,710	203,000
Notes payable	(1,099,971)	—	—
Long-term debt -current installments	289,723	(900,624)	(200,000)
Floor plan notes payable	(7,739,233)	(22,962,163)	(3,986,435)
Accounts payable	(2,688,690)	(1,896,668)	(219,293)
Income taxes	1,828,234	(620,489)	(1,207,745)
Accrued expenses and other liabilities	(1,508,6 22)	(585,940)	(495,032)
Increase in working capital	$10,290,971	$ 1,709	$ 1,120,019

NOTES TO CONSOLIDATED FINANCIAL STATEMENTS

December 31, 1986, 1985 and 1984

Note 1
Summary of Significant Accounting Policies

Principles of Consolidation and Nature of Business

The consolidated financial statements include the accounts of Manufactured Homes, Inc. and all subsidiaries, each wholly-owned, and hereafter referred to collectively as the "Company." All significant intercompany items are eliminated.

The Company is engaged principally in the retail sale of new and used manufactured single-family homes.

Inventories

Inventories are stated at the lower of cost or market, with cost being determined using the specific unit method for new and used manufactured homes and average cost for materials and supplies.

Property, Plant and Equipment

Depreciation of property, plant and equipment is provided principally by the straight-line method over the estimated useful lives of the respective assets. Amortization of leasehold improvements is provided by the straight-line method over the shorter of the lease terms or the estimated useful lives of the improvements.

Income Taxes

Deferred income taxes are recognized for income and expense items that are reported in different periods for financial reporting and income tax purposes.

Income Recognition

A sale is recognized when payment is received or, in the case of credit sales, when a down payment (generally 10% of the sales price) is received and the Company and the customer enter into an installment contract. Installment contracts are normally payable over periods ranging from 120 to 180 months. Credit sales represent the majority of the Company's sales.

Under existing financing arrangements, the majority of installment contracts are sold, with recourse to unrelated financial institutions at an agreed upon rate which is below the contractual interest rate of the installment contract. At the time of sale, the Company receives immediate payment for the stated principal amount of the installment contract and a portion of the finance participation resulting from the interest rate differential. The remainder of the interest rate differential is retained by the financial institution as security against credit losses and is paid to the Company in proportion to customer payments received by the financial institution. The Company accounts for these transactions as sales in accordance with Statement of Financial Accounting Standards No. 77, "Reporting by Transferors for Transfers of Receivables with Recourse," and recognizes finance participation income equal to the difference between the contractual interest rates of the installment contracts and the agreed upon rates to the financial institutions; the portion retained by the financial institutions is discounted for estimated time of collection and carried at its present value (see Note 2).

Reserve for Losses on Credit Sales

Estimated losses arising from the recourse provisions of the Company's financing arrangements with unrelated financial institutions are provided for currently based on historical loss experience and current economic conditions and consist of estimated future rebates of finance participation income due to prepayment or repossession, estimated future losses on installment contracts repurchased from financial institutions and estimated future losses on installment contracts transferred to new purchasers in lieu of repossession. Actual losses are charged to the reserve when incurred.

Excess of Costs over Net Assets of Acquired Companies

The excess of costs over net assets of acquired companies is being amortized over 30 years on the straight-line method.

Earnings per Share

Primary earnings per share are based on the weighted average number of common and common equivalent shares outstanding. Such average shares are as follows:

Years Ended December 31,	1986	1985	1984
Outstanding shares	3,660,048	3,488,968	3,488,968
Equivalent shares	204,113	313,725	—
	3,864,161	3,802,693	3,488,968

The equivalent shares in 1986 and 1985 represent the shares issuable upon exercise of stock options and warrants after the assumed repurchase of common shares with the related proceeds at the average price during the period. Common equivalent shares were not considered in 1984 as the resulting dilution was insignificant.

Fully diluted earnings per share are based on the weighted average number of common and common equivalent shares outstanding plus the common shares issuable upon the assumed conversion of the convertible subordinated notes and elimination of the applicable interest expense less related income tax benefit. In determining equivalent shares, the assumed repurchase of common shares is at the higher of the average or period-end price.

Note 2
Accounting Change

Prior to 1985, the Company recognized finance participation income without discounting for the estimated time of collection of the portion retained by the unrelated financial institutions as security against credit losses. However, in 1985 the Company adopted the practice whereby the portion of finance participation income retained by the financial institutions is recorded at its present value based upon estimated time of collection. The Company believes the new method is preferable since it more accurately reflects the value of the finance participation receivable at the date the installment contracts are sold to the financial institutions.

As a result of this change, earnings in 1985, before the cumulative effect of the change on prior years,

were decreased by $538,466 ($.14 per share). Net earnings were further decreased by $504,571 ($.13 per share), which represents the cumulative effect of the change on prior years. Proforma net earnings and earnings per share amounts reflecting retroactive application of the change are shown in the consolidated statements of earnings.

Note 3
Acquisitions

On January 6, 1984, Manufactured Homes, Inc. acquired the outstanding common stock of Tri-County Homes, Inc., a retailer of manufactured housing located in eastern North Carolina. The purchase agreement required cash payments of $400,000 and potential earn-out payments of $600,000, all earned at December 31, 1984. The acquisition has been accounted for as a purchase and, accordingly, the operations of Tri-County are included in the consolidated financial statements of Manufactured Homes, Inc. beginning in 1984. Effective March 22, 1985, Manufactured Homes, Inc. acquired the outstanding common stock of Country Squire Mobile Homes, Inc., a retailer of manufactured housing located principally in South Carolina. The purchase agreement required cash payments of $873,000 and includes potential earn-out payments of $1,960,000 over the period 1985 to 1990. The potential earn-out is based on a percentage of Country Squire's pre-tax earnings as defined. At December 31, 1986, $642,947 ($396,000 in 1986 and $246,947 in 1985) of the potential earn-out had been earned and recorded as an adjustment of the purchase price. The acquisition has been accounted for as a purchase and, accordingly, the operations of Country Squire are included in the consolidated financial statements of Manufactured Homes, Inc. since March 22, 1985. The following unaudited proforma data presents the results of operations of the Company and Country Squire as if the acquisition had occurred at January 1, 1984.

Years Ended December 31,	1985	1984
Total revenues	$87,729,677	$59,696,534
Net earnings	3,090,464	2,812,632
Net Earnings per share:		
Primary	$ .81	$ .81
Fully diluted	$ .80	$ .81

In September 1986, Manufactured Homes, Inc. acquired the outstanding common stock of two companies engaged in the retail sale of manufactured homes. The purchase agreements required aggregate cash payments of $151,000 and potential earn-out payments of $874,000 over the period 1987 to 1992. The potential earn-outs are based on a percentage of the respective companies' pre-tax earnings as defined. The acquisitions have been accounted for as purchases and, accordingly, their operations, which are not material, are included in the consolidated financial statements of Manufactured Homes, Inc., since September 1986. At date of acquisition, one company had operating loss carryforwards of $612,049 and to the extent utilized, the income tax reductions will be accounted for as adjustments of the purchase price. At December 31, 1986, $324,510 (tax benefit of $159,226) of the carryforwards had been utilized.

The net assets, exclusive of working capital of $806,363 in 1985 and deficits in working capital of $1,109,080 in 1986 and $140,604 in 1984, of the acquired companies were as follows:

Years Ended December 31,	1986	1985	1984
Finance participation receivable	$ 323,931	$1,337,147	$1,172,853
Property, plant and equipment	169,092	747,092	131,367
Other assets	493,089	23,403	61,016
Long-term debt	(202,752)	(353,527)	(70,423)
Reserve for losses on credit sales	(436,665)	(1,675,000)	(74,615)
Other liabilities	—	(679,524)	—
Excess of costs over net assets of acquired companies	939,240	1,022,588	—
	$1,285,935	$ 422,179	$1,220,198

Note 4
Other Receivables

Other receivables consist of the following:

December 31,	1986	1985
Manufacturers' volume bonuses	$1,979,021	$1,557,029
Sundry	1,767,842	500,645
	$3,746,863	$2,057,674

Note 5
Inventories

Inventories consist of the following:

December 31,	1986	1985
New manufactured homes	$31,920,134	$22,766,030
Used manufactured homes	4,971,040	2,068,099
Materials and supplies	1,272,538	794,027
	$38,163,712	$25,628,156

Note 6
Property, Plant and Equipment

The cost and estimated useful lives of the major classifications of property, plant and equipment are as follows:

	Estimated Useful Life	December 31,	
		1986	1985
Land	—	$ 735,329	$ 620,083
Buildings	15–20 yrs.	1,660,321	849,427
Manufactured homes— office units	5–7 yrs.	1,048,571	1,013,543
Leasehold improvements	3–5 yrs.	615,319	
Furniture & equipment	3–10 yrs.	1,921,101	1,108,123
Vehicles	3–5 yrs.	1,485,222	1,124,154
Signs	3–7 yrs.	38,409	185,196
		$7,504,272	$5,467,164

Manufactured Homes

Note 7
Reserve for Losses on Credit Sales

An analysis of the reserve for losses on credit sales follows:

Years Ended December 31,	1986	1985	1984
Balance at beginning of year	$1,863,992	$ 406,394	$197,165
Amount at date of acquisition applicable to acquired companies, less actual charges of $69,236 in 1986 and $604,403 in 1985	367,429	1,070,597	74,615
Provision for losses	3,777,900	793,497	253,004
Actual charges	(3,009,321)	(406,496)	(118,390)
Balance at end of year	$3,000,000	$1,863,992	$406,394

Note 8
Accrued Expenses and Other Liabilities

A summary of accrued expenses and other liabilities follows:

December 31,	1986	1985
Payroll and related costs	$1,580,235	$ 697,287
Other	1,151,689	526,015
	$2,731,924	$1,223,302

Note 9
Floor Plan Notes Payable

A substantial portion of the Company's new manufactured home inventories are financed through floor plan arrangements with certain unrelated financial institutions. A summary of floor plan notes payable follows:

December 31,	Rate	Floor Plan Lines	1986	1985
General Electric Credit Corporation	Prime + 1.75 (9.25%)	$27,052,000	$22,601,520	$17,183,988
ITT Diversified Credit Corporation	Prime + 2.00 (9.50%)	7,200,000	5,869,438	5,224,373
CIT Financial Services	Prime + 2.00 (9.50%)	4,000,000	3,958,932	1,761,854
Whirlpool Acceptance Corporation	Prime + 1.50 (9.00%)	1,500,000	1,210,586	—
U.S. Home Acceptance	Prime (7.50%)	1,000,000	36,680	815,066
Citicorp Acceptance Company, Inc.	Prime + 2.00 (9.50%)	975,000	—	1,706,728
Others	Various	1,850,000	1,530,230	776,144
		$43,577,000	$35,207,386	$27,468,153

The floor plan liability at December 31, 1986 is collateralized by inventories and contract proceeds receivable from financial institutions. The floor plan arrangements generally require periodic partial repayments with the unpaid balance due upon sale of the related collateral.

The weighted average interest rate paid on the outstanding floor plan liability was 10.9%, 11.0%, and 14.7% for 1986, 1985, and 1984, respectively. The maximum amount outstanding at any month end during each year was $35,207,386 for 1986, $27,468,153 for 1985, and $4,508,319 for 1984, with a weighted average balance outstanding for each year of approximately $25,500,000, $16,000,000 and $3,750,000, respectively.

Note 10
Long-Term Debt

A summary of long-term debt follows:

December 31,	1986	1985
9% convertible subordinated notes payable, due in annual installments of $1,800,000 beginning May 15, 1992 through May 15, 2001	$18,000,000	—
Note payable, due in monthly installments of $66,667 through October 1, 1987, interest at prime rate (7½% at December 31, 1986) and collateralized by property, plant and equipment with a depreciated cost of $1,160,640	666,670	1,466,667
Obligation payable in January 1988, interest at the prime rate (7½% at December 31, 1986) and collateralized by the common stock of Country Squire Mobile Homes, Inc. (Note 3)	396,000	—
Obligation payable in annual installments of $200,000 through April 15, 1987, repaid in 1986	—	400,000
Various notes payable, due in monthly installments, including interest at rates ranging from 8% to 18%	358,218	316,500
	19,420,888	2,183,167
Less current installments	810,901	1,100,624
	$18,609,987	$1,082,543

The aggregate annual maturities of the long-term debt for the five years following December 31, 1986 are: 1987, $810,901; 1988, $508,497; 1989, $53,498; 1990, $33,255; 1991, $14,737.

Pursuant to an agreement dated April 25, 1986 (the "1986 Agreement"), the Company sold its Convertible Subordinated Notes due May 15, 2001, in the amount of $18,000,000 to two lenders. The proceeds from these notes have been used principally to reduce floor plan notes payable. The notes are convertible into shares of the Company's common stock at the conversion price of $17.50 per share. The conversion price is subject to adjustment in the event of stock dividends, stock splits, payment of extraordinary distributions, granting of options or sale of additional shares of common stock. The notes are subject to prepayment at the option of the Company between October 28, 1986 and May 15, 1996 at 100% of par if for a specified period preceding the written notice of prepayment the closing market price per share of the Company's common stock is equal to or greater than a percentage of the conversion price. Such percentage decreases from 200% through May 15, 1989 to 110% at May 15, 2001. The 1986 Agreement contains various restrictive covenants which include, among other things, maintenance of a minimum level of working capital as defined, maintenance of a minimum level of net earnings available for fixed charges as defined, consolidated current assets as defined, equal or greater than senior debt, payment of cash dividends and the creation of additional indebtedness.

Manufactured Homes

Subsequent to December 31, 1986 and pursuant to an agreement dated February 13, 1987 (the "1987 Agreement"), the Company sold the Prudential Insurance Company of America Series A and Series B Senior notes in the aggregate of $25,000,000. The Series A notes in the amount of $15,000,000 bear interest at the rate of 8.64% and are due February 15, 1990. The Series B notes in the amount of $10,000,000 bear interest at the rate of 9.42% and are due February 15, 1992. The proceeds from these notes have been used partially to reduce floor plan notes payable and the remainder added to corporate funds. The 1987 Agreement also contains restrictive financial covenants. The 1987 Agreement financial covenants were changed to reflect more accurately the Company's current financial structure.

Concurrent with the execution of the 1987 Agreement, the financial covenants contained in the 1986 Agreement were amended to conform to the covenants in the 1987 Agreement. At December 31, 1986, the Company was in compliance with the various restrictive covenants in the 1986 Agreement with the exception of the net earnings available for fixed charges covenant. The Company was in compliance with all of the restrictive covenants in the 1986 Agreement, as amended. Retained earnings available for the payment of cash dividends amounted to $1,516,712 at December 31, 1986.

Note 11
Income Taxes

Income taxes are reflected in the consolidated statements of earnings as follows:

Years Ended December 31,	1986	1985	1984
Before cumulative effect of change in accounting principle	$2,020,695	$3,327,224	$2,457,000
Cumulative effect on prior years of change in accounting principle	—	(449,989)	—
	$2,020,695	$2,877,235	$2,457,000

Components of income tax expense (benefit) are as follows:

Years Ended December 31,	1986	1985	1984
Current:			
State	$ 550,653	$ 342,085	$ 166,000
Federal	3,942,668	2,366,685	1,075,000
	4,493,321	2,708,770	1,241,000
Deferred:			
State	(305,198)	20,529	143,000
Federal	(2,167,428)	147,936	1,073,000
	(2,472,626)	168,465	1,216,000
	$2,020,695	$2,877,235	$2,457,000

A reconciliation of the statutory Federal income tax rate with the Company's actual income tax rate follows:

Years Ended December 31,	1986	1985	1984
Statutory Federal income tax rate	46.0%	46.0%	46.0%
State income tax rate less applicable Federal income tax benefit	3.2	3.2	3.2
Investment and jobs tax credit	—	(1.2)	(.4)
Nontaxable items – net	1.1	(.2)	.2
Other – net	(.5)	(.6)	(1.3)
Actual income tax rate	49.8%	47.2%	47.7%

The sources of deferred income tax expenses (benefits) and their tax effects are as follows:

Years Ended December 31,	1986	1985	1984
Provision for losses on credit sales	$(1,622,079)	$743,032	$705,000
Finance participation income	(778,939)	(521,030)	453,000
Operating loss and tax credit carryforwards	—	—	244,000
Manufacturers' volume bonuses	(105,058)	(32,062)	(203,000)
Depreciation	103,519	50,415	17,000
Accrued compensation	63,027	(101,434)	—
Allowance for doubtful accounts	—	29,544	—
Other – net	(133,096)	—	—
	$(2,472,626)	$168,465	$1,216,000

The operating loss and tax credit carryforwards in 1984 represent the reinstatement of deferred tax credit recognized in previous years for financial reporting purposes.

The Tax Reform act of 1986 will benefit the Company through a reduction of the statutory Federal income tax rate.

Note 12
Common Stock

In connection with a public offering of common stock in 1983, the Company sold to the primary underwriter warrants to purchase 142,500 shares of common stock at a price equal to 120% of the public offering price. The warrants are exercisable for a four-year period beginning in 1984 at $3.84 per share. On June 14, 1983, the Board of Directors approved an Incentive Stock Option Plan and reserved 608,900 shares of the Company's authorized common stock for award to officers, directors and key employees. Under the Plan, options are granted at the discretion of a committee appointed by the Board of Directors and may be either incentive stock options or nonqualified stock options. Incentive options must be at a price equal to or greater than fair market value at date of grant. Nonqualified options may be at a price lower

than fair market value at date of grant. The Plan expires June 13, 1993.

Activity and price information regarding the plan follows:

	Shares	Option Price Range
Balance December 31, 1983	104,750	$2.40– $3.20
Granted	119,250	$2.40– $3.75
Canceled	(20,500)	$3.20
Balance December 31, 1984	203,500	$2.40– $3.75
Granted	297,600	$4.06–$11.25
Canceled	(5,250)	$2.40– $3.75
Balance December 31, 1985	495,850	$2.40–$11.25
Granted	32,300	$11.00–$17.50
Exercised	(245,000)	$2.40– $4.06
Canceled	(18,250)	$2.70–$10.38
Balance December 31, 1986	264,900	$2.40–$17.50

At December 31, 1986, options for 17,000 shares were currently exercisable. The remaining options become exercisable through the expiration date of the Plan. The excess, if any, of the fair market value at date of grant over the exercise price of nonqualified options is considered compensation and is charged to operations as earned. For 1986 and 1985, the charge to operations was $142,000 and $206,000, respectively. No options were granted at prices lower than fair market value prior to 1985.

At December 31, 1986, 1,534,971 shares of the Company's authorized common stock were reserved for issuance as follows: 142,500 shares for the outstanding warrants, 363,900 shares for the Incentive Stock Option Plan, and 1,028,571 shares for the convertible subordinated notes.

Note 13
Commitments and Contingent Liabilities

The Company leases office space, the majority of its retail sales centers and certain equipment under noncancellable operating leases that expire over the next five years. Total rental expense under such leases amounted to $1,335,809 in 1986, $888,719 in 1985, and $433,759 in 1984. Approximately 10%, 18%, and 22%, respectively, of such amounts were paid to the Company's majority stockholder and the officers of certain subsidiaries.

Manufactured Homes

Future minimum payments under noncancellable operating leases as of December 31, 1986 follow:

Year Ending December 31,	Minimum Payments
1987	$1,298,346
1988	787,572
1989	498,572
1990	312,510
1991	192,912
	$3,089,912

At December 31, 1986 the Company was contingently liable as guarantor on approximately $180 million (net) of installment sales contracts sold to financial institutions on a recourse basis. [Case writer's note: This contingent liability was $150 million at December 31, 1985, $116 million at December 31, 1984, and $45 million at December 31, 1983.]

Note 14
Supplementary Income Statement Information

Advertising costs amounted to $1,569,658, $1,021,978 and $311,285 in 1986, 1985 and 1984, respectively. Maintenance and repairs, depreciation and amortization of intangible assets, preoperating costs and similar deferrals, taxes, other than payroll and income taxes, and royalties did not exceed 1% of revenues in 1986, 1985 or 1984.

REPORT OF INDEPENDENT CERTIFIED PUBLIC ACCOUNTANTS

THE BOARD OF DIRECTORS AND STOCKHOLDERS MANUFACTURED HOMES, INC.:

We have examined the consolidated balance sheets of Manufactured Homes, Inc. and subsidiaries as of December 31, 1986 and 1985 and the related consolidated statements of earnings, stockholders' equity and changes in financial position for each of the years in the three-year period ended December 31, 1986. Our examinations were made in accordance with generally accepted auditing standards and, accordingly, included such tests of the accounting records and such other auditing procedures as we considered necessary in the circumstances.

In our opinion, the aforementioned consolidated financial statements present fairly the financial position of Manufactured Homes, Inc. and subsidiaries at December 31, 1986 and 1985 and the results of their operations and the changes in their financial position for each of the years in the three-year period ended December 31, 1986, in conformity with generally accepted accounting principles consistently applied during the period except for the change, with which we concur, in the method of recording the uncollected portion of finance participation income as explained in Note 2 to the consolidated financial statements.

PEAT, MARWICK, MITCHELL & CO.
Charlotte, North Carolina
March 10, 1987

EXHIBIT 3

Manufactured Homes, Consolidated Financial Statements for the First Nine Months of 1987

CONSOLIDATED BALANCE SHEETS (unaudited)

	September 30, 1987	December 31, 1986
ASSETS		
Current Assets:		
Cash and cash equivalents:		
Cash and temporary investments (includes) $5,212,849 of restricted cash in 1987	$9,311,240	$2,486,024
Contract proceeds receivable from financial institutions	17,435,191	11,496,098
Total cash and cash equivalents	26,746,431	13,982,102
Finance participation receivable - current portion	4,572,042	2,691,497
Deferred finance participation income	(1,208,275)	(801,511)
Net finance participation receivable	3,363,767	1,889,986
Installment sales contracts held for resale (less unearned interest of $3,648,675)	2,382,573	—
Other receivables	6,343,052	3,746,863
Refundable income taxes	—	778,971
Inventories	41,638,452	38,163,712
Prepaid expenses	587,749	538,419
Deferred income taxes	1,000,262	761,262
Total current assets	82,062,286	59,861,315
Finance participation receivable - noncurrent portion	25,020,194	16,128,799
Deferred finance participation income	(5,984,910)	(3,923,178)
Net finance participation receivable	19,035,284	12,205,621
Property, plant and equipment, at cost	9,248,065	7,504,272
Accumulated depreciation and amortization	(3,166,445)	(2,410,812)
Net property, plant and equipment	6,081,620	5,093,460
Deferred income taxes	1,847,735	—
Excess of costs over net assets of acquired companies, less amortization	2,130,099	2,107,874
Other assets	1,446,657	2,109,533
	$112,603,681	$81,377,803

(continued)

Manufactured Homes

Manufactured Homes

	September 30, 1987	December 31, 1986
LIABILITIES AND STOCKHOLDERS' EQUITY		
Current liabilities:		
Notes payable	$ —	$ 1,099,971
Long-term debt—current installments	90,038	810,901
Floor plan notes payable.	28,306,796	35,207,386
Accounts payable	8,181,736	4,899,250
Income taxes	2,469,015	—
Accrued expenses and other liabilities	5,351,963	2,731,924
Total current liabilities	44,399,548	44,749,432
Long-term debt - noncurrent installments	43,000,000	18,609,987
Reserve for losses on credit sales	4,850,000	3,000,000
Deferred income taxes	—	851,265
Total liabilities	92,249,548	67,210,684
Stockholder's equity:		
Common stock—$.50 par value per share; authorized 10,000 shares; issued and outstanding 3,777,168 shares in 1987 and 3,733,968 in 1986	1,888,584	1,866,984
Additional paid-in capital	3,830,314	3,508,351
Retained earnings	14,635,235	8,791,784
Total stockholders' equity	20,354,133	14,167,119
	$112,603,681	$81,377,803

CONSOLIDATED STATEMENT OF EARNINGS (unaudited)

	Three Months Ended September 30,		Nine Months Ended September 30,	
	1987	1986	1987	1986
Revenues:				
Net sales	$44,590,244	$29,464,161	$126,599,392	$76,396,868
Finance participation income	8,439,473	3,277,085	18,895,975	8,629,223
Insurance commissions	291,868	180,870	976,128	465,577
Interest	373,415	98,327	925,116	230,602
Other	534,916	121,378	786,971	221,448
Total revenues	54,229,916	33,141,821	148,183,582	85,943,718
Costs and expenses:				
Cost of sales	36,325,647	23,741,484	101,997,757	61,554,367
Selling, general and administrative	10,806,534	5,905,930	27,973,865	14,823,385
Provision for losses on credit sales	1,096,027	294,716	3,203,913	772,417
Interest	1,568,906	877,531	4,416,596	2,303,482
Total costs and expenses	49,797,114	30,819,661	137,592,131	79,453,651
Earnings before income taxes	4,432,802	2,322,160	10,591,451	6,490,067
Income taxes	2,038,000	1,145,000	4,748,000	3,109,000
Net earnings	$2,394,302	$1,177,160	$5,843,451	$3,381,067
Net earnings per share:				
Primary	$ .60	$ .30	$ 1.48	$ .87
Fully diluted	$ .53	$ .28	$ 1.31	$ .83

Manufactured Homes

Manufactured Homes

CONSOLIDATED STATEMENTS OF CHANGES IN FINANCIAL POSITION (unaudited)

	Nine Months Ended September 30	
	1987	**1986**
Working capital was provided by:		
Operations:		
Net earnings	$ 5,843,451	$ 3,381,067
Adjustments for items not requiring (providing) working capital:		
Depreciation and amortization	921,388	664,769
Noncurrent deferred income taxes	(2,699,000)	(345,000)
Provision for losses on credit sales, net of actual changes	1,850,000	(318,539)
Issuance of nonqualified stock options	39,000	106,500
Finance participation income	(18,895,975)	(8,629,223)
Collections and net change in noncurrent portion of finance participation receivable	12,066,312	5,019,381
Working capital used by operations	(874,824)	(121,045)
Proceeds from long-term debt	25,000,000	18,000,000
Exercise of stock options	304,563	1,060,805
Decrease in other assets	662,876	—
	25,092,615	18,939,760
Working capital was used for:		
Net assets, exclusive of working capital, of acquired companies:		
Finance participation receivable	—	349,749
Property and equipment	—	212,716
Other assets	—	509,514
Long-term debt	—	(257,571)
Reserve for losses on credit sales	—	(436,664)
Deferred income taxes	—	78,486
Excess of costs over net assets of acquired companies	—	867,849
	—	1,324,079
Additions to property, plant and equipment	1,851,773	1,365,703
Current installments and repayment of long-term debt	609,987	1,015,876
Additions to other assets and excess costs	80,000	879,665
	2,541,760	4,585,323
Increase in working capital	$22,550,855	$14,354,437
Changes in working capital, by component:		
Cash and cash equivalents	$12,764,329	$ 6,425,144
Finance participation receivable - current portion	1,473,781	239,967
Installment sales contracts held for resale	2,382,573	—
Other receivables	2,596,189	2,818,093
Refundable income taxes	(778,971)	—
Inventories	3,474,740	6,923,301
Prepaid expenses	49,330	59,791
Deferred income taxes	239,000	52,001
Notes payable	1,099,971	(1,391,500)
Long-term debt - current installments	720,863	167,046
Floor plan notes payable	6,900,590	1,424,866
Accounts payable	3,282,486)	(2,811,331)
Income taxes	(2,469,015)	1,820,226
Accrued expenses and other liabilities	(2,620,039)	(1,373,167)
Increase in working capital	$22,550,855	$14,354,437

Notes to Consolidated Financial Statements

1. Pursuant to an agreement dated February 13, 1987, the Company sold to Prudential Insurance Company of America Series A and Series B Senior notes in the aggregate of $25,000,000. The Series A notes in the amount of $15,000,000 bear interest at the rate of 8.64% and are due February 15, 1990. The Series B notes in the amount of $10,000,000 bear interest at the rate of 9.42% and are due February 15, 1992. The proceeds from these notes have been used partially to reduce floor plan notes payable and to fund the Company's finance subsidiary with the remainder added to working capital.

2. On August 18, 1987, the Company's finance subsidiary sold, with recourse, a portfolio of retail installment sales contracts with a principal balance of approximately $8,300,000 to an unrelated financial institution. As a result, the Company recognized, in the third quarter, finance participation income, net of discounts and estimated future servicing costs, of $1,688,690. The terms of the sale required the Company to provide to the unrelated financial institution as security against credit losses, an irrevocable reducing letter of credit in the amount of $3,000,000 secured by a six-month renewable certificate of deposit equal in amount to the letter of credit. At September 30, 1987, approximately $2,200,000 of the proceeds from the sale was held in an escrow account pending receipt, from the appropriate state agencies, of the titles to certain of the new and pre-owned homes securing the retail installment sales contracts in accordance with the terms of the sale.

3. Primary earnings per share are based on the weighted average number of common and common equivalent shares outstanding. Such average shares are as follows:

	Three Months Ended September 30,		Nine Months Ended September 30,	
	1987	1986	1987	1986
Outstanding shares	3,773,894	3,726,427	3,758,245	3,635,137
Equivalent shares	205,159	195,979	187,848	272,150
	3,979,053	3,922,406	3,946,093	3,907,287

The equivalent shares represent shares issuable upon exercise of stock options and warrants after the assumed repurchase of common shares with the related proceeds at the average price during the period.

Fully diluted earnings per share are based on the weighted average number of common and common equivalent shares outstanding plus the common shares issuable upon the assumed conversion of the convertible subordinated notes and elimination of the applicable interest expense less related income tax benefit. In determining equivalent shares, the assumed repurchase of common shares is at the higher of the average or period-end price.

4. Certain amounts in the 1986 financial statements have been reclassified to conform to the presentation adopted in 1987.

5. In the opinion of management, all adjustments which are necessary for a fair presentation of operating results are reflected in the accompanying interim financial statements. All such adjustments are considered to be of a normal recurring nature.

Manufactured Homes

MANAGEMENT'S DISCUSSION AND ANALYSIS OF FINANCIAL CONDITION AND RESULTS OF OPERATIONS

Results of Operations

The Company's net sales for the three-month period ended September 30, 1987 were $44,590,244 compared to $29,464,161 for the comparable period of 1986, an increase of 51%. Net sales for the nine-month period ended September 30, 1987 were $126,599,392 compared to $76,396,868 for the comparable period of 1986, an increase of 66%. These increases are due primarily to the acquisitions in September 1986 of Jeff Brown Homes, Inc., with nine retail sales centers, and Piggy Bank Homes of Alabama, Inc., with six retail sales centers, and the opening of 24 additional retail centers between September 30, 1986 and September 30, 1987. In addition, the average number of homes sold per retail sales center for the three-month and the nine-month periods ended September 30, 1987 increased by 28% and 20% respectively, over the corresponding periods of 1986.

Finance participation income for both the three-month and the nine-month periods ended September 30, 1987 was greater as a percentage of net sales than in the comparable periods of 1986 due primarily to improved financing terms from third-party finance sources and the sale in August 1987 of a portfolio of retail installment sales contracts with a principal balance of approximately $8,300,000, which resulted in finance participation income of $1,688,690 net of discounts and estimated future servicing costs. This portfolio consisted of retail installment sales contracts originated during 1987 and the fourth quarter of 1986. Insurance commissions increased as a percentage of net sales due to added emphasis being placed on this revenue source. Interest income increased significantly due to an improved cash position in 1987 and the interest earned on retail installment sales contracts while held in the Company's finance subsidiary. Other income increased primarily due to a gain of $400,000 recognized in September 1987 on the cancellation of a lease on one of the Company's sales centers.

Cost of sales increased as a percentage of net sales for the three-month period ended September 30, 1987 as compared to the corresponding period of 1986 primarily as a result of extremely competitive market conditions. For the nine-month period ended September 30, 1987, cost of sales as a percentage of net sales was unchanged from the comparable period of 1986. Selling, general and administrative expenses were higher, as a percentage of total revenues, for both the three-month and nine-month periods ended September 30, 1987 as a result of expenses incurred for the following activities: the acquisitions in September 1986 of Piggy Bank Homes of Alabama, Inc. and Jeff Brown Homes, Inc.; the segregation and expanded operations of MANH Independent Retailers Corp. and AAA Mobile Homes, Inc. as separate subsidiaries of the Company; the increased number of retail sales centers; and the establishment in October 1986 of the Company's finance subsidiary.

The provision for losses on credit sales, as a percentage of total revenues, increased significantly for both the three-month and nine-month periods ended September 30,1987 as compared to the corresponding periods of 1986, primarily as a result of industry-wide problems which became evident in the second half of 1986 and which caused the Company to incur increased costs relating to the prepayment of retail installment sales contracts, the repossession of homes and the resale of repossessed homes.

Interest rates were generally lower in 1987; however, total interest expense increased significantly in 1987 due to increased borrowings to support additional retail sales centers and to fund the activities of the Company's finance subsidiary.

Liquidity and Capital Resources

Liquidity and capital resources were greater at September 30, 1987 than at September 30, 1986 due to the sale in February 1987 of $25,000,000 of unsecured senior notes due in 1990 and 1992 bearing interest at a blended rate of 8.95% and to increased floor plan lines of credit. At September 30, 1987, the Company had available $3,000,000 in a bank line of credit and approximately $18,500,000 in unused floor plan lines of credit. In addition, the Company filed a registration statement with the Securities and Exchange Commission on September 22, 1987 for the proposed sale by the Company of 1,200,000 shares of its previously unissued common stock. Due to recent events in the financial market place, the status of this proposed sale is now uncertain.

The Tax Reform Act of 1986 is benefiting the Company through a reduction of the corporate income tax rate. However, beginning January 1, 1987, the Act required the Company to change from the reserve method to the direct write-off method for providing for losses on credit sales, which is requiring the Company to accelerate the payment of federal income taxes. However, the Company believes that funds to be generated by operations, combined with financial resources and credit lines currently available, will be sufficient to satisfy capital needs for current operations.

Manufactured Homes

Revenue Analysis

Revenues are economic resources earned during a time period. Firms earn revenues from a variety of different sources. Manufacturers of consumer goods earn revenues from sales of their products to distributors and to consumers. Banks generate revenues from interest earned from loans to borrowers. Insurance companies receive premiums from policyholders. Lawyers receive fees from providing services to clients. Leasing companies generate income from leasing assets to lessees.

Analysis of revenues focuses on assessing when it is appropriate to recognize revenues in the financial statements. Should they be recorded when the service is provided or the product is shipped? Should they be recorded when cash is received from the customer? Or should they be recorded after cash is received and the customer has indicated that the product or service was satisfactory?

Revenue recognition occurs when two critical uncertainties are resolved: the product or service has been provided, and cash collection is reasonably likely. Management typically has the best information on these uncertainties. However, given management's reporting incentives and the limitations of accounting rules discussed in Chapter 3, there are opportunities for analysis of revenues by financial statement users.

In this chapter, we overview the revenue recognition rule, discuss types of transactions where application of this rule has proven challenging, and identify the key risks and opportunities for revenue analysis by users of financial statements.

THE REVENUE RECOGNITION RULE

As discussed in Chapter 1, cash accounting usually does not provide the most informative or relevant way of measuring a firm's performance. For example, in some transactions where the firm has received cash, it has yet to fulfill any of its contractual obligations to the customer. In other cases, it has provided the full service or product to the customer but has yet to receive cash. For both these types of transactions, accountants argue that cash receipts from customers typically do not reflect the most relevant measure of revenue performance for the business.

Accrual accounting attempts to reflect the economic substance of a firm's revenue performance by formulating two criteria for revenue recognition. As Figure 6-1 shows,

Figure 6-1 Criteria for Revenue Recognition and Implementation Challenges

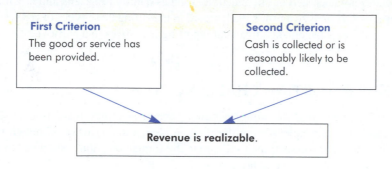

the first criterion deals with uncertainty over whether the earnings process is essentially complete, that is, whether the firm has provided all, or substantially all, of the goods or services to be delivered to the customer. The second criterion focuses on uncertainty over whether cash is likely to be received. If both these criteria are satisfied, revenue is recognizable.

For corporate managers and external users of financial statements, the above two criteria are likely to generate questions about whether effective business processes or third-party contracts are in place to manage the inherent risks. For example, firms can manage the risk that substantially all the goods and services have been delivered to the customer through effective quality programs to reduce the risk of product returns and warranties, or by sales contracts that limit customer returns and warranties. The collectibility risk can be managed through effective credit analysis or by transferring receivables to a third party.

Managers are likely to have the best information about the processes in place to manage revenue risks, but they are also likely to have incentives to manage reported earnings. Consequently, analysis of revenues helps financial statement users independently assess the reporting risks underlying revenues. Also, under accounting rules, a transaction either satisfies or does not satisfy the revenue recognition criteria. Revenue analysis allows financial statement users to better understand where on the "product/service delivery–collectibility" continuum a transaction lies.

There are several ways that financial statement users can analyze the uncertainties associated with revenue recognition. They can evaluate the processes used to manage risks that revenues are unearned or uncollectible, such as quality programs and credit analysis. They can also analyze a firm's track record in managing these types of risks. Finally, they can analyze management's financial reporting incentives in a particular period.

REVENUE REPORTING CHALLENGES

To provide a deeper understanding of how to analyze revenue recognition risks, we discuss challenges in implementing the revenue recognition criteria. Although we use specific industries or transactions to illustrate the implementation challenges, the conceptual issues apply at a general level.

Challenge One: Customers Pay in Advance

For some businesses, customers pay in advance of receiving the service or product. Examples include magazine subscriptions, insurance policies, and service contracts. For these types of products, there is no uncertainty about collectibility. The only question is when the revenue will be earned.

If revenues are recognized prior to the service delivery process, there is a risk that subsequent costs incurred are larger than expected, particularly if dissatisfied purchasers demand additional work or reimbursement from the seller. Indeed, given management's reporting incentives, users of financial reports are likely to be concerned that early revenue recognition provides management with the opportunity to boost current earnings by shading product quality and underreporting the cost of returns, reducing the credibility of financial reports. Of course, if accountants wait for all uncertainties associated with sales to be fully resolved, financial statements are likely to provide tardy information on the firm's performance.

Below we discuss revenue recognition rules for service contracts and property-casualty insurance policies. These examples illustrate revenue recognition issues for contracts where cash is received prior to product delivery or provision of the service.

EXAMPLE: SERVICE CONTRACTS.   Many firms provide service contracts for products that they sell. In some cases, they actually charge customers a fee for the service contract. For example, some consumer electronics chains sell service contracts separately from the sale of the product. Customers then pay a fee to secure protection for an extended period. In other cases, the service contract is included as a part of the purchase price of the product. Such is typically the case for manufacturers' warranties on new automobiles.

How should revenue be recognized on these contracts? Should they be recorded at the sale of the product, prorated over the warranty period, recognized when service is required, or deferred until the end of the contract period?

Let's first consider cases where the service contract can be purchased separately from the product. At this time, the product sale can be recognized; but since product servicing has yet to be provided, there are likely to be many uncertainties about the frequency and cost of future service claims. As a result, generally accepted accounting principles require firms to record service revenues during the contract period rather than when the contract is signed.

For service contracts that are included as a part of the purchase price, it is difficult to separate the price of the product from the price of the warranty. They are sold as a package. Indeed, some customers may buy the package primarily because of the service agreement rather than the product itself. For such sales, the seller typically recognizes revenue at delivery of the product or service. Most of the uncertainties associated with the sale (collectibility and the product's cost) have been resolved at this point. The only outstanding uncertainty is the future service contract claims against the seller. If the frequency and cost of claims can be predicted with reasonable certainty, revenues from the bundled product and service are recognized at the sale of the product. An estimate of the expected cost of servicing the contracts is then recorded as an expense.

EXAMPLE: PROPERTY CASUALTY INSURANCE POLICIES. Property casualty companies provide policyholders with insurance against certain risks, such as property damage from fire or natural disaster, automobile damage from an accident, or personal injury as a result of accidents. Policyholders typically pay insurance premiums at the beginning of the coverage period. Claims are then reported when damage or injury occurs.

When should property casualty firms recognize revenue on insurance contracts? Revenue could be reported when a customer is billed or pays. Alternatively, it could be recognized during (or at the end of) the contractual coverage period. Finally, it could be recognized when the costs of meeting reported claims are known or payments are made.

Property casualty firms face no collectibility risk, since premiums are received from policyholders at the beginning of the contract period. However, as discussed in Chapter 5, there are considerable uncertainties about the timing and cost of the claims to be covered. Some claims are not reported until subsequent periods. In addition, the amounts of the payments due for current and unreported claims are often not resolved for several years. Given these uncertainties, a case could be made for deferring revenue recognition until there is assurance that all claim reports have been made and the cost of the claims is known. However, insurance companies are in the business of managing risk. They hire actuaries to analyze the historical frequencies and costs of claims. Given these estimates and the law of large numbers, property casualty firms are able to make reasonable estimates of expected claim costs. As a result, SFAS 60 requires that they recognize revenue during the contract period and make an estimate of the expected costs of meeting both reported and unreported claims for that period.

Key Analysis Questions

When customers pay in advance of delivery of a product or service, accounting rules typically require revenues to be deferred. However, if revenues can be recognized, managers are required to make reasonable forecasts of the costs of delivering the product or service. This raises the following questions for financial analysts:

- Are management's costs estimates comparable to those for prior years? If not, why does management expect costs to be unusually high or low? For example, has the firm changed its marketing strategy, or has there been a change in the mix of its customers?
- How accurate have management's estimates been for prior years? Does the firm appear to systematically over- or underestimate these types of costs?
- How do the firm's estimates compare to those for other firms in the same line of business? If there are differences, does the firm have a different strategy from its competitors that could explain the cost differences. For example, are there differences in customer base, location, or product mix that are consistent with the cost estimate differences?

Challenge Two: Products or Services Provided over Multiple Periods

It can also be difficult to assess whether to recognize revenues for products or services that are provided over multiple years. These may or may not be paid in advance. Examples include long-term construction contracts and airline ticket sales with frequent flyer miles attached. The challenge for these types of contracts is to decide how to allocate revenue over the contractual period.

Typically, long-term contracts face two types of uncertainties: (1) a risk that purchasers will be dissatisfied with the quality of future work or service and demand additional work or reimbursement, and (2) a risk that the cost of providing the future service will be greater than anticipated. Both these types of risk raise concerns for financial statement users that revenue recognized prior to full completion of the service provides a misleading indicator of the value created by the completed product or service.

How, then, should revenues be recorded on these types of contracts? Should they be recorded as the service is being performed or the product manufactured, which presumably helps external readers of financial reports assess interim results? Alternatively, should revenues be deferred until the full product or service has been completed and all uncertainties have been resolved?

Below we discuss long-term construction contracts and frequent flyer contracts to better understand the issues and the way that they are typically handled in financial reporting.

EXAMPLE: LONG-TERM CONSTRUCTION CONTRACTS.   In February 1999, Turkmenistan awarded a $2.5 billion contract to an American consortium that included Bechtel Enterprises and General Electric to build a pipeline for bringing natural gas out of the Caspian Sea region. How should revenues under this contract be recorded? Conceptually, two methods can be considered. The more conservative method, the completed contract method, records the revenues when the contract is actually completed. Bechtel and GE would then show costs of construction as an asset, Construction in Progress, until the construction is complete. These costs would then be matched against the $2.5 billion of revenues.

The second approach, the percentage of completion method, recognizes revenues on a contract as construction progresses. The percentage of construction progress for a given year is estimated by the ratio of construction costs incurred during that year relative to total estimated costs of contract completion. This percentage of total contract revenues is then recognized as revenues for the year. Construction costs for the year are actual costs incurred.

Under U.S. GAAP, construction firms are expected to use the percentage of completion method if "estimates of the cost to complete and extent of progress toward completion of long-term contracts are reasonably dependable" (Accounting Research Bulletin 45). Of course, implementation of this rule requires management judgment, potentially creating an opportunity for earnings management.

In the Bechtel-GE example, the consortium faces many uncertainties. Funding for the pipeline is unlikely to be finalized until the former Soviet republic solves a territorial dispute with Azerbaijan, and until the five Caspian Sea nations (Turkmenistan, Azerbaijan, Kazakhstan, Russia, and Iran) agree on the division of the sea's rich reserves, potentially delaying the start of construction. These uncertainties imply that there are also likely to be serious political risks associated with the project that could cause delays and cost overruns once construction begins. As a result, Bechtel and GE are likely to have to record the transaction under the completed contract method.

EXAMPLE: FREQUENT FLYER MILES.   As discussed in Chapter 5, most airlines have frequent flyer programs that enable customers to earn awards for free flights, flight upgrades, hotel stays, and car rentals. For example, under United Airlines' Star Alliance reward system, passengers earn one free mile for each mile flown on United or its partner airlines (Air Canada, Lufthansa, SAS, and Thai). Passengers who fly for 25,000 miles can redeem their bonus miles for a free economy class round-trip ticket within the continental U.S.

Given its frequent flyer program, how should United record the purchase of a round-trip ticket from London to Boston for $750? This ticket sale provides the passenger with round-trip passage from Boston to London. But it also provides the passenger with 5000 bonus miles.

Two methods of recording the ticket sale can be considered. The first views passengers as purchasing two tickets—the first for a flight at the time the ticket is purchased, and the second for a possible flight at some future date. Under this approach, revenues are split between those earned for the current flight and those deferred to the future in the event the passenger redeems the bonus miles for another flight. The second approach views the award miles program as a form of promotion to attract passengers and records the incremental costs expected to be incurred to provide the promotion service, such as fuel, baggage handling, and meal costs. This method was discussed in Chapter 5. Both methods are used by airlines throughout the world. United Airlines uses the second method, the incremental cost approach.

Key Analysis Questions

Accounting for products or services provided over multiple periods is particularly challenging when revenues are recognized prior to completion of the product or service. Managers are then required to either forecast the costs of completion or estimate revenues that are earned and those that are deferred. These challenges raise the following questions for financial analysts:

- What are the risks associated with working on multi-period contracts? These could include political risks, weather risks, competitive risks, forecasting risks, and so forth. How is the firm managing these risks? What is its track record in managing these risks? Are the risks likely to be severe enough that the firm should defer recognizing revenues until the project is completed?
- How does management break apart current period revenues from future revenues in multi-period contracts? What assumptions and estimates are inherent in this analysis? What is the basis for these estimates? Are they based on historical data or industry data? How relevant is the data used for this analysis? Has the firm changed its strategy or operations significantly over time? Does it follow a different strategy from its competitors?
- Does accounting require management to forecast the full cost of a multi-period program? If so, what types of costs are included in the analysis and what types are excluded? What information does management use as a basis for their forecasts—internal budgets, industry data, historical data, etc.? How accurate have management's forecasts of costs been for prior years? If cost forecasts are systematically under- or over-budget, what are the implications for performance reported in the current period?

Challenge Three: Products or Services Sold but Residual Rights Retained by Seller

The third area where challenges arise in revenue recognition is where the seller retains some ongoing rights in the product or service sold. For example, a firm sells its receivables to a bank, but the bank has recourse against the seller if the creditor fails to pay off the receivable. Has the receivable been sold or has the firm simply borrowed against its receivables? Alternatively, if a firm signs a long-term agreement to lease equipment from the manufacturer but the manufacturer retains the residual rights to the equipment, has the equipment been sold or has it been rented?

To determine which of the above approaches best reflects the economics of the transaction, analysts need to understand the risks that are borne by the parties involved and how those risks are managed. Accounting standards frequently attempt to regulate the reporting of these types of transactions. However, the transactions frequently arrange for risks to be shared by both parties involved, making accounting complex. Receivable sales and long-term leasing contracts are discussed further to illustrate the reporting challenges for these types of transactions.

EXAMPLE: RECEIVABLE SALE WITH RECOURSE.   Many companies sell receivables to banks, financial institutions, or public investors as a way to accelerate the collection of cash. Two forms of sale are typically used: factoring and securitization. Under factoring, a finance company or bank purchases the rights to the cash flows under the receivable. Under securitization, a portfolio of receivables (such as credit card, auto loan, or mortgage receivables) is packaged into securities that represent claims on the interest and principal payments under the receivables. These securities are then sold to multiple buyers.

Securitization as a form of financing has become increasingly popular. For example, on February 17, 1999, the *Financial Times* reported that many Japanese finance houses have been launching "asset-backed securities, which allow consumer finance companies, among others, to remove assets from their balance sheets. These assets, typically equipment leases, car purchase loans and other types of consumer receivables, are transferred to a 'special purpose vehicle,' which stands legally at arm's-length from its originator. The special purpose vehicle launches a bond, often rated AAA because it is backed by the collateral of the asset's cash flow (such as repayments on car loans)."

How should these types of transactions be recorded? One approach is to view the receivables as having been sold at a gain or loss, depending on any difference between the interest rate on the receivable and the rate charged by the bank. Under this treatment, the seller creates a reserve to reflect any default and prepayment risks borne by the seller. Alternatively, the contract can be viewed as a bank loan where the receivables are a form of collateral.

Which of these two approaches best captures the economics of the transaction? Have the receivables really been sold, or should we consider the transaction as a bank loan using the receivables as collateral? To answer this question, we have to understand the potential risks faced by the seller. These include default and prepayment risks. Default risk arises if the receivables subsequently default and the bank is forced to recover from the seller. Prepayment risk arises if the receivables are fixed rate notes and interest rates subsequently fall. Receivables are then likely to be refinanced through alternative financing sources at lower interest rates. As a result, the seller of the receivables will no longer receive any spread difference between the interest rate on the note and the rate charged by the bank. Accounting rules in the U.S. (SFAS 77) argue that receivables sold with recourse can only be accounted for as a sale if (a) the seller gives up control of the economic benefits associated with the receivable, (b) the seller can make a reliable estimate of any obligations due to the default and prepayment risks, and (c) the buyer of the receivables cannot require the seller to repurchase the receivables. Otherwise, the transaction should be treated as a loan.

EXAMPLE: SALES-TYPE LEASE AGREEMENTS.   IBM sells mainframe computers to its customers under two different contractual arrangements. First, the customer can purchase the computer using either its own funds or financing through a third party. Second, the customer can sign a long-term lease agreement with IBM for use of the computer for much of its useful life. At the end of the lease term, IBM retains the residual value of the asset.

The first of these options (outright sale) is straightforward. However, it is more complex to determine how to record the other contractual arrangement. A long-term lease contract is very similar in form to an outright sale. IBM sells the use of the computer to the lessee for much of its useful life. However, instead of requiring the customer to raise external financing for the purchase, IBM agrees to provide financing. At the end of the lease term, IBM retains some residual claim to the computer. Should this transaction be viewed as a rental agreement or as a sale? Under a rental agreement, the lessor continues to own the asset and rents it to the lessee for the lease term.

Financial reporting for leases attempts to reflect these different types of lease arrangements. The critical accounting question is whether the lease terms are equivalent to the sale of the asset or to a rental agreement. In substance, a lease can be thought of as the equivalent of a sale if the lessee bears most of the risks normally associated with ownership. Thus, if the IBM customer contracts to use the computer for the bulk of its life, it bears much of the loss in value from obsolescence. The lease is then equivalent to a sale. Alternatively, if IBM bears most of these risks, the contract is more like a rental agreement.

Accounting rules in the U.S. are intended to reflect these differences in the nature of lease contracts. Under SFAS 13, a lease transaction is viewed as equivalent to a sale if any of the following conditions hold: (1) ownership of the asset is transferred to the lessee at the end of the lease term; (2) the lessee has the option to purchase the asset for a bargain price at the end of the lease term; (3) the lease term is 75 percent or more of the asset's expected useful life; or (4) the present value of the lease payments is 90 percent or more of the fair value of the asset.

Lease contracts that satisfy the criteria for an effective sale for accounting purposes are recorded as sales-type leases. For IBM, revenues from the sale would be recognized at the present value of the lease payments. This would also be shown as a receivable— Investment in Sales-Type Leases—on IBM's balance sheet. The expected residual value of the computer at the end of the lease term would be removed from inventory and included in the asset Investment in Sales-Type Leases. Finally, the balance of the book value of the computer would be removed from inventory and recorded as the cost of goods sold. The markup on the computer "sale" would then be reflected in the gross profit. In subsequent periods, the lease payments received by the lessor are separated into interest income and principal repayments of the note receivable.

Lease contracts that do not qualify as an effective sale for accounting purposes are termed operating leases. The lessor then reports rental income throughout the lease term and continues to depreciate the cost of the asset.

Key Analysis Questions

Accounting can become complex when a seller retains a residual value in a product or service. Managers are then required to determine whether the asset has been sold and, if so, how to value the residual owned by the seller. For financial analysts, the following questions are likely to arise:

- What are the residual risks borne by the seller? What factors affect these risks? Does the seller have control over these risks?
- What processes does the seller have in place to manage its residual risks? How effective are these processes?
- What have been the historical outcomes of risks borne by the seller relative to forecasts? If these risks have been poorly managed, where on the financial statements are they reflected? Have historical forecasts of the seller's residual risks systematically over- or understated subsequent realizations?
- What has been the seller's experience in managing its residual risks relative to other firms in its industry? If its historical experience has been different from its industry peers, does it follow a different strategy, or target different customers?
- If the firm does not have a strong track record in managing and forecasting residual risks, is it appropriate to view the transaction as a sale? Accounting rules typically require that a transaction either be recorded as a sale or that revenue be deferred. As a result, among the transactions that meet the requirements for current revenue recognition, some are closer to satisfying the minimum requirements than others. Where on this continuum do the transactions being analyzed lie?

Challenge Four: Credit-Worthiness of Customer

Many firms provide credit to their customers. In most instances, customers are expected to pay for the product or service within thirty days of billing. However, for some businesses, sellers provide long-term financing.

Transactions where there are significant credit risks for the seller raise a number of questions for financial statement users. Does the seller have a system in place to evaluate and manage credit risks of customers? Has the firm done a good job of managing credit risk in the past? Is past success in managing credit risk likely to be a good indicator of the future?

Credit risk can be particularly difficult to analyze if (a) customers have experienced a change in circumstances, (b) sales growth has led to a change in the mix of a firm's customers, or (c) the seller has an innovative strategy that makes it difficult to use historical data to assess credit risk. The following two transactions illustrate these points and the challenges of assessing collectibility.

EXAMPLE: REAL ESTATE TRANSACTIONS. Real estate companies frequently provide long-term financing for their customers. A customer may put down 5 percent of the full purchase price of a property and arrange a mortgage with the seller to cover the remaining 95 percent. If the buyer is unable to pay off the loan, the seller can reclaim possession of the property, resell it, and use the proceeds to cover the remaining balance on the mortgage. This transaction raises several questions about collectibility. First, is the initial 5 percent payment refundable? If so, the buyer can potentially renege on the contract with no penalty. Second, is the owner's equity in the property sufficient to provide some assurance to the seller that the buyer is likely to be committed to meeting the payments, particularly if the property value subsequently declines? For example, if the property in the above transaction declines in value by 20 percent, a buyer with only a 5 percent equity stake has a strong incentive to return the property to the seller. The buyer then loses the equity investment, but avoids further losses that would arise from continuing to make mortgage payments.

Accounting standards attempt to capture the above risks. Under SFAS 66, retail land sales can be recognized as revenue only if all of the following conditions are met:

1. The buyer signs a legally binding contract for the land purchase and pays a non-refundable down payment of 10 percent or more of the sales price.
2. The seller's collection experience on similar sales indicates that at least 90 percent of the receivables will be collected in full. A down payment of 20 percent or more is an acceptable substitute for this test.
3. The seller's receivable for the property is not subject to subordination of new loans.
4. The seller is not obliged to construct amenities or other facilities or to make other improvements to the property.

If a real estate contract satisfies the above requirements for recognizing a property sale, the seller can recognize the full price of the land as revenue. Otherwise, accounting rules require that revenue be recognized on a cash basis.

EXAMPLE: SUBPRIME LENDING. The subprime lending industry is a relatively recent phenomenon. Subprime lenders provide consumer credit to individuals who have incomplete or poor credit records and who are unable to obtain financing from traditional bank financing. Subprime lenders thus provide consumer credit through credit cards, automobile financing, and home equity loans. Yields on these loans and service fees tend to be high.

Of course, there are significant risks associated with these loans, notably a higher default rate than traditional lending. To manage these risks, subprime lenders attempt to stratify the additional default risk inherent in the loans and to price them accordingly.

Key Analysis Questions

Credit risks require management to estimate the effect of default risks, raising the following questions for financial analysts:

- What is the seller's business strategy and how does that strategy affect its ability to manage credit risks? For example, does the firm use low-cost financing as a form of marketing for its product? Alternatively, does it offer low prices on its product and make money on financing? What are the risks of these different strategies?
- Do the accounting rules governing whether a transaction is a sale factor in all of the risks faced by the seller? Are there risks that are not considered in accounting rules? If so, how serious are these risks? How do firms manage these risks?
- Does the seller have a credit process in place to help manage default risk? This process will access customers' credit histories, job security, assets, and other liabilities. From this information, the seller can adequately assess the risks and price the loan accordingly.
- Is the estimated provision for doubtful debts consistent with historical data and with industry norms? If the provision appears to be lower than these norms, what factors explain the differences? For example, has the firm changed its strategy, or does it follow a different strategy from other firms in the industry, making these norms less reliable benchmarks? Is it growing rapidly and selling to different types of customers than historically? If so, are these new customers likely to be more or less risky than the current portfolio mix?

Challenge Five: Refunds for Dissatisfied Customers

Questions about cash collection can also arise when firms provide open-ended offers to refund returned merchandise from dissatisfied customers. Such is frequently the case for magazine and textbook publishers. It can also arise for some manufacturers and retailers.

For example, L. L. Bean, the mail-order clothing retailer, provides its customers the following assurance: "Our products are guaranteed to give 100% satisfaction in every way. Return anything purchased from us at any time if it proves otherwise. We will replace it, refund your purchase price or credit your credit card. We do not want you to have anything from L. L. Bean that is not completely satisfactory." This assurance, of course, creates a risk for the company if it fails to deliver on its customer satisfaction pledge.

How do firms manage return risks? The most straightforward way is to have a product or service that is attractive to customers. As a result, these types of offers tend to make sense only for firms that follow a differentiated strategy, offering their customers a high-quality product or service at full price. However, even for these firms, it can be difficult to manage the risks associated with returns. For example, consider L. L. Bean's risks from returns by customers who bought incorrectly sized clothing. The company can provide clear directions to customers on how to estimate their sizes, but it cannot eliminate these types of returns. At best, the customer will want to replace the clothing for the correct size. However, if the desired size is out of stock, the company has to refund the purchase price. Given the seasonal nature of the clothing industry, this type of risk may be largely out of L. L. Bean's control.

How are customer dissatisfaction and return risks reflected in financial reporting? Typically, the sale is recognized at point of delivery of the product or service, and at the end of the period an estimate is made for the cost of returns, requiring the exercise of management judgment. However, SFAS 48 recognizes that this approach only works if "the amount of future returns can be reasonably estimated." If such is not the case, the seller cannot recognize revenues until the return privilege has effectively expired.

Key Analysis Questions

Businesses where there are significant risks of customer returns and refunds raise a number of questions for financial analysts.

- How does the selling firm position its business relative to competitors and how does that strategy relate to its ability to manage return risks?
- Does the seller have a process in place to help manage return risk? This process could include customer satisfaction and/or product/service quality programs to limit the likelihood of returns.
- Is the estimated allowance for returns consistent with historical data and with industry norms? If the allowance is lower than these norms, what factors explain the differences? For example, has the firm changed its strategy, or does it follow a different strategy from other firms in the industry, making these norms less reliable benchmarks? Is it growing rapidly and selling to different types of customers than historically? Has there been any change in product quality or customer satisfaction with the firm's product or service that is likely to impact returns?

SUMMARY

In this chapter, we overviewed the revenue recognition rule and discussed its implications for analysis of revenues by financial statement users. Under the rule, revenues can be recognized only if (1) the seller has provided all, or substantially all, of the goods or services to be delivered to the customer, and (2) the customer has paid cash or is expected to pay cash with reasonable certainty.

For certain types of transactions, implementing this rule can be challenging. For example, it can be difficult to assess whether revenues have been earned if:

1. Customers pay for a product or service prior to its delivery, as in the case of magazine subscriptions, property and casualty insurance policies, and service contracts.
2. Products or services are provided over multiple years, as is the case for long-term construction contracts and frequent flyer awards.
3. Products or services are sold with some residual rights retained by the seller, reflected in sales of receivables with recourse and lease agreements.
4. Sellers of products or services provide their customers with long-term financing, as in the case of some real estate developers.
5. Sellers provide an open-ended offer to refund dissatisfied customers.

In general, corporate managers of the selling firm are likely to have the best information on whether revenue has been earned and cash is likely to be received from the customer. Revenues (net of estimates of costs for default and returns) then potentially provide users of financial statements with information on managers' assessment of these risks. However, the value of this information has to be tempered by management's incentive to report favorable information on its stewardship of the firm. This provides a role for analysis of revenues. Such analysis involves independently assessing whether revenues have been earned, and whether cash is likely to be collected.

DISCUSSION QUESTIONS

1. A customer pays $1,000 in advance for a service agreement. What are the financial statement effects of this transaction if (a) revenue is recognized at receipt of cash, and (b) revenue is recognized at delivery of the product? What forecasts, if any, do you have to make to complete the recording of this transaction? What factors would determine which of these two approaches is appropriate? As a financial analyst, what questions would you raise with the firm's CFO?
2. A firm signs a long-term contract to construct a building for $10,000,000. The building is to be completed in two years at a cost of $8,000,000. At the end of the first year, $6,000,000 of costs has been incurred. Under the contract terms, the customer pays for the building during the first year. What are the financial statement effects of this transaction if (a) revenue is recognized under the completed contract method, and (b) revenue is recognized using the percentage of completion method? What fore-

casts, if any, do you have to make to complete the recording of this transaction? What factors would determine which of these two approaches is appropriate? As a financial analyst, what questions would you raise with the firm's CFO?

3. United Airlines sells a round-trip ticket for a flight from Boston to London for $750. The customer also receives 5,000 award miles, equivalent to 20 percent of the miles required for a free domestic flight. United expects 20 percent of its customers to redeem awards for future air travel, and the average forgone revenues from these flights to be $400 per passenger. Finally, United estimates that the incremental costs associated with redemption of frequent flyer awards amount to $100 per passenger. What are the financial statement effects of this transaction if (a) the incremental cost approach is used, and (b) revenue is recognized using the deferred revenue approach? What forecasts, if any, do you have to make to complete the recording of this transaction? What factors would determine which of these two approaches is appropriate? As a financial analyst, what questions would you raise with the firm's CFO?

4. A firm sells $200,000 of interest-bearing two-year notes receivable to a bank, with recourse, for $208,978. The interest rate on the notes is 10 percent, and the bank's effective interest rate is 7.5 percent. What are the financial statement effects of this transaction if (a) the receivable is viewed as sold, and (b) the receivable is viewed as providing collateral for a bank loan? What forecasts, if any, do you have to make to complete the recording of this transaction? What factors would determine which of these two approaches is appropriate? As a financial analyst, what questions would you raise with the firm's CFO?

5. Consider a lessor that sells the right to use a depreciable asset, with a book value of $1,500, to a customer for two years for $1,000 per year, payable at the beginning of the year. At the end of the lease term, the rights to the asset revert to the seller. Assuming a discount rate of 10 percent, the present value of the lease payments is $1,909. What are the financial statement effects of this transaction if (a) revenue is recognized under the sales-type lease approach, and (b) revenue is recognized using the operating lease method? What forecasts, if any, do you have to make to complete the recording of this transaction? What factors would determine which of these two approaches is appropriate? As a financial analyst, what questions would you raise with the firm's CFO?

6. A real estate developer sells land parcels to its customers and provides them with financing. In 2000, the first year of operation, the firm signed new land sale contracts for $25,000,000. This land had originally been acquired for $20,000,000, implying a gross margin of 20 percent. Customer receipts for the year were $8,000,000 for deposits on property sold and $1,000,000 in principal repayments under financing agreements with customers. What are the financial statement effects of this transaction if (a) revenue is recognized at sale, and (b) revenue is recognized when cash is received? What forecasts, if any, do you have to make to complete the recording of this transaction? What factors would determine which of these two approaches is appropriate? As a financial analyst, what questions would you raise with the firm's CFO?

7. A publishing company delivers 130,000 copies of a new textbook to bookstores during the year. The bookstores pay the publisher $10 per book, but have the right to be reimbursed for any books returned within one year. The cost of the books to the publisher is $5 per book. What are the financial statement effects of this transaction if (a) revenue is recognized at sale, and (b) revenue is recognized when return rights expire? What forecasts, if any, do you have to make to complete the recording of this transaction? What factors would determine which of these two approaches is appropriate? As a financial analyst, what questions would you raise with the firm's CFO?

In August 1990 Lawrence J. Ellison, CEO of Oracle Systems Corporation, was facing increasing pressure from analysts about the method the company used to recognize revenue in its financial reports. Analysts' major concerns were clearly articulated by a senior technology analyst at Hambrecht & Quist, Inc. in San Francisco:

> *Under Oracle's current set of accounting rules, Oracle can recognize any revenue they believe will be shipped within the next twelve months. . . . Many other software firms have moved to booking only the revenue that has been shipped.*

Given its aggressive revenue-recognition policy and relatively high amount of accounts receivable, many analysts argued that Oracle's stock was a risky buy. As a result, the company's stock price had plummeted from a high of $56 in March to around $27 in mid-August. This poor stock performance concerned Larry Ellison for two reasons. First, he worried that the firm might become a takeover candidate, and second that the low price made it expensive for the firm to raise new equity capital to finance its future growth.

ORACLE'S BUSINESS AND PERFORMANCE

Since its formation in California in June 1977, Oracle Systems Corporation has grown rapidly to become the world's largest supplier of database management software. Its principal product is the ORACLE relational database management system, which runs on a broad range of computers, including mainframes, minicomputers, microcomputers, and personal computers. The company also develops and distributes a wide array of products to interface with its database system, including applications in financial reporting, manufacturing management, computer aided systems engineering, computer network communications, and office automation. Finally, Oracle offers extensive maintenance, consulting, training, and systems integration services to support its products.

Oracle's leadership in developing software for database management has enabled it to achieve impressive financial growth. As reported in Exhibit 1, the company's sales grew from $282 million in 1988 to $971 million two years later. Larry Ellison was proud of this rapid growth and committed to its continuance. He often referred to Genghis Khan as his inspiration in crushing competitors and achieving growth.

This case was prepared for class discussion by Cholthicha Srivisal and Paul M. Healy of the MIT Sloan School of Management.

The primary factors underlying Oracle's strong performance have been its successes in R&D and its committed sales force. The firm's R&D triumphs are proudly noted in the 1990 annual report:

> In 1979, we delivered ORACLE, the world's first relational database management system and the first product based on SQL. In 1983, ORACLE was the first database management system to run on mainframes, minicomputers, and PCs. In 1986, ORACLE was the first database management system with distributed capability, making access to data on a network of computers as easy as access on a single computer.
>
> We continued our tradition of technology leadership in 1990, with three key achievements in the area of client-server computing. First, we delivered software that allows client programs to automatically adapt to the different graphical user interfaces on PCs, Macintoshes, and workstations. Second, we delivered our complete family of accounting applications running as client programs networked to an ORACLE database server. Third, the ORACLE database server set performance records of over 400 transactions per second on mainframes, 200 transactions per second on minicomputers, and 20 transactions per second on PCs.

Oracle's sales force has also been responsible for its success. The sales force is compensated on the basis of sales, giving it a strong incentive to aggressively court large corporate customers. In some cases salespeople even have been known to offer extended payment terms to a potentially valuable customer to close a sale.

Oracle's growth slowed in early 1990. In March the firm announced a 54 percent jump in quarterly revenues (relative to 1989's results)—but only a 1 percent rise in earnings (see Exhibit 2 for quarterly results for 1989 and 1990). Management explained that several factors contributed to this poor performance. First, the company had recently redrawn its sales territories and, as a result, for several months salespeople had become unsure of their new responsibilities, leaving some customers dissatisfied. Second, there were problems with a number of new products, such as Oracle Financials, which were released before all major bugs could be fixed. However, the stock market was unimpressed by these explanations, and the firm's stock price dropped by 31 percent with the earnings announcement.

REVENUE RECOGNITION

The deterioration in its financial performance prompted analysts to question Oracle's method of recognizing revenues. For example, one analyst commented:

> Oracle's accounting practices might have played a role in the low net income results. The top line went up over 50%, though the net bottom line did not do so well, because Oracle's running more cash than it should be as a result of financial mismanagement. The company's aggressive revenue-recognition policy and relatively high amount of accounts receivables make the stock risky.

Oracle Systems Corporation

Oracle's major revenues come from licensing software products to end users, and from sublicensing agreements with original equipment manufacturers (OEMs) and software value-added relicensors (VARs). Initial license fees for the ORACLE database management system range from $199 to over $5,500 on micro- and personal computers, and from $5,100 to approximately $342,000 on mini- and mainframe computers. License fees for Oracle Financial and Oracle Government Financial products range from $20,000 to $513,000, depending on the platform and number of users. A customer may obtain additional licenses at the same site at a discount. Oracle recognizes revenues from these licenses when a contract has been signed with a financially sound customer, even though shipment of products has not occurred.

OEM agreements are negotiated on a case-by-case basis. However, under a typical contract Oracle receives an initial nonrefundable fee (payable either upon signing the contract or within 30 days of signing) and sublicense fees based on the number of copies distributed. Under VAR agreements the company charges a development license fee on top of the initial nonrefundable fee, and it receives sublicense fees based on the number of copies distributed. Sublicense fees are usually a percentage of Oracle's list price. The initial nonrefundable payments and development license fees under these arrangements are recorded as revenue when the contracts are signed. Sublicense fees are recorded when they are received from the OEM or VAR.

Oracle also receives revenues from maintenance agreements under which it provides technical support and telephone consultation on the use of the products and problem resolution, system updates for software products, and user documentation. Maintenance fees generally run for one year and are payable at the end of the maintenance period. They range from 7.5 percent to 22 percent of the current list price of the appropriate license. These fees are recorded as unearned revenue when the maintenance contract is signed and are reflected as revenue ratably over the contract period.

The major questions about Oracle's revenue recognition concern the way the firm recognizes revenues on license fees. There is no currently accepted standard for accounting for these types of revenues.[1] However, Oracle tends to be one of the more aggressive reporters. The firm's days receivable exceeds 160 days, substantially higher than the average of 62 days receivable for other software developers (see Exhibit 3 for a summary of days receivable for other major software developers in 1989 and 1990). As a result, some analysts argue that the firm should recognize revenue when software is delivered rather than when a contract is signed, consistent with the accounting treatment for the sale of products. In addition, the collectibility of license fees is considered questionable by some analysts, who have urged the firm to recognize revenue only when there is a reasonable basis for estimating the degree of collectibility of a receivable. Estimates by Oracle's controller indicate that if Oracle were to change to a more conservative revenue recognition policy, the firm's days receivable would fall to about 120 days.

---

1. *The Financial Accounting Standards Board was considering the issue of revenue recognition for software developers at this time. It was widely expected that the Board would make a pronouncement on the topic early in 1991.*

MANAGEMENT'S CONCERNS

Oracle's management was concerned about analysts' opinions and the downturn in the firm's stock. The company had lost credibility with investors and customers due to its recent poor performance and its controversial accounting policies.

One of the items on the agenda at the upcoming board meeting was to consider proposals for changing the firm's revenue recognition method and for dealing with its communication challenge. Ellison knew that his opinion on this question would be influential. As he saw it, the company had three alternatives. One was to modify the recognition of license fees so that revenue would be recognized only when substantially all the company's contractual obligations had been performed. However, he worried that such a change would have a negative impact on the firm's bottom line and further depress the stock price. A second possibility was to wait until the FASB announced its position on software revenue recognition before making any changes. Finally, the company could make no change and vigorously defend its current accounting method. Ellison carefully considered which alternative made the most sense for the firm.

QUESTIONS

1. What factors might have led analysts to question Oracle Systems' method of revenue recognition in mid-1990? Are these legitimate concerns?
2. Estimate the earnings impact for Oracle from recognizing revenue at delivery, rather than when a contract is signed.
3. What accounting or communication changes would you recommend to Oracle's Board of Directors?

EXHIBIT 1
Oracle Systems Corporation – Consolidated Financial Statements

CONSOLIDATED BALANCE SHEETS
As of May 31, 1990 and 1989 (in $000, except per share data)

	1990	1989
ASSETS		
CURRENT ASSETS:		
Cash and cash equivalents	$ 44,848	$ 44,893
Short-term investments	4,980	4,500
Receivables		
Trade, net of allowance for doubtful accounts of $28,445 in 1990 and $16,829 in 1989	468,071	261,989
Other	28,899	16,175
Prepaid expenses and supplies	22,459	9,376
Total current assets	569,257	336,933
PROPERTY, net	171,945	94,455
COMPUTER SOFTWARE DEVELOPMENT COSTS, net of accumulated amortization of $14,365 in 1990 and $6,180 in 1989	33,396	13,942
OTHER ASSETS	12,649	14,879
TOTAL ASSETS	$787,247	$460,209
LIABILITIES AND STOCKHOLDERS' EQUITY		
CURRENT LIABILITIES:		
Notes payable to banks	$ 31,236	$ 9,747
Current maturities of long-term debt	11,265	13,587
Accounts payable	64,922	51,582
Income taxes payable	18,254	14,836
Accrued compensation and related benefits	61,164	39,063
Customer advances and unearned revenues	42,121	15,403
Other accrued liabilities	32,417	23,400
Sales tax payable	22,193	8,608
Deferred income taxes	—	2,107
Total current liabilities	283,572	178,333
LONG-TERM DEBT	89,129	33,506
OTHER LONG-TERM LIABILITIES	4,936	5,702
DEFERRED INCOME TAXES	22,025	12,114
STOCKHOLDERS' EQUITY:		
Common stock, $.01 par value-authorized, 200,000,000 shares; outstanding: 131,138,302 shares in 1990 and 126,933,288 shares in 1989	388	346
Additional paid-in capital	118,715	84,931
Retained earnings	267,475	150,065
Accumulated foreign currency translation adjustments	1,007	(4,788)
Total stockholders' equity	387,585	230,554
TOTAL LIABILITIES AND STOCKHOLDERS' EQUITY	$787,247	$460,209

Oracle Systems Corporation

CONSOLIDATED STATEMENTS OF INCOME
For the Years Ended May 31, 1990 to 1988 (in $000, except per share data)

	1990	1989	1988
REVENUES			
Licenses	$689,898	$417,825	$205,435
Services	280,946	165,848	76,678
Total revenues	970,844	583,673	282,113
OPERATING EXPENSES			
Sales and marketing	465,074	272,812	124,148
Cost of services	160,426	100,987	51,241
Research and development	88,291	52,570	25,708
General and administrative	67,258	34,344	17,121
Total operating expenses	781,049	460,713	218,218
OPERATING INCOME	189,795	122,960	63,895
OTHER INCOME (EXPENSE):			
Interest income	3,772	2,724	2,472
Interest expense	(12,096)	(4,318)	(1,540)
Other income (expense)	(8,811)	(1,121)	152
Total other income (expense)	(17,135)	(2,715)	1,084
INCOME BEFORE PROVISION FOR INCOME TAXES	172,660	120,245	64,979
PROVISION FOR INCOME TAXES	55,250	38,479	22,093
NET INCOME	$117,410	$81,766	$42,886
EARNINGS PER SHARE	$ .86	$ .61	$ .32
NUMBER OF COMMON AND COMMON EQUIVALENT SHARES OUTSTANDING	136,826	135,066	132,950

Oracle Systems Corporation

Oracle Systems Corporation

CONSOLIDATED STATEMENTS OF CASH FLOWS
For the Years Ended May 31, 1990 to 1988 (in $000)

	1990	1989	1988
CASH FLOWS FROM OPERATING ACTIVITIES			
Net income	$117,410	$ 81,766	$ 42,886
Adjustments to reconcile net income to net cash provided by operating activities:			
Depreciation and amortization	44,078	23,156	12,973
Provision for doubtful accounts	16,625	9,211	4,839
Increase in receivables	(227,046)	(149,900)	(74,777)
Increase in prepaid expenses & supplies	(12,834)	(5,684)	(1,458)
Increase in accounts payable	12,491	25,236	12,854
Increase income taxes payable	3,002	6,821	7,940
Increase in other accrued liabilities	42,166	38,057	21,420
Increase in customer advances and unearned revenues	25,786	6,496	5,682
Increase (decrease) in deferred taxes	7,728	(10,857)	8,170
Increase (decrease) in other non-current liabilities	(766)	1,938	—
Net cash provided by operating activities	28,640	26,240	40,529
CASH FLOWS FROM INVESTING ACTIVITIES			
Increase in short-term investments	(480)	2,998	(7,498)
Capital expenditures	(89,275)	(68,428)	(30,959)
Capitalization of computer software development costs	(27,639)	(10,526)	(4,447)
Increase in other assets	(1,116)	(2,084)	(481)
Purchase of a business	—	(6,650)	—
Net cash used for investing activities	(118,510)	(84,690)	(43,385)
CASH FLOWS FROM FINANCING ACTIVITIES			
Notes payable to banks	21,156	10,305	(169)
Proceeds from issuance of long-term debt	68,530	37,539	1,445
Payments of long-term debt	(34,239)	(6,205)	(3,638)
Proceeds from common stock issued	18,460	11,060	4,712
Tax benefits from stock options	15,366	10,593	3,992
Net cash provided by financing activities	89,273	63,292	6,342
EFFECT OF EXCHANGE RATE CHANGES ON CASH	552	(1,061)	69
NET INCREASE (DECREASE) IN CASH	**(45)**	**3,781**	3,555
CASH: BEGINNING OF YEAR	44,893	41,112	37,557
CASH: END OF YEAR	$44,848	$44,893	$41,112

EXCERPTS FROM NOTES TO CONSOLIDATED FINANCIAL STATEMENTS

1. Organization and Significant Accounting Policies

Organization

Oracle Systems Corporation (the Company) develops and markets computer software products used for database management, applications development, decision support, programmer tools, computer network communication, end user applications, and office automation. The Company offers maintenance, consulting, and training services in support of its clients' use of its software products.

Basis of Financial Statements

The consolidated financial statements include the Company and its subsidiaries. All transactions and balances between the companies are eliminated.

Business Combination

In November 1988, the Company's subsidiary, Oracle Complex Systems Corporation, acquired all of the outstanding shares of Falcon Systems, Inc., a systems integrator, for $13,714,000 in cash and $4,600,000 in notes which become due November 1, 1991. The acquisition was accounted for as a purchase and the excess of the cost over the fair value of assets acquired was $5,648,000, which is being amortized over 5 years on a straight-line method. Pro forma results of operations, assuming the acquisition had taken place June 1, 1987, would not differ materially from the Company's actual results of operations.

Software Development Costs

Effective June 1, 1986, the Company began capitalizing internally generated software development costs in compliance with Statement of Financial Accounting Standards No. 86, "Accounting for the Costs of Computer Software to be Sold, Leased or Otherwise Marketed." Capitalization of computer software development costs begins upon the establishment of technological feasibility for the product. Capitalized software development costs amounted to $27,639,000, $10,526,000, and $4,447,000 in fiscal 1990, 1989, and 1988, respectively.

Amortization of capitalized computer software development costs begins when the products are available for general release to customers, and is computed product by product as the greater of: (a) the ratio of current gross revenues for a product to the total of current and anticipated future gross revenues for the product, or (b) the straight-line method over the remaining estimated economic life of the product. Currently, estimated economic lives of 24 months are used in the calculation of amortization of these capitalized costs. Amortization amounted to $8,185,000, $3,504,000, and $2,345,000 for fiscal years ended May 31, 1990, 1989, and 1988, respectively, and is included in sales and marketing expenses.

Statements of Cash Flows

The Company paid income taxes in the amount of $33,731,000, $29,006,000, and $711,000 and interest expense of $8,026,000, $4,274,000 and $1,540,000 during the fiscal years ended 1990, 1989, and 1988, respectively. The Company purchased equipment under capital lease obligations in the amount of $17,616,000, $4,692,000, and $4,108,000 in fiscal 1990, 1989 and 1988, respectively.

Oracle Systems Corporation

Revenue Recognition

The Company generates several types of revenue including the following:

License and Sublicense fees. The Company licenses ORACLE products to end users under license agreements. The Company also has entered into agreements whereby the Company licenses Oracle products and receives license and sublicense fees from original equipment manufacturers (OEMs) and software value-added relicensors (VARs). The minimum amount of license and sublicense fees specified in the agreements is recognized either upon shipment of the product or at the time such agreements are effective (which in most instances is the date of the agreement) if the customer is creditworthy and the terms of the agreement are such that the amounts are due within one year and are nonrefundable, and the agreements are noncancellable. The Company recognizes revenue at such time as it has substantially performed all of its contractual obligations. Additional sublicense fees are subsequently recognized as revenue at the time such fees are reported to the Company by the OEMs and VARs.

Maintenance Agreements. Maintenance agreements generally call for the Company to provide technical support and certain systems updates to customers. Revenue related to providing technical support is recognized proportionately over the maintenance period, which in most instances is one year, while the revenue related to systems updates is recognized at the beginning of each maintenance period.

Consulting, Training, and Other Services. The Company provides consulting services to its customers; revenue from such services is generally recognized under the percentage of completion method.

2. Short-Term Debt

Short term debt (in $000) consists of:	Year Ended May 31	
	1990	1989
Unsecured revolving lines of credit	$18,198	$5,955
Other	13,038	3,792
Total	$31,236	$9,747

At May 31, 1990, the Company had short-term unsecured revolving lines of credit with two banks providing for borrowings aggregating $42,000,000, of which $18,198,000 was outstanding. These lines expire in September 1990 ($2,000,000), November 1990 ($10,000,000), and January 1991 ($30,000,000). Interest on these borrowings is based on varying rates pegged to the banks' prime rate, cost of funds, or LIBOR. The Company also had other unsecured short-term indebtedness to banks of $13,038,000 at May 31, 1990, payable upon demand. The average interest rate on short-term borrowings was 9.4% at May 31, 1990.

The Company is required to maintain certain financial ratios under the line of credit agreements. The Company was in compliance with these financial covenants at May 31, 1990.

3. Long-Term Debt

At May 31, 1990, the Company had long-term unsecured revolving lines of credit with four banks providing for borrowings aggregating $135,000,000, of which $61,460,000 was outstanding. Of the $61,460,000 outstanding, $58,210,000 was classified as long-term debt and $3,250,000 was classified as current maturities of long-term debt. These lines of credit expire in December 1991 ($60,000,000), March 1992 ($15,000,000), July 1992 ($20,000,000), January 1991 ($20,000,000), and March 1991 ($20,000,000). The Company has the option to convert $20,000,000 of its line expiring in January of 1991 and $8,000,000 of that expiring in March of 1991 into two term loans which would mature in 1993. Interest on these borrowings vary based on the banks' cost of funds rates. At May 31, 1990 the interest rate on outstanding domestic and foreign currency borrowings ranged from 8.6% to 15.6%. The aggregate amount available under these lines of credit at May 31, 1990 was $73,540,000.

Under the line-of-credit agreements, the Company is required to maintain certain financial ratios. At May 31, 1990 the Company was in compliance with these financial covenants.

Subsequent to May 31, 1990, the Company obtained two additional unsecured revolving lines of credit, one which expires May 1992 ($20,000,000) and one which expires January 1991 ($20,000,000).

4. Stockholders' Equity

Stock Option Plan
The Company's stock option plan provides for the issuance of incentives stock options to employees of the Company and nonqualified options to employees, directors, consultants, and independent contractors of the Company. Under the terms of this plan, options to purchase up to 23,335,624 shares of Common Stock may be granted at not less than fair market value, are immediately exercisable, become vested as established by the Board (generally ratably over four to five years), and generally expire ten years from the date of grant. The Company has the right to repurchase shares issued upon the exercise of unvested options at the exercise price paid by the stockholder should the stockholder leave the Company prior to the scheduled vesting date. At May 31, 1990, 271,300 shares of Common Stock outstanding were subject to such repurchase rights. Options to purchase 5,005,720 common shares were vested at May 31, 1990.

Non-Plan Options
In addition to the above option plan, nonqualified stock options to purchase a total of 5,712,000 common shares have been granted to employees and directors of the Company. These options were granted at the fair market value as determined by the Board of Directors, became exercisable immediately, vest either immediately (for directors) or ratably over a period of up to five years (for individuals other than directors) and generally expire ten years from the date of grant. The Company has the right to repurchase shares issued upon the exercise of unvested options at the exercise price paid by the stockholder should the stockholder leave the Company prior to the scheduled vesting date. Options to purchase 160,000 common shares were vested as of May 31, 1990.

As of May 31, 1990, the Company had reserved 11,135,194 shares of Common Stock for exercise of options.

Stock Purchase Plan

In October 1987, the Company adopted an Employee Stock Purchase Plan and reserved 8,000,000 shares of Common Stock for issuance thereunder. Under this plan, the Company's employees may purchase shares of Common Stock at a price per share that is 85% of the lesser of the fair market value as of the beginning or the end of the semi-annual option period. Through May 31, 1990, 2,326,772 shares have been issued and 5,673,228 shares are reserved for future issuances under this plan.

REPORT OF INDEPENDENT PUBLIC ACCOUNTANTS

To Oracle Systems Corporation:

We have audited the accompanying consolidated balance sheets of Oracle Systems Corporation (a Delaware corporation) and subsidiaries as of May 31, 1990 and 1989 and the related consolidated statements of income, stockholders' equity, and cash flows for each of the three years in the period ended May 31, 1990. These financial statements are the responsibility of the company's management. Our responsibility is to express an opinion on these financial statements based on our audits. We conducted our audits in accordance with generally accepted auditing standards. Those standards require that we plan and perform the audit to obtain reasonable assurance about whether the financial statements are free of material misstatement. An audit includes examining, on a test basis, evidence supporting the amounts and disclosures in the financial statements. An audit also includes assessing the accounting principles used and significant estimates made by management, as well as evaluating the overall financial statement presentation. We believe that our audits provide a reasonable basis for our opinion.

In our opinion, the financial statements referred to above present fairly, in all material respects, the financial position of Oracle Systems Corporation and subsidiaries as of May 31, 1990 and 1989 and the results of their operations and their cash flows for each of the three years in the period ended May 31, 1990, in conformity with generally accepted accounting principles.

Our audits were made for the purpose of forming an opinion on the basic financial statements taken as a whole. The schedules listed under Item 14(a)2. are presented for purposes of complying with the Securities and Exchange Commission's rules and are not part of the basic financial statements. These schedules have been subjected to the auditing procedures applied in the audit of the basic financial statements and, in our opinion, fairly state in all material respects the financial data required to be set forth therein in relation to the basic financial statements taken as a whole

ARTHUR ANDERSEN & CO.
SAN JOSE, CALIFORNIA
JULY 9, 1990

EXHIBIT 2

Oracle Systems Corporation – Review of Quarterly Results in Fiscal 1989 and 1990 (in $000 except per share data)

	Fiscal 1990 Quarter Ended			
	Aug. 31 1989	Nov. 30 1989	Feb. 28 1990	May 31 1990
Revenues	$175,490	$209,023	$236,165	$350,166
Net income	11,679	28,491	24,282	52,958
Earnings per share[a]	$ .09	$ .21	$ .18	$ .39

	Fiscal 1989 Quarter Ended			
	Aug. 31 1988	Nov. 30 1988	Feb. 28 1989	May 31 1989
Revenues	$90,639	$123,745	$153,354	$215,935
Net income	7,067	17,189	23,964	33,546
Earnings per share[a]	$ .05	$ .13	$ .18	$ .25

a. Adjusted to reflect the two-for-one stock splits in the third quarter of fiscal 1988 and the first quarter of fiscal 1990.

EXHIBIT 3

Days Receivable for Selected Companies in the Software Industry for 1989–90

Company	1989	1990
Borland International Corp.	49	45
Lotus Development Corp.	64	64
Microsoft Corp.	51	56
Novell Corp.	85	81
Average	62	62

Expense Analysis

Expenses are the economic resources that have been consumed or have declined in value. Firms incur expenses to acquire or produce products or services that are sold. In addition, expenses are incurred for marketing (including advertising costs, sales force salaries and commissions, and salaries of marketing management), for managing the firm (salaries of the head office staff and depreciation on headquarters), for the cost of any debt financing, for taxes, and for realized and unrealized declines in asset values.

Analysis of expenses focuses on assessing when expenses should be recognized in the financial statements. Should they be recognized when the resources are used? Should they be recognized when the firm is billed for resources? Should they be recognized when payment for resources is made? Or should they be reported when the revenues generated from using the resources are recognized?

The key principles in accounting that dictate how expenses are recorded are matching and conservatism. Under these principles, resources directly associated with revenues are recorded in the same period as revenues are recognized. Resources that are more closely associated with a specific period are recorded in that period. Finally, all other costs are recognized as an expense when they are incurred or can be reasonably estimated.

Challenges in recognizing expenses arise when resources provide benefits over multiple periods, when resources have been consumed but there is uncertainty about the timing and amount of payment, when the value of resources consumed is difficult to define, and when resources have declined in value. These challenges give rise to opportunities for financial analysis of expenses.

MATCHING AND CONSERVATISM

Cash outlays are a poor indicator of resource use when a firm acquires (and pays for) resources but has yet to use them, or when a firm uses resources but has yet to pay for them. Indeed, recognizing resource use at the outlay of cash can be misleading and can provide perverse incentives for managers to improve reported performance by deferring payments for resources. This incentive to delay making cash outlays is likely to be magnified for big-ticket items, such as purchases of assets that provide benefits for multiple periods.

Figure 7-1 Criteria for Recognizing Expenses and Implementation Challenges

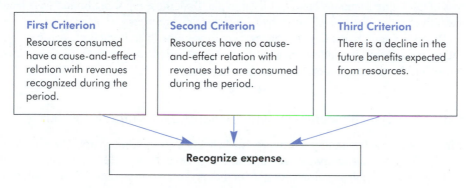

First Criterion	Second Criterion	Third Criterion
Resources consumed have a cause-and-effect relation with revenues recognized during the period.	Resources have no cause-and-effect relation with revenues but are consumed during the period.	There is a decline in the future benefits expected from resources.

Recognize expense.

Challenging Transactions
1. Resources provide benefits over multiple periods.
2. Resources are consumed, but the timing and amount of future payments is uncertain.
3. The value of resources consumed is difficult to define.
4. Unused resources have declined in value.

Accrual accounting relies on the matching and conservatism principles to determine the cost of resources used. As shown in Figure 7-1, these principles classify expenses into three types. First, the matching principle views expenses as the cost of consumed resources that have a cause-and-effect relation with revenues. These include the cost of materials consumed in manufacturing a product or the cost of acquiring merchandise by retailers. Matching therefore makes it easier for financial statement readers to assess whether a firm's products or services are profitable. The cost of resources that have no clear cause-and-effect relation to revenues are recorded as expenses during the period they are consumed. Examples include general administration and marketing costs. Finally, under the conservatism principle, accountants require firms to record expenses when there is a decline in the future benefits expected to be generated by resources, or when it becomes difficult to estimate benefits with reasonable certainty. Write-downs of impaired assets are one such form of expense.

EXPENSE REPORTING CHALLENGES

Four types of resource uses are particularly challenging from a financial reporting viewpoint. These arise when resources have benefits across multiple accounting periods, when resources are consumed but the timing and amount of payment is uncertain, when the value of resources consumed is difficult to define, and when unused resources have declined in value. Considerable management judgment is involved in recording these types of expenses. Managers are likely to have better information on the cost of resources consumed by the firm during the period, but they are also self-interested. Further, accounting rules sometimes require certain outlays to be recorded as an expense, regardless of the future economic benefits they provide. Both these reporting limitations create incentives for analysis of expenses by financial statement users.

Below we analyze the key challenges in implementing the criteria for expense recognition and use specific industries and types of transactions to illustrate the key points. However, the challenges discussed are quite general.

Challenge One: Resources Provide Benefits over Multiple Periods

Many resources acquired by a firm provide benefits over multiple years. These include outlays for plant and equipment, research and development, advertising, and drilling oil and gas wells. A challenge in accounting for these types of transactions is how to allocate the cost of these types of resources over multiple periods. Should it be allocated equally over their useful life? Or should it be recorded conservatively as an expense when it is incurred? The matching principle argues for spreading out the cost of a resource over its expected life if it has a clear and reasonably certain cause-and-effect relation with future revenues. Alternatively, if the cause-and-effect relation is unclear or highly uncertain, the resource cost is recognized as an expense in the period incurred.

To illustrate the issues in reporting for outlays for resources with multi-period benefits, we discuss the financial reporting treatment of fixed asset depreciation, goodwill amortization, research and development outlays, and advertising outlays.

EXAMPLE: FIXED ASSET DEPRECIATION.   Fixed assets include plant, buildings, manufacturing equipment, computer equipment, automobiles, and furnishings, all of which have multi-year lives. There is typically little question that these resources are expected to directly or indirectly help generate future revenues for the firm. Thus, the cause-and-effect relation between outlays for such resources and future revenues is typically reasonably certain.

It is more challenging, however, to assess how the cost of these types of resources should be matched with future revenues. Generally accepted accounting rules require managers to make estimates of the expected useful lives of these assets and their expected salvage values at the end of their lives. These estimates are then used to allocate the cost of the fixed assets over their useful lives in a systematic manner.

Assets' useful lives are determined by the risk of technological obsolescence and physical use. Managers' estimates of these effects are therefore likely to depend on their firms' business strategies and their prior experience in operating, managing, and reselling similar assets. For example, in 1998 Delta Air Lines depreciated new aircraft over 25 years and estimated salvage values at 5 percent of cost. In contrast, Singapore Airlines estimated the life of aircraft at 10 years and salvage values at 20 percent of cost. These estimates partially reflect differences in the two airlines' business strategies. Singapore Airlines targets business travelers who are typically less price conscious and demand reliable service. In contrast, Delta focuses more on economy travelers who are highly price-sensitive and for whom on-time arrival is less critical. As a result, the two airlines follow very different operating strategies for their aircraft. Singapore Airlines replaces older aircraft regularly to maintain a relatively new fleet. This reduces the risk of flight delays for maintenance problems, enabling the company to have high on-time arrival rates. In contrast, Delta holds its aircraft longer, lowering its equipment outlays, but at the cost of increased maintenance and lower on-time arrival rates. These differences in operations are reflected in the depreciation estimates made by the two companies. Of course, there may be other factors that influence management's estimates for the two companies. For example, Delta is likely to face more pressure to report profits for owners since it is 100 percent publicly owned. In contrast, Singapore Airlines is majority owned by the Singapore government.

A variety of depreciation methods are permitted under generally accepted accounting rules. The standard method used for financial reporting in the U.S. is straight-line depreciation, which allocates the depreciable cost (defined as purchase price less estimated salvage value) equally over the asset's estimated useful life. More than 90 percent of all publicly owned firms in the U.S. use this method. Outside the U.S., many companies employ accelerated depreciation, in conformance with their tax reporting method.[1] Accelerated depreciation generates higher depreciation expenses than the straight-line method in the early years of an asset's life, and lower expenses toward the end of its life. A third depreciation method, the units of production method, is used for assets whose lives can be measured in physical units. The depreciation expense for a given year is then the cost of the asset multiplied by the percentage of lifelong physical capacity used during that period. This method is commonly used by natural resource companies to record depreciation on production assets whose useful lives are tied to the resource capacity at a particular mine or well site.

Management uses its judgment in estimating asset lives and salvage values and in selecting depreciation methods. Thus, there is a risk that depreciation expenses reflect management's reporting incentives as well as the economics of the business.

EXAMPLE: GOODWILL AMORTIZATION. As discussed in Chapter 4, when a firm acquires another firm and accounts for the acquisition using purchase accounting, goodwill is recorded. Goodwill represents the premium paid for the target's intangible assets. These assets include brand names, research and development, customer base, superior management, well trained employees, patents, and other sources of superior performance.

For several reasons, the cause-and-effect relation between purchased goodwill resources and future revenues is less obvious than for fixed assets. First, the particular source of the future benefits to be derived from goodwill is less clear than for fixed assets. Second, goodwill can represent any overpayment by the acquirer for the target's business as well as payment for intangibles. As a result of these uncertainties, goodwill amortization policies permitted by standard setters have differed across countries. For example, in the Netherlands goodwill is not amortized against income at all, but is written off against shareholders' equity at the completion of the acquisition. Goodwill is amortized on a straight-line basis over a maximum of forty years in the U.S., five years in Japan, and four years in Germany. In the U.K., goodwill is reported as an asset, but does not have to be amortized at all if it has not been impaired.

The expected value and economic life of goodwill depend on a number of factors. First, they depend on the ability of acquiring management to price the intangible assets of the target appropriately, avoiding overpayment. Second, they depend on acquiring management's ability to integrate the target firm without destroying intangible assets that it purchased, such as superior management, existing customers, or key employees. Finally, the value and expected life depend on the strategy and strategy implementation capabilities of the new firm, which can either leverage or destroy the target firm's intangible assets.[2]

To illustrate, Cooper Industries, a diversified company operating in the electrical, hand-tool, automotive, and energy equipment businesses, acquired Cameron Iron Works, a manufacturer of oil and gas machinery, for $967 million in 1989.[3] Cooper's strategy was to acquire manufacturing businesses, strengthen their management, and improve their reporting and control systems. However, several problems arose with this strategy and its implementation at Cameron. First, Cooper's expertise was in understanding manufacturing. Its management mistakenly believed that this was critical to Cameron's success. Only after the acquisition did it learn that service and marketing were the key performance drivers for Cameron. Second, in implementing the acquisition, Cooper became preoccupied with control, making it difficult for management at Cameron to run its business. As a result, Cooper took $440 to $750 million of write-downs related to the acquisition, and it divested Cameron in 1994.

Given management's self-interest in communicating to investors that an acquisition is successful and the challenge in estimating future benefits from outlays for goodwill, there is a risk that managers making value-decreasing acquisitions will fail to recognize any deterioration in goodwill values on a timely basis. Equally, for acquisitions that do create shareholder value, accounting rules for goodwill amortization often do a poor job of reflecting merger benefits, since many countries require firms to amortize goodwill even if the asset has not declined in value.

EXAMPLE: RESEARCH AND DEVELOPMENT OUTLAYS.   Research and development outlays are intended to create value for the firm in future periods. This suggests that they should be expensed in the same periods as when the new product revenues they are expected to generate are recognized. However, research and development (R&D) is a highly uncertain process. There are typically many failed projects for every successful one. As a result, accounting rules in most countries require R&D outlays to be expensed as incurred (see SFAS 2).[4]

In the U.S., there are several exceptions to the rule requiring expensing of R&D. First, completed R&D that is purchased from another company is capitalized and amortized over its useful life (see SFAS 68). Second, software development costs are capitalized upon completion of a detailed program design plan or working model. Amortization of this asset for a particular year is proportional to the project revenues generated during that year relative to total expected project revenues (see SFAS 86).[5]

The rules on capitalizing and amortizing outlays for completed R&D and software development provide management with opportunity to exercise judgment in financial reporting. Management can potentially use this judgment to match R&D costs with revenues they generate. Alternatively, it can misuse this judgment to accelerate or defer earnings, either in their assessments of the types of outlays that satisfy the criteria for capitalization and amortization against future revenues, or in the estimates of future lives of any outlays to be amortized.[6]

The diversity in reporting practice on these issues is likely to raise questions for users of financial reports. For example, Microsoft, the most successful software developer in the world, expenses all software development outlays immediately. In contrast, Peoplesoft, one of the smaller players in the software industry, capitalizes its development costs and amortizes them over three years. Is Microsoft being conservative in its reporting? Is Peoplesoft reporting aggressively? Or do the two firms have very different models of developing software consistent with their reporting differences?

Analysis is also important for firms whose managers have no opportunity to exercise judgment in reporting on R&D outlays. For example, firms in the R&D-intensive pharmaceutical industry are required to expense all R&D outlays immediately. For these firms, financial reporting does not help investors discriminate between firms with the most and the least effective research labs, a critical issue for evaluating the performance of management and for valuation. As a result, analysts research other sources of information on firms' research capabilities and successes, such as patent filings and FDA approvals.

EXAMPLE: ADVERTISING OUTLAYS.   Advertising outlays create an even greater challenge for financial reporting than R&D. As discussed in Chapter 4, companies such as Coca-Cola have been able to create long-term sustainable economic rents from advertising their products. However, it is often unclear what link, if any, exists between advertising outlays in a period and future revenues.

To illustrate the difficulty in linking a firm's advertising program to long-term revenues, consider Microsoft's $220 million campaign to launch Windows 95. The role of this campaign in the success of the new product is difficult to estimate. Because of the company's dominant position in its market, there was widespread public interest in the product well before the first paid advertisement for Windows appeared on August 24, 1995. *The Wall Street Journal* estimated that 3,000 headlines, 6,852 stories, and over 3 million words had been dedicated to Windows 95 during the period July 1 to August 24, 1995. In addition, during the launch week, Microsoft engaged in a series of publicity stunts to promote the new product. A 600-foot Windows 95 banner was hung from the CN Tower in Toronto, the Empire State Building was lit in the colors of the Windows 95 logo, and the company paid *The London Times* to distribute an entire day's run of 1.5 million copies free. What was the role of these promotions relative to the $220 million advertising campaign in making the product a market success?

As shown by the Windows 95 example, the long-term effectiveness of a firm's advertising is typically difficult to assess because so many other factors aside from the company's advertising strategy are likely to influence its campaign effectiveness. Intervening factors include the firm's own pricing and promotion decisions, the price, promotion, and advertising responses of competitors, the market position of the firm relative to its competitors, and the stage of the product market (growing, mature, or declining). Given the difficulty in quantifying these effects and isolating any cause-and-effect relation between advertising outlays and future revenues, accounting standards typically require advertising expenditures to be expensed as incurred.

However, for several industries it is possible to link some forms of marketing outlays and future revenues. For example, life insurance companies pay commissions to compensate sales representatives for signing up new policyholders. The benefits of these contracts can be short-term (for property-casualty insurers) or long-term (for life insurers). As a result, SFAS 60 and SFAS 120 require insurers to capitalize these outlays and to expense them over the life of the contract.

Direct response advertising costs are another type of advertising outlay where it may be possible to establish a link between outlays and future revenues. Credit card companies, telephone companies, Internet service providers, satellite television providers, magazine publishers, and membership service companies spend heavily on direct response advertising to attract new members. Many of these firms can document the sign-up rates from their programs, as well as the rates of membership renewal. Indeed, many of these firms use market research to target customers that are most likely to sign up and subsequently renew their memberships. Consequently, accounting standards (see Statement of Practice 93-7) permit firms to capitalize these types of costs provided they can document that (a) customers have responded directly to the advertising campaign, and (b) future benefits from the expenditures are reasonably certain. The first requirement can be satisfied by use of coded order forms, coupons, or response cards. The second can be satisfied by reference to historical data on membership renewals. Of course, there are always risks that future renewals will not follow historical patterns, perhaps due to increased competition or to customer disappointments over service.

Key Analysis Questions

The above discussion indicates that management sometimes has an opportunity to use judgment to expense resources that provide value over multiple periods. In addition, accounting standards for reporting on some of these resources require all firms to immediately expense outlays. This makes it more difficult for analysts to distinguish firms that are able to create multi-period benefits from these outlays from firms that are not. As a result, the following questions are likely to be useful for analysts:

- What assumptions are made by management to amortize resources with multi-period benefits? Are these assumptions consistent with the firm's business strategy? How do they compare to assumptions made by other firms in the industry? If there are significant differences, what factors can explain these differences?

- Has the firm changed its amortization assumptions over time? What factors explain these decisions? For example, is it following a different business or operating model?

- Is there evidence that management has consistently over- or underamortized long-lived assets? Such evidence includes systematic reporting of gains (or losses) on asset sales, or persistent asset write-downs.

- What is the value and reliability of benefits expected from capitalized current period outlays? These are affected by the firm's position in its product market and the sustainability of that position. For example, if the firm records significant goodwill as a result of an acquisition, is there an economic basis for this asset, or did the acquirer overpay for the target?

- If accounting standards require outlays for intangible resources to be expensed as incurred, analysts may want to discount the effect of these expenses on earnings, particularly for firms that appear to be capable of creating long-term value from these outlays. This requires an analysis of the expected benefits and associated risks from these outlays. Does the firm have a track record of creating new products through its R&D labs, or brand names through its marketing campaigns?

Challenge Two: The Timing and Amount of Payment for Resources Is Uncertain

Some transactions require firms to make long-term commitments for resources that have no long-term benefits to the firm. For example, many firms offer pension and other post-retirement benefits to their employees. Firms also incur long-term obligations to pay for the cleanup of environmental hazards for which they are responsible. These obligations represent expenses, since they provide no future benefit to the firm. Any benefits have already been realized in either the current period or prior periods. However, they are challenging to record, since the timing and amount of the obligations is frequently uncertain.

How should these types of commitments be recorded? Should an expense be estimated for the expected obligation or for the present value of the expected obligation? If so, how should errors in management's forecasts of these obligations and interest rates be reflected? Alternatively, should recording the expense be delayed until the timing and amount of the obligation can be determined more accurately?

To illustrate the challenges associated with recording expenses for long-term obligations with no future benefits, we discuss the accounting for pension and post-retirement benefits and environmental obligations.

EXAMPLE: PENSIONS AND OTHER POST-RETIREMENT BENEFITS.   Many firms offer employees a pension plan and other forms of post-retirement benefits. Typically, employees are entitled to receive some form of benefit after working for a firm for a minimum period. Thereafter, the magnitude of the benefits typically increases for each year the employee works.

As discussed in Chapter 5, companies are required to estimate liabilities for the expected future obligations under pension and post-retirement plans. This is a significant challenge for recording the liability associated with defined benefit plans, where an employer guarantees certain future levels of benefits for employees.[7] For these types of plans, managers have to forecast current employees' future working lives with the firm, their life expectancies, retirement ages, and the expected cost of the future benefits. These data are used to estimate the present value of the expected future benefits for all current employees. This value is amortized as a benefit expense by using a straight-line method over the employees' expected working lives with the firm. In addition, the benefit expense reflects increases in the value of the obligation as employees get closer to receiving benefits (an interest effect) and decreases as any assets invested by the company to fund the benefit plan increase in value. Expenses are also adjusted as management revises its forecasts of future plan commitments. Of course, under this approach, management has considerable judgment in estimating the annual benefit cost.

Estimating the cost of obligations provided under such plans is challenging for management. However, it does ensure that the risks associated with the plans, such as uncertainty over employee turnover, medical cost inflation, and employee life expectancy, are reflected in the financial statements. It is likely to be important for management and for external users of financial statements to understand the implications of these risks and the value of the benefits provided to employees.

EXAMPLE: ENVIRONMENTAL COSTS.   As discussed in Chapter 5, the Comprehensive Environmental Response, Compensation, and Liability Act (CERCLA) empowers the federal government to make those responsible for the improper disposal of hazardous waste at the nation's worst hazardous waste sites bear the cost of cleanup. The challenges in measuring environmental liabilities, namely the difficulties in estimating the cost of the cleanup and in assessing how the cleanup cost will be shared by the parties associated with the site, also make it challenging to record an expense. How should the expense be recorded? For example, should it be recorded as a one-time charge at the same time as the liability is recorded, or should it be spread out over the cleanup period? Should it be shown as an extraordinary item, as a non-operating item, or as a part of normal operations?

As noted in Chapter 5, a liability must be recorded when much of the uncertainty over the cost of cleanup and the firm's responsibility have been resolved (see SFAS 5 and Statement of Position 96-1). The Statement of Position also requires firms to recognize the full cost of cleanup as an operating expense when the liability is recorded. Cleanup costs cannot be considered extraordinary or included in the "other income and expense" category. Of course, if these costs are large and unlikely to be ongoing, analysts may want to consider them separately from operating income in order to improve the forecasts of future operating earnings.

Key Analysis Questions

Considerable management judgment is involved in estimating the costs for future obligations that are uncertain in timing and amount. In addition, for some of these costs, accounting standards do not require an expense to be recorded because the amount is too uncertain, making it difficult to assess which firms' costs are likely to be understated. As a result, the following questions are likely to be useful for financial analysts:

- What assumptions are made by management to recognize the cost of uncertain future obligations? Have these assumptions changed in relation to prior years? If so, what factors explain this change? For example, has the firm altered its benefit plans or its business operations? If management changed the discount rate used to compute the present value of pension obligations, has there been a comparable change in interest rates?
- Are there any differences in the firm's assumptions for estimating the costs of uncertain future obligations in relation to other firms in the same industry? If so, what factors can explain these differences? Does the firm have a different relationship with the suppliers of these resources?
- Is there any evidence that the firm's managers have a record of systematically over- or underestimating costs for long-term obligations?
- How seriously are a firm's expenses likely to be affected by accounting standards that delay recording costs for future obligations because of uncertainty in estimating the future outlays, such as the cost of environmental liabilities? How does the firm manage these risks? Are there indicator variables that can be used to help identify firms with high and low risks?

Challenge Three: It Is Difficult to Define the Value of Resources Consumed

Some types of resources used to generate revenues are difficult to value. For example, inventory is purchased or manufactured at different prices and then has to be matched to revenues. Which inventory units should be reported as a cost of sales and which should be reported as inventory? Executive stock options also raise questions about the value of the resources consumed in return for the options, and the timing of when these costs should be treated as an expense. We discuss how these types of resources are recorded and the challenges involved.

EXAMPLE: COST OF SALES.   If a firm purchases or manufactures products at different costs and then sells some of those units, it faces a question of determining the cost of the units that were sold and the cost of units remaining in inventory. Costs of merchandise purchased or produced can differ over time if there is inflation in the economy or if there is a demand or supply shock for the firm's merchandise or inputs. Manufacturing costs can also vary over time if the firm changes the number of units it produces. Since capacity costs of production are fixed in the short run, these costs will be allocated over more or less units, affecting unit costs.

For some types of products, the valuation of the cost of sales and inventory can be easily resolved, since the specific units that are purchased and sold are identifiable. Such is the case for auto dealerships. New and used cars are identifiable by make, model, color, year, accessories, and if necessary by vehicle identification number. Consequently, when a vehicle is sold, management can identify its specific cost to match against the sales revenue.

However, for most businesses it is not feasible to specifically identify each unit purchased and sold. For example, a large automobile manufacturer that purchases thousands of inputs to make a new automobile would find it inefficient to keep track of the cost of each specific part. Consequently, some other form of accounting is required to estimate the cost of sales.

The approach taken by accountants is to make an assumption about how products flow from inventory to cost of sales. Three major methods are permitted. The first, called the last-in-first-out method (or LIFO), assumes that the last units purchased or manufactured are the first units to be sold. This method therefore matches recent costs with revenues, leading some to argue that it gives a better indication of the firm's future profit margins than do the other methods.[8] However, it can also lead to inventory valuations that are long out of date, and it provides the potential for management to temporarily boost profits by reducing inventory levels, thereby selling merchandise carried at old costs.

The second method is the first-in-first-out (or FIFO) method. This approach assumes that the first units purchased or manufactured are the first to be sold. The advantage to this approach is that it ensures that inventories are valued at recent costs. However, it makes it more difficult to interpret profit margins, since margins include holding gains on units purchased at old cost levels.

The third approach, the average cost method, is a compromise between LIFO and FIFO. It values the cost of sales and inventory at the average cost of units purchased or manufactured.

Several points are worth noting about inventory valuation. First, the particular method followed does not have to represent the actual physical flow of merchandise from the warehouse. Thus, a company that bakes bread can report under the LIFO method, but it would not follow such an approach for managing its physical inventory. Second, the LIFO method cannot be used in some countries. For example, it is not permitted under U.K., French, or Canadian accounting. Third, in the U.S., tax factors are a consideration for managers deciding which method to use for financial reporting. Tax rules require that the method used for financial reporting must also be used for tax reporting. Consequently, firms in industries with increasing factor or merchandise costs have tax incentives to select the LIFO method, since it lowers the present value of their tax obligations. For firms in industries with declining factor or merchandise costs, there are tax advantages from using FIFO.

In summary, the valuation of the cost of sales provides several opportunities for managers to exercise judgment in financial reporting. Managers can select the inventory flow method, increase or reduce production to allocate capacity costs over more or less units, or, if the firm uses LIFO, deplete inventory to match old costs against revenues.[9]

EXAMPLE: EXECUTIVE STOCK OPTION COMPENSATION.   In the U.S., most public companies provide stock option remuneration to top executives. A stock option permits an executive to purchase stock at a given price, known as the exercise or strike price, at some point in the future, known as the exercise or expiration date. For example, Walt Disney Company's 1999 proxy statement disclosed that on September 30, 1996, the Compensation Committee granted the firm's CEO, Michael Eisner, the option to purchase 15,000,000 Disney shares at an exercise price of $21.10, the stock price when the option was granted. The option expires on September 30, 2008. At fiscal year-end on September 30, 1998, Disney's stock price was $25.375.

Stock option compensation, like that reported for Michael Eisner, is intended to provide top management with a powerful incentive to maximize shareholder value, since managers get to share in any upside in the stock price. For several reasons, options are a more popular form of compensation than straight stock awards. They protect management against downside risk from holding the stock. Compensation that imposes downside risk on risk-averse managers can induce them to be more cautious in their decisions than owners would like. Also, stock option compensation is often tax advantageous relative to stock awards.[10]

The challenging question for financial reporting is how to record these forms of compensation. Should an expense be recorded for these types of compensation awards, or is it too difficult to estimate their value? If an expense is to be recorded, when should it be shown and at what value? Should the value of the compensation be recognized when the award is granted? If so, what is its value? Should the compensation cost be shown throughout the option exercise period? Again, what is the value of the compensation provided? Should compensation be recorded when the options are exercised and the value of shares awarded is known? Should the compensation expense be recognized when management actually sells the shares awarded under option grants?

Prior to 1995, U.S. firms were required under APB Opinion 25 to use the "intrinsic value" method of reporting for option grants. Under this approach, a compensation expense was recorded for the difference between the market price of the stock at the date the option was granted and its exercise price. However, since most options had an exercise price equal to the stock price at the grant date, no compensation expense was reported. In 1995 the FASB released an Exposure Draft on stock option compensation, recommending the "fair value" method to value options. This involved creating at the grant date a deferred compensation expense for the market value of options awarded, estimated using Black-Scholes or binomial option-valuation models.[11] The compensation expense, reflecting compensation effectively earned by managers from option awards, is then recorded by amortizing the deferred compensation expense over the option's vesting period.

Considerable controversy surrounded the stock option exposure draft, and the FASB decided to tone down its recommendation. The final standard, SFAS 123, permitted managers to decide whether to report under APB 25 or SFAS 123. However, if a firm elects to use APB 25, it is also required to disclose the fair value of options awarded in its footnotes.[12]

Key Analysis Questions

When it is difficult to define the value of resources consumed, accounting rules have to either suggest definitive methods that can be used to estimate resource consumption, or permit management to exercise judgment in recording their consumption. Both outcomes create an opportunity for financial analysis of expenses. Some questions that are likely to arise for financial analysts include the following:

- What method does management use to account for and value the cost of sales, stock option compensation, and other expenses for resources whose use is difficult to value? Has this method changed over time? Does the firm use the same method as other firms in the industry? If the method used differs over time or across firms in the industry, what factors are likely to explain this difference? Has the firm changed its business strategy or is it following a different model for value creation than its competitors that could explain any method differences? Has it changed its tax status or tax management strategy? Or does it appear to be trying to report positive performance to the capital market?

- What earnings effects, if any, arise from the accounting methods used to value the cost of sales, stock options, and other expenses for resources that are difficult to value? For example, are there any one-time effects on the cost of sales from LIFO inventory liquidations? How do changes in production capacity utilization affect the cost of sales? If firms use FIFO or average cost methods to record the cost of sales, how are future margins likely to be affected by any recent increases in input prices? If the firm uses the "intrinsic value" method to record option expenses, what would have been the effect of using the "fair value" approach? Is management being compensated appropriately, given the firm's performance?

Challenge Four: Unused Resources Decline in Value

The final challenge in recording expenses arises for unused resources whose values change over time. In most cases the financial reporting implications of these value changes are based on the application of the conservatism principle. This principle holds that permanent declines in resource values should be recorded as a loss, but if values have increased, no gain should be recognized until the resource is sold. The issues are the same as those discussed for asset impairments in Chapter 4. Below we discuss the expense reporting challenges for changes in values of operating assets and financial instruments.

EXAMPLE: OPERATING ASSET IMPAIRMENTS.   As discussed in Chapter 4, the conservatism principle requires that an asset whose value is impaired should be written down to its market value, below cost. For example, in December 1997, following a disappointing performance in its core business, Eastman Kodak recorded a $1.5 billion restructuring charge. Of this amount, $428 million was for asset impairments (7 percent of pre-written-down fixed assets), and $165 million was for inventory write-downs (12 percent of pre-written-down inventory). The remainder was primarily to reflect the severance costs for 16,100 personnel to be laid off.

The challenge in recognizing losses from asset impairments is that it is often difficult to assess whether an asset has been impaired and, if so, the amount of the loss. Accounting for asset impairments in the U.S. is regulated by SFAS 121. Under this standard, firms are required to review assets for impairment whenever there is a change in the firm's circumstances or an indication that the book value cannot be recovered. Changes in circumstances can arise if the asset is used less extensively or in a different manner, if legal or regulatory changes affect the asset's value, or if the firm has a history of cash-flow losses. If management's forecast of the undiscounted future cash flows associated with an asset is less than its book value, the asset is required to be written down to fair value and a loss recognized.

The decision to recognize an impairment loss and the estimation of the value of the loss under SFAS 121 involves considerable management judgment. Management must decide what level of asset grouping is appropriate for evaluating asset impairments.[13] It must also forecast and value the expected future cash flows from these assets.

In late 1998 the SEC expressed concern about management abuse of its reporting judgment for asset impairments. Arthur Levitt, Chairman of the SEC, articulated this concern as follows: "When earnings take a major hit, the theory goes that Wall Street will look beyond a one-time loss and focus only on future earnings. And if these charges are conservatively estimated with a little extra cushioning, that so-called estimate is miraculously reborn as income when estimates change or future earnings fall short."[14]

EXAMPLE: CHANGES IN VALUE OF FINANCIAL INSTRUMENTS.   As discussed in Chapter 4, firms are required to record at fair values their financial instruments that are held as investments and are intended to be sold or are available for sale. A key question is whether gains and losses on these types of investment should be reflected in the income statement or charged directly to owners' equity. Current rules require that if a firm holds an instrument as a store of cash and intends to sell it, the unrealized fair value of gains and losses must be shown as a part of income. If the instrument is available for sale, only realized gains and losses are shown in income. Financial instruments that are potentially available for sale are valued at fair values. Unrealized gains or losses are recorded as a part of the comprehensive income and are not included in the income statement.[15] Finally, instruments expected to be held to maturity are valued at historical cost, and only realized gains and losses are reported in the income statement. However, as noted earlier, these distinctions based on management's intentions are not relevant from an economic perspective. Analysts should, therefore, regard both realized and unrealized gains as relevant for evaluating management's performance.

Firms with financial instruments that are held for hedging purposes are also required to record the instruments at fair values (see Chapter 4). The income effect of marking these types of instruments to market depends on the purpose of ownership. If the purpose is to hedge changes in the fair value of another item, fair value gains and losses on both the hedge item and the financial instrument are included in income. However, if the instrument is held to hedge fluctuations in expected future cash inflows or outflows, fair value gains and losses on the effective portion of the hedge are deferred and included in income only when the cash flows are reported. Fair value gains and losses on the ineffective portion of the hedge are included in income immediately.

Key Analysis Questions

The management judgment involved in estimating impairments of operating assets and changes in values of financial instruments raises a number of questions for financial analysts. They include the following:

- For operating assets, is the timing and amount of any asset impairment charge taken by management consistent with changes in the firm's operating performance and the performance of other firms in the same industry? Does management appear to have delayed recording a loss from asset impairment?
- Does management appear to have over- or understated prior impairment losses on operating assets, thereby making it difficult to evaluate future performance? Has the firm consistently reported impairment losses, indicating an unwillingness to appreciate the full extent of the impairment?
- What is the basis for the estimation of the fair value of the impaired operating resource? For example, is the valuation based on an independent appraisal, or is it a management estimate?

- For financial instruments, what is management's purpose for owning the financial instruments? Is that purpose consistent with shareholders' interests? For example, is the firm hedging risks for shareholders' benefits or for managers?
- What is the extent of unrealized gains and losses on holding financial instruments, regardless of whether they are reported in the income statement? What factors explain any significant gains or losses? For example, does management appear to be using financial instruments to hedge risks or to take on additional risk? Is this decision consistent with shareholders' interests? Are there appropriate controls in place to avoid excessive risks being taken?

SUMMARY

The recording of a firm's expenses is determined primarily by the matching and conservatism principles. Under these principles, three classes of expenses arise:

1. Costs of consumed resources that have a cause-and-effect relation with revenues and are matched with revenues;
2. Costs of resources that have no clear cause-and-effect relation to revenues and are recorded as expenses during the period they are consumed; and
3. Costs from declines in the future benefits expected to be generated by resources, which are recorded when the decline in value occurs.

For certain types of transactions, implementing these principles can be challenging. For example, it can be difficult to assess whether to record expenses if:

1. Resources acquired by a firm provide benefits over multiple years, such as for fixed assets, goodwill, research and development outlays, and advertising.
2. Firms make uncertain long-term commitments for resources that have no long-term benefits to the firm. This arises for pension and other post-retirement benefits and for environmental liabilities.
3. Resources used to generate revenues are difficult to value, as in the cost of sales and executive stock options.
4. Unused resources have declined in value over time, such as for operating and financial asset impairments.

In general, corporate managers are likely to have the best information to estimate expenses for the period. However, their incentives to report favorable information on their stewardship of the firm raise questions for users of financial information about the reliability of management's estimates. In addition, accounting standards require all firms to expense certain types of outlays, such as R&D, even though they generate future benefits for successful firms. This creates another role for financial analysis: to understand how accounting standards affect reported performance for different firms.

DISCUSSION QUESTIONS

1. A firm purchases an asset for $10,000,000. Management forecasts that the asset will have an expected life of ten years and a salvage value of 5 percent. What are the financial statement effects from recording depreciation for this asset in the first two years of its life if financial reporting depreciation is recorded under (a) the straight-line method, and (b) the double-declining balance method? As a financial analyst, what questions would you raise with the firm's CFO about its depreciation policy?

2. On February 9, 1996, Walt Disney Co. acquired Capital Cities/ABC Inc. for $10.1 billion in cash and 155 million shares of Disney valued at $8.8 billion, based on the stock price at the date the transaction was announced. Disney estimated that goodwill under the acquisitions would amount to $19 billion. What forecasts does Disney's management have to make to record amortization of this goodwill? What factors would underlie these forecasts? As a financial analyst, what questions would you raise with the firm's CFO about the amortization of goodwill?

3. In 1997 Peoplesoft, a software company, presented the following footnote information in its annual report:

    The Company capitalizes software purchased from third parties if the related software product under development has reached technological feasibility or if there are alternative future uses for the purchased software, provided that capitalized amounts will be realized over a period not exceeding five years. In addition, the Company capitalizes certain internally incurred costs, consisting of salaries, related payroll taxes and benefits, and an allocation of indirect costs related to developing computer software products. Costs incurred prior to the establishment of technological feasibility are charged to product development expense. The establishment of technological feasibility and the ongoing assessment of recoverability of capitalized software development costs require considerable judgment by management with respect to certain external factors, including, but not limited to, anticipated future revenues, estimated economic life and changes in software and hardware technologies. Upon the general release of the software product to customers, capitalization ceases and such costs are amortized (using the straight-line method) on a product by product basis over the estimated life, which is generally three years. All other research and development expenditures are charged to research and development expense in the period incurred.

    Capitalized software costs and accumulated amortization at December 31, 1995, 1996 and 1997 were as follows (in thousands):

	1995	1996	1997
Capitalized software:			
Internal development costs	$7,016	$10,737	$13,232
Purchased from third parties	5,137	6,832	6,832
	12,153	17,569	20,064
Accumulated amortization	(4,811)	(6,396)	(10,358)
	$7,342	$11,173	$9,706

How much did Peoplesoft capitalize for software costs in 1996? How much was capitalized in 1997? How much did Peoplesoft record as amortization expense for software costs in 1997? What was the amortization expense in 1996? If Peoplesoft had never capitalized any software research and development outlays, how would its earnings before taxes have been affected in 1997? What would have been the effect for 1996? Why is the earnings effect of expensing versus capitalizing different in 1996 versus 1997? Microsoft does not capitalize any software costs. Why might Peoplesoft choose to capitalize some of its software costs and Microsoft expense all its costs? As a financial analyst, what questions would you raise with Peoplesoft's CFO about the firm's policy for amortizing software development costs?

4. Procter and Gamble is a consumer products firm that owns such brands as Pampers diapers, Crisco vegetable shortening, Tide laundry detergent, and Crest toothpaste. In its 1998 annual report, the company reported: "Worldwide marketing, research and administrative expenses were $10.04 billion compared to $9.77 billion in the prior year. This equates to 27.0 percent of sales, compared with 27.3 percent in the prior year." As a financial analyst, what questions would you raise with the firm's CFO about the advertising and research and administrative costs for 1998? As the CFO of Procter and Gamble, what other information would you recommend the firm include in its annual report on these outlays?

5. A firm hires a 27-year-old MBA at a salary of $85,000 for the first year. It also agrees to provide a pension upon retirement at age sixty-five and estimates that the present value of that pension is $150,000. What forecasts did management have to make to estimate this value? What factors determine how much of the pension cost is recognized as an expense at the end of the employee's first year of service? As a financial analyst, what questions would you raise with the firm's CFO about its pension costs?

6. In the contingent liability section of its 1998 annual report, Dow Chemical Company reported the following:

Accruals for environmental matters are recorded when it is probable that a liability has been incurred and the amount of the liability can be reasonably estimated, based on current law and existing technologies. The Company had accrued $364 million at December 31, 1998, for environmental matters, including $9 million for the remediation of Superfund sites. This is management's best estimate of the costs for remediation and restoration with respect to environmental matters for which the Company has accrued liabilities, although the ultimate cost with respect to these particular *matters could range up to twice that amount. Inherent uncertainties exist in these es-timates primarily due to unknown conditions, changing governmental regulations and legal standards regarding liability, and evolving technologies for handling site remediation and restoration. It is the opinion of the Company's management that the possibility is remote that costs in excess of those accrued or disclosed will have a ma-terial adverse impact on the Company's consolidated financial statements.*

As a financial analyst, what questions would you raise with the firm's CFO about the firm's environmental disclosures?

7. Eastman Kodak reported the following information on inventory valuation in its 1998 annual report:

(In millions)	1998	1997
At FIFO or average cost (approximates current cost)	$ 907	$ 788
Work in process	569	538
Raw materials and supplies	439	460
	1,915	1,786
LIFO reserve	(491)	(534)
Total	$1,424	$1,252

Kodak reported that its cost of sales was $72.93 million for 1998. What would the firm's cost of sales have been if it had valued inventory exclusively under the FIFO method? What factors are likely to be relevant to Kodak in setting its inventory val-uation policies? As a financial analyst, what questions would you raise with the firm's CFO about the firm's inventory valuation and cost of sales?

8. In its 1998 annual report, Eastman Kodak reported the following information on its stock option program:

Pro forma net earnings and earnings per share information, as required by SFAS No. 123, "Accounting for Stock-Based Compensation," has been determined as if the Company had accounted for employee stock options under SFAS No. 123's fair value method. The fair value of these options was estimated at grant date using a Black-Scholes option pricing model.

For purposes of pro forma disclosures, the estimated fair value of the options is am-ortized to expense over the options' vesting period (2–3 years). The Company's pro forma information follows:

Year Ended December 31 (In millions, except per share data)

	1998	1997	1996
Net earnings (loss):			
As reported	$1,390	$ 5	$1,288
Pro forma	1,272	(52)	1,262
Basic earnings (loss) per share:			
As reported	$4.30	$.01	$3.82
Pro forma	3.93	(.16)	3.74

Is stock option compensation a material item for Kodak? As a financial analyst, what questions would you raise with the firm's CFO about this disclosure?

9. In a meeting of the Board of Directors over a proposal to restructure, a firm's CEO states: "I recommend we take as large a charge against current earnings as our auditors will permit, since Wall Street will love us for being tough. Further, in future years our earnings will look improved, giving us a long-term boost from the current hit." Do you agree with these comments? Explain why or why not.

10. The CFO of a large bank argues: "It is ridiculous to recognize any fair-value gains or losses on our debt instruments that we intend holding to maturity. Since we intend holding these securities, we are insulated from the whims of the market." Do you agree? Explain why or why not. Given your answer, what are the implications for financial analysts following the company?

NOTES

1. The most common accelerated depreciation method is called double-declining-balance. Under this approach, the depreciation expense in any year is twice the straight-line rate multiplied by the book value of the asset in question. For example, under this method an asset with a five-year life and an initial cost of $100,000 depreciates $40,000 in year one ($100,000 × .4), $24,000 in year two ($60,000 × .4), and so on.

2. P. Healy, K. Palepu, and R. Ruback, "Which Takeovers Are Profitable—Strategic or Financial?" *Sloan Management Review*, Summer 1997, find that acquisitions add value for approximately one-third of the 50 largest acquisitions during the early 1980s.

3. See Steven N. Kaplan, Mark L. Mitchell, and Karen H. Wruck, "A Clinical Exploration of Value Creation and Destruction in Acquisitions: Organizational Design, Incentives, and Internal Capital Markets," working paper, (July 1997), Harvard Business School.

4. Accounting rules in the U.S., the U.K., Canada, and Germany require expensing R&D outlays. Expensing is the norm in Japan and France, even though capitalization is permitted.

5. E. Eccher, "The Value Relevance of Software Capitalized Costs," working paper, 1998, MIT, finds that the amortization of capitalized software development costs provides investors with valuable information on management's estimate of the future revenues for the software. D. Aboody and B. Lev, "The Value-Relevance of Intangibles: The Case of Software Capitalization," 1998, working paper, University of California, Los Angeles, and New York University, find that investors value capitalized software assets and changes in their values. They conclude that management judgment in capitalizing software development costs does not adversely affect the quality of reported earnings.

6. P. Healy, S. Myers, and C. Howe, "R&D Accounting and the Tradeoff Between Relevance and Objectivity," working paper, 1999, Harvard University and MIT, show that, even if managers abuse reporting judgment by delaying writing down R&D assets, accounting methods that capitalize R&D and write-off costs of unsuccessful projects provide better information for investors on firm values than do expense rules.

7. Defined contribution plans, where companies agree to contribute fixed amounts today to cover future benefits, require very little forecasting to estimate their annual cost, since the firm's obligation is limited to its annual obligation to contribute to the employees' retirement funds.

8. Consistent with this view, R. Jennings, P. Simko, and R. Thompson, "Does LIFO Inventory Accounting Improve the Income Statement at the Expense of the Balance Sheet?" *Journal of Accounting Research* 34, No. 1 (1996), find that LIFO earnings are more related to equity values than non-LIFO earnings.

9. Research findings indicate that management's inventory method decisions are related to tax considerations, (see R. Hagerman and M. Zmijewski, "Some Economic Determinants of Accounting Policy Choice," *Journal of Accounting and Economics* 1, 1979, and B. Cushing and M. LeClere, "Evidence on the Determinants of Inventory Accounting Policy," *The Accounting Review* 67, No. 2, 1992), corporate governance (see G. Niehaus, "Ownership Structure and Inventory Method Choice," *The Accounting Review* 64, No. 2, 1989), and firm characteristics such as R&D and labor intensity (see R. Bowen, L. DuCharme, and D. Shores, "Stakeholders' Implicit Claims and Accounting Method Choice, *Journal of Accounting and Economics* 20, No. 3, 1995).

10. See M. Scholes and M. Wolfson, *Taxes and Business Strategy: A Planning Approach,* Englewood Cliffs, NJ: Prentice-Hall, 1992, Chapter 10.

11. The Black-Scholes option-pricing model estimates the value of an option as a nonlinear function of the exercise price, the remaining time to expiration, the estimated variance of the underlying stock, and the risk-free interest rate. Studies of the valuation of executive stock options include T. Hemmer, S. Matsunaga, and T. Shevlin, "Optimal Exercise and the Cost of Granting Employee Stock Options with a Reload Provision," *Journal of Accounting Research* 36, No. 2 (1998), C. Cuny and P. Jorion, "Valuing Executive Stock Options with Endogenous Departure," *Journal of Accounting and Economics* 20, No. 2; and S. Huddart, "Employee Stock Options," *Journal of Accounting and Economics* 18, No. 2.

12. P. DeChow, A. Hutton, and R. Sloan, "Economic Consequences of Accounting for Stock-Based Compensation," *Journal of Accounting Research*, Supplement, 1996, find evidence that lobbying against SFAS 123 was motivated by concerns about reporting higher levels of executive compensation.

13. J. Francis, D. Hanna, and L. Vincent, "Causes and Effects of Discretionary Asset Write-Offs," *Journal of Accounting Research* 34 (1996), Supplement, find that management is more likely to exercise judgment in its self-interest for goodwill write-offs and restructuring charges than for inventory or PP&E write-offs.

14. Arthur Levitt, "The Numbers Game," remarks at NYU Center for Law and Business, New York, September 28, 1998. Consistent with this concern, J. Elliott and D. Hanna, "Repeated Accounting Write-Offs and the Information Content of Earnings," *Journal of Accounting Research* 34 (1996), Supplement, find evidence that the market reacts to unexpected earnings declines in the quarter subsequent to large write-downs.

15. See Chapter 8 for a discussion of comprehensive income.

P*re-paid Legal plans are designed to help middle-income Americans have affordable access to quality legal assistance.*

Pre-Paid Legal Services Corporate Vision

Harland C. Stonecipher founded Pre-Paid Legal Services, Inc. (PPLS) in 1972 after an expensive encounter with lawyers stemming from an automobile accident. PPLS sold legal expense insurance that provided for partial payment of legal fees in connection with the defense of certain civil and criminal actions. The company went public in 1979 and grew rapidly throughout the 1980s as an increasing number of Americans subscribed to legal service insurance (see Exhibit 1). In 1998 the company had membership revenues of $110 million, earnings of $30.2 million, and end-of-year book equity of $101.1 million. In May 1999 it began trading on the New York Stock Exchange, and in August 1999 its market capitalization reached $738 million, an increase of 101 percent over the previous year.

Despite its strong financial performance, opinions about the future of Pre-Paid Legal Services varied widely among U.S. equity analysts in the period late 1997 to mid-1999. The company was highly recommended by a number of analysts, but there was also persistent short selling of the stock.[1] Short sellers' primary concern about the company was outlined in a *Fortune* article in late 1997. The business publication alleged that the company was using an inappropriate method of accounting for sales commissions. As a result of this uncertainty, the company's stock price fluctuated widely from a high of $40.50 to a low of $13.50 between late 1997 and mid-1999.

BUSINESS DESCRIPTION

PPLS offered its customers (termed members) a wide range of legal insurance. The most popular plan, The Family Plan, accounted for 94 percent of all memberships in 1998. This plan provided reimbursement for a broad range of legal expenses incurred by mem-

Professor Paul M. Healy and Teaching Fellow Jacob Cohen J.D. prepared this case as the basis for class discussion rather than to illustrate either effective or ineffective handling of an administrative situation. Copyright © 1999 by the President and Fellows of Harvard College. Harvard Business School case 9-100-037.

1. *A short seller borrows stock certificates from a brokerage firm and sells the stocks on the open market. If the stock price declines, the short seller can buy back stock, cover his loan from the brokerage firm, and earn a profit. Of course, if the price increases, the short seller takes a loss.*

bers and their spouses, including will preparation, document review and letter writing, some of the legal costs associated with employment-related trial defense, traffic violations, and Internal Revenue Service audits.[2] The Family Plan specified limits on the number of hours of attorney time that a member was entitled to receive for many of these services. It also provided a 25 percent discount on attorney rates for the purchase of any legal services over and above those provided under the insurance contract.

PPLS's membership premiums in 1998 averaged $19.08 per month (or $229 per year). Premiums were typically paid on a monthly basis either by automatic charges to the member's credit card or through employee payroll deductions. The premiums were generally guaranteed renewable and noncancelable except for fraud, nonpayment of premiums, or upon written request by a member. The annual membership renewal rate in 1998 was high; 75 percent of members at the beginning of 1998 were still members at the end of the year. At March 31, 1999, PPLS had 648,475 active members, and membership had been increasing at about 40 percent per year.

Marketing of Services

PPLS marketed its memberships through a multilevel marketing program that encouraged buyers to become salespeople. Members that sought to become sales associates paid the company a fee, typically $65, to cover the cost of training materials, training meetings, and home office support services. Registered sales associates sold the company's services to their friends and business associates. The most successful even recruited and developed their own sales forces. In 1998 PPLS generated 76 percent of its annual sales from the roughly 150,000 members registered as sales associates. The remaining 24 percent of sales were generated through arrangements with insurance and service companies with established sales forces, such as CNA and Primerica Financial Services.

Sales associates were compensated on a commission basis (see Exhibit 2). Prior to 1995, associates that signed up a new member received a commission of 70 percent of the first year premium, and a 16 percent commission for subsequent year renewals. First-year commissions were paid in advance whereas renewal commissions were paid as premiums were received. For example, if a new member signed up at a premium of $229 per year, the associate responsible for the sale received a first-year commission of $160 (0.70 × $229) at sign up. If the member renewed in subsequent years, the sales associate received a monthly commission of $3.04 (0.16 × $19).

After 1995 PPLS modified its commission formula to a flat 25 percent commission for both initial year and subsequent renewal memberships. To retain and attract sales associates, PPLS advanced the sales associate three years of commission on every new membership sold. If a membership lapsed before the advances had been recovered, PPLS deducted 50 percent of any unearned advances from future commissions to the relevant associate.

----

2. *Legal services specifically excluded from coverage included domestic matters, bankruptcy, deliberate criminal acts, alcohol or drug-related matters, business matters, and pre-existing conditions.*

Claim Cost Management

PPLS had historically offered two forms of legal services, each with very different implications for managing legal claim costs. The first form of service, termed open panel, allowed members to use their own attorney to provide legal services available under their policy. Members' attorneys were reimbursed for their services using a payment schedule that reflected "usual, reasonable and customary fees" for a particular service and geographic area.

The second form of service, closed panel memberships, required members to access legal services through a network of independent attorneys that were under contract with PPLS. These provider attorneys were paid a fixed monthly fee on a per capita basis to provide services to plan members living within the state in which the attorney was licensed to practice. PPLS contracted with one large, highly rated legal firm in each of its 36 major markets. These were selected after a detailed review by PPLS management. Martindale-Hubbell, a legal rating firm, typically rated PPLS's provider attorneys AV, its highest rating.

Average costs of membership claims in 1998 were 33 percent of membership premiums, and management reported that these costs were expected to remain at around 35 percent in the future.

FINANCIAL PERFORMANCE

PPLS reported record financial performance in the period 1997 and 1998 (see Exhibit 3 for summary financial data). Membership revenues during this period grew by an average of 52 percent per year, net income grew by 61 percent per year, and operating cash flows grew 270 percent per year. The firm's financial performance for the first six months of 1999 continued to be strong. Membership revenues grew by 20 percent, earnings by 54 percent, and operating cash flows by 138 percent (from $2.4 million to $5.7 million).

As a result of the company's growth performance, a number of equity analysts that followed the stock recommended it to their clients. For example, David Strasser of Salomon Brothers issued strong buy recommendations for PPLS in August 1997 and commented on the stock as follows:

> We reiterate our Strong Buy recommendation on the shares of Pre-Paid Legal Services, Inc. . . . We have recently increased our one-year price to $34 from $26. We did this for several reasons. First, the company continues to demonstrate consistent earnings growth, in line with Wall Street estimates, which gives us greater visibility of our projected 36% growth rate. . . . We are also encouraged by the company's ability to generate positive operating cash flow while still growing revenues 53%. This positive cash flow is indicative of the seasoned membership base that generates cash in spite of the company's policy of paying commission advances to its associates for new sales. We continue to believe that the company will announce an alliance with a major insurance company to sell the company's

products. This would essentially double the size of the company's productive sales force and increase overall visibility of the prepaid legal product.[3]

ACCOUNTING DISPUTE

Despite its strong financial performance, in late 1997 PPLS was a target of short selling. On November 24, 1997, *Fortune* published an article titled "Will Pre-Paid Keep Growing?" The article cited short seller Robert Olstein of Olstein's Financial Alert Fund, who explained that his concern arose because "PPLS's accounting for commissions is unrealistic and not in accordance with economic reality."[4] The *Fortune* article noted:

> *Rather than record the commissions as an instant hit to earnings, Pre-Paid spreads them out over a three-year period. Such deferrals, the shorts argue, make today's earnings growth look stronger than it really is. In the first half of this year, for example, if the company had swallowed commissions when they were paid, it would have shown little if any earnings growth—certainly not a level of growth to justify the stock's trading at nearly 40 times earnings.*
>
> *Plus, trouble could emerge if the company's cancellation rate on its policies increases and it can't somehow recover the commissions it has already paid. Pre-Paid shrugs this off, arguing that its historic cancellation rate is a manageable 24%. And, Harp (PPLS's CEO) boasts, "I can predict this business more precisely than anybody you want to mention."*
>
> *Maybe so, but the company's own figures, disclosed in SEC filings, show that the rate is on an upward trend. The filings also state that Pre-Paid's cancellation rate will rise if newly written policies make up a greater portion of its business, and the company warns (deep in its 10-K annual report) that it experienced a "significant increase" in sales of new contracts last year. Unless this shift is offset by "other factors," the 10-K says, financial performance could be severely hurt. In other words, Olstein contends, Pre-Paid may face a big write-off at some point.*

Exhibit 4 presents the company's footnote disclosure on its method of accounting for sales commissions.

MANAGEMENT RESPONSE

PPLS argued that its policy of accounting for commissions resulted in a commission expense that was more consistent with the collection of the premiums generated by the sale of such contracts. In addition, between October 1998 and June 1999, management ac-

---

3. *Analyst Report, David Strasser, Salomon Brothers, August 1997.*

4. *Herb Greenberg, "Will Pre-Paid Keep Growing? A Company's HMO-Style Approach to Legal Services Has Won It Plenty of Fans —And a Soaring Price. But Shortsellers Say the Numbers Don't Add Up," Fortune, November 24, 1997.*

quired 1,384,440 of the firm's shares on the open market at an average price of $28 per share.[5]

Nonetheless, concern over the company's accounting persisted. In late June 1999, short sales were 6.5 percent of outstanding shares, more than four times the level of typical companies.[6] The company's stock traded at $26.63, well off its yearly high of $39.25 and the all-time high of $40.50.

Rick Nelson, an analyst at Furman Selz, summed up the market sentiment this way: "Insiders feel they've got a company that's trading well off its high where the operating fundamentals are going gangbusters. But the shorts have caught on the notion that from a cash flow standpoint, the company just can't handle the growth, and that their business model itself will come back to haunt them."[7]

QUESTIONS

1. Based on the post-1995 commission formula, calculate the commission that would be earned by a sales associate who sold a Family Plan with a $19 per month premium. How much would the company attempt to recover from the sales associate if the customer chose not to renew the contract after two years?
2. How should PPLS account for the above transactions?
3. Who do you think has it right? *Fortune* or PPLS's management? Why?
4. What actions could PPLS's management take to change the unease among key investors about the firm's accounting and its business model?

Pre-Paid Legal Services

5. Quicken.com, "Insider Trading in Pre-Paid Legal Services."

6. "Uncovered Short Positions Rise on Big Board and Amex," The New York Times, June 22, 1999.

7. Ian Mount, "The Long and Short of It," SmartMoney.com, May 25, 1999.

Pre-Paid Legal Services

EXHIBIT 1
Number of Subscribers to Legal Service Plans in the U.S.,
1981 to 1997

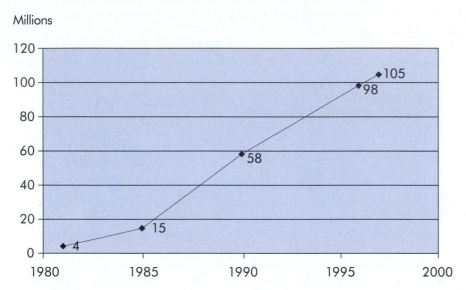

Millions

The above estimates were developed by The National Resources Center for Consumer Legal Services (NRC) and reported by PPLS in its 1998 10-K Report. NRC estimates included free member plans sponsored by labor unions, the American Association for Retired Persons, the National Education Association, and military services, as well as employer-paid plans. PPLS estimated that 10 percent of the total legal insurance market was covered by plans comparable to those provided by PPLS. The other major companies servicing this market were Hyatt Legal Services, ARAG Group, LawPhone, National Legal Plan, and the Signature Group. The NRC estimated that in 1997 the market share of these firms (and PPLS) was 79 percent. The market share of PPLS alone was estimated at 15 percent.

Source: Pre-Paid Legal Annual Report, 1998.

EXHIBIT 2
Summary of Commission Rates and Timing of Payment for PPLS

	First-Year Commission	Subsequent Year Commissions
Pre-1995:		
Commission rate	70% of subscription	16% of subscription
Timing of payment	At customer sign-up	Monthly
1995:		
Commission rate	25% of subscription	25% of subscription
Timing of payment	Advance of three years' worth of commissions at customer sign-up	None for first three years, then monthly

EXHIBIT 3
Summary Financial information for Pre-Paid Legal Services

(in $000)	Year ended December 31			
	1998	**1997**	**1996**	**1995**
Membership revenues	$110,003	$76,688	$50,582	$31,290
Net income	30,210	18,790	12,470	7,312
Cash from operations	$9,895	$7,733	$942	$548
Total assets	$167,903	$91,912	$57,532	$35,629
Book value of equity	101,304	70,511	45,474	29,740
New memberships sold	391,827	283,723	194,483	109,922
Period-end memberships in force	603,017	425,381	294,151	203,535

Source: Annual Reports, 1995–98.

EXHIBIT 4
Financial Footnotes Disclosure of Commission Advance from 1998 10-K

Commission Advances represent the unearned portion of the commissions advanced to Associates on the sales of Memberships. Commissions are earned as premiums are collected, usually on a monthly basis. The Company reduces commission advances as premiums are paid and commissions earned. Unearned commission advances on lapsed Memberships are recovered through collection of premiums on an associate's active Memberships. At December 31, 1998 and 1997, the Company had an allowance of $4.0 million and $3.7 million, respectively, to provide for estimated uncollectible balances. The Company charges interest at the prime rate on unearned commission advances relating to Memberships that canceled subsequent to the advance being made.

Data on Commission Advances reported in PPLS's 1995–98 annual reports are as follows:

(in $000)	Year ended December 31			
	1998	**1997**	**1996**	**1995**
Commission advances — current	$21,224	$15,705	$9,108	$3,923
Noncurrent commission advances, net	60,661	38,038	21,744	8,548

Entity Accounting Analysis

For financial reporting purposes, an entity is an organization that controls some economic resources. Entities can take many different forms: they can be individuals, partnerships (such as many professional firms), private or public corporations, divisions of corporations, private nonprofit organizations, and government departments.

Business entity analysis involves understanding how the boundaries of entities are defined to better evaluate how they are performing. For financial reporting purposes, an entity's boundaries can be specified narrowly, using a strict legal definition. Such an approach has been popular in Germany and Japan until relatively recently. However, it frequently fails to provide investors with comprehensive information on the legal entity's risks and performance. Accountants and analysts therefore typically take a broader view of the entity. This approach focuses on the resources over which managers have control, rather than the legal entity.

Entity analysis is important for shareholders because it clarifies which resources they have a claim over and how those resources are performing. Three specific concerns arise for shareholders in entity analysis. First, does the firm have hidden commitments or hidden losses arising from its investments in other firms? Second, is management siphoning off resources to other entities that they can control? This can arise if a firm sells to or buys from related parties that are largely owned by management. Finally, is management overinvesting in "pet projects" that generate low or negative returns for shareholders? Entity analysis attempts to answer these questions by understanding how an entity is defined, what resources it controls, how it performs, what related-party transactions it undertakes, and how its business segments perform.

Many firms have sizable and complex relations with other companies that create financial reporting challenges. These include stock investments, stakes in research and development limited partnerships, and franchising arrangements. For these types of business relations, a critical accounting challenge is to decide whether financial performance of the two companies should be aggregated as if the firms were a single entity, or reported for each unit separately. If performance is aggregated, a follow-up question for analysts is to evaluate how the separate entities are performing, particularly if they are in very different business segments. The answer to this question is particularly challenging if the entities buy goods and services from one another.

ENTITY REPORTING CHALLENGES

As shown in Figure 8-1, the critical entity challenge in financial reporting is deciding how an entity is to be defined. From an economic perspective, if one firm has complete

Figure 8-1 Criteria for Aggregating Performance of Units and Implementation Issues

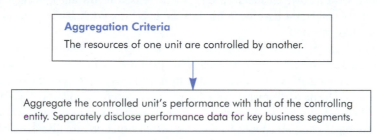

Aggregation Criteria

The resources of one unit are controlled by another.

Aggregate the controlled unit's performance with that of the controlling entity. Separately disclose performance data for key business segments.

Challenging Transactions

1. A firm has partial control over another.
2. Control is difficult to measure.
3. Defining and measuring performance for core business segments is difficult.

control over the resources of another, the two can be considered to be a single entity. Of course, many firms have only partial rather than complete control over the resources of another. One entity question for financial reporting is therefore determining whether one firm's level of control over another is sufficient to justify viewing the two as a single entity. A second challenge is that, for some business relations, it is difficult to measure the extent of one firm's control over another.

The decision to account for two or more firms as a single entity for financial reporting purposes does not eliminate investors' demand for information on each of the subunits, particularly if they are in dissimilar businesses. Consequently, firms with different businesses report summary financial information for each segment. Of course, segment reporting has its own complications. How are segments defined? How is segment performance measured when there are transactions between segments?

Challenge One: Partial Control

For many company investments, the purchaser clearly acquires control of another entity. For example, on June 25, 1999, Lucent Technologies Inc., the leading maker of telephone equipment, agreed to acquire 100 percent of the stock of Nexabit Networks, a private company that developed high-speed switches for moving data traffic on telecommunications networks. Lucent's offer was for nearly $900 million in stock. By offering to acquire 100 percent of Nexabit's stock, Lucent ensured that it would have complete control over Nexabit's assets.

Typically, when one firm owns more than 50 percent of the voting stock of another, it has control. In this case, it is required to combine or consolidate the performance of the acquiree with its own financial results. As discussed below and in Chapter 4, two methods of consolidation have been used in the U.S., the pooling-of-interests method and the purchase method.

An acquirer can also exercise considerable control over an acquiree when it owns less than 50 percent of its voting stock. At what point, then, should one firm be viewed as having control over another? Should an investing firm with less than 50 percent ownership in another consolidate its performance with that of the acquiree? In addition, for some business combinations, it can be difficult to ascertain who has control over whom. How should these types of combinations be reported? Both situations are discussed below.

EXAMPLE: INVESTMENTS OF LESS THAN 50 PERCENT INTEREST.   On May 19, 1999, Amazon.com, a leading Internet retailer specializing in books, music, and videos, announced that it had acquired a 35 percent stake in Homegrocer.com, an online grocery delivery service in Portland and Seattle, for $42.5 million. Amazon.com announced that its investment would allow Homegrocer.com to accelerate its expansion into new cities. How should Amazon.com record this investment? How much control, if any, does the company have over Homegrocer.com? Should Amazon.com consolidate its results with those of Homegrocer.com?

Assessing whether a company has control over the resources of another is clearly subjective. It depends on the percentage ownership acquired, the purpose of the acquisition, as well as the voting strength of the other owners. Accounting rules in the U.S. (APB 18 and FASB Interpretation 35) recognize this ambiguity and require firms to use the equity method to report investments where an investor has "significant influence" over the operations of another firm but lacks control.[1] The equity method is effectively a "one-line consolidation." It provides a way of recognizing that there is a middle ground between full consolidation and treating an investment as a marketable security.

Under the equity method, the investor reports its share of the other company's earnings (less any goodwill amortization or depreciation on written-up assets) in a separate line item in its income statement. In other words, the investor's bottom-line earnings under the equity method are identical to those under purchase accounting, even though the details presented in the income statement differ. In the balance sheet, the investor reports the investment asset as a one-line item at cost plus its share of undistributed profits since acquisition.

The FASB notes that prima facie evidence of "significant influence" is the ownership of more than 20 percent and less than 50 percent of another company's common voting stock. However, the 20 percent minimum threshold is not intended to be a hard-and-fast rule. An investor with a stake of less than 20 percent in another company may be viewed as having significant influence, and an acquirer with a stake of more than 20 percent may not. In February 1999, the FASB proposed modifying the 50 percent threshold that had been used to distinguish whether a firm has significant influence or outright control over another. Under the proposal, some firms with less than 50 percent ownership stakes but effective control over another entity may be required to consolidate the entities, rather than using the equity method to record their investments.

The accounting rules that define the boundaries of an entity permit managers to exercise judgment in deciding how to define the firm's boundaries. Managers certainly have the best information on the nature of the relation between their firm and other companies. However, the rules also provide opportunities for managers to use their discretion to window-dress their firms' reported performance. For example, if managers classify the securities as "available for sale" rather than as investments reported under the equity method, income statement effects from the investment are limited to dividend income.

EXAMPLE: WHO CONTROLS WHOM?   For some combinations it is difficult to infer who controls whom. For example, on April 6, 1998, Citicorp and Travelers Group announced an agreement to merge to become a global financial service provider. The merged firm, Citigroup Inc., served over 100 million customers in 100 countries around the world and had interests in traditional banking, consumer finance, credit cards, investment banking, securities brokerage and asset management, and property casualty and life insurance. Under the merger, each company's shareholders owned 50 percent of the combined firm. Citicorp shareholders exchanged each of their shares for 2.5 shares of Citigroup, whereas Travelers shareholders retained their existing shares, which automatically became shares of the new company. The new firm also announced that John S. Reed, Citicorp's Chairman and CEO, and Sanford I. Weill, the chairman and CEO of Travelers, would serve as cochairmen and coCEOs of the merged firm.

In the Citicorp-Travelers combination, it is not clear which company is the acquirer and which the acquired. How, then, should accounting reflect this combination? The boundaries of the new entity are clear. But what is the value of its assets, liabilities, revenues, and expenses? Given the difficulty in identifying which party is the acquirer, accountants have historically simply summed up the two firms' financial statements. Under this approach, called "pooling-of-interests," the consolidated financials are the aggregated book values of the two firms' individual statements.

In contrast to the Citicorp-Travelers merger, most combinations do have an identifiable acquirer and target. For these types of investments, investors want to know how much the acquirer paid for the target firm and whether the investment creates value for shareholders. The pooling-of-interests approach does a poor job of providing this type of information, since it consolidates the two firms' financial statements at their book values. Acquirers typically pay a considerable premium over book value, and even over pre-acquisition market value, to take control over other companies.

The second method of consolidation, called purchase accounting, provides more relevant information by combining the target firm's assets and liabilities into the balance sheet of the acquirer at their market values. Any difference between the price the acquirer paid for the target firm's equity and the market value of the separable net assets is then reported as goodwill. Goodwill is subsequently amortized over as many as 40 years, or in some countries is written off if there is evidence of impairment.

One challenge in accounting for business combinations has been in assessing when pooling-of-interests or when purchase values provide more relevant information for investors. Under APB 16, firms were required to use the pooling method when both partners had been autonomous companies for more than two years, the deal was largely a stock swap, voting and dividend rights for shareholders were unchanged, and there were no major asset sales for at least two years following the combination. Otherwise, acquisitions have to be accounted for using the purchase method. However, in April 1999, the FASB proposed new rules that would require all mergers and acquisitions to be reported using the purchase method and would limit the maximum life of goodwill to twenty years.

Key Analysis Questions

Several opportunities for financial analysis arise from the difficulty in assessing whether one company has control over another. First, accounting rules provide management with some latitude in entity reporting. Management can use this discretion to ensure that financial statements reflect the underlying entity's performance. However, it can also seek to omit important resources or commitments from the firm's financial statements. Second, accounting rules require a firm to consolidate, to use the equity method, or to mark an investment to market. In contrast, the degree of control that one company has over another lies on a continuum between no control and complete control. Consequently, the information generated by entity accounting rules is unlikely to reflect all of the subtleties associated with control. Given these challenges, the following questions are likely to be useful for analysts:

- What are a firm's major investments in other companies? What percentage of these companys' stock does it own? Who are the other key owners of the same firms, and how much stock do they own? Is there other evidence of a firm's control over others, such as representation on the boards of directors?
- What are the assets and leverage of related companies that are not consolidated? Does the investor's management appear to be using its reporting discretion to keep key resources and commitments off the balance sheet? What is the performance of related companies that are not accounted for using the equity method? What are the investor management's incentives for this reporting choice?
- How have significant acquisitions been recorded? Does management of the acquirer appear to have used the pooling-of-interests method to avoid showing the full cost of the acquisition? If so, what was the effective cost of the acquisition? Has it generated an adequate return for shareholders? If the purchase method has been used, has the acquirer been forced to write down the value of the assets it acquired?

Challenge Two: Control Is Difficult to Measure

Certain complex business relations, such as research and development (R&D) limited partnerships and franchise agreements, raise questions about whether one party in the relation effectively has control over the other, or whether the two parties are separate entities. Also, in some situations, a firm's managers but not its stockholders have control over another company.

EXAMPLE: R&D LIMITED PARTNERSHIPS.   In 1997 Dura Pharmaceuticals Inc., a company that developed respiratory drugs, formed a limited partnership with Spiros Development II Inc. to raise capital for development of a new form of pulmonary drug delivery process. Under the partnership agreement, Spiros II made a $94 million public offering of a package of securities that included its own callable common stock (valued at $81.3 million) and warrants for Dura's common stock (valued at $12.7 million). Dura also invested $75 million in Spiros II. In exchange for the warrants and $75 million investment, Dura received an option to purchase Spiros II's callable common stock at prices that increase over time, as well as the exclusive rights to any products developed. Spiros then uses these funds to acquire research from Dura to develop the new products.

The contractual relationship between Dura and Spiros II is called an R&D limited partnership. Under this type of relationship, one general partner (in this case Dura) performs the research, and the limited partners (public investors in this case) supply financing. The arrangement differs from more traditional equity financing in that the limited investors receive a claim on only the specific research project covered in the agreement. In contrast, if Dura were to raise the funding itself through a public offer of its own stock, the new shareholders would have a claim on all of Dura's research output. The arrangement also provides a way for Dura to offload some of the risks associated with specific research projects. Dura effectively reduces its exposure to development failures and in return shares the upside if a drug is developed and becomes a market success.

How should Dura's relation with Spiros II be recorded? Does Dura exercise control over Spiros? If it does, then Spiros is effectively a Dura subsidiary. If it does not, Spiros can be considered a separate entity. A key question for investors is to understand how much of the project's risk and upside has been sold by Dura. If most of the risk resides with Spiros II's public owners, it is inappropriate to consolidate the two firms. Alternatively, if most of the risk resides with Dura, consolidation of Spiros II's results with those of Dura's is more likely to give investors an accurate understanding of Dura's performance.

Historically, the decision to consolidate Spiros II has been determined by Dura's ownership of Spiros II's stock. If Dura owns more than 50 percent of Spiros II's voting stock, it is required to consolidate; otherwise it is not. However, in 1999 the FASB suggested broadening the definition of control. Under the proposed approach, control is likely to be defined as "the ability to derive benefits from the use of individual assets" (of another firm) "in essentially the same way a controlling entity can direct the use of its own assets." Evidence of control is likely to include domination of another entity's board of directors, ability to obtain a majority voting interest in another entity through ownership of convertible securities, a sole general-partner interest in a limited partnership, and the ability to dissolve an entity and assume control of its assets. This broader view of control would almost surely require Dura to consolidate Spiros II, both because it is the general partner in a limited partnership and because it has an option to acquire Spiros II.

It is interesting to consider Dura's reporting of its relation with Spiros in its 1997 annual report. The key transactions are recorded as follows:

- The initial $75 million contribution to Spiros II is reported as a Purchase Option Expense, included in Dura's income statement.
- The warrants issued as part of Spiros II's public offering are included in Dura's Additional Paid-In Capital and Warrants Proceeds Receivable recorded on its balance sheet.
- Annual payments from Spiros II for contracted research are recorded as contract revenues by Dura and effectively offset the research costs of the development program.
- Finally, when Dura has exercised its option to acquire limited partners in similar earlier agreements, it has written off much of the outlay as purchased R&D.

The fact that R&D limited partnerships permit R&D risks to be shared between partners along a continuum, whereas consolidation is a binary decision, implies that it is difficult for accountants to fully capture the risk-sharing complexities involved in these types of relations. As a result, they provide an opportunity for analysts to add value by clearly identifying how the partners share risks and rewards under the agreement, and whether these events are portrayed in the financial statements.

EXAMPLE: FRANCHISE OPERATIONS.   Franchising is a popular organizational form in the U.S., where franchise operations employ more than 8 million people and account for more than 30 percent of all retail sales. Franchise companies include McDonalds, Burger King, Kentucky Fried Chicken, Pizza Hut, Holiday Inn, Marriott, Avis, Hertz, H&R Block, and 7 Eleven Stores.

A typical franchise arrangement works as follows. A franchisor sells the right to operate a retail operation in a given location to a franchisee. The franchisee typically pays an initial franchise fee to cover such services as management training, advertising and promotion, site selection assistance, bookkeeping services, and construction supervision. Franchisees are also frequently required to purchase critical equipment and supplies from the franchisor, and to pay annual fees that vary with franchise sales. Finally, franchise agreements often provide the franchisor with the right to purchase profitable or unsuccessful franchise operations.

Franchising is viewed as an effective organizational form because it provides the franchisee with some of the rights and incentives associated with ownership. Of course, there are also potential problems arising from franchising. For example, franchisees can underinvest in quality and free ride on the franchisor's reputation. Franchise arrangements also make it cumbersome to coordinate corporate-wide changes in product offerings and strategy. Finally, franchisees are often concerned that after they have invested in establishing a market in a particular location, the franchisor will sell another (competing) franchise outlet in the same location.

The accounting entity question that arises for franchise arrangements is whether the franchisor effectively has control over the franchisees and should therefore consolidate their performance with its own. Several factors suggest that franchisors do have considerable control over franchisees. First, as noted above, franchise contracts give franchisors significant control over the franchisee's business operations by requiring them to maintain certain quality standards and to acquire supplies from the franchisor. Second, many franchisors have the right to acquire successful and also unsuccessful franchisees. Finally, franchisors often provide significant financing to franchisees or guarantee their debt.

Given the considerable control exercised by franchisors over franchisees, some have argued in favor of considering franchise operations as a system, rather than as independent franchisor and franchisee entities. Consolidated reports for a franchise system would provide information on the overall profitability of the business concept. This type of information could be very valuable to investors, particularly if franchisors do not operate any established franchise outlets. However, consolidation fails to provide information on that portion of the rewards of the franchise system that go to the franchisor. Successful franchisors, after all, are likely to capitalize on their brand name by writing franchise contracts that ensure that they, rather than the franchisees, earn most of the rents from the system. This potentially creates a challenge for financial reporting, since if the franchisor demands too much of the franchisee, it is likely to fail and have to be acquired by the franchisor.

Because of the limitations of considering franchise operations as a system, franchisors typically do not consolidate franchisees. Under SFAS 45, franchisors are required to defer recognizing revenues from initial franchise fees until all services have been performed. These services could include the guarantee of debt or the control of the franchisee's operations. However, these rules do not require franchisors to provide key data on the performance of their franchisees. This information is likely to be critical to help investors evaluate whether the concept is successful and whether the franchisor has been too demanding in its contractual relations with franchisees. As a result, there is considerable scope for financial analysis of franchise operations.

EXAMPLE: MANAGEMENT CONTROL OF A RELATED PARTY.   Some companies have business relations with other companies that are owned by management. For example, on November 17, 1997, Zaitun Bhd, a Malaysian personal care products company, proposed acquiring a piece of land for RM36 million from Benua Rezeki Sdn Bhd. Benua Rezeki Sdn Bhd was partially owned by two of the directors of Zaitun (Datuk Mohd Kamal Mohd Eusuff and Aisha Mohd Eusuff). On December 31, 1997, Zaitun put down a deposit on the land for RM18 million, which was 50 percent of the total amount.

For the public owners of Zaitun, this type of transaction raised questions about whether the proposed price for the land was a fair market price, or whether Zaitun overpaid for the land, permitting the Zaitun directors to benefit at the expense of the company's external owners. In subsequent developments (on April 15, 1998), Zaitun canceled the sale agreement and agreed to refund the deposit.

In the case of related-party transactions, external shareholders do not have any control over the related party. Consequently, there is no justification for aggregating the performance of the two parties. The challenge for shareholders is to understand management's incentives in these types of transactions. This can be assessed by comparing management's stake in the related party and in the company it is managing. If management owns more in the related party than it owns in the company it manages, there are potential conflicts of interest. Shareholders are then interested in understanding the magnitude of the related-party transactions and their profitability for the related party versus the company. Not surprisingly, almost all countries require companies to make disclosures of related-party transactions to ensure that shareholders have full information on any potential management conflicts of interest. It is interesting to note that on September 26, 1998, the Malaysian Securities Commission reprimanded Zaitun for failing to disclose the related-party land sale.

Key Analysis Questions

Complex business relations between companies can make it difficult to measure whether one firm has control over another. Financial analysts can add value by understanding the details of these types of relations and their potential financial implications. The following questions are likely to be useful for this purpose:

- Does a firm have complex and/or unusual relations with other firms, such as those discussed above for franchising and R&D limited partnerships? If so, what is the primary purpose of these relations? Is it for risk management, for raising capital, for keeping core assets and commitments off the balance sheet, or for managing earnings?
- Does it make sense to consolidate the performance of related entities that have complex business relations? If not, what other information is needed and available to fully understand the financial implications of the relations?
- How is the company using the business relation to manage risk? If it has an option to acquire another company, how is it exercising that option? Is it exercising it in a way that is consistent with its stated purpose?
- Does the company have any related party transactions? If so, who are the related parties? What governance mechanisms protect the rights of external stockholders? Is there any evidence that resources are being siphoned out of the company in related party transactions at the expense of external stockholders?

Challenge Three: Defining and Measuring
Core Business Units' Performance

For firms in diverse businesses, consolidated information provides investors with a good overview of the performance of the entire entity. However, investors are also likely to be interested in understanding how the separate business units are performing. Consequently, diversified companies provide disaggregated data on the performance of their major business segments in the financial statement footnotes.

Segment reporting generates a number of measurement challenges. First, there are many different ways of defining business segments, making it difficult to compare performance of supposedly similar segments across firms or even over time for the same firm. Second, analysis is particularly challenging for firms with financial services segments whose business models are very different from those of the other operating segments. Finally, if there are transactions between business segments involving intercompany transfer prices, it can be difficult to evaluate the performance of individual segments.

EXAMPLE: DEFINING BUSINESS SEGMENTS.   Managers have traditionally been able to exercise considerable judgment in deciding how to define business units for segment reporting. A number of factors affect how business segments are organized. They can be structured to create operating and management synergies between units with overlapping development, production, or distribution processes. For example, in its 1998 annual report, Eastman Kodak disclosed separate information for four segments that were primarily defined by the imaging needs of the company's main customer groups: Consumer Imaging, Kodak Professional, Health Imaging, and Other Imaging. The Consumer Imaging segment produced film, paper, chemicals, cameras, photoprocessing equipment, and photoprocessing services for consumers. The Kodak Professional segment catered to professional customers. The Health Imaging segment manufactured medical film and processing equipment. Finally, the Other Imaging segment was a catch-all for Kodak's many other imaging businesses, including motion picture film, copiers, microfilm equipment, printers, scanners, and other business equipment.

Segment definitions can also reflect management's desire to conceal information that it regards as sensitive. For example, prior to 1998, Merck & Co. Inc. operated two primary businesses, Merck Pharmaceutical and Merck-Medco Managed Care, but avoided reporting any segment data on the two. Merck Pharmaceutical discovered, developed, manufactured, and marketed prescription drugs for treating human disorders, whereas Merck-Medco generated revenues from filling and managing prescriptions and health management programs. Merck's management was concerned that reporting segment data for these two businesses would make its pricing strategies more transparent to customers, potentially reducing the firm's future bargaining power in its negotiations with medical providers. However, in 1998 it was required to report segment data for the two businesses to satisfy new FASB rules on segment disclosures.

Finally, segment definitions can be used by management as a way of concealing from investors the poor performance in one or more business units. For example, management may be particularly sensitive about poor performance of a recent acquisition and may elect to combine it with a strong performer for segment reporting purposes.

In 1998 the FASB attempted to reduce the degree of management judgment in the definition of reporting segments. SFAS 131 defined segments for financial reporting using a "management" approach. Under this approach, firms were required to report segment data for significant business units whose "separate financial information is . . . regularly reviewed by the chief operating decision makers in deciding how to allocate resources and in assessing performance."[2] A significant segment is one whose assets, revenues, or profits comprise at least 10 percent of consolidated assets, revenues, or profits. The standard requires companies to disclose revenues, profits, and assets for core segments.

The overall impact of the FASB standard on segment disclosures has yet to be analyzed. However, it has had an effect on reporting by some companies. For example, as noted above, Merck expanded its segment disclosures to report data for both Merck Pharmaceutical and Merck-Medco Managed Care. In addition, prior to 1998, IBM only reported revenues for its business segments. Some analysts speculated that this decision was made to avoid disclosing large losses in the personal computing segment. In 1998 IBM adopted SFAS 131 and began reporting operating profit data for all its segments. The results showed that the company had a sizable loss in 1998 in its Personal Systems segment (a pretax loss of $1.0 billion on revenues of $12.8 billion).

EXAMPLE: FINANCE COMPANIES.   Another challenge in analyzing segment data arises for companies with leasing, real estate, financing, or insurance subsidiaries. The economic model for these companies is quite different from those for retail, manufacturing, or other service companies. Many firms with finance subsidiaries argue that consolidation of such "nonhomogeneous" operations distorts the parent's key ratios, particularly leverage, working capital ratios, and gross margins. For example, consider the impact of IBM's finance subsidiary on its performance. In 1998 the finance subsidiary had assets of $40.1 billion versus $46 billion for the parent, and pretax profit margins of 32 percent versus 11 percent for the company as a whole. It also had significantly higher leverage than the parent company. These factors made it difficult to compare the performance of IBM with that of other computer companies that had no such finance subsidiary.

Prior to SFAS 94, many U.S. companies elected to account for finance subsidiaries using the equity method rather than full consolidation. Frequently, a summary income statement and balance sheet for the finance subsidiary were also disclosed. SFAS 94 stopped this practice and required that finance companies be consolidated. Companies that provided separate financial statements for finance subsidiaries were required to continue this practice.

The question of whether to use consolidated or segment information to best evaluate firms with finance subsidiaries is a complex one. Many companies with finance subsidiaries provide additional disclosure to help analysts benchmark core segments with the performance of companies that operate as stand-alone entities.[3] However, this approach ignores any interactions that occur between operating and finance segments. For example, some companies use finance subsidiaries to provide low-cost financing to their customers, affecting pricing and selling strategies for the other segments. Comparing segment performance data for these firms to that of other firms in the same industries is likely to uncover this strategy. It is then important to analyze consolidated data to understand the performance of the entire portfolio of services provided to customers.

EXAMPLE: INTERSEGMENT TRANSACTIONS.   The final challenge for segment reporting comes from intersegment transactions, such as intersegment sales and allocation of common costs across segments. SFAS 131 requires companies to use the same transfer prices and cost allocations for segment reporting that are used internally. However, this permits management to have considerable control over the reported performance of both segments. For example, by setting a relatively high transfer price, management can enhance the reported performance of the selling segment at the expense of the buying one.

Many factors can influence managers' transfer pricing decisions. These include facilitating the efficient allocation of resources within the enterprise, motivating segment management, optimizing taxes, and affecting reported financial performance. It is therefore difficult to know how to interpret segment performance when there are high levels of intersegment sales. Is one segment outperforming its industry peers because of the firm's transfer pricing policy? If so, what are management's motives for such a policy?

Similarly, the allocation of common costs can give rise to difficulty in interpreting segment performance. Does one segment outperform its peers because it receives a relatively low allocation of a common cost? If so, what are management's motives for this policy? Does the firm simply have a poor cost allocation system? Or is management attempting to understate the performance of one of its segments? What are the potential internal implications of the firm's cost allocation approach?

Key Analysis Questions

The challenge in defining business segments and measuring their performance provides several opportunities for financial analysis. Given management's control over the way the firm is structured and segments are reported, analysts can add value by evaluating the way the firm's business segments are defined as well as the reported performance for each segment. The following questions are likely to be useful for analyzing segment data:

- What are a multibusiness firm's major businesses? How are these aggregated into segments for reporting purposes? Does management appear to have aggregated segment data in such a way that it avoids presenting information for

an important part of its operations? If so, is management legitimately concerned that these data are proprietary, or is it concealing poor-performing
units?

• What are the business relations between segments? This question is the heart
of the firm's corporate strategy. How do these relations affect intersegment
transactions? Does a firm use one segment to subsidize the customers of another? What are the financial effects of these intercompany transactions and
customer subsidies? How useful are segment data, given the relations between segments?

• What is the performance of segments relative to other firms in the same industries? Is management propping up poor-performing segments at the expense of other business units?

SUMMARY

The entity principle defines the boundaries of the firm for financial reporting purposes.
When one firm has control over the resources of another, it consolidates the performance
of the two firms as if they were a single entity, using either the purchase method or the
pooling-of-interests method. If it does not have control but has significant influence over
the other firm, it reports its investment using the equity method of "one-line consolidation."

Control has typically been assessed when one company owns more than 50 percent
of the voting stock of another. One company is viewed as having significant influence
over another when it owns between 20 percent and 50 percent of its voting stock. However, as we have seen in this chapter, the implementation of these entity principles is not
always straightforward. The key implementation challenges arise when:

1. One company is able to control or have significant influence over another without
owning more than 50 percent or 20 percent, respectively, of its stock.
2. It is difficult to assess who has control over whom in a business combination.
3. There are complex business relations between firms that are difficult to classify
using the traditional definitions of control. These include R&D limited partnerships and franchise arrangements.

For firms that consolidate the operations of multibusiness units, investors are also interested in the separate performance of each business unit. Firms therefore report segment data in their financial statement footnotes. Segment reporting poses a number of
challenges. First, there are multiple ways of defining segments, making it difficult to
compare segments across firms or even for the same firm over time. Second, managers
often create multibusiness segments because they believe that there are opportunities for
synergies. For example, some companies use finance subsidiaries to subsidize customers

of operating divisions. Other companies have significant intersegment transactions. In either case, it is difficult to know how to interpret segment data, since it is subject to cross-subsidies, transfer prices, and cost allocations that would not arise for single business firms.

Both entity accounting rules and segment disclosures provide opportunities for financial analysts to evaluate a firm's entity accounting. The rules for measuring control have traditionally permitted management to avoid consolidating some types of firms where it has effective control. Rules on pooling-of-interests have permitted some firms to use the pooling method to avoid including the real cost of an acquisition in its financial statements. The entity questions raised by these rules and practices enable analysts to add value by assessing whether a firm's accounting presents an accurate picture of its entire operations. If not, analysts can attempt to estimate the effect of consolidation. For segment disclosures, analysts can add value by assessing the quality of management's segment definitions, given the firm's businesses. They can also assess the relevance of segment data for business analysis, given the extent of intersegment transactions and subsidies across segments.

DISCUSSION QUESTIONS

1. The Coca-Cola Company owns 42 percent of Coca-Cola Enterprises, the largest soft-drink bottler in the world. On December 31, 1998, The Coca-Cola Company reported the following information in its financial statement footnotes:

    "The excess of our equity in the underlying net assets of Coca-Cola Enterprises over our investment is primarily amortized on a straight-line basis over 40 years. The balance of this excess, net of amortization, was approximately $442 million at December 31, 1998. A summary of financial information for Coca-Cola Enterprises is as follows (in millions):

December 31,	1998	1997
Current assets	$ 2,285	$ 1,813
Noncurrent assets	18,847	15,674
Total assets	$21,132	$17,487
Current liabilities	$3,397	$3,032
Noncurrent liabilities	15,297	12,673
Total liabilities	$18,694	$15,705
Share-owners' equity	$2,438	$1,782
Company equity investment	$584	$184
Operating revenues	$13,414	$11,278
Cost of goods sold	8,391	7,096

(*continued*)

December 31,	1998	1997
Gross profit	$5,023	$4,182
Operating income	$869	$720
Net income	$142	$171
Net income available to common share owners	$141	$169
Company equity income	$51	$59

"Our net concentrate/syrup sales to Coca-Cola Enterprises were $3.1 billion in 1998. Coca-Cola Enterprises purchases sweeteners through our Company. . . . These transactions amounted to $252 million in 1998."

Show the 1998 financial statement effects of reporting Coca-Cola Enterprises using the equity method for The Coca-Cola Company. How much control does The Coca-Cola Company have over Coca-Cola Enterprises? Is the equity method the most appropriate method for recording this investment?

2. On April 22, 1999, MediaOne Group and AT&T agreed to merge. Under the merger, MediaOne Group's shareowners will receive .95 of a share of AT&T common stock and $30.85 in cash for each share of MediaOne Group. The total package of cash and stock was valued at $85 per share. MediaOne has 604.4 million shares outstanding.

Income Statement December 31, 1998 (in $ millions)	AT&T	MediaOne
Revenues		
Business Services	$23,611	—
Consumer Services	22,885	—
Wireless Services	5,406	$361
Broadband and Internet Services	—	2,491
Other and Corporate	1,321	30
Total Revenues	**53,223**	**2,882**
Operating Expenses	45,736	3,121
Total Operating Income (Loss)	**7,487**	**(239)**
Other income, net	1,247	3,368
Earnings (Loss) Before Interest and Taxes	**8,734**	**3,129**
Interest expense	427	491
Income from Continuing Operations Before Income Taxes	**8,307**	**2,638**
Provision for income taxes	3,072	1,208

Income Statement

December 31, 1998 (in $ millions)	AT&T	MediaOne
Income (Loss) from Continuing Operations	**5,235**	**1,430**
Income from discontinued operations	10	25,208
Gain on sale of discontinued operations	1,290	
Extraordinary loss	137	333
Net Income	**$ 6,398**	**$26,305**

Balance Sheet

December 31, 1998 (in $ millions)	AT&T	MediaOne
Assets		
Total Current Assets	$14,118	$1,200
Property, plant and equipment, net of accumulated depreciation	26,903	4,069
Licensing costs, net of accumulated amortization	7,948	
Investments	4,434	9,705
Prepaid pension costs	2,074	
Goodwill	2,205	11,647
Other assets	1,868	1,571
Total Assets	**$59,550**	**$28,192**
Liabilities and Equity		
Short-term debt	1,171	569
Other current liabilities	14,271	1,045
Total Current Liabilities	**15,442**	**1,614**
Long-term debt	5,556	4,853
Deferred credits and other	12,921	6,676
Minority interest in consolidated subsidiaries	109	1,099
Preferred stock		1,161
Common shareowners' equity	25,522	12,789
Total Liabilities and Equity	**$59,550**	**$28,192**

If MediaOne's asset book values are approximately equal to their market values, how much goodwill did AT&T pay for MediaOne? Prepare a pro forma income statement and balance sheet for the merged firm for 1998.

3. As discussed in the chapter, on April 6, 1998, Citicorp and Travelers Group announced an agreement to merge to become Citigroup Inc., a global financial service provider. Under the merger, each company's shareholders owned 50 percent of the

combined firm. Citicorp shareholders exchanged each of their shares for 2.5 shares of Citigroup, whereas Travelers shareholders retained their existing shares, which automatically became shares of the new company.

The financial statements for Citicorp and Travelers for 1997, the year prior to the merger, are as follows:

Income Statement **December 31, 1997 (in $ millions)**	**Citicorp**	**Travelers**
Revenues		
Interest and dividends	$21,164	$16,214
Insurance premiums		8,995
Commissions and fees	5,817	5,119
Other	7,716	7,281
Total Revenues	**34,697**	**37,609**
Expenses		
Interest	13,081	11,443
Provision for credit losses	1,907	277
Insurance benefits and claims		7,714
Other operating costs	13,987	13,163
Total Expenses	**28,975**	**32,597**
Income Before Taxes	**5,722**	**5,012**
Income taxes	2,131	1,696
Minority interest		212
Net Income	**$ 3,591**	**$ 3,104**

Balance Sheet **December 31, 1997 (in $ millions)**	**Citicorp**	**Travelers**
Assets		
Cash	$ 8,585	$ 4,033
Deposits with banks	13,049	—
Securities and real estate investments	33,361	171,568
Trading account assets	40,356	139,732
Loans	181,712	—
Receivables	3,288	21,360
Other	30,546	49,862
Total Assets	**$310,897**	**$386,555**

Balance Sheet
December 31, 1997 (in $ millions)

	Citicorp	Travelers
Liabilities and Equity		
Deposits	$199,121	—
Trading account liabilities	30,986	$ 96,166
Securities sold under repurchase agreements	—	120,921
Insurance reserves	—	43,782
Long-term debt	19,785	28,352
Other	39,809	76,441
Preferred stock	1,903	1,450
Common shareholders' equity	19,293	19,443
Total Liabilities and Equity	**$310,897**	**$386,555**

Estimate the pro forma income, common shareholders' equity, and total assets for Citigroup in 1997, using the pooling-of interests method. What concerns would you have as a shareholder about Citigroup using the pooling-of-interests method? What criteria would you use as an analyst to decide when, if ever, the pooling-of-interests method is an appropriate method of recording a business combination between two firms? Does the Citicorp-Travelers merger satisfy these criteria?

4. Review the financial statement effects for the Dura investments in Spiros II described in the chapter. How would these effects be reflected in Dura's books if its investment were consolidated?

5. Below is the segment disclosure reported by General Electric in its 1998 annual report.

In addition, General Electric provided the following information about the businesses comprising CECS:

"Consumer services — private-label and bank credit card loans, personal loans, time sales and revolving credit and inventory financing for retail merchants, auto leasing and inventory financing, mortgage servicing, and consumer savings and insurance services.

Equipment management — leases, loans, sales and asset management services for portfolios of commercial and transportation equipment, including aircraft, trailers, auto fleets, modular space units, railroad rolling stock, data processing equipment, containers used on ocean-going vessels, satellites.

Mid-market financing — loans, financing and operating leases and other services for middle-market customers, including manufacturers, distributors and end users, for a variety of equipment that includes vehicles, corporate aircraft, data processing equipment, medical and diagnostic equipment, and equipment used in construction, manufacturing, office applications, electronics and telecommunications activities.

Revenues for the years ended December 31

(in millions)	Total revenues 1998	1997	1996	Intersegment revenues 1998	1997	1996	External revenues 1998	1997	1996
GE									
Aircraft Engines	$ 10,294	$ 7,799	$ 6,302	$ 292	$101	$ 86	$ 10,002	$ 7,698	$ 6,216
Appliances	5,619	5,801	5,586	12	12	5	5,607	5,789	5,581
Industrial Products and Systems	11,222	10,984	10,401	479	491	453	10,743	10,493	9,948
NBC	5,269	5,153	5,232	—	—	—	5,269	5,153	5,232
Plastics	6,633	6,695	6,509	20	24	22	6,613	6,671	6,487
Power Systems	8,466	7,915	7,643	166	80	67	8,300	7,835	7,576
Technical Products and Services	5,323	4,861	4,700	14	18	23	5,309	4,843	4,677
All Other	264	308	291	—	—	—	264	308	291
Eliminations	(1,367)	(1,176)	(1,032)	(983)	(726)	(656)	(384)	(450)	(376)
Total GE segment revenues	51,723	48,340	45,632	—	—	—	51,723	48,340	45,632
Corporate items [a]	507	2,919	1,116	—	—	—	507	2,919	1,116
GECS net earnings	3,796	3,256	2,817	—	—	—	3,796	3,256	2,817
Total GE	56,026	54,515	49,565	—	—	—	56,026	54,515	49,565
GECS	48,694	39,931	32,713	—	—	—	48,694	39,931	32,713
Eliminations	(4,251)	(3,606)	(3,099)	—	—	—	(4,251)	(3,606)	(3,099)
Consolidated revenues	$100,469	$90,840	$79,179	$ —	$ —	$ —	$100,469	$90,840	$79,179

GE revenues include income from sales of goods and services to customers and other income. Sales from one Company component to another generally are priced at equivalent commercial selling prices.

(a) Includes revenues of $944 million and $789 million in 1997 and 1998, respectively, from an appliance distribution affiliate that was deconsolidated in 1998. Also includes $1,538 million in 1997 from exchanging preferred stock in Lockheed Martin Corporation for the stock of a newly formed subsidiary.

(in millions)	Assets at December 31 1998	1997	1996	Property, plant and equipment additions (including equipment leased to others) For the years ended December 31 1998	1997	1996	Depreciation and amortization (including goodwill and other intangibles) For the years ended December 31 1998	1997	1996
GE									
Aircraft Engines	$ 8,866	$ 8,895	$ 5,423	$ 480	$ 729	$ 551	$ 398	$ 292	$ 282
Appliances	2,436	2,354	2,399	150	83	168	137	131	123
Industrial Products and Systems	6,466	6,672	6,574	428	487	450	440	408	362
NBC	3,264	3,050	3,007	105	116	176	127	142	121
Plastics	9,813	8,890	9,130	722	618	748	591	494	552
Power Systems	7,253	6,182	6,322	246	215	185	215	199	184
Technical Products and Services	3,858	2,438	2,245	254	189	154	143	137	123
All Other	189	224	239	—	—	—	52	46	40
Total GE segments	42,145	38,705	35,339	2,385	2,437	2,432	2,103	1,849	1,787
Investments in GECS	19,727	17,239	14,276	—	—	—	—	—	—
Corporate items and eliminations [a]	12,798	11,482	10,310	158	129	114	189	180	176
Total GE	74,670	67,426	59,925	2,543	2,566	2,546	2,292	2,029	1,963
GECS	303,297	255,408	227,419	8,110	7,320	5,762	3,568	3,240	2,805
Eliminations	(22,032)	(18,822)	(14,942)	—	—	—	—	—	—
Consolidated totals	$355,935	$304,012	$272,402	$10,653	$9,886	$8,308	$5,860	$5,269	$4,768

Additions to property, plant and equipment include amounts relating to principal businesses purchased.

(a) Depreciation and amortization includes $84 million of unallocated RCA goodwill amortization in 1998, 1997 and 1996 that relates to NBC.

Specialized financing — loans and financing leases for major capital assets, including industrial facilities and equipment and energy-related facilities; commercial and residential real estate loans and investments; and loans to and investments in public and private entities in diverse industries.

Specialty insurance — U.S. and international multiple-line property and casualty reinsurance; certain directly written specialty insurance and life reinsurance; financial guaranty insurance, principally on municipal bonds and structured finance issues; private mortgage insurance; and creditor insurance covering international customer loan repayments.

Very few of the products financed by GECS are manufactured by GE's segment."

How useful is GE's segment information? What do you learn from this information that you cannot learn from the consolidated results? How important is GECS to GE's overall performance? What other information would you want to have to analyze the performance of GECS?

NOTES

1. Most countries outside the U.S. follow similar reporting practices for controlling and "influential" investments in other companies. However, these practices are relatively recent in some countries, including Germany and Japan, where parent companies formerly reported using a strict legal definition of an entity.

2. SFAS No 131, *Disclosures About Segments of Enterprise and Related Information.*

3. Gilson et al. (1999) show that since financial analysts specialize by industry and it is not economical for investment brokers to have more than one analyst follow a single firm, firms with diverse segments are underfollowed and undervalued relative to stand-alone entities. See Gilson, Healy, Noe, and Palepu, "Changes in Organizational Form and Capital Market Intermediation: Analyst Coverage After Stock Breakups," working paper, Harvard Business School, 1999.

In technology, things that have a high payoff are very risky. You need the ability to pursue risky ventures and yet not risk the company. If that means pursuing a lot of little things instead of one big thing, so be it—especially if the one big thing never panned out.

George Hatsopolous
Forbes, 11/16/87

In early July 1994, research analyst John Kolmanoff was considering the recent performance of Thermo Electron (NYSE: TMO), a technology creation company with an impressive track record for capitalizing on internally developed and externally acquired research. In the past, Kolmanoff had strongly recommended Thermo Electron to his clients, and many had profited from its extraordinary price appreciation during the last five years (see Exhibit 1). However, the firm's stock had recently been lagging the S&P 500, declining 19 percent for the six months ended June 30, 1994 (versus only a 10 percent decline for the S&P 500). This decline had been accompanied by an increase in short positions in the stock, and by criticism of the company's accounting. As a result of these developments, Kolmanoff decided that it was time to reconsider the company.

COMPANY BACKGROUND

Dr. George Hatsopolous founded Thermo Electron in 1956 in his Belmont, Massachusetts, garage using a $50,000 loan from his friend Peter Nomikos, heir to a Greek shipping fortune. A graduate student at the Massachusetts Institute of Technology, Hatsopolous hoped to capitalize on his doctoral research by commercializing the process of converting heat directly into electricity without moving parts. Two years later his prototype was completed and was widely acclaimed in the popular press as a breakthrough. One article proclaimed that the invention could be used to power satellites, military equipment, and even motor vehicles. Money flowed in from the venture capital community and the federal government. Although the process subsequently proved to be uneconomical, the research led to several spillover products which were economically viable, and which formed the basis for Thermo Electron's early success.

Souren G. Ouzounian and Professor Paul M. Healy prepared this case as the basis for class discussion rather than to illustrate either effective or ineffective handling of an administrative situation. We are also grateful to Don McAllister for his helpful input. Copyright © 1999 by the President and Fellows of Harvard College. Harvard Business School case 9-100-057.

During the 1960s the company provided contract research for public utilities and government agencies such as NASA, the U.S. Air Force, and the now defunct Atomic Energy Commission. In 1971, when the U.S. Congress required car manufacturers to monitor exhaust emissions, no instruments with the required precision were available. Dr. Hatsopolous saw the opportunity this presented and quickly contacted Ford Motor Company to offer his company's services in developing the new instruments. At the time Ford was skeptical of Thermo Electron's ability to complete the contract, but the instruments were delivered on time, ahead of any competitors. As a result, many other auto companies came to Thermo Electron for the same devices. This infant instruments business grew to become Thermo Instrument Systems, Inc.

The company continued to grow rapidly in the 1980s and early 1990s by developing a wide range of innovative new products. These included a portable device for detecting plastic bombs, a portable drug detector used by customs agents and police, a cardiac assist device to keep patients alive while awaiting transplants, the first commercial detector and analyzer for nitrosamines (carcinogens), a portable remediation system that removes gasoline from contaminated soil, soil-analysis instrumentation for the Environmental Protection Agency, a home-use radon detector kit, and the first commercially practical instrument for monitoring concentrations of NO_2. Other recent innovations included mammography systems, paper-recycling and papermaking equipment, alternative energy systems, industrial process equipment, and a number of other specialized products.

While much of Thermo Electron's research success was internally generated at the company's own research labs, it was not afraid to buy other developers. For example, in 1989 it acquired a San Diego-based laser lab. At the time of the acquisition the lab relied almost exclusively on the shrinking Star Wars budget for funding. Following a remarkable transformation, it developed a painless method to remove unwanted hair using laser technology, and as a result of a spinout in 1991, became ThermoTrex. But not all of the company acquisitions were so successful. A small metal-plate company that had been acquired ended up costing Thermo Electron $18 million, and an environmental engineering company acquired in 1988 cost $6 million.

MANAGEMENT PHILOSOPHY AND CORPORATE STRUCTURE

Thermo Electron mirrored the psyche of its founder, Dr. George Hatsopolous, whose talents spanned many fields—he is an inventor, teacher, self-taught economist, and CEO. He has used the Socratic method to encourage organizational learning and growth, and fostered an open-door policy for employees to discuss problems and ideas.

The almost 9,000-person company was unique in several other ways. First, it had always retained the right to use the technology it developed. This permitted it to use the technology created for one project as a springboard for new ventures. At times this policy was costly, and the firm undertook research at a reduced fee to retain the rights to the technology.

Thermo Electron Corporation

Thermo Electron's corporate structure, designed by Dr. Hatsopolous and his brother John Hatsopolous, the Company's Chief Financial Officer, was also a unique feature of the business. The firm sold a minority interest to the public in subsidiaries that focused on the best ideas and products that came from the parent company's R&D labs. The parent company typically kept between 70 and 80 percent of the stock in these "spinouts," but the units functioned as independent companies with their own management and their own shareholders. As John Hatsopolous explained, "The plan is simple: let employees develop an idea, spend some time and money testing the quality and market potential of the product, then set up a subsidiary and let it grow."[1]

The first unit to be "spun out" was Thermedics, which was sold in August 1983 for $2.51 per share. In March 1994, Thermedic's stock was valued at $12.13. In mid-1994 Thermo Electron had nine "pups," as the spinouts became known on Wall Street. Most had performed well following the initial offering. (See Exhibit 2 for details of stock performance of these units following the spinouts). For example, Thermo Instrument Systems, Inc., which grew out of the successful instrument project with Ford and which was spun out in 1986, was initially sold for $3.56 per share and in mid-1994 sold for more than $32.

There were several differences between the spinout concept pioneered by Thermo Electron and the more traditional spinoffs. First, under a traditional spinoff all of the subsidiary's equity was distributed to either the parent-company shareholders or to new shareholders through an Initial Public Offering (IPO). In the Thermo spinout the parent company sold off only a minority stake in the division, either through an IPO, a private placement, or both. Second, traditional spinoffs typically arose when the parent wanted to raise cash, to reduce debt obligations, or to rid itself of poor-performing units and focus on its "core" competencies. Consequently, announcements of spinoffs tended to have a negative impact on the parent company stock.[2] In contrast, announcements of spinouts, or "equity carve-outs" as they are sometimes called, usually had a positive 2 to 3 percent effect on the stock of the parent company. Theo Melas-Kyriazi, Thermo's treasurer explained, "We don't sell poor performers, the dogs; we sell our core technologies."[3] The cash generated from these sales was then used to provide working capital for the spun-out units.

Dr. Hatsopolous believed that the company's spinout strategy enabled it to combine the vibrancy of a small high-growth start-up with the financial stability and research strength of an established company. The structure provided strong incentives for management and key researchers, who were rewarded with stock options in the newly created publicly traded subsidiaries. As a result, there was virtually no turnover among key employees at Thermo Electron. In addition, Dr. Hatsopolous was convinced that, by creating a series of "pure plays" on specific technologies, the firm helped investors to better understand its business, and hence lowered its cost of raising capital.

....

1. Boston Business Journal 13, November 19, 1993, Sec. 1:3.

2. See Schipper and Smith, Journal of Financial Economics, 1986: 153–186.

3. Wall Street Journal, August 5, 1993: 1.

Accounting for Spinouts

One issue that arose from the spinout strategy was how to account for the spinouts. There was no FASB ruling on this accounting practice. However, two options were available to Thermo Electron: (1) record any realized gain or loss on sale of shares in the spun-out unit as an increase or decrease in equity reserves; or (2) report any gain or loss in the income statement. The footnotes in the annual report explained that Thermo Electron followed the second of these options:

> *At the time a subsidiary sells its stock to unrelated parties at a price in excess of its book value, the Company's net investment in that subsidiary increases. If at that time the subsidiary is an operating entity and not engaged principally in research and development, the Company records the increase as a gain.*
>
> *If gains have been recognized on issuance of a subsidiary's stock and shares of the subsidiary are subsequently repurchased by the subsidiary or by the Company, gain recognition does not occur on issuances subsequent to the date of repurchase until such time as shares have been issued in an amount equivalent to the number of repurchased shares.*

The impact of this accounting decision was significant. Since the first spinout in 1983, 50 percent or more of the firm's net income arose from gains on spinouts. For example, in 1993 the gain on sale (both before and after tax effects) was $39.9 million, compared to net income of $76.6 million.

Management believed that the accounting policy has been critical in helping the company raise funds, since it enabled the firm to generate smooth earnings growth in its income statement. However, analysts remained concerned about the quality of the firm's earnings.

Recent Financial Performance

In *Fortune* magazine's 1994 ranking of the nation's top 500 industrial companies, Thermo Electron was ranked number one for largest growth in earnings per share from 1983 to 1993. The company also ranked twenty-ninth on the *Fortune* list of firms with the highest total return to investors over for the last ten years. "We attribute our success in large part to our strategy of spinning out promising businesses that serve energy, environmental, and biomedical markets," said Dr. Hatsopolous. "By forming these entities, we are able to tap the capital markets and create an entrepreneurial environment that spurs ingenuity."[4]

For its fiscal year ended January 1, 1994, Thermo Electron reported its ninth consecutive year of record financial performance. Its revenues were $1.2 billion and income before an accounting change was $76.6 million, or $1.75 per share. See Exhibit 3 for a

4. Wall Street Journal, *August 5, 1993: 1.*

Thermo Electron Corporation

ten-year summary of the company's financial data and Exhibit 4 for its most recent financial statements.

Despite its impressive record, John Kolmanoff was uncertain about whether he should continue to recommend the stock to his clients. Many analysts were forecasting that the company's earnings would grow at a rate of 18 to 22 percent for the next five years. Given the stock price in early July 1994 of $24.75, the company was trading at 1.38 times its book value. However, others were more cautious, and questioned the quality of the firm's earnings, given that much of its income was derived from gains on spinouts. Short sales in the company's stock had grown 21 percent in the previous six months, to approximately 11 percent of its outstanding stock. Given the mixed opinions on the company, Kolmanoff decided that he should undertake a complete review of its business, accounting, and valuation.[5]

QUESTIONS

1. Evaluate how Thermo Electron's strategy for spinning out its R&D units affects its long-term success. What factors are critical to the success of this strategy, and what are the risks the company faces?
2. Examine Thermo Electron's accounting policies. What is the quality of the firm's earnings?
3. Analyze Thermo Electron's financial performance for 1991, 1992, and 1993, using financial ratio analysis. How is the company managing its cash flows for 1993? Is the company effectively managing its business risks?
4. What is the value of the shares retained by Thermo Electron in spun-out subsidiaries? What is the market value of Thermo Electron itself? What factors explain the difference between these values?

---

5. In early July 1994, Thermo Electron's equity beta was 1.1, the 3-month Treasury Bill rate was 4.2%, and the 30-year Government Bond Rate was 7.68%.

EXHIBIT 1
Five-Year Summary of Stock Performance: Thermo Electron and SPX

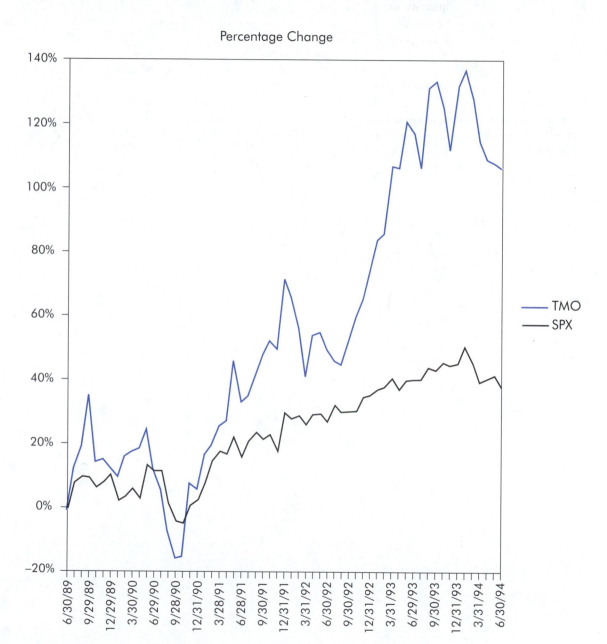

Percentage Change

TMO
SPX

Thermo Electron Corporation

Thermo Electron Corporation

EXHIBIT 2
Stock Performance for Thermo Electron Spinouts

Company	IPO Date	Split-adjusted IPO Price	3/3/94 Price	3/3/94 Shares Outstanding	CAGR
Thermedics	8/10/83	$2.51	$12.13	31,978	15.40%
Thermo Instrument Systems	8/5/86	3.56	32.25	45,865	31.70
Thermo Process Systems	8/21/86	1.83	9.00	16,041	22.00
Thermo Power	6/26/87	8.50	8.75	12,232	0.50
Thermo Cardiosystems[a]	1/12/89	2.27	19.25	n/a	51.70
Thermo Voltek	3/19/90	2.56	9.00	3,929	36.90
ThermoTrex	7/24/91	7.92	15.50	17,093	25.10
Thermo Fibertek	11/2/92	8.00	14.63	26,832	82.90
Thermo Remediation[b]	12/16/93	12.50	14.13	6,503	15.00

a. Reflects combined ownership by Thermo Electron and Thermedics
b. Reflects ownership by Thermo Process
Source: Centre for Research in Security Prices.

EXHIBIT 3
Thermo Electron Ten-Year Financial Summary

(in millions except per-share amounts)	1993[a]	1992[b]	1991[c]	1990[d]	1989	1988	1987	1986	1985	1984
Revenues	$1,249.7	$ 949.0	$ 805.5	$720.7	$623.0	$540.7	$419.9	$359.1	$286.2	$253.3
Costs and Expenses:										
Cost of revenues	755.5	609.0	533.6	465.3	424.2	359.6	280.3	244.8	194.9	172.6
Expenses for R&D and new lines of business	87.0	62.3	52.6	54.0	46.4	43.2	31.4	26.5	21.5	21.6
Selling, general and administrative expenses	283.6	209.4	177.3	163.1	130.0	113.7	91.5	72.7	56.9	48.2
Costs associated with divisional and product restructuring	8.3	—	3.7	1.0	2.2	0.9	3.5	7.1	4.3	0.1
	1,134.4	880.7	767.2	683.4	602.8	517.4	406.7	351.1	277.6	242.5
Gain on Issuance of Stock by Subsidiaries	39.9	30.2	27.4	20.3	16.8	6.0	16.1	15.9	9.1	—
Other Income (Expense), Net	(24.1)	3.5	13.5	2.3	3.3	4.5	(0.6)	(3.3)	(4.7)	(5.1)
Income Before Income Taxes, Minority Interest, and Cumulative Effect of Change in Accounting Principle	131.1	102.0	79.2	59.9	40.3	33.8	28.7	20.6	13.0	5.7
Provision for Income Taxes	33.4	27.5	24.8	17.8	10.4	9.0	6.0	4.0	2.5	0.1
Minority Interest Expense	21.1	13.9	7.3	7.1	3.3	2.0	1.9	0.5	(0.1)	(0.1)
Income Before Cumulative Effect of Change in Accounting Principle	76.6	60.6	47.1	35.0	26.6	22.8	20.8	16.1	10.6	5.7
Cumulative Effect of Change in Accounting Principle, Net of Tax[e]	—	1.4	—	—	—	—	—	—	—	—
Net Income	$76.6	$59.2	$ 47.1	$ 35.0	$ 26.6	$ 22.8	$ 20.8	$ 16.1	$ 10.6	$ 5.7
Earnings per Share Before Cumulative Effect of Change in Accounting Principle:										
Primary	$ 1.75	$ 1.51	$ 1.31	$1.09	$ .86	$ .77	$ .68	$ .55	$ .42	$ .24
Fully diluted	$ 1.57	$ 1.41	$ 1.23	$1.03	$ .84	$ .75	$ .67	$ .54	$ .41	$ .23
Earnings per Share:										
Primary	$ 1.75	$ .48	$ 1.31	$1.09	$ .86	$ .77	$ .68	$ .55	$ .42	$ .24
Fully diluted	$ 1.57	$ 1.38	$ 1.23	$1.03	$ .84	$ .75	$ .67	$ .54	$ .41	$ .23
Balance Sheet Data:										
Working capital	$ 828.3	$ 503.4	$ 463.5	$241.4	$276.0	$218.8	$210.9	$124.3	$ 79.1	$ 51.3
Total assets	2,473.7	1,818.3	1,199.5	904.4	664.1	524.4	460.8	332.6	240.9	208.0
Net assets related to construction projects	9.4	23.8	29.4	—	—	—	—	—	—	—
Long-term obligations	647.5	494.2	255.0	210.0	176.9	152.7	135.7	61.4	49.1	47.5
Minority interest	277.7	164.3	122.5	83.9	51.8	22.6	25.8	20.1	6.6	1.3
Common stock of subsidiaries subject to redemption	14.5	5.5	5.5	8.7	13.1	—	—	—	—	—
Shareholders' investment	858.5	552.9	480.9	310.2	226.4	194.3	173.5	153.1	106.7	87.8

a. Reflects the February 1993 acquisition of Spectra-Physics Analytical and the Company's 1993 public offering of common stock for net proceeds of $246.0 million.

b. Reflects the August 1992 acquisition of Nicoles Instrument Corporation and the issuance of $260.0 million principal amount of convertible debentures.

c. Reflects the issuance of $164.0 million principal amount of convertible debentures.

d. Reflects the May 1990 acquisition of Finnigan Corporation.

e. Reflects the adoption in fiscal 1992 of Statement of Financial Accounting Standards No. 106, "Accounting for Post-retirement Benefits Other Than Pensions."

Thermo Electron Corporation

Thermo Electron Corporation

EXHIBIT 4

Thermo Electron Summarized Financial Statements

CONSOLIDATED INCOME STATEMENT

(in thousands except per-share amounts)	1993	1992	1991
Revenues:			
Product sales and revenues	$1,103,558	$ 808,928	$ 666,565
Service revenues	121,987	114,268	112,003
Research and development contract revenues	24,173	25,776	26,916
	1,249,718	948,972	805,484
Costs and Expenses:			
Cost of products	664,201	521,668	444,273
Cost of services	91,292	87,307	89,347
Expenses for research and development and new lines of business[a]	87,027	62,343	52,609
Selling, general and administrative expenses	283,390	209,392	177,304
Costs associated with division and product (Note 11)	8,261	—	3,709
	1,134,371	880,710	767,242
Gain on Issuance of Stock by Subsidiaries (Note 9)	39,863	30,212	27,367
Other Income (Expense), Net (Note 10)	(24,091)	3,496	13,564
Income Before Income Taxes, Minority Interest, and Cumulative Effect of Change in Accounting Principle	131,119	101,970	79,173
Provision for Income Taxes (Note 8)	33,400	27,474	24,850
Minority Interest Expense	21,086	13,902	7,269
Income Before Cumulative Effect of Change in Accounting Principle	76,633	60,594	47,054
Cumulative Effect of Change in Accounting Principle, Net of Tax (Note 7)	—	1,438	—
Net Income	$ 76,633	$ 59,156	$ 47,054
Earnings per Share Before Cumulative Effect of Change in Accounting Principle:			
Primary	$ 1.75	$ 1.51	$ 1.31
Fully diluted	$ 1.57	$ 1.41	$ 1.23
Earnings per Share:			
Primary	$ 1.75	$ 1.48	$ 1.31
Fully diluted	$ 1.57	$ 1.38	$ 1.23
Weighted Average Shares:			
Primary	43,779	40,049	35,836
Fully diluted	55,520	47,163	41,711

a. Includes costs of: Research and development contracts	$ 20,435	$ 19,426	$ 21,196
Internally funded research and development	58,943	38,675	26,171
Other expenses for new lines of business	7,649	4,242	5,242
	$ 87,027	$ 62,343	$ 52,609

CONSOLIDATED BALANCE SHEET

(in thousands except per-share amounts)	1993	1992
ASSETS		
Current Assets:		
Cash and cash equivalents	$ 325,744	$ 190,601
Short-term investments, at cost (quoted market value of $377,183 and $180,060)	374,450	178,101
Accounts receivable, less allowances of $14,129 and $11,341	267,377	204,750
Unbilled contract costs and fees	32,574	25,941
Inventories:		
Work in process and finished goods	82,385	60,629
Raw materials and supplies	110,437	106,619
Prepaid income taxes (Note 8)	39,258	54,377
Prepaid expenses	12,318	8,716
	1,244,543	829,734
Assets Related to Projects Under Construction:		
Restricted funds (quoted market value of $34,100 and $95,639)	34,100	95,348
Facilities under construction	128,040	133,876
	162,140	229,224
Property, Plant and Equipment, at Cost:		
Land	40,570	35,729
Buildings	116,895	99,502
Alternative-energy facilities	199,800	30,554
Machinery, equipment and leasehold improvements	224,629	205,508
	581,894	371,293
Less: Accumulated depreciation and amortization	134,423	113,383
	447,471	257,910
Long-term Marketable Securities, at Cost (quoted market value of $45,125 and $45,731)	43,630	44,497
Other Assets	102,347	92,870
Cost in Excess of Net Assets of Acquired Companies (Note 2)	473,579	364,030
	$2,473,710	$1,818,265

Thermo Electron Corporation

Thermo Electron Corporation

CONSOLIDATED BALANCE SHEET (continued)

(in thousands except per-share amounts)	1993	1992
LIABILITIES AND SHAREHOLDERS' INVESTMENT		
Current Liabilities:		
Notes payable	$ 45,851	$ 22,034
Accounts payable	85,278	69,473
Billings in excess of contract costs and fees	8,564	7,987
Accrued payroll and employee benefits	49,029	45,115
Accrued income taxes (Note 8)	7,713	9,796
Accrued installation and warranty costs	26,049	17,179
Other accrued expenses (Note 2)	193,762	154,786
	416,246	326,370
Deferred Income Taxes (Note 8)	48,387	34,171
Other Deferred Items	58,152	35,500
Liabilities Related to Projects Under Construction (Note 5):		
Payables and accrued expenses	10,680	5,874
Tax-exempt obligations	142,069	199,536
	152,749	205,410
Long-term Obligations (Note 5):		
Senior convertible obligations	275,000	260,000
Subordinated convertible obligations	238,386	199,829
Nonrecourse tax-exempt obligations	108,800	—
Other	25,275	34,323
	647,461	494,152
Minority Interest	277,681	164,293
Commitments and Contingencies (Note 6)		
Common Stock of Subsidiaries Subject to Redemption ($15,390 and $5,468 redemption values)	14,511	5,468
Shareholders' Investment (Notes 3 and 4):		
Preferred stock, $100 par value, 50,000 shares authorized; none issued		
Common stock, $1 par value, 100,000,000 shares authorized; 47,950,580 and 27,099,598 shares issued	47,951	27,100
Capital in excess of par value	467,076	257,105
Retained earnings	362,138	285,505
	877,165	569,710
Treasury stock at cost, 31,898 and 85,342 shares	(1,212)	(3,810)
Cumulative translation adjustment	(13,591)	(7,949)
Deferred compensation (Note 7)	(3,839)	(5,050)
	858,523	552,901
	$2,473,710	$1,818,265

CONSOLIDATED CASH FLOW STATEMENT

(in thousands)	1993	1992	1991
OPERATING ACTIVITIES:			
Net income	$ 76,633	$ 59,156	$ 47,054
Adjustments to reconcile net income to net cash provided by operating activities:			
Cumulative effect of change in accounting principle (Note 7)	—	1,438	—
Depreciation and amortization	42,356	29,228	23,391
Costs associated with divisional and product restructuring (Note 11)	8,261	—	3,709
Equity in losses of unconsolidated subsidiaries	21,076	3,948	1,663
Provision for losses on accounts receivable	2,675	2,021	3,020
Increase in deferred income taxes	13,888	12,273	169
Gain on sale of investments	(2,469)	(4,968)	(7,622)
Gain on issuance of stock by subsidiaries (Note 9)	(39,863)	(30,212)	(27,367)
Minority interest expense	21,086	13,902	7,269
Other noncash expenses	7,850	11,549	6,804
Changes in current accounts, excluding the effects of acquisitions:			
Accounts receivable	(43,171)	(10,763)	(10,220)
Inventories	(6,525)	(4,753)	8,224
Other current assets	(230)	(9,860)	5,276
Accounts payable	10,014	(2,479)	(10,140)
Other current liabilities	15,355	(15,363)	(11,684)
Other	(198)	(175)	(142)
Net cash provided by operating activities	126,738	54,942	39,404
INVESTING ACTIVITIES:			
Acquisitions, net of cash acquired (Note 2)	(142,962)	(251,738)	(7,552)
Purchases of property, plant and equipment	(56,580)	(60,007)	(33,469)
Purchases of long-term investments	(20,573)	(70,340)	(21,278)
Proceeds from sale of short-term investments	16,651	35,899	15,814
(Increase) decrease in short-term investments	(193,894)	68,260	(175,701)
Increase in assets related to construction projects	(3,781)	(132,971)	(67,790)
Other	1,848	313	(4,834)
Net cash used in investment activities	(399,291)	(410,584)	(294,810)
FINANCING ACTIVITIES:			
Proceeds from issuance of long-term obligations	102,151	255,694	162,273
Repayment and repurchase of long-term obligations	(11,732)	(27,415)	(10,493)
Proceeds from issuance of tax-exempt obligations	—	133,536	66,000
Proceeds from issuance of Company and subsidiary common stock	378,790	100,749	64,947
Purchases of Company and subsidiary common stock	(57,198)	(45,334)	(11,663)
Other	(941)	485	(430)
Net cash provided by financing activities	411,070	417,715	270,634
Exchange Rate Effect on Cash	(3,374)	(2,424)	(2,499)
Increase in Cash and Cash Equivalents	135,143	59,649	12,729
Cash and Cash Equivalents at Beginning of Year	190,601	130,952	118,223
Cash and Cash Equivalents at End of Year	$325,744	$190,601	$130,952
CASH PAID FOR:			
Interest	$ 29,438	$ 18,287	$ 15,426
Income taxes	$ 9,699	$ 16,593	$ 15,723
NONCASH ACTIVITIES:			
Conversions of convertible obligations	$ 50,403	$ 13,863	$109,865
Subsidiary stock issued for acquired business (Note 2)	$ —	$ 9,673	$ 1,026
Purchase of electric-generating facility through assumption of debt	$ 66,900	$ —	$ —

Thermo Electron Corporation

Thermo Electron Corporation

SELECTED NOTES TO CONSOLIDATED FINANCIAL STATEMENTS

1. SIGNIFICANT ACCOUNTING POLICIES

Principles of Consolidation

The accompanying consolidated financial statements include the accounts of Thermo Electron Corporation and its majority- and wholly owned subsidiaries (the Company). All material intercompany accounts and transactions have been eliminated. Majority-owned public subsidiaries include Thermedics, Inc., Thermo Instrument Systems, Inc., Thermo Process Systems Inc., Thermo Power Corporation, ThermoTrex Corporation, and Thermo Fibertek Inc. Thermo Cardiosystems Inc. and Thermo Voltek Corp. are majority-owned public subsidiaries of Thermedics. Thermo Remediation Inc. is a majority-owned public subsidiary of Thermo Process. Thermo Energy Systems Corporation is a majority-owned, privately held subsidiary of the Company; ThermoLase Inc. is a majority-owned, privately held subsidiary of TherTrex; and J. Amerika N.V. is a majority-owned, privately held subsidiary of Thermo Process. The Company accounts for investments in businesses in which it owns between 20% and 50% under the equity method.

Fiscal Year

The Company has adopted a fiscal year ending the Saturday nearest December 31. References to 1993, 1992, and 1991 are for the fiscal years ended January 1, 1994, January 1, 1992, and December 28, 1991, respectively. Fiscal years 1993 and 1991 each included 52 weeks; 1992 included 53 weeks.

Revenue Recognition

For the majority of its operations, the Company recognizes revenues based upon shipment of its products or completion of services rendered. The Company provides a reserve for its estimate of warranty and installation costs at the time of shipment. Revenues and profits on substantially all contracts are recognized using the percentage-of-completion method. Revenues recorded under the percentage-of-completion method were $176,727,000 in 1993, $186,407,000 in 1992, and $173,210,000 in 1991. The percentage of completion is determined by relating either the actual costs or actual labor, respectively, to be incurred on each other. If a loss is indicated on any contract in process, a provision is made currently for the entire loss. The Company's contracts generally provide for billing of customers upon attainment of certain milestones specified in each contract. Revenues earned on contracts in process in excess of billings are classified as "Unbilled contract costs and fees," and amounts billed in excess of revenues earned are classified as "Billings in excess of contract costs and fees" in the accompanying balance sheet. There are no significant amounts included in the accompanying balance sheet that are not expected to be recovered from existing contracts at current contract values or that are not expected to be collected within one year, including amounts that are billed but not paid under retainage provisions.

Gain on Issuance of Stock by Subsidiaries

At the time a subsidiary sells its stock to unrelated parties at a price in excess of its book value, the Company's net investment in that subsidiary increases. If at that time the subsidiary is an operating entity and not engaged principally in research and development, the Company records the increase as a gain.

If gains have been recognized on issuances of a subsidiary's stock and shares of the subsidiary are subsequently repurchased by the subsidiary or the Company, gain recognition does not occur on issuances subsequent to the date of a repurchase until such time as shares have been issued in an amount equivalent to the number of repurchased shares. Such transactions are reflected as equity transactions and the net effect of these transactions is reflected in the accompanying statement of shareholders' investment as "Effect of majority-owned subsidiaries' common stock transactions."

Income Taxes

The Company adopted Statement of Financial Accounting Standards (SFAS) No. 109, "Accounting for Income Taxes," as of the beginning of 1992. Under SFAS No. 109, deferred income taxes are recognized based on the expected future tax consequences of differences between the financial statement basis and the tax basis of assets and liabilities calculated using enacted tax rates in effect for the year in which the differences are expected to be reflected in the tax return. Prior to 1992, the Company recorded income taxes on timing differences between financial statement and tax treatment of income and expenses under Accounting Principles Board Opinion No. 11. The implementation of SFAS No. 109 and the effect of adoption were not material to the Company's financial statements.

Earnings per Share

Primary earnings per share have been computed based on the weighted average number of common shares outstanding during the year. Because the effect of common stock equivalents was not material, they have been excluded from the primary earnings per share calculation. Fully diluted earnings per share assumes the effect of the conversion of the Company's dilutive convertible obligations and elimination of the related interest expense, the exercise of stock options, and their related income tax effects.

Stock Splits

All share and per share information has been restated to reflect a three-for-two stock split, effected in the form of a 50% stock dividend that was distributed in October 1993.

In addition, all share and per share information pertaining to Thermedics, Thermo Instrument, ThermoTrex, and Thermo Voltek has been restated to reflect three-for-two stock splits, effected in the form of 50% stock dividends, that were distributed in 1993. All share and per share information pertaining to Thermo Cardiosystems and ThermoLase has been restated to reflect two-for-one stock splits, effected in the form of 100% stock dividends, that was distributed for Thermo Cardiosystems in 1993 and will be effected for ThermoLase on March 15, 1994.

Cash and Cash Equivalents

Cash equivalents consist principally of U.S. government agency securities, bank time deposits, and commercial paper purchased with an original maturity of three months or less. These investments are carried at cost. The fair market value of cash and cash equivalents was $325,823,000 and $191,004,000 at January 1, 1994 and January 2, 1993, respectively.

Short- and Long-term Investments

Short- and long-term investments consist principally of corporate notes and U.S. government agency securities. Securities with an original maturity of greater than three months, which the Company intends to hold for less than one year, are classified as short-term. Securities that are intended to be held for more than one year are classified as long-term. These investments are carried at the lower of cost or market value.

In May 1993, the Financial Accounting Standards Board issued SFAS No. 115, "Accounting for Certain Investments in Debt and Equity Securities." SFAS No. 115 requires that marketable equity and debt securities considered trading securities be accounted for at market value with the difference between cost and market value recorded currently in the statement of income; that securities considered available for sale be accounted for at market value, with the difference between cost and market value, net of related tax effects, recorded currently as a component of shareholders' investment; and that debt securities considered held-to-maturity be recorded at amortized cost. The Company is required to adopt SFAS No. 115 at the beginning of fiscal 1994. Management believes that the marketable equity and debt securities in the accompanying balance sheet will be considered available-for-sale and that the adoption of SFAS No. 115 will result in a total increase to shareholders' investment of approximately $2,600,000.

Inventories

Inventories are stated at the lower of cost (on a first-in, first-out or weighted average basis) or market value and include materials, labor, and manufacturing overhead.

Property, Plant and Equipment

The costs of additions and improvements are capitalized, while maintenance and repairs are charged to expense as incurred. The Company provides for depreciation and amortization using the straight-line method over the estimated useful lives of the property as follows: buildings and improvements—10 to 40 years; alternative-energy facilities—25 years, machinery and equipment—3 to 20 years; and lease-hold improvements—the shorter of the term of the lease or the life of the asset.

1. SIGNIFICANT ACCOUNTING POLICIES (continued)

Assets Related to Projects Under Construction

"Facilities under construction" in the accompanying 1992 balance sheet included an alternative-energy facility that was under construction in Delano, California. This facility was completed in 1993 and is included in "Alternative-energy facilities" in the accompanying 1993 balance sheet. "Facilities under construction" in fiscal 1993 and 1992 include a waste-recycling facility located in San Diego County, California. Construction costs for this facility were capitalized as incurred. Construction was completed in early 1994.

"Restricted funds" in the accompanying balance sheet represents unexpended proceeds from the issuance of tax-exempt obligations (Note 5), which are invested principally in U.S. government agency securities and municipal tax-exempt obligations. These investments are carried at the lower of cost or market value.

In August 1993, the Company agreed, in exchange for a cash settlement, to terminate a power sales agreement between a subsidiary of the Company and a utility. The power sales agreement required the utility to purchase the power to be generated by the Company's 55-megawatt natural gas cogeneration facility under development on Staten Island, New York. Under the termination agreement, the Company received $9.0 million in August 1993, with subsequent payments to be made as follows: $3.6 million in 1994; $2.7 million in 1995; $1.8 million in 1996; and $0.9 million in 1997. The Company will be obligated to return $8.2 million of this settlement if the Company elects to proceed with the Staten Island facility and it achieves commercial operation before January 1, 2000. Accordingly, the Company has deferred recognition of $8.2 million of revenues, pending final determination of the project's status. During 1993, the Company recorded revenues of $9.8 million and segment income of $5.4 million from the termination of the power sales agreement.

Other Assets

"Other assets" in the accompanying balance sheet include capitalized costs associated with the Company's operation of certain alternative-energy power plants, as well as the cost of acquired trademarks, patents, and other identifiable intangible assets. These assets are being amortized using the straight-line method over their estimated useful lives, which range from 4 to 20 years. These assets were $41,252,000 and $49,646,000, net of accumulated amortization of $16,699,000 and $11,002,000, at year-end 1993 and 1992, respectively.

Cost in Excess of Net Assets of Acquired Companies

The excess of cost over the fair value of net assets of acquired businesses is amortized using the straight-line method principally over 40 years. Accumulated amortization was $32,439,000 and $20,954,000 at year-end 1993 and 1992, respectively. The Company continually assesses whether a change in circumstances has occurred subsequent to an acquisition that would indicate that the future useful life of the asset should be revised. The Company considers the future earnings potential of the acquired business in assessing the recoverability of this asset.

Common Stock of Subsidiaries Subject to Redemption

In March 1993, ThermoLase sold 3,078,000 units at $5 per unit, each unit consisting of one share of ThermoLase common stock and one redemption right. A redemption right allows holders to redeem ThermoLase common stock for $5 per share, and is exercisable in December 1996 and 1997. The redemption rights are guaranteed on a subordinated basis by the Company.

"Common stock of subsidiaries subject to redemption" in the accompanying 1992 balance sheet represents amounts associated with redemption rights outstanding that were issued in connection with the Thermo Cardiosystms 1989 initial public offering and were guaranteed on a subordinated basis by the Company. These redemption rights expired at the end of 1993 and, as a result, the Company transferred $5,468,000 of "Common stock of subsidiary subject to redemption" to "Minority interest" and "Capital in excess of par value."

Foreign Currency

All assets and liabilities of the Company's foreign

subsidiaries are translated at year-end exchange rates, and revenues and expenses are translated at average exchange rates for the year in accordance with SFAS No. 52, "Foreign Currency Translation." Resulting translation adjustments are reflected as a separate component of shareholders' investment titled "Cumulative translation adjustment." Foreign currency transaction gains and losses are included in the accompanying statement of income and are not material for the three years presented.

Presentation

Certain amounts in 1992 and 1991 have been reclassified to conform to the 1993 financial statement presentation.

2. ACQUISITIONS

In February 1993, Thermo Instrument acquired Spectra-Physics Analytical, a manufacturer of liquid chromatography and capillary electrophoresis analytical instruments, for $6.7 million in cash. In 1993, the Company's majority-owned subsidiaries made several other acquisitions for $76.5 million in cash.

In 1992, Thermo Instruments acquired Nicolet Instrument Corporation. The total purchase price to the Company was approximately $175 million. Nicolet designs, manufactures, and markets instrumentation for a broad range of analytical chemistry, neurodiagnostic, and electronic engineering problem-solving applications in science and industry.

In 1992, the Company's majority-owned subsidiaries made several other acquisitions for $77.7 million in cash, assumption of debt in the amount of $7.3 million, prepayment of debt in the amount of $1.5 million, and issuance of common stock and stock options of a majority-owned subsidiary valued at approximately $12.3 million.

These acquisitions have been accounted for as purchases and their results of operations have been included in the accompanying financial statements from their respective dates of acquisition. The aggregate cost of these acquisitions exceeded the estimated fair value of the acquired net assets by $325 million, which is being amortized principally over 40 years. Allocation of the purchase price was based on the fair value of the net assets acquired and, for acquisitions completed in fiscal 1993, is subject to adjustment.

Based on unaudited data, the following table presents selected financial information for the Company, Spectra-Physics Analytical, and Nicolet on a pro forma basis, assuming the companies had been combined since the beginning of 1992. Net income and earnings per share are shown before Nicolet's discontinued operations, which occurred in fiscal 1992. The effect on the Company's financial statements of the acquisitions not included in the pro forma data was not significant.

(In thousands, except per share amounts)	1993	1992
Revenues	$1,257,523	$1,105,907
Earnings per share before cumulative effect of change in accounting principal:	75,631	43,016
Primary	1.73	1.07
Fully diluted	1.55	1.04

9. TRANSACTIONS IN STOCK OF SUBSIDIARIES

"Gain on issuance of stock by subsidiaries" in the accompanying statement of income results primarily from the following transactions:

1993

Public offering of 3,225,000 shares of Thermedics common stock at $10.00 per share for net proceeds of $29,980,000 resulted in a gain of $10,707,000. Public offering of 4,312,500 shares of Thermo Power common stock at $9.00 per share for net proceeds of $35,998,000 resulted in a gain of $10,578,000.

Private placements of 2,062,500 shares of ThermoTrex common stock at $11.17 and $14.50 per share for net proceeds of $27,463,000 resulted in a gain of $11,400,000.

Thermo Electron Corporation

9. TRANSACTIONS IN STOCK OF SUBSIDIARIES (continued)

Private placement of 200,000 shares and initial public offering of 1,100,000 shares of Thermo Remediation at $9.89 and $12.50 per share, respectively, for net proceeds of $14,554,000 resulted in a gain of $4,239,000.

Conversion of $7,270,000 of Thermedics 6½% subordinated convertible debentures convertible at $10.42 per share into 697.919 shares of Thermedics common stock resulted in a gain of $2,506,000.

1992

Private placement of 2,709,356 shares and initial public offering of 3,000,000 shares of Thermo Fibertek common stock at $6.70 to $8.00 per share in net proceeds at $39,748,000 resulted in a gain of $34,303,000.

Issuance of 1,566,480 restricted shares of ThermoTrex common stock valued at $6.17 per share, or $9,673,000 to acquire Lorad Corporation resulted in a gain of $3,081,000.

Private placement of 375,000 shares of ThermoTrex common stock at $10.67 per share for net proceeds of $3,556,000 resulted in a gain of $1,745,000.

1991

Conversion of $9,099,000 of Thermo Instrument 6% and 6½% subordinated convertible debentures convertible at $12.19 and $10.83 per share, respectively, into 766.786 shares of Thermo Instrument common stock resulted in a gain of $3,707,000.

Conversion of $6,200,000 of Thermo Process 6½% subordinated convertible debentures convertible at $10.33 per share into 600.191 shares of Thermo Process common stock resulted in a gain of $3,043,000.

Repurchases of $3,700,000 of Thermedics 6½% subordinated convertible debentures convertible at $10.42 per share for $941,000 in cash and 367,500 shares of Thermedics common stock valued at $7.14 per share, or $2,623,000, resulted in a gain of $1,010,000.

Private placement of 1,660,197 shares and initial public offering of 2,250,000 shares of ThermoTrex common stock at $5.55 and $8.00 per share, respectively, for net proceeds of $24,764,000 resulted in a gain of $13,958,000.

Private placement of 1,591,549 shares of common stock of J. Amerika N.V. at 6.00 Dutch guilders per share for net proceeds of $4,573,000 resulted in a gain of $2,148,000.

Sale of 244,200 shares of Thermo Cardiosystems common stock by Thermedics at an average price of $8.43 per share for net proceeds of $2,040,000 resulted in a taxable gain of $1,958,000.

The Company's ownership percentage in these subsidiaries changed primarily as a result of the transactions listed above, as well as the Company's purchases of shares of majority-owned subsidiary stock, the subsidiaries' purchases of their own stock, the sale of subsidiaries' stock by the Company or by the subsidiaries under employees' and directors' stock plans or in other transactions, and the conversion of convertible obligations held by the Company, its subsidiaries, or by third parties.

The Company's ownership percentages at year-end were as follows:

	1993	1992	1991
Thermo Instrument	81%	81%	80%
Thermo Fibertek	80%	80%	100%
Thermedics	52%	59%	59%
Thermo Power	52%	81%	81%
ThermoTrex	55%	62%	70%
Thermo Process	72%	71%	71%
Thermo Energy Systems	88%	87%	87%
Thermo Cardiosystems (a)	57%	58%	55%
Thermo Voltek (a)	67%	57%	52%
Thermo Remediation (b)	67%	85%	93%
ThermoLase (c)	81%	100%	100%

(a) Reflects combined ownership by Thermo Electron and Thermedics.
(b) Reflects ownership by Thermo Process.
(c) Reflects ownership by ThermoTrex.

REPORT OF INDEPENDENT AUDITORS

To the Shareholders and Board of Directors of Thermo Electron Corporation:

We have audited the accompanying consolidated balance sheet of Thermo Electron Corporation (a Delaware corporation) and subsidiaries as of January 1, 1994 and January 2, 1993, and the related consolidated statements of income, shareholders, investment, and cash flows for each of the three years in the period ended January 1, 1994. These consolidated financial statements are the responsibility of the Company's management. Our responsibility is to express an opinion on these consolidated financial statements based on our audits.

We conducted our audits in accordance with generally accepted auditing standards. Those standards require that we plan and perform the audit to obtain reasonable assurance about whether the financial statements are free of material misstatement. An audit includes examining, on a test basis, evidence supporting the amounts and disclosures in the financial statements. An audit also includes assessing the accounting principles used and significant estimates made by management, as well as evaluating the overall financial statement presentation. We believe that our audits provide a reasonable basis for our opinion.

In our opinion, the consolidated financial statements referred to above present fairly, in all material aspects, the financial position of Thermo Electron Corporation and subsidiaries as of January 1, 1994 and January 2, 1993, and the results of their operations and their cash flows for each of the three years in the period ended January 1, 1994, in conformity with generally accepted accounting principles.

As discussed in Note 7 to the consolidated financial statements, effective December 29, 1991, the Company has changed its method of accounting for post-retirement benefits other than pensions.

Arthur Andersen & Co.

Boston, Massachusetts
February 17, 1994

MANAGEMENT DISCUSSION AND ANALYSIS

Overview

The Company develops and manufactures a broad range of products that are sold worldwide. The Company expands its products and services by developing and commercializing its own core technologies and by making strategic acquisitions of complementary businesses. The majority of the Company's businesses fall into three broad market segments: environmental, energy, and selected health and safety instrumentation.

An important component of the Company's strategy is to establish leading positions in its markets through the application of proprietary technology, whether developed internally or acquired. A key contributor to the growth of the Company's segment income (as defined in the results of operations below), particularly over the last two years, has been the ability to identify attractive acquisition opportunities, complete those acquisitions, and derive a growing income contribution from these newly acquired businesses as they are integrated into the Company's business segments.

The Company seeks to minimize its dependence on any specific product or market by maintaining and diversifying its portfolio of businesses and technologies. Similarly, the Company's goal is to maintain a balance in its businesses between those affected by various regulatory cycles and those more dependent on the general level of economic activity. To date, the Company's overall financial performance has been relatively unaffected by the recession in the U.S. economy in 1991 and 1992 and the general economic weakness in Europe and Japan in 1992 and 1993. This is due in large part to strong contributions from newly acquired businesses and the continued strength of businesses primarily driven by environmental regulation. Although the Company is diversified in terms of technology, product offerings, and geographic markets served, the future financial performance of the Company as a whole depends upon, among other factors, the strength of worldwide economies and the continued adoption and diligent enforcement of environmental regulations.

Thermo Electron Corporation

Thermo Electron Corporation

The Company believes that maintaining an entrepreneurial atmosphere is essential to its continued growth and development. In order to preserve this atmosphere, the Company adopted in 1983 a strategy of spinning out certain of its businesses into separate subsidiaries and having these subsidiaries sell a minority interest to outside investors. The Company believes that this strategy provides additional motivation and incentives for the management of the subsidiaries through the establishment of subsidiary-level stock option incentive programs, as well as capital to support the subsidiaries' growth. As a result of the sale of stock by subsidiaries, the issuance of shares by subsidiaries upon conversion of indebtedness, and similar transactions, the Company records gains that represent the increase in the Company's net investment in the subsidiaries and are classified as "Gain on issuance of stock by subsidiaries" in the accompanying statement of income. These gains have represented a substantial portion of the net income reported by the Company in recent years. Although the Company expects to continue this strategy in the future, its goal is to continue increasing segment income over the next few years so that gains generated by sales of stock by its subsidiaries will represent a decreasing portion of net income. The size and timing of these transactions are dependent on market and other conditions that are beyond the Company's control. Accordingly, there can be no assurance that the Company will be able to generate gains from such transactions in the future.

OTHER INFORMATION

(In thousands)	1993	1992	1991
Revenues:			
Thermo Instrument Systems, Inc.	$ 584,176	$ 423,199	$ 338,747
Thermo Fibertek Inc.	137,088	125,577	124,731
Thermedics Inc. (a)	80,220	45,778	32,295
Thermo Power Corporation	77,360	43,904	29,131
ThermoTrex Corporation	54,329	19,843	16,801
Thermo Process Systems Inc. (b)	53,839	47,082	50,632
	987,012	705,383	592,337
Wholly and majority-owned nonpublic companies	262,706	243,589	213,147
	$1,249,718	$ 948,972	$ 805,484
Segment Income(c):			
Thermo Instrument Systems Inc.	$ 96,786	$ 63,373	$ 49,742
Thermo Fibertek Inc.	15,902	15,716	14,652
Thermedics Inc. (a)	8,292	841	(3,048)
Thermo Power Corporation	2,707	715	(3,158)
ThermoTrex Corporation	485	(1,185)	(113)
Thermo Process Systems Inc. (b)	1,338	371	(1,487)
	125,510	79,831	56,588
Wholly and majority-owned nonpublic companies	17,122	7,237	7,315
	142,632	87,068	63,903
Equity in Losses of Unconsolidated Subsidiaries	(21,076)	(3,948)	(1,663)
Corporate	9,563	18,850	16,933
Income Before Income Taxes, Minority Interest, and Cumulative Effect of Change in Accounting Principle	$131,119	$101,970	$ 79,173

(a) Includes Thermo Cardiosystems Inc. and Thermo Voltek Corp.

(b) Includes Thermo Remediation Inc.

(c) Segment income is income before corporate general and administrative expenses, costs associated with divisional and product restructuring, other income and expense, minority interest expense, and income taxes.

COMMON STOCK MARKET INFORMATION

The following table shows the market range for the Company's common stock based on reported sales prices on the New York Stock Exchange (symbol TMO) for 1993 and 1992. Prices have been restated to reflect a three-for-two stock split distributed in October 1993.

Quarter	1993		1992	
	High	Low	High	Low
First	$38	$31⅓	$31⅔	$26¼
Second	41⅙	36⅓	29¹⁄₁₂	25⅙
Third	43¼	37¼	28⅓	25
Fourth	43	38⅛	31½	26½

The closing market price on the New York Stock Exchange for the Company's common stock on February 25, 1994, was 39½ per share.

DIVIDEND POLICY

The Company has never paid cash dividends and does not expect to pay cash dividends in the foreseeable future because its policy has been to use earnings to finance expansion and growth. Payments of dividends will rest within the discretion of the Board of Directors and will depend upon, among other factors, the Company's earnings, capital requirements, and financial condition.

As of February 25, 1994, the Company had 6,406 holders of record of its common stock. This does not include holdings in street or nominee names.

Common stock of the following majority-owned public subsidiaries is traded on the American Stock Exchange: Thermedics Inc. (TMD; Thermo Instrument Systems Inc. (THI); Thermo Power Corporation (THP); Thermo Process Systems Inc. (TPI); Thermo Voltek Corp. (TVL); ThermoTrex Corporation (TKN); Thermo Fibertek Inc. (TFT); and Thermo Remediation Inc. (THN).

Thermo Electron Corporation

9 chapter

The goal of financial analysis is to assess the performance of a firm in the context of its stated goals and strategy. There are two principal tools of financial analysis: ratio analysis and cash flow analysis. Ratio analysis involves assessing how various line items in a firm's financial statements relate to one another. Cash flow analysis allows the analyst to examine the firm's liquidity, and how the firm is managing its operating, investment, and financing cash flows.

Financial analysis is used in a variety of contexts. Ratio analysis of a company's present and past performance provides the foundation for making forecasts of future performance. As we will discuss in later chapters, financial forecasting is useful in company valuation, credit evaluation, financial distress prediction, security analysis, mergers and acquisitions analysis, and corporate financial policy analysis.

RATIO ANALYSIS

The value of a firm is determined by its profitability and growth. As shown in Figure 9-1, the firm's growth and profitability are influenced by its product market and financial market strategies. The product market strategy is implemented through the firm's competitive strategy, operating policies, and investment decisions. Financial market strategies are implemented through financing and dividend policies.

Thus, the four levers managers can use to achieve their growth and profit targets are: (1) operating management, (2) investment management, (3) financing strategy, and (4) dividend policies. The objective of ratio analysis is to evaluate the effectiveness of the firm's policies in each of these areas. Effective ratio analysis involves relating the financial numbers to the underlying business factors in as much detail as possible. While ratio analysis may not give all the answers to an analyst regarding the firm's performance, it will help the analyst frame questions for further probing.

In ratio analysis, the analyst can (1) compare ratios for a firm over several years (a time-series comparison), (2) compare ratios for the firm and other firms in the industry (cross-sectional comparison), and/or (3) compare ratios to some absolute benchmark. In a time-series comparison, the analyst can hold firm-specific factors constant and examine the effectiveness of a firm's strategy over time. Cross-sectional comparison facilitates examining the relative performance of a firm within its industry, holding industry-level factors constant. For most ratios, there are no absolute benchmarks. The exceptions are measures of rates of return, which can be compared to the cost of the capital associ-

Figure 9-1 Drivers of a Firm's Profitability and Growth

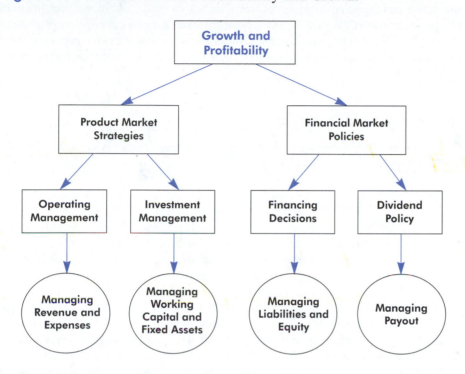

ated with the investment. For example, subject to distortions caused by accounting, the rate of return on equity (ROE) can be compared to the cost of equity capital.

In the discussion below, we will illustrate these approaches using the example of Nordstrom, Inc., a prominent U.S. retailer. We will compare Nordstrom's ratios for the fiscal year ending January 31, 1999, with its own ratios for the fiscal year ending January 31, 1998, and with the ratios for TJX Companies, Inc., another U.S. retailer, for the fiscal year ending January 31, 1999.[1]

Nordstrom is a leading fashion specialty retailer, offering a wide variety of high-end apparel, shoes, and accessories for men, women, and children. The company pursues a strategy of high quality, extraordinary service, and premium price. Dissatisfied with the inconsistent earnings performance in recent years, the company's management has focused in the last two years on improving its profit performance. We will use the financial statements for the year ending January 31, 1999, to examine how successful the management has been in achieving this objective. TJX Companies pursues a strategy quite different from Nordstrom's: it operates off-price apparel and home fashions retail stores through its T.J. Maxx and Marshalls stores. The company's strategy is to offer brand-name goods at 20–60 percent below department store regular prices. The company seeks to accomplish this by buying opportunistically and by operating with a highly efficient distribution network and low cost structure. Nordstrom and TJX seem to follow different investment and financing strategies as well. Nordstrom makes significant investment in its stores whereas TJX leases its stores. Nordstrom has a credit card operation whereas TJX does not. We will illustrate how these differences between the two companies affect their ratios. We will also try to see which strategy is delivering better performance for shareholders.

Measuring Overall Profitability

The starting point for a systematic analysis of a firm's performance is its return on equity (ROE), defined as:

$$\text{ROE} = \frac{\text{Net income}}{\text{Shareholder's equity}}$$

ROE is a comprehensive indicator of a firm's performance because it provides an indication of how well managers are employing the funds invested by the firm's shareholders to generate returns. On average over long periods, large publicly traded firms in the U.S. generate ROEs in the range of 11 to 13 percent.

In the long run, the value of the firm's equity is determined by the relationship between its ROE and its cost of equity capital.[2] That is, those firms that are expected over the long run to generate ROEs in excess of the cost of equity capital should have market values in excess of book value, and vice versa. (We will return to this point in more detail in the chapter on valuation.)

A comparison of ROE with the cost of capital is useful not only for contemplating the value of the firm but also in considering the path of future profitability. The generation of consistent supernormal profitability will, absent significant barriers to entry, attract competition. For that reason, ROEs tend over time to be driven by competitive forces toward a "normal" level—the cost of equity capital. Thus, one can think of the cost of equity capital as establishing a benchmark for the ROE that would be observed in a long-run competitive equilibrium. Deviations from this level arise for two general reasons. One is the industry conditions and competitive strategy that cause a firm to generate supernormal (or subnormal) economic profits, at least over the short run. The second is distortions due to accounting.

Table 9-1 shows the ROE based on reported earnings for Nordstrom and TJX.

Table 9-1 Return on Equity for Nordstrom and TJX

Ratio	Nordstrom 1998	Nordstrom 1997	TJX 1998
Return on equity	15.6%	12.6%	34.5%

Nordstrom's ROE showed a significant improvement, from 12.6 percent to 15.6 percent, between 1997 and 1998. This indicates that Nordstrom's strategy of focusing on profit improvement is beginning to show positive results. Compared to the historical trends of ROE in the economy, Nordstrom's 1997 performance can be viewed as being just about average. Further, its ROE in 1997 is barely adequate to cover reasonable estimates of its equity cost of capital. The three percentage points increase in ROE in 1998 allowed Nordstrom to comfortably exceed both these benchmarks.[3] Unfortunately, despite the improvement in 1998, Nordstrom's performance is still far behind TJX's ROE of 34.5 percent. At that performance, TJX was earning excess returns relative to both the historical trends in ROE in the U.S. economy, as well as its own ROE. TJX's superior performance relative to Nordstrom is reflected in the difference in the two companies' ratio of market value of equity to its book value. As of June 1999, Nordstrom's market value to book value ratio was 3.6, while the same ratio for TJX was 8.6.

Decomposing Profitability: Traditional Approach

A company's ROE is affected by two factors: how profitably it employs its assets and how big the firm's asset base is relative to shareholders' investment. To understand the effect of these two factors, ROE can be decomposed into return on assets (ROA) and a measure of financial leverage, as follows:

$$\text{ROE} = \text{ROA} \times \text{Financial leverage}$$

$$= \frac{\text{Net income}}{\text{Assets}} \times \frac{\text{Assets}}{\text{Shareholders' equity}}$$

ROA tells us how much profit a company is able to generate for each dollar of assets invested. Financial leverage indicates how many dollars of assets the firm is able to deploy for each dollar invested by its shareholders.

The return on assets itself can be decomposed as a product of two factors:

$$\text{ROA} = \frac{\text{Net income}}{\text{Sales}} \times \frac{\text{Sales}}{\text{Assets}}$$

The ratio of net income to sales is called net profit margin or return on sales (ROS); the ratio of sales to assets is known as asset turnover. The profit margin ratio indicates how much the company is able to keep as profits for each dollar of sales it makes. Asset turnover indicates how many sales dollars the firm is able to generate for each dollar of its assets.

Table 9-2 displays the three drivers of ROE for our retail firms: net profit margins, asset turnover, and financial leverage. Nordstrom's ROE increased from 12.6 percent to 15.6 percent. This increase is largely driven by an increase in its financial leverage and, to a lesser extent, by a small increase in its net profit margin. In fact, its return on equity in 1998 was hurt by a decline in its asset turnover. TJX's superior ROE seems to be driven

Table 9-2 Traditional Decomposition of ROE

Ratio	Nordstrom 1998	Nordstrom 1997	TJX 1998
Net profit margin (ROS)	4.1%	3.85%	5.3%
× Asset turnover	1.61	1.68	2.89
= Return on assets (ROA)	6.6%	6.5%	15.3%
× Financial leverage	2.37	1.95	2.25
= Return on equity (ROE)	15.6%	12.6%	34.5%

by higher profit margins and better asset utilization; TJX was able to achieve higher ROE than Nordstrom even though it has a slightly lower financial leverage ratio.

Decomposing Profitability: Alternative Approach

Even though the above approach is popularly used to decompose a firm's ROE, it has several limitations. In the computation of ROA, the denominator includes the assets claimed by all providers of capital to the firm, but the numerator includes only the earnings available to equity holders. The assets themselves include both operating assets and financial assets such as cash and short-term investments. Further, net income includes income from operating activities, as well as interest income and expense, which are consequences of financing decisions. Often it is useful to distinguish between these two sources of performance. Finally, the financial leverage ratio used above does not recognize the fact that a firm's cash and short-term investments are in essence "negative debt" because they can be used to pay down the debt on the company's balance sheet.[4] These issues are addressed by an alternative approach to decomposing ROE discussed below.[5]

Before discussing this alternative ROE decomposition approach, we need to define some terminology used in this section as well as in the rest of this chapter. This terminology is given in Table 9-3.

We use the terms defined in Table 9-3 to decompose ROE in the following manner:

$$
\begin{aligned}
\text{ROE} \;=\;& \frac{\text{NOPAT}}{\text{Equity}} - \frac{(\text{Net interest expense after tax})}{\text{Equity}} \\[2mm]
=\;& \frac{\text{NOPAT}}{\text{Net assets}} \times \frac{\text{Net assets}}{\text{Equity}} - \frac{\text{Net interest expense after tax}}{\text{Net debt}} \times \frac{\text{Net debt}}{\text{Equity}} \\[2mm]
=\;& \frac{\text{NOPAT}}{\text{Net assets}} \times \left(1 + \frac{\text{Net debt}}{\text{Equity}}\right) - \frac{\text{Net interest expense after tax}}{\text{Net debt}} \times \frac{\text{Net debt}}{\text{Equity}} \\[2mm]
=\;& \text{Operating ROA} + (\text{Operating ROA} - \text{Effective interest rate after tax}) \\
& \times \text{Net financial leverage} \\[2mm]
=\;& \text{Operating ROA} + \text{Spread} \times \text{Net financial leverage}
\end{aligned}
$$

Table 9-3 Definitions of Accounting Items Used in Ratio Analysis

Item	Definition
Net interest expense after tax	(Interest expense – Interest income) × (1 – Tax rate)
Net operating profit after taxes (NOPAT)	Net income + Net interest expense after tax
Operating working capital	(Current assets – Cash and marketable securities) – (Current liabilities – Short-term debt and current portion of long-term debt)
Net long-term assets	Total long-term assets – Non-interest-bearing long-term liabilities
Net debt	Total interest bearing liabilities – Cash and marketable securities
Net assets	Operating working capital + Net long-term assets
Net capital	Net debt + Shareholders' equity

Operating ROA is a measure of how profitably a company is able to deploy its operating assets to generate operating profits. This would be a company's ROE if it were financed with all equity. Spread is the incremental economic effect from introducing debt into the capital structure. This economic effect of borrowing is positive as long as the return on operating assets is greater than the cost of borrowing. Firms that do not earn adequate operating returns to pay for interest cost reduce their ROE by borrowing. Both the positive and negative effect is magnified by the extent to which a firm borrows relative to its equity base. The ratio of net debt to equity provides a measure of this net financial leverage. A firm's spread times its net financial leverage, therefore, provides a measure of the financial leverage gain to the shareholders.

Operating ROA can be further decomposed into NOPAT margin and operating asset turnover as follows:

$$\text{Operating ROA} = \frac{\text{NOPAT}}{\text{Sales}} \times \frac{\text{Sales}}{\text{Net assets}}$$

NOPAT margin is a measure of how profitable a company's sales are from an operating perspective. Operating asset turnover measures the extent to which a company is able to use its operating assets to generate sales.

Table 9-4 presents the decomposition of ROE for Nordstrom and TJX. The ratios in this table show that there is a significant difference between Nordstrom's ROA and operating ROA. In 1998, for example, Nordstrom's ROA was 6.6 percent, and its operating ROA was 11.7 percent. This difference in ROA and operating ROA is even more remarkable for TJX: its ROA in 1998 was 15.3 percent whereas the operating ROA was 43 percent. Because TJX had a large amount of non-interest-bearing liabilities and short-term investments, its operating ROA is dramatically larger than its ROA. This shows that, for at least some firms, it is important to adjust the simple ROA to take into account interest expense, interest income, and financial assets.

Table 9-4 Distinguishing Operating and Financing Components in ROE Decomposition

Ratio	Nordstrom 1998	Nordstrom 1997	TJX 1998
Net operating profit margin	4.7%	4.3%	5.3%
× Net operating asset turnover	2.49	2.27	8.11
= Operating ROA	11.7%	9.8%	43.0%
Spread	7.3%	6.4%	42.9%
× Net financial leverage	0.54	0.45	(0.20)
= Financial leverage gain	3.9%	2.8%	(8.5)%
ROE = Operating ROA + Financial leverage gain	15.6%	12.6%	34.5%

The appropriate benchmark for evaluating operating ROA is the weighted average cost of debt and equity capital, or WACC. In the long run, the value of the firm's assets is determined by where operating ROA stands relative to this norm. Moreover, over the long run and absent some barrier to competitive forces, operating ROA will tend to be pushed towards the weighted average cost of capital. Since the WACC is lower than the cost of equity capital, operating ROA tends to be pushed to a level lower than that to which ROE tends. The average operating ROA for large firms in the U.S., over long periods of time, is in the range of 9 to 11 percent. Nordstrom's operating ROA in 1997 and 1998 is in this range, indicating that its operating performance is about average. At 43 percent, TJX's operating ROA is far larger than Nordstrom's and also the U.S. industrial average and any reasonable estimates of TJX's weighted average cost of capital. This dramatic superior operating performance of TJX would have been obscured by using the simple ROA measure.[6]

TJX dominates Nordstrom in terms of both operating drivers of ROE—it has a better NOPAT margin and a dramatically higher operating asset turnover. TJX's higher operating asset turnover is primarily a result of its strategy of renting its stores, unlike Nordstrom, which owns many of its stores. What is surprising is TJX's higher NOPAT margin, which suggests that Nordstrom is unable to price its merchandise high enough to recoup the cost of its high service strategy.

Nordstrom is able to create shareholder value through its financing strategy. In 1997 the spread between Nordstrom's operating ROA and its after-tax interest cost was 6.4 percent; its net debt as a percent of its equity was 45 percent. Both these factors contributed to a net increment of 2.8 percent to its ROE. Thus, while the Nordstrom's operating ROA in 1997 was 9.8 percent, its ROE was 12.6 percent. In 1998 Nordstrom's spread increased to 7.3 percent, its net financial leverage went up to 0.54, leading to a 3.9 percent net increment to ROE due to its debt policy. With an operating ROA of 11.7 percent in that year, its ROE in 1998 went up to 15.6 percent.

Even though TJX had a very high spread in 1998, it did not exploit this advantage due an inefficient financial strategy. Because the company had a large cash balance in 1998, in effect it had *negative* net financial leverage. As a result, the company had a lower ROE than its operating ROA. As a result of its ineffective financial management, even though TJX's operating ROA in 1998 was almost four times as large as Nordstrom's, its ROE was only about twice as large as Nordstrom's in that year.

Assessing Operating Management: Decomposing Net Profit Margins

A firm's net profit margin or return on sales (ROS) shows the profitability of the company's operating activities. Further decomposition of a firm's ROS allows an analyst to assess the efficiency of the firm's operating management. A popular tool used in this analysis is the common-sized income statement in which all the line items are expressed as a ratio of sales revenues.

Common-sized income statements make it possible to compare trends in income statement relationships over time for the firm, and trends across different firms in the industry. Income statement analysis allows the analyst to ask the following types of questions: (1) Are the company's margins consistent with its stated competitive strategy? For example, a differentiation strategy should usually lead to higher gross margins than a low cost strategy. (2) Are the company's margins changing? Why? What are the underlying business causes—changes in competition, changes in input costs, or poor overhead cost management? (3) Is the company managing its overhead and administrative costs well? What are the business activities driving these costs? Are these activities necessary?

To illustrate how the income statement analysis can be used, common-sized income statements for Nordstrom and TJX are shown in Table 9-5. The table also shows some commonly used profitability ratios. We will use the information in Table 9-5 to investigate why Nordstrom had a net income margin (or return on sales) of 4.1 percent in 1998 and 3.8 percent in 1997, while TJX had a net margin of 5.3 percent.

GROSS PROFIT MARGINS.   The difference between a firm's sales and cost of sales is gross profit. Gross profit margin is an indication of the extent to which revenues exceed direct costs associated with sales, and it is computed as:

$$\text{Gross profit margin} \quad = \quad \frac{\text{Sales} \ - \ \text{Cost of sales}}{\text{Sales}}$$

Gross margin is influenced by two factors: (1) the price premium that a firm's products or services command in the marketplace and (2) the efficiency of the firm's procurement and production process. The price premium a firm's products or services can command is influenced by the degree of competition and the extent to which its products are unique. The firm's cost of sales can be low when it can purchase its inputs at a lower cost than competitors and/or run its production processes more efficiently. This is generally the case when a firm has a low-cost strategy.

Table 9-5 Common-Sized Income Statement and Profitability Ratios

	Nordstrom 1998	Nordstrom 1997	TJX 1998
Line Items as a Percent of Sales			
Sales	100%	100%	100%
Cost of Sales	(66.5)	(67.9)	(74.9)
Selling, general, and admin. expense	(28.0)	(27.3)	(16.2)
Other income/expense	2.1	2.2	—
Net interest expense/income	(0.9)	(0.7)	—
Income taxes	(2.6)	(2.5)	(3.4)
Unusual gains/losses, net of taxes	—	—	(0.1)
Net Income	4.1%	3.8%	5.3%
Key Profitability Ratios			
Gross profit margin	33.5%	32.1%	25.1%
EBITDA margin	10.4%	9.7%	10.6%
NOPAT margin	4.7%	4.3%	5.3%
Net Margin	4.1%	3.8%	5.3%

Table 9-5 indicates that Nordstrom's gross margin in 1998 increased slightly to 33.5 percent, validating the company's stated intention in its annual report of focusing on profitability. Consistent with Nordstrom's premium price strategy, its gross margins in both 1998 and 1997 were significantly higher than TJX's gross margin in 1998, which stood at 25.1 percent.

SELLING, GENERAL, AND ADMINISTRATIVE EXPENSES.   A company's selling, general, and administrative (SG&A) expenses are influenced by the operating activities it has to undertake to implement its competitive strategy. As discussed in Chapter 2, firms with differentiation strategies have to undertake activities to achieve differentiation. A company competing on the basis of quality and rapid introduction of new products is likely to have higher R&D costs relative to a company competing purely on a cost basis. Similarly, a company that attempts to build a brand image, distribute its products through full-service retailers, and provide significant customer service is likely to have higher selling and administration costs relative to a company that sells through warehouse retailers or direct mail and does not provide much customer support.

A company's SG&A expenses are also influenced by the efficiency with which it manages its overhead activities. The control of operating expenses is likely to be especially important for firms competing on the basis of low cost. However, even for differentiators, it is important to assess whether the cost of differentiation is commensurate with the price premium earned in the marketplace.

Several ratios in Table 9-5 allow us to evaluate the effectiveness with which Nordstrom and TJX were managing their SG&A expenses. First, the ratio of SG&A expense to sales shows how much a company is spending to generate each sales dollar. We see that Nordstrom has a significantly higher ratio of SG&A to sales than does TJX. This should not be surprising given that TJX pursues a low-cost off-price strategy whereas Nordstrom pursues a high service strategy. However, despite its stated goal to manage its profitability better, Nordstrom did not improve its cost management: its SG&A expense as a percent of sales increased marginally from 27.3 percent in 1997 to 28 percent in 1998.

Given that Nordstrom and TJX are pursuing radically different pricing, merchandising, and service strategies, it is not surprising that they have very different cost structures. As a percent of sales, Nordstrom's cost of sales is lower, and its SG&A expense is higher. The question is, when both these costs are netted out, which company is performing better? Two ratios provide useful signals here: net operating profit margin ratio and EBITDA margin:

$$\text{NOPAT margin} = \frac{\text{NOPAT}}{\text{Sales}}$$

$$\text{EBITDA margin} = \frac{\text{Earnings before interest, taxes, depreciation, and amortization}}{\text{Sales}}$$

NOPAT margin provides a comprehensive indication of the operating performance of a company because it reflects all operating policies and eliminates the effects of debt policy. EBITDA margin provides similar information, except that it excludes depreciation and amortization expense, a significant noncash operating expense. Some analysts prefer to use EBITDA margin because they believe that it focuses on "cash" operating items. While this is to some extent true, it can be potentially misleading for two reasons. EBITDA is not a strictly cash concept because sales, cost of sales, and SG&A expenses often include non-cash items. Also, depreciation is a real operating expense, and it reflects to some extent the consumption of resources. Therefore, ignoring it can be misleading.

From Table 9-5 we see that Nordstrom's NOPAT margin has improved a little between 1997 and 1998. However, even with this improvement, the company is able to retain only 4.7 cents in net operating profits for each dollar of sales, whereas TJX is able to retain 5.3 cents. TJX also has a slightly better EBITDA margin than Nordstrom, but the difference seems insignificant. However, this comparison is potentially misleading because TJX leases most of its stores while Nordstrom owns its; TJX's leasing expense is included in the EBITDA calculation, but Nordstrom's store depreciation is excluded. This is an example of how EBITDA margin can sometimes be misleading.

TAX EXPENSE.   Taxes are an important element of firms' total expenses. Through a wide variety of tax planning techniques, firms can attempt to reduce their tax expenses.[7] There are two measures one can use to evaluate a firm's tax expense. One is the ratio of tax expense to sales, and the other is the ratio of tax expense to earnings before taxes (also known as average tax rate). The firm's tax footnote provides a detailed account of why its average tax rate differs from the statutory tax rate.

When evaluating a firm's tax planning, the analyst should ask two questions: (1) Are the company's tax policies sustainable, or is the current tax rate influenced by one-time tax credits? (2) Do the firm's tax planning strategies lead to other business costs? For example, if the operations are located in tax havens, how does this affect the company's profit margins and asset utilization? Are the benefits of tax planning strategies (reduced taxes) greater than the increased business costs?

Table 9-5 shows that Nordstrom's tax rate did not change significantly between 1997 and 1998. Nordstrom's taxes as a percent of sales were somewhat lower than TJX's. An important reason for this is that TJX's pretax profits as a percent of sales were higher. In fact, the average tax rate (ratio of tax expense to pretax profits) for both Nordstrom and TJX were the same, 39 percent.

In summary, we conclude that Nordstrom's small improvement in return on sales is primarily driven by a reduction in its cost of sales. In all other areas, Nordstrom's performance either stayed the same or worsened a bit. TJX is able to earn a superior return on its sales despite following an off-price strategy because it is able to save significantly on its SG&A expenses.

Evaluating Investment Management: Decomposing Asset Turnover

Asset turnover is the second driver of a company's return on equity. Since firms invest considerable resources in their assets, using them productively is critical to overall profitability. A detailed analysis of asset turnover allows the analyst to evaluate the effectiveness of a firm's investment management.

There are two primary areas of asset management: (1) working capital management and (2) management of long-term assets. Working capital is defined as the difference between a firm's current assets and current liabilities. However, this definition does not distinguish between operating components (such as accounts receivable, inventory, and accounts payable) and the financing components (such as cash, marketable securities, and notes payable). An alternative measure that makes this distinction is operating working capital, as defined in Table 9-3:

Operating working capital = (Current assets − cash and marketable securities)
  − (Current liabilities − Short-term and current portion of long-term debt)

WORKING CAPITAL MANAGEMENT.   The components of operating working capital that analysts primarily focus on are accounts receivable, inventory, and accounts payable. A certain amount of investment in working capital is necessary for the firm to run its normal operations. For example, a firm's credit policies and distribution policies determine its optimal level of accounts receivable. The nature of the production process and the need for buffer stocks determine the optimal level of inventory. Finally, accounts payable is a routine source of financing for the firm's working capital, and payment practices in an industry determine the normal level of accounts payable.

The following ratios are useful in analyzing a firm's working capital management: operating working capital as a percent of sales, operating working capital turnover, accounts receivable turnover, inventory turnover, and accounts payable turnover. The turnover ratios can also be expressed in number of days of activity that the operating working capital (and its components) can support. The definitions of these ratios are given below.

$$\text{Operating working capital-to-sales ratio} = \frac{\text{Operating working capital}}{\text{Sales}}$$

$$\text{Operating working capital turnover} = \frac{\text{Sales}}{\text{Operating working capital}}$$

$$\text{Accounts receivable turnover} = \frac{\text{Sales}}{\text{Accounts receivable}}$$

$$\text{Inventory turnover} = \frac{\text{Cost of goods sold}}{\text{Inventory}}$$

$$\text{Accounts payable turnover} = \frac{\text{Purchases}}{\text{Accounts payable}} \quad or \quad \frac{\text{Cost of goods sold}}{\text{Accounts payable}}$$

$$\text{Days' receivables} = \frac{\text{Accounts receivable}}{\text{Average sales per day}}$$

$$\text{Days' inventory} = \frac{\text{Inventory}}{\text{Average cost of goods sold per day}}$$

$$\text{Days' payables} = \frac{\text{Accounts payable}}{\text{Average purchases (or cost of goods sold) per day}}$$

Operating working capital turnover indicates how many dollars of sales a firm is able to generate for each dollar invested in its operating working capital. Accounts receivable turnover, inventory turnover, and accounts payable turnover allow the analyst to examine how productively the three principal components of working capital are being used. Days' receivables, days' inventory, and days' payables are another way to evaluate the efficiency of a firm's working capital management.[8]

LONG-TERM ASSETS MANAGEMENT. Another area of investment management concerns the utilization of a firm's long-term assets. It is useful to define a firm's investment in long-term assets as follows:

Net long-term assets =
    (Total long-term assets − Non-interest-bearing long-term liabilities)

Long-term assets generally consist of net property, plant, and equipment (PP&E), intangible assets such as goodwill, and other assets. Non-interest-bearing long-term liabilities include such items as deferred taxes. We define net long-term assets and net working capital in such a way that their sum, net operating assets, is equal to the sum of net debt and equity, or net capital. This is consistent with the way we defined operating ROA earlier in the chapter.

The efficiency with which a firm uses its net long-term assets is measured by the following two ratios: net long-term assets as a percent of sales and net long-term asset turnover. Net long-term asset turnover is defined as:

$$\text{Net long-term asset turnover} \quad = \quad \frac{\text{Sales}}{\text{Net long-term assets}}$$

Property plant and equipment (PP&E) is the most important long-term asset in a firm's balance sheet. The efficiency with which a firm's PP&E is used is measured by the ratio of PP&E to sales, or by the PP&E turnover ratio:

$$\text{PP\&E turnover} \quad = \quad \frac{\text{Sales}}{\text{Net property, plant, and equipment}}$$

The ratios listed above allow the analyst to explore a number of business questions in four general areas: (1) How well does the company manage its inventory? Does the company use modern manufacturing techniques? Does it have good vendor and logistics management systems? If inventory ratios are changing, what is the underlying business reason? Are new products being planned? Is there a mismatch between the demand forecasts and actual sales? (2) How well does the company manage its credit policies? Are these policies consistent with its marketing strategy? Is the company artificially increasing sales by loading the distribution channels? (3) Is the company taking advantage of trade credit? Is it relying too much on trade credit? If so, what are the implicit costs? (4) Are the company's investment in plant and equipment consistent with its competitive strategy? Does the company have a sound policy of acquisitions and divestitures?

Table 9-6 shows the asset turnover ratios for Nordstrom and TJX. Nordstrom achieved an improvement in its working capital management between 1997 and 1998, as can be seen from a reduction of operating working capital as a percent of sales and an increase in operating working capital turnover. This improvement is attributable to a reduction in accounts receivable and better inventory management. There was also a marginal improvement in its accounts payable days as well. In contrast, Nordstrom's long-term asset utilization did not improve in 1998: its net long-term asset turnover and PP&E turnover show marginal declines. In its annual report, Nordstrom acknowledges that the sales from stores that it operated for more than a year (also called same-store sales) showed a small decline in 1998 because management was focusing on controlling inventory to cut costs.

TJX achieved dramatically better asset utilization ratios in 1998 relative to Nordstrom. TJX was able to invest a negligible amount of money in its operating working capital by taking full advantage of trade credit from its vendors and by delaying payment of some of its operating expenses. Also, because TJX has no credit card operations of its own, it is able to collect its receivables in 3 days, in contrast to Nordstrom's 43 receivable days. TJX is also managing its inventory more efficiently, perhaps because of its more focused merchandising strategy. Finally, because TJX uses operating leases to rent its stores, it has significantly lower capital tied up in its stores. As a result, its PP&E turn-

Table 9-6 Asset Management Ratios

Ratio	Nordstrom 1998	Nordstrom 1997	TJX 1998
Operating working capital/Sales	16.2%	20.8%	(0.3)%
Net long-term assets/Sales	24.0%	23.2%	12.6%
PP&E/Sales	27.1%	25.8%	9.5%
Operating working capital turnover	6.17	4.81	Not meaningful
Net long-term assets turnover	4.17	4.31	7.94
PP&E turnover	3.69	3.88	10.52
Accounts receivable turnover	8.56	7.30	117.9
Inventory turnover	4.46	3.99	5.0
Accounts payable turnover	9.85	10.26	9.6
Days' accounts receivable	42.6	50	3.1
Days' inventory	81.8	91.5	73
Days' accounts payable	37.1	35.6	38

over is almost three times as much as Nordstrom's. One should, however, be cautious in interpreting this difference between the two companies, because, as TJX discloses in its footnotes, it owes a substantial amount of money in the coming years on noncancelable operating leases. TJX's financial statements do not fully recognize its potential investment in its stores through these noncancelable leases, potentially inflating its operating asset turns.

Evaluating Financial Management: Financial Leverage

Financial leverage enables a firm to have an asset base larger than its equity. The firm can augment its equity through borrowing and the creation of other liabilities like accounts payable, accrued liabilities, and deferred taxes. Financial leverage increases a firm's ROE as long as the cost of the liabilities is less than the return from investing these funds. In this respect, it is important to distinguish between interest-bearing liabilities such as notes payable, other forms of short-term debt and long-term debt, which carry an explicit interest charge, and other forms of liabilities. Some of these other forms of liability, such as accounts payable or deferred taxes, do not carry any interest charge at all. Other liabilities, such as capital lease obligations or pension obligations, carry an implicit interest charge. Finally, some firms carry large cash balances or investments in marketable securities. These balances reduce a firm's net debt because conceptually the firm can pay down its debt using its cash and short-term investments.

While a firm's shareholders can potentially benefit from financial leverage, it can also increase their risk. Unlike equity, liabilities have predefined payment terms, and the firm faces risk of financial distress if it fails to meet these commitments. There are a number of ratios to evaluate the degree of risk arising from a firm's financial leverage.

CURRENT LIABILITIES AND SHORT-TERM LIQUIDITY.   The following ratios are useful in evaluating the risk related to a firm's current liabilities:

$$\text{Current ratio} = \frac{\text{Current assets}}{\text{Current liabilities}}$$

$$\text{Quick ratio} = \frac{\text{Cash + Short-term investments + Accounts receivable}}{\text{Current liabilities}}$$

$$\text{Cash ratio} = \frac{\text{Cash + Marketable securities}}{\text{Current liabilities}}$$

$$\text{Operating cash flow ratio} = \frac{\text{Cash flow from operations}}{\text{Current liabilities}}$$

All the above ratios attempt to measure the firm's ability to repay its current liabilities. The first three compare a firm's current liabilities with its short-term assets that can be used to repay the current liabilities. The fourth ratio focuses on the ability of the firm's operations to generate the resources needed to repay its current liabilities.

Since both current assets and current liabilities have comparable duration, the current ratio is a key index of a firm's short-term liquidity. Analysts view a current ratio of more than one to be an indication that the firm can cover its current liabilities from the cash realized from its current assets. However, the firm can face a short-term liquidity problem even with a current ratio exceeding one when some of its current assets are not easy to liquidate. Quick ratio and cash ratio capture the firm's ability to cover its current liabilities from liquid assets. Quick ratio assumes that the firm's accounts receivable are liquid. This is true in industries where the credit-worthiness of the customers is beyond dispute, or when receivables are collected in a very short period. However, when these conditions do not prevail, cash ratio, which considers only cash and marketable securities, is a better indication of a firm's ability to cover its current liabilities in an emergency. Operating cash flow is another measure of the firm's ability to cover its current liabilities from cash generated from operations of the firm.

The liquidity ratios for Nordstrom and TJX are shown in Table 9-7. Nordstrom's liquidity situation in 1998 was comfortable when measured in terms of current ratio or quick ratio. Both these ratios improved in 1998. Because Nordstrom accumulated a large cash balance and improved its cash flow from operations through better inventory management in 1998, its cash ratio and operating cash flow ratio also show dramatic improvement in 1998. All this is good news for Nordstrom's short-term creditors. TJX also has a comfortable liquidity position, thanks to its large cash balance and a sound operating cash flow. Because of its tight management of operating working capital, however,

Table 9-7 Liquidity Ratios

Ratio	Nordstrom 1998	Nordstrom 1997	TJX 1998
Current ratio	2.19	1.71	1.33
Quick ratio	1.08	0.73	0.40
Cash ratio	0.31	0.03	0.35
Operating cash flow ratio	0.78	0.32	0.49

TJX's current and quick ratios are smaller than Nordstrom's. If TXJ were to pay out its cash balance, its liquidity ratios would show a significant decline.

DEBT AND LONG-TERM SOLVENCY. A company's financial leverage is also influenced by its debt financing policy. There are several potential benefits from debt financing. First, debt is typically cheaper than equity because the firm promises predefined payment terms to debt holders. Second, in most countries, interest on debt financing is tax deductible whereas dividends to shareholders are not tax deductible. Third, debt financing can impose discipline on the firm's management and motivate it to reduce wasteful expenditures. Fourth, it is often easier for management to communicate their proprietary information on the firm's strategies and prospects to private lenders than to public capital markets. Such communication can potentially reduce a firm's cost of capital. For all these reasons, it is optimal for firms to use at least some debt in their capital structure. Too much reliance on debt financing, however, is potentially costly to the firm's shareholders. The firm will face financial distress if it defaults on the interest and principal payments. Debt holders also impose covenants on the firm, restricting the firm's operating, investment, and financing decisions.

The optimal capital structure for a firm is determined primarily by its business risk. A firm's cash flows are highly predictable when there is little competition or there is little threat of technological changes. Such firms have low business risk, and hence they can rely heavily on debt financing. In contrast, if a firm's operating cash flows are highly volatile and its capital expenditure needs are unpredictable, it may have to rely primarily on equity financing. Managers' attitude towards risk and financial flexibility also often determine a firm's debt policies.

There are a number of ratios which help the analyst in this area. To evaluate the mix of debt and equity in a firm's capital structure, the following ratios are useful:

$$\text{Liabilities-to-equity ratio} \quad = \quad \frac{\text{Total liabilities}}{\text{Shareholders' equity}}$$

$$\text{Debt-to-equity ratio} \quad = \quad \frac{\text{Short-term debt} + \text{Long-term debt}}{\text{Shareholders' equity}}$$

$$\text{Net-debt-to-equity ratio} \quad = \quad \frac{\text{Short-term debt} + \text{Long-term debt} - \text{Cash and marketable securities}}{\text{Shareholders' equity}}$$

$$\text{Debt-to-capital ratio} \quad = \quad \frac{\text{Short-term debt} + \text{Long-term debt}}{\text{Short-term debt} + \text{Long-term debt} + \text{Shareholders' equity}}$$

$$\text{Net-debt-to-net-capital ratio} \quad = \quad \frac{\text{Interest bearing liabilities} - \text{Cash and marketable securities}}{\text{Interest bearing liabilities} - \text{Cash and marketable securities} + \text{Shareholders' equity}}$$

The first ratio restates the assets-to-equity ratio (one of the three primary ratios underlying ROE) by subtracting one from it. The second ratio provides an indication of how many dollars of debt financing the firm is using for each dollar invested by its shareholders. The third ratio uses net debt, which is total debt minus cash and marketable securities, as the measure of a firm's borrowings. The fourth and fifth ratios measure debt as a proportion of total capital. In calculating all the above ratios, it is important to include all interest bearing obligations, whether the interest charge is explicit or implicit. Recall that examples of line items which carry an implicit interest charge include capital lease obligations and pension obligations. Analysts sometimes include any potential off-balance-sheet obligations that a firm may have, such as noncancelable operating leases, in the definition of a firm's debt.

The ease with which a firm can meet its interest payments is an indication of the degree of risk associated with its debt policy. The interest coverage ratio provides a measure of this construct:

$$\text{Interest coverage (earnings basis)} \quad = \quad \frac{\text{Net income} + \text{Interest expense} + \text{Tax expense}}{\text{Interest expense}}$$

$$\text{Interest coverage (cash flow basis)} \quad = \quad \frac{\text{Cash flow from operations} + \text{Interest expense} + \text{Taxes paid}}{\text{Interest expense}}$$

One can also calculate coverage ratios that measure a firm's ability to measure all fixed financial obligations, such as interest payment, lease payments and debt repayments, by appropriately redefining the numerator in the above ratios. In doing so, it is important to remember that while some fixed charge payments, such as interest and lease rentals, are paid with pretax dollars, others payments, such as debt repayments, are made with after-tax dollars.

The earnings-based coverage ratio indicates the dollars of earnings available for each dollar of required interest payment; the cash-flow-based coverage ratio indicates the dollars of cash generated by operations for each dollar of required interest payment. In both these ratios, the denominator is the interest expense. In the numerator, we add taxes back because taxes are computed only after interest expense is deducted. A coverage ratio of one implies that the firm is barely covering its interest expense through its operating activities, which is a very risky situation. The larger the coverage ratio, the greater the cushion the firm has to meet interest obligations.

Key Analysis Questions

Some of the business questions to ask when the analyst is examining a firm's debt policies are:

- Does the company have enough debt? Is it exploiting the potential benefits of debt—interest tax shields, management discipline, and easier communication?
- Does the company have too much debt given its business risk? What type of debt covenant restrictions does the firm face? Is it bearing the costs of too much debt, risking potential financial distress and reduced business flexibility?
- What is the company doing with the borrowed funds? Investing in working capital? Investing in fixed assets? Are these investments profitable?
- Is the company borrowing money to pay dividends? If so, what is the justification?

We show debt and coverage ratios for Nordstrom and TJX in Table 9-8. While Nordstrom recorded an increase in its liabilities-to-equity and debt-to-equity ratios, its net financial leverage after taking into account its increased cash balance in 1998 shows little increase. The company's interest coverage also remained at comfortable levels. All these ratios suggest that Nordstrom has been following a fairly conservative debt policy.

Table 9-8 Debt and Coverage Ratios

Ratio	Nordstrom 1998	Nordstrom 1997	TJX 1998
Liabilities to equity	1.37	0.95	1.25
Debt to equity	0.72	0.46	0.18
Net debt to equity	0.54	0.48	(0.20)
Debt to capital	0.42	0.38	0.15
Net debt to net capital	0.35	0.31	(0.25)
Net debt to equity, including operating lease obligations	Not available	Not available	1.19
Interest coverage (earnings based)	8.2	9.6	410
Interest coverage (cash flow based)	16.4	13.4	541.2
Fixed charges coverage, including lease payments (earnings based)	4.6	4.8	3.17
Fixed charges coverage, including lease payments (cash flow based)	8.7	6.2	3.87

TJX's debt ratios confirm that it is primarily relying on non-interest-bearing liabilities such as accounts payable and accrued expenses to finance its operations. Given its large cash balance, its net debt is in fact negative. Its interest coverage ratios are extraordinarily high. However, this picture changes when one considers the fact that TJX relies heavily on operating leases for its stores. If the present value of minimum lease rental obligations is added to TJX's net debt, its net-debt-to-equity ratio increases dramatically. Similarly, when one includes minimum rental payments in the fixed charge coverage ratio, TJX's coverage drops dramatically. This illustrates the importance of considering off-balance-sheet obligations in analyzing a company's financial management.

RATIOS OF DISAGGREGATED DATA.   So far we have discussed how to compute ratios using information in the financial statements. Often, analysts probe the above ratios further by using disaggregated financial and physical data. For example, for a multibusiness company, one could analyze the information by individual business segments. Such an analysis can reveal potential differences in the performance of each business unit, allowing the analyst to pinpoint areas where a company's strategy is working and where it is not. It is also possible to probe financial ratios further by computing ratios of physical data pertaining to a company's operations. The appropriate physical data to look at varies from industry to industry. As an example in retailing, one could compute productivity statistics such as sales per store, sales per square foot, customer transactions per store, and amount of sale per customer transactions; in the hotel industry, room occupancy rates provide important information; in the cellular telephone industry, acquisition cost per new subscriber and subscriber retention rate are important. These disaggregated ratios are particularly useful for young firms and young industries (for example, the Internet firms) where accounting data may not fully capture the business economics due to conservative accounting rules.

Putting It All Together: Assessing Sustainable Growth Rate

Analysts often use the concept of sustainable growth as a way to evaluate a firm's ratios in a comprehensive manner. A firm's sustainable growth rate is defined as:

$$\text{Sustainable growth rate} \quad = \quad \text{ROE} \times (1 - \text{Dividend payout ratio})$$

We already discussed the analysis of ROE in the previous four sections. The dividend payout ratio is defined as:

$$\text{Dividend payout ratio} \quad = \quad \frac{\text{Cash dividends paid}}{\text{Net income}}$$

A firm's dividend payout ratio is a measure of its dividend policy. As we discuss in detail in Chapter X, firms pay dividends for several reasons. Dividends are a way for the firm to return to its shareholders any cash generated in excess of its operating and investment needs. When there are information asymmetries between a firm's managers and its shareholders, dividend payments can serve as a signal to shareholders about managers' expectation of the firm's future prospects. Firms may also pay dividends to attract a certain type of shareholder base.

Sustainable growth rate is the rate at which a firm can grow while keeping its profitability and financial policies unchanged. A firm's return on equity and its dividend payout policy determine the pool of funds available for growth. Of course, the firm can grow at a rate different from its sustainable growth rate if its profitability, payout policy, or financial leverage changes. Therefore, the sustainable growth rate provides a benchmark against which a firm's growth plans can be evaluated. Figure 9-2 shows how a firm's sustainable growth rate can be linked to all the ratios discussed in this chapter. These linkages allow an analyst to examine the drivers of a firm's current sustainable growth rate. If the firm intends to grow at a higher rate than its sustainable growth rate, one could

Figure 9-2 Sustainable Growth Rate Framework for Financial Ratio Analysis

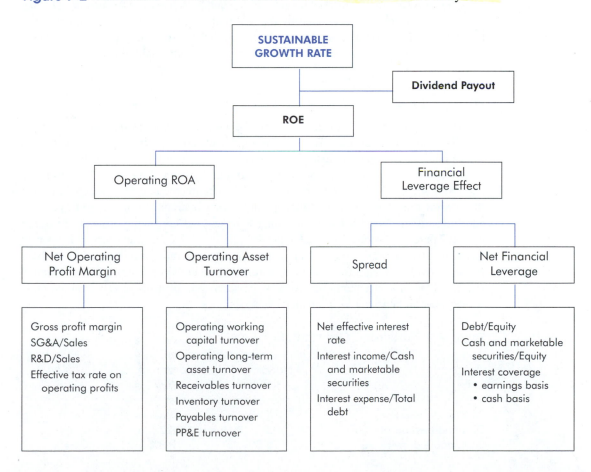

assess which of the ratios are likely to change in the process. This analysis can lead to asking business questions such as: Where is the change going to take place? Is management expecting profitability to increase? Or asset productivity to improve? Are these expectations realistic? Is the firm planning for these changes? If the profitability is not likely to go up, will the firm increase its financial leverage, or cut dividends? What is the likely impact of these financial policy changes?

Table 9-9 shows the sustainable growth rate and its components for Nordstrom and TJX. Nordstrom had a lower ROE and a higher dividend payout ratio relative to TJX, leading to a significantly lower sustainable growth rate in both 1998 and 1997. However, Nordstrom improved its sustainable growth rate because of its improved ROE and a marginal decline in its payout ratio.

Nordstrom's actual growth rate in 1998 in sales, assets, and liabilities was lower than its sustainable growth rate in 1997. In 1998 Nordstrom's sales grew by 3.6 percent, net operating assets declined by 5.3 percent, and its net debt grew by 6.9 percent. These differences in Nordstrom's sustainable growth rate and its actual growth rates in sales, net assets, and net debt are reconciled by the fact that Nordstrom reduced its equity base through significant stock repurchases. Nordstrom has the room to grow in future years at much higher levels without altering its operating and financial policies.

Historical Patterns of Ratios for U.S. Nonfinancial Firms

To provide a benchmark for analysis, Table 9-10 reports historical values of the key ratios discussed in this chapter. These ratios are calculated using financial statement data for all nonfinancial publicly listed U.S. companies. The table shows the values of ROE, its key components, and the sustainable growth rate for each of the years 1979 to 1998, and the average for this twenty-year period. The data in the table show that the average ROE during this period has been 11.2 percent, average operating ROA has been 9 percent, and the average spread between operating ROA and net borrowing costs after tax has been 2.7 percent. Average sustainable growth rate for U.S. companies during this period has been 4.6 percent. Of course, an individual company's ratios might depart from these economy-wide averages for a number of reasons, including industry effects, company strategies, and management effectiveness. Nonetheless, the average values in the table serve as useful benchmarks in financial analysis.

Table 9-9 Sustainable Growth Rate

Ratio	Nordstrom 1998	Nordstrom 1997	TJX 1998
ROE	15.6%	12.6%	34.5%
Dividend payout ratio	0.21	0.22	0.09
Sustainable growth rate	12.3%	9.8%	31.4%

Table 9-10 Historical Values of Key Financial Ratios

Year	ROE	NOPAT Margin	Operating Asset Turnover	Operating ROA	Spread	Net Financial Leverage	Sustainable Growth Rate
1979	14.7%	7.2%	1.77	11.5%	5.4%	0.57	8.8%
1980	13.9%	7.0%	1.81	11.3%	4.3%	0.58	8.0%
1981	13.5%	7.4%	1.77	11.3%	3.7%	0.59	7.5%
1982	10.5%	6.8%	1.61	9.4%	1.7%	0.60	4.2%
1983	10.5%	6.9%	1.61	9.6%	1.6%	0.53	4.2%
1984	12.4%	7.4%	1.64	10.6%	3.1%	0.56	6.1%
1985	9.6%	6.4%	1.61	8.7%	1.4%	0.60	3.2%
1986	8.8%	6.4%	1.51	8.1%	0.9%	0.65	1.9%
1987	11.6%	7.4%	1.52	9.8%	2.7%	0.69	4.7%
1988	13.5%	8.2%	1.42	10.0%	3.7%	0.93	5.9%
1989	12.5%	8.1%	1.40	9.5%	2.9%	1.03	5.3%
1990	10.4%	7.1%	1.42	8.3%	1.9%	1.06	3.3%
1991	6.5%	5.7%	1.41	6.3%	0.1%	1.01	−0.5%
1992	3.1%	3.9%	1.49	4.2%	−1.3%	1.03	−4.0%
1993	6.8%	4.9%	1.51	5.9%	0.8%	1.00	−0.2%
1994	12.9%	6.7%	1.57	9.1%	4.0%	0.92	6.3%
1995	11.7%	6.3%	1.58	8.5%	3.3%	0.93	4.8%
1996	13.7%	7.1%	1.56	9.7%	4.7%	0.85	7.6%
1997	12.9%	6.7%	1.55	9.1%	4.2%	0.88	6.9%
1998	13.7%	7.0%	1.45	8.9%	4.4%	0.93	7.9%
Average	11.2%	6.7%	1.56	9.0%	2.7%	0.80	4.6%

Source: Financial statement data for all nonfinancial companies publicly traded in the U.S., listed in the Compustat files.

CASH FLOW ANALYSIS

Ratio analysis discussed above focused on analyzing a firm's income statement (net profit margin analysis) or its balance sheet (asset turnover and financial leverage). The analyst can get further insights into the firm's operating, investing, and financing policies by examining its cash flows. Cash flow analysis also provides an indication of the quality of the information in the firm's income statement and balance sheet. As before, we will illustrate the concepts discussed in this section using Nordstrom's and TJX's cash flows.

Cash Flow and Funds Flow Statements

All U.S. companies are required to include a statement of cash flows in their financial statements under Statement of Financial Accounts Standard No. 95 (SFAS 95). In the reported cash flow statement, firms classify their cash flows into three categories: cash flow from operations, cash flow related to investments, and cash flow related to financing activities. Cash flow from operations is the cash generated by the firm from the sale of goods and services after paying for the cost of inputs and operations. Cash flow related to investment activities shows the cash paid for capital expenditures, intercorporate investments, acquisitions, and cash received from the sales of long-term assets. Cash flow related to financing activities shows the cash raised from (or paid to) the firm's stockholders and debt holders.

Firms use two cash flow statement formats: the direct format and the indirect format. The key difference between the two formats is the way they report cash flow from operating activities. In the direct cash flow format, which is used by only a small number of firms in practice, operating cash receipts and disbursements are reported directly. In the indirect format, firms derive their operating cash flows by making adjustments to net income. Because the indirect format links the cash flow statement with the firm's income statement and balance sheet, many analysts and managers find this format more useful. As a result, the FASB required firms using the direct format to report operating cash flows in the indirect format as well.

Recall from Chapter 3 that net income differs from operating cash flows because revenues and expenses are measured on an accrual basis. There are two types of accruals embedded in net income. First, there are current accruals like credit sales and unpaid expenses. Current accruals result in changes in a firm's current assets (such as accounts receivable, inventory, prepaid expenses) and current liabilities (such as accounts payable and accrued liabilities). The second type of accruals included in the income statement is noncurrent accruals such as depreciation, deferred taxes, and equity income from unconsolidated subsidiaries. To derive cash flow from operations from net income, adjustments have to be made for both these types of accruals. In addition, adjustments have to be made for nonoperating gains included in net income such as profits from asset sales.

Most firms outside the U.S. report a funds flow statement rather than a cash flow statement of the type described above. Prior to SFAS 95, U.S. firms also reported a similar statement. Funds flow statements show working capital flows, not cash flows. It is useful for analysts to know how to convert a funds flow statement into a cash flow statement.

Funds flow statements typically provide information on a firm's working capital from operations, defined as net income adjusted for noncurrent accruals, and gains from the sale of long-term assets. As discussed above, cash flow from operations essentially involves a third adjustment, the adjustment for current accruals. Thus, it is relatively straightforward to convert working capital from operations to cash flow from operations by making the relevant adjustments for current accruals related to operations.

Information on current accruals can be obtained by examining changes in a firm's current assets and current liabilities Typically, operating accruals represent changes in all the current asset accounts other than cash and cash equivalents, and changes in all the current liabilities other than notes payable and the current portion of long-term debt.[9] Cash from operations can be calculated as:

Working capital from operations
- Increase (or + decrease) in accounts receivable
- Increase (or + decrease) in inventory
- Increase (or + decrease) in other current assets excluding cash and cash equivalents
+ Increase (or − decrease) in accounts payable
+ Increase (or − decrease) in other current liabilities excluding debt.

Funds flow statements also often do not classify investment and financing flows. In such a case, the analyst has to classify the line items in the funds flow statement into these two categories by evaluating the nature of the business transactions that give rise to the flow represented by the line items.

Analyzing Cash Flow Information

Cash flow analysis can be used to address a variety of questions regarding a firm's cash flow dynamics:

- How strong is the firm's internal cash flow generation? Is the cash flow from operations positive or negative? If it is negative, why? Is it because the company is growing? Is it because its operations are unprofitable? Or is it having difficulty managing its working capital properly?
- Does the company have the ability to meet its short-term financial obligations, such as interest payments, from its operating cash flow? Can it continue to meet these obligations without reducing its operating flexibility?
- How much cash did the company invest in growth? Are these investments consistent with its business strategy? Did the company use internal cash flow to finance growth, or did it rely on external financing?
- Did the company pay dividends from internal free cash flow, or did it have to rely on external financing? If the company had to fund its dividends from external sources, is the company's dividend policy sustainable?
- What type of external financing does the company rely on? Equity, short-term debt, or long-term debt? Is the financing consistent with the company's overall business risk?
- Does the company have excess cash flow after making capital investments? Is it a long-term trend? What plans does management have to deploy the free cash flow?

While the information in reported cash flow statements can be used to answer the above questions directly in the case of some firms, it may not be easy to do so always for a number of reasons. First, even though SFAS 95 provides broad guidelines on the format of a cash flow statement, there is still significant variation across firms in how cash flow data are disclosed. Therefore, to facilitate a systematic analysis and comparison across firms, analysts often recast the information in the cash flow statement using their own cash flow model. Second, firms include interest expense and interest income in computing their cash flow from operating activities. However, these two items are not strictly related to a firm's operations. Interest expense is a function of financial leverage, and interest income is derived from financial assets rather than operating assets. Therefore, it is useful to restate the cash flow statement to take this into account.

Analysts use a number of different approaches to restate the cash flow data. One such model is shown in Table 9-11. This presents cash flow from operations in two stages. The first step computes cash flow from operations before operating working capital investments. In computing this cash flow, the model excludes interest expense and interest income. To compute this number starting with a firm's net income, an analyst adds back three types of items: (1) after-tax net interest expense because this is a financing item that will be considered later, (2) nonoperating gains or losses typically arising out of asset disposals or asset write-offs because these items are investment related and will be considered later, and (3) long-term operating accruals such as depreciation and deferred taxes because these are noncash operating charges.

Several factors affect a firm's ability to generate positive cash flow from operations. Healthy firms that are in a steady state should generate more cash from their customers than they spend on operating expenses. In contrast, growing firms, especially those investing cash in research and development, advertising and marketing, or building an organization to sustain future growth, may experience negative operating cash flow. Firms' working capital management also affects whether they generate positive cash flow from operations. Firms in the growing stage typically invest some cash flow in operating working capital items like accounts receivable, inventories, and accounts payable. Net investments in working capital are a function of firms' credit policies (accounts receivable), payment policies (payables, prepaid expenses, and accrued liabilities), and expected growth in sales (inventories). Thus, in interpreting firms' cash flow from operations after working capital, it is important to keep in mind their growth strategy, industry characteristics, and credit policies.

The cash flow analysis model next focuses on cash flows related to long-term investments. These investments take the form of capital expenditures, intercorporate investments, and mergers and acquisitions. Any positive operating cash flow after making operating working capital investments allows the firm to pursue long-term growth opportunities. If the firm's operating cash flows after working capital investments are not sufficient to finance its long-term investments, it has to rely on external financing to fund its growth. Such firms have less flexibility to pursue long-term investments than those that can fund their growth internally. There are both costs and benefits from being able to fund growth internally. The cost is that managers can use the internally generated free cash flow to fund unprofitable investments; such wasteful capital expenditures are less likely if managers are forced to rely on external capital suppliers. Reliance on external capital markets may make it difficult for managers to undertake long-term risky investments if it is not easy to communicate to the capital markets the benefits from such investments.

Any excess cash flow after these long-term investments is free cash flow that is available for both debt holders and equity holders. Payments to debt holders include interest payments and principal payments. Firms with negative free cash flow have to borrow

Table 9-11 Cash Flow Analysis

Line Item	Nordstrom 1998	Nordstrom 1997	TJX 1998
Net income (dollars in millions)	206.7	186.2	420.6
After-tax net interest expense (income)	30.6	22.3	1.1
Nonoperating losses (gains)	—	—	6.0
Long-term operating accruals	186.7	156.9	139.3
Operating cash flow before working capital investments	**424.0**	**365.4**	**567.0**
Net (investments in) or liquidation of operating working capital	199.1	(45.0)	73.3
Operating cash flow before investment in long-term assets	**623.1**	**320.4**	**640.3**
Net (investment in) or liquidation of operating long-term assets	(259.3)	(257.7)	(198.3)
Free cash flow available to debt and equity	**363.8**	**62.7**	**442**
After-tax net interest (expense) or income	(30.6)	(22.3)	(1.1)
Net debt (repayment) or issuance	258.1	140.4	(23.4)
Free cash flow available to equity	**591.3**	**180.8**	**417.5**
Dividend (payments)	(44.1)	(41.2)	(38.1)
Net stock (repurchase) or issuance	(330.6)	(143.1)	(322.6)
Net increase (decrease) in cash balance	**216.6**	**(3.5)**	**56.8**

additional funds to meet their interest and debt repayment obligations, or cut some of their investments in working capital or long-term investments, or issue additional equity. This situation is clearly financially risky for the firm.

Cash flow after payments to debt holders is free cash flow available to equity holders. Payments to equity holders consist of dividend payments and stock repurchases. If firms pay dividends despite negative free cash flow to equity holders, they are borrowing money to pay dividends. While this may be feasible in the short term, it is not prudent for a firm to pay dividends to equity holders unless it has a positive free cash flow on a sustained basis. On the other hand, firms that have a large free cash flow after debt payments run the risk of wasting that money on unproductive investments to pursue growth for its own sake. An analyst, therefore, should carefully examine the investment plans of such firms.

The model in Table 9-11 suggests that the analyst should focus on a number of cash flow measures: (1) cash flow from operations before investment in working capital and interest payments, to examine whether or not the firm is able to generate a cash surplus from its operations, (2) cash flow from operations after investment in working capital, to assess how the firm's working capital is being managed and whether or not it has the flexibility to invest in long-term assets for future growth, (3) free cash flow available to debt and equity holders, to assess a firm's ability to meet its interest and principal payments, and (4) free cash flow available to equity holders, to assess the firm's financial ability to sustain its dividend policy and to identify potential agency problems from excess free cash flow. These measures have to be evaluated in the context of the company's business, its growth strategy, and its financial policies. Further, changes in these measures from year to year provide valuable information on the stability of the cash flow dynamics of the firm.

> ## Key Analysis Questions
>
> The cash flow model in Table 9-11 can be also used to assess a firm's earnings quality, as discussed in Chapter 3. The reconciliation of a firm's net income with its cash flow from operations facilitates this exercise. Some of the questions an analyst can probe in this respect are:
>
> - Are there significant differences between a firm's net income and its operating cash flow? Is it possible to clearly identify the sources of this difference? Which accounting policies contribute to this difference? Are there any one-time events contributing to this difference?
> - Is the relationship between cash flow and net income changing over time? Why? Is it because of changes in business conditions or because of changes in the firm's accounting policies and estimates?
> - What is the time lag between the recognition of revenues and expenses and the receipt and disbursement of cash flows? What type of uncertainties need to be resolved in between?
> - Are the changes in receivables, inventories, and payables normal? If not, is there adequate explanation for the changes?

Finally, as we will discuss in Chapter 12, free cash flow available to debt and equity and free cash flow available to equity are critical inputs into the cash-flow-based valuation of firms' assets and equity, respectively.

Analysis of Nordstrom's Cash Flow

Nordstrom and TJX reported their cash flows using the indirect cash flow statement. Table 9-11 recasts these statements so that we can analyze the two companies' cash flow dynamics, as discussed above.

Cash flow analysis presented in Table 9-11 shows Nordstrom had an operating cash flow before working capital investments of $424 million in 1998, a substantial improvement from $365.4 million in 1997. The difference between earnings and these cash flows is primarily attributable to the depreciation and amortization charge included in the company's income statement. In 1998 Nordstrom managed to squeeze an additional $199 million from its operating working capital, primarily by reducing its investment in accounts receivable and inventory. This contrasts with a net operating working capital investment of $45 million in 1997. As a result of this, the company had an operating cash flow before long-term investments to the tune of $623 million in 1998, more than adequate to meet its total investment in long-term assets. Nordstrom thus had $363.8 million of free cash flow available to debt and equity holders in 1998, compared to a total of only $62.7 million in 1997. Both in 1997 and 1998, the company was a net borrower. As a result, there was considerable free cash flow available to equity holders in both years. The company utilized this free cash flow to pay its regular dividends and also buy back stock in both the years. The difference between the two years, however, is that in 1998 the company had adequate internal cash flow to pay dividends and buy back stock, while in 1997 the company could not have made these payments to equity holders either without borrowing or without cutting its long-term investments. Clearly, Nordstrom's cash flow improved significantly in 1998.

TJX also had a very strong cash flow situation in 1998. It had $567 million in operating cash flow before working capital investments. TJX was also able to reduce its investments in operating working capital. There is, however, a significant difference between the way investments in working capital appear to have been managed by TJX and Nordstrom. While Nordstrom reduced its investments in inventory and accounts receivable, TJX stretched its payables and accrued expenses. Similar to Nordstrom, TJX was able to fund all its long-term investments in operating assets from its own operating cash flow. As a result, TJX had $442 million in free cash flow available to debt and equity holders. From this, the company paid out approximately $25 million in interest and principal to its debt holders and $360.7 million in dividends and stock repurchases to its equity holders, leaving a cash increase of about $57 million.

SUMMARY

This chapter presents two key tools of financial analysis: ratio analysis and cash flow analysis. Both these tools allow the analyst to examine a firm's performance and its financial condition, given its strategy and goals. Ratio analysis involves assessing the firm's income statement and balance sheet data. Cash flow analysis relies on the firm's cash flow statement.

The starting point for ratio analysis is the company's ROE. The next step is to evaluate the three drivers of ROE, which are net profit margin, asset turnover, and financial leverage. Net profit margin reflects a firm's operating management, asset turnover reflects its investment management, and financial leverage reflects its liability management. Each of these areas can be further probed by examining a number of ratios. For example, common-sized income statement analysis allows a detailed examination of a firm's net margins. Similarly, turnover of key working capital accounts like accounts receivable, inventory, and accounts payable, and turnover of the firm's fixed assets allow further examination of a firm's asset turnover. Finally, short-term liquidity ratios, debt policy ratios, and coverage ratios provide a means of examining a firm's financial leverage.

A firm's sustainable growth rate—the rate at which it can grow without altering its operating, investment, and financing policies—is determined by its ROE and its dividend policy. Therefore, the concept of sustainable growth provides a way to integrate the ratio analysis and to evaluate whether or not a firm's growth strategy is sustainable. If a firm's plans call for growing at a rate above its current sustainable rate, then the analyst can examine which of the firm's ratios is likely to change in the future.

Cash flow analysis supplements ratio analysis in examining a firm's operating activities, investment management, and financial risks. Firms in the U.S. are currently required to report a cash flow statement summarizing their operating, investment, and financing cash flows. Firms in other countries typically report working capital flows, but it is possible to use this information to create a cash flow statement.

Since there are wide variations across firms in the way cash flow data are reported, analysts often use a standard format to recast cash flow data. We discussed in this chapter one such cash flow model. This model allows the analyst to assess whether a firm's operations generate cash flow before investments in operating working capital, and how much cash is being invested in the firm's working capital. It also enables the analyst to calculate the firm's free cash flow after making long-term investments, which is an indication of the firm's ability to meet its debt and dividend payments. Finally, the cash flow analysis shows how the firm is financing itself, and whether or not its financing patterns are too risky.

The insights gained from analyzing a firm's financial ratios and its cash flows are valuable in forecasts of the firm's future prospects, a topic we address in the chapter.

DISCUSSION QUESTIONS

1. Which of the following types of firms do you expect to have particularly high or low asset turnover? Explain why.
   - a supermarket
   - a pharmaceutical company
   - a jewelry retailer
   - a steel company
2. Which of the following types of firms do you expect to have high or low sales margins? Why?
   - a supermarket
   - a pharmaceutical company
   - a jewelry retailer
   - a software company
3. James Broker, an analyst with an established brokerage firm, comments: "The critical number I look at for any company is operating cash flow. If cash flows are less than earnings, I consider a company to be a poor performer and a poor investment prospect." Do you agree with this assessment? Why or why not?

4. In 1995 Chrysler has a return on equity of 20 percent, whereas Ford's return is only 8 percent. Use the decomposed ROE framework to provide possible reasons for this difference.

5. Joe Investor claims: "A company cannot grow faster than its sustainable growth rate." True or false? Explain why.

6. What are the reasons for a firm having lower cash from operations than working capital from operations? What are the possible interpretations of these reasons?

7. ABC Company recognizes revenue at the point of shipment. Management decides to increase sales for the current quarter by filling all customer orders. Explain what impact this decision will have on:
   - Days receivable for the current quarter
   - Days receivable for the next quarter
   - Sales growth for the current quarter
   - Sales growth for the next quarter
   - Return on sales for the current quarter
   - Return on sales for the next quarter

8. What ratios would you use to evaluate operating leverage for a firm?

9. What are the potential benchmarks that you could use to compare a company's financial ratios? What are the pros and cons of these alternatives?

10. In a period of rising prices, how would the following ratios be affected by the accounting decision to select LIFO, rather than FIFO, for inventory valuation?
   - Gross margin
   - Current ratio
   - Asset turnover
   - Debt-to-equity ratio
   - Average tax rate

NOTES

1. We will call the fiscal year ending January 1999 as the year 1998, and the fiscal year ending January 1998 as the year 1997.

2. In computing ROE, one can either use the beginning equity, ending equity, or an average of the two. Conceptually, the average equity is appropriate, particularly for rapidly growing companies. However, for most companies, this computational choice makes little difference as long as the analyst is consistent. Therefore, in practice, most analysts use ending balances for simplicity. This comment applies to all ratios discussed in this chapter where one of the items in the ratio is a flow variable (items in the income statement or cash flow statement) and the other item is a stock variable (items in the balance sheet). Throughout this chapter, we use the ending balances of the stock variables for computational simplicity.

3. We discuss in greater detail in Chapter 12 how to estimate a company's cost of equity capital. The equity beta for both Nordstrom and TJX was close to one in 1999, and the yield on long-term treasury bonds was approximately 6 percent. If one assumes a risk premium of 6 percent, the two firms' cost of equity is 12 percent; if the risk premium is assumed to be 8 percent, then their

cost of equity is 14 percent. Lower assumed risk premium will, of course, lead to lower estimates of equity capital.

4. Strictly speaking, part of a cash balance is needed to run the firm's operations, so only the excess cash balance should be viewed as negative debt. However, firms do not provide information on excess cash, so we subtract all cash balance in our definitions and computations below. An alternative possibility is to subtract only short-term investments and ignore the cash balance completely.

5. See "Ratio Analysis and Valuation," by Doron Nissim and Stephen Penman, unpublished manuscript, March 1999, for a more detailed description of this approach.

6. TJX has a small amount of debt and a cash balance larger than its debt. Therefore, its weighted average cost of capital is likely to be similar to its cost of equity. We will discuss in Chapter 12 how to estimate a company's weighted average cost of capital.

7. See *Taxes and Business Strategy,* by Myron Scholes and Mark Wolfson, Englewood Cliffs, NJ: Prentice-Hall, 1992.

8. There are a number of issues related to the calculation of these ratios in practice. First, in calculating all the turnover ratios, the assets used in the calculations can either be year-end values or an average of the beginning and ending balances in a year. We use the year-end values here for simplicity. Second, strictly speaking, one should use credit sales to calculate accounts receivable turnover and days' receivables. However, since it is usually difficult to obtain data on credit sales, total sales are used instead. Similarly, in calculating accounts payable turnover or days' payables, cost of goods sold is substituted for purchases for data availability reasons.

9. Changes in cash and marketable securities are excluded because this is the amount being explained by the cash flow statement. Changes in short-term debt and the current portion of long-term debt are excluded because these accounts represent financing flows, not operating flows.

T*he difference between a company with a concept and one without is the difference between a stock that sells for 20 times earnings and one that sells for 10 times earnings. The Home Depot is definitely a concept stock, and it has the multiple to prove it – 27-28 times likely earnings in the current fiscal year ending this month. On the face of it, The Home Depot might seem like a tough one for the concept-mongers to work with. It's a chain of hardware stores. But, as we noted in our last visit to the company in the spring of '83, these hardware stores are huge warehouse outlets – 60,000 to 80,000 feet in space. You can fit an awful lot of saws in these and still have plenty of room left over to knock together a very decent concept.*

And in truth, the warehouse notion is the hottest thing in retailing these days. The Home Depot buys in quantum quantities, which means that its suppliers are eager to keep within its good graces and hence provide it with a lot of extra service. The company, as it happens, is masterful in promotion and pricing. The last time we counted, it had 22 stores, all of them located where the sun shines all the time.

Growth has been sizzling. Revenues, a mere $22 million in fiscal '80, shot past the quarter billion mark three years later. As to earnings, they have climbed from two cents in fiscal '80 to an estimated 60 cents in the fiscal year coming to an end [in January 1985].

Its many boosters in the Street, moreover, anticipate more of the same as far as the bullish eye can see. They're confidently estimating 30% growth in the new fiscal year as well. Could be. But while we share their esteem for the company's merchandising skills and imagination, we're as bemused now as we were the first time we looked at The Home Depot by its rich multiple. Maybe a little more now than then.[1]

The above report appeared on January 21, 1985, in "Up & Down Wall Street," a regular column in *Barron's* financial weekly.

COMPANY BACKGROUND

Bernard Marcus and Arthur Blank founded The Home Depot in 1978 to bring the warehouse retailing concept to the home center industry. The company operated retail "do-

This case was prepared by Professor Krishna Palepu as the basis for class discussion rather than to illustrate either effective or ineffective handling of an administrative situation. Copyright © 1988 by the President and Fellows of Harvard College. Harvard Business School case 9-188-148.

1. Reprinted with permission from *Barron's*, January 21, 1985.

The Home Depot

it-yourself" (DIY) warehouse stores which sold a wide assortment of building materials and home improvement products. Sales, which were on a cash-and-carry basis, were concentrated in the home remodeling market. The company targeted as its customers individual homeowners and small contractors.

The Home Depot's strategy had several important elements. The company offered low and competitive prices, a feature central to the warehouse retailing concept. The Home Depot's stores, usually in suburbs, were also the warehouses, with inventory stacked over merchandise displayed on industrial racks. The warehouse format of the stores kept the overhead low and allowed the company to pass the savings to customers. Costs were further reduced by emphasizing higher volume and lower margins with a high inventory turnover. While offering low prices, The Home Depot was careful not to sacrifice the depth of merchandise and the quality of products offered for sale.

To ensure that the right products were stocked at all times, each Home Depot store carried approximately $4,500,000 of inventory, at retail, consisting of approximately 25,000 separate stock-keeping units. All these items were kept on the sales floor of the store, thus increasing convenience to the customer and minimizing out-of-stock occurrences. The company also assured its customers that the products sold by it were of the best quality. The Home Depot offered nationally advertised brands as well as lesser known brands carefully chosen by the company's merchandise managers. Every product sold by The Home Depot was guaranteed by either the manufacturer or by the company itself.

The Home Depot complemented the above merchandising strategy with excellent sales assistance. Since the great majority of the company's customers were individual homeowners with no prior experience in their home improvement projects, The Home Depot considered its employees' technical knowledge and service orientation to be very important to its marketing success. The company pursued a number of policies to address this need. Approximately 90% of the company's employees were on a full-time basis. To attract and retain a strong sales force, the company maintained salary and wage levels above those of its competitors. All the floor sales personnel attended special training sessions to gain thorough knowledge of the company's home improvement products and their basic applications. This training enabled them to answer shoppers' questions and help customers in choosing equipment and material appropriate for their projects. Often, the expert advice the sales personnel provided created a bond that resulted in continuous contact with the customer throughout the duration of the customer's project.

Finally, to attract customers, The Home Depot pursued an aggressive advertising program utilizing newspapers, television, radio, and direct mail catalogues. The company's advertising stressed promotional pricing, the broad assortment and depth of its merchandise, and the assistance provided by its sales personnel. The company also sponsored in-store demonstrations of do-it-yourself techniques and product uses. To increase customers' shopping convenience, The Home Depot's stores were open seven days a week, including weekday evenings.

Fortune magazine commented on The Home Depot's strategy as follows:

Warehouse stores typically offer shoppers deep discounts with minimal service and back-to-basics ambiance. The Home Depot's outlets have all the charm of a freight yard and predictably low prices. But they also offer unusually helpful customer service. Although warehouse retailing looks simple, it is not: As discounting cuts into gross profit margins, the merchant must carefully control buying, merchandising, and inventory costs. Throwing in service, which is expensive and hard to systematize, makes the job even tougher. In the do-it-yourself (DIY) segment of the industry — which includes old-style hardware stores, building supply warehouses, and the everything-under-one-roof home centers — The Home Depot is the only company that has successfully brought off the union of low prices and high service.[2]

The Home Depot's strategy was successful in fueling an impressive growth in the company's operations. The first three Home Depot stores, opened in Atlanta in 1979, were a quick success. From this modest beginning, the company grew rapidly and went public in 1981. The company's stock initially traded over-the-counter and was listed on the New York Stock Exchange in April 1984. Several new stores were opened in markets throughout the Sunbelt, and the number of stores operated by The Home Depot grew from 3 in 1979 to 50 by the end of fiscal 1985. As a result, sales grew from $7 million in 1979 to $700 million in 1985. Exhibit 1 provides a summary of the growth in the company's operations. The company's stock price performance during 1985 is summarized in Exhibit 2.

INDUSTRY AND COMPETITION

The home improvement industry was large and growing during the 1980s. The industry sales totaled approximately $80 billion in 1985 and strong industry growth was expected to continue, especially in the do-it-yourself (DIY) segment, which had grown at a compounded annual rate of 14 percent over the last 15 years. With the number of two-wage-earner households growing, there was an increase in families' average disposable income, making it possible to increase the frequency and magnitude of home improvement projects. Further, many homeowners were undertaking these projects by themselves rather than hiring a contractor. Research conducted by the Do-It-Yourself Institute, an industry trade group, showed that DIY activities had become America's second most popular leisure-time activity after watching television.

The success of warehouse retailing pioneered by The Home Depot attracted a number of other companies into the industry. Among the store chains currently operating in the industry were Builders Square (a division of K Mart), Mr. HOW (a division of Service Merchandise), The Home Club (a division of Zayre Corp.), Payless Cashways (a division of W.R. Grace), and Hechinger Co. Most of these store chains were relatively new and not yet achieving significant profitability.

....

2. *Reprinted with permission from Fortune, February 1988, p. 73.*

Among The Home Depot's competitors, the most successful was Hechinger, which had operated hardware stores for a long time and recently entered the do-it-yourself segment of the industry. Using a strategy quite different from The Home Depot's, Hechinger ran gleaming upscale stores and aimed at high profit margins. As of the end of fiscal 1985, the company operated 55 stores, located primarily in southeastern states. Hechinger announced that it planned to expand its sales by 20 to 25 percent a year by adding 10 to 14 stores a year. A summary of Hechinger's recent financial performance is presented in Exhibit 3.

THE HOME DEPOT'S FUTURE

While The Home Depot had achieved rapid growth every year since its inception, fiscal 1985 was probably the most important in the company's seven-year history. During 1985 the company implemented its most ambitious expansion plan to date by adding 20 new stores in eight new markets. Nine of these stores were acquired from Bowater, a competing store chain which was in financial difficulty. As The Home Depot engaged in major expansion, its revenues rose 62 percent from $432 million in fiscal 1984 to $700 million in 1985. However, the company's earnings declined in 1985 from the record levels achieved during the previous fiscal year. In fiscal 1985, The Home Depot earned $8.2 million, or $0.33 per share, as compared with $14.1 million or $0.56 per share in fiscal 1984.

Bernard Marcus, The Home Depot's chairman and chief executive officer, commented on the company's performance as follows:

Fiscal 1985 was a year of rapid expansion and continued growth for The Home Depot. Feeling the time was ripe for us to enhance our share of the do-it-yourself market, we seized the opportunity to make a significant investment in our long-term future. At the same time, we recognized that our short-term profit growth would be affected.

The Home Depot's 1985 annual report (Exhibit 4) provided more details on the firm's financial performance during the year.

As fiscal 1985 came to a close, The Home Depot faced some critical issues. The competition in the do-it-yourself industry was heating up. The fight for market dominance was expected to result in pressure on margins, and industry analysts expected only the strongest and most capable firms in the industry to survive. Also, The Home Depot had announced plans for further expansion that included the opening of nine new stores in 1986. The company estimated that site acquisition and construction would cost about $6.6 million for each new store, and investment in inventory (net of vendor financing) would require an additional $1.8 million per store. The company needed significant additional financing to implement these plans.

Home Depot relied on external financing—both debt and equity—to fund its growth in 1984 and 1985. However, the significant drop in its stock price in 1985 made further equity financing less attractive. While the company could borrow from its line of credit, it had to make sure that it could satisfy the interest coverage requirements (see Note 3 in Exhibit 4 for a discussion of debt covenant restrictions). Clearly, generating more cash from its own operations would be the best way for Home Depot to invest in its growth on a sustainable basis.

QUESTIONS

1. Evaluate Home Depot's business strategy. Do you think it is a viable strategy in the long run?
2. Analyze Home Depot's financial performance during the fiscal years 1983–1985. Compare Home Depot's performance in this period with Hechinger's performance. (You may use the ratios and the cash flow analysis in Exhibit 3 in this summary.)
3. How productive were Home Depot's stores in the fiscal years 1983–1985? (You may use the statistics in Exhibit 1 in this analysis.)
4. Home Depot's stock price dropped by 23 percent between January 1985 and February 1986, making it difficult for the company to rely on equity capital to finance its growth. Covenants on existing debt (discussed in Note 3 of Exhibit 4) restrict the magnitude of the company's future borrowing. Given these constraints, what specific actions should Home Depot take with respect to its current operations and growth strategy? How can the company improve its operating performance? Should the company change its strategy? If so, how?

The Home Depot

The Home Depot

EXHIBIT 1
The Home Depot, Inc. – Summary of Performance During Fiscal Years 1981–1985

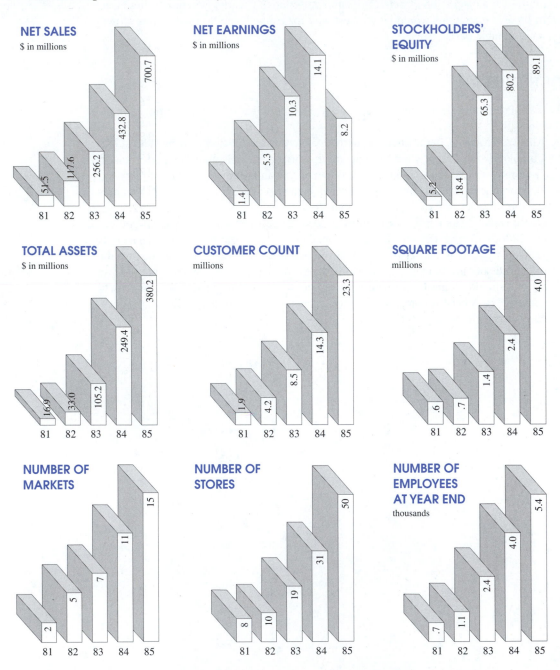

NET SALES
$ in millions

51.5 — 81
117.6 — 82
256.2 — 83
432.8 — 84
700.7 — 85

NET EARNINGS
$ in millions

1.4 — 81
5.3 — 82
10.3 — 83
14.1 — 84
8.2 — 85

STOCKHOLDERS' EQUITY
$ in millions

5.2 — 81
18.4 — 82
65.3 — 83
80.2 — 84
89.1 — 85

TOTAL ASSETS
$ in millions

16.9 — 81
33.0 — 82
105.2 — 83
249.4 — 84
380.2 — 85

CUSTOMER COUNT
millions

1.9 — 81
4.2 — 82
8.5 — 83
14.3 — 84
23.3 — 85

SQUARE FOOTAGE
millions

.6 — 81
.7 — 82
1.4 — 83
2.4 — 84
4.0 — 85

NUMBER OF MARKETS

2 — 81
5 — 82
7 — 83
11 — 84
15 — 85

NUMBER OF STORES

8 — 81
10 — 82
19 — 83
31 — 84
50 — 85

NUMBER OF EMPLOYEES AT YEAR END
thousands

.7 — 81
1.1 — 82
2.4 — 83
4.0 — 84
5.4 — 85

EXHIBIT 2

The Home Depot's Common Stock Price and Standard & Poor's 500
Composite Index from January 1985 to February 1986

Date	Home Depot Stock Price	S&P 500 Composite Index
1/2/85	$17.125	165.4
2/1/85	16.375	178.6
3/1/85	19.000	183.2
4/1/85	17.000	181.3
5/1/85	18.000	178.4
6/3/85	16.125	189.3
7/1/85	13.000	192.4
8/1/85	12.625	192.1
9/2/85	11.875	197.9
10/1/85	11.375	185.1
11/1/85	10.750	191.5
12/2/85	11.000	200.5
1/2/86	12.625	209.6
2/3/86	13.125	214.0
Cumulative Return:	–23.4%	29.4%

The Home Depot's ß = 1.3 (Value Line estimate).

The Home Depot

EXHIBIT 3

The Home Depot, Inc. – Summary of Financial Performance of Hechinger Company

I. HECHINGER'S FINANCIAL RATIOS

	Year Ending		
	February 1, 1986	February 2, 1985	January 28, 1984
Profit Before Taxes/Sales (%)	7.80	9.40	9.80
× Sales/Average Assets	1.48	1.72	2.02
× Average Assets/Average Equity	2.21	2.12	1.79
× (1 – Average Tax Rate)	0.62	0.55	0.54
= Return on Equity (%)	15.80	18.90	19.10
× (1 – Dividend Payout Ratio)	0.93	0.95	0.95
= Sustainable Growth Rate (%)	14.70	18.00	18.10
Gross Profit/Sales (%)	29.30	30.10	32.10
Selling, General and Administrative Expenses/Sales (%)	21.60	21.10	22.90
Interest Expenses/Sales (%)	2.10	1.30	0.70
Interest Income/Sales (%)	2.20	1.70	1.30
Inventory Turnover	4.50	4.50	4.40
Average Collection Period[a] (Days)	32.00	33.00	35.00
Average Accounts Payable Period[b] (Days)	58.00	61.00	63.00

a. Assumed 365 days in the fiscal year.
b. Payables also include accrued wages and expenses. Purchases are computed as cost of sales plus increase in inventory during the year. Assumed 365 days in the fiscal year.

II. HECHINGER'S CASH FLOW

	Year Ending		
(Dollars in Thousands)	February 1, 1986	February 2, 1985	January 28, 1984
Cash Provided from Operations			
Net earnings	$23,111	$20,923	$16,243
Items not requiring the use of cash or marketable securities:			
Depreciation and amortization	6,594	4,622	3,429
Deferred income taxes	1,375	2,040	1,515
Deferred rent expense	2,321	2,064	1,463
	33,401	**29,649**	**22,650**
Cash Invested in Operations			
Accounts receivable	4,657	7,905	7,954
Merchandise inventories	17,998	8,045	20,596
Other current assets	4,891	3,760	1,304
Accounts payable and accrued expenses	(6,620)	(12,099)	(9,767)
Taxes on income – current	285	3,031	(575)
	21,211	**10,642**	**19,512**
Net Cash Provided from Operations	**12,190**	**19,007**	**3,138**
Cash Used for Investment Activities			
Expenditures for property, furniture and equipment, net of disposals, and other assets	**(36,037)**	**(25,531)**	**(16,346)**
Cash Used to Pay Dividends to Shareholders	**(1,550)**	**(1,091)**	**(868)**
Cash Provided from Financing Activities			
Proceeds from public offering of 8½% converted subordinated debentures, net of expenses	—	85,010	—
Proceeds from public offering of common stock net of expenses	28,969	—	13,439
Proceeds from sale and leaseback transactions under operating leases	—	8,338	6,874
Increase (decrease) in long-term debt	—	(4,750)	6,366
Decrease in short-term debt	—	—	(318)
Exercise of stock options including income tax benefit	180	674	611
Decrease in capital lease obligations	(311)	(280)	(254)
	28,838	**88,992**	**26,718**
Increase in Cash and Marketable Securities	**$ 3,441**	**$81,377**	**$12,642**

The Home Depot

The Home Depot

EXHIBIT 4
The Home Depot, Inc.—Abridged Annual Report for Fiscal Year 1985

A Letter to Our Shareholders:

Fiscal 1985 was a year of rapid expansion and continued growth for The Home Depot. Feeling the time was ripe for us to enhance our share of the do-it-yourself market, we seized the opportunity to make a significant investment in our long-term future. At the same time, we recognized that our short-term profit growth would be affected.

The Home Depot intends to be the dominant factor in every market we serve. The key to our success has been that upon entering a new market, we make a substantial commitment—opening multiple stores, providing excellent customer service, creating highly visible promotions, and growing the entire market. We turn the novice into a do-it-yourselfer and enable the expert to do more for less money.

From shortly before the end of fiscal 1984 to the close of fiscal 1985, The Home Depot entered eight new markets—Dallas, Houston, Jacksonville, San Diego, Los Angeles, Shreveport, Baton Rouge and Mobile—in a period of approximately 13 months. In that time, the number of Home Depot stores rose dramatically, from 22 to 50, including 9 stores acquired in the Bowater acquisition which had not been in our original plan. Twenty of these stores were opened during the past fiscal year alone. During this time span, we have become the only national warehouse retailing chain serving markets across the Sunbelt.

This expansion program required a tremendous investment of capital expenditures and inventory, as well as in personnel. As a result, our net earnings declined from record levels achieved during the previous fiscal year. In fiscal 1985, The Home Depot earned $8,219,000, or $.33 per share, as compared with $14,122,000, or $.56 per share, in fiscal 1984. However, as The Home Depot engaged in this major thrust forward, it also increased its market share and market presence as revenues rose 62% from $432,779,000 in fiscal 1984 to $700,729,000 in fiscal 1985.

Despite our significant investments, we still continue to be in a very strong financial condition. In December, The Home Depot replaced a prior $100 million bank credit line with an eight-year decreasing revolving credit agreement of $200 million. In addition, we are pursuing sale-and-leaseback negotiations for an aggregate of approximately $50 million for ten of our stores. These sources of additional funds, along with internally generated cash flow, will provide us with an ample financial foundation to continue to underwrite our growth over the next several years.

We are also quite proud that The Home Depot achieved its substantial gain in sales and market share in what turned out to be a very difficult year for our industry and retailing in general. The do-it-yourself "warehouse" industry, which we pioneered only a few short years ago, has recently attracted many competitors, some of whom have already fallen by the wayside, having mistaken our dramatic success as a path towards easy profits. Now the industry is faced with a situation when only the strongest and most capable will survive. As this process continues, we expect to encounter additional cost competition in the fight for market dominance. However, with our strengths—both financial and our successful ability to develop a loyal customer base—we are confident that The Home Depot will emerge an even stronger company.

We have never doubted The Home Depot's ability to be a leader in our business. We have the market dominance, the superior retailing concepts and the necessary foundation of experienced management. Further, we have the determination to maintain our position.

Looking at some of our markets individually, clearly our most difficult environment has been in Houston, where the oil-related economy is undergoing painful contractions combined with particularly fierce industry competition. This has caused our newly-opened stores to operate at a sub par level. In Dallas/Fort Worth, the stores we acquired at the end of fiscal 1984 have not yet generated the profits we expect. Such difficult market conditions demand a flexible reaction both in merchandising and operations. Recognizing the future potential of both of these markets, our management team is addressing the issues and feels confident that the final outcome will be positive.

In the other markets entered this year, the situation has been considerably more positive. There, our stores are experiencing growth much closer to our historical patterns.

In support of our California and Arizona operations, a West Coast division was inaugurated to facilitate a timely response to the demands of that marketplace. With management personnel in place, this division is now responsible for the merchandising and operations of all stores in the western states.

Other highlights of the past year's activities include the progress we have made in expanding our management team, and the computer systems we installed into our operations to enhance our efficiency.

During the year, we completed the store price lookup phase of our management information system. This facilitates tracking individual items' sales through our registers, resulting in a more concise method of inventory reorder and margin management with the information now available.

During the coming year we will be testing a perpetual inventory tie-in with our price look-up system, eliminating pricing of our merchandise at the store level. The latter is being tested in several stores presently and hopefully will be expanded to include all of our stores by year end. This will have a significant effect on labor productivity at the store level.

The Home Depot is always looking for ways in which to do things better, priding ourselves on our flexibility and ability to innovate and to react to changing conditions. Whether it is a matter of developing state-of-the-art computer systems, reevaluating our store layouts or adapting to fast-changing markets and new types of merchandising, flexibility has always been a Home Depot characteristic.

In fiscal 1986, The Home Depot will continue to expand, but at a much more moderate pace. We plan to open nine new stores. These stores will be in existing markets except for two locations in the new market of San Jose, California.

When we open stores in existing markets, sharing advertising costs and operational expenses, we achieve a faster return than stores in new markets. With this in mind, in January 1986, we withdrew from the Detroit market and delayed the opening of stores in San Francisco. These stores were targeted for a substantial initial loss in earnings that would have been necessary to achieve market dominance. From our standpoint, these new markets would have had the combined effect of diluting our personnel and negatively affecting our earnings.

It has always been Home Depot's philosophy to maintain orderly growth and achieve market dominance as we expand to new markets. Indeed, growth for growth's sake has never been and never will be our objective. We intend to invest prudently and expand aggressively in our business and our markets only when such expenditures meet our criteria for long-term profitability.

We are quite optimistic about our company's future—both for fiscal 1986 and for the years to follow. Essential to this optimism is the fact that The Home Depot has consistently proven that we can grow the market in every geographical area we enter. Simply, this means that we do not have to take business away from hardware stores and other existing home-improvement outlets, but rather, to create new do-it-yourselfers out of those who have never done their own home improvements.

Our philosophy is to educate our customers on how to be do-it-yourselfers. Our customers have come to expect The Home Depot's knowledgeable sales staff to guide them through any project they care to undertake, whether it be installing kitchen cabinets, constructing a deck, or building an entire house. Our sales staff knows how to complete each project, what tools and material to include, and how to sell our customers everything they need.

The Home Depot traditionally holds clinics for its customers in such skills as electrical wiring, carpentry, and plumbing, to name a few. Upon the successful completion of such clinics, our customers are confident in themselves and in The Home Depot. This confidence allows them to attempt increasingly advanced and complex home improvements.

Concerning our facilities, Home Depot's warehouse retailing concept allows us to carry a truly fantastic selection of merchandise and offer it at the lowest possible prices. Each of our stores ranges from about 65,000 to over 100,000 square feet of selling space, with an additional 4,000 to 10,000 square feet of outdoor selling area. In these large stores, we are able to stock all the materials and tools needed to build a house from scratch, and to landscape its grounds. With each store functioning as its own warehouse, with a capacity of over 25,000 different items, we are able to keep our prices at a minimum while providing the greatest selection of building materials and name brand merchandise.

For the majority of Americans, their home is their most valuable asset. It is an asset that consistently appreciates. It is also an asset in need of ongoing care and maintenance. By becoming do-it-yourselfers, homeowners can significantly enhance the value of their homes. We at The Home Depot have found that by successfully delivering this message, we have created loyal and satisfied customers. And by maintaining leadership in our markets, we have established a sound basis on which to build a future of growth with profitability.

The Home Depot management and staff are dedicated to the proposition that we are—and will remain—America's leading do-it-yourself retailer.

Bernard Marcus
Chairman and
Chief Executive Officer

Arthur M. Blank
President and
Chief Operating Officer

CONSOLIDATED STATEMENTS OF EARNINGS

	Fiscal Year Ended		
	February 2, 1986 (52 weeks)	February 3, 1985 (53 weeks)	January 29, 1984 (52 weeks)
Net Sales (note 2)	$700,729,000	$432,779,000	$256,184,000
Cost of Merchandise Sold	519,272,000	318,460,000	186,170,000
Gross Profit	181,457,000	114,319,000	70,014,000
Operating Expenses:			
Selling and store operating expenses	134,354,000	74,447,000	43,514,000
Preopening expenses	7,521,000	1,917,000	2,456,000
General and administrative expenses	20,555,000	12,817,000	7,376,000
Total Operating Expenses	162,430,000	89,181,000	53,346,000
Operating Income	19,027,000	25,138,000	16,668,000
Other Income (Expense):			
Net gain on disposition of property and equipment (note 7)	1,317,000	—	—
Interest income	1,481,000	5,236,000	2,422,000
Interest expense (note 3)	(10,206,000)	(4,122,000)	(104,000)
	(7,408,000)	1,114,000	2,318,000
Earnings Before Income Taxes	11,619,000	26,252,000	18,986,000
Income Taxes (note 4)	3,400,000	12,130,000	8,725,000
Net Earnings	$ 8,219,000	$ 14,122,000	$ 10,261,000
Earnings per Common and Common Equivalent Share (note 5)	$ .33	$ .56	$ .41
Weighted Average Number of Common and Common Equivalent Shares	25,247,000	25,302,000	24,834,000

The Home Depot

The Home Depot

CONSOLIDATED BALANCE SHEETS

	February 2, 1986	February 3, 1985
ASSETS		
Current Assets:		
Cash, including time deposits of $43,374,000 in 1985	$ 9,671,000	$ 52,062,000
Accounts receivable, net (note 7)	21,505,000	9,365,000
Refundable income taxes	3,659,000	—
Merchandise inventories	152,700,000	84,046,000
Prepaid expenses	2,526,000	1,939,000
Total current assets	190,061,000	147,412,000
Property and Equipment, at Cost (note 3):		
Land	44,396,000	30,044,000
Buildings	38,005,000	3,728,000
Furniture, fixtures, and equipment	34,786,000	18,162,000
Leasehold improvements	23,748,000	11,743,000
Construction in progress	27,694,000	14,039,000
	168,629,000	77,716,000
Less accumulated depreciation and amortization	7,813,000	4,139,000
Net property and equipment	160,816,000	73,577,000
Cost in Excess of the Fair Value of Net Assets Acquired, net of accumulated amortization of $730,000 in 1985 and $93,000 in 1984 (note 2)	24,561,000	25,198,000
Other	4,755,000	3,177,000
	$380,193,000	$249,364,000
LIABILITIES AND STOCKHOLDERS' EQUITY		
Current Liabilities:		
Accounts payable	$ 53,881,000	$ 32,356,000
Accrued salaries and related expenses	5,397,000	3,819,000
Other accrued expenses	13,950,000	10,214,000
Income taxes payable (note 4)	—	626,000
Current portion of long-term debt (note 3)	10,382,000	287,000
Total current liabilities	83,610,000	47,302,000
Long-Term Debt, Excluding Current Installments (note 3):		
Convertible subordinated debentures	100,250,000	100,250,000
Other long-term debt	99,693,000	17,692,000
	$199,943,000	$117,942,000

(continued)

	February 2, 1986	February 3, 1985
Other Liabilities	**861,000**	1,320,000
Deferred Income Taxes (note 4)	**6,687,000**	2,586,000
Stockholders' Equity (note 5):		
Common stock, par value $.05. Authorized: 50,000,000 shares; issued and outstanding – 25,150,063 shares at February 2, 1986 and 25,055,188 shares at February 3, 1985	**1,258,000**	1,253,000
Paid-in capital	**48,900,000**	48,246,000
Retained earnings	**38,934,000**	30,715,000
Total stockholders' equity	**89,092,000**	80,214,000
Commitments and Contingencies (notes 5, 6 and 8)	**$380,193,000**	$249,364,000

CONSOLIDATED STATEMENTS OF CHANGES IN FINANCIAL POSITION

	Fiscal Year Ended		
	February 2, 1986	February 3, 1985	January 29, 1984
Sources of Working Capital:			
Net earnings	**$8,219,000**	$14,122,000	$ 10,261,000
Items which do not use working capital:			
Depreciation and amortization of property and equipment	**4,376,000**	2,275,000	903,000
Deferred income taxes	**3,612,000**	1,508,000	713,000
Amortization of cost in excess of the fair value of net assets required	**637,000**	93,000	—
Net gain on disposition of property and equipment	**(1,317,000)**	—	—
Other	**180,000**	77,000	59,000
Working capital provided by operations	**15,707,000**	18,075,000	11,936,000
Proceeds from disposition of property and equipment	**9,469,000**	861,000	3,000
Proceeds from long-term borrowings	**92,400,000**	120,350,000	4,200,000
Proceeds from sale of common stock, net	**659,000**	814,000	36,663,000
	$118,235,000	$140,100,000	$ 52,802,000

(continued)

The Home Depot

CONSOLIDATED STATEMENTS OF CHANGES IN FINANCIAL POSITION (continued)

	Fiscal Year Ended		
	February 2, 1986	February 3, 1985	January 29, 1984
Uses of Working Capital:			
Additions to property and equipment	$ 99,767,000	$50,769,000	$ 16,081,000
Current installments and repayments of long-term debt	10,399,000	6,792,000	52,000
Acquisition of Bowater Home Center, Inc., net of working capital of $9,227,000 (note 2):			
Property and equipment	—	4,815,000	—
Cost in excess of the fair value of net assets acquired	—	25,291,000	—
Other assets, net of liabilities	—	(913,000)	—
Other, net	1,728,000	2,554,000	252,000
Increase in working capital	6,341,000	50,792,000	36,417,000
	$118,235,000	$140,100,000	$ 52,802,000
Changes in Components of Working Capital:			
Increase (decrease) in current assets:			
Cash	(42,391,000)	$29,894,000	$ 13,917,000
Receivables, net	15,799,000	7,170,000	1,567,000
Merchandise inventories	68,654,000	25,334,000	41,137,000
Prepaid expenses	587,000	1,206,000	227,000
	42,649,000	63,604,000	56,848,000
Increase (decrease) in current liabilities:			
Accounts payable	21,525,000	10,505,000	17,150,000
Accrued salaries and related expenses	1,578,000	(93,000)	2,524,000
Other accrued expenses	3,736,000	2,824,000	341,000
Income taxes payable	(626,000)	(657,000)	406,000
Current portion of long-term debt	10,095,000	233,000	10,000
	36,308,000	12,812,000	20,431,000
Increase in Working Capital	$ 6,341,000	$ 50,792,000	$ 36,417,000

SELECTED FINANCIAL DATA

	Fiscal Year Ended				
	February 2, 1986	February 3, 1985[a]	January 29, 1984	January 30, 1983	January 31, 1982
Selected Consolidated Statement of Earnings Data:					
Net sales	**$700,729,000**	$432,779,000	$256,184,000	$117,645,000	$51,542,000
Gross profit	**181,457,000**	114,319,000	70,014,000	33,358,000	14,735,000
Earnings before income taxes and extraordinary item	**11,619,000**	26,252,000	18,986,000	9,870,000	1,963,000
Earnings before extraordinary item	**8,219,000**	14,122,000	10,261,000	5,315,000	1,211,000
Extraordinary item-reduction of income taxes arising from carryforward of prior years' operating losses	—	—	—	—	234,000
Net earnings	**$ 8,219,000**	$ 14,122,000	$10,261,000	$5,315,000	$1,445,000
Per Common and Common Equivalent Share:					
Earnings before extraordinary item	**$ .33**	$ .56	$ .41	$ .24	$.06
Extraordinary item	—	—	—	—	.01
Net earnings	**$ .33**	$ .56	$ .41	$ .24	$ .07
Weighted average number of common and common equivalent shares	**25,247,000**	25,302,000	24,834,000	22,233,000	21,050,000
Selected Consolidated Balance Sheet Data:					
Working capital	**$106,451,000**	$100,110,000	$ 49,318,000	$ 12,901,000	$ 5,502,000
Total assets	**380,193,000**	249,364,000	105,230,000	33,014,000	16,906,000
Long-term debt	**199,943,000**	117,942,000	4,384,000	236,000	3,738,000
Stockholders' equity	**89,092,000**	80,214,000	65,278,000	18,354,000	5,024,000

a. 53-week fiscal year; all others were 52-week fiscal years.

The Home Depot

MANAGEMENT'S DISCUSSION AND ANALYSIS OF RESULTS OF OPERATIONS AND FINANCIAL CONDITION

The data below reflect the percentage relationship between sales and major categories in the Consolidated Statements of Earnings and selected sales data of the percentage change in the dollar amounts of each of the items.

	Fiscal Year[a]			Percentage Increase (Decrease) of Dollar Amounts	
	1985	1984	1983	**1985 v. 1984**	1984 v. 1983
Selected Consolidated Statements of Earnings Data:					
Net sales	**100.0%**	100.0%	100.0%	**61.9%**	68.9%
Gross profit	**25.9**	26.4	27.3	**58.7**	63.3
Cost and expenses:					
Selling and store operating	**19.2**	17.2	17.0	**80.5**	71.1
Preopening	**1.1**	.4	.9	**292.3**	(21.9)
General and administrative	**2.9**	3.0	2.9	**60.4**	73.8
Net gain on disposition of property and equipment	**(.2)**	—	—	**—**	—
Interest income	**(.2)**	(1.2)	(.9)	**(71.7)**	116.2
Interest expense	**1.4**	.9	—	**147.6**	3,863.5
	24.2	20.3	19.9	**92.9**	72.6
Earnings before income taxes	**1.7**	6.1	7.4	**(55.7)**	38.3
Income taxes	**.5**	2.8	3.4	**(72.0)**	39.0
Net earnings	**1.2%**	3.3%	4.0%	**(41.8%)**	37.6%
Selected Consolidated Sales Data:					
Number of customer transactions	**23,324,000**	14,256,000	8,479.000	**63.6%**	68.1%
Average amount of sale per transaction	**$30.04**	$30.36	$30.21	**(1.1)**	.5
Weighted average weekly sales per operating store	**$ 342,500**	$ 365,500	$ 360,300	**(6.3)**	1.4

a. Fiscal years 1985, 1984 and 1983 refer to the fiscal years ended February 2, 1986, February 3, 1985 and January 29, 1984, respectively. Fiscal 1984 consisted of 53 weeks while 1985 and 1983 each consisted of 52 weeks.

Results of Operations

For an understanding of the significant factors that influenced the Company's performance during the past three fiscal years, the following discussion should be read in conjunction with the consolidated financial statements appearing elsewhere in this annual report.

Fiscal Year Ended February 2, 1986 Compared to February 3, 1985

Net sales in fiscal year 1985 increased 62% from $432,779,000 to $700,729,000. The growth is attributable to several factors. First, the Company opened 20 new stores during 1985 and closed one store. Second, second-year sales increases were realized from the three new stores opened in 1984 and from the nine former Bowater Home Center stores acquired during 1984. Third, comparable store sales increases of 2.3% were achieved despite comparing the 52-week 1985 fiscal year to the sales of the 53-week 1984 fiscal year, due in part to the number of customer transactions increasing by 64%. Finally, the weighted average weekly sales per operating store declined 6% in 1985 due to the significant increase in the ratio of the number of new stores to total stores in operation—new stores have a lower sales rate than mature stores until they establish market share.

Gross profit in 1985 increased 59% from $114,319,000 to $181,457,000. This increase was due to the increased sales and was partially offset by a reduction in the gross profit margin from 26.4% to 25.9%. The reduction is primarily due to lower margins achieved while establishing market presence in new markets.

Cost and expenses increased 93% during 1985 and, as a percent of sales, increased from 20.3% to 24.2%. The increase in selling and store operating, preopening expenses and net interest expense is due to the opening of 20 new stores, the costs associated with the former Bowater Home Center stores, and the related cost of building market share. The large percentage of new stores which have lower sales but fixed occupancy and certain minimum operating expenses tends to cause the percentage of selling and store operating costs to increase as a percentage of sales. The net gain on disposition of property and equipment is discussed fully in note 7 to the financial statements.

Earnings before income taxes decreased 56% from $26,252,000 to $11,619,000 resulting from the increase in operating expenses to support the Company's expansion program. The Company's effective income tax rate declined from 46.2% to 29.3% resulting from an increase in investment and other tax credits as a percentage of the total tax provision. As a percentage of sales, earnings decreased from 3.3% in 1984 to 1.2% in 1985 due to the increase in operating expenses as discussed above.

Fiscal Year Ended February 3, 1985 Compared to January 29, 1984

Net sales in fiscal 1984 increased 69% from $256,184,000 to $432,779,000. The growth was attributable to several factors. First, the company opened three new stores during fiscal 1984. Second, the Company had sales of $9,755,000 from the nine former Bowater Home Center stores acquired on December 3, 1984. Third, second-year sales increases were realized from the nine stores opened during fiscal 1983. Fourth, comparable store sales increases of 14% were due in part to 53 weeks in fiscal 1984 compared to 52 weeks in fiscal 1983 and in part to the number of customer transactions increasing by 63%. Finally, excluding the sales of the former Bowater Home Center stores, the weighted average weekly sales per operating store increased 6% to $383,500 in fiscal 1984.

Gross profit in fiscal 1984 increased 63% from $70,014,000 to $114,319,000. This net increase was due to the increased sales and was partially offset by a reduction in the gross profit margin from 27.3% to 26.4%. The reduction in the gross profit percentage is largely the result of the purchase of a high proportion of promoted merchandise by customers in the second quarter.

Costs and expenses increased 73% during fiscal 1984. As a percent of sales, costs and expenses increased from 19.9% to 20.3% due to increased selling, store operating, general and administrative expenses. This planned increase was in preparation of the Company's future expansion. Interest expense increased significantly as a result of the

The Home Depot

issuance of substantial debt during fiscal 1984 to fund the Company's expansion. These increases were partially offset by reduced preopening expenses and increased interest income resulting from temporary investment of the proceeds of the debt financing.

Earnings before income taxes increased 38% from $18,986,000 to $26,252,000 resulting from the factors discussed above. Such pretax earnings, however, were reduced by a loss from the Bowater stores of approximately $1,900,000 from date of acquisition (December 1984) to year end. The Company's effective income tax rate increased slightly from 46.0% to 46.2% resulting principally from less investment and other tax credits as a percentage of the total tax provision. As a percentage of sales, earnings decreased from 4.0% in fiscal 1983 to 3.3% in fiscal 1984. The decline is a result of the company's reduced gross profit percentage and increases in the operating expenses discussed above.

Impact of Inflation and Changing Prices

Although the Company cannot accurately determine the precise effect of inflation on its operations, it does not believe inflation has had a material effect on sales or results of operations. The Company has complied with the reporting requirements of the Financial Accounting Standards Board Statement No. 33 in note 10 to the financial statements. Due to the experimental techniques, subjective estimates and assumptions, and the incomplete presentation required by this accounting pronouncement, the Company questions the value of the required reporting.

Liquidity and Capital Resources

Cash flow generated from existing store operations provided the Company with a significant source of liquidity since sales are on a cash-and-carry basis. In addition, a significant portion of the Company's inventory is financed under vendor credit terms. The Company has supplemented its operating cash flow from time to time with bank credit and equity and debt financing. During fiscal 1985, $88,000,000 of working capital was provided by the revolving bank credit line, $4,400,000 from industrial revenue bonds, and approximately $15,707,000 from operations. In addition, during fiscal 1985, the Company entered into a new credit agreement for a $200,000,000 revolving credit facility with a group of banks.

The Company has announced plans to open nine new stores during fiscal 1986, two in the new market of northern California and the balance in existing markets. The cost of this store expansion program will depend upon, among other factors, the extent to which the Company is able to lease second-use store space as opposed to acquiring leases or sites and having stores constructed to its own specifications. The Company estimates that approximately $6,600,000 per store will be required to acquire sites and construct facilities to the Company's specifications and that approximately $1,700,000 will be required to open a store in leased space plus any additional costs of acquiring the lease. These estimates include costs for site acquisition, construction expenditures, fixtures and equipment, and in-store minicomputers and point-of-sale terminals. In addition, each new store will require approximately $1,800,000 to finance inventories, net of vendor financing. The Company believes it has the ability to finance these expenditures through existing cash resources, current bank lines of credit which include a $200,000,000 eight-year revolving credit agreement, funds generated from operations, and other forms of financing, including but not limited to various forms of real estate financing and unsecured borrowings.

NOTES TO CONSOLIDATED FINANCIAL STATEMENTS

1. Summary of Significant Accounting Policies

Fiscal Year

The Company's fiscal year ends on the Sunday closest to the last day of January and usually consists of 52 weeks. Every five or six years, however, there is a 53-week year. The fiscal year ended February 2, 1986 (1985) consisted of 52 weeks, the year ended February 3, 1985 (1984) consisted of 53 weeks and the year ended January 29, 1984 (1983) consisted of 52 weeks.

Principles of Consolidation

The consolidated financial statements include the accounts of the Company and its wholly owned subsidiary. All significant intercompany transactions have been eliminated in consolidation. Certain reclassifications were made to the 1984 balance sheet to conform to current year presentation.

Merchandise Inventories

Inventories are stated at the lower of cost (first-in, first-out) or market, as determined by the retail inventory method.

Depreciation and Amortization

The Company's buildings, furniture, fixtures, and equipment are depreciated using the straight-line method over the estimated useful lives of the assets. Improvements to leased premises are amortized on the straight-line method over the life of the lease or the useful life of the improvement, whichever is shorter.

Investment Tax Credit

Investment tax credits are recorded as a reduction of Federal income taxes in the year the credits are realized.

Store Preopening Costs

Non-capital expenditures associated with opening new stores are charged to expense as incurred.

Earnings Per Common and Common Equivalent Share

Earnings per common and common equivalent share are based on the weighted average number of shares and equivalents outstanding. Common equivalent shares used in the calculation of earnings per share represent shares granted under the Company's employee stock option plan and employee stock purchase plan.

Shares issuable upon conversion of the 8½% convertible subordinated debentures are also common stock equivalents. Shares issuable upon conversion of the 9% convertible subordinated debentures would only be included in the computation of fully diluted earnings per share. However, neither shares issuable upon conversion of the 8½% nor the 9% convertible debentures were dilutive in any year presented, and thus neither were considered in the earnings per share computations.

The Home Depot

2. Acquisition

On December 3, 1984 the Company acquired the outstanding capital stock of Bowater Home Center, Inc. (Bowater) for approximately $38,420,000 including costs incurred in connection with the acquisition. Bowater operated nine retail home center stores primarily in the Dallas, Texas metropolitan area. The acquisition was accounted for by the purchase method and, accordingly, results of operations have been included with those of the Company from the date of acquisition. Cost in excess of the fair value of net assets acquired amounted to approximately $25,291,000, which is being amortized over forty years from date of acquisition using the straight-line method.

The following table summarizes, on a pro forma, unaudited basis, the estimated combined results of operations of the Company and Bowater for the years ended February 3, 1985 and January 29, 1984, as though the acquisition were made at the beginning of fiscal year 1983. This pro forma information does not purport to be indicative of the results of operations which would have actually been obtained if the acquisition had been effective on the dates indicated.

	Fiscal Year Ended	
	February 3, 1985	January 29, 1984*
	(Unaudited)	
Net sales	$482,752,000	$274,660,000
Net earnings	9,009,000	6,913,000
Earnings per common and common equivalent share	.36	.28

*Includes the operations and pro forma adjustments from the date of inception of Bowater's operations in August, 1983.

3. Long-Term Debt and Lines of Credit

Long-term debt consists of the following:

	February 2, 1986	February 3, 1985
8½% convertible subordinated debentures, due July 1, 2009, convertible into shares of common stock of the Company at a conversion price of $26.50 per share. The debentures are redeemable by the Company at a premium from July 1, 1986 to July 1, 1995, will retire 70% of the issue prior to maturity. Interest is payable semi-annually.	$86,250,000	$86,250,000
9% convertible subordinated debentures, due December 15, 1999, convertible into shares of common stock of the Company at a conversion price of $16.90 per share. The debentures are redeemable by the Company at a premium from December 15, 1986 to December 15, 1994. An annual mandatory sinking fund of $2,000,000 per year is required from 1994 to 1998. Interest is payable semi-annually.	14,000,000	14,000,000
Total convertible subordinated debentures	**100,250,000**	100,250,000

	February 2, 1986	February 3, 1985
Revolving credit agreement. Interest may be fixed for any portion outstanding for up to 180 days, at the Company's option, based on a CD rate plus ¾%, the LIBOR rate plus ½% or at the prime rate.	88,000,000	—
*Variable Rate Industrial Revenue Bond (see note 7)	10,100,000	10,100,000
*Variable Rate Industrial Revenue Bond, secured by a letter of credit, payable in sinking fund installments from December 1, 1991 through December 1, 2010	4,400,000	—
9⅝% Industrial Revenue Bond, secured by a letter of credit, payable on December 1, 1993, with interest payable semi-annually	4,200,000	4,200,000
*Variable Rate Industrial Revenue Bond, secured by land, payable in annual installments of $233,000 with interest payable semi-annually	3,267,000	3,500,000
Other	108,000	179,000
Total long-term debt	210,325,000	118,229,000
Less current portion	10,382,000	287,000
Long-term debt, excluding current portion	$199,943,000	$117,942,000

*The interest rates on the variable rate industrial revenue bonds are related to various short-term municipal money market composite rates.

Maturities of long-term debt are approximately $10,382,000 for fiscal 1986 and $234,000 for each of the next four subsequent years.

During the fiscal year ended February 2, 1986, the Company entered into a new unsecured revolving line of credit for a maximum of $200,000,000, subject to certain limitations, of which $88,000,000 is outstanding at year-end. Commitment amounts under the agreement decrease by $15,000,000 on July 31, 1990, by $20,000,000 each six months from that date through January 31, 1993, by $35,000,000 on July 31, 1993, and with the remaining $50,000,000 commitment expiring on January 31, 1994. Maximum borrowings outstanding within the commitment limits may not exceed specified percentages of inventories, land and buildings, and fixtures and equipment, all as defined in the Agreement. Under certain conditions, the commitments may be extended and/or increased. An annual commitment fee of ¼% to ⅜% is required to be paid on the unused portion of the revolving line of credit. Interest rates specified may be increased by a maximum of ⅜ of 1% based on specified ratios of interest rate coverage and debt to equity.

Under the revolving credit agreement, the Company is required, among other things, to maintain during fiscal year 1985 a minimum tangible net worth (defined to include the convertible subordinated debentures) of $150,000,000 (increasing annually to $213,165,000 by January 3, 1989), a debt to tangible net worth ratio of no more than 2 to 1, a current ratio of not less than 1.5 to 1, and a ratio of earnings before interest expense and income taxes to interest expense, net, of not less than 2 to 1. The Company was in compliance with all restrictive covenants as of February 2, 1986. The restrictive covenants related to the letter of credit agreements securing the industrial revenue bonds and the convertible subordinated debentures are no more restrictive than those under the revolving line of credit agreement.

The Home Depot

Interest expense in the accompanying consolidated statements of earnings is net of interest capitalized of $3,429,000 in fiscal 1985 and $1,462,000 in fiscal 1984.

4. Income Taxes

The provision for income taxes consists of the following:

| | Fiscal Year Ended | | |
	February 1, 1986	February 3, 1985	January 29, 1984
Current:			
Federal	$(578,000)	$9,083,000	$6,916,000
State	366,000	1,539,000	1,096,000
	(212,000)	10,622,000	8,012,000
Deferred:			
Federal	3,306,000	1,464,000	713,000
State	306,000	44,000	—
	3,612,000	1,508,000	713,000
Total	$3,400,000	$12,130,000	$8,725,000

The effective tax rates for fiscal 1985, 1984, and 1983 were 29.3%, 46.2%, and 46.0%, respectively. A reconciliation of income tax expense at Federal statutory rates to actual tax expense for the applicable fiscal years follows:

| | Fiscal Year Ended | | |
	February 2, 1986	February 3, 1985	January 29, 1984
Income taxes at Federal statutory rate, net of surtax exemption	$5,345,000	$12,076,000	$8,734,000
State income taxes, net of Federal income tax benefit	363,000	855,000	592,000
Investment and targeted jobs tax credits	(2,308,000)	(800,000)	(747,000)
Other, net	—	(1,000)	146,000
	$3,400,000	$12,130,000	$8,725,000

Deferred income taxes arise from differences in the timing of reporting income for financial statement and income tax purposes. The sources of these differences and the tax effect of each are as follows:

	Fiscal Year Ended		
	February 2, 1986	February 3, 1985	January 29, 1984
Accelerated depreciation	**$2,526,000**	$1,159,000	$713,000
Interest capitalization	**855,000**	349,000	—
Other, net	**231,000**	—	—
	$3,612,000	$1,508,000	$713,000

5. Leases

The Company leases certain retail locations, office, and warehouse and distribution space, equipment, and vehicles under operating leases. All leases will expire within the next 25 years; however, it can be expected that in the normal course of business, leases will be renewed or replaced. Total rent expense, net of minor sublease income for the fiscal years ended February 2, 1986, February 3, 1985 and January 29, 1984 amounted to approximately $12,737,000, $6,718,000 and $4,233,000, respectively. Under the building leases, real estate taxes, insurance, maintenance, and operating expenses applicable to the leased property are obligations of the Company. Certain of the store leases provide for contingent rentals based on percentages of sales in excess of specified minimums. Contingent rentals for fiscal years ended February 2, 1986, February 3, 1985 and January 29, 1984 were approximately $650,000, $545,000 and $111,000.

The approximate future minimum lease payments under operating leases at February 2, 1986 are as follows:

Fiscal Year	
1986	**$ 16,093,000**
1987	16,668,000
1988	16,345,000
1989	16,086,000
1990	16,129,000
Thereafter	171,455,000
	$252,776,000

7. Disposition of Property and Equipment

During the fourth quarter of fiscal year 1985, the Company disposed of certain properties and equipment at a net gain of $1,317,000. The properties represented real estate located in Detroit, Houston and Tucson, and the equipment represented the trade-in of cash registers of current generation point of sale equipment. Under the terms of the Detroit real estate sale, the purchaser will either assume the bond obligations of the Company of $10,100,000 after February 2, 1986 or pay the Company the funds disbursed under the bonds in order for the Company to prepay the total amount outstanding. Included in accounts receivable at February 2, 1986 is $13,800,000 related to these transactions.

8. Commitments and Contingencies

At February 2, 1986, the Company was contingently liable for approximately $5,300,000 under outstanding letters of credit issued in connection with purchase commitments.

The Company has litigation arising from the normal course of business. In management's opinion, this litigation will not materially affect the Company's financial condition.

9. Quarterly Financial Data (Unaudited)

The following is a summary of the unaudited quarterly results of operations for fiscal years ended February 2, 1986 and February 3, 1985:

	Net Sales	Gross Profit	Net Earnings	Net Earnings per Common and Common Equivalent Share
Fiscal year ended February 2, 1986:				
First Quarter	$145,048,000	$ 36,380,000	$ 1,945,000	$ .08
Second Quarter	174,239,000	45,572,000	2,499,000	.10
Third Quarter	177,718,000	46,764,000	1,188,000	.05
Fourth Quarter	203,724,000	52,741,000	2,587,000	.10
	$700,729,000	$181,457,000	$ 8,219,000	$ .33
Fiscal year ended February 3, 1985:				
First Quarter	$ 95,872,000	$ 25,026,000	$ 3,437,000	$ .14
Second Quarter	119,068,000	29,185,000	3,808,000	.15
Third Quarter	100,459,000	27,658,000	3,280,000	.13
Fourth Quarter	117,380,000	32,450,000	3,597,000	.14
	$432,779,000	$114,319,000	$14,122,000	$ .56

AUDITORS' REPORT

The Board of Directors and Stockholders,
The Home Depot, Inc.:

We have examined the consolidated balance sheets of The Home Depot, Inc. and subsidiary as of February 2, 1986 and February 3, 1985 and the related consolidated statements of earnings, stockholders' equity, and changes in financial position for each of the years in the three-year period ended February 2, 1986. Our examinations were made in accordance with generally accepted auditing standards, and, accordingly, included such tests of the accounting records and such other auditing procedures as we considered necessary in the circumstances.

In our opinion, the aforementioned consolidated financial statements present fairly the financial position of The Home Depot, Inc. and subsidiary at February 2, 1986 and February 3, 1985, and the results of their operations and the changes in their financial position for each of the years in the three-year period ended February 2, 1986, in conformity with generally accepted accounting principles applied on a consistent basis.

PEAT, MARWICK, MITCHELL & CO.
Atlanta, Georgia
March 24, 1986

The Home Depot

Prospective Analysis: Forecasting

Most financial statement analysis tasks are undertaken with a forward-looking decision in mind—and much of the time, it is useful to summarize the view developed in the analysis with an explicit forecast. Managers need forecasts for planning and to provide performance targets; analysts need forecasts to help communicate their views of the firm's prospects to investors; bankers and debt market participants need forecasts to assess the likelihood of loan repayment. Moreover, there are a variety of contexts (including but not limited to security analysis) where the forecast is usefully summarized in the form of an estimate of the firm's value—an estimate that, after all, can be viewed as the best attempt to reflect in a single summary statistic the manager's or analyst's view of the firm's prospects.

Prospective analysis includes two tasks—forecasting and valuation—that together represent approaches to explicitly summarizing the analyst's forward-looking views. In this chapter, we focus on forecasting. Valuation is the topic of the following two chapters. The key concepts discussed in this chapter are again illustrated using analysts' forecasts for Nordstrom.

RELATION OF FORECASTING TO OTHER ANALYSES

Forecasting is not so much a separate analysis as it is a way of summarizing what has been learned through business strategy analysis, accounting analysis, and financial analysis. For example, a projection of the future performance of Nordstrom as of early 1999 must be grounded ultimately in an understanding of questions such as:

- *From business strategy analysis:* What will Nordstrom's recent focus on restructuring to enhance shareholder value mean for future margins and sales volume? What will it imply about the need for working capital and capital expenditures?
- *From accounting analysis:* Are there any aspects of Nordstrom's accounting that suggest past earnings and assets are overstated, or expenses or liabilities are overstated? If so, what are the implications for future accounting statements?
- *From financial analysis:* What are the sources of the improvement in Nordstrom's margin in 1998? Is the improvement sustainable? Has Nordstrom's shift in business strategy translated into improvements in asset utilization in 1998? Can any such improvements in efficiency be sustained or enhanced? Will Nordstrom change its debt policy?

The upshot is that a forecast can be no better than the business strategy analysis, accounting analysis, and financial analysis underlying it. However, there are certain techniques and knowledge that can help a manager or analyst to structure the best possible forecast, conditional on what has been learned in the previous steps. Below, we summarize an approach to structuring the forecast, some information useful in getting started, and some detailed steps used to forecast earnings, balance sheet data, and cash flows.

THE TECHNIQUES OF FORECASTING

The Overall Structure of the Forecast

The best way to forecast future performance is to do it comprehensively—producing not only an earnings forecast, but a forecast of cash flows and the balance sheet as well. A comprehensive approach is useful, even in cases where one might be interested primarily in a single facet of performance, because it guards against unrealistic implicit assumptions. For example, if an analyst forecasts growth in sales and earnings for several years without explicit consideration of the required increases in working capital and plant assets and the associated financing, the forecast might possibly imbed unreasonable assumptions about asset turnover, leverage, or equity capital infusions.

A comprehensive approach involves many forecasts, but in most cases they are all linked to the behavior of a few key "drivers." The drivers vary according to the type of business involved, but for businesses outside the financial services sector, the sales forecast is nearly always one of the key drivers; profit margin is another. When asset turnover is expected to remain stable—as is often realistic—working capital accounts and investment in plant should track the growth in sales closely. Most major expenses also track sales, subject to expected shifts in profit margins. By linking forecasts of such amounts to the sales forecast, one can avoid internal inconsistencies and unrealistic implicit assumptions.

In some contexts, the manager or analyst is interested ultimately in a forecast of cash flows, not earnings per se. Nevertheless, even forecasts of cash flows tend to be grounded in practice on forecasts of accounting numbers, including sales and earnings. Of course, it would be possible in principle to move *directly* to forecasts of cash flows—inflows from customers, outflows to suppliers and laborers, and so forth—and in some businesses, this is a convenient way to proceed. In most cases, however, the growth prospects and profitability of the firm are more readily framed in terms of accrual-based sales and operating earnings. These amounts can then be converted to cash flow measures by adjusting for the effects of noncash expenses and expenditures for working capital and plant.

Getting Started: Points of Departure

Every forecast has, at least implicitly, an initial "benchmark" or point of departure—some notion of how a particular amount, such as sales or earnings, would be expected to behave in the absence of detailed information. For example, in beginning to contemplate 1999 profitability for Nordstrom, one must start somewhere. A possibility is to begin with the 1998 performance. Another starting point might be 1998 performance adjusted for recent trends. A third possibility that might seem reasonable—but one that generally turns out not to be very useful—is the average performance over several prior years.

By the time one has completed a business strategy analysis, an accounting analysis, and a detailed financial analysis, the resulting forecast might differ significantly from the original point of departure. Nevertheless, simply for purposes of having a starting point that can help anchor the detailed analysis, it is useful to know how certain key financial statistics behave "on average."

In the case of some key statistics, such as earnings, a point of departure or benchmark based only on prior behavior of the number is more powerful than one might expect. Research demonstrates that some such benchmarks for earnings are not much less accurate than the forecasts of professional security analysts, who have access to a rich information set. (We return to this point in more detail below.) Thus, the benchmark is often not only a good starting point, but also close to the amount forecast after detailed analysis. Large departures from the benchmark could be justified only in cases where the firm's situation is demonstrably unusual.

Reasonable points of departure for forecasts of key accounting numbers can be based on the evidence summarized below. Such evidence may also be useful for checking the reasonableness of a completed forecast.

THE BEHAVIOR OF SALES GROWTH.   Sales growth rates tend to be "mean-reverting": firms with above-average or below-average rates of sales growth tend to revert over time to a "normal" level (historically in the range of 7 to 9 percent for U.S. firms) within no more than three to ten years. Figure 10-1 documents this effect for U.S. firms for 1979–1998. All firms are ranked in terms of their sales growth in 1979 (year 1) and formed into five portfolios based on the relative ranking of their sales growth in that year. Firms in portfolio 1 have the top twenty percent of rankings in terms of their sales growth in 1979, and those in portfolio 2 fall into the next twenty percent; those in portfolio 5 have the bottom twenty percent sales growth ranks. The sales growth rates of each of the five portfolios plotted in Figure 10-1 in year +1 to year +10 are averaged across three experiments. The sales growth rates of firms in each of these five portfolios are traced from 1979 through the subsequent nine years (years 2 to 10). The same experiment is repeated with 1984 and then 1989 as the base year (year 1).

The figure shows that the group of firms with the highest growth initially—sales growth rates of more than 50 percent—experience a decline to about 6 percent growth rate within three years and are never above 13 percent in the next seven years. Those with the lowest initial growth experience an increase to about 8 percent growth rate by year 5, and never fall below 5 percent after that. All five portfolios, irrespective of their starting growth levels, revert to "normal" levels of sales growth of between 7 and 9 percent within five years.

Figure 10-1   Behavior of Sales Growth over Time for U.S. Companies for 1979–1998

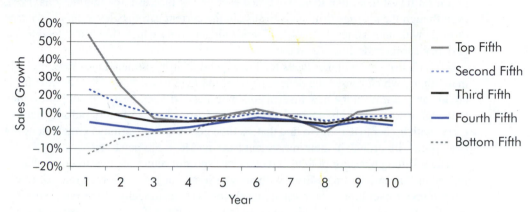

One explanation for the pattern of sales growth seen in Figure 10-1 is that as industries and companies mature, their growth rate slows down due to demand saturation and intra-industry competition. Therefore, even when a firm is growing rapidly at present, it is generally unrealistic to extrapolate the current high growth indefinitely. Of course, how quickly a firm's growth rate reverts to the average depends on the characteristics of its industry and its own competitive position within an industry.

THE BEHAVIOR OF EARNINGS.   Earnings have been shown, on average, to follow a process that can be approximated by a "random walk" or "random walk with drift"; thus, the prior year's earnings is a good starting point in considering future earnings potential. As will be explained in more detail later in the chapter, it is reasonable to adjust this simple benchmark for the earnings changes of the most recent quarter (that is, changes versus the comparable quarter of the prior year after controlling for the long-run trend in the series). Even a simple random walk forecast—one that predicts next year's earnings will be equal to last year's earnings—is surprisingly useful. One study documents that professional analysts' year-ahead forecasts are only 22 percent more accurate (on average) than a simple random walk forecast.[1] Thus, a final earnings forecast will *usually* not differ dramatically from a random walk benchmark.

   The implication of the evidence is that, in beginning to contemplate future earnings possibilities, a useful number to start with is last year's earnings; the average level of earnings over several prior years is not. Long-term trends in earnings tend to be sustained on average, and so they are also worthy of consideration. If quarterly data are also considered, then some consideration should usually be given to any departures from the long-run trend that occurred in the most recent quarter. For most firms, these most recent changes tend to be partially repeated in subsequent quarters.[2]

THE BEHAVIOR OF RETURNS ON EQUITY.   Given that prior earnings serves as a useful benchmark for future earnings, one might expect the same to be true of rates of return on investment, like ROE. That, however, is not the case, for two reasons. First, even though the *average* firm tends to sustain the current earnings level, this is not true of firms with unusual levels of ROE. Firms with abnormally high (low) ROE tend to experience earnings declines (increases).[3]

Second, firms with higher ROEs tend to expand their investment bases more quickly than others, which causes the denominator of the ROE to increase. Of course, if firms could earn returns on the new investments that match the returns on the old ones, then the level of ROE would be maintained. However, firms have difficulty pulling that off. Firms with higher ROEs tend to find that, as time goes by, their earnings growth does not keep pace with growth in their investment base, and ROE ultimately falls.

The resulting behavior of ROE and other measures of return on investment is characterized as "mean-reverting": firms with above-average or below-average rates of return tend to revert over time to a "normal" level (for ROE, historically in the range of 10 to 15 percent for U.S. firms) within no more than ten years.[4] Figure 10-2 documents this effect for U.S. firms for 1979–1998. All firms are ranked in terms of their ROE in 1979 (year 1) and formed into five portfolios. Firms in portfolio 1 have the top twenty percent ROE rankings in 1979, those in portfolio 2 fall into the next twenty percent, and those in portfolio 5 have the bottom twenty percent sales growth ranks. The average ROE of firms in each of these five portfolios is then traced through nine subsequent years (years 2 to 10). The same experiment is repeated with 1984 and 1989 as the base year (year 1), and the subsequent years as years +2 to +10. Figure 10-2 plots the average ROE of each of the five portfolios in years 1 to 10 averaged across these three experiments.

The most profitable group of firms initially—with average ROEs of 27 percent—experience a decline to 17 percent within three years. By year 10, this group of firms has an ROE of 14 percent. Those with the lowest initial ROEs (–33 percent) experience an increase in ROE until they reach a level of 13 percent in year 10. Three of the five portfolios record an average ROE in the range of 13 to 15 percent by year 10, even though they start out in year 1 with a wide range of average ROEs.

The pattern in Figure 10-2 is not a coincidence; it is exactly what the economics of competition would predict. The tendency of high ROEs to fall is a reflection of high profitability attracting competition; the tendency of low ROEs to rise reflects the mobility of capital away from unproductive ventures toward more profitable ones.

Despite the general tendencies documented in Figure 10-2, there are some firms whose ROEs may remain above or below normal levels for long periods of time. In some cases, the phenomenon reflects the strength of a sustainable competitive advantage (e.g., Wal-Mart), but in other cases, it is purely an artifact of conservative accounting methods. A good example of the latter phenomenon in the U.S. is pharmaceutical firms, whose major economic asset (the intangible value of research and development) is not recorded on the balance sheet and is therefore excluded from the denominator of ROE. For those firms, one could reasonably expect high ROEs—in excess of 20 percent—over the long run, even in the face of strong competitive forces.

Figure 10-2 Behavior of ROE over Time for U.S. Companies for 1979–1998

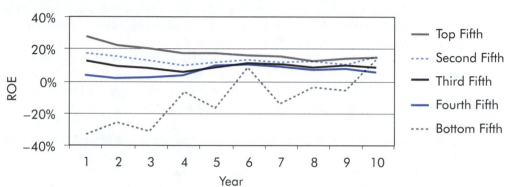

THE BEHAVIOR OF COMPONENTS OF ROE.   The behavior of rates of return on equity can be analyzed further by looking at the behavior of its key components. Recall from Chapter 9 that ROEs and profit margins are linked as follows:

$$\text{ROE} = \text{Operating ROA} + (\text{Operating ROA} - \text{Net interest rate after tax})$$
$$\times \text{Net financial leverage}$$

$$= \text{NOPAT margin} \times \text{Operating asset turnover} + \text{Spread}$$
$$\times \text{Net financial leverage}$$

The time-series behavior of the components of ROE for U.S. industrial companies for 1979–1998 are shown in a series of figures in the appendix to this chapter. The major conclusions from these figures are: Operating asset turnover tends to be rather stable, in part because it is so much a function of the technology of the industry. Net financial leverage also tends to be stable, simply because management policies on capital structure aren't often changed. NOPAT margin and spread stand out as the most variable component of ROE; if the forces of competition drive abnormal ROEs toward more normal levels, the change is most likely to arrive in the form of changes in profit margins and the spread. The change in spread is itself driven by changes in NOPAT margin, since the cost of borrowing is likely to remain stable if leverage remains stable.

To summarize, profit margins, like ROEs, tend to be driven by competition to "normal" levels over time. However, what constitutes normal varies widely according to the technology employed within an industry and the corporate strategy pursued by the firm—both of which influence turnover and leverage.[5] In a fully competitive equilibrium, profit margins should remain high for firms that must operate with a low turnover, and vice versa.

The implication of the above discussion of rates of return and margins is that a reasonable point of departure for a forecast of such a statistic should consider more than just the most recent observation. One should also consider whether that rate or margin is above or below a normal level. If so, then absent detailed information to the contrary, one would expect some movement over time to that norm. Of course, this central tendency might be overcome in some cases—for example, where the firm has erected barriers to competition that can protect margins, even for extended periods. The lesson from the evidence, however, is that such cases are unusual.

In contrast to rates of return and margins, it is reasonable to assume that asset turnover, financial leverage, and net interest rate remain constant over time. Unless there is an explicit change in technology or financial policy being contemplated for future periods, a reasonable point of departure for assumptions for these variables is the current period level.

As we proceed below with the steps involved in producing a detailed forecast, the reader will note that we draw on the above knowledge of the behavior of accounting numbers to some extent. However, it is important to keep in mind that a knowledge of *average* behavior will not fit all firms well. The art of financial statements analysis requires not only knowing what the "normal" patterns are but also expertise in identifying those firms that will *not* follow the norm.

ELEMENTS OF THE DETAILED FORECAST

Here we summarize steps that could be followed in producing a comprehensive forecast. The discussion assumes that the firm being analyzed is among the vast majority for which the forecast would reasonably be anchored by a sales forecast.

The Sales Forecast

The first step in most forecasting exercises is the sales prediction. There is no generally accepted approach to forecasting sales; the approach should be tailored to the context and should reflect the factors considered in the prior steps of the analysis. For example, for a large retail firm, a sales forecast would normally consider the prior year's sales, increases due purely to expansion of the number of retail outlets, and "comparable store growth," which captures growth in sales in already-existing stores. The forecast of growth might consider such factors as customer acceptance of new product lines, marketing plans, changes in pricing strategies, competitors' behavior, and the expected state of the economy. Another possible approach—and one that may represent the only feasible approach when little history exists—is to estimate the size of the target market, project the degree of market penetration, and then consider how quickly that degree of penetration can be achieved.

Table 10-1 presents a forecast of sales and earnings for Nordstrom for the fiscal year ending January 31, 2000 (fiscal 1999), produced by an analyst at Morgan Stanley in December 1998. At the time these forecasts were made, the analyst had information on Nordstrom's actual performance for the first three quarters of 1998 but not for the entire 1998 fiscal year. As a result, some of the assumptions are driven by the actual perfor-

Table 10-1 Analyst's Forecast of 1999 Income Statement for Nordstrom

	1999 Forecast		1998 Actual	
	$ Millions	% of Sales	$ Millions	% of Sales
Total sales	5627	100.0	5028	100.0
Cost of sales	3760	66.8	3345	66.5
SG&A expense	1537	27.3	1405	28.0
Other income	107	2.1	107	2.1
Earnings before interest and taxes	437	7.8	385	7.7
Net operating profit after taxes (NOPAT)	**275**	**4.9**	**238**	**4.7**
Net interest expense after taxes	**37**	**0.7**	**31**	**0.6**
Net Income	**238**	**4.2**	**207**	**4.1**

Tax expense forecasted by the analyst has been allocated to operations and interest expense.

Source: "Nordstrom: Shareholders should be as satisfied as customers," by B. Missett et al., Morgan Stanley Dean Witter, December 2, 1998.

mance in 1997 rather than the performance in 1998. The actual results for 1998 are also shown in the table for comparison.

The 1999 sales growth forecast is significantly larger than the 6 percent growth rate in 1998, and similar to the growth rate in 1997. In commenting on the forecast, the analyst recognized at least two factors that might support a more optimistic outlook on sales. He viewed the comparable store sales growth in 1998 to be unusually low (in fact, negative) as resulting from Nordstrom's focus in that year on better inventory management and reducing markdowns. The analyst expected the comparable store sales in 1999 to bounce back to a higher level, 3 percent, but below the level of 4 percent in 1997. The rest of the sales growth in 1999 is forecasted to come from opening new stores.

The Morgan Stanley forecast appears to be based largely on analysis that views the firm as a whole. An alternative approach—not feasible for all firms—is to build a sales forecast on a product line-by-product line basis, or by major business segments of a firm

The Forecast of Expenses and Earnings

Expenses should be forecast item by item, since different expenses may be driven by different factors. However, most major expenses are clearly related to sales and are therefore naturally framed as fractions of sales. These include cost of sales and SG&A expenses. R&D need not track current sales closely; however, R&D generally tracks sales at least roughly over the long run. Other expenses are more closely related to drivers other than sales. Interest expense is driven by debt levels and interest rates. Depreciation expense should be forecast in a way consistent with the firm's depreciation policy; under straight-line depreciation, the expense would tend to be a fairly stable fraction of beginning depreciable plant. Tax provisions are driven by pretax income and factors (such as tax rates applicable to certain foreign subsidiaries) that have a permanent impact on tax payments. Equity in the income of affiliates is determined by whatever drives the affiliate's earnings.

In the case of Nordstrom, the two largest expenses—cost of sales and SG&A expense—were forecast by the analyst as fractions of sales (see Table10-1). Cost of sales was expected to marginally decrease as a fraction of sales, causing the gross margin percentage to increase to 33.5 percent from 33.2 percent. This projected increase is a continuation of the margin improvement in 1998, a reflection of the view that management's new strategy will continue to cut purchase costs. SG&A is also expected to decrease from 28 percent to 27.3 percent. Here, the analyst assumed that the SG&A costs increased temporarily in 1998 and that they will return in 1999 to the levels experienced in 1997 and 1996.

The analyst appears to assume that the net interest expense and other income will remain approximately unchanged as a percent of sales. Tax expense is projected as 39.4 percent of pretax income—35 percent for federal and 4.4 percent for state taxes.

The forecasts of sales and expenses produce an expected net margin of 4.2 percent, a small improvement over the 1998 net margin of 4.1 percent. The analyst is betting that Nordstrom's emphasis on cost cutting and value-based management will continue to produce improvements in the company's bottom line.

The Forecast of Balance Sheet Accounts

Since various balance sheet accounts may be driven by different factors, they are usually best forecast individually. However, several asset accounts, including operating working capital accounts and operating long-term assets, are driven over the long run by sales activity. Thus, these accounts can be forecast as fractions of sales, allowing for any expected changes in the efficiency of asset utilization. If management plans for capital expenditures are known, they would clearly be useful in forecasting plant assets. Liability and equity accounts will depend on a variety of factors, including policies on capital structure, dividends, and stock repurchases.

While it is useful to project balance sheet accounts in detail for some purposes, it may be adequate sometimes to project a summary balance sheet that contains major categories of assets and liabilities along the lines discussed in the financial analysis chapter—operating working capital, net operating long-term assets, net debt, and shareholders' equity. Such projections are useful for valuing a company. One simple approach to projecting a summary balance sheet is as follows:

First, one can project operating working capital and operating long-term assets by making assumptions about these two asset categories as a fraction of sales. The sum of these two items is net operating assets. Next, by making an assumption about net financial leverage (ratio of net debt to equity), one can project the amount of debt and equity needed to support these net operating assets. Therefore, to project summary balance sheets, one needs to make only three critical assumptions: ratio of operating working capital to sales, ratio of operating long-term assets to sales, and the ratio of net debt to equity.

Table 10-2 presents Morgan Stanley Dean Witter analysts' forecast (as of December 1998) of the 1999 balance sheet for Nordstrom. The balance sheet accounts on the asset side are primarily driven by the analyst's assumptions on Nordstrom's turnover ratios assets. The analyst assumed, for 1999 relative to the levels achieved in 1998, higher levels of accounts receivable and inventory and lower levels of accounts payable . Since these forecasts were made prior to the release of the fourth quarter results for 1998, they do not reflect the unexpected significant reduction in working capital achieved by Nordstrom in that quarter. The forecast on net property, plant, and equipment is based on an assumption that capital expenditures will be slightly lower in 1999 relative to 1998, and that the depreciation expense will remain the same as a proportion of gross PP&E. Recall that the analyst made an assumption regarding the number of new stores that will be opened in 1999 in making the sales forecast, and it is presumably the basis for the capital

Table 10-2 Analyst's Forecast of Nordstrom's 1999 Balance Sheet

	1999 Forecast		1998 Actual	
Net Operating Assets	$ Millions	% of Sales	$ Millions	% of Sales
Accounts receivable	771	13.7	587	11.7
Inventory	902	16.0	750	14.9
Other operating current assets	96	1.7	102	2.0
Accounts payable	(373)	(6.6)	(340)	(6.8)
Other operating current liabilities	(338)	(6.0)	(287)	(5.7)
Operating working capital	**1058**	**18.8**	**812**	**16.1**
PP&E, net	1479	26.3	1362	27.1
Other long-term assets	18	0.3	73	1.5
Other operating long-term liabilities	(179)	(3.2)	(225)	(4.5)
Net operating long-term assets	**1318**	**23.4**	**1210**	**24.1**
Total net operating assets	**2376**	**42.2**	**2022**	**40.2**

		% of Net		% of Net
Net Capital	$ Millions	Capital	$ Millions	Capital
Total short-term and long-term debt	959	40.4	946	46.8
Cash and short-term investments	(15.4)	(0.7)	(241)	(11.9)
Net debt	**945**	**39.7**	**705**	**34.9**
Total shareholders' equity	**1431**	**60.3**	**1317**	**65.1**
Total net capital	**2376**	**100.0**	**2022**	**100.0**

Source: "Nordstrom: Shareholders should be as satisfied as customers," by B. Missett et al., Morgan Stanley Dean Witter, December 2, 1998.

expenditure assumption. The end result of these assumptions was that the net PP&E turnover was forecasted to decline somewhat from the level in 1998. The analyst had to make assumptions on a few other smaller line items—other operating current assets and liabilities, and other operating long-term assets and liabilities. These assumptions were not explained by the analyst.

To forecast net debt and equity, the analyst had to assume a ratio of net debt to net capital (or equivalently, net debt to equity). In 1998 Nordstrom had a ratio of approximately 35 percent net debt to equity. The analyst assumed that this ratio will increase to about 40 percent in 1999. The relatively low net debt ratio in 1998 is due to an unusually large cash balance that Nordstrom built up in 1998. The forecast assumes that Nordstrom will use that cash to reduce its debt or to buy back stock. Therefore, the 1999 forecasted balance sheet has 40.4 percent total debt to net capital and 0.7 percent cash to net capital, and 60.3 percent equity to net capital, whereas the 1998 ratios were 46.8 percent debt to net capital, 11.9 percent cash to net capital, and 65.1 percent equity to net capital.

The forecasted balance sheet and income statement for Nordstrom imply an increase in the company's ROE from 15.6 percent in 1998 to 16.6 percent in 1999. This increase in ROE is driven by an assumed increase in net profit margin from 4.1 to 4.2 percent, a decrease in operating asset turnover from 2.49 to 2.37, and an increase in net operating assets to equity from 1.54 to 1.66 (or equivalently, an increase in net debt to equity from 0.54 to 0.66). These forecasts assume that Nordstrom will continue its recently adopted strategy of emphasizing profitability and shareholder value.

An alternative approach to balance sheet projection is to assume the *change* in each balance sheet account is linked to the *change* in sales. For example, one might forecast that inventory balances will increase by 15 to 20 percent of sales increases. The weakness of this approach is that it takes the beginning balances as given and adjusts from those points. This is problematic because working capital accounts at a given point in time often reflect some unusual deviation from the norm (for example, beginning-of-year accruals might have ballooned, depending on where payday falls on the calendar). More important, the firm's strategy may suggest a shift from the beginning-of-year position.

The Forecast of Cash Flows

The forecast of earnings and balance sheet accounts implies a forecast of cash flows. Table 10-3 shows the projection of cash flows for Nordstrom for 1999, using the cash flow analysis model discussed in Chapter 9. These forecasts are based on the projected balance sheet for 1999 and the actual balance sheet for 1998, as shown in Table 10-2.[6]

The cash flow forecasts begin with the projected income for 1998. To this we add back projected after-tax net interest expense and depreciation to arrive at operating cash flow before working capital investments. The forecasted operating cash flow before working capital for 1999 is slightly higher than in 1998. The projected working capital levels at the end of 1999 imply a net investment of $246 million. Notice how this differs from a significant reduction in working capital in 1998. The level of PP&E and other

Table 10-3 Analyst's Forecasts of Nordstrom's 1999 Cash Flows

	1999 Forecast $ Millions	1998 Actual $ Millions
Net income	238	207
After-tax net interest expense	37	31
Depreciation and other long-term operating accruals	196	187
Operating cash flow before investment in working capital	**471**	**425**
Net investment in operating working capital	(246)	199
Operating cash flow	**225**	**623**
Net investment in long-term operating assets and liabilities	(304)	(259)
Free cash flow available to debt and equity	**(79)**	**364**
After-tax net interest expense	(37)	(31)
Net debt (repayment) or issuance	13	258
Free cash flow available to equity	**(103)**	**591**
Cash dividends and repurchase of common stock	(123)	(375)
Net cash increase (decrease)	**(202)**	**216**
Ending cash balance	(226)	241

Source: Forecasted balance sheet for 1999 from "Nordstrom: Shareholders should be as satisfied as customers," by B. Missett et. al., Morgan Stanley Dean Witter, December 2, 1998, and the actual balance sheet for 1998 issued by Nordstrom.

operating long-term assets and liabilities implies a net investment of $304 million, leading to a cash flow deficit of $79 million. After-tax interest payment was projected to be 37 million dollars. Total debt is projected to be $13 million higher at the end of 1999 relative to the 1998 actual level. Thus, there is a projected 103-million-dollar cash flow deficit before dividends and stock repurchases. Despite this deficit, Nordstrom is projected to make a 123-million-dollar payout to equity holders in the form of dividends and share buybacks because of the large cash balance available at the end of 1998. The net result is a decrease in cash balance from $241 million to $15 million.

SENSITIVITY ANALYSIS

The projections discussed thus far represent nothing more than a "best guess." Managers and analysts are typically interested in a broader range of possibilities. For example, in considering the likelihood that short-term financing will be necessary, it would be wise to produce projections based on a more pessimistic view of profit margins and asset turnover. Alternatively, an analyst estimating the value of Nordstrom should consider the sensitivity of the estimate to the key assumptions about sales growth, profit margins, and asset utilization. What if Nordstrom's emphasis on profitability results in less sales growth than anticipated? What if the anticipated improvements in profit margins do not materialize?

There is no limit to the number of possible scenarios that can be considered. One systematic approach to sensitivity analysis is to start with the key assumptions underlying a set of forecasts and then examine the sensitivity to the assumptions with greatest uncertainty in a given situation. For example, if a company has experienced a variable pattern of gross margins in the past, it is important to make projections using a range of margins. Alternatively, if a company has announced a significant change in its expansion strategy, asset utilization assumptions might be more uncertain. In determining where to invest one's time in performing sensitivity analysis, it is therefore important to consider historical patterns of performance, changes in industry conditions, and changes in a company's competitive strategy.

Seasonality and Interim Forecasts

Thus far, we have concerned ourselves with annual forecasts. However, especially for security analysts in the U.S., forecasting is very much a quarterly game. Forecasting quarter by quarter raises a new set of questions. How important is seasonality? What is a useful point of departure—the most recent quarter's performance? The comparable quarter of the prior year? Some combination of the two? How should quarterly data be used in producing an annual forecast? Does the item-by-item approach to forecasting used for annual data apply equally well to quarterly data? Full consideration of these questions lies outside the scope of this chapter, but we can begin to answer some of them.

Seasonality is a more important phenomenon in sales and earning behavior than one might guess. It is present for more than just the retail sector firms that benefit from holiday sales. Seasonality also results from weather-related phenomena (e.g., for electric and gas utilities, construction firms, and motorcycle manufacturers), new product introduction patterns (e.g., for the automobile industry), and other factors. Analysis of the time series behavior of earnings for U.S. firms suggests that at least some seasonality is present in nearly every major industry.

The implication for forecasting is that one cannot focus only on performance of the most recent quarter as a point of departure. In fact, the evidence suggests that, in forecasting earnings, if one had to choose only one quarter's performance as a point of departure, it would be the comparable quarter of the prior year, not the most recent quarter. Note how this finding is consistent with the reports of analysts or the financial press; when they discuss a quarterly earnings announcement, it is nearly always evaluated relative to the performance of the comparable quarter of the prior year, not the most recent quarter.

Research has produced models that forecast sales, earnings, or EPS based solely on prior quarters' observations. Such models are not used by many analysts, since analysts have access to much more information than such simple models contain. However, the models are useful for helping those unfamiliar with the behavior earnings data to understand how it tends to evolve through time. Such an understanding can provide useful general background, a point of departure in forecasting that can be adjusted to reflect details not revealed in the history of earnings, or a "reasonableness" check on a detailed forecast.

Using Q_t to denote earnings (or EPS) for quarter t, and $E(Q_t)$ as its expected value, one model of the earnings process that fits well across a variety of industries is the so-called Foster model[7]:

$$E(Q_t) = Q_{t-4} + \delta + \phi(Q_{t-1} - Q_{t-5})$$

Foster shows that a model of the same form also works well with sales data.

The form of the Foster model confirms the importance of seasonality because it shows that the starting point for a forecast for quarter t is the earnings four quarters ago, Q_{t-4}. It states that, when constrained to using only prior earnings data, a reasonable forecast of earnings for quarter t includes the following elements:

the earnings of the comparable quarter of the prior year (Q_{t-4});

a long-run trend in year-to-year quarterly earnings increases (δ);

a fraction (ϕ) of the year-to-year increase in quarterly earnings experienced most recently ($Q_{t-1} - Q_{t-5}$).

The parameters δ and ϕ can easily be estimated for a given firm with a simple linear regression model available in most spreadsheet software.[8] For most firms, the parameter ϕ tends to be in the range of .25 to .50, indicating that 25 to 50 percent of an increase in quarterly earnings tends to persist in the form of another increase in the subsequent quarter. The parameter δ reflects, in part, the average year-to-year change in quarterly earnings over past years, and it varies considerably from firm to firm.

Research indicates that the Foster model produces one-quarter-ahead forecasts that are off, on average, by $.30 to $.35 per share.[9] Such a degree of accuracy stacks up surprisingly well with that of security analysts, who obviously have access to much information ignored in the model. As one would expect, most of the evidence supports analysts' being more accurate, but the models are good enough to be "in the ball park" in most circumstances. Thus, while it would certainly be unwise to rely completely on such a naïve model, an understanding of the typical earnings behavior reflected by the model is useful.

Nordstrom's quarterly EPS for years prior to 1999 behaved as shown in Table 10-4. Note the strong presence of seasonality. The second and fourth quarters of each year have higher earnings than the other two quarters; the fourth quarter of the year has been the strongest in every year except 1989, 1991, and 1996.

If we used the Foster model to forecast EPS for the first quarter of 1999, we would start with EPS of the comparable quarter of 1998, or $0.215. We would then expect some additional upward trend in EPS, and a partial repetition of the most recent quarter's in-

Table 10-4 Nordstrom's Quarterly Primary EPS, 1988–1998

Fiscal Year	EPS Quarter 1	EPS Quarter 2	EPS Quarter 3	EPS Quarter 4
1988	0.120	0.225	0.120	0.290
1989	0.140	0.235	0.135	0.195
1990	0.080	0.220	0.125	0.285
1991	0.155	0.305	0.120	0.250
1992	0.130	0.255	0.145	0.305
1993	0.070	0.260	0.155	0.370
1994	0.195	0.385	0.230	0.425
1995	0.170	0.325	0.180	0.335
1996	0.160	0.275	0.210	0.265
1997	0.205	0.380	0.235	0.380
1998	0.215	0.470	0.270	0.470

crease ($0.470 − $0.270). More specifically, when the parameters δ and ϕ are estimated with the data in Table 10-4 [10], the Foster model predicts EPS of $0.255:

$$
\begin{aligned}
E(Q_t) &= Q_{t-4} + 0.01 + 0.44(Q_{t-1} - Q_{t-5}) \\
&= 0.215 + 0.01 + 0.44(0.470 - 0.380) = 0.255
\end{aligned}
$$

The model can be extended to forecast earnings two quarters ahead, and even to produce a forecast for all quarters of the next year. The issue that arises here is that, in forecasting earnings two quarters ahead, one needs earnings one quarter ahead, and that quarter's earnings are still unknown. The proper resolution of the issue is to substitute the forecast of next quarter's earnings. Our forecast of earnings for Nordstrom for the second quarter of 1999, based on data through the fourth quarter of 1998, would be $0.408:

$$
\begin{aligned}
E(Q_{t+1}) &= Q_{t-3} + 0.01 + 0.44[E(Q_t) - Q_{t-4}] \\
&= 0.380 + 0.01 + 0.44(0.255 - 0.215)
\end{aligned}
$$

The $0.255 forecast for the first quarter of 1999, naïve as it is, is not far from the 0.220 actual EPS for Nordstrom in that quarter. Part of the reason that the naïve model produces a higher forecast is that Nordstrom had an unusually strong fourth quarter in 1998. The model assumes that 44 percent of the EPS increase of the most recent quarter will carry forward into 1999, but that increase reflected a one-time effect of the company's shift in strategy. The Foster model is not intended as a potential substitute for the hard work of producing a detailed forecast. Forecasting quarterly earnings should be done using the same approach used earlier for annual earnings—a line-item by line-item projection. However, the model does remind us of some important issues. First, it underscores that, due to seasonality, a reasonable starting point in quarterly forecasting is usually the comparable quarter of the prior year, not the most recent quarter. Second, it indicates that recent increases in profitability should *usually* not be extrapolated fully into the future—for Nordstrom's EPS, only 44 percent of such changes, on average, tend to persist.

SUMMARY

Forecasting represents the first step of prospective analysis and serves to summarize the forward-looking view that emanates from business strategy analysis, accounting analysis, and financial analysis. Although not every financial statement analysis is accompanied by such an explicit summarization of a view of the future, forecasting is still a key tool for managers, consultants, security analysts, investment bankers, commercial bankers and other credit analysts, and others.

The best approach to forecasting future performance is to do it comprehensively—producing not only an earnings forecast but a forecast of cash flows and the balance sheet as well. Such a comprehensive approach provides a guard against internal inconsistencies and unrealistic implicit assumptions. The approach described here involved line-by-line analysis, so as to recognize that different items on the income statement and balance sheet are influenced by different drivers. Nevertheless, it remains the case that a few key projections—such as sales growth and profit margin—usually drive most of the projected numbers.

The forecasting process should be embedded in an understanding of how various financial statistics tend to behave on average, and what might cause a firm to deviate from that average. Absent detailed information to the contrary, one would expect sales and earnings numbers to persist at their current levels, adjusted for overall trends of recent years. However, rates of return on investment (ROEs) tend, over several years, to move from abnormal to normal levels—close to the cost of equity capital—as the forces of competition come to play. Profit margins also tend to shift to normal levels, but for this statistic, "normal" varies widely across firms and industries, depending on the levels of asset turnover and leverage. Some firms are capable of creating barriers to entry that enable them to fight these tendencies toward normal returns, even for many years, but such firms are the unusual cases.

For some purposes, including short-term planning and security analysis, forecasts for quarterly periods are desirable. One important feature of quarterly data is seasonality; at least some seasonality exists in the sales and earnings data of nearly every industry. An understanding of a firm's within-year peaks and valleys is a necessary ingredient of a good forecast of performance on a quarterly basis.

There are a variety of contexts (including but not limited to security analysis) where the forecast is usefully summarized in the form of an estimate of the firm's value—an estimate that, after all, can be viewed as the best attempt to reflect in a single summary statistic the manager's or analyst's view of the firm's prospects. That process of converting a forecast into a value estimate is labeled valuation. It is to that topic that we turn in the following chapter.

APPENDIX:
The Behavior of Components of ROE

In Figure 10-2, we show that the ROEs tend to be mean reverting. In this appendix, we show the behavior of the key components of ROE—operating ROA, operating margin, operating asset turnover, spread, and net financial leverage. These ratios are computed using the same portfolio approach described in the chapter, based on the data for all U.S. industrial firms for the time period 1978–1998.

Figure A-1 Behavior of Operating ROA for U.S. Industrial Firms for 1978–1998

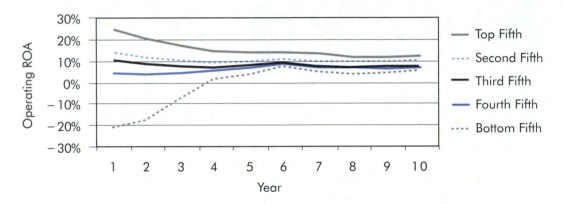

Figure A-2 Behavior of Operating Margin for U.S. Industrial Firms for 1978–1998

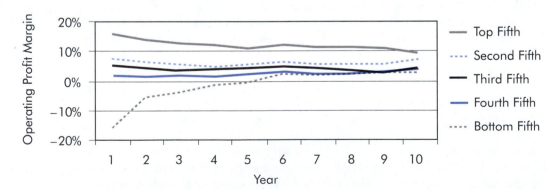

Figure A-3 Behavior of Operating Asset Turnover for U.S. Industrial Firms for 1978–1998

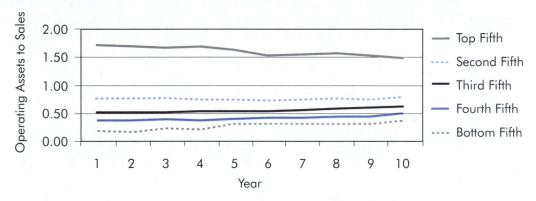

Figure A-4 Behavior of Operating Asset Turnover for U.S. Industrial Firms for 1978–1998

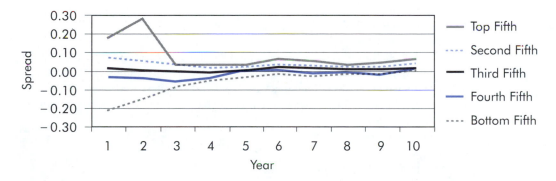

Figure A-5 Behavior of Operating Asset Turnover for U.S. Industrial Firms for 1978–1998

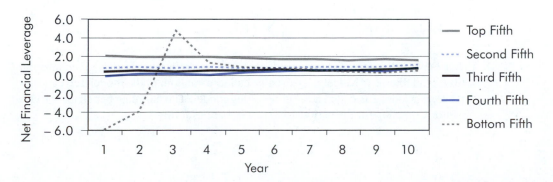

DISCUSSION QUESTIONS

1. Merck is one of the largest pharmaceutical firms in the world. In the period 1985 to 1995 Merck consistently earned higher ROEs than the pharmaceutical industry as a whole. As a pharmaceutical analyst, what factors would you consider to be important in making projections of future ROEs for Merck? In particular, what factors would lead you to expect Merck to continue to be a superior performer in its industry, and what factors would lead you to expect Merck's future performance to revert to that of the industry as a whole?

2. John Right, an analyst with Stock Pickers Inc., claims: "It is not worth my time to develop detailed forecasts of sales growth, profit margins, etcetera, to make earnings projections. I can be almost as accurate, at virtually no cost, using the random walk model to forecast earnings." What is the random walk model? Do you agree or disagree with John Right's forecast strategy? Why or why not?

3. Which of the following types of businesses do you expect to show a high degree of seasonality in quarterly earnings? Explain why.
   - a supermarket
   - a pharmaceutical company
   - a software company
   - an auto manufacturer
   - a clothing retailer

4. What factors are likely to drive a firm's outlays for new capital (such as plant, property, and equipment) and for working capital (such as receivables and inventory)? What ratios would you use to help generate forecasts of these outlays?

5. How would the following events (reported this year) affect your forecasts of a firm's future net income?
   - an asset write-down
   - a merger or acquisition
   - the sale of a major division
   - the initiation of dividend payments

6. Consider the following two earnings forecasting models:

   Model 1: $E_t(EPS_{t+1}) = EPS_t$

   Model 2: $E_t(EPS_{t+1}) = \dfrac{1}{5}\sum_{t=1}^{5} EPS_t$

   $E_t(EPS)$ is the expected forecast of earnings per share for year $t+1$, given information available at t. Model 1 is usually called a random walk model for earnings, whereas Model 2 is called a mean-reverting model. The earnings per share for Ford Motor Company for the period 1990 to 1994 are as follows:

Year	1990	1991	1992	1993	1994
EPS	$0.93	$(2.40)	$(0.73)	$2.27	$4.97

a. What would be the 1995 forecast for earnings per share for each model?

b. Actual earnings per share for Ford in 1995 were $3.58. Given this information, what would be the 1996 forecast for earnings per share for each model? Why do the two models generate quite different forecasts? Which do you think would better describe earnings per share patterns? Why?

7. Joe Fatcat, an investment banker, states: "It is not worth my while to worry about detailed long-term forecasts. Instead, I use the following approach when forecasting cash flows beyond three years. I assume that sales grow at the rate of inflation, capital expenditures are equal to depreciation, and that net profit margins and working capital to sales ratios stay constant." What pattern of return on equity is implied by these assumptions? Is this reasonable?

NOTES

1. See Patricia O'Brien, "Analysts' Forecasts as Earnings Expectations," *Journal of Accounting and Economics* (January 1988): 53–83.

2. See George Foster, "Quarterly Accounting Data: Time Series Properties and Predictive Ability Results," *The Accounting Review* (January 1977): 1–21.

3. See Robert Freeman, James Ohlson, and Stephen Penman, "Book Rate-of-Return and Prediction of Earnings Changes: An Empirical Investigation," *Journal of Accounting Research* (Autumn 1982): 639–653.

4. See Stephen H. Penman, "An Evaluation of Accounting Rate-of-Return," *Journal of Accounting, Auditing, and Finance* (Spring 1991): 233–256; Eugene Fama and Kenneth French, "Size and Book-to-Market Factors in Earnings and Returns," *Journal of Finance* (March 1995): 131–156; and Victor Bernard, "Accounting-Based Valuation Methods: Evidence on the Market-to-Book Anomaly and Implications for Financial Statements Analysis," University of Michigan working paper (1994). Ignoring the effects of accounting artifacts, ROEs should be driven in a competitive equilibrium to a level approximating the cost of equity capital.

5. A "normal" profit margin is that which, when multiplied by the turnover achievable within an industry and with a viable corporate strategy, yields a return on investment that just covers the cost of capital. However, as mentioned above, accounting artifacts can cause returns on investment to deviate from the cost of capital for long periods, even in a competitive equilibrium.

6. When the Morgan Stanley Dean Witter analyst was making the presentation in December 1998, the actual balance sheet for 1998 was not available. Therefore, in the analyst's report, cash flow projections were based on projected balance sheets for both 1998 and 1999. Since we present cash flow forecasts implied by the actual balance sheet for 1998 and the projected balance sheet for 1999, the figures in Table 10-3 differ from the cash flow forecasts in the analyst's report.

7. See Foster (1977). A somewhat more accurate model is furnished by Brown and Rozeff, but it requires interactive statistical techniques for estimation. Lawrence D. Brown and Michael Rozeff, "Univariate Time Series Models of Quarterly Accounting Earnings per Share," *Journal of Accounting Research* (Spring 1979): 179–189.

8. To estimate the model, we write in terms of realized earnings (as opposed to expected earnings) and move Q_{t-4} to the left-hand side:

$$Q_t - Q_{t-4} = \delta + \phi(Q_{t-1} - Q_{t-5}) + e_t$$

We now have a regression where $(Q_t - Q_{t-4})$ is the dependent variable, and its lagged value— $(Q_{t-1} - Q_{t-5})$—is the independent variable. Thus, to estimate the equation, prior earnings data must first be expressed in terms of year-to-year changes; the change for one quarter is then regressed against the change for the most recent quarter. The intercept provides an estimate of δ, and the slope is an estimate of ϕ. The equation is typically estimated using 24 to 40 quarters of prior earnings data.

9. See O'Brien (1988).

10. See footnote 8 for a description of the estimation process. The series for the dependent variable would be $(0.47 - 0.38)$, $(0.27 - 0.235)$, $(0.47 - 0.38)$, and so on. The series for the independent variable would be the corresponding lagged values: $(0.27 - 0.235)$, $(0.47 - 0.38)$, $(0.215 - 0.205)$, and so on.

Ina McKinsey, an active investor in the stock market, was intrigued by the following brokerage report recommendation of Maxwell Shoe Company:

> *Maxwell Shoe reported fourth quarter earnings per share on an operating basis of $0.33, slightly above our estimate of $0.32. Operating EPS for fiscal 1998 was $1.37. Including the final one-time tax benefit related to the company's secondary offering, net EPS was $0.36 for the fourth quarter and $1.44 for the year.*
>
> *The company's backlog was up 10.4%, lower than previous quarters but still very solid given the tough retail conditions. . . . We remain very positive toward Maxwell Shoe given the brand's performance in a challenging retail environment, management's execution, and its low-cost sourcing capabilities.*
>
> *We are adjusting our 1999 EPS estimate to $1.50 from $1.55 due mostly to higher tax rate and weighted average share count assumptions. Additionally, we are increasing our revenue estimates to $188 million from $182 million. The company is trading at only 8.0 times our fiscal 1999 estimate, which is a discount to the industry. Additionally, the company has no debt and has about $2.00 per share of cash on its balance sheet. We reiterate our Strong Buy rating.*
>
> S. A. Richter et al., of Tucker Anthony
& R. L. Day, December 18, 1998

This analyst report reminded McKinsey of another equally bullish evaluation of Maxwell she read a few months ago in *Barron's* (see Exhibit 1). As it was becoming increasingly difficult to find undervalued stocks in the current bull market, McKinsey decided to investigate Maxwell Shoe further.

COMPANY BACKGROUND[1]

Maxwell Shoe was originally a closeout footwear business founded in 1949. It was incorporated as Maxwell Shoe Company, Inc. in 1976. During the late 1980s, the company began focusing on designing, developing, and marketing full lines of branded women's footwear. The company went public with a listing on the NASD in 1994.

....

Professor Krishna G. Palepu prepared this case as the basis for class discussion rather than to illustrate either effective or ineffective handling of an administrative situation. Copyright © 1999 by the President and Fellows of Harvard College. Harvard Business School case 9-100-038.

1. Material in this section is drawn from Maxwell's 1998 10-K report.

In 1998 the company offered casual and dress footwear for women in the moderately priced market segment ($20 to $90 price range) under Mootsies Tootsies, Sam & Libby, and Jones New York brand names. The company also designed and developed private label footwear for selected retailers under their own brand name, or under the names of J.G. Hook or Dockers. Substantially all of the company's products were manufactured overseas by independent factories in low-cost locations such as China.

Maxwell sold its footwear primarily to department stores, specialty stores, catalog retailers, and cable television shopping channels. In April 1997 the company entered into a joint venture with Butler Group LLC, a wholly owned subsidiary of General Electric Capital Corporation, to operate approximately 130 retail Sam & Libby and Jones New York women's footwear stores through a company called SLJ Retail. Maxwell owned 49 percent of SLJ Retail, the rest being owned by GE Capital.

Since 1987, when Maxwell first focused on its branded footwear strategy, it has reported sales and profit increases every year. The company attributed this financial success to the following strengths: established brand recognition by consumers, strong manufacturing relationships with overseas manufacturers and buying agents, emphasis on high volume, moderately priced footwear, and comprehensive customer relationships enhanced through electronic data interchange (EDI) systems.

The company expected to build on this competitive advantage, and grow in future by enhancing its current brands, by increasing its private label business, and by acquiring new brands as consolidation in the fragmented footwear industry continued.

FINANCIAL PERFORMANCE

Maxwell reported for the year ending October 21, 1998, $165.6 million in revenues and 13.3 million in profits (see Exhibit 2 for the company's balance sheet, income statement, and cash flow statement for the year). The company's revenues and profits grew at average rates of 16 percent and 24 percent during the previous three years. The corresponding five-year sales and profit growth rates for the footwear industry as a whole were 17 percent and 9 percent.

Until the middle of July 1998, Maxwell's financial performance was mirrored by the company's stock price performance (see Exhibit 3). The company's share price increased from about $5 in 1995 to a peak of $19 by July 1998. However, in the subsequent months, the company's share price began to drop, ending at $11 by December 1998. Analysts attributed this share price decline to overall concerns with the footwear industry, which was expected to grow at a relatively modest rate in future because of cheap imports from Asia and relatively flat consumption patterns. Analysts, however, expected Maxwell to do better than the industry because of its focus on the moderate price segment and its heavy reliance on low-cost overseas manufacturing. For example, Tucker Anthony's analysts stated:

Investors' concerns rest with the challenging footwear industry, tough retail environment and overall inventory concerns. While we believe the footwear sector will continue to underperform as a group, we believe Maxwell's shares currently discount investor's concerns. If the company continues to perform as we estimate, we believe the risk/reward ratio is very attractive at the current levels.[2]

Ina McKinsey was wondering how she should go about evaluating the analysts' view that Maxwell is an undervalued stock.

QUESTIONS

1. What set of assumptions regarding Maxwell's future growth rate, return on equity, and cost of equity are consistent with its observed stock price in December 1998? Which of these assumptions are you most comfortable with and least comfortable with?
2. Do you agree with *Barron's* assessment that Maxwell's stock was undervalued in December 1998?
3. What is your estimate of the intrinsic value of Maxwell's stock?

Maxwell Shoe Company

EXHIBIT 1
Barron's Article on Maxwell Shoe Company

BEST FOOT FORWARD

By Rhonda Brammer
Barron's, September 28, 1998

As somebody or other once said, Trouble is only opportunity in work clothes. Which could be a motto of our pal Scott Black, who runs Delphi Management up in Boston. A shrewd contrarian and first-rate value manager of the old school (yes, book and p/e do matter), Scott talks a mile a minute, can recite vital statistics on over 100 names in his portfolio (without crib sheets) and, here's the amazing part, he actually gets the numbers right.

These days, many a small-cap manager is pretty glum—and no wonder, with the Russell 2000 off 15% for the year, compared with an 8% gain for the S&P 500. But, we're happy to report, when we checked in with Scott, he was positively upbeat.

Sure, small stocks have been "annihilated," he concedes. Worse still, in his eyes at least, Delphi is down 4% for the year (he hates to lose money). But the definite bright spot: "We're buying companies—and I am talking about decent companies—at 10 and 11 times earnings."

Which is how we got to talking about Maxwell Shoe.

Founded half a century ago, when Maxwell Blum started a closeout footwear business, Maxwell Shoe today boasts sales of over $160 million. The company designs and markets casual and dress shoes for women—and to a lesser extent, kids—under several brand names, carefully targeting each brand to a specific segment of the market.

Shoes in the Mootsies Tootsies line, for example, which chips in almost half of revenue, are designed to appeal to women 18 to 34. They sell for $25 to $40 a pair and might be found at Kohl's or Mercantile Stores. The slightly pricier Sam & Libby line—about 10% of sales—are targeted at women 21 to 35, sell for $35–$50 a pair, and might wind up at Rich's or Robinson-May. The relatively upscale Jones New York brand—some 25% of revenue—are designed for women over 30. A pair fetches $65 to $90 and you might see them in the window at Macy's or Lord & Taylor.

Most of Maxwell's shoes are made in China, though some of the Jones New York Line are manufactured in Spain and Italy. To leverage its offshore experience, Maxwell makes private label shoes for others, which account for roughly the balance of sales.

Now there's no denying, footwear is a slow-growing, fiercely competitive business— one that isn't likely to prosper in a sluggish economy. Global players, like Nike and Reebok, moreover, have already been hard hit by weakness in Asia.

But there's no reason, Black argues, that shares of Maxwell Shoe, which recently traded over 23, should have been hammered to 12.

"People group them all together," he shrugs. "But this is no Nike where, at the margin, they were dependent on Japan and the Far East for their growth."

Indeed, Maxwell's results sparkle.

In fiscal '97, ending October, sales grew by 28% to 134 million, while net rose over 50%, to $9 million, or $1.09 a share. In the first nine months, ended July, sales advanced 27%, while net climbed 44%, to $9.8 million, or $1.08 a share. For all of fiscal '98, Black's looking for $1.35–$1.40 a share.

Book value is over $8 and the company is debt-free—something Black likes. "If the economy turns south," he quips, "at least they live to fight another day."

Worth noting, too—at least for those who remember Maxwell from years back—is that the Class B voting stock, controlled by the Blum family, was eliminated via a stock offering this spring.

Looking ahead to fiscal 1999 (and assuming a 33% tax rate), Black sees Maxwell earning $1.65 a share. Which works out to P/E of 7.3.

"That's one third of the market multiple," he stresses, "and for a company with a legitimate 20% growth rate."

Of course, shoe companies rarely command sexy multiples. But even putting a humble P/E of 12 on Black's estimate translates into a stock price of $20.

Maxwell Shoe Company

EXHIBIT 2
Maxwell's Abridged Financial Statements

MAXWELL SHOE COMPANY, INC.—BALANCE SHEET ($ millions)

	31-Oct-98	31-Oct-97	31-Oct-96
Assets			
Cash and cash equivalents	18.7	3.1	10.4
Accounts receivable, net	35.7	28.6	16.9
Inventory	22.9	20.1	12.2
Prepaid expenses	1.6	0.3	0.1
Deferred income taxes	1.1	1.5	0.8
Total Current Assets	**80.0**	**53.6**	**40.4**
Property, plant and equipment	8.7	3.0	2.5
Accumulated depreciation and amortization	−2.5	−1.7	−1.5
Property plant and equipment, net	6.2	1.3	1.0
Trademarks and other assets, net	4.8	5.1	5.5
Total Assets	**91.0**	**60.1**	**46.9**
Liabilities			
Accounts payable	3.8	2.2	0.9
Current portion of capital leases	0.1	0.1	0.1
Accrued expenses and other current liabilities	6.2	6.9	3.8
Total Current Liabilities	**10.2**	**9.2**	**4.8**
Capitalized lease obligations	0.2	0.3	0.5
Deferred taxes	1.3	0.0	0.0
Total Liabilities	**11.7**	**9.5**	**5.3**
Stockholders' Equity			
Common stock	0.1	0.1	0.1
Additional paid-in capital	43.0	27.3	27.3
Retained earnings	36.5	23.2	14.2
Deferred compensation	−0.3	0.0	0.0
Total Shareholders' Equity	**79.3**	**50.6**	**41.6**
Total Liabilities and Shareholders' Equity	**91.0**	**60.1**	**46.9**
Shares outstanding	8.8	2.5	2.5

Note: some numbers may not add up because of rounding errors.

Maxwell Shoe Company

MAXWELL SHOE COMPANY, INC.—ANNUAL INCOME STATEMENT ($ millions)

Handwritten notes in right margin:
5 yr sales growth - Industry 17%
5-yr profit growth - Industry - 9%

	31-Oct-98	31-Oct-97	31-Oct-96
Total sales	165.9 *(16%)*	134.2 *(29%)*	104.3
Cost of goods sold	121.0	98.2	79.9
Gross profit	44.9	36.0	24.4
Selling expense	10.2	7.9	5.6
General and administrative expense	14.9	13.1	9.8
Total operating expenses	25.1	21.0	15.4
Interest expense	–0.0	–0.1	–0.0
Other income-net	0.2	–0.3	0.6
Pretax income	20.0	14.6	9.6
Income taxes	6.6	5.5	3.6
Net income	13.4	9.1	6.0
Basic EPS	1.61	1.19	0.78
Shares to calculate basic EPS (millions)	8.2	7.6	7.6
Diluted EPS	1.44	1.06	0.72
Shares used to calculate diluted EPS (millions)	9.2	8.5	8.3

Note: some numbers may not add up because of rounding errors.

MAXWELL SHOE COMPWANY, INC.—STATEMENT OF CASH FLOWS ($ millions)

	31-Oct-98	31-Oct-97	31-Oct-96
Net income	13.3	9.0	5.9
Depreciation	1.2	0.7	0.2
Deferred taxes	1.9	–0.7	0.2
Other noncash items	0.1	0.1	0.1
Changes in operating current assets and liabilities	–9.7	–15.6	3.0
Cash from operations	6.8	–6.5	9.4
Capital expenditures	–5.7	–0.7	–5.6
Cash from investing	–5.7	–0.7	–5.6
Purchase or sale of stock	14.5	0.0	0.0
Payment of capital lease obligations	–0.1	–0.1	–0.2
Cash from financing	14.4	–0.1	–0.2
Net change in cash	15.5	–7.3	3.6
Cash interest paid	0.0	0.1	0.0
Cash taxes paid	4.8	6.8	2.4

Vertical text in right margin: Maxwell Shoe Company

Maxwell Shoe Company

EXHIBIT 3
Maxwell Shoe Company, Inc.—Monthly Stock Price History

Month	Month End Closing Price
December 1998	10.938
November 1998	11.875
October 1998	11.750
September 1998	11.875
August 1998	13.125
July 1998	19.375
June 1998	19.875
May 1998	19.625
April 1998	17.750
March 1998	15.813
February 1998	15.750
January 1998	14.125
December 1997	10.750
November 1997	13.625
October 1997	13.125
September 1997	15.000
August 1997	11.000
July 1997	10.500
June 1997	12.250
May 1997	9.250
April 1997	8.250
March 1997	7.875
February 1997	7.625
January 1997	7.375
December 1996	6.625
November 1996	7.250
October 1996	6.625
September 1996	6.313
August 1996	6.125
July 1996	6.000
June 1996	7.750
May 1996	6.500
April 1996	5.000
March 1996	5.000
February 1996	5.000
January 1996	5.250

Maxwell's equity beta was estimated to be 0.81.
The yield on 30-year treasury bonds in December 1998 was approximately 5%.
Source: One Source Information Services, Inc.

11
chapter

Prospective Analysis: Valuation Theory and Concepts

The previous chapter introduced forecasting, the first stage of prospective analysis. In this and the following chapter we describe the second and final stage of prospective analysis, valuation. This chapter focuses on valuation theory and concepts, and the following chapter discusses implementation issues.

Valuation is the process of converting a forecast into an estimate of the value of the firm or some component of the firm. At some level, nearly every business decision involves valuation (at least implicitly). Within the firm, capital budgeting involves consideration of how a particular project will affect firm value. Strategic planning focuses on how value is influenced by larger sets of actions. Outside the firm, security analysts conduct valuation to support their buy/sell decisions, and potential acquirers (often with the assistance of their investment bankers) estimate the value of target firms and the synergies they might offer. Valuation is necessary to price an initial public offering and to inform parties to sales, estate settlements, and divisions of property involving ongoing business concerns. Even credit analysts, who typically do not explicitly estimate firm value, must at least implicitly consider the value of the firm's equity "cushion" if they are to maintain a complete view of the risk associated with lending activity.

In practice, a wide variety of valuation approaches are employed. For example, in evaluating the fairness of a takeover bid, investment bankers commonly use five to ten different methods of valuation. Among the available methods are the following:

- *Discounted dividends.* This approach expresses the value of the firm's equity as the present value of forecasted future dividends.
- *Discounted abnormal earnings.* Under this approach the value of the firm's equity is expressed as the sum of its book value and discounted forecasts of "abnormal" earnings.
- *Valuation based on price multiples.* Under this approach a current measure of performance or single forecast of performance is converted into a value through application of some price multiple for other presumably comparable firms. For example, firm value can be estimated by applying a price-to-earnings ratio to a forecast of the firm's earnings for the coming year. Other commonly used multiples include price-to-book ratios and price-to-sales ratios.
- *Discounted cash flow (DCF) analysis.* This approach involves the production of detailed, multiple-year forecasts of cash flows. The forecasts are then discounted at the firm's estimated cost of capital to arrive at an estimated present value.

All of the above approaches can be structured in two ways. The first is to directly value the equity of the firm, since this is usually the variable the analyst is directly interested in estimating. The second is to value the assets of the firm, that is, the claims of equity and net debt, and to then deduct the value of net debt to arrive at the final equity estimate. Theoretically, both approaches should generate the same values. However, as we will see in the following chapter, there are implementation issues in reconciling the approaches. In this chapter we illustrate valuation using an all-equity firm to simplify the discussion. However, where appropriate we discuss the theoretical issues in valuing the firm's assets.

From a theoretical perspective, shareholder value is the present value of future dividend payoffs. This definition can be implemented by forecasting and discounting future dividends directly. However, it can also be framed by recasting dividends in terms of earnings and book values, or in terms of free cash flows to shareholders. These methods are developed throughout the chapter, and their pros and cons discussed.

Valuation using multiples is also discussed. Multiples are a popular method of valuation because, unlike the discounted dividend, discounted abnormal earnings, and discounted cash flow methods, they do not require analysts to make multiyear forecasts. However, the identification of comparable firms is a serious challenge in implementing the multiple approach. The chapter discusses how the discounted abnormal earnings valuation approach can be recast to generate firm-specific estimates of two popular multiples, value-to-book and value-earnings ratios. Value-to book multiples are shown to be a function of future abnormal ROEs, book value growth, and the firm's cost of equity. Value-earnings multiples are driven by the same factors and also the current ROE.

DEFINING VALUE FOR SHAREHOLDERS

How should shareholders think about the value of their equity claims on a firm? Finance theory holds that the value of any financial claim is simply the present value of the cash payoffs that its claim holders receive. Since shareholders receive cash payoffs from a company in the form of dividends, the value of their equity is the present value of future dividends (including any liquidating dividend).

Equity value   =   PV of expected future dividends

If we denote the expected future dividend for a given year as DIV and r_e as the cost of equity capital (the relevant discount rate), the stock value is as follows:

$$\text{Equity value} \;=\; \frac{DIV_1}{(1 + r_e)} \;+\; \frac{DIV_2}{(1 + r_e)^2} \;+\; \frac{DIV_3}{(1 + r_e)^3} \;+\; \dots$$

Notice that the valuation formula views a firm as having an indefinite life. Of course, in reality firms go bankrupt and get taken over. In these situations, shareholders effectively receive a terminating dividend on their stock.

If a firm had a constant dividend growth rate (g^d) indefinitely, its value would simplify to the following formula:

$$\text{Equity value} \quad = \quad \frac{DIV_1}{r_e - g^d}$$

To better understand how the discounted dividend approach works, consider the following example. At the beginning of year 0 Down Under Company raises $60 million of equity and uses the proceeds to buy a fixed asset. Operating profits before depreciation (all received in cash) and dividends for the company are expected to be $40 million in year 1, $50 million in year 2, and $60 million in year 3, at which point the company terminates. The firm pays no taxes. If the cost of equity capital for this firm is 10%, the value of the firm's equity is computed as follows:

Year	Dividend	PV Factor	PV of Dividend
1	$40m	0.9091	$36.4m
2	50	0.8264	41.3
3	60	0.7513	45.1
Equity value			$122.8m

The above valuation formula is called the dividend discount model. It forms the basis for most of the popular theoretical approaches for stock valuation. The remainder of the chapter discusses how this model can be recast to generate the discounted abnormal earnings and discounted cash flow models of value.

THE DISCOUNTED ABNORMAL EARNINGS VALUATION METHOD

As discussed in Chapter 3, there is a link between dividends and earnings. If all equity effects (other than capital transactions) flow through the income statement,[1] the expected book value of equity for existing shareholders at the end of year one (BVE_1) is simply the book value at the beginning of the year (BVE_0) plus expected net income (NI_1) less expected dividends (DIV_1).[2] This relation can be rewritten as follows:

$$DIV_1 \quad = \quad NI_1 + BVE_0 - BVE_1$$

By substituting this identity for dividends into the dividend discount formula and rearranging the terms, stock value can be rewritten as follows[3]:

$$\text{Equity value} \quad = \quad \text{Book value of equity} + \text{PV of expected future abnormal earnings}$$

Abnormal earnings are net income adjusted for a capital charge computed as the discount rate multiplied by the beginning book value of equity. Abnormal earnings therefore make an adjustment to reflect the fact that accountants do not recognize any opportunity cost for equity funds used. Thus, the discounted abnormal earnings valuation formula is:

$$\text{Equity value} = BVE_0 + \frac{NI_1 - r_e \cdot BVE_0}{(1 + r_e)} + \frac{NI_2 - r_e \cdot BVE_1}{(1 + r_e)^2} + \frac{NI_3 - r_e \cdot BVE_2}{(1 + r_e)^3} + \ldots$$

As noted earlier, equity values can also be estimated by valuing the firm's assets and then deducting its net debt. Under the earnings-based approach, this implies that the value of the assets is:

$$\text{Asset value} = BVA_0 + \frac{NOPAT_1 - WACC \cdot BVA_0}{(1 + WACC)} + \frac{NOPAT_2 - WACC \cdot BVA_1}{(1 + WACC)^2} + \ldots$$

BVA is the book value of the firm's assets, NOPAT is net operating profit (before interest) after tax, and WACC is the firm's weighted-average cost of debt and equity. From this asset value the analyst can deduct the market value of net debt to generate an estimate of the value of equity.

The earnings-based formulation has intuitive appeal. It implies that if a firm can earn only a normal rate of return on its book value, then investors should be willing to pay no more than book value for the stock. Investors should pay more or less than book value if earnings are above or below this normal level. Thus, the deviation of a firm's market value from book value depends on its ability to generate "abnormal earnings." The formulation also implies that a firm's stock value reflects the cost of its existing net assets (that is, its book equity) plus the net present value of future growth options (represented by cumulative abnormal earnings).

Key Analysis Questions

Valuation of equity (debt plus equity) under the discounted abnormal earnings method requires the analyst to answer the following questions:

- What are expected future net income (NOPAT) and book values of equity (assets) over a finite forecast horizon (usually 5 to 10 years)?
- What are expected future abnormal earnings (NOPAT), after deducting a capital charge from forecasts of net income (NOPAT)? The capital charge is the firm's cost of equity (WACC) multiplied by beginning book equity (assets).
- What is expected future abnormal net income (NOPAT) beyond the final year of the forecast horizon (called the "terminal year") based on some simplifying assumption?
- What is the present value of abnormal earnings (NOPAT) discounted at the cost of equity capital (WACC)?

> • What is the estimated value of equity, computed by adding the current book value of equity (assets) to the cumulated present value of future abnormal earnings (NOPAT)? Are there nonoperating assets held by the firm that have been ignored in the previous abnormal earnings (NOPAT) forecasts (e.g., marketable securities or real estate held for sale)? If so, their values should be included in the equity estimate.

To illustrate the earnings-based valuation approach, let's return to the Down Under Company example. Since the company is an all-equity firm, the value of the firm's equity and its assets (debt plus equity) are the same. If the company depreciates its fixed assets using the straight-line method, its beginning book equity, earnings, abnormal earnings, and valuation will be as follows:

Year	Beginning Book Value	Earnings	Abnormal Earnings	PV Factor	PV of Abnormal Earnings
1	$60m	$20m	$14m	0.9091	$12.7m
2	40	30	26	0.8264	21.5
3	20	40	38	0.7513	28.6
Cumulative PV of abnormal earnings					62.8
+ Beginning book value					60.0
= Equity value					$122.8m

This stock valuation of $122.8 million is identical to the value estimated when the expected future dividends are discounted directly.

Recent research shows that abnormal earnings estimates of value outperform traditional multiples, such as price-earnings ratios, price-to-book ratios, and dividend yields, for predicting future stock movements.[4] Firms with high abnormal earnings model estimates of value relative to current price show positive abnormal future stock returns, whereas firms with low estimated value-to-price ratios have negative abnormal stock performance.

Accounting Methods and Discounted Abnormal Earnings

It may seem odd that firm value can be expressed as a function of accounting numbers. After all, accounting methods per se should have no influence on firm value (except as those choices influence the analyst's view of future real performance). Yet the valuation approach used here is based on numbers—earnings and book value—that vary with accounting method choices. How, then, can the valuation approach deliver correct estimates?

It turns out that because accounting choices affect *both* earnings *and* book value, and because of the self-correcting nature of double-entry bookkeeping (all "distortions" of accounting must ultimately reverse), estimated values based on the discounted abnormal earnings method will not be affected by accounting choices per se. For example, assume that Down Under Company's managers choose to be conservative and expense some unusual costs that could have been capitalized as inventory at year 1, causing earnings and ending book value to be lower by $10 million. This inventory is then sold in year 2. For the time being, let's say the accounting choice has no influence on the analyst's view of the firm's real performance.

Managers' choice reduces abnormal earnings in year 1 and book value at the beginning of year 2 by $10 million. However, future earnings will be higher, for two reasons. First, future earnings will be higher (by $10 million) when the inventory is sold in year 2 at a lower cost of sales. Second, the benchmark for normal earnings (based on book value of equity) will be lower by $10 million. The $10 million decline in abnormal earnings in year 1 is perfectly offset (on a present value basis) by the $11 million higher abnormal earnings in year 2. As a result, the value of Down Under Company under conservative reporting is identical to the value under the earlier accounting method ($122.8 million).

Year	Beginning Book Value	Earnings	Abnormal Earnings	PV Factor	PV of Abnormal Earnings
1	$60m	$10m	$ 4m	0.9091	$ 3.6m
2	30	40	37	0.8264	30.6
3	20	40	38	0.7513	28.6
Cumulative PV of abnormal earnings					62.8
+ Beginning book value					60.0
= Equity value					$122.8m

Consequently, provided the analyst is aware of biases in accounting data as a result of the use of aggressive or conservative accounting choices by management, abnormal earnings-based valuations are unaffected by the variation in accounting decisions. This implies that strategic and accounting analyses are critical precursors to abnormal earnings valuation. The strategic and accounting analysis tools help the analyst to identify whether abnormal earnings arise from sustainable competitive advantage or from unsustainable accounting manipulations. For example, consider the implications of failing to understand the reasons for a decline in earnings from a change in inventory policy for Down Under Company. If the analyst mistakenly interpreted the decline as indicating that the firm was having difficulty moving its inventory, rather than that it had used conservative accounting, she might reduce expectations of future earnings. The estimated value of the firm would then be lower than that reported in our example.

VALUATION USING PRICE MULTIPLES

Valuations based on price multiples are widely used by analysts. The primary reason for their popularity is their simplicity. Unlike the discounted abnormal earnings, discounted dividend, and discounted cash flow methods, they do not require detailed multiple-year forecasts about a variety of parameters, including growth, profitability, and cost of capital.

Valuation using multiples involves the following steps:

Step 1: Select a measure of performance or value (e.g., earnings, sales, cash flows, book equity, book assets) as the basis for multiple calculations.

Step 2: Estimate price multiples for comparable firms using the measure of performance or value.

Step 3: Apply the comparable firm multiple to the performance or value measure of the firm being analyzed.

Under this approach, the analyst relies on the market to undertake the difficult task of considering the short- and long-term prospects for growth and profitability and their implications for the values of the "comparable" firms. Then the analyst *assumes* that the pricing of those other firms is applicable to the firm at hand.

On the surface, using multiples seems straightforward. Unfortunately, in practice it is not as simple as it would appear. Identification of "comparable" firms is often quite difficult. There are also some choices to be made concerning how multiples will be calculated. Finally, explaining why multiples vary across firms, and how applicable another firm's multiple is to the one at hand, requires a sound understanding of the determinants of each multiple.

Selecting Comparable Firms

Ideally, price multiples used in a comparable firm analysis are those for firms with similar operating and financial characteristics. Firms within the same industry are the most obvious candidates. However, even within narrowly defined industries, it is often difficult to find multiples for similar firms. Many firms are in multiple industries, making it difficult to identify representative benchmarks. In addition, firms within the same industry frequently have different strategies, growth opportunities, and profitability, creating comparability problems.

One way of dealing with these issues is to average across *all* firms in the industry. The analyst implicitly hopes that the various sources of noncomparability "cancel out," so that the firm being valued is comparable to a "typical" industry member. Another approach is to focus on only those firms within the industry that are most similar.

For example, consider using multiples to value Nordstrom. Dow Jones Interactive classifies the company in the Retail: Apparel industry. On July 16, 1999, Dow Jones reported that the industry price-earnings ratio was 24.0 and the average price-to-book ratio was 6.36 percent. In contrast, Nordstrom had a price-earnings ratio of 27.3 and a price-to-book ratio of 4.49 percent.

However, Dow Jones reported that Nordstrom's competitors could be narrowed to the following firms: Ann Taylor, Brown Shoe, Dayton Hudson, Donna Karan, Dillards, Federated Department Stores, The Gap, Lands' End, The Limited, Mens Wearhouse, Neiman Marcus, May Department Stores, JC Penney, Saks, Spiegel, and Talbots. These include other firms that Dow Jones classified in the Retail: Apparel industry and several firms in the Retail: Broadline segment. The average price-earnings ratio for these direct competitors was 55.9 and the average price-to-book ratio was 3.81. Clearly, the market expects that Nordstrom's future performance will differ somewhat from that of the Retail: Apparel industry as a whole, and from that of its direct competitors.

Multiples for Firms with Poor Performance

Price multiples can be affected when the denominator variable is performing poorly. This is especially common when the denominator is a flow measure, such as earnings or cash flows. For example, Donna Karan, one of Nordstrom's competitors, had earnings per share of only 0.01 in 1998 and a price-earnings ratio of 434.4.

What are analysts' options for handling the problems for multiples created by transitory shocks to the denominator? One option is to simply exclude firms with large transitory effects from the set of comparable firms. If Donna Karan is excluded from Nordstrom's peer set, the average benchmark price-earnings ratio declines from 55.9 to 30.7. Alternatively, if the poor performance is due to a transitory shock, such as a write-off or special item, the transitory effect can be excluded from computation of the multiple. For Donna Karan this is not possible, since the temporary poor performance is not attributable to any single event. Finally, the analyst can use a denominator that is a forecast of future performance rather than a past measure. Multiples based on forecasts are termed *leading* multiples, whereas those based on historical data are called *trailing* multiples. Leading multiples are less likely to include one-time gains and losses in the denominator, simply because such items are difficult to anticipate. For Donna Karan, *First Call* reported that analysts expected 1999 earnings to be $0.27, implying a leading price-earnings multiple of only 16.1.

Adjusting Multiples for Leverage

Price multiples should be calculated in a way that preserves consistency between the numerator and denominator. Consistency is an issue for those ratios where the denominator reflects performance *before* servicing debt. Examples include the price-to-sales multiple and any multiple of operating earnings or operating cash flows. When calculating these multiples, the numerator should include not just the market value of equity, but the value of debt as well.

DETERMINANTS OF VALUE-TO-BOOK
AND VALUE-EARNINGS MULTIPLES

Even across relatively closely related firms, price multiples can vary considerably. Careful analysis of this variation requires consideration of factors that might explain why one firm's multiples should be higher than those of benchmark firms. We therefore return to the abnormal earnings valuation method and show how it provides insights into differences in value-to-book and value-to-earnings multiples across firms

If the abnormal earnings formula is scaled by book value, the left-hand side becomes the equity value-to-book ratio, as opposed to the equity value itself. The right-hand side variables are now earnings deflated by book value, or our old friend return on equity (*ROE*), discussed in Chapter 9.[5] The valuation formula becomes:

$$\text{Equity value-to-book ratio} = 1 + \frac{ROE_1 - r_e}{(1 + r_e)} + \frac{(ROE_2 - r_e)(1 + gbve_1)}{(1 + r_e)^2}$$

$$+ \frac{(ROE_3 - r_e)(1 + gbve_1)(1 + gbve_2)}{(1 + r_e)^3} + \cdots$$

where $gbve_t$ = growth in book value (*BVE*) from year t-1 to year t or

$$\frac{BVE_t - BVE_{t-1}}{BVE_{t-1}}$$

The formulation implies that a firm's equity value-to-book ratio is a function of three factors: its future abnormal ROEs, its growth in book equity, and its cost of equity capital. Abnormal ROE is defined as ROE less the cost of equity capital ($ROE - r_e$). Firms with positive abnormal ROE are able to invest their net assets to create value for shareholders, and have price-to-book ratios greater than one. Firms that are unable to generate returns greater than the cost of capital have ratios below one.

The magnitude of a firm's value-to-book multiple also depends on the amount of growth in book value. Firms can grow their equity base by issuing new equity or by re-investing profits. If this new equity is invested in positive valued projects for shareholders, that is projects with ROEs that exceed the cost of capital, the firm will boost its equity value-to-book multiple. Of course, for firms with ROEs that are less than the cost of capital, equity growth further lowers the multiple.

The valuation task can now be framed in terms of two key questions about the firm's "value drivers":

- How much greater (or smaller) than normal will the firm's ROE be?
- How quickly will the firm's investment base (book value) grow?

If desired, the equation can be rewritten so that future ROEs are expressed as the product of their components: profit margins, sales turnover, and leverage. Thus, the approach permits us to build directly on projections of the same accounting numbers utilized in financial analysis (see Chapter 9) without the need to convert projections of those numbers into cash flows. Yet in the end, the estimate of value should be the same as that from the dividend discount model.[6]

It is also possible to structure the multiple valuation as the debt plus equity value-to-book assets ratio by scaling the abnormal NOPAT formula by book value of net operating assets. The valuation formula then becomes:

$$\text{Debt plus equity value-to-book ratio} = 1 + \frac{ROA_1 - WACC}{(1 + WACC)} + \frac{(ROA_2 - WACC)(1 + gbva)}{(1 + WACC)^2}$$

$$+ \frac{(ROA_3 - WACC)(1 + gbva_1)(1 + gbva_2)}{(1 + WACC)^3} + \dots$$

where ROA = operating return on assets = NOPAT/(Operating working capital + Net long-term assets)

$WACC$ = weighted average cost of debt and equity

$gbva_n$ = growth in book value of assets (BVA) from year t-1 to year t or

$$\frac{BVA_t - BVA_{t-1}}{BVA_{t-1}}$$

The value of a firm's debt and equity to net operating assets multiple therefore depends on its ability to generate asset returns that exceed its WACC, and its ability to grow its asset base. The value of equity under this approach is then the estimated multiple times the current book value of assets less the market value of debt.

Returning to the Down Under Company example, the implied equity value-to-book multiple can be estimated as follows:

	Year 1	Year 2	Year 3
Beginning book value	$60m	$40m	$20m
Earnings	$20m	$30m	$40m
ROE	33%	75%	200%
– Cost of capital	10%	10%	10%
= Abnormal ROE	23%	65%	190%
× (1+ cumulative book value growth)	1.00	0.67	0.33
= Abnormal ROE scaled by book value growth	23%	43%	63%
× PV factor	0.9091	0.8264	0.7513
= PV of abnormal ROE scaled by book value growth	21.2%	35.8%	47.6%
Cumulative PV of abnormal ROE scaled by book value growth	104.6%		
+ 1.00	100.0		
= Equity value-to-book multiple	204.6%		

The equity value-to-book multiple for Down Under is therefore 204.6 percent, and the implied stock value is $122.8 ($60 · 2.046), once again identical to the dividend discount model value. Recall that Down Under is an all-equity firm, so that the abnormal ROE and abnormal ROA structures for valuing the firm are the same.

The equity value-to-book formulation can also be used to construct the equity value-earnings multiple as follows:

$$\text{Equity value-to-earnings multiple} = \text{Equity value-to-book multiple} \times \frac{\text{Book value of equity}}{\text{Earnings}}$$

$$= \frac{\text{Equity value-to-book multiple}}{\text{ROE}}$$

In other words, the same factors that drive a firm's equity value-to-book multiple also explain its equity value-earnings multiple. The key difference between the two multiples is that the value-earnings multiple is affected by the firm's current level of ROE performance, whereas the value-to-book multiple is not. Firms with low current ROEs therefore have very high value-earnings multiples and vice versa. If a firm has a zero or negative ROE, its PE multiple is not defined. Value-earnings multiples are therefore more volatile than value-to-book multiples.

The following data for a subset of firms in the Retail: Apparel industry illustrate the relation between ROE, equity growth, the price-to-book ratio, and the price-earnings ratio:

Company	ROE	Book Value Growth	Price-to-Book Ratio	Price-Earnings Ratio
The Gap	48.5%	–1%	2327%	50.1
The Limited	88.9%	9%	346%	5.5
Saks	2.1%	83%	262%	74.8
Donna Karan	0.2%	0%	135%	434.4

Both the price-to-book and price-earnings ratios are high for The Gap. Investors therefore expect that in the future The Gap will generate even higher ROEs than its current high level (48 percent). In contrast, the Limited has a high price-to-book ratio (346 percent) but a low price-earnings ratio. This indicates that investors expect that The Limited will continue to generate positive abnormal ROEs, but that the current level of ROE (89 percent) is not sustainable. Saks has a price-to-book ratio of 262 percent, indicating that investors expect it to earn abnormal ROEs. However, it has a high price-earnings multiple (75), suggesting that the current low ROE (2 percent) is considered temporary. Finally, Donna Karan has a relatively low price-to-book ratio (135 percent) but a high price-earnings multiple. Investors apparently do not expect Donna Karan's poor performance to persist, but they also do not believe that the company will be able to sustain high abnormal ROEs.

Key Analysis Questions

To value a firm using multiples, an analyst has to assess the quality of the variable used as the multiple basis, and to determine the appropriate peer firms to include in the benchmark multiple. Analysts are therefore likely to be interested in answering the following questions:

- What is the expected future growth in the variable to be used as the basis for the multiple? For example, if the variable is earnings, has the firm made conservative or aggressive accounting choices that are likely to unwind in the coming years? If the multiple is book value, what is the sustainability of the firm's growth and ROE? What is the dynamics of the firm's industry and product market? Is it a market leader in a high growth industry, or is it in a mature industry with fewer growth prospects? How is the firm's future performance likely to be affected by competition or potential entry in the industry?
- Who are the most suitable peer companies to include in the benchmark multiple computation? Have these firms had comparable growth (earnings or book values), profitability, and quality of earnings as the firm being analyzed? Do they have the same risk characteristics?

SHORTCUT FORMS OF EARNINGS-BASED VALUATION

The discounted abnormal earnings valuation formula can be simplified by making assumptions about the relation between a firm's current and future abnormal earnings. Similarly, the equity value-to-book formula can be simplified by making assumptions about long-term ROEs and growth.

1. Relation Between Current and Future Abnormal Earnings

Several assumptions about the relation between current and future net income are popular for simplifying the abnormal earnings model. First, abnormal earnings are assumed to follow a random walk. The random walk model for abnormal earnings implies that an analyst's best guess about future expected abnormal earnings are current abnormal earnings. The model assumes that past shocks to abnormal earnings persist forever, but that future shocks are random or unpredictable. The random walk model can be written as follows:

$$\text{Forecasted } AE_1 \quad = \quad AE_0$$

Forecasted AE_1 is the forecast of next year's abnormal earnings and AE_0 is current period abnormal earnings. Under the model, forecasted abnormal earnings for two years ahead are simply abnormal earnings in year one, or once again current abnormal earnings. In other words, the best guess of abnormal earnings in any future year is just current abnormal earnings.[7]

How does the above assumption about future abnormal earnings simplify the discounted abnormal earnings valuation model? If abnormal earnings follow a random walk, all future forecasts of abnormal earnings are simply current abnormal earnings. It is then possible to rewrite value as follows:

$$\text{Stock value} \;=\; BVE_0 \;+\; \frac{AE_0}{r_e}$$

The stock value is the book value of equity at the end of the year, plus current abnormal earnings divided by the cost of capital.

Of course, in reality shocks to abnormal earnings are unlikely to persist forever. Firms that have positive shocks are likely to attract competitors that will reduce opportunities for future abnormal performance. Firms with negative abnormal earnings shocks are likely to fail or to be acquired by other firms that can manage their resources more effectively. The persistence of abnormal performance will therefore depend on strategic factors, such as barriers to entry and switching costs, discussed in Chapter 2. To reflect this, analysts frequently assume that current shocks to abnormal earnings decay over time. Under this assumption, abnormal earnings are said to follow an autoregressive model. Forecasted abnormal earnings are then:

$$\text{Forecasted } AE_1 \;=\; \beta AE_0$$

β is a parameter that captures the speed with which abnormal earnings decay over time. If there is no decay, β is one and abnormal earnings follow a random walk. If β is zero, abnormal earnings decay completely within one year. Estimates of β using actual company data indicate that for a typical U.S. firm, β is approximately 0.6. However, it varies by industry, and is smaller for firms with large accruals and one-time accounting charges.[8]

The autoregressive model implies that stock values can again be written as a function of current abnormal earnings and book values[9]:

$$\text{Stock value} \;=\; BVE_0 \;+\; \frac{\beta AE_0}{1 + r_e - \beta}$$

This formulation implies that stock values are simply the sum of current book value plus current abnormal earnings weighted by the cost of equity capital and persistence in abnormal earnings.

2. ROE and Growth Simplifications

It is also possible to make simplifications about long-term ROEs and equity growth to reduce forecast horizons for estimating the equity value-to-book multiple. Firms' long-term ROEs are affected by such factors as barriers to entry in their industries, change in production or delivery technologies, and quality of management. As discussed in Chapter 10, these factors tend to force abnormal ROEs to decay over time. One way to model this decay is to assume that ROEs follow a mean reverting process. Forecasted ROE in one period's time then takes the following form:

$$\text{Forecasted } ROE_1 = ROE_0 + \beta(ROE_0 - \overline{ROE})$$

$\overline{ROE}$ is the steady state ROE (either the firm's cost of capital or the long-term industry ROE) and β is a "speed of adjustment factor" that reflects how quickly it takes the ROE to revert to its steady state.[10]

Growth rates are affected by several factors. First, the size of the firm is important. Small firms can sustain very high growth rates for an extended period, whereas large firms find it more difficult to do so. Second, firms with high rates of growth are likely to attract competitors, which reduces their growth rates. As discussed in Chapter 10, book value growth rates for real firms exhibit considerable reversion to the mean.

The long-term patterns in ROE and book equity growth rates imply that for most companies there is limited value in making forecasts for valuation beyond a relatively short horizon, three to five years. Powerful economic forces tend to lead firms with superior or inferior performance early in the forecast horizon to revert to a level that is comparable to that of other firms in the industry or the economy. For a firm in steady state, that is, expected to have a stable ROE and book equity growth rate (*gbve*), the value-to-book multiple formula simplifies to the following:

$$\text{Equity value-to-book multiple} = 1 + \frac{ROE_0 - r_e}{r_e - gbve}$$

Consistent with this simplified model, there is a strong relation between price-to-book ratios and current ROEs. Figure 11-1 shows the relation between these variables for firms in the Retail: Apparel industry as reported by Dow Jones Interactive on July 16, 1999. The correlation between the two variables is 45 percent. Two firms, The Limited

Figure 11-1 Relation Between ROE and Price-to-Book Multiples

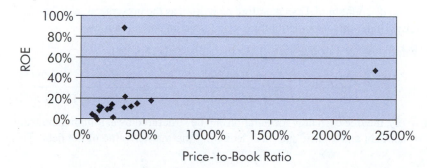

and The Gap, have ROEs that are considerably higher than those for other firms in the industry (88 percent and 48 percent, respectively). Earnings for The Limited include a $1.7 million special gain from the spin-off of a subsidiary, indicating that the high ROE is unlikely to be sustained. Absent this gain, The Limited's ROE would be approximately 14 percent, in keeping with its price-to-book value. The Gap has shown a steady increase in earnings during the last four years. Its high price-to-book ratio suggests that investors expect this level of performance to be sustainable.

Of course, analysts can make a variety of simplifying assumptions about a firm's ROE and growth. For example, they can assume that they decay slowly or rapidly to the cost of capital and the growth rate for the economy. They can assume that the rates decay to the industry or economy average ROEs and book value growth rates. The valuation formula can easily be modified to accommodate these assumptions

THE DISCOUNTED CASH FLOW MODEL

The final valuation method discussed here is the discounted cash flow approach. This is the valuation method taught in most finance classes. Like the abnormal earnings approach, it is derived from the dividend discount model. It is based on the insight that dividends can be recast as free cash flows,[11] that is:

$$\text{Dividends} \;=\; \text{Operating cash flow} \;-\; \text{Capital outlays} \;+\; \text{Net cash flows from debt owners}$$

As discussed in Chapter 9, operating cash flows to equity holders are simply net income plus depreciation less changes in working capital accruals. Capital outlays are capital expenditures less asset sales. Finally, net cash flows from debt owners are issues of new debt less retirements less the after-tax cost of interest. By rearranging these terms, the free cash flows to equity can be written as follows:

$$\text{Dividends} \;=\; \text{Free cash flows to equity} \;=\; NI - \Delta BVA + \Delta BVND$$

where NI is net income, ΔBVA is the change in book value of operating net assets (including changes in working capital plus capital expenditures less depreciation expense), and $\Delta BVND$ is the change in book value of net debt (interest-bearing debt less excess cash).

The dividend discount model can therefore be written as the present value of free cash flows to equity. Under this formulation firm value is estimated as follows:

$$
\begin{aligned}
\text{Equity value} \;&=\; \text{PV of free cash flows to equity claim holders} \\
&=\; \frac{NI_1 - \Delta BVA_1 + \Delta BVND_1}{(1 + r_e)} + \frac{NI_2 - \Delta BVA_2 + \Delta BVND_2}{(1 + r_e)^2} + \cdots
\end{aligned}
$$

Alternatively, the free cash flow formulation can be structured by estimating the value of claims to net debt and equity, and then deducting the market value of net debt. This approach is more widely used in practice, because it does not require explicit forecasts of changes in debt balances.[12] The value of debt plus equity is then:

Debt plus equity value $\;=\;$ PV of free cash flows to net debt and equity claim holders

$$= \frac{NOPAT_1 - \Delta BVA_1}{(1 + WACC)} + \frac{NOPAT_2 - \Delta BVA_2}{(1 + WACC)^2} + \ldots$$

Valuation under the discounted cash flow method therefore involves the following steps:

Step 1: Forecast free cash flows available to equity holders (or to debt and equity holders) over a finite forecast horizon (usually 5 to 10 years).

Step 2: Forecast free cash flows beyond the terminal year based on some simplifying assumption.

Step 3: Discount free cash flows to equity holders (debt plus equity holders) at the cost of equity (weighted average cost of capital). The discounted amount represents the estimated value of free cash flows available to equity (debt and equity holders as a group).

Returning to the Down Under Company example, there is no debt, so that the free cash flows to owners are simply the operating profits before depreciation. Since Down Under is an all-equity firm, its WACC is the cost of equity (10 percent), and the present value of the free cash flows is as follows:

Year	Free Cash Flows	PV Factor	PV of Free Cash Flows
1	$40m	0.9091	$36.4m
2	50	0.8264	41.3
3	60	0.7513	45.1
Equity value			$122.8m

COMPARING VALUATION METHODS

We have discussed three methods of valuation derived from the dividend discount model: discounted dividends, discounted abnormal earnings (or abnormal ROEs), and discounted cash flows. What are the pluses and minuses of these approaches? Since the methods are all derived from the same underlying model, no one version can be considered superior to the others. As long as analysts make the same assumptions about firm fundamentals, value estimates under all four methods will be identical.

However, there are several important differences between the models that are worth noting:

- they focus the analyst's task on different issues;
- they require different levels of structure for valuation analysis; and
- they have different implications for the estimation of terminal values.

Focus on Different Issues

The methods frame the valuation task differently and can in practice focus the analyst's attention on different issues. The earnings-based approaches frame the issues in terms of accounting data such as earnings and book values. Analysts spend considerable time analyzing historical income statements and balance sheets, and their primary forecasts are typically for these variables.

Defining values in terms of ROEs has the added advantage that it focuses analysts' attention on ROE, the same key measure of performance that is decomposed in a standard financial analysis. Further, because ROEs control for firm scale it is likely to be easier for analysts to evaluate the reasonableness of their forecasts by benchmarking them with ROEs of other firms in the industry and the economy. This type of benchmarking is more challenging for free cash flows and abnormal earnings.

Differences in Required Structure

The methods differ in the amount of analysis and structure required for valuation. The discounted abnormal earnings and ROE methods require analysts to construct both proforma income statements and balance sheets to forecast future earnings and book values. In contrast, the discounted cash flow method requires analysts to forecast income statements and changes in working capital and long-term assets to generate free cash flows. Finally, the discounted dividend method requires analysts to forecast dividends.

The discounted abnormal earnings, ROE, and free cash flow models all require more structure for analysis than the discounted dividend approach. They therefore help analysts to avoid structural inconsistencies in their forecasts of future dividends by specifically allowing for firms' future performance and investment opportunities. Similarly, the discounted abnormal earnings/ROE method requires more structure and work than the discounted cash flow method to build full proforma balance sheets. This permits analysts to avoid inconsistencies in the firm's financial structure.

Differences in Terminal Value Implications

A third difference between the methods is in the effort required for estimating terminal values. Terminal value estimates for the abnormal earnings and ROE methods tend to represent a much smaller fraction of total value than under the discounted cash flow or dividend methods. On the surface, this would appear to mitigate concerns about the aspect of valuation that leaves the analyst most uncomfortable. Is this apparent advantage real? As explained below, the answer turns on how well value is already reflected in the accountant's book value.

The abnormal earnings valuation does not eliminate the discounted cash flow terminal value problem, but it does reframe it. Discounted cash flow terminal values include the present value of *all* expected cash flows beyond the forecast horizon. Under abnormal earnings valuation, that value is broken into two parts: the present values of *normal* earnings and *abnormal* earnings beyond the terminal year. The terminal value in the abnormal earnings technique includes only the *abnormal* earnings. The present value of *normal* earnings is already reflected in the original book value or growth in book value over the forecast horizon.

The abnormal earnings approach, then, recognizes that current book value and earnings over the forecast horizon already reflect many of the cash flows expected to arrive after the forecast horizon. The approach builds directly on accrual accounting. For example, under accrual accounting, book equity can be thought of as the minimum recoverable future benefits attributable to the firm's net assets. In addition, revenues are typically realized when earned, not when cash is received. The discounted cash flow approach, on the other hand, "unravels" all of the accruals, spreads the resulting cash flows over longer horizons, and then reconstructs its own "accruals" in the form of discounted expectations of future cash flows. The essential difference between the two approaches is that abnormal earnings valuation recognizes that the accrual process may already have performed a portion of the valuation task, whereas the discounted cash flow approach ultimately moves back to the primitive cash flows underlying the accruals.

The usefulness of the accounting-based perspective thus hinges on how well the accrual process reflects future cash flows. The approach is most convenient when the accrual process is "unbiased," so that earnings can be abnormal only as the result of economic rents, and not as a product of accounting itself.[13] The forecast horizon then extends to the point where the firm is expected to approach a competitive equilibrium and earn only normal earnings on its projects. Subsequent abnormal earnings would be zero, and the terminal value at that point would be zero. In this extreme case, *all* of the firm's value is reflected in the book value and earnings projected over the forecast horizon.

Of course, accounting rarely works so well. For example, in most countries research and development costs are expensed, and book values fail to reflect any research and development assets. As a result, firms that spend heavily on research and development—such as pharmaceuticals—tend on average to generate abnormally high earnings even in the face of stiff competition. Purely as an artifact of research and development accounting, abnormal earnings would be expected to remain positive indefinitely for such firms, and the terminal value could represent a substantial fraction of total value.

If desired, the analyst can alter the accounting approach used by the firm in his/her own projections. "Better" accounting would be viewed as that which reflects a larger fraction of the firm's value in book values and earnings over the forecast horizon.[14] This same view underlies analysts' attempts to "normalize" earnings; the adjusted numbers are intended to provide better indications of value, even though they reflect performance only over a short horizon.

Recent research has focused on the performance of earnings-based valuation relative to discounted cash flow and discounted dividend methods. The findings indicate that over relatively short forecast horizons, ten years or less, valuation estimates using the abnormal earnings approach generate more precise estimates of value than either the discounted dividend or discounted cash flow models. This advantage for the earnings-based approach persists for firms with conservative or aggressive accounting, indicating that accrual accounting in the U.S. does a reasonably good job of reflecting future cash flows.[15]

Key Analysis Questions

The above discussion on the trade-offs between different methods of valuing a company raises several questions for analysts about how to compare methods and to consider which is likely to be most reliable for their analysis:

- What are the key performance parameters that the analyst forecasts? Is more attention given to forecasting accounting variables, such as earnings and book values, or to forecasting cash flow variables?
- Has the analyst linked forecasted income statements and balance sheets? If not, is there any inconsistency between the two statements, or in the implications of the assumptions for future performance? If so, what is the source of this inconsistency and does it affect discounted earnings-based and discounted cash flow methods similarly?
- How well does the firm's accounting capture its underlying assets and obligations? Does it do a good enough job that we can rely on book values as the basis for long-term forecasts? Alternatively, does the firm rely heavily on off-balance-sheet assets, such as R&D, which make book values a poor lower bound on long-term performance?
- Has the analyst made very different assumptions about long-term performance in the terminal value computations under the different valuation methods? If so, which set of assumptions is more plausible given the firm's industry and its competitive positioning?

SUMMARY

Valuation is the process by which forecasts of performance are converted into estimates of price. A variety of valuation techniques are employed in practice, and there is no single method that clearly dominates others. In fact, since each technique involves different advantages and disadvantages, there are gains to considering several approaches simultaneously.

For shareholders, a stock's value is the present value of future dividends. This chapter described three valuation techniques directly based on this dividend discount definition of value: discounted dividends, discounted abnormal earnings/ROEs, and discounted free cash flows. The discounted dividend method attempts to forecast dividends directly. The abnormal earnings approach expresses the value of a firm's equity as book value plus discounted expectations of future abnormal earnings. Finally, the discounted cash flow method represents a firm's stock value by expected future free cash flows discounted at the cost of capital.

Although these three methods were derived from the same dividend discount model, they frame the valuation task differently. In practice they focus the analyst's attention on different issues and require different levels of structure in developing forecasts of the underlying primitive, future dividends.

Price multiple valuation methods were also discussed. Under these approaches, analysts estimate ratios of current price to historical or forecasted measures of performance for comparable firms. The benchmarks are then used to value the performance of the firm being analyzed. Multiples have traditionally been popular, primarily because they do not require analysts to make multiyear forecasts of performance. However, it can be difficult to identify comparable firms to use as benchmarks. Even across highly related firms, there are differences in performance that are likely to affect their multiples.

The chapter discussed the relation between two popular multiples, value-to-book and value-earnings ratios, and the discounted abnormal earnings valuation. The resulting formulations indicate that value-to-book multiples are a function of future abnormal ROEs, book value growth, and the firm's cost of equity. The value-earnings multiple is a function of the same factors, and also the current ROE.

APPENDIX:
Reconciling the Discounted Dividends and Discounted Abnormal Earnings Models

To derive the earnings-based valuation from the dividend discount model consider the following two-period valuation:

$$\text{Equity value} = \frac{DIV_1}{(1 + r_e)} + \frac{DIV_2}{(1 + r_e)^2}$$

With clean surplus accounting, dividends (DIV) can be expressed as a function of net income (NI), and the book value of equity (BVE):

$$DIV_t = NI_t + BVE_{t-1} - BVE_t$$

Substituting this expression into the dividend discount model yields the following:

$$\text{Equity value} = \frac{NI_1 + BVE_0 - BVE_1}{(1 + r_e)} + \frac{NI_2 + BVE_1 - BVE_2}{(1 + r_e)^2}$$

This can be rewritten as follows:

$$\text{Equity value} = \frac{NI_1 - r_e BVE_0 + BVE_0(1 + r_e) - BVE_1}{(1 + r_e)}$$

$$+ \frac{NI_2 - r_e BVE_1 + BVE_1(1 + r_e) - BVE_2}{(1 + r_e)^2}$$

$$= BVE_0 + \frac{NI_1 - r_e BVE_0}{(1 + r_e)} + \frac{NI_2 - r_e BVE_1}{(1 + r_e)^2} - \frac{BVE_2}{(1 + r_e)^2}$$

The value of equity is therefore the current book value plus the present value of future abnormal earnings. As the forecast horizon expands, the final term (the present value of liquidating book value) becomes inconsequential.

DISCUSSION QUESTIONS

1. Joe Watts, an analyst at EMH Securities, states: "I don't know why anyone would ever try to value earnings. Obviously, the market knows that earnings can be manipulated and only values cash flows." Discuss.

2. Explain why terminal values in accounting-based valuation are significantly less than those for DCF valuation.

3. Manufactured Earnings is a "darling" of Wall Street analysts. Its current market price is $15 per share, and its book value is $5 per share. Analysts forecast that the firm's book value will grow by 10 percent per year indefinitely, and the cost of equity is 15 percent. Given these facts, what is the market's expectation of the firm's long-term average ROE?

4. Given the information in question (3), what will be Manufactured Earnings' stock price if the market revises its expectations of long-term average ROE to 20 percent?

5. Analysts reassess Manufactured Earnings' future performance as follows: growth in book value increases to 12 percent per year, but the ROE of the incremental book value is only 15 percent. What is the impact on the market-to-book ratio?

6. How can a company with a high ROE have a low PE ratio?

7. What type of companies have:
   a. a high PE and a low market-to-book ratio?
   b. a high PE ratio and a high market-to-book ratio?
   c. a low PE and a high market-to-book ratio?
   d. a low PE and a low market-to-book ratio?

8. Free cash flows (FCF) used in DCF valuations discussed in the chapter are defined as follows:

   FCF to debt and equity = Earnings before interest and taxes × (1 − tax rate)
   + Depreciation and deferred taxes − Capital
   expenditures −/+ Increase/decrease in working capital

$$\text{FCF to equity } = \text{ Net income } + \text{ Depreciation and deferred taxes } - \text{ Capital}$$
$$\text{expenditures } -/+ \text{ Increase/decrease in working capital}$$
$$+/- \text{ Increase/decrease in debt}$$

Which of the following items affect free cash flows to debt and equity holders? Which affect free cash flows to equity alone? Explain why and how.

- An increase in accounts receivable
- A decrease in gross margins
- An increase in property, plant and equipment
- An increase in inventory
- Interest expense
- An increase in prepaid expenses
- An increase in notes payable to the bank

9. Starite Company is valued at $20 per share. Analysts expect that it will generate free cash flows to equity of $4 per share for the foreseeable future. What is the firm's implied cost of equity capital?

10. Janet Stringer argues that "the DCF valuation method has increased managers' focus on short-term rather than long-term performance, since the discounting process places much heavier weight on short-term cash flows than long-term ones." Comment.

NOTES

1. The incorporation of all noncapital equity transactions into income is called clean surplus accounting. It is analogous to comprehensive income, the concept defined in FAS 130.

2. Changes in book value also include new capital contributions. However, the dividend discount model assumes that new capital is issued at fair value. As a result, any incremental book value from capital issues is exactly offset by the discounted value of future dividends to new shareholders. Capital transactions therefore do not affect firm valuation.

3. Appendix A provides a simple proof of the earnings-based valuation formula.

4. See C. Lee and J. Myers, "What is the Intrinsic Value of the Dow?," Cornell University, working paper, 1997.

5. There is an important difference between the way ROE is defined in the value-to-book formulation and the way it is defined in Chapter 9. The valuation formula defines ROE as return on beginning equity, whereas in our ratio discussion we used return on ending or return on average equity.

6. It may seem surprising that one can estimate value with no explicit attention to two of the cash flow streams considered in DCF analysis: investments in working capital and capital expenditures. The accounting-based technique recognizes that these investments cannot possibly contribute to value without impacting abnormal earnings, and that therefore only their earnings impacts need be considered. For example, the benefit of an increase in inventory turnover surfaces in terms of its impact on ROE (and thus, abnormal earnings), without the need to consider explicitly the cash flow impacts involved.

7. It is also possible to include a drift term in the model, allowing earnings to grow by a constant amount, or at a constant rate each period.

8. See P. M. Dechow, A. P. Hutton, and R. G. Sloan, "An empirical assessment of the residual income valuation model," *Journal of Accounting and Economics* 23, January 1999.

9. This formulation is a variant of a model proposed by James Ohlson, "Earnings, book values, and dividends in security valuation," *Contemporary Accounting Research* 11, Spring 1995. Ohlson includes in his forecasts of future abnormal earnings a variable that reflects relevant information other than current abnormal earnings. This variable then also appears in the stock valuation formula. Empirical research by Dechow, Hutton, and Sloan indicates that financial analysts' forecasts of abnormal earnings do reflect considerable information other than current abnormal earnings, and that this information is useful for valuation.

10. This specification is similar to the model for dividends developed by J. Lintner, "Distribution of incomes of corporations among dividends, retained earnings, and taxes," *American Economic Review* 46 (May 1956): 97–113.

11. In practice, firms do not have to pay out all of their free cash flows as dividends; they can retain surplus cash in the business. The conditions under which a firm's dividend decision affects its value are discussed by M. H. Miller and F. Modigliani in "Dividend Policy, Growth and the Valuation of Shares," *Journal of Business* 34 (October 1961): 411–433.

12. A good forecast, however, would be grounded in an understanding of these changes as well as all other key elements of the firm's financial picture. The changes in financing cash flows are particularly critical for firms that anticipate changing their capital structure.

13. Unbiased accounting is that which, in a competitive equilibrium, produces an expected ROE equal to the cost of capital. The actual ROE thus reveals the presence of economic rents. Market-value accounting is a special case of unbiased accounting that produces an expected ROE equal to the cost of capital, even when the firm is *not* in a competitive equilibrium. That is, market-value accounting reflects the present value of future economic rents in book value, driving the expected ROEs to a normal level. For a discussion of unbiased and biased accounting, see G. Feltham and J. Ohlson, "Valuation and Clean Surplus Accounting for Operating and Financial Activities," *Contemporary Accounting Research* 11, No. 2 (Spring 1995): 689–731.

14. In his book on EVA valuation, Bennett Stewart (1994) recommends a number of accounting adjustments, including the capitalization of research and development.

15. S. Penman and T. Sougiannis, "A Comparison of Dividend, Cash Flow, and Earnings Approaches to Equity Valuation," *The Accounting Review*, compares the valuation methods using actual realizations of earnings, cash flows, and dividends to estimate prices. J. Francis, P. Olsson, and D. Oswald, "Comparing Accuracy and Explainability of Dividend, Free Cash Flow and Abnormal Earnings Equity Valuation Models," 1997, University of Chicago working paper, estimates values using *Value Line* forecasts.

I n late January 1991, Didier Pineau-Valencienne, CEO and Chairman of the French firm Groupe Schneider, was frustrated at his lack of success in building a closer working relationship between his company and Square D, Schneider's American counterpart in the electrical equipment industry. Convinced that a global market was developing for electrical equipment, Pineau-Valencienne believed that Schneider needed to become a major player in the U.S. market to maintain its future competitive position. Given the lack of success in partnering with Square D, he was considering the option of acquiring the company.

THE ELECTRICAL EQUIPMENT INDUSTRY

The electrical equipment industry generates revenue from new construction as well as from the maintenance of existing equipment. Demand for both closely follows general economic conditions. The 1990 economic slump hit the electrical manufacturing segment in the United States severely. However, by early 1991 analysts expected prospects for the industry to brighten with the predicted upturn in the economy and the construction market.

Two related trends dominated the industry in 1990: globalization and industry concentration. The first of these has led many U.S. firms to expand internationally to take advantage of market growth in Western Europe and Pacific Rim countries. These international opportunities have been enhanced by the globalization of product standards in the industry. The most widely accepted standards in the U.S. were developed by the National Electrical Manufacturers Association (NEMA). European products conformed to a different set of standards, developed by the International Electrical Commission (IEC) in Geneva. However, many in the industry expected that the move toward a unified Europe, set for 1992, would ultimately lead IEC standards to become dominant in the world.

The second major trend in the industry, concentration of manufacturing and research capabilities, resulted from increasing costs of development and production as well as from globalization. The development of a new product line costs between $46 million

This case was prepared by Edouard De Vitry D'Avaucourt, under the supervision of Professor Paul Healy. Additional comments and information were provided by Professors Paul Asquith from the MIT Sloan School of Management and Anant Sundaram from the Amos Tuck School.

and $74 million (FF 250 million to FF 400 million). Globalization of markets and product standards enabled firms to take advantage of economies of scale, using their expertise and technologies to create common products for domestic and international markets.

SQUARE D COMPANY

Square D is a major supplier of electrical equipment, services, and systems in the U.S. (see Exhibit 1 for Square D's U.S. market shares). The company was incorporated in 1903 and has grown steadily since then. It currently owns and operates 18 manufacturing plants in 11 foreign countries. Operations are concentrated in two segments: electrical distribution and industrial control. The electrical distribution segment manufactures products and systems used to transmit electricity from power lines to outlets for residential, commercial, industrial, or other types of buildings. The industrial control segment manufactures products and provides services to control power used by electrical devices or processes.

One of Square D's strengths is its network of independent electrical distributors, or wholesalers, which market its products. Individual distributors, selected by Square D, provide products and services to all types of clients (contractors, utilities, industrial users, and original equipment manufacturers). This extensive network is the result of many years of relationship building, and is the envy of most of Square D's competitors.

Square D's major competitors include ABB, Westinghouse, Siemens, Allen Bradley, General Electric, and Schneider (through its subsidiaries Télémécanique and Merlin Gerin). These companies compete across a number of segments. In late 1990, *US Industrial Outlook* ranked Square D second in the U.S. industrial control business after Allen Bradley. In electrical distribution, the company ranks third in the U.S. market behind Westinghouse and General Electric.

Square D has had an impressive financial track record—it has been profitable for each of the last 59 years. In the mid-1980s, however, company performance indicators began to deteriorate, prompting the Board to make a change in top management. Jerre Stead joined Square D as president and COO in 1987, was elected CEO in 1988, and was appointed Chairman of the Board in 1989. Stead led a revitalization plan to restore the company's performance and help it face the new industry challenges. Under the plan the following restructuring changes were made:

- Some facilities in the U.S. and Canada were closed, and others were consolidated.
- The firm's businesses were reorganized into three externally focused sectors serving industrial control, electrical distribution, and international markets.
- The resources generated by redeployments and disposal of operations not closely related to the core were used to strengthen core businesses.

Thanks to these efforts, Square D weathered the 1990 recession better than many of its competitors. In 1990 Square D's sales were $1.7 billion (see Exhibit 2 for financial statements), 71 percent in the electrical distribution segment (85 percent of operating earnings) and 29 percent in the industrial control segment (15 percent of operating earnings). By early 1991 analysts were expressing optimism about the industry's prospects for late 1991 and 1992, especially those for Square D. *Value Line* noted that "a stronger economy, a rebound in housing, and positive operating leverage . . . could enable earnings per share to surge to $5.50 or so in 1992 (from $4.73 in 1990)."

GROUPE SCHNEIDER

Schneider was founded in October 1886 as a partnership and was transformed into a corporation (société anonyme) in 1966. It is one of the largest industrial groups in France and is ranked 184 in Fortune's 500 (worldwide ranking).

In 1981, with the arrival of Pineau-Valencienne as chairman and CEO of the group, Schneider embarked on an ambitious restructuring program. The first stage of the program was to divest all loss-making businesses (shipbuilding, railways, and telephone equipment), which had historically generated much of the firm's sales. The sale of these businesses allowed the group to simplify its operational structure and to strengthen its finances. In the second stage of the restructuring Schneider focused on two core businesses:

- Electrical equipment manufacturing for power distribution and automation of industrial complexes (56 percent of sales, 85 percent of operating profits in 1990)
- Electrical building contracting (44 percent of sales, 15 percent of operating profits in 1990)

As a result of the restructuring efforts, Schneider transformed itself from a diversified holding company into an industrial group focused on electrical equipment, engineering, and contracting. The company was organized around four major industrial subsidiaries:

- *Merlin Gerin*—Manufacturer of high-, medium-, and low-voltage equipment, as well as process control systems
- *Télémécanique*—Manufacturer of automation systems and equipment
- *Jeumont Schneider*—Manufacturer of electrical and electronic engineering equipment
- *Spie Batignolles*—Provider of electrical contracting and civil engineering services

With sales of 51 billion francs (financial statements are presented in Exhibit 3) and 85,000 employees throughout the world in 1990, Schneider ranked second or third in most segments of the global electrical equipment industry.

In the late 1980s, Pineau-Valencienne became convinced that the industry was moving more toward a global industry. In his communications with analysts, he emphasized that IEC standards would gain influence in the U.S. and would become the worldwide standard. In addition, he believed that increasing R&D and manufacturing costs would encourage international concentration. Consequently, Schneider began a third restructuring stage—geographical diversification. This move was initiated with two major acquisitions in 1989:

- Spie Batignolles acquired 15 percent of DAVY, the leading British engineering company.
- Schneider acquired a controlling interest in Federal Pioneer, the leading Canadian electrical equipment manufacturer.

The Relationship Between Schneider and Square D

Schneider became interested in Square D in 1988. In September 1988, Pineau-Valencienne arranged a meeting between the top executives of the two companies, during which Schneider presented its vision of a possible joint venture. After this presentation, operational meetings were scheduled from fall 1988 to spring 1989 to determine the product lines most suitable for such a joint venture. To protect the information exchanged, the companies entered into a confidentiality agreement in late October 1988. This restricted the use and public disclosure of confidential information received during the discussions, but it did not contain any "standstill" provisions limiting purchase of securities or business combination proposals.

Very early in the negotiations it became clear that the two CEOs diverged in their understanding of the nature of the relationship. Pineau-Valencienne had hoped that Schneider would acquire an equity position in Square D to cement the relationship. Stead, however, made it very clear that he did not welcome this, and requested that Square D's independence be respected. In correspondence on September 25, 1989, Pineau-Valencienne made his views very clear, connecting the future of the joint venture discussions to Square D's agreeing to Schneider acquiring a 20 percent interest in Square D. As a result, joint venture discussions between the two firms terminated. Frustrated over this standstill, in September 1990 Pineau-Valencienne indicated to Stead that Schneider's interests in Square D had changed from a joint venture to a "friendly cash merger transaction." Square D's Board subsequently became increasingly hostile to Schneider's proposals.

At the same time that Schneider was making overtures to Square D, Square D was organizing legal defenses against hostile takeovers. In 1989 it moved to Delaware, where state laws require hostile bidders to have a minimum of 85 percent of the shares tendered to effect a takeover. In addition, it created poison pill amendments to fight potential unsolicited bids, including a Common Stock Purchase Plan (see Exhibit 4 for details).

During November 1990, unusual activity was noticeable in Square D's stock. Rumors of a takeover led to a jump in volume and increased the share price from $36.50 on October 22 to $49.75 on November 7 (see Exhibit 5). On November 6, 1990, Stead discussed the unusual activity in a phone conversation with Pineau-Valencienne, who expressed an interest in having the opportunity to propose a transaction to Square D if any other parties were given such an opportunity.

On February 1, 1991, *Value Line Investments Survey* made the following comments:

Square D stock is trading on takeover speculation, as it has for the past three months. Square D has several attractions (including positions in selected electrical equipment markets), and could well be a tempting takeover target, especially to a foreign company trying to establish or to enlarge a market presence in the U.S. An acquirer might be willing to pay $70 a share or more for the company. But after three months of unusually heavy trading in the stock, during which time all of its outstanding shares theoretically have changed hands, no evidence of a pending buyout attempt has appeared. If none is eventually forthcoming, we'd expect the stock to gradually drift lower, perhaps to the range of $40–$45 a share. At this juncture, only speculative investors should be holding these shares.

Potential Acquisition of Square D

One option that Pineau-Valencienne was considering was to make a bid for Square D. After two years of contacts with Square D, he had a number of ideas for synergies and sources of value that could result from a full combination of the two companies. These included:

- Rationalizing R&D efforts between the two companies and sharing the benefits of existing technologies;
- Providing access to larger distribution channels for both companies;
- Rationalizing manufacturing capabilities; and
- Expanding Square D's product lines by selling products developed by Télémécanique or Merlin Gerin.

Lazard Frères, the financial advisor of Schneider, was asked to analyze the stand-alone value of Square D as well as its value to Schneider. To determine Square D's stand-alone value, Lazard Frères prepared a set of base assumptions for the firm's future performance as an independent entity. They projected that (a) sales would grow 3.5 percent in 1991 and 7 percent per year thereafter; (b) EBIT would be 15–16 percent of sales; (c) net working capital would continue to be 11–13 percent of sales; (d) projected capital expenditures would be 5 percent of sales; and (e) depreciation expenses would remain at 4 percent of sales between 1991 and 1997, and 4.3 percent thereafter. Based on the synergies between Schneider and Square D, Lazard Frères estimated that Square D could save approximately $60 million per year in expenses (after tax) if it were combined with Schneider. In addition, the disposal of some of Square D's unrelated assets could generate $150 million in cash. Other data relevant to the valuation of Square D is presented in Exhibit 6.

One other issue that Pineau-Valencienne was concerned about in a possible acquisition of Square D was its effect on Schneider's income. Under French accounting, Schneider would have to amortize goodwill, regardless of whether the offer was cash or stock-financed. Lazard Frères estimated that asset and liability revaluations under an acquisition would be minimal, implying that there would be significant goodwill amortization charges, even if the maximum period of 40 years was chosen. Pineau-Valencienne expected that many analysts would react negatively to the resulting dilution of earnings.

Didier Pineau-Valencienne felt he had to make a quick decision. There were rumors that Square D already had been approached by a number of other companies about a business combination. Pineau-Valencienne was very concerned that other competitors could gain control of Square D, leaving Schneider with few opportunities to gain access to the U.S. market.

QUESTIONS

1. Assess and discuss the strategic fit between Square D and Schneider. What are the economic pros and cons of a combination?
2. Evaluate the base assumptions Lazard Frères made for valuing Square D.
3. Estimate the value of Square D as an independent company. What is the company worth to Schneider?
4. What would be the effect of the acquisition on Schneider's future earnings, assuming that it was forced to pay the full value of Square D? Should Schneider be concerned about this effect?
5. If you were Mr. Pineau-Valencienne in late January 1991, what would you do? Would you offer a bid for Square D? If so, how much would you bid, and would you make your offer friendly or hostile?

EXHIBIT 1
Schneider and Square D Market Shares, U.S. and Europe

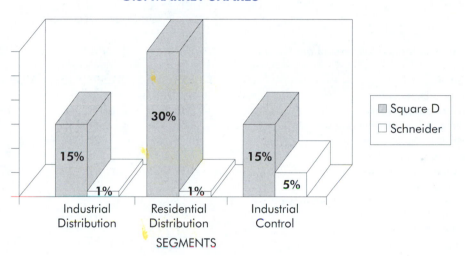

U.S. MARKET SHARES

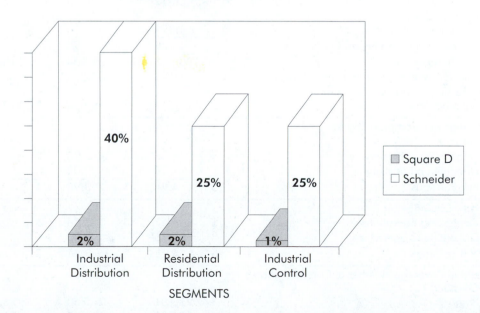

EUROPEAN MARKET SHARES

Schneider and Square D

EXHIBIT 2
Selected Pages from Square D's 1990 Annual Report

CONSOLIDATED FINANCIAL STATEMENTS

CONSOLIDATED STATEMENTS OF NET EARNINGS

	Year Ended December 31		
(Amounts in thousands, except per share)	1990	1989	1988
Net Sales	$1,653,319	$1,598,688	$1,497,772
Costs and Expenses:			
Cost of products sold	1,088,977	1,027,348	979,591
Selling, administrative and general	385,903	369,726	338,962
Restructuring charge	—	26,320	—
Operating Earnings	178,439	175,294	179,219
Non-Operating Income	34,740	17,106	17,255
Interest Expense	(28,760)	(31,438)	(22,082)
Earnings from Continuing Operations before Income Taxes	184,419	160,962	174,392
Provision for Income Taxes	67,773	59,856	63,310
Earnings from Continuing Operations	116,646	101,106	111,082
Discontinued Operations:			
(Loss) earnings from operations, net of income tax (benefit) expense: 1990—$(1,188); 1989—$(1,086); 1988—$3,831	(312)	798	7,852
Gain on disposal, net of other provisions; net of income taxes of $1,865	4,391	—	—
Earnings from Discontinued Operations	4,079	798	7,852
Net Earnings	120,725	101,904	118,934
Preferred Dividend, Net of Income Taxes	6,176	3,300	—
Net Earnings Available for Common Shareholders	$ 114,549	$ 98,604	$ 118,934
Earnings per Common Share:			
Primary:			
Continuing operations	$ 4.76	$ 3.95	$ 4.15
Discontinued operations	.18	.03	.29
Net Earnings	$ 4.94	$ 3.98	$ 4.44
Fully Diluted:			
Continuing operations	$ 4.57	$ 3.88	$ 4.13
Discontinued operations	.16	.03	.29
Net Earnings	$ 4.73	$ 3.91	$ 4.42
Weighted Average Number of Common Shares Outstanding:			
Primary	23,181	24,763	26,776
Fully diluted	25,088	25,809	27,016

CONSOLIDATED BALANCE SHEETS

	December 31,	
(Dollars in thousands, except per share)	1990	1989

ASSETS

Current Assets:

Cash and short-term investments	$ 244,933	$ 66,348
Receivables, less allowances (1990—$23,759; 1989—$18,556)	305,241	314,123
Inventories	159,109	151,316
Prepaid expenses	12,664	15,206
Prepaid income taxes	4,714	—
Deferred income tax benefit	34,988	26,459
Net assets of discontinued operation	—	117,116
Total Current Assets	761,649	690,568
Investment in Leveraged Leases	137,182	133,344
Property, Plant and Equipment:		
Land	24,477	22,216
Buildings and improvements	222,105	212,992
Equipment	552,785	501,531
Property, Plant and Equipment—at cost	799,367	736,739
Less accumulated depreciation	349,265	318,261
Property, Plant and Equipment—net	450,102	418,478
Net Assets of Discontinued Operations	36,681	52,949
Excess of Purchase Price Over Net Assets of Businesses Acquired, Less Amortization (1990—$13,769; 1989— $12,978)	51,391	50,528
Other Assets	22,744	26,718
Total Assets	$1,459,749	$1,372,585

LIABILITIES AND COMMON SHAREHOLDERS' EQUITY

Current Liabilities:

Short-term debt	$ 123,871	$ 263,730
Current maturities of long-term debt	15,067	10,174
Accounts payable and accrued expenses	220,575	200,686
Income taxes	—	10,327
Dividends payable	12,633	11,893
Total Current Liabilities	372,146	496,810
Long-Term Debt	244,820	123,420
Deferred Income Taxes	82,381	74,464
Deferred Income Taxes—Leveraged Leases	127,699	112,473
Other Liabilities	14,000	—
Minority Interest	10,941	9,295
Preferred Stock, No Par Value, Authorized 6,000,000 Shares; Issued 1,709,402 Shares, Outstanding 1,701,822 Shares, Cumulative Series A ESOP Convertible Preferred Stock	$ 124,568	$ 125,000

(continued)

Schneider and Square D

Schneider and Square D

(Dollars in thousands, except per share)	December 31, 1990	1989
Note Receivable from ESOP Trust	(25,000)	(125,000)
Unearned ESOP Compensation	(95,400)	—
Common Shareholders' Equity:		
Common stock, par value $1.66²/₃, authorized 100,000,000 shares	49,601	49,409
Additional paid-in capital	130,401	120,211
Retained earnings	773,126	713,225
Cumulative translation adjustments	3,262	(8,788)
Treasury stock—at cost	(352,796)	(317,934)
Total Common Shareholders' Equity	603,594	556,123
Total Liabilities and Common Shareholders' Equity	$1,459,749	$1,372,585

CONSOLIDATED STATEMENTS OF CASH FLOWS

(Dollars in thousands)	Year Ended December 31, 1990	1989	1988
Cash and Short-Term Investments at January 1	$ 66,348	$ 65,855	$ 94,488
Cash and Short-Term Investments Were Provided from (Used for):			
Operating Activities:			
Earnings from Continuing Operations	116,646	101,106	111,082
Add (deduct) non-cash items included in earnings from continuing operations:			
Depreciation and amortization	59,300	49,443	45,174
Deferred income taxes	1,707	(25,147)	(8,506)
Deferred income taxes—leveraged leases	15,226	23,445	25,683
(Gain) loss on sale of property, plant and equipment	(1,011)	1,936	657
(Gain) loss on foreign exchange	(2,222)	964	(52)
Minority interest	1,646	985	1,047
Other credits to earnings—net	—	(15)	(63)
Current Items (net of effects of purchase of businesses):			
Receivables	13,501	(58,515)	(20,789)
Inventories	(1,285)	26,568	(52,795)
Prepaid expenses	2,769	12,027	1,635
Accounts payable and accrued expenses	(7,312)	16,736	20,316
Income taxes	(15,253)	(3,319)	8,243
Net cash provided from continuing operations	183,712	146,214	131,632
Net cash (used for) provided from discontinued operations	(484)	2,971	721
Net cash provided from operating activities	183,228	149,185	132,353

(Dollars in thousands)	Year Ended December 31,		
	1990	1989	1988
Investing Activities:			
Increase in investment in leveraged leases	$ (3,838)	$ (2,876)	$ (4,829)
Purchase of businesses, net of $103 of cash acquired	—	(9,271)	—
Property additions	(83,117)	(80,024)	(70,419)
Proceeds from sale of business	175,476	—	—
Proceeds from sale of property, plant and equipment	21,774	6,186	14,222
Decrease (increase) in other investments	1,281	(12,794)	24,692
Net cash provided from (used for) investing activities	111,576	(98,779)	(36,334)
Financing Activities:			
Net (decrease) increase in short-term debt	(143,983)	142,262	44,430
Increase in long-term debt	27,883	614	11,066
Reductions in long-term debt	(14,412)	(21,580)	(17,910)
Proceeds of note receivable from ESOP trust	125,000	—	—
Loan to ESOP trust	(25,000)	—	—
Cash dividends paid on common stock	(50,128)	(50,590)	(54,601)
Cash dividends paid on preferred stock	(9,956)	(5,000)	—
Common stock issued	6,602	8,929	6,349
Purchase of treasury stock	(34,916)	(126,778)	(111,394)
Redemption of preferred stock	(432)	—	—
Treasury stock issued	54	114	256
Net cash used for financing activities	(119,288)	(52,029)	(121,804)
Effect of Exchange Rate Changes on Cash	3,069	2,116	(2,848)
Net Increase (Decrease) in Cash and Short-Term Investments	178,585	493	(28,633)
Cash and Short-Term Investments at December 31	$244,933	$ 66,348	$ 65,855

See accompanying notes to consolidated financial statements.

Schneider and Square D

Schneider and Square D

NOTES TO CONSOLIDATED FINANCIAL STATEMENTS

(Dollars in thousands, except per share)

A. *Summary of Significant Accounting Policies*

Principles of Consolidation

The financial statements include the accounts of the company and all majority-owned subsidiaries. Investments in unconsolidated affiliates are accounted for by the equity method. All significant intercompany accounts and transactions have been eliminated. The statements are based on years ended December 31, except for substantially all international subsidiaries whose fiscal years end November 30.

Cash and Short-Term Investments

Cash consists of cash in banks and time deposits. Short-term investments consist of a variety of highly liquid short-term instruments with purchased maturities of generally three months or less. Short-term investments are carried at cost, which approximates market.

Inventories

Inventories are stated at the lower of cost or market. Cost of inventories is determined using the last-in, first-out (LIFO) method for substantially all domestic inventories and certain international inventories. The first-in, first-out (FIFO) method is used for substantially all international inventories.

Property, Plant and Equipment

Depreciation of property, plant and equipment is provided on a straight-line basis over the estimated useful lives of the assets. Accelerated methods are used for income tax purposes.

Businesses Acquired

The excess of purchase price over net assets of businesses acquired is amortized on a straight-line basis over not more than forty years.

Income Taxes

Income taxes are accounted for in accordance with APB No. 11. The Financial Accounting Standards Board has issued Statement No. 96, which will change the accounting for income taxes; the company will adopt this statement no later than January 1, 1992.

Off-Balance Sheet Financial Instruments

The company enters into a variety of financial instruments in the management of its exposure to changes in interest rates and foreign currency rates. These instruments include interest rate swap agreements and foreign exchange contracts. These financial instruments do not represent a material off-balance sheet risk in relation to the financial statements.

Earnings per Common Share

Primary earnings per common share are determined by dividing the weighted average number of common shares outstanding during the year into net earnings after deducting after-tax dividends attributable to preferred shares. Common share equivalents in the form of stock options and convertible debt are excluded from the calculation since they do not have a material dilutive effect on per share figures. Fully diluted earnings per share reflect the conversion of all convertible preferred stock and common stock equivalents into common stock.

Reclassifications

Certain amounts in the 1989 and 1988 financial statements have been reclassified to conform to the current year's financial statement presentation.

B. Discontinued Operations

As of June 30, 1990, the company reported its General Semiconductor Industries (GSI) business as a discontinued operation, and as of September 30, 1989, the company reported its Yates Industries (Yates) copper foil business as a discontinued operation. Accordingly, the consolidated financial statements of the company have been reclassified to report separately the net assets and operating results of these discontinued operations. Financial results for periods prior to the dates of discontinuance have been restated to reflect continuing operations.

In January 1990, the company concluded the sale of its Yates operations in Europe and its 50 percent joint venture interest in Japan. In April 1990, the company completed the sale of its Yates operation in Bordentown, N.J. Total gross proceeds from the sale of all Yates operations were $175,476. The proceeds from the sale of Yates operations and the associated costs approximated management's original estimates. Management is actively pursuing the sale of the GSI business.

A gain from the sale of Yates, offset by provisions for a loss on the prospective sale of GSI and costs associated with other previously discontinued businesses, resulted in a gain of $4,391, net of income taxes, in the second quarter of 1990 from discontinued operations. The gain on the sale of Yates is net of a $14,000 provision for long-term environmental costs. The gain from the sale of Yates' foreign locations included a gain of $6,895 from the recognition of cumulative translation adjustments.

Net assets of discontinued operations were $36,681 and $170,065 at December 31, 1990 and 1989, respectively. These amounts consist of current assets; property, plant and equipment; other noncurrent assets; and current and concurrent liabilities.

Sales applicable to the discontinued operations prior to the dates of discontinuance were $16,158, $124,121 and $159,000 in 1990, 1989 and 1988, respectively. Interest expense of $249, $2,730 and $2,246, net of income taxes, was allocated to the discontinued operations prior to dates of discontinuance based on net assets for 1990, 1989 and 1988, respectively. The operating results of GSI from the date of discontinuance to December 31, 1990 were immaterial.

C. Restructuring Charge

In 1989, a restructuring charge of $17,511 net of taxes, or $.71 per share, was incurred by the company as a part of a plan to rationalize and improve profitability of several

Schneider and Square D

businesses and product lines both in the United States and abroad. The charge is principally comprised of costs associated with product, facility and organizational rationalization of the electrical distribution segment; product rationalization of the industrial control segment; plant consolidation and organizational restructuring in Canada; reorganization in Europe; and marketing restructuring.

D. Acquisitions

In 1989, the company acquired Crisp Automation, Inc. of Dublin, Ohio. Crisp Automation is a designer of process controls and factory automation systems and operates as part of the Square D Automation Products business. Also in 1989, the company acquired Electrical Specialty Products (ESP) of Montevallo, Alabama. ESP is a manufacturer of electrical connectors and operates as part of the Square D Connectors business. These acquisitions were accounted for as purchases; their sales and net earnings for the periods prior to the dates of acquisition were not material.

G. Inventories

Inventories valued by the last-in, first-out (LIFO) method aggregated $83,941 and $65,017 at December 31, 1990 and 1989, respectively. If the first-in, first-out (FIFO) method had been used, inventories would have been $138,120 and $140,076 higher than reported in the accompanying consolidated balance sheets at December 31, 1990 and 1989, respectively.

Inventories are maintained by element of cost; therefore, it is not practical to determine major classes such as finished goods, work in process and raw materials.

H. Lease Commitments

The company rents various warehouse and office facilities and certain equipment, principally computers and vehicles, under lease arrangements classified as operating leases.

Future minimum rental payments under noncancelable operating leases with initial terms of one year or more as of December 31, 1990 are:

1991	$10,160
1992	7,266
1993	5,520
1994	4,473
1995	975
Remainder	1,224
Total	$29,618

J. Debt

Long-term debt consists of:

	1990	1989
ESOP Notes, 7.7%, due on various dates to 2004	$120,400	$ —
Senior Notes, 10.0%, due 1995	75,000	75,000
Industrial Revenue Bonds, 5.6% to 8.8%, due on various dates to 2004	25,715	26,610
First Mortgage Notes, 9.0% to 9.2%, due on various dates to 2009	10,825	11,119
Subordinated Convertible Notes, 9.0%, due 1992 (net of unamortized discount at 13.0%: 1990—$220, 1989—$376)	2,787	4,096
Payable to banks; average rate 1990—13.8%, 1989—10.3%; due on various dates to 1996	1,114	2,423
Other debt: average rate 1990—14.4%, 1989—12.7%; due on various dates to 2000	24,046	14,346
Subtotal	259,887	133,594
Less current maturities	15,067	10,174
Total	$244,820	$123,420

The aggregate annual maturities of long-term debt for the years 1991 through 1995 are $15,067, $14,642, $14,968, $13,877 and $82,187, respectively.

The Employee Stock Ownership Plan (ESOP) Notes include $25,000 of direct borrowings by the company, the proceeds from which have been advanced in the form of a loan to the company's ESOP. Direct borrowings of the ESOP, aggregating $95,400 as of December 31, 1990, have been guaranteed by the company and accordingly, are reported as long-term debt of the company. See Note Q for further discussion.

Industrial Revenue Bonds of $9,115 and the First Mortgage Notes are secured by the property and equipment acquired with the proceeds of the financings.

The Subordinated Convertible Notes are convertible at a rate of 28.57 shares for each one thousand dollars of principal. The company has reserved 85,934 shares of common stock for the conversion.

The company has entered into revolving credit agreements in which twelve of its principal banks participate. The agreements provide for up to $180,000 of revolving credit through 1994. The credit is available in both the domestic and euro markets.

Short-term debt includes bank borrowings of $33,611 and $19,438 and commercial paper of $70,260 and $214,292 at December 31, 1990 and 1989, respectively. Additionally, short-term debt includes a master note agreement of $20,000 and $30,000 at December 31, 1990 and 1989, respectively.

The company has additional unused short-term lines of credit which aggregated $69,501 at December 31, 1990.

Schneider and Square D

K. Income Taxes

Pre-tax income from continuing operations is as follows:

	1990	1989	1988
United States	$163,674	$142,855	$155,453
International	20,745	18,107	18,939
Total	$184,419	$160,962	$174.392

Income tax provisions for continuing operations are as follows:

	1990	1989	1988
Current:			
U.S. Federal	$ 33,452	$ 46,784	$ 35,261
International	7,999	4,752	3,989
State	9,037	9,902	6,625
	50,488	61,438	45,875
Deferred:			
U.S. Federal	17,189	(1,375)	17,475
International	(869)	1,479	228
State	965	(1,686)	(268)
	17,285	(1,582)	17,435
Total	$ 67,773	$ 59,856	$ 63,310

The components of the deferred income tax provision are as follows:

	1990	1989	1988
Leasing subsidiary income	$ 17,077	$ 22,502	$ 25,256
401(k) contributions	4,383	—	—
State tax	965	(1,686)	(268)
Tax over book depreciation	2,535	1,301	751
Deferred taxable income on installment sales	—	(13,006)	(5,615)
Alternative minimum tax	—	8,484	1,634
Funding of group health insurance trust	—	(6,863)	(11,634)
Restructuring charge	—	(4,510)	—
Other	(7,675)	(7,804)	7,311
Deferred Income Tax Expense (Benefit)	$ 17,285	$ (1,582)	$ 17,435

A reconciliation between the statutory and effective tax rates for continuing operations is as follows:

	1990	1989	1988
U.S. Federal statutory rate	34.0%	34.0%	34.0%
State income taxes, net of Federal benefit	3.6	3.4	2.4
Rate reduction	—	—	(2.5)
U.S. tax on international dividend	0.4	0.3	4.2
International rate differential	0.1	(0.9)	(2.6)
Leasing subsidiary	(0.1)	(0.2)	(0.8)
Restructuring charge	—	0.6	—
Other	(1.3)	—	1.6
Effective tax rate	36.7%	37.2%	36.3%

No provisions have been made for possible international withholding and U.S. income taxes payable on the distribution of approximately $120,009 of undistributed earnings which have been or will be reinvested abroad or are expected to be returned to the United States in tax-free distributions. Provisions for taxes have been made for all earnings which the company presently plans to repatriate.

L. Supplementary Earnings Statement Information

	1990	1989	1988
Non-Operating Income:			
Interest income	$25,501	$14,497	$9,666
Settlement of lawsuit	5,695	—	—
Income from leveraged leases	5,273	6,694	8,219
Gain (loss) on sale of property, plant and equipment	1,005	(1,933)	(673)
Other non-operating (expense) income	(2,734)	(2,152)	43
Total	$34,740	$17,106	$17,255
Research and Development	$55,384	$44,720	$46,533
Maintenance and Repairs	47,328	49,572	47,131
Advertising	26,584	25,933	19,586
Rents	22,857	23,238	19,958
Foreign Currency Transaction (Loss) Gain	(1,423)	292	2,343

O. Pension Plans

The company's domestic operations maintain several pension plans, primarily defined benefit pension plans covering substantially all employees for normal retirement benefits at age 65. Defined benefits for salaried employees are based on a final average compensation formula and hourly plans are based on an amount per year of service formula. The company makes annual contributions to the plans in accordance with ERISA and IRS regulations, including amortization of past service cost over the average remaining service life of active employees.

In 1989 the company adopted SFAS No. 87 for its significant international pension plans. For the company's international pension plans that have not adopted SFAS No. 87, the excess of vested benefits over fund assets is insignificant. The company makes annual contributions to the plans in accordance with the laws and regulations of the respective international taxing jurisdictions in which the company operates.

Components of net periodic pension cost for the company's domestic and international pension plans consist of the following:

	1990	1989	1988
Service cost—benefits earned during period	$12,409	$11,039	$9,515
Net deferral and amortization	(42,253)	24,976	(11,621)
Interest on projected benefit obligation	28,547	25,796	25,414
Actual return on plan assets	10,809	(55,795)	(14,388)
Net periodic pension cost	$ 9,512	$ 6,016	$ 8,920

The net periodic pension cost attributable to the company's significant international pension plans was $843 and $1,000 in 1990 and 1989, respectively.

The following tables set forth the company's domestic and international pension plans' funded status and amounts recognized in the company's balance sheet at December 31:

	Overfunded Plans		Underfunded Plans	
	1990	1989	1990	1989
Actuarial present value of benefit obligations:				
Vested employees	$(193,615)	$(194,793)	$(96,325)	$(90,466)
Non-vested employees	(12,169)	(6,073)	(15,407)	(3,251)
Total accumulated benefit obligation	(205,784)	(200,866)	(111,732)	(93,717)
Additional amounts related to projected salary increases	(35,705)	(45,637)	(3,949)	(3,095)
Projected benefit obligation	(241,489)	(246,503)	(115,681)	(96,812)
Fair value of plan assets (primarily common equities and fixed income instruments)	245,953	267,184	75,493	68,884
Projected benefit obligation less than (in excess of) plan assets	4,464	20,681	(40,188)	(27,928)
Unrecognized net (gain) loss	(7,583)	(15,018)	9,451	8,442
Unrecognized prior service cost	(6,374)	(6,934)	17,281	4,673
Unrecognized net liability existing at the date of initial adoption of SFAS No. 87	6,604	1,682	1,378	4,569
(Accrued) Prepaid Pension Cost	$ (2,889)	$ 411	$(12,078)	$(10,244)

The economic assumptions used in determining the actuarial present value of the projected benefit obligation of the domestic plans were:

	1990	1989
Weighted average discount rate	9.0%	8.3%
Rate of increase in future compensation levels	5.3	5.3
Rate of return on plan assets	10.0	10.0

The assumed rates for the company's international plans, which reflect the economic conditions of each plan, generally varied from U.S. rates by 1.0 percent to 2.0 percent.

Total pension expense for all plans was $10,914, $8,073 and $12,962 for 1990, 1989 and 1988, respectively. Actuarial assumptions were revised in 1990, 1989 and 1988 principally to update the investment return and rates of pay increase to levels more reflective of current economic conditions. These and other changes increased pension expense in 1990 by approximately $920 and reduced pension expense in 1989 and 1988 by approximately $5,838 and $1,218, respectively.

P. Post-Retirement Benefits

The company provides health plan coverage and life insurance benefits for retired employees of substantially all of its domestic operations. Substantially all of the company's employees may become eligible for these benefits when they retire from active employment with the company. The cost of retiree health coverage is recognized as an expense when claims are paid. The cost of life insurance benefits is recognized as an expense as premiums are paid. These costs totaled $6,165 in 1990, $5,075 in 1989 and $3,982 in 1988.

The Financial Accounting Standards Board has issued Statement of Financial Accounting Standards No. 106, "Employers' Accounting for Post-Retirement Benefits Other Than Pensions." This Statement will require accrual of post-retirement benefits during the years an employee provides services. While the impact of this new standard has not been fully determined, the change will result in significantly greater expense being recognized for these benefits. The company plans to adopt this Statement in 1993.

T. Segment and Geographic Information

The company is engaged in the manufacture and sale of electrical distribution products, systems and services and industrial control products, systems and services, and operates in virtually every major marketing area in the world. Major manufacturing plants are located throughout the United States and in Europe, Latin America, Canada, Australia and Thailand.

The electrical distribution segment primarily consists of the manufacture and sale of products, systems and services used in the distribution of electricity. Distribution equipment is used principally in distributing electricity from the end of transmission lines to points of utilization within residential, commercial, industrial or other types of buildings. Distribution products include industrial molded case circuit breakers, miniature circuit breakers, load centers, safety switches, metering devices, switchboards, panelboards, motor control centers, low and medium voltage switchgear, busways and raceways, dry type transformers and power and cast resin transformers.

Schneider and Square D

Schneider and Square D

The industrial control segment mainly consists of the manufacture and sale of control products, systems and services that control the electricity used in the operation of power utilization devices or processes. Control equipment includes motor starters, contactors, push buttons, adjustable frequency motor controllers and sensors. Other products in this segment include programmable controllers, cell controllers, electronic computerized control and data-gathering systems, uninterruptible power systems, power protection equipment, infrared radiation thermometers and pyrometers and snap dome switches and keyboards.

Substantially all products of the electrical distribution and industrial control segments are marketed through the company's own marketing organization and distributed through a system of strategically located warehouses. The majority of all sales are made directly to authorized electrical distributors who, in turn, market the products to electrical contractors, electrical utilities, large industrial plants and other classes of trade.

Sales between geographic areas and industry segments are based on prices approximating current market values. Net sales to a group of customers under common control, for both industry segments, were $161,015 in 1990, $161,156 in 1989 and $176,700 in 1988.

Financial information by industry segment for the three years ended December 31, 1990 is summarized as follows:

Industry Segments	1990	1989	1988
Sales			
Electrical Distribution:			
Unaffiliated customers	$1,170,420	$1,117,619	$1,057,359
Intercompany	18,203	13,083	10,484
	1,188,623	1,130,702	1,067,843
Industrial Control:			
Unaffiliated customers	482,899	481,069	440,413
Intercompany	63,919	51,923	49,244
	546,818	532,992	489,657
Eliminations	(82,122)	(65,006)	(59,728)
Consolidated	$1,653,319	$1,598,688	$1,497,772
Operating Earnings			
Electrical Distribution	$ 152,280	$ 143,541	$ 138,229
Industrial Control	26,302	31,614	40,046
Eliminations	(143)	139	944
Consolidated	$ 178,439	$ 175,294	$ 179,219
Identifiable Assets			
Electrical Distribution	$ 920,781	$ 755,253	$ 701,973
Industrial Control	503,079	447,913	418,247
Eliminations	(792)	(646)	(835)
Identifiable Assets of Continuing Operations	$1,423,068	$1,202,520	$1,119,385
Net Assets of Discontinued Operations	36,681	170,065	181,338
Consolidated	$1,459,749	$1,372,585	$1,300,723

Industry Segments	1990	1989	1988
Depreciation and Amortization Expense			
Electrical Distribution	$ 36,688	$ 29,815	$ 26,345
Industrial Control	22,612	19,628	18,829
Capital Additions			
Electrical Distribution	$ 54,763	$ 50,323	$ 43,980
Industrial Control	39,125	30,125	27,975

Effective September 30, 1989, the company changed its reportable segments from Electrical Equipment and Electronic Products to Electrical Distribution Products, Systems and Services and Industrial Control Products, Systems and Services.

Financial information by geographic area for the three years ended December 31, 1990 is summarized as follows:

Geographic Areas	1990	1989	1988
Sales			
United States:			
Unaffiliated customers	$1,332,390	$1,321,769	$1,256,009
Intercompany	73,646	62,253	47,479
	1,406,036	1,384,022	1,303,488
Europe:			
Unaffiliated customers	138,836	115,678	105,471
Intercompany	22,617	23,691	25,207
	161,453	139,369	130,678
Latin America:			
Unaffiliated customers	78,867	68,178	53,242
Intercompany	1,300	1,217	1,761
	80,167	69,395	55,003
Other International			
Unaffiliated customers	103,226	93,063	83,050
Intercompany	447	256	620
	103,673	93,319	83,670
Eliminations	(98,010)	(87,417)	(75,067)
Consolidated	$1,653,319	$1,598,688	$1,497,772
Operating Earnings			
United States	$ 164,155	$ 163,202	$ 156,791
Europe	3,555	212	4,098
Latin America	10,445	12,547	11,212
Other International	650	(463)	3,942
Eliminations	(366)	(204)	3,176
Consolidated	$ 178,439	$ 175,294	$ 179,219

Schneider and Square D

(continued)

Schneider and Square D

Geographic Areas	1990	1989	1988
Identifiable Assets			
United States	$1,131,085	$ 952,865	$ 883,334
Europe	158,637	120,483	109,297
Latin America	65,847	62,171	62,924
Other International	70,203	69,357	64,886
Eliminations	(2,704)	(2,356)	(1,056)
Identifiable Assets of Continuing Operations	1,423,068	1,202,520	1,119,385
Net Assets of Discontinued Operations	36,681	170,065	181,338
Consolidated	$1,459,749	$1,372,585	$1,300,723

SELECTED FINANCIAL DATA

	1990	1989	1988	1987	1986	1985
Summary of Operations						
Net sales	$1,653,319	$1,598,688	$1,497,772	$1,330,784	$1,274,932	$1,223,193
Cost of products sold	1,088,977	1,027,348	979,591	838,749	820,457	787,310
Selling, administrative and general expenses	385,903	369,726	338,962	287,386	267,066	237,790
Restructuring charge	—	26,320	—	11,192	—	—
Non-operating income	34,740	17,106	17,255	17,590	26,670	14,486
Interest expense	28,760	31,438	22,082	19,699	24,977	21,191
Earnings from continuing operations before income taxes	184,419	160,962	174,392	191,348	189,102	191,388
Provision for income taxes	67,773	59,856	63,310	75,736	85,191	89,465
Earnings from continuing operations	116,646	101,106	111,082	115,612	103,911	101,923
Earnings (loss) from discontinued operations, net of income taxes	4,079	798	7,852	(5,611)	(4,983)	(14,735)
Net earnings	120,725	101,904	118,934	110,001	98,928	87,188
Financial Information						
Working capital	$ 389,503	$ 193,758	$ 178,399	$ 192,693	$ 204,083	$ 202,076
Property, plant and equipment—at cost	799,367	736,739	673,946	630,754	606,757	570,538
Total assets	1,459,749	1,372,585	1,300,723	1,252,819	1,178,826	1,118,473
Long-term debt	244,820	123,420	135,467	141,085	166,389	201,028
Common shareholders' equity	603,594	556,123	636,029	679,711	670,789	606,139
Capital additions	93,888	80,448	71,955	35,356	71,617	61,880
Depreciation and amortization	59,300	49,443	45,174	42,277	38,548	32,430

SELECTED FINANCIAL DATA (continued)

	1990	1989	1988	1987	1986	1985
Share Data						
Earnings per common share:						
Primary:						
Continuing operations	$4.76	$3.95	$4.15	$4.01	$3.59	$3.53
Discontinued operations	.18	.03	.29	(.19)	(.17)	(.51)
Net earnings	4.94	3,98	4.44	3.82	3.42	3.02
Fully diluted:						
Continuing operations	4.57	3.88	4.13	3.98	3.56	3.50
Discontinued operations	.16	.03	.29	(.19)	(.17)	(.50)
Net earnings	4.73	3.91	4.42	3.79	3.39	3.00
Cash dividends declared per common share	2.20	2.00	1.94	1.86	1.84	1.84
Common shares outstanding at December 31	22,886	23,489	25,691	27,660	28,966	28,864
Common shareholders' equity per share	$26.37	$23.68	$24.76	$24.57	$23.16	$21.00
Key Financial Relationships						
Gross profit	34.1%	35.7%	34.6%	37.0%	35.6%	35.6%
Current ratio	2.0:1	1.4:1	1.5:1	1.7:1	1.9:1	1.8:1
Average total debt to average total equity	66.2%	55.7%	38.2%	29.0%	39.2%	40.5%
Average long-term debt to average capital	23.3%	13.6%	15.6%	16.7%	22.0%	19.8%

All financial data for the periods prior to 1990 have been restated for discontinued operations.

All financial data for the periods prior to 1988 have been restated for the consolidation of a majority-owned subsidiary.

Schneider and Square D

Schneider and Square D

EXHIBIT 3

Schneider Financial Statements and Accounting Policies

STATEMENT OF INCOME

(in FF million for the year ended December 31)	1990	1989	1988
Net sales	**49,884**	**45,127**	**40,493**
Cost of goods sold, personnel and administrative expenses	(44,978)	(41,008)	(36,766)
Depreciation and amortization	(1,565)	(1,166)	(1,272)
Operating expenses	**(46,543)**	**(42,174)**	**(38,038)**
Operating income	**3,341**	**2,953**	**2,455**
Interest expense – net	(832)	(757)	(182)
Income before non-recurring items, amortization of goodwill, taxes and minority interest	**2,509**	**2,196**	**2,273**
Non-recurring items:			
Gains on disposition of assets – net	419	550	484
Other non-recurring income and expense – net	(367)	(343)	(642)
Income before taxes, employee profit-sharing, amortization of goodwill and minority interests	**2,561**	**2,403**	**2,115**
Employee profit-sharing	(158)	(130)	(126)
Income taxes	(802)	(912)	(701)
Net income of fully consolidated companies before amortization of goodwill	**1,601**	**1,361**	**1,288**
Amortization of goodwill	(236)	(235)	(345)
Net income of fully consolidated companies	**1,365**	**1,126**	**943**
Group's share of income of companies accounted for by the equity method	**4**	**17**	**(53)**
Minority interests	(445)	(266)	(330)
Net income (Schneider SA share)	**924**	**877**	**560**
Net income (Schneider SA share) per share – in FF	62.96	63.06	48.85
Net income (Schneider SA share) per share after dilution – in FF	61.65	60.53	N/A

BALANCE SHEET

(in FF million for the year ended December 31)	1990	1989	1988
ASSETS			
Current Assets			
Cash and equivalents	1,841.3	3,400.3	1,579.6
Marketable securities	3,020.9	1,924.3	1,243.7
Accounts receivable – trade	14,597.4	14,987.3	13,998.5
Other receivables and prepaid expenses	4,738.1	3,876.5	4,054.9
Deferred taxes	407.5	290.2	236.9
Inventories and work in process	7,712.6	7,159.0	29,715.3
Total current assets	**32,317.8**	**31,637.6**	**50,828.9**
Non-Current Assets			
Property, plant and equipment	14,293.9	13,107.5	12,019.7
Accumulated depreciation	(6,691.5)	(6,365.6)	(6,409.5)
Property, plant and equipment – net	7,602.4	6,741.9	5,610.2
Investments accounted for by the equity method	175.9	135.7	244.9
Other equity investments	1,727.9	571.3	684.6
Other investments	573.0	618.3	909.8
Total investments	2,476.8	1,325.3	1,839.3
Intangible assets – net	147.5	153.5	115.0
Goodwill – net	7,032.8	6,087.8	5,596.8
Total non-current assets	**17,259.5**	**14,308.5**	**13,161.3**
Total assets	**49,577.3**	**45,946.1**	**63,990.2**
LIABILITIES AND SHAREHOLDERS' EQUITY			
Current Liabilities			
Accounts payable – trade	9,867.9	9,614.6	8,440.8
Taxes and benefits payable	4,822.5	4,795.8	3,748.4
Other payables and accrued liabilities	5,230.4	4,332.2	3,405.5
Short-term debt	3,120.5	3,165.8	3,081.3
Customer prepayments	2,509.5	3,848.3	27,606.1
Total current liabilities	**25,547.2**	**25,756.7**	**46,282.1**
Long-term debt	9,958.4	7,345.9	7,712.1
of which: convertible bonds	3,950.2	1,108.8	500.5
Provisions for contingencies	3,942.6	3,890.0	3,758.8
Invested Capital	**24,030.1**	**20,189.4**	**17,708.1**
Capital stock	1,414.4	1,397.2	1,146.3
Retained earnings	6,091.1	5,344.6	3,046.6
Shareholders' Equity	**7,505.5**	**6,741.8**	**4,192.9**
Minority interests	2,623.6	2,211.7	2,044.3
Total shareholders' equity and minority interests	**10,129.1**	**8,953.5**	**6,237.2**
Total liabilities and shareholders' equity	**49,577.3**	**45,946.1**	**63,990.2**

Schneider and Square D

Schneider and Square D

STATEMENT OF CASH FLOWS

(in FF million for the year ended December 31)	1990	1989
I. Operating activities		
Net income of fully consolidated companies	1,368.5	1,143.7
Depreciation, amortization and provisions, net of recoveries	2,164.0	2,283.0
(Gains) on disposals of assets	(418.7)	(550.1)
Others	(0.8)	(28.7)
Net cash provided by operating activities before changes in operating assets and liabilities	**3,113.0**	**2,847.9**
Decrease (increase) in accounts receivable	(944.4)	1,170.4
Inventories and work in process	675.4	(1,708.6)
Increase (decrease) in accounts payable	578.7	(16.3)
Other current assets and liabilities	(1,681.4)	736.0
Net change in operating assets and liabilities	**(1,371.7)**	**181.5**
Net cash provided by operating activities	**1,741.3**	**3,029.4**
II. Investing activities		
Disposals of fixed assets	712.9	1,394.8
Purchases of property, plant and equipment and intangible assets	(2,589.5)	(2,154.3)
Financial investments	(2,788.2)	(1,068.8)
Other long-term investments	125.5	13.4
Net cash used in investing activities	**(4,539.3)**	**(1,814.9)**
III. Financing activities		
Reduction in long-term debt	(1,626.4)	(3,045.2)
New borrowings	1,508.7	2,435.1
Convertible bonds issued	2,655.6	634.7
Common stock issued	71.9	1,877.0
Dividends paid:		
Schneider SA shareholders	(174.6)	(126.1)
Minority interests	(116.5)	(69.7)
Net cash provided by financing activities	**2,318.7**	**1,705.8**
IV. Net effect of exchange rate and other changes	**13.8**	**178.5**
Net increase (decrease) in cash and cash equivalents (I + II + III + IV)	**(465.5)**	**3,098.8**
Cash and cash equivalents at beginning of year	**3,424.9**	**326.1**
at end of year	**2,959.4**	**3,424.9**

The following notes are an integral part of these financial statements.

SELECTED NOTES TO FINANCIAL STATEMENTS

1. ACCOUNTING PRINCIPLES

The consolidated financial statements of Schneider SA have been prepared in accordance with French generally accepted accounting principles and with the international accounting principles recommended by the International Accounting Standards Committee (I.A.S.C.). The differences between these principles and U.S. GAAP are explained in Note l.m), below.

The financial statements of consolidated subsidiaries, which are prepared in accordance with accounting principles generally accepted in the countries in which they operate, have been restated in accordance with the principles applied by the Group.

a) Consolidation principles

All significant companies that are controlled directly or indirectly by Schneider SA have been fully consolidated.

Companies over which Schneider SA exercises significant influence have been accounted for by the equity method.

As an exception to the above principles, Banque Morhange, in which the Group holds a majority interest but whose operations are not material in relation to the Group as a whole, has also been consolidated by the equity method.

In accordance with French generally accepted accounting principles, joint ventures in which the Group is the managing partner are fully consolidated by Schneider SA, after deducting the other partners' share in the income or loss of the joint venture. In cases where the Group is not the managing shareholder, only Schneider SA's share of the income or loss is accounted for, except for two contracts which are consolidated by the proportional method.

Goodwill is amortized out of income over a maximum of forty years based on estimated useful life.

b) Translation of the financial statements of foreign subsidiaries

The financial statements of foreign subsidiaries are translated into French francs as follows:

- Assets and liabilities are translated at year-end exchange rates;
- Income statement and cash flow items are translated at average exchange rates.

Differences arising on translation are recorded under shareholders' equity.

c) Translation of foreign currency transactions

With the exception of the transactions described below, foreign currency debts and receivables are translated into French francs at year-end exchange rates. As allowed under French law, translation differences are recorded in the income statement under interest income and expense.

Exchange gains as well as carrybacks and carryforwards related to forward purchases and sales of foreign currency used to hedge the Group's trading commitments are deferred and recognized at the same time as the gain or loss on the underlying transaction.

Gains and losses on unhedged forward currency transactions are credited or charged to income. The gain or loss corresponds to the difference between the forward exchange rate provided for in the contract and the exchange rate prevailing at year end for purchases and sales made in the same currency and according to the same term.

In cases where a speculative currency position is considered to exist due to the future interest on fixed to variable currency swaps, the interest is discounted on the basis of the fixed rate and stated at the exchange rate prevailing at year end for cash transactions. The translation difference is credited or charged to income.

d) Financial instruments based on exchange and interest rates

The Group uses financial instruments based on exchange and interest rates. The methods used to account for these instruments are described above.

Schneider and Square D

e) Long-term contracts

Income from long-term contracts is recognized by the percentage-of-completion method, based on the financial status of the contract. Probable losses upon completion of a given contract are provided for in full as soon as they become known. The cost of work in process includes costs relating directly to the contracts and a percentage of overheads.

The estimated cost of the remaining work on contracts expected to generate a loss does not take account of any income from claims, except where such claims have been accepted by the customer and the latter has no major financing problems. Contracts in progress are therefore stated at the lower of cost or realizable value.

In accordance with the logic underlying the percentage-of-completion method, work in process is matched with customer prepayments received upon presentation of a schedule of work performed to date. However, prepayments in connection with the work in process include:
- Prepayments to finance production;
- Prepayments for work in process on contracts which are still in the early stages and for which it is not possible to make any estimate of probable income or losses; and
- Contracts scheduled to last less than twelve months.

f) Research and development expenditures

Internally-financed research and development expenditures are charged to income for the period.

g) Deferred taxes

Deferred taxes corresponding to timing differences between the recognition of income and expenses in the consolidated financial statements and for tax purposes are accounted for by the liability method.

h) Provisions for retirement bonuses

The Group's liability for retirement bonuses is calculated taking into account projected future compensation levels. The method used is in accordance with the Financial Accounting Standards Board (FASB) Statement of Financial Accounting Standards No. 87.

Part of the Group's liability for retirement bonuses is provided for and part is funded by an insured plan. The provisions are calculated for all eligible employees and the same discount and indexation rates are used for all Group companies that have adopted this method. For the insured plan, the current value of the plan assets has been calculated and provision has been made for any unfunded liability.

i) Marketable securities

Almost all marketable securities represent conventional short-term instruments (commercial paper, mutual funds and related securities). They are stated at cost. In the case of bonds and other debt instruments, cost includes accrued interest.

j) Inventories and work in process

Inventories and work in process are stated at weighted average cost. Any difference between cost and realizable value is provided for.

The cost of work in process, semi-finished and finished products includes direct materials and labor costs, sub-contracting costs incurred up to the balance sheet date and a percentage of production overheads

k) Property, plant and equipment

Land, buildings and equipment are stated at cost. Assets held at the time of a legal revaluation are stated at revalued cost. An equivalent amount is recorded in shareholders' equity, under retained earnings or revaluation reserve, and is written back to income in an amount matching the corresponding depreciation and disposals, so that the revaluation has no impact on income.

In the case of subsidiaries operating in high-inflation countries, the impact of legal revaluations is eliminated on consolidation and the resulting translation differences are recorded in retained earnings.

Property, plant and equipment is depreciated on a straight-line basis over the estimated useful lives of the assets.

Property, plant and equipment acquired under a capital lease is capitalized on the basis of the cost of the asset concerned and depreciated in accordance with the above principles. An obligation in the same amount is recorded on the liabilities side of the balance sheet.

l) Non-consolidated equity investments and other investments

Non-consolidated equity investments and other investments are stated at cost, except for investments held at the time of the 1977 legal revaluation. Each year, the carrying value is compared to fair value and any difference is provided for. Fair value is determined by reference to the Group's share in the underlying net assets, the expected future profitability and business prospects of the investee company, and – in the case of listed securities – the market value of the stock.

m) Differences between Schneider SA accounting principles and U.S. GAAP

The main differences between the accounting principles described above and U.S. GAAP are as follows:

Write-ups

As mentioned in Note l.k. above, the Company has performed certain write-ups which are contrary to U.S. GAAP. The write-ups have no impact on income but do affect shareholders' equity.

Consolidation

As indicated in Note a, Banque Morhange, whose operations are not material in relation to the Group as a whole, has been accounted for by the equity method.

Provisions for contingencies

In U.S. GAAP, the part of these provisions related to operating cycles would be considered as accrued liabilities.

Customer prepayments

In the consolidated financial statements, customer prepayments are recorded as a separate component of current liabilities. Under U.S. GAAP, work in process in an amount equal to the cost of the work performed for which no income or loss has been recognized.

Deferred taxes

In December 1987, the FASB issued a new standard concerning the accounting treatment of deferred taxes. The application of this standard is not compulsory in 1990. The Company has not yet decided the date at which it will start applying this standard and, in view of the complexity of the new rules, has not determined the impact that its application would have had on the 1990 financial statements as presented.

Non-recurring income and expense

Non-recurring income and expense includes items that the Company considers to be non-recurring but that would be treated as operating income and expense under U.S. GAAP. In addition, under U.S. GAAP, the amortization of goodwill would have been accounted for under income from continuing operations.

These reclassifications would have the following impact on income from continuing operations:

(in FF million)	**1990**	1989
Income from continuing operations, before tax	**2,509**	2,196
Non-recurring income other than extraordinary items	**(237)**	85
Amortization of goodwill	**(236)**	(235)
Income from continuing operations, before tax, according to U.S. GAAP	**2,036**	2,046

EXHIBIT 4
Square D Common Stock Purchase Plan

The firm's Articles of Incorporation were modified in August 1988 as follows:

The Company adopted a new Share Purchase Rights Plan and declared a dividend distribution of one new common purchase right on each outstanding share of Square D common stock. The rights are exercisable only if someone acquires 20 percent or more of the company's common stock or announces a tender offer. At any time a person or group acquires 20 percent or more of the company's outstanding common stock and prior to that person acquiring 50 percent or more of the company's common stock, the company may exchange the rights (other than rights owned by such 20 percent or greater shareholder) in whole or in part for one share of common stock per right. If a person or group acquires 20 percent or more of the common stock, or certain events occur, each right not owned by the 20 percent or greater shareholder becomes exercisable for the number of shares of the company having a market value of twice the exercise price of the right. If the company is acquired in a merger or other business combination transaction or 50 percent or more of its assets or earning power are sold at any time after the rights become exercisable, the rights entitle a holder to buy a number of shares of common stock of the acquiring company having a market value of twice the exercise price of each right.

EXHIBIT 5

Selected Square D Stock Data for the Fourth Quarter 1990[a]

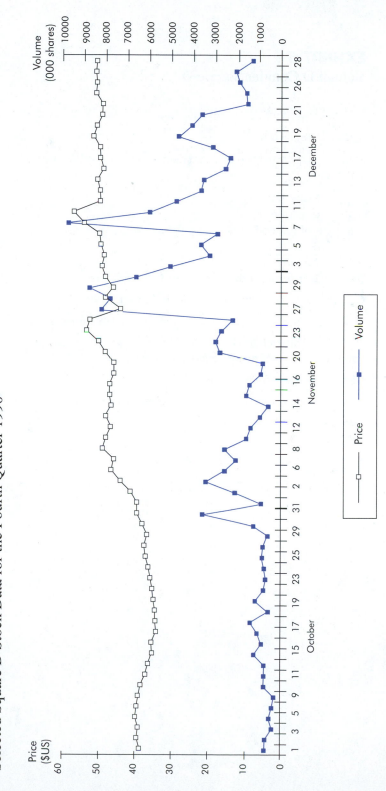

a. In late 1990, approximately 23 million shares were outstanding.

Schneider and Square D

EXHIBIT 6
Valuation Data for Square D

Square D equity beta	0.95
Moody's corporate bond average yield in February 1991 for major ratings:	
Aaa	8.83%
Aa	9.16%
A	9.38%
Ba	10.07%
Prime rate in February 1991	8.8%
Treasury bills rates in February 1991 (3 months)	6.0%
Government 30-year treasuries rates in February 1991	8.25%
Square D commercial paper rating in February 1991 (on a scale from P3 to P1, P1 being the best rating)	P1
Square D corporate bonds rating in February 1991	Aa3
US federal statutory tax rate in 1990	34.0%
State income tax rate, net of federal benefit in 1990	3.6%

Prospective Analysis: Valuation Implementation

To move from the valuation theory discussed in the previous chapter to the actual task of valuing a company, one has to deal with a number of issues. First, the analyst needs to make forecasts of financial performance stated in terms of dividends, earnings, and book values, or free cash flows over the life of the firm. As a practical matter, the forecasting task is often divided into two subcomponents—detailed forecasts over a finite number of years and a forecast of "terminal value," which represents a summary forecast of performance beyond the period of detailed forecasts. Second, the analyst needs to estimate the cost of capital to discount these forecasts. We discuss these issues in this chapter, and provide guidance on how to deal with them.

DETAILED FORECASTS OF PERFORMANCE

The horizon over which detailed forecasts are to be made is itself a choice variable. We will discuss later in this chapter how the analyst might make this choice. Once it is made, the next step is to consider the set of assumptions regarding a firm's performance that are needed to arrive at the forecasts. We described in Chapter 10 the general framework of financial forecasting. Since valuation involves forecasting over a long time horizon, it is not practical to forecast all the line items in a company's financial statements. Instead, the analyst has to focus on the key elements of a firm's performance.

The key to sound forecasts, of course, is that the underlying assumptions are grounded in a company's business reality. Strategy analysis provides a critical understanding of a company's value proposition, and whether or not current performance is likely to be sustainable in future. Accounting analysis and ratio analysis provide a deep understanding of a company's current performance, and whether the ratios themselves are reliable indicators of performance. It is, therefore, important to see the valuation forecasts as a continuation of the earlier steps in business analysis rather than as a discreet and unconnected exercise from the rest of the analysis.

A common practice for generating valuation forecasts is to begin with assumptions about the following six key performance drivers of a company in each time period: (1) the sales growth rate over the prior year, (2) the ratio of net operating profit after tax to sales, (3) the ratio of after-tax net interest expense to net debt, (4) the ratio of net operating working capital to sales, (5) the ratio of net operating long-term assets to sales, and (6) the ratio of net debt to net capital. All the balance sheet items in these ratios are beginning-of-period balances, and all the income statement items are for a given time period.[1] Together, these six assumptions are sufficient to forecast a company's income statement, balance sheet, cash flows, and return on equity.[2] To forecast abnormal net operating profit after tax and abnormal earnings, we also need to estimate the firm's cost of capital.

We discussed in Chapter 9 the definition of the items used in the above ratios—net operating profit after tax (NOPAT), after-tax interest expense, net operating working capital, net operating long-term assets, net debt, and net capital. These are recapped in Table 12-1.

Table 12-1 Definitions of Financial Items Used in Valuation Forecasts

Variable	Definition
Net operating profit after tax (NOPAT)	Net income + Net Interest Expense × (1 − Tax rate)
After-tax net interest expense	(Interest expense − Interest income) × (1 − Tax rate)
Net operating working capital	(Current assets − Excess cash and short-term investments) − (Current liabilities − Interest-bearing current liabilities) where excess cash is the cash on the balance sheet less cash needed for supporting operations
Net operating long-term assets	(Long-term assets − Non-interest-bearing long-term liabilities)
Net debt	All interest-bearing liabilities − Excess cash
Net capital	Net debt + Shareholders' equity
Operating assets	Net operating working capital + Net operating long-term assets

To illustrate the mechanics of forecasting, we show an example in Table 12-2. The example is for Sigma Inc., with sales of $1,000 million in 1998 and net assets of $715 million ($275 million net operating working capital, and $440 million long-term operating assets) at the end of 1998. The table shows Sigma's actual balance sheet at the beginning of 1999, forecasts of summary income statements for 1999 to 2003, and forecasts of beginning balance sheets for 2000 to 2004.

The forecasted financial statements are based on the following assumptions:
(1) Sales will grow each year at a rate of 10 percent from 1999 to 2003. Sales in 2004 will grow at 3.5 percent in 2004. (This assumption will be discussed and altered later.) Sales growth forecast is based on the past pattern of sales for the company, expected growth in industry sales, and the company's strategic position within the industry;
(2) The ratio of NOPAT to sales will be 14 percent in 1999, and will decline by 1 percentage point each year to 10 percent in 2003. The initial level of assumed NOPAT reflects the company's strategy and its past operating performance. The decline in NOPAT margins reflects the expected increase in competitive forces in this time period;

(3) The ratio of after-tax net interest expense to net debt is 5 percent. This is based on the expected interest rates given the company's capital structure policy (which will be discussed later) and forecasted tax rate;

(4) The ratio of net operating working capital (at the beginning of the year) to sales (during the year) is 25 percent. Net working capital includes an operating cash balance of 1 percent of sales;

(5) The ratio of net long-term assets (at the beginning of the year) to sales (during the year) is 40 percent. This assumption reflects the pattern of asset turnover in the past, expected depreciation and amortization policies, expected capital expenditures, and expected increases in deferred tax liability; and

(6) Net debt is assumed to be 40 percent of net capital, based on the company's business risk and financing strategy. Net debt includes any cash and marketable securities balances that are not required to support operations.

Table 12-2 Forecasts for Valuation of Sigma Inc. from 1999 to 2003

($ millions)	1999	2000	2001	2002	2003	2004
Income Statement						
Sales	$1,100	$1,210	$1,331	$1,464	$1,611	$1,667
Net operating profit after tax (NOPAT)	121	121	120	117	113	
After-tax net interest expense	14	16	17	19	21	
Net income	$107	$105	$103	$98	$92	
Balance Sheet (at the beginning of the year)						
Net operating working capital	$275	$303	$333	$366	$ 403	$417
Net long-term assets	440	484	532	586	644	667
Total net assets	$715	$787	$865	$952	$1,047	$1,083
Net debt	286	315	346	381	419	433
Shareholders' equity	429	472	519	571	628	650
Total net capital	$715	$787	$865	$952	$1,047	$1,083

Note: The 1999 balance sheet shows the actual balances at the beginning of the year; the balance sheets for the rest of the years are forecasts of the beginning-of-year balances. Income statements for each year show the forecasted amounts during that year. To forecast the balance sheet for the beginning of 2004, it is assumed that there will be 3.5 percent sales growth in 2004. The 2004 beginning balance sheet forecasts will change under different growth rate assumptions beyond 2003, as discussed later.

Table 12-3 shows the performance forecasts implied by the financial statement forecasts in Table 12-2. Six performance forecasts, which can be used as input into the valuation exercise, are shown: abnormal operating ROA, abnormal ROE, abnormal NOPAT, abnormal earnings, free cash flows to debt and equity holders, and free cash flows to equity holders implied by the forecasted income statement and balance sheet. The following definitions are used in the calculations:

(1) Abnormal operating ROA is the difference between operating ROA and the weighted average cost of debt and equity (WACC), where operating ROA is the ratio of NOPAT during the year to net assets at the beginning of the year;

(2) Abnormal ROE is the difference between ROE and cost of equity, where ROE is the ratio of net income to beginning-of-year equity;

(3) Abnormal NOPAT is NOPAT less total net capital at the beginning of the year times the weighted average cost of capital;

(4) Abnormal earnings is net income less shareholders' equity at the beginning of the year times cost of equity;

(5) Free cash flows to debt and equity are NOPAT less the increase in operating working capital less the increase in net long-term assets; and

(6) Free cash flow to equity is net income less the increase in operating working capital less the increase in net long-term assets plus the increase in net debt.

The weighted average cost of capital (WACC) used is 9.2 percent based on an assumed equity cost of capital of 12 percent, a 5 percent after-tax net interest rate on debt, and a 40 percent ratio of debt to net capital. Recall that the net interest rate and capital structure assumptions are among the six assumptions made earlier for forecasting income statements and balance sheets. Here we needed to make an additional assumption about the firm's cost of equity capital. We will discuss later in the chapter how to make assumptions regarding a company's equity capital.

Recall that the balance sheet at the beginning of 2004 shown in Table 12-2 is based on the assumption that sales in 2004 will grow at 3.5 percent. If we assume a low growth in sales, the assumed incremental investments in working capital and long-term assets in 2003 will also be low. As a result, cash flows to debt and equity and cash flows to equity shown in 2003 will show a significant jump in 2003, as shown in Table 12-3. If we assumed a larger growth rate in 2004 and beyond, free cash flows in 2003 will jump by a smaller amount. As discussed in Chapter 11, the performance variables forecasted in Table 12-3 are key inputs into the valuation process. Operating ROA, abnormal NOPAT, and free cash flow to debt and equity can be used to value Sigma's net capital

Table 12-3 Performance Forecasts for Sigma, Inc.

	1999	2000	2001	2002	2003
Abnormal operating ROA	7.7%	6.2%	4.6%	3.1%	1.6%
Abnormal ROE	12.9%	10.3%	7.7%	5.2%	2.6%
Abnormal NOPAT (millions)	$55.2	$48.6	$40.2	$29.2	$16.4
Abnormal earnings (millions)	$55.2	$48.6	$40.2	$29.6	$16.4
Free cash flow to debt and equity (millions)	$49.5	$42.4	$33.3	$22	$76.1
Free cash flow to equity (millions)	$63.8	$58.1	$50.6	$41	$69.8

(or net assets); ROE, abnormal earnings, and free cash flow to equity can be used in valuing Sigma's equity.

Table 12-4 shows present values of the performance variables by year. Present values of abnormal NOPAT and free cash flow to debt and equity are computed using a WACC of 9.2 percent; present values of abnormal earnings and free cash flow to equity are computed using a cost of equity of 12 percent. To calculate the present values of abnormal operating ROA and abnormal ROE, the values for each year are first multiplied by the corresponding growth factor, as shown in the formulae in Chapter 11, and then they are discounted using a WACC of 9.2 percent and cost of equity of 12 percent, respectively.

To complete the valuation task, however, we also need to estimate the terminal value of Sigma at the end of the detailed forecasting horizon, the end of year 2003. We will, therefore, turn to the discussion of how to estimate terminal values next.

Table 12-4 Present Values of Performance Forecasts for Sigma, Inc.

	1999	2000	2001	2002	2003	Total for 1999–2000
Discount factor for asset flows	0.916	0.839	0.768	0.703	0.644	N/A
Discount factor for equity flows	0.893	0.797	0.712	0.636	0.567	N/A
Growth factor	1.000	1.100	1.210	1.331	1.464	N/A
PV of abnormal operating ROA	0.071	0.057	0.043	0.029	0.015	0.215
PV of abnormal ROE	0.115	0.090	0.067	0.044	0.022	0.338
PV of abnormal NOPAT (millions)	$50.6	$40.8	$30.9	$20.8	$10.6	$153.7
PV of abnormal earnings (millions)	$49.3	$38.8	$28.6	$18.8	$9.3	$144.8
PV of free cash flow to debt and equity (millions)	$45.3	$35.5	$25.6	$15.4	$49.0	$170.8
PV of free cash flow to equity (millions)	$57.0	$46.3	$36.0	$26.1	$39.6	$205

Notes:
1. Discount factor for asset flows and equity flows are computed using WACC (9.2 percent) and cost of equity (12 percent). The value for year t is equal to $1/(1+r)^t$ where r is the appropriate discount rate.
2. Growth factor is computed using the assumed sales growth rate of 10 percent in all the years. The value for year t is equal to $(1+g)^{t-1}$.
3. Present values of abnormal operating ROA and abnormal ROE are equal to their respective values in each year times the growth factor times the appropriate discount factor.
4. Present values of abnormal NOPAT, abnormal earnings, free cash flow to debt and equity, and free cash flow to equity are equal to their respective values in each year times the appropriate discount factor.

TERMINAL VALUES

The forecasts in Table 12-2 extend only through the year 2003, and thus we label 2003 the "terminal year." (Selection of an appropriate terminal year is discussed later.) Terminal value is essentially the present value of either abnormal earnings or free cash flows occurring beyond the terminal year. Since this involves forecasting performance over the remainder of the firm's life, the analyst must adopt some assumption that simplifies the process of forecasting. Below, we discuss a variety of alternative approaches to this task.

Terminal Values with the Competitive Equilibrium Assumption

Table 12-2 projects that until the year 2003, Sigma's sales, earnings, and cash flows from operations will all grow at an annual rate of 10 percent. What should we assume beyond 2003? Is it reasonable to assume a continuation of the 10 percent growth rate? Is some other pattern more reasonable?

One thing that seems clear is that continuation of a 10 percent sales growth rate is unrealistic over a very long horizon. That rate would likely outstrip inflation in the dollar and the real growth rate of the world economy. Over many years, it would imply that Sigma would grow to a size greater than that of all other firms in the world combined. But what would be a suitable alternative assumption? Should we expect the firm's sales growth rate to ultimately settle down to the rate of inflation? Or to a higher rate, such as the nominal GNP growth rate? Or to something else?

Ultimately, to answer these questions, one must consider how much longer the rate of growth in industry sales can outstrip the general growth in the world economy, and how long Sigma's competitive advantages can enable it to grow faster than the overall industry. Clearly, looking six or more years into the future, any forecasts of sales growth rates are likely to be subject to considerable error.

Fortunately, in many if not most situations, how we deal with the seemingly imponderable questions about long-range growth in sales simply *does not matter very much!* In fact, under plausible economic assumptions, there is no practical need to consider sales growth beyond the terminal year. Such growth may be *irrelevant,* so far as the firm's current value is concerned!

How can long-range growth in sales *not* matter? The reasoning revolves around the forces of competition. Competition tends to constrain a firm's ability to identify, on a consistent basis, growth opportunities that generate supernormal profits. (Recall the evidence in Chapter 10 concerning the reversion of ROEs to normal levels over horizons of five to ten years.) Certainly, a firm may at a point in time maintain a competitive advantage that permits it to achieve returns in excess of the cost of capital. When that advantage is protected with patents or a strong brand name, the firm may even be able to maintain it for many years, perhaps indefinitely. With hindsight, we know that some such firms—like Coca-Cola and Wal-Mart—were able not only to maintain their competitive edge, but to expand it across dramatically increasing investment bases. But in the face of competition, one would typically not expect a firm to extend its supernormal profitability to new *additional* projects *year after year.* Ultimately, we would expect high profits to attract enough competition to drive the firm's return down to a normal level. Each new project would generate cash flows with a present value no greater than the cost of the investment—the investment would be a "zero net present value" project. Since the benefits of the project are offset by its costs, it does nothing to enhance the current value of the firm, and the associated growth can be ignored.

Table 12-5 presents a simple illustration to clarify the point. In it we consider a wide range of growth in sales for the year 2004: no growth at all, 5 percent growth, and 10 percent growth. The NOPAT margin is assumed to drop to 5.98 percent; all other assumptions (including the cost of equity) are expected to remain the same as in the years 1999 to 2003. Under these assumptions, the table shows that the sales growth—whether zero, 5 percent, or 10 percent—does *nothing* to enhance the current value of the firm.

The key assumption is that the NOPAT margin is 5.98 percent of sales. Under that assumption, Sigma's operating ROA is equal to its weighted average cost of capital, its ROE is equal to its cost of equity, and the firm earns no abnormal NOPAT or abnormal earnings. While the firm generates positive free cash flows, they are just sufficient to cover the capital charge on the investments in working capital and long-term assets required to generate the incremental sales. These conclusions remain unchanged whatever is the growth rate in sales.

The assumption about the NOPAT margin is not arbitrary, but based on the notion that over the long run, competitive forces drive margins to the point of costs. Margins any higher than this attract competition and force margins down. Margins below this level drive investment away until margins recover.

When we invoke the competitive equilibrium assumption during the terminal years, it is straightforward to determine what the terminal values will be. These are shown in Table 12-6, assuming a sales growth of 3.5 percent in 2004 and beyond. Since abnormal NOPAT and abnormal earnings are zero in years beyond 2003, terminal values for these

Table 12-5 Sigma's Financial Forecasts Beyond the Terminal Year
Under Alternative Growth Assumptions and No Abnormal Earnings

	Forecasted Financial Performance in 2004 and Beyond		
Assumed sales growth	0%	5%	10%
Assumed NOPAT margin	5.98%	5.98%	5.98%
Sales (millions)	$1,611	$1,691	$1,772
NOPAT (millions)	$96	$101	$106
Net income (millions)	$75	$79	$83
Assets at the beginning of the year (millions)	$1,047	$1,099	$1,152
Equity at the beginning of the year (millions)	$628	$660	$691
Abnormal operating ROA	0%	0%	0%
Abnormal ROE	0%	0%	0%
Abnormal NOPAT	$0	$0	$0
Abnormal earnings	$0	$0	$0

two variables are zero. Since free cash flows are essentially equal to the capital charge, terminal values for free cash flow to capital and free cash flow to equity are the same as the book values of capital and equity in Table 12-2, respectively.

Terminal value estimation does not *require* this "competitive equilibrium assumption." If the analyst expects that supernormal margins can be extended to new markets for many years, it can be accommodated within the context of a valuation analysis. At a minimum, as we will discuss in the next section, the analyst may expect that supernormal margins can be maintained on the existing sales base, or on markets that grow at the rate of inflation. However, the important lesson here is that the rate of growth in *sales* beyond the forecast horizon is *not* a relevant consideration *unless* the analyst believes that the growth can be achieved while generating supernormal margins—and competition may make that a difficult trick to pull off.

Table 12-6 Sigma's Terminal Values with No Abnormal Earnings Beyond the Terminal Year

Valuation attribute	Present value of flows beyond 2003 (at the beginning of 2004)	Present value of flows beyond 2003 (at the beginning of 1999), or Terminal value
Abnormal operating ROA	0	0
Abnormal ROE	0	0
Abnormal NOPAT	0	0
Abnormal earnings	0	0
Free cash flow to debt and equity (millions)	Book value of net assets at the beginning of 2004 = $1,083	$1083 / (1.092)^5 = \$697.8$
Free cash flow to equity (millions)	Book value of equity at the beginning of 2004 = $650	$650 / (1.12)^5 = \$368.9$

Terminal Values with Competitive Equilibrium Assumption Only on Incremental Sales

An alternative version of the competitive equilibrium assumption is to assume that Sigma will continue to earn abnormal earnings forever on the sales it had in 2003, but there will be no abnormal earnings on any incremental sales beyond that level. That is, the NOPAT margin in 2004 and beyond will remain at 7 percent on the sales level achieved in 2003; the NOPAT margin on any incremental sales will be 5.98 percent, leading to zero incremental value from these sales.

If we invoke the competitive equilibrium assumption on incremental sales for years beyond 2004, then it does not matter what sales growth rate we use beyond that year, and we may as well simplify our arithmetic by treating sales *as if* they will be constant at the year 2003 level. Then operating ROA, ROE, NOPAT, net income, free cash flow to debt and equity, and free cash flow to equity will all remain constant at the year 2003 level.[3]

Under this scenario, it is simple to estimate the terminal value, by dividing the 2003 level of each of the variables by the appropriate discount rate. Again assuming a cost of equity of 12 percent and a WACC of 9.2 percent, the estimated terminal values at the beginning of 2004 are shown in Table 12-7. As one should expect, terminal values in Table 12-7 are higher than those reported in Table 12-6. This is entirely due to the fact that we are now assuming that the firm can retain its superior performance on its existing base of sales indefinitely.

Table 12-7 Sigma's Terminal Values with Abnormal Earnings on Existing Sales Only

Valuation attribute	Present value of flows beyond 2003 (at the beginning of 2004)	Present value of flows beyond 2003 (at the beginning of 1999), or Terminal value
Abnormal operating ROA	$[0.016 \times (1.1)^4 \times 1.0]/0.092$ $= 0.25$	$0.25/(1.092)^5$ $= 0.161$
Abnormal ROE	$[0.026 \times (1.1)^4 \times 1.0]/0.12$ $= 0.319$	$0.319/(1.12)^5$ $= 0.181$
Abnormal NOPAT (millions)	$16.4/0.092 = \$178.3$	$178.3/(1.092)^5 = \$114.8$
Abnormal earnings (millions)	$16.4/0.12 = \$137$	$137/(1.12)^5 = \$78$
Free cash flow to debt and equity (millions)	$113/0.092 = \$1,228$	$1228/(1.092)^5 = \$791$
Free cash flow to equity (millions)	$92/0.12 = \$767$	$767/(1.12)^5 = \$435$

Terminal Value with Persistent Abnormal Performance and Growth

The approaches described above each appeal in some way to the "competitive equilibrium assumption." However, there are circumstances where the analyst is willing to assume that the firm may defy competitive forces and earn abnormal rates of return on new projects for many years. If the analyst believes supernormal profitability can be extended to larger markets for many years, one possibility is to project earnings and cash flows over a longer horizon, until the competitive equilibrium assumption can reasonably be invoked.

Another possibility is to project growth in abnormal earnings or cash flows at some constant rate. Consider the following. By treating Sigma as if its competitive advantage can be maintained only on the *nominal* sales level achieved in the year 2003, we were previously assuming that in *real* terms, its competitive advantage will shrink. Let's say that the analyst expects Sigma to maintain its advantage (through supplies of new and more advanced products to a similar customer base) on a sales base that remains constant in *real* terms—that grows beyond the year 2003 at the expected long-run inflation rate of 3.5 percent. The computations implied by these assumptions are described below. The approach is more aggressive than the one described earlier, but it may be more realistic. After all, there is no obvious reason why the *real* size of the investment base on which Sigma earns abnormal returns should depend on inflation rates.

The approach just described still relies to some extent on the competitive equilibrium assumption. The assumption is now invoked to suggest that supernormal profitability can be extended only to an investment base that remains constant in real terms. However, there is nothing about the valuation method that requires *any* reliance on the competitive equilibrium assumption. The calculations described below could be used with *any* rate of growth in sales. The question is not whether the arithmetic is available to handle such an approach, but rather how realistic it is.

Let's stay with the approach that assumes Sigma will extend its supernormal margins to sales that grow beyond 2003 at the rate of inflation. How would abnormal earnings and free cash flows beyond 2003 behave?

Table 12-8 projects performance for the years 2003 through 2006, assuming that sales increase by 3.5 percent, NOPAT margin is 7 percent in 2004 and beyond, and that all other performance assumptions remain the same as in Table 12-2. The balance sheet for the beginning of 2004 shown in Table 12-7 differs from that in table 12-2 because the latter reflects the assumption that sales will grow at 3.5 percent in 2004, whereas the

Table 12-8 Forecast of Sigma's Free Cash Flows Beyond 2000, with 3.5 Percent Sales Growth and Abnormal Profit Margins

	2003	2004	2005	2006
Sales growth	10%	3.5%	3.5%	3.5%
Sales (millions)	$1,611	$1,667	$1,725	$1,786
NOPAT (millions)	$113	$117	$121	$125
Net income (millions)	$92	$95	$98	$102
Net assets (millions)	$1,047	$1,083	$1,121	$1,161
Equity (millions)	$628	$650	$673	$696
Abnormal operating ROA	1.6%	1.6%	1.6%	1.6%
Abnormal ROE	2.6%	2.6%	2.6%	2.6%
Abnormal NOPAT (millions)	$16.4	$17.0	$17.6	$18.2
Abnormal earnings (millions)	$16.4	$17.0	$17.6	$18.2
Free cash flow to debt and equity (millions)	$76.1	$78.8	$81.5	$84.4
Free cash flow to equity (millions)	$69.8	$72.3	$74.8	$77.4

former assumes that the growth rate is 0 percent. So the free cash flows shown in Table 12-7 for 2003 are different from those shown in Table 12-2.

Beyond 2003, which is our terminal year, as the sales growth rate remains constant at 3.5 percent, abnormal earnings, free cash flows, and book values of assets and equity also grow at a constant rate of 3.5 percent. This is simply because we held all other performance ratios constant in this period. As a result, abnormal operating ROA and abnormal ROE remain constant at the same rate as in the terminal year.

The above exercise shows that, when we assume that the abnormal performance persists at the same level as in the terminal year, projecting abnormal earnings and free cash flows is a simple matter of growing them at the assumed sales growth rate. Since the rate of abnormal earnings and cash flows growth is constant beginning in 2004, it is also straightforward to discount those flows. For a given discount rate r, any flow stream growing at the constant rate g can be discounted by dividing the flows in the first year by the amount $(r - g)$. The resulting terminal value calculations are shown in Table 12–9.

Table 12-9 Sigma's Terminal Values with Persistent Abnormal Earnings and Sales Growth

Valuation attribute	Present value of flows beyond 2003 (at the beginning of 2004)	Present value of flows beyond 2003 (at the beginning of 1999), or Terminal Value
Abnormal operating ROA	$[0.016 \times (1.1)^4 \times 1.035] / (0.092 - 0.035)$ $= 0.417$	$0.417/(1.092)^5$ $= 0.269$
Abnormal ROE	$[0.026 \times (1.1)^4 \times 1.035] / (0.12 - 0.035)$ $= 0.466$	$0.466/(1.12)^5$ $= 0.265$
Abnormal NOPAT (millions)	$17/(0.092 - 0.035) = \$298.2$	$298.2/(1.092)^5 = \$192.0$
Abnormal earnings (millions)	$17/(0.12 - 0.035) = \$200$	$200/(1.12)^5 = \$113.5$
Free cash flow to debt and equity (millions)	$78.8/(0.092 - 0.035) = \$1,382.5$	$1382.5/(1.092)^5 = \$890.3$
Free cash flow to equity (millions)	$72.3/(0.12 - 0.025) = \$850.6$	$850.6/(1.12)^5 = \$482.6$

Terminal Value Based on a Price Multiple

A popular approach to terminal value calculation is to apply a multiple to abnormal earnings, cash flows, or book values of the terminal period. The approach is not as ad hoc as it might at first appear. Note that under the assumption of no sales growth, abnormal earnings or cash flows beyond 2003 remain constant. Capitalizing these flows in perpetuity by dividing by the cost of capital, as shown in Table 12-7, is equivalent to multiplying them by the inverse of the cost of capital. For example, capitalizing free cash flows to equity at 12 percent is equivalent to assuming a terminal cash flow multiple of 8.3. Thus, applying a multiple in this range is similar to discounting all free cash flows beyond 2003, while invoking the competitive equilibrium assumption on incremental sales.

The mistake to avoid here is to capitalize the future abnormal earnings or cash flows using a multiple that is too high. The earnings or cash flow multiples might be high currently because the market anticipates abnormally profitable growth. However, once that growth is realized, the PE multiple should fall to a normal level. It is that normal PE, applicable to a stable firm, or one that can grow only through zero net present value projects, that should be used in the terminal value calculation. Thus, multiples in the range of 7 to 11—close to the reciprocal of cost of equity and WACC—should be used here. Higher multiples are justifiable only when the terminal year is closer and there are still abnormally profitable growth opportunities beyond that point.

Terminal values can also be based on book value multiples. The computations for abnormal operating ROA and ROE in Table 12-7 suggest that the value of Sigma's assets and equity at the end of 2003 will be in the range of 1.2 to 1.3 times their book value. These multiples will be higher if one assumes abnormal profitability on future growth also, as shown in Table 12-8.

Selecting the Terminal Year

A question begged by the above discussion is how long to make the detailed forecast horizon. When the competitive equilibrium assumption is used, the answer is whatever time is required for the firm's returns on incremental investment projects to reach that equilibrium—an issue that turns on the sustainability of the firm's competitive advantage. As indicated in Chapter 10, historical evidence indicates that most firms in the U.S. should expect ROEs to revert to normal levels within five to ten years. But for the typical firm, we can justify ending the forecast horizon even earlier—note that the return on *incremental* investment can be normal even while the return on *total* investment (and therefore ROE) remains abnormal. Thus, a five- to ten-year forecast horizon should be *more* than sufficient for most firms. Exceptions would include firms so well insulated from competition (perhaps due to the power of a brand name) that they can extend their investment base to new markets for many years and still expect to generate supernormal returns. In 1999 the Wrigley Company, producer of chewing gum, is still extending its brand name to untapped markets in other nations, and appears to be such a firm.

In the case of Sigma, the terminal year used is five years beyond the current one. Table 12-2 shows that the return on capital (in this case, ROE) is forecast to decline only gradually over these five years, from the unusually high 25 percent in 1999 to a level that holds steady at 14.6 percent by 2003. If NOPAT margins could be maintained at the projected 7 percent on ever-increasing sales, this high ROE could be achieved even on new investment in 2004 and beyond. However, even a slight decline in the NOPAT margin to about 6 percent would, in the face of continued 10 percent sales growth, be enough to render the return on the *incremental* investment to be no higher than the cost of capital. Thus, the performance we have already projected for the terminal year 2003 is not far removed from a competitive equilibrium, and extending the forecast horizon by a few more years would have little impact on the calculated value. Even if we project continuation of the 7 percent NOPAT margin through 2009 with 10 percent annual sales increases (and with the competitive equilibrium assumption invoked thereafter), the final estimated firm value would increase only marginally. Large changes in the value estimate would arise only if the analyst is willing to assume abnormal rates of return on investments well into the twenty-first century. In light of historical patterns for corporate performance, such an assumption would have to be based on a strong belief in Sigma's continued competitive advantage. The upshot is that an analyst could argue that the terminal year used for Sigma should be extended from the fifth year to, say, the tenth year or even a few years beyond that point, depending on the perceived sustainability of its competitive advantage. However, because Sigma is already assumed to be close to a competitive equilibrium in 2003, the final value estimate would not be particularly sensitive to this change.

COMPUTING A DISCOUNT RATE

Thus far, the discount rates used have been offered without explanation. How would they be estimated by the analyst?

To value a company's assets, the analyst discounts the cash flows available to both debt and equity holders. The proper discount rate to use is therefore the weighted average cost of capital (WACC). The WACC is calculated by weighting the costs of debt and equity capital according to their respective market values:

$$\text{WACC} = \frac{V_d}{V_d + V_e} r_d (1 - T) + \frac{V_e}{V_d + V_e} r_e$$

where V_d = the market value of debt and V_e = the market value of equity

r_d = the cost of debt capital

r_e = the cost of equity capital

T = the tax rate reflecting the marginal tax benefit of interest

Weighting the Costs of Debt and Equity

The weights assigned to debt and equity represent their respective fractions of total capital provided, measured in terms of market values. Computing a market value for debt should not be difficult. It is reasonable to use book values if interest rates have not changed significantly since the time the debt was issued. Otherwise, the value of the debt can be estimated by discounting the future payouts at current market rates of interest applicable to the firm.

What is included in debt? Should short-term as well as long-term debt be included? Should payables and accruals be included? The answer is revealed by considering how we calculated free cash flows. Those free cash flows are the returns to the providers of the capital to which the WACC applies. The cash flows are those available *before* servicing short-term and long-term debt—indicating that both short-term and long-term debt should be considered a part of capital when computing the WACC. Servicing of other liabilities, such as accounts payable or accruals, should already have been considered as we computed free cash flows. Thus, internal consistency requires that operating liabilities not be considered a part of capital when computing the WACC.

The tricky problem we face is assigning a market value to equity. That is the very amount we are trying to estimate in the first place! How can the analyst possibly assign a market value to equity at this intermediate stage, given that the estimate will not be known until all steps in the DCF analysis are completed?

One common approach to the problem is to insert "target" ratios of debt to capital $[V_d / (V_d + V_e)]$ and equity to capital $[V_e / (V_d + V_e)]$ at this point. For example, one might expect that a firm will, over the long run, maintain a capital structure that is 40 percent debt and 60 percent equity. The long-run focus is reasonable because we are discounting cash flows over a long horizon.

Another way around the problem is to use book value of equity as a starting point as a weight for purposes of calculating an initial estimate of the WACC, which in turn can be used in the discounting process to generate an initial estimate of the value of equity. That initial estimate can then be used in place of the guess to arrive at a new WACC, and a second estimate of the value of equity can be produced. This process can be repeated until the value used to calculate the WACC and the final estimated value converge. In this chapter, we use book value debt and equity to estimate a company's WACC.

ESTIMATING THE COST OF DEBT.   The cost of debt (r_d) should be based on current market rates of interest. For privately held debt, such rates are not quoted, but stated interest rates may provide a suitable substitute if interest rates have not changed much since the debt was issued. The cost of debt should be expressed on a net-of-tax basis, because it is after-tax cash flows that are being discounted. In most settings, the market rate of interest can be converted to a net-of-tax basis by multiplying by one minus the marginal corporate tax rate.

ESTIMATING THE COST OF EQUITY.   Estimating the cost of equity (r_e) can be difficult, and a full discussion of the topic lies beyond the scope of this chapter. At any rate, even an extended discussion would not supply answers to all the questions that might be raised in this area, because the field of finance is in a state of flux over what constitutes an appropriate measure of the cost of equity.

One possibility is to use the capital asset pricing model (CAPM), which expresses the cost of equity as the sum of a required return on riskless assets, plus a premium for systematic risk:

$$r_e = r_f + \beta[E(r_m) - r_f]$$

where r_f is the riskless rate;

$[E(r_m) - r_f]$ is the risk premium expected for the market as a whole, expressed as the excess of the expected return on the market index over the riskless rate; and β is the systematic risk of the equity.

To compute r_e, one must estimate three parameters: the riskless rate, r_f; the market risk premium $[E(r_m) - r_f]$, and systematic risk, β. For r_f, analysts often use the rate on intermediate-term treasury bonds, based on the observation that it is cash flows beyond the short term that are being discounted.[4] When r_f is measured in that way, then average common stock returns (based on the returns to the Standard and Poor's 500 index) have exceeded that rate by 7.6 percent over the 1926–1998 period (Ibbotson Associates [1998]).[5] This excess return constitutes an estimate of the market risk premium $[E(r_m) - r_f]$. Finally, systematic risk (β) reflects the sensitivity of the firm's value to economy-wide market movements.[6]

Although the above CAPM is often used to estimate the cost of capital, the evidence indicates that the model is incomplete. Assuming stocks are priced competitively, stock returns should be expected just to compensate investors for the cost of their capital. Thus, long run average returns should be close to the cost of capital, and should (according to the CAPM) vary across stocks according to their systematic risk. However, factors beyond just systematic risk seem to play some role in explaining variation in long-run average returns. The most important such factor is labeled the "size effect": smaller firms (as measured by market capitalization) tend to generate higher returns in subsequent periods. Why this is so is unclear; it could either indicate that smaller firms are riskier than indicated by the CAPM, or that they are underpriced at the point their market capitalization is measured, or some combination of both. Average stock returns for U.S. firms (including NYSE, AMEX, and NASDAQ firms) varied across size deciles from 1926–1993 as shown in Table 12-10.

Table 12-10 Stock Returns and Firm Size

Size decile	Market value of largest company in decile, in 1998 (millions of dollars)	Average annual stock return, 1926–1998	Fraction of total NYSE value represented by decile (in 1998)
1-small	$ 10,764.3	21.0%	0.1%
2	27,647.9	17.9	0.3
3	53,218.4	17.1	0.7
4	78,601.4	16.0	1.0
5	114,517.6	15.6	1.4
6	170,846.6	15.5	2.1
7	273,895.7	14.8	3.3
8	476,920.5	14.1	5.8
9	1,052,131.2	13.7	12.8
10-large	5,985,553.1	12.1	72.6

Source: Ibbotson Associates (1998).

The table indicates that, historically, investors in firms in the top two deciles of the size distribution have realized returns of only 12.1 to 13.7 percent. Note, however, that if we use firm size as an indicator of the cost of capital, we are implicitly assuming that large size is indicative of lower risk. Yet, finance theorists have not developed a well-accepted explanation for why that should be the case.

One method for combining the cost of capital estimates is based on the CAPM and the "size effect."[7] The approach calls for adjustment of the CAPM-based cost of capital, based on the difference between the average return on the market index used in the CAPM (the Standard and Poor's 500) and the average return on firms of size comparable to the firm being evaluated. The resulting cost of capital is:

$$r_e = r_f + \beta[E(r_m) - r_f] + r_{size}$$

In light of the continuing debate on how to measure the cost of capital, it is not surprising that managers and analysts often consider a range of estimates. In particular, there has been considerable debate in recent times about whether or not the historical risk premium of 7.6 percent is valid today. Many analysts argue that a variety of changes in the U.S. economy make the historical risk premium an invalid basis for forecasting expected risk premium going forward. Some recent academic research has provided evidence that suggests that the expected risk premium in the market in recent years has declined substantially, to the range of 3 to 4 percent.[8] Since this debate is still unresolved, it is prudent for analysts to use a range of risk premium estimates in computing a firm's cost of capital.

To estimate the cost of capital for Sigma, we start with the assumption that its after-tax cost of debt is 5 percent, its cost of equity is 12 percent using the CAPM model, and the market risk premium is 7.6 percent. The weighted average cost of capital of 9.2 is computed using book value weights of 40 percent debt and 60 percent equity. Clearly, this estimate is only a starting point, and the analyst can change the estimate by changing the assumed market risk premium as well as using an iterative approach discussed above to refine the weights used in computing WACC.

COMPUTING ESTIMATED VALUES

We show below the estimated value of Sigma's assets and equity, each using three different methods. Value of assets is estimated using abnormal operating ROA, abnormal NOPAT, and free cash flows to debt and equity. Value of equity is estimated using operating ROE, abnormal NOPAT, and free cash flow to equity. These values are computed using the financial forecasts and the terminal value forecasts with sales growth of 10 percent from 1999 to 2003, terminal growth rate of 3.5 percent, and abnormal profits in terminal years persisting at the year 2003 level. Asset values are estimated with a WACC of 9.2 percent, and equity values are estimated with a cost of equity of 12 percent.

ABNORMAL RETURNS METHOD

Estimated value of assets = Book value of net assets at the beginning of 1999
$\times$ (1 + PV of abnormal operating ROA for 1999–2003
+ Terminal value)
= $715 million $\times$ (1 + 0.215 + 0.269)
= $715 million $\times$ (1.484)
= $1,061.1 million

Estimated value of equity = Book value of equity at the beginning of 1999
$\times$ (1 + PV of abnormal ROE for 1999–2003 +
Terminal value beyond 2003)
= $429 million $\times$ (1 + 0.338 + 0.265)
= $429 million $\times$ (1.603)
= $687.7 million

ABNORMAL EARNINGS METHOD

Estimated value of assets = Book value of assets at the beginning of 1999
+ PV of abnormal NOPAT for 1999–2003
+ Terminal value beyond 2003
= $715 million + $153.7 million + $192 million
= $1,060.7 million

Estimated value of equity = Book value of equity at the beginning of 1999
+ PV of abnormal earnings for 1999–2003
+ Terminal value beyond 2003
= $429 million + $144.8 million + $113.5 million
= $687.3 million

FREE CASH FLOW METHOD

Estimated value of assets = PV of free cash flow to debt and equity for 1999–2003
+ Terminal value beyond 2003
= $170.8 million + $890.3 million
= $1,061.1 million

Estimated value of equity = PV of free cash flow to equity for 1999–2003
+ Terminal value beyond 2003
= $205 million + $482.6 million
= $687.6 million

Value estimates presented above show that the abnormal returns method, abnormal earnings method, and the free cash flow method result in the same value estimates (except for small differences due to rounding errors)—the estimated value of Sigma's assets is about $1061 million, and the estimated value of its equity is about $687 million.[9] Note also that Sigma's terminal value represents a significantly larger fraction of the total value of assets and equity under the free cash flow method relative to the other methods. As discussed in Chapter 11, this is due to the fact that the abnormal returns and earnings methods rely on a company's book value of assets and equity, so the terminal value estimates are estimates of incremental values over book values. In contrast, the free cash flow approach ignores the book values, so the terminal value forecasts are estimates of total value during this period.

The primary calculations in the above estimates treat all flows as if they arrive at the end of the year. Of course, they are likely to arrive throughout the year. If we assume for the sake of simplicity that cash flows will arrive mid-year, then we should adjust our value estimates upward by the amount $\left[1 + \left(\frac{r}{2}\right)\right]$, where r is the discount rate.

Other Practical Issues in Valuation

The above discussion provides a blueprint for doing valuation. However, in practice, the analyst has to deal with a number of other issues that have an important effect on the valuation task. We discuss below three frequently encountered complications—accounting distortions, negative book values, and excess cash.

DEALING WITH ACCOUNTING DISTORTIONS.   We know from the discussion in Chapter 11 that accounting methods per se should have no influence on firm value (except as those choices influence the analyst's view of future real performance). Yet the abnormal returns and earnings valuation approaches used here are based on numbers—earnings and book value—that vary with accounting method choices. How, then, can the valuation approach deliver correct estimates?

Because accounting choices must affect *both* earnings *and* book value, and because of the self-correcting nature of double-entry bookkeeping (all "distortions" of accounting must ultimately reverse), estimated values will not be affected by accounting choices, *as long as the analyst recognizes the accounting distortions.*[10] As an example, let's assume that managers are aggressive in their accounting choices, choosing to provide for a lower allowance for uncollected receivables even though they have information to the contrary, thus causing the current period's abnormal earnings and the ending book value to be higher by $100. For the time being, let's say the accounting choice has no influence on the analyst's view of the firm's real performance. That is, the analyst is assumed to recognize that management's current estimate of future customer defaults is artificially lower and can make accurate forecasts of future defaults.

Our accounting-based valuation approach starts with the current period's abnormal earnings, which are $100 higher as a result of the accounting choice. However, the choice also causes future abnormal earnings to be lower, for two reasons. First, future earnings will be lower (by $100) in a later period, when the customer actually defaults on the payments and receivables will have to be written off. Second, in the meantime, the benchmark for normal earnings, the book value of equity, will be higher by $100. Let's say the accounts receivables are not written off until two years after the current period. Then assuming a discount rate of 13 percent and the impact of the current aggressive accounting, the subsequent write-down on our calculation of value is as follows:

	Dollar Impact	Present Value
Increase in current abnormal earnings (and book value)	$100	$100.00
Decrease in abnormal earnings of year 1, due to higher book value (.13 × $100)	−13	÷ 1.13 = −11.50
Decrease in abnormal earnings of year 2, due to higher book value (.13 × $100)	−13	
due to lower earnings from accounts receivable write-off	−100	
	−113	÷ 1.13² = −88.50
Impact of accounting choice on present value		$0.00

The impact of the higher current abnormal earnings and the lower future abnormal earnings offset exactly, leaving no impact of the current underestimation of the allowance for uncollected receivables on estimated firm value.

The above discussion makes it appear as if the analyst would be indifferent to the accounting methods used. There is an important reason why this is not necessarily true. When a company uses "biased" accounting—either conservative or aggressive—the analyst is forced to expend resources doing accounting analyses of the sort described in Chapter 3. These additional analysis costs are avoided for firms if the accounting is "unbiased".

If a thorough analysis is not performed, a firm's accounting choices can, in general, influence analysts' perceptions of the real performance of the firm and hence the forecasts of future performance. In the above example, the managers' allowance and receivables estimates, if taken at face value, will influence the analyst's forecasts of future earnings and cash flows. If so, the accounting choice per se would affect expectations of future earnings and cash flows in ways beyond those considered above. The estimated value of the firm would presumably be higher—but it would still be the same regardless of whether the valuation is based on DCF or discounted abnormal earnings.[11]

An analyst who encounters biased accounting has two choices—either to adjust current earnings and book values to eliminate manager's accounting biases, or to recognize these biases and adjust future forecasts accordingly. Both approaches lead to the same estimated firm value. For example, in the above illustration, a simple way to deal with manager's underestimation of current default allowance is to increase the allowance and to decrease the current period's abnormal earnings by $100. Alternatively, as shown above, the analyst could forecast the write-off two periods from now. Which of the two approaches is followed will have an important impact on what fraction of the firm's value is captured within the forecast horizon, and what remains in the terminal value.

Holding forecasting horizon and future growth opportunities constant, higher accounting quality allows a higher fraction of a firm's value to be captured by the current book value and the abnormal earnings within the forecasting horizon. Accounting can be of low quality either because it is unreliable or because it is extremely conservative. If accounting reliability is a concern, the analyst has to expend resources on "accounting adjustments." If accounting is conservative, the analyst is forced to increase the forecasting horizon to capture a given fraction of a firm's value, or to rely on relatively more uncertain terminal values estimates for a large fraction of the estimated value.

DEALING WITH NEGATIVE BOOK VALUES.   A number of firms have negative earnings and book values of book equity. One category of firms with negative equity are those in the start-up phase, or in high-technology industries. These firms incur large investments whose payoff is uncertain. Accountants write off these investments as a matter of conservatism, leading to negative book equity. Examples of firms in this situation include biotechnology firms, Internet firms, telecommunication firms, and other high-technology firms. A second category of firms with negative book equity are those that are performing poorly, resulting in cumulative losses exceeding the original investment by the shareholders.

Negative book equity makes it difficult to use the accounting-based approach to value a firm's equity. There are several possible ways to get around this problem. The first approach is to value the firm's assets (using, for example, abnormal operating ROA, or abnormal NOPAT) rather than equity. Then, based on an estimate of the value of the firm's debt, one can estimate the equity value. Another alternative is to "undo" accountants' conservatism by capitalizing the investment expenditures written off. This is possible if the analyst is able to establish that these expenditures are value creating. A third alternative, feasible for publicly traded firms, is to start from the observed stock and work backwards. Using reasonable estimates of cost of equity and steady-state growth rate, the analyst can calculate the average long-term level of abnormal earnings needed to justify the observed stock price. Then the analytical task can be framed in terms of examining the feasibility of achieving this abnormal earnings "target."

It is important to note that the value of firms with negative book equity often consists of a significant option value. For example, the value of high-tech firms is not only driven by the expected earnings from their current technologies, but also the payoff from technology options embedded in their research and development efforts. Similarly, the value of troubled companies is driven to some extent by the "abandonment option"—shareholders with limited liability can put the firm to debt holders and creditors. One can use the options theory framework to estimate the value of these "real options."

DEALING WITH EXCESS CASH AND EXCESS CASH FLOW.   Firms with excess cash balances, or large free cash flows, also pose a valuation challenge. In our valuation projections in Table 12-2, we implicitly assumed that cash beyond the level required to finance a company's operations will be paid out to the firm's shareholders. If a firm has a large excess cash balance (after taking into account the firm's operating needs and the financial leverage policy) on its balance sheet at the beginning of the forecasting period, our approach requires that the excess cash balance is treated as a one-time cash payout to the shareholders. This payout can simply be added to the estimated value of the firm from the rest of the calculations. On an ongoing basis, excess cash flows are assumed to be paid out to shareholders either in the form of dividends or stock repurchases. Notice that these cash flows are already incorporated into the valuation process when they are earned, so there is no need to take them into account when they are paid out.

It is important to recognize that both the accounting-based valuation and the discounted cash flow valuation assume a dividend payout that can potentially vary from period to period. This dividend policy assumption is required as long as one wishes to assume a constant level of financial leverage, a constant cost of equity, and a constant level of weighted average cost of capital used in the valuation calculations. As discussed in a later chapter, firms rarely have such a variable dividend policy in practice. However, this in itself does not make the valuation approaches invalid, as long as a firm's dividend policy does not affect its value. That is, the valuation approaches assume that the well-known Modigliani-Miller theorem regarding the irrelevance of dividends holds.

A firm's dividend policy can affect its value if managers do not invest firms' free cash flows optimally. For example, if a firm's managers are likely to use excess cash to undertake value-destroying acquisitions, then our approach overestimates the firm's value. If the analyst has these types of concerns about a firm, one approach is to first estimate the firm according to the approach described earlier and then adjust the estimated value for whatever agency costs the firm's managers may impose on its investors. One approach to evaluating whether or not a firm suffers from severe agency costs is to examine how effective its corporate governance processes are.

SUMMARY

We illustrate in this chapter how to apply the valuation theory discussed in Chapter 11. The chapter discusses the set of business and financial assumptions one needs to make to conduct the valuation exercise. It also illustrates the mechanics of making detailed valuation forecasts and terminal values of earnings, free cash flows, and accounting rates of return. We also discuss how to compute cost of equity and the weighted average cost of capital. Using a detailed example, we show how a firm's equity values and asset values can be computed using earnings, cash flows, and rates of return. Finally, the chapter raises and discusses ways to deal with some commonly encountered practical issues, including accounting distortions, negative book values, and excess cash balances.

DISCUSSION QUESTIONS

1. Verify the forecasts in Table 12-2. How will the forecasts change if the assumed growth rate in sales from 1999 to 2003 is changed to 15 percent (and all the other assumptions are kept unchanged)?
2. Recalculate the forecasts in Table 12-2 assuming that the NOPAT profit margin declines by 1.5 percent per year (keep all the other assumptions unchanged).

3. Recalculate the forecasts in Table 12-2 assuming that the ratio of net operating working capital to sales is 30 percent, and the ratio of net long-term assets to sales is 50 percent. Keep all the other assumptions unchanged.

4. Calculate Sigma's dividend payments in the years 1999–2003 implicitly assumed in the projections in Table 12-2. How will these payments change if the ratio of net debt to net capital is changed from 40 percent to 50 percent?

5. Verify the present value calculations in Table 12-3. How will the present values in the table change if the cost of equity changes to 15 percent?

6. Verify the terminal value calculations in Table 12-9. How will the terminal values in Table 12-9 change if the sales growth in years 2004 and beyond is 5 percent (keeping all the other assumptions in the table unchanged)?

7. Calculate the proportion of terminal values to total estimated values of equity and assets under the abnormal earnings method and the discounted cash flow method. Why are these proportions different?

8. Can accounting analysis improve accounting-based valuations? Explain why or why not.

9. Can accounting distortions, if not recognized by an analyst, affect cash flow-based valuations? Construct a numerical example to verify your answer.

10. Nancy Smith says she is uncomfortable making the assumption that Sigma's dividend payout will vary from year to year. If she makes a constant dividend payout assumption, what changes does she have to make in her other valuation assumptions to make them internally consistent with each other?

NOTES

1. As discussed in Chapter 9, using the beginning-of-period balances in these ratios ensures that operating activities such as sales and expenses in a time period are compared to the resources available at the beginning of the time period. In practice, it may not make much difference for companies which are not growing rapidly if the end-of-period balances are used.

2. An alternative approach to making projections involves starting with a beginning balance sheet, making assumptions about asset turnover to forecast sales, NOPAT margin, and after-tax interest rate assumptions to project net income, a book value growth rate assumption to project ending book value, and a debt-to-equity ratio assumption to project total capital and assets at the end of the year. The approach discussed in this chapter, which starts with a sales growth assumption, is more traditional. However, it requires a one-time restructuring of the beginning balance sheet to conform to the rest of the assumptions.

3. Recall that the balance sheet at the beginning of 2004 shown in Table 12-2 is based on the assumption that sales in 2004 will growth at 3.5 percent. This balance sheet has to be recalculated with zero sales growth to re-estimate the cash flows in 2003. Then the free cash flow to debt and equity in 2003 will be $113 million and the free cash flow to equity will be $92 million.

4. See T. Copeland, T. Koller, and J. Murrin, *Valuation: Measuring and Managing the Value of Companies*, 2nd Edition (New York: John Wiley & Sons, 1994). Theory calls for the use of a short-term rate, but if that rate is used here, a difficult practical question rises: how does one reflect the premium required for expected inflation over long horizons? While the premium could, in

principle, be treated as a portion of the term $[E(r_m) - r_f]$, it is probably easier to use an intermediate- or long-term riskless rate that presumably reflects expected inflation.

5. The average return reported here is the arithmetic mean, as opposed to the geometric mean. Ibbotson and Associates explain why this estimate is appropriate in this context (see *Stocks, Bonds, Bills, and Inflation*, 1998 Yearbook, Chicago).

6. One way to estimate systematic risk is to regress the firm's stock returns over some recent time period against the returns on the market index. The slope coefficient represents an estimate of β. More fundamentally, systematic risk depends on how sensitive the firm's operating profits are to shifts in economy-wide activity, and the firm's degree of leverage. Financial analysis that assesses these operating and financial risks should be useful in arriving at reasonable estimates of β.

7. Ibbotson and Associates, op. cit.

8. See "Toward an Implied Cost of Capital" by William R. Gebhardt, Charles M. C. Lee, and Bhaskaran Swaminathan, Cornell University, working paper, 1999; and "The Equity Premium Is Much Lower Than You Think It Is: Empirical Estimates from a New Approach" by James Claus and Jacob Thomas, Columbia University, working paper, 1999.

9. Analysts often estimate the value of a firm's assets and then estimate the value of equity by subtracting the book value of debt from the estimated asset value. Notice that for Sigma this approach leads to an estimated value of equity that is somewhat different from the equity value estimated directly. This difference is attributable to the fact that the WACC estimate here is based on book values of debt and equity, rather than market values. Unfortunately, as discussed earlier, it is difficult in practice to avoid this problem because WACC estimates based on market value leverage ratio are hard to implement. Our recommendation, therefore, is to estimate equity values directly, as illustrated here.

10. Valuation based on discounted abnormal earnings does require one property of the forecasts: that they be consistent with "clean surplus accounting." Such accounting requires the following relation:

End-of-period book value =

Beginning book value + earnings − dividends ± capital contributions/withdrawals

Clean surplus accounting rules out situations where some gain or loss is excluded from earnings but is still used to adjust the book value of equity. For example, under U.S. GAAP, gains and losses on foreign currency translations are handled this way. In applying the valuation technique described here, the analyst would need to deviate from GAAP in producing forecasts and treat such gains/losses as a part of earnings. However, the technique does *not* require that clean surplus accounting has been applied *in the past*—so the existing book value, based on U.S. GAAP or any other set of principles, can still serve as the starting point. All the analyst needs to do is apply clean surplus accounting in his/her forecasts. That much is not only easy but is usually the natural thing to do anyway.

11. It is important to recognize that when the analyst uses the "indirect" cash flow forecasting method, undetected accounting biases can influence not only future earnings forecasts but also future free cash flow forecasts. In the current example, since accounts receivables are overstated, the analyst will assume that they will be collected as cash in some future period, leading to a higher future cash flow estimate.

Brenda Curtis, a buy-side analyst focusing on retail stocks, has watched her favorite industry suffer through turmoil and retrenchment during 1991. But while the industry faltered and Macy's filed for bankruptcy, one retailer—The Gap—was busy generating an almost-unheard-of ROE of 40 percent for the year ended January 1992. This San Francisco based marketer of casual clothing was labeled as "the nation's hottest retailer" by *Business Week* (March 9, 1992, cover story). Curtis has decided to take a harder look at The Gap to see what all the fuss is about.

The Gap's lofty P/E ratio of 35 and price-to-book ratio of 12 (based on a price in the $55 range) suggest that investors expect even more good things from The Gap in the future. Duff and Phelps analyst Carol I. Palmer labels The Gap a "buy," noting that relative to 1993 earnings forecasts, the P/E multiple was not unusually high, and yet five-year earnings growth was forecast "conservatively" at 17 percent, well above the 13 percent forecasted growth rate for the market as a whole. In speaking about The Gap's valuation, Palmer notes the following:

> *Discounting only five years of Gap cash flows (using a weighted average discount rate) and adding the residual value (present value of cash flows from 1996 on) and subtracting debt, we obtain a fair market value of $30 per share. However, since we feel strongly that The Gap is a long-term growth company, it is, therefore, appropriate to discount years beyond the next five, using a weighted average discount rate, into the "fair price"; a ten-year time frame yields a fair market value of $55 per share. Note also that our forecast of fundamentals is conservative by the standards of both consensus opinion and the Company itself.*[1]

Palmer's optimism about the long run is buttressed by her view of The Gap's position within the industry. Few if any retailers had been so successful in recent years in executing their strategy and establishing their "look":

> *The Gap has established itself as a trend-setter in casual wear, at good prices, for younger consumers. Excellent management, systems, and merchandising support a continued leadership position. . . . We think the Company has mastered the right*

Prepared by Professor Victor L. Bernard, with the assistance of Elise Kartchmar. This case is based upon publicly available information. It was prepared as a basis for class discussion and is not intended to illustrate either an effective or ineffective management of a business situation.

1. *Duff and Phelps Company Analysis (April 1992). Duff & Phelps does not disclose the cost of capital estimate used in their model. However, analysts estimate The Gap's beta at approximately 1.30. Intermediate-term government bonds are yielding approximately 6.3 percent.*

The Gap

mix of value-added, fashion merchandise and quality staples. This mix, combined with highly focused image-management (advertising, store layout, and locations), has made The Gap the definition of correctness in casual wear for a broad demographic group.[2]

Ironically, The Gap's notable success may be its greatest source of concern. *Business Week* notes that:

. . . plenty of rivals are regrouping to compete. Department store executives preach to employees about the need to "Gap-ize" the colors, fibers, and display of their wares. . . . Giorgio Armani is looking to skim The Gap's biggest-spending customers with its new A/X Armani Exchanges, which offer stripped-down fashions with a European look at prices much lower than those at the top of Armani's line. . . . The Limited Inc. has Gap-like "relaxed fit" jeans, sold in some stores with a sales tag whose design is strikingly like The Gap's. . . . Dayton Hudson is experimenting with a chain called Everyday Hero that will have a distinctly Gap-like approach.[3]

Despite concerns about competitive forces in the retail industry, analyst Curtis is intrigued enough by Palmer's optimism to press on with her investigation of The Gap. The following paragraphs summarize the information at her disposal.

BUSINESS AT THE GAP

The Gap, Inc. is a specialty retailer of casual and active apparel for men, women, and children. Incorporated in 1969 as a retailer of Levi's jeans, records, and tapes, The Gap was restructured in 1984 under the guidance of merchandiser Mickey Drexler. Under Drexler, The Gap sought to provide stylish yet affordable apparel, primarily for the 20- to 45-year-old customer. GapKids was introduced in 1986 to serve the market for boys and girls aged 2 through 12. Selected GapKids stores include "babyGap" sections offering clothing for infants and toddlers. The Gap also owns Banana Republic, Inc., another specialty retailer emphasizing rugged and casual men's and women's apparel.

Gap, GapKids, and Banana Republic stores are located primarily in shopping malls throughout the U.S. As of April 1992, there were 1226 such stores, 1176 of which were located in the U.S. The remainder were located in Canada and the U.K.

Drexler's motto for The Gap is "Good style, good quality, good value." Analyst Palmer characterized The Gap's formula this way:

. . . mostly staple/commodity apparel, with some differentiated fashion merchandise, at highly competitive prices (given the reliable quality), in convenient locations; while the s.k.u. count is limited, the inventory is deep. To summarize, using The Gap's self-description: "intensely focused."[4]

---

2. *Ibid.*

3. *Business Week, March 9, 1992, pp. 63–64.*

4. *Duff and Phelps Company Analysis (April 1992)*

The Gap's formula begins with its own New York designers, Lisa Schultz and John Fumiatti, who attempt to anticipate consumer desires for clothing that is stylish but basic, and faithful to The Gap "look." The Gap relies more on the vision of its designers and quick market tests than on quantitative consumer research. Designs are created approximately one year in advance of sale, in sufficient numbers to assure that Gap stores will receive a new collection of styles every two months; older clothing still unsold at that point is moved out quickly by slashing prices.

All clothing is manufactured under The Gap's private label, by over 450 suppliers. To control manufacturing quality, The Gap establishes specifications for each order and maintains a staff of 200 inspectors at the factory sites. In 1991, 38 percent of the clothing was produced domestically, and the rest in Hong Kong and other foreign countries. No single manufacturer accounted for more than 5 percent of the supply.

The Gap maintains little replenishment merchandise at the retail outlets. Instead, large inventories are maintained in distribution centers in California, Kentucky, Canada, the U.K., and (beginning in 1992) Maryland. Point-of-sale scanners permit tracking of inventory needs at each retail outlet, so that distribution centers can replenish stock quickly.

Gap stores are usually leased in shopping malls and are company-controlled, not franchised. Most Gap stores tend to be small by industry standards—often no more than 4000 square feet—but many of the newer outlets are larger: about 7000 square feet. They are more sparse than some specialty clothing outlets, but are well-lit, clean, and "shopper friendly," with wide aisles and readily accessible merchandise. Store layout and operations are controlled tightly by the corporation; one observer states that "there's no more room for creative expression at a Gap store than there is at a McDonald's— maybe less."[5] Each week, store windows and displays are rearranged, according to a specified company design, to maintain a fresh, new look even to frequent customers.

The Gap "look" is reinforced through advertising in lifestyle and fashion magazines, and in various outdoor media: bus shelters, mass transit posters, telephone kiosks, and so forth. Advertising campaigns are designed by The Gap's own in-house staff. The ads feature such well-known faces as Spike Lee, Joan Didion, and James Dean. Some of the black-and-white prints used in this campaign have won advertising awards. In 1991, The Gap kicked off a black-and-white television ad campaign, and intended to expand this campaign in 1992. Advertising costs were 1.5 percent, 1.2 percent, and 1.4 percent of sales in fiscal 1989, 1990, and 1991. Comparable amounts for direct competitors, such as the Limited, are not available.

Growth at The Gap has been phenomenal. Sales, which stood at about $850 million in 1986, rose to $2.5 billion in 1991. Over that same period, annual earnings rose from $68 million to $230 million. In 1991, The Gap brand became the Number 2 private label in the clothing business, behind Levi Strauss.

Much of the sales growth at The Gap has resulted from new store openings; the number of stores rose from 960 in 1989 to 1092 in 1990, and to 1216 in 1991. In addition, however, much growth is attributable to enhanced utilization of existing floor space.

The Gap

5. *Business Week, March 9, 1992, p. 61*

The Gap

Sales per square foot increased from $250 in 1986 to $481 in 1991; comparable store growth (i.e., growth ignoring the effects of new store openings and expansions) has been much higher than that of competitors. Below is a comparison of growth at The Gap with each of two competitors, The Limited and Petrie Stores. The Limited Inc. (owner of The Limited Stores, Express, Lane Bryant, Victoria's Secret, Structure, and others) was the second-fastest growing specialty retailer in fiscal 1991, behind The Gap. Petrie Stores (owner of Petrie's, Marianne's, Stuarts, and others), was among the more slowly growing firms in the specialty retail category.

	Sales ($ billions)			Sales per Square Foot ($)			Comparable Store Growth		
	Gap	Limited	Petrie	Gap	Limited	Petrie	Gap	Limited	Petrie
1991	2.519	6.281	1.355	481	302	N/D	13%	3%	3.5%
1990	1.933	5.376	1.282	438	309	N/D	14%	3%	1.7%
1989	1.587	4.750	1.258	389	323	N/D	15%	9%	2.0%
1986	0.848	3.223	1.198	250	277	N/D	12%	18%	N/D

N/D = not publicly disclosed

INDUSTRY CONDITIONS AND COMPETITION

The Gap's performance in the early 1990s was highly unusual within the retail sector. Retail businesses were hit hard by weak consumer confidence and a slowly growing economy. In real terms, sales declined from 1989 to 1990, and again from 1990 to 1991. Particularly hard hit were department stores, which experienced "probably the most trying period in [their] history."[6] Performance by general merchandisers was stronger, but still not overly impressive; ROEs for a composite of general merchandisers (K-Mart, Penney's, Sears, and Wal-Mart) averaged about 12 to 15 percent over the 1987–1991 period, not much different from the average for U.S. corporations in a typical year. Profitability at speciality retailers was highly variable, but healthy on average. ROEs for a specialty retailer composite (Gap, Limited, Melville, Nordstrom, and Petrie) ranged from 20 to 23 percent in 1987–1991.

Those firms who managed to find paths to profitability were the so-called "power retailers" or "New Wave retailers."[7] Included in this category were some specialty retailers (e.g., The Gap, The Limited, and Toys-R-Us) and other general merchandisers, including discount retailer Wal-Mart. The innovations that made these firms successful were varied, and included higher-margin niche strategies as well as everyday low pricing

6. *Standard and Poor's Industry Surveys, June 4, 1992, p. R77.*

7. *Ibid., p. R81. The term "New Wave" retailer is attributed to Dr. Carl Steidtmann, Chief Economist of Management Horizons, a division of Price Waterhouse.*

("value pricing") strategies. Most success stories, however, involved high inventory turns and high sales volume per square foot.

The Gap's 1991 10-K characterizes the specialty retail industry as "highly competitive," and acknowledges that the success of the Company's operations has increased the likelihood of imitation. Indeed, *Fortune* magazine states that "If imitation is the sincerest form of you-know-what, then The Gap is in the middle of an outright lovefest."[8]

On the subject of competition within the industry, Gap Chairman and CEO Donald Fisher says, "We don't worry. We have a distinct advantage in our name, our merchandise, and the number and location of our stores."[9] Is President Drexler worried? "Sure, but hey look, there aren't too many secrets in this business. It's just going to make us run a little harder."[10]

OUTLOOK

In their 1991 Letter to Shareholders, President Drexler and CEO Fisher described The Gap's outlook as follows:

Our challenges for 1992 and beyond begin with increasing market share through continued sales growth. To start working toward this goal we will open approximately 135 new stores in 1992. We will also continue the program to expand our locations by enlarging approximately 100 existing stores.

Along with building new stores and larger stores, . . . we plan to continue to grow our business through a concerted effort to increase consumer awareness of our four brands—Gap, GapKids, babyGap, and Banana Republic.

The Gap has stated goals of at least 20 percent annual sales and EPS growth; 30 percent ROE; and pretax margins of 10.5 to 11 percent. The growth is to be supported through capital expenditures of over $200 million per year beyond 1992.[11] In the foreseeable future, most of this will be devoted to investment in the U.S. However, international sales may become increasingly important. By the end of 1993, The Gap expects to have approximately 100 stores outside the U.S., primarily in Canada, but with an increasing presence in the U.K. Longer term, there is some possibility of expansion to Europe and Asia.

Analyst Michael Schiffman rated The Gap a strong buy, based on his optimism about short-run earnings performance, but still expressed some reasons to constrain enthusiasm about the long run:

The Gap has been a big beneficiary of changes in spending habits in the 1990s. Recessionary times have altered consumers' attitudes over the last couple of years. Expensive, impressive "labels" are out; value is in. . . . In the current environment, consumers have decided that a logo is not worth the extra cost.

8. Fortune, *December 2, 1991, p. 106.*

9. Business Week, *March 9, 1992, p. 60.*

10. Fortune, *op. cit.*

11. *Duff and Phelps Company Analysis (April 1992).*

The Gap

Will these changes be long-lasting? That remains to be seen. It's not clear to us that people's attitudes have been permanently altered; that when prosperity returns, they will still flock to this retailer's stores in search of good quality at a value price. That's not to say the market for good-quality apparel at prices most people can afford to pay will disappear. We just don't think it will continue to grow by leaps and bounds over the next 3 to 5 years.[12]

Analyst Carol Palmer was more optimistic:

. . . The big question is whether The Gap can continue its recent record of success; more precisely, is its formula one for this recession (in which white-collar boomers are tightening their belts) or one for the decade of the '90s?

The market's worst fear about The Gap appears to be that, in an economic recovery, shoppers will trade up from The Gap for casual wear. In our opinion, consumers will merely complement Gap-shopping with more traditionally upscale shopping as they sense themselves gaining purchasing power. We think a better economy should serve to bolster The Gap's formidable consumer franchise.[13]

QUESTIONS

1. The Gap's return on equity for fiscal 1991 was extraordinarily high. Analyze the company's profitability, relative to prior years and relative to the competition. Which components of profitability provided the Gap with its "edge" in 1991? What appear to be the sources of that edge, and what does that suggest about The Gap's business strategy? What is your assessment of the sustainability of the company's profitability?
2. Forecast earnings and cash flows for The Gap for fiscal 1992.
3. With its stock price standing at $55 per share in early 1992, what must the market have in mind for The Gap? Using a valuation model—based either on discounted cash flow or discounted abnormal earnings—infer what possible combinations of profitability, growth, and cost of capital would be necessary to justify such a price.
4. Compare your assessment of prospects for profitability at The Gap with those reflected in the market price.

---

12. *Value Line report (February 28, 1992).*

13. *Duff and Phelps Company Analysis (April 1992).*

EXHIBIT 1
Excerpts from The Gap's 1991 Annual Report

MANAGEMENT'S DISCUSSION AND ANALYSIS OF RESULTS OF OPERATIONS AND FINANCIAL CONDITION

RESULTS OF OPERATIONS

Net Sales

	Fiscal Year Ended		
	Feb. 1, 1992 (Fiscal 1991) 52 Weeks	Feb. 2, 1991 (Fiscal 1990) 52 Weeks	Feb. 3, 1990 (Fiscal 1989) 53 Weeks
Net Sales ($000)	$2,518,893	$1,933,780	$1,586,596
Total sales growth	30%	22%	27%
Growth in comparable store sales (52-week basis)	13%	14%	15%
Number of			
New stores	139	152	98
Expanded stores	79	56	7
Closed stores	15	20	38

The opening of new stores (less the effect of stores closed), and the expansion of existing stores, as well as the increase in comparable store sales contributed to total sales growth for the fiscal years 1991, 1990 and 1989.

Net sales per average square foot increased to $481 in 1991 from $438 in 1990 and $389 in 1989. Over the past two years, the Company has increased the average size of its new stores and expanded the size of some of its existing stores. This has resulted in a net increase in total square footage of 18% in 1991 and 17% in 1990.

Cost of Goods Sold and Occupancy Expenses

Cost of goods sold and occupancy expenses decreased as a percentage of net sales to 62.3% in 1991 from 64.2% in 1990 and 65.9% in 1989. The 1.9% decrease in 1991 was primarily a result of an increase in merchandise margins as a percentage of net sales. The 1.7% decrease in 1990 was the result of higher merchandise margins, somewhat offset by an increase in occupancy expenses as a percentage of net sales.

Operating Expenses

Operating expenses as a percentage of net sales were 22.9%, 23.4% and 22.9% for fiscal years 1991, 1990 and 1989. The .5% decrease in 1991 from 1990 was primarily due to lower payroll costs as a percentage of net sales, which reflected the positive leverage achieved on expenses through sales growth. The .5% increase in 1990 from 1989 was largely attributable to costs associated with the write off of fixed assets for store expansions and relocations.

Net Interest Expense

Net interest expense was $3,523,000 and $1,435,000 and $2,760,000 for fiscal years 1991, 1990 and 1989. The increase in 1991 over 1990 of $2,088,000 was due to increases in average net borrowings and average net interest rates. The decrease in 1990 from 1989 of $1,325,000 reflected lower average net borrowings and lower average net interest rates.

Hemisphere Closure

During the fourth quarter of 1989, the Company closed its Hemisphere stores resulting in a pretax charge to earnings of $10,785,000 ($.05 per share after tax). This charge represented the write down of related property and equipment, inventory, fourth quarter operating loss and a provision for occupancy expenses.

Income Taxes

The effective tax rate was 38.0% in 1991 compared with 39.0% in 1990 and 40.0% in 1989. The 1.0% decrease in the effective tax rate for 1991 was primarily due to a reduction in state taxes and net foreign taxes as a percentage of earnings before income taxes. The 1.0% decrease in 1990 was primarily due to a reduction in state taxes as a percentage of earnings before income taxes.

LIQUIDITY AND CAPITAL RESOURCES

The following sets forth certain measures of the Company's liquidity:

	Fiscal Year		
	1991	1990	1989
Cash provided by operating activities ($000)	$333,696	$256,892	$118,093
Working capital ($000)	$235,537	$101,518	$129,139
Current ratio	1.71:1	1.39:1	1.69:1
Debt to equity ratio	.12:1	.04:1	.06:1

In 1991, capital expenditures totaled $227 million, net of construction allowances and dispositions (representing the addition of 139 new stores, the expansion of 79 stores and the remodeling of certain existing stores) which resulted in a net increase in store space of 876,100 square feet. The expenditures also included the construction of the Maryland distribution facility and an offsite data center. Capital expenditures were $200 million in 1990 and $94 million in 1989, a net increase in store space of 705,700 square feet in 1990 and 177,300 square feet in 1989.

In fiscal year 1992, the Company expects capital expenditures to total approximately $230 million, net of construction allowances, representing the addition of approximately 135 stores, the expansion of approximately 100 stores, and the remodeling of certain existing stores. Planned expenditures also include costs for administrative facilities and equipment. The Company expects to fund such capital expenditures by a combination of anticipated cash flow from operations, normal trade credit arrangements, and bank and other borrowings. New stores are generally expected to be leased.

In February 1991, the Company issued $75 million of 8.87% Senior Notes which are due in February 1995. Interest is payable quarterly. The Senior Notes are redeemable, in whole or in part, at any time after February 22, 1993, at the option of the Company.

The Company has a credit agreement which provides for a $250 million revolving credit facility until March 1995, at which time any outstanding borrowings can be converted to a four-year term loan. In addition, the credit agreement provides for the issuance of letters of credit during the three-year revolving period for up to $300 million at any one time.

Under the Company's 1988 program to repurchase up to 12,000,000 shares of its common stock, 40,460 shares were repurchased in 1991 for $1,004,000. To date, 10,484,528 shares have been repurchased for $92,454,000. Share amounts have been restated to reflect the two-for-one splits of common stock to stockholders of record on June 17, 1991 and September 17, 1990.

PER SHARE DATA

	Market Prices(a)				Cash Dividends(a)	
Fiscal	1991		1990		1991	1990
	High	Low	High	Low		
1st Quarter	$31 1/2	$20	$17 3/8	$12 5/32	$.062	$.048
2nd Quarter	36 1/8	20 9/16	17 3/8	13 21/32	.080	.048
3rd Quarter	47 1/2	34 3/4	14 1/32	10 3/32	.080	.062
4th Quarter	59	44 3/4	21 1/4	13 1/4	.080	.062
Year					$.302	$.22

The principal markets on which the Company's stock is traded are the New York and Pacific Stock Exchanges. The number of holders of record of the Company's common stock as of April 3, 1992 was 4,311.

(a) Restated to reflect the 2-for-1 splits of common stock to stockholders of record on June 17, 1991 and September 17, 1990.

CONSOLIDATED STATEMENTS OF EARNINGS

($000 except per share amounts)	Fiscal 1991 52 Weeks		Fiscal 1990 52 Weeks		Fiscal 1989 53 Weeks	
Net sales	$2,518,893	100.0%	$1,933,780	100.0%	$1,586,596	100.0%
Costs and expenses						
Cost of goods sold and occupancy expenses	1,568,921	62.3%	1,241,243	64.2%	1,046,236	65.9%
Operating expenses	575,686	22.9%	454,180	23.4%	364,101	22.9%
Interest expense (net)	3,523	.1%	1,435	.1%	2,760	.2%
Hemisphere closure	—	—	—	—	10,785	.7%
Earnings before income taxes	370,763	14.7%	236,922	12.3%	162,714	10.3%
Income taxes	140,890	5.6%	92,400	4.8%	65,086	4.1%
Net earnings	$ 229,873	9.1%	$ 144,522	7.5%	$ 97,628	6.2%
Weighted average number of shares	142,139,577		141,500,888		141,080,200	
Earnings per share	$ 1.62	$ 1.02	$ .69			

See notes to consolidated financial statements.

The Gap

CONSOLIDATED BALANCE SHEETS

($000)	February 1, 1992	February 2, 1991
ASSETS		
Current Assets		
Cash and equivalents	$192,585	$66,716
Accounts receivable	7,962	9,609
Merchandise inventory	313,899	247,462
Prepaid expenses and other	51,402	41,268
Total Current Assets	565,848	365,055
Property and Equipment		
Leasehold improvements	394,835	289,266
Furniture and equipment	255,665	178,109
Construction-in-progress	86,967	60,992
	737,467	528,367
Accumulated depreciation and amortization	(189,727)	(144,819)
	547,740	385,548
Lease rights and other assets	33,826	28,297
Total Assets	$1,147,414	$776,900
LIABILITIES AND STOCKHOLDERS' EQUITY		
Current Liabilities		
Accounts payable	$ 158,317	$115,282
Accrued expenses	135,333	102,341
Income taxes payable	32,104	32,725
Current installments on long-term debt	2,500	12,500
Other current liabilities	2,057	689
Total Current Liabilities	330,311	263,537
Long-Term Liabilities		
Long-term debt	77,500	5,000
Other liabilities	16,773	18,945
Deferred lease credits	45,042	23,685
	139,315	47,630
Stockholders' Equity		
Common stock $.05 par value		
Authorized 240,000,000 shares; issued 153,007,862 and 151,708,098		
shares; outstanding 142,523,334 and 141,264,030 shares	7,650	7,585
Additional paid-in capital	124,683	91,185
Retained earnings	654,858	466,111
Foreign currency translation adjustment	575	5,667
Restricted stock plan deferred compensation	(17,524)	(13,365)
Treasury stock, at cost	(92,454)	(91,450)
	677,788	465,733
Total Liabilities and Stockholders' Equity	$1,147,414	$776,900

See notes to consolidated financial statements.

The Gap

CONSOLIDATED STATEMENTS OF CASH FLOWS

($000)	Fiscal 1991 52 Weeks	Fiscal 1990 52 Weeks	Fiscal 1989 53 Weeks
Cash Flows from Operating Activities			
Net earnings	$229,873	$144,522	$ 97,628
Adjustments to reconcile net earnings to net cash provided by operating activities			
Depreciation and amortization	82,133	61,473	43,769
Hemisphere closure	—	—	6,522
Deferred income taxes	(7,045)	(5,637)	(4,134)
Change in operating assets and liabilities			
Accounts receivable	1,643	(3,807)	108
Merchandise inventory	(66,559)	(3,980)	(50,214)
Prepaid expenses and other	(5,557)	(2,969)	(15,953)
Accounts payable	43,220	20,481	12,897
Accrued expenses	33,417	26,910	19,393
Income taxes payable	(574)	18,022	(27)
Other current liabilities	1,368	(26)	13
Other long-term liabilities	420	(2,802)	3,910
Deferred lease credits	21,357	4,705	4,181
Net cash provided by operating activities	333,696	256,892	118,093
Cash Flows from Investing Activities			
Net purchases of property and equipment	(236,521)	(193,734)	(88,398)
Net lease rights	(7,802)	(5,883)	(5,868)
Other assets	(1,382)	1,423	10,628
Net cash used for investing activities	(245,705)	(198,194)	(83,638)
Cash Flows from Financing Activities			
Issuance of long-term debt	75,000	—	—
Payments on long-term debt	(12,500)	(2,500)	(2,000)
Issuance of common stock	20,036	10,189	4,262
Repurchase of common stock	—	—	(213)
Purchase of treasury stock	(1,004)	(10,076)	(21,446)
Cash dividends paid	(41,126)	(29,625)	(22,857)
Net cash provided by (used for) financing activities	40,406	(32,012)	(42,254)
Effect of exchange rate changes on cash	(2,528)	1,245	219
Net increase (decrease) in cash and equivalents	125,869	27,931	(7,580)
Cash and equivalents at beginning of year	66,716	38,785	46,365
Cash and equivalents at end of year	$192,585	$ 66,716	$ 38,785

See notes to consolidated financial statements.

The Gap

NOTES TO CONSOLIDATED FINANCIAL STATEMENTS

For the Fifty-Two Weeks ended February 1, 1992 (Fiscal 1991), the Fifty-Two Weeks ended February 2, 1991 (Fiscal 1990) and the Fifty-Three Weeks ended February 3, 1990 (Fiscal 1989).

NOTE A: SUMMARY OF SIGNIFICANT ACCOUNTING POLICIES

The Company is an international specialty retailer selling casual and contemporary apparel. The consolidated financial statements include the accounts of the Company and its subsidiaries. Intercompany accounts and transactions have been eliminated.

Cash and equivalents represent cash and short-term, highly liquid investments with maturities of three months or less.

Merchandise inventory is stated at the lower of FIFO (first-in, first-out) cost or market.

Property and equipment are stated at cost. Depreciation and amortization are computed using the straight-line method over the estimated useful lives of the related assets or lease terms, whichever is less.

Lease rights are recorded at cost and are amortized over 12 years or the lives of the respective leases, whichever is less.

Costs associated with the opening of new stores are charged against earnings as incurred.

Deferred taxes are provided for those items reported in different periods for income tax and financial statement purposes. Tax credits reduce the current provision for income taxes in the year they are realized. The Company is required to adopt Statement of Financial Accounting Standards No. 109, Accounting for Income Taxes, during fiscal 1993. The impact on the current financial statements would have been immaterial if early adoption had been elected.

Foreign currency translation adjustments result from translating foreign subsidiaries' assets and liabilities to U.S. dollars using the exchange rates in effect at the balance sheet date. Resulting translation adjustments are included in stockholders' equity. Results of foreign operations are translated using the average exchange rates during the period.

Restricted stock awards represent deferred compensation and are shown as a reduction of stockholders' equity.

Earnings per share are based upon the weighted average number of shares of common stock outstanding during the period.

Certain reclassifications have been made to the 1990 and 1989 financial statements to conform with the classifications used in the 1991 financial statements.

NOTE B: LONG-TERM DEBT AND OTHER CREDIT ARRANGEMENTS

Long-Term Debt

($000)	Feb. 1, 1992	Feb. 2, 1991
8.87% Senior Notes, due February 1995	$75,000	$ —
Term Loan Agreement, unsecured, due in equal annual installments through July 1993	5,000	7,500
9.46% unsecured Term Loan due August 1991	—	10,000
	80,000	17,500
Less current installments	(2,500)	(12,500)
	$77,500	$ 5,000

Interest on the Senior Notes is payable quarterly. The Senior Notes are redeemable, in whole or in part, at anytime after February 22, 1993, at the option of the Company.

Interest on the Term Loan Agreement is at prime plus one-quarter of 1% or at LIBOR plus three-quarters of 1%, at the Company's option.

Other Credit Arrangements

The Company has a credit agreement with a syndicated bank group which provides for a $250 million revolving credit facility until March 2, 1995 at which time any outstanding borrowings can be converted to a four-year term loan. The revolving credit facility contains both auction and fixed spread borrowing options and serves as a back-up for the issuance of commercial paper. In addition, the credit agreement provides for the issuance of letters of credit during the three-year revolving period of up to $300 million at any one time.

At February 1,1992, the Company had outstanding letters of credit totaling $148,634,000.

Borrowings under the Company's loan and credit agreements are subject to the Company maintaining certain levels of tangible net worth and financial ratios. Under the most restrictive covenant of these agreements, $376,918,000 of retained earnings were available for the payment of cash dividends at February 1, 1992.

Gross interest payments were $7,593,000, $4,477,000 and $4,501,000 in fiscal 1991,1990 and 1989.

NOTE C: INCOME TAXES

Income taxes consisted of the following:

($000)	Fiscal 1991 52 Weeks	Fiscal 1990 52 Weeks	Fiscal 1989 53 Weeks
Currently Payable			
Federal income taxes	$125,181	$79,951	$55,236
Less tax credits	(6,879)	(1,392)	(1,282)
	118,302	78,559	53,954
State income taxes	24,354	18,011	15,604
Foreign income taxes	6,733	2,142	1,731
	149,389	98,712	71,289
Deferred			
Federal	(9,920)	(5,879)	(4,471)
State	1,421	(433)	(1,732)
	(8,499)	(6,312)	(6,203)
Total provision	$140,890	$92,400	$65,086

The foreign component of earnings before income taxes in fiscal 1991,1990 and 1989 was $31,174,000, $23,377,000 and $11,974,000. Deferred federal and applicable state income taxes, net of applicable foreign tax credits, have not been provided for the undistributed earnings of foreign subsidiaries (approximately $38,791,000 at February 1, 1992) because the Company intends to permanently reinvest such undistributed earnings abroad.

The difference between the effective income tax rate and the United States federal income tax rate is summarized as follows:

	Fiscal 1991 52 Weeks	Fiscal 1990 52 Weeks	Fiscal 1989 53 Weeks
Federal tax rate	34.0%	34.0%	34.0%
State income taxes, less federal benefit	4.8	5.1	5.6
Other	(.8)	(.1)	.4
Effective tax rate	38.0%	39.0%	40.0%

In fiscal 1990 and 1989, accelerated depreciation decreased deferred tax assets by $4,719,000 and $2,797,000. In fiscal 1989, deferred compensation increased deferred tax assets by $4,547,000.

Income tax payments were $135,370,000, $74,790,000 and $73,682,000 in fiscal 1991,1990 and 1989.

NOTE D: LEASES

The Company leases substantially all of its store premises, distribution and office facilities.

Leases relating to store premises, distribution and office facilities expire at various dates through 2025. The aggregate minimum annual lease payments under leases in effect on February 1, 1992 are as follows:

Fiscal Year	($000)
1992	$ 143,780
1993	139,434
1994	134,414
1995	129,422
1996	125,761
Thereafter	624,070
Total minimum lease commitment	$1,296,881

For leases which contain predetermined fixed escalations of the minimum rentals, the Company recognizes the related rental expense on a straight-line basis and includes the difference between the expense charged to income and amounts payable under the leases in deferred lease credits. At February 1, 1992 and February 2, 1991, this liability amounted to $27,400,000 and $19,700,000.

Cash or rent abatements received upon entering into certain store leases are recognized on a straight-line basis as a reduction to rent expense over the lease term. The unamortized portion is included in deferred lease credits.

Some of the leases relating to stores in operation at February 1, 1992 contain renewal options for periods ranging up to 20 years. Most leases also provide for payment of operating expenses, real estate taxes, and for additional rent based on a percentage of sales. No lease directly imposes any restrictions relating to leasing in other locations (other than radius clauses).

The Gap

Net rental expense for all operating leases was as follows:

	Fiscal 1991 52 Weeks	Fiscal 1990 52 Weeks	Fiscal 1989 53 Weeks
Minimum rentals	$137,721	$106,754	$ 88,386
Contingent rentals	30,473	24,666	20,463
	$168,194	$131,420	$108,849

NOTE I: QUARTERLY FINANCIAL INFORMATION (UNAUDITED)

Fiscal 1991 Quarter Ended

($000 except per share amounts)	May 4, 1991	Aug. 3, 1991	Nov. 2, 1991	Feb.1, 1992	Fiscal 1991
Net sales	$490,300	$523,056	$702,052	$803,485	$2,518,893
Gross profit	183,254	179,413	277,731	309,574	949,972
Net earnings	40,913	34,222	70,796	83,942	229,873
Net earnings per share	.29	.24	.50	.59	1.62

Fiscal 1990 Quarter Ended

($000 except per share amounts)	May 5, 1990	Aug. 4, 1990	Nov. 3, 1990	Feb. 2, 1991	Fiscal 1990
Net sales	$402,368	$404,996	$501,690	$624,726	$1,933,780
Gross profit	132,575	131,127	196,283	232,552	692,537
Net earnings	21,154	19,162	47,726	56,480	144,522
Net earnings per share	.15	.14	.33	.40	1.02

The Gap

EXHIBIT 2

Comparative Five-Year Financial Summaries for The Gap, The Limited, and Specialty Retailers

THE GAP, INC.

INCOME STATEMENT

($ millions)	Jan. 1992	Jan. 1991	Jan. 1990	Jan. 1989	Jan. 1988
Sales	$2,519	$1,934	$1,587	$1,252	$1,062
Cost of Goods Sold	1,499	1,190	1,008	814	654
Gross Profit	1,020	744	578	438	408
Selling, General, and Administrative Expense	576	454	364	271	254
Operating Income Before Depreciation	444	290	214	167	154
Depreciation & Amortization	70	51	38	31	25
Operating Profit	374	238	176	136	129
Interest Expense	4	1	3	3	4
Shut-down and Restructuring Costs	0	0	−11	−7	0
Pretax Income	371	237	163	126	125
Total Income Taxes	141	92	65	52	55
Net Income	$ 230	$ 145	$ 98	$ 74	$ 70
Earnings per Share	$1.62	$1.02	$0.69	$0.51	$0.49
Dividends per Share	$0.30	$0.22	$0.17	$0.13	$0.13

Note: Depreciation and amortization above is less than that disclosed in The Gap's cash flow statement because it excludes amortization of deferred compensation.

The Gap

BALANCE SHEET

($ millions)	Jan. 1992	Jan. 1991	Jan. 1990	Jan. 1989	Jan. 1988
ASSETS					
Cash & Equivalents	$ 193	$ 67	$ 38	$ 46	$ 32
Net Receivables	8	10	6	6	9
Inventories	314	248	244	193	195
Other Current Assets	51	41	29	13	23
Total Current Assets	566	365	317	258	259
Gross Plant, Property & Equipment	738	528	352	286	234
Accumulated Depreciation	190	145	114	95	77
Net Plant, Property & Equipment	548	384	238	191	157
Other Assets	34	29	25	32	19
TOTAL ASSETS	1,147	777	580	481	434
LIABILITIES					
Long-Term Debt Due in One Year	3	13	3	2	2
Notes Payable	0	0	0	0	5
Accounts Payable	158	115	94	81	68
Taxes Payable	32	33	15	15	6
Accrued Expenses	135	102	75	53	47
Other Current Liabilities	2	1	1	1	1
Total Current Liabilities	330	264	187	152	129
Long-Term Debt	78	5	18	20	12
Other Liabilities	62	43	37	33	21
TOTAL LIABILITIES	470	311	242	205	161
EQUITY					
Common Stock	8	4	2	2	2
Capital Surplus	125	95	73	57	51
Retained Earnings	638	458	345	277	221
Less: Treasury Stock	93	92	81	60	0
TOTAL EQUITY	678	466	338	276	273
TOTAL LIABILITIES & EQUITY	$1,147	$777	$580	$481	$434

The Gap

THE LIMITED, INC.

COMMON SIZE INCOME STATEMENT

	Jan. 1992	Jan. 1991	Jan. 1990	Jan. 1989	Jan. 1988
Sales	1.000	1.000	1.000	1.000	1.000
CGS	0.658	0.640	0.640	0.654	0.671
Gross Profit	0.342	0.360	0.360	0.346	0.329
SGA	0.193	0.196	0.194	0.200	0.186
Operating Income Before Depreciation	0.149	0.164	0.165	0.146	0.143
Depreciation and Amortization	0.035	0.034	0.034	0.033	0.030
Operating Profit	0.113	0.130	0.132	0.112	0.113
Interest Expense	0.010	0.011	0.012	0.015	0.011
Non-op. and Special Items	0.002	0.002	0.001	−0.002	0.003
Pretax Income	0.105	0.122	0.121	0.095	0.105
Income Taxes	0.041	0.047	0.048	0.036	0.040
Minority Interest	0.000	0.000	0.000	0.000	0.000
Income Before Extra Items	0.064	0.074	0.073	0.059	0.065
Extra Items and Discontinued Operations	0.000	0.000	0.000	0.000	0.000
Net Income	0.064	0.074	0.073	0.059	0.065
EBI/Sales	0.070	0.080	0.080	0.068	
Asset Turnover	1.997	2.032	2.081	2.226	
Leverage = assets/equity (average)	1.830	1.889	2.087	2.228	
Net Income/EBI	0.913	0.921	0.909	0.866	
ROE = product of above	0.235	0.285	0.317	0.293	
ROA = EBI/Assets	0.140	0.163	0.167	0.152	
Sustainable Growth	0.175	0.222	0.264	0.241	

EBI = earnings before interest, net of assumed 40% tax effect.
Sustainable growth rate is equal to ROE, multiplied by earnings retention rate.

SELECTED FINANCIAL STATEMENT DATA

(millions of $)	Jan. 1992	Jan. 1991	Jan. 1990	Jan. 1989	Jan. 1988
Net Receivables	736	670	596	532	95
Inventory	730	585	482	407	354
Net Property and Equipment	1,657	1,395	1,173	1,067	889
Total Assets	3,419	2,872	2,419	2,146	1,588
Total Equity	1,877	1,560	1,241	946	729
Sales	6,281	5,376	4,750	4,155	3,616
Cost of Goods Sold	4,133	3,440	3,041	2,717	2,426
Selling, General, & Admin. Expense	1,212	1,056	923	832	672
Operating Income Before Depreciation	935	880	785	606	518
Net Income	403	398	347	245	235

Part 2 Business Analysis and Valuation Tools

SPECIALTY RETAILERS INDUSTRY COMPOSITE

(including Gap, Limited, Melville, Petrie, and Nordstrom)

COMMON SIZE INCOME STATEMENT

	Jan. 1992	Jan. 1991	Jan. 1990	Jan. 1989	Jan. 1988
Sales	1.000	1.000	1.000	1.000	1.000
CGS	0.638	0.635	0.630	0.632	0.637
Gross Profit	0.362	0.365	0.370	0.368	0.363
SGA	0.252	0.253	0.251	0.253	0.250
Operating Income Before Depreciation	0.110	0.112	0.119	0.115	0.113
Depreciation and Amortization	0.026	0.025	0.024	0.024	0.023
Operating Profit	0.084	0.087	0.094	0.091	0.090
Interest Expense	0.007	0.008	0.008	0.008	0.009
Non-op and Special Items	0.005	0.005	0.004	0.004	0.009
Pretax Income	0.082	0.085	0.091	0.087	0.091
Income Taxes	0.032	0.030	0.033	0.031	0.035
Minority Interest	0.002	0.002	0.002	0.003	0.003
Income Before Extra Items	0.049	0.052	0.056	0.053	0.053
Extra Items and Discontinued Operations	0.000	0.000	0.000	0.004	0.000
Net Income	0.049	0.052	0.056	0.057	0.053
EBI/Sales	0.053	0.057	0.060	0.061	
Asset Turnover	2.141	2.153	2.175	2.190	
Leverage = Assets/equity (average)	1.874	1.889	1.869	1.860	
Net income/EBI	0.919	0.919	0.923	0.921	
ROE = Product of above	0.196	0.211	0.226	0.230	
ROA = EBI/Assets	0.114	0.122	0.131	0.134	
Sustainable Growth	0.058	0.062	0.058	0.054	

EBI = earnings before interest, net of assumed 40% tax effect.
Sustainable growth = ROE × earnings retention rate.

SELECTED FINANCIAL STATEMENT DATA

(millions of $)	Jan. 1992	Jan. 1991	Jan. 1990	Jan. 1989	Jan. 1988
Net Receivables	1,604	1,430	1,290	1,156	631
Inventory	3,578	3,067	2,558	2,316	1,986
Net Property and Equipment	4,456	3,874	3,200	2,878	2,476
Total Assets	11,588	10,104	8,635	7,749	6,622
Total Equity	6,230	5,344	4,576	4,192	3,534
Sales	23,220	20,172	17,819	15,734	13,771
Cost of Goods Sold	14,804	12,817	11,226	9,946	8,769
Selling, General, & Administrative Expense	5,855	5,096	4,480	3,984	3,442
Operating Income Before Depreciation	2,561	2,259	2,113	1,805	1,560
Net Income	1,132	1,047	990	889	730

The Gap

p a r t 3

Business Analysis and Valuation Applications

Equity Security Analysis

Equity security analysis is the evaluation of a firm and its prospects from the perspective of a current or potential investor in the firm's stock. Security analysis is one step in a larger investment process that involves (1) establishing the objectives of the investor or fund, (2) forming expectations about the future returns and risks of individual securities, and then (3) combining individual securities into portfolios to maximize progress toward the investment objectives.

Security analysis is the foundation for the second step, projecting future returns and assessing risk. Security analysis is typically conducted with an eye towards identification of mispriced securities, in hopes of generating returns that more than compensate the investor for risk. However, that need not be the case. For analysts who do not have a comparative advantage in identifying mispriced securities, the focus should be on gaining an appreciation for how a security would affect the risk of a given portfolio, and whether it fits the profile that the portfolio is designed to maintain.

Security analysis is undertaken by individual investors, by analysts at brokerage houses (sell-side analysts), by analysts that work at the direction of funds managers for various institutions (buy-side analysts), and others. The institutions employing buy-side analysts include mutual funds, pension funds, insurance companies, universities, and others.

A variety of questions are dealt with in security analysis:

- A sell-side analyst asks: How do my forecasts compare to those of the analysts' consensus? Is the observed market price consistent with that consensus? Given my expectations for the firm, does this stock appear to be mispriced? Should I recommend this stock as a buy, a sell, or a hold?
- A buy-side analyst for a "value stock fund" offered to mutual fund investors asks: Does this stock possess the characteristics we seek in our fund? That is, does it have a relatively low ratio of price to earnings, book value, and other fundamental indicators? Do its prospects for earnings improvement suggest good potential for high future returns on the stock?
- An individual investor asks: Does this stock offer the risk profile that suits my investment objectives? Does it enhance my ability to diversify the risk of my portfolio? Is the firm's dividend payout rate low enough to help shield me from taxes while I continue to hold the stock?

As the above questions underscore, there is more to security analysis than estimating the value of stocks. Nevertheless, for most sell-side and buy-side analysts, the key goal remains the identification of mispriced stocks.

INVESTOR OBJECTIVES

The investment objectives of individual savers in the economy are highly idiosyncratic. For any given saver they depend on such factors as income, age, wealth, tolerance for risk, and tax status. For example, savers with many years until retirement are likely to prefer to have a relatively large share of their portfolio invested in equities, which offer a higher expected return but high short-term variability. Investors in high tax brackets are likely to prefer to have a large share of their portfolio in stocks that generate tax-deferred capital gains rather than stocks that pay dividends or interest-bearing securities.

Mutual funds (or unit trusts as they are termed in some countries) have become popular investment vehicles for savers to achieve their investment objectives. Mutual funds sell shares in professionally managed portfolios that invest in specific types of stocks and/or fixed income securities. They therefore provide a low-cost way for savers to invest in a portfolio of securities that reflects their particular appetite for risk.

The major classes of mutual funds include (1) money market funds that invest in CDs and treasury bills, (2) bond funds that invest in debt instruments, (3) equity funds that invest in equity securities, (4) balanced funds that hold money market, bond, and equity securities, and (5) real estate funds that invest in commercial real estate. Within the bond and equities classes of funds, however, there are wide ranges of fund types. For example, bond funds include:

- *Corporate bond funds* that invest in investment-grade rated corporate debt instruments
- *High yield funds* that invest in non-investment-grade rated corporate debt
- *Mortgage funds* that invest in mortgage-backed securities
- *Municipal funds* that invest in municipal debt instruments and which generate income that can be nontaxable

Equity funds include:

- *Income funds* that invest in stocks that are expected to generate dividend income
- *Growth funds* that invest in stocks expected to generate long-term capital gains
- *Income and growth funds* that invest in stocks that provide a balance of dividend and capital gains
- *Value funds* that invest in equities that are considered to be undervalued
- *Short funds* that sell equity securities short that are considered to be overvalued
- *Index funds* that invest in stocks that track a particular market index, such as the S&P 500
- *Sector funds* that invest in stocks in a particular industry segment, such as the technology or health sciences sectors
- *Regional funds* that invest in equities from a particular country or geographic region, such as Japan, Europe, or the Asia-Pacific region

The focus of this chapter is on analysis for equity securities.

EQUITY SECURITY ANALYSIS AND MARKET EFFICIENCY

How a security analyst should invest his or her time depends on how quickly and efficiently information flows through markets and becomes reflected in security prices. In the extreme, information would be reflected in security prices fully and immediately upon its release. This is essentially the condition posited by the *efficient markets hypothesis.* This hypothesis states that security prices reflect all available information, as if such information could be costlessly digested and translated immmediately into demands for buys or sells without regard to frictions imposed by transactions costs. Under such conditions, it would be impossible to identify mispriced securities on the basis of public information.

In a world of efficient markets, the expected return on any equity security is just enough to compensate investors for the unavoidable risk the security involves. Unavoidable risk is that which cannot be "diversified away" simply by holding a portfolio of many securities. Given efficient markets, the investor's strategy shifts away from the search for mispriced securities and focuses instead on maintaining a well diversified portfolio. Aside from this, the investor must arrive at the desired balance between risky securities and short-term government bonds. The desired balance depends on how much risk the investor is willing to bear for a given increase in expected returns.

The above discussion implies that investors who accept that stock prices already reflect available information have no need for analysis involving a search for mispriced securities. Of course, if all investors adopted this attitude, no such analysis would be conducted, mispricing would go uncorrected, and markets would no longer be efficient! This is why the efficient markets hypothesis cannot represent an equilibrium in a strict sense. In equilibrium, there must be just enough mispricing to provide incentives for the investment of resources in security analysis.

The existence of some mispricing, even in equilibrium, does not imply that it is sensible for just anyone to engage in security analysis. Instead, it suggests that securities analysis is subject to the same laws of supply and demand faced in all other competitive industries: it will be rewarding only for those with the strongest comparative advantage. How many analysts are in that category depends on a number of factors, including the liquidity of a firm's stock and investor interest in the company.[1] For example, there are about 40 sell-side professional analysts who follow IBM, a company with a highly liquid stock and considerable investor interest. There are many other buy-side analysts who track the firm on their own account without issuing any formal reports to outsiders. For the smallest publicly traded firms in the U.S., there is typically no formal following by analysts, and would-be investors and their advisors are left to themselves to conduct securities analysis.

Market Efficiency and the Role of Financial Statement Analysis

The degree of market efficiency that arises from competition among analysts and other market agents is an empirical issue addressed by a large body of research spanning the last three decades. Such research has important implications for the role of financial statements in security analysis. Consider, for example, the implications of an extremely efficient market, where information is fully impounded in prices within minutes of its revelation. In such a market, agents could profit from digesting financial statement information in two ways. First, the information would be useful to the select few who receive newly-announced financial data, interpret it quickly, and trade on it within minutes. Second, and probably more important, the information would be useful for gaining an understanding of the firm, so as to place the analyst in a better position to interpret other news (from financial statements as well as other sources) as it arrives.

On the other hand, if securities prices fail to reflect financial statement data fully, even days or months after its public revelation, there is a third way in which market agents could profit from such data. That is to create trading strategies designed to exploit any systematic ways in which the publicly available data are ignored or discounted in the price-setting process.

Market Efficiency and Managers' Financial Reporting Strategies

The degree to which markets are efficient also has implications for managers' approaches to communicating with their investment communities. The issue becomes most important when the firm pursues an unusual strategy, or when the usual interpretation of financial statements would be misleading in the firm's context. In such a case, the communication avenues managers can successfully pursue depend not only on management's credibility, but also on the degree of understanding present in the investment community. We will return to the issue of management communications in more detail in Chapter 17.

Evidence of Market Efficiency

There is an abundance of evidence consistent with a high degree of efficiency in the primary U.S. securities markets.[2] In fact, during the 1960s and 1970s, the evidence was so one-sided that the efficient markets hypothesis gained widespread acceptance within the academic community and had a major impact on the practicing community as well.

Evidence pointing to very efficient securities markets comes in several forms:

- When information is announced publicly, the markets react *very* quickly.
- It is difficult to identify specific funds or analysts who have consistently generated abnormally high returns.
- A number of studies suggest that stock prices reflect a rather sophisticated level of fundamental analysis.

While a large body of evidence consistent with efficiency exists, recent years have witnessed a re-examination of the once widely accepted thinking. A sampling of the research includes the following:

- On the issue of the speed of stock price response to news, a number of studies suggest that even though prices react quickly, the initial reaction tends to be incomplete.[3]
- A number of studies point to trading strategies that could have been used to outperform market averages.[4]
- Some related evidence—still subject to ongoing debate about its proper interpretation—suggests that, even though market prices reflect some relatively sophisticated analyses, prices still do not fully reflect all the information that could be garnered from publicly available financial statements.[5]

The controversy over the efficiency of securities markets is unlikely to end soon. However, there are some lessons that are accepted by most researchers. First, securities markets not only reflect publicly available information, they also anticipate much of it before it is released. The open question is what fraction of the response remains to be impounded in price once the day of the public release comes to a close. Second, even in most studies that suggest inefficiency, the degree of mispricing is relatively small for large stocks.

Finally, even if some of the evidence is currently difficult to align with the efficient markets hypothesis, it remains a useful benchmark (at a minimum) for thinking about the behavior of security prices. The hypothesis will continue to play that role unless it can be replaced by a more complete theory. Some researchers are developing theories that encompass the existence of market agents who trade for inexplicable reasons, and prices that differ from so-called "fundamental values," even in equilibrium.

APPROACHES TO FUND MANAGEMENT AND SECURITIES ANALYSIS

Approaches used in practice to manage funds and analyze securities are quite varied. One dimension of variation is the extent to which the investments are actively or passively managed. Another variation is whether a quantitative or a traditional fundamental approach is used. Security analysts also vary considerably in terms of whether they produce formal or informal valuations of the firm.

Active Versus Passive Management

Active portfolio management relies heavily on security analysis to identify mispriced securities. The passive portfolio manager serves as a price taker, avoiding the costs of security analysis and turnover while typically seeking to hold a portfolio designed to match some overall market index or sector performance. Combined approaches are also possible. For example, one may actively manage 20 percent of a fund balance while passively managing the remainder. The widespread growth of passively managed funds in the U.S. over the past twenty years serves as testimony to many fund managers' belief that earning superior returns is a difficult thing to do.

Quantitative Versus Traditional Fundamental Analysis

Actively managed funds must depend on some form of security analysis. Some funds employ "technical analysis," which attempts to predict stock price movements on the basis of market indicators (prior stock price movements, volume, etc.). In contrast, "fundamental analysis," the primary approach to security analysis, attempts to evaluate the current market price relative to projections of the firm's future earnings and cash-flow generating potential. Fundamental analysis involves all the steps described in the previous chapters of this book: business strategy analysis, accounting analysis, financial analysis, and prospective analysis (forecasting and valuation).

In recent years, some analysts have supplemented traditional fundamental analysis, which involves a substantial amount of subjective judgment, with more quantitative approaches. The quantitative approaches themselves are quite varied. Some involve simply "screening" stocks on the basis of some set of factors, such as trends in analysts' earnings revisions, price-earnings ratios, price-book ratios, and so on. Whether such approaches are useful depends on the degree of market efficiency relative to the screens.

Quantitative approaches can also involve implementation of some formal model to predict future stock returns. Longstanding statistical techniques such as regression analysis and probit analysis can be used, as can more recently developed, computer-intensive techniques such as neural network analysis. Again, the success of these approaches depends on the degree of market efficiency and whether the analysis can exploit information in ways not otherwise available to market agents as a group.

Quantitative approaches play a more important role in security analysis today than they did a decade or two ago. However, by and large, analysts still rely primarily on the kind of fundamental analysis involving complex human judgments, as outlined in our earlier chapters.

Formal Versus Informal Valuation

Full-scale, formal valuations based on the methods described in Chapter 11 have become more common, especially in recent years. However, less formal approaches are also possible. For example, an analyst can compare his or her long-term earnings projection with the consensus forecast to generate a buy or sell recommendation. Alternatively, an analyst might recommend a stock because his or her earnings forecast appears relatively high in comparison to the current price. Another possible approach might be labeled "marginalist." This approach involves no attempt to value the firm. The analyst simply assumes that if he or she has unearthed favorable (unfavorable) information believed not to be recognized by others, the stock should be bought (sold).

Unlike many security analysts, investment bankers produce formal valuations as a matter of course. Investment bankers, who estimate values for purposes of bringing a private firm to the public market, for evaluating a merger or buyout proposal, or for purposes of periodic managerial review, must document their valuation in a way that can readily be communicated to management and (if necessary) to the courts.

THE PROCESS OF A COMPREHENSIVE SECURITY ANALYSIS

Given the variety of approaches practiced in security analysis, it is impossible to summarize all of them here. Instead, we briefly outline steps to be included in a comprehensive security analysis. The amount of attention focused on any given step varies among analysts.

Selection of Candidates for Analysis

No analyst can effectively investigate more than a small fraction of the securities on a major exchange, and thus some approach to narrowing the focus must be employed. Sell-side analysts are often organized within an investment house by industry or sector. Thus, they tend to be constrained in their choices of firms to follow. However, from the perspective of a fund manager or an investment firm as a whole, there is usually the freedom to focus on any firm or sector.

As noted earlier, funds typically specialize in investing in stocks with certain risk profiles or characteristics (e.g., growth stocks, "value" stocks, technology stocks, cyclical stocks). Managers of these types of funds seek to focus the energies of their analysts on identifying stocks that fit their fund objective In addition, individual investors who seek to maintain a well diversified portfolio without holding many stocks also need information about the nature of a firm's risks.

An alternative approach to stock selection is to screen firms on the basis of some hypothesis about mispricing—perhaps with follow-up detailed analysis of stocks that meet the specified criteria. For example, one fund managed by a large U.S. insurance company screens stocks on the basis of recent "earnings momentum," as reflected in revisions in the earnings projections of sell-side and buy-side analysts. Upward revisions trigger investigations for possible purchase. The fund operates on the belief that earnings momentum is a positive signal of future price movements. Another fund complements the earnings momentum screen with one based on recent short-term stock price movements, in the hopes of identifying earnings revisions not yet reflected in stock prices.

Key Analysis Questions

Depending on whether fund managers follow a strategy of targeting stocks with specific types of characteristics, or of screening stocks that appear to be mispriced, the following types of questions are likely to be useful:

- What is the risk profile of a firm? How volatile is its earnings stream and stock price? What are the key possible bad outcomes in the future? What is the upside potential? How closely linked are the firm's risks to the health of the overall economy? Are the risks largely diversifiable, or are they systematic?
- Does the firm possess the characteristics of a growth stock? What is the expected pattern of sales and earnings growth for the coming years? Is the firm reinvesting most or all of its earnings?
- Does the firm match the characteristics desired by "income funds"? Is it a mature or maturing company, prepared to "harvest" profits and distribute them in the form of high dividends?
- Is the firm a candidate for a "value fund"? Does it offer measures of earnings, cash flow, and book value that are high relative to the price? What specific screening rules can be implemented to identify misvalued stocks?

Inferring Market Expectations

If the security analysis is conducted with an eye toward the identification of mispricing, it must ultimately involve a comparison of the analyst's expectations with those of "the market." One possibility is to view the observed stock price as the reflection of market expectations and to compare the analyst's own estimate of value with that price. However, a stock price is only a "summary statistic." It is useful to have a more detailed idea of the market's expectations about a firm's future performance, expressed in terms of sales, earnings, and other measures. For example, assume that an analyst has developed potentially unrecognized information about near-term sales. Whether in fact the information is unrecognized, and whether it indicates that a "buy" recommendation is appropriate, can be easily determined if the analyst knows the market consensus sales forecast.

Around the world, a number of agencies summarize analysts' forecasts of sales and earnings. Forecasts for the next year or two are commonly available, and for many firms, a "long-run" earnings growth projection is also available—typically for three to five years. In the U.S., some agencies provide continuous on-line updates to such data, so that if an analyst revises a forecast, that can be made known to fund managers and other analysts within seconds.

As useful as analysts' forecasts of sales and earnings are, they do not represent a complete description of expectations about future performance, and there is no guarantee that consensus analyst forecasts are the same as those reflected in market prices. Further, financial analysts typically forecast performance for only a few years, so that even if these do reflect market expectations, it is helpful to understand what types of long-term forecasts are reflected in stock prices. Armed with the model in Chapters 11 and 12 that expressed price as a function of future cash flows or earnings, an analyst can draw some educated inferences about the expectations embedded in stock prices.

For example, consider the valuation of IBM. On July 28, 1999, IBM's stock price was $126.25. At this time analysts were forecasting that the company's earnings per share would grow by 19 percent to $3.91 in 1999, by 15 percent to $4.51 in 2000, and by a further 24 percent to $5.60 in 2001. However, analysts did not provide detailed forecasts of earnings growth beyond 2001. What then are the market's implicit assumptions about the short-term and long-term earnings growth for IBM?

By altering the amounts for key value drivers and arriving at combinations that generate an estimated value equal to the observed market price, the analyst can infer what the market might have been expecting for IBM in mid-1999. Table 13-1 summarizes the combinations of earnings growth, book value growth, and cost of capital that generate prices higher, lower, and at the market price. The lightly shaded cells represent combinations of assumptions that are consistent with market prices close to the observed price (in the range of $123 to $127).

IBM has an equity beta of 1.2. Given long-term government bond rates of 5 percent and a market risk premium of 3–4 percent, IBM's cost of equity capital probably lies between 8 percent and 10 percent. In addition, the company's growth in book value has been relatively stable at 4–6 percent for the last three years, which is close to the historical long-term book value growth rate for the economy. A critical question for estimating the market's assessment of IBM's performance is to estimate when its strong earnings growth will conclude and revert to the same level as average firms in the economy, historically around 4 percent. The analysis reported in Table 13-1 assumes that IBM's superior earnings growth persists for five years, until 2003, and then reverts to the economy average.

Table 13-1 Alternative Assumptions About Value Drivers for IBM, Including Combinations Consistent with Observed Market Price of $26

	Average annual earnings and book value growth, 1999 to 2003					
	Earnings growth =15%		Earnings growth = 20%		Earnings growth = 25%	
	Book value growth = 4%	Book value growth = 6%	Book value growth = 4%	Book value growth = 6%	Book value growth = 4%	Book value growth = 6%
Implied earnings per share in 2003	$6.62	$6.62	$8.19	$8.19	$10.04	$10.04
Implied ROE in 2003	55%	51%	68%	63%	83%	77%
Implied price, based on cost of capital of:						
8%	$127	$125	$157	$155	$193	$192
9%	$101	$99	$125	$123	$153	$151
10%	$83	$82	$103	$101	$126	$124

Table 13-1 shows several combinations of assumptions that are consistent with an observed market price of $126. One is 15 percent earnings growth for the next five years and an equity cost of capital of 8 percent. Under these assumptions, earnings per share will effectively double in the next five years, from $3.29 in 1998 to $6.62 in 2003. In addition, IBM's return on equity soars from 33 percent in 1998 to between 51 and 55 percent, depending on the rate of growth in book value. It is interesting to note that changes in the book value growth rate do not have a strong impact on the valuation. Other combinations of assumptions that generate a value consistent with the market price include (1) a five-year earnings growth of 20 percent and a 9 percent cost of capital, and (2) a five-year growth rate of 25 percent and a 10 percent cost of capital. Of course, these assumptions imply that IBM will earn extremely high returns on equity by 2003, between 63 and 83 percent.

Security analysis need not involve such a detailed attempt to infer market expectations. However, whether the analysis is made explicit or not, a good analyst understands what economic scenarios could plausibly be reflected in the observed price

Key Analysis Questions

By using the discounted abnormal earnings/ROE valuation model, analysts can infer the market's expectations for a firm's future performance. This permits analysts to ask whether the market is over- or undervaluing a company. Typical questions that analysts might ask from this analysis include the following:

- What are the market's assumptions about long-term ROE and growth? For example, is the market forecasting that the company can grow its earnings without a corresponding level of expansion in its asset base (and hence equity)? If so, how long can this persist?
- How do changes in the cost of capital affect the market's assessment of the firm's future performance? If the market's expectations seem to be unexpectedly high or low, has the market reassessed the company's risk? If so, is this change plausible?

Developing the Analyst's Expectations

Ultimately, a security analyst must compare his or her own view of a stock with the view embedded in the market price. The analyst's own view is generated using the same tools discussed in Chapters 2 through 12: business strategy analysis, accounting analysis, financial analysis, and prospective analysis. The final product of this work is, of course, a forecast of the firm's future earnings and cash flows and an estimate of the firm's value. However, that final product is less important than the understanding of the business and its industry that the analysis provides. It is such understanding that enables the analyst to interpret new information as it arrives and to infer its implications.

Key Analysis Questions

In developing expectations about the firm's future performance using the financial analysis tools discussed throughout this book, the analyst is likely to ask the following types of questions:

- How profitable is the firm? In light of industry conditions, the firm's corporate strategy, and its barriers to competition, how sustainable is that rate of profitability?
- What are the opportunities for growth for this firm?
- How risky is this firm? How vulnerable are operations to general economic downturns? How highly levered is the firm? What does the riskiness of the firm imply about its cost of capital?
- How do answers to the above questions compare to the expectations embedded in the observed stock price?

The Final Product of Security Analysis

For financial analysts, the final product of security analysis is a recommendation to buy, sell, or hold the stock (or some more refined ranking). The recommendation is supported by a set of forecasts and a report summarizing the foundation for the recommendation. Analysts' reports often delve into significant detail and include an assessment of a firm's business as well as a line-by-line income statement, balance sheet, and cash flow forecasts for one or more years.

FINANCIAL STATEMENT DATA AND SECURITY PRICES

While security analysis clearly involves much information beyond the financial statements, those statements play an important role. Much research over the past three decades has helped describe the role of financial statement data in the setting of security prices. An understanding of that role provides an appreciation for the importance of that data in security analysis, as well as market agents' ability to digest such data.

A thorough review of research on financial statement data and security prices lies well outside the scope of this chapter. However, we can summarize a few of the key findings from the literature.

Earnings and book value are good indicators of stock prices.

Accounting earnings and book values ignore important aspects of the firm's economic landscape, are subject to distortion by managers, and are not adjusted for inflation in the U.S. and most other countries. One could (and the financial press frequently does) reasonably question whether accounting numbers are good indicators of the expected cash flows that should drive stock prices.

It turns out that, in spite of the widely discussed shortcomings of accounting systems, earnings and book value offer a good reflection of much of the information in security prices. In the U.S., the combination of book value (per-share) and earnings explains, in a typical year, nearly two-thirds of the cross-sectional variation in stock prices.[6] Such a finding indicates that book value and earnings provide good starting points for predicting the cash flows that should drive prices.

That book value and earnings do not summarize the information in prices more completely should not be surprising. There are a number of factors that influence prices that accounting systems are not designed to capture well, including, for example, the value of brand assets, growth opportunities, and research and development.

Explaining variation in the *level* of a firm's stock prices is one thing; explaining stock returns, which depend on *changes* in those levels, is quite another. The latter is clearly the more challenging task. It is necessary to not only identify factors that explain value, but also to determine to what extent information about the factors became known to market agents within the interval over which the price changes are measured. Researchers have in fact had difficulty explaining more than a small fraction of the variance in stock returns over years or shorter intervals. Earnings data are the most powerful of the factors that have been studied, but even so, the explanatory power is relatively low. A combination of earnings and earnings changes (both expressed relative to price at the beginning of the year) explains only about 5–15 percent of the variation in annual stock returns.[7]

To summarize, the picture that emerges is that earnings data provide somewhat noisy indicators of value—good enough to approximate whether the stock price should be closer to, say, $10 than $5, but not sufficiently precise to provide clear indications of whether that price level might have changed by, for example, 10 percent rather than 5 percent over the past year. Thus, while the earnings number is a good starting point for analysis, more information is certainly required to track stock prices.

Market agents can anticipate much of the information in earnings.

To say that financial statement data *reflect* much of the information in prices does not necessarily mean that when those data are reported, they convey *new* information. Indeed, market agents have access to a variety of information sources more timely than financial statements, and they use these sources to anticipate the data ultimately revealed in financial statements.

Figure 13-1 describes the extent to which the key financial statement datum—earnings—is anticipated by market agents.[8] In the figure, firms are divided into 10 groups, based on the extent to which quarterly earnings have changed from prior quarters. (The earnings change is labeled SUE, for standardized unexpected earnings.) The importance of the earnings information is evident in how much the stock price performance differs across the groups. The top performers experience a three-month stock price increase

Figure 13-1 Stock Price Movements Before and After Quarterly Earnings Announcements

Stock return relative to control group (%)

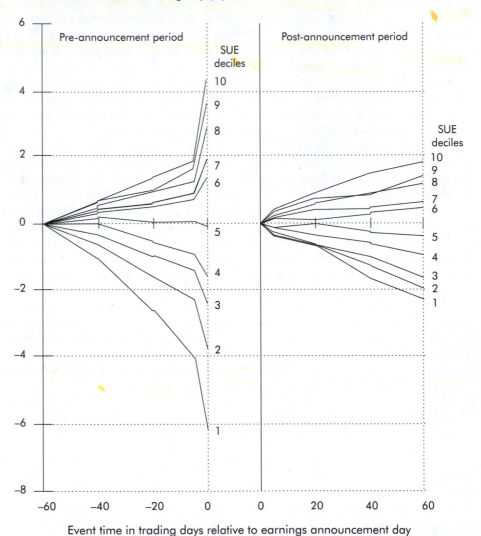

Event time in trading days relative to earnings announcement day

Explanation: Firms are grouped into ten portfolios based on "standardized unexpected earnings," or SUE: actual earnings less a statistical forecast, and scaled by the standard deviation of past unexpected earnings. Stock returns (less those for a size control group) are then cumulated over the 60 days before and after the earnings announcement for each of the ten groups.

4.2 percent greater than a control group, while those at the bottom underperform by 6.1 percent. However, note that most (about 60 percent) of this movement occurs *before* the week of the earnings announcement. This underscores that there are sources more timely than earnings that reflect the same information that will ultimately be reflected in earnings.

How does the market anticipate the earnings announcement? In some cases, management itself reveals information. For example, management makes statements to the press and in financial analysts' meetings about the firm's progress. That information should improve market agents' ability to forecast earnings. Sometimes management will make explicit statements about the range in which earnings are likely to be. Even in the absence of such direct information channels, however, it should be possible to anticipate to some extent how well a firm is performing. One could learn through discussions with retail outlets, suppliers, competitors, and industry news sources. Even general information about the state of the economy and the industry should permit more educated guesses about how well a firm is performing.

The findings summarized in Figure 13-1 offer an important lesson for security analysts. Specifically, it's not good enough to be aware of earnings as soon as they are announced. A good analyst also tracks more timely information sources.

A final comment on Figure 13-1 pertains to stock price movements *after* the earnings are announced. Note that for those firms with earnings increases, the stock prices continue to rise, and for those with earnings decreases, the prices continue to fall (relative to the control group). This is the phenomenon that was mentioned briefly in the section on market efficiency. The figure suggests that even though most of the response to earnings occurs on a timely basis, some portion appears to be delayed.

Financial statement details matter.

Throughout our discussion of business strategy analysis, accounting analysis, financial analysis, and prospective analysis, we drew on financial statement information beyond simply earnings. Moreover, in the chapters on accounting analysis, we pointed to a number of items in the financials that could temper one's view of the quality of earnings. Assuming market agents are capable of conducting similar analyses, we would expect stock prices to reflect financial statement details beyond just earnings.

A large number of studies have examined the relation between stock prices and financial statement data beyond earnings. For example, one study focused on roughly a dozen financial statement variables that could be useful in assessing the quality of earnings: disproportionate inventory and receivables buildups, increases in gross margin percentage, and other factors.[9] The results confirm that stock prices reflect such variables. In other words, one can explain variation in stock prices better when armed not just with earnings but also with the factors that help analysts interpret the quality of earnings.

Many studies have also examined the extent to which footnote disclosures are related to stock price behavior. For example, one study examined the extent to which unrealized gains in banks' investment portfolios are reflected in stock prices.[10] The conclusion of most studies in this area is that prices at least approximately reflect the details in footnotes. Thus, the evidence is consistent with the footnotes presenting important data and with analysts "doing their homework." Whether market agents do a *complete* job of digesting footnote data is less clear.

Research on the relation of stock prices to financial statement details continues, and many of the questions in the area remain unsettled.[11] A few general comments on the current state of understanding can be offered. First, many financial statement details are important, in the sense that they reflect factors that drive stock prices. Second, whether market agents learn about such details from the financial statements themselves or from more timely sources is difficult to know. (Most studies are not sharp enough to answer this question.) Third, whether stock prices reflect financial statement details completely and immediately remains a subject of debate, with studies on both sides of the issue. One implication of the research for security analysts is that to stay abreast of the market one must be able to gather and interpret the kind of information reflected in the financial statement details—either by going directly to the statements or (preferably) to more timely sources.

SUMMARY

Equity security analysis is the evaluation of a firm and its prospects from the perspective of a current or potential investor in the firm's stock. Security analysis is one component of a larger investment process that involves (1) establishing the objectives of the investor or fund, (2) forming expectations about the future returns and risks of individual securities, and then (3) combining individual securities into portfolios to maximize progress toward the investment objectives.

Some security analysis is devoted primarily to assuring that a stock possesses the proper risk profile and other desired characteristics prior to inclusion in an investor's portfolio. However, especially for many professional buy-side and sell-side security analysts, the analysis is also directed toward the identification of mispriced securities. In equilibrium, such activity will be rewarding for those with the strongest comparative advantage. They will be the ones able to identify any mispricing at the lowest cost and exert pressure on the price to correct the mispricing. What kinds of efforts are productive in this domain depends on the degree of market efficiency. A large body of evidence exists that is supportive of a high degree of efficiency in the U.S. market, but recent evidence has reopened the debate on this issue.

In practice, a wide variety of approaches to fund management and security analysis are employed. However, at the core of the analyses are the same steps outlined in Chapters 2 through 12 of this book: business strategy analysis, accounting analysis, financial analysis, and prospective analysis (forecasting and valuation). For the professional analyst, the final product of the work is, of course, a forecast of the firm's future earnings and cash flows, and an estimate of the firm's value. However, that final product is less important than the understanding of the business and its industry, which the analysis provides. It is such understanding that positions the analyst to interpret new information as it arrives and infer its implications.

While security analysis clearly involves much information beyond the financial statements, those statements play an important role. Much research over the past three decades has helped describe the role of financial statement data in the setting of security prices. The research shows conclusively that financial statements reflect much of the information that drives prices. However, whether market agents acquire the information directly from the financial statements themselves or from more timely sources is less clear. Much of the information in financial statements appears to be anticipated before its release. Finally, whether stock prices reflect financial statement details completely and immediately remains a subject of debate. One implication of the research for security analysts is that to stay abreast of the market, one must be able to gather and interpret the kind of information reflected in the financial statement details—either by going directly to the statements or (preferably) to more timely sources.

DISCUSSION QUESTIONS

1. Despite many years of research, the evidence on market efficiency described in this chapter appears to be inconclusive. Some argue that this is because researchers have been unable to link company fundamentals to stock prices precisely. Comment.

2. Geoffrey Henley, a professor of finance, states: "The capital market is efficient. I don't know why anyone would bother devoting their time to following individual stocks and doing fundamental analysis. The best approach is to buy and hold a well-diversified portfolio of stocks." Do you agree? Why or why not?

3. What is the difference between fundamental and technical analysis? Can you think of any trading strategies that use technical analysis? What are the underlying assumptions made by these strategies?

4. Investment funds follow many different types of investment strategies. Income funds focus on stocks with high dividend yields, growth funds invest in stocks that are expected to have high capital appreciation, value funds follow stocks that are considered to be undervalued, and short funds bet against stocks they consider to be overvalued. What types of investors are likely to be attracted to each of these types of funds? Why?

5. Three months ago, Intergalactic Software Company went public. You are a sophisticated investor who devotes time to fundamental analysis as a way of identifying mispriced stocks. Which of the following characteristics would you focus on in deciding whether to follow this stock?
   - The market capitalization
   - The average number of shares traded per day
   - The bid–ask spread for the stock
   - Whether the underwriter that brought the firm public is a Top Five investment banking firm
   - Whether its audit company is a Big Six firm
   - Whether there are analysts from major brokerage firms following the company
   - Whether the stock is held mostly by retail or institutional investors

6. There are two major types of financial analysts: buy-side and sell-side. Buy-side analysts work for investment firms and make stock recommendations that are available only to the management of funds within that firm. Sell-side analysts work for brokerage firms and make recommendations that are used to sell stock to the brokerage firms' clients, which include individual investors and managers of investment funds. What would be the differences in tasks and motivations of these two types of analysts?

7. Many market participants believe that sell-side analysts are too optimistic in their recommendations to buy stocks, and too slow to recommend sells. What factors might explain this bias?

8. Joe Klein is an analyst for an investment banking firm that offers both underwriting and brokerage services. Joe sends you a highly favorable report on a stock that his firm recently helped go public and for which it currently makes the market. What are the potential advantages and disadvantages in relying on Joe's report in deciding whether to buy the stock?

9. Intergalactic Software Company's stock has a market price of $20 per share and a book value of $12 per share. If its cost of equity capital is 15 percent and its book value is expected to grow at 5 percent per year indefinitely, what is the market's assessment of its steady state return on equity? If the stock price increases to $35 and the market does not expect the firm's growth rate to change, what is the revised steady state ROE? If instead the price increase was due to an increase in the market's assessments about long-term book value growth, rather than long-term ROE, what would the price revision imply for the steady state growth rate?

10. Joe states: "I can see how ratio analysis and valuation help me do fundamental analysis, but I don't see the value of doing strategy analysis." Can you explain to him how strategy analysis could be potentially useful?

NOTES

1. See R. Bhushan, "Firm characteristics and analyst following," *Journal of Accounting and Economics* 11, Nos. 2/5 (July 1989): 255–275, and P. O'Brien and R. Bhushan, "Analyst following and instititional ownership," *Journal of Accounting Research* 28, (1990): 55–xx.

2. For a recent review of evidence on market efficiency, see Eugene Fama, "Efficient Capital Markets: II," *Journal of Finance* (December 1991): 1575–1618.

3. For example, see V. Bernard and J. Thomas, "Evidence that Stock Prices Do Not Fully Reflect the Implications of Current Earnings for Future Earnings," *Journal of Accounting and Economics* (December 1990): 305–341.

4. A good example, in which a "value stock" strategy is examined, is in Josef Lakonishok, Andre Shleifer, and Robert Vishny, "Contrarian Investment, Extrapolation, and Risk," *Journal of Finance* (December 1994): 1541–1578.

5. For example, see J. Ou and S. Penman, "Financial Statement Analysis and the Prediction of Stock Returns," *Journal of Accounting and Economics* (November 1989a): 295–330; R. Holthausen and D. Larcker, "The Prediction of Stock Returns Using Financial Statement Information,"

Journal of Accounting and Economics (June/September 1992): 373–412; and Richard Sloan, "Do Stock Prices Fully Reflect Information in Accruals and Cash Flows about Future Earnings?" *The Accounting Review* 71, No. 3: 298–325.

6. On average across time, 66 percent of the variance in price per share is explained by book value per share and the rank of earnings per share. See Victor Bernard, "Accounting-Based Valuation, the Determinants of Market-to-Book Ratios, and Implications for Financial Statements Analysis," working paper, University of Michigan (January 1994).

7. For two of several discussions of research in this area, see Baruch Lev, "On the Usefulness of Earnings and Earning Research: Lessons and Directions from Two Decades of Empirical Research," *Journal of Accounting Research*, supplement 1989: 153–197; and Peter Easton, Trevor Harris, and James Ohlson, "Aggregate Accounting Earnings Can Explain Most of Security Returns," *Journal of Accounting and Economics* (June/September 1992): 119–142.

8. V. Bernard and J. Thomas, "Post-Earnings-Announcement Drift: Delayed Price Response or Risk Premium?" *Journal of Accounting Research* (Supplement 1989): 1–36. For seminal work on the timeliness of earnings information, see R. Ball and P. Brown, "An Empirical Evaluation of Accounting Income Numbers," *Journal of Accounting Research* (Autumn 1968): 159–178; and William H. Beaver, "The Information Content of Annual Earnings Announcements," *Journal of Accounting Research* (Supplement, 1968), 67–92.

9. Baruch Lev and Ramu Thiagarajan, "Fundamental Information Analysis," *Journal of Accounting Research* (Autumn 1993): 190–215.

10. M. Barth, "Fair value accounting: Evidence from investment securities and the market valuation of banks," *The Accounting Review* (January 1994), 1–25.

11. For some incomplete reviews of work in this area, see Victor Bernard, "Capital Markets Research in Accounting During the 1980's: A Critical Review," in *The State of Accounting Research As We Enter the 1990's,* Thomas J. Frecka, editor. (Urbana: University of Illinois Press, 1989): 72–120; and Victor Bernard and Katherine Schipper, "Recognition and Disclosure in Financial Reporting," working paper, University of Michigan (November 1994).

T*here are some great bargains to be had in paging stocks, analysts say. The sector, bruised repeatedly since the start of the year, got kicked again when technology stocks plummeted recently, and for no good reason. . . . One stock—Arch Communications—is an absolute bargain. "One of the most beaten up stocks is Arch, and there is no reason for it," said Christopher Larsen of NatWest Securities.*

The paging industry has been deluged with bad news in the last six months, from management turmoil and broken bank covenants to broad worries of a rise in interest rates and of paging being eclipsed by a new generation of mobile phones. . . . Arch stock has fallen from a trading range of $22–$26 early in the year to as low as $12 in recent sessions . . . but analysts are adamant the sector has a bright future.

Reuters Financial Service, July 29, 1996[1]

COMPANY BACKGROUND

Founded in 1986, Arch Communications Group Inc. was the third largest paging company in the U.S. serving nearly three million subscribers. Arch offered paging services and equipment on local, regional, and nationwide (40 states) bases, and in 180 of the 200 largest U.S. cities.

Arch followed a strategy that consisted of three primary elements: low prices, standard and reliable technologies, and prompt and efficient service delivery. Arch offered competitively priced messaging services and was able to do so because of its own low cost structure. Arch's low costs were drawn from economies of scale in its operations and the size of its subscriber base. Second, for the majority of its paging services, Arch avoided using experimental paging technologies. Rather, Arch endorsed paging technologies that might not be the latest or most advanced but were consistently predictable and dependable. When it came to pioneering new technologies, Arch prefered to let other

Research Associate Sarayu Srinivasan prepared this case under the supervision of Professor Krishna G. Palepu as the basis for class discussion rather than to illustrate either effective or ineffective handling of an administrative situation. *This case benefited significantly from the insights of analyst John Adams.* Copyright © 1997 by the President and Fellows of Harvard College. Harvard Business School case 9-197-047.

1. Nick Louth, "Talking Point—Bargains Shine in Paging Stocks," *Reuters Financial Service, July 29, 1996.*

companies lead and take the risks. Finally, Arch strove to consistently deliver reliable and immediate service by its choice of technologies and protocols,[2] and by expanding its networks and their capacities to accommodate and expedite message flow. Arch believed that fast, reliable, and efficient message delivery was the core objective of paging and critical to generating and retaining customers.

Arch was one of the industry's fastest growing paging providers, seeking growth through a blend of strategic acquisitions and internal additions. The firm had grown from a local provider to a national one, traditionally concentrating on serving small and medium sized markets with low pager penetration rates. Now Arch was also entering major metropolitan markets, in an effort to establish a nationwide footprint.

In Arch's industry, financial performance was commonly assessed by analyzing operating cash flows or EBITDA.[3] Most paging companies were not able to show positive earnings, and net losses were considered an ordinary near-term industry phenomenon. These losses in part resulted from the large capital expenditures, heavy debt financing, and high depreciation rates common to the sector. Analysts expected earnings to turn positive when networks matured and infrastructure spending slowed. Performance evaluation for the present was, therefore, based on EBITDA. Arch's EBITDA grew 162.6 percent from $18 million in 1994 to $47.2 million in 1995. Net revenues also grew: 124.7 percent from $63.1 million in 1994 to $141.8 million in 1995. Subscriber numbers grew from 538,000 in 1994 to 2,006,000 in 1995. (Exhibit 4 shows Arch's financial statements.)

On November 13, 1995, Arch stock was trading at $29.62. Five months later, in March 1996, the stock had fallen to $23. By July 1996, Arch's stock price had dropped to $12.50 per share. The plunge in the stock's value had paralleled the falls in prices of most paging sector stocks. Analysts, however, felt Arch was still a sound investment, suffering from "guilt by association" due to the poor performance of fellow companies in its sector, and investor misunderstanding of industry dynamics. Despite the falls in price, analysts continued to recommend investing in Arch stock, rating it a "buy."

THE U.S. PAGING INDUSTRY

Introduced in the 1950s, pagers were compact, portable, one-way wireless messaging devices used for mobile communication. Pagers were first used almost exclusively by the business sector and time sensitive professionals such as doctors and law enforcement personnel. But by 1995, the paging industry had revenues over $4.1 billion, 34.5 million paging subscribers (eight million units added in 1995), and a 13 percent pager penetration rate of the population.

....

2. *Pager protocol is the set of rules defining a network's capacity and the rate at which data travels through it.*

3. *EBITDA (Earnings Before Interest Taxes Depreciation & Amortization) is the paging industry's measure of financial performance. This metric is the basis for a firms's valuation by industry equity analysts and is important in a company's ability to secure financing.*

Arch Communications Group

Most pagers worked on the same basic technology. Each pager had an identification number and was basically a receiver always tuned to a specific radio frequency listening for messages directed to its number among a constant broadcast of messages. To page a user, a caller dialed the pager's identification number by phone and left a voice[4] or text message with either an operator or an automated system. The pager user was then alerted of message receipt by the broadcast of a paging signal (tone) to the pager. Users then called the operator or checked the pager to retrieve the message.

There were four pager types:

Tone. The simplest type alerted by tone. Users called an answering service for messages.

Digital/Numeric. Digitals displayed numeric messages, usually a phone number where the caller could be reached. Digitals alerted by tone or vibration (for loud or quiet alerts), and screened and stored numbers. In 1995, digitals accounted for 85 percent of all pagers in use.

Alphanumeric. These pagers had both numeric and text messaging, eliminating message retrieval. The pagers' text capability allowed for immediate user action. These accounted for only 10 percent of the market but were the fastest growing segment.

Tone/Voice. These pagers delivered voice messages after tone alerts, and made up 3 percent of the market. Average retail price per pager was $57 for tone, $77 for digital, $138 for alphanumeric, and $189 for tone/voice.[5] Pagers had an estimated 4–5-year life.

The two main industry participants were pager manufacturers and paging service providers (paging companies). Most pagers were made by one of a few major manufacturers. In 1994 Motorola had produced 83 percent of all pagers in service, while NEC (another manufacturer) had produced 12 percent.[6] Motorola's dominance was based on its ability to consistently meet service providers' delivery schedules, its reliable equipment, and strong brand. Most equipment was distributed and activated by service providers, and most service providers sourced equipment mainly from a major maker.

Paging companies provided paging service and also leased and sold pagers. In 1995–1996 the three largest service providers, PageNet, MobileComm, and Arch, together served 45 percent of the total paging market. Over half the market was served by the 8–10 largest companies, while the rest of the market was served by small local providers. While most paging was regional, nationwide service was also available. Rarely, companies had "roaming" agreements, fee-based contracts between providers to serve users that entered areas not covered by their provider, as was common practice in the cellular industry. On average, it cost $11.00 per month to use a service. Users were charged fixed periodic fees, regardless of usage, that included pager rental but not special fees such as

4. *Voice messages, while easy to use, occupy large airtime on a provider's limited frequency.*

5. *MTA-EMCI,* State of the U.S. Paging Industry: 1996

6. *1995 NATA,* Telecommunications Market Review and Forecast.

Arch Communications Group

excess use charges. The most costly service was alphanumeric, followed by tone/voice, digital, and tone only.

In 1995 only three companies offered nationwide service as it consumed a lot of bandwidth,[7] was not widely demanded, and might require market frequency compatibility if the provider did not have a nationwide license. Nationwide licenses, because they operated on one frequency, were useful to large providers that had many resellers because they eliminated the need to coordinate equipment, infrastructure, and frequencies from market to market. Nationwide service was used mostly by business travelers. Providers also offered nationwide service to differentiate themselves.

Distribution

There were three distribution channels: direct, retail, and reseller. Retail and resellers were indirect channels and were becoming very important as consumers became a growing market segment. In 1994 30 percent of all new pagers added were through resellers.

DIRECT DISTRIBUTION.   Equipment and service were acquired by subscribers directly from service providers. Providers bought pagers from the manufacturer and leased or sold pagers to subscribers, more commonly leasing, in addition to providing service. Leasing contributed to the large costs borne by providers: equipment, maintenance, and replacement tied up large sums of cash as 25 percent of a company's pagers were replaced each year. Increasingly, however, subscribers opted to own their pagers (28 percent owned pagers in 1989; 52 percent by 1994). "Churn"[8] in this channel was the lowest across channels, roughly 3 percent per month. The providers bore all expenses, but produced the highest average revenue per unit (ARPU) because it sold direct. This channel had the highest cash flow per subscriber and was the most profitable channel for providers.

RETAIL.   Equipment and service acquired through retailers were usually subject to mark-ups to compensate the retailer who did not work for the equipment maker or service provider. After the sale, the subscriber became the service provider's client and had no further contact with the retailer. Provider ARPU was equal to that from the direct channel, but churn was the highest among channels.

RESELLERS.   Resellers purchased equipment and service directly from the provider and resold to their own clients. Resellers bore the full costs of service and equipment and

---

7. *Bandwidth is the volume of information per unit time that a transmission medium can handle. Larger bandwidth means more information can be transmitted in a given time period and at a faster speed.*

8. *Churn is the rate at which subscribers leave service providers by switching providers, subscribing at introductory costs and then dumping the provider at the end of the promotion, skipping payments, and other voluntary or involuntary service deactivation. Churn is higher among consumers than business users.*

Arch Communications Group

supplied providers with the lowest ARPU. Low revenue, however, was accompanied by low costs, and thus higher cash flow margins for the providers. Churn was zero, because the provider only focused on net additions.

Substitute Products

CELLULAR PHONES.   Two-way cell phone communication had analysts continually predicting the demise of paging, yet in 1995 pagers had 34.5 million subscribers to the 32 million cellular subscribers. Several factors explained pager dominance. First, $56 per month for cell service made $11 per month paging service the lowest cost form of wireless messaging. Cell users were also charged per incoming or outgoing call, and if they went out of their service area. Second, cell phones had a shorter battery life (a few hours) than the multiple-month pager battery life. Third, pagers were also cell complements, used as screening devices for the phones. Fourth, pagers helped manage cell costs. Cell users generally made rather than received calls (over 85 percent of all cell calls were outbound), and left phones off to conserve batteries and control costs, using pagers to get messages. Cell phones were, however, becoming smaller, less costly, and more feature laden (including longer battery lives and silent alerts). Cell phones also had a unique value as emergency situation devices.

PERSONAL COMMUNICATION SERVICES (PCS).   PCS was a generic term used for a range of advanced mobile communication technologies. PCS used a larger spectrum (range of sound wave frequencies) that could be either narrowband (NPCS) for advanced paging technologies like two-way paging, or broadband (BPCS), which supported the more costly and spectrum consumptive technologies cell service was based on. Narrowband providers could offer advanced services and have more reliable networks. NPCS and BPCS offerings were feared to cannibalize or destroy current paging networks.

MOBILE SATELLITE COMMUNICATIONS.   Satellites served subscribers not served by land or cellular systems, and nonconsumer markets. Satellites offered wireless services over vast geographic areas with minimal ongoing capital costs for the provider. Profitable satellite-based global wireless services could be developed, and already satellite providers had started to eye the consumer market.

Paging subscribers had grown 27 percent per year from 1990–1995. Large paging companies had even higher subscriber growth rates. This growth was fueled by the market shift from business to consumer, changing user perceptions of pagers, falling product and service prices, and an expanding variety of product and service options. The historical images of pagers as costly professional items or illegal drug trade tools were fading: nearly 65 percent of new owners used pagers as personal "lifestyle management" tools. Increasingly time constrained and busy consumers demanding both accessibility and mobility relied on pagers as integrative tools. But, despite such high growth, service providers had slim margins. Paging was capital intensive and companies needed large recurrent capital injections. Infrastructure and equipment accounted for the two largest capital outlays.

COMPETITION IN THE PAGING INDUSTRY IN THE 1990s

From 1994 to 1996 the Federal Communications Commission (FCC), the regulatory authority over the airwaves, allocated limited radio spectrum to be auctioned off by license for various wireless services. The auctions debuted licenses for bandwidth supporting advanced services, such as PCS. Bidders for and winners of the new licenses were subject to FCC determined regulations meant to limit bidding to only serious investors, promote rigorous competition, and ensure effective use of spectrum. These rules included limiting the number of different PCS channels a provider could own to three, restricting license transfers, and requiring providers to show pro forma construction plans.

For auctioning purposes, spectrum suitable for paging was divided into four geographic service areas: nationwide, regional (comprised of five regions each with 20 percent of the U.S. population), MTAs (51 major trading areas), and BTAs (493 basic trading areas). Each service area was allotted channels of frequency requiring operating licenses. A total of 7 MHz of spectrum[9] was available or already being used by paging companies, approximately 4 MHz of which was for advanced paging. Commonly, 25 kHz of one-way frequency supported numerous local and regional providers using a variety of protocols. The same channel in different markets could be occupied by many providers.

By 1995 the nationwide and regional auctions had taken place. (MTA and BTA licenses were to be auctioned in 1996.) The auctions sold licenses for eleven nationwide channels and 30 regional channels (six channels in each region). In each region two and four of the six channels respectively were identical so that a provider could acquire the same channel in each of the five regions and thus have the coverage of a nationwide license without actually bidding on one. MTAs would have a total of 561 licenses available (51 MTAs × 11 licenses) and BTAs, 2,958 licenses (493 BTAs × 6 licenses).

The number of providers in a market was technically limited by the number of operating licenses issued for that market. But since license holders could sell portions of their spectrum to resellers, the number of providers a market could physically accommodate and the spectrum's capacity defined the true number of firms operating in a market. Licenses could also be bought by a group of companies, so that multiple providers could operate on the same license in the same area.

The minimum provider investment necessary to start a paging company varied by the technology, protocols, and licenses used. In 1996 the minimum outlay for a simple one-way nationwide network was approximately $200 million dollars.[10] A nationwide license would cost an additional $25 million dollars. A regional network of the same

----

9. MHz (megahertz) is a unit of frequency comprised of a million hertz. 1 hertz = 1 cycle per second. 1 MHz = 1,000 kHz (kilohertz).

10. This scenario assumed the network used FLEX protocol and 1,000 radio transmitters to broadcast messages.

Arch Communications Group

specifications, with licenses, would cost approximately $40 million. Larger, better capitalized providers, therefore, had advantages.

While the six largest providers served over 60 percent of the market, the remainder of the industry was highly fragmented. Competition was intense at all levels, and since service was hard to differentiate, it rested on the linked elements of cost, data delivery, and price. Low costs, in a high fixed cost industry, were achieved by "loading" infrastructure, that is, piling as many subscribers as possible onto an existing network. Allocating costs over a large subscriber base lowered per-unit costs and could be reflected in pricing. Loading, however, swelled the number of messages that had to travel the network, increased transmission time, and delayed messages to the end user. In paging, rapid message delivery was critical. Low prices drew subscribers, but long term loyalty was a function of the ability to deliver data immediately. Providers could manage these components by upgrading to faster protocols or adding spectrum.

In the pursuit of scale and spectrum, a pan-industry rush of mergers took place in the 1980s and 1990s. In one decade, providers consolidated from 1,000 to 500 with 8–10 large regional or national companies. By 1996, however, merging pains, management mismatches, concern over the merger wave ending, delays in deployment of NPCS networks, and fears that PCS would cannibalize paging and that no room was left for internal growth, caused sector morale to go down.

Arch's Largest Competitors, 1990s

PAGENET.   Founded in 1981, PageNet was the largest and fastest growing provider in the U.S. with service in all 50 states, the U.S. Virgin Islands, and Puerto Rico. PageNet was considered a trend setter (first to add a million units via internal growth), the low cost leader, and the most successful company in the industry (160 percent the size of its closest competitor). PageNet had 7.8 million subscribers (20 percent of the industry base), adding 2.3 million subscribers in 1995 (350,000 by acquisition).

PageNet's growth strategy focused primarily on addition through internal growth. Due to this strategy, PageNet did not have the acquisition problem of consolidating networks of different frequencies or back office systems. PageNet's strategy of aggressive pricing policies, reliable service, and emphasis on direct sales (largest industry sales force with 1,000 people and 6,000 resellers) was executed by decentralized management. PageNet owned the most spectrum of any provider. The company built a 24-hour support/distribution center and a National Accounts Division to provide one contact point to large, national clients and to forge and manage such alliances.

PageNet regularly entered partnership and distribution agreements to expand its client base. Sprint, MCI, and GTE were PageNet clients who resold services to their own clients. Partners could market services under their own or PageNet's brand and could customize agreements. With Sprint and MCI, PageNet handled shipping, customer service, and pager leasing. Sprint and MCI oversaw advertising, billing, and marketing. Subscribers were unaware they were dealing with PageNet at all. GTE was a typical reseller, owning its pagers and handling its own customer service and billing. Reseller churn impacted PageNet's subscriber numbers but not its revenues.

PageNet's future projects included the first commercial wireless pocket answering machine, dubbed VoiceNow, which was in its final testing stages. PageNet was also expanding its business overseas through its recently formed international division.

MOBILECOMM.   MobileComm was the second largest provider of paging services (4.4 million subscribers) with local, regional, and national service in the 50 states, Canada, and the Caribbean. MobileComm served 97 of the top 100 largest metropolitan markets. In 1996 MobileMedia acquired (and renamed itself) MobileComm for $930 million (the largest industry acquisition), netting 1.8 million subscribers and consolidating revenues of $323 million.

MobileComm's acquisitions aimed at establishing national presence in one-way and two-way networks (it had two nationwide PCS licenses), growing sales distribution capability to retail channels, and adding spectrum. MobileComm's internal growth plan emphasized high sales productivity and strategic alliances. After the MobileMedia merger, MobileComm began centralizing back office functions (all credit and collection tasks in one place) and building two service centers (in Texas and Maryland) that provided 24-hour customer service and billing support.

By mid-1996 MobileComm was the victim of high churn: 3.8 percent (industry average: 2–3 percent). This was due to network congestion[11] that delayed message delivery during peak hours in major markets and a rise in resellers on its networks. MobileComm was also still trying to cut duplicate back office/support expenses from the merger. In late 1996 MobileComm changed its entire upper management. The restructuring slowed the already troubled integration and Texas center project. Standard & Poor's downgraded its rating on MobileComm's $460 million debt. MobileComm was bound by its creditors to raise $100 million in equity capital by year's end.

OTHER PROVIDERS.   The fourth largest provider, Metrocall, gained scale by a series of fast acquisitions, but would expend considerable resources to mold the various parts into one entity, while also attempting to integrate new management. American Paging, the seventh largest player, was undergoing a large restructuring which included a management turnover. The restructuring was blamed for the drop in subscriber additions and weak operating performance the firm experienced.

The fifth largest provider, ProNet, had followed a fast grow strategy that focused on dense urban markets. Despite acquisitions, doubling subscribers in one year, creating reseller programs to drive long-term internal growth, and one of the lowest cost structures, ProNet announced mid-1996 that, due to price concessions to resellers, it would be unable to grow cash flow for several quarters. Standard & Poor's lowered ProNet's credit rating. Consequently, ProNet saw its stock dumped.

....

11. MobileComm had the industry's largest alphanumeric subscriber base (14 percent of its subscribers used alphanumerics). High revenue alphanumeric paging, however, uses four to five times the capacity of numeric paging, congesting and over-trafficking the paging networks they occupy.

Arch Communications Group

Arch Communications Group

ARCH'S PERFORMANCE, POSITION, AND FUTURE

Arch offered local, regional, and nationwide service, every pager type, and also special services such as voice mail. In 1995 87 percent of Arch's in-service pagers were digital display, 7 percent were alphanumeric, 2 percent tone only, and 2 percent tone/voice. Arch owned, leased, and provided service to 45 percent of its in-service pagers and provided service only to the remainder (30 percent of which were subscriber owned pagers, 25 percent reseller owned).

Arch owned and was developing two nationwide channels (acquired primarily to expand its regional services), but had followed a unique service strategy of offering nationwide paging through a network of affiliates. When a subscriber using Arch's nationwide paging left one affiliate's market and entered another, he/she called a toll-free number that would prompt the user's pager to become active and receive messages (on the affiliate's channel) in the new market.

Arch acquired 60 percent of its subscribers through direct distribution (direct sales and firm owned stores). Direct distribution was a more expensive channel by which to add subscribers, but gave Arch an ARPU higher than the industry average. The indirect channel (comprised of low cost, low ARPU resellers and high ARPU retailers) contributed the remaining 40 percent of subscribers.

Over the past few years, Arch had shown a decline in monthly ARPU. This was because the number of subscriber or reseller owned pagers for which Arch received no recurring rental fee had increased more than 25 percent over the past few years. Secondly, over the same period, the percentage of new pagers in service added through indirect channels (mostly resellers who purchased bulk airtime at discount) had increased. Finally, the decline in paging service retail prices, resulting from pressure on pricing due to increased competition and growth, also drove revenues down. Arch's revenue decline mirrored an industry-wide decline. While some observers were alarmed by the sustained declines, others measured operating performance by EBITDA rather than revenues and paid little attention to the drop. Revenue declines ignored both the differences in operating margins from different distribution channels and the fact that paging was a volume driven, fixed cost business and that spreading those costs over a large base had a positive impact on margins.

Arch generated most of its revenues by charging subscribers fixed periodic fees. As long as subscribers remained in service, the recurring payments constituted an income stream free of additional selling expenses. Arch's net losses were mostly due to the interest on debt incurred to finance growth, and the large depreciation and amortization charges related to assets. Arch required considerable funds to service debt, finance acquisitions, fund expansion and upkeep of existing operations, and cover pager and paging system expenditures. The company's capital expenditures had increased from $10.5 million in 1992 to over $60.6 million in 1995 and were expected to reach the $100 million mark in 1996. These expenditures were supported by cash from operations, equity issues, and debt. At the end of 1995 Arch had assets totaling $785.3 million. The company expected to generate positive cash flow by 1998.

During 1995 Arch had several important accomplishments: it made six acquisitions of which the $540 million USA Mobile (second largest industry acquisition) and Westlink (substantially adding to Arch's nationwide presence) helped push it from the industry's tenth to third largest company; added 1.1 million subscribers (acquisition) and 366,000 subscribers (internal growth—tripling quarterly internal growth); expanded service from 13 to 40 states; grew EBITDA from $18 million in 1994 to $47.2 million; grew total revenues 114.2 percent to $141.8 million (and grew net revenue by 124.7 percent); and raised over $300 million in new debt and equity capital. These results crowned seventeen consecutive quarters of net revenue and cash flow increases in an industry where such measures were expected to remain weak for the foreseeable future. Table A shows selected Arch financial highlights.

Table A Arch Financial Highlights

	Year Ended 12/31/95	Year Ended 12/31/94	Year Ended 12/31/93
Net revenues	$141,809,000	$63,116,000	$41,277,000
Earnings before interest, taxes, depreciation and amortization (EBITDA)	47,186,000	17,969,000	11,315,000
Net income (loss)	(36,602,000)	(6,462,000)	(5,725,000)
Per share data:			
Weighted average shares	13,498,000	7,183,000	7,125,000
EBITDA	$ 3.50	$ 2.50	$ 1.59
Net Income (loss)	$(2.72)	$(0.90)	$(0.80)
Ending subscriber units in service	2,006,000	538,000	254,000

Source: Arch 1995 Annual Report

Strategy

Arch followed a strategy that emphasized low prices, proven technologies, and reliable delivery of service. Arch's management team, headed by CEO C. Edward Baker Jr., was considered to have the longest successful management track record in the public paging industry. Arch's decentralized management structure allowed it to control costs, smoothly consolidate acquisitions, and respond to subscriber needs quickly.

As one of the industry's lowest cost providers, Arch was able to price competitively, sustaining its cost structure by consolidating operating functions, using fast transmission systems, and spreading costs by taking advantage of economies of scale arising from pursuing large scale.

Arch offered its subscribers no frills paging services based on standard and tested technologies that could be depended upon to deliver messages reliably and quickly with none of the potential hiccups that services based on new or experimental technologies might present. Arch did, however, keep up with emerging paging technologies by investing in a consortium that was developing advanced paging services. Scott Hoyt, Arch

Arch Communications Group

Marketing V.P., explained, "This industry will eat you alive if you're wrong as a technology innovator. We prefer to take advantage of other people's mistakes." Hoyt added that Arch considered itself a "fast follower."[12]

While Arch's subscriber numbers seemed to attest to reliable and timely message delivery, some of Arch's clients did not agree. In August 1996, Arch had a 2½ hour service outage in Portland, Maine. Further, due to a computer glitch, many serviceless subscribers failed to receive notification from Arch that their pagers were down. Portland Police Chief Michael Chitwood, whose department used eighteen Arch pagers for emergency pagers, said, "To be down for two and a half hours without being notified is crazy. We are talking about public safety here."[13]

Growth

Arch's growth strategy combined internal growth (developing markets and extending out into adjacent or existing markets) and a series of acquisitions. The acquired companies were all characterized by what were considered sound operating performance track records. By 1996 Arch had the second highest absolute subscriber growth rate in the industry and had felt few growing pains.

Internal growth, which was over 40 percent in 1995 (higher than industry growth), was driven by market development and penetration, and expanding marketing activities and sales. Arch had traditionally entered small and medium sized markets with lower rates of pager penetration because of the greater growth opportunities these markets offered. Increasingly, however, Arch also concentrated on strengthening its nationwide presence, entering and establishing itself in major metropolitan areas and larger markets by both using service agreements with other paging carriers and extending its national footprint through acquisitions (bypassing buying a nationwide license).

Arch's acquisitions were made to expand subscriber base, geographic operations, and spectrum without deploying new networks. Most of Arch's acquisitions fell into one of three groups: (1) acquisitions that primarily expanded geographic reach and were likely to be in adjoining markets, (2) acquisitions that operated in Arch's markets and would be folded into Arch, and (3) acquisitions, mostly in nonadjacent markets, made for strategic purposes that extended Arch's physical reach and added new markets. The company had experienced few of the acquisition integration difficulties that had plagued its competitors and the industry. Arch CEO Baker tried to explain their success:

> *We've certainly learned a great deal as we've done thirty-two acquisitions. . . We've put in place a program called the SOAP [Standard Operating and Accounting Practices] package, so that every time we make an acquisition, we put a team together that very rapidly and efficiently implements this package at all of our acquired targets. It's really a proven methodology for quickly and efficiently integrating these acquired properties. Arch was very fortunate with our latest and*

12. Audrey Choi, "Arch Builds Strong Paging Business Slowly But Surely," Wall Street Journal, August 22, 1996.

13. Ibid.

largest acquisitions, because the most difficult thing that you encounter when you integrate companies is integrating the backroom operations—your accounting, your customer support, and your operating systems. We were fortunate enough in those two most recent acquisitions to have bought companies who were using the same billing, customer support, and operating packages that we were.[14]

Arch also actively attempted to increase the capacity of its existing infrastructure and network by upgrading to faster protocols. Protocol upgrades allowed messages to travel the network faster, increasing the network's subscriber carrying capacity. Faster protocols eliminated the need to purchase additional spectrum or invest in dispatching new networks. One past example was the company's upgrade to a protocol called FLEX. The upgrade doubled capacity without the substantial capital outlay acquiring new spectrum would entail. Future upgrade plans included acquiring a protocol called ReFLEX25, a two-way messaging protocol being developed by Motorola.

Competitive Position

Arch faced competition from at least one other paging company in every market it operated in. Although no single company competed with Arch in all its markets, some competitors held nationwide licenses so that they could potentially enter all of Arch's markets.

Arch believed that competition for subscribers rested on quality of service, geographic coverage, and price, and felt itself competitive on these dimensions. In response to the competitive threat of cellular technology, Arch CEO Baker had this to say:

Broadband PCS [cellular] is not going to affect our growth. . . We have people on the street utilizing APC's [a cellular/PCS firm operating in Arch markets] BPCS network for messaging, and it doesn't work well. . .   And there is absolutely no way, in our view, that it is going to affect the growth of messaging. It doesn't perform well; you've got coverage problems; there are penetration problems; you've got battery life issues. All the things that we've talked about, and others have written about, are proving themselves to be true with respect to how messaging will perform over broadband PCS networks. . . Metrocall [a paging provider in APC's market] posted record growth and has not experienced a single customer loss to APC.[15]

Arch invested in new wireless technologies such as wireless data delivery, two-way messaging, voice paging, and narrowband PCS by acquiring shares in a consortium of companies that owned five regional NPCS licenses. In this way Arch would have a stake in emerging technologies with comparatively small capital investments and risk. Despite such forays into emanating technologies, Arch remained loyal to its proven technology strategy.

....

14. Sarah E. Reynolds, "Staying True to the Company's Vision," Worcester Business Journal, April 29, 1996.

15. Lehman Brothers, Analysts Report, Arch Communications, August 6, 1996.

Arch Communications Group

Future

To maintain a competitive edge, Arch intended to pursue several future strategic initiatives, including strengthening distribution channels, increasing the capacity to serve more customers through expansion of its two national paging channels, building more efficient support infrastructure by expanding the national sales and customer service operations, and continued investment into select technologies.[16] Arch also planned to use the extra capacity it would acquire from its protocol upgrades to build up its alphanumeric subscriber base.

Arch's acquisitions to date had been free of the troubles that had traditionally accrued to acquiring companies. Arch intended to continue its acquisitions, but there was no guarantee that the pattern of smooth integration would be sustainable. Future acquisitions could be difficult to identify, troublesome to integrate, and demand excessive financial resources and managerial focus. Factors outside the company's control also threatened to affect growth strategies, and included prevailing economic conditions and interest rates, competitive and regulatory environments, technological advances, and the ability to attract and retain professionals.

Despite Arch's stock price of $12.50 per share in July 1996—a drop of more than 100 percent from its trading range at the year's start—analysts remained bullish about the stock (see Exhibit 1 for stock movements). John Adams, an analyst at Wessels, Arnold & Henderson, explained how analysts valued paging companies and might arrive at valuations different from the market's in a report on the paging industry:

> When valuing paging companies, analysts do not use P/E multiples on current earnings because there is usually no positive earnings stream from which a multiple can be derived, at least not near-term. Therefore, analysts typically value stock with either a discounted cash flow analysis and/or with an unlevered valuation approach which adjusts the market value of comparative companies for various capital structures (debt and cash in particular) thus permitting an apples-to-apples multiples comparison to operating cash flow or EBITDA.[17]

In his August 1996 report, Adams presented a detailed valuation of Arch using the discounted cash flow analysis (Exhibit 2). For comparison, Exhibit 3 shows Adams's valuation of other paging industry stocks. Based on his analysis, Adams was optimistic about Arch's future:

> We continue to rate Arch's stock Buy-Aggressive Growth. Arch reported an impressive second quarter. . . As far as we can tell the company has not been plagued with any operating problems in 1996. . . We believe Arch continues to do an excellent job of managing its business. . . The company continues to show tremendous momentum in its subscriber base and operating cash. . . There are absolutely no fundamental problems that we can detect in Arch's operating model.[18]

---

16. *Arch 1995 Annual Report.*

17. *John Adam's* Wireless Communications Industry Report, *Wessels, Arnold & Henderson, Vol. I, Sept. 1995.*

18. *John Adams,* Wireless Communications, *Wessels, Arnold & Henderson, August, 1, 1996.*

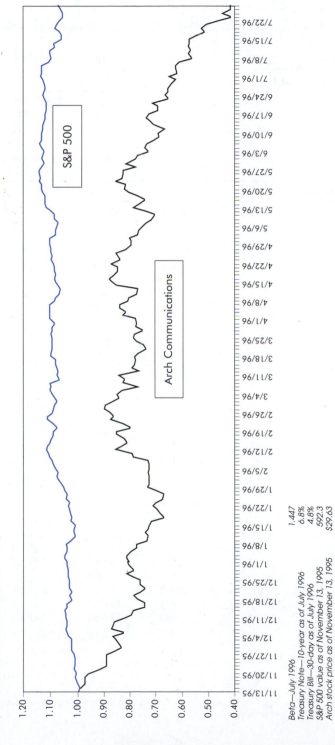

EXHIBIT 1

Arch Communications Stock Price vs. S&P 500, November 13, 1995–July 26, 1996

(Both Rebased to 1.00 at 11/13/95)

Beta—July 1996	1.447
Treasury Note—10-year as of July 1996	6.8%
Treasury Bill—30-day as of July 1996	4.8%
S&P 500 value as of November 13, 1995	592.3
Arch stock price as of November 13, 1995	$29.63

Source: Adapted from Datastream International by case writer.

EXHIBIT 2

Arch Communications Cash Flow Analysis (in millions, except paging units and per share information)

Fiscal Year: December	1995	1996E	1997E	1998E	1999E	2000E
Subscriber Trends (paging units):						
Beginning pagers	538,000	2,006,000	3,121,000	3,826,000	4,667,720	5,507,910
Net additions	1,468,000	1,115,000	705,000	841,720	840,190	826,186
Ending pagers	2,006,000	3,121,000	3,826,000	4,667,720	5,507,910	6,334,096
% change	272.9	55.6	22.6	22.0	18.0	15.0
Average revenue/unit/month	$11.00	$8.95	$8.29	$7.88	$7.48	$7.19
% change	—	NM	(7.3)	(5.0)	(5.0)	(4.0)
Consolidated Income Statement:						
Net revenues	$141.8	$283.2	$355.6	$444.5	$502.7	$557.7
% change	—	99.7	25.6	25.0	13.1	11.0
EBITDA (operating c.f.)	**47.2**	**102.4**	**135.9**	**171.4**	**198.0**	**225.5**
Cash flow margin (%)	33.3	36.2	38.2	38.6	39.4	40.4
Depreciation and amortization	60.2	155.7	195.6	254.9	269.7	278.7
Operating income	(13.0)	(53.3)	(59.7)	(83.4)	(71.7)	(53.2)
Interest expense	22.5	77.7	96.0	100.8	105.7	108.0
Pretax income	(39.5)	(131.0)	(155.6)	(184.2)	(177.3)	(161.2)
Taxes	(4.6)	0.0	0.0	0.0	0.0	0.0
Net income	(34.9)	(131.0)	(155.6)	(184.2)	(177.3)	(161.2)
EPS ($/share)	($2.59)	($6.51)	($7.60)	($8.82)	($8.32)	($7.42)
Cash Flow Analysis:						
EBITDA	$47.2	$102.4	$135.9	$171.4	$198.0	$225.5
Taxes	(4.6)	0.0	0.0	0.0	0.0	0.0
Capital expenditures	446.8	428.8	111.7	114.9	113.7	114.3
Pre-interest free c.f.	(395.0)	(326.4)	24.2	56.5	84.3	111.2
Interest expense	22.5	77.7	96.0	100.8	105.7	108.0
Free cash flow	(417.6)	(404.1)	(71.8)	(44.2)	(21.4)	3.2
Valuation (discounted cash flow analysis):						
PV (pre-interest free c.f.)	($134.4)	$275.6	$777.3	$948.2	$1,078.5	$1,132.4
PV final year EBITDA (10X)	854.1	972.7	1,107.7	1,261.4	1,436.5	1,635.9
Less net long-term debt	453.4	857.5	929.3	973.5	994.9	991.7
Plus PCS license	6.5	6.5	6.5	6.5	6.5	6.5
Net value	272.8	397.2	962.2	1,242.6	1,526.6	1,783.1
Net value per share	NM	NM	$47.00	$59.50	$71.67	$82.07
Fair price per share	**NM**	**NM**	**$37.60**	**$47.60**	**$57.33**	**$65.65**
Average shares	13.5	20.1	20.5	20.9	21.3	21.7
Net debt per subsidiary	$226	$275	$243	$209	$181	$157
WACC*—13.9%						

What Arch's stock is worth in one year ($ per share)

*WACC assumes 7% risk free rate of return, 7% market risk premium, 1.6 Arch beta, 11% borrowing rate, and 40% equity/60% debt mix.
Source: John Adams and Wessels, Arnold & Henderson.

Arch Communications Group

EXHIBIT 2 *(continued)*

Fiscal Year: December	2001E	2002E	2003E	2004E	2005E
Subscriber Trends (paging units):					
Beginning pagers	6,334,096	7,157,529	7,944,857	8,659,894	9,266,086
Net additions	823,432	787,328	715,037	606,193	463,304
Ending pagers	7,157,529	7,944,857	8,659,894	9,266,086	9,729,391
% change	13.0	11.0	9.0	7.0	5.0
Average revenue/unit/month	$6.97	$6.76	$6.63	$6.49	$6.36
% change	(3.0)	(3.0)	(2.0)	(2.0)	(2.0)
Consolidated Income Statement:					
Net revenues	$611.9	$659.4	$704.7	$739.2	$760.7
% change	9.7	7.8	6.9	4.9	2.9
EBITDA (operating c.f.)	**255.2**	**283.9**	**312.7**	**337.5**	**356.8**
Cash flow margin (%)	41.7	43.1	44.4	45.7	46.9
Depreciation and amortization	286.8	217.8	170.8	125.3	118.6
Operating income	(31.6)	66.1	141.9	212.2	238.2
Interest expense	107.7	103.8	95.9	83.1	65.1
Pretax income	(139.3)	(37.7)	46.0	129.1	173.1
Taxes	0.0	0.0	0.0	0.0	0.0
Net income	(139.3)	(37.7)	46.0	129.1	173.1
EPS ($/share)	($6.28)	($1.67)	$1.99	$5.49	$7.22
Cash Flow Analysis:					
EBITDA	$255.2	$283.9	$312.7	$337.5	$356.8
Taxes	0.0	0.0	0.0	0.0	0.0
Capital expenditures	112.5	108.4	100.2	90.4	79.5
Pre-interest free c.f.	142.7	175.5	212.5	247.1	227.3
Interest expense	107.7	103.8	95.9	83.1	65.1
Free cash flow	35.0	71.7	116.4	164.0	212.2
Valuation (discounted cash flow analysis):					
Average shares	22.2	22.6	23.1	23.5	24.0

Arch Communications Group

Arch Communications Group

EXHIBIT 3
Paging Sector Valuations, 1995

March 21, 1996	ACOM[a]	APGR[b]	APP[c]	MBLM[d]	MCLL[e]	PAGE[f]	PNET[g]	Average
Stock price	$10.75	$23.00	$6.50	$21.00	$19.00	$25.25	$24.25	—
Year-to-date % change	-7%	-4%	6%	-5%	1%	6%	-17%	
Subscribers:				December Quarter				
Subscriber base	529,450	2,006,000	784,500	2,369,101	944,013	6,737,907	856,302	
ARPU, paging	$10.85	$9.70	$10.17	$10.26	$8.51	$7.86	$6.40	$9.11
AOCPU, paging	$8.79	$6.13	$8.40	$7.41	$6.41	$4.93	$4.41	$6.64
EBITDA/subscriber	$2.06	$3.57	$1.77	$2.85	$2.10	$2.92	$1.99	$2.47
Selling costs/net addition	NM	$64	NM	$72	$69	$32	$65	$60
Churn	2.9%	2.0%	2.5%	3.4%	2.6%	1.3%	1.6%	2.3%
Reseller base	46%	50%	38%	37%	42%	45%	68%	47%
Direct base	54%	50%	62%	63%	58%	55%	32%	53%
Current Growth Rate:				December Quarter				
Subscriber growth	145%	273%	20%	64%	25%	53%	142%	103%
Revenue growth	47%	224%	14%	53%	26%	38%	76%	68%
EBITDA growth	84%	303%	-5%	82%	-5%	44%	51%	79%
Margin Analysis (total company):				December Quarter				
Net revenues	100%	100%	100%	100%	100%	100%	100%	100%
Service, rental & main. exp.	47%	20%	28%	35%	32%	20%	23%	29%
Selling expense	23%	17%	17%	19%	18%	12%	17%	18%
General and administrative	17%	26%	38%	18%	25%	31%	27%	26%
EBITDA	12%	37%	17%	28%	25%	37%	31%	27%
Depreciation and amortization	34%	55%	28%	29%	43%	27%	44%	37%
Quarter End Ratio and Balance Sheet Analysis:				September Quarter				
Receivable turn (days)	34.9	22.2	43.3	30.9	54.2	19.7	43.4	35.5
Long-term debt/capital	46%	62%	67%	58%	39%	106%	59%	63%
EBITDA/interest ratio	0.9	1.8	4.5	1.5	2.6	2.2	1.8	2.2
Net debt/EBITDA ratio	2.4	5.3	5.0	4.3	0.3	3.8	4.1	3.6
Net debt/subscriber	$39	$226	$106	$144	$7	$133	$104	$108
Quarter end net debt (mil.)	$21	$453	$83	$341	$7	$894	$89	
Value of PCS license (mil.)	$2	$7	$55	$54	$0	$197	$0	—

☐ = strengths

(continued)

March 21, 1996	ACOM[a]	APGR[b]	APP[c]	MBLM[d]	MCLL[e]	PAGE[f]	PNET[g]	Average
EBITDA Trends:								
EBITDA 1995 ($ mil.)	$4.7	$47.2	$15.7	$61.7	$27.8	$201.1	$18.4	—
EBITDA 1996E ($ mil.)	$15.1	$102.4	$20.3	$177.1	$33.8	$252.3	$27.7	—
EBITDA 1997E ($ mil.)	$22.6	$135.9	$28.5	$207.5	$43.0	$305.7	$34.2	—
Enterprise Value/EBITDA Ratio (adjusted for cash value of PCS licenses):								
1994	19.9	14.3	9.0	14.4	15.8	21.8	9.9	15.0
1995	38.7	18.9	10.6	27.8	11.0	16.6	13.4	19.6
1996E[h]	15.6	12.9	10.1	11.0	11.4	13.6	10.7	12.2
1997E	11.2	10.3	8.8	10.0	9.3	12.0	8.9	10.1
YE 1996 Enterprise value/subscriber	$308	$422	$236	$408	$266	$402	$238	$326
Discounted CF Valuation (per share):								
PMV beginning 1996	$24.92	NM	$10.66	$0.00	$29.90	$36.49	$38.62	—
PMV beginning 1997	$32.03	$47.00	$12.26	$39.91	$39.94	$41.98	$55.07	—
Fair price beginning 1996	$19.93	NM	$8.53	NM	$23.92	$29.19	$30.90	—
Fair price year-end 1996	$25.62	$37.60	$9.81	$31.93	$31.95	$33.59	$44.06	—
Appreciation potential	138%	63%	51%	52%	68%	33%	82%	—
Other:								
Subscribers, YE 1996	766,450	3,121,000	864,500	4,774,101	1,446,013	9,129,907	1,244,802	—
Net debt, YE 1995 (mil.)	$85	$453	$91	$920	$28	$952	$90	—
Net debt, YE 1996 (mil.)	$125	$858	$128	$1,015	$103	$1,271	$121	—
Net debt, YE 1997 (mil.)	$141	$929	$172	$1,131	$118	$1,697	$127	—
Net Debt per sub., YE 1996	$163	$275	$148	$213	$71	$139	$98	$158
1996 Cap-X/1997 EBITDA ratio	1.5	3.2	1.8	5.3	2.2	1.3	2.4	2.5
Market cap. (mil.)	$113	$467	$131	$987	$281	$2,598	$175	—
Shares outstanding, YE 1995	9.21	19.38	20.03	40.35	14.63	102.25	6.47	—
Shares outstanding, YE 1996	10.50	20.32	20.10	47.00	14.80	102.90	7.20	—
Shares outstanding, YE 1997	10.59	20.57	20.38	47.44	14.93	104.14	7.30	—
Insider stock ownshp. (mil. shs.)	1.80	1.97	16.54	15.52	5.52	3.96	0.76	—
Insider options (mil. shs.)	0.18	0.18	0.34	0.56	0.33	1.42	0.26	—

Source: John Adams and Wessels, Arnold & Henderson.

Note: In calculating PageNet's enterprise/EBITDA ratio we add back the expected $17 million impact from VoiceNow in 1996.

Ticker Symbols: [a]A+Network. [b]Arch Communications. [c]American Paging Inc. [d]MobileMedia. [e]Metrocall. [f]PageNet. [g]ProNet.
[h]Arch pro forma enterprise multiple 10.9 × 1996 EBITDA.

Arch Communications Group

Arch Communications Group

EXHIBIT 4

Arch Communications Group Abridged 1995 Annual Report

TO OUR SHAREHOLDERS:

Arch Communications Group, Inc. enjoyed unprecedented success in 1995, a year marked by explosive growth which propelled the Company into the top tier of the narrowband wireless communications industry. In this year of extraordinary growth, Arch's subscriber base increased nearly four-fold to more than 2.0 million subscribers from 538,000 at the end of 1994. Arch also produced record financial results in 1995. We now have produced 17 consecutive record quarters of sequential increases in net revenues and cash flows.

To support Arch's rapid growth we raised more than $300 million in new capital including $46 million from a public offering of common stock, and $225 million in a bank credit facility. This capital will be used for acquisitions and capital expenditures. Our ability to raise this amount of capital is a reflection of Arch's past success and future promise.

Unprecedented Growth

Arch's internal growth rate during 1995 was among the highest in the industry. This was the fourth consecutive year in which we produced almost twice as many net new customers from internal distribution channels as we had produced the previous year. During 1995 the Company tripled its quarterly internal growth from approximately 50,000 net new customers per quarter to more than 150,000. We view our 366,000 new subscribers added in 1995 as validation of our strategy for internal growth.

Acquisitions also played a significant role in our growth for the year. We closed six transactions this year which increased our subscribers by over 1.1 million. The most significant acquisition was that of USA Mobile. The $540 million transaction is the second largest in the history of the paging industry and added 959,000 subscribers to Arch.

Record Financial Performance

Financial performance in the wireless communications industry is measured primarily by operat-ing cash flow or "EBITDA" (Earnings Before Interest, Taxes, Depreciation and Amortization). This performance measure is the basis for a company's valuation by the equity markets and an important criterion for a company's ability to secure financing. Arch achieved a record increase of EBITDA from a $20 million annualized rate at year end 1994 to more than $80 million on an annualized basis at year end 1995.

Arch's net revenues in 1995 increased 125% to $141.8 million from the $63.1 million level for 1994. Net revenues are the sum of service and product sales less cost of product sales, which is the standard presentation method in the paging industry. Our shareholder equity base, or market capitalization, increased from $135 million to $500 million.

Industry Consolidation

Arch continues to play a major role in our industry's accelerating consolidation. To date, we have completed 32 acquisitions. These acquisitions have allowed Arch to increase shareholder value by increasing our operating leverage and expanding our access to new geographic markets.

In addition to the major acquisition of USA Mobile, Arch made five other acquisitions in 1995. These consisted of The Beeper Company of America, Inc. with operations in Texas, California, and Georgia; Beta Tele-Page, Inc., with operations in Texas; Data Transmission, Inc., with operations in Georgia; Groome Enterprises, Inc., with operations in Louisiana; and Professional Paging and Radio, Inc. with operations in Florida.

At year end Arch entered into an agreement to acquire Westlink Holdings, Inc. for $340 million. This transaction is expected to close in the second quarter of 1996. Pro forma for the Westlink acquisition, Arch has 2.5 million subscribers, operating in 38 states and is the third largest paging company in the United States. Additionally, we expect our annualized EBITDA to be more than $100 million following the close.

Arch Communications Group

Narrowband Personal Communications Services (NPCS)

We believe that NPCS holds promise as a platform for new narrowband wireless messaging services. Arch is well positioned to participate in this new generation of messaging services as a result of two strategic investments.

Our first investment was made in PCS Development Corporation (PCSD), a company in which Arch played a significant role in its beginnings. PCSD was formed to bid in the Federal Communications Commission 1994 auction for NPCS licenses. PCSD was a successful bidder at the auctions and acquired a national license for paired 50 KHz inbound/50 KHz outbound frequencies. These frequencies are ideally suited for voice paging and wireless data service applications. Through Arch's 10% equity position and its seat on PCSD's Board of Directors, we believe Arch will have the opportunity to offer exciting new NPCS service offerings in the future.

Our second strategic investment results from the upcoming acquisition of Westlink Holdings, Inc. As a part of this transaction, Arch will acquire a 49% equity interest in Benbow PCS Ventures. Benbow is licensed for paired 50 KHz outbound/12.5 KHz inbound frequencies that cover over half of the United States. Benbow's licenses are expected to enhance Arch's ability to be a full participant in the evolving market of NPCS.

Human Resources

As Arch's business has grown significantly in 1995, so has the depth and strength of our management team. With the acquisition of USA Mobile, Stan Sech joined us as president of USA Mobile, now our largest division. Stan brings many years of management experience in paging. Tony Ott was appointed vice president, Information Services. Tony brings to Arch over 20 years of experience in information services and telecommunications. Bob Alperin joined Arch as vice president, Business Development. Bob will be focused on expanding our strategic alliances, developing new distribution partnerships and assisting with future acquisitions. Carol Burns was named director, Human Resources. Carol has over 14 years of experience in the human resources field. We are pleased to welcome these key leaders to the Arch team.

In Conclusion

1995 was the most eventful year in Arch's history. In addition to setting records in all key operating and financial measures, we achieved the size and national geographic presence required for our future success. I want to thank all Arch team members for their dedication, commitment and high performance levels which have been so critical to our track record of operating excellence. And although all of us at Arch are proud of past accomplishments, our motivation comes from our bright prospects for the future.

C.E. Baker, Jr.

Chairman of the Board, President and Chief Executive Officer

March 12, 1996

MANAGEMENT'S DISCUSSION AND ANALYSIS OF FINANCIAL CONDITION AND RESULTS OF OPERATIONS

Overview

Arch is a leading provider of wireless messaging services, primarily paging services, and had 2.0 million pagers in service as of December 31, 1995. From September 1, 1991 through December 31, 1995, Arch's total subscriber base grew at a compound rate on an annualized basis of 89.1% and its compound rate of internal subscriber base growth (excluding pagers added through acquisitions) on an annualized basis was 52.8%.

Arch derives the majority of its revenues from fixed periodic (usually monthly) fees, not dependent on usage, charged to subscribers for paging services. As long as a subscriber remains on service, operating results benefit from the recurring payments of the fixed periodic fees without incurrence of additional selling expenses by Arch. Arch's service, rental and maintenance revenues and the related expenses exhibit substantially similar growth trends. Arch's average paging revenue per subscriber has declined over the past three years for two principal reasons: (i) the percentage of subscriber-owned and reseller-owned pagers for which Arch receives no recurring equipment rental revenues has increased from 29% of pagers in service at August 31, 1992 to 55% of pagers in service at December 31, 1995; and (ii) the percentage of net new pagers in service added to Arch's subscriber base through indirect channels has increased from 3% in the year ended August 31, 1992 to 49% in the year ended December 31, 1995. Most of the indirect channel additions are derived from resellers who purchase air time from Arch at wholesale prices. The reduction in average paging revenue per subscriber resulting from these trends has been more than offset by the elimination of associated expenses so that Arch's margins have improved over such period.

Arch's total revenues have increased from $35.2 million in the year ended August 31, 1992 to $67.2 million in the year ended August 31, 1994, and from $75.9 million in the year ended December 31, 1994 to $162.6 million in the year ended December 31, 1995. Over the same period, through operating efficiencies and economies of scale, Arch has been able to reduce its per pager operating costs to enhance its competitive position in its markets. Due to the rapid growth in its subscriber base, Arch has incurred significant selling expenses, which are charged to operations in the year incurred. Arch has reported net losses of $6.7 million, $5.7 million, $5.1 million, $3.3 million, $6.5 million, and $36.6 million in the years ended August 31, 1992, 1993, and 1994, the four months ended December 31, 1994 and the years ended December 31, 1994 and 1995, respectively, as a result of significant depreciation and amortization expenses related to acquired and developed assets and interest charges associated with indebtedness. However, as its subscriber base has grown, Arch's operating results have improved, as evidenced by an increase in its EBITDA from $9.8 million in the year ended August 31, 1992 to $16.0 million in the year ended August 31, 1994, and from $18.0 million in the year ended December 31, 1994 to $47.2 million in the year ended December 31, 1995.

EBITDA is a standard measure of financial performance in the paging industry and also is one of the financial measures used to calculate whether Arch and its subsidiaries are in compliance with the covenants under their respective indebtedness, but should not be construed as an alternative to operating income or cash flows from operating activities as determined in accordance with generally accepted accounting principles. Arch's financial objective is to increase its EBITDA, as such earnings are a significant source of funds for servicing indebtedness and for investment in continued growth, including purchase of pagers and paging system equipment construction and expansion of paging systems, and possible acquisitions.

On October 17, 1994, Arch announced that it was changing its fiscal year end from August 31 to December 31. Arch filed a transitional report on Form 10-K with audited financial statements for the period September 1, 1994 through December 31, 1994 and has elected to include herein, for comparative purposes, unaudited financial statements for the period September 1, 1993 through December 31, 1993. Arch's quarterly and annual reporting is now based on its new fiscal year end of December 31.

Results of Operations

The table on the facing page presents certain items from Arch's Consolidated Statements of Operations as a percentage of net revenue (total revenue less cost of products sold) and certain other information for periods indicated.

Year Ended December 31, 1995 Compared with Year Ended December 31, 1994

Total revenue increased $86.7 million, or 114.2%, to $162.6 million in the year ended December 31, 1995 from $75.9 million the year ended December 31, 1994 and net revenues increased $78.7 million, or 124.7%, from $63.1 million to $141.8 million over the same period. Service, rental and maintenance revenues, which consist primarily of recurring revenues associated with the sale or lease of pagers, increased $77.0 million, or 125.2%, to $138.5 million in the year ended December 31, 1995 from $61.5 million in the year ended December 31, 1994. These increases in revenues were due primarily to the increase in the number of pagers in service from 538,000 at December

	Year Ended August 31,		Four Months Ended December 31,		Year Ended December 31,	
	1993	1994	1993	1994	1994	1995
Total revenues	109.8%	117.7%	111.7%	120.1%	120.3%	114.7%
Cost of products sold	(9.8)	(17.7)	(11.7)	(20.1)	(20.3)	(14.7)
Net revenues	100.0	100.0	100.0	100.0	100.0	100.0
Operating expenses:						
Service, rental and maintenance	23.1	23.0	22.8	22.4	22.8	20.9
Selling	17.7	17.9	17.6	18.6	18.3	17.3
General and administrative	31.8	31.0	31.8	30.1	30.5	28.5
Depreciation and amortization	33.3	29.8	32.0	29.5	29.0	42.5
Operating income (loss)	(5.9)%	(1.7)%	(4.2)%	(0.6)%	(0.6)%	(9.2)%
Net income (loss)	(13.9)%	(8.9)%	(10.8)%	(14.0)%	(10.2)%	(25.8)%
EBITDA	27.4%	28.1%	27.8%	28.9%	28.5%	33.3%
Annual service, rental and maintenance expenses per pager	$ 48	$41	$44	$33	$35	$28
Selling cost per net new pager in service	$105	$74	$90	$68	$69	$67

31, 1994 to 2,006,000 at December 31, 1995. Acquisitions of paging companies added 1,102,000 pagers in service, with the remaining 366,000 pagers added through internal growth. Maintenance revenues represented less than 10% of total service, rental and maintenance revenues in the years ended December 31, 1994 and 1995. Arch does not differentiate between service and rental revenues. Product sales, less cost of products sold, increased 110.7% to $3.3 million in the year ended December 31, 1995 from $1.6 million in the year ended December 31, 1994 as a result of a greater number of pager unit sales.

Service, rental and maintenance expenses, which consist primarily of telephone line and site rental expenses, increased to $29.7 million (20.9% of net revenues) in the year ended December 31, 1995 from $14.4 million (22.8% of net revenues) in the year ended December 31, 1994. The increase in absolute dollars was due primarily to increased expenses associated with system expansions and the provision of paging services to a greater number of subscribers. The decrease as a percentage of revenues resulted from the increase in Arch's subscriber base described above. As existing paging systems became more populated through the addition of new subscribers, the fixed costs of operating these paging systems are spread over a greater subscriber base. Annualized service, rental and maintenance expenses per subscriber decreased to $28 in the

year ended December 31, 1995 from $35 in the year ended December 31, 1994.

Selling expenses increased to $24.5 million (17.3% of net revenues) in the year ended December 31, 1995 from $11.5 million (18.3% of net revenues) in the year ended December 31, 1994. The increase in selling expenses was due to the addition of sales personnel to support continued growth in the subscriber base, as the number of net new pagers in service resulting from internal growth increased by 117.9% from the year ended December 31, 1994 to the year ended December 31, 1995. Arch's selling cost per net new pager in service decreased to $67 in the year ended December 31, 1995 from $69 in the year ended December 31, 1994. Most selling expenses are directly related to the number of net new subscribers added. Therefore, such expenses may increase in the future if pagers in service are added at a more rapid rate than in the past.

General and administrative expenses increased to $40.4 million (28.5% of net revenues) in the year ended December 31, 1995 from $19.2 million (30.5% of net revenues) in the year ended December 31, 1994. The increase in absolute dollars was due primarily to increased expenses associated with supporting more pagers in service.

Depreciation and amortization expenses increased to $60.2 million (42.5% of net revenues) in the year ended December 31, 1995 from $18.3

Arch Communications Group

million (29.0% of net revenues) in the year ended December 31, 1994. These expenses reflect Arch's acquisitions of paging businesses, accounted for as purchases, and continued investment in pagers and other system expansion equipment to support continued growth. As a result of its September 1995 acquisition of USA Mobile, which also was accounted for under the purchase method of accounting, Arch expects its depreciation and amortization expenses to increase by approximately $70 million annually through the year ending December 31, 2002. Arch's pending acquisition of Westlink, if completed, will result in further significant increases in Arch's future depreciation and amortization expenses.

Operating loss increased to $13.0 million in the year ended December 31, 1995 from $0.4 million in the year ended December 31, 1994 as a result of the factors outlined above.

Net interest expense increased to $22.5 million in the year ended December 31, 1995 from $5.0 million in the year ended December 31, 1994. The increase was attributable to an increase in Arch's outstanding debt and higher interest rates. Arch expects its future interest expense to increase significantly as a result of additional debt incurred in connection with its September 1995 acquisition of USA Mobile, its pending Westlink acquisition, and other acquisitions.

During the year ended December 31, 1995, Arch recognized an income tax benefit of $4.6 million representing the tax benefit of operating losses subsequent to September 7, 1995 which were available to offset previously established deferred tax liabilities arising from Arch's acquisition of USA Mobile. Arch expects to recognize the $28.9 million balance of such tax benefit in the year ending December 31, 1996.

During the year ended December 31, 1995, Arch recognized an extraordinary charge of $1.7 million, representing the write-off of unamortized deferred financing costs associated with the prepayment of indebtedness under a prior credit facility in May 1995. During the year ended December 31, 1994, Arch recognized an extraordinary charge of $1.1 million, representing the write-off of unamortized deferred financing costs associated with the

prepayment of indebtedness under a prior credit facility in September 1994.

Net loss increased to $36.6 million in the year ended December 31, 1995 from $6.5 million in the year ended December 31, 1994 as a result of the factors outlined above. Included in the net loss for the year ended December 31, 1995 was a charge of $4.0 million representing Arch's pro rata share of USA Mobile's net loss for the period of time from Arch's acquisition of its initial 37% interest in USA Mobile on May 16, 1995 through the completion of Arch's acquisition of USA Mobile on September 7, 1995. The increases in depreciation and amortization expenses attributable to Arch's September 1995 acquisition of USA Mobile and its pending acquisition of Westlink, as described above, will increase Arch's future net losses (or decrease its future net income, if any).

EBITDA increased 162.6% to $47.2 million (33.3% of net revenues) in the year ended December 31, 1995 from $18.0 million (28.5% of net revenues) in the year ended December 31, 1994 as a result of the factors outlined above.

Recent and Pending Acquisitions

In September 1995, Arch completed its acquisition of USA Mobile for aggregate consideration of $582.2 million, consisting of $88.9 million in cash (including direct transaction cost), 7,599,493 shares of common stock valued at $209.0 million on the date of completion and the assumption of liabilities of $284.3 million, including $241.2 million of long-term debt. The acquisition was completed in two steps. The first step, Arch acquired an aggregate of 5,450,000 shares of USA Mobile common stock, representing approximately 37% of USA Mobile's then outstanding capital stock, in a tender offer completed in May 1995 for $15.40 per share. On September 7, 1995, Arch completed its acquisition of USA Mobile through the merger of Arch with and into USA Mobile. In accordance with generally accepted accounting principles, Arch was treated as the acquirer in such transaction for accounting and financial reporting purposes. See Note 2 to Consolidated Financial Statements.

During 1995, Arch also completed five additional acquisitions for aggregate consideration of $36.1 million in cash plus the issuance of 395,000 shares of common stock valued at $6.9 million on the date of completion. See Note 2 to Arch's Consolidated Financial Statements.

In December 1995, Arch entered into a definitive agreement to acquire Westlink for approximately $340 million in cash, subject to adjustment by the amount of certain budgeted or approved capital expenditures made by Westlink prior to the closing less the increase in Westlink's bank indebtedness between December 17, 1995 and the closing.

Arch has pursued and intends to continue to pursue acquisitions of paging businesses as part of its growth strategy. As a result, Arch evaluates acquisition opportunities on an ongoing basis and from time to time is engaged in discussions with respect to possible acquisitions. On December 5, 1995, Arch entered into a letter of intent to acquire a paging business for $14.0 million, subject to adjustment, of which $7.5 million would be paid in cash and $6.5 million would be paid through the issuance of unregistered common stock. The acquisition is subject to the execution of a definitive purchase agreement, regulatory approvals and other conditions, and no assurance can be given that the acquisition will be completed.

Sources of Funds

Arch's net cash provided by operating activities was $7.9 million, $8.7 million, $14.8 million, $4.7 million, $14.2 million, and $14.7 million in the years ended August 31, 1992, 1993 and 1994, and four months ended December 31, 1994 and the years ended December 31, 1994 and 1995, respectively.

In February 1995, Arch completed a public offering of 4,600,000 shares of common stock, of which 2,701,296 shares were sold by Arch for net proceeds of $46.2 million and 1,898,704 shares were sold by certain stockholders of Arch (including 1,295,000 shares sold by the former owners of certain paging businesses acquired by Arch). Arch used its proceeds to repay borrowings of $46.2 million under a prior credit facility.

On February 7, 1996, the Company commenced an offer (the "Conversion Offer") to pay a cash premium of $110 for each $1,000 principal amount of the Company's 6-3/4% Convertible Sub-

ordinated Debentures due 2003 ("Arch Convertible Debentures") converted into common stock at $16.75 per share. Effective upon the expiration of the Conversion Offer at 12:00 midnight, Eastern Time, on March 6, 1996, the Company accepted for conversion $14,121,000 in principal amount of Arch Convertible Debentures in exchange for an aggregate of approximately 843,000 shares of common stock and $1.6 million in cash.

On March 12, 1996, Arch completed a public offering of 10-7/8% Senior Discount Notes due 2008 (the Senior Discount Notes) in the aggregate principal amount of $467.4 million ($275.0 million initial accreted value). Interest does not accrue on the Senior Discount Notes prior to March 15, 2001. Commencing September 15, 2001, interest on the Senior Discount Notes is payable semi-annually at an annual rate of 10-7/8%. The $266.1 million net proceeds from the issuance of the Senior Discount Notes, after deducting underwriting discounts and commissions and offering expenses, will be used principally to fund a portion of the purchase price of Arch's pending acquisition of Westlink. Pending completion of Westlink acquisition, Arch used $225.0 million of the net proceeds to repay existing indebtedness under Arch's credit facilities, with the remainder primarily invested in short-term, interest-bearing instruments. See Notes 3 and 9 to Arch's Consolidated Financial Statements.

Future Capital Needs

The Company's business strategy requires the availability of substantial funds to finance the continued development and further growth and expansion of its operations, including the Company's pending acquisition of Westlink and other possible acquisitions. The amount of capital required by the Company will depend upon a number of factors, including subscriber growth, technical developments, marketing and sales expenses, competitive conditions, acquisition strategy and acquisition opportunities. No assurance can be given that additional equity or debt financing will be available to the Company on acceptable terms, if at all. The unavailability of sufficient financing when needed would have a material adverse effect on the Company.

Arch Communications Group

CONSOLIDATED BALANCE SHEETS

In 1994 Arch changed its fiscal year end from August 31 to December 31. Included herein are statements covering the period from September 1 to December 31, 1994. Arch's financial reporting is now based on its new fiscal year end of December 31.

December 31, (in thousands, except share amounts)	1994	1995
Assets		
Current assets:		
Cash	$ 2,351	$ 3,643
Accounts receivable (less reserves of $707 and $2,125 in 1994 and 1995, respectively)	4,632	14,278
Inventories	—	11,801
Due from employees	47	41
Prepaid expenses and other	1,453	3,908
Total current assets	8,483	33,671
Property and equipment, at cost:		
Land, buildings, and improvements	3,333	6,813
Paging and computer equipment	73,992	191,461
Furniture, fixtures, and vehicles	2,935	7,362
	80,260	205,636
Less accumulated depreciation and amortization	23,130	36,390
Property and equipment, net	57,130	169,246
Intangible and other assets (less accumulated amortization of $14,255 and $44,915 in 1994 and 1995, respectively)	52,245	582,459
	$117,858	$785,376
Liabilities and Stockholders' Equity		
Current liabilities:		
Current maturities of long-term debt	$ 86	$ 166
Accounts payable	8,567	22,463
Accrued expenses	3,044	8,947
Accrued interest	391	7,845
Customer deposits	1,182	5,258
Deferred revenue	1,800	4,493
Total current liabilities	15,070	49,172
Long-term debt, less current maturities	93,420	457,044
Deferred income taxes	—	28,900
Commitments (Note 6)		
Redeemable preferred stock	—	3,376
Stockholders' equity:		
Preferred stock—$.01 par value, authorized 10,000,000 shares, no shares issued	—	—
Common stock—$.01 par value, authorized 75,000,000 shares, issued and outstanding: 8,058,665, and 19,653,031 shares in 1994 and 1995 respectively	81	197
Additional paid-in capital	60,823	334,825
Accumulated deficit	(51,536)	(88,138)
Total stockholders' equity	9,368	246,884
	$117,858	$785,376

The accompanying notes are an integral part of these consolidated financial statements.

CONSOLIDATED STATEMENT OF OPERATIONS

In 1994 Arch changed its fiscal year end from August 31 to December 31. Included herein are statements covering the period from September 1 to December 31, 1994. Arch's financial reporting is now based on its new fiscal year end of December 31.

(in thousands, except share and per amounts)	Years Ended August 31,		Four Months Ended December 31,		Year Ended December 31,
	1993	1994	1993 (unaudited)	1994	1995
Service, rental and maintenance revenues	$ 39,610	$ 55,139	$ 16,457	$ 22,847	$ 138,466
Product sales	5,698	12,108	2,912	5,178	24,132
Total revenues	45,308	67,247	19,369	28,025	162,598
Cost of products sold	(4,031)	(10,124)	(2,027)	(4,690)	(20,789)
	41,277	57,123	17,342	23,335	141,809
Operating expenses:					
Service, rental and maintenance	9,532	13,123	3,959	5,231	29,673
Selling	7,307	10,243	3,058	4,338	24,502
General and administrative	13,123	17,717	5,510	7,022	40,448
Depreciation and amortization	13,764	16,997	5,549	6,873	60,205
Total operating expenses	43,726	58,080	18,076	23,464	154,828
Operating income (loss)	(2,449)	(957)	(734)	(129)	(13,019)
Interest expense	(3,036)	(4,221)	(1,138)	(2,009)	(22,560)
Interest income	175	109	6	16	38
Equity in loss of affiliate	—	—	—	—	(3,977)
Income (loss) before income tax benefit and extraordinary item	(5,310)	(5,069)	(1,866)	(2,122)	(39,518)
Benefit from income taxes	—	—	—	—	4,600
Income (loss) before extraordinary item	(5,310)	(5,069)	(1,866)	(2,122)	(34,918)
Extraordinary charge from early extinguishment of debt	(415)	—	—	(1,137)	(1,684)
Net income (loss)	(5,725)	(5,069)	(1,866)	(3,259)	(36,602)
Accretion of redeemable preferred stock	—	—	—	—	(102)
Net income (loss) to common stockholders	$ (5,725)	$ (5,069)	$ (1,866)	$ (3,259)	$ (36,704)
Income (loss) per common share before extraordinary item	$ (.74)	$ (.71)	$ (.26)	$ (.29)	$ (2.59)
Extraordinary charge from early extinguishment of debt	(.06)	—	—	(.16)	(.12)
Accretion of redeemable preferred stock	—	—	—	—	(.01)
Net income (loss) per common share	$ (.80)	$ (.71)	$ (.26)	$ (.45)	$ (2.72)
Weighted average number of common shares outstanding	7,125,164	7,153,044	7,149,136	7,238,624	13,497,734

The accompanying notes are an integral part of these consolidated financial statements.

Arch Communications Group

Arch Communications Group

CONSOLIDATED STATEMENT OF CASH FLOWS

In 1994 Arch changed its fiscal year end from August 31 to December 31. Included herein are statements covering the period from September 1 to December 31, 1994. Arch's financial reporting is now based on its new fiscal year end of December 31.

(in thousands)	Years Ended August 31,		Four Months Ended December 31,		Year Ended December 31,
	1993	1994	1993 (unaudited)	1994	1995
Cash flows from operating activities:					
Net income (loss)	$ (5,725)	$ (5,069)	$ (1,866)	$ (3,259)	$(36,602)
Adjustments to reconcile net income (loss) to net cash provided by operating activities:					
Depreciation and amortization	13,764	16,997	5,549	6,873	60,205
Deferred tax benefit	—	—	—	—	(4,600)
Extraordinary charge from early extinguishment of debt	415	—	—	1,137	1,684
Equity in loss of affiliate	—	—	—	—	3,977
Accretion of discount on subordinated note	70	—	—	—	—
Accounts receivable loss provision	873	1,239	389	649	3,915
Changes in assets and liabilities, net of effect from acquisitions of paging companies:					
Accounts receivable	(1,296)	(2,683)	(929)	(855)	(9,582)
Inventories	—	—	—	—	(3,176)
Due from employees	8	16	15	2	6
Prepaid expenses and other	(419)	(197)	(164)	(156)	(517)
Accounts payable	23	2,633	2,143	2,338	3,535
Accrued expenses	681	1,093	108	(1,382)	(5,089)
Accrued interest	(143)	523	123	(279)	1,003
Customer deposits	81	248	10	(173)	262
Deferred revenue	389	(19)	(72)	(215)	(272)
Net cash provided by operating activities	8,721	14,781	5,306	4,680	14,749
Cash flows from investing activities:					
Additions to property and equipment, net	(16,607)	(21,506)	(5,340)	(9,438)	(45,331)
Additions to intangible and other assets	(4,246)	(4,151)	(2,146)	(5,841)	(15,137)
Acquisition of paging companies, net of cash acquired	(10,145)	(3,325)	—	(15,085)	(132,081)
Net cash used for investing activities	(30,998)	(28,982)	(7,486)	(30,364)	(192,549)
Cash flows from financing activities:					
Issuance of long-term debt	13,323	40,225	35,225	58,872	191,617
Repayment of long-term debt	(2,061)	(25,791)	(24,125)	(32,776)	(63,705)
Net proceeds from sale of common stock	6	202	190	12	51,180
Net cash provided by financing activities	11,268	14,636	11,290	26,108	179,092
Net increase (decrease) in cash & equivalents	(11,009)	435	9,110	424	1,292
Cash, beginning of period	12,501	1,492	1,492	1,927	2,351
Cash, end of period	$ 1,492	$ 1,927	$ 10,602	$ 2,351	$ 3,643

The accompanying notes are an integral part of these consolidated financial statements.

NOTES TO CONSOLIDATED FINANCIAL STATEMENTS

1. Organizational and Significant Accounting Policies

Organization Arch Communication Group, Inc. (Arch) is a leading provider of wireless messaging services, primarily paging services.

Principles of consolidation The accompanying consolidating financial statements include the accounts of Arch and its wholly-owned subsidiaries. All significant inter-company accounts and transactions have been eliminated.

Revenue recognition Arch recognizes revenue under rental and service agreements with customers as the related services are performed. Maintenance revenues and related costs are recognized ratably over the respective terms of the agreements. Sales of equipment are recognized upon delivery. Commissions are recognized as an expense when incurred.

Inventories Inventories consist of new pagers which are held specifically for resale. Inventories are stated at the lower of cost or market, with cost determined on a first-in, first-out basis.

Property and equipment Effective June 1, 1993, Arch changed its estimate of the useful life of pagers from five years to four years. This change was made to better reflect the estimated period during which pagers will produce equipment rental revenue. The change had the effect of increasing depreciation expense and net loss by approximately $700,000 ($.10 per share) in the quarter ended August 31, 1993.

Effective October 1, 1995, Arch changed its estimate of the useful life of pagers from four years to three years. This change was made to better reflect the estimated period during which pagers will produce equipment rental revenue. The change did not have a material effect on depreciation expense or net loss in the quarter ended December 31, 1995.

Pagers sold or otherwise retired are removed from the accounts at their net book value using the first-in, first-out method.

Arch provides for depreciation and amortization using the straight-line method over the following estimated useful lives:

Asset Classification	Estimated Useful Life
Buildings and improvements	20 Years
Leasehold improvements	Lease Term
Paging and computer equipment	3-8 Years
Furniture and fixtures	5-8 Years
Vehicles	3 Years

Intangible and other assets Intangible and other assets, net of accumulated amortization, are composed of the following at December 31, 1994 and 1995:

(in thousands)	1994	1995
Purchased subscriber lists	$ 5,675	$ 96,686
Purchased FCC licenses	22,886	174,533
Goodwill	12,722	283,814
Non-competition agreements	963	5,321
Deferred financing costs	3,867	6,012
Investment In PCS Development Corporation	1,419	6,500
Other	4,713	9,593
	$52,245	$582,459

Subscriber lists, Federal Communications Commission (FCC) licenses and goodwill are amortized over their estimated useful lives, ranging from five to ten years using the straight-line method. Non-competition agreements are amortized over the terms of the agreements using the straight-line method. Other assets consist of contract rights, organizational and FCC application and development costs, which are amortized using the straight-line method over their estimated useful lives not exceeding ten years. Development costs include non-recurring, direct costs incurred in the development and expansion of paging systems, and are amortized over a two-year period.

Deferred financing costs incurred in connection with Arch's credit agreements (see Note 3) are being amortized over periods not to exceed the terms of the related agreements. As credit agreements are amended or renegotiated, unamortized deferred financing costs are written off as an extraordinary charge. For the four months ended December 31, 1994, a charge of $1,137,000 was recognized, and an additional charge of $1,684,000 was recognized in the second quarter of 1995 in connection with the closing of a new credit facility in May 1995.

On November 8, 1994, PCS Development Corporation (PCSD) was successful in acquiring the rights to a two-way paging license in five designated regions in the United States in the FCC narrowband wireless spectrum auction. Upon completion of the Merger, Arch's equity interest in PCSD became 17.47% but was subsequently diluted to 10.5%. As of December 31, 1995, Arch's investment in PCSD totaled $6.5 million.

Arch evaluates the realizability of goodwill and other intangible assets based on estimated cash flows to be generated from each of such assets as compared to the original estimates used in measuring the assets. To the extent impairment is identified, Arch recognizes a write-down. To date, Arch has not had any such impairments.

Fair value of financial instruments   Arch's financial instruments, as defined under Statement of Financial Accounting Standards (SFAS) No. 107, include its cash and its debt financing. The fair value of cash is equal to the carrying value at December 31, 1995.

As discussed in Note 3, Arch's debt financing consists primarily of (1) senior bank debt, (2) fixed rate senior notes, and (3) convertible subordinated debentures. Arch considers the fair value of senior bank debt to be equal to the carrying value since the related facilities bear a current market rate of interest. Arch is unable to determine the fair value of the convertible subordinated debentures due to the specific terms and conversion features available in their respective agreements. These various facilities were negotiated with creditors based on the facts and circumstances available at the time the debt was incurred. Since Arch has undergone significant change over the past year, management is unable to determine what rates and terms would be available currently.

Arch's fixed rate senior notes are traded publicly. The following depicts the fair value of this debt based on the current market quotes as of December 31, 1995:

Description (in thousands)	Carrying Value	Fair Value
9-1/2% Senior Notes due 2004 of USA Mobile II	$125,000	$129,000
14% Senior Notes due 2004 of USA Mobile II	100,000	111,000

Net income (loss) per common share   Net income (loss) per common share is based on the weighted average number of common shares outstanding. Shares of stock issuable pursuant to stock options and upon conversion of the subordinated debentures (see Note 3) have not been considered, as their effect would be antidilutive.

Use of estimates   The preparation of financial statements in conformity with generally accepted accounting principles requires management to make estimates and assumptions that affect the reported amounts of assets and liabilities and disclosure of contingent assets and liabilities at the date of the financial statements and the reported amounts of revenues and expenses during the reported period. Actual results could differ from those estimates.

Unaudited interim consolidated financial statements   The consolidated statements of operations and cash flows for the four months ended December 31, 1993 are unaudited and, in the opinion of Arch's management, include all adjustments, consisting of normal, recurring adjustments, necessary for a fair presentation of Arch's consolidated financial position, results of operations, and cash flows. The results of operations for the four months ended December 31, 1993 are not necessarily indicative of the results of any other period.

Change in year end   In October 1994, Arch changed its fiscal year end from August 31 to December 31. Arch's quarterly and annual reporting is now based on Arch's new fiscal year end.

Reclassifications   Certain amounts of prior periods were reclassified to conform to the 1995 presentation.

2. Acquisitions

During the year ended August 31, 1993, Arch acquired, in separate transactions, four paging systems located in New York, New Hampshire, and

Maine for an aggregate purchase price of approximately $10,100,000.

During the year ended August 31, 1994, Arch acquired a paging system located in Rhode Island for approximately $3,325,000.

During the four months ended December 31, 1994, Arch acquired in separate transactions the paging assets of a system located in Florida and the stock of a paging company located in Illinois and Wisconsin for an aggregate purchase price of approximately $31 million including 900,000 shares of Arch common stock valued at $15.9 million. In connection with the stock acquisition, the fair value of assets acquired was approximately $33 million less liabilities assumed of approximately $2 million. In December 1994, Arch purchased certain paging system assets and frequencies from BellSouth Telecommunications, Inc. for approximately $500,000 in cash.

On September 7, 1995, Arch completed its acquisition of USA Mobile Communications Holdings, Inc. (USA Mobile). The acquisition was completed in two steps. First, in May 1995, Arch acquired approximately 37%, or 5,450,000 shares, of USA Mobile's then outstanding common stock for $83.9 million in cash, funded by borrowings under the Arch Enterprises Credit Facility (see Note 3). Second, on September 7, 1995, the acquisition was completed through the merger of Arch with and into USA Mobile (the Merger). Upon consummation of the Merger, USA Mobile was renamed Arch Communications Group, Inc. In the Merger, each share of USA Mobile's outstanding common stock was exchanged for Arch common stock on a .8020-for-one-basis (an aggregate of 7,599,493 shares of Arch common stock) and the 5,450,000 USA Mobile shares purchased by Arch in May 1995 were retired. Outstanding shares of USA Mobile's Series

A Redeemable Preferred Stock remained outstanding and were not otherwise affected by the Merger (see Note 4).

Arch is treated as the acquirer in the Merger for accounting and financial reporting purposes. The aggregate consideration paid or exchanged in the Merger was $582.2 million, consisting of cash paid of $88.9 million, including direct transaction costs, 7,599,493 shares of Arch common stock valued at $209.0 million and the assumption of liabilities of $284.3 million, including $241.2 million of long-term debt.

During the year ended December 31, 1995, Arch completed five acquisitions of paging companies, in addition to the Merger, for purchase prices aggregating approximately $43.0 million, consisting of cash of $36.1 million and 395,000 shares of Arch common stock valued at $6.9 million. Goodwill resulting from the acquisitions and the Merger is being amortized over a ten-year period using the straight-line method.

These acquisitions have been accounted for as purchases, and the results of their operations have been included in the consolidated financial statements from the dates of the respective acquisitions. The following unaudited pro forma summary presents the consolidated results of operations as if the acquisitions had occurred at the beginning of the periods presented, after giving effect to certain adjustments, including depreciation and amortization of acquired assets and interest expense on acquisition debt. These pro forma results have been prepared for comparative purposes only and do not purport to be indicative of what would have occurred had the acquisitions been made at the beginning of the period presented, or of results that may occur in the future.

(unaudited)	Year Ended August 31, 1994	Four Months Ended December 31, 1993	Four Months Ended December 31, 1994	Year Ended December 31, 1995
Revenues	$155,566	$42,093	$67,512	$249,507
Income (loss) before extraordinary item	(75,523)	(25,161)	(25,188)	(71,806)
Net income (loss)	(75,523)	(25,161)	(26,325)	(73,490)
Net income (loss) per common share	(4.71)	(1.57)	(1.64)	(3.93)

On December 17, 1995, Arch entered into a definitive stock purchase agreement to acquire Westlink Holdings, Inc. for approximately $340 million in cash subject to adjustment by the amount of certain budgeted or approved capital expenditures made by Westlink prior to the closing less the increase in Westlink's bank indebtedness between December 17, 1995 and the closing. This acquisition is subject to closing conditions, including FCC approval.

3. Long-Term Debt

Long-term debt consisted of the following at December 31, 1994 and 1995:

(in thousands)	1994	1995
Senior bank debt	$58,872	$204,500
9-1/2% Senior Notes due 2004 of USA Mobile II	—	125,000
14% Senior Notes due 2004 of USA Mobile II	—	100,000
Convertible subordinated debentures	34,475	27,485
Non-competition agreement obligations	135	210
Capital lease obligations	24	15
	93,506	457,210
Less-current maturities	86	166
Long-term debt	$93,420	$457,044

9. Subsequent Events

On March 6, 1996, the holders of $14.1 million principal amount of Arch Convertible Debentures (see Note 3) elected to convert their Arch Convertible Debentures into Arch common stock at a conversion price of $16.75 per share and received approximately 843,000 shares of Arch common stock, together with a $1.6 million cash premium.

On March 12, 1996, Arch completed a public offering of 10-7/8% Senior Discount Notes due 2008 (the Senior Discount Notes) in the aggregate principal amount of $467.4 million ($275.0 million initial accreted value). Interest does not accrue on the Senior Discount Notes prior to March 15, 2001. Commencing September 15, 2001, interest on the Senior Discount Notes is payable semi-annually at an annual rate of 10-7/8%. The $266.1 million net proceeds from the issuance of the Senior Discount Notes, after deducting underwriting discounts and commissions and offering expenses, principally will be used to fund a portion of the purchase price of Arch's pending acquisition of Westlink (see Note 2). Pending completion of the Westlink acquisition, Arch used $225.0 million of the net proceeds to repay existing indebtedness under Arch's credit facilities, with the remainder primarily invested in short-term, interest-bearing instruments.

REPORT OF INDEPENDENT PUBLIC ACCOUNTS

To Arch Communications Group, Inc:

We have audited the accompanying consolidated balance sheets of Arch Communications Group, Inc. (a Delaware corporation) and subsidiaries as of December 31, 1994 and 1995 and the related consolidated statements of operations, stockholders' equity (deficit) and cash flows for each of the two years in the period ended August 31, 1994, for the four months ended December 31, 1994 and the year ended December 31, 1995. These financial statements are the responsibility of Arch's management. Our responsibility is to express an opinion on these financial statements based on our audit.

We conducted our audit in accordance with generally accepted accounting standards. Those standards require that we plan and perform the audit to obtain reasonable assurance about whether the financial statements are free of material misstatement. An audit includes examining, on a test basis, evidence supporting the amounts and disclosures in the financial statements. An audit also includes assessing the accounting principles used and significant estimates made by management, as well as evaluating the overall financial statement presentation. We believe that our audits provide a reasonable basis for our opinion.

In our opinion, the financial statements referred to above present fairly, in all material respects, the financial position of Arch Communications Group, Inc. and subsidiaries as of December 31, 1994 and 1995 and the results of their operations and their cash flows for each of the two years in the period ended August 31, 1994, for the four months ended December 31, 1994 and the year ended December 31, 1995, in conformity with generally accepted accounting principals.

Arthur Andersen LLP

Boston, Massachusetts
February 15, 1996 (except with respect to Note 9 as to which the date is March 12, 1996)

Credit Analysis and Distress Prediction

Credit analysis is the evaluation of a firm from the perspective of a holder or potential holder of its debt, including trade payables, loans, and public debt securities. A key element of credit analysis is the prediction of the likelihood a firm will face financial distress.

Credit analysis is involved in a wide variety of decision contexts:

- A potential supplier asks: Should I sell products or services to this firm? The associated credit will be extended only for a short period, but the amount is large and I should have some assurance that collection risks are manageable.
- A commercial banker asks: Should we extend a loan to this firm? If so, how should it be structured? How should it be priced?
- If the loan is granted, the banker must later ask: Are we still providing the services, including credit, that this firm needs? Is the firm still in compliance with the loan terms? If not, is there a need to restructure the loan, and if so, how? Is the situation serious enough to call for accelerating the repayment of the loan?
- A pension fund manager, insurance company, or other investor asks: Are these debt securities a sound investment? What is the probability that the firm will face distress and default on the debt? Does the yield provide adequate compensation for the default risk involved?
- An investor contemplating purchase of debt securities in default asks: How likely is it that this firm can be turned around? In light of the high yield on this debt, relative to its current price, can I accept the risk that the debt will not be repaid in full?

Although credit analysis is typically viewed from the perspective of the financier, it is obviously important to the borrower as well:

- A manager of a small firm asks: What are our options for credit financing? Would the firm qualify for bank financing? If so, what type of financing would be possible? How costly would it be? Would the terms of the financing constrain our flexibility?
- A manager of a large firm asks: "What are our options for credit financing? Is the firm strong enough to raise funds in the public market? If so, what is our debt rating likely to be? What required yield would that rating imply?

Finally, there are third parties—those other than borrowers and lenders—who are interested in the general issue of how likely it is that a firm will avoid financial distress:

- An auditor asks: How likely is it that this firm will survive beyond the short run? In evaluating the firm's financials, should I consider it a going concern?
- An actual or potential employee asks: How confident can I be that this firm will be able to offer employment over the long term?
- A potential customer asks: What assurance is there that this firm will survive to provide warranty services, replacement parts, product updates, and other services?
- A competitor asks: Will this firm survive the current industry shakeout? What are the implications of potential financial distress at this firm for my pricing and market share?

THE MARKET FOR CREDIT

An understanding of credit analysis requires an appreciation for the various players in the market for credit. We describe those players briefly here.

Suppliers of Credit

The major suppliers in the market for credit are described below.

COMMERCIAL BANKS.   Commercial banks are very important players in the market for credit. Since banks tend to provide a range of services to a client, and have intimate knowledge of the client and its operations, they have a comparative advantage in extending credit in settings where (1) knowledge gained through close contact with management reduces the perceived riskiness of the credit and (2) credit risk can be contained through careful monitoring of the firm.

A constraint on bank lending operations is that the credit risk be relatively low, so that the bank's loan portfolio will be of acceptably high quality to bank regulators. Because of the importance of maintaining public confidence in the banking sector and the desire to shield government deposit insurance from risk, governments have incentives to constrain banks' exposure to credit risk. Banks also tend to shield themselves from the risk of shifts in interest rates by avoiding fixed-rate loans with long maturities. Since most of banks' capital comes from short-term deposits, such long-term loans leave them exposed to increases in interest rates, unless the risk can be hedged with derivatives. Thus, banks are less likely to play a role when a firm requires a very long-term commitment to financing. However, in some such cases they assist in providing a placement of the debt with, say, an insurance company, a pension fund, or a group of private investors.

OTHER FINANCIAL INSTITUTIONS.   Banks face competition in the commercial lending market from a variety of sources. In the U.S., there is competition from savings and loans, even though the latter are relatively more involved in financing mortgages. Finance companies compete with banks in the market for asset-based lending (i.e., the secured financing of specific assets, such as receivables, inventory, or equipment). Insurance companies are involved in a variety of lending activities. Since life insurance companies face obligations of a long-term nature, they often seek investments of long duration (e.g., long-term bonds or loans to support large, long-term commercial real estate and development projects). Investment bankers are prepared to place debt securities with private investors or in the public markets (discussed below). Various government agencies are another source of credit.

PUBLIC DEBT MARKETS.   Some firms have the size, strength, and credibility necessary to bypass the banking sector and seek financing directly from investors, either through sales of commercial paper or through the issuance of bonds. Such debt issues are facilitated by the assignment of a debt rating. In the U.S., Moody's and Standard and Poor's are the two largest rating agencies. A firm's debt rating influences the yield that must be offered to sell the debt instruments. After the debt issue, the rating agencies continue to monitor the firm's financial condition. Changes in the rating are associated with fluctuation in the price of the securities.

Banks often provide financing in tandem with a public debt issue or other source of financing. In highly-levered transactions, such as leveraged buyouts, banks commonly provide financing along with a public debt issue that would have a lower priority in case of bankruptcy. The bank's "senior financing" would typically be scheduled for earlier retirement than the public debt, and it would carry a lower yield. For smaller or startup firms, banks often provide credit in conjunction with equity financing from venture capitalists. Note that in the case of both the leveraged buyout and the startup company, the bank helps provide the cash needed to make the deal happen, but does so in a way that shields it from risks that would be unacceptably high in the banking sector.

SELLERS WHO PROVIDE FINANCING.   Another sector of the market for credit are manufacturers and other suppliers of goods and services. As a matter of course, such firms tend to finance their customers' purchases on an unsecured basis for periods of 30 to 60 days. Suppliers will, on occasion, also agree to provide more extended financing, usually with the support of a secured note. A supplier may be willing to grant such a loan in the expectation that the creditor will survive a cash shortage and remain an important customer in the future. However, the customer would typically seek such an arrangement only if bank financing is unavailable, because it could constrain flexibility in selecting among and/or negotiating with suppliers.

THE CREDIT ANALYSIS PROCESS

At first blush, credit analysis might appear less difficult than the valuation task discussed in Chapters 11 and 12. After all, a potential creditor ultimately cares only about whether the firm is strong enough to pay its debts at the scheduled times. The firm's exact value, its upside potential, or its distance from the threshold of credit-worthiness may not appear so important. Viewed in that way, credit analysis may seem more like a "zero-one" decision: either the credit is extended, or it is not.

It turns out, however, that credit analysis involves more than "just" establishing credit-worthiness. First, there are ranges of credit-worthiness, and it is important to understand where a firm lies within that range for purposes of pricing and structuring a loan. Moreover, if the creditor is a bank or other financial institution with an expected continuing relationship with the borrower, the borrower's upside potential is important, even though downside risk must be the primary consideration in credit analysis. A firm that offers growth potential also offers opportunities for income-generating financial services.

Given this broader view of credit analysis, it should not be surprising that it involves most of the same issues already discussed in the prior chapters on business strategy analysis, accounting analysis, financial analysis, and prospective analysis. Perhaps the greatest difference is that credit analysis rarely involves any explicit attempt to estimate the value of the firm's equity. However, the determinants of that value are relevant in credit analysis, because a larger equity cushion translates into lower risk for the creditor.

Below we describe one series of steps that is used by commercial lenders in credit analysis. Of course, not all commercial lenders follow the same process, but the steps are representative of typical approaches. The approach used by commercial lenders is of interest in its own right and illustrates a comprehensive credit analysis. However, analysis by others who grant credit often differs. For example, even when a manufacturer conducts some credit analysis prior to granting credit to a customer, it is typically much less extensive than the analysis conducted by a banker because the credit is very short-term and the manufacturer is willing to bear some credit risk in the interest of generating a profit on the sale.

We present the steps in a particular order, but they are in fact all interdependent. Thus, analysis at one step may need to be rethought, depending on the analysis at some later step.

Step 1: Consider the Nature and Purpose of the Loan

Understanding the purpose of a loan is important not just for deciding whether it should be granted, but also for structuring the loan. Loans might be required for only a few months, for several years, or even as a permanent part of a firm's capital structure. Loans might be used for replacement of other financing, to support working capital needs, or to finance the acquisition of long-term assets or another firm.

The required amount of the loan must also be established. In the case of small and medium-sized companies, a banker would typically prefer to be the sole financier of the business, in which case the loan would have to be large enough to retire existing debt. The preference for serving as the sole financier is not just to gain an advantage in providing a menu of financial services to the firm. It also reflects the desirability of not permitting another creditor to maintain a superior interest that would give it a higher priority in case of bankruptcy. If other creditors are willing to subordinate their positions to the bank, that would of course be acceptable so far as the bank is concerned.

Often the commercial lender deals with firms that may have parent-subsidiary relations. The question of to whom one should lend then arises. The answer is usually the entity that owns the assets that will serve as collateral (or that could serve as such if needed in the future). If this entity is the subsidiary and the parent presents some financial strength independent of the subsidiary, a guarantee of the parent could be considered.

Step 2: Consider the Type of Loan and Available Security

The type of loan considered is a function of not only its purpose, but also the financial strength of the borrower. Thus, to some extent, the loan type will be dictated by the financial analysis described in the following step in the process. Some of the possibilities are as follows:

- *Open line of credit.* An open line of credit permits the borrower to receive cash up to some specified maximum on an as-needed basis for a specified term, such as one year. To maintain this option, the borrower pays a fee (e.g., 3/8 of 1 percent) on the unused balance, in addition to the interest on any used amount. An open line of credit is useful in cases where the borrower's cash needs are difficult to anticipate.
- *Revolving line of credit.* When it is clear that a firm will need credit beyond the short run, financing may be provided in the form of a "revolver." Sometimes used to support working capital needs, the borrower is scheduled to make payments as the operating cycle proceeds and inventory and receivables are converted to cash. However, it is also expected that cash will continue to be advanced so long as the borrower remains in good standing. In addition to interest on amounts outstanding, a fee is charged on the unused line.
- *Working capital loan.* Such a loan is used to finance inventory and receivables, and is usually secured. The maximum loan balance may be tied to the balance of the working capital accounts. For example, the loan may be allowed to rise to no more than 80 percent of receivables less than 60 days old.
- *Term loan.* Term loans are used for long-term needs and are often secured with long-term assets, such as plant or equipment. Typically, the loan will be amortized, requiring periodic payments to reduce the loan balance.
- *Mortgage loan.* Mortgages support the financing of real estate, have long terms, and require periodic amortization of the loan balance.
- *Lease financing.* Lease financing can be used to facilitate the acquisition of any asset, but is most commonly used for equipment, including vehicles. Leases may be structured over periods of 1 to 15 years, depending on the life of the underlying asset.

Much bank lending is done on a secured basis, especially with smaller and more highly levered companies. Security will be required unless the loan is short-term and the borrower exposes the bank to minimal default risk. When security is required, one consideration is whether the amount of available security is sufficient to support the loan. The amount that a bank will lend on given security involves business judgment, and it depends on a variety of factors that affect the liquidity of the security in the context of a situation where the firm is distressed. The following are some rules of thumb often applied in commercial lending to various categories of security:

- *Receivables.* Accounts receivable are usually considered the most desirable form of security because they are the most liquid. One large regional bank allows loans of 50 to 80 percent of the balance of nondelinquent accounts. The percentage applied is lower when (1) there are many small accounts that would be costly to collect in the case the firm is distressed; (2) there are a few very large accounts, such that problems with a single customer could be serious; and/or (3) the customer's financial health is closely related to that of the borrower, so that collectibility is endangered just when the borrower is in default. On the latter score, banks often refuse to accept receivables from affiliates as effective security.
- *Inventory.* The desirability of inventory as security varies widely. The best case scenario is inventory consisting of a common commodity that can easily be sold to other parties if the borrower defaults. More specialized inventory, with appeal to only a limited set of buyers, or inventory that is costly to store or transport, is less desirable. The large regional bank mentioned above lends up to 60 percent on raw materials, 50 percent on finished goods, and 20 percent on work in process.
- *Machinery and equipment.* Machinery and equipment is less desirable as collateral. It is likely to be used, and it must be stored, insured, and marketed. Keeping the costs of these activities in mind, banks typically will loan only up to 50 percent of the estimated value of such assets in a forced sale, such as an auction.
- *Real estate.* The value of real estate as collateral varies considerably. Banks will often lend up to 80 percent of the appraised value of readily salable real estate. However, a factory designed for a unique purpose would be much less desirable.

When security is required to make a loan viable, a commercial lender will estimate the amounts that could be loaned on each of the assets available as security. Unless the amount exceeds the required loan balance, the loan would not be extended.

Even when a loan is not secured initially, a bank can require a "negative pledge" on the firm's assets—a pledge that the firm will not use the assets as security for any other creditor. In that case, if the borrower begins to experience difficulty and defaults on the loan, and if there are no other creditors in the picture, the bank can demand the loan become secured if it is to remain outstanding.

Step 3: Analyze the Potential Borrower's Financial Status

This portion of the analysis involves all the steps discussed in our chapters on business strategy analysis, accounting analysis, and financial analysis. The emphasis, however, is on the firm's ability to service the debt at the scheduled rate. The focus of the analysis depends on the type of financing under consideration. For example, if a short-term loan is considered to support seasonal fluctuations in inventory, the emphasis would be on the ability of the firm to convert the inventory into cash on a timely basis. In contrast, a term loan to support plant and equipment must be made with confidence in the long-run earnings prospects of the firm.

Key Analysis Questions

Some of the questions to be addressed in analyzing a potential borrower's financial status include the following:

- *Business strategy analysis*:
  How does this business work? Why is it valuable? What is its strategy for sustaining or enhancing that value? How well qualified is the management to carry out that strategy effectively? Is the viability of the business highly dependent on the talents of the existing management team?
- *Accounting analysis*:
  How well do the firm's financial statements reflect its underlying economic reality? Are there reasons to believe that the firm's performance is stronger or weaker than reported profitability would suggest? Are there sizable off-balance-sheet liabilities (e.g., operating leases) that would affect the potential borrower's ability to repay the loan?
- *Financial analysis*:
  Is the firm's level of profitability unusually high or low? What are the sources of any unusual degree of profitability? How sustainable are they? What risks are associated with the operating profit stream?

  How highly levered is the firm?

  What is the firm's funds flow picture? What are its major sources and uses of funds? Are funds required to finance expected growth? How great are fund flows expected to be, relative to the debt service required? Given the possible volatility in those fund flows, how likely is it that they could fall to a level insufficient to service debt and meet other commitments?

Ultimately, the key question in the financial analysis is how likely it is that cash flows will be sufficient to repay the loan. With that question in mind, lenders focus much attention on solvency ratios: the magnitude of various measures of profits and cash flows relative to debt service and other requirements. To the extent such a ratio exceeds one, it indicates the "margin of safety" the lender faces. When such a ratio is combined with an assessment of the variance in its numerator, it provides an indication of the probability of nonpayment.

Ratio analysis from the perspective of a creditor differs somewhat from that of an owner. For example, there is greater emphasis on cash flows and earnings available to *all* claimants (not just owners) *before* taxes (since interest is tax-deductible and paid out of pretax dollars). To illustrate, the creditor's perspective is apparent in the following solvency ratio, called the "funds flow coverage ratio":

$$\text{Funds flow coverage} = \frac{\text{EBIT} + \text{Depreciation}}{\text{Interest} + \dfrac{\text{Debt repayment}}{(1 - \text{tax rate})} + \dfrac{\text{Preferred dividends}}{(1 - \text{tax rate})}}$$

We see earnings before both interest and taxes in the numerator. This measures the numerator in a way that can be compared directly to the interest expense in the denominator, because interest expense is paid out of pretax dollars. In contrast, any payment of principal scheduled for a given year is nondeductible and must be made out of after-tax profits. In essence, with a 50 percent tax rate, one dollar of principal payment is "twice as expensive" as a one-dollar interest payment. Scaling the payment of principal by (1 − tax rate) accounts for this. The same idea applies to preferred dividends, which are not tax deductible.

The funds flow coverage ratio provides an indication of how comfortably the funds flow can cover unavoidable expenditures. The ratio excludes payments such as common dividends and capital expenditures on the premise that they could be reduced to zero to make debt payments if necessary.[1] Clearly, however, if the firm is to survive in the long run, funds flow must be sufficient to not only service debt but also maintain plant assets. Thus, long-run survival requires a funds flow coverage ratio well in excess of 1.[2]

It would be overly simplistic to establish any particular threshold above which a ratio indicates a loan is justified. However, a creditor clearly wants to be in a position to be repaid on schedule, even when the borrower faces a reasonably foreseeable difficulty. That argues for lending only when the funds flow coverage is expected to exceed 1, even in a recession scenario—and higher if some allowance for capital expenditures is prudent.

The financial analysis should produce more than an assessment of the risk of nonpayment. It should also identify the nature of the significant risks. At many commercial banks, it is standard operating procedure to summarize the analysis of the firm by listing the key risks that could lead to default and factors that could be used to control those risks if the loan were made. That information can be used in structuring the detailed terms of the loan so as to trigger default when problems arise, at a stage early enough to permit corrective action.

Step 4: Utilize Forecasts to Assess Payment Prospects

Already implicit in some of the above discussion is a forward-looking view of the firm's ability to service the loan. Good credit analysis should also be supported by explicit forecasts. The basis for such forecasts is usually management, but, not surprisingly, lenders do not accept such forecasts without question.

In forecasting, a variety of scenarios should be considered—including not just a "best guess" but also a "pessimistic" scenario. Ideally, the firm should be strong enough to repay the loan even in this scenario. Ironically, it is not necessarily a decline in sales that presents the greatest risk to the lender. If managers can respond quickly to a sales dropoff, it should be accompanied by a liquidation of receivables and inventory, which enhances cash flow for a given level of earnings. The nightmare scenario is one that involves large negative profit margins, perhaps because managers are caught by surprise by a downturn in demand and are forced to liquidate inventory at substantially reduced prices.

At times, it is possible to reconsider the structure of a loan so as to permit it to "cash flow." That is, the term of the loan might be extended, or the amortization pattern changed. Often, a bank will grant a loan with the expectation that it will be continually renewed, thus becoming a permanent part of the firm's financial structure. (Such a loan is labeled an "evergreen.") In that case, the loan will still be written as if it is due within the short term, and the bank must assure itself of a viable "exit strategy." However, the firm would be expected to service the loan by simply covering interest payments.

Step 5: Assemble the Detailed Loan Structure, Including Loan Covenants

If the analysis thus far indicates that a loan is in order, it is then time to pull together the detailed structure: type of loan, repayment schedule, loan covenants, and pricing. The first two items were discussed above. Here we discuss loan covenants and pricing.

WRITING LOAN COVENANTS.   Loan covenants specify mutual expectations of the borrower and lender by specifying actions the borrower will and will not take. Some covenants require certain actions (such as regular provision of financial statements); others preclude certain actions (such as undertaking an acquisition without the permission of the lender); still others require maintenance of certain financial ratios. Violation of a covenant represents an event of default that could cause immediate acceleration of the debt payment, but in most cases the lender uses the default as an opportunity to re-examine the situation and either waive the violation or renegotiate the loan.

Loan covenants must strike a balance between protecting the interests of the lender and providing the flexibility management needs to run the business. The covenants represent a mechanism for insuring that the business will remain as strong as the two parties anticipated at the time the loan was granted. Thus, required financial ratios are typically based on the levels that existed at that time, perhaps with some allowance for deterioration but often with some expected improvement over time.

The particular covenants included in the agreement should contain the significant risks identified in the financial analysis, or to at least provide early warning that such risks are surfacing. Some commonly used financial covenants include:

- *Maintenance of minimum net worth.* This covenant assures that the firm will maintain an "equity cushion" to protect the lender. Covenants typically require a level of net worth rather than a particular level of income. In the final analysis, the lender may not care whether that net worth is maintained by generating income, cutting dividends, or issuing new equity. Tying the covenant to net worth offers the firm the flexibility to use any of these avenues to avoid default.
- *Minimum coverage ratio.* Especially in the case of a long-term loan, such as a term loan, the lender may want to supplement a net worth covenant with one based on

coverage of interest or total debt service. The funds flow coverage ratio presented above would be an example. Maintenance of some minimum coverage helps assure that the ability of the firm to generate funds internally is strong enough to justify the long-term nature of the loan.

- *Maximum ratio of total liabilities to net worth.* This ratio constrains the risk of high leverage and prevents growth without either retaining earnings or infusing equity.
- *Minimum net working capital balance or current ratio.* Constraints on this ratio force a firm to maintain its liquidity by using cash generated from operations to retire current liabilities (as opposed to acquiring long-lived assets).
- *Maximum ratio of capital expenditures to earnings before depreciation.* Constraints on this ratio help prevent the firm from investing in growth (including the illiquid assets necessary to support growth) unless such growth can be financed internally, with some margin remaining for debt service.

In addition to such financial covenants, loans sometimes place restrictions on other borrowing activity, pledging of assets to other lenders, selling of substantial parts of assets, engaging in mergers or acquisitions, and payment of dividends.

Covenants are included in not only private lending agreements with banks, insurance companies, and others, but also in public debt agreements. However, public debt agreements tend to have less restrictive covenants, for two reasons. First, negotiations resulting from a violation of public debt covenants are costly (possibly involving not just the trustee, but also bondholders), and so they are written to be triggered only in serious circumstances. Second, public debt is usually issued by stronger, more creditworthy firms. (The primary exception would be high-yield debt issued in conjunction with leveraged buyouts.) For the most financially healthy firms, with strong debt ratings, very few covenants will be used—only those necessary to limit dramatic changes in the firm's operations, such as a major merger or acquisition.

LOAN PRICING. A detailed discussion of loan pricing falls outside the scope of this text. The essence of pricing is to assure that the yield on the loan is sufficient to cover (1) the lender's cost of borrowed funds; (2) the lender's costs of administering and servicing the loan; (3) a premium for exposure to default risk; and (4) at least a normal return on the equity capital necessary to support the lending operation. The price is often stated in terms of a deviation from a bank's prime rate—the rate charged to stronger borrowers. For example, a loan might be granted at prime plus 1½ percent. An alternative base is LIBOR, or the London Interbank Offer Rate, the rate at which large banks from various nations lend large blocks of funds to each other.

Banks compete actively for commercial lending business, and it is rare that a yield includes more than 2 percentage points to cover the cost of default risk. If the spread to cover default risk is, say, 1 percent, and the bank recovers only 50 percent of amounts due on loans that turn out bad, then the bank can afford only 2 percent of their loans to fall into that category. This underscores how important it is for banks to conduct a thorough analysis and to contain the riskiness of their loan portfolio.

FINANCIAL STATEMENT ANALYSIS AND PUBLIC DEBT

Fundamentally, the issues involved in analysis of public debt are no different from those of bank loans and other private debt issues. Institutionally, however, the contexts are different. Bankers can maintain very close relations with clients so as to form an initial assessment of their credit risk and monitor their activities during the loan period. In the case of public debt, the investors are distanced from the issuer. To a large extent, they must depend on professional debt analysts, including debt raters, to assess the riskiness of the debt and monitor the firm's ongoing activities. Such analysts and debt raters thus serve an important function in closing the information gap between issuers and investors.

The Meaning of Debt Ratings

As indicated above, the two major debt rating agencies in the U.S. are Moody's and Standard and Poor's. Using the Standard and Poor's labeling system, the highest possible rating is AAA. Firms with this rating are large and have strong and steady earnings and little leverage. Only about 1 to 2 percent of the public industrial companies rated by Standard & Poor's have the financial strength to merit this rating. Among the few are Merck, General Electric, and Johnson & Johnson—all among the largest, most profitable firms in the world. Proceeding downward from AAA, the ratings are AA, A, BBB, BB, B, CCC, CC, C, and D, where "D" indicates debt in default. To be considered investment grade, a firm must achieve a rating of BBB or higher. Many funds are precluded by their charters from investing in any bonds below that grade. Table 14-1 presents examples of firms in rating categories AAA through CCC, as well as average values for selected financial ratios across all firms in each category.

Note that even to achieve a grade of BBB is difficult. Delta Airlines, one of the largest airlines in the U.S., was rated as "only" BBB—barely investment grade—in 1998. Overall, firms in the BBB class are only moderately leveraged, with about 45 percent of long-term capitalization coming in the form of debt. Earnings tend to be relatively strong, as indicated by a pretax interest coverage (EBIT/interest) of 3.0 and a cash flow debt coverage (cash flow from operations/total debt) of nearly 34 percent.

Firms with below investment-grade ratings tend to face some significant risk, even though many are quite profitable. Table 14-1 places Northwest Airlines in the BB category. In 1998 Northwest was the fourth largest airline carrier in the U.S. However, it had suffered from a recent pilot strike and declining demand in Asia, a key international market. The B category includes Apple Computer, Greyhound Lines, and Loehmanns, all of which had faced recent financial difficulty. The CCC category includes firms whose debt is 80 percent of long-term capital, on average. An illustrative CCC firm is Oxford Health Plans, a health benefit plan provider. Oxford Health Plans came close to bankruptcy in 1997 after computer malfunctions and poor financial controls led to massive delays in claims processing and customer dissatisfaction.

Table 14-1 Debt Ratings in December 1998: Example Firms and Median Financial Ratios by Category

S&P debt rating	Example firms in 1998	Percentage of public industrials given same rating by S&P	Median ratios for overall category in 1998 (industrials only)			
			Pretax return on long-term capital	Pretax interest coverage	Cash flow from operations to total debt	Long-term debt to total capital
AAA	General Electric Johnson & Johnson Merck and Co.	1.9%	35.3%	11.6 times	100.1%	9.7%
AA	McDonald's Corp. J. P. Morgan Wal-Mart Stores, Inc.	7.0	25.0	7.2	59.8	29.4
A	Ford Motor Company General Motors Sears Roebuck & Co.	21.8	16.6	4.8	34/3	39.0
BBB	Delta Airlines MCI Communications	28.2	12.6	3.0	24.8	45.0
BB	Northwest Airlines RJR Nabisco	21.0	11.1	1.9	11.1	59.5
B	Apple Computer Greyhound Lines Loehmanns	18.3	7.4	0.7	3.1	78.4
CCC	Oxford Health Plans Trans World Airlines	1.7	−5.3	−1.7	−17.3	80.8

Source: Standard and Poor's Compustat, 1998.

Factors That Drive Debt Ratings

Research demonstrates that some of the variation in debt ratings can be explained as a function of selected financial statement ratios, even as used within a quantitative model that incorporates no subjective human judgment. Some debt rating agencies rely heavily on quantitative models, and such models are commonly used by insurance companies, banks, and others to assist in the evaluation of the riskiness of debt issues for which a public rating is not available.

Table 14-2 lists the factors used by three different firms in their quantitative debt-rating models. The firms include one insurance company and one bank, which use the models in their private placement activities, and an investment research firm, which employs

Table 14-2 Factors Used in Quantitative Models of Debt Ratings

	Firm 1	Firm 2	Firm 3
Profitability measures	Return on long-term capital	Return on long-term capital	Return on long-term capital
Leverage measures	Long-term debt to capitalization	Long-term debt to capitalization Total debt to total capital	Long-term debt to capitalization
Profitability and leverage	Interest coverage Cash flow to long-term debt	Interest coverage Cash flow to long-term debt	Fixed charge coverage Coverage of short-term debt and fixed charges
Firm size	Sales	Total assets	
Other		Standard deviation of return Subordination status	

the model in evaluating its own debt purchases and holdings. In each case, profitability and leverage play an important role in the rating. One firm also uses firm size as an indicator, with larger size associated with higher ratings.

Several researchers have estimated quantitative models used for debt ratings. Two of these models, developed by Kaplan and Urwitz and shown in Table 14-3, highlight the relative importance of the factors.[3] Model 1 has the greater ability to explain variation in bond ratings. However, it includes some factors based on stock market data, which are not available for all firms. Model 2 is based solely on financial statement data.

The factors in Table 14-3 are listed in the order of their statistical significance in Model 1. An interesting feature is that the most important factor explaining debt ratings is not a financial ratio at all—it is simply firm size! Large firms tend to get better ratings than small firms. Whether the debt is subordinated or unsubordinated is next most important, followed by a leverage indicator. Profitability appears less important, but in part that reflects the presence in the model of multiple factors (ROA and interest coverage) that capture profitability. It is only the explanatory power that is *unique* to a given variable that is indicated by the ranking in Table 14-3. Explanatory power common to the two variables is not considered.

When applied to a sample of bonds that were not used in the estimation process, the Kaplan-Urwitz model (1) predicted the rating category correctly in 44 of 64 cases, or 63 percent of the time. Where it erred, the model was never off by more than one category, and in about half of those cases its prediction was more consistent with the market yield on the debt than was the actual debt rating. The discrepancies between actual ratings and those estimated using the Kaplan-Urwitz model indicate that rating agencies incorporate

Table 14-3 Kaplan-Urwitz Models of Debt Ratings

Firm or debt characteristic	Variable reflecting characteristic	Coefficients	
		Model 1	Model 2
	Model intercept	5.67	4.41
Firm size	Total assets[a]	.0010	.0012
Subordination status of debt	1 = subordinated; 0 = unsubordinated	–2.36	–2.56
Leverage	Long-term debt to total assets	–2.85	–2.72
Systematic risk	Market model beta, indicating sensitivity of stock price to market-wide movements (1 = average)[b]	–.87	NA
Profitability	Net income to total assets	5.13	6.40
Unsystematic risk	Standard deviation of residual from market model (average = .10)[b]	–2.90	NA
Riskiness of profit stream	Coefficient of variation in net income over 5 years (standard deviation/mean)	NA	–.53
Interest coverage	Pretax funds flow before interest to interest expense	.007	.006

The score from the model is converted to a bond rating as follows:
If score > 6.76, predict AAA
   score > 5.19, predict AA
   score > 3.28, predict A
   score > 1.57, predict BBB
   score < 0.00, predict BB

a.   *The coefficient in the Kaplan-Urwitz model was estimated at .005 (Model 1) and .006 (Model 2). Its scale has been adjusted to reflect that the estimates were based on assets measured in dollars from the 1960s and 1970s. Given that $1 from 1970 is approximately equivalent to $5 in 1995, the original coefficient estimate has been divided by 5.*
b.   *Market model is estimated by regressing stock returns against the return on the market index, using monthly data for prior five years.*

factors other than financial ratios in their analysis. These are likely to include the types of strategic, accounting, and prospective analyses discussed throughout this book.

Given that debt ratings can be explained reasonably well in terms of a handful of financial ratios, one might question whether ratings convey any *news* to investors—anything that could not already have been garnered from publicly available financial data. The answer to the question is yes, at least in the case of debt rating downgrades. That is, downgrades are greeted with drops in both bond and stock prices.[4] To be sure, the capital markets anticipate much of the information reflected in rating changes. However, that is not surprising, given that the changes often represent reactions to recent known events, and that the rating agencies typically indicate in advance that a change is being considered.

PREDICTION OF DISTRESS AND TURNAROUND

The key task in credit analysis is assessing the probability that a firm will face financial distress and fail to repay a loan. A related analysis, relevant once a firm begins to face distress, involves considering whether it can be turned around. In this section, we consider evidence on the predictability of these states.

The prediction of either distress or turnaround is a complex, difficult, and subjective task that involves all of the steps of analysis discussed throughout this book: business strategy analysis, accounting analysis, financial analysis, and prospective analysis. Purely quantitative models of the process can rarely serve as substitutes for the hard work the analysis involves. However, research on such models does offer some insight into which financial indicators are most useful in the task. Moreover, there are some settings where extensive credit checks are too costly to justify, and where quantitative distress prediction models are useful. For example, the commercially available "Zeta" model is used by some manufacturers and other firms to assess the credit-worthiness of their customers.[5]

Several distress prediction models have been developed over the years.[6] They are similar to the debt rating models, but instead of predicting ratings, they predict whether a firm will face some state of distress within one year, typically defined as bankruptcy. One study suggests that the factors most useful (on a stand-alone basis) in predicting bankruptcy one year in advance are[7]:

1. Profitability $= \left[\dfrac{\text{Net income}}{\text{Net worth}} \right]$

2. Volatility $= \left[\text{Standard deviation of} \left(\dfrac{\text{Net income}}{\text{Net worth}} \right) \right]$

3. Financial leverage $= \left[\dfrac{\text{Market value of equity}}{(\text{Market value of equity} + \text{Book value of debt})} \right]$

The evidence indicates that the key to whether a firm will face distress is its level of profitability, the volatility of that profitability, and how much leverage it faces. Interestingly, liquidity measures turn out to be much less important. Current liquidity won't save an unhealthy firm if it is losing money at a fast pace.

Of course, if one were interested in predicting distress, there would be no need to restrict attention to one variable at a time. A number of multi-factor models have been designed to predict financial distress. One such model is the Altman Z-score model[8]:

$$Z = .717(X_1) + .847(X_2) + 3.11(X_3) + .420(X_4) + .998(X_5)$$

where X_1 = net working capital/total assets
X_2 = retained earnings/total assets
X_3 = EBIT/total assets
X_4 = shareholders' equity/total liabilities
X_5 = sales/total assets

The model predicts bankruptcy when Z < 1.20. The range between 1.20 and 2.90 is labeled the "gray area."

The following table presents calculations for two companies, Northwest Airlines and Merck:

	Model Coefficient	Northwest Airlines		Merck	
		Ratios	Score	Ratios	Score
Net working capital/assets	0.717	−0.15	−0.108	0.13	0.093
Retained earnings/Total assets	0.847	−0.06	−0.051	0.63	0.534
EBIT/Total assets	3.11	−0.01	−0.031	0.26	0.809
Shareholders' equity/Total liabilities	0.42	−0.02	−0.008	0.67	0.281
Sales/Total assets	0.998	0.88	0.878	0.84	0.838
			0.680		2.555

As noted earlier, in 1998 Northwest Airlines experienced a significant decline in revenues and profits as a result of a costly pilot strike and a downturn in demand from Asia. Consequently, it is not surprising to see that the model rates Northwest's likelihood of failure as quite high. Merck's financial performance ratios are much healthier than for Northwest Airlines. However, it is interesting to note that the model rates Merck as in the "gray area." Of course, Merck is a highly successful company. Its relatively low model score reflects limitations of the model and the method of accounting for its most significant asset, R&D, rather than performance.

Such models have some ability to predict failing and surviving firms. Altman reports that when the model was applied to a holdout sample containing 33 failed and 33 non-failed firms (the same proportion used to estimate the model), it correctly predicted the outcome in 63 of 66 cases. However, the performance of the model would degrade substantially if applied to a holdout sample where the proportion of failed and nonfailed firms was not forced to be the same as that used to estimate the model.

As reflected in the Merck analysis, simple distress prediction models like the Altman model cannot serve effectively as a replacement for in-depth analysis of the kind discussed throughout this book. But they provide a useful reminder of the power of financial statement data to summarize important dimensions of the firm's performance. Even in the absence of direct information about management expertise, corporate strategy, engineering know-how, and market position, financial ratios can reveal much about who will make it and who will not.

SUMMARY

Credit analysis is the evaluation of a firm from the perspective of a holder or potential holder of its debt. Credit analysis is important to a wide variety of economic agents—not just bankers and other financial intermediaries, but also public debt analysts, industrial companies, service companies, and others.

At the heart of credit analysis lie the same techniques described in Chapters 2 through 10: business strategy analysis, accounting analysis, financial analysis, and portions of prospective analysis. The purpose of the analysis is not just to assess the likelihood that a potential borrower will fail to repay the loan. It is also important to identify the nature of the key risks involved, and how the loan might be structured to mitigate or control those risks. A well-structured loan provides the lender with a viable "exit strategy," even in the case of default. A key to this structure is properly designed accounting-based covenants.

Fundamentally, the issues involved in analysis of public debt are no different from those involved in evaluating bank loans or other private debt. Institutionally, however, the contexts are different. Investors in public debt are usually not close to the borrower and must rely on other agents, including debt raters and other analysts, to assess credit-worthiness. Debt ratings, which depend heavily on firm size and financial measures of performance, have an important influence on the market yields that must be offered to issue debt.

The key task in credit analysis is the assessment of the probability of default. The task is complex, difficult, and to some extent, subjective. A small number of key financial ratios can help predict financial distress with some accuracy. The most important financial indicators for this purpose are profitability, volatility of profits, and leverage. However, the models cannot replace the in-depth forms of analysis discussed in this book.

DISCUSSION QUESTIONS

1. What are the critical performance dimensions for (a) a retailer and (b) a financial services company that should be considered in credit analysis? What ratios would you suggest looking at for each of these dimensions?

2. Why would a company pay to have its public debt rated by a major rating agency (such as Moody's or Standard and Poor's)? Why might a firm decide not to have its debt rated?

3. Some have argued that the market for original-issue junk bonds developed in the late 1970s as a result of a failure in the rating process. Proponents of this argument suggest that rating agencies rated companies too harshly at the low end of the rating scale, denying investment grade status to some deserving companies. What are proponents of this argument effectively assuming were the incentives of rating agencies? What economic forces could give rise to this incentive?

4. Many debt agreements require borrowers to obtain the permission of the lender before undertaking a major acquisition or asset sale. Why would the lender want to include this type of restriction?

5. Betty Li, the CFO of a company applying for a new loan, argues: "I will never agree to a debt covenant that restricts my ability to pay dividends to my shareholders, because it reduces shareholder wealth." Do you agree with this argument?

6. Cambridge Construction Company follows the percentage-of-completion method for reporting long-term contract revenues. The percentage of completion is based on the cost of materials shipped to the project site as a percentage of total expected material costs. Cambridge's major debt agreement includes restrictions on net worth, interest coverage, and minimum working capital requirements. A leading analyst claims that "the company is buying its way out of these covenants by spending cash and buying materials, even when they are not needed." Explain how this may be possible.

7. Can Cambridge improve its Z score by behaving as the analyst claims in Question 6? Is this change consistent with economic reality?

8. A banker argues: "I avoid lending to companies with negative cash from operations because they are too risky." Is this a sensible lending policy?

9. A leading retailer finds itself in a financial bind. It doesn't have sufficient cash flow from operations to finance its growth, and is close to violating the maximum debt-to-assets ratio allowed by its covenants. The Vice-President for Marketing suggests: "We can raise cash for our growth by selling the existing stores and leasing them back. This source of financing is cheap, since it avoids violating either the debt-to-assets or interest coverage ratios in our covenants." Do you agree with his analysis? Why or why not? As the firm's banker, how would you view this arrangement?

NOTES

1. The same is true of preferred dividends. However, when preferred stock is cumulative, any dividends missed must be paid later, when and if the firm returns to profitability.

2. Other relevant coverage ratios are discussed in Chapter 9.

3. Robert Kaplan and G. Urwitz, "Statistical Models of Bond Ratings: A Methodological Inquiry," *Journal of Business* (April 1979): 231–261.

4. See Robert Holthausen and Richard Leftwich, "The Effect of Bond Rating Changes on Common Stock Prices," *Journal of Financial Economics* (September 1986): 57–90; and John Hand, Robert Holthausen, and Richard Leftwich, "The Effect of Bond Rating Announcements on Bond and Stock Prices," *Journal of Finance* (June 1992): 733–752.

5. See Edward Altman, *Corporate Financial Distress,* New York: John Wiley, 1983.

6. See Edward Altman, "Financial Ratios, Discriminant Analysis, and the Prediction of Corporate Bankruptcy," *Journal of Finance* (September 1968): 589–609; Altman, 1983, op. cit.; William Beaver, "Financial Ratios as Predictors of Distress," *Journal of Accounting Research,* supplement, 1966: 71–111; James Ohlson, "Financial Ratios and the Probabilistic Prediction of Bankruptcy," *Journal of Accounting Research* (Spring 1980): 109–131; and Mark Zmijewski, "Predicting Corporate Bankruptcy: An Empirical Comparison of the Extant Financial Distress Models," working paper, SUNY at Buffalo, 1983.

7. Zmijewski, op. cit.

8. Altman, 1983, op. cit.

In mid-April 1996 Sarah Kim, a senior lending officer at a major U.S. bank, was considering Adelphia Communications Corporation, the seventh largest U.S. cable provider. Adelphia had applied to the bank for a $690 million financing arrangement, consisting of a $540 million revolving credit facility and a $150 million term loan facility. The funds provided by this arrangement would be used to pay down existing bank debt, and to finance Adelphia's upgrade of its cable system.

Kim had no prior experience with the cable industry, and was surprised to find that Adelphia was highly unprofitable and already had extraordinarily high leverage. As a result, her initial thought was to reject Adelphia's request out of hand. However, she decided that she should first spend some time understanding the cable business. This would then provide a better basis for considering Adelphia's request.

THE U.S. CABLE INDUSTRY

Created in 1948 as a "community antenna" system for rural areas with weak broadcast signals, cable television grew steadily through the mid-1970s. However, the night of September 30, 1975, when Muhammad Ali's 14-round boxing fight with Joe Frazier in Manila was transmitted live to cable subscribers, changed the industry forever. Thereafter, subscribership growth spread rapidly to urban areas. By the mid-1990s the cable industry provided services to 63 percent of U.S. households with TVs. Earnings before interest, taxes, depreciation, and amortization (known as EBITDA or "cash flow") per subscriber were $169.85 in 1994, and industry EBITDA and revenues were $9.93 billion and $22.6 billion respectively.

Cable television systems offered subscribers a package of video services including local network channels; public, government, and educational channels; and premium news, sports, family entertainment, music, weather, and shopping channels. Subscribers could also view recent movies, live and taped concerts, sports events, and other programming on a pay-per-event basis. Cable television providers were awarded a franchise to provide these services by state or local government authorities for a defined period. In return, they paid the authorities an annual franchise fee of up to 5 percent of gross revenues.

Professor Paul Healy prepared this case as the basis for class discussion rather than to illustrate effective or ineffective handling of an administrative situation. The case has benefited from the help of Lucca Fabri and comments of Michael Schwartz, Liz Kramer, and Holly Holtz. Copyright © 1997 by the President and Fellows of Harvard College. Harvard Business School case 9-198-031.

Once they received a franchise to provide services to a community, cable operators made large upfront expenditures for laying cable to subscriber neighborhoods and for broadcast equipment. These initial system outlays generally acted as a barrier to entry for competitors.[1] Cable laying costs ranged from $10,000 per mile in rural areas to as much as $300,000 per mile in major cities where cables have to be laid underground. In addition to the initial capital outlays, cable operators incurred costs for program content from the major networks (ABC, NBC, CBS, and Fox) as well as pay-TV programmers such as Disney, Turner Broadcasting, and Time Warner.

Cable operator revenues were typically generated from monthly subscriber fees for programming, as well as fees for special pay-per-view services and installations. These fees had been regulated by the Federal Commerce Commission (FCC). The Cable Communications Policy Act of 1984 deregulated basic service rates for systems in communities meeting the FCC's definition of effective competition. However, the 1992 Cable Act contained a new definition of effective competition, and subjected almost all U.S. cable systems to regulation of basic service rates.

By the mid-1990s, growth in sign-ups of new subscribers had begun to flatten out and the industry was facing a number of important changes. These included the increased consolidation of many of the small cable providers, significant new regulations in the telecommunications industry, the development of competing forms of multichannel networks, and the opportunity for cable operators to provide subscribers access to the Internet.

Industry Consolidation

Consolidation of the cable industry began in the late 1980s, as operators sought to gain benefits from programming discounts and improved capital utilization. Thus began a race to accumulate market share, primarily through acquisition. In 1993 and 1994 $43 billion of acquisitions took place in the broadcasting industry, many among cable operators. The average acquisition cost per subscriber in 1994 was $1,869. Many of these acquisitions were financed with debt, increasing the financial burdens of the largest operators. The six leading multiple system operators, or MSOs, which emerged from this consolidation—TCI, Time Warner, Continental Cablevision, Comcast, Cox Communications, and Cablevision Systems—had a 63 percent share of the cable market in 1996. Exhibit 1 reports revenues, EBITDA, capital expenditures, debt obligations, and subscriber base for each of these firms.

New Telecommunications Regulations

The telecommunications Act of 1996 had several implications for the cable industry. It permitted cable companies to offer local telephone services using their cable infrastruc-

---

1. *Although franchise agreements were generally nonexclusive, only a few communities had more than one cable company serving the same subscribers. Allentown, Pennsylvania was one such community.*

Adelphia Communications Corporation

ture. It was estimated that an investment of $40 to $90 could make a household's cable plug phone-ready. Furthermore, long-distance telephone carriers were eager to supply their know-how and exchanges to cable operators. This potential growth opportunity was offset by new rules permitting telephone companies to offer entertainment services to their own customers. Finally, the new regulations eliminated rate regulation in the cable industry as of March 31, 1999. The regulations therefore created new opportunities for cable companies, but raised the prospect of competition from telephone companies.

New Forms of Multichannel Networks

Competition for the cable industry had intensified with the successful introduction of several alternative video delivery systems, direct-to-home satellite and wireless cable. Direct Broadcast Satellite (or DBS) used powerful satellites to transmit up to 175 digital channels to 18-inch satellite receivers mounted on its subscribers' homes at a price competitive with traditional cable. DBS systems had higher quality digital broadcasts and a larger array of channels than traditional cable, but did not include coverage of local networks. The major providers of DBS systems were DirecTV (owned by Hughes), Echostar, and Primestar (owned by TCI). DirecTV and Echostar sold subscribers satellite dishes and receivers for $150 to $400 whereas Primestar rented this equipment to users. Other companies entering the market included long-distance telephone giant AT&T, which purchased a 2.5 percent stake in DirecTV for $137.5 million in January 1996. AT&T planned to market DirecTV to its 90-million customer base, and had the option to acquire up to 27.5 percent of DirecTV at a discount tied to the number of new customers that it signed up. In addition, MCI and Rupert Murdoch's News Corporation formed a joint venture to use DBS to provide up to 170 digital channels of entertainment to all 50 states.

Wireless cable or MMDS (Multichannel Multipoint Distribution Service) systems used a line-of-sight microwave network to send video signals to subscribers. MMDS systems avoided the expensive construction costs of DBS and cable systems. Like DBS, they did not require municipal franchises to operate and were free of several of the more burdensome cable regulations. The downside of MMDS systems was their limited analog capacity (a maximum of 33 channels), "rain fade," and the fact that the signal could not be clearly received in "shadow" areas. The early entrants in this market include Bell Atlantic, NYNEX, and Pacific Telesis.

The increased competition, particularly from DBS, had generated different responses within the cable industry. Time Warner and TCI announced that they would continue using one-way digital technology. However, Comcast, Cox, and Cablevision began upgrading their systems to permit two-way transmissions. Two-way data transmission required cable and electronic equipment capable of delivering a signal from the customer back to the cable operator's headend. This permitted full interactive video services to be offered to subscribers. Of course, it also required cable companies to make significant new capital investments.

Internet Access

Cable modems enabled operators to deliver high speed access to the Internet and other on-line services using their existing cable infrastructure. This cable data service would be available at speeds up to 300 times faster than that available from 28.8 kilobit-per-second telephone modems. Although this service would require users to have a computer equipped with an ethernet card and an adjunct cable modem, it did not use the phone line, required no log-on, and permitted connections to multiple services simultaneously.

ADELPHIA COMMUNICATIONS CORPORATION

John J. Rigas, the current chairman, president, chief executive officer and majority stockholder of Adelphia, was one of the earliest pioneers in cable television, creating his first system in Coudersport, Pennsylvania in 1952. Since then Adelphia had grown steadily by acquiring and developing municipal cable television franchises. In 1986 the company made an initial public offering to raise new external equity capital, although the company remained firmly in the control of the Rigas Family. Stock price performance of Adelphia is reported in Exhibit 2.

Adelphia's cable systems were organized into seven regional clusters: Western New York, Virginia, Western Pennsylvania, New England, Eastern Pennsylvania, Ohio, and Coastal New Jersey. Further details on these clusters are provided in Exhibit 3. The clusters were located primarily in suburban areas of large and medium-sized cities within the 50 largest television markets. Adelphia also created an eighth regional cluster in Southeastern Florida as a result of a joint venture with Olympus Communications, L.P. Adelphia owned 50 percent of Olympus and was the managing general partner.

From 1992 to 1996 Adelphia's subscriber base grew from 1.4 million to 2.0. Seventy-five percent of this growth was generated from acquisitions and the remaining 25 percent was from internal growth. As reported in Adelphia's financial statements, shown in Exhibit 4, the company's revenues and EBITDA also grew significantly in this period. Revenues grew on average 12 percent per year to $403 million, and EBITDA grew by an average of 9 percent per year to $247 million.

Adelphia planned to provide expanded local telephone services to its subscribers through its subsidiary, Hyperion Telecommunications, Inc. Management anticipated that the Telecommunications Act of 1996 would expand the market opportunities for Hyperion by removing legal barriers to entering local telephone markets. In the markets where Hyperion's networks were currently operating or were under construction, the market opportunity was estimated to be approximately $4.8 billion, substantially all of which was currently provided by the incumbent local exchange carrier.

Like many of the major cable operators, Adelphia had begun upgrading the technical capabilities of its cable plant. All of the firm's current systems had a minimum 35-channel capacity and were capable of delivering one-way data transmission and digital video services. In addition, over 94 percent of its subscribers could receive pay-per-view programming. However, in most of its recent upgrades, Adelphia had used fiber optic cable as an alternative to the formerly used coaxial cable. Fiber optic cable provided increased reliability, improved bandwidth, and easier implementation of two-way data transmission. This would allow the Company to offer additional video programming services, and to meet transmission requirements for high-definition television, digital television, high-speed data on the Internet, and telephone services. Exhibit 5 summarizes the status of the firm's cable plant as of March 31, 1996.

The Lending Decision

Much of Adelphia's external subscriber acquisition and cable replacement had been financed with debt. As a result, Adelphia's ratio of debt to assets in 1996 was 1.85. Despite this high leverage, management expected that it would need additional debt financing to continue upgrading its cable technology. Management forecasted that capital expenditures in 1997 would be somewhat higher than the $100 million outlay for 1996. To ensure that it had the financial resources to meet these outlays the firm applied to a major bank for a $690 million financing arrangement, consisting of a $540 million revolving credit facility to mature December 31, 2003 and a $150 million term loan facility maturing December 31, 2004. The firm proposed using $480 million of the revolving credit facility to repay existing bank loans, and the remainder for new plant upgrades.

Interest rates on Adelphia's existing bank loans had been based on either the Eurodollar rate, the prime rate, or the Federal funds rate. On top of these base rates the banks had charged a margin of from 0.5 to 2.5 percent depending upon Adelphia's senior funded debt ratio. Interest on current revolving credit agreements were set at either prime plus 0 to 1.5 percent, the certificate of deposit rate plus 1.25 to 2.75 percent, or the LIBOR rate plus 1 to 2.5 percent. The weighted average interest rate on notes payable to banks and institutions at March 31, 1996, was 8.36 percent.

The firm's existing revolving credit agreement provided for collateral against the company's investments and in some cases its cable assets. These agreements also required Adelphia and its subsidiaries to maintain certain financial ratios and limited the firm's additional borrowings, investments, transactions with affiliates and other subsidiaries, and the payment of dividends by the subsidiaries.

After reviewing the industry and Adelphia's financial performance, Sarah Kim was unsure whether she should approve the loan request. The cable business seemed to be at a turning point in its history, and Adelphia was one of the weaker firms in the industry. If she did decide to approve the firm's request, Sarah would have to make a recommendation on how the loan should be structured, on the interest rate the bank should charge, and on the covenants that should be built into the loan agreement.

QUESTIONS

1. Evaluate Adelphia's business strategy. What are the company's key business risks?
2. Do you think the company's financial strategy is appropriate, given its business?
3. Given the changes in the cable industry, is the company's financing strategy still appropriate?
4. Should Sarah Kim grant the loan to Adelphia? What would be the appropriate terms (in terms of interest rate, covenants, other security requirements)?
5. What financing options should Adelphia pursue if the bank does not grant the loan?

EXHIBIT 1

Performance of Major U.S. Cable Companies

Twelve Months Ending June 30, 1996:	EBITDA (millions)	Capital Outlays (millions)	Interest Expense (millions)	Debt to EBITDA	Subscribers (millions)
TCI	$2,111	$1,957	$1,053	6.3	14.5
Time Warner	1,480	1,700	1,562	6.7	11.8
Continental Cablevision	717	599	431	7.8	4.2
Comcast	1,105	567	542	6.5	4.2
Cox Communications	542	484	133	4.8	3.2
Cablevision Systems	436	346	350	6.4	2.7

Source: Salomon Bros., *Business Week..*

EXHIBIT 2

Adelphia Communications Corporation Stock Price Performance,
March 1993 to March 1996

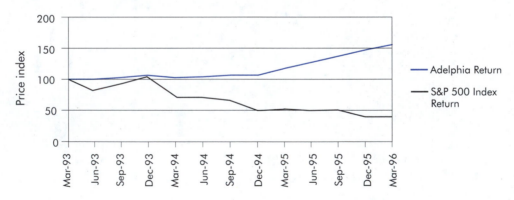

Source: Bloomberg.

EXHIBIT 3

Adelphia Communications Corporation, Summary of Subscriber Data as of March 31, 1996

	Homes Passed in District	Basic Subscribers	Basic Penetration	Premium Units	Premium Penetration as % of Total Subscribers
Western New York	368,071	254,121	69.0%	148,814	58.6%
New England	260,542	183,819	70.6	108,517	59.0
Virginia	336,261	245,748	73.1	111,245	45.3
Western Pennsylvania	252,013	184,291	73.1	72,488	39.3
Ohio	168,332	121,960	72.5	66,131	54.2
Coastal New Jersey	125,646	98,304	78.2	53,917	54.9
Eastern Pennsylvania	159,872	113,016	70.7	83,854	74.2
Southeastern Florida	808,683	551,377	68.2	237,842	43.1
	2,479,420	1,752,636	Avg. 70.7%	882,808	Avg. 50.4%

Source: Adelphia Communications Corporation 10-K.

Adelphia Communications Corporation

Adelphia Communications Corporation

EXHIBIT 4
Adelphia Communications Corporation, Abridged 1996 Annual Report

SELECTED CONSOLIDATED FINANCIAL DATA

(Dollars in thousands, except per-share amounts)

The selected consolidated financial data as of and for each of the five years in the period ended March 31, 1996 have been derived from the audited consolidated financial statements of the Company.

	Year Ended March 31,				
	1992	**1993**	**1994**	**1995**	**1996**
Statement of Operations Data:					
Revenues	$273,630	$305,222	$319,045	$361,505	$403,597
Direct operating and programming expenses	74,787	82,377	90,547	106,993	124,116
Selling, general, and administrative expenses	44,427	49,468	52,801	63,487	68,357
Operating income before depreciation, amortization, and rate regulation expenses	154,416	173,377	175,697	191,025	211,124
Depreciation and amortization	84,817	90,406	89,402	97,602	111,031
Rate regulation charge	—	—	—	—	5,300
Operating income	69,599	82,971	86,295	93,423	94,793
Interest income from affiliates	3,085	5,216	9,188	11,112	10,623
Other income (expenses)	968	1,447	(299)	1,453	-
Priority investment income[a]	22,300	22,300	22,300	22,300	28,852
Cash interest expense	(129,237)	(164,695)	(180,456)	(180,942)	(194,403)
Noncash interest expense	(35,602)	(164)	(1,680)	(14,756)	(16,288)
Equity in loss of joint ventures	(52,718)	(46,841)	(30,054)	(44,349)	(46,257)
Loss before income taxes, extraordinary loss and cumulative effect of change in accounting principle[b]	(121,605)	(99,766)	(94,706)	(111,759)	(122,680)
Income tax (expense) benefit	—	(3,143)	(2,742)	5,475	2,786
Loss before extraordinary loss and cumulative effect of change in accounting principle	(121,605)	(102,909)	(97,448)	(106,284)	(119,894)
Extraordinary loss on early retirement of debt[b]	—	(14,386)	(752)	—	—
Cumulative effect of change in accounting for income taxes[b]	—	(59,500)	(89,660)	—	—
Net loss	($121,605)	($176,795)	($187,860)	($106,284)	($119,894)
Loss per weighted average share of common stock before extraordinary loss and cumulative effect of change in accounting principle	$ (8.80)	$ (6.80)	$ (5.66)	$ (4.32)	$ (4.56)
Net loss per weighed average share of common stock	(8.80)	(11.68)	(10.91)	(4.32)	(4.56)
Cash dividends declared per common share	—	—	—	—	—

(continued)

SELECTED CONSOLIDATED FINANCIAL DATA (*continued*)

| | \multicolumn{5}{c}{Year Ended March 31,} |
	1992	1993	1994	1995	1996
Other Data:					
EBITDA[d]	$ 180,769	$ 202,340	$ 207,936	$ 225,890	$ 257,999
Balance Sheet Data:					
Cash and cash equivalents	$ 11,173	$ 38,671	$ 74,075	$ 5,045	$ 10,809
Investment in and amounts due from (to) Olympus[a]	64,972	7,692	9,977	11,943	(33,656)
Total assets	925,791	949,593	1,073,846	1,267,291	1,333,923
Total debt	1,554,270	1,731,099	1,793,711	2,021,610	2,175,473
Debt net of cash[c]	1,543,097	1,692,428	1,719,636	2,016,565	2,164,664
Stockholders' equity (deficiency)	(713,544)	(868,614)	(918,064)	(1,011,575)	(1,128,239)

(a) On March 28, 1996, ACP Holdings, Inc. ("ACP"), a wholly owned subsidiary and managing general partner of Olympus Communications, L.P. ("Olympus"), various Telesat Entities ("Telesat"), wholly owned subsidiaries of FPL Group Inc., Olympus, Adelphia and certain shareholders of Adelphia entered into an agreement which provided for a distribution of Adelphia of $40,000 and the repayment of certain amounts owed Telesat totaling $20,000. See "Management's Discussion and Analysis of Financial Condition and Results of Operations" for further details. Investment in and amounts due from Olympus at March 31, 1996 are comprised of the following:

Gross investment in PLP interests and general partners' equity	$298,402
Excess of ascribed value of contributed property over historical cost	(98,303)
Cumulative equity in net loss of Olympus	(359,584)
Additional investment in Olympus—net of distributions	65,922
Investment in Olympus	(93,563)
Amounts due from Olympus	59,907
	$(33,656)

(b) "Extraordinary loss" relates to loss on the early retirement of debt. "Cumulative Effect of Change in Accounting Principle" refers to a change in accounting principle for Olympus and the Company. Effective January 1, 1993 and April 1, 1993, respectively. Olympus and the Company adopted the provisions of Statement of Financial Accounting Standards ("SFAS") No. 109, "Accounting for Income Taxes," which requires an asset and liability approach for financial accounting and reporting for income taxes. SFAS No. 109 resulted in the cumulative recognition of an additional liability by Olympus and the Company of $59,500 and $89,660, respectively.

(c) Represents total debt less cash and cash equivalents.

(d) Earnings before interest, income taxes, depreciation and amortization, equity in loss of joint ventures, other noncash charges, extraordinary loss and cumulative effect of change in accounting principle ("EBITDA"). EBITDA and similar measurements of cash flow are commonly used in the cable television industry to analyze and compare cable television companies on the basis of operating performance, leverage and liquidity. While EBITDA is not an alternative indicator of operating performance to operating income as defined by generally accepted accounting principles, the Company's management believes EBITDA is a meaningful measure of performance as substantially all of the Company's financing agreements contain financial covenants based on EBITDA.

Adelphia Communications Corporation

Adelphia Communications Corporation

MANAGEMENT'S DISCUSSION AND ANALYSIS OF FINANCIAL CONDITION AND RESULTS OF OPERATIONS

(Dollars in thousands)

Results of Operations

GENERAL

Adelphia Communications Corporation and its subsidiaries ("Adelphia" or the "Company") earned substantially all of its revenues in each of the last three fiscal years from monthly subscriber fees for basic, satellite, premium and ancillary services (such as installations and equipment rentals), local and national advertising sales, pay-per-view programming, home shopping networks and competitive local exchange carrier ("CLEC") telecommunications services. Certain changes in the way the Company offers and charges for subscriber services were implemented as of September 1, 1993 under the 1992 Cable Act and under the Company's revised method of offering certain services. See "Regulatory and Competitive Matters."

The changes in Adelphia's results of operations for the years ended March 31, 1995 and 1996, compared to the same period of the prior year, were primarily the result of acquisitions, expanding existing cable television operations and, for the year ended March 31, 1996, the impact of increased advertising sales and other service offerings as well as an increase in cable rates which became effective October 1, 1995.

The high level of depreciation and amortization associated with the significant number of acquisitions in recent years, the recent upgrading and expansion of systems and interest costs associated with financing activities will continue to have a negative impact on the reported results of operations. Also, significant charges for depreciation, amortization and interest are expected to be incurred in the future by the Olympus joint venture, which will also adversely impact Adelphia's future results of operations. Adelphia expects to report net losses for the next several years.

An 89% owned unrestricted subsidiary of the Company, Hyperion Telecommunications, Inc. ("Hyperion"), together with its subsidiaries owns certain investments in CLEC joint ventures and manages those ventures. Hyperion is an unrestricted subsidiary for purposes of the Company's indentures. Excluding the impact of Hyperion's operating results, the Company's EBITDA (see definition below) would increase by $1,941, $2,138, and $2,254 for the years ended March 31, 1994, 1995, and 1996, respectively. On April 14, 1996, Hyperion realized gross proceeds of $175,265 upon issuance of notes and warrants (see "Liquidity and Capital Resources").

The following table is derived from Adelphia's Consolidated Financial Statements and sets for the historical percentage relationship of operating income contained in such financial statements for the years indicated.

	Percentage of Revenues for Year Ended March 31,		
	1994	**1995**	**1996**
Revenues	100.0%	100.0%	100.0%
Operating expenses:			
Direct operating and programming	28.4%	29.6%	30.8%
Selling, general and administrative	16.5%	17.6%	16.9%
Operating income before depreciation, amortization, and rate regulation expenses	55.1%	52.8%	52.3%
Depreciation and amortization	28.0%	27.0%	27.5%
Rate regulation	0.0%	0.0%	1.3%
Operating income	27.1%	25.8%	23.5%

COMPARISON OF THE YEARS ENDED MARCH 31, 1994, 1995 AND 1996

Revenues.

Revenues increased approximately 13.3% for the year ended March 31, 1995 and 11.6% for the year ended March 31, 1996 compared with the prior fiscal year. The increases were attributable to the following:

	Year Ended March 31,	
	1995	1996
Acquisitions	87%	36%
Basic subscriber growth	10%	20%
Rate increases	0%	20%
Advertising sales and other services	3%	24%

Effective October 1, 1995, certain rate increases related to regulated cable services were implemented in substantially all of the Company's systems. No rate increases were implemented during the 1995 fiscal year. Advertising revenues and revenues derived from other strategic service offerings such as paging and CLEC services also had a positive impact on revenues for the year ended March 31, 1996.

Direct Operating and Programming Expenses.

Direct operating and programming expenses, which are mainly basic and premium programming costs and technical expenses, increased 18.2% and 16.0% for the years ended March 31, 1995 and 1996, respectively, compared with the respective prior years. Such increases were primarily due to increased operating expenses from acquired systems, increased programming costs and incremental costs associated with increased subscribers. Because of regulatory limitations on the timing and extent to which costs increases may be passed on to customers, operating and programming expenses during the fiscal years ended 1995 and 1996 have increased at a greater magnitude than corresponding revenue increases. As a result of recent FCC regulatory rulemaking decisions, the Company intends to implement a systematic program of rate increases to reverse this trend. Consistent with such a program, the Company intends to increase rates in most markets, in accordance with FCC guidelines, during the second quarter of fiscal 1997.

Selling, General, and Administrative Expenses.

These expenses, which are mainly comprised of costs related to system offices, customer service representatives, and sales and administrative employees, increased 20.2% and 7.7% in the years ended March 31, 1995 and 1996, respectively, compared with the respective prior years. The increases were primarily due to incremental costs associated with acquisitions, subscriber growth and implementation of the 1992 Cable Act and regulations thereunder. Selling, general and administrative expenses increased as a percentage of revenues for the year ended March 31, 1995, as compared with fiscal 1994, primarily due to wage and benefit increases without a corresponding increase in revenues as a result of the rate freeze enacted by the 1992 Cable Act. For the year ended March 31, 1996, selling, general and administrative expenses decreased as a percentage of revenues compared to the prior year, primarily due to the favorable impact on revenues of the above mentioned October 1, 1995 rate increases.

Operating Income Before Depreciation, Amortization and Rate Regulation Expenses.

Operating income before depreciation, amortization and rate regulation settlement was $175,697, $191,025 and $211,124 for the years ended March 31, 1994, 1995 and 1996, respectively. The increase for the year ended March 31, 1995 was due primarily to the impact of acquisitions, offset by cost increases at a rate greater than increases in revenues due largely to the above noted rate freeze. For the year ended March 31, 1996, the increase is attributable to a combination of acquisitions, an increase in subscriber rates, internal subscriber growth and the expansion of advertising and other non-cable services, partially offset by increased programming, general and administrative costs.

Rate Regulation Expenses.

The fiscal year ended March 31, 1996 includes a $5,300 charge representing management's estimate of the total costs associated with the resolution of subscriber rate disputes. Such costs include, (i) an estimate of credits to be extended to customers in future periods of up to $2,700 (ii) legal and other

Adelphia Communications Corporation

costs incurred during the fiscal year ended March 31, 1996, and (iii) an estimate of legal and other costs to be incurred associated with the ultimate resolution of this matter.

Depreciation and Amortization.

Depreciation and amortization was higher for the years ended March 31, 1995 and 1996, compared with the respective prior year, primarily due to increased depreciation and amortization related to acquisitions consummated during the years ended March 31, 1994, 1995, and 1996 as well as increased capital expenditures made during the past several years.

Priority Investment Income.

Priority investment income is comprised of payments received from Olympus of accrued priority return on the Company's investment in PLP Interests in Olympus. Priority investment income increased during the year ended March 31, 1996 as compared with the prior two fiscal years due to increased payments by Olympus.

EBITDA.

EBITDA (earnings before interest, income taxes, depreciation and amortization, equity in loss of joint ventures, other non-cash charges, extraordinary loss and cumulative effect of change in accounting principle) amounted to $207,936, $225,890 and $247,999 for the years ended March 31, 1994, 1995 and 1996, respectively. The increase of 8.6% and 9.8% for the years ended March 31, 1995 and 1996, compared with the respective prior fiscal years is primarily due to the acquisition of cable systems during the years ended March 31, 1995 and 1996 and increased priority investment income from Olympus during the year ended March 31, 1996. Increased revenues and operating expenses for the years ended March 31, 1995 and 1996, compared with the respective prior years, primarily reflect the impact of acquisitions consummated during fiscal 1995 and 1996. While EBITDA is not an alternative to operating income as defined by generally accepted accounting principles, the Company's management believes EBITDA is a meaningful measure of performance as substantially all of the Com-

pany's financing agreements contain financial covenants based on EBITDA.

Interest Expense.

Interest expense increased approximately 7.4% and 7.7% for the years ended March 31, 1995 and 1996, respectively, compared with the respective prior year. Approximately 56% of the increase for fiscal 1995 was due to additional interest cost associated with incremental debt related to acquisitions. For the year ended March 31, 1996, interest expense increased due to incremental debt outstanding during the period, partially offset by a decrease in the average interest rate on outstanding debt during fiscal 1996 compared with the prior fiscal year. Approximately 27% of the increase in interest expense in fiscal 1996 as compared with the prior year was attributable to incremental debt related to acquisitions. Interest expense includes non-cash accretion of original issue discount and non-cash interest expense totaling $1,680, $14,756, and $16,288 for the years ended March 31, 1994, 1995 and 1996, respectively.

Equity in Loss of Joint Ventures.

The equity in loss of joint ventures represents primarily (i) the Company's pro rata share of Olympus' losses and the accretion requirements of Olympus' preferred limited partner interests, and (ii) Hyperion's pro rata share of its less than majority owned partnerships' operating losses. The increase in the year ended March 31, 1995, compared with the prior year, is primarily attributable to the impact of the sale by Olympus of Northeast Cable and lower operating margins at Olympus. The increase in the loss during the year ended March 31, 1996, compared with the prior year, is due to an increase in the losses of certain investments in the CLEC business in which the Company is a less than majority partner partially offset by improved operating performance in the Olympus partnership.

Net Loss.

The Company reported net losses of $187,860, $106,284 and $119,894 for the years ended March 31, 1994, 1995 and 1996, respectively. Net loss for fiscal 1994 included the cumulative effect of the change in accounting for income taxes by the

Company of $89,660. Excluding the effect of this item, net loss increased by $8,084 for fiscal 1995 compared with the prior fiscal year. The increase in net loss in fiscal 1995 when compared with fiscal 1994 was primarily due to an increase in the equity in net loss of joint ventures (primarily Olympus) and higher non-cash interest expense, partially offset by higher operating income. The increase in net loss of $13,610 in fiscal 1996 when compared with the prior year was due primarily to an increase in interest expense and the impact of rate regulation expenses, partially offset by an increased operating income and priority investment income from Olympus.

Liquidity and Capital Resources.

The cable television business is capital intensive and typically requires continual financing for the construction, modernization, maintenance, expansion and acquisition of cable systems. During the three fiscal years in the period ended March 31, 1996, the Company committed substantial capital resources for these purposes and for investments in Olympus and other affiliates and entities. These expenditures were funded through long-term borrowings and, to a lesser extent, internally generated funds. The Company's ability to generate cash to meet its future needs will depend generally on its results of operations and the continued availability of external financing.

Capital Expenditures.

The Company has developed an innovative fiber-to-feeder network architecture which is designed to increase channel capacity and minimize future capital expenditures, while positioning the Company to take advantage of future opportunities. Management believes its capital expenditures program has resulted in higher levels of channel capacity and addressability in comparison to other cable television operators.

Capital expenditures for the years ended March 31, 1994, 1995, and 1996, were $75,894, $92,082 and $100,089, respectively. The increase in capital expenditures for fiscal 1994, 1995, and 1996, compared to each respective prior year, was primarily due to the acceleration of the rebuilding of plant using fiber-to-feeder technology, and expendi-

tures related to faster than expected growth of Hyperion. Management expects capital expenditures for fiscal 1997 to be somewhat higher than fiscal 1996 due to the further expansion of cable plant rebuilds and due to further expansion by Hyperion.

Financing Activities.

The Company's financing strategy has been to maintain its public long-term debt at the parent holding company level while the Company's consolidated subsidiaries have their own senior and subordinated credit arrangements with banks and insurance companies. The Company's ability to generate cash adequate to meet its future needs will depend generally on its results of operations and the continued availability of external financing. During the three-year period ended March 31, 1996, the Company funded its working capital requirements, capital expenditures, and investments in Olympus and other affiliates and entities through long-term borrowings primarily from banks and insurance companies, short-term borrowings, internally generated funds and the issuance of parent company public debt and equity. The Company generally has funded the principal and interest obligations on its long-term borrowings from banks and insurance companies by refinancing the principal with new loans or through the issuance of parent company debt securities, and by paying the interest out of internally generated funds. Adelphia has funded the interest obligations on its public borrowings from internally generated funds.

Most of Adelphia's directly-owned subsidiaries have their own senior credit agreements with banks and/or insurance companies. Typically, borrowings under these agreements are collateralized by the stock in and, in some cases, by the assets of the borrowing subsidiary and its subsidiaries and, in some cases, are guaranteed by such subsidiary's subsidiaries. At March 31, 1996, an aggregate of $1,096,675 in borrowings was outstanding under these agreements. These agreements contain certain provisions which, among other things, provide for limitations on borrowings of and investments by the borrowing subsidiaries, transactions between the borrowing subsidiaries and Adelphia and its other subsidiaries and affiliates, and the payment of dividends and fees by the borrowing subsidiaries. Sev-

Adelphia Communications Corporation

eral of these agreements also contain certain cross-default provisions relating to Adelphia or other subsidiaries. These agreements also require the maintenance of certain financial ratios by the borrowing subsidiaries. In addition, at March 31, 1996, an aggregate of $128,000 in subordinated and unsecured borrowings by Adelphia's subsidiaries was outstanding under credit agreements containing limitations and restrictions similar to those mentioned above. See Note 3 to the Adelphia Communications Corporation Consolidated Financial Statements. The Company is in compliance with the financial covenants and related financial ratio requirements contained in its various credit agreements, based on operation results for the period ended March 31, 1996.

INDEPENDENT AUDITOR'S REPORT

Adelphia Communications Corporation:

We have audited the accompanying consolidated balance sheets of Adelphia Communications Corporation and subsidiaries as of March 31, 1995 and 1996, and the related consolidated statements of operations, stockholders' equity (deficiency) and cash flows for each of the three years in the period ended March 31, 1996. These financial statements are the responsibility of the Company's management. Our responsibility is to express an opinion on the financial statements based on our audits.

We conducted our audits in accordance with generally accepted auditing standards. Those standards required that we plan and perform the audit to obtain reasonable assurance about whether the financial statements are free of material misstatements. An audit includes examining, on a test basis, evidence supporting the amounts and disclosures in the financial statements. An audit also includes assessing the accounting principles used and significant estimates made by management, as well as evaluating the overall financial statement presentation. We believe that our audits provide a reasonable basis for our opinion.

In our opinion, such consolidated financial statements present fairly, in all material respects, the financial position of Adelphia Communications Corporation and subsidiaries at March 31, 1995 and 1996, and the results of their operations and their cash flows for each of the three years in the period ended March 31, 1996 in conformity with generally accepted accounting principles.

As discussed in Note 7 to the consolidated financial statements, effective April 1, 1993, the Company changed its method of accounting for income taxes.

DELOITTE & TOUCHE LLP
Pittsburgh, Pennsylvania
June 28, 1996

CONSOLIDATED BALANCE SHEETS
(Dollars in thousands, except per-share amounts)

	Year Ended March 31,	
	1995	**1996**
Assets:		
Cable television systems, at cost, net of accumulated depreciation and amortization		
Property, plant and equipment	$ 518,405	$ 560,376
Intangible assets	546,116	568,898
Total	1,064,521	1,129,274
Cash and cash equivalents	5,045	10,809
Investments	48,968	68,147
Preferred equity investment in Managed Partnership	18,338	18,338
Subscriber receivables—net	20,433	23,803
Prepaid expenses and other assets—net	48,352	52,658
Related party investments and receivables—net	61,634	30,894
Total	$1,267,291	$1,333,923
Liabilities and Stockholders' Equity (Deficiency):		
Notes payable of subsidiaries to banks and institutions	$1,086,350	$1,224,675
12-1/2% Senior Notes due 2002	400,000	400,000
10-1/4 Senior Notes due 2000	99,011	99,158
11-7/8 Senior Debentures due 2004	124,470	124,502
9-7/8 Senior Debentures due 2005	127,994	128,118
9-1/2 Senior Pay-In-Kind Notes due 2004	164,370	180,357
Other debt	19,415	18,663
Accounts payable	42,872	66,668
Subscriber advance payments and deposits	16,494	14,706
Accrued interest and other liabilities	87,751	99,106
	110,139	106,209
Total Liabilities	2,278,866	2,462,162
Commitments and contingencies (Note 4)		
Stockholders' equity (deficiency):		
Class A Common Stock, $.01 par value, 50,000,000 and 200,000,000 shares authorized, respectively; 14,906,691 and 15,364,009 shares outstanding respectively	149	154
Class B Common Stock, $.01 par value, 25,000,000 shares authorized and 10,944,476 shares outstanding	109	109
Additional paid-in capital	211,190	214,415
Accumulated deficit	(1,223,023)	(1,342,917)
Total Stockholders' Equity (Deficiency)	(1,011,575)	(1,128,239)
TOTAL	$1,267,291	$1,333,923

Adelphia Communications Corporation

Adelphia Communications Corporation

CONSOLIDATED STATEMENT OF OPERATIONS
(Dollars in thousands, except per-share amounts)

	Year Ended March 31,		
	1994	**1995**	**1996**
Revenues	$ 319,045	$ 361,505	$ 403,597
Operating expenses:			
Direct operating and programming	90,547	106,993	124,116
Selling, general and administrative	52,801	63,487	68,357
Depreciation and amortization	89,402	97,602	111,031
Rate regulation	—	—	5,300
Total	232,750	268,082	308,804
Operating income	86,295	93,423	94,793
Other income (expense):			
Interest income from affiliates	9,188	11,112	10,623
Other income	(299)	1,453	—
Priority investment income from Olympus	22,300	22,300	28,852
Interest expense	(182,136)	(195,698)	(210,691)
Equity in loss of joint ventures	(30,054)	(44,349)	(46,257)
Total	(181,001)	(205,182)	(217,473)
Loss before income taxes, extraordinary loss and cumulative effect of change in accounting principle	(94,706)	(111,759)	(122,680)
Income tax (expense) benefit	(2,742)	5,475	2,786
Loss before extraordinary loss and cumulative effect of change in accounting principle	(97,448)	(106,284)	(119,894)
Extraordinary loss on early retirement of debt	(752)	—	—
Cumulative effect of change in accounting for income taxes	(89,660)	—	—
Net loss	$(187,860)	$(106,284)	$(119,894)
Loss per weighted average share of common stock before extraordinary loss and cumulative effect of change in accounting principle	$ (5.66)	$ (4.32)	$ (4.56)
Extraordinary loss per weighted average share of change in accounting for income taxes	(0.04)	—	—
Cumulative effect per weighted average share of change in accounting for income taxes	(5.21)	—	—
Net loss per weighted average share of common stock	$ (10.91)	$ (4.32)	$ (4.56)
Weighted average shares of common stock outstanding (in thousands)	17,221	24,628	26,305

See notes to consolidated financial statements.

CONSOLIDATED STATEMENTS OF CASH FLOWS

(Dollars in thousands)

	Year Ended March 31,		
	1994	**1995**	**1996**
Cash flows from operating activities:			
Net loss	$(187,860)	$(106,284)	$(119,894)
Adjustments to reconcile net loss to net cash provided by operating activities:			
Depreciation	56,370	66,064	70,890
Amortization	33,032	31,538	40,141
Noncash interest expense	1,680	14,756	16,288
Equity in loss of joint ventures	30,054	44,349	46,257
Rate regulation	—	—	2,700
Extraordinary loss on debt retirement	752	—	—
Loss on disposal of property	1,051	—	—
Cumulative effect of change in accounting for income taxes	89,660	—	—
Increase (decrease) in deferred income taxes, net of effects of acquisitions	2,061	(5,975)	(3,930)
Changes in operating assets and liabilities, net of effects of acquisitions and divestitures:			
Subscriber receivables	(155)	(478)	(3,370)
Prepaid expenses and other assets	(16,288)	(21,152)	(14,465)
Accounts payable	5,871	14,789	23,796
Subscriber advance payments and deposits	(1,134)	699	(1,788)
Accrued interests and other liabilities	11,858	10,630	7,662
Net cash provided by operating activities	26,952	48,936	64,287
Cash flows from investing activities:			
Cable television systems acquired	(21,681)	(70,256)	(60,804)
Expenditures for property, plant and equipment	(75,894)	(92,082)	(100,089)
Investments in other joint ventures	(8,890)	(38,891)	(24,333)
Preferred equity investment in Management Partnership	(18,338)	—	—
Amounts invested in and advanced to Olympus and related parties	(45,285)	(46,046)	(4,236)
Alternate access rights acquired	(27,000)	—	—
Net cash used for investing activities	(197,088)	(247,275)	(189,462)
Cash flows from financing activities:			
Proceeds from debt	744,770	155,314	273,508
Repayments of debt	(690,232)	(38,107)	(138,694)
Costs associated with debt financing	(4,961)	(2,759)	(3,875)
Issuance of Class A Common Stock	155,963	14,861	—
Net cash provided by financing activities	205,540	129,309	130,939
Increase (decrease) in cash and cash equivalents	35,404	(69,030)	5,764
Cash and cash equivalents, beginning of year	38,671	74,075	5,045
Cash and cash equivalents, end of year	$ 74,075	$ 5,045	$ 10,809
Supplemental disclosure of cash flow activity—			
Cash payments for interest	$ 178,840	$193,206	$198,369

See notes to consolidated financial statements.

Adelphia Communications Corporation

SELECTED NOTES TO CONSOLIDATED FINANCIAL STATEMENTS

(Dollars in thousands, except per-share amounts)

1. The Company and Summary of Significant Accounting Policies:

The Company and Basis for Consolidation

Adelphia Communications Corporation and subsidiaries ("Adelphia") owns, operates, and manages cable television systems and other related telecommunication businesses. Adelphia's operations consist primarily of selling video programming which is distributed to subscribers for a monthly fee through a network of fiber optic and coaxial cables. These services are offered in the respective franchise areas under the name Adelphia Cable Communications.

The consolidated financial statements include the accounts of Adelphia and its more than 50% owned subsidiaries. All significant intercompany accounts and transactions have been eliminated in consolidation.

During the years ended March 31, 1995 and 1996, Adelphia consummated several relationships, each of which was accounted for using the purchase method. Accordingly, the financial results of each acquisition have been included in the consolidated results of Adelphia effective with the date acquired. A description of the acquisitions is provided below.

On June 16, 1994, Adelphia invested $34,000 in TMC Holdings Corporation ("THC"), the parent of Tele-Media Company of Western Connecticut. THC owns cable television systems which, at the acquisition date, served approximately 43,000 subscribers in western Connecticut. The investment in THC provides Adelphia with a $30,000 preferred equity interest in THC and a 75% non-voting common equity interest with a liquidation preference to the remaining 25% common stock ownership interest in THC. Adelphia has the right to convert such interest to a 75% voting common equity interest, with a liquidation preference to the remaining shareholders' 25% common stock ownership interest on demand subject to certain regulatory approvals. Debt

assumed, included in notes payable of subsidiaries to banks and institutions, was $52,000 at closing.

On June 30, 1994, Adelphia acquired from Olympus 85% of the common stock of Northeast Cable, Inc. ("Northeast") for a purchase price of $31,875. Northeast owns cable television systems which, at the acquisition date, served approximately 36,500 subscribers in eastern Pennsylvania. Of the purchase price, $16,000 was paid in cash and the remainder resulted in a decrease in Adelphia's receivable from Olympus. Debt assumed, included in notes payable of subsidiaries to banks and institutions, was $42,300 at closing.

On January 10, 1995, Adelphia issued 399,087 shares of Class A Common Stock in connection with the merger of a wholly-owned subsidiary of Adelphia into Oxford Cablevision, Inc. ("Oxford"), one of the Terry Family cable systems. At the acquisition date, Oxford served approximately 4,200 subscribers located in the North Carolina counties of Granville and Warren.

On January 31, 1995, Adelphia acquired a majority equity position in Tele-Media Company of Martha's Vineyard, L.P. for $11,775, a cable system which, at the acquisition data, served approximately 7,000 subscribers located in Martha's Vineyard, Massachusetts.

On April 12, 1995, Adelphia acquired cable systems from Clear Channels Cable TV Company located in Kittanning, New Bethlehem, and Freeport, Pennsylvania for $17,456. These systems served approximately 10,700 subscribers at the date of acquisition.

On January 9, 1996, Adelphia completed the acquisition of the cable system of Eastern Telecom Corporation and Robinson Cable TV, Inc. These systems served approximately 24,000 subscribers located in western Pennsylvania at the acquisition date and were purchased for an aggregate price of $43,000.

Investment in Olympus Joint Venture Partnership

The investment in the Olympus joint venture partnership comprises both limited and general partner interests. The general partner interest represents a 50% voting interest in Olympus Communications, L.P. ("Olympus") and is being accounted for using the equity method. Under this method, Adelphia's investment, initially recorded at the historical cost of contributed property, is adjusted for subsequent capital contributions and its share of the losses of the partnership as well as its share of the accretion requirements of the partnership's interests. The limited partner interest represents a preferred interest ("PLP interests") entitled to a 16.5% annual return.

The PLP interests are nonvoting, are senior to claims of certain other partner interests, and provide for an annual priority return of 16.5%. Olympus is not required to pay the entire 16.5% return currently and priority return on PLP interests is recognized as income by Adelphia when received. Correspondingly, equity in net loss of Olympus excludes accumulated unpaid priority return (see Note 2).

Subscriber Revenues

Subscriber revenues are recorded in the month the service is provided.

Property, Plant and Equipment

Property, plant and equipment are comprised of the following:

	March 31,	
	1995	1996
Operating plant and equipment	$ 786,917	$ 863,957
Real estate and improvements	46,453	51,147
Support equipment	28,242	30,076
Construction in progress	77,026	105,158
	938,638	1,050,338
Accumulated depreciation	(420,233)	(489,962)
	$ 518,405	$ 560,376

Depreciation is computed on the straight-line method using estimated useful lives of 5 to 12 years for operating plant and equipment and 3 to 20 years for support equipment and buildings. Additions to property, plant and equipment are recorded at cost which includes amounts for material, applicable labor and overhead, and interest. Capitalized interest amounted to $1,345, $1,736, and $1,766 for the years ended March 31, 1994, 1995, and 1996, respectively.

Intangible Assets

Intangible assets, net of accumulated amortization, are comprised of the following:

	March 31,	
	1995	1996
Purchased franchises	$ 493,249	$ 465,983
Goodwill	38,805	58,377
Non-compete agreements	13,495	11,240
Purchased subscriber lists	567	33,298
	$ 546,116	$ 568,898

A portion of the aggregate purchase price of cable television systems acquired has been allocated to purchased franchises, purchased subscriber lists, goodwill and non-compete agreements. Purchased franchises and goodwill are amortized on the straight-line method over 40 years. Purchased subscriber lists are amortized on the straight-line method of periods which range from 5 to 10 years. Non-compete agreements are amortized on the straight-line method over their contractual lives which range from 4 to 12 years. Accumulated amortization of intangible assets amounted to $107,914 and $137,012 at March 31, 1995 and 1996, respectively.

Cash and Cash Equivalents

Adelphia considers all highly liquid investments with original maturities of three months or less to be cash equivalents. Interest on liquid investments was $2,020, $1,230 and $1,859 for the years ended March 31, 1994, 1995, and 1996, respectively.

Investments

The equity method of accounting is generally used to account for investments in affiliates which are greater than 20% but not more than 50% owned. Under this method, Adelphia's initial investment is recorded at cost and subsequently adjusted for the amount of its equity in the net income or losses of its affiliates. Dividends or other distributions are recorded as a reduction of Adelphia's investment.

Investments in affiliates accounted for using the equity method generally reflect Adelphia's equity in their underlying assets.

Investments in entities in which Adelphia's ownership is less than 20% and investments greater than 20% in which Adelphia does not influence the operating or financial decisions of the entity are generally accounted for using the cost method. Under the cost method, Adelphia's initial investment is recorded at cost and subsequently adjusted for the amount of its equity in net income or losses of the investee only to the extent distributed by the investee as dividends or other distributions. Dividends received in excess of earnings subsequent to the date the investment was made are recorded as reductions of the cost of the investment.

The balance of Adelphia's investment is as follows:

	March 31,	
	1995	1996
Investments accounted for using the equity method:		
Gross investment:		
Alternate access ventures	15,764	$28,754
Page Call, Inc.	6,915	11,187
Other	2,847	800
Cumulative equity in net losses	(1,458)	(6,814)
Total	24,068	33,927
Investments accounted for using the cost method:		
Niagara Frontier Hockey, L.P.	15,000	22,681
Commonwealth Security, Inc.	4,200	4,200
SuperCable	3,000	3,171
Other	2,700	4,168
Total	24,900	34,220
Total investments	$48,968	$68,147

On April 12, 1994, Adelphia purchased for $15,000 (i) convertible preferred units in Niagara Frontier Hockey, L.P. (the "Sabres Partnership"), which owns the Buffalo Sabres National Hockey League ("NHL") franchise, convertible to a 34% equity interest and (ii) warrants allowing Adelphia to increase its interest to 40%. Adelphia has also committed to advance $12,500 to the Sabres Partnership in the form of 14% convertible capital funding notes. In connection with the $12,500 commitment, Adelphia's convertible preferred units'

return has been increased to 14%. During the year ended March 31, 1996, the Company funded $7,681 of the $12,500 and by April 24, 1996 the entire $12,500 had been funded. The Sabres Partnership manages and will receive allocations of profits, losses, and distributions from the Marine Midland Arena, a new sports and entertainment facility expected to be completed by the opening of the 1996-1997 NHL season. Adelphia believes this investment will be a competitive advantage in the Buffalo cable television market.

Subscriber Receivables

An allowance of doubtful accounts of $3,503 and $1,216 has been deducted from subscriber receivables at March 31, 1995 and 1996, respectively. The decrease in the allowance for doubtful accounts as of March 31, 1996 resulted from a change in procedure for writing off doubtful accounts. This change had no effect on bad debt expense.

Amortization of Other Assets and Debt Discounts

Deferred debt financing costs, included in prepaid expenses and other assets, and debt discounts, a reduction of the carrying amount of the debt, are amortized over the term of the related debt. The unamortized amounts included in prepaid expenses and other assets were $23,355 and $25,274 at March 31, 1995 and 1996, respectively.

Asset Impairments

Adelphia periodically reviews the carrying value of its long-lived assets for impairment whenever events or changes in circumstances indicate that the carrying value of assets may not be recoverable. Measurement of any impairment would include a comparison of estimated future operating cash flows anticipated to be generated during the remaining life of the assets with their carrying value. An impairment loss would be recognized as the amount by which the carrying value of the assets exceeds their fair value.

Noncash Financing and Investing Activities

Capital leases entered into during the year ended March 31, 1994 totaled $7,186. There were no material capital leases entered into the years ended March 31, 1995 and 1996. Reference is made to Notes 1, 2, 5 and 9 for descriptions of additional non-cash financing and investing activities.

Derivative Financial Instruments

Net settlement amounts under interest rate swap agreements are recorded as adjustments to interest expense during the period incurred.

Use of Estimates in the Preparation of Financial Statements

The preparation of financial statements in conformity with generally accepted accounting principles requires management to make estimates and assumptions that affect the reported amounts of assets and liabilities and disclosure of contingent assets and liabilities at the date of the financial statements and the reported amounts of revenues and expenses during the reporting period. Actual results could differ from those estimates.

Reclassification

Certain 1994 and 1995 amounts have been reclassified for comparability with the 1996 presentation.

3. Debt:

Notes Payable of Subsidiaries to Banks and Institutions

Notes payable of subsidiaries to banks and institutions are comprised of the following:

Borrowings under most of these credit arrangements of subsidiaries are collateralized by a pledge of the stock in their respective subsidiaries, and, in some cases, by assets. These agreements stipulate, among other things, limitations on additional borrowings, investments, transactions with affiliates and other subsidiaries, and the payment of dividends and fees by the subsidiaries. They also require maintenance of certain financial ratios by the subsidiaries. Several of the subsidiaries' agreements, along with the notes of the parent company, contain cross default provisions. At March 31, 1996 approximately $219,000 of the net assets of subsidiaries would be permitted to be transferred to the parent company in the form of dividends, priority return and loans without the prior approval of the lenders based upon the results of operations of such subsidiaries for the quarter ended March 31, 1996. The subsidiaries are permitted to pay fees to the parent company or other subsidiaries. Such fees are limited to a percentage of the subsidiaries' revenues.

Bank debt interest rates are based upon one or more of the following rates at the option of Adelphia: prime rate plus 0% to 1.5%; certificate of deposit rate plus 1.25% to 2.75%; or LIBOR rate plus 1% to 2.5%. At March 31, 1995 and 1996, the weighted average interest rate on notes payable to banks and institutions was 9.33% and 8.36%, respectively. The rates on 36% of Adelphia's notes payable to banks and institutions were fixed for at least one year through the terms of the notes or interest rate swap agreements.

	March 31,	
	1995	1996
Credit agreements with banks payable through 2003 (weighted average interest rate 8.16% and 7.51% at March 31, 1995 and 1996, respectively)	$ 584,250	$ 758,975
10.66% Senior Secured Notes due 1996 through 1999	250,000	245,000
9.95% Senior Secured Notes due through 1997	9,600	3,200
10.80% Senior Secured Notes due 1996 through 2000	45,000	36,000
10.50% Senior Secured Notes due 1997 through 2001	16,000	16,000
9.73% Senior Secured Notes due 1998 through 2001	37,500	37,500
10.25% Senior Subordinated Notes due 1996 through 1998	72,000	56,000
11.85% Senior Subordinated Notes due 1998 through 2000	60,000	60,000
11.13% Senior Subordinated Notes due 1999 through 2002	12,000	12,000
	$1,086,350	$1,224,675

Adelphia Communications Corporation

12 1/2% Senior Notes Due 2002

On May 14, 1992, Adelphia issued at face value to the public $400,000 aggregate principal amount of unsecured 12 1/2% Senior Notes due May 15, 2002. Interest is due on the notes semiannually. The notes, which are effectively subordinated to all liabilities of the subsidiaries, contain restrictions on, among other things, the incurrence of indebtedness, mergers and sale of assets, certain restricted payments by Adelphia, investments in affiliates and certain other affiliate transactions. The notes further require that Adelphia maintain a debt to annualized operating cash flow ratio of not greater than 8.75 to 1.00, based on the latest fiscal quarter, exclusive of the incurrence of $50,000 in additional indebtedness which is not subject to the required ratio. Adelphia may redeem the notes in whole or in part on or after May 15, 1997, at 106% of principal, declining to 100% of principal on or after May 15, 1999.

10 1/4% Senior Notes Due 2000

On July 28, 1993, Adelphia issued $110,000 aggregate principal amount of unsecured 10 1/4% Senior Notes due July 2000. Interest is due on the notes semiannually. The notes, which are effectively subordinated to all liabilities of the subsidiaries, contain restrictions and covenants similar to the restrictions on the 12 1/2% Senior Notes. The notes are not callable prior to the maturity date of July 15, 2000. During fiscal 1995, $10,000 of notes were retired through open market purchases.

11 7/8% Senior Debentures Due 2004

On September 10, 1992, Adelphia issued to the public $125,000 aggregate principal amount of unsecured 11 7/8% Senior Debentures due September 2004. Interest is due on the debentures semiannually. The debentures, which are effectively subordinated to all liabilities of the subsidiaries, contain restrictions and covenants similar to the restrictions on the 12 1/2% Senior Notes. Adelphia may redeem the debentures in whole or in part on or after September 15, 1999, at 104.5% of principal, declining to 100% of principal on or after September 15, 2002.

9 7/8% Senior Debentures Due 2005

On March 11, 1993, Adelphia issued 9 7/8% Senior Debentures due March 2005 in the aggregate principal amount of $130,000. Interest on the debentures is payable semi-annually. The debentures, which are effectively subordinated to all liabilities of the subsidiaries, contain restrictions and covenants similar to the restrictions on the 12 1/2% Senior Notes. The debentures are not redeemable prior to the maturity date of March 1, 2005.

9 1/2% Senior Pay-in-Kind Notes Due 2004

On February 15, 1994, Adelphia issued $150,000 aggregate 9 1/2% Senior Pay-in-Kind Notes due February 2004. On or prior to February 1999, all interest on the notes, which is due semi-annually, may at the option of Adelphia be paid in cash or through the issuance of additional notes valued at 100% of their principal amount. The notes will bear cash interest from February 1999 through maturity. The notes, which are effectively subordinated to all liabilities of the subsidiaries, contain restrictions and covenants similar to the 12 1/2% Senior Notes. Adelphia may redeem the notes in whole or in part on or after February 15, 1999, at 103.56% of principal, declining to 100% of principal on or after February 15, 2002.

13% Senior Subordinated Notes Due 1996

On February 14, 1994, Adelphia redeemed all of the 13% Senior Subordinated Notes for 100% of the $100,000 aggregate principal amount.

Maturities of Debt

Maturities of debt for the five years after March 31, 1996 are as follows:

1997	$127,906
1998	177,475
1999	162,791
2000	82,483
2001	157,381

The maturities of debt listed above have been adjusted to reflect changed maturity dates resulting from repayment of certain debt during April 1996 from borrowings under a new credit facility (see

Note 11). Management intends to fund its requirements for maturities of debt through borrowings under new and existing credit arrangements and internally generated funds. Changing conditions in the financial markets may have an impact on how Adelphia will refinance its debt in the future.

Interest Rate Swaps and Caps

Adelphia has entered into interest rate swap agreements and interest rate cap agreements with banks, Olympus and Managed Entities to reduce the impact of changes in interest rates on its debt. Several of Adelphia's credit arrangements include provisions which require interest rate protection for a portion of its debt. Adelphia enters into pay-fixed agreements to effectively convert a portion of its variable-rate debt to fixed-rate debt to reduce the risk of incurring higher interest costs due to rising interest rates. Adelphia enters into receive-fixed agreements to effectively convert a portion of its fixed-rate debt to a variable-rate debt which is indexed to LIBOR rates to reduce the risk of incurring higher interest costs in periods of falling interest rates. Interest rate cap agreements are used to reduce the impact of increases in interest rates on variable rate debt. Adelphia is exposed to credit loss in the event of nonperformance by the banks, by Olympus or by the Managed Entities. Adelphia does not expect any such nonperformance. The following table summarizes the notional amounts of outstanding and weighted average interest rate data, based on variable rates in effect at March 31, 1995 and 1996, for all swaps and caps which expire 1996 through 1998.

	March 31,	
	1995	**1996**
Pay Fixed Swaps:		
Notional amount	$396,000	$416,000
Average receive rate	6.19%	5.68%
Average pay rate	7.50%	7.94%
Receive Fixed Swaps:		
Notional amount	$406,000	$108,500
Average receive rate	6.77%	6.66%
Average pay rate	6.30%	5.74%
Interest Rate Caps:		
Notional amount		$ 50,000
Average cap rate		9.00%

During fiscal 1996, Adelphia received $11,526 upon termination of several interest rate swap agreements having a stated notional principal amount of $270,000. The amount received will be amortized as a reduction of interest expense through November 1998. At March 31, 1996, the unamortized balance is $10,027. Also during fiscal 1996, the Company received $4,900 and assumed the obligations as a counterparty under certain interest rate swap agreements with Olympus. These interest rate swap agreements have a notional principal amount of $140,000 and expire through November 1998.

7. Taxes on Income:

Adelphia and its corporate subsidiaries file a consolidated federal income tax return, which includes its share of the subsidiary partnerships and joint venture partnership results. At March 31, 1996, Adelphia had net operating loss carryforwards for federal income tax purposes of approximately $1.1 billion expiring through 2011. Depreciation and amortization expense differs for tax and financial statement purposes due to the use of prescribed periods rather than useful lives for tax purposes and also as a result of differences between tax basis and book basis of certain acquisitions.

Adelphia adopted Statement of Financial Accounting Standards ("SFAS") No. 109, "Accounting for Income Taxes," effective April 1, 1993. Under SFAS No. 109, deferred tax assets and liabilities are recognized for differences between the financial statement amounts of assets and liabilities and their respective tax bases. The cumulative effect of adopting SFAS No. 109 at April 1, 1993 was to increase the net loss by $89,660 for the year ended March 31, 1994. The effect of adopting SFAS No. 109 on loss before extraordinary loss and cumulative effect of a change in accounting principle was not significant for the year ended March 31, 1994.

As a result of applying SFAS No. 109, $110,498 of previously unrecorded deferred tax benefits from operating loss carryforwards incurred by Adelphia were recognized at April 1, 1993 as part of the cumulative effect of adopting the statement. Under prior accounting, a portion of these

Adelphia Communications Corporation

benefits would have been recognized as a reduction of income tax expense from continuing operations in the year ended March 31, 1994.

The tax effects of significant items comprising Adelphia's net deferred tax liability are as follows:

| | April 1, 1993 | March 31, | | |
		1994	1995	1996
Deferred tax liabilities:				
Differences between book and tax basis of property, plant and equipment and intangible assets	$192,444	$210,816	$232,639	$234,312
Other	8,401	9,703	11,783	—
Subtotal	200,845	220,519	244,422	234,312
Deferred tax assets:				
Reserves not currently deductible	687	15,576	12,326	14,467
Operating loss carryforwards	307,001	337,924	381,377	415,121
	307,688	353,500	393,703	429,588
Valuation allowance	(196,503)	(224,702)	(259,420)	(301,485)
Subtotal	111,185	128,798	134,283	128,103
Net deferred tax liability	$ 89,660	$ 91,721	$110,139	$106,209

The net change in the valuation allowance for the years ended March 31, 1995 and 1996 was an increase of $34,718 and $42,065, respectively.

Income tax (expense) benefit for the years ended March 31, 1994, 1995, and 1996 is as follows:

| | Year Ended March 31, | | |
	1994	1995	1996
Current	$(681)	$(500)	$(1,144)
Deferred	(2,061)	5,975	3,930
Total	$(2,742)	$5,475	$2,786

A reconciliation of the statutory federal income tax rate and Adelphia's effective income tax rate is as follows:

| | Year Ended March 31, | | |
	1994	1995	1996
Statutory federal income tax return	35%	35%	35%
Change in valuation allowance	(30%)	(31%)	(37%)
State taxes, net of federal benefit	(2%)	4%	(1%)
Other	(6%)	(3%)	5%
Effective income tax (expense) benefit rate	(3%)	5%	2%

8. *Disclosures about Fair Value of Financial Instruments:*

Included in Adelphia's financial instrument portfolio are cash, notes payable, debentures and interest rate swaps and caps. The carrying values of notes payable approximate their fair values at March 31, 1995 and 1996. The carrying cost of the public notes and debentures at March 31, 1995 and 1996 of $915,845 and $932,135, respectively, exceeded their fair value by $95,628 and $1,420, respectively. At March 31, 1995 and 1996, Adelphia would have been required to pay approximately $6,929 and $14,225, respectively, to settle its interest rate swap and cap agreements, representing the excess of carrying cost over fair value of these agreements. The fair values of the debt and interest rate swaps and caps were based upon quoted market prices of similar instruments or on rates available to Adelphia for instruments of the same remaining maturities.

EXHIBIT 5

Adelphia Communications Corporation, Status of Cable Plant—
March 31, 1996

Cable Plant Characteristics:	
Plant miles	34,429
Fiber route miles	3,015
Fiber strand miles	65,020
Fiber nodes	1,948
Homes passed per fiber node	1,273
Channel Capacity (plant miles):	
Less than 400 Mhz	8,592
400 Mhz up to 550 Mhz	15,724
550 Mhz or more	10,113
Total plant miles	34,429
Channel Capacity (percent of plant miles):	
Less than 400 Mhz	25.0%
400 Mhz up to 550 Mhz	45.6%
550 Mhz or more	29.4%
Total plant miles	100.0%
Services Capability (as a percent of total plant miles):	
Digital video	100.0%
Interactive video	23.4%
One-way data transmission	100.0%
Two-way data transmission	23.4%
Residential telephone	9.0%

Mergers and Acquisitions

Mergers and acquisitions have long been a popular form of corporate investment, particularly in countries with Anglo-American forms of capital markets. There is no question that these transactions provide a healthy return to target stockholders. However, their value to acquiring shareholders is less understood. Many skeptics point out that given the hefty premiums paid to target stockholders, acquisitions tend to be negative-valued investments for acquiring stockholders.[1]

A number of questions can be examined using financial analysis for mergers and acquisitions:

- Securities analysts can ask: Does a proposed acquisition create value for the acquiring firm's stockholders?
- Risk arbitrageurs can ask: What is the likelihood that a hostile takeover offer will ultimately succeed, and are there other potential acquirers likely to enter the bidding?
- Acquiring management can ask: Does this target fit our business strategy? If so, what is it worth to us, and how can we make an offer that can be successful?
- Target management can ask: Is the acquirer's offer a reasonable one for our stockholders? Are there other potential acquirers that would value our company more than the current bidder?
- Investment bankers can ask: How can we identify potential targets that are likely to be a good match for our clients? And how should we value target firms when we are asked to issue fairness opinions?

In this chapter we focus primarily on the use of financial statement data and analysis directed at evaluating whether a merger creates value for the acquiring firm's stockholders. However, our discussion can also be applied to these other merger contexts.

Our discussion of whether acquisitions create value for acquirers focuses on evaluating motivations for acquisitions, the pricing of offers, and the methods of financing, as well as assessing the likelihood that an offer will be successful. Throughout the chapter we use AT&T's $7.5 billion acquisition of NCR in 1991 to illustrate how financial analysis can be used in a merger context.[2]

MOTIVATION FOR MERGER OR ACQUISITION

There are a variety of reasons that firms merge or acquire other firms. Some acquiring managers may want to increase their own power and prestige. Others, however, realize that business combinations provide an opportunity to create new economic value for their stockholders. New value can be created in the following ways:

1. *Taking Advantage of Economies of Scale*. Mergers are often justified as a means of providing the two participating firms with increased economies of scale. Economies of scale arise when one firm can perform a function more efficiently than two. For example, AT&T and NCR both design and manufacture UNIX-based personal computers. Following a merger, they will probably be able to take advantage of economies of scale in research and development by reducing the number of researchers working on similar new products. The combined firm may also be able to economize on management costs, including accounting and corporate finance functions and corporate management.

2. *Improving Target Management.* Another common motivation for acquisition is to improve target management. A firm is likely to be a target if it has systematically underperformed its industry. Historical poor performance could be due to bad luck, but it could also be due to the firm's managers making poor investment and operating decisions, or deliberately pursuing goals which increase their personal power but cost stockholders.

3. *Combining Complementary Resources.* Firms may decide that a merger will create value by combining complementary resources of the two partners. For example, a merger between a firm with a strong research and development unit, such as AT&T, and a firm in the same industry with a strong distribution unit, such as NCR, may benefit both firms. Of course, they could both separately invest to strengthen their respective distribution and R&D units. However, it may well be cheaper to combine resources through a merger.

4. *Capturing Tax Benefits.* In the U.S. the 1986 Tax Reform Act eliminated many of the tax benefits from mergers and acquisitions. However, several merger tax benefits remain. The major benefit is the acquisition of operating tax losses. If a firm does not expect to earn sufficient profits to fully utilize operating loss carryforward benefits, it may decide to buy another firm which is earning profits. The operating losses and loss carryforwards of the acquirer can then be offset against the target's taxable income.[3] A second tax benefit often attributed to mergers is the tax shield that comes from increasing leverage for the target firm. This was particularly relevant for leveraged buyouts in the 1980s.[4]

5. *Providing Low-Cost Financing to a Financially Constrained Target.* If capital markets are imperfect, perhaps because of information asymmetries between management and outside investors, firms can face capital constraints. Information problems are likely to be especially severe for newly formed, high-growth firms. These firms can be difficult for outside investors to value since they have short track records, and their financial statements provide little insight into the value of their growth opportunities. Further, since they typically have to rely on external funds to finance their growth, capital market constraints for high-growth firms are likely to affect their ability to undertake profitable new projects. Public capital markets are therefore likely to be costly sources of funds for these types of firms.

An acquirer that understands the business and is willing to provide a steady source of finance may therefore be able to add value.[5]

6. *Increasing Product-Market Rents.* Firms also can have incentives to merge to increase product-market rents. By merging and becoming a dominant firm in the industry, two smaller firms can collude to restrict their output and raise prices, thereby increasing their profits. This circumvents problems that arise in cartels of independent firms, where firms have incentives to cheat on the cartel and increase their output.

While product-market rents make sense for firms as a motive for merging, the two partners are unlikely to announce their intentions when they explain the merger to their investors, since most countries have antitrust laws which regulate mergers between two firms in the same industry. For example, in the U.S. there are three major antitrust statutes—The Sherman Act of 1890, The Clayton Act of 1914, and The Hart Scott Rodino Act of 1976.

While many of the motivations for acquisitions are likely to create new economic value for shareholders, some are not. Firms that are flush with cash but have few new profitable investment opportunities are particularly prone to using their surplus cash to make acquisitions. Stockholders of these firms would probably prefer that managers pay out any surplus or "free" cash flows as dividends, or use the funds to repurchase their firm's stock. However, these options reduce the size of the firm and the assets under management's control. Management may therefore prefer to invest the free cash flows to buy new companies, even if they are not valued by stockholders. Of course, managers will never announce that they are buying a firm because they are reluctant to pay out funds to stockholders. They may explain the merger using one of the motivations discussed above, or they may argue that they are buying the target at a bargain price.

Another motivation for mergers that is valued by managers but not stockholders is diversification. Diversification was a popular motivation for acquisitions in the 1960s and early 1970s. Acquirers sought to dampen their earnings volatility by buying firms in unrelated businesses. Diversification as a motive for acquisitions has since been widely discredited. Modern finance theorists point out that in a well functioning capital market, investors can diversify for themselves and do not need managers to do so for them. In addition, diversification has been criticized for leading firms to lose sight of their major competitive strengths and to expand into businesses where they do not have expertise.[6]

Key Analysis Questions

In evaluating a proposed merger, analysts are interested in determining whether the merger creates new wealth for acquiring and target stockholders, or whether it is motivated by managers' desires to increase their own power and prestige. Key questions for financial analysis are likely to include:

- *What is the motivation(s) for an acquisition and any anticipated benefits through public disclosures by acquirers or targets?*
- *What are the industries of the target and acquirer?* Are the firms related horizontally or vertically? How close are the business relations between them? If the businesses are unrelated, is the acquirer cash-rich and reluctant to return free cash flows to stockholders?
- *What are the key operational strengths of the target and the acquirer?* Are these strengths complementary? For example, does one firm have a renowned research group and the other a strong distribution network?
- *Is the acquisition a friendly one, supported by target management, or hostile?* A hostile takeover is more likely to occur for targets with poor-performing management who oppose the acquisition to preserve its job.
- *What is the premerger performance of the two firms?* Performance metrics are likely to include ROE, gross margins, general and administrative expenses to sales, and working capital management ratios. On the basis of these measures, is the target a poor performer in its industry, implying that there are opportunities for improved management? Is the acquirer in a declining industry and searching for new directions?
- *What is the tax position of both firms?* What are the average and marginal current tax rates for the target and the acquirer? Does the acquirer have operating loss carryforwards and the target taxable profits?

This analysis should help the analyst understand what specific benefits, if any, the merger is likely to generate.

Motivation for AT&T's Acquisition

Prior to 1984, AT&T was a regulated utility providing telephone services and manufacturing-related equipment. However, in 1982 the company signed a Consent Agreement with the Department of Justice (DOJ) to divest its Bell operating companies, which provided short-distance telephone services. This agreement followed eight years of negotiations with the DOJ over allegations that AT&T monopolized the telephone services and telephone equipment industries. In return for agreeing to this divestiture, AT&T was granted permission to enter the computer industry, which had previously been off-limits to the company.

Management argued that the Consent Agreement permitted the firm to concentrate on linking its telecommunications with computer and information services. The company could finally begin to take advantage of advances in computer science, particularly the development of UNIX operating systems that had been made at its renowned research park, Bell Labs. However, prior to 1990, the company had not been particularly successful in implementing this strategy. The financial press estimated that the firm's computer operations lost at least $2 billion between 1984 and 1990. Losses for 1990 alone were estimated at between $10 million and $300 million on sales of $1.5 billion.

AT&T's management decided that the best approach to its computer problems involved increasing its presence in computer operations and began searching for a suitable acquisition candidate. NCR, which had a corporate culture similar to AT&T's, emerged as the ideal target from this search. It also had compatible product lines and a similar policy of using UNIX operating systems. However, NCR was stronger than AT&T in networking and had an international computer marketing presence and customer base. Consistent with its desire to use NCR to develop its expertise in computer operations, AT&T announced that it would combine both companies' computer operations under NCR's management.

In summary, given AT&T's strategy of combining telecommunications and computer technologies and services, the acquisition of NCR appeared to make some economic sense. However, some analysts who were critical of AT&T's overall strategy argued that the acquisition would probably not create value for AT&T's stockholders, and that AT&T should concede that its entry into the computer business was a costly mistake.

ACQUISITION PRICING

A well thought-out economic motivation for a merger or acquisition is a necessary but not sufficient condition for it to create value for acquiring stockholders. The acquirer must be careful to avoid overpaying for the target. Overpayment makes the transaction highly desirable and profitable for target stockholders, but it diminishes the value of the deal to acquiring stockholders. A financial analyst can use the following methods to assess whether the acquiring firm is overpaying for the target.

Analyzing Premium Offered to Target Stockholders

One popular way to assess whether the acquirer is overpaying for a target is to compare the premium offered to target stockholders to premiums offered in similar transactions. If the acquirer offers a relatively high premium, the analyst is typically led to conclude that the transaction is less likely to create value for acquiring stockholders.

Premiums differ significantly for friendly and hostile acquisitions. Premiums tend to be about 30 percent higher for hostile deals than for friendly offers, implying that hostile acquirers are more likely to overpay for a target.[7] There are several reasons for this. First, a friendly acquirer has access to the internal records of the target, making it much less likely that it will be surprised by hidden liabilities or problems once it has completed the deal. In contrast, a hostile acquirer does not have this advantage in valuing the target and is forced to make assumptions, which may later turn out to be false. Second, the delays that typically accompany a hostile acquisition often provide opportunities for competing bidders to make an offer for the target, leading to a bidding war.

Comparing a target's premium to values for similar types of transactions is straight-forward to compute, but it has several practical problems. First, it is not obvious how to define a comparable transaction. Figure 15-1 shows the mean and median premiums paid for U.S. targets between 1989 and 1998 relative to stock prices one week prior to the first acquisition announcement. Average premiums have been approximately 40 percent and medians around 30 percent during this period. However, there is considerable variation across transactions, making it difficult to use these estimates as a benchmark.

A second problem in using premiums offered to target stockholders to assess whether an acquirer overpaid is that measured premiums can be misleading if an offer is antici-pated by investors. The stock price run-up for the target will then tend to make estimates of the premium appear relatively low. This limitation can be partially offset by using tar-get stock prices one month prior to the acquisition offer as the basis for calculating pre-miums. However, in some cases offers may have been anticipated for even longer than one month.

Finally, using target premiums to assess whether an acquirer overpaid ignores the value of the target to the acquirer after the acquisition. This value can be viewed as:

Value of target after acquisition = Value as independent firm + Value of merger benefits

The value of the target before acquisition is the present value of the free cash flows for the target if it were to remain an independent entity. This is likely to be somewhat different from the firm's stock price prior to any merger announcement, since the pre-takeover price is a weighted average of the value of the firm as an independent unit and its value in the event of a takeover. The benefits of the merger include such effects as improvements in target operating performance from economies of scale, improved man-agement, or tax benefits, as well as any spillover benefits to the acquirer from the acqui-sition. Clearly, acquirers will be willing to pay higher premiums for targets which are expected to generate higher merger benefits. Thus, examining the premium alone cannot determine whether the acquisition creates value for acquiring stockholders.

Figure 15-1 Premium Paid for Mergers and Acquisitions in the Period 1989 to 1998

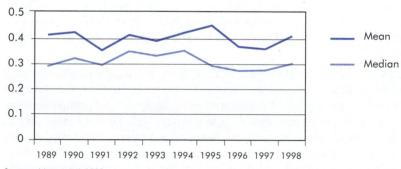

Source: *Mergerstat*, 1999.

Analyzing Value of the Target to the Acquirer

A second and more reliable way of assessing whether the acquirer has overpaid for the target is to compare the offer price to the estimated value of the target to the acquirer. This latter value can be computed using the valuation techniques discussed in Chapters 11 and 12. The most popular methods of valuation used for mergers and acquisitions are earnings multiples and discounted cash flows. Since a comprehensive discussion of these techniques is provided earlier in the book, we focus here on implementation issues that arise for valuing targets in mergers and acquisitions. We recommend first computing the value of the target as an independent firm. This provides a way of checking whether the valuation assumptions are reasonable, since for publicly listed targets we can compare our estimate with premerger market prices. It also provides a useful benchmark for thinking about how the target's performance, and hence its value, is likely to change once it is acquired.

EARNINGS MULTIPLES.   To estimate the value of a target to an acquirer using earnings multiples, we have to forecast earnings for the target and decide on an appropriate earnings multiple.

Step One: Forecasting Earnings. Earnings forecasts are usually made by first forecasting next year's net income for the target, assuming no acquisition. Historical sales growth rates, gross margins, and average tax rates are useful in building a pro forma income model. Once we have forecasted the income for the target prior to an acquisition, we can incorporate into the pro forma model any improvements in earnings performance that we expect to result from the acquisition. Performance improvements can be modeled as:

- Higher operating margins through economies of scale in purchasing, or increased market power;
- Reductions in expenses as a result of consolidating research and development staffs, sales forces, and/or administration; or
- Lower average tax rates from taking advantage of operating tax loss carryforwards.

Forecasting earnings after acquisition requires some caution since, as we discuss later, an acquisition accounted for using purchase accounting will typically lead to increased goodwill amortization and depreciation expenses for revalued assets after the acquisition. These effects should be ignored in estimating future earnings for price-earnings valuation.

Step Two: Determining Price-Earnings Multiple. How do we determine the earnings multiple to be applied to our earnings forecasts? If the target firm is listed, it may be tempting to use the preacquisition price-earnings multiple to value postmerger earnings. However, there are several limitations to this approach. First, for many targets, earnings growth expectations are likely to change after a merger, implying that there will be a difference between the pre- and postmerger price-earnings multiples. Postmerger earnings should then be valued using a multiple for firms with comparable growth and risk characteristics. (See discussion in Chapter 11.) A second problem is that premerger price-earnings multiples are unavailable for unlisted targets. Once again, it becomes necessary to decide which types of listed firms are likely to be good comparables. Finally, if a premerger price-earnings multiple is appropriate for valuing postmerger earnings, care is required to ensure that the multiple is calculated prior to any acquisition announcement, since the price will increase in anticipation of the premium to be paid to target stockholders.

The following table summarizes how price-earnings multiples are used to value a target firm before an acquisition (assuming it will remain an independent entity), and to estimate the value of a target to a potential acquirer:

Summary of Price-Earnings Valuation for Targets

Value of target as an independent firm	Target earnings forecast for the next year, assuming no change in ownership, multiplied by its *premerger* PE multiple.
Value of target to potential acquirer	Target *revised* earnings forecast for the next year, incorporating the effect of any operational changes made by the acquirer, multiplied by its *postmerger* PE multiple.

LIMITATIONS OF PRICE-EARNINGS VALUATION.   As explained in Chapter 11, there are serious limitations to using earnings multiples for valuation. In addition to these limitations, the method has several more that are specific to merger valuations:

1. PE multiples assume that merger performance improvements come either from an immediate increase in earnings or from an increase in earnings growth (and hence an increase in the postmerger PE ratio). In reality, improvements and savings can come in many forms—gradual increases in earnings from implementing new operating policies, elimination of overinvestment, better management of working capital, or paying out excess cash to stockholders. These types of improvements are not naturally reflected in PE multiples.
2. PE models do not easily incorporate any spillover benefits from an acquisition for the acquirer, since they focus on valuing the earnings of the target.

DISCOUNTED CASH FLOWS OR ABNORMAL EARNINGS.   As discussed in Chapters 11 and 12, we can also value a company using the discounted abnormal earnings and discounted free cash flow methods. These require us to first forecast the abnormal earnings or free cash flows for the firm and then discount them at the cost of capital.

Step One: Forecast Abnormal Earnings/Free Cash Flows. A pro forma model of expected future income and cash flows for the firm provides the basis for forecasting abnormal earnings/free cash flows. As a starting point, the model should be constructed under the assumption that the target remains an independent firm. The model should reflect our best estimates of future sales growth, cost structures, working capital needs, investment and research and development needs, and cash requirements for known debt retirements, developed from financial analysis of the target. The abnormal earnings method requires that we forecast abnormal earnings or net operating profit after tax (NOPAT) for as long as the firm expects new investment projects to earn more than their cost of capital. Under the free cash flow approach, the pro forma model will forecast free cash flows to either the firm or to equity, typically for a period of five to ten years. Once we have a model of the abnormal earnings or free cash flows, we can incorporate any improvements in earnings/free cash flows that we expect to result from the acquisition. These will include the cost savings, cash received from asset sales, benefits from eliminating overinvestment, improved working capital management, and paying out excess cash to stockholders.

Step Two: Compute the Discount Rate. If we are valuing the target's postacquisition abnormal NOPAT or cash flows to the firm, the appropriate discount rate is the weighted average cost of capital for the target, using its expected *postacquisition* capital structure. Alternatively, if the target equity cash flows are being valued directly or if we are valuing abnormal earnings, the appropriate discount rate is the target's *postacquisition cost of equity* rather than its weighted average cost of capital (WACC). Two common mistakes are to use the acquirer's cost of capital or the target's *preacquisition* cost of capital to value the postmerger abnormal earnings/cash flows from the target.

The computation of the target's postacquisition cost of capital can be complicated if the acquirer plans to make a change to the target's capital structure after the acquisition, since the target's costs of debt and equity will change. However, the net effect of these changes on the weighted average cost of capital is likely to be quite small unless the revision in leverage has a significant effect on the target's interest tax shields or its likelihood of financial distress.

The following table summarizes how the discounted abnormal earnings/cash flow methods can be used to value a target before an acquisition (assuming it will remain an independent entity), and to estimate the value of a target firm to a potential acquirer.

Summary of Discounted Abnormal Earnings/Cash Flow Valuation for Targets

Value of target without an acquisition	(a) Present value of abnormal earnings/free cash flows to target equity assuming no acquisition, discounted at *premerger* cost of equity; or
	(b) Present value of abnormal NOPAT/free cash flows to target debt and equity assuming no acquisition, discounted at *premerger* WACC, less value of debt; or
Value of target to potential acquirer	(a) Present value of abnormal earnings/free cash flows to target equity, *including benefits from merger,* discounted at *postmerger* cost of equity; or

(b) Present value of abnormal NOPAT/free cash flows to target, *including benefits from merger,* discounted at *post-merger* WACC, less value of debt

....

Step Three: Analyze Sensitivity. Once we have estimated the expected value of a target, we will want to examine the sensitivity of our estimate to changes in the model assumptions. For example, answering the following questions can help the analyst assess the risks associated with an acquisition.

- What happens to the value of the target if it takes longer than expected for the benefits of the acquisition to materialize?
- What happens to the value of the target if the acquisition prompts its primary competitors to respond by also making an acquisition? Will such a response affect our plans and estimates?

Key Analysis Questions

To analyze the pricing of an acquisition, the analyst is interested in assessing the value of the acquisition benefits to be generated by the acquirer relative to the price paid to target stockholders. Analysts are therefore likely to be interested in answers to the following questions:

- What is the premium that the acquirer paid for the target's stock? What does this premium imply for the acquirer in terms of future performance improvements to justify the premium?
- What are the likely performance improvements that management expects to generate from the acquisition? For example, are there likely to be increases in the revenues for the merged firm from new products, increased prices, or better distribution of existing products? Alternatively, are there cost savings as a result of taking advantage of economies of scale, improved efficiency, or a lower cost of capital for the target?
- What is the value of any performance improvements? Values can be estimated using multiples or discounted earnings/cash flow methods.

AT&T's Pricing of NCR

AT&T's $7.5 billion price for NCR represents a 120 percent premium to target stockholders (adjusted for market-wide changes during the merger negotiation period). This is certainly substantially higher than typical premiums during this period and in part reflects opposition to the acquisition from NCR's management. AT&T's initial offer for the firm was $85 per share. The final price, which was accepted by target management, was $110.

AT&T's pricing of NCR also appears to be aggressive in terms of traditional forms of valuation. At the time of the announcement of AT&T's offer, the typical PE value for firms in the computer industry was 12.9 and NCR's PE was 11.5, yet AT&T's final offer valued NCR at 18 times current earnings. If these benefits are realized immediately, the total annual performance improvements from the acquisition for the new firm is equivalent to 50 percent of NCR's premerger earnings, a challenging target. Of course AT&T's management believed some of these benefits would come from increased earnings from its own operations.

The market reaction to acquisition announcements suggests that analysts believed that AT&T overpaid for NCR—AT&T's stock price dropped by 13 percent (again adjusted for market-wide changes), or $4.9 billion, during the negotiation period. Given the $3.7 billion premium that AT&T paid for NCR, this decline in AT&T equity implies that analysts believed that AT&T would actually destroy value in NCR! Subsequent short-term financial results for AT&T's computer operations (which includes NCR) support the market's skepticism. NCR's 1991 earnings were $100 million (26 percent) below projections made to AT&T. AT&T's loss from computer operations in 1993 was $99 million (including a $190 million restructuring charge). For the first quarter of 1994 the firm reported an operating loss of $61 million (including another restructuring charge of $120 million).

NCR continued to show poor performance through 1995, with losses reportedly as high as $2 million per day. Consequently, in 1995 AT&T announced that it would take a $1.6 billion write-off of its NCR assets. In 1996 AT&T decided to reposition itself as a communications services company. As part of the accompanying restructuring, it spun off NCR to its shareholders. The newly listed NCR was valued at $3.5 billion, less than half of the $7.5 billion that AT&T had paid for the company.

In summary, it appears from preliminary results and market assessments of the acquisition that AT&T overpaid for NCR. Indeed, the market believed that AT&T would actually destroy NCR's value as an independent firm, raising questions about the merits of AT&T's overall technology strategy.

ACQUISITION FINANCING

Even if an acquisition is undertaken to create new economic value and is priced judiciously, it may still destroy shareholder value if it is inappropriately financed. Several financing options are available to acquirers, including issuing stock or warrants to target stockholders, or acquiring target stock using surplus cash or proceeds from new debt. The trade-offs between these options from the standpoint of target stockholders usually hinge on their tax and transaction cost implications. For acquirers, they can affect the firm's capital structure and the financial reporting of the transaction and provide new information to investors.

As we discuss below, the financing preferences of target and acquiring stockholders can diverge. Financing arrangements can therefore increase or reduce the attractiveness of an acquisition from the standpoint of acquiring stockholders. As a result, a complete analysis of an acquisition will include an examination of the implications of the financing arrangements for the acquirer.

Effect of Form of Financing on Target Stockholders

As noted above, the key financing considerations for target stockholders are the tax and transaction cost implications of the acquirer's offer.

TAX EFFECTS OF DIFFERENT FORMS OF CONSIDERATION.   Target stockholders care about the after-tax value of any offer they receive for their shares. In the U.S., whenever target stockholders receive cash for their shares, they are required to pay capital gains tax on the difference between the takeover offer price and their original purchase price. Alternatively, if they receive shares in the acquirer as consideration and the acquisition is undertaken as a tax-free reorganization, they can defer any taxes on the capital gain until they sell the new shares.

   U.S. tax laws appear to cause target stockholders to prefer a stock offer to a cash one. This is certainly likely to be the case for a target founder who still has a significant stake in the company. If the company's stock price has appreciated over its life, the founder will face a substantial capital gains tax on a cash offer and will therefore probably prefer to receive stock in the acquiring firm. However, cash and stock offers can be tax-neutral for some groups of stockholders. For example, consider the tax implications for risk arbitrageurs, who take a short-term position in a company that is a takeover candidate in the hope that other bidders will emerge and increase the takeover price. They have no intention of holding stock in the acquirer once the takeover is completed, and will pay ordinary income tax on any short-term trading gain. Cash and stock offers therefore have identical after-tax values for risk arbitrageurs. Similarly, tax-exempt institutions are likely to be indifferent to whether an offer is in cash or stock.

TRANSACTION COSTS AND THE FORM OF FINANCING.   Transaction costs are another factor related to the form of financing that can be relevant to target stockholders. Transaction costs are incurred when target stockholders sell any stock received as consideration for their shares in the target. These costs will not be faced by target stockholders if the bidder offers them cash. Transaction costs are unlikely to be significant for investors who intend to hold the acquirer's stock following a stock acquisition. However, they may be relevant for investors who intend to sell, such as risk arbitrageurs.

Effect of Form of Financing on Acquiring Stockholders

For acquiring stockholders, the costs and benefits of different financing options usually depend on how the offer affects their firm's capital structure, any information effects associated with different forms of financing, and the accounting methods of recording the acquisition.

CAPITAL STRUCTURE EFFECTS OF FORM OF FINANCING. In acquisitions where debt financing or surplus cash are the primary form of consideration for target shares, the acquisition increases the financial leverage of the acquirer. This increase in leverage may be part of the acquisition strategy, since one way an acquirer can add value to an inefficient firm is to lower its taxes by increasing interest tax shields. However, in many acquisitions an increase in postacquisition leverage is a side effect of the method of financing and not part of a deliberate tax-minimizing strategy. The increase in leverage can then potentially reduce shareholder value for the acquirer by increasing the risk of financial distress.

To assess whether an acquisition leads an acquirer to have too much leverage, financial analysts can assess the acquirer's financial risk following the proposed acquisition by these methods:

- Assessing the pro forma financial risks for the acquirer under the proposed financing plan. Popular measures of financial risk include debt-to-equity and interest-coverage ratios, as well as projections of cash flows available to meet debt repayments. The ratios can be compared to similar performance metrics for the acquiring and target firms' industries. Do postmerger ratios indicate that the firm's probability of financial distress has increased significantly?
- Examining whether there are important off-balance-sheet liabilities for the target and/or acquirer which are not included in the pro forma ratio and cash flow analysis of postacquisition financial risk.
- Determining whether the pro forma assets for the acquirer are largely intangible, and therefore sensitive to financial distress. Measures of intangible assets include such ratios as market to book equity and tangible assets to the market value of equity.

INFORMATION PROBLEMS AND THE FORM OF FINANCING. As we discuss in Chapter 16, information asymmetries between managers and external investors can make managers reluctant to raise equity to finance new projects. Managers' reluctance arises from their fear that investors will interpret the decision as an indication that the firm's stock is overvalued. In the short term, this effect can lead managers to deviate from the firm's long-term optimal mix of debt and equity. As a result, acquirers are likely to prefer to use internal funds or debt to finance an acquisition, since these forms of consideration are less likely to be interpreted negatively by investors.[8]

The information effects imply that firms forced to use stock financing are likely to face a stock price decline when investors learn of the method of financing.[9] From the viewpoint of financial analysts, the financing announcement may therefore provide valuable news about the preacquisition value of the acquirer. However, it should have no implications for analysis of whether the acquisition creates value for acquiring shareholders, since the news reflected in the financing announcement is about the *preacquisition* value of the acquirer and not about the *postacquisition* value of the target to the acquirer.

A second information problem arises if the acquiring management does not have good information about the target. Stock financing then provides a way for acquiring stockholders to share the information risks with target shareholders. If the acquirer finds out after the acquisition that the value of the target is less than previously anticipated, the accompanying decline in the acquirer's equity price will be partially borne by target stockholders who continue to hold the acquirer's stock. In contrast, if the target's shares were acquired in a cash offer, any postacquisition loss would be fully borne by the acquirer's original stockholders. The risk-sharing benefits from using stock financing appears to be widely recognized for acquisitions of private companies, where public information on the target is largely unavailable. In practice, it appears to be considered less important for acquisitions of large public corporations.

FORM OF FINANCING AND POSTACQUISITION ACCOUNTING.   Finally, the form of financing has an effect on the acquirer's financial statements following the acquisition. Two methods of reporting for the acquisition are permitted under U.S. accounting—purchase and pooling of interests.[10]

Under the *purchase method,* the acquirer writes up the assets of the target to their market value, and records the difference between the purchase price and the market value of the target's tangible net assets as goodwill. In the U.S. and most other countries, goodwill is subsequently amortized to earnings over a period of from 5 to 40 years.

The *pooling-of-interests method* of accounting for mergers, which is rarely used outside the U.S., requires acquirers to show the target's assets, liabilities, and equity at their original book values. Thus, no goodwill is recorded, and subsequent earnings need not be reduced by the amortization of goodwill.

An acquirer's decision on a method of financing an acquisition largely determines its method of accounting for the transaction. A number of conditions must be satisfied for an acquirer to use the pooling-of-interests method to account for an acquisition. If these conditions are not satisfied, the acquirer is required to use purchase accounting. The most significant of these conditions are that: (1) the acquirer issues voting common shares (not cash) in exchange for substantially all of the voting common shares (at least 90 percent) of the acquired company; and (2) the acquisition occurs in a single transaction.

Some managers seem to believe that there is a benefit to shareholders from using the pooling-of-interests method for recording an acquisition. They argue that investors use earnings to value a firm's stock. Since the pooling-of-interests method leads to higher earnings than the purchase method by avoiding amortization of goodwill (at least until the asset is fully depleted), pooling must therefore lead to higher stock prices. However, while the two methods do have different earnings implications for the firm, they do not lead to different cash flows. They therefore do not alter the economic value of the firm.[11] Thus, for the financial analyst, the choice of financing largely determines the accounting methods used to prepare an acquirer's pro forma balance sheets and income statements. But these accounting effects are not relevant to the question of whether the acquisition creates value for acquiring stockholders.

Key Analysis Questions

The form of financing has important tax and transaction cost implications for target stockholders. It can also have important capital structure, information, and merger accounting implications for acquirers. From the perspective of the analyst, the effect of any corporate tax benefits from debt financing should already be reflected in the valuation of the target. Information and accounting effects are not relevant to the value of the acquisition. However, the analyst does need to consider whether demands by target stockholders for consideration in cash lead the acquirer to have a postacquisition capital structure which increases the risk of financial distress to a point that is detrimental for stockholders. Thus, part of the analyst's task is to determine how it affects the acquirer's capital structure and its risks of financial distress by asking the following questions:

- What is the leverage for the newly created firm? How does this compare to leverage for comparable firms in the industry?
- What are the projected future cash flows for the merged firm? Are these sufficient to meet the firm's debt commitments? How much of a cushion does the firm have if future cash flows are lower than expected? Is the firm's debt level so high that it is likely to impair its ability to finance profitable future investments if future cash flows are below expectations?
- Does management appear to be excessively concerned about financing the acquisition in a way that ensures the pooling of interests method can be used to account for the acquisition? If so, what are management's motivations? Is the firm failing to take advantage of interest tax shields to merely avoid future goodwill charges?

AT&T's Financing of NCR

AT&T offered NCR's shareholders the right to exchange 100 percent of their shares for AT&T stock, valued at $110 per NCR share, unless AT&T was not satisfied that an all-stock merger could be accounted for as a pooling of interests. In that case, target stockholders would exchange 40 percent of their shares for AT&T stock and 60 percent for cash, where both stock and cash were valued at $110 per share. High and low collars were added to the stock deal to ensure that NCR's stockholders were protected in the event of a decline in AT&T's stock price. In either event the acquisition was to be treated as a tax-free purchase of stock.

AT&T's offer is unusual because it indicates that the firm had a strong preference for having the acquisition accounted for under the pooling-of-interests method. AT&T's managers argued that it was important for the firm to use pooling-of-interests accounting to avoid any goodwill amortization, which would hurt the firm's earnings and stock price. And certainly, goodwill amortization would have hurt earnings: pro forma estimates indicate that 1990 earnings per share for AT&T (including the earnings of NCR) would have been $2.42 under the pooling-of-interests method and only $1.97 under the purchase method. However, it is not so obvious that this earnings decline would have affected the stock price.

In summary, AT&T chose to finance NCR with a 100 percent stock offer, primarily to ensure that it could use pooling-of-interests accounting. Because this is a very conservative approach, the financing of the acquisition does not impose additional financial risks on AT&T's stockholders. However, AT&T's explanation of the offer should raise questions for analysts about whether the form of the offer really maximized value for AT&T's existing shareholders.

ACQUISITION OUTCOME

The final question of interest to the analyst evaluating a potential acquisition is whether it will indeed be completed. If an acquisition has a clear value-based motive, the target is priced appropriately, and its proposed financing does not create unnecessary financial risks for the acquirer, it may still fail because the target receives a higher competing bid or because of opposition from entrenched target management. Therefore, to evaluate the likelihood that an offer will be accepted, the financial analyst has to understand whether there are potential competing bidders who could pay an even higher premium to target stockholders than is currently offered. They also have to consider whether target managers are entrenched and, to protect their jobs, likely to oppose an offer.

Other Potential Acquirers

- If there are other potential bidders for a target, especially ones who place a higher value on the target, there is a strong possibility that the bidder in question will be unsuccessful. Target management and stockholders have an incentive to delay accepting the initial offer to give potential competitors time to also submit a bid. From the perspective of the initial bidder, this means that the offer could potentially reduce stockholder value by the cost of making the offer (including substantial investment banking and legal fees). In practice, a losing bidder can usually recoup these losses, and sometimes even make healthy profits from selling to the successful acquirer any shares it has accumulated in the target.

Key Analysis Questions

The financial analyst can determine whether there are other potential acquirers for a target and how they value the target by asking the following questions:

- Are there other firms that could also implement the initial bidder's acquisition strategy? For example, if this strategy relies on developing benefits from

complementary assets, look for potential bidders who also have assets complementary to the target. If the goal of the acquisition is to replace inefficient
management, what other firms in the target's industry could provide management expertise?
- Who are the acquirer's major competitors? Could any of these firms provide
an even better fit for the target?

Target Management Entrenchment

If target managers are entrenched and fearful for their jobs, it is likely that they will oppose a bidder's offer. Some firms have implemented "golden parachutes" for top managers to counteract their concerns about job security at the time of an offer. Golden
parachutes provide top managers of a target firm with attractive compensation rewards
should the firm get taken over. However, many firms do not have such schemes, and opposition to an offer from entrenched management is a very real possibility.

While the existence of takeover defenses for a target indicates that its management is
likely to fight a bidding firm's offer, defenses have typically not prevented an acquisition
from taking place. Instead, they tend to cause delays, which increase the likelihood that
there will be competing offers made for the target, including offers by friendly parties solicited by target management, called "white knights." Takeover defenses therefore increase
the likelihood that the bidder in question will be outbid for the target, or that it will have to
increase its offer significantly to win a bidding contest. Given these risks, some have argued that acquirers are now less likely to embark on a potentially hostile acquisition.

Key Analysis Questions

To assess whether the target firm's management is entrenched, and therefore likely
to oppose an acquisition, analysts can ask the following questions:

- Does the target firm have takeover defenses designed to protect management? Many such defenses were used during the turbulent 1980s, when hostile acquisitions were at their peak. Some of the most widely adopted include
poison pills, staggered boards, super-majority rules, dual-class recapitaliza-
tions, fair-price provisions, ESOP plans, and changes in firms' states of incorporation to states with more restrictive anti-takeover laws.
- Has the target been a poor performer relative to other firms in its industry? If
so, management's job security is likely to be threatened by a takeover, leading it to oppose any offers.
- Is there a golden parachute plan in place for target management? Golden
parachutes provide attractive compensation for management in the event of a
takeover to deter opposition to a takeover for job security reasons.

Analysis of Outcome of AT&T's Offer for NCR

AT&T had good reason to be concerned about the outcome of an offer for NCR. NCR had rejected AT&T's preliminary friendly offers made to the company before any public announcement, indicating that target management intended to oppose the offer and use whatever anti-takeover measures were at their disposal. NCR followed up this opposition by creating a qualified ESOP and announcing a special dividend of $1 and a $.02 per share regular dividend increase, all intended to prohibit AT&T from using pooling of interests to account for the acquisition. NCR's opposition certainly increased the likelihood that either AT&T would overpay for NCR, or that it would be forced to drop its offer. No competing offers for NCR emerged, probably because the high price offered by AT&T scared off any competitors. The acquisition was finally completed on September 19, 1991, ten months after AT&T's initial offer.

SUMMARY

This chapter summarizes how financial statement data and analysis can be used by financial analysts interested in evaluating whether an acquisition creates value for an acquiring firm's stockholders. Obviously, much of this discussion is also likely to be relevant to other merger participants, including target and acquiring management and their investment banks.

For the external analyst, the first task is to identify the acquirer's acquisition strategy. We discuss a number of strategies. Some of these are consistent with maximizing acquirer value, including acquisitions to: take advantage of economies of scale; improve target management; combine complementary resources; capture tax benefits; provide low-cost financing to financially constrained targets; and increase product-market rents.

However, other strategies appear to benefit managers more than stockholders. For example, some unprofitable acquisitions are made because managers are reluctant to return free cash flows to shareholders, or because managers want to lower the firm's earnings volatility by diversifying into unrelated businesses.

The financial analyst's second task is to assess whether the acquirer is offering a reasonable price for the target. Even if the acquirer's strategy is based on increasing shareholder value, it can overpay for the target. Target stockholders will then be well rewarded but at the expense of acquiring stockholders. We show how the ratio, pro forma, and valuation techniques discussed earlier in the book can all be used to assess the worth of the target to the acquirer.

The method of financing an offer is also relevant to a financial analyst's review of an acquisition proposal. If a proposed acquisition is financed with surplus cash or new debt, it increases the acquirer's financial risk. Financial analysts can use ratio analysis of the acquirer's postacquisition balance sheet and pro forma estimates of cash flow volatility and interest coverage to assess whether demands by target stockholders for consideration in cash lead the acquirer to increase its risk of financial distress.

Finally, the financial analyst is interested in assessing whether a merger is likely to be completed once the initial offer is made, and at what price. This requires the analyst to determine whether there are other potential bidders, and whether target management is entrenched and likely to oppose a bidder's offer.

DISCUSSION QUESTIONS

1. Mary Saxon, a Dutch investment banker, is advising a local client on a potential foreign acquisition in the U.S. Currently, there is a competing cash bid for the target by a U.S. competitor. However, Saxon argues that the target should be worth more to the Dutch client than to the U.S. competitor, since Dutch accounting rules permit the considerable goodwill from the transaction to be written off against owners' equity, thus avoiding any ongoing charges against income. In contrast, U.S. rules require goodwill to be written off over 40 years or less. What would you recommend to the Dutch bidder?

2. During the early 1990s there was a noticeable increase in mergers and acquisitions between firms in different countries (termed cross-border acquisitions). What factors could explain this increase? What special issues can arise in executing a cross-border acquisition and in ultimately meeting your objectives for a successful combination?

3. In the 1980s leveraged buyouts (LBOs) were a popular form of acquisition. Under a leveraged buyout, a buyout group (which frequently includes target management) makes an offer to buy the target firm at a premium over its current price. The buyout group finances much of the acquisition with debt capital, leading the target to become a highly leveraged private company following the acquisition.
   a. What types of firms would make ideal candidates for LBOs? Why?
   b. How might the acquirer add sufficient value to the target to justify a high buyout premium?

4. Kim Silverman, CFO of the First Public Bank Company, notes: "We are fortunate to have a cost of capital of only 10 percent. We want to leverage this advantage by acquiring other banks that have a higher cost of funds. I believe that we can add significant value to these banks by using our lower cost financing." Do you agree with Silverman's analysis? Why or why not?

5. The Boston Tea Company plans to acquire Hi Flavor Soda Co. for $60 per share, a 50 percent premium over current market price. John E. Grey, the CFO of Boston Tea, argues that this valuation can easily be justified, using a price-earnings analysis. "Boston Tea has a price-earnings ratio of 15, and we expect that we will be able to generate long-term earnings for Hi Flavor Soda of $5 per share. This implies that Hi Flavor is worth $75 to us, well below our $60 offer price." Do you agree with this analysis? What are Grey's key assumptions?

6. You have been hired by GS Investment Bank to work in the merger department. The analysis required for all potential acquisitions includes an examination of the target

for any off-balance-sheet assets or liabilities that have to be factored into the valuation. Prepare a checklist for your examination.

7. Company T is currently valued at $50 in the market. A potential acquirer, A, believes that it can add value in two ways: $15 of value can be added through better working capital management, and an additional $10 of value can be generated by making available a unique technology to expand T's new product offerings. In a competitive bidding contest, how much of this additional value will A have to pay out to T's shareholders to emerge as the winner?

8. In 1995 Disney acquired ABC television at a significant premium. Disney's management justified much of this premium by arguing that the acquisition would guarantee access for Disney's programs on ABC's television stations. Evaluate the economic merits of this claim.

9. A leading oil exploration company decides to acquire an Internet company at a 50 percent premium. The acquirer argues that this move creates value for its own stockholders because it can use its excess cash flows from the oil business to help finance growth in the new Internet segment. Evaluate the economic merits of this claim.

10. a. How would the following ratios differ for a company that used the purchase method to account for an acquisition versus the pooling-of-interests method in the year following the acquisition?
    • Return on sales
    • Return on assets
    • Asset turnover
   b. Two years after the acquisition, the company decides that it was a failure and sells the target at a price substantially below its original price but above the original book value. What effect will this transaction have on the earnings of the acquirer in the two cases (purchase versus pooling)?

NOTES

1. In a review of studies of merger returns, Michael Jensen and Richard Ruback, "The Market for Corporate Control: The Scientific Evidence," *Journal of Financial Economics* 11, (April 1983): 5–50, conclude that target shareholders earn positive returns from takeovers, but that acquiring shareholders only break even.

2. Much of our discussion is based on analysis of the acquisition presented by Thomas Lys and Linda Vincent in "An Analysis of the Value Destruction in AT&T's Acquisition of NCR," *Journal of Financial Economics* 39, No. 2–3 (Oct./Nov. 1995): 353–379.

3. Of course, another possibility is for the profitable firm to acquire the unprofitable one. However, in the U.S., the IRS will disallow the use of tax loss carryforwards by an acquirer if it appears that an acquisition was tax-motivated.

4. See Steven Kaplan, "Management Buyouts: Evidence on Taxes as a Source of Value," *Journal of Finance* 44 (1989): 611–632.

5. Krishna Palepu, "Predicting takeover targets: A methodological and empirical analysis," *Journal of Accounting and Economics* 8, No. 1 (March 1986): 3–36.

6. Chapter 2 discusses the pros and cons of corporate diversification, and evidence on its implications for firm performance.

7. See Paul Healy, Krishna Palepu, and Richard Ruback, "Which Mergers Are Profitable—Strategic or Financial?," *Sloan Management Review* 38, No. 4 (Summer 1997): 45–58.

8. See Stewart Myers and Nicholas Majluf, "Corporate Financing and Investment Decisions When Firms Have Information That Investors Do Not," *Journal of Financial Economics* (June 1984): 187–221.

9. For evidence see Nicholas Travlos, "Corporate takeover bids, methods of payments, and bidding firms' stock returns," *Journal of Finance* 42 (1987): 943–963.

10. In 1999 the Financial Accounting Standards Board voted to eliminate the use of the pooling of interests method.

11. However, pooling-of-interests may make it more difficult to assess whether an acquisition is generating positive value for the acquiring firm's stockholders, since the acquired assets are not reflected at market values. Managers that make acquisitions that are likely to be unprofitable may therefore prefer to use the pooling method.

Pharmacia & Upjohn will be a powerful new competitor in the global pharmaceutical industry. For both Pharmacia and Upjohn, this merger is a bold strategic move to build a highly competitive company as the worldwide pharmaceutical industry continues to consolidate. The new company will be positioned to attain its goals of revenue growth above the industry average and operating margins exceeding 25% by 1998.

> Jan Ekberg, President and CEO of Pharmacia
> Proposed Chairman of Pharmacia & Upjohn

This is a merger that truly constitutes far more than the sum of the parts. The new company will be able to take full advantage of uniquely complementary geographic reach, product portfolio, pipeline and R&D strengths. As a result of the merger, Pharmacia & Upjohn will have extensive financial and operating resources, market scope and earnings potential. Consequently, we fully expect the new company to achieve additional growth in expected 1996 EPS as well as acceleration of future earnings growth. Above all, Pharmacia & Upjohn is expected to generate significantly enhanced value for shareholders.

> John L. Zabriskie, Ph.D., Chairman and CEO of Upjohn
> Proposed President and CEO of Pharmacia & Upjohn

On August 20, 1995, The Upjohn Company and Pharmacia AB, two pharmaceutical companies incorporated in the U.S. and Sweden, respectively, announced that they were forming a "merger of equals." With combined sales of nearly $7 billion, the new company would be the ninth largest pharmaceutical company in the world. Management and major shareholders alike seemed excited by the deal. William U. Parfet, great-grandson of founder W. E. Upjohn and a company director, stated, "We recognize we're being distanced from our heritage, and that tugs at you, but this is absolutely the right thing for Upjohn to do in today's environment, and John Zabriskie is really the key."[1]

THE UPJOHN COMPANY

The Upjohn Company, founded in 1886, developed, manufactured, and sold prescription and nonprescription pharmaceuticals (68 percent of sales), animal health products (10

Research Associate James Weber prepared this case under the supervision of Professors Amy Patricia Hutton and Krishna Palepu as the basis for class discussion rather than to illustrate either effective or ineffective handling of an administrative situation. Copyright © 1996 by the President and Fellows of Harvard College. Harvard Business School case 9-197-034.

1. Keith Naughton and Heidi Dawley, "Upjohn Finally Makes It to The Big Leagues," Business Week, September 4, 1995.

percent), and bulk pharmaceutical chemicals and other products (22 percent). Upjohn maintained headquarters in Kalamazoo, Michigan, and owned research, manufacturing, and distribution facilities throughout the world. In 1994 Upjohn had sales of $3.3 billion of which 59 percent were U.S. sales, 20 percent European, 13 percent Japanese and Pacific Rim, and 8 percent in other countries. Sales were down 2 percent from the previous year while net income, at $491 million, was up 25 percent. Upjohn employed 16,900 worldwide.[2]

The proposed merger with Pharmacia was an attempt by Upjohn to address a number of the strategic problems it faced. While some of these problems affected the industry as a whole, others were specific to Upjohn. For the industry, the increasing strength of cost-conscious buyers such as hospital networks, Health Maintenance Organizations (HMOs), and insurers, was putting downward pressure on pharmaceutical companies' margins. In an effort to maintain margins, drug companies were consolidating in order to reduce costs and obtain economies of scale. For Upjohn, a number of its patents had expired on key products resulting in stiff competition from lower priced generic drugs. Upjohn had fewer products than it would have liked in its product development pipeline with which to replace these older drugs. Further, Upjohn was weak in foreign sales, a market segment that made up approximately two-thirds of the world market for pharmaceutical products. Finally, Upjohn's stock price had been stagnant over the six months preceding the merger announcement and the company was rumored to be a potential takeover target.

THE PHARMACEUTICAL INDUSTRY

The worldwide prescription drug market was estimated at $252 billion in 1994 and was expected to grow by 6 percent in 1995. North America was the largest segment ($79 billion), followed by Europe ($77 billion) and Japan ($49 billion). Even with the ongoing consolidation among pharmaceutical firms, the industry was still highly fragmented with many competitors. Glaxo Wellcome, the largest firm in the industry in mid-1995, had pharmaceutical sales of just under $12 billion, while the top ten firms in pharmaceutical sales had a 28 percent market share and the top 50 firms had just over 60 percent.[3] Further, in an industry where companies needed large markets to cover high development costs, the sales of many companies were concentrated in one or two markets.

Prior to the late 1980s, drug companies had greater power in relation to drug buyers. Drug company salespeople contacted doctors directly and sold them on the superior benefits of their company's products. Doctors were largely free to prescribe medications of their choosing and they frequently chose the branded products that were developed by the major pharmaceutical companies and with which they were most familiar. Payers—

---

2. *The Upjohn Company 1994 Annual Report.*

3. Medical & Healthcare Marketplace Guide, *11th Edition, p. 55.*

mostly insurance companies, employers, and governments—had little choice other than to pay for what doctors prescribed. In this market, drug companies continuously raised prices on their products and most companies were able to increase earnings over 10 percent yearly. Some observers felt that this high historical profitability in the industry had led to significant excess capacity in production and bloated administration staffing.

Since the late 1980s, significant change had been occurring in the pharmaceutical industry. Most of this change was a direct result of pressures from buyers to reduce the costs of health care. The high prices charged by the pharmaceutical companies for prescription drugs made them an obvious target. Buyers of pharmaceutical products were consolidating into increasingly larger entities and gaining power relative to suppliers. Drug purchasing decisions were increasingly being made by plan administrators and pharmaceutical benefit management (PBM) firms, with a strong eye on cost, rather than by individual doctors.

PBM companies served as intermediaries between pharmaceutical companies and large drug purchasers such as HMOs, hospital networks, and insurance companies. Both PBMs and individual plan administrators were able to negotiate lower prices through bulk purchases. These bulk purchases were made possible by the large numbers of patients they were buying for, and by the ability to limit the number of different drugs purchased by requiring doctors to prescribe only drugs that appeared on approved lists called formularies. The large drug buyers also sought to limit the number of suppliers they purchased from by purchasing from large suppliers that could provide many different drug products.

Generic Drugs and Patents

The new pharmaceutical environment opened the door for producers of generic drugs. Under the old system, doctors and patients tended to select well-known branded drugs even when generic drugs were available. By the mid-1990s, drug buyers were requiring the use of lower cost drugs wherever possible and doctors were required to justify their use of higher cost drugs whenever lower cost alternatives were available. Further, doctors working for HMOs and other medical plans often had financial incentives to prescribe generic products.

The development and use of generic drugs became possible once patent protection had expired on the branded product that had opened the market. While some branded products seemed to have unreasonably high prices, the pharmaceutical companies that developed the branded products argued that the high cost of R&D and the long regulatory approval process justified such prices. Bringing a new drug to the market could take fifteen years and cost between $350 million and $600 million.[4] Generic producers did not have these costs, nor did they have the advertising expenditures associated with branded

....
4. *Eric Reguly,* Drug Firms Take the Merger Treatment to Stay Healthy, *Times Newspapers Limited, August 22, 1995.*

drugs; thus, generic drugs typically were priced at one-half the price of their branded equivalents. In 1995 generic drug makers had a 40 percent U.S. market share, up from 23 percent in 1980. By the late 1990s, it was estimated that generics would control two-thirds of the market.[5] In an effort to limit lost sales, some branded drug producers, including Upjohn, had begun selling generic drugs that copied their own branded products.

Drugs coming off patent were a significant issue in the pharmaceutical industry. Between 1996 and 2000, drugs generating $15 billion in sales would lose patent protection and become open for generic competition.[6] The concern for the branded producers was that there were few blockbuster drugs, those with expected sales of over $500 million, in the development pipeline to replace the lost sales due to generics. A key reason for this was that the chronic diseases that had yet to be solved, and that affected large numbers of people, were only poorly understood. Thus, breakthrough drugs for chronic diseases were not expected until perhaps early in the next century. There were few diseases such as diabetes where an individual could be successfully treated by pharmaceuticals for a lifetime. The difficulty in developing new drugs had led to industry R&D expenditures of nearly 19 percent of sales in 1994, up from less than 16 percent in 1990.[7]

The Industry's Response to the New Environment

In the face of the economic changes occurring in the industry, pharmaceutical companies began making significant changes in their operations, strategies, and organizations. The first step that many companies took was to rationalize their operations in search of efficiency gains. Downsizing, restructuring, and the closing of plants had been the order of the day. Further, companies were selling off their nonpharmaceutical businesses to focus on their core activities. The use of a "disease management" approach to health care was growing. Disease management involved focusing on all facets of an illness from prevention to diagnostics and treatment in an effort to offer a complete care package that was of higher quality and lower cost than a piecemeal approach. For drug companies, this often meant joint ventures with medical device companies and even medical care providers.

The most dramatic change in the industry, however, was the ongoing consolidation. Nearly $70 billion in mergers and acquisitions occurred in the two years prior to the Upjohn-Pharmacia announcement. Further, while the top ten companies had less than a 30 percent market share in 1995, they were expected to have a near 50 percent market share by the turn of the century. Between 1993 and 1994, the consolidation trend, along with company downsizing efforts, had led to the elimination of over 60,000 jobs in the industry worldwide.[8]

5. Health Care Products & Services, *Standard & Poor's Industry Surveys, 1995, p. 26.*

6. *Ibid.*

7. *Marketplace Guide, 11th Edition, p. 66.*

8. Health Care Products 1995, *p. 4.*

Pharmaceutical companies were consolidating through both vertical and horizontal integration. The vertical integration was an attempt to move closer to the patients by merging with or acquiring major drug buyers, PBMs, HMOs, and other large networks. By integrating vertically, drug companies were seeking access to patients and inclusion on drug formularies.

The horizontal integration of drug companies was being driven by a number of factors. First, buyer strength was increasing through consolidation in this segment of the market as well. Second, the cost to develop new drugs was rising, making it difficult for many companies to go it alone. Third, pharmaceutical markets were becoming increasingly worldwide as more countries sought to improve their health care systems, and as drug companies looked for larger markets over which to spread their costs. Companies weaker in some markets than in others were seeking to join with companies in a similar situation, but with different markets so that the combined company would be strong in all markets. Fourth, under pressure to reduce costs, drug companies were seeking efficiency gains through economies of scale. And last, companies with weak product development pipelines were looking for new products to sell.

Examples of horizontal integration were both more numerous and larger in size than those of vertical integration. Further, horizontal integration was the more "proven" strategy. However, some analysts believed that vertical integration was the more significant trend for the longer term structure of the industry.

The Industry's Future

Despite the increasing competitive pressures faced by individual companies, the long-term economic factors appeared positive for the industry as a whole. Several of these factors pointed towards a growing industry and the increased use of pharmaceuticals: the population had been aging, particularly in the U.S.; an increasing number of health insurance plans covered prescription drugs; the use of pharmaceutical products tended to be more cost effective than hospitalization; an increasing number of countries were attempting to improve their health care systems; and finally, the pharmaceutical industry was relatively recession proof.

UPJOHN'S POSITION

Upjohn operated in several market segments. Its pharmaceutical product sales were divided into six areas: central nervous system; steroids, anti-inflammatory, and analgesic; reproductive and women's health; critical care, transplant, and cancer; infectious disease; and metabolic. Although primarily in human prescription and nonprescription drugs, Upjohn was the world's ninth largest producer of animal pharmaceuticals. The company also had significant bulk pharmaceutical chemical sales and had spent some $100 million on two new production facilities in 1994. Upjohn's top ten human pharmaceutical products accounted for approximately 56 percent of company sales (see Table A).

The Uphohn Company

The Upjohn Company

Table A Upjohn's 1994 Top Selling Human Pharmaceutical Products[9]

Product	Description	1994 Sales ($ millions)	Percent Increase (Decrease) 1994 over 1993
Xanax	Anti-Anxiety/Panic Disorder	$ 342	(45.2)%
Micronase	Oral Anti-Diabetes	271	(4.2)
Cleocin	Antibiotic	248	6.4
Provera	Sex Hormone	211	2.4
Solu-Medrol	Injectable Steroid	153	7.7
Depo-Provera	Injectable Contraceptive	134	86.1
Ibuprofen	Analgesic, Anti-Inflammatory	129	3.2
Rogaine	Hair Loss Treatment	122	10.9
Ansaid	Anti-Inflammatory	105	(14.6)
Halcion	Hypnotic Sleep Induction	104	(14.0)
Total Top 10		1819	(10.8)
Other Products	Various	1456	11.9
Total All Products		3275	(1.9)

To a certain extent, Upjohn's problems were not unique: the problems it faced were those typical to many companies in the industry. As the world's nineteenth largest pharmaceutical company, Upjohn was a mid-sized company in an industry where success was increasingly characterized by larger companies and by small innovative companies. Middle tier companies such as Upjohn were at a disadvantage to their larger competitors in dealing with major buyers. Upjohn was particularly hard hit by the loss of patent protection on four key drugs and the ensuing generic competition that led to a $400 million decline in sales on these products. For one of these drugs, Xanax, Upjohn's highest selling product, generics were selling at 20 percent of Xanax's price prior to patent expiration. Despite the loss of Xanax sales dollars, Upjohn was able to maintain approximately 80 percent of its Xanax unit volume sales by the introduction of its own generic equivalent. Upjohn was also weak in international sales. This was particularly true in Europe, a market approximately the same size as the U.S. market but where Upjohn had sales of only one-third its U.S. sales. Further, there were significantly better opportunities for sales growth in overseas markets than in the more highly competitive U.S. market.

Another problem faced by Upjohn was a weak product development pipeline. While the company claimed its pipeline was "one of the strongest in Upjohn's history, with ten compounds in late-stage development,"[10] analysts noted that none of these new drugs were expected to be blockbusters. The weak pipeline remained despite Upjohn spending

9. *Pharmacia & Upjohn Merger Prospectus, September 15, 1995; Upjohn's 1994 Annual Report;* and Joseph P. Riccardo and Scott J. Shevick, Analyst Report, The Merger: Upjohn Co., Pharmacia AB, *Bear Stearns & Co. Inc., September 18, 1995.*

10. *The Upjohn Company 1994 Annual Report, p. 4.*

18.5 percent of sales or $607 million on R&D in 1994. On the positive side, 25 percent of 1994 sales were from products introduced since 1992, and between 1990 and 1994, Upjohn had cut in half the time necessary to move a product through its R&D pipeline.

In January 1993, Upjohn hired John Zabriskie as its new CEO. Zabriskie, who arrived at Upjohn after nearly 30 years at Merck, then the industry's largest company, began a number of initiatives aimed at improving Upjohn's performance. These initiatives included cutting costs, particularly in marketing and administration, reducing the workforce by some 1,300 people,[11] selling off non-core activities, such as the Asgrow Seed Company and part interest in a chicken breeding venture, and consolidating sixteen divisions into three—R&D, manufacturing, and marketing. (For more details, see Exhibit 1: Upjohn Company - 1994 Letter to Shareholders and Financial Review.)

THE PHARMACIA MERGER

Given the strategic problems Upjohn faced in the changing pharmaceuticals market, and the general belief that size was an important factor in determining success, the company's announcement of the proposed merger was of little surprise.

Details of the Merger

The proposed merger had Upjohn and Pharmacia executing a tax-free exchange of shares (pooling of interests) to create a new company named Pharmacia & Upjohn, Inc. One Upjohn share would be exchanged for 1.45 shares in the new company, while Pharmacia shares would be exchanged one-for-one. (See Exhibit 2: Abridged Merger Prospectus.) The new company would have 504 million shares outstanding, with 248 million held by Upjohn shareholders and 255 million held by Pharmacia owners. In the new company, Upjohn's Zabriskie would be the President and CEO while Pharmacia's Jan Ekberg would serve as Nonexecutive Chairman. An Upjohn executive would serve as CFO. Pharmacia & Upjohn's board of directors would be formed from an equal number of current Upjohn and Pharmacia board members. Pharmacia & Upjohn would have corporate headquarters in London and operational headquarters in Kalamazoo, Michigan; Stockholm/Uppsala, Sweden; and Milan, Italy. A special meeting of Upjohn stockholders was to be held on October 17, 1995, to vote on the proposed merger. The merger had the unanimous support of Upjohn's board of directors. Exhibit 3 shows data on the stock prices of Upjohn and Pharmacia around the merger announcement.

Pharmacia

Pharmacia was the world's eighteenth largest pharmaceutical company, with 1994 sales of $3.4 billion. Headquartered in Sweden, the firm's predecessor, Procordia AB, was

---

11. *Between 1988 and 1994, Upjohn had eliminated 4,600 jobs.*

The Uphohn Company

part of a state holding company along with a number of unrelated businesses until the late 1980s. Between 1989 and 1993, the company evolved through a series of mergers and acquisitions to become primarily an international health care company focused in pharmaceutical products. During this period, Procordia also divested a significant portion of its lines of branded consumer products and changed its name to Pharmacia. Following the 1993 acquisition of the Italian firm FICE, with its approximately $900 million in sales, Pharmacia sales were 59 percent in Europe, 16 percent in each of North America and Japan, and 9 percent in the rest of the world. Only 8 percent of Pharmacia sales were in their home country. At the end of 1994, Pharmacia employed 18,600 individuals worldwide.

Pharmacia was a market leader in several product areas including cancer treatment, growth hormones, cataract surgery products, intravenous nutrition, allergy diagnostics, smoking cessation, and chemicals for biotechnology R&D. See Table B for information on Pharmacia's top selling products which accounted for 44 percent of company sales.

In an effort to combine the several companies that had formed Pharmacia, and to better meet the increased competition in the pharmaceuticals industry, Pharmacia had undergone significant restructuring between 1993 and 1995. This restructuring included: a consolidation and reduction in the size of the combined sales and marketing organizations; rationalizing production facilities, including a reduction from 52 to 43 plants and the planned reduction in plants to 22 by 1998; the elimination of some 1,300 jobs, mainly from the middle management ranks; and a refocusing of R&D onto fewer projects in fewer areas.

Table B Pharmacia's 1994 Top Selling Human Pharmaceutical Products[12]

Product	Description	1994 Sales ($ millions)	Percent Increase (Decrease) 1994 over 1993
Genotropin	Growth Hormone	$ 335	1.2%
Healon	Cataract Surgery Aid	208	(1.9)
Farmorubicin	Anticancer	191	11.7
Allergy Diagnostics	Blood Tests for Allergies	175	8.7
Adriamycin	Anticancer	140	6.1
Sermion	Senility Disorders	105	(2.8)
Nicorette	Smoking Cessation	105	1.9
Fragmin	Blood Clot Treatments	100	(8.3)
Intralipid	Intravenous Nutrition	88	1.1
Salazopyrin	Inflammatory Bowel Disease	84	9.1
Total Top 10		1531	2.7
Other Products	Various	1921	(3.4)
Total All Products		3452	(0.7)

12. *Pharmacia & Upjohn Merger Prospectus, September 15, 1995; Pharmacia's 1994 Annual Report;* and Joseph P. Riccardo and Scott J. Shevick, Analyst Report, The Merger: Upjohn Co., Pharmacia AB, *Bear Stearns & Co. Inc., September 18, 1995.*

Pharmacia's business strategy was somewhat different than the typical pharmaceutical company. The industry in general pursued the broad general practitioner market segment while Pharmacia focused on the smaller segment of hospitals and specialists. Pharmacia had no blockbuster drugs in its product development pipeline, partly as a result of this niche-market strategy, but rather relied on a larger number of products with smaller potential sales. Further, at least one analyst believed that Pharmacia stock was somewhat undervalued because of the lack of a high-profile blockbuster drug in the pipeline.[13]

The Combined Companies

The August 20 merger announcement described the combined company as follows:

> The company, named Pharmacia & Upjohn, Inc., would have had combined 1994 sales of nearly $7 billion, with prescription pharmaceutical sales placing it in the top ten in the worldwide industry. Annual research and development expenditures will exceed $1 billion, also in the top tier of the pharmaceutical industry. The complementary geographical strengths of the two companies will give Pharmacia & Upjohn sales ranking among the top five pharmaceutical companies in Europe, top 15 in North America, and top 20 in Japan (also among the top two or three non-Japanese companies in Japan). Pharmacia & Upjohn will have a broad product portfolio with sales exceeding $500 million in six key therapeutic areas. Sales growth in Pharmacia & Upjohn, led by 28 product introduction and line extensions in the next three years and deeper penetration of existing markets, is expected to exceed industry averages. Projected annual operating cost synergies of over $500 million, more than 85% of which are expected to be in effect by the end of 1996, are anticipated to further contribute to increased earnings and a strong balance sheet as well as provide flexibility to take advantage of further growth opportunities.

According to company management, the combination of Upjohn and Pharmacia would create a company better prepared to compete in the changing environment of the pharmaceuticals industry. Specifically, a merger with Pharmacia would strengthen Upjohn in terms of market presence, R&D, geographic reach, product portfolio, cost synergies, financial position and growth, and provide the management experience necessary to succeed. (See Exhibit 3 for the stock market reaction to the merger announcement.)

MARKET PRESENCE.   Pharmacia & Upjohn would become the world's ninth largest pharmaceutical company. In a world increasingly dominated by large buyers looking to deal with fewer suppliers, the general belief in the industry was "bigger is better."

....

13. *Analysts Report*, Pharmacia, *Auerbach Grayson & Company*, July 7, 1995.

The Uphohn Company

R&D.   The increasing cost of developing new pharmaceutical products was making it more difficult for smaller companies. Some analysts believed that $1 billion in yearly R&D expenditures was becoming a minimum threshold for continued long-term success. Upjohn alone had been spending above the industry average for R&D, but was still significantly short of this threshold. The addition of Pharmacia would enable Upjohn to reach this level. Further, although Pharmacia's pipeline was not in the industry's top tier and did not contain potential blockbusters, it did have several products expected to begin making moderate contributions to sales growth in the 1995 to 1997 period, and had several more potential products further back in the pipeline.

GEOGRAPHIC REACH.   Upjohn alone was weak in the world's second and third largest markets, Europe and Japan. While some drugs were tailored to specific markets, most could be used worldwide, and particularly in the top three markets. Thus, as the cost of developing drugs rose, it became increasingly important to be able to access the world market. Improving Upjohn's position outside of the U.S. would require market specific drugs, but more important it required a developed sales and marketing organization with good contacts among the many buyers in these markets. Pharmacia provided both, particularly since Europe, which was Upjohn's weakness, was Pharmacia's strongest market.

PRODUCT PORTFOLIO.   One of the key benefits of the merger for Upjohn was the addition of Pharmacia's products. The combined companies would have sales of over $500 million in each of six areas. In five of Upjohn's top selling product areas (central nervous system; reproductive and women's health; critical care, transplant, and cancer; infectious disease; and metabolics) Pharmacia added strong products of their own, potential products to be introduced within a few years, or better access to key markets. Further, the addition of Pharmacia's over-the-counter products, such as Nicorette and Nicotrol for smoking cessation, the laxative Microlax, and various dietary supplements, to Upjohn's Motrin IB pain reliever, Kaopectate for diarrhea, Dramamine for motion sickness, and Unicap vitamins, may give this area a critical mass that it lacked at both companies individually. Also, Pharmacia added additional experience in moving products from being prescription drugs to over-the-counter products. This could prove useful as Upjohn attempted to make this switch with several of their products in various world markets.

COST SYNERGIES.   The combined companies had announced $500 million in expected operating cost synergies as a result of the merger with some 85 percent of the reductions in place by the end of 1996. One analyst estimated that one-half of the savings would come from Selling, General, and Administrative expenses and one-quarter each from manufacturing expenses and R&D expenses.[14] A part of these savings was to be the reduction of over 4,000 jobs.

....

14. Joseph P. Riccardo and Scott J. Shevick, *Analyst Report*, The Merger: Upjohn Co., Pharmacia AB, *Bear Stearns & Co. Inc.*, September 18, 1995.

FINANCIAL POSITION.   The combined company would have a strong balance sheet. Because this was a pooling of interests merger financed by stock, there would be no acquisition-related interest costs or amortization of goodwill. Further, because it was one of the least leveraged companies in the industry, Pharmacia & Upjohn would be able to pursue future growth opportunities without severe financial constraints.

GROWTH.   In addition to growth by acquisition, management expected the addition of Pharmacia would increase the growth of the existing company. Although in mid-1995 Pharmacia was growing faster than Upjohn, both companies were growing at below industry average rates. However, management believed that because Pharmacia's sales organization was strong where Upjohn's was weak, the combined companies would grow faster than either would separately—even faster than the industry average.

MANAGEMENT EXPERIENCE.   While Upjohn had management skilled in rationalizing operations, Pharmacia management brought critical skills in terms of integrating merged or acquired companies, having done so several times since the late 1980s. In particular, with the 1993 acquisition of FICE, Pharmacia had to restructure the company and combine and reduce its manufacturing, sales, and marketing organizations, as would be necessary with the proposed merger. The potential of the new company could not fully be realized unless it was successful in combining different operations and cultures to create effective and efficient functional units.

The Decision

As the date of the shareholders meeting approached, Upjohn's shareholders were trying to decide whether to approve the proposed merger with Pharmacia. Many observers saw the merger as a significant step toward addressing Upjohn's strategic problems, and in the days following the announcement several investment firms raised their recommendations on Upjohn stock from neutral to outperform. However, it was not clear that the proposed deal was the best one available for the shareholders. Difficult questions remained to be answered.

A merger with Pharmacia appeared to make Upjohn a top tier firm. However, merging two companies of this size from different countries and with different cultures might be more complex than management believed. Was $500 million in cost synergies obtainable by the merger of two companies that had already achieved significant improvements in margins through rationalization efforts over the preceding few years? Even though Pharmacia's sales force was strong in Europe and Japan, there were questions about whether that sales force had the right contacts to achieve the sales increase that Upjohn was expecting. Further, Upjohn's product development pipeline had no blockbuster products and the addition of Pharmacia did not solve this problem. Were blockbuster drugs necessary for success, or was a relatively large number of lower potential products sufficient? Was Pharmacia the right partner with which to merge? Might

The Uphohn Company

Upjohn be better off acquiring rather than merging? Or perhaps shareholders would receive a higher premium by having Upjohn be acquired by some other firm. Finally, assuming Pharmacia was a good merger partner, was the stock exchange ratio a fair one for shareholders?

These questions were complicated by the fact that this might very well be an interim step for Upjohn if they hoped to remain a top tier player in the industry. The proposed merger would make Pharmacia & Upjohn a top ten company in 1995, but they might not be able to hold that position because other top companies were likely to merge and/or had potential blockbuster drugs in their pipelines.

EXHIBIT 1

Upjohn Company - 1994 Letter to Shareholders of Financial Review

TO OUR SHAREHOLDERS:

In 1994, The Upjohn Company sharpened its focus and directed its resources toward a long-range strategy for growth. We began re-examining everything we do to find ways to do things better. We sold non-core businesses and initiated the re-engineering of our supply (manufacturing), sales and marketing and research and development operations. We redirected our sales and marketing efforts to exploit growth opportunities around the world. We continued to concentrate our research and development on major unmet medical needs. Through these key initiatives, we have strengthened our prospects for increasing the company's long-term performance and value.

We pursued these initiatives during one of the most challenging years in our company's history, balancing our efforts to establish long-term programs and priorities and the need to achieve a respectable financial performance today. Our sales for 1994 reached $3.3 billion, slightly below 1993 levels. Net earnings were $491 million in 1994, compared to $392 million in 1993. Earnings from continuing operations (before restructuring and unusual items and the cumulative effect of accounting changes) were $489 million, compared to $575 million in 1993. These results met our goal and exceeded external expectations.

Four of our largest-selling products—XANAX, HALCION, MICRONASE and ANSAID—lost U.S. patent protection, resulting in a $400 million decline in sales from intense generic competition. We offset substantially all of this loss in revenue with new-product sales, strong growth in international markets and a generics effort of our own. Our generics strategy helped us retain 83 percent of the dispensed new prescriptions for XANAX and alprazolam in the U.S. anti-anxiety market in 1994. While this competition will continue, we have a unique array of products in our pipeline aimed at penetrating new, specialized markets.

As we strengthen our product portfolio, we are rationalizing and consolidating our manufacturing sites

worldwide to reduce excess capacity and operating costs in the years ahead. We also sold Asgrow Seed Company and our chicken-breeding joint venture, enabling us to focus on our core human and animal health pharmaceutical businesses. Our re-engineering and cost-containment efforts, including work-force reductions, contributed $75 million to operating earnings in 1994.

We are accelerating growth of our international business, which now contributes 44 percent of our total sales. We received 199 international product registrations in 1994. A joint venture in China, a growing presence in Central and Eastern Europe, and a return to Argentina and Brazil positions Upjohn to take maximum advantage of some of the world's fastest-growing markets.

We restructured our U.S. pharmaceutical sales and marketing operations to focus on integrated health care systems, HMOs, business coalitions, insurance providers and other emerging large customers in medical specialty areas. We formed Greenstone Healthcare Solutions to add the dimension of comprehensive disease management and analysis services to our traditional role of researcher, manufacturer and marketer of health care products.

Of course, the key to our company's long-term performance remains research and development. Our 1994 investment in R&D was $607 million, or 18.5 percent of sales, a rate above the industry average. This investment, along with a relentless discovery focus and accelerated development pace, comprises our commitment to create new products with high value and line extensions that maximize the value of our existing products.

Our current R&D pipeline is one of the strongest in Upjohn's history, with 10 compounds in late-stage development. We expect to file 10 New Drug Applications in the U.S. between 1994 and 1996. Over the last five years, we have reduced by more than 50 percent the time it takes to move a product through the R&D pipeline. Our R&D strategy is sharply focused, concentrating on 30 high-potential projects.

The Upjohn Company

The Uphohn Company

We are seeking unique products targeted at conditions for which adequate treatment is unavailable. Our pipeline includes promising compounds in late-stage development for cancer, certain types of stroke, head and spinal cord injuries and AIDS.

Upjohn's plan for dramatically improving its performance in the short-term and eventually moving into an industry leadership position is clear. By controlling costs and re-engineering our processes, we are finding better, more efficient ways to operate our business. By focusing on our customers and taking advantage of global opportunities in emerging markets, we are effectively adapting to the changing marketplace. By targeting our R&D efforts on major unmet medical needs and accelerating product development on a global scale, we are creating opportunities for the decades ahead. We are a company on the move. We are confident that these strategic initiatives in every area of the company have positioned us to take advantage of future opportunities.

I would like to thank our 16,900 employees worldwide for their hard work and dedication. Together, we demonstrated in 1994 what our employees can do when we believe in ourselves. I am proud of what our employees have accomplished and look forward to working with them to achieve our vision for growth in the years ahead.

John L. Zabriskie, Ph.D.
Chairman of the Board and
Chief Executive Officer

March 3, 1995

OVERVIEW OF CONSOLIDATED RESULTS

Dollars in millions, except per-share data	1994	% Change	1993	% Change	1992
Total revenue	$3,344.5	(1%)	$3,380.5	3%	$3,284.7
Operating income	599.4	30	459.5	(31)	662.7
Earnings from continuing operations before income taxes and minority equity	643.3	34	480.0	(29)	671.9
Earnings from continuing operations	489.1	23	396.4	(25)	527.0
Net earnings	490.8	25	392.4	21	324.3
Net earnings per common share:					
Primary	$ 2.76	27	$ 2.18	22	$ 1.78
Fully diluted	$ 2.68	26	$ 2.13	22	$ 1.74

When comparing year-to-year earnings, accounting changes and restructuring recorded in each of the prior two years should be considered. In 1993, the company made two accounting changes: the adoption of calendar-year reporting for subsidiaries formerly reporting on a fiscal year and the adoption of Statement of Financial Accounting Standards (SFAS) No. 112 relating to postemployement benefits. The cumulative effect of these changes reduced 1993 net earnings by $18.9 million ($.11 per share). In 1992, the company adopted SFAS No. 106 relating to the postretirement benefit costs other than pensions and SFAS No. 109 relating to accounting for income taxes. The cumulative effect of these accounting changes reduced net earnings by $223 million ($1.26 per share).

In 1993, the company recorded restructuring charges that reduced operating income by $209 million ($155 million, or $.89 per share after tax), primarily associated with a worldwide work-force reduction, the write-down of certain assets and the reduction of excess manufacturing capacity. In 1992, restructuring charges of $22 million ($13.4 million, or $.08 per share after tax) were made to reflect the cost of a special voluntary early retirement program.

Several actions were taken to increase the company's focus on its core pharmaceutical business, including the 1994 divestitures of the Asgrow Seed Company and the company's interest in a chicken-breeding joint venture and the 1993 divestiture of Asgrow Florida Company. Both the sales of the Asgrow Seed Company and Asgrow Florida Company have been reported as discontinued operations. Accordingly, certain prior-period financial data have been restated to reflect only the continuing operations of the company.

With the sale of three agricultural segment operations identified above, the company has elected to report its business operations as a single industry segment—Pharmaceutical Products. This industry designation more accurately reflects the ongoing operations of the company. Prior-year data presented in this review also reflect the single Pharmaceutical Products industry segment.

Product Sales

The table below provides a year-to-year comparison of consolidated net sales by major pharmaceutical product group[15]:

dated sales for 1994 were down as the result of a 3 percent decline in price, offset in part by a 1 percent benefit from foreign exchange. Volume was unchanged.

The current year decline in worldwide sales of central nervous system agents was the result of intense generic competition against XANAX, the anti-anxiety agent, which lost U.S. patent protection in October 1993. The U.S. decline in sales of XANAX was offset somewhat by sales of the company's generic anti-anxiety agent alprazolam. In international markets, XANAX continued to record good growth. Sales of HALCION Tablets (triazolam), the sleep inducing agents, were also down in the U.S. largely due to the loss of U.S. patent protection in October 1993. Sales of HALCION in international markets were up in 1994, reversing the trend of decline encountered over the past few years. The decline in sales of central nervous system agents is expected to continue in 1995. The 1993 decrease from 1992 sales levels also resulted from the loss of U.S. patent protections, offset somewhat by the launch of generic versions of XANAX and HALCION.

Dollars in millions	1994	% Change	1993	% Change	1992
Central nervous system	$ 455.3	(39%)	$ 749.7	(4%)	$ 783.3
Steroids, anti-inflammatory and analgesic	413.4	2	406.5	(4)	422.1
Reproductive and women's health	511.1	41	362.5	24	292.6
Critical care, transplant and cancer	412.1	8	383.1	11	344.3
Infectious disease	439.0	11	394.0	14	346.4
Animal health	336.2	1	332.6	4	320.7
Other products and materials	707.9	(1)	711.6	(5)	746.8
Consolidated net sales	$3,275.0	(2)	3,340.0	3	$3,256.2

Consolidated domestic sales of pharmaceutical products in 1994 decreased 10 percent to $1,847 million from $2,046 million in 1993, and compared to $2,003 million in 1992. Domestic sales in 1994 were 56 percent of total consolidated sales, down from 61 and 62 percent in 1993 and 1992, respectively. International sales in 1994 were $1,428 million, up 10 percent from $1,294 million in 1993 and compared to $1,253 million in 1992. Consoli-

15. Prior-year data have been conformed to current year product group classification.

The Upjohn Company

The Uphohn Company

The 1994 growth in steroids, anti-inflammatory and analgesic product group was let by MOTRIN IB, the over-the-counter nonsteroidal analgesic agent, which continued to perform well in a very competitive market. This performance resulted in part from a 1993 agreement that provided access to new-product technology and product-line extensions. This and other products sales gains offset the decline in U.S. sales of ANSAID Tablets (flurbiprofen), which resulted from generic competition encountered in late 1994. U.S. patent protection for ANSAID was lost in February 1993.

Sales of reproductive and women's health products recorded strong, benefiting from the addition of OGEN, the estrogen replacement therapy acquired in late 1993. Sales of DEPO-PROVERA, the injectable contraceptive, continued to record strong increases in both U.S. and international markets. Combined worldwide sales of PROVERA Products (medroxy-progesterone), the progestational agents, were up for the year in spite of a moderate decline in the U.S. due to increasing generic competition. CAVERJECT, for erectile dysfunction, was approved for sale in 12 countries in 1994 and also contributed to sales.

International sales of SOLU-MEDROL, the injectable steroid, and other MEDROL Products led the growth in the critical care, transplant and cancer product group. Sales of ATGAM, the immunosuppressant, were up slightly for the year. In 1994, the company completed a series of agreements with Yakult Honsha Co. Ltd. for the rights to develop and market the anti-cancer compound irinotecan for several indications in the U.S., Canada, and Latin America. Clinical development of this compound is currently in process.

VANTIN, the broad-spectrum oral antibiotic sold primarily in the U.S., led the growth in the infectious disease product group. Sales of CLEOCIN (DALACIN in international markets), the family of antibiotic products, demonstrated good growth in international markets but declined in the U.S. Sales of CLEOCIN T Products (clindamycin topical) were down for the year due to U.S. generic competition.

In the animal health product group, PIRSUE, introduced late in 1993 for the treatment of mastitis, and LUTALYSE, the fertility-control agent, both provided 1994 sales growth. Sales of MGA, the feed additive, were flat. Sales of NAXCEL (EXCENEL in international markets), the antibiotic, were up in international markets and down slightly in the U.S. due to a lower-than-average cattle population. Sales of lincomycin and companion animal products were down in 1994.

In other products and materials category, GLYNASE Press Tab, the oral anti-diabetes agent, continued to record good growth in the U.S. Sales of MICRONASE Tablets (glyburide), the oral anti-diabetes agents, were down significantly from 1993 levels as a result of the loss of U.S. market exclusivity in the second quarter of 1994. While the company will continue to sell its generic glyburide to minimize the effect of third-party generic competition, it is anticipated that combined sales of MICRONASE and glyburide will decline in 1995. Sales of ROGAINE, the treatment for hair loss, were up for the year. The consumer products CORTAID, the anti-itch medication; DOXIDAN and SURFAK, the treatments for constipation; and DRAMAMINE, the treatment for motion sickness, all demonstrated good growth, while sales of KAOPECTATE, the treatment for diarrhea, were down for the year.

Other Operating Revenue

Operating income for 1994 benefited from marketing alliance agreements with Burroughs-Wellcome Co. for the promotion of their product ZOVIRAX, and with Hoechst-Roussel Pharmaceuticals Inc. (HRPI) to market and detail their product ALTACE. The agreement with Burroughs-Wellcome expires at the end of 1995. An agreement has been reached with HRPI to sell the company's rights relating to ALTACE effective January 1, 1995.

Cost and Expenses

Consolidated operating expenses, stated as a percent of sales, were as follows:

	1994	1993	1992
Cost of products sold	25.7%	23.5%	23.2%
Research and development	18.5	18.3	17.0
Marketing and administrative	39.5	39.4	39.7
Restructuring		6.3	0.7
Operating income	18.3	13.8	20.4

The rise in 1994 cost of products sold compared to that of the prior two years is the result of a change in product mix, which is primarily due to U.S. generic competition encountered with the major products identified previously. Compared to the products that lost patent protection, the company's generic equivalents and other products have lower gross margins. The decline is also due to a higher percentage of total worldwide pharmaceutical product sales in international markets where the company's products generally carry lower gross margins.

Expenditures for research and development in 1994 were up slightly as a percent of sales from 1993 due primarily to the timing of expenses related to large clinical programs. Both 1994 and 1993 research and development expenditures are significantly higher than in 1992 due to the continuing costs associated with accelerated development of FREEDOX IV Solution (tirilazad mesylate) and other compounds.

In December 1994, further enrollment in the North American clinical trial of FREEDOX for severe to moderate head injury was suspended pending further analysis of an unexplained difference in mortality rates. At the time of suspension, enrollment in this trial was 98 percent complete. The results were unexpected because a fully-enrolled study in Europe showed no signs of the effects encountered in the North American trial. The company will continue to medically evaluate patients in both the North American and European trials for six months following treatment. The data from both trials will be analyzed to assess the therapeutic benefit of FREEDOX in the treatment of severe to moderate head injury and to determine the reason for the difference in mortality encountered in the North American trial. Analysis of the results of other clinical trials of FREEDOX for subarachnoid hemorrhage, spinal cord injury and stroke has not identified any safety concerns and these trials will continue.

Marketing and administrative expense as a percent of sales in 1994 was comparable to both 1993 and 1992. Savings from the 1993 and 1992 restructurings realized in this expense category were offset by increases in other costs related to various marketing programs and by other expenses. A portion of the increased costs in 1994 resulted from new-product marketing expenses related to LUVOX, the treatment

for obsessive-compulsive disorder, which will be sold in the U.S. LUVOX is a product of Solvay Pharmaceuticals Inc. Unfavorable foreign exchange comparisons in certain international markets also added to this expense category in 1994.

The restructuring plan announced in October 1993 was in the process of being implemented during 1994. At the beginning of 1994, approximately 400 employees had left the company under the 1993 restructuring, while at the end of 1994 that number had increased to approximately 1,100. Certain elements of the 1993 plan are still in the process of implementation. All aspects of the 1992 plan had been implemented by the end of 1993. The gross combined benefit to 1995 earnings from the 1992 and 1993 restructurings is expected to be approximately $120 million. The benefit is expected to increase moderately after 1995 when all aspects of the 1993 restructuring plan are fully implemented.

Earnings before taxes and minority equity from the company's operation in Europe of $44 million were up significantly in 1994 from a loss of $39 million and earnings of $11 million in 1993 and 1992, respectively. This improvement is the result of increased sales volume, a net favorable effect from exchange and savings from expense reductions. The 1993 European measure was depressed largely due to unfavorable exchange and the costs of restructuring. Sales increased in Japan largely as the result of favorable exchange, which was partially offset by continuing price erosion in that market. Restructuring did not have a significant adverse effect on earnings in the Japan and Pacific geographic area in 1993. In other international markets, increases in sales volume, which were offset somewhat by exchange, and expense savings led to the significant increase in earnings before taxes from 1993 levels. The cost of restructuring reduced earnings in other international markets in 1993.

Nonoperating Income and Expense

The favorable interest income to interest expense relationships have increased in each of the years 1992 through 1994. Nonoperating income in 1994 also benefited from the favorable resolution of a coverage dispute with an insurance carrier and the gain on the sale of a joint venture. The 1993 measure includes a nonoperating gain on the sale of a cough/cold medicine trademark. There were no such gains in 1992.

Income Taxes

The effective tax rate for 1994 was 24 percent, compared to 17.5 percent and 21.7 percent in 1993 and 1992, respectively. When the tax benefits related to restructuring are excluded, the 1993 rate would have been 22 percent. The increase in 1994 is the result of a higher proportion of earnings from international operations, which are taxed at relatively higher rates, and a lower proportion of total earnings from operations in Puerto Rico. The major products encountering U.S. generic competition are manufactured in Puerto Rico.

The Omnibus Budget Reconciliation Act of 1993 will have a significant impact on the company's net earnings beginning in 1995. The Act ultimately reduces tax benefits from operations in Puerto Rico under Section 936 of the Internal Revenue Code by 60 percent. The change had little effect on the tax rate for 1994.

SFAS No. 109 was adopted effective January 1, 1992. The cumulative effect of this accounting change was a favorable adjustment to 1992 net earnings of $13 million, resulting primarily from adjusting deferred tax balances to reflect current tax rates.

Financial Condition

	1994	1993	1992
Working capital (millions)	$1,011	$678	$582
Current ratio	1.9	1.7	1.5
Debt to total capitalization	26.0%	28.1%	30.3%
Return on average equity- continuing operations before accounting changes	21.9%	19.3%	26.2%

The significant increase in working capital and the corresponding improvement in the current ratio were largely the result of the year-end 1994 receipt of the proceeds from the sale of the Asgrow Seed Company which were temporarily invested in cash equivalents. Also contributing to the improvement in these measures was the increase in short-term investments, which were classified on the balance sheet as other current assets. The company recently

announced a common stock repurchase program, to be completed in 1995, which will utilize approximately $300 million. The working capital increase and improvement in the current ratio realized at the end of 1993 was because the proceeds of medium-term notes had been used during the year to reduce outstanding commercial paper.

The 1994 ratio of debt to total capitalization benefited from the increase in total shareholders' equity when compared to a consistent level of year-to-year total borrowing. The improvement in 1993 when compared to 1992, resulted from lower total debt.

The 1994 improvement in return on average equity before accounting changes was due to the favorable earnings comparison. Net earnings in 1993 and 1992 were reduced by the after-tax expense associated with restructuring, totaling $154.6 and $13.4 million, respectively. Excluding the cost of restructurings, return on average equity would have been 27.5 percent in 1993 and 27.9 percent in 1992.

Net cash provided by operations was $710 million in 1994 compared to $780 million and $597 million in 1993 and 1992, respectively. Significant adjustments were made to 1993 cash provided by net earnings to reflect the non-cash effects of restructuring charges. Spending against the related restructuring reserves reduced the 1994 measure by $72 million. This spending was primarily the result of the reduction in personnel and is expected to be less than $35 million in 1995. Cash provided by 1992 net earnings was adjusted to reflect the non-cash effects of a restructuring and a significant accounting change. Nonoperating uses of cash in 1994 included purchase of investments; the addition of property, plant and equipment; the payment of dividends to shareholders; and the purchase of treasury stock. The largest source of cash from nonoperating activities was realized from the sale of the Asgrow Seed Company.

In 1993, proceeds of a $200 million 5.875% debt issue under a 1993 shelf registration were utilized to redeem $200 million 8% notes that were called at par on July 1, 1993. Medium-term borrowing at the end of 1994 was unchanged from 1993 at $466 million and compared to $138 million in 1992. The company had $134 million available for future borrowing under the 1993 and 1991 shelf registrations at the end of 1994.

The company utilizes derivative financial instruments in conjunction with its foreign currency risk management programs. These programs employ over-the-counter forward exchange contracts and purchased foreign currency options to hedge existing net transaction exposure and certain existing obligations in several subsidiary locations. These exposures arise both from intercompany and third-party transactions. Foreign currency options are occasionally utilized to hedge anticipated transactions. Risk of loss in the hedging of anticipated transactions is minimized through the exclusive use of purchased foreign currency options.

The hedging activities seek to protect operating results and cash flows from the potential adverse effects of foreign currency fluctuations. This is done by offsetting the gains or losses on the underlying exposures with losses and gains on the instruments utilized to create the hedge. The company does not utilize derivative financial instruments for trading purposes.

The company is obligated to make contributions to certain employee benefit programs and may elect to continue funding one other program. The company's cash flow requirements under the Employee Stock Ownership Plan will begin to accelerate in 1996 from current levels, and there will be a minimum contribution required for the U.S. pension plan of approximately $25 million. In each of the years 1992 through 1994, the company has made contributions to a Voluntary Employee Benefit Association to partially prefund postretirement benefit obligations. Future contributions are discretionary.

The company has committed to make a series of investments in a company that intends to manufacture a hemoglobin-based oxygen carrier as certain progress goals are met.

The company's future cash provided by operations and borrowing capacity are expected to cover normal cash flow needs and planned capital additions for the foreseeable future, despite the adverse effects of the expiration of patents and other product protection discussed below.

Patent Expirations

A U.S. Food and Drug Administration (FDA) moratorium on the approval of Abbreviated New Drug Applications (ANDAs) for products containing glyburide, the generic name for MICRONASE, expired in May 1994. Patent protection of ANSAID, CLEOCIN T, XANAX, and HALCION expired in 1993. No significant patent protection remains on PROVERA. The company began marketing generic equivalents for most of these products in 1993 and 1994. U.S. sales of these six products, including that of the generic equivalents, declined from $1,068 million in 1993 to $672 million in 1994. While it is anticipated that sales of these products will continue to decrease over the next several years, the decline is expected to be lower than that experienced in 1994.

FDA moratoriums on the approval of ANDAs protect exclusivity for GLYNASE until March 1995 and for DEPO-PROVERA until November 1995. U.S. patent protection for ROGAINE will expire in February 1996.

Sales growth of other existing products, the acquisition and development of new products, the marketing of generic equivalents, and efforts to control costs and enhance revenues are expected to offset much of the effects of the loss of patent and ANDA protection. Therefore, the combined earnings impact of the patent expirations, offset by these strategies and actions, are not expected to be as severe in 1995 as in 1994. Earnings in years subsequent to 1995 depend on the success of new products and the strategies noted above.

Other Items

The company is subject to environmental legislation and regulation. Environmental compliance costs, including capital expenditures related to future productions, have been increasing each year. Spending at the Kalamazoo, Mich., production site is expected in the near future related to groundwater remediation and improved control of surface water discharges.

Other projects related to the prevention, mitigation and elimination of environmental effects are being planned and implemented worldwide.

The company is involved in several administrative

The Uphohn Company

The Uphohn Company

and judicial proceedings relating to environmental matters, including actions brought by the U.S. Environmental Protection Agency (EPA) and state environmental agencies for cleanup at approximately 40 "Superfund" or comparable sites, including the West KL Avenue Landfill in Kalamazoo County, Mich. The company's estimate of the ultimate cost to be incurred in connection with these environmental situations could change due to the potential existence of joint and several liability, possible recovery from other potentially responsible parties, the levels of cleanup to be required and the technologies to be employed. An accrual has been recorded, but added costs could be incurred in connection with the various remedial actions. Although the company cannot predict the outcome of these matters, the ultimate liability should not have a material effect on the company's consolidated financial position; and unless there is a significant deviation from the histor-

ical patterns of resolution of such issues, the ultimate liability should not have a material adverse effect on the company's results of operations or liquidity.

Studies directed toward a final remediation plan for the site of the company's discontinued industrial chemical operations in North Haven, Conn., are in process. Issues related to removal of a sludge pile located on the site due to zoning violations have been resolved with the town. The final plan of remediation of the pile will be worked out among the company, the Connecticut Department of Environmental Protection and the U.S. EPA with input from the public. The company cannot at the present time predict the final resolution of the sludge pile issue and has not established any reserves for the cost of off-site disposal. The company believes that it has established sufficient reserves to cover the costs of other remedial activities that may be required.

Selected Financial Data (Dollar amounts in millions, except per-share data)

Years ended December 31	1994	1993	1992	1991	1990
Operating revenue	$3,344.5	$3,380.5	$3,284.7	$3,057.9	$2,675.3
Earnings from continuing operations before cumulative effect of accounting changes[a]	489.1	396.4	527.0	521.5	435.9
Earnings per share from continuing operations before cumulative effect of accounting changes[a]	2.75	2.20	2.92	2.87	2.36
Dividends declared per share	1.48	1.48	1.42	1.26	1.04
Total assets	5,162.5	4,811.9	4,513.1	4,053.9	3,578.8
Long-term debt	521.0	526.8	402.9	295.5	274.6

(a) Relating to January 1, 1993 accounting changes resulting in a net charge of $18.9 or $.11 per share and to January 1, 1992 accounting changes resulting in a net charge of $222.9 or $1.26 per share.

EXHIBIT 2
Abridged Merger Prospectus

UNAUDITED CONDENSED PRO FORMA COMBINED FINANCIAL STATEMENTS

The following unaudited condensed pro forma combined balance sheet as of June 30, 1995, and the unaudited condensed pro forma combined statements of earnings for the years ended December 31, 1994, 1993, and 1992 and the six-month periods ended June 30, 1995 and 1994 have been prepared to illustrate the estimated effects of the proposed combination of Pharmacia and Upjohn in accordance with U.S. GAAP under the "pooling of interrests" method of accounting. A condition in order to account for the merger as a "pooling of interests" under U.S. GAAP is that there must at a minimum be an exchange of at least 90% of the outstanding common stock of each of Upjohn and Pharmacia. The Combination will occur through the formation of the company which will issue an assumed 503,722,558 shares of New Common Stock and an assumed 7,263 shares of New Preferred Stock, which will be exchanged for all of the outstanding Pharmacia Securities and shares of Upjohn Common Stock and Upjohn Preferred Stock. The Unaudited Condensed Pro Forma Combined Balance Sheet as of June 30, 1995 was prepared as if the Combination was consummated at June 30, 1995. The Unaudited Condensed Pro Forma Combined Statements of Earnings for the years ended December 31, 1994, 1993 and 1992 and the six-month periods ended June 30, 1995 and 1994 were prepared as if the Combination was consummated as of January 1, 1992. The unaudited condensed pro forma combined financial statements are based on the historical consolidated financial statements of Pharmacia and Upjohn giving effect to the Combination under the assumptions and adjustments outlined in the accompanying Notes to Unaudited Condensed Pro Forma Combined Financial Statements.

The unaudited condensed pro forma combined financial statements have been prepared in accordance with U.S. GAAP. The financial statements of Pharmacia have been converted from Swedish GAAP to U.S. GAAP and translated into U.S. dollars

for purposes of this presentation (see Note 1 of the Notes to unaudited condensed pro forma combined financial statements.) Swedish GAAP differs in certain significant respects from U.S. GAAP. A reconciliation of net income and shareholders' equity of Pharmacia from Swedish GAAP to U.S. GAAP is presented in Note 25 to the Consolidated Financial Statements of Pharmacia.

The unaudited condensed pro forma combined financial statements do not give effect to certain restructuring and rationalization costs expected to be incurred following the Combination. The management of the company presently is considering the nature and extent of the charges to be so incurred. Such costs presently cannot be reasonably predicted in a manner sufficient to quantify the amount and timing of such charges under U.S. GAAP. Upon final determination, a substantial charge or charges will be recorded during 1995 and/or 1996 and be reflected in the company's statement of earnings as a non-recurring charge or charges to operations in accordance with the U.S. GAAP. The actual payments to implement the restructuring and rationalization are expected to be made over a two- to three-year period. In addition, although the company expects to realize cost reductions from the Combination and the restructuring and rationalization, no effect has been given in the company's unaudited condensed pro forma combined financial statements to any such benefits.

The unaudited condensed pro forma combined financial statements are provided for illustrative purposes only and do not purport to represent what the financial position or results of operations of the company would actually have been if the Combination had in fact occurred on the dates indicated or to project the financial position or results of operations for any future date or period. The unaudited pro forma combined financial statements should be read in conjunction with the notes thereto and the consolidated financial statements of Pharmacia and

The Upjohn Company

Upjohn and the related notes thereto contained elsewhere herein.

The Combination Agreement provides that each outstanding Pharmacia Class A Common Share, Pharmacia Class B Common Share and ADS representing one Pharmacia Class A Common Share will be exchanged for one share of New Common Stock or SDS, each outstanding share of Upjohn Common Stock will be exchanged for 1.45 shares of New Common Stock and each outstanding share of Upjohn Preferred Stock will be exchanged for one share of New Preferred Stock. The precise number of outstanding shares cannot be determined until the Effective Date. For purposes of the unaudited condensed pro forma financial statements, the actual number of shares of capital stock of Pharmacia and Upjohn issued and outstanding at June 30, 1995 has been used to calculate the issuance of shares of New Common Stock and New Preferred Stock pursuant to the Offer and the Merger.

The Uphohn Company

UNAUDITED CONDENSED PRO FORMA COMBINED BALANCE SHEET, JUNE 30, 1995

(dollar amounts in thousands)	Historical	
	Pharmacia (Note 1)	Upjohn
Current assets:		
Cash and cash equivalents	$ 198,141	$ 303,914
Short-term investments	900,929	328,443
Trade accounts receivable (net)	913,046	671,767
Inventories	500,379	502,172
Deferred income taxes and other	286,541	335,584
Total current assets	2,799,036	2,141,880
Investments	127,367	598,254
Property, plant and equipment, at cost	2,359,380	3,203,532
Less allowance for depreciation	(1,035,456)	(1,351,189)
Net property, plant and equipment	1,323,924	1,852,343
Other noncurrent assets	119,656	426,390
Intangibles (net)	1,592,702	224,719
Total assets	$5,962,685	$5,243,586
Current liabilities:		
Accounts payable, accrued liabilities and dividends payable	$ 732,392	$ 297,119
Short-term borrowings, including current maturities of long-term debt	700,034	60,285
Income taxes payable	180,103	226,702
Other	179,140	494,967
Total current liabilities	1,791,669	1,079,073
Long-term debt	85,508	515,005
Guaranteed of ESOP debt		267,200
Postretirement benefit cost	15,040	374,607
Deferred income taxes and other noncurrent liabilities	609,401	505,322
Shareholders' equity:		
Preferred stock	—	292,719
Common stock	880,413	190,590
Capital in excess of par value, statutory reserves and other	1,755,034	97,291
Retained earnings	825,620	2,891,048
ESOP deferred compensation and note receivable from ESOP trust	—	(273,430)
Treasury stock, at cost	—	(695,839)
Total shareholders' equity	3,461,067	2,502,379
Total liabilities and shareholders' equity	$5,962,685	$5,243,586

(continued)

UNAUDITED CONDENSED PRO FORMA COMBINED BALANCE SHEET, JUNE 30, 1995 (*cont.*)

(dollar amounts in thousands)	Pro Forma Adjustments	Combined
Current assets:		
Cash and cash equivalents (Note 2)	$ (69,000)	$ 433,055
Short-term investments		1,229,372
Trade accounts receivable (net)		1,584,813
Inventories		1,002,551
Deferred income taxes and other		622,125
Total current assets	(69,000)	4,871,916
Investments		725,621
Property, plant and equipment, at cost		5,562,912
Less allowance for depreciation		(2,386,645)
Net property, plant and equipment		3,176,267
Other noncurrent assets		546,046
Intangibles (net)		1,817,421
Total assets	$(69,000)	$11,137,271
Current liabilities:		
Accounts payable, accrued liabilities and dividends payable		$1,029,511
Short-term borrowings, including current maturities of long-term debt		760,319
Income taxes payable		406,805
Other		674,107
Total current liabilities		2,870,742
Long-term debt		600,513
Guaranteed of ESOP debt		267,200
Postretirement benefit cost		389,647
Deferred income taxes and other noncurrent liabilities		1,114,723
Shareholders' equity:		
Preferred stock (Note 3d)	$(292,719)	292,719
(Note 3d)	292,719	
Common stock (Note 3a)	(880,413)	5,038
(Note 3a)	2,558	
(Note 3b)	(190,590)	
(Note 3b)	2,480	
Capital in excess of par value, statutory reserves and other		
(Note 3a)	877,855	2,222,451
(Note 3b)	188,110	
(Note 3c)	(695,839)	
Retained earnings (Note 2)	(69,000)	3,647,668
ESOP deferred compensation and note receivable from ESOP trust		(273,430)
Treasury stock, at cost (Note 3c)	695,839	
Total shareholders' equity	(69,000)	5,894,446
Total liabilities and shareholders' equity	$(69,000)	$11,137,271

The accompanying notes are an integral part of the unaudited condensed pro forma combined financial statements.

UNAUDITED CONDENSED PRO FORMA COMBINED STATEMENT OF EARNINGS
FOR THE SIX MONTHS ENDED JUNE 30, 1995

(dollar amounts in thousands, except per share amounts)	Historical		Pro Forma Combined
	Pharmacia (Note 1)	Upjohn	
Operating revenue:			
Net sales	$1,808,125	$1,643,446	$3,451,571
Other revenue	21,117	74,123	95,240
Total	1,829,242	1,717,569	3,546,811
Operating costs and expenses:			
Cost of products sold	525,735	446,828	972,563
Research and development	289,324	290,809	580,133
Marketing and administrative	681,085	628,153	1,309,238
Restructuring, rationalization and merger-related costs	11,853	—	11,853
Total	1,507,997	1,365,790	2,873,787
Operating income	321,245	351,779	673,024
Interest income	57,900	40,690	98,590
Interest expense	(32,015)	(12,988)	(45,003)
Foreign exchange	(23,160)	(1,147)	(24,307)
Other (net)	—	(1,557)	(1,557)
Earnings from continuing operations before income taxes	323,970	376,777	700,747
Provision for income taxes	131,740	109,300	241,040
Earnings from continuing operations	192,230	267,477	459,707
Dividends on preferred stock (net of tax)	—	6,186	6,186
Earnings from continuing operations available for common shareholders	$192,230	$261,291	$453,521
Primary earnings from continuing operations per common share (Note 4)			$0.90
Fully diluted earnings from continuing operations per common share (Note 4)			$0.88
Weighted average equivalent shares used in primary per-share calculation (Note 4)			506,277
Weighted average equivalent shares used in fully diluted per share calculation (Note 4)			519,694

The accompanying notes are an integral part of the unaudited condensed pro forma combined financial statements.

The Upjohn Company

The Uphohn Company

UNAUDITED CONDENSED PRO FORMA COMBINED STATEMENT OF EARNINGS FOR THE SIX MONTHS ENDED JUNE 30, 1994

(dollar amounts in thousands, except per share amounts)	Historical		Pro Forma Combined
	Pharmacia (Note 1)	Upjohn	
Operating revenue:			
Net sales	$1,730,358	$1,619,350	$3,349,708
Other revenue	23,276	24,507	47,783
Total	1,753,634	1,643,857	3,397,491
Operating costs and expenses:			
Cost of products sold	507,002	420,558	927,560
Research and development	233,995	303,091	537,086
Marketing and administrative	692,472	617,982	1,310,454
Total	1,433,469	1,341,631	2,775,100
Operating income	320,165	302,226	622,391
Interest income	45,286	27,356	72,642
Interest expense	(46,045)	(12,671)	(58,716)
Foreign exchange	4,933	(2,079)	2,854
Other (net)	(126)	(374)	(500)
Earnings from continuing operations before income taxes	324,213	314,458	638,671
Provision for income taxes	137,629	72,500	210,129
Earnings from continuing operations	186,584	241,958	428,542
Dividends on preferred stock (net of tax)	—	6,126	6,126
Earnings from continuing operations available for common shareholders	$186,584	$235,832	$422,416
Primary earnings from continuing operations per common share (Note 4)			$0.84
Fully diluted earnings from continuing operations per common share (Note 4)			$0.82
Weighted average equivalent shares used in primary share calculation (Note 4)			505,360
Weighted average equivalent shares used in fully diluted per share calculation (Note 4)			518,197

The accompanying notes are an integral part of the unaudited condensed pro forma combined financial statements.

UNAUDITED CONDENSED PRO FORMA COMBINED STATEMENT OF EARNINGS
FOR THE YEAR ENDED DECEMBER 31, 1994

(dollar amounts in thousands, except per share amounts)	Historical Pharmacia (Note 1)	Upjohn	Pro Forma Combined
Operating revenue:			
Net sales	$3,429,364	$3,274,996	$6,704,360
Other revenue	48,880	69,542	118,422
Total	3,478,244	3,344,538	6,822,782
Operating costs and expenses:			
Cost of products sold	1,046,702	843,152	1,889,854
Research and development	490,081	607,187	1,097,268
Marketing and administrative	1,357,367	1,294,752	2,652,119
Restructuring, rationalization and merger-related costs	19,837	—	19,837
Total	2,913,987	2,745,091	5,659,078
Operating income	564,257	599,447	1,163,704
Interest income	97,630	59,624	157,254
Interest expense	(87,517)	(24,600)	(112,117)
Foreign exchange	23,208	(1,087)	22,121
Other (net)	30,210	10,104	40,314
Earnings from continuing operations before income taxes	627,788	643,488	1,271,276
Provision for income taxes	283,425	154,400	437,825
Earnings from continuing operations	344,363	489,088	833,451
Dividends on preferred stock (net of tax)	—	12,291	12,291
Earnings from continuing operations available for common shareholders	$344,363	$476,797	$821,160
Primary earnings from continuing operations per common share (Note 4)			$1.62
Fully diluted earnings from continuing operations per common share (Note 4)			$1.60
Weighted average equivalent shares used in primary share calculation (Note 4)			505,432
Weighted average equivalent shares used in fully diluted per share calculation (Note 4)			518,363

The accompanying notes are an integral part of the unaudited condensed pro forma combined financial statements.

The Upjohn Company

The Uphohn Company

UNAUDITED CONDENSED PRO FORMA COMBINED STATEMENT OF EARNINGS
FOR THE YEAR ENDED DECEMBER 31, 1993

| (dollar amounts in thousands, except per share amounts) | Historical | | Pro Forma Combined |
	Pharmacia (Note 1)	Upjohn	
Operating revenue:			
Net sales	$3,167,530	$3,339,957	$6,507,487
Other revenue	12,692	40,579	53,271
Total	3,180,222	3,380,536	6,560,758
Operating costs and expenses:			
Cost of products sold	1,038,665	783,590	1,822,255
Research and development	481,591	612,490	1,094,081
Marketing and administrative	1,330,111	1,316,138	2,646,249
Restructuring, rationalization and merger-related costs	59,869	208,789	268,658
Total	2,910,236	2,921,007	5,831,243
Operating income	269,986	459,529	729,515
Interest income	176,529	50,789	227,318
Interest expense	(151,018)	(31,496)	(182,514)
Foreign exchange	2,308	(4,556)	(2,248)
Other (net)	(641)	6,306	5,665
Earnings from continuing operations before income taxes	297,164	480,572	777,736
Provision for income taxes	132,942	84,201	217,143
Earnings from continuing operations	164,222	396,371	560,593
Dividends on preferred stock (net of tax)	—	12,125	12,125
Earnings from continuing operations available for common shareholders	$164,222	$384,246	$548,468
Primary earnings from continuing operations per common share (Note 4)			$1.08
Fully diluted earnings from continuing operations per common share (Note 4)			$1.07
Weighted average equivalent shares used in primary share calculation (Note 4)			506,414
Weighted average equivalent shares used in fully diluted per share calculation (Note 4)			519,256

The accompanying notes are an integral part of the unaudited condensed pro forma combined financial statements.

UNAUDITED CONDENSED PRO FORMA COMBINED STATEMENT OF EARNINGS
FOR THE YEAR ENDED DECEMBER 31, 1992

(dollar amounts in thousands, except per share amounts)	Historical Pharmacia (Note 1)	Upjohn	Pro Forma Combined
Operating revenue:			
Net sales	$2,653,657	$3,256,188	$5,909,845
Other revenue	—	28,560	28,560
Total	2,653,657	3,284,748	5,938,405
Operating costs and expenses:			
Cost of products sold	868,863	754,483	1,623,346
Research and development	344,367	553,297	897,664
Marketing and administrative	1,142,560	1,292,204	2,434,764
Restructuring, rationalization and merger-related costs	24,221	22,055	46,276
Total	2,380,011	2,622,039	5,002,050
Operating income	273,646	662,709	936,355
Interest income	197,547	50,054	247,601
Interest expense	(104,270)	(31,253)	(135,523)
Foreign exchange	(95,166)	(3,397)	(98,563)
Other (net)	2,748	(5,223)	(2,475)
Earnings from continuing operations before income taxes	274,505	672,890	947,395
Provision for income taxes	97,743	145,900	243,643
Earnings from continuing operations	176,762	526,990	703,752
Dividends on preferred stock (net of tax)	—	12,084	12,084
Earnings from continuing operations available for common shareholders	$176,762	$514,906	$691,668
Primary earnings from continuing operations per common share (Note 4)			$1.36
Fully diluted earnings from continuing operations per common share (Note 4)			$1.34
Weighted average equivalent shares used in primary share calculation (Note 4)			508,565
Weighted average equivalent shares used in fully diluted per share calculation (Note 4)			521,446

The accompanying notes are an integral part of the unaudited condensed pro forma combined financial statements.

The Upjohn Company

PHARMACIA AND UPJOHN, INC.—NOTES TO UNAUDITED CONDENSED PRO FORMA COMBINED FINANCIAL STATEMENTS
(dollar amounts in thousands, except per share data)

The unaudited condensed pro forma combined financial statements have been prepared to reflect the Combination of Pharmacia and Upjohn through the formation of the company which will issue an assumed 503,722,558 shares of New Common Stock and an assumed 7,263 shares of New Preferred Stock, which will be exchanged for all of the outstanding Pharmacia Securities and shares of Upjohn Common Stock and the Upjohn Preferred Stock. The Combination is accounted for under the pooling-of-interests method of accounting in accordance with U.S. GAAP.

Note 1

The historical Pharmacia consolidated financial statements included elsewhere herein have been prepared in accordance with Swedish GAAP and denominated in Swedish kroner with a reconciliation of net income and stockholders' equity to U.S. GAAP included in the Notes to the consolidated financial statements. See "Note 25 to the Consolidated Financial Statements of Pharmacia." The Pharmacia historical financial information included in these unaudited condensed pro forma combined financial statements has been presented in accordance with U.S. GAAP and translated into U.S. dollars at a rate of $1 = SEK 7.2625 as of June 30, 1995 and using the weighted average rate of exchange for the six-month periods ended June 30, 1995 and 1994, and for the years ended December 31, 1994, 1993 and 1992 of $1 = SEK 7.3402.

Note 2

To record estimated expenses associated with the Combination, which include, without limitation, fees and expenses of investment bankers, legal counsel, accountants and consultants incurred by Pharmacia and Upjohn in connection with or related to the authorization, preparation, negotiation and execution of the Combination Agreement and the preparation, printing, filing and mailing of this Prospectus including solicitation of stockholder approvals and all other matters related to closing the Transactions.

Note 3

To record the issuance of shares of New Common Stock, and 7,263 shares of New Preferred Stock in exchange for the outstanding Pharmacia Securities, the outstanding shares of Upjohn Common Stock (at an exchange ratio of 1.45 to 1) as set forth below, and 7,263 outstanding shares of Upjohn Preferred Stock.

	Pharmacia
Pharmacia Class A Common Shares outstanding (par value SEK 25)	164,724,715
Pharmacia Class B Common Shares outstanding (par value SEK 25)	91,027,398
Upjohn Common Stock outstanding (par value $1.00)	—
	255,752,113
Exchange ratio to New Common Stock (par value $.01)	1.00
	255,752,113

(continued)

	Upjohn
Pharmacia Class A Common Shares outstanding (par value SEK 25)	—
Pharmacia Class B Common Shares outstanding (par value SEK 25)	—
Upjohn Common Stock outstanding (par value $1.00)	171,014,100
	171,014,100
Exchange ratio to New Common Stock (par value $.01)	1.45
	247,970,445
New Common Stock to be issued	503,722,558

Note 3a

Record issuance of New Common Stock to Pharmacia stockholders.

Note 3b

Record issuance of new Common Stock to Upjohn stockholders.

Note 3c

Record cancellation of Upjohn treasury stock pursuant to the Combination Agreement.

Note 3d

Record exchange of Upjohn's Preferred Stock for New Preferred Stock (an exchange ratio of 1:1) pursuant to the Combination Agreement.

Note 4

Primary earnings from continuing operations per share are computed by dividing earnings from continuing operations available to holders of New Common Stock by the weighted average of common shares outstanding based on the share exchange ratio (including common share equivalents, principally stock options). Fully diluted earnings from continuing operations per share have been computed assuming that all of the convertible preferred stock and convertible debenture loans are converted into common shares.

The Upjohn Company

The Uphohn Company

EXHIBIT 3

Upjohn Pharmacia Merger Announcement—August 20, 1995

A   Upjohn Stock Price and Trading Volume

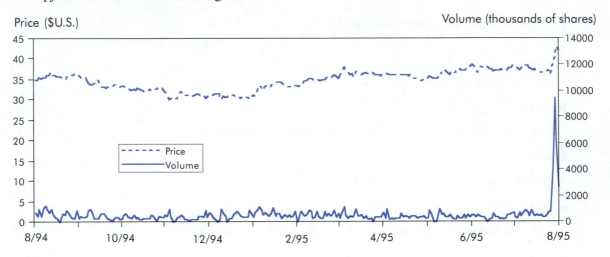

B   Pharmacia Stock Price and Trading Volume

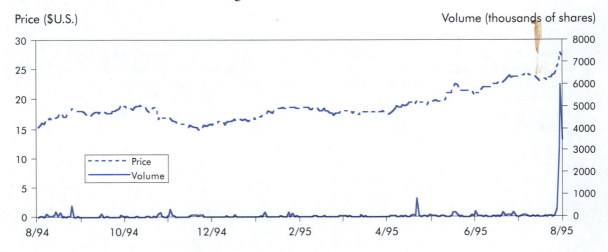

C   Upjohn and Pharmacia Daily Stock Returns on Trading Days
Surrounding the Merger Announcement

	Upjohn	Pharmacia
3 days prior to announcement	+0.34%	+1.54%
2 days prior to announcement	-2.36	+1.08
1 day prior to announcement	+9.31	+4.63
1 day after announcement	+2.84	+4.43
2 days after announcement	+5.52	+5.21
3 days after announcement	-2.33	-2.23

Source: Datastream International.

D   Valuation Data at Announcement

Upjohn's share price on August 18, 1995	$39.63
Pharmacia's share price on August 18, 1995	$25.38
Upjohn's Beta	0.95
Pharmacia's Beta	0.91
US T-Bills, 30 day, August 1995	5.3%
30-Year US Treasury Bonds	6.9%

The Uphohn Company

16 chapter

Corporate Financing Policies

In this chapter, we discuss how firms set their capital structure and dividend policies to maximize shareholder value. There is a strong relation between these two decisions. For example, a firm's decision to retain internally-generated funds rather than paying them out as a dividend can also be thought of as a financing decision. It is not surprising, therefore, to find that many of the factors that are important in setting capital structure (such as taxes, costs of financial distress, agency costs, and information costs) are also relevant for dividend policy decisions. In the following sections we discuss these factors, how they affect capital structure and dividend policy, as well as how the financial analysis tools, discussed in Part 2 of this book, can be used to evaluate capital structure and dividend policy decisions.

A variety of questions are dealt with in analysis of corporate financing policies:

- Securities analysts can ask: Given its capital structure and dividend policy, how should we position a firm in our fund—as a growth or income stock?
- Takeover specialists can ask: Can we improve stockholder value for a firm by changing its financial leverage or by increasing dividend payouts to owners?
- Management can ask: Have we selected a capital structure and dividend policy which supports our business objectives?
- Credit analysts can ask: What risks do we face in lending to this company, given its business and current financial leverage?

Throughout our discussion, we take the perspective of an external analyst who is evaluating whether a firm has selected a capital structure and dividend policy that maximize shareholder value. However, our discussion obviously also applies to management's decisions about what debt and dividend policies it should implement.

FACTORS THAT DETERMINE FIRMS' DEBT POLICIES

As discussed in Chapter 9, a firm's debt policy can be represented by comparing its net debt, defined as interest-bearing debt less excess cash and marketable securities, and its equity. In practice, since it is difficult to estimate excess cash and marketable securities, analysts typically use total cash and marketable securities as a proxy. For example, consider the debt policies for Merck, a large pharmaceutical company, and American Water Works, a large utility, for the year ended December 31, 1998, reported in Table 16-1.

Table 16-1 Net Interest-Bearing Debt for Merck and American Water Works for the Year ended December 31, 1998

	Merck	American Water Works
Interest-bearing debt	$ 3,220.8	$,2247.9
Less: cash and short-term investments	3,355.7	39.1
Net debt	(134.9)	2,208.8
Book shareholders' equity	12,801.8	1,290.9
Net interest-bearing debt to book equity	–1%	171%

Merck actually has more liquid assets (cash and marketable securities) than debt. As a result, it has almost no net debt. In contrast, American Water Works has a ratio of net debt to book equity of 171 percent. Throughout the chapter we will examine factors that are relevant to the financing differences for these firms.

When financial analysts evaluate a firm's capital structure, two related questions typically emerge. First, in the long term, what is the best mix of debt and equity for creating stockholder value? And second, if managers are considering new investment initiatives in the short-term, what type of financing should they use? Two popular models of capital structure provide help in thinking about these questions. The static model of capital structure examines how trade-offs between the benefits and costs of debt determine a firm's long-term optimal mix of debt and equity. And the dynamic model examines how information effects can lead a firm to deviate from its long-term optimal capital structure as it seeks financing for new investments. We discuss both models, since they have somewhat different implications for thinking about capital structure.

THE OPTIMAL LONG-TERM MIX OF DEBT AND EQUITY

To determine the best long-term mix of debt and equity capital for a firm, we need to consider the benefits and costs of financial leverage. By trading off these benefits and costs, we can decide whether a firm should be financed mostly with equity or mostly with debt.

Benefits of Leverage

The major benefits of financial leverage typically include corporate tax shields on interest and improved incentives for management.

CORPORATE INTEREST TAX SHIELDS.   In the U.S., and in many other countries for that matter, tax laws provide a form of government subsidy for debt financing which does not exist for equity financing. This arises from the corporate tax deductibility of interest against income. No such corporate tax shield is available for dividend payments or for retained earnings. Debt financing therefore has an advantage over equity, since the interest tax shields under debt provide additional income to debt and equity holders. This higher income translates directly into higher firm values for leveraged firms in relation to unleveraged firms.

Some practitioners and theorists have pointed out that the corporate tax benefit from debt financing is potentially offset by a personal tax disadvantage of debt.[1] That is, since the holders of debt must pay relatively high tax rates on interest income, they require that corporations offer high pretax yields on debt. This disadvantage is particularly severe when interest income is taxed at a higher rate than capital gains on equity. However, under current U.S. tax laws, personal tax rates on interest income and capital gains are identical, implying that personal tax effects are unlikely to eliminate the corporate tax benefits of debt.

Therefore, the corporate tax benefits from debt financing should encourage firms with high effective tax rates and few forms of tax shield other than interest to have highly leveraged capital structures. In contrast, firms that have tax shield substitutes for interest, such as depreciation, or that have operating loss carryforwards and hence do not expect to pay taxes, should have capital structures that are largely equity.

Key Analysis Questions

To evaluate the tax effects of additional debt, analysts can use accounting, financial ratio, and prospective analysis to answer the following types of questions:

- What is a firm's average income tax rate? How does this rate compare with the average tax rate and financial leverage for its major competitors?
- What portion of a firm's tax expense is deferred taxes versus current taxes?
- What is the firm's marginal corporate tax rate likely to be?
- Does the firm have tax loss carryforwards or other tax benefits? How long are they expected to continue?
- What noninterest tax shields are currently available to the firm? For example, are there sizable tax shields from accelerated depreciation?
- Based on pro forma income and cash flow statements, what are our estimates for the firm's taxable income for the next five to ten years? What noninterest tax shields are available to the firm? Finally, what would be the tax savings from using some debt financing?

MANAGEMENT INCENTIVES FOR VALUE CREATION. A second benefit of debt financing is that it focuses management on value creation, thus reducing conflicts of interest between managers and shareholders. Conflicts of interest can arise when managers make investments that are of little value to stockholders and/or spend the firm's funds on perks, such as overly spacious office buildings and lavish corporate jets. Firms are particularly prone to these temptations when they are flush with cash but have few promising new investment opportunities, often referred to as a "free cash flow" situation. These firms' stockholders would generally prefer that their managers pay out any free cash flows as dividends or use the funds to repurchase stock. However, these options reduce the size of the firm and the assets under management's control. Management may therefore invest the free cash flows in new projects, even if they are not valued by stockholders, or spend the cash flows on management perks.

How can debt help reduce management's incentives to overinvest and to overspend on perks? The primary way is by reducing resources available to fund these types of outlays, since firms with relatively high leverage face pressures to generate cash flows to meet payments of interest and principal.

The debt introduced as a result of the 1988 leveraged buyout of RJR Nabisco was viewed by many as an example of debt creating pressure for management to refocus on value creation for stockholders. Under this view, the incentive problems facing the company stemmed from the high cash flows it generated in the tobacco business and the low investment opportunities in this line of business given the decline in popularity of smoking in the U.S. The increased debt taken with the LBO forced RJR Nabisco's management to eliminate unnecessary perks, such as corporate jets and parties with famous sports stars, to slow diversification into the food industry, and to cancel unprofitable projects such as the smokeless cigarette.

Key Analysis Questions

Financial ratio and prospective analysis can help analysts assess whether there are currently free cash flow inefficiencies at a firm as well as risks of future inefficiencies. Symptoms of excessive management perks and investment in unprofitable projects include the following:

- *Does the firm have high ratios of general and administrative expenses and overhead to sales?* If its ratios are higher than those for its major competitors, one possibility is that management is wasting money on perks.
- *Is the firm making significant new investments in unrelated areas?* If it is difficult to rationalize these new investments, there might be a free cash flow problem.
- *Does the firm have high levels of expected operating cash flows* (net of essential capital expenditures and debt retirements) from pro forma income and cash flow statements?
- *Does the firm have poor management incentives to create additional shareholder value,* evidenced by a weak linkage between management compensation and firm performance?

Costs of Leverage: Financial Distress

As a firm increases its leverage, it increases the likelihood of financial distress, where it is unable to meet interest or principal repayment obligations to creditors. This may force the firm to declare bankruptcy or to agree to restructure its financial claims.

Financial distress can be expensive, since restructurings of a firm's ownership claims typically involve costly legal negotiations. It can also be difficult for distressed firms to raise capital to undertake profitable new investment opportunities. Finally, financial distress can intensify conflicts of interest between stockholders and the firm's debtholders, increasing the cost of debt financing.

LEGAL COSTS OF FINANCIAL DISTRESS.   When a firm is in serious financial distress, its owners' claims are likely to be restructured. This can take place under formal bankruptcy proceedings or out of bankruptcy. Restructurings are likely to be costly, since the parties involved have to hire lawyers, bankers, and accountants to represent their interests, and they have to pay court costs if there are formal legal proceedings. These are often called the *direct* costs of financial distress.

COSTS OF FORGONE INVESTMENT OPPORTUNITIES.   When a firm is in financial distress and particularly when it is in bankruptcy, it may be very difficult for it to raise additional capital for new investments, even though they may be profitable for all the firm's owners. In some cases, bankrupt firms are run by court-appointed trustees, who are unlikely to take on risky new investments—profitable or not. Even for a firm whose management supports new investment, the firm is likely to be capital constrained. Creditors are unlikely to approve the sale of nonessential assets unless the proceeds are used to first repay their claims. Potential new investors and creditors will be wary of the firm because they do not want to become embroiled in the legal disputes themselves. Thus, in all likelihood the firm will be unable to make significant new investments, potentially diminishing its value.

COSTS OF CONFLICTS BETWEEN CREDITORS AND STOCKHOLDERS.   When a firm is performing well, both creditors' and stockholders' interests are likely to coincide. Both want the firm's managers to take all investments which increase the value of the firm. However, when the firm is in financial difficulty, conflicts can arise between different classes of owners. Creditors become concerned about whether the firm will be able to meet its interest and principal commitments. Shareholders become concerned that their equity will revert to the creditors if the firm is unable to meet its outstanding obligations. Thus, managers are likely to face increased pressure to make decisions which serve the interests of only one form of owner, typically stockholders, rather than making decisions in the best interests of all owners. For example, managers have incentives to issue additional debt with equal or higher priority, to invest in riskier assets, or to pay liquidating dividends, since these actions reduce the value of outstanding creditors' claims and benefit stockholders. When it is costly to completely eliminate this type of game playing, creditors will simply reduce the amount they are willing to pay the firm for the debt when it is issued, increasing the costs of borrowing for the firm's stockholders.

OVERALL EFFECTS OF FINANCIAL DISTRESS.   The costs of financial distress discussed above offset the tax and monitoring benefits of debt. As a result, firms that are more likely to fall into financial distress or for which the costs of financial distress are especially high should have relatively low financial leverage. Firms are more likely to fall into financial distress if they have high business risks, that is, if their revenues and earnings before interest are highly sensitive to fluctuations in the economy. Financial distress costs are also likely to be relatively high for firms whose assets are easily destroyed in financial distress. For example, firms with human capital and brand intangibles are particularly sensitive to financial distress since dissatisfied employees and customers can leave or seek alternative suppliers. In contrast, firms with tangible assets can sell their assets if they get into financial distress, providing additional security for lenders and lowering the costs of financial distress. Firms with intangible assets are therefore less likely to be highly leveraged than firms whose assets are mostly tangible.

These factors probably largely explain why Merck and American Water Works, the two companies discussed at the beginning of the chapter, have such different financing policies. Merck probably keeps its leverage low because many of its core assets are intangibles, such as research staff and sales force representatives. These types of assets can easily be lost if Merck gets into financial difficulty as a result of too much leverage. In all likelihood, management would be forced to cut back on R&D and marketing, leading the most talented researchers and sales representatives to be attracted by offers from competitors. Merck can reduce these risks by having very low leverage.

In contrast, American Water Works is a utility. It has very stable cash flows since its revenues are regulated. In addition, its major asset is its physical plant, which is less likely to diminish in value if it gets into financial distress. If the debt holders ended up as the new owners of the firm following financial distress, they could continue to use the existing assets. American Water Works can therefore take advantage of the tax benefits from corporate debt without bearing a high cost of financial distress.

Key Analysis Questions

The above discussion implies that a firm's optimal financial leverage will depend on its underlying business risks and asset types. If the firm's business risks are relatively high or its assets can be easily destroyed by financial distress, changing the mix of debt and equity toward more debt may actually destroy shareholder value. Analysts can use ratio, cash flow, and pro forma analysis to assess a firm's business risks and whether its assets are easily destroyed by financial distress. Their analysis should focus on:

- *Comparing indicators of business risk for the firm and other firms in its industry with the economy.* Popular indicators of business risk include the ratio of fixed operating expenses (such as depreciation on plant and equipment) to sales, the volatility of return on assets, as well as the relation between indicators of the firm's performance and indicators of performance for the economy as a whole.
- *Examining the competitive nature of the industry.* For firms in a highly competitive industry, performance is very sensitive to changes in strategy by competitors.
- *Determining whether the firm's assets are largely intangible and therefore sensitive to financial distress,* using such ratios as market to book equity.

Determining the Long-Term Optimal Mix of Debt and Equity

The above discussion implies that the optimal mix of debt and equity for a firm can be estimated by trading off the corporate interest tax shield and monitoring benefits of debt against the costs of financial distress. As the firm becomes more highly leveraged, the costs of leverage presumably begin to outweigh the tax and monitoring benefits of debt.

However, there are several practical difficulties in trying to estimate a firm's optimal financial leverage. One difficulty is quantifying some of the costs and benefits of leverage. For example, it is not easy to value the expected costs of financial distress or any management incentive benefits from debt. There are no easy answers to this problem. The best that we can do is to qualitatively assess whether the firm faces free cash flow problems, and whether it faces high business risks and has assets that are easily destroyed by financial distress. These qualitative assessments can then be used to adjust the more easily quantified tax benefits from debt to determine whether the firm's financial leverage should be relatively high, low, or somewhere in between.

A second practical difficulty in deciding whether a firm should have high, low, or medium financial leverage is quantifying what we mean by high, low, and medium. One way to resolve this question is to use indicators of financial leverage, such as debt-to-equity ratios, for the market as a whole as a guide on leverage ranges.

To provide a rough sense of what companies usually consider to be high and low financial leverage, Table 16-2 shows median debt-to-market-equity and debt-to-book-equity ratios for selected U.S. industries in 1998. Median ratios are reported for all listed companies and for NYSE companies.

Median debt-to-market-equity ratios are highest for the hotel, steel, and water supply industries. The core assets for firms in these industries include physical equipment and property that are readily transferable to debt holders in the event of financial distress. In addition, firms in these industries are typically not highly sensitive to economy risk. In contrast, the software and pharmaceutical industries' core assets are their research staffs.

Table 16-2 Median Net Interest-Bearing Debt to Market Equity and Net Interest-Bearing Debt to Book Equity for Selected U.S. Industries in 1998

Industry	Net Interest-Bearing Debt to Market Equity		Net Interest-Bearing Debt to Book Equity	
	All Listed Firms	NYSE Firms	All Listed Firms	NYSE Firms
Computer Software	–8%	0%	–52%	–12%
Pharmaceutical	–7%	1%	–43%	1%
Retail Stores	3%	46%	13%	75%
Water Supply	50%	49%	100%	108%
Steel Works	85%	46%	55%	38%
Hotels & Motels	107%	75%	126%	108%

Ownership of these types of assets cannot be easily transferred to debt holders if the firm is in financial distress. Researchers are likely to leave for greener pastures if their budgets are cut. As a result, firms in this industry have relatively conservative capital structures.

It is also interesting to note that NYSE firms tend to have less extreme leverage than non-NYSE firms in the same industries. For example, NYSE firms have lower leverage in the steel and hotel industries, and higher leverage in the software and pharmaceutical industries than for all firms. The retail industry appears to have relatively low leverage for all firms but quite high leverage for NYSE firms. This reflects the fact that NYSE retail stores tend to be large department stores that offer a broad range of merchandise and are more likely to be diversified geographically.

The net debt-to-book-equity ratios by and large tell a similar story to the debt-to-market-equity ratios. They reflect the fact that most firms have market-to-book-equity ratios greater than one both because companies generally invest in projects that add value for stockholders and because some types of assets, such as R&D, are typically not reflected in book equity. Note that this is not true for the steel industry, which has a negative market-to-book ratio, reflecting disappointing performance by many firms in the industry.

THE FINANCING OF NEW PROJECTS

The second model of capital structure focuses on how firms make new financing decisions. Proponents of this dynamic model argue that there can be short-term frictions in capital markets which cause deviations from long-run optimal capital structure. One source of friction arises when managers have better information about their firm's future performance than outside investors. This could lead managers to deviate from their long-term optimal capital structure as they seek financing for new investments.

To see how information asymmetries between outside investors and management can create market imperfections and potentially affect short-term capital structure decisions, consider management's options for financing a proprietary new project that it expects to be profitable. One financing option is to use retained earnings to cover the investment outlay. However, what if the firm has no retained earnings available today? If it pays dividends, it could perhaps cut dividends to help pay for the project. But as we discuss later, investors usually interpret a dividend cut as an indication that the firm's management anticipates poor future performance. A dividend cut is therefore likely to lead to a stock price decline, which management would probably prefer to avoid. Also, many firms do not pay dividends.

A second financing option is to borrow additional funds to finance the project. However, if the firm is already highly leveraged, the tax shield benefits from debt are likely to be relatively modest and the potential costs of financial distress relatively high, making additional borrowing unattractive.

The final financing option available to the firm is to issue new equity. However, if investors know that management has superior information on the firm's value, they are likely to interpret an equity offer as an indication that management believes that the firm's stock price is higher than the intrinsic value of the firm.[2] The announcement of an equity offer is therefore likely to lead to a drop in the price of the firm's stock, raising the firm's cost of capital, and potentially leading management to abandon a perfectly good project.

The above discussion implies that if the firm has internal cash flows available or is not already highly leveraged, it is relatively straightforward for it to arrange financing for the new project. Otherwise, management has to decide whether it is worthwhile undertaking the new project, given the costs of cutting dividends, issuing additional debt, or issuing equity to finance the project. The information costs of raising funds through these means lead managers to have a "pecking order" for new financing. Managers first use internal cash to fund investments, and only if this is unavailable do they resort to external financing. Further, if they have to use external financing, managers first use debt financing. New equity issues are used only as a last resort because of the difficulties that investors have in interpreting these issues.[3]

One way for management to mitigate the information problems of using external financing is to ensure that the firm has financial slack. Management can create financial slack by reinvesting free cash flows in marketable securities, so that it doesn't have to go to the capital market to finance a new project. It could also choose to have relatively low levels of debt, so that the firm can borrow easily in the future.

In summary, information asymmetries between managers and external investors can make managers reluctant to raise new equity to finance new projects. Managers' reluctance arises from their fear that investors will interpret the decision as an indication that the firm's stock is overvalued. In the short-term, this effect can lead managers to deviate from the firm's long-term optimal mix of debt and equity.

Key Analysis Questions

The above discussion implies that in the short term management should attempt to finance new projects primarily with retained earnings. Further, it suggests that management would be well advised to maintain financial slack to ensure that it is not forced to use costly external financing. To assess a firm's financing options, we would ask the following types of questions:

- What is the value of current cash reserves (not required for day-to-day working capital needs) that could be used for new capital outlays? What operating cash resources are expected to become available in the coming few years? Do these internal resources cover the firm's expected cash needs for new investment and working capital?
- How do the firm's future cash needs for investment change as its operating performance deteriorates or improves? Are its investment opportunities relatively fixed, or are they related to current operating cash flow performance? Investment opportunities for many firms decline during a recession and increase during booms, enabling them to consistently use internal funds for financing. However, firms with stable investment needs should build financial slack during booms so that they can support investment during busts.
- If internal funds are not readily available, what opportunities does the firm have to raise low-cost debt financing? Normally, a firm which has virtually zero debt could do this without difficulty. However, if it is in a volatile industry or has mostly intangible assets, debt financing may be costly.
- If the firm has to raise costly equity capital, are there ways to focus investors on the value of the firm's assets and investment opportunities to lower any information asymmetries between managers and investors? For example, management might be able to disclose additional information about the value of existing assets, and the uses and expected returns from the new funds.

Summary of Debt Policy

There are no easy ways to quantify the best mix of debt and equity for a firm and its best financing options. However, some general principles are likely to be useful in thinking about these questions. We have seen that the benefits from debt financing are likely to be highest for firms with:

high marginal tax rates and few noninterest tax shields, making interest tax shields from debt valuable;

high, stable income/cash flows and few new investment opportunities, increasing the monitoring value of debt and reducing the likelihood that the firm will fall into financial distress or require costly external financing for new projects; and high tangible assets that are not easily destroyed by financial distress.

The financial analysis tools developed in Part 2 of the book are useful in rating a firm's interest tax shield benefits, its business risk and investment opportunities, and its major asset types. This information can then be used to judge whether there are benefits from debt or whether the firm would be better off using equity financing to support its business strategies.

FACTORS THAT DETERMINE FIRMS' DIVIDEND POLICIES

To assess a firm's dividend policy, analysts typically examine its dividend payout, its dividend yield, and any stock repurchases. Dividend payout is defined as cash dividends as a percentage of income available to common shareholders, and reflects the extent to which a company pays out profits or retains them for reinvestment. Dividend yield is dividends per share as a percentage of the current stock price, and indicates the current dividend return earned by shareholders. Finally, stock repurchases are relevant because many companies use repurchases of their own stock as an alternative way of returning cash to shareholders. Table 16-3 provides information on these variables for Merck and American Water Works.

Table 16-3 Dividend Policy for Merck and American Water Works for the Year Ended December 31, 1998

	Merck	American Water Works
Dividend payout	1.3%	2.9%
Dividend yield	44%	55%
Cash dividends	$2,253.1m	$69.8m
Stock repurchases	$3,625.5m	$2.4m

Merck appears to be following a more conservative dividend policy. It has a lower payout than American Water Works, and a lower dividend yield. However, Merck also has a significant stock repurchase program, whereas American Water Works does not. After including stock repurchases, Merck effectively paid out more than 100 percent of its income to shareholders in 1998.

What factors should a firm consider when setting its dividend policy? Do investors prefer firms to pay out profits as dividends or to retain them for reinvestment? As we noted above, many of the factors that affect dividends are similar to those examined in the section on capital structure decisions. This should not be too surprising, since a firm's dividend policies also affect its financing decisions. Thus, dividends provide a means of reducing free cash flow inefficiencies. They also have tax implications for investors and can reduce a firm's financial slack. Finally, lending contracts can affect a firm's dividend payouts to protect lenders' interests.

Below we discuss the factors that are relevant to managers' dividend decisions and how financial analysis tools can be used in this decision process.

Dividends as a Way of Reducing Free Cash Flow Inefficiencies

As we discussed earlier, conflicts of interest between managers and shareholders can affect a firm's optimal capital structure; they also have implications for dividend policy decisions. Stockholders of a firm with free cash flows and few profitable investment opportunities want managers to adopt a dividend policy with high payouts. This will deter managers from growing the firm by reinvesting the free cash flows in new projects that are not valued by stockholders or from spending the free cash flows on management perks. In addition, if managers of a firm with free cash flows wish to fund a new project, most stockholders would prefer that they do so by raising new external capital rather than cutting dividends. Stockholders can then assess whether the project is genuinely profitable or simply one of management's pet projects.

Key Analysis Questions

Earlier we discussed how ratio and cash flow analysis can help analysts assess whether a firm faces free cash flow inefficiencies, and how pro forma analysis can help indicate the likelihood of future free cash flow problems. The same analysis and questions can be used to decide whether a firm should initiate dividends.

Tax Costs of Dividends

What are the implications for dividend policy if dividends and capital gains are taxed, particularly at different rates? Classical models of the tax effects of dividends predict that if the capital gains tax rate is less than the rate on dividend income, investors will prefer that the firm either pay no dividends, so that they subsequently take gains as capital accumulation, or that the firm undertakes a stock repurchase, which qualifies as a capital distribution. Even if capital gains are slightly higher than dividend tax rates, investors are still likely to prefer capital gains to dividends, since they do not actually have to realize their capital gains. They can delay selling their shares and thereby defer paying the taxes on any capital appreciation. The longer investors wait before selling their stock, the lower the value of the capital gains tax. Only if capital gains tax rates are substantially higher than the rates on ordinary income are investors likely to favor dividend distributions over capital gains.

Today many practitioners and theorists believe that taxes play only a minor role in determining a firm's dividend policy, since a firm can attract investors with different tax preferences. Thus, a firm that wishes to pay high dividend rates will attract stockholders that are tax-exempt institutions, which do not pay taxes on dividend income. In contrast, a firm that prefers to pay low dividend rates will attract stockholders who have high marginal tax rates and prefer capital gains to dividend income.

Dividends and Financial Slack

We discussed earlier how managers' information advantage over dispersed investors can increase a firm's cost of external funds. One way to avoid having to raise costly external funds is to have a conservative dividend policy which creates financial slack in the organization. By paying only a small percentage of income as dividends and reinvesting the free cash flows in marketable securities, management reduces the likelihood that the firm will have to go to the capital market to finance a new project.

Managers of firms with high intangible assets and growth opportunities are particularly likely to have an information advantage over dispersed investors, since accounting information for these types of firms is frequently a poor indicator of future performance. Accountants, for example, do not attempt to value R&D, intangibles, or growth opportunities. These types of firms are therefore more likely to face information problems and capital market constraints. To compound this problem, high-growth firms are typically heavily dependent on external financing, since they are not usually able to fund all new investments internally. Any capital market constraints are therefore likely to affect their ability to undertake profitable new projects.

Because paying dividends reduces financial slack and is thus costly, a firm's dividend policy can help management communicate effectively with external investors. Investors recognize that managers will only increase their firm's dividend rate if they anticipate that the payout does not have a serious effect on the firm's future financing options. Thus, the decision to increase dividends can help investors appreciate management's optimism about the firm's future performance and its ability to finance growth.[4]

Key Analysis Questions

As discussed earlier for debt policy, the financial analysis tools discussed in Part 2 of the book can help analysts assess how much financial slack a firm should maintain. The same analysis and questions are relevant to dividend policy analysis. Based on the answers to the earlier questions, analysts can assess whether the firm's projected cash needs for new investments are stable in relation to its operating cash flows. If so, it makes sense for management not to pursue too high a dividend payout and to build financial slack during boom periods to help fund investments during busts. Similarly, if the firm's ability to raise low-cost debt is limited because it is in a volatile industry or has mostly intangible assets, management is likely to avoid high dividend payouts to reduce the risk that it will have to raise high-cost external capital in the future or even forego a profitable new project.

Lending Constraints and Dividend Policy

One of the concerns of a firm's creditors is that when the firm is in financial distress, managers will pay a large dividend to stockholders. This problem is likely to be particularly severe for a firm with highly liquid assets, since its managers can pay a large dividend without selling assets. To limit these types of games, managers agree to restrict dividend payments to stockholders. Such dividend covenants usually require the firm to maintain certain minimum levels of retained earnings and current asset balances, which effectively limit dividend payments when it is facing financial difficulties. However, these constraints on dividend policy are unlikely to be severe for a profitable firm.

Determining Optimal Dividend Payouts

One question that arises in using the above factors to determine dividend policy is defining what we mean by high, low, and medium dividend payouts. To provide a rough sense of what companies usually consider to be high and low dividend payouts and yields, Table 16-4 shows median dividend payout ratios and dividend yields for selected U.S. industries in 1998. Median ratios are reported for all listed companies and for NYSE companies.

It is interesting to note that many U.S. listed companies do not pay any dividends. This is particularly true for non-NYSE firms, which probably have more attractive growth opportunities. The highest payouts tend to be made by public utilities, such as natural gas, water, and electric services. For these firms the median payouts tend to be roughly 60–70 percent and yields are between 3.6 percent and 4.8 percent. In contrast, firms in highly competitive industries with substantial reinvestment opportunities, such as software and pharmaceutical, tend to have very low dividend payouts and dividend yields.

Returning to the cases of Merck and American Water Works presented earlier, it is interesting to see that Merck has a higher dividend payout ratio than its industry median

Table 16-4 Median Dividend Payout Ratio and Dividend Yield for Selected U.S. Industries in 1998

Industry	Dividend Payout Ratio		Dividend Yield	
	All Listed Firms	NYSE Firms	All Listed Firms	NYSE Firms
Computer Software	0%	0%	0.0%	0.0%
Retail Stores	0%	18%	0.0%	0.7%
Pharmaceutical	0%	23%	0.0%	0.8%
Natural Gas	58%	58%	3.6%	3.6%
Water Supply	70%	69%	3.7%	3.9%
Electric Services	71%	71%	4.8%	4.7%

(44 percent versus 23 percent). When stock repurchases are included, Merck actually paid out more than 100 percent of its 1998 profits. Apparently the company believes that it does not have to reinvest all of its profits to maintain its high rate of success in drug development. It is also interesting to note that Merck uses stock repurchases as an important way to return funds to shareholders. One potential explanation for this is that Merck does not want to commit to the current high rate of payout indefinitely. Its dividend payout therefore represents its long-term payout commitment, and repurchases are used for temporary increases in that rate.

A Summary of Dividend Policy

Just as it is difficult to provide a simple formula to compute a firm's optimal capital structure, it is difficult to formalize the optimal dividend policy. However, we are able to identify several factors that appear to be important:

- High-growth firms should have low dividend payout ratios, and they should use their internally generated funds for reinvestment. This minimizes any costs from capital market constraints on financing growth options.
- Firms with high and stable operating cash flows and few investment opportunities should have high dividend payouts to reduce managers' incentives to reinvest free cash flows in unprofitable ventures.
- Firms should probably not worry too much about tax factors in setting dividend policy. Whatever their policy, they will be able to attract a clientele of investors. Firms that select high dividend payouts will attract tax-exempt institutions or corporations, and firms that pay low or no dividends will attract individuals in high tax brackets.
- Firms' financial covenants can have an impact on their dividend policy decisions. Firms will try to avoid being too close to their constraints in order to minimize the possibility of cutting their dividend.

SUMMARY

This chapter examined how firms make optimal capital structure and dividend decisions. We show that a firm's optimal long-term capital structure is largely determined by its expected tax status, business risks, and types of assets. The benefits from debt financing are expected to be highest for firms with: high marginal tax rates and few non-interest tax shields, making interest tax shields valuable; high, stable income/cash flows and few new investment opportunities, increasing the monitoring value of debt and reducing the likelihood that the firm will fall into financial distress; and high tangible assets that are not easily destroyed by financial distress.

We also show that, in the short-term, managers can deviate from their long-term optimal capital structure when they seek financing for new investments. In particular, managers are reluctant to raise external financing, especially new equity, for fear that outside investors will interpret their action as meaning that the firm is overvalued. This information problem has implications for how much financial slack a firm is likely to need to avoid facing these types of information problems.

   Optimal dividend policy is determined by many of the same factors—firms' business risks and their types of assets. Thus, dividend rates should be highest for firms with high and stable cash flows and few investment opportunities. By paying out relatively high dividends, these firms reduce the risk of managers investing free cash flows in unprofitable projects. Conversely, firms with low, volatile cash flows and attractive investment opportunities, such as start-up firms, should have relatively low dividend payouts. By reinvesting operating cash flows and reducing the amount of external financing required for new projects, these firms reduce their costs of financing.

   Financial statement analysis can be used to better understand a firm's business risks, its expected tax status, and whether its assets are primarily assets in place or growth opportunities. Useful tools for assessing whether a firm's current capital structure and dividend policies maximize shareholder value include accounting analysis to determine off-balance-sheet liabilities, ratio analysis to help understand a firm's business risks, and cash flow and pro forma analysis to explore current and likely future investment needs.

DISCUSSION QUESTIONS

1. Financial analysts typically measure financial leverage as the ratio of debt to equity. However, there is less agreement on how to measure debt, or even equity. How would you treat the following items in computing this ratio? Justify your answers.
   • Revolving credit agreement with bank
   • Cash and marketable securities
   • Deferred tax liabilities
   • Preferred stock
   • Convertible debt

2. Until 1987 Master Limited Partnerships (MLPs) were treated as partnerships for tax purposes. This meant that no corporate taxes were paid by the entity. Instead, taxes were paid by partners (at their individual tax rates) on entity profits (both distributed and undistributed). The marginal tax rate for corporations in 1987 was 34 percent, compared to 33 percent for individuals in the highest tax bracket.
   a. If an entity distributes all after-tax earnings as dividends and generates before-tax earnings of $10 million, what would be the distribution to owners (after entity and personal taxes) if it is organized as (1) a corporation and (2) an MLP?
   b. What would be the optimal capital structure for the MLP discussed in (a)? Justify your answer.
   c. What types of dividend policy do you expect the MLP to follow? Why?

3. Finance theory implies that the debt-to-equity ratio should be computed using the market values of debt and equity. However, most financial analysts use book val-

ues of debt and equity to compute a firm's financial leverage. What are the limitations of using book values rather than market values for comparing leverage across industries or firms? For what types of industries/firms are book values likely to be most misleading?

4. One important driver of a firm's capital structure and dividend policy decisions is its business risk. What ratios would you look at to assess business risk? Name two industries with very high business risk and two industries with very low business risk.

5. U.S. public companies with "low" leverage have an interest-bearing net debt-to-equity ratio of 0 percent or less, firms with "medium" leverage have a ratio between 1 and 62 percent, and "high" leverage firms have a ratio of 63 percent or more. Given these data, how would you classify the following firms in terms of their optimal debt-to-equity ratio (high, medium, or low)?
   - a successful pharmaceutical company
   - an electric utility
   - a manufacturer of consumer durables
   - a commercial bank
   - a start-up software company

6. A rapidly growing Internet company, recently listed on NASDAQ, needs to raise additional capital to finance new research and development. What financing options are available, and what are the trade-offs between each?

7. The following table reports (in millions) earnings, dividends, capital expenditures, and R&D for Intel for the period 1990–95:

Year	Net Income	Dividends	Capital Expenditures	R&D
1990	$650	$0	$680	$517
1991	819	0	948	618
1992	1,067	43	1,228	780
1993	2,295	88	1,933	970
1994	2,288	100	2,441	1,111
1995	3,566	133	3,550	1,296

What are the dividend payout rates for Intel during these years? Is this payout policy consistent with the factors expected to drive dividend policy, as discussed in the chapter? What factors do you expect would lead Intel's management to increase its dividend payout? How do you expect the stock market to react to such a decision?

8. U.S. public companies with "low" dividend payouts have payout ratios of 0 percent or less, firms with "medium" payouts have ratios between 1 and 48 percent, and "high" payout firms have a ratio of 49 percent or more. Given these data, how would you classify the following firms in terms of their optimal payout policy (high, medium, or low)?

- a successful pharmaceutical company
- an electric utility
- a manufacturer of consumer durables
- a commercial bank
- a start-up software company

9. It is frequently argued that Japanese and German companies can afford to have more financial leverage and to follow lower dividend payout policies than U.S. companies because they are largely owned by financial institutions that have long-term horizons. Does this argument make economic sense? If so, explain why, and if not, why not. What other factors might explain differences in capital structure and dividend policy across countries.

10. In 1990 U.S. tax law increased capital gains rates from 20 percent to the same level as ordinary income rates, between 28 and 34 percent. What implications does this change have for corporate dividend policy and capital structure?

NOTES

1. See Merton Miller, "Debt and Taxes," *Journal of Finance* 32 (May 1977): 261–276.

2. Paul Healy and Krishna Palepu in "Earnings and Risk Changes Surrounding Primary Stock Offers," *Journal of Accounting Research* (Spring 1990): 25–49, find that announcements of stock issues are interpreted by investors as a signal from management that the firm is riskier than investors expected.

3. These issues are discussed by Stewart Myers and Nicholas Majluf in "Corporate Financing and Investment Decisions When Firms Have Information That Investors Do Not Have," *Journal of Financial Economics* (June 1984): 187–221.

4. Findings by Paul Healy and Krishna Palepu in "Earnings Information Conveyed by Dividend Initiations and Omissions," *Journal of Financial Economics* (1988): 149–175, indicate that investors interpret announcements of dividends initiations and omissions as managers' forecasts of future earnings performance.

In March 1989 Stuart Bell, Executive Vice President and CFO of CUC International, Inc., was concerned that the company's stock was seriously undervalued. He attributed the undervaluation to the investment community's concern about the quality of CUC's earnings:

> *I am afraid our accounting is misunderstood by many investors. Recently, we have been forced to spend a lot of top management time and energy defending our policy in analysts' meetings. As a result we have been unable to focus investors' attention on our innovative business strategy and the tremendous cash-flow generating potential of our business. Concerns about our earnings quality are scaring new institutional investors from investing in our business. Many money managers tell me that they love our business concept but are afraid to buy our stock because they are worried about our accounting. The accounting is also giving short sellers an excuse to scare our current investors and drive down the stock price.*

While Bell was convinced that CUC's accounting was appropriate, he wondered whether it was actually hurting, rather than helping, the company. What, if anything, should CUC do to shore up investors' confidence in the company?

BUSINESS HISTORY AND OPERATIONS

CUC International, located in Stamford, Connecticut, was a membership-based consumer services company. CUC marketed its membership programs to credit cardholders of major financial, retailing, and oil companies, including Chase Manhattan, Citibank, Sears, JC Penney, and Amoco. The company was formed in 1973 as Comp-U-Card of America, went public in 1983, and was renamed CUC International in 1987. As a result of its strong performance, the company was included in *Inc.* magazine's list of the fastest growing public companies in 1984 and 1986.

CUC's most popular product was Shoppers Advantage, introduced in 1981. Consumers paid an annual membership fee for this service, which entitled them to call the company's operators on a toll-free line, or to use on-line computer access seven days a week

This case was prepared by Professor Paul Healy of M.I.T. Sloan School and Professor Krishna Palepu of Harvard Business School as the basis for class discussion rather than to illustrate either effective or ineffective handling of an administrative situation. Copyright © 1992 by the President and Fellows of Harvard College. Harvard Business School case 9-192-099.

to inquire about, price, and/or buy brand-name products. Shoppers Advantage offered more than 250,000 brand-name and specialty items. Many members used the service principally as a reference for comparison pricing, not necessarily to purchase items directly. The company's large membership base allowed it to negotiate attractive discounts on the products offered in its catalog. As a result, the company guaranteed its subscribers the lowest prices available on goods it sold. If a member, after purchasing merchandise through CUC, sent an advertisement from an authorized dealer with a lower price within 30 days of placing an order, the company agreed to refund the difference. Members' purchase orders were executed through independent vendors who shipped the merchandise directly to customers, enabling the company to carry no inventory.

The firm acquired a large share of its new members through agreements with major credit card issuers, who provided CUC access to its list of cardholders. These individuals were solicited by three direct marketing approaches: billing statement inserts, solo mailings, and telemarketing. In billing statement insert programs, membership applications were enclosed in the monthly billing statements of credit card issuers. Solo mailings were membership offers mailed directly. Telemarketing involved following up mailings with telephone calls to explain membership offers further. CUC paid 10 percent to 20 percent of initial and renewal membership fees as a commission to the credit card company.

CUC incurred a large one-time cost for new member solicitations. Because only a small fraction of people reached through direct mail solicitations purchased the service, membership acquisition costs typically exceeded membership fees in the first year. For example, in 1989 the annual membership fee for Shoppers Advantage was $39, the average solicitation cost per new member was $29.37, commissions to the credit card companies were $6.63, and the average operating service cost per member was $5.00. Thus on average for each new member acquired, CUC incurred a cash outflow of $2 in the first year.

Members subscribed to Shoppers Advantage for a single year at a time. Renewals were automatically billed each year through the credit card company, and members could elect to cancel the service. There were thus no direct solicitation costs for renewing members. In 1989 CUC had a net cash inflow of $27.37 for each renewing member—membership fees were $39, and the commissions to the credit card companies and operating service costs totaled $11.63.[1] Membership renewal rates were therefore a key determinant of the profitability of the Shoppers Advantage program. The average annual renewal rate for Shoppers Advantage in recent years was 71 percent, making the program very profitable. This average was based on eight years' experience with the product since 1981.

CUC capitalized on its Shoppers Advantage experience by introducing a variety of other membership-based products. These included: (1) Travellers Advantage—a travel membership created in 1988 to provide subscribers access to database information and reservations on discount airline travel, hotels and auto rental, tours, and cruises; (2) AutoVantage—provided subscribers with new car price and performance summaries,

1. The figures in this and the previous paragraph are from an analyst report by Brian E. Stack of Advest, Inc. dated October 30, 1989.

CUC International

used car valuations, and parts and service discounts; and (3) Premier Dining—a service introduced in 1989 that offered subscribers two-for-one dining at mid- to upscale restaurants in major U.S. cities. The company made large marketing investments to build memberships in these new programs.

CUC's management explained the key elements of its business strategy as follows:

The company's expansion has been built on a foundation of creating, developing, and marketing a broad array of valuable services to consumers. . . . Aggressive marketing is an important strength. We sell our goods and services directly to millions of customers of major credit card issuers. Because our consumer services are a natural enhancement to personal financial services, more than 40 of the top 50 money center banks and a growing number of retailers and oil companies find it advantageous to work with CUC. . . . As competition heats up in the financial services industry, demand for CUC's services is likely to increase. Credit card issuers rely upon our services to draw new customers, increase card use, and raise average balances. They also use our services to differentiate their cards from others, and to tailor what they offer to appeal to different life-style and geographic preferences. Finally, card issuers benefit from the stream of membership commissions they receive from CUC.[2]

By December 1988, CUC had approximately 12 million members enrolled in its programs. Revenues had grown from $45 million in the year ending January 31, 1984 (fiscal year 1984) to $198 million in the year ending January 31, 1988 (fiscal 1988), and earnings had grown from $3 million to $17 million during this period. Exhibits 3 and 4 present the financial statements for the year ended January 31, 1988, and for the nine months ended October 31, 1988. Management expected the company to continue its rapid growth in the future, with revenues for the fiscal year ending January 31, 1989 projected to be approximately $270 million.

THE FINANCIAL REPORTING CONTROVERSY

CUC's management decided that because current marketing outlays provided significant future benefits, the company should capitalize membership solicitation costs in its financial statements, and amortize them over three years at rates of 40 percent, 30 percent, and 30 percent. This choice was endorsed by Ernst & Whinney, the company's auditors, and by the Securities and Exchange Commission when the company went public.

While it was unusual to capitalize marketing costs, CUC's managers believed that this decision was justified given the nature of the company's business and their confidence in future renewal rates. Bell explained the rationale behind CUC's accounting choice:

Many companies spend money on acquiring plant and equipment, and they capitalize these costs. Our business does not require major investments in plant and equipment. Instead, it requires investments in membership acquisitions. Because

---

2. Source: CUC's 1988 Annual Report.

our membership renewal rates are so high and steady, I believe that it is important for accounting to reflect future benefits from spending money on membership acquisition in the current period. While expensing these costs is conservative, it fails to reflect their true nature.

In its accounting choice, CUC's management could not obtain much guidance from other companies' practices. Magazine publishers typically expensed costs of acquiring new subscribers, whereas insurance companies capitalized policy acquisition costs. Safecard Services, Inc., a credit-card registration company which also incurred large outlays for membership acquisition, capitalized its membership acquisition costs and amortized them over a ten-year period.

When CUC made the initial public stock offering, it had only a limited following among analysts and institutional investors. As the company grew larger, it sought to broaden its investor base. Some analysts, however, were concerned that capitalized marketing costs would subsequently have to be written off as losses because of high uncertainty about future renewal rates. They argued that deferring current marketing costs lowered the firm's earnings quality.

Analysts' concerns about the firm's accounting for marketing costs may have arisen from their experience with Safecard Services Inc. Safecard's capitalization of membership acquisition costs had been the subject of considerable controversy in the financial press. Safecard's decision to write off deferred marketing costs in 1987 may have heightened analysts' concerns about the value of CUC's capitalized marketing costs.

By early 1989 the company's stock had become a target of short sellers and its price began to suffer. As shown in Exhibit 1, short positions in the company rose from approximately 157,000 in November 1988 to more than 2,000,000 in March 1989.[3] While the stock market was generally on the upswing, CUC's stock price declined from $19.3 at the beginning of January 1988 to $16.3 at the beginning of March 1989. Exhibit 2 shows the stock price performance for CUC relative to the performance of the value-weighted OTC market index between January 1, 1988, and March 1, 1989. During this period CUC's stock price declined by 50 percent relative to the market. *Value Line Investment Survey* commented in its report on CUC dated March 17, 1989:

> *CUC International shares have taken a beating. The stock has fallen more than 35% since our last report three months ago. Wall Street's concern over the company's accounting methods . . . contributed to the stock price decline.*

Management believed that the decline in CUC's stock performance could not be explained by either disappointing current operating performance or by forecasts of slower growth. Quarterly revenues and earnings grew steadily throughout 1988, and were consistent with *Value Line* analyst forecasts. In its March 18, 1988, report, *Value Line* forecasted that the company would have earnings of $5.5 million, $6 million, and $6.6 million in the quarters ending in April 1988, July 1988, and October 1988. Actual earnings in these quarters were $6 million, $6.6 million, and $6.9 million, respectively. The

3. *Source:* Barron's Financial Weekly *(Down Jones News Service).*

company projected that its growth would continue in the future—sales were projected to grow by 30 percent per year and operating cash flows would grow by 60 percent per year during the next five years. Finally, the firm was able to fund its substantial marketing outlays solely from operating cash flows during this period.

POSSIBLE MANAGEMENT RESPONSES

At least three options were available to CUC's management in responding to investors' concerns. One approach would be to adopt a more conservative policy to account for membership acquisition costs. By writing off previously capitalized expenses and adopting a policy of expensing future outlays as incurred, the firm would eliminate the major source of analysts' criticisms. However, such a move would seriously affect the company's balance sheet and income statement. More importantly, the accounting change would be unlikely to help management convince investors that current marketing outlays have future benefits.

An alternative strategy would be to provide expanded disclosure to justify the firm's capitalization of membership acquisition costs. This approach would involve identifying what type of information is likely to be most relevant and credible to investors. Further, it would require assessing whether the additional disclosures would provide proprietary information to competitors.

Finally, CUC could use corporate finance policies to enhance its stock price. Investors typically interpret cash payouts in the form of dividends and share repurchases as an indication of management's optimism about the firm's future cash flows. Such payouts, however, need to be planned in the context of the firm's investment needs for membership acquisitions.

One of the items on the agenda of CUC's upcoming board meeting was to consider proposals for dealing with the firm's communication challenge. Stu Bell was wondering which of the above options he should recommend.

QUESTIONS

1. What are the key success factors for CUC? How well does the company's management address them?
2. Is CUC's policy of capitalizing membership acquisition costs appropriate? Does this policy make the income statement more or less likely to reflect the company's operating performance?
3. Evaluate CUC's cash flow. Is the company financially healthy?
4. Why do you think CUC's investors are so concerned? Is CUC's stock undervalued?
5. CUC's CFO Stu Bell was considering a large stock repurchase or one-time dividend payment, financed by debt, as a way to improve investor confidence. Do you think this is a good idea? What is the maximum amount the company can borrow to finance this initiative without taking undue financial risk?
6. Assuming that CUC implements the stock repurchase or dividend payment plan, should the company do anything with respect to its accounting for membership acquisition costs?

EXHIBIT 1

CUC International Shares Sold Short from January 1988 to March 1989

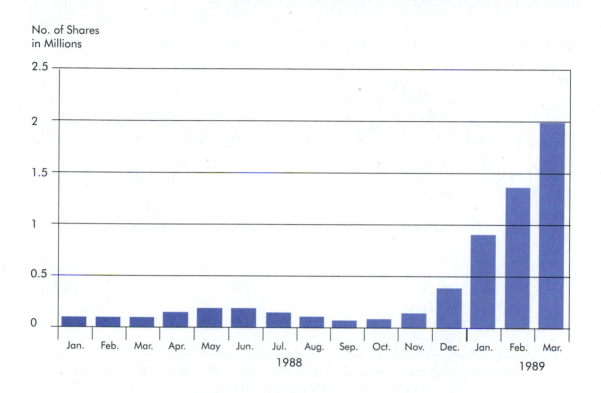

No. of Shares
in Millions

CUC International

EXHIBIT 2

Cumulative Difference in Stock Returns for CUC International and the OTC Market Index in the Period January 4, 1988, to March 9, 1989

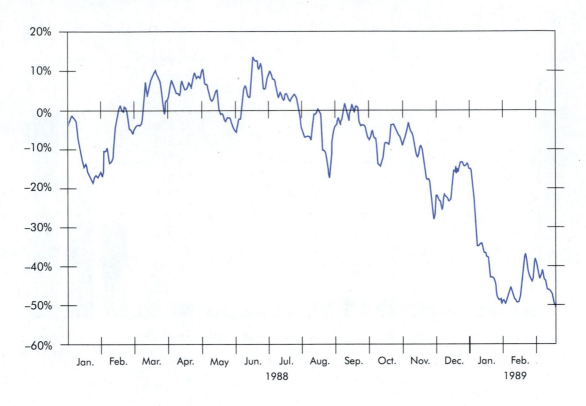

EXHIBIT 3

CUC International, Abridged Annual Report for the Year Ended January 31, 1988

CONSOLIDATED BALANCE SHEET

	January 31	
(Dollar amounts in thousands)	1988	1987
ASSETS		
Current Assets		
Cash and cash equivalents	$ 25,953	$ 14,810
Receivables, less allowance of $613 and $405	33,201	24,209
Prepaid expenses and other	3,468	3,288
Total Current Assets	62,622	42,307
Deferred membership charges, net	22,078	13,112
Prepaid solicitation costs	17,089	4,915
Prepaid commissions	6,267	8,127
Contract renewal rights, net	27,944	30,443
Excess of cost over net assets acquired, net	33,301	19,066
Properties, net	16,048	10,074
Other	1,519	4,416
Total Assets	$186,868	$132,460
LIABILITIES AND SHAREHOLDERS' EQUITY		
Current Liabilities		
Members' deposits	$ 4,997	$ 4,340
Accounts payable and accrued expenses	36,063	16,446
Federal and state income taxes	423	
Current portion of long-term obligations	1,404	5,011
Total Current Liabilities	42,887	25,797
Convertible subordinated debentures	12,000	22,000
Long-term obligations	3,767	5,120
Deferred income taxes	14,624	6,073
Other	1,229	1,268
Total Liabilities	74,507	60,258
Shareholders' Equity		
Common stock-par value $.01 per share; authorized 50 million shares; issued 19,683,567 and 17,820,338	197	178
Additional paid-in capital	82,271	59,550
Retained earnings	32,420	14,997
Treasury stock—398,230 and 398,091 shares, at cost	(2,527)	(2,523)
Total Shareholders' Equity	112,361	72,202
Total Liabilities and Shareholders' Equity	$186,868	$132,460

CUC International

CUC International

CONSOLIDATED STATEMENT OF INCOME

	Year Ended January 31		
(Dollar amounts in thousands, except per share amounts)	1988	1987	1986
Revenues			
Membership and service fees	$195,277	$138,149	$84,123
Other	3,180	3,610	3,342
Total Revenues	198,457	141,759	87,465
Expenses			
Operating	64,092	43,248	26,729
Marketing	68,937	56,496	35,042
General and administrative	31,729	23,342	14,572
Interest	2,259	2,663	1,507
Total Expenses	167,017	125,749	77,850
Operating Income	31,440	16,010	9,615
Acquisition costs			2,348
Income Before Income Taxes and Extraordinary Credit	31,440	16,010	7,267
Provision for income taxes	14,017	7,350	4,435
Income Before Extraordinary Credit	17,423	8,660	2,832
Extraordinary credit-utilization of tax loss carryforwards		1,041	3,589
Net Income	$ 17,423	$ 9,701	$ 6,421
Income Per Common Share			
Income before extraordinary credit	$.90	$.49	$.18
Extraordinary credit		.06	.23
Net Income Per Common Share	$.90	$.55	$.41

CONSOLIDATED STATEMENT OF CASH FLOWS

(Dollar amounts in thousands)	1988	1987	1986
Operating Activities			
Net income	$17,423	$ 9,701	$ 6,421
Adjustments to reconcile net income to net cash provided by operating activities:			
Amortization of membership acquisition costs	44,641	35,501	20,237
Amortization of prepaid commissions	1,860	2,029	2,081
Amortization of contract rights and excess cost	3,423	2,199	
Deferred income taxes	11,712	5,553	442
Depreciation	2,506	2,582	1,969
Extraordinary credit and loss from discontinued operations			(1,475)
Change in operating assets and liabilities, net of acquisitions:			
Net (increase) decrease in receivables	(8,049)	(6,747)	3,795
Net increase (decrease) in members' deposits, accounts payable and accrued expenses and federal and state income taxes	12,755	(3,649)	(586)
Deferred membership income	9,629	14,366	9,052
Membership acquisition costs	(63,236)	(43,720)	(42,564)
Prepaid solicitation costs	(12,174)	(4,915)	
Prepaid commissions			(409)
Other, net	2,576	(1,748)	39
Net cash from (used in) operating activities	23,066	11,152	(998)
Investing Activities			
Acquisitions, net of cash acquired	(4,625)	(18,341)	
Acquisitions of properties	(7,586)	(5,078)	(4,345)
Proceeds from disposal of properties net of $3.2 million note receivable		783	
Disposals of marketable securities		1,933	2,724
Other, net			240
Net cash from (used in) investing activities	(12,211)	(20,703)	(1,381)
Financing Activities			
Issuance of Common Stock	5,326	6,220	613

CUC International

CONSOLIDATED STATEMENT OF CASH FLOWS (continued)

(Dollar amounts in thousands)	1988	1987	1986
Issuance of convertible subordinated debentures			15,000
Purchase of treasury stock		(2,377)	
Repayments of long-term obligations	(4,960)	(2,955)	(795)
Other, net	(78)		
Net cash from financing activities	288	888	14,818
Net Increase (Decrease) in Cash and Cash Equivalents	11,143	(8,663)	12,439
Cash and cash equivalents at beginning of year	14,810	23,473	11,034
Cash and cash equivalents at end of year	$25,953	$14,810	$23,473

Year Ended January 31

NOTES TO CONSOLIDATED FINANCIAL STATEMENTS

Note 1. Summary of Significant Accounting Policies

Principles of Consolidation: The consolidated financial statements include the accounts of CUC International Inc. (formerly Comp-U-Card International Incorporated) and its wholly-owned subsidiaries. The Company operates in one business segment, providing a variety of services through individual, financial institution, credit union and group memberships. All significant intercompany transactions have been eliminated in consolidation.

Deferred Membership Charges, Net: Deferred membership charges is comprised of (in thousands):

January 31,	1988	1987
Deferred membership income	$(52,834)	$(43,205)
Unamortized membership acquisition costs	74,912	56,317
Deferred membership charges, net	$ 22,078	$ 13,112

The related membership fees and membership acquisition costs have been between $30 and $39 per individual member during the years ended January 31, 1988 and 1987. In addition, the annual renewal costs have remained between ten and twenty percent of annual membership fees for the same period.

Renewal costs consist principally of charges from sponsoring institutions and are amortized over the renewal period. Individual memberships are principally for a one-year period. These membership fees are recorded, as deferred membership income, upon acceptance of membership, net of estimated cancellations, and pro-rated over the membership period. The related initial membership acquisition costs are recorded as incurred and charged to operations as membership fees are recognized, allowing for renewals, over a three-year period. Such costs are amortized commencing with the beginning of the membership period, at the annual rate of 40%, 30% and 30%, respectively. Membership renewal rates are dependent upon the nature of the benefits and services provided by the Company in its various membership programs. Through January 31, 1988, membership renewal rates have been sufficient to generate future revenue in excess of deferred membership acquisition costs over the remaining amortization period.

Amortization of membership acquisition costs, including deferred renewal costs, amounted to $44.6 million, $35.5 million and $20.2 million for the years ended January 31, 1988, 1987, and 1986, respectively.

Prepaid Solicitation Costs: Prepaid solicitation costs consist of initial membership acquisition costs pertaining to membership solicitation programs that were in process at year end. Accordingly, no membership fees had been received or recognized at year end.

Prepaid Commissions: Prepaid commissions consist of the amount to be paid in connection with the termination of contracts with the Company's field sales force ($4.9 million and $5.8 million at January 31, 1988 and 1987, respectively) and the termination of special compensation agreements with an officer and former officer ($1.3 million and $1.6 million at January 31, 1988 and 1987, respectively). The amount relating to the termination of the field sales force is being amortized, using the straight-line method, over eight years and the amount relating to the termination of the special compensation agreement is being amortized ratably over ten years.

Contract Renewal Rights: Contract renewal rights represent the value assigned to contracts acquired in acquisitions and are being amortized over 9 to 16 years using the straight-line method.

Excess of Cost Over Net Assets Acquired: The excess of cost over net assets acquired is being amortized over 15 to 25 years using the straight-line method.

Earnings Per Share: Amounts per share have been computed using the weighted average number of common and common equivalent shares outstanding. The weighted average number of common and common equivalent shares outstanding was 19.4 million, 17.8 million and 15.8 million for the years ended January 31, 1988, 1987, and 1986, respectively. Fully diluted earnings per share did not differ significantly from primary earnings per share in any year.

Statement of Cash Flows: The Company adopted Financial Accounting Standards Board (FASB) "Statement of Cash Flows" in its fiscal 1988 financial statements and restated previously reported statements of changes in financial position for fiscal years 1987 and 1986. For purposes of the consolidated statement of cash flows, the Company considers all investments with a maturity of three months or less to be cash equivalents.

FINANCIAL HIGHLIGHTS

(In thousands, except per share amounts)

Year Ended January 31	1988	1987	1986	1985	1984
Total Revenues	$198,457	$141,759	$87,465	$65,947	$45,468
Net Income	17,423	9,701	6,421	4,214	3,184
Per Common Share:					
Net Income	$ .90	$ .55	$ .41	$ .28	$ .23
Book Value	5.83	4.14	2.33	1.94	1.70
Shareholders' Equity	$112,361	$ 72,202	$34,859	$28,673	$24,806
Number of Active Members	10,000	8,400	4,700	1,200	450

REPORT OF INDEPENDENT AUDITORS

Ernst & Whinney

Six Landmark Square, Suite 500
Stamford, Connecticut 06901

Board of Directors and Shareholders
CUC International Inc.
Stamford, Connecticut

We have examined the consolidated balance sheet of CUC International Inc. as of January 31, 1988 and 1987, and the related consolidated statements of income, shareholders' equity and cash flows for each of the three years in the period ended January 31, 1988. Our examinations were made in accordance with generally accepted auditing standards and, accordingly, included such tests of the accounting records and such other auditing procedures as we considered necessary in the circumstances.

In our opinion, the consolidated financial statements referred to above present fairly the consolidated financial position of CUC International Inc. at January 31, 1988 and 1987, and the consolidated results of operations and cash flows for each of the three years in the period ended January 31, 1988, in conformity with generally accepted principles applied on a consistent basis.

Ernst & Whinney

Stamford, Connecticut
March 30, 1988

EXHIBIT 4

CUC International, Abridged Interim Financial Statements for Nine
Months Ended October 31, 1988

CONSOLIDATED BALANCE SHEET

(Dollar amounts in thousands)	October 31, 1988 (unaudited)	January 31, 1988
ASSETS		
Current Assets		
Cash and cash equivalents	$ 32,003	$ 25,953
Receivables	38,118	33,201
Other	4,164	3,468
Total Current Assets	74,285	62,622
Deferred membership charges, net	37,223	22,078
Prepaid solicitation costs	25,538	17,089
Prepaid commissions	5,397	6,267
Contract renewal rights and intangible assets, net	64,419	61,245
Properties, net	19,805	16,048
Other	2,040	1,519
Total Assets	$228,707	$186,868

CUC International

CONSOLIDATED BALANCE SHEET (continued)

(Dollar amounts in thousands)	October 31, 1988 (unaudited)	January 31, 1988
LIABILITIES AND SHAREHOLDERS' EQUITY		
Current Liabilities		
Members' deposits	$ 4,485	$ 4,997
Accounts payable and accrued expenses	50,017	36,063
Federal and state income taxes	1,264	423
Current portion of long-term obligations	1,494	1,404
Total Current Liabilities	57,260	42,887
Convertible subordinated debentures	12,000	12,000
Long-term obligations	2,673	3,767
Deferred income taxes	16,844	14,624
Other	1,402	1,229
Total Liabilities	90,179	74,507
Shareholders' Equity		
Common Stock	203	197
Other shareholders' equity	138,325	112,164
Total Shareholders' Equity	138,528	112,361
Total Liabilities and Shareholders' Equity	$228,707	$186,868

CUC International

CONSOLIDATED INCOME STATEMENT
(unaudited)

(In thousands, except per share amounts)	Three Months Ended October 31		Nine Months Ended October 31	
	1988	1987	1988	1987
Revenues				
Membership and service fees	$70,131	$50,696	$192,016	$143,409
Other	938	386	2,297	1,693
Total Revenues	71,069	51,082	194,313	145,102
Expenses				
Operating	24,320	16,258	64,123	47,608
Marketing	23,524	17,761	65,647	50,625
General and administrative	11,787	8,721	32,363	25,097
Total Expenses	59,631	42,740	162,133	123,330
Operating Income	11,438	8,342	32,180	21,772
Provision for income taxes	4,577	3,672	12,854	9,591
Net Income	$ 6,861	$ 4,670	$ 19,326	$ 12,181
Net Income Per Common Share	$.33	$.24	$.93	$.63
Weighted Average Number of Common and Common Equivalent Shares Outstanding	20,752	19,665	20,870	19,231

CUC International

Management Communications

Management communication is increasingly important as firms invest in complex product and production technologies and in intangible assets such as research and development. These outlays can be quite difficult for outsiders to value, since they do not have access to the same data as management. As we discuss in this chapter, financial reports provide a low-cost way for management to communicate with investors. However, financial reports are not always effective as a communication vehicle. We therefore examine how alternative forms of communication can be used by management to mitigate information problems with external investors.

Several questions can be addressed by analyzing management's communication strategy:

- Management can ask: Is our current communication strategy effective in helping investors understand the firm's business strategy and expected future performance, thereby ensuring that our stock price is not seriously over- or undervalued?
- Securities analysts can ask: Do management's communications provide us with credible information that is useful for forecasting a firm's future performance? What types of information can we reasonably expect management to provide us? And how should we interpret information provided by management?

Throughout this book we have focussed primarily on showing how financial statement data can be helpful for *analysts* and *outside investors* in making a variety of decisions. In this chapter we change our emphasis and focus primarily on *management's* use of financial analysis to help communicate effectively with external users. However, as we note above, analysis of management's communication strategy is also likely to be useful to securities analysts.

COMMUNICATING WITH INVESTORS

Some managers argue that communication problems are not worth worrying about. They maintain that as long as managers make investment and operating decisions that enhance shareholder value, investors will value their performance and the firm's stock accordingly. While this is true in the long run, since all information is eventually public, it may not hold in the short- or even medium-term. If investors do not have access to the same information as management, they will probably find it difficult to value new and innovative investments. In an efficient capital market, they will not consistently over- or undervalue these new investments, but their valuations will tend to be noisy. This can make stock prices relatively noisy, leading management at various times to consider their firms to be either seriously over-or undervalued.

Does it matter if a firm's stock is over- or undervalued for a period? Most managers would prefer to not have their stock undervalued, since it makes it more costly to raise new financing. They may also worry that undervaluation is likely to increase the chance of a takeover by a hostile acquirer, with an accompanying reduction in their job security. Managers of firms that are overvalued may be concerned about the market's assessment, since they are legally liable for failing to disclose information relevant to investors.[1] They may therefore not wish to see their stock seriously overvalued, even though over-valuation provides opportunities to issue new equity at favorable rates.

A Word of Caution

It is natural that many managers believe that firms are undervalued by the capital market. This frequently occurs because it is difficult for managers to be realistic about their company's future performance. After all, it is part of their job to sell the company to new employees, customers, suppliers, and investors. In addition, forecasting the firm's future performance objectively requires them to judge their own capabilities as managers. Thus, many managers may argue that investors are uninformed and that their firm is un-dervalued. Only some can back that up with solid evidence.

If management decides that the firm does face a genuine information problem, it can be-gin to consider whether and how this could be redressed. Is the problem potentially serious enough that it is worth doing something to alter investors' perceptions? Or is the problem likely to resolve itself within a short period? Does the firm have plans to raise new equity or to use equity to acquire another company? Is management's job security threatened? As we discuss below, there is a wide range of options for management in this situation.

Key Analysis Questions

We recommend that before jumping to the conclusion that their firm is under-valued, managers should analyze their firm's performance and compare their own forecasts of future performance with those of analysts, using the following approach:

- *Is there a significant difference between internal management forecasts of future earnings and cash flows and those of outside analysts?*
- *Do any differences between managers' and analysts' forecasts arise because of different expectations about economy-wide performance?* Managers may understand their own businesses better than analysts, but they may not be any better at forecasting macroeconomic conditions.

> • *Can managers identify any factors that might explain a difference between analysts' and managers' forecasts of future performance?* For example, are analysts unaware of positive new R&D results, do they have different information about customer responses to new products and marketing campaigns, etc.? These types of differences could indicate that the firm faces an information problem.

Example: Communication Issues for FPIC Insurance Group

FPIC Insurance Group Inc. is the largest provider of liability insurance for doctors and hospitals in Florida. In the period 1996 to 1998, FPIC reported stable returns on equity of 13.8 percent, average growth in both revenues and net income of 28 percent, and growth in book equity of 2.8 percent. On December 31, 1998, the firm had a book value per share of $15.85, a price-to-book value of 2.23, a price to earnings multiple of 15.9, and an equity beta of 1.57.

In August 1999, the firm's stock price declined from $45.25 to $14.25. The stock decline began on August 10, the day the company reported a 48 percent jump in second-quarter profits to $7.4 million. The earnings increase was in part attributable to the FPIC's Florida Physicians unit releasing $8.1 million in reserves it had set aside against future claims, compared with $4 million in the year-ago quarter. In addition, the company reported higher-than-expected claims in a health insurance plan offered to Florida Dental Association members.

Reuters reported that the stock price decline reflected investors' concern about the quality of the firm's earnings. However, in response FPIC spokeswoman Amy D. Ryan stated, "As far as we're concerned, we had a great quarter." The company's chief operating officer, John Byers, argued that the company's decision to release the unit's reserves was normal business practice and based on its expectations of future claims. In response to the higher than expected dental claims, the company announced that it had increased its rates for this insurance.

The sharp decline in its price raises questions about the valuation of the company's stock. On September 9, 1999, the price-to-book ratio was less than one, and the price-to-earnings multiple was 6.0. The market therefore expected that the company would generate a return on equity somewhat lower than its cost of capital. FPIC's management appeared to be puzzled by the sharp drop in price and argued that the market was undervaluing the firm. However, before this can be concluded, a number of questions need to answered:

• Was the firm previously overvalued? If so, what forces were behind the market's high valuation of the company? If the market expected the company to continue to grow at 2.8 percent, to generate a 13.8 percent return on equity, and the firm's cost of capital is 11.3 percent (consistent with a market risk premium of 4 percent and a risk free rate of 5 percent), FPIC would be worth around $20.50. Why then was the stock valued at $45 early in August? Had management been painting too rosy a picture for the company's future in its meetings with analysts?

- What events explain the company's sudden drop in stock value? As noted above, the primary question for analysts was the quality of the firm's earnings. However, management needs to have a deeper understanding of these issues.
- If management believes that the firm is actually undervalued, what options are available to correct the market's view of the company?

COMMUNICATION THROUGH FINANCIAL REPORTING

Financial reports are the least costly and the most popular format for management communication. Below we discuss the role of financial reporting as a means of investor communication, the institutions that make accounting information credible, and when it is likely to be ineffective.

Accounting as a Means of Management Communication

As we discussed in Chapters 3 to 8, financial reports are an important medium for management communication with external investors. Reports provide investors with an explanation of how their money has been invested, a summary of the performance of those investments, and a discussion of how current performance fits within the firm's overall philosophy and strategy.

Accounting reports not only provide a record of past transactions, they also reflect management estimates and forecasts of the future. For example, they include estimates of bad debts, forecasts of the lives of tangible assets, and implicit forecasts that outlays will generate future cash flow benefits that exceed their cost. Since management is likely to be in a position to make forecasts of these future events that are more accurate than those of external investors, financial reports are a potentially useful form of communicating with investors. However, investors are also likely to be skeptical of reports prepared by management, since managers have conflicts of interest in providing information that will be used to assess their own performance.

Investors' Concerns about the Credibility of Accounting Communication

It is difficult for managers to be truly impartial in providing external investors with information about their firm's performance. Management has a natural incentive to want to "sell" the company, in part because that is its job and in part because it is reluctant to provide information that jeopardizes its own job security. Reporting consistently poor earnings increases the likelihood that top management will be replaced, either by the board of directors or by an acquirer who takes over the firm to improve its management.[2] Consequently, investors sometimes believe that accounting communications lack credibility.

Factors that Increase the Credibility of Accounting Communication

A number of mechanisms mitigate conflicts of interest in financial reporting and increase the credibility of accounting information that is communicated to stockholders. These include accounting standards, auditing, monitoring of management by financial analysts, and management reputation.

ACCOUNTING STANDARDS AND AUDITING.   Accounting standards, such as those promulgated by the Financial Accounting Standards Board (FASB) and the Securities Exchange Commission (SEC) in the U.S., provide guidelines for managers on how to make accounting decisions and provide outside investors with a way of interpreting these decisions. Uniform accounting standards attempt to reduce managers' ability to record similar economic transactions in different ways, either over time or across firms. Compliance with these standards is enforced by external auditors who attempt to ensure that managers' estimates are reasonable. Auditors therefore reduce the likelihood of earnings management.

MONITORING BY FINANCIAL ANALYSTS.   Financial intermediaries, such as analysts, also limit management's ability to manage earnings. Financial analysts specialize in developing firm- and industry-specific knowledge, enabling them to assess the quality of a firm's reported numbers and to make any necessary adjustments. Analysts evaluate the appropriateness of management's forecasts implicit in accounting method choices and reported accruals. This requires a thorough understanding of the firm's business and the relevant accounting rules used in the preparation of its financial reports. Superior analysts adjust reported accrual numbers, if necessary, to reflect economic reality, perhaps by using the cash flow statement and the footnote disclosures.

Analysts' business and technical expertise as well as their legal liability and incentives differ from those of auditors. Consequently, analyst reports can provide information to investors on whether the firm's accounting decisions are appropriate, or whether managers are overstating the firm's economic performance to protect their jobs.[3]

MANAGEMENT REPUTATION.   A third factor that can counteract external investors' natural skepticism about financial reporting is management reputation. Managers that expect to have an ongoing relation with external investors and financial intermediaries may be able to build a track record for unbiased financial reporting. By making accounting estimates and judgments that are supported by subsequent performance, managers can demonstrate their competence and reliability to investors and analysts. As a result, managers' future judgments and accounting estimates are more likely to be viewed as credible sources of information.

Limitations of Financial Reporting for Investor Communication

While accounting standards, auditing, monitoring of management by financial analysts, and management concerns about its reputation increase the credibility and informativeness of financial reports, these mechanisms are far from perfect. Consequently, there are times when financial reporting breaks down as a means for management to communicate with external investors. These breakdowns can arise when: (1) there are no accounting rules to guide practice or the existing rules do not distinguish between poor and successful performers, (2) auditors and analysts do not have the expertise to judge new products or business opportunities, or (3) management faces credibility problems.

ACCOUNTING RULES.   Despite the rapid increase in new accounting standards, accounting rules frequently do not distinguish between good and poor performers. For example, current accounting rules do not permit managers to show on their balance sheets in a timely fashion the benefits of investments in quality improvements, human resource development programs, research and development (with the exception of software development costs), and customer service.

Some of the problems with accounting standards arise because it takes time for standard setters to develop appropriate standards for many new types of economic transactions. Other difficulties arise because standards are the result of compromises between different interest groups (e.g., auditors, investors, corporate managers, and regulators).

AUDITOR AND ANALYST EXPERTISE.   While auditors and analysts have access to proprietary information, they do not have the same understanding of the firm's business as managers. The divergence between managers' and auditors'/analysts' business assessments is likely to be most severe for firms with distinctive business strategies, or firms that operate in emerging industries. In addition, auditors' decisions in these circumstances are likely to be dominated by concerns about legal liability, hampering management's ability to use financial reports to communicate effectively with investors.

MANAGEMENT CREDIBILITY.   When is management likely to face credibility problems with investors? There is very little evidence on this question. However, we expect that managers of new firms, firms with volatile earnings, firms in financial distress, and firms with poor track records in communicating with investors will find it difficult to be seen as credible reporters.

If management has a credibility problem, financial reports are likely to be viewed with much skepticism. Investors will see financial reporting estimates that increase income as evidence that management is padding earnings. This makes it very difficult for management to use financial reports to communicate positive news about future performance.

Example: Accounting Communication for FPIC Insurance Group

FPIC Insurance Group's key financial reporting estimates are for loss reserves for insurance claims using actuarial analysis of its own and other insurers' claims histories.

At the end of fiscal year 1998, FPIC reported a loss reserve of $242.3 million. In its 10-K, the management warns that "the uncertainties inherent in estimating ultimate losses on the basis of past experience have grown significantly in recent years, principally as a result of judicial expansion of liability standards and expansive interpretations of insurance contracts. These uncertainties may be further affected by, among other factors, changes in the rate of inflation and changes in the propensities of individuals to file claims. The inherent uncertainty of establishing reserves is relatively greater for companies writing long-tail casualty insurance."

To help investors assess its track record in making loss estimates, FPIC is required to provide a detailed breakdown of changes in loss estimates from prior years given actual claim losses. These data indicate that FPIC has actually been quite conservative in prior years' forecasts, and has historically incurred fewer losses than it had initially predicted.

It is interesting to note that the area that raised questions for investors about FPIC's record was precisely its conservative estimation of loss reserves and their subsequent reversal. By being conservative, management may have raised questions about its ability to forecast losses reliably in the future.

Key Analysis Questions

For management interested in understanding how effectively the firm's financial reports help it communicate with outside investors, the following questions are likely to provide a useful starting point:

- What are the key business risks that have to be managed effectively? What processes and controls are in place to manage these risks?
- How are the firm's key business risks reflected in the financial statements? For example, credit risks are reflected in the bad debt allowance, and product quality risks are reflected in allowances for product returns and the method of revenue recognition. For these types of risks, what message is the firm sending on the management of these risks through its estimates or choices of accounting methods? Has the firm been unable to deliver on the forecasts underlying these choices, through writeoffs or accounting method changes? Alternatively, does the market seem to be ignoring the message underlying the firm's financial reporting choices, indicating a lack of credibility?
- How does the firm communicate about key risks that cannot be reflected in accounting estimates or methods? For example, if technological innovation risk is critical for a company, it is unable to reflect how well it is managing this risk through research and development in its financial statements. However, that does not mean that investors will not have questions about this business issue.

OTHER FORMS OF COMMUNICATING WITH INVESTORS

Given the limitations of accounting standards, auditing, and monitoring by financial analysts, as well as the reporting credibility problems faced by management, firms that wish to communicate effectively with external investors are often forced to use alternative media. Below we discuss three alternative ways that managers can communicate with external investors and analysts: meetings with analysts to publicize the firm, expanded voluntary disclosure, and using financing policies to signal management expectations. These forms of communication are typically not mutually exclusive. For example, at meetings with analysts, management usually discloses additional information that is helpful in valuing the firm.

Analyst Meetings

One popular way for managers to help mitigate communication problems is to meet regularly with financial analysts that follow the firm. At these meetings, management will field questions about the firm's current financial performance as well discuss its future business plans. As noted above, management typically provides additional disclosures to analysts at these meetings. In addition to holding analyst meetings, many firms appoint a director of public relations, who provides further regular contact with analysts seeking more information on the firm.

In the last five years, conference calls have become a popular forum for management to communicate with financial analysts. Recent research finds that firms are more likely to host calls if they are in industries where financial statement data fail to capture key business fundamentals on a timely basis.[4] In addition, conference calls themselves appear to provide new information to analysts about a firm's performance and future prospects.[5]

Voluntary Disclosure

One way for managers to improve the credibility of their financial reporting is through voluntary disclosure. Accounting rules usually prescribe minimum disclosure requirements, but they do not restrict managers from voluntarily providing additional information. These could include an articulation of the company's long-term strategy, specification of nonfinancial leading indicators which are useful in judging the effectiveness of the strategy implementation, explanation of the relation between the leading indicators and future profits, and forecasts of future performance. Voluntary disclosures can be reported in the firm's annual report, in brochures created to describe the firm to investors, in management meetings with analysts, or in investor relations responses to information requests.[6]

One constraint on expanded disclosure is the competitive dynamics in product markets. Disclosure of proprietary information on strategies and their expected economic consequences may hurt the firm's competitive position. Managers then face a trade-off between providing information that is useful to investors in assessing the firm's economic performance, and withholding information to maximize the firm's product market advantage.

A second constraint in providing voluntary disclosure is management's legal liability. Forecasts and voluntary disclosures can potentially be used by dissatisfied shareholders to bring civil action against management for providing misleading information. This seems ironic, since voluntary disclosures should provide investors with additional information. Unfortunately, it can be difficult for courts to decide whether managers' disclosures were good-faith estimates of uncertain future events which later do not materialize, or whether management manipulated the market. Consequently, many corporate legal departments recommend against management providing much voluntary disclosure.

Finally, management credibility can limit a firm's incentives to provide voluntary disclosures. If management faces a credibility problem in financial reporting, any voluntary disclosures it provides are also likely to be viewed skeptically. In particular, investors may be concerned about what management is not telling them, particularly since such disclosures are not audited.

Selected Financial Policies

Managers can also use financing policies to communicate effectively with external investors. Financial policies that are useful in this respect include dividend payouts, stock repurchases, financing choices, and hedging strategies. One important difference between this type of communication and additional disclosure is that the firm does not provide potentially proprietary information to competitors. The signal therefore indicates to competitors that a firm's management is bullish on its future, but it does not provide any details.

DIVIDEND PAYOUT POLICIES.   As we discussed in Chapter 16, a firm's cash payout decisions can provide information to investors on managers' assessments of the firm's future prospects. This arises because dividend payouts tend to be sticky, in the sense that managers are reluctant to cut dividends. Thus, managers will only increase dividends when they are confident that they are able to sustain the increased rate in future years. Consequently, investors interpret dividend increases as signals of managers' confidence in the quality of current and future earnings.[7]

STOCK REPURCHASES.   In some countries, such as the U.S. and the U.K., managers can use stock repurchases to communicate with external investors. Under a stock repurchase, the firm buys back its own stock, either through a purchase on the open market, through a tender offer, or through a negotiated purchase with a large stockholder. Of course a stock repurchase, particularly a tender offer repurchase, is an expensive way for management to communicate with outside investors. Firms typically pay a hefty premium to acquire their shares in tender offer repurchases, potentially diluting the value of the shares that are not tendered or not accepted for tender. In addition, the fees to investment banks, lawyers, and share solicitation fees are not trivial. Given these costs, it is not surprising that research findings indicate that stock repurchases are effective signals to investors about the level and risk of future earnings performance.[8] Research findings also suggest that firms that use stock repurchases to communicate with investors have accounting assets that reflect less of firm value and have high general information asymmetry.[9]

FINANCING CHOICES.   Firms that have problems communicating with external investors may be able to use financing choices to reduce them. For example, a firm that is unwilling to provide proprietary information to help dispersed public investors value it may be willing to provide such information to a knowledgeable private investor—which can become a large stockholder/creditor—or a bank that agrees to provide the company with a significant new loan. A firm with credibility problems in financial reporting can sell stock or issue debt to an informed private investor such as a large customer who has superior information about the quality of its product or service.

Such changes in financing and ownership can mitigate communication problems in two ways. First, the terms of the new financing arrangement and the credibility of the new lender or stockholder can provide investors with information to reassess the value of the firm. Second, the accompanying increased concentration of ownership and the role of large block holders in corporate governance can have a positive effect on valuation. If investors are concerned about management's incentives to increase shareholder value, the presence of a new block shareholder or significant creditor on the board can be reassuring. This type of monitoring arises in leveraged buyouts, start-ups backed by venture capital, and in firms with equity partnership investments. In Japanese and German corporations, it may also arise because large banks own both debt and equity and have close working relationships with firms' managers.

Of course, in the extreme, management can decide that the best option for the firm is to no longer continue operating as a public company. This can be accomplished by a management buyout, where a buyout group (including management) leverages its own investment (using bank or public debt finance), buys the firm, and takes it private. The buyout firm hopes to run the firm for several years and then take the company public again, hopefully with a track record of improved performance that enables investors to value the firm more effectively.

HEDGING.   An important source of mispricing arises if investors are unable to distinguish between unexpected changes in reported earnings due to management performance and transitory shocks that are beyond managers' control (e.g., foreign currency translation gains and losses). Managers can counteract these effects by hedging such "accounting" risks. Even though hedging is costly, it may be valuable if it reduces information problems that potentially lead to misvaluation.

Example: Other Communications for FPIC Insurance Group

On August 12, 1999, FPIC Insurance Group announced that it would immediately begin purchasing shares of its common stock. As many as 429,000 shares were to be repurchased under the program. The company argued that the dramatic drop in its stock price was unwarranted and that its stock was now greatly undervalued. William R. Russell, president and chief executive officer of FPIC stated: "We believe the recent drop in our stock price may be linked to certain changes in our reserving policy that were described in our earnings release. We believe that our reserving policy is now and has always been appropriate. We believe that the market has overreacted and that FPIC continues to be an excellent long-term investment. Our repurchases . . . reflect our commitment to enhance shareholder value." (Reuters, August 12, 1999)

The repurchase temporarily arrested FPIC's stock price slide. The price recovered from $21 to around $26 during the repurchase period. However, this effect was temporary, and the price subsequently fell further to $14.25.

Key Analysis Questions

For management considering whether to use financing policies to communicate more effectively with investors, the following questions are likely to provide a useful starting point for analysis:

- Have other potentially less costly actions, such as expanded disclosure or accounting communication, been considered? If not, would these alternatives provide a lower cost means of communication? Alternatively, if management is concerned about providing proprietary information to competitors, or has low credibility, these alternatives may not be effective.
  Does the firm have sufficient free cash flow to be able to implement a share repurchase program or to increase dividends? If so, these may be feasible options. If the firm has excess cash available today but expects to be constrained in the future, a stock repurchase may be more effective. Alternatively, if management expects to have some excess cash available each year, a dividend increase may be in order.
- Is the firm cash constrained and unable to increase disclosure for proprietary reasons? If so, management may want to consider changing the mix of owners as a way of indicating to investors that another informed outsider is bullish on the company. Of course, one possibility is for management itself to increase its stake in the company.

SUMMARY

This chapter discussed firms' strategies for communicating with investors. Communication with investors can be useful because managers typically have better information on their firm's current and expected future performance than outside analysts and investors. By communicating effectively with investors, management can potentially reduce this information gap, lowering the likelihood that the stock will be mispriced or volatile. This can be important for firms that wish to raise new capital, avoid takeovers, or whose management is concerned that its true job performance is not reflected in the firm's stock.

The typical way for firms to communicate with investors is through financial reporting. Accounting standards and auditing make the reporting process a way for managers to not only provide information about the firm's current performance, but to indicate, through accounting estimates, where they believe the firm is headed in the future. However, financial reports are not always able to convey the types of forward looking information that investors need. Accounting standards often do not permit firms to capitalize outlays that provide significant future benefits to the firm, such as R&D outlays.

A second way that management can communicate with investors is through non-accounting means. We discussed several such mechanisms, including: meeting with financial analysts to explain the firm's strategy, current performance and outlook; disclosing additional information, both quantitative and qualitative, to provide investors with similar information as management's; and using financial policies (such as stock repurchases, dividend increases, and hedging) to help signal management's optimism about the firm's future performance.

In this chapter we have stressed the importance of communicating effectively with investors. However, firms also have to communicate with other stakeholders, including employees, customers, suppliers, and regulatory bodies. Many of the same principles discussed here can also be applied to management communication with these other stakeholders.

DISCUSSION QUESTIONS

1. Apple's inventory increased from $1 billion on December 29, 1994, to $1.95 billion one year later. In contrast, sales for the fourth quarter in each of these years increased from $2 billion to $2.6 billion. What is the implied annualized inventory turnover for Apple for these years? What different interpretations about future performance could a financial analyst infer from this change? What information could Apple's management provide to investors to clarify the change in inventory turnover? What are the costs and benefits to Apple from disclosing this information?

2. a. What are likely to be the long-term critical success factors for the following types of firms?
    - a high technology company, such as Microsoft
    - a large low-cost retailer, such as Kmart

   b. How useful is financial accounting data for evaluating how well these two companies are managing their critical success factors? What other types of information would be useful in your evaluation? What are the costs and benefits to these companies from disclosing this type of information to investors?

3. Management frequently objects to disclosing additional information on the grounds that it is proprietary. Consider the recent FASB proposals on expanding disclosures on (a) executive stock compensation and (b) business segment performance. Many corporate managers expressed strong opposition to both proposals. What are the potential proprietary costs from expanded disclosures in each of these areas? If you conclude that proprietary costs are relatively low for either, what alternative explanations do you have for management's opposition?

4. Financial reporting rules in many countries outside the U.S. (e.g., the U.K., Australia, New Zealand, and France) permit management to revalue fixed assets (and in some cases even intangible assets) which have increased in value. Revaluations are typically based on estimates of realizable value made by management or independent valuers. Do you expect that these accounting standards will make earnings and book values more or less useful to investors? Explain why or why not. How can management make these types of disclosures more credible?

5. Under a management buyout, the top management of a firm offers to buy the company from its stockholders, usually at a premium over its current stock price. The management team puts up its own capital to finance the acquisition, with additional financing typically coming from a private buyout firm and private debt. If management is interested in making such an offer for its firm in the near future, what are its financial reporting incentives? How do these differ from the incentives of management that are not interested in a buyout?

6. You are approached by the management of a small start-up company that is planning to go public. The founders are unsure about how aggressive they should be in their accounting decisions as they come to the market. John Smith, the CEO, asserts: "We might as well take full advantage of any discretion offered by accounting rules, since the market will be expecting us to do so." What are the pros and cons of this strategy?

7. Two years after a successful public offering, the CEO of a bio-technology company is concerned about stock market uncertainty surrounding the potential of new drugs in the development pipeline. In his discussion with you, the CEO notes that even though they have recently made significant progress in their internal R&D efforts, the stock has performed poorly. What options does he have to help convince investors of the value of the new products? Which of these options are likely to be feasible?

8. Why might the CEO of the bio-technology firm discussed in Question 7 be concerned about the firm being undervalued? Would the CEO be equally concerned if the stock is overvalued? Do you believe that the CEO would attempt to correct the market's perception in this overvaluation case?

9. When companies decide to shift from private to public financing by making an initial public offering for their stock, they are likely to face increased costs of investor communications. Given this additional cost, why would firms opt to go public?

10. German firms are traditionally financed by banks, which have representatives on the companies' boards. How would communication challenges differ for these firms relative to U.S. firms, which rely more on public financing?

NOTES

1. Douglas J. Skinner, "Earnings disclosures and stockholder lawsuits," *Journal of Accounting and Economics* (Nov. 1997): 249–283, finds that firms with bad earnings news tend to predisclose this information, perhaps to reduce the cost of litigation that inevitably follows bad news quarters.

2. Kevin J. Murphy and Jerold L. Zimmerman, "Financial Performance Surrounding CEO Turnover," *Journal of Accounting and Economics* 16 (January/April/July 1993): 273–315, find a strong relation between CEO turnover and earnings-based performance.

3. For example, George Foster, "Rambo IX: Briloff and the Capital Market," *Journal of Accounting, Auditing & Finance* 2, No. 4 (Fall 1987): 409–429, finds firms that are criticized for their accounting by Abraham J. Briloff on average suffer a 5 percent decline in their stock price.

4. See Sarah Tasker, "Voluntary Disclosure as a Response to Low Accounting Quality: Evidence from Quarterly Conference Call Usage," *Review of Accounting Studies*, forthcoming.

5. See Richard Frankel, Marilyn Johnson, and Douglas Skinner, "An Empirical Examination of Conference Calls as a Voluntary Disclosure Medium," working paper, University of Michigan, 1997.

6. Recent research on voluntary disclosure includes Mark Lang and Russell Lundholm, "Cross-Sectional Determinants of Analysts' Ratings of Corporate Disclosures," *Journal of Accounting Research* 31 (Autumn 1993): 246–271; Lang and Lundholm, "Corporate Disclosure Policy and Analysts," *The Accounting Review* 71 (October 1996): 467–492; M. Welker, "Disclosure Policy, Information Asymmetry and Liquidity in Equity Markets," *Contemporary Accounting Research* (Spring 1995); Christine Botosan, "The Impact of Annual Report Disclosure Level on Investor Base and the Cost of Capital," *The Accounting Review* (July 1997): 323–350; and Paul Healy, Amy Hutton, and Krishna Palepu, "Stock Performance and Intermediation Changes Surrounding Sustained Increases in Disclosure," *Contemporary Accounting Research*, forthcoming. This research finds that firms are more likely to provide high levels of disclosure if they have strong earnings performance, issue securities, have more analyst following, and have less dispersion in analyst forecasts. In addition, firms with high levels of disclosure policies tend to have a lower cost of capital and bid-ask spread. Finally, firms that increase disclosure have accompanying increases in stock returns, institutional ownership, analyst following, and stock liquidity.

7. Findings by Paul Healy and Krishna Palepu in "Earnings Information Conveyed by Dividend Initiations and Omissions," *Journal of Financial Economics* 21 (1988): 149–175, indicate that investors interpret announcements of dividend initiations and omissions as managers' forecasts of future earnings performance.

8. See Larry Dann, Ronald Masulis, and David Mayers, "Repurchase Tender Offers and Earnings Information," *Journal of Accounting & Economics* (Sept. 1991): 217–252, and Michael Hertzel and Prem Jain, "Earnings and Risk Changes Around Stock Repurchases," *Journal of Accounting & Economics* (Sept. 1991): 253–276.

9. See Mary Barth and Ron Kasznik, "Share Repurchase Decisions and Market Reaction: Accounting, Information Asymmetry, and Investment Opportunities," working paper, Stanford University, 1996.

On July 7, 1995, Sensormatic said earnings would be substantially below expectations and below last year's fourth quarter. Also troublesome was an August 31 announcement that the release of 1995 results would be delayed, pending an extended audit by Ernst & Young that is to be completed by mid-September. [Sensormatic] says it doesn't believe there will be any "major write-offs." [However], Wall Street short-sellers, who thrive on signs of accounting shenanigans, have targeted the company. [They argued that] Sensormatic's revenue accounting, while permissible under generally accepted accounting principles, was "overly aggressive." While that put pressure on the stock, it was the July 7 announcement that caused the stock to fall to $23 from a high of $36 two days earlier.[1]

Business Week, 9/18/95

BUSINESS HISTORY AND OPERATIONS

Overview

Ronald Assaf, CEO of Sensormatic, founded Sensormatic in 1965 after a burglary in his grocery store in Akron, Ohio. His idea was a security device that would deter shoplifting. With the help of two scientists, Assaf developed a semiconductor device encased in a plastic tag that could be attached to clothing. The tag, which must be removed with a special tool, operates in conjunction with a transmitter of microwave signals near the store exit. When the thief tries to leave the store, the microwave signal sets off an alarm.

Incorporated in 1968, Sensormatic grew steadily. For 39 consecutive quarters prior to July 1995 Sensormatic reported revenue and earnings growth of 20 percent or more. In 1995 Sensormatic reported sales of $860 million and net income of $73 million. Sensormatic's tags guarded everything from stereos at Macy's department stores to shampoo at CVS drugstores and lumber at the Home Depot. Hospitals used Sensormatic's equipment to prevent babies from being snatched from nurseries.

Doctoral Candidate James Jinho Chang and Professor Krishna G. Palepu prepared this case as the basis for class discussion rather than to illustrate either effective or ineffective handling of an administrative situation. Professor Amy Patricia Hutton provided helpful comments. Copyright © 1997 by the President and Fellows of Harvard College. Harvard Business School case 9-197-041.

1. Excerpts from *"This anti-theft company is feeling insecure,"* Business Week, *September 18, 1995.*

With diversification through acquisition, Sensormatic became an integrated supplier of electronic security systems to retail, commercial, industrial, and governmental markets. Sensormatic manufactured and marketed electronic article surveillance (EAS), closed circuit television (CCTV) systems, and Access Control systems. In fiscal 1995, revenues from EAS accounted for 57 percent of Sensormatic's total revenues and revenues from CCTV and Access Control accounted for 34 percent of total revenues. Sensormatic's products were marketed by a worldwide sales and service organization complemented by a broad network of business partners, independent distributors, and dealers. Sensormatic was appointed as an electronic security supplier for the 1996 Olympics.

Electronic Security Industry[2]

There were two theft-prevention methods: to monitor articles and to monitor people. The electronic security industry, based on EAS, monitored articles, and CCTV/Access Control systems monitored people. EAS, CCTV, and Access Control systems were used by retailers to deter shoplifting and internal theft. Inventory shrinkage was often the second largest variable operating expense of retailers, after payroll costs, and normally ranged from 1 to 5 percent of sales.

EAS systems consisted of two components: detectable security circuits embedded in tags, which were attached to the articles to be protected; and electronic detection equipment, referred to as sensors, usually located in the exit path. By 1995 the EAS market reported about $1 billion sales and was estimated to grow at 20 percent annually. The ultimate market size of EAS was estimated to be $2.5 billion. The fast industry growth was due to several factors: improved technology capabilities of loss prevention devices, lower costs of electronic security systems, the rising cost of security staff labor, and an increased need for open display of product. Major players in the EAS industry included Sensormatic, Checkpoint Systems, and 3M in the U.S. as well as Esselte Meto and Nedap B.V. in Europe. In 1995 Sensormatic was the world's largest provider of electronic anti-theft technology.

EAS products were first used by retailers to protect soft goods (e.g., apparel merchandise). Due to subsequent technological advances, applications for hard goods merchandise, which was generally packaged, also became economical and effective. Hard goods retailers such as drugstores, supermarkets, home improvements centers, and video stores increasingly became users of EAS products.

Sensormatic and Checkpoint competed primarily in the hard goods market, which accounted for 40 percent of Sensormatic's total revenues. Even though Sensormatic and Checkpoint had expanded the installation of EAS substantially, EAS penetration into hard goods stores was still low in 1995. The drugstore penetration by EAS was only 41

---

2. *Some of the material in this section is drawn from a report on checkpoint systems by Barry J. Peter, Deutsche Morgan Grenfell Inc., October 24, 1996.*

percent of the 38,150 drugstores in the U.S. Penetration in the supermarket industry (five times the size of the drugstore market) was just beginning. Only 4 percent of a total of 125,000 stores in the U.S. supermarket industry used EAS in 1995. Currently Sensormatic and Checkpoint split the EAS market in the supermarket industry evenly.

EAS sales are comprised of one-time sales and recurring revenues. Installation of an EAS sensor in the exit path (one-time sale) was charged at $40,000 per store with a 50 percent gross margin. Recurring revenues included disposable tags used by hard goods retailers. Each supermarket was expected to use 175,000 antitheft tags annually. Each antitheft tag was sold at $0.035 with gross margin approximately 70 percent. The recurring revenues from tags could grow from 25 to 50 percent of total revenues within the next three years.[3]

Checkpoint Systems, Sensormatic's main domestic competitor, was a popular supplier to the drugstore industry for many years (71 percent market share in 1995) because it was a first mover and a low cost provider. With revenues of approximately $204 million in 1995, Checkpoint had less resources than Sensormatic did. However, Checkpoint's competitive position was supported by its manufacturing know-how and, to a lesser degree, its technology and patents. Checkpoint believed that its manufacturing efficiencies gave it a significant cost advantage over its competitors. Checkpoint expected that volume increases would result in a further decrease of product cost. Checkpoint's strategy was to continue to increase its sales penetration in existing markets and to develop a significant presence in new geographic markets.

Checkpoint's current technology advantage was its reliable scan-deactivation of hidden tags. This technology deactivates hidden tags as salespeople check out customers' shopping items. Sensormatic was offering a different technology, a pass-around system that did not have the deactivation process. Under the pass-around system, merchandise is passed around a pair of sensors located at the checkout lane and only the customers go through the sensors. Problems of the pass-around system were tag pollution (tags which were not deactivated might cause false alarms at other stores) and higher capital costs (one pair of sensors per checkout lane rather than one per store). However, Checkpoint's scan-deactivation technology was not likely to be a sustainable advantage because Sensormatic was expected to develop the same technology in the near future.

The new trend in the EAS industry was source tagging, where disposable tags were packaged into consumer products at the point of manufacturing. The application of tags in an automated factory rather than at retailers' stores reduced labor costs. Source tagging increased tagging compliance and its feature of being hidden inside the package improved effectiveness. The ultimate market size for source tagging was believed to be in the neighborhood of 20–30 billion tags annually.

Most companies producing EAS expanded not only domestically but also internationally. EAS sales in Europe and Latin America had increased substantially. Industry experts forecasted that there was a great growth opportunity for EAS sales in the Asia/Pacific market.

---

3. *Excerpts from Deutsche Morgan Grenfell Analyst Report.*

CCTV products were used to protect against inventory shrinkage in retail businesses, and for the protection and monitoring of personnel and assets in office and manufacturing complexes. CCTV systems could be used alone or in combination with EAS and Access Control. The electronic door lock Access Control systems allowed employees with clearance to have free access and movement around the plant and offices without the need for constant checks or locked doors.

CCTV and Access Control markets were estimated to have $2–$3 billion combined annual sales. These businesses were also benefiting from the increasing costs of labor intensive methods (such as hiring security guards). The companies in CCTV and Access Control systems competed on the basis of product performance, multiple technologies, service, and price. CCTV and Access Control systems markets were highly fragmented with numerous providers, including Philips, Panasonic, CardKey, and Westinghouse Electronic Corporation, and there were few significant entry barriers. Firms with greater financial and other resources could enter into direct competition with existing companies.

Sensormatic's Strategies

GROWTH STRATEGY.   Sensormatic's key element for growth was to expand its product line and geographic market presence through acquisitions. Acquisitions were intended to strengthen Sensormatic's core business by increasing its ability to distribute its products and achieving synergy in the combined companies. In fiscal 1993, Sensormatic acquired Automated Loss Prevention Systems (ALPS), a large European distributor of EAS, and Security Tag Systems, Inc. (Security Tag), a U.S. manufacturer and distributor of loss prevention products. In 1995 Sensormatic acquired Knogo's overseas operations through a stock exchange.

The acquisitions of ALPS, Security Tag, and Knogo resulted in goodwill of approximately $223 million, $47 million, and $114 million, respectively, which were being amortized over 40 years. Sensormatic believed that this goodwill at the end of fiscal 1995 would be fully recoverable because the acquisitions were made to enhance the revenue and profit potential for the indefinite future of these companies by increasing efficiencies, and realizing synergies with Sensormatic's own core businesses.

The acquisition of direct and indirect distribution channels helped Sensormatic to reach a wide range of potential customers worldwide. Sensormatic applied the same approach used in penetrating the U.S. commercial/industrial market to developing a presence in this market in Europe. The company felt that not only its wide geographical presence but also its broad product portfolio provided it with a competitive advantage; if a company used an EAS from Sensormatic, it was also likely to choose Sensormatic for other related security products such as CCTV and Access Control since compatibility was an issue. Honeywell, Toshiba, Panasonic, Lux Products, Monsanto, and GTE were companies that had used Sensormatic's EAS and chose CCTV/Access Control systems from Sensormatic.

However, Sensormatic's management felt that the company had grown faster than its management and organization. The integration of the Knogo European operations was slower and costlier than planned. The rapid growth in sales, product diversity, and the demands of integrating acquired businesses outpaced the growth in corporate infrastructure and systems, resulting in adverse bottom-line figures in 1995 as expenses grew significantly faster than revenues.

MARKETING STRATEGY.   Sensormatic's major retail customers included Blockbuster Video, Sears Roebuck, Kmart, Wal-Mart, J.C. Penney, CVS, and Crown Books. Retail customers did not want to pay cash for the purchase of anti-theft systems until they achieved the benefits (payback period for the typical installation was six months).

A key element of Sensormatic's marketing strategy was to increase market penetration by providing alternative financing options to its retail customers (i.e., vendor financing). Sensormatic's management believed that this strategy gave the company a significant competitive advantage and helped it rapidly penetrate markets and increase customer loyalty. The longer-term financing arrangements were limited to products which had long useful lives (i.e., not offered with the sale of products such as disposable tags).

In order to finance customer receivables, Sensormatic entered into an agreement with a third-party financing institution whereby it could sell (with recourse) or assign (without recourse) certain pre-approved U.S. accounts receivables. This program also provided Sensormatic with the expertise of outside parties who were fully dedicated to the business of collecting receivables.

Checkpoint, a main competitor of Sensormatic, did not depend much on long-term financing arrangements, such as installment sales and deferred payment sales, to increase revenue. At Checkpoint, the only sales transactions made under long-term financing arrangements were sales-type leases, which accounted for a minor percentage of total sales in 1995. However, Sensormatic believed that Checkpoint would build up long-term receivables over time as Checkpoint received large orders from discount stores.

ACCOUNTING CONTROVERSY

Accounting Policy

SALES UNDER LONG-TERM FINANCING ARRANGEMENTS.   Sensormatic recognized revenue when a customer took title of the product, even though payments were sometimes not received for a considerable period of time thereafter. The longer term financing arrangements offered by the company included the following (see Exhibit 1 for the accounting method of alternative financing options, as reported by Sensormatic):

Installment sales. One financing option offered by Sensormatic, primarily to U.S. retail customers, was installment sales. Under this option, the purchase price was payable in equal installments, normally monthly, over the period of the sales contract, from one to five years. The stream of scheduled payments was discounted to its present value, using a market rate of interest. This amount was recognized as sales revenue at the date of shipment. Legal title to the equipment passed to the customer upon shipment, but Sensormatic normally retained a security interest in the equipment to secure the receivable. The total amount of installment sales receivables on Sensormatic's balance sheet represented total outstanding installment sales receivables less unearned interest income, unearned maintenance fees, and an allowance for doubtful accounts.

Deferred payment sales (extended credit terms). A second financing option offered primarily to U.S. retail customers was deferred payment sales, under which the payment date was delayed for a specific period, more than 90 days but not more than 365 days after the product shipment date. The accounting treatment was the same as was used with installment sales—the sales revenue was discounted, using a market rate of interest, to its present value at the date of shipment. The deferred receivables on the balance sheet represented the gross receivable less unearned interest income and an allowance for doubtful accounts.

Sales-type leases. A third alternative was sales-type leases, offered primarily to European retail customers. Under this option, the Company's equipment was leased to the customer for a period generally running between 60 and 72 months. During the term of these leases, which were noncancelable, all of the benefits and risks of ownership were effectively transferred from Sensormatic to the lessee. The sales revenue recognized on sales-type leases was the present value of the stream of scheduled payments, using a market rate of interest. The amount reported on Sensormatic's balance sheet as "net investment in sales-type leases" represents total lease payments less unearned interest income, unearned maintenance fees, and an allowance for doubtful accounts.[4]

SALES OF RECEIVABLES TO FINANCIAL INSTITUTIONS.   Sensormatic financed its investments in receivables and leases by transferring them to financing institutions. These receivables and leases were *sold with recourse* or *assigned without recourse*.

Sales of Receivables with Recourse. When receivables and leases were sold with recourse, Sensormatic was obligated to repurchase the receivables and leases, if customers were delinquent in their scheduled payments beyond a defined period of time. Once receivables were sold (with recourse) to a third party, these receivables were removed from Sensormatic's balance sheet.

Related to the receivables sold with recourse, Sensormatic accrued a liability for estimated future losses due to the default of customer payments and the repurchase of receivables from financial institutions. At June 30, 1994, the company accrued loss con-

....

4. *Excerpts from White Paper, Sensormatic Electronics Corporation, September 1995.*

tingencies of $1.3 million related to $199.8 million of receivables and leases sold to and outstanding with the financing institutions which were subject to repurchase.[5] In fiscal 1995, Sensormatic repurchased approximately $13 million of receivables/leases sold with recourse to financing institutions, of which approximately $8.6 million was outstanding on Sensormatic's balance sheet at June 30, 1995. Upon repurchase, these receivables were accounted for by recording the specific receivables or sales-type leases on the balance sheet and an allowance for doubtful accounts, if necessary.

Sales of Receivables Without Recourse. Sensormatic also had agreements with third-party financing institutions whereby the company assigned receivables without recourse. Under this agreement, Sensormatic did not have an obligation to repurchase the receivables assigned, even if customers were delinquent in scheduled payments. When Sensormatic assigned receivables (without recourse) to a third party, these receivables were eliminated from Sensormatic's balance sheet. No liability was accrued with respect to the receivables assigned, because Sensormatic would not incur any loss even if there was a default.

The receivables sold or assigned usually carried fixed interest rates. However, Sensormatic sold them to the financing institution at a floating rate indexed to one month LIBOR. Any differential in interest (fixed vs. floating) was either paid or received by Sensormatic. In order to manage the interest rate risk associated with the receivables sold, Sensormatic entered into interest rate instruments such as floating to fixed interest rate swaps. This resulted in offsetting interest rate differential payments or receipts.

Barron's Criticism

In March 1995, *Barron's*, a widely circulated financial weekly, issued an article criticizing Sensormatic's accounting policies as aggressive. The article explained[6]:

> . . . *while the 35% gain in revenues and 33% increase in net income that Sensormatic reported for its fiscal first half are right on the pace it maintained for all of fiscal 1994, a close reading of its financials raises the suspicion that it has had to make increasingly aggressive accounting assumptions to stay on that track.*
>
> . . . *Sensormatic's stated policy is to use its balance-sheet heft as a marketing tool by offering new customers a variety of flexible deferred payment arrangements. Thus, it carries a big chunk of receivables on its balance sheet, as well as sales-type lease arrangements. And, to turn some of that business into cash, it sells part of its receivables, generally with recourse, to third parties.*
>
> *What's notable is that while the receivables on its books increased roughly in line with sales, to $174.5 million [2nd quarter of fiscal year 1995] from $127.6*

5. Sensormatic disclosed the amount of accrued loss contingencies in 1994 but did not disclose it in the 1995 Annual Report.

6. Excerpts from Barron's Financial Weekly, March 20, 1995.

million [4th quarter of fiscal year 1994] between June and December, the amount it expensed as a reserve for doubtful accounts stayed flat at $10.4 million and thus dropped, in percentage terms, to 6% from 8% of receivables. A back-of-the-envelope calculation is that, had the reserve stayed at 8%, pretax charges against Sensormatic's income would have risen by roughly $3.5 million . . .

Moreover, the receivables and leases it had sold to and outstanding with third parties climbed over that stretch to $273.5 million [2nd quarter of fiscal year 1995] from $199.9 million [4th quarter of fiscal year 1994]. Yet the loss contingencies Sensormatic accrued on those grew by all of $500,000 to $1.8 million [2nd quarter of fiscal year 1995]. That amounted to 1% of outstandings, a puny percentage under any circumstances. But it seems downright skimpy considering the seemingly endless chain of store closings, restructurings and bankruptcies that shapes the history of the industry from which Sensormatic draws most of its customers. Not to mention the fact that last fiscal year, it ended up repaying nearly $13 million, or 5%, of the funds it was advanced for receivables—mostly because customers turned out to be deadbeats.

. . . If Sensormatic's business and prospects are as good as it would have the Street believe, why push the numbers?

It's worth noting, in that context, that while Sensormatic insiders still own well over a million of its shares, they've blown out all 157,500 shares that they've acquired through the exercise of options over the past year. And they've sold an additional 115,600 shares, at prices ranging from 28 and a fraction all the way up to the stock's all-time high of 39. . . .

Sensormatic's Response

In response to the criticism of *Barron's*, Sensormatic's management argued that the company followed U.S. GAAP and that their accounting policies were consistent with the practice of many companies in the EAS industry. Also, Sensormatic issued a "white paper" which explained its accounting policies in detail (see Exhibit 1).

The white paper tried to answer why the allowance for doubtful accounts did not increase proportionately with revenue growth. Sensormatic's management explained[7]:

The Company as well as many financial analysts believe that the ratio of allowance for doubtful accounts to revenue is far less meaningful than 1) the ratio of the provision for doubtful accounts to total revenues (expense to revenue) and 2) the ratio of allowance for doubtful accounts to outstanding receivables and sales-type leases. The Company routinely reviews the credit quality of each customer before an order is accepted. Thereafter, the Company continues to evaluate the collectibility of the accounts and provides for estimated uncollectible amounts. At

7. *Excerpts from White Paper, Sensormatic Electronics Corporation, September 1995.*

Sensormatic Electronics Corporation

such time, an expense is recorded which reflects the Company's best estimate of the amount which will not be collected. As shown in Exhibit 2, the bad debt expense as a percentage of revenue has remained fairly constant from fiscal 1993 to fiscal 1995, at approximately 1.9 percent.

The Company evaluates the total allowance for doubtful accounts on a quarterly basis to ensure that it is adequate, based on recent payment patterns, write-off amounts, etc., and records additional bad debt expense, if necessary. As shown in Exhibit 3, the allowance for doubtful accounts from fiscal 1993 to fiscal 1995 has remained constantly between five and six percent of receivables outstanding.

The Company's evaluation of the allowance for doubtful accounts is influenced by several factors. First, the aging profile of the accounts receivable outstanding —amounts past due for more than 30, 60, 90 days, etc.—at quarter-end is somewhat longer in the Company's presentation and appears to give more cause for concern about aging and ultimate collection than is warranted. While the aging profile may show amounts that are technically 30, 60 or even 90 days past due, internal approvals and processing of accounts payable for many retailers normally take between 30 and 90 days, resulting in more aged accounts receivables outstanding. In addition, like many other companies which do business with retailers, the Company has experienced a historical pattern of longer payment cycles by major retail customers. Delayed payments are often a business practice by large retailers, and not an indication of credit unworthiness. Through working to accelerate collection of receivables, the Company historically has accepted the longer collection cycles as part of its strategy to maintain and further penetrate this important market segment. The lost interest income due to the delayed payment is just another cost factor that is considered by the Company in the pricing of its products.

Second, as Sensormatic's sales to larger, relatively high creditworthy customers have increased, the required allowance for doubtful accounts, as a percentage of total sales, has decreased. In addition, a number of European customers have agreed to a payment arrangement on sales-type leases whereby a direct debit is made to the customer's bank account on scheduled dates. This is a common practice in Europe.

A third factor relates to acquisitions. Receivables acquired through acquisitions, such as those of Knogo in the most recent fiscal year, are initially recorded net of allowance for doubtful accounts, as is required by U.S. GAAP. This lowers the percentage relationship between the allowance for doubtful accounts and receivables in the year of the acquisition relative to prior years.

Finally, the Company normally retains a security interest in most underlying equipment for which a deferred or installment receivable is outstanding, and it retains legal title to equipment under a sales-type lease agreement. In either case, if necessary, the Company can repossess, refurbish and resell the equipment. The high resale value of used equipment enables Sensormatic to resell the repossessed equipment and substantially reduce its ultimate loss on the receivable or lease.

With respect to the Sensormatic's risks of repurchasing receivables and leases, Sensormatic argued that, based on its experiences, some form of payment program could be worked out with the customer. Sensormatic's management explained[8]:

The Company establishes a liability, reported in Accrued Liabilities, for estimated future losses attributable to a risk of default. This liability is generally based on a portfolio basis rather than on a specific identification approach and is, as a percentage of outstanding receivables and leases, much lower than allowances for doubtful accounts relating to receivables and leases on the balance sheet. Even if the receivable or lease is repurchased, the Company's experience is that in many cases, some form of payment program can be worked out with the customer. An example which illustrates this is the case of Macy's Department Store. When Macy's filed for bankruptcy in early 1992 under Chapter 11 (reorganization), the Company repurchased the Macy's installment sales receivable it had sold to a financing institution (approximately $7 million). The Company recorded the receivable on its balance sheet and an allowance for doubtful account based on its best estimate of the potential ultimate loss from default. Ultimately, the Company did not incur any such loss. Even while under Chapter 11, Macy's was allowed to continue making scheduled payments to Sensormatic and recently paid off its obligation ahead of schedule. In addition, Macy's made a number of additional purchases of Sensormatic EAS equipment while still in bankruptcy.

RECENT DEVELOPMENTS

Since Barron's criticism of Sensormatic's accounting policy in March 1995, short interest in Sensormatic shares increased to 4 million shares (out of 73 million shares outstanding) at the end of June 1995 (see Exhibit 5 for the trend of Sensormatic shares sold short). On July 7, 1995, with the pressure of short-sellers' criticism in the background, Sensormatic announced that its fourth-quarter earnings would be substantially lower than analysts' earnings forecast. Sensormatic never had a down quarter in the prior ten years. Sensormatic's management stated that costs related to higher expenses and Sensormatic's acquisition of rival Knogo Corporation's overseas electronics security business for $103 million in stock in January 1995 contributed to lower earnings. On the day of this announcement, Sensormatic shares fell $12 3/8 to close at $23. The 35 percent drop was the biggest percentage decline among U.S. stocks on that day.

A few weeks later, on August 31, Sensormatic announced that its fiscal 1995 result would be delayed pending an extended audit by Ernst & Young. The expanded audit focused on two specific accounting issues: (1) shifting revenue between reporting periods and (2) one-time expenses related to the Knogo acquisition. Upon the announcement of extended audit, Sensormatic share price dropped by a further 17 percent.

---

8. *Ibid.*

Sandwiched between the bad news in early July and the bad news in late August, moreover, was the disclosure of shareholder class-action lawsuits. Three shareholders filed lawsuits after the stock drop in July, claiming the company lowered reserves for risky accounts while its revenues and receivables increased dramatically. According to these lawsuits, Sensormatic made earnings look better by lowering reserves for doubtful accounts.

However, some investors believed that the bad news could not overshadow the underlying strengths of Sensormatic's business. On September 15, 1995, billionaire investor George Soros filed forms with the Securities and Exchange Commission disclosing his 6 percent stake, valued at about $104 million, in Sensormatic.

On October 3, 1995, Sensormatic released financial results for the fourth quarter and fiscal year 1995, following the completion of an expanded audit. The expanded audit identified two accounting problems. First, in certain instances, the company booked sales in a quarter for products that were physically shipped several days following the quarter's end. Correcting for this error would shift $35 million in revenues from fiscal 1995 to 1996. Second, related to Sensormatic's acquisition of Knogo Corporation's international operations, the company capitalized items that should have been expensed. The company was estimated to take a one-time nonrecurring charge of about $8 million in fiscal 1995 to correct for this error.

Sensormatic's management stated that the extended audit results suggested that improper accounting was not material to Sensormatic. One analyst said, "It is definitely a sigh of relief that this accounting issue is behind us. The disaster many feared—and some hoped for—didn't occur."[9] With no major surprises, on October 3, 1995, Sensormatic's share slipped 12 cents to $22.88 in normal trading volume.

After the expanded audit was over, Assaf, the CEO and chairman of Sensormatic, stated:

> The fourth-quarter earnings disappointment, the audit adjustments, and the third-quarter restatement demonstrate a need to better assure compliance with our financial and administrative controls. However, the accounting issues related to extended audit are different from the attack made by short-sellers. [Short-sellers] have been attacking our accounting for a year, and there is nothing wrong with our accounting [related to short-sellers' arguments].[10]

On October 5, 1995, Sensormatic issued a 20-page white paper, as a response to allegations that Sensormatic's accounting methods did not give an accurate picture of the company's financial position. At the end of October, 1995, Sensormatic's share price remained at $21 and had a short position of 6 million shares (see Exhibits 4 and 5).

....

9. Excerpts from the Wall Street Journal, October 3, 1995.

10. Short-sellers sell borrowed shares of stock, betting the price will fall so they can profit when they buy the shares back later. Short-selling is inherently riskier than ordinary investing. If you sell a stock short, the share price can rise an unlimited amount, allowing the potential for unlimited losses. If you buy a stock "long"—betting the price will go up—you can only lose what you invested.

EXHIBIT 1

Sensormatic Electronics Corporation:
Example of Accounting Treatment of Alternative Revenue Transactions

CONTRACT TERMS

Date of Contract: 1/1/95   Date of Shipment: 1/15/95   Date of Installation: 2/15/95

	Accounts Receivable	Deferred Receivable	Installment Receivable	Sales-Type Leases
Contract Price:				
Sales Price	$1,000	$1,000	$1,000	n/a
Monthly Payments	n/a	n/a	$20.50	$21.00
Stated Interest Rate	n/a	n/a	8.50%	none
Payment Terms:				
Single Payment due	3/15/95	7/15/95	n/a	n/a
Monthly Payments due:				
# of months	n/a	n/a	60	60
Final payment due	n/a	n/a	1/15/00	1/15/00

Market Interest Rate				
(Based on Length of Contract)	n/a	6%	9.50%	9.50%

Income Statement Recognition (for Quarter ended 3/31/95)				
Revenue	$1,000	$971	$976	$1,000
Cost	450	450	450	450
Gross Profit	$550	$521	$526	$550

Balance Sheet Recognition (at June 30, 1995)				
Account Receivable	$1,000			
Deferred Receivable		$971		
Installment Receivable			$976	
Net Investment in Sales-Type Lease				$1,000

Source: White Paper, Sensormatic Electronics Corp., September 1995.

Sensormatic Electronics Corporation

EXHIBIT 2
Bad Debt Expense as a Percent of Revenues

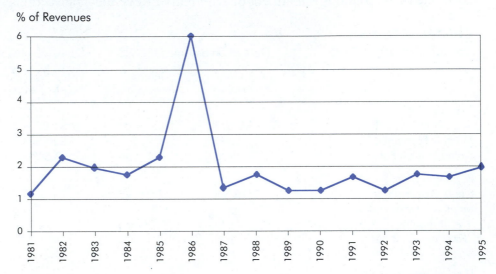

Source: White Paper, Sensormatic Electronics Corp., September 1995.

EXHIBIT 3
Year-End Allowance as a Percent of Gross Receivables

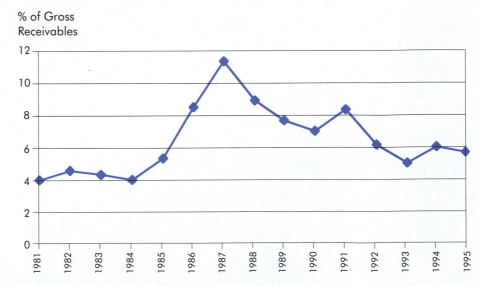

Source: White Paper, Sensormatic Electronics Corp., September 1995.

Sensormatic Electronics Corporation

EXHIBIT 4

Sensormatic's Share Price from October 1994 to October 1995

Source: White Paper, Sensormatic Electronics Corp., September 1995.

EXHIBIT 5

Sensormatic Shares Sold Short from October 1994 to October 1995

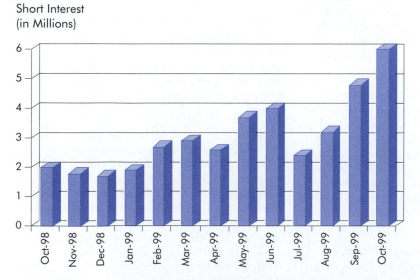

Source: White Paper, Sensormatic Electronics Corp., September 1995.

EXHIBIT 6

Data for Valuation

Sensormatic equity beta*	1.10
Treasury bill rate in December 1995 (3 months)**	5.08%
Government 30-year treasuries rate in December 1995**	6.75%
Sensormatic corporate bond average yield**	8.21%
US federal statutory tax rate in 1995	34%

* Source: Value Line Investment Survey, October 20, 1995

** Source: Bloomberg Financial Analysis

EXHIBIT 7

Sensormatic Electronics 1995 Annual Report - Edited

LETTER TO SHAREHOLDERS, CUSTOMERS AND EMPLOYEES:

Fiscal 1995 was a year of both successes and disappointments for Sensormatic. The successes we achieved were significant, and provide us with great confidence for the future. Revenue grew 36 percent, with increases across the board—18 percent for U.S. retail, 53 percent for Asia/Pacific, 40 percent for Europe and 36 percent for exports to Latin America, Eastern Europe and the Middle East. Most impressively, revenues for our commercial/industrial business grew 73 percent to $213 million worldwide and now account for approximately one-fourth of our businesses, compared with just 3 percent five years ago.

This revenue growth clearly demonstrates the strength of our business in all segments of the electronic security industry. We have almost doubled our business over the past two years and before that, doubled it more than two times in nine years. We have grown from a single-focus retail loss prevention company to a large, diversified operation providing turnkey, integrated electronic security systems for retail and commercial/industrial establishments across the globe.

In 1995 we continued to make the investments required of a leader. We strengthened our product

and market breadth with strategic acquisitions, including the operations of Knogo Corporation outside North America; Software House, Inc., a leading supplier of high-end Access Control systems; Case Security Limited, a leading supplier of security systems to the U.K. financial industry; and Glen Industrial Communications, Inc., one of the leading U.S. systems integrators.

We introduced new products using innovative technology, including Rapid Pad II, an improved, lower-cost Ultra-Max deactivator; a new line of Video Managers that can integrate CCTV systems with any PC or software system; and SensorStrip, a new electromagnetic label designed for source tagging in Europe.

To better serve our customers, we implemented a "Customer Care" program company wide. In the U.S., this includes a fully computerized Customer Response Center, providing 24-hour access to Sensormatic's sales and service organizations; a "Help Desk," providing expert technical and product information to Sensormatic representatives; and a national Operations Group to service customers when product installations extend beyond regional lines. We are undertaking similar initiatives interna-

Sensormatic Electronics Corporation

tionally. In addition, we increased the number of customer service engineers supporting our global customer base to over 1,600 worldwide.

To continue building our commercial/industrial business, we restructured our product companies—Robot Research, American Dynamics, Software House and Continental Instruments—into the Security Product Division (SPD). With a single organization, we will be better able to coordinate, control and expand our product offerings to our dealers. In April, we established the first non-U.S. office of SPD in Paris, which will serve as the headquarters of SPD's European operations.

Despite our customer and product successes, which generated impressive revenue growth, we failed to meet our earnings targets this year. Our fourth quarter earnings shortfall and an extensive year-end examination by our auditors graphically demonstrated that in focusing on revenue growth, we have grown the Company faster than the management organization. As a consequence, we stretched our management resources—with adverse bottom-line results.

Contributing to our disappointing results were the following:

Expenses grew significantly faster than revenues, particularly in the second half of the fiscal year.

The integration of the Knogo European operations was slower and more costly than anticipated.

Revenues from three of our four international units were below forecast, impacting overall margins.

A downward restatement of our third quarter results was required primarily due to the premature recognition of revenue on certain shipments made after quarter-end and on certain shipments subject to non-standard contractual terms.

As a result of these problems, we initiated immediate corrective action.

We centralized all financial activities that formerly reported to the individual Business Units. This will provide for closer corporate control, as well as improve the speed of reporting.

We are implementing a company-wide expense reduction program, intended to reduce corporate operating expenses by 10 percent.

We are increasing throughput at our Irish production plant to increase margins.

We initiated programs to improve inventory turns and accelerated the collection of receivables. Improving our cash flow and reducing debt and related interest expense is a key priority.

Most importantly, we are pleased to announce the appointment of Bob Vanourek as President and Chief Operating Officer. Previously, Bob was President and Chief Executive Officer of Recognition International, Inc., an international provider of document processing hardware, software and services. He has more than 25 years' experience in marketing and general management, including eight years at Pitney Bowes and several years' experience in our industry. We welcome Bob and look forward to his contributions to Sensormatic's continued growth in the months and years to come.

Despite the disappointments of the past year, the fundamentals of our business remain strong. Our market is large and growing. Our leadership position is intact. As we address the financial and administrative issues described above, we will continue to pursue our many growth opportunities by:

• Increasing global market penetration;

• Accelerating source tagging;

• Building and marketing our systems integration capabilities for both retail and commercial/industrial customers.

And finally, to help shareholders better understand the uniqueness of our business and measure our progress against the objectives outlined above, with this annual report, we have expanded the discussion of our lines of business and the presentation of our financial results. We are committed to achieving and maintaining the highest standards of performance in all aspects of our business—for employees, customers, and fellow investors.

Ronald G. Assaf
Chairman of the Board and Chief Executive Officer

October 16, 1995

Sensormatic Electronics Corporation

MANAGEMENT'S DISCUSSION AND ANALYSIS OF FINANCIAL CONDITION AND RESULTS OF OPERATIONS (edited by the casewriters)

The Company's consolidated financial statements present a consolidation of its worldwide operations. This discussion supplements the detailed information presented in the Consolidated Financial Statements and Notes thereto and is intended to assist the reader in understanding the financial results and condition of the Company.

Overview

Consolidated revenues increased 36% in fiscal 1995 compared to fiscal 1994, and 35% and 57% in fiscal 1994 and 1993, respectively, over the prior years, representing an annual compounded growth rate of 42% over the last three fiscal years. This growth rate is largely attributable to successfully implementing a strategy of product, customer and geographic market diversification. More than 52% of fiscal 1995 revenues were generated from outside of the United States.

The Company's increased internal product research, development and engineering activities resulting in a broad array of new proprietary products, as well as selected strategic acquisitions over the last several years, have been a key element in the diversification strategy. The Company invested $25.5 million in fiscal 1995, and anticipates investing approximately $31.0 million in fiscal 1996, in research and product development and engineering support. These activities will contribute to broadening product lines and expanding product applications. Introduction of new products into the market place will be made in accordance with its strategic marketing plans.

Additionally, the Company has made a number of strategic acquisitions over the last several years including Security Tag Systems, Inc. (Security Tag), a U.S.-based manufacturer and marketer of loss prevention products, Software House, Inc. (Software House), a premier U.S.-based developer of high-end Access Control and integrated security systems, Robot Research Inc. (Robot Research), a U.S. manufacturer of sophisticated CCTV equipment, and Case Security Limited (Case Security), a distributor of visual security systems, and Automated Loss Pre-

vention Systems (ALPS), as well as the merger with Knogo Corporation's operations outside of the U.S., Puerto Rico and Canada (Knogo), all under the diversification strategy (see Note 11 to Notes to Consolidated Financial Statements).

The acquisitions of Knogo and ALPS significantly broadened the Company's presence and direct distribution capacity in Europe. The acquisitions of Software House, Robot Research and Case Security, as well as American Dynamics and Continental Instruments Corporation in fiscal 1991 and 1990, respectively, broadened the Company's customer base by adding new proprietary products and distribution channels aimed at commercial, industrial and other non-retail customers.

Another strategy is to focus on expanding the Company's base of recurring revenues. Recurring revenues are generated from sales of disposable labels to the hard goods retailers, maintenance agreements entered into in connection with the sale or lease of systems, and rental revenues from operating leases. The latter is a particular focus of the marketing efforts of certain European and Asia/Pacific subsidiaries. In fiscal 1995, recurring revenues were approximately $152 million compared to approximately $120 million and $106 million in fiscal 1994 and 1993, respectively. The sale of disposable labels to the hard goods retailers is the fastest growing component of the recurring revenue stream, growing from less than $4 million in fiscal 1988 to approximately $76 million in fiscal 1995, an annual compounded growth rate of over 52%.

In fiscal 1993, the Company took a major step in its efforts to increase future recurring label revenues through the introduction of its Universal Product Protection (UPPSM) program. Under this program (also referred to as source labeling), EAS labels are incorporated into or affixed to the merchandise to be protected during the process of manufacturing, packaging or distribution rather than at the retail store. At June 30, 1995, over 500 manufacturers and suppliers located worldwide applied the Company's labels to merchandise delivered to retailers' stores. The Company has been working with a number of its retailer customers around the world, from various segments of the soft and hard goods retail marketplace (including retailers from the music, home improvement centers and discount industries), as well as strategic suppliers and manufacturers, to accelerate this initiative.

Operating income in fiscal 1995 decreased 7% from fiscal 1994. This was primarily a result of a 51% increase in selling, customer service and administrative and research, development and engineering expenses (increasing as a percentage of revenue to 46% in fiscal 1995 from 41% in fiscal 1994), including approximately $6.0 million of expenses related to acquisitions, primarily the merger with Knogo. This was partially offset by a 36% increase in product sales earning gross margins of 54% (consistent with fiscal 1994). Operating income as a percentage of total revenues decreased to 11% compared to 16% in fiscal 1994. Operating income in fiscal 1994 increased 48% over fiscal 1993. Growth in operating income outpaced the revenue growth as a result of improved gross margins and a reduction in operating expenses.

Income from continuing operations decreased 3% in fiscal 1995 and increased 33% in fiscal 1994 as a result of the matters discussed above. In addition net income was $74 million for fiscal 1995 compared to $72 million for fiscal 1994. Fiscal 1995 net income included the effects of a $4.1 million reduction of income taxes payable relating to a previously discontinued business, which reserve was no longer required.

Financial Condition

During fiscal 1995, cash and marketable securities increased $16 million primarily due to: (a) increased short-term borrowings ($105 million); (b) proceeds from issuance of Common Stock pursuant to employee benefit plans ($13 million); and (c) a net decrease in deferred and installment receivables and sales-type leases ($14 million). These were offset in part by (a) increased inventory available for sale ($63 million); (b) capital expenditures ($63 million); and (c) the payment of dividends on Common Stock ($16 million).

Total receivables and sales-type leases increased from $309 million at June 30, 1994 to $401 million

at June 30, 1995 principally as a result of the higher level of business in fiscal 1995 and from the acquisition of Knogo (approximately $37 million acquired at December 29, 1994); offset in part by an increase in sales of receivables and sales-type leases to third party financing institutions (described further below).

The Company has historically had a high level of receivables and sales-type leases outstanding, measured as a percentage of revenues. This results in part from a key element of the Company's marketing strategy, based on its size and financial strength, to increase market penetration by providing alternative financing options to its retail customers (i.e., vendor financing). This strategy has given the Company a significant competitive advantage and has helped the Company penetrate markets and increase customer loyalty and commitment to Sensormatic. The ability to pursue such a strategy results from the Company's relatively high profit margins, strong balance sheet, and its ability to sell receivables and leases to financing institutions.

Additionally, like other companies which do business with retailers, the Company has experienced an historical pattern of delayed payments by certain major retail customers which has extended the Company's receivables aging profile. Internal approvals and processing of accounts payable for many retailers normally take between 30 and 90 days, which has extended its receivables aging profile. In addition, further delays in payments are often a business practice by large retailers, and not an indication of credit unworthiness. Though working to accelerate collection of receivables, the Company historically has accepted the longer collection cycles as part of its strategy to maintain and further penetrate this important market segment. The lost interest income due to the delayed payment is another cost factor that is considered by the Company in the pricing of the product.

The Company continues to manage its receivables and sales-type leases by, among other things, using third-party servicing agents to enhance the efficiency of its billing and collection practices and expanding the number and use of relationships with third-party financing institutions to sell or assign receivables and sales-type leases (see Note 2. of Notes to Consolidated Financial Statements). The results of these ongoing efforts have been to reduce the average collection time and to provide the Company with the flexibility to convert its receivables and sales-type leases into cash as needed. The Company received proceeds of $458 million and $271 million from the sale and assignment of receivables and sales-type leases in fiscal 1995 and 1994, respectively (net of repurchases due to customer non-payment of approximately $14 million and $13 million, respectively).

Finally, short-term receivables from the Company's slower paying retail customers are becoming a relatively smaller part of its overall business as a result of 1) the expansion of the Company's source labeling program, whereby Sensormatic sells labels to vendors and manufacturers who apply the labels prior to shipment to the retailer; and 2) the continued growth of the commercial/ industrial customer base which is made up of customers which (i) tend to be the higher end commercial/industrial users with higher credit ratings than many retailers and (ii) a closely monitored network of third-party dealers and distributors. In adding this new commercial/ industrial customer base to the Company's historical retail customer base, the Company has developed a base of generally faster paying customers.

The Company believes its total allowance for doubtful accounts for receivables and sales-type leases, and its related reserve for receivables and sales-type leases sold to financing institutions which are subject to full or partial recourse, are adequate after taking into account, among other things: (a) the aging of its receivables and sales-type leases (including those repurchased or subject to repurchase from financing institutions); (b) the payment history of its customers; (c) the Company's security interest in equipment financed under deferred and installment sales contracts and the Company's retention of title in equipment under sales-type leases; (d) its ability to re-market such equipment if needed; (e) the prospects of its collection efforts; and (f) its relationship with major retail customers. Additionally, with the broadening of the Company's customer base both geographically and to include hard goods retailers, and commercial and industrial customers, the Company's historical concentration in soft goods retailers is being reduced.

Inventories at June 30, 1995 increased $77 million over June 30, 1994 to meet increased forecasted production and sales levels and reduce the risk of inventory shortages resulting from the rapid growth in market demand. Other property, plant and equipment increased $44 million primarily due to the purchases of additional production equipment in Florida and Puerto Rico and the start-up of the manufacturing facility in Ireland. Deferred income taxes, patents and other assets increased $42 million primarily as a result of increased deferred income taxes and other assets principally related to companies acquired in fiscal 1995.

Total stockholders' equity at June 30, 1995 increased $225 million over the June 30, 1994 balance, to $953 million, principally as a result of the issuance of 4.6 million shares of Common Stock (aggregating $149 million) in connection with acquisitions, and net income.

Total debt increased $108 million over the June 30, 1994 balance, to $327 million, primarily as a result of an increase in short-term credit line borrowings and other debt (approximately $23 million of Knogo debt was incurred as part of the merger). The debt-to-total capitalization ratio was .26 to 1 at June 30, 1995 compared to .23 to 1 at June 30, 1994.

The Company estimates capital requirements for fiscal 1996 to include capital expenditures for new production equipment and a facility to consolidate the Company's research and product development, engineering support, and certain corporate marketing and administrative personnel and equipment at approximately $30 million, and expenditures for research and product development and engineering support at approximately $31 million. Such capital requirements and other expenditures will be funded through operating activities (including sale of receivables and sales-type leases), existing cash and marketable securities and worldwide credit lines (see Note 6. of Notes to Consolidated Financial Statements).

Additionally, future niche acquisitions, a fundamental element of the Company's diversification and growth strategy, may be funded, when deemed appropriate, through the issuance of shares of Sensormatic Common Stock. The Company maintains a shelf registration statement filed with the Securities and Exchange Commission under which the Company is able to issue up to 4.5 million shares of its Common Stock (approximately 2.5 million shares remain available).

Results from Continuing Operations

Revenues. Consolidated revenues for fiscal 1995 were $889 million, a 36% increase from $656 million in fiscal 1994. The revenue growth in 1995 resulted principally from: (a) increased EAS revenues, particularly from the Ultra-Max product line, primarily for hard goods retail customers and used in source labeling programs; (b) increased CCTV product volume from retailers; (c) increased volume from the U.S.-based Commercial/Industrial Group; and (d) the foreign exchange effect on the international subsidiaries' local currency revenues when translated into U.S. dollars for financial statement purposes caused by the weaker average U.S. dollar (relative to the international subsidiaries' local currencies, in the aggregate) throughout fiscal 1995 compared to fiscal 1994 (approximately $3 million).

Consolidated revenues from the EAS product lines for retail customers increased 25% to $511 million in fiscal 1995 compared to $406 million in fiscal 1994. This increase resulted principally from a 47% volume increase from the Ultra-Max product line and the inclusion in the last six months of fiscal 1995 of revenues from the Knogo product line ($29 million). Revenues from the CCTV product lines for retailers exceeded $112 million compared to $72 million in fiscal 1994. Revenues from the Commercial/Industrial Group (including installation revenues) increased 83%, to $143 million compared to $78 million in fiscal 1994, due primarily to the sale of CCTV and Access Control products to non-retail customers, and incremental revenue from recent acquisitions. Revenues from the Company's CamEra™ systems increased 38% to $66 million in fiscal 1995 compared to $48 million in fiscal 1994. The Company generated $256 million of revenue in fiscal 1995 from all of its CCTV products and systems combined, worldwide.

International revenues were $468 million, $333 million and $267 million in fiscal 1995, 1994 and 1993, respectively, and included revenues of the European subsidiaries of $386 million, $275 million and $232 million, respectively.

In fiscal 1994, consolidated revenues increased $169 million (35%) compared to fiscal 1993 principally as a result of increased revenue from the Ultra-Max product line, inclusion of revenue from the Security Tag EAS and Ink Tag® product lines, increased revenues from the sale of CCTV products to retailers, and increased revenues from the Commercial/Industrial Group; offset in part by the foreign exchange effect caused by the stronger average U.S. dollar (approximately $34 million).

In fiscal 1993, consolidated revenues increased $177 million (57%) compared to fiscal 1992 principally as a result of the inclusion of revenues generated from ALPS products, increased worldwide revenues in every EAS product line for the hard goods retailers, increased revenues from the sale of CCTV products to retailers and increased revenues from the Commercial/Industrial Group.

Operating Costs and Expenses. Operating costs and expenses in fiscal 1995 increased to 89% of consolidated revenues, compared with 84% in fiscal 1994 and 85% in fiscal 1993. The reduced operating margin in fiscal 1995 was due primarily to: 1) higher than budgeted selling and customer service expenses (in part due to the opening of a distribution center and a customer response center in the U.S., and activities associated with the expansion of the source labeling program); 2) significant integration costs and expenses related to acquisitions, primarily Knogo (approximately $6 million); 3) costs associated with the opening of the manufacturing facility in Ireland; and 4) expenses associated with the Company's sponsorship of the 1996 Summer Olympics.

Gross margin on product sales in fiscal 1995 remained at 54% compared to fiscal 1994. Gross margin on product sales in fiscal 1994 increased to 54% from 53% in fiscal 1993, primarily from improved gross margins on certain EAS and CCTV product lines (resulting from improved manufacturing efficiencies) and the inclusion of the manufacturer's gross margin (as a result of the acquisition of Security Tag) on the Security Tag product line; offset in part by a relative increase in sales of lower margin products (such as CCTV products and labels) compared to fiscal 1993.

Sensormatic Electronics Corporation

Total selling and customer service, administrative, research, development and engineering expenses (operating expenses) for fiscal 1995 increased to 46%, as a percentage of total consolidated revenues, from 41% in fiscal 1994, and increased 51% over fiscal 1994, primarily as a result of higher selling and customer service expenses including significant integration costs of the Knogo operations in Europe. The increases in operating expenses include the foreign exchange effect caused by the weaker average U.S. dollar (approximately $15 million). Operating expenses in fiscal 1994 and 1993 increased 31% and 62% over the respective prior fiscal year primarily as a result of the higher levels of business (including the effect of the ALPS acquisition in fiscal 1993) and an increase in research, development and engineering expenses of 31% and 20% over the respective prior years; offset in part by the foreign exchange effect caused by the stronger average U.S. dollar in fiscal 1994 compared to 1993 ($14 million).

Other Income (Expenses). Interest income increased by $3 million in fiscal 1995 principally due to higher amounts of sales-type leases and deferred and installment receivables outstanding throughout fiscal 1995 compared to fiscal 1994. Interest income declined by $3 million in fiscal 1994 due primarily to a decline in long-term interest rates throughout the year earned on higher amounts of sales-type leases and deferred and installment receivables. In fiscal 1993 interest income increased by $10 million principally due to interest income earned on sales-type leases acquired in connection with the ALPS acquisition and higher amounts of deferred and installment receivables.

Interest expense increased by $6 million, $4 million and $7 million in fiscal 1995, 1994 and 1993, respectively, due to higher levels of net short-term bank borrowings used to fund (i) increases in the Company's working capital (including the longer-term receivables and sales-type leases) and (ii) in fiscal 1995, debt assumed as part of the acquisition of Knogo and increased long-term debt in fiscal 1993, incurred with respect to the acquisition of ALPS. As previously mentioned, the Company entered into three-year interest rate swaps in fiscal 1993 to lower its current interest expense on the $135 million 8.21% Senior Notes by exchanging their fixed interest rate for a floating interest rate

based on six month LIBOR rates (throughout the term of the swap agreements) in order to take advantage of the then lower prevailing short-term interest rates. The effective rate on the Senior Notes was approximately 9.2%, 6.8% and 6.8% in fiscal 1995, 1994 and 1993 through the use of these swap agreements.

Income Taxes

The effective consolidated tax rate on income from continuing operations was 22% for fiscal 1995, and 25% for both fiscal 1994 and 1993. The fiscal 1995 effective tax rate was negatively affected by (i) earnings of the Company's international subsidiaries which are subject to statutory tax rates generally higher than the U.S. effective rate, (ii) increases in U.S. earnings not qualifying for U.S./Puerto Rico "Section 936" tax benefits (see Note 5. Of Notes to Consolidated Financial Statements) and (iii) increases in amortization of costs in excess of net assets acquired (substantially all of which are non-deductible for income tax purposes). However, these effects were offset by an adjustment of prior years' tax accruals which were no longer required. In addition to the items above, changes in U.S. and Puerto Rico tax law related to the Company's operations in Puerto Rico (effective for fiscal 1995), as well as potentially more adverse changes presently being considered by the U.S. Congress, will continue to exert upward pressure on the Company's effective tax rate. Legislation proposals in the U.S. Congress in recent years have sought to limit or phase out the favorable tax status in Puerto Rico. The potential effect of these items is continually being examined by the Company in order to develop strategies to minimize their effect.

Discontinued Operations

In fiscal 1995, the Company recorded a $4.1 million reduction in income tax liabilities related to a previously discontinued business which was no longer required.

Net Income

Consolidated net income for fiscal 1995, 1994 and 1993 increased $2 million, $18 million and $23 million compared to their respective prior years, representing an annual compounded rate of growth of 33% over the last three fiscal years, due principally to the factors discussed above.

CONSOLIDATED BALANCE SHEETS
June 30, 1995 and 1994 (In thousands, except par value amounts)

	1995	1994
ASSETS		
Cash and marketable securities (including marketable securities of $26,727 in 1995 and $33,618 in 1994)	$ 70,307	$ 54,542
Accounts receivable, net	221,873	134,517
Deferred and installment receivables, net	67,843	64,375
Net investment in sales-type leases	110,942	109,607
Inventories, net	240,807	163,906
Revenue equipment, less accumulated depreciation of $46,439 in 1995 and $36,183 in 1994	49,920	58,326
Other property, plant and equipment, net	150,957	107,152
Deferred income taxes, patents and other assets, less accumulated amortization of $17,685 in 1995 and $13,114 in 1994	161,614	120,061
Costs in excess of net assets acquired, less accumulated amortization of $29,863 in 1995 and $17,930 in 1994	496,641	343,017
	$1,570,904	$1,155,503
LIABILITIES AND STOCKHOLDERS' EQUITY		
Accounts payable	$ 63,314	$ 40,884
Accrued liabilities	209,091	143,067
Accrued and deferred income taxes payable	19,059	24,687
Debt	326,710	219,173
Commitments and contingencies		
Stockholders' equity:		
Preferred stock, $.01 par value, 10,000 shares authorized, none issued; Common stock, $.01 par value, 125,000 shares authorized, 73,023 and 67,612 shares outstanding in 1995 and 1994, respectively	713,866	546,577
Retained earnings	295,680	237,553
Treasury stock at cost and other, 1,095 shares in 1995 and 1,162 shares in 1994	(13,222)	(10,835)
Currency translation adjustments	(43,594)	(45,603)
Total stockholders' equity	952,730	727,692
	$1,570,904	$1,155,503

Sensormatic Electronics Corporation

Sensormatic Electronics Corporation

CONSOLIDATED STATEMENTS OF INCOME
June 30, 1995, 1994 and 1993 (In thousands, except par value amounts)

	1995	1994	1993
Revenues:			
Sales	$762,375	$557,393	$398,122
Rentals	50,601	46,566	46,021
Other	76,107	52,007	43,176
Total revenues	889,083	655,966	487,319
Operating costs and expenses:			
Costs of sales	353,990	256,003	188,138
Depreciation on revenue equipment	16,327	14,974	15,394
Selling, customer service & administrative	383,583	251,933	192,077
Research, development and engineering	22,666	18,023	13,739
Amortization of intangible assets	14,598	10,246	6,963
Total operating costs and expenses	791,164	551,179	416,311
Operating income	97,919	104,787	71,008
Other income (expenses):			
Interest income	17,221	14,262	17,114
Interest expense	(28,989)	(22,711)	(18,656)
Other, net	2,900	(373)	2,518
Total other income (expenses)	(8,868)	(8,822)	976
Income from continuing operations before income taxes	89,051	95,965	71,984
Provision for income taxes	19,500	23,900	17,900
Income from continuing operations	69,551	72,065	54,084
Discontinued operations - adjustment of prior year amounts (Note 5.)	4,100	—	—
Net income	$ 73,651	$ 72,065	$ 54,084
Primary earnings per common share:			
Continuing operations	$ .97	$ 1.16	$ .97
Discontinued operations	.05	—	—
Net income	$ 1.02	$ 1.16	$ .97
Fully diluted earnings per common share:			
Continuing operations	$ .97	$ 1.13	$ .93
Discontinued operations	.05	—	—
Net income	$ 1.02	$ 1.13	$ .93

CONSOLIDATED STATEMENTS OF CASH FLOWS

June 30, 1995, 1994 and 1993 (In thousands, except par value amounts)

	1995	1994	1993
Cash flows from operating activities:			
Income from continuing operations	$69,551	$72,065	$54,084
Adjustments to reconcile income from continuing operations to net cash provided by (used in) operating activities:			
Depreciation	26,705	22,603	21,446
Amortization	14,615	11,681	7,917
Other non-cash charges to operations, net	19,993	11,502	9,508
Net changes in operating assets and liabilities, net of effects of acquisitions:			
Inventories	(63,589)	(56,333)	(6,299)
Net investment in sales-type leases	17,194	(42,269)	(9,824)
Accounts receivable and receivables from financing institutions	(77,294)	(23,858)	(52,742)
Deferred and installment receivables	(3,099)	(9,268)	12,277
Other assets	(9,497)	(31,345)	1,541
Accrued liabilities	3,197	13,506	14,320
Accounts payable	15,108	10,801	(2,778)
Income taxes	(3,830)	7,473	12,631
Net cash provided by (used in) operating activities	9,054	(13,442)	62,081
Cash flows from investing activities:			
Capital expenditures	(62,972)	(51,835)	(26,735)
Purchases of marketable securities	(843)	(18,178)	(8,921)
Maturities of marketable securities	7,717	13,294	24,262
Increase in revenue equipment and available for lease	(3,959)	(17,033)	(35,177)
Acquisitions (net of cash acquired of $6,687 in 1995, $1,135 in 1994 and $8,223 in 1993)	(9,587)	(11,467)	(299,342)
Other, net	5,696	5,676	2,837
Net cash used in investing activities	(63,948)	(79,543)	(343,076)
Cash flows from financing activities:			
Bank borrowings and other debt	105,370	30,500	128,271
Proceeds from issuances of common stock under employee benefit plans and for acquisitions	12,902	17,167	212,154
Cash dividends	(15,524)	(12,530)	(10,588)
Repayments of bank borrowings and other debt	(25,198)	(10,329)	(109,934)
Issuance of Senior Notes, net	—	—	134,111
Net cash provided by financing activities	77,550	24,808	354,014
Net increase (decrease) in cash	22,656	(68,177)	73,019
Cash at beginning of year	20,924	89,101	16,082
Cash at end of period	43,580	20,924	89,101
Marketable securities at end of year	26,727	33,618	28,798
Cash and marketable securities at end of year	$ 70,307	$54,542	$117,899

Sensormatic Electronics Corporation

NOTES TO CONSOLIDATED FINANCIAL STATEMENTS

Note 1. *Summary of significant accounting policies*

a. Basis of presentation. The Consolidated Financial Statements include the accounts of Sensormatic Electronics Corporation and all of its subsidiaries (the Company). All significant intercompany balances and transactions have been eliminated.

The accompanying Consolidated Balance Sheets are presented in a format which does not segregate current assets and current liabilities. As a result of the constantly changing mix of inventories and revenue equipment sold and leased, including sales of equipment originally installed under lease contracts, it is not possible to accurately determine the amount of revenue equipment that will be sold and thus realized currently. The Company believes presentation of its financial position in the non-classified format avoids misunderstandings as to the relationships of current and non-current assets and liabilities. However, information with respect to the current and non-current nature of certain assets and liabilities is included in Notes below.

b. Cash and marketable securities. The Company classifies cash equivalents (highly liquid investments with a maturity of three months or less when acquired) as cash. Effective July 1, 1994, the Company adopted FASB Statement No. 115 "Accounting for Certain Investments in Debt and Equity Securities." In accordance with FASB 115, the Company has classified certain of its non-equity investments as available-for-sale securities which are carried at market value (versus cost or amortized cost prior to the adoption of FASB 115). Unrealized gains and losses are recorded, net of tax, in Stockholders' equity ($0.3 million loss at June 30, 1995).

c. Inventories. Inventories are stated at the lower of cost (first-in, first-out) or market.

d. Revenue equipment and other property, plant and equipment. Revenue equipment (principally equipment on lease) and other property, plant and equipment (including assets acquired under capital leases) are recorded at cost and depreciated using the straight-line method over their estimated useful lives (4 years and 6 years for revenue equipment, 10 years through 40 years for buildings and

improvements and 3 years through 10 years for other property, plant and equipment).

e. Revenue recognition. Revenue from sales of equipment is recognized when a customer takes title to the product, in accordance with the terms agreed upon by the parties (i.e. "FOB Shipping Point," "FOB Destination," acceptance of a customer order to purchase presently installed equipment or acceptance by a third party leasing company of an operating lease and the related equipment). Payment terms are either cash and/or acceptance of deferred term (i.e., extended payment terms normally not greater than 365 days) or installment obligations (generally with terms of 60 months) subject to stated or imputed interest, and are generally secured. Revenue from sales-type leases (primarily with terms of 60 months or greater) is recognized as a "sale" upon receipt of a customer order and shipment in an amount equal to the present value of the minimum rental payments under the fixed non-cancelable lease term. Interest income on deferred and installment obligations and net investment in sales-type leases is recognized over the term of the contract using the effective interest method.

The Company also leases equipment under long-term operating leases (primarily leases with terms of 36 to 54 months) which are generally non-cancelable. Rental revenues are recognized as earned over the term of the lease. Minimum future rentals on non-cancelable operating leases at June 30, 1995 aggregated (in millions) $107.2 and are due as follows: 1996 - $32.4; 1997 - $25.8; 1998 - $22.0; 1999 - $15.5 and 2000 - $11.5.

Service revenues are recognized as earned and maintenance revenues are recognized ratably over the service contract term.

f. Research, development and engineering. In fiscal 1995, 1994 and 1993 "Research, development and engineering" included research and development expenses of $18.2 million, $14.7 million and $11.9 million, respectively.

g. Accounting for currency translation and transactions. The Company's international subsidiaries' assets and liabilities are translated into U.S. dollars at the rate of exchange in effect at their balance sheet dates and their revenues, costs and expenses are translated into U.S. dollars at the average rate of exchange in effect during their respective fiscal years. Translation adjustments resulting therefrom and transaction gains or losses attributable to certain intercompany transactions are excluded from results of operations and accumulated in a separate component of consolidated stockholders' equity. Gains and losses attributable to other intercompany transactions are included in results of operations.

The Company has a policy of not hedging its investment in the net assets of its international subsidiaries (aggregating $370 million and $250 million at June 30, 1995 and 1994, respectively, primarily located in 15 countries in Europe) against exchange rate fluctuations due to the high economic costs of such a program and the long-term nature of its investments. The gains and losses resulting from these exchange rate fluctuations ($2.0 million and $15.9 million net gain in fiscal 1995 and fiscal 1994, respectively) are excluded from results of operations and accumulated in a separate component of consolidated stockholders' equity.

The Company has a policy of purchasing forward exchange contracts (forward contracts) and options designated to hedge certain identifiable, foreign currency anticipatory, intercompany commitments. Forward contracts and options are stated at cost, if any. Market value gains or losses resulting from such forward contracts and options, and from the related hedged commitments, occurring in periods prior to the period in which they are settled, are deferred, to be recognized in the period when they are settled. Cash flows resulting from the settlement of the forward contracts and options are included in cash provided by operating activities.

Net currency exchange gains (losses) in fiscal 1995, 1994 and 1993 resulting from the settlement of intercompany transfers of products manufactured in Florida and Puerto Rico and sold to certain international subsidiaries were (in millions) $3.0, $0.7 and ($0.1), respectively. Additionally, non-recurring net currency exchange gains of $2.2 million and $1.3 million were recognized in fiscal 1995 and 1993, respectively, after the Knogo and ALPS acquisitions. Net currency exchange gains are included in "Other income (expenses)" in the Consolidated Statements of Income.

h. *Intangible assets.* Patents, stated at cost, are amortized using the straight-line method over 17 years. Costs in excess of net assets acquired are amortized using the straight-line method over 20 to 40 years. The carrying value of costs in excess of net assets acquired (or goodwill) will be reviewed if the facts and circumstances suggest that it may be impaired. If this review indicates the goodwill will not be fully recoverable over the remaining amortization period, as determined based on the estimated undiscounted cash flows of the assets acquired, the carrying value of the goodwill will be adjusted accordingly. (See Notes 1k. and 11.)

i. *Interest rate instruments.* The differential to be paid or received on interest rate swap agreements and interest rate cap agreements (interest rate instruments) is accrued as interest rates change and is recognized as an adjustment to interest expense. Premiums paid or received for the early termination of interest rate instruments will be amortized into interest expense over the remaining original term of the instruments should the Company elect to terminate any of the interest rate instruments prior to their expiration date. Interest rate instruments are stated at cost, if any.

j. *Primary and fully diluted earnings per common share.* Primary earnings per common share is calculated based on the weighted average number of common shares and dilutive common stock equivalents outstanding during the period. Common stock equivalents include stock options issued under employee benefit plans and common stock warrants. Fully diluted earnings per common share in 1993 and 1994 included the if-converted dilutive effect of the 7% Convertible Subordinated Debentures due in 2001 which were fully converted in May 1994.

k. *Prospective accounting changes.* In March 1995, FASB Statement No. 121 "Accounting for the Impairment of Long-Lived Assets and for Long-Lived Assets to Be Disposed Of" was issued. FASB 121 requires impairment losses to be recorded on long-lived assets (e.g., revenue equipment, property, plant and equipment, patents and costs in excess of net assets acquired related to such assets) used in operations when impairment indicators are present and the undiscounted cash flows estimated to be generated

Sensormatic Electronics Corporation

by those assets are less than the assets' carrying amount. FASB 121 also addresses the accounting for long-lived assets that are expected to be disposed of.

The Company will adopt the provisions of FASB 121 in the first quarter of fiscal 1996 and, based on current circumstances, does not believe the effect of adoption will be material.

In July 1995, the Emerging Issues Task Force (EITF) reached a consensus which narrows the scope of intercompany foreign currency commitments which are eligible to be hedged for financial reporting purposes. This applies to transactions arising after July 21, 1995. The Company has not completed the complex analyses and comprehensive study of this matter to either estimate its current or future effect on the Company's operating results or hedging strategy. However, the Company believes it can modify its current hedging practices in order to comply with the new consensus without having a materially adverse effect on its financial condition.

l. Reclassifications. Certain amounts in the prior years' Consolidated Financial Statements have been reclassified to conform to the current fiscal year's presentation.

Note 2. Receivables and net investment in sales-type leases

Accounts receivable are stated net of an allowance for doubtful accounts of $13.5 million and $10.4 million at June 30, 1995 and 1994, respectively.

Net deferred receivables ($24.5 million and $30.5 million outstanding at June 30, 1995 and 1994, respectively) and installment receivables are stated net of the following (at June 30, in millions):

	1995	1994
Allowance for doubtful accounts	$ 5.5	$ 6.4
Unearned interest and maintenance	$ 24.4	$19.5

The Company leases equipment under sales-type lease agreements expiring in various years through 2002. The net investment in sales-type leases consisted of the following (at June 30, in millions):

	1995	1994
Minimum lease payments receivable	$168.8	$151.6
Allowance for uncollectible minimum lease payments	(7.5)	(3.4)
Unearned interest and maintenance	(50.4)	(38.6)
	$110.9	$109.6

Net receivables and sales-type leases at June 30, 1995 are due as follows (in millions): 1996 - $252.0 and 21.2; 1997 - $12.7 and $22.8; 1998 - $11.8 and $21.8; 1999 - $8.9 and $21.3; 2000 - $4.4 and $18.2, respectively, and with respect to sales-type leases (in millions): $5.6 thereafter.

The Company has agreements with third-party financing institutions whereby certain installment receivables in the United States (U.S.) and sales-type leases in Europe together with certain related rights are sold to the financing institutions. Under such agreements, should certain events occur (principally related to customer non-payment or other customer-related defaults), the Company is obligated to repurchase the specific receivables and sales-type leases.

Under the principal agreement in the U.S., the Company sells fixed interest rate receivables to the financing institution. Under such agreement, the financing institution earns interest throughout the term of the receivables at a floating rate of interest indexed to one month LIBOR. Any resulting differential in interest caused by the varying interest rates (variance amounts) is either paid or received by the Company. In order to manage the risk associated with the variance amounts, the Company enters into interest rate instruments for notional amounts (on a portfolio basis) equal to the outstanding principal amounts of receivables sold. This results in offsetting interest rate differential payments or receipts thereby limiting the variance amounts paid or received by the Company.

Additionally, the Company has an agreement with a third-party financing institution whereby the Company may assign certain pre-approved U.S. accounts receivable. At June 30, 1995 and 1994, receivables assigned and outstanding under such agreement were $79.7 million and $57.9 million, respectively, (substantially all of which were not subject to recourse resulting from the customer's inability to pay) of which the financing institution had advanced in anticipation of their collection $74.6 million and $50 million, respectively, to the Company (bearing interest at fluctuating rates, 6.5% and 4.9% at June 30, 1995 and 1994, respectively).

The Company received proceeds of $458.1 million and $270.5 million upon the sale and assignment of receivables and leases under these agreements in fiscal 1995 and 1994, respectively (net of repurchases due to customer non-payment of approximately $12.6 million and $12.8 million, respectively). The uncollected principal balance of receivables and leases sold which is subject to varying amounts of recourse totaled $333.0 million and 199.8 million at June 30, 1995 and 1994, respectively. Adequate reserves have been provided for receivables and leases sold and are included in accrued liabilities.

At June 30, 1995 balances due from financing institutions under these agreements aggregated $8.2 million, are due within one year and are included in "Deferred income taxes, patents and other assets."

At June 30, 1995 and 1994, there were receivables (including those subject to recourse) due from the following sectors of the U.S. retail market which represented a concentration of credit risk to the Company: department and discount stores 1995 - $48.9 million and 1994 - $40.5 million; supermarkets 1995 - $31.9 million and 1994 - $26.2 million; and specialty stores 1995 - $26.2 million and 1994 - $30.7 million. Assuming the obligors under these receivables were to fail to completely perform according to the terms of the receivables at June 30, 1995, the Company estimates it would have incurred a loss with respect to each retail market of approximately $36.1 million, $21.1 million and $21.2 million, respectively, representing the amount of the receivables less any related allowance for doubtful accounts and the estimated realizable value of the collateralized equipment securing these receivables. The Company minimizes its exposure to credit risk through its credit review procedures, collection practices, and its policy of retaining a security interest in the underlying equipment and ability to re-market such repossessed equipment.

The activity in the allowance for doubtful accounts related to receivables and sales-type leases during fiscal 1995, 1994 and 1993 is as follows (in millions):

	1995	1994	1993
Beginning of year	$20.1	$13.5	$10.6
Additions charged to income	19.6	11.0	8.8
Amounts written off, net	(15.5)	(6.1)	(5.6)
Other (including currency translation)	2.2	1.7	(0.3)
Balance at end of year	$26.4	$20.1	$13.5

Note 5. Income taxes

Effective July 1, 1993, the Company adopted FASB Statement No. 109 "Accounting for Income Taxes" (FASB 109). As permitted by FASB 109, the Company elected not to restate the financial statements of any prior periods. The cumulative effect of the change was not material and therefore no adjustment was separately reported in the Consolidated Statement of Income for the year ended June 30, 1994.

The United States (including Puerto Rico) and international components of income from continuing operations before income taxes are as follows (in millions):

	1995	1994	1993
United States	$62.8	$65.7	$49.8
International	26.2	30.3	22.2
	$89.0	$96.0	$72.0

The components of the provision for income taxes on income from continuing operations before income taxes are as follows (in millions):

	Current	Deferred	Total
1995:			
U.S. Federal	$ 2.0	$ 4.6	$ 6.6
International	3.2	10.0	13.2
Other	—	(0.3)	(0.3)
	$5.2	$14.3	$19.5
1994:			
U.S. Federal	$ 5.6	$ 2.1	$ 7.7
International	12.3	3.1	15.4
Other	1.4	(0.6)	0.8
	$19.3	$ 4.6	$23.9
1993:			
U.S. Federal	$ 8.4	$ (4.1)	$ 4.3
International	11.0	(0.2)	10.8
Other	3.3	(0.5)	2.8
	$22.7	$ (4.8)	$17.9

Sensormatic Electronics Corporation

Sensormatic Electronics Corporation

The deferred provision is presented net of a tax benefit of $20 million for 1995, and $4.1 million for 1994, relating to net operating losses. A reconciliation between the statutory U.S. Federal income tax rate and the consolidated effective tax rate on income from continuing operations before income taxes is as follows:

	1995	1994	1993
Statutory rate	35.0%	35.0%	34.5%
Benefits due to tax exempt earnings and investment income of the Puerto Rico operations	(10.2)	(9.5)	(12.0)
Amortization of costs in excess of net assets acquired	4.6	2.7	2.7
Adjustment of prior years' accruals	(4.9)	(3.4)	—
Other	(2.6)	0.1	(0.3)
	21.9%	24.9%	24.9%

Note 9. Commitments, contingencies and other matters

a. *Commitments.* The Company leases certain operating plant and equipment. The future lease commitments for plant and equipment and other assets at June 30, 1995 aggregated $48.2 million and are due as follows (in millions): 1996 - $12.0; 1997 - $11.7; 1998 - $5.8; 1999 - $3.6; 2000 - $2.3 and $12.8 thereafter. Rent expense was charged to operations as follows (in millions): 1995 - $10.4; 1994 - $10.2 and 1993 - $4.7.

b. *Contingent royalty payments.* In connection with certain acquisitions, the Company pays royalties (ranging from 3% to 10%) on revenues generated by the acquired businesses for periods expiring in 1996 through 2004. Such contingent payments, when incurred, will be recorded as additional cost of the related acquisitions and amortized over the remaining amortization period. Royalty payments in fiscal 1995, 1994 and 1993 were $13.3 million, $7.6 million and $5.6 million, respectively.

c. *Litigation.* In July, August and September 1995, thirteen actions were filed by alleged shareholders of the Company following announcements by the Company that its earnings for the quarter and year ended June 30, 1995, would be substantially below expectations and, in the more recent actions and a complaint amendment, that the scope of the Com-

pany's year-end audit had been expanded. The various complaints allege, among other things, that the Company and certain of its directors and officers who are named as defendants issued false and misleading statements about the Company's business prospects, failed to follow appropriate accounting practices, and failed to disclose adverse information. One of the complaints also alleges, among other things, that the Company failed to disclose hazards affecting individuals wearing pacemakers allegedly caused by certain of its products. The claimants are seeking class certification, rescissory damages and/or unspecified compensatory damages, as well as interest, costs and various fees and expenses, on behalf of themselves and other putative class members who purchased the Company's common stock or related securities during the respective class periods alleged by their complaints. In one of the actions, allegedly brought on behalf of Company shareholders who obtained their shares in the Company's merger with Knogo Corporation, the relief sought also includes rescission of the vote on that merger. Also in September 1995, three derivative actions were filed against the Company and its directors for breach of fiduciary duties, mismanagement and waste of corporate assets. Those claimants are seeking, among other relief, restitution and/or damages in favor of the Company and imposition of a constructive trust. The Company intends to vigorously defend against the actions. The ultimate outcome of these actions cannot presently be determined. Accordingly, no provision for any liability that may result has been made in the consolidated financial statements.

d. *Restatement of interim financial statements.* In fiscal 1995, revenues related to certain shipments that were recorded incorrectly in fiscal 1995 were identified and were reported to the Audit Committee of the Board of Directors by the Company's independent certified public accountants. The Audit Committee authorized an expansion of the scope of the fiscal 1995 audit and retained independent counsel to assist in the investigation of this matter. The results of the investigation concluded that certain accounting irregularities resulted in incorrectly recording revenues and related costs and expenses for certain product shipments in each quarter of 1995, 1994 and 1993. These shipments included both product shipments actually made after the end of each quarter as well as shipments subject to nonstandard contractual terms. In addition, during fiscal 1995, certain expenses were incorrectly capitalized during the third and fourth quarters of fiscal 1995 as an element of the purchase price of Knogo Corporation. After carefully evaluating the findings, the Company concluded the financial statements for the third quarter of fiscal 1995 required restatement. (See Note 13.) Further, the Company concluded the effects of these matters on fiscal 1993, on fiscal 1994 and the quarters therein and on the first and second quarters of fiscal 1995 were such that restatement of the financial statements of such periods was not required.

Note 11. Acquisitions

On December 29, 1994, the Company acquired the operations outside of the United States, Puerto Rico and Canada of Knogo Corporation ("Knogo") for approximately 3.1 million shares of the Company's Common Stock (with a value of approximately $100 million). Based on the preliminary purchase price allocation, the significant identifiable assets acquired and liabilities assumed and/or incurred in connection with the Knogo acquisition were as follows:

Cash and marketable securities	$ 5.8
Accounts receivable, net	18.7
Net investment in sales-type leases	17.8
Inventories, net	12.5
Deferred income taxes, patents and other assets net	26.0
Accrued liabilities	54.0
Debt	23.5

In fiscal 1993, the Company acquired Automated Loss Prevention Systems (ALPS), a large European distributor of EAS and CCTV products, and Security Tag Systems, Inc. (Security Tag), a U.S.- based manufacturer and marketer of loss prevention products, for an aggregate amount of approximately $323 million consisting of approximately $280 million (funded with net proceeds of approximately $194.8 million from the issuance of 12.6 million shares of its Common Stock and from borrowings under a short-term credit facility) and 1.5 million shares of the Company's Common Stock (with a value of

approximately $43 million). The acquisitions of Knogo, ALPS and Security Tag resulted in costs in excess of net assets acquired of approximately $114 million, $223 million and $47 million, respectively (based on a preliminary allocation of the Knogo purchase price), which are being amortized using the straight-line method over 40 years. These acquisitions were accounted for under the purchase method and the respective subsidiaries were consolidated in the Company's financial statements from their respective dates of acquisition.

The Company's unaudited pro forma consolidated condensed statements of income for fiscal 1995, 1994 and 1993, assuming the acquisitions of Knogo (fiscal 1995 and 1994), ALPS (fiscal 1993) and Security Tag (fiscal 1993) were effected at the beginning of each year, are summarized as follows (in millions, except per share data):

	1995	1994	1993
Total revenues	$922.3	$726.1	$510.2
Income from continuing operations before income taxes	89.6	108.7	72.3
Net income	73.7	79.3	53.9
Primary earnings per common share	$1.00	$1.22	$ .91
Fully diluted earnings per common share	$ .99	$1.16	$ .89

This pro forma information does not purport to be indicative of the results which may have been obtained had the acquisitions been consummated at the dates assumed (see the financial statements and other information related to Knogo in the Company's Current Report on Form 8-K filed January 11, 1995, as amended on Form 8-K/A filed January 27, 1995).

In connection with acquisitions during fiscal 1995, 1994 and 1993, the market value of the assets acquired was as follows (in millions):

	1995	1994	1993
Cash paid (net of cash acquired)	$ 9.6	$11.5	$299.3
Liabilities assumed and/or incurred	101.1	13.2	76.6
Common stock	149.3	31.0	43.4
Market value of assets acquired	$260.0	$55.7	$419.3

DIRECTORS OF THE COMPANY

Ronald G. Assaf
Chairman of the Board and
Chief Executive Director

Robert A. Vanourek
President and Chief Operating
Officer

Thomas V. Buffet*
Vice Chairman of the Board,
President, Chipper Investments
Retired Chairman of the Board
and Chief Executive Officer of
Automated Security

Jerome M. LeWine
Partner, Christy & Viener
Attorney at Law

James E. Lineberger
Chairman of the Executive
Committee
Partner, Lineberger & Co. Private
Investment Firm

Dr. Arthur G. Milnes*
Professor Emeritus, Electrical
Engineering Department
Carnegie-Mellon University

John T. Ray, Jr.*
Senior Vice President
ASC Division
H.B. Fuller Company

Timothy P. Hartman
Chairman of Nations Bank of
Texas, Private Investor

* Member of the Audit Committee

Sensormatic Electronics Corporation

REPORT OF INDEPENDENT CERTIFIED PUBLIC ACCOUNTANTS

The Board of Directors

Sensormatic Electronics Corporation

We have audited the accompanying consolidated balance sheets of Sensormatic Electronics Corporation as of June 30, 1995 and 1994, and the related consolidated statements of income, stockholders' equity, and cash flows for each of the three years in the period ended June 30, 1995. These financial statements are the responsibility of the Company's management. Our responsibility is to express an opinion on these financial statements based on our audits.

We conducted our audits in accordance with generally accepted auditing standards. Those standards require that we plan and perform the audit to obtain reasonable assurance about whether the financial statements are free of material misstatement. An audit includes examining, on a test basis, evidence supporting the amounts and disclosures in the financial statements. An audit also includes assessing the accounting principles used and significant estimates made by management, as well as evaluating the overall financial statement presentation. We believe that our audits provide a reasonable basis for our opinion.

In our opinion, the consolidated financial statements referred to above present fairly, in all material respects, the consolidated financial position of Sensormatic Electronics Corporation at June 30, 1995 and 1994, and the consolidated results of their operations and their cash flows for each of the three years in the period ended June 30, 1995, in conformity with generally accepted accounting principles.

As discussed in Note 9. to the consolidated financial statements, the Company is a defendant in various lawsuits brought by alleged shareholders claiming, among other things, violations of federal securities laws. The Company strongly disputes these charges and intends to vigorously defend against these lawsuits. The ultimate outcome of the litigation cannot presently be determined. Accordingly, no provision for any liability that may result has been made in the consolidated financial statements.

As discussed in Note 5. to the consolidated financial statements, in 1994 the Company changed its method of accounting for income taxes.

ERNST & YOUNG LLP

West Palm Beach, Florida
September 30, 1995

p a r t 4

Additional Cases

Anacomp, Inc.

Brierly Investments Limited

The City of New York

Comdisco, Inc. (A)

Comdisco, Inc. (B)

CompUSA

The Computer Industry in 1992

Debt Ratings in the Chemical Industry

Donna Karan International Inc.

Echlin Versus SPX

Kansas City Zephyrs Baseball Club, Inc.

The Murray Ohio Manufacturing Company

Olympic Financial Ltd.

Revco D.S., Inc.

O n September 10, 1982, Anacomp, a computer software company, re-leased its first annual report after being listed on the New York Stock Exchange. Prior to 1982, the company's stock was traded on the over-the-counter market. In the annual report Anacomp's management outlined the company's strategy for new software systems development:

> Anacomp is committed to being the world's leading supplier of software and services to the banking industry. Anacomp and its subsidiaries have licensed software products, sold data processing services, or entered into software consulting agreements with more than 200 billion-dollar financial institutions around the world. But the bank marketplace is changing rapidly. Regulatory and technological changes are blurring the distinctions between banks and other financial institutions. Bank customers—both retail and wholesale—are becoming more sophisticated and more demanding. Bankers require computer systems which encourage total customer relationships, adapt quickly to product changes, and meet requirements of round-the-clock banking.

> Since 1979, Anacomp has been developing a totally new generation of banking computer software systems to serve those evolving needs. Anacomp's software development effort is one the most substantial ever undertaken by an independent computer services vendor. It is based on an Anacomp innovation—the software R&D partnership—and on the philosophy of getting prospective customers involved in developing the software products they will eventually use.

> In 1979, when its net worth was $10 million, Anacomp recognized the opportunity to develop at a cost of $12 million a major new IBM-based real-time retail banking system. The development was expected to take several years to complete. Anacomp selected the limited partnership alternative to buffer the company's stockholders from the financial risks involved. To help assure the development of a superior product, Anacomp also sought the participation of a cross-section of major financial institutions—the ultimate users of the bank product. To induce these banks to become co-developers, it was necessary to show that the required funding was in place and that Anacomp's commitment was firmly established. A

1

limited partnership was the best way to induce four "primary development banks" to contribute collectively $6 million and 24 software development people for two years to the project.

The same considerations were present in each of the four subsequent partnerships—BANKSERV 10000, CEFT, CDA, and CIBS. Each partnership assumed development risks; except for BANKSERV 10000, each project involved several major banks acting as co-developers with Anacomp. Any product developed becomes the property of the partnership. Anacomp has the option to purchase the products but is under no obligation to exercise this option; Anacomp did purchase the CIS and BANKSERV 10000 systems in 1982. In total, more than $60 million has been raised since 1979 for investment in the development of new wholesale and retail banking software products.

COMPANY BACKGROUND

Anacomp, Inc., based in Indianapolis, Indiana, began as a computer and data services company in 1969. The company was founded by Ronald Palamara, a Ph.D. in computer sciences. Among the computer services offered by the company were the design and implementation of computer software systems and the management of customers' computer facilities. The company also operated customers' data centers, offered data processing and microfilming services, and sold micrographic equipment. The company viewed that its future growth would primarily come from the design and development of software for the banking industry.

Prior to 1980, the company's principal proprietary software system for commercial banks and thrift institutions was the Customer Integrated/Reference File (CI/RF) system. CI/RF integrated a customer's banking relationships—such as checking, savings, loans, etc.—and incorporated them into a single record. The system was utilized by banks in 20 states throughout the United States, including Manufacturers Hanover Trust and Sumitomo Bank of California. The system and software primarily used a computer language designed for computers manufactured by NCR Corporation.

Beginning in 1980 Anacomp announced plans to develop a number of new software systems for the banking and financial services industry. For the retail banking industry the company was developing two new products: the Continuous Integrated System (CIS) and the BANKSERVE 10000 system. CIS was claimed to be the first on-line real-time retail banking transactions processing system designed for IBM computers. The BANK-SERVE 10000 system would allow banks to share networks of point-of-sale terminals or automated teller machines on a national or regional basis.

Anacomp had also announced plans to develop a full line of software systems to help banks deal more efficiently with their wholesale customers—companies, institutions, and other banks. The Corporate Electronic Funds Transfer (CEFT) system was expected to combine three banking functions: an electronic funds transfer mechanism that would take payments from external sources, a money transfer component which would automate the bank's internal paying and receiving functions, and a corporate funds control

Anacomp

component which would allow the bank to monitor its own cash position and the cash position of each customer. The Corporate Deposit and Analysis (CDA) system, another wholesale banking product that Anacomp targeted for development, was expected to automate the bank's depository relationships with large corporations and other banks.

In August 1982 the company announced that it was initiating the development of yet another new software system, Corporate International Banking System (CIBS). CIBS was the most complex system the company planned to date, and was intended to help a large international bank automate certain internal treasury operations, generate complete information on the bank's foreign currency positions, and automate the processing of letters of credit and documentary credit collections.

Anacomp's management believed that the above software systems, if successfully developed and implemented, would enable the company to become a leading supplier of software and services to the banking industry.

INDUSTRY AND COMPETITION[1]

The computer services industry was marked by very rapid growth. In 1981, computer service revenues totaled $18.9 billion, up 23 percent from $15.4 billion a year, according to INPUT, a leading international consulting firm. INPUT had estimated that the industry growth rate between 1981 and 1986 would be approximately 23 percent per annum.

There were three major segments of the computer services industry: processing services, professional services, and software products. The companies in the processing area offered customers access to a large computer facility in which batch processing, remote computing services, and facilities management services were performed. This segment accounted for 57 percent of total computer services revenues in 1981 and was expected to grow at a compound annual rate of 17 percent between 1981 and 1986. The companies in the professional services segment provided customers alternatives to in-house data processing. These services included custom-made computer systems and programming to perform specialized tasks, as well as the management of data processing facilities. The professional services segment, which accounted for 23 percent of total computer services industry revenues in 1981, was expected to grow 29 percent annually from 1981 to 1986. Software products, the third segment of the software services industry, was the fastest-growing sector. Software products consist of instructions that guide computer equipment through tasks. This segment was expected to grow at an annual compound growth rate of 33 percent between 1981 and 1986.

The high growth rates of the computer services industry were being fueled by the large number of computers installed and customers' realization of the value computer services can have in lifting their productivity. Hardware, the premiere growth area of the 1960s and 1970s, had since taken on a commodity-like status as a result of progressively lower manufacturing costs. Computer services, on the other hand, increased in value and in price.

------

1. *Material in this section is drawn from Standard and Poor's industry surveys on office equipment systems and services, October 21, 1982.*

The computer services industry in 1982 consisted of some 5,000 companies ranging from small software operations to giants such as IBM and Control Data Corporation. Smaller companies in the industry generally concentrated on serving particular market niches; their performance depended on factors influencing these small sectors.

There was active competition in each of the areas of services provided by Anacomp. In the computer service area, Anacomp competed with other computer service companies, manufacturers of mainframe computers, and companies developing in-house computer service capabilities. In the data center service business, Anacomp competed with other data processing and micrographic service companies. Anacomp believed that the services performed by it represented only a small portion of the market in each of the fields it operated.

The computer services industry was subject to rapid technological change requiring constant adaptation to provide competitive service. Competition in the computer services industry was based primarily on technical capability and expertise, pricing, quality of work, and ability to meet system development deadlines. In the other areas of Anacomp's business, competition was based upon the reliability and timeliness of the services and products provided.

TOP MANAGEMENT

The names, ages, and current and former positions of Anacomp's executive officers in September 1982 were as follows:

Ronald D. Palamara, Ph.D., age 42, has served as Chairman and President for more than the past five years.

Stanley E. Hirschfeld, age 47, became Senior Vice President of Corporate Development during 1981. For more than the prior five years, he served as Vice President-Finance and Secretary of Anacomp.

Ralph C. McAuley, age 47, became President of Anacomp's Computer Services group during 1981. For more than the five prior years, he served as Vice President of Data Processing Services.

John J. Flanigan, age 42, became Group Vice President of Data Services in 1981. During the prior five-year period, he served as Vice President of Data Processing Services.

Christopher Duffy, age 44, became Vice President and Chief Administrative Officer during 1981. For more than the five prior years, he served as Vice President and General Manager of an Indianapolis television station.

Myles Hannan, age 44, became Vice President-Finance, General Counsel and Secretary during 1981. During 1979 and 1980, he served as Vice President-Law and Administration for Delaware North Companies, Incorporated. For more than the prior two years he served as Vice President-Legal and Staff Divisions of the Stop & Shop Companies, Inc.

William C. Ater, age 40, became Vice President of Administration during 1981. During 1979 and 1980, he served as Anacomp's Vice President of Bank Data Processing. For more than the prior two years, he served in various computer management positions with NCR Corporation.

As of the end of fiscal 1981, all officers and directors as a group owned 15.1 percent of Anacomp's common stock and were paid $2.9 million in cash and cash equivalent forms of remuneration during the year.

NEW SOFTWARE SYSTEMS DEVELOPMENT

Anacomp organized and financed its new software development in a unique manner. During the fiscal year ended June 30, 1980, Anacomp initiated the development of a major new computer software system called Continuous Integrated System (CIS) to be marketed to major financial institutions. According to Anacomp's management, CIS would represent a major advance over the company's current CI/RF system.

Anacomp stated that, in view of the anticipated significant development expenditure for the CIS system, the company had entered into an agreement in November 1979 with a limited partnership, RTS Associates. Under this agreement, Anacomp agreed to develop the CIS system on behalf of the partnership. In return, RTS agreed to pay a development fee of $6 million, of which $2.2 million was paid in 1980. Upon completion of the development of the CIS system, Anacomp agreed to market CIS for five years on a commission basis. Anacomp also had the option to acquire all rights to the CIS system at the greater of its appraised fair market value or RTS's investment plus a fixed profit. RTS had the right to extend Anacomp's five-year marketing agreement an additional five years or to cancel it if Anacomp did not use its best efforts to market CIS.

RTS Associates' payments for the CIS development expenses were financed by (1) an investment of $1.444 million by the partners, (2) a $3.25 million bank loan to RTS, secured by bank letters of credit and personal guarantees of the limited partners, and (3) a $2.2 million loan to RTS, personally guaranteed by the limited partners, from Anacomp, with interest at 11 percent per annum payable quarterly through December 31, 1981, and with principal and interest payable thereafter in 84 equal monthly installments. In addition, if the CIS development expenses exceeded $6 million and therefore RTS was required to pay further development fees, Anacomp agreed to loan RTS, without recourse to the limited partners, up to $1.5 million to complete the CIS system.

Several officers and directors of Anacomp were affiliated with the corporate general partner of RTS, and were also investors in the limited partnership arrangement. Ronald Palamara, Chairman of the Board and President of Anacomp, and three other directors of Anacomp, were also directors and officers of the corporate general partner of RTS. The ownership interest of Anacomp's officers and directors in the limited partnership amounted to 38.5% of the total.

During the fiscal year 1981, thirteen major banks, including the National Bank of North America in New York, the Shawmut National Bank in Boston, Provident National Bank in Philadelphia, and the First National Bank in Kansas City, contracted with Anacomp to participate as advisory banks in the CIS project for a nonrefundable fee of

$150,000 each. The arrangement permitted each bank to review the project during development and provide input regarding changes to enhance the ultimate marketability of CIS.

In June 1982, Anacomp announced that the CIS system development was completed. The company also announced that it purchased the system from RTS Associates for $16 million.

FINANCIAL PERFORMANCE

After reporting a strong increase in revenues and profits from 1978 to 1981, Anacomp reported a slower revenue growth and a decline in profits in fiscal 1982. Dr. Palamara commented that the 1982 performance was a short-term aberration, and that the company's long-term strategy and prospects were sound:

> *Fiscal 1982 marked the beginning of one era and the end of another for Anacomp. A new era began with five events having tremendous long-term significance for Anacomp: the purchase of two major software products, the completion of our most significant acquisition, an offering of $50 million in convertible debentures, the formation of history's largest software research and development partnership, and Anacomp's listing on the New York Stock Exchange. Thus, despite a difficult fourth quarter which was affected by several non-recurring items and resulted in lower earnings for the year, fiscal 1982 was perhaps the most significant year of achievements in Anacomp's history.*
>
> *Judged solely by the numbers, of course, 1982 does not seem especially memorable. . . . In terms of positioning the company for future growth, however, 1982 may well be remembered as the most significant year in Anacomp's history. . . .*
>
> *We believe that Anacomp's performance in future years will demonstrate that the company is well along in its evolution from a small, explosive-growth firm to a nationally recognized market leader.*

Dr. Palamara projected record financial results in fiscal 1983. He also assured investors that Anacomp would place renewed emphasis on improving the company's profitability and reducing its financial leverage.

Exhibit 1 shows Anacomp's stock price data around the time of its 1982 results. An abridged version of the company's annual report is presented in Exhibit 2.

QUESTIONS

1. Evaluate Anacomp's new product development strategy. What are the risks and benefits of this strategy for Anacomp's shareholders?
2. How is Anacomp's accounting influenced by the way the company organizes and finances its new product development?
3. Compare Anacomp's cash flow performance with its accounting performance. What is your evaluation of the company's financial condition?
4. What is your assessment of Anacomp's future?

EXHIBIT 1

Anacomp—Stock Price and Trading Volume Data

Trading	Anacomp Trading Volume (thousands)	Anacomp Closing Price (dollars)	S&P 500 Composite Closing
9/1/82	109	10.875	118.25
9/2/82	92	10.875	120.38
9/3/82	437	11.125	122.68
9/7/82	120	10.875	121.37
9/8/82	231	11.000	122.20
9/9/82	230	10.750	121.97
9/10/82	417	10.625	120.97
9/13/82	284	10.375	122.24

Anacomp's common stock beta = 1.3 (Value Line estimate)

STOCK TRADING INFORMATION

	Stock Price		
	High	Low	Cash Dividends
Fiscal Year 1981			
First quarter	$15.63	$10.63	$.026
Second quarter	19.88	13.75	.026
Third quarter	16.50	12.75	.026
Fourth quarter	18.38	15.13	.030
Fiscal Year 1982			
First quarter	16.63	11.25	.030
Second quarter	14.00	11.88	.030
Third quarter	12.25	10.00	.030
Fourth quarter	13.38	10.88	.030

OTHER INFORMATION

Interest rate on 3-month Treasury bills:	8.2%
Interest rate on 20-year government bonds:	12.2%
P/E ratio for Standard & Poor's 400 Industrials:	23.2

Anacomp

Anacomp

EXHIBIT 2

Anacomp, Inc.—Abridged 1982 Annual Report

To our Shareholders

Fiscal 1982 marked the beginning of one era and the end of another for Anacomp.

A new era began with five events having tremendous long-term significance for Anacomp: the purchase of two major software products, the completion of our most significant acquisition, an offering of $50 million in convertible debentures, the formation of history's largest software research and development partnership and Anacomp's listing on the New York Stock Exchange. Thus, despite a difficult fourth quarter which was affected by several non-recurring items and resulted in lower earnings for the year, fiscal 1982 was perhaps the most significant year of achievements in Anacomp's history.

Judged solely by the numbers, of course, 1982 does not seem especially memorable. Although revenues rose slightly over 1981, earnings per share declined due to the impact of fourth quarter results, which reflected several one-time changes and short-term factors. These factors are described in detail in our fourth quarter report.

In terms of positioning the company for future growth, however, 1982 may well be remembered as the most significant year in Anacomp's history.

- In January, Anacomp completed a $50 million offering of 13⅞ percent convertible subordinated debentures which, after an original issue discount, increased the company's working capital position by $41 million.

- Listing on the New York Stock Exchange in April recognized Anacomp's stature in the computer services industry and provided the opportunity for greater visibility as the computer reaches out to new, worldwide markets.

- During June of the year, Anacomp purchased two major retail banking software systems which we had been developing for investment partnerships. CIS, a totally integrated system that we believe will revolutionize retail banking in the 1980s, was purchased for nearly $16 million. CIS has already attracted a financial commitment from nearly 35 banks, seven of which had signed substantial license agreements by the end of the year. BANKSERV® 10000, a system to provide banks with a new level of electronic transaction switching and processing capabilities, was purchased for $2.3 million.

- Also during June, Anacomp signed an agreement with IBM Corporation which gives us the capability to be a primary source of supply for a bank's branch automation requirements.

- The acquisition of 24 micrographic data imaging centers from DSI Corporation and Kalvar Corporation in May provided the ability to deliver Anacomp services to an even broader base of regular, repetitive customers, and the opportunity to offer new services through an expanded delivery system.

- After the close of the fiscal year, funding for the CIBS research and development partnership was completed with the closing of the final portion of $26.25 million in partnership interests. The partnership will contract with Anacomp to develop CIBS, Corporate International Banking System, a complex software system for use by large banks and other financial institutions engaged in international business.

We believe Anacomp's performance in future years will demonstrate that the company is well along in its evolution from a small, explosive-growth firm to a nationally recognized market leader.

To ensure that Anacomp's evolution will result in a stable company, with performance attractive to investors, Anacomp will be placing renewed emphasis in several areas. These areas will include our rate of return, where we anticipate achieving a superior return on investment from the maturation of software projects, existing operations, plus the addition of quality investments.

We also expect to reduce our leverage ratio over the next few years by calling our convertible debt, when this becomes practical, and by taking other appropriate measures. We will continue to employ strategic planning approaches in all our business units. Lastly, we will seek out those acquisitions which blend with our long-term goals.

We have projected record financial results in fiscal 1983 as the company asserts its leadership in bank software and micrographic data imaging. We appreciate the continued support of our stockholders and employees which makes that goal achievable.

Sincerely,

Ronald D. Palamara, Ph.D.
President and Chairman of the Board

September 10, 1982

MANAGEMENT'S DISCUSSION AND ANALYSIS OF FINANCIAL CONDITION AND RESULTS OF OPERATIONS

Anacomp, Inc. and Subsidiaries

General

In September 1980, Anacomp completed a public offering of $30,000,000 of 9½% Convertible Subordinated Debentures due 2000. In January 1981, Anacomp completed an offering outside the United States of $12,500,000 of 9% Convertible Subordinated Debentures due 1996, with warrants to purchase a like amount of debentures. In January 1982, Anacomp completed the public offering of $50,000,000 of 13⅞% Convertible Subordinated Debentures due 2002. The Debentures were offered at an original issue discount of 15%, with net proceeds of $41,125,000, and carry an effective cost of 16.6%. The cash from these offerings has been used to finance the expansion of receivables and unbilled revenues, to retire long-term debt, to provide funds for acquisitions, and to increase working capital. During the past three years, Anacomp has completed the acquisition of eleven business entities. The acquisitions and the debenture offerings accounted for the major changes in Anacomp's financial condition and results of operations.

Financial Condition and Liquidity

During 1982, working capital increased $1,949,000. The major source of working capital, other than operations, was the increase in long-term debt, primarily the result of the

January offering of $50,000,000 of debentures and to a lesser extent the exercise of warrants to purchase $1,289,000 of additional 9% debentures. The major use of working capital was the purchase of computer software systems from limited partnerships. Other major uses of working capital were the purchase of marketable securities held as long-term investments, the retirement of long-term debt, and additions of fixed assets. During the year, cash was used to finance the increase in unbilled revenues, to purchase 92% of the shares of DSI Corporation, and to pay certain software development costs. As a result, the current ratio at June 30, 1982, is 2.40, compared to 3.84 at June 30, 1981. At June 30, 1982, Anacomp had $35,000,000 of available but unused lines of credit that could be used if needed to provide short-term financing. Negotiations are currently being held with a group of banks to establish a revolving credit arrangement which will replace the existing lines of credit.

At the present time, Anacomp has no major commitments to acquire assets or facilities which will require a substantial outlay of working capital. It is anticipated that the current acquisition program will continue in the future as opportunities present themselves.

Anacomp currently expects to incur approximately $6,000,000 during 1983 on enhancements to a computer software system, of which approximately $3,000,000 is expected to be funded by others. The project is being undertaken because the results will yield a product with improved marketability, which at the same time will meet commitments to certain customers.

Operations—Fiscal 1982 Compared to 1981

Revenues for 1982 increased only 3% over fiscal 1981, with the increase being generated primarily by internal growth and the addition of internally generated projects. Software development projects, especially two new projects contracted for by major banks and limited partnerships, and higher levels of sales of minicomputers and microcomputers and related software, contributed the largest portion of the increase. Revenues were also increased by certain data centers. These increases, along with smaller increases in other areas, were largely offset by reduced revenue being generated by other data centers as a result of a consolidation of certain operations.

Total operating costs and expenses increased 10.4% during fiscal 1982. Personnel costs and outside services costs associated with the increased software development activity were the major factors in the increase. Other contributors to the increase were higher supply costs, equipment-related costs, and the cost of computer hardware sales, each caused by higher levels of activity. Also, amortization of purchased software added to the overall increase, along with generally higher prices for all purchased goods and services. These increases were partially offset by cost reductions from the synergism obtained from prior acquisitions, a reduction in costs as a result of consolidating certain administrative functions and, in the third quarter, from the recovery of previously recorded expenses.

Margins for the current periods were substantially lower than the prior year due to the emphasis on completing large systems development projects as opposed to generating new license fees for other products. Margins earned on development work have typically been less than those earned from software licensing and related activities. The reduction in revenue in certain data centers has also tended to reduce margins, as the revenue losses have preceded to some extent the current cost reduction and consolidation efforts.

Interest expense increased in the convertible year as a result of the interest on the 9½% Convertible Subordinated Debentures offered during fiscal 1981 and the 13⅞%

Convertible Subordinated Debentures offered in January 1982. Interest income was derived from investing the proceeds from these offerings not otherwise utilized. Due to the uses of cash mentioned previously and a lowering of interest rates on investments, interest income decreased throughout the current period.

The extraordinary credit arose from the sale of a branch office which had been acquired in 1981 in a transaction accounted for as a pooling of interests. The amount of the credit is the gain realized, net of related income taxes.

The provision for income taxes reflects the normal tax relating to the income reported for financial statement purpose4 after recognizing the impact of investment tax credits, non-deductible expenses, and the effect of interest due from the under-depositing of tax payments as a result of the denial of a request for a change in certain reporting policies for tax purposes.

Fiscal 1981 Compared to 1980

Of the $34,725,000 increase in revenue, the major portion was attributable to acquisitions included for the first time in 1981, or for the full period in 1981, plus internal growth generated by those acquisitions. Other changes in revenue for the year resulted primarily from new software development sales and non-recurring licensing agreements (especially from new software systems for banks, financed in part by limited partnerships), offset in part by reduced revenues due to declining activity in certain data centers and the completion of certain non-repetitive software projects.

Direct costs of service and equipment increased 54%, primarily from the costs associated with the recent acquisitions plus increased expenses required to support increased software development, and rising costs for personnel and other services. Selling, general and administrative expenses increased 17% from the costs associated with the recent acquisitions plus the expenses necessary to manage the rapidly growing company and from rising personnel costs. The increases in other direct operating and selling, general and administrative costs were offset in part by a savings of approximately $1,255,000 being realized during 1981 due to a change in the funding of Anacomp's contribution to the Thrift Plan for Employees.

Interest income increased from interest earned by cash investment programs and from the interest earned on notes receivable.

Interest expense increased primarily from the interest on the recently issued 9% and 9½% Convertible Subordinated Debentures, with other increases from debt incurred to finance acquisitions and interest on short-term borrowings, offset somewhat by lower interest on the 10% Convertible Subordinated Debentures due to conversions to equity.

Other income included the gain from a transaction with Kalvar which resulted from an agreement whereby Anacomp sold to Kalvar its Kalvar preferred stock for Kalvar common stock and sold its option to acquire additional Kalvar common stock in exchange for a promissory note from Kalvar.

The provision for income taxes reflects the normal tax relating to the income reported for financial statement purposes after giving effect to the benefits obtained from investment tax credits and from the exclusion of dividend income. The expected tax rate for fiscal 1981 was revised downward during the fourth quarter as a result of a large capital gain arising primarily from the transaction with Kalvar.

Anacomp

SELECTED FINANCIAL DATA

Anacomp, Inc., and Subsidiaries

(dollars in thousands, except per share amounts)	1982	1981	1980	1979	1978
For the year ended June 30					
Revenues	$109,599	$106,368	$71,643	$41,662	$23,433
Income before provision for income taxes and extraordinary credit	3,622	13,997	7,787	5,045	3,154
Income before extraordinary credit	2,779	7,938	4,627	2,704	1,542
Net income	4,609	7,938	4,627	2,704	1,542
Earnings per common and common equivalent share:					
Income before extraordinary credit	$.30	$.87	$.70	$.57	$.39
Net income	.50	.87	.70	.57	.39
Earnings per common share assuming full dilution:					
Income before extraordinary credit	$.29	$.83	$.66	$.51	$.32
Net income	.48	.83	.66	.51	.32
Cash dividends declared per common share	.12	.11	.10	.09	.06
As of June 30					
Current assets	$ 99,044	$ 75,453	$33,453	$16,200	$ 9,869
Current liabilities	41,276	19,634	22,079	11,452	3,561
Working capital	7,768	55,819	11,374	4,748	6,308
Total assets	211,660	130,798	76,950	30,069	14,182
Long-term debt	105,208	50,591	10,608	8,162	3,993
Stockholders' equity	61,035	55,891	44,077	10,211	6,639
Book value per common share	$6.59	$6.18	$5.56	$2.14	$1.55
Number of employees	2,300	2,000	1,800	895	430
Number of holders of common stock	7,930	5,575	3,810	1,955	1,225

CONSOLIDATED BALANCE SHEET

Anacomp, Inc. and Subsidiaries

	June 30	
(dollars in thousands, except per share amounts)	1982	1981
Assets		
Current assets:		
Cash (including temporary investments)	$ 34,519	$29,392
Accounts and notes receivable, less allowances for doubtful accounts of $1,915 and $1,210, respectively	25,284	23,216
Unbilled revenues	18,534	15,863
Inventories	4,469	3,014
Deferred CIBS development costs (Note 3)	5,647	—
Prepaid expenses (including income taxes of $3,018 and $1,242, respectively)	10,591	3,968
Total current assets	99,044	75,453
Property and equipment, at cost less accumulated depreciation and amortization of $10,189 and $8,660, respectively	25,112	14,930
Cost of computer software systems purchased, less accumulated depreciation of $1,584 and $186, respectively	20,363	1,747
Excess of purchase price over net assets of businesses acquired, less accumulated amortization of $2,319 and $1,285, respectively	42,646	24,291
Other assets	24,495	14,377
	$211,660	$130,798

(continued)

Anacomp

Anacomp

CONSOLIDATED BALANCE SHEET (continued)

	June 30	
(dollars in thousands, except per share amounts)	1982	1981
Liabilities and Stockholders' Equity		
Current liabilities:		
Notes payable, banks	$ 14,000	$ —
Current portion of long-term debt	2,907	2,359
Accounts payable	8,151	8,787
Accrued salaries, wages and bonuses	4,604	3,863
Accrued interest payable	5,129	1,747
Income taxes	—	419
Other accrued liabilities	6,485	2,459
Total current liabilities	41,276	19,634
Long-term debt, net of current portion:		
Convertible subordinated debentures	86,274	43,340
Other long-term debt	18,934	7,251
Total long-term debt	105,208	50,591
Deferred income taxes	3,177	4,015
Minority interest	964	667
Stockholder's equity:		
Preferred stock—$1 par value, authorized 1,000,000 shares, none issued	—	—
Common stock—$1 par value, authorized 25,000,000 shares, 9,256,544 and 9,042,722 issued, respectively	9,257	9,043
Capital in excess of par value of common stock	37,305	35,207
Unrealized losses on marketable securities	(899)	(233)
Retained earnings	15,372	11,874
Total stockholders' equity	61,035	55,891
	$211,660	$130,798

CONSOLIDATED STATEMENT OF INCOME

Anacomp, Inc., and Subsidiaries

(dollars in thousands, except per share amounts)	Year Ended June 30		
	1982	1981	1980
Revenues			
Services provided	$88,045	$87,304	$58,781
Equipment sold	21,554	19,064	12,862
	109,599	106,368	71,643
Operating costs and expenses			
Costs of services provided	67,302	62,464	40,342
Costs of equipment sold	16,764	13,900	9,172
Selling, general and administrative expenses	19,888	17,821	15,284
	103,954	94,185	64,798
	5,645	12,183	6,845
Interest income	5,525	3,204	485
Interest expense	(8,158)	(4,090)	(1,381)
Other, net	610	2,700	1,838
	(2,023)	1,814	942
Income before provision for income taxes and extraordinary credit	3,622	13,997	7,787
Provision for income taxes	843	6,059	3,160
Income before extraordinary credit	2,779	7,938	4,627
Extraordinary credit, net of related tax	1,830	—	—
Net income	$ 4,609	$ 7,938	$ 4,627
Earnings per common and common equivalent share			
Income before extraordinary credit	$.30	$.87	$.70
Extraordinary credit	.20	—	—
Net income	$.50	$.87	$.70
Earnings per common share assuming full dilution			
Income before extraordinary credit	$.29	$.83	$.66
Extraordinary credit	.19	—	—
Net income	$.48	$.83	$.66
Cash dividends declared per share	$.12	$.11	$.10

Anacomp

Anacomp

CONSOLIDATED STATEMENT OF CHANGES IN FINANCIAL POSITION

Anacomp, Inc., and Subsidiaries

(dollars in thousands)	Year Ended June 30		
	1982	1981	1980
Working capital was provided by:			
Income before extraordinary credit	$2,779	$7,938	$4,627
Charges to income not requiring an outlay of working capital:			
Depreciation and amortization	6,708	4,368	3,026
Deferred income taxes	(1,314)	3,951	2
Other	143	416	331
Working capital provided by operations	8,316	16,673	7,986
Working capital provided by extraordinary credit	742	—	—
Dispositions of property and equipment	702	218	2,001
Decrease in investment in Computer Micrographics, Inc.	—	—	1,733
Long-term debt incurred	55,680	43,636	7,158
Issuances of common stock	2,236	4,813	28,371
Other	3,224	1,024	(84)
	70,900	66,364	47,165
Working capital was applied to:			
Additions to property and equipment	11,172	3,533	5,171
Excess of purchase price over net assets of businesses acquired	19,791	4,172	18,900
Noncurrent assets of companies acquired in purchase transactions	5,315	1,088	4,593
Noncurrent liabilities of businesses acquired in purchase transactions	(2,892)	(1,040)	(2,199)
Purchase of computer software systems	20,014	1,734	—
Increase in investments	6,099	4,806	2,027
Increase in other assets	4,441	1,977	4,443
Reduction of long-term debt	3,900	4,693	6,911
Cash dividends declared	1,111	956	693
	68,951	21,919	40,539
	$ 1,949	$44,445	$ 6,626

(continued)

	Year Ended June 30		
(dollars in thousands)	1982	1981	1980
Increase in working capital represented by:			
Increase (decrease) in current assets:			
Cash (including temporary investments)	$5,127	$24,649	$1,484
Accounts and notes receivable	2,068	6,841	8,333
Unbilled revenues	2,671	7,283	5,605
Inventories	1,455	513	1,383
Deferred CIBS development costs	5,647	—	—
Prepaid expenses	6,623	2,714	448
Decrease (increase) in current liabilities:			
Notes payable	(14,000)	4,000	(3,250)
Current portion of long-term debt	(548)	791	(315)
Accounts payable	636	(1,022)	(4,716)
Accrued salaries, wages and bonuses	(741)	(1,185)	(683)
Accrued interest payable	(3,382)	(1,639)	(48)
Income taxes	419	1,162	286
Other accrued liabilities	(4,026)	338	(1,901)
Increase in working capital	$ 1,949	$44,445	$6,626

The accompanying notes are an integral part of the consolidated financial statements.

Anacomp

NOTES TO CONSOLIDATED FINANCIAL STATEMENTS

Anacomp, Inc. and Subsidiaries
(dollars in thousands, except per share amounts)

Note 1. Summary of Significant Accounting Policies

Consolidation

The consolidated financial statements include the accounts of Anacomp, Inc. ("Anacomp") and its majority-owned subsidiaries except Anacomp Leasing Company, Inc., an immaterial wholly-owned subsidiary, which is reflected in the equity method in the accompanying financial statements. Intercompany transactions have been eliminated. Certain amounts in the 1981 and 1980 financial statements have been reclassified to conform to the 1982 presentation.

Revenue Recognition

Revenues are generally recognized as follows:

(1) Data preparation, data processing, facility management and computer output microfilm ("COM") services and sales are recognized as the services are performed or products are shipped.

(2) Revenues from granting perpetual licenses of existing software systems which do not require substantial modification are recognized at the time the license agreement is executed, if collectibility is reasonably assured and the software system is delivered to the customer.

(3) Revenues from contracts for development and/or modifications to existing software systems are recognized under methods which approximate the percentage-of-completion method, except for revenues from development contracts with certain limited partnerships which are reported on the completed contract method, other than immaterial amounts reported for 1980 (see Note 3). Losses on such contracts are recognized when identified.

Revenue recognized under items (2) and (3) may precede the date at which the customer may be billed pursuant to the contract terms. Substantially all unbilled revenue is collected in the year subsequent to the year revenue is recognized.

The subject of revenue recognition for development contracts with limited partnerships including certain arrangements described in (3) above is presently under review by the Financial Accounting Standards Board (FASB). Anacomp will comply with any Statement of Financial Standards issued by the FASB. In April, 1982, the FASB issued an exposure draft entitled "Research and Development Arrangements." Anacomp believes that it is in substantial compliance with the exposure draft, and that approval of the draft by the FASB would not result in an adjustment to the amounts presented in the financial statements.

Inventories

Inventories are stated at the lower of cost or market, cost being determined primarily on the specific identification basis. The cost of the inventories is distributed as follows:

	June 30		
	1982	1981	1980
Equipment held for resale	$3,084	$1,899	$1,315
Operating supplies	1,385	1,115	1,186
	$4,469	$3,014	$2,501

Purchased Computer Software Systems

Purchased computer software systems held for licensing to others are earned at cost less accumulated depreciation. Depreciation is recorded over the estimated marketing lives of the software, and is computed based on the greater of the amount calculated using either a percent-of-revenue or the straight-line method. The percent-of-revenue method is based on the total estimated future revenues expected to be derived from sales of the software, while straight-line depreciation is provided using estimated marketing lives of five to ten years.

Amortization of Excess Purchase Price over Net Assets

Excess of purchase price over net assets of business acquired is amortized on the straight-line method over the estimated useful life, currently ranging from five to twenty years, if determined, and over 40 years if life is indeterminate.

Earnings per Share

The computation of earnings per common and common equivalent share is based upon the weighted average number of common shares outstanding during the year plus (in years in which they have a dilutive effect) the effect of common shares contingently issuable, primarily from stock options, conversion of subordinated debentures issued during fiscal 1981 and, for 1980, common shares purchased in July 1980, in connection with an employment agreement (see Note 13). Interest expense, net of taxes, on the subordinated debentures is added to net income in the computation of earnings per common and common equivalent share.

The fully diluted per share computation reflects the effect of common shares contingently issuable upon conversion of each convertible subordinated debenture outstanding in years in which such conversions would cause dilution. Interest expense, net of income taxes, on the debentures assumed to be converted is added to net income in the computation of fully diluted earnings per share. Fully diluted earnings per share also reflects additional dilution related to stock options due to the use of the year-end market price, when higher than the average price for the year.

The weighted average number of common and common equivalent shares used to compute earnings per share is 9,281,640, 9,425,788 and 6,624,955 for 1982, 1981 and 1980, respectively. The average number of shares used to compute earnings per common share assuming full dilution is 9,667,794, 11,457,335 and 7,149,132 for the respective years. The numbers of shares for all years are adjusted for all stock splits and stock dividends declared.

Vacation Pay

In November 1980, the Financial Accounting Standards Board issued Statement of Financial Accounting Standards No. 43 (SFAS No. 43), "Accounting for Compensated Absences," which requires the accrual of vacation pay earned but not taken. The provisions of SFAS No. 43 require the restatement of prior periods and therefore the cumulative effect as of July 1, 1979, is shown as an adjustment to retained earnings at that date. The effect of this change was to reduce net income by $97 ($.01 per share) in 1982, $72 ($.01 per share) in 1981 and $273 ($.03 per share) in 1980.

Note 3. Major Software Products and Related Party Transactions

CIS

In June 1982, Anacomp purchased for $16,000 a major new computer software system called CIS (Continuous Integrated System) developed by Anacomp for RTS Associates ("RTS"), a limited partnership formed in 1979. Several officers and directors of Anacomp who are affiliated with RTS's general partner are also investors in RTS, aggregating approximately 39% of the combined general and limited partnership units. The remaining partnership interests are owned by persons not affiliated with Anacomp. Anacomp contracted to develop the system on a best-efforts basis, and RTS agreed to pay a development fee of $6,000, of which $4,750 was paid through 1981, and an additional $1,250 during 1982. RTS paid Anacomp an additional $1,500 after actual costs to Anacomp exceeded $6,000. Anacomp had previously loaned $2,200 to RTS, personally guaranteed by the limited partners, and loaned the additional $1,500 as provided for in the development agreement. RTS paid all such loans in full out of the proceeds of the sale of the CIS system.

Concurrent with the development of CIS for the RTS partnership, a complimentary project was being developed for four CIS Primary Development Banks. Each bank committed $1,500 to fund modifications of the CIS project to conform to their specific requirements and thereby obtained a nonexclusive license to CIS as so modified. Under the terms of the Primary Development Bank agreements, 10% of any revenue from licensing CIS to others will accrue to each of the banks until such time as their entire $1,500 development fee has been recovered. At June 30, 1982, seven other banks had entered into, or committed to enter into, license agreements for CIS.

During 1981 and 1982, twenty major banks contracted with Anacomp to participate as Advisory Development Banks on the CIS project for a nonrefundable fee of $150. The fee permits each bank to review the project during development and provide input, which is not binding to Anacomp, regarding changes which would enhance the marketability of CIS. Anacomp defers a portion of this fee which will be recognized as services are provided to the participating banks throughout the terms of their contracts.

EFT

During fiscal 1981, Anacomp initiated and completed development of a new computer software switching system called H-10000 to be marketed to major financial institutions. Anacomp entered into an agreement with EFT Partners, Ltd. ("EFT"), a limited partnership formed in the fall of 1980. Several officers and directors of Anacomp purchased limited partnership units in EFT, aggregating approximately 31% of the partnership units, and Kranzley & Co., a wholly-owned subsidiary of Anacomp, was the general partner. The remaining limited partnership interests were owned by persons not affiliated with Anacomp. Anacomp agreed to develop and market the system, and EFT agreed to pay a development fee of $1,000, of which $910 was paid during 1981 and an additional $90 during 1982. The contract was reported on the completed contract basis; revenue and profits were recognized upon completion during the fourth quarter of 1981. In June 1982, Kranzley & Co. exercised its right under the purchase option to buy the interests of the limited partners at the appraised fair market value for the H-10000 system of $2,300.

CEFT

During fiscal 1981, Anacomp entered into an agreement with CEFT Partners, Ltd. ("CEFT"), a limited partnership formed in December 1980, and primary development banks to jointly develop a new computer funds transfer software system to be marketed to major financial institutions. Certain officers, directors and employees of Anacomp purchased limited partnership units in CEFT aggregating approximately 9% of the limited partnership units. The remaining partnership interest and the general partnership interest are owned by persons not affiliated with Anacomp.

Under the development agreement, Anacomp agreed to develop the new system on a best-effort basis. The agreement permits Anacomp to contract with primary development banks to provide development fees up to $1,000 in addition to the $2,100 development fee to be paid by the partnership. In June 1981, the general partner agreed to permit Anacomp to increase the bank fees allowable to $2,000 on this project. Contracts with five banks aggregating $2,000 have been completed.

Anacomp has acquired rights to a system owned by a major bank at a cost of $500 to assist and expedite the completion of the system. A portion of this cost has been charged to expense as a system development cost and the remainder is being amortized over the expected marketing life of the purchased system in its unmodified form.

The system was certified as being complete in July 1982, and Anacomp has agreed to market it for seven years on an exclusive commission basis. Anacomp has the option to acquire all rights to the system at the greater of (a) fair market value or (b) $3,000 to $5,000, depending on the date the option is exercised. Revenues earned on this software development project were $3,150 and $942 during fiscal 1981 and 1982.

CBS

During fiscal 1981, Anacomp entered into an agreement with CBS Partners, Ltd. ("CBS"), a limited partnership formed in April 1981, and primary development banks to jointly develop a wholesale banking computer software system to be marketed to major financial institutions. Certain officers, directors and employees of Anacomp purchased limited partnership units in the partnership aggregating approximately 20% of the limited partnership units. The remaining limited partnership interest and the general partnership interest are owned by persons not affiliated with Anacomp. Under the development agreement, Anacomp agreed to develop the new system on a best-efforts basis. The agreement permits Anacomp to contract with primary development banks to provide development fees up to $3,750 in addition to the $4,500 development fee to be paid by the partnership. Contracts with three banks aggregating $3,750 have been completed.

Anacomp has acquired rights to a wholesale banking system owned by a major bank at a cost of $1,350 to assist and expedite the completion of the system. A portion of this cost is being charged to expense as a system development cost and the remainder is being amortized over the expected marketing life of the purchased system in its unmodified form.

Upon completion of the system, Anacomp has agreed to market it for seven years on an exclusive commission basis. Anacomp has the option to acquire all rights to CBS at the greater of (a) fair market value or (b) $7,000 to $9,000, depending on the date the option is exercised. Revenues earned on this software development project were $2,620 and $4,319 during 1981 and 1982.

CIBS

Subsequent to June 30, 1982, Anacomp entered into an agreement with CIBS Partners, Limited ("CIBS"), a limited partnership formed in April 1981, to develop new software systems for large banks engaged in international business. Certain officers, directors and employees of Anacomp purchased limited partnership units in CIBS aggregating approximately 6.5% of the limited partnership units. The remaining limited partnership interests are owned by persons not affiliated with Anacomp. Anacomp is the sole holder of $400 of the non-voting preferred stock of the corporate general partner. The partnership payments under the development agreements are to be funded with $26,250 of partners' capital investment.

Under the development agreement, Anacomp has agreed to develop the new systems on a best-efforts basis. The agreement permits Anacomp to contract with primary development banks to provide development fees up to $12,000 in addition to the $23,000 development fee to be paid by the partnership. A contract with one bank for $500 has been completed.

Upon completion of the systems, Anacomp has agreed to lease the systems for five years on an exclusive basis at rental based on a percentage of license fees generated. Anacomp has the option to acquire all rights to the systems during the three-year period commencing one year after completion of the systems at total prices ranging from $46,400 to $59,700, plus a share of licensing fees generated thereafter, depending on the year in which the option is exercised.

At June 30, 1982, the Company considered the funding for this project to be imminent. Accordingly, costs of $5,647, including $2,750 to acquire rights to certain software incurred in commencing the development of CIBS, were deferred until such time as project funding became available in August 1982. Such costs will be charged to operations in fiscal 1983.

Other

During fiscal 1980, a group of officers and directors of Anacomp formed a limited partnership which purchased a computer system and leased it to Anacomp at a competitive rental rate. In May 1982, the Company purchased the computer equipment from the partnership for $1,167, which was its appraised value.

Note 5. Cash, Cash Investments and Short-Term Borrowings

Cash balances at June 30, 1982 and 1981, include temporary investments of $34,380 and $26,550, respectively, at costs which approximate market value. Of the amounts invested at June 20, 1982, $10,000 is pledged as collateral for the short-term borrowings from banks of $10,000 and is restricted as to withdrawal.

At June 20, 1982, Anacomp has short-term lines of credit from banks in the amount of $39,000, of which $35,000 is unused. Anacomp has agreed to maintain compensating balances, not restricted as to withdrawal, on certain of these lines. The average of compensating balances on these lines was approximately 5% of the available lines during fiscal 1982.

Note 7. Other Assets

The following comprise other assets:

	June 30	
	1982	1981
Investment in Kalvar Corporation, including $1,028 note receivable in both years and income bond and preferred stock in 1982	$ 6,428	$ 3,398
Marketable securities valued at the lower of cost or market	6,068	3,665
Notes receivable, RTS Associates	—	2,095
Notes receivable, other	4,132	400
Employment and non-compete agreements, less accumulated amortization of $1,297 and $848, respectively	491	737
Deferred debenture costs, less accumulated amortization of $313 and $152, respectively	3,470	2,026
Deferred charges, other	3,906	2,056
	$24,495	$14,377

Note 8. Long-Term Debt

Long-term debt is comprised of the following:

	June 30	
	1982	1981
10% Convertible Subordinated Debentures due November 1, 1988	$ 758	$ 915
9½% Convertible Subordinated Debentures due September 1, 2000	29,925	29,925
9% Convertible Subordinated Debentures due January 15, 1996	13,789	12,500
13⅞% Convertible Subordinated Debentures due January 15, 2002 (net of unamortized original issue discount of $7,440	42,560	—
Notes payable to banks at an average rate of 15.5% at June 30, 1982, due in installments to 1985	12,880	1,436
Other	8,203	8,174
	108,115	52,950
Less current portion	2,907	2,359
	$105,208	$50,591

Other debt includes equipment purchase notes, debtor to finance acquisitions, mortgages and obligations under capitalized financial leases. These items have effective costs of 9¾% to 15% and are payable in installments over varying periods extending to 2006. Shares representing substantially all of the operations of DSI are pledged as collateral for a note with a discounted balance of $2,793 at June 30, 1982. At June 30, 1982, processing equipment with an aggregate book value of approximately $3,600 is pledged as collateral under certain of the debt agreements.

Anacomp is guarantor of a bank loan to Anacomp's wholly-owned leasing subsidiary. At June 30, 1982, the balance of the debt being guaranteed is $480.

At June 30, 1982, the aggregate maturities of long-term debt through fiscal year 1987 are: 1983, $2,907; 1984, $12,972; 1985, $3,482; 1986, $347; and 1987, $219.

Note 9. Capital Stock

Stock Dividends and Stock Splits

The Board of Directors declared the following stock dividends and stock splits during the three years ended June 30, 1982:

January, 1980—five-for-four stock split
March, 1981—five-for-four stock split

All applicable share and per share amounts have been restated to reflect the stock dividends and stock splits. All conversion prices and stock option data have also been adjusted to give effect to the stock dividends and stock split.

Note 10. Segment Information

Anacomp operates in two business segments—data center services and computer services. Data center services consist of providing computer output microfilm ("COM") and computer processing for banks and credit unions through a network of branch offices, where Anacomp's equipment and personnel process data for numerous customers at each branch site. Computer services consist of providing computer software, primarily to large financial institutions, and managing computer facilities for large customers, primarily state and local governments.

	Year Ended June 30, 1982			Year Ended June 30, 1981		
	Consolidated	Data Center Services	Computer Services	Consolidated	Data Center Services	Computer Services
Revenues	$109,599	$67,418	$42,181	$106,368	$67,899	$38,469
Operating profit	12,451	8,504	3,947	18,191	7,294	10,897
Income before taxes	3,622			13,997		
Depreciation and amortization	6,054	3,636	2,418	3,859	2,527	1,332
Corporate depreciation and amortization	654			509		

	June 30, 1982			June 30, 1981		
Identifiable assets	$155,039	$84,785	$70,254	$93,737	$57,332	$36,405
Corporate assets	56,621			37,061		
	$211,660			$130,798		

Approximately 19% of Anacomp's fiscal 1982 consolidated revenues were provided by major computer services contracts which extend beyond one year, including those contracts in process discussed in Note 3. Contracts of this type provided 18% of the 1981 and 20% of the 1980 revenue. This included system licensing and modification contracts, which accounted for 13% of revenues in 1982, 11% in 1981 and 1980, and facility management arrangements, which accounted for 6% of revenue in 1982, 7% in 1981 and 9% in 1980.

Revenues from various federal, state and local government agencies amounted to approximately 11% of revenue in 1982 and 1981, and 14% in 1980.

Note 11. Income Taxes

Deferred taxes are provided where differences exist between the period in which transactions affect taxable income and the period in which they enter into the determination of income for financial reporting purposes. Investment tax credits are reflected in income in the year realized by reducing the current provision for federal taxes on income.

The following table sets forth the components of the provision for income taxes:

Year ended June 30,	1982	1981	1980
Charge equivalent to realized tax benefits of pre-acquisition losses of acquired companies	$ 67	$ 164	$ 250
Charge equivalent to realized tax benefits from early disposition of shares issued under qualified stock option and stock purchase plans	76	252	81
Charge equivalent to realized tax benefits from certain acquisition expenditures	276	—	—
Taxes currently payable:			
Federal	2,536	1,034	2,263
State	889	602	377
Deferred	(3,001)	4,007	189
	$ 843	$6,059	$3,160

The deferred income tax effects of timing differences are as follows:

Year ended June 30,	1982	1981	1980
Excess of tax over book depreciation	$1,906	$265	$189
Use of cash basis accounting for tax purposes	(3,830)	3,830	—
Accrued interest on convertible debentures	(1,282)	(436)	—
Election of installment sale for tax purposes	506	(8)	—
Deferred income of foreign subsidiary	109	187	—
Deferred income of DISC	(156)	140	—
Transfer from deferred to currently payable	(264)	—	—
Other	10	29	—
	$(3,001)	$4,007	$189

The following is a reconciliation of income taxes calculated at the United States federal statutory rate to the provision for income taxes:

Year Ended June 30,	1982	1981	1980
Provision for taxes on income at statutory rate	$1,666	$6,439	$3,582
Investment tax credit	(1,950)	(333)	(377)
State income taxes, net of federal income tax benefit	569	325	204
Nondeductible amortization of intangible assets	474	332	169
Difference between capital gain and statutory tax rates	—	(316)	(269)
Dividend deduction of 85% of dividend income	(119)	(179)	—
Interest on tax deposits, net of federal income tax benefit	302	—	—
Other	(99)	(209)	(149)
	$ 843	$6,059	$3,160

At June 30, 1982, certain subsidiaries of Anacomp have net operating loss carry-forwards of approximately $1,997. The carryforwards pertain to preacquisition losses of the subsidiaries and therefore can be utilized only to the extent that the subsidiaries produce taxable income in the future. Any tax benefit resulting from the utilization of these carryforwards will reduce the intangible assets recorded at the time of purchase of the subsidiaries. The carryforwards expire in the following fiscal years: 1992, $357; 1993, $774; 1994, $514; and 1995, $352.

Note 12. Other Income and Extraordinary Credit

Year Ended June 30,	1982	1981	1980
Gain (loss) on transaction with Kalvar	$(725)	$ 898	$1,567
Gain on sale of certain assets	630	855	25
Other	705	947	246
	$610	$2,700	$1,838

The extraordinary credit in 1982 arose from the sale of a branch office which had been acquired in 1981 as part of an acquisition accounted for as a pooling of interests. The gain was $2,541 before income taxes, determined at the capital gains rate of $711.

Note 13. Lease and Other Commitments

Anacomp has commitments under long-term operating leases, principally for building space, covering periods generally up to five years. The following summarizes by year the future minimum lease payments due within the next five years and under all noncancellable operating lease obligations which extend beyond one year.

Anacomp

Fiscal	As of June 30
1983	$3,933
1984	3,159
1985	2,362
1986	1,605
1987	565
1988 and thereafter	626
Total minimum payments required	$12,250

Anacomp and Dr. Ronald D. Palamara, president and chairman of Anacomp, are parties to a March 27, 1980, employment and noncompetition agreement pursuant to which Anacomp agreed (a) to pay Dr. Palamara commencing July 1, 1980, a base annual salary of $125 plus an amount equal to 3.54% of Anacomp's annual income before income taxes in excess of $1,000, (b) to make a one-time payment of $430 in July, 1980, to Dr. Palamara for his agreement not to compete with Anacomp for three years following any termination of service with Anacomp and (c) to sell Dr. Palamara, in July, 1980, 428,688 shares of Anacomp common stock for a consideration of $6.08 per share, that being the per share market price on the date of the agreement. Of the $6.08 per share consideration, Dr. Palamara agreed to pay $1.22 per share and granted Anacomp a right of first refusal to purchase such shares upon any resale by Dr. Palamara or subsequent holders at $4.86 below the sale price, $4.86 being the balance of the $6.08 per share consideration.

Note 15. Supplementary Income Statement Information

Supplementary income statement information follows.

Year ended June 30,	1982	1981	1980
Maintenance and repairs	$4,475	$3,738	$2,271
Depreciation and amortization of property, equipment and purchased computer software systems	$4,789	$2,938	$2,246
Amortization of intangible assets	$1,919	$1,430	$780
Taxes other than payroll and income taxes	$1,000	$507	$410
Rents	$7,503	$8,084	$4,819

REPORT OF INDEPENDENT ACCOUNTANTS

To the Board of Directors and Stockholders of Anacomp, Inc.

We have examined the consolidated balance sheet of Anacomp, Inc. and Subsidiaries as of June 30, 1982 and 1981, and the related consolidated statements of income, stockholders' equity, and changes in financial position for each of the three years in the period ended June 30, 1982. Our examinations were made in accordance with generally accepted auditing standards and, accordingly, included such tests of the accounting records and such other auditing procedures as we considered necessary in the circumstances.

In our opinion, the financial statements referred to above present fairly the consolidated financial position of Anacomp, Inc. and Subsidiaries as of June 30, 1982 and 1981, and the consolidated results of their operations and changes in financial position for each of the three years in the period ended June 30, 1982, in conformity with generally accepted accounting principles applied on a consistent basis, after restatement for the change, with which we concur, in the method of accounting for vacation pay as described in Note 1 to the financial statements.

Coopers & Lybrand

Indianapolis, Indiana
September 1982

Anacomp

In late 1995, Paul Collins, the CEO of Brierley Investments Limited (BIL), was concerned that the company's stock was increasingly being undervalued in the New Zealand market. In a discussion in the 1995 annual report, he stated:

We have been disappointed with [our] share price. In 1991 I made a prediction that in 1995 the share price would be $2 after having paid $1 billion in cash dividends. While we have been largely successful on the dividend front, the growth in share price has not been achieved. That prediction was based on my confidence of a substantial, sustainable lift in the Company's performance which has been achieved—profits have more than doubled, operating earnings from investments have been significantly increased, debt levels have been slashed and new investments such as Sky City and Sealord provide the foundation for future growth.

Throughout 1995 the company's stock price had steadily climbed from NZ$1.10 at the beginning of the year to a close of NZ$1.20, well below the firm's target of NZ$2. This performance also lagged the New Zealand stock market, which had grown by 20 percent during the same period. BIL had an equity beta of 0.85 and an estimated cost of equity of 13 percent in June 1995.

BUSINESS

BIL was formed in Wellington, New Zealand, in 1961 by Ron Brierley to invest in undervalued assets. The company acquired an Australian subsidiary in 1964 and was first listed on the New Zealand Stock Exchange in 1970. Brierley's grew rapidly throughout the 1960s, 70s and 80s: by 1987 its assets under management were almost NZ$11.3 billion, owners' equity was NZ$1.8 billion, and net income was NZ$342 million. The company was arguably the most successful firm in New Zealand during this period, growing into the nation's third largest publicly traded company.

BIL owed its success to its management's ability to identify companies that were either undervalued or poorly managed. BIL would acquire a stake in these companies, replace poor management, and wait until the market appreciated the real strategic value of the business. Consequently, BIL generated income from two sources: the operations of companies in which it owned stock and the sale of its investments at a price different from purchase. BIL thus performed the same role of corporate investor and takeover specialist in New Zealand as T. Boone Pickens and Carl Icahn performed in the United States, and Sir James Goldsmith and Lord Hanson performed in the United Kingdom.

1990 proved to be a critical turning point for BIL. During that year it embarked on a successful takeover of Mount Charlotte Investments PLC, the UK's second largest hotelier. Mount Charlotte owned 104 hotels under its own name, including 24 located in London, as well as Hospitality Inns and the recently acquired Thistle Hotels. BIL initially acquired an 11 percent stake in Mount Charlotte in 1988, and gradually increased its stake to 30 percent. The Gulf War in 1991 presented the firm with the opportunity to purchase an additional 10 percent from the Kuwait Investment Office. As a result of this holding, BIL was required by The City Code on Takeovers and Mergers to make an offer to all remaining shareholders. Upon successful acquisition of the remaining shares outstanding, BIL sold a 30 percent stake in Mount Charlotte to the Government of Singapore. As a result of its acquisition of Mount Charlotte, at the year ended June 30 1991, NZ$5.2 billion of BIL's assets were invested in the U.K. hotelier, a NZ$4.2 billion increase over the prior year.

Almost immediately after the acquisition, performance at Mount Charlotte deteriorated. The Gulf War adversely affected tourism in London, driving down occupancy rates in Mount Charlotte's London hotels from 80 to 62 percent in 1991. A severe recession in the United Kingdom during the early 1990s led to a steady decline in revenues for Mount Charlotte through 1994. Financial information on Mount Charlotte is reported in Exhibit 1. This poor performance acted as a drag on BIL's performance during the same period. Financial information for BIL is presented in Exhibit 2.

Following the Mount Charlotte acquisition, BIL's management vowed to focus the firm's investment activity in Australia and New Zealand, where it had been more consistently successful, and restricted any future investments to no more than 20 percent of shareholders' funds. Its New Zealand investments in the 1990s proved more successful. For example, it acquired stakes in Air New Zealand (the largest domestic and international airline in New Zealand), Sealord Products (New Zealand's largest seafood catching, processing, and marketing company), Carter Holt (the country's largest plantation forest owner), Skellerup (a diversified manufacturing and distribution company), and Sky City (a newly created casino company). Each of these companies showed significant improvements in operating performance and market valuation following their acquisition by BIL. For example, the NZ$326 million investment in Carter Holt was sold for NZ$468 million. The Sky City investment of NZ$152 million generated sale proceeds of NZ$122 and a remaining interest valued at more than NZ$300 million.

New Zealand Accounting

The most obvious difference between New Zealand and U.S. financial reports was their format. Income Statements were called Profit and Loss Accounts, and typically did not separately report revenues, cost of sales, and SG&A expenses (even in footnote disclosures). The cash flow statement used the direct method of reporting Cash from Operating

Activities, showing cash inflows and outflows rather than the reconciliation of net income and cash from operations (which was reported in a footnote).

New Zealand accounting standards relating to investments were quite similar to those used in the United States. For example, BIL investments of less than 20 percent stakes in publicly traded companies were recorded at market values, similar to U.S. GAAP treatment of securities available for sale. However, in New Zealand any unrealized holding gains or losses were shown on the balance sheet in the liabilities section under the title "Investment Fluctuation" and were only transferred to income when the gains or losses were realized. Under U.S. GAAP, unrealized gains and losses were included as a reserve in owners' equity, and were also included in net income when realized. Investments in associate companies, where ownership is between 20 and 50 percent, were recorded using the equity method. Investments of more than a 50 percent stake were consolidated using the purchase method. Pooling of interests was not permitted in New Zealand. For BIL this implied that the investment in Mount Charlotte was fully consolidated, and the interest of the Government of Singapore was included as a minority interest on both BIL's balance sheet and income statement.

FINANCIAL ANALYSTS' QUESTIONS

Given the lackluster performance of BIL's stock, many analysts were cautious in their recommendations. For example, in October 1995 Raymond Webb of ANZ McCaughan, stated that:

> As we see it, ultimately the only way for BIL management to end the long period of underperformance is to realign the portfolio by extracting value and then capital from those assets which are underperforming, and by reinvesting in assets with more identifiable growth prospects. . . . We recommend that clients seeking short-term gains look elsewhere and that longer term investors underweight BIL until the company's performance justifies rerating.

By late 1995, many analysts were anticipating that the firm would soon sell all or some of its stake in Mount Charlotte. The key question was what would the firm do with the proceeds. Many analysts advocated a targeted share repurchase program, which would effectively downsize the firm.

MANAGEMENT RESPONSES

In response to the firm's stagnant stock price, in 1995 BIL's management attempted to show how value had been created for stockholders by reporting estimates of intrinsic value of the business. Intrinsic values were estimated by summing the market values of shares owned in listed companies and discounted cash flow estimates of market values of nonlisted shares, and deducting outstanding liabilities. In the firm's 1995 Annual Report, Paul Collins committed that "Over the next three years, BIL's objective is to increase its intrinsic value by NZ$2 billion, equivalent to an 18 percent per annum increase on the June 1995 intrinsic value of NZ$3.7 billion (NZ$1.25 per share)."

Management considered that this goal would be achievable provided the market recognized the value that BIL created in capitalizing on undervalued businesses as an investor and takeover specialist. As Paul Collins considered this challenge, he wondered what tangible actions would best help the market appreciate the firm's operating and trading performance in the New Zealand market during the five preceding years. One approach would be to separate out the financial results for Mount Charlotte from the remainder of the firm's investments, so that analysts could better appreciate its exceptional performance. A second approach would be to undertake a stock repurchase program using the firm's $874 million in cash and marketable securities. Finally, the firm had been approached by a consortium of Malaysian investors interested in acquiring a stake in BIL. Paul Collins wondered whether New Zealand analysts would view such an agreement positively.

QUESTIONS

1. What are BIL's critical success factors and risks?
2. What are the likely benefits and limitations of management using the "intrinsic value" metric as a way to report on BIL's business? If you were management, would you use this metric? Explain.
3. Analyze BIL's financial performance for 1995 using financial ratio analysis. How is the company managing its cash flows for 1995? What would be the firm's ROE on its Mount Charlotte investment versus all of its other investments? What assumptions do you need to make for these estimates? Does it make sense to separate the Mount Charlotte and non-Mount Charlotte ROEs to evaluate BIL performance? Explain.
4. Using the ROE valuation technique, estimate what assumptions the market is making about the company's future performance. Do you believe that these assumptions are realistic? Why? Use your estimate of the ROE for the non-Mount Charlotte operations to estimate what the company would be worth if it sold its Mount Charlotte operations in 1996 at book value and distributed the proceeds to shareholders.
5. Given your analysis in the above questions, what would you recommend to management as a way of helping the market to assess BIL's likely future performance? Why?

EXHIBIT 1

Mount Charlotte Investments PLC, Five-Year Record from December 25, 1990, to December 25, 1994[a]

(£000)	1994	1993	1992	1991	1990
Revenues	241,215	214,090	217,285	226,128	241,659
Operating profit	74,275	60,352	60,346	72,613	88,427
Profit on sale of properties	—	—	—	—	765
Profit before interest	74,275	60,352	60,346	72,613	89,192
Interest expense	51,119	52,975	59,326	71,075	42,576
Profit before taxes	23,156	7,377	1,020	1,538	46,616
Taxes	3,254	3,008	1,100	—	(3,475)
Profit after taxes	26,410	10,385	2,120	1,538	43,141
Dividends	—	—	—	—	4,673
Retained profit	26,410	10,385	2,120	1,538	38,468
Shareholders' equity	1,184,950	1,158,540	1,148,155	1,126,035	1,101,363
Earnings per share	2.81p	1.11p	0.23p	0.17p	4.89p
Return on sales	30.8%	28.2%	27.8%	32.1%	36.6%

a. BIL and Mount Charlotte have different year ends: BIL is June 30 whereas Mount Charlotte is December 25. Consequently, on June 30 each year BIL consolidates Mount Charlotte results reported for the prior year ended December 25.

Brierley Investments Limited

EXHIBIT 2
Brierley Investments Limited, Selections from 1995 Annual Report
(all amounts are reported in New Zealand dollars)

CHIEF EXECUTIVE'S REVIEW

It is pleasing to report a record profit of $431.7 million. While only marginally ahead of last year, it nevertheless represents another milestone for the Group. In particular the record results of the last two years underscore the quantum leap which the Group has made since the early 1990s when profits of $212 million, $251 million and $271 million were reported in 1991, 1992 and 1993 respectively. As importantly, the underlying quality of the assets today, in terms of both current and potential earnings and cash flow, has been significantly enhanced, providing a solid platform for future growth in value.

In a review such as this it is easy to dwell on the year's highlights and there have been many. These include the rapid progress on the construction of Sky City casino together with its independent financing and selldown of BIL's holding from 80% to 51%, the continuing improvement in the profitability of Mount Charlotte, an outstanding performance from Air New Zealand and the successful foray into and exit from Wilson & Horton to name but a few. I will comment on these and other highlights in my review of BIL's trading and investment activities.

BIL's financial position continues to strengthen. While total assets of $9.4 billion show little change on last year's $9.1 billion, the underlying profitability of individual assets has materially improved. In addition, the recent sales of shareholdings in Carter Holt Harvey and Wilson & Horton have resulted in the Group being highly liquid with cash deposits at balance date of $874 million. At the same time debt maturing within one year of $922 million has been extended on to a term basis with the average maturity profile for senior debt now exceeding seven years. Overall, net debt to total capitalisation was steady at 32%, which further reduces to 26% if the capital notes of $449 million are treated as quasi-equity rather than debt.

In the early 1990s, the opportunity for BIL to maximise shareholder value was severely constrained due to high debt levels and inadequate profitability. Today the situation is reversed and the Group now has substantial financial flexibility and is well placed to best optimise shareholder value.

The term *shareholder value* is now widely referred to in investor circles and forums. As an investment company, BIL has always been acutely aware of what constitutes value. In our own planning processes we focus not so much on the underlying book net worth of BIL but rather our assessment of BIL's intrinsic value and the strategies required to ensure that there is continuing growth in that value. More recently we have also given considerable thought as to the actions which the Company can take to best ensure that the value which is created is mirrored in tangible shareholder returns—whether it be from higher share prices, cash dividends or share buy backs.

VALUE CREATION
While the notion of value creation is a fundamental underlying business principle, it is particularly relevant in the context of an investment company such as BIL.

In its simplest form, value creation comes back to quality asset management:
- existing assets—increasing returns while at the same time minimising the capital required to achieve these returns;
- new investment—careful evaluation of and commitment to new investment;
- harvesting—where appropriate, selling assets when returns can be maximised and the funds more effectively invested elsewhere;
- minimising risk—by focusing on core management competencies and maximising comparative advantages in the geographic regions in which we invest.

While the financial statements measure the movement in value in an accounting sense, the resultant answer, while in itself a precise number, does not normally represent the underlying intrinsic value of the business or in other words what is today's market value. While assessing the intrinsic value is a more difficult and somewhat imprecise exercise, it is nevertheless highly relevant for an investment company. In BIL's case intrinsic value is established by reference to the underlying market value of listed securities and the discounted earnings and cash flows of unlisted assets. No account is taken of the very real but somewhat more intangible assets such as the Group's tax losses, skilled people resources or its strong balance sheet and resultant capacity to make new investments.

Over the next three years, BIL's objective is to increase its intrinsic value by $2 billion equivalent to an 18% per annum increase on the June 1995 intrinsic value of $3.7 billion ($1.25 per share). In assessing whether this target is credible and achievable it is necessary to review where BIL has come from, its current position and future direction. In this regard during the last decade there have been two watershed events for BIL. The first was the sharemarket crash in October 1987 and the second, the acquisition of Mount Charlotte Investments in late 1990. Each of these events had a fundamental impact on the intrinsic value and external perception of BIL and it is, therefore, relevant to use these periods for comparative purposes:

MOVEMENT IN INTRINSIC VALUE

$ millions	December 1987– June 1991	June 1991– June 1995	June 1995– June 1998
Opening Intrinsic Value	2,045	3,107	3,717
New Capital	422	293	—
	2,467	3,400	3,717
Increase in Intrinsic Value	1,061	1,622	2,000
Foreign Currency Translation	—	(540)	—
	3,528	4,482	5,717
Cash Dividends	(421)	(765)	(717)
Closing Intrinsic Value	$3,107	$3,717	$5,000

$ millions	June 1991	June 1995
Reported Profit	1185[#]	1,334[*]
Book Value	3,231	3,605
Market Capitalisation	2,857	3,335

[#]3½ years   [*]4 years

In the 1991 to 1995 period, BIL's intrinsic value grew by $1.62 billion. Adjusted to New Zealand dollars, value grew by $1.08 billion or 9% per annum. This simple statistic hides three key issues:

- With the benefit of hindsight, the June 1991 assessment of BIL's intrinsic value was somewhat flattering given the weak economic activity and capital markets which subsequently eventuated in 1992 and 1993. This is evidenced in the performances of many of the Group companies at that time. By way of example, Mount Charlotte was on course for a virtual break even result (1995: £35 million), Air New Zealand's operating profit was $18 million (1995: $286 million), Skellerup's earnings before interest and tax were $12 million (1995: $64 million) and funding costs and overheads were $378 million (1995: $130 million). There are other similar examples such as Magnum Corporation and Carter Holt Harvey but the simple reality is that the then market capitalisation of BIL gave the Company more credit than it deserved, whereas today the reverse is the case.

- Although Mount Charlotte's operating returns have reflected its continuing outperformance of the UK hotel industry, depressed trading conditions until 1994 and its own high level of indebtedness have resulted in inadequate returns to BIL. While the price paid in 1990 would represent good investment value if made in 1995, it does not compensate for holding costs and foreign currency movements which have denied the Group additional growth in intrinsic value of in excess of $1 billion.

- Foreign exchange—70% of BIL's Parent Company assets are invested internationally which is roughly equivalent to all the Group's shareholders' funds being invested offshore. During the last four years the New Zealand dollar has appreciated by 25% against the currencies of the countries in which we invest. As a consequence BIL's overall returns have been higher in those countries but lower on translation to New Zealand dollars. To put it another way, notwithstanding the strong New Zealand dollar and with 70% of the Group's assets invested offshore, the value of the Company has still grown by over $1 billion in New Zealand dollar terms—a considerable achievement given both the quality of the assets and the financial position of BIL in 1991. In reality the growth in value of $1 billion was largely achieved over the last two years as the weak economic conditions and capital markets which prevailed throughout 1992 and 1993 depressed profits and asset values at that time. Strong economic growth over the last two years and a more robust outlook have contributed to a sharp rise in corporate cash flows and profits. These factors have yet to be fully reflected in asset values and augur well for growth in BIL's intrinsic value.

Looking to the future we have every confidence that we can continue to create value as we have done in the past. Factors which underpin this confidence include:

- BIL's sustainable profit (after funding costs and overheads but before investment surpluses) is now $225 million per annum and will rise to $300 million per annum in 1997. This compares to $70 million in 1991.

- Over the last eight years in what can best be described as challenging times in equity markets, BIL has achieved investment surpluses (net of ordinary dividends, tax provisions, write-offs and minority interests) of $2,083 million or an average of $260 million per annum. In the first two months of the 1995/96 year, over $80 million in investment surpluses have already been generated.

- BIL is well placed in its core Australia/New Zealand markets with very little competition and a great deal of knowledge and expertise. With its strong financial position BIL is well positioned to take advantage of the relatively static investment markets in these countries.

- BIL's reported earnings for the last two years total $862 million. Assuming a continuation of but no improvement in this trend over the next three years, earnings of $1.3 billion or 65% of the targeted $2 billion would be the outcome. This takes no account of the growth potential in the wider BIL Group or any new investment strategies.
- Intrinsic values at June 1995 have been conservatively assessed. Mount Charlotte achieving its profit forecasts and Air New Zealand being re-rated to 80% of the average market P/E would alone contribute the balance of $700.million or 35% of the $2 billion target.

Obviously, achieving expectations such as these to some degree depends on macro economic factors beyond BIL's control. For the above scenarios it is assumed that inflation, bond yields and economic growth rates in the major economies in which we operate will remain around present levels. It also assumes no major change to BIL's capital structure.

MARKET VALUE

While BIL has a clear raison d'être and a proven ability to create value, it is axiomatic that such value creation be represented in a tangible way in shareholder returns. In 1991 I stated that our objective over the next four years was to make BIL a $2 stock, equivalent to a stock market valuation of $5 billion after paying our shareholders an additional $1 billion in cash dividends.

While we have largely succeeded on the dividend front, we have fallen well short on the share price. While there are various mitigating factors such as the stronger New Zealand dollar and an equity market much weaker than anticipated, BIL's own improved performance, particularly over the last two years, has so far resulted in only a modest re-rating by the market.

In my first year as Chief Executive in 1985/86, the Company's market capitalisation peaked at around $5 billion. At that time shareholders' funds were $939 million and profit $179 million. Notwithstanding BIL's impressive performance at that time, the then market capitalisation assumed an unrealistic growth potential and earning capacity. Today we have the opposite situation. Shareholders' funds (including convertible notes) are $3.6 billion, a record profit of $432 million has been achieved, the Company's growth prospects are sound yet today's market capitalisation is only $3.3 billion.

While some broking houses have moved to a more dynamic basis of valuation for BIL, many still rate the Company on their assessment of BIL's underlying static asset value today and then deduct a discount on the basis that BIL operates in a similar manner to a unit trust.

This valuation approach ignores BIL's active asset management, the very real achievements of the last few years, the substantial improvement in the quality and sustainable earnings mix of the asset base and, in particular, the strength and flexibility now inherent in the Company's overall financial position. In short, BIL is given no premium for future earnings or asset value appreciation which is a fundamental premise in any equity investment. In earlier years these attributes would have resulted in a substantially higher share price. Today's lower share price is perhaps as much a reflection of the implications arising from the Mount Charlotte acquisition five years ago as it is a more restrained view on investment companies generally given the collapse of many of our so termed pretenders in the late 1980s. However, for whatever reason, the share price today is what it is. While BIL's principal objective is to put "runs on the board" and create value, as important an objective is for shareholders to reap the benefit of that enhanced value. In this regard, it is important to understand BIL's view on an optimum level of capital.

Brierley Investments Limited

OPTIMUM LEVEL OF CAPITAL

In March 1995 the well known investor Warren Buffett, Chairman of Berkshire Hathaway in the United States, commented that:

" . . . a fat wallet, however, is the enemy of superior investment results . . . We now consider a security for purchase only if we can deploy at least US$100 million in it."

BIL's optimum capital requirement is defined by our existing asset base and overall financial position, the opportunities within the regions in which we invest and the people resources available to the Group. While the level of capital required is a somewhat imprecise calculation and will change over time, our present view is that given the Group's current mix of assets and available opportunities, the present level of capital is appropriate. There are two significant factors which could change this view. Firstly, over the next three years we envisage significant growth in the overall value of the Group. To the extent this materialises and there are limited value adding investment opportunities available, the Group could have excess capital.

Secondly, the Group's largest asset is its investment in Mount Charlotte. To put this in context, if Mount Charlotte was sold today at book value for cash, the Parent Company would have $1 billion in cash and no senior debt. Under this scenario the Group could also find itself with excess capital, again the overall level dependent on the extent to which attractive new investment opportunities are available.

Our present view on Mount Charlotte is that it will achieve a significant lift in its earnings in each of the next three years. While Mount Charlotte has detracted from BIL's value over the last four years, its sale in 1995, based on current earnings, would not be in the best interest of BIL shareholders. However, given this investment is too large in the context of one company, one sector and one country, it will be regularly reviewed and, when appropriate, BIL's stake will be reduced.

In the context of an optimum level of capital, an important investment option for BIL will be the ability to buy back and cancel its own shares. The Chairman's Report refers to the adoption of a new Constitution which will provide the Company with the flexibility to undertake share buy backs if and when it is considered in the best interests of all shareholders to do so.

In the introduction to this review I indicated that BIL has two simple objectives:
- to grow the underlying intrinsic value of BIL; and
- to ensure that such growth is reflected in shareholders' hands through increased returns.

Each is important in its own right with the first largely dictating the extent to which the second can be achieved. Management is absolutely committed to both objectives and will take whatever steps are necessary in pursuit of their achievement.

INVESTMENT ACTIVITIES

While investment returns are an important component of BIL's overall profit, the profitable realisation of any specific investment is often not in itself a noteworthy occasion. By the time an investment is sold, its underlying value is usually readily apparent and identifiable, with the marketplace generally having recognised the merits of BIL's original investment decision.

A good case in point was the sale in 1995 of the Group's residual holding in Carter Holt Harvey for $468 million resulting in a surplus of $142 million. The initial investment in Carter Holt Harvey was made in 1990. Around that time its own acquisition strategies had resulted in it becoming heavily indebted and out of favour with the market. While

BIL's involvement is well documented and the success of that investment now widely recognised, the reality is that the initial investment was viewed sceptically by the market as, somewhat ironically, was the final selldown—but for quite different reasons.

As a contrarian value-based investor we were delighted with our investment in Carter Holt Harvey which, over time, averaged some $500 million and realised in excess of $1 billion.

The investment highlight of the year was unquestionably the purchase and subsequent sale of a 28% interest in New Zealand's pre-eminent publishing company Wilson & Horton. After an extensive evaluation process BIL acquired its interest in November 1994 at $9.50 per share and a total outlay of $265 million, with the intention of being a long-term shareholder. Subsequent to the acquisition, discussions were held with the company's directors who expressed their preference for a major shareholder to be an existing newspaper industry participant. BIL agreed to work with the company to identify a suitable shareholder and to sell its shareholding, provided the price reflected the strategic value of the shareholding and the real underlying value of the company. The sale process introduced a number of potential buyers who concurred with our view on value and resulted in BIL selling its shareholding for a profit of $65 million. The outcome has already proven to be of significant benefit to all Wilson & Horton shareholders with the company's new dividend policy ensuring that the longer term share price more fully reflects the underlying value of the company.

A more recent outcome and one which will be accounted for in the 1995/96 financial year is the recent completion of the partial selldown of the Group's interest in Auckland casino owner, Sky City. With construction now well advanced and the casino due to open in early 1996, we arranged $300 million in external debt facilities based on equity of $186 million. Having completed this financing, BIL offered 29% of the total capital for sale by way of a private placement. The selldown in July valued Sky City's equity at $425 million and resulted in a profit to BIL of $65 million. BIL retains a 50.6% interest which, based on recent sales, now has a market value of $278 million, which compares favourably to its book value of $95 million.

OUTLOOK

There are three key determinants to BIL's future prospects:

- current investments—a careful review of current investments highlights the opportunity to grow cashflow and earnings and hence enhance value in each of the regions in which the Group operates with the gross trading contribution forecast to rise from $290 million in 1995 to over $400 million in 1997;
- strong financial position—there will always be new investment opportunities available in any market environment. While careful evaluation of, and commitment to, each new investment is a fundamental prerequisite, as important is maintaining a strong financial position which will enable BIL to take advantage of these opportunities; and
- people—the importance of a capable team cannot be underestimated. BIL is appropriately resourced with well motivated, highly skilled people, enabling us to add value to existing investments and create value from new investments.

BIL is well positioned to continue to enhance shareholder value in the future as it has in the past. While the present market capitalisation is a source of disappointment, we nevertheless are committed to ensuring that the value created is represented in a tangible form in the hands of individual shareholders.

Brierley Investments Limited

Brierley Investments Limited

FINANCIAL SUMMARY

	BIL Holding	Net Profit		Sales		Total Assets		Shareholders' Funds	
		1995 millions	1994 millions	**1995 millions**	1994 millions	**1995 millions**	1994 millions	**1995 millions**	1994 millions
New Zealand									
Air New Zealand Ltd	42%	**$260.2**	$190.7	**$2,888**	$2,598	**$3,107**	$2,915	**$1,274**	$1,198
LWR Industries Ltd	66%	**$12.6**	$13.2	**$152**	$157	**$98**	$97	**$65**	$60
Sealord Products Group	50%	**$32.3**	$23.5	**$307**	$301	**$325**	$320	**$158**	$128
Skellerup Group Ltd	30%	**$44.4**	$25.4	**$828**	$646	**$519**	$421	**$217**	$177
Tasman Agriculture Ltd**	52%	**$6.1**	$5.5	**$17**	$15	**$203**	$155	**$154**	$108
Union Shipping Group Ltd	50%	**$14.7**	$15.3	**$137**	$152	**$126**	$107	**$74**	$71
Australia									
Australian Consolidated Investments Ltd	96%	**A$9.8**	A$85.4	**A$797**	—	**A$893**	A$440	**A$298**	A$280
The Austotel Trust	100%	**A$7.2**	A$5.1	**A$351**	A$321	**A$319**	A$391	**A$125**	A$122
Asia									
Paul Y.—ITC Construction Holdings Ltd*	21%	**HK$230.4**	HK$201.9	**HK$3,965**	HK$2,074	**HK$3,094**	HK$2,039	**HK$1,004**	HK$611
United States									
Associated Hosts Inc+	100%	**US$(5.5)**	US$(4.5)	**US$58**	US$57	**US$55**	US$62	**US$34**	US$29
Everest & Jennings International Ltd ++	85%	**US$(9.7)**	US$(55.7)	**US$79.4**	US$94.5	**US$62**	US$59	**US$(16)**	US$(7)
Molokai Ranch Ltd	100%	**US$(4.8)**	US$(1.0)	**US$3**	US$5	**US$187**	US$181	**US$175**	US$172
United Kingdom									
Mount Charlotte Investments Plc ++	70%	**£26.4**	£10.4	**£241**	£214	**£1,880**	£1,853	**£1,185**	£1,159

BIL holding percentages as at 11 September 1995

*   Balance date 31 March

**   Balance date 31 May

+   Balance date 30 September

++ Balance date 31 December

COMPARATIVE FINANCIAL REVIEW

	Consolidated				
	1995 **$000**	1994 $000	1993 $000	1992 $000	1991 $000
Profits					
Net Operating Surplus	**381,356**	378,162	222,860	354,829	303,741
Less					
Taxation	**1.883**	(2,771)	(12,920)	55,392	50,044
Minority Interests	**38,786**	38,861	23,099	11,696	63,147
Unrealised Reduction in Value of Investment Properties	—	—	18,960	—	—
Add					
Equity Earnings	**91,083**	88,005	77,623	(36,631)	21,183
Profit Attributable to the Group	**431,770**	430,077	271,344'	251,110	211,733
Less					
Cash Dividends	**226,747**	151,988	160,033	225,564	161,676
Profit Retained in the Group	**$205,023**	$278,089	$111,311	$25,546	$50,057
Capital Funds					
Issued Capital	**1,328,701**	1,302,882	1,253,135	1,253,135	1,253,135
Reserves and Retained Earnings	**2,006,410**	1,917,245	1,762,689	2,012,206	1,977,724
Total Shareholders' Funds	**3,335,111**	3,220,127	3,015,824	3,265,341	3,230,859
Minority Interests in Subsidiary Companies	**1,138,725**	1,129,278	1,190,180	1,409,895	1,030,091
Capital Notes	**449,219**	461,838	168,239	—	—
Convertible Notes	**269,414**	269,414	269,414	—	—
Subordinated Debt	—	74,085	736,575	866,918	372,394
Investment Fluctuation	**10,999**	252,995	17,155	63,740	21,024
Surplus on Acquisitions	**386,568**	420.925	454,026	566,178	457,992
Total Capital Funds	**$5.590,036**	$5,828,662	$5,851,413	$6,172,072	$5,112,260
Represented By					
Fixed Assets	**5,712,567**	5,938,367	5,991,068	7,502,037	6,320,079
Investments and Intangibles	**2,200,187**	2,261,430	2,244,149	2,191,372	2,128,494
Current Assets	**1,507,710**	948,593	1,746,941	1,600,456	3,500,918
Total Assets	**9,420,464**	9,148,390	9,982,158	11,293,865	11,949,491
Miscellaneous Contingencies	**273,849**	319,662	334,153	499,808	468,522
Term Liabilities	**2,720,263**	1,302,619	2,205,993	2,946,632	3,112,251
Current Liabilities	**836,316**	1,697,447	1,590,599	1,675.353	3,256,458
	$5,590,036	$5,828,662	$5,851,413	$6,172,072	$5,112,260
Statistics					
Adjusted Earnings per 50c Ordinary Share	**15.4c**	15.8c	10.8c	10.0c	10.5c
Adjusted Dividend per 50c Ordinary Share	**9.0c**	9.0c	9.0c	9.0c	9.0c
Net Asset Backing per 50c Ordinary Share	**$1.26**	$1.24	$1.20	$1.30	$1.29
Rate of Net Profit Earned on Year-end Ordi- nary Capital	**32.5%**	33.0%	21.7%	20.0%	16.9%
Rate of Net Profit Earned on Average Share- holders' Funds	**13.2%**	13.8%	8.6%	7.7%	7.1%

Brierley Investments Limited

Brierley Investments Limited

CONSOLIDATED PROFIT AND LOSS ACCOUNT

For the year ended 30 June 1995	1995 $000	1994 $000
Net Operating Surplus (13)	381,356	378,162
Less		
Taxation (14)	1,883	(2,771)
Consolidated Net Profit After Taxation	379,473	380,933
Less		
Share of Profits Applicable to Minority Interests	38,786	38,861
	340,687	342,072
Add		
Equity Earnings (15)	91,083	88,005
Profit Attributable to the Group (4) (16)	$431,770	$430,077

CONSOLIDATED BALANCE SHEET

As at 30 June 1995		**1995** **$000**	1994 $000
CAPITAL FUNDS			
Authorised Capital (1)		**$2,000,000**	$2,000,000
Issued Capital (1)	**1,328,701**		1,302,882
Reserves (2) (3)	**(31,686)**		129,414
Retained Earnings (4)	**2,038,096**		1,787,831
Total Shareholders' Funds		**3,335,111**	3,220,127
OTHER CAPITAL FUNDS			
Minority Interests in Subsidiary Companies	**1,138,725**		1,129,278
Capital Notes (5)	**449,219**		461,838
Convertible Notes (6)	**269,414**		269,414
Subordinated Debt	**—**		74,085
Investment Fluctuation	**10,999**		252,995
Surplus on Acquisitions	**386,568**		420,925
Total Other Capital Funds		**2,254,925**	2,608,535
Total Capital Funds		**5,590,036**	5,828,662
MISCELLANEOUS CONTINGENCIES		**273,849**	319,662
TERM LIABILITIES (7)			
Loans and Advances		**2,720,263**	1,302,619
CURRENT LIABILITIES (8)			
Bank Overdrafts	**126,109**		71,408
Creditors	**563,537**		558,593
Loans and Advances	**144,427**		1,066,362
Provision for Taxation	**2,243**		1,084
		836,316	1,697,447
		$9,420,464	$9,148,390
FIXED ASSETS (9)			
Land and Buildings	**5,412,658**		5,550,105
Plant, Vehicles and Fittings	**299,909**		388,262
		5,712,567	5,938,367
INVESTMENTS (10)			
Shares in –			
Public Companies	**535,069**		950,650
Associate Companies	**931,365**		648,620
Other Investments	**733,753**		662,160
		2,200,187	2,261,430
CURRENT ASSETS (11)			
Cash and Marketable Securities	**874,312**		327,824
Debtors	**364,748**		434,681
Short-term Investments	**27,521**		11,143
Inventories	**241,129**		174,945
		1,507,710	948,593
		$9,420,464	$9,148,390

Brierley Investments Limited

CONSOLIDATED STATEMENT OF CASH FLOWS

For the year ended 30 June 1995	1995 $000	1994 $000
Cash Flows from Operating Activities		
Received from Customers	2,450,876	1,640,717
Interest Received	54,363	111,449
Dividends Received	123,808	52,400
Paid to Suppliers and Employees	(2,256,180)	(1,457,359)
Interest Paid	(275,555)	(363,388)
Tax Paid	(7,074)	20,456
Other	62,991	138,427
Total Operating Cash Flows (21)	153,229	142,702
Cash Flows from Investing Activities (20)		
Sale of Fixed Assets	94,614	13,233
Sale of Investments	941,965	1,154,846
Loans and Advances Repaid	723	2,000
Purchase of Fixed Assets	(278,761)	(230,702)
Interest Paid Capitalised	(14,345)	—
Purchase of Investments	(971,048)	(684,310)
Loans and Advances	(11,069)	—
Other	114,687)	153,902
Total Investing Cash Flows	(123,234)	408,969
Cash Flows from Financing Activities (20)		
Issue of Shares and Capital Notes	58,672	317,517
Borrowings	2,455,015	899,537
Repayment of Borrowings	(1,821,023)	(2,197,576)
Dividends Paid	(178,968)	(138,576)
Other	(28,384)	—
Total Financing Cash Flows	485,312	(1,119,098)
Net Change in Cash	515,307	(567,427)
Opening Cash	256,416	839,798
Effect of Acquisition and Disposal of Subsidiaries	(16,183)	5,232
Effect of Exchange Rate Changes on Cash	(7,337)	(21,187)
Closing Cash	$748,203	$256,416
Closing Cash Comprises		
Cash and Marketable Securities (11)	874,312	327,824
Bank Overdrafts (8)	(126,109)	(71,408)
	$748,203	$256,416

STATEMENT OF ACCOUNTING POLICIES

GENERAL ACCOUNTING POLICIES

The following general accounting policies have been adopted in these financial statements which have been prepared on a going concern basis:

historical cost adjusted by the revaluation of certain assets;

accrual accounting to match expenses with revenues

The financial statements have been prepared under the requirements of the Companies Act 1955 and Financial Reporting Act 1993.

PARTICULAR ACCOUNTING POLICIES

(a) Principles of Consolidation

(i) *Subsidiaries*

The Group financial statements include the financial statements of all subsidiaries, being companies which Brierley Investments Limited control either directly, indirectly or beneficially.

The financial statements of subsidiaries are included in the Group financial statements using the purchase method.

All material inter-company balances and profits resulting from intra-group transactions have been eliminated.

Where subsidiaries are acquired during the year, their results are included from the date of acquisition, while for subsidiaries disposed of during the year, their results are included to the date of disposal.

Date of acquisition is either the date on which the title to the asset passes, or in respect of listed public companies, the date of the last published financial statements, from which the acquisition price is determined.

(ii) *Associate Companies*

An associate company is one in which the Group has an equity interest of between 20% and 50% and has the capacity to significantly influence the policies of that company.

The financial statements of associate companies are included in the Group financial statements using the equity method with the Group's share of associate companies' profits reflected in the consolidated profit and loss account.

(iii) *Details of Subsidiary and Associate Companies*

Details of subsidiary and associate companies are listed in the Group Investments section of the Annual Report. Subsidiary and associate company results are included for the period to the Group balance date except as follows:

	Last Balance Date	Period Included
Paul Y. — ITC Construction Holdings Limited	31 March 1995	Year to 31 March 1995
Steego Corporation	30 April 1995	Year to 30 April 1995
Tasman Agriculture Limited	31 May 1995	Year to 31 May 1995

(iv) *Joint Ventures*

The following joint ventures are included in the Group financial statements on a proportionate basis:

AsiaPower Developments

Sealord Products Group

(b) Balance on Acquisition

On the acquisition of a subsidiary or associate company the fair value of net identifiable assets is ascertained. The difference between the fair value and the cost of investment in the subsidiary or associate company is brought to account either as a surplus or goodwill on acquisition.

Goodwill is amortised by systematic charges against income over the appropriate periods in which benefits are expected to be realised, but not exceeding 20 years. The periods over which the amounts are to be amortised are subject to annual review.

Surplus on acquisitions is included under "Other Capital Funds" on the balance sheet and is released to the profit and loss account as and

Brierley Investments Limited

when the assets to which it relates are disposed of.

(c) Fixed Assets

Fixed assets are recorded at cost of purchase or at adjusted fair values. Investment properties are recorded at their net current value determined by reference to independent valuations. Net changes in the value of investment properties are recorded in the profit and loss account.

(d) Depreciation

Fixed assets are depreciated on a straight-line or diminishing value basis over their estimated economic lives.

Where depreciation is not charged by an overseas subsidiary, its policy has been consistently applied in the preparation of the Group financial statements.

Depreciation sales are:

Buildings	1%–5%
Plant, Vehicles and Fittings	4%–33⅓%

(e) Investments

(i) *Listed Public Securities*

Investments in shares in listed public companies are recorded at market value based on official stock exchange quotations at balance date. The difference between market value and cost is shown in "Investment Fluctuation," which is included in the profit and loss account when realised.

Unrealised losses in the value of investments are taken to the profit and loss account where the diminution is considered to be permanent.

(ii) *Other Investments*

All other investments are included at cost or valuation.

(f) Inventories

Inventories are valued at lower of cost or net realisable value including a share of fixed and variable overheads where appropriate. Cost is determined using various methods including specific identification, average cost, first in first out and standard cost.

(g) Debtors

Debtors are shown at their expected realisable value.

(h) Foreign Currency

Overseas investments and balances payable in foreign currency to and by the Group have been included in the Group financial statements at rates ruling at balance date. Where transactions have been hedged by way of obtaining forward exchange cover over the balances outstanding they are converted at the forward rate.

The assets, liabilities and operating results of overseas subsidiaries are translated at balance date rates. Foreign exchange movements on independent foreign operations, and any offsetting foreign exchange movement on monetary assets or liabilities designated as a hedge of an independent foreign operation, are taken to the Foreign Currency Translation Reserve.

All other exchange differences, including differences arising on the conversion of short-term and long-term monetary items, whether realised or unrealised, are taken directly to the profit and loss account.

Exchange rates used at balance date:

A	$0.94	=	NZ$1.00
SFr	0.77	=	NZ$1.00
HK	$5.16	=	NZ$1.00
US	$0.67	=	NZ$1.00
Stg	£0.42	=	NZ$1.00

(i) Taxation

Taxation has been provided in the financial statements on the basis of the estimated taxation payable on the taxable income by each member company of the Group after taking advantage of all available deductions and concessions.

The deferred tax provision is calculated using the liability method, resulting from short-term differences between profits computed for tax purposes and profits as stated in the financial statements. Provision is not made for timing differences unless a liability is expected to arise in the foreseeable future.

Deferred tax assets of subsidiaries are recognised where the individual subsidiary is able to justify the deferred tax assets. Deferred tax liabilities of individual subsidiaries are recognised if the subsidiary is unable to use Group tax losses available.

(j) Sales

Group sales represent sales to outside parties by the trading subsidiaries and do not include dividends, interest or other investment income. The amount of investment income is disclosed in Note 16 to these financial statements.

(k) Bonus Shares in Lieu of Dividends

The premium on bonus shares issued in lieu of dividends on the election of shareholders has been recognised in the Share Premium Reserve.

(l) Changes in Accounting Policies

There have been no material changes in accounting policies during the year. All policies have been applied on a consistent basis with previous years.

(m) Comparative Figures

Certain comparative figures have been restated to reflect changes in presentation.

12 SEGMENTED ASSETS AND SALES

			Consolidated	
	1995			1994
	Assets	**Sales**	Assets	Sales
	$000	**$000**	$000	$000
By Activity Segment:				
Energy and Oil Royalties	274,335	—	287,990	—
Engineering, Construction and Property	559,591	9,504	572,387	180,987
Food and Beverages	203,419	153,480	326,878	376,658
Hotels	4,540,850	600,406	4,865,027	590,055
Investment	1,059,496	—	1,233,406	—
Manufacturing	309,582	326,114	373,711	157,055
Transport	752,496	136,953	559,466	152,309
Wholesale and Retail	215,929	849,788	11,688	14,315
Other	630,454	500,080	590,013	113,881
	8,546,152	2,576,325	8,820,566	1,585,260
Cash and Marketable Securities	874,312	—	327,824	—
	$9,420,464	$2,576,325	$9,148,390	$1,585,260
By Geographic Segment:				
New Zealand	1,848,934	481,096	1,965,868	724,555
Australia	1,151,317	1,224,339	977,473	—
Asia	294,514	—	222,658	151,028
United States	612,556	270,484	698,535	119,622
United Kingdom	4,638,831	600,406	4,956,032	590,055
	8,546,152	2,576,325	8,820,566	1,585,260
Cash and Marketable Securities	874,312	—	327,824	—
	$9,420,464	$2,576,325	$9,148,390	$1,585,260

The increase in sales in the current year is principally due to the acquisition of Vox Holdings Pty Limited.

Brierley Investments Limited

Brierley Investments Limited

14 TAXATION

		Consolidated
	1995	1994
	$000	$000
Net Operating Surplus	**381,356**	378,162
Taxation at 33%	**125,847**	124,793
Adjusted by the Tax Effect of:		
Non-assessable Dividend Income	**(27,918)**	(3,660)
Other Non-assessable Revenues	**(17,001)**	(33,055)
Non-deductible Expenses	**109,636**	76,257
Deductible Items Carried Forward/(Brought Forward)	**(187,283)**	(160,162)
Income at Other Tax Rates	**(4,546)**	(1,765)
Under/(Over) Provisions in Prior Years	**(1,470)**	(9,870)
Other	**4,618**	4,691
	$1,883	$(2,771)
Taxation Charged/(Credited)—New Zealand	**3,802**	6,981
Taxation Charged(Credited)—Other Countries	**(1,919)**	(9,752
	$1,883	$(2,771)
Current Taxation	**4,050**	(2,443)
Deferred Taxation	**(2,167)**	(328)
	$1,883	$ (2,771)
Deferred Taxation		
Opening Balance	**(2,553)**	1,501
Deferred Taxation in Profit and Loss Account	**(2,167)**	(328)
Other Movements	**1,248**	(3,726)
	$(3,472)	$(2,553)

The Group currently has tax losses available to carry forward and offset against future assessable income in several jurisdictions. The tax benefit of these losses is only recognised to the extent of deferred tax liabilities.

Revenue authorities are currently conducting investigations into the Group which makes the accurate quantification of the unrecognised tax benefit of the tax losses uncertain. The Group considers that there are sufficient tax losses to offset both adjustments arising as a result of these investigations and deferred tax liabilities.

Imputation Credits

Parent Company	**4,560**	4,560
Subsidiary Companies	**47,778**	15,863
Minority Interest Share in Subsidiary Companies	**(8,385)**	(12,233)
	$43,953	$8,190

16 PROFIT ATTRIBUTABLE TO THE GROUP

			Consolidated	
By Activity Segment:	**Operating Surplus $000**	**Net Interest $000**	**1995 Total $000**	1994 Total $000
Trading Activities				
Energy and Oil Royalties	33,342	—	33,342	120,597
Engineering, Construction and Property	7,867	(627)	7,240	9,363
Food and Beverages	24,853	(8,597)	16,256	20,171
Forestry	—	—	—	27,982
Hotels	192,281	(100,449)	91,832	41,534
Manufacturing	24,971	(7,982)	16,989	19,133
Transport	129,058	(4,230)	124,828	87,179
Wholesale and Retail	(7,938)	1,315	(6,623)	768
Other	20,923	(15,042)	5,881	(8,552)
Trading Contribution	425,357	(135,612)	289,745	318,175
Taxation and Minority Interests			(41,674)	(35,080)
Net Trading Contribution			248,071	283,095
Investment Activities				
Dividend Income			92,711	7,933
Surplus on Sale of Assets and Investments			209,501	269,663
Other Income			13,825	5,252
Investment Contribution			316,037	282,848
Taxation and Minority Interests			1,005	(1,010)
Net Investment Contribution			317,042	281,838

					Consolidated	
By Geographic Segment:	**New Zealand**	**Australia**	**Asia**	**United States**	**United Kingdom**	**1995 Total $000**	1994 Total $000
Trading Contribution	172,253	34,962	13,665	(22,967)	91,832	289,745	318,175
Investment Contribution	246,094	34,933	15,088	1,838	18,084	316,037	282,848
Total Contribution	418,347	69,895	28,753	(21,129)	109,916	605,782	601,023
Taxation and Minority Interests						(40,669)	(36,090)
Funding Costs and Overheads						(133,343)	(134,856)
Profit Attributable to the Group						$431,770	$430,077

Trading Activities reflects the results of the trading subsidiary and associate companies. Investment Activities reflects the results of the respective holding companies in New Zealand, Australia and Hong Kong.

Brierley Investments Limited

Brierley Investments Limited

AUDITORS' REPORT

KPMG Peat Marwick
Chartered Accountants

AUDIT REPORT TO THE SHAREHOLDERS OF BRIERLEY INVESTMENTS LIMITED

We have audited the financial statements on pages 61 to 82. The financial statements provide information about the past financial performance and financial position of the Company and Group as at 30 June 1995. This information is stated in accordance with the accounting policies set out on pages 65 and 66.

Directors' Responsibilities
The Directors are responsible for the preparation of financial statements which give a true and fair view of the financial position of the Company and Group as at 30 June 1995 and of the results of the Company and the Group's operations and cash flows for the year ended 30 June 1995.

Auditors' Responsibilities
It is our responsibility to express an independent opinion on the financial statements presented by the Directors and report our opinion to you.

Basis of Opinion
An audit includes examining, on a test basis, evidence relevant to the amounts and disclosures in the financial statements. It also includes assessing:
- the significant estimates and judgements made by the Directors in the preparation of the financial statements; and
- whether the accounting policies are appropriate to the Company and Group's circumstances, consistently applied and adequately disclosed.

We conducted our audit in accordance with generally accepted auditing standards in New Zealand. We planned and performed our audit so as to obtain all the information and explanations which we considered necessary in order to provide us with sufficient evidence to give reasonable assurance that the financial statements are free from material misstatements, whether caused by fraud or error. In forming our opinion we also evaluated the overall adequacy of the presentation of information in the financial statements.

Other than in our capacity as auditors we have no relationship with or interests in the Company or any of its Subsidiaries.

Unqualified Opinion
We have obtained all the information and explanations we have required.

In our opinion:
- proper accounting records have been kept by the Company as far as appears from our examination of those records; and
- the financial statements on pages 61 to 82:
  - comply with generally accepted accounting practice
  - give a true and fair view of the financial position of the Company and Group as at 30 June 1995 and the results of the Company and the Group's operations and cash flows for the year ended on that date.

Our audit was completed on 6 September 1995 and our unqualified opinion is expressed as at that date.

KPMG Peat Marwick
Wellington, New Zealand

Ln July 1996 Moody's Investors Service was reviewing the ratings for the general obligation bonds of the City of New York. With a population of approximately 7.3 million, New York was the largest city in the United States and an international business and cultural center. Its key industries included banking, securities, life insurance, communications, publishing, printing, fashion design, apparel manufacture, retailing, and construction. In addition, the City was the leading tourist destination in the United States.

New York's economy was closely linked to national economic events. Thus, in the early 1990s, it experienced a decline in employment and real gross product. Growth picked up in the period 1992 to 1994, but slowed after 1995. The City's general obligation bonds were rated Baa1, the lowest rated investment grade bonds.

Moody's review included an analysis of the challenges facing U.S. municipalities generally, as well as an examination of the financial performance of New York. At the completion of the review, Moody's had to decide whether to upgrade, downgrade, or maintain the City's current rating.

FINANCIAL CHALLENGES FOR MUNICIPALITIES

Municipal governments typically provided a range of services to local communities, including legislative, executive, and judicial functions. They also offered a range of other services, such as primary and secondary education, public safety (police and fire), public works (streets, sewers, and sanitation), public welfare, public transportation, airports, utilities (water and power), colleges, hospitals, corrections facilities, community development, and parks and recreation facilities. To fund these activities, municipal governments received support from state and federal governments, property and other forms of taxes, charges for various services, and utility revenues.

Municipal governments grew dramatically after World War II, from 2.8 million employees in 1945 to 7.4 million in 1970 and 10 million in 1987. This level of employment exceeded that for the combined state and federal civilian governments.

During the 1990s municipalities faced a number of financial challenges, including deteriorating infrastructure, stagnant revenues accompanied by increasing cost structures,

Professor Paul M. Healy prepared this case as the basis for class discussion rather than to illustrate either effective or ineffective handling of an administrative situation. The case has benefited from the comments of Jack Miller and Elizabeth Krahmer. Copyright © 1998 by the President and Fellows of Harvard College. Harvard Business School case 9-198-030.

unfunded mandates from federal and state governments to provide additional services, pressures to increase the quality of public services provided (without increasing costs), and competition between municipalities to attract new businesses.

Much of the infrastructure for older U.S. cities such as New York was provided during the Depression. For example, the public works projects of the New Deal provided for the construction of municipal roads, bridges, and some public buildings. The 1970s saw a shift from maintenance and replacement of this infrastructure to increased social services. As a result, infrastructure deteriorated and by the early 1990s often required replacement.

A second financial challenge facing older U.S. municipalities arose from stagnant revenue bases and increased cost structures. Many municipalities in the Northeast and the Midwest had stable or declining populations, and had seen key businesses move to less costly areas of the country. As a result, their revenue base was stagnant. Compounding this problem, their costs had escalated during the 1980s and early 1990s. For example, medical costs increased at rates significantly higher than inflation during this period. This increased significantly the cost of medical benefits for municipal employees, as well as the cost of providing health services to older and poorer residents through public hospital systems.

A third factor affecting municipal governments had been the increase in unfunded state and federal government mandates to provide additional services. For example, state and federal governments required local governments to accept increased responsibility for undertaking such services as police and safety, mass transit, housing for the indigent, and special education, without necessarily providing the full funding for these services.

The 1980s and 1990s also saw increased product and service quality in many areas of the private sector. For example, there were significant product improvements in the computer and auto industries, faster customer response times due to overnight delivery, faxes, and E-mail, as well as opportunities for home shopping and banking. Taxpayers frequently expected the same types of quality improvements in public services, leading to a growing expectations gap between taxpayers and public service providers about the quality and cost of services. As a result, there was widespread pressure on local governments to improve productivity and to make existing resources stretch further.

Finally, there was increased competition among local governments to attract new businesses to their community. In many cases, local governments offered tax incentives and commitments to provide infrastructure to companies considering locating in their communities. For example, in late September 1993, after months of negotiations with at least 30 states and municipalities which were willing to provide attractive location packages, Mercedes-Benz announced that it had decided on Tuscaloosa, Alabama, as the site of its new $300 million plant. The plant, which was expected to open in 1997, would employ 1,500 and manufacture 60,000 sport utility vehicles per year. The city of Tuscaloosa committed as much as $30 million for land acquisition and site preparation; Mercedes would be allowed to buy this package for $100 million, implying that the deal cost local taxpayers roughly $20,000 per new job.

FINANCIAL REPORTING BY MUNICIPALITIES

Financial reporting standards for municipalities were developed by the Government Accounting Standards Board (GASB), as well as by the Financial Accounting Standards Board (FASB) and municipal laws. There were a number of differences between financial reporting for municipalities and reporting by for-profit organizations. Some of these differences were differences in terminology. For example, the income statement was called the Statement of Revenues and Expenditures and Changes in Fund Balances, and owners equity was termed the "fund balance" in government organizations. However, there were also substantive differences, including the use of fund accounting and modifications to accrual accounting.

Fund Accounting

Fund accounting required separate funds reports to be maintained to account and report for many of the different activities of government. For example, separate statements were typically created for the local public hospital, for new capital projects, for debt service, for public employee pension funds, and for general government operations. Each of these activities was viewed as a separate entity or "fund" and received its own allocation of resources. For many funds these resources were restricted, and could only be used for specific purposes. Separate financial reports are therefore prepared for each fund account so that users can monitor whether the resources allocated to the funds were used in the way intended.

For municipalities there are three major classes of funds: governmental funds, proprietary funds, and fiduciary funds.

Governmental funds included the general fund (where resources were unrestricted), special revenue funds (which were restricted to outlays for specific purposes other than major capital projects), capital project funds (where funds were restricted to use for capital expenditures), and debt service funds (used to accumulate funds to pay interest and principal on outstanding debt).

Proprietary funds were for activities that were intended to be operated like a business. They included enterprise funds (such as hospitals and water and sewer operations), which provided goods and services to outside parties and which were intended to be self-supporting. Proprietary funds were also created for operations that provided goods or services for other parts of the government.

Fiduciary funds were assets held by a government unit in trust. They typically included pension funds for government employees.

Financial statements for municipalities presented separate results for all three classes of funds. Also, separate group accounts were reported for debt obligations and fixed assets.

Modifications to Accrual Accounting

For proprietary funds, the traditional accrual accounting system was used. However, for governmental funds several modifications to accrual accounting were made. These

City of New York

modifications (for revenue recognition, accrual of interest, and depreciation), made governmental fund accounting closer to a cash basis of accounting than accrual accounting.

The first key difference between governmental accounting and traditional accrual accounting was that revenues for governmental funds were reported when they become measurable and available, rather than when they were earned. For example, property taxes were recognized as revenue when levied rather than when they were earned. A second major difference was that interest on long-term debt was not recorded until it became due, rather than when it was accrued. Thus, if quarterly interest payments on municipal bonds outstanding were due on January 31, a municipality with a December 31 year-end would not accrue interest owed to bondholders for the months of November and December. Finally, while depreciation was recorded for business-like activities (proprietary funds), for governmental funds new capital outlays were effectively expensed. As a result, the balance sheet for the principal government fund, the general fund, typically included only current assets and liabilities.

THE CITY OF NEW YORK'S FINANCES

New York City had a checkered financial history. In February 1975, the New York Urban Development Corporation was unable to repay a $100 million short-term note to Chase Manhattan Bank. This triggered a crisis that resulted in the City being shut out of the credit market. Its bleak prospects eventually forced bankers, unions, and government to work together to reach an agreement. City management took on three sacred cows (low transit fares, CUNY tuition, and subsidized housing); a special agency, the Municipal Assistance Corporation of the City of New York (MAC) was created as a vehicle to issue new municipal debt; State legislators agreed to provide a 28 percent increase in intergovernmental aid; the banks deferred debt and interest payments and provided additional financing; and municipal employees accepted short-term pay cuts and layoffs (many through attrition) and agreed that their pension fund would invest in new MAC debt.

Subsequent analysis attributed the City's financial collapse to a dramatic increase in short-term debt (from $747 million to $4.5 billion in only six years). The New York State Charter Revision Commission explained that:

Since 1970-71 every expense budget has been balanced with an array of gimmicks—revenue accruals, capitalization of expenses, raiding reserves, appropriation of illusory fund balances, suspension of payments, carry-forward of deficits and questionable receivables, and finally, the creation of a public benefit corporation whose purpose is to borrow funds to bail out the expense budget.[1]

As a result of the management and budgetary changes discussed above, by 1981 the City had balanced its budget again, and has since recovered from the financial crisis.

-----

1. *See R. Herzlinger,* Public Sector Accounting, *Prentice-Hall, Englewood Cliffs, NJ, 1996, p. 316.*

Exhibit 1 presents General Fund Revenues and Expenditures for the City during the period 1992 to 1996, the 1996 budget, footnotes, and management discussion of performance. Revenues were generated from a variety of sources, including real estate taxes, sales taxes, income taxes, as well as funding from the federal and state governments. As reported in Exhibit 2, in 1996 real estate tax rates for the City were 10.37 percent of assessed property values, and 1.88 percent of their market values. This difference reflects the City's practice of assessing property at less than its full market value.[2] The ratio of the assessed value of property to its market value (called the Special Equalization Ratio) had declined steadily from 29.7 percent in 1993 to 22.1 percent in 1996.

Sales taxes arose from the City's 4 percent sales tax as well as the state's 4.25 percent retail sales tax. In addition, the City levied a personal income tax on residents and on earnings made in the City for nonresidents, and a corporate income tax on companies doing business in the city. Other revenues were generated by fees paid to the City for issuing licenses, permits, and franchises; interest income; tuition fees from city-run colleges and universities; and rents collected from city-owned property and airports. In 1995 the City included in Other Revenues $200 million from the recovery of prior year FICA overpayments for Social Security and Medicare, as well as $120 million from the sale of upstate jails to the state. Other revenues in 1996 included one-time receipts of $170 million from the New York City Health and Hospitals Corporation, and $28 million from the New York City Housing Financing Agency.

Most of the federal and state funding provided to the City was in the form of categorical grants, which were earmarked for specific activities. These included expenditures for welfare, education, higher education, health and mental health, community development, job training programs, housing, and criminal justice. The City also received a modest amount of unrestricted federal and state aid, which could be used for general-purpose expenditures. However, this support had been declining.

The City's major General Fund expenditures were for social services, education, public safety, debt service, health, and pensions. As reported in Exhibit 1, the difference between General Fund revenues and expenditures, the General Fund surplus, was $5 million for the three years 1994–1996. However, this surplus did not tell the whole story, since the City was required to balance its budget each year. The reported surplus therefore included discretionary transfers and expenditures used to cover a deficit or to eliminate any surplus. Operating surpluses before discretionary transfers and expenditures were $570 million, $371 million, $72 million, $71 million, and $229 million in the period 1991 to 1996.

New York's financial plan for the period 1997 to 2000, presented in Exhibit 3, shows a steadily growing gap between General Fund revenues and expenditures. By 2000 this gap was projected to be $3.4 billion. To meet this deficit the City had embarked on a series of programs to contain costs and increase revenues. The new programs were

2. Revenues from real estate taxes are limited by the New York State Constitution, which requires real estate revenues to be no more than 2.5 percent of the average market value of real estate for the most recent five years.

City of New York

expected to provide revenues and cost savings by reducing entitlements, by restructuring City government through consolidating and privatizing operations, by increasing federal and state aid, and by selling assets. In addition, for 1997 the City projected a savings of $150 million in pension fund costs from changing the actuarial assumption on investment earnings.

Other studies, however, suggested that the City's problems may be more serious than official projections. For example, a May 1996 report by the City Comptroller identified between $1.176 billion and $1.546 billion of potential risks for the 1997 forecasts. These included uncertainties about $100 million of assumed state aid, $160 million in proposed revisions to Medicaid benefits, $40 million from changes in entitlement programs, $319 million in airport-related payments which had been the subject of ongoing unsuccessful negotiation, and as much as $400 million from unidentified cuts in education. These concerns were echoed in staff reports from the OSDC and the Control Board. The OSDC report, published in May 1996, concluded that the City had a structural imbalance, and only succeeds in balancing the 1997 budget by including $1.4 billion of one-time items. The study pointed out that the City's structural problems did not appear to have diminished by workforce reductions of more than 20,000 employees, the lowering of public assistance and Medicaid costs, and the scaling back of tax reduction proposals.

In addition to its 1996 operating outlays of $32 billion, the City made capital outlays of $3.8 billion. These were financed through the issuance of bonds by the City and City agencies, as well as by state and federal grants. Exhibit 4 provides a breakdown of Capital Expenditures for the period 1992 to 1996, as well as long-term projections of capital outlays required to maintain and improve the City's infrastructure. These included outlays for mass transit facilities, sewers, bridges and tunnels, and investments to improve the City's operating productivity. The four-year Capital Commitment Plan for the period 1997 to 2000 projected that in 1997 the City would make commitments for capital projects of $4.3 billion, and would have capital expenditures of $3.7 billion.

As required by its charter, the City reported on the condition of fixed assets, and recommended maintenance expenditures and capital outlays needed to ensure assets were in a good state of repair. The report suggested that the City is letting its fixed assets deteriorate. Actual maintenance outlays in the previous five years had been only 33 percent of recommended levels, and the four year Capital Commitment Plan projected a continuance of this pattern for the period 1997 to 2000. In addition, budgeted capital expenditures in the Capital Plan were only 63 percent of those recommended.

Bond Rating Review

As shown in Exhibit 5, at December 31, 1996, the City had $30.3 billion of debt outstanding. This included debt for the City itself, MAC, and City-guaranteed debt. On a per capita basis the City's debt had increased from $2,202 in 1989 to $3,901 in 1995, outpacing the growth in pretax personal income of City residents.

The New York State constitution required that the City's debt outstanding be less than 10 percent of the average market value of taxable real estate for the last five years, and that debt raised to fund low-rent housing, low-income nursing homes, and urban renewal be less than 2 percent of taxable real estate for the previous five years. The City's projections indicated that by 1998 its debt outstanding would exceed the general debt limit. As a result, the City was proposing state legislation to create the new Infrastructure Finance Authority. The Infrastructure Finance Authority would be permitted to issue debt that would not be subject to the constitutional limit.

Throughout 1996 the City's $25.9 billion of general obligation bonds had been rated Baa1 and A– by Moody's and Fitch Investors Service, respectively. However, Standard & Poor's had downgraded their rating from A– to BBB+, and Moody's and Fitch were also contemplating a downgrade. Additional information on Moody's ratings as well as the relation between yields and ratings are presented in Exhibit 6. During 1996 the City issued $5.3 billion of general obligation bonds, using $2.7 billion to refinance outstanding bonds. Yields on 30-year City debt peaked in 1995 at 6.65 percent and declined to 6.18 percent by March 1996. The City's debt traded 53 basis points over the Bond Buyer 20 Bond Index in July 1995, but this spread had declined to 48 basis points by June 1996.

QUESTIONS

1. Who are the key constituents participating in municipal governments? What challenges do they create for New York City?
2. What are the key performance indicators that you would consider in reviewing the performance of The City of New York for Moody's municipal bond ratings? How has The City performed on these dimensions? What concerns, if any, do you have about its recent performance?
3. Given your analysis in Question 1, what is your assessment of the reasonableness of the assumptions underlying The City's projections made in its four-year plan?
4. Would you recommend downrating The City's General Obligation bonds?

EXHIBIT 1

The City of New York Condensed Financial Statements—General Fund Revenues
and Expenditures, 1992–1996

(in millions)	Adopted Budget 1996	1996	1995	Actual 1994	1993	1992
General Fund Revenues						
Taxes (net of refunds):						
Real estate	$7,274	$7,100	$7,474	$7,773	$7,886	$7,818
Sales and use	3,097	3,111	3,013	2,855	2,739	2,621
Income	6,502	6,808	6,015	6,281	5,751	5,389
Other	1,029	1,095	1,184	1,206	1,204	1,221
	17,902	18,114	17,686	18,115	17,580	17,049
Federal, State and Other Aid:						
Categorical	9,891	10,880	10,733	10,143	9,535	8,880
Unrestricted	549	621	603	667	707	826
	10,440	11,501	11,336	10,810	10,242	9,706
Other than Taxes and Aid:						
Charges for services	1,253	1,312	1,298	1,277	1,304	1,195
Other revenues	1,578	1,118	1,244	1,127	961	1,039
OTB transfers	30	26	27	24	29	33
	2,861	2,456	2,569	2,428	2,294	2,267
Total Revenues	31,203	32,071	31,591	31,353	30,116	29,022
General Fund Expenditures						
General government	$811	$855	$853	$875	$862	$853
Public safety and judicial	4,226	4,446	4,121	3,846	3,759	3,586
Board of Education	7,286	7,835	7,863	7,561	7,213	6,626
City University	363	348	348	353	571	459
Social services	7,522	7,901	8,112	8,030	7,430	7,108
Environmental protection	1,096	1,138	1,120	1,156	1,094	989
Transportation services	667	732	933	981	1,023	1,044
Parks, recreation, cultural	239	244	240	238	229	202
Housing	399	455	527	590	516	541
Health (including HHC)	1,544	1,829	1,737	1,620	1,452	1,276
Libraries	176	253	168	172	146	129
Pensions	1,555	1,356	1,273	1,274	1,427	1,370
Judgments and claims	279	309	251	271	231	232
Fringe and other benefits	1,227	1,581	1,444	1,552	1,492	1,378
Other	948	210	307	375	267	257
Transfers for debt service	2,865	2,574	2,289	2,454	2,440	2,968
Total Expenditures	31,203	32,066	31,586	31,348	30,152	29,018
Surplus (deficit)	0	5	5	5	(36)	4

Source: The City of New York, Comprehensive Annual Financial Report of the Comptroller for the Fiscal Year Ended June 30, 1996.

FOOTNOTES

Statement of General Fund Revenues and Expenditures

(1) The City's results of operations refer to the City's General Fund revenues and transfers reduced by expenditures and transfers. The revenues and assets of Proprietary Funds included in the City's audited financial statements do not constitute revenues and assets of the City's General Fund, and, accordingly, the revenues of such funds, other than net OTB revenues, are not included in the City's results of operations. Expenditures required to be made by the City with respect to such Proprietary Funds are included in the City's results of operations.

(2) In October 1993, the City reported a General Fund operating surplus of $5,079,000 for the 1993 fiscal year as reported in accordance with then applicable GAAP. The City has been required to restate its fiscal year 1993 financial statements because the City has implemented for the 1994 fiscal year Governmental Accounting Standards Board ("GASB") Statement Number 22, which provides for a change in the method of recognizing certain tax receipts. For purposes of presenting comparative financial statements for the 1994 fiscal year, the City was required to restate the fiscal year 1993 statements as if the Statement were adopted in fiscal year 1993. Accordingly, for purposes of presenting fiscal year 1993 financial statements on a comparative basis, the opening fund balance of fiscal year 1993 was restated from $82,974,000 to $311,435,000 and the surplus for the 1993 fiscal year was restated from $5,079,000 to $(36,025,000).

(3) Real Estate Tax for the 1992, 1993, 1994, 1995 and 1996 fiscal years includes $131 million, $128 million, $147.5 million, and $150 million, respectively, of Criminal Justice fund revenues. Real Estate Tax for fiscal years 1994, 1995 and 1996 also includes $201 million and $223 million from the sale of the City's delinquent tax receivables outstanding as of May 31, 1994 and April 1, 1995, and $182 million from the sale of property tax liens, respectively.

(4) Revenues include amounts paid and expected to be paid to the City Municipal Assistance Corp. (MAC) by the State from sales tax receipts, stock transfer tax receipts and State per capita aid otherwise payable by the State to the City. Pursuant to State statute, these revenues flow directly from the State to MAC, and flow to the City only to the extent not required by MAC for debt service, reserve fund requirements and for operating expenses. The City includes such revenues as City revenues and reports the amount retained by MAC from such revenues as "MAC Debt Service Funding," although the City has no control over the statutory application of such revenues to the extent MAC requires them. Estimates of City "Debt Service" include, and estimates of "MAC Debt Service Funding" are reduced by, payments to the City of debt service on City obligations held by MAC. Other Taxes include transfers of net OTB revenues. Other Taxes for the 1992 fiscal year includes $1.5 million of Criminal Justice Fund revenues from the City lottery.

(5) The General Fund surplus is the surplus after discretionary transfers and expenditures. The City had General Fund operating surpluses of $71 million, $72 million, $371 million and $570 million before discretionary transfers and expenditures for the 1995, 1994, 1993, and 1992 fiscal years, respectively. The Financial Plan projects a discretionary transfer of $243 million for the 1996 fiscal year. The expenditures and discretionary transfers made by the City after the adoption of its fiscal year 1996 and fiscal year 1995 budgets follow:

(in millions)	1996	1995
Transfer to the General Debt Service Fund of real estate taxes collected in excess of the amount needed to finance debt service	$106	$66
Adv. cash subsidiaries to Transit Authority	44	—
Adv. cash subsidiaries to Library System	74	—
Total expenditures and discretionary surplus	224	66
Reported operating surplus	5	5
Total operating surplus	$229	$71

Final results for any given fiscal year may differ greatly from that year's Adopted Budget. The following table shows how actuals for fiscal year 1996 differ from the Adopted Budget:

	Amount (in millions)
Additional resources:	
Federal categorical aid above budget	$524
State categorical aid above budget	148
Unrestricted federal and state aid above budget	72
Higher revenues from tax collections, excluding property tax refunds	387
Interest income above budget	23
Lower pension contributions	199
Lower subsidy payments to the Health & Hospitals Corporation	88
Release by the Municipal Assistance Corp. of sales tax monies above targets in the Adopted Budget	145
Lower debt service costs due to bond refundings	64
Sale of Mitchell Lama mortgages	265
Higher collection of licenses, permits and privileges revenues	14
Total additional resources	$1929
Enabled the City to:	
Withstand higher than anticipated refunds of property taxes	$174
Withstand reduction of FY95 budgeted surplus to be used to fund FY96 expenditures	129
Provide for future debt service costs	106
Provide for increased overtime costs	81
Provide for increased judgment and claims costs	19
Higher grant costs paid to recipients of the Home Relief program	185
Provide for increased Medicaid expenditures	512
Provide for prepayment of FY97 subsidy to the Library System	74
Provide for prepayment of FY97 subsidy to the Transit Authority	44
Provide for increased subsidy for reduced fares for schoolchildren	45
Withstand lower collection of anticipated federal aid	75

(continued)

	Amount (in millions)
Withstand lower collection of anticipated state aid	50
Withstand lower collection of revenues from firms and forfeitures	40
Withstand higher provision for disallowances of federal and state aid	25
Withstand lower than anticipated transfers from OTB Corp	5
Withstand postponement of the sale of City assets	32
Withstand lower than anticipated collection and settlement of back rent from the Port Authority for the Municipal Airports	103
Withstand other overspending and revenue below budget	225
Total	1,924
Reported surplus	$5

MANAGEMENT DISCUSSION:
STATEMENT OF GENERAL FUND REVENUES AND EXPENDITURES

Total tax revenue increased by $428 million, or 2.4%, to $18,114 billion in fiscal year 1996. Collections of real estate taxes in fiscal year 1996 were 91.7% of the current fiscal year's tax levy of $7.871 billion. The delinquency rate (an important indicator of fiscal health) was 3.8% in fiscal year 1996, down from 5.0% in fiscal year 1995. Real estate tax collections remained constant at $7.5 billion in fiscal year 1996. The tax levy remained constant as well, $7.9 billion in fiscal years 1995 and 1996.

Revenues from economically sensitive taxes on general sales, personal income, general and financial corporation and unincorporated business income increased 9.6% in fiscal year 1996; these taxes decreased 1.7% in fiscal year 1995. Individually, the taxes changed as follows: general sales tax revenues up 4.6%, the financial corporation tax up 27.6%, unincorporated business income tax up 25.6%, personal income tax up 8.8%, and general corporation tax up 11.4%. The large increase in Financial Corporation Tax is predominantly due to the strength of the City's Wall Street sector and to loan growth stemming from a cut in the Federal Funds rate.

Federal, state and other categorical aid grew $147 million (1.4%) in fiscal year 1996 over 1995. Unrestricted aid increased 3.0% from the fiscal year 1995 level.

General fund expenditures and other financing uses in fiscal year 1996 including transfers for debt service, increased $480 million (1.5%) over fiscal year 1995, to $32.066 billion.

Excluding transfers for debt service, expenditures in fiscal year 1996 increased by 0.7% over fiscal year 1995. Personal service expenditures including pensions and fringes increased 2.1% in fiscal year 1996. Employee salaries and wages in fiscal year 1996 increased 1.9% over fiscal year 1995; health insurance expenditures increased by 9.4% and Social Security increased by 2.9%. Overtime expenditures increased 3.1% to $436 million from $423 million in fiscal year 1995; pension costs increased 2.6% from fiscal 1995, to $1.415 billion. The number of full-time City employees was 236,674 on June

30, 1996, an increase of 2,065 from June 30, 1995. The most significant headcount increases occurred in the Fire Department (3,393), the Police Department (549), the Department of Corrections (288) and the Department of Finance (254). The most significant decreases occurred in the Board of Education (1,407), the Department of Homeless Services (365), and the Department of Housing and Preservation and Development (126). Other than personal services related expenditures excluding Medicaid, Welfare and Debt Service increased 4.8% in fiscal year 1996 over fiscal year 1995.

Transfers for debt service on long-term debt increased by $285 million, or 12.5%, to $2,574 billion in fiscal year 1996.

STATEMENT OF SOURCES AND USES OF CASH 1995–96 (in millions)

	1996	1995
Summary of General Fund Operations		
Revenues	$32,071	$31,591
Expenditures Before Transfers	(29,492)	(29,297)
Surplus Before Debt Service and Other Transfers	2,579	2,294
Transfers for Debt Service and Other Purposes	(2,574)	(2,289)
Surplus from General Fund Operations	5	5
Adjustments to Bring Operations to a Cash Basis		
Increase in Payables	1,659	1,305
Increase in Receivables	(967)	(897)
Provision for Disallowances of Federal and State Aid	40	21
Less Disallowances Paid	(28)	(10)
Cash Provided by Operations	709	424
Other Sources of Cash		
Proceeds from Sale of City Bonds	2,594	2,242
Decrease (Increase) in Amounts Restricted Pending Expenditure	(282)	221
Seasonal Borrowings	2,400	2,200
Total Other Sources of Cash	4,712	4,663
Other Uses of Cash		
Repayment of Seasonal Borrowings	(2,400)	(2,200)
Federal and State Financed Capital Disbursements	(375)	(331)
Less Reimbursements	244	810
City-Financed Capital Construction	(3,421)	(3,344)
Increase in Other	258	427
Total Other Uses of Cash	(5,694)	(4,638)
Net Increase (Decrease) in Cash	(273)	449
Cash, Beginning of Year	748	299
Cash, End of Year	$475	$748

EXHIBIT 2

Real Estate Tax Levies, Values, and Tax Collections, The City of New York

Comparison of Real Estate Tax Levies, Tax Limits, and Tax Rates

Fiscal Year	Total Levy	Operating Limit[a]	Rate per $100 of Full Valuation	Average Tax Rate per $100 of Assessed Valuation
1993	$8,392.5	$11,945.0	$1.60	$10.59
1994	8,113.2	13,853.8	1.30	10.37
1995	7,889.8	13,446.5	1.14	10.37
1996	7,871.4	8,633.4	1.88	10.37
1997	7,835.1	7,857.3	2.46	10.37

a. The State Constitution limits the amount of revenue which the City can raise from the real estate tax for operating purposes ("the operating limit") to 2.5% of the average full value of taxable real estate in the City for the current and the last four years less interest on temporary debt and the aggregate amount of business improvement district charges subject to the 2.5% tax limitation. The most recent calculation of the operating limit does not fully reflect the current downturn in the real estate market, which is expected to lower the operating limit in the future.

Billable Assessed and Full Value of Taxable Real Estate

Fiscal Year	Billable Assessed Valuation of Taxable Real Estate (in millions)	÷	Special Equalization Ratio	=	Full Valuation (in millions)
1993	$79,370.6		0.2965		$267,691.6
1994	78,364.6		0.2627		298,304.4
1995	76,202.4		0.2384		319,641.1
1996	76,029.4		0.2209		344,180.3
1997	75,668.5		0.2069		365,724.8

Real Estate Tax Collections and Delinquencies

Fiscal Year	Tax Levy (in millions)	Tax Collections as Percentage of Tax Levy	Delinquent at Fiscal Year End (in millions)	Delinquency as Percentage of Tax Levy
1990	$6,872.4	94.7%	$230.2	3.35%
1991	7,681.3	93.7	315.7	4.11
1992	8,318.8	93.1	370.2	4.45
1993	8,392.5	92.5	411.2	4.90
1994	8,113.2	92.7	403.4	4.97
1995	7,889.8	93.5	381.6	4.84
1996	7,871.4	93.4	288.9	3.67

City of New York

EXHIBIT 3
The City of New York Financial Plan, 1997–2000

(in millions)	Fiscal Year			
	1997	1998	1999	2000
Revenues				
Taxes:				
General property tax	$ 7,088	$ 7,244	$ 7,469	$ 7,752
Other taxes	10,407	10,837	11,352	11,897
Tax audit revenue	659	659	659	659
Tax reduction program	(25)	(188)	(366)	(432)
Miscellaneous revenues	4,468	3,549	3,117	2,894
Unrestricted intergovernmental aid	523	510	509	513
Anticipated state actions	50	—	—	—
Other categorical grants	293	275	281	280
Interfund revenues	260	260	258	256
Less: Intracity revenues	(647)	(647)	(646)	(644)
Disallowances against categorical grants	(15)	(15)	(15)	(15)
Total City Funds	$23,061	$22,484	$22,618	$23,160
Federal categorical grants	3,771	3,600	3,586	3,582
State categorical grants	6,149	6,071	6,106	6,087
Total Revenues	$32,981	$32,155	$32,310	32,829
Expenditures				
Personal service	$16,237	$16,813	$17,612	$18,812
Other than personal service	14,128	14,064	14,256	14,271
Debt service	2,735	3,015	3,124	3,241
MAC debt service funding	328	394	423	370
General reserve	200	200	200	200
Total Expenditures	$33,628	$34,486	$35,615	$36,894
Less: Intracity Expenses	(647)	(647)	(646)	(644)
Net Total Expenditures	$32,981	$33,839	$34,969	$36,250
Deficit	$0	$1,684	$2,959	$3,421

EXHIBIT 4

The City of New York Actual and Planned Capital Outlays, 1992-2000

Actual Capital Outlays (in millions)

	1996	1995	1994	1993	1992
Education	$ 812	$ 881	$ 727	$ 758	$ 686
Environmental protection	1,135	819	768	934	1,046
Transportation	554	444	423	341	364
Transit authority	218	150	221	250	330
Housing	246	292	387	431	639
All other	831	1,108	817	903	828
Total Expenditures	$3,796	$3,694	$3,343	$3,617	$3,893

Capital Commitment Plan, 1997–2000 (in millions)

	1997	1998	1999	2000
Education	$ 713	$ 859	$ 799	$1,392
Environmental protection	1,385	1,270	1,488	518
Transportation	760	643	671	590
Transit authority	497	231	231	231
Housing	311	267	317	382
Sanitation	185	604	167	361
City operations/Facilities	1,321	630	650	587
Economic and port development	71	46	35	44
Reserve for unattained commitments	(449)	(107)	(300)	(244)
Total Commitments	$4,793	$4,443	$4,058	$3,861
Total Expenditures	$4,255	$3,958	$4,114	$4,179

City of New York

MANAGEMENT DISCUSSION OF CAPITAL PROJECTS

Capital expenditures increased by $102 million to $3.8 billion in fiscal year 1996, or 2.8% more than in fiscal year 1995 and approximately 2.5% less than just four years ago. Expenditures on the infrastructure component of the Capital Budget were $2.1 billion in fiscal year 1996, $873 million more than in fiscal year 1995. Expenditures for environmental protection (excluding sanitation) accounted for 48.6% of the total spent on infrastructure in fiscal year 1996. Expenditures for mass transit in fiscal year 1996 accounted for 10.6% of the total expenditures on infrastructure. The amount expended on the City's water distribution and sewage collection system in fiscal year 1996 was $1.0 billion.

In October 1990, the City completed a project to inventory the major portions of its physical plant. The first citywide and individual agency report was published in fiscal year 1991, which has been updated yearly. It provides the City with a comprehensive assessment of the condition of its major assets, the projected costs necessary to restore these assets to a state of good repair and schedules detailing the maintenance required to maintain the assets' structural integrity. The City estimates costs for repairs, replacements, and major maintenance for fiscal years 1997 through 2000 to be $4.3 billion.

EXHIBIT 5
The City of New York Debt

City of New York

Combined Net City Debt

(in millions)	1996	1995	1994	1993	1992
Net City debt	$25,052	$23,258	$21,531	$19,424	$17,916
Net MAC debt	3,936	4,033	4,215	4,470	4,657
Net Samurai debt	200	200	200	200	—
Total City, MAC and Samurai Debt	29,188	27,491	25,946	24,094	22,573
City guaranteed debt	1,155	1,104	1,114	733	745
Combined Net City Debt	$30,343	$28,595	$27,060	$24,827	$23,318

City, MAC, and City-Guaranteed Proprietary Corporation Debt Service

Fiscal Years	Principal on City Long-Term Debt	Interest on City Long-Term Debt	City-Guaranteed Debt	Required MAC Funding	Total
1996	$ 22,718	$ 150,987	$ 22,560	$ 425,310	$ 621,575
1997	1,220,995	1,493,357	110,015	570,498	3,394,865
1998	1,206,764	1,401,147	116,997	583,535	3,308,443
1999	1,133,395	1,329,846	125,751	602,079	3,191,071
2000	1,072,079	1,271,698	125,749	537,438	3,006,964
2001	1,072,637	1,218,150	125,634	537,621	2,954,042
2002–2147	19,111,773	11,693,985	1,644,505	3,766,678	36,216,941
Total	$24,840,361	$18,559,170	$2,271,211	$7,023,159	$52,693,901

City, MAC, and City-Guaranteed Proprietary Corporation Debt

Fiscal Year	Debt per Capita	Debt per Capita as Percent of Personal Income per Capita	Debt as Percent of Assessed Value of Taxable Property	Debt as Percent of Full Value of Taxable Property
1989	$2,202	9.96%	25.4%	4.6%
1990	2,490	10.49	26.0	4.5
1991	2,917	11.93	28.0	4.5
1992	3,192	12.14	28.5	4.1
1993	3,389	12.51	31.3	3.9
1994	3,691	n.a.	35.2	4.4
1995	3,901	n.a.	36.9	4.1

City of New York

EXHIBIT 6
Moody's Investor Service, Inc.—Bond Ratings

Rating	Description of Rating	Average Yield, December 20, 1995
Aaa	Best quality or "gilt edge," with the smallest degree of investment risk. Interest payments are protected by large or exceptionally stable margin and principal is secure. Protective elements can be visualized and are most unlikely to impair strong position of such issues.	5.38%
Aa	High quality by all standards. Together with the Aaa group they comprise high grade bonds. They are rated lower than the best bonds because margins of protection may not be as large, fluctuation of protective elements may be of greater amplitude, or risks appear somewhat larger than in Aaa securities.	5.50%
A	Upper medium grade obligations. Security to principal and interest is considered adequate, but are susceptible to impairment sometime in the future.	5.55%
Baa	Medium grade obligations, i.e., they are neither highly protected nor poorly secured. Interest payments and principal security appear adequate for the present but certain protective elements may be lacking or unreliable over any great length of time. Such bonds lack outstanding investment characteristics and have speculative characteristics.	5.70%
Ba	Judged to have speculative elements; their future cannot be considered as well assured. Often the protection of interest and principal payments may be very moderate, and not well safeguarded during good and bad times over the future. Uncertainty of position characterizes bonds in this class.	n.a.
B	Lack characteristics of desirable investment. Assurance of interest and principal payments or maintenance of other terms of the contract over any long period of time may be small.	n.a.
Caa	Poor standing. Such issues may be in default or there may be present elements of danger with respect to principal or interest.	n.a.
Ca	Speculative in a high degree. Such issues are often in default or have other marked shortcomings.	n.a.
C	Lowest rated class of bonds. Issues so rated have extremely poor prospects of ever attaining any real investment standing.	n.a.

Source: *Moody's Bond Record*, Moody's Investors Service, New York.

Comdisco Inc., the world's leading independent lessor of IBM computers, would seem like a company Wall Street ought to love. Annual revenues are up fourfold since 1978, to an estimated $600 million in the fiscal year that ended September 30. Earnings per share have grown at an even more torrid tempo, and return on shareholders' equity is running at an estimated 35%. Yet at a recent price of $37, the stock was selling at 15 times projected earnings in fiscal 1984—a tepid multiple for a company whose earnings could grow at a 30% clip over the next five years.

⋮

Just about the only thing wrong with Comdisco is the tainted reputation that computer-leasing companies acquired as a result of the well-known bankruptcies of OPM Leasing and Itel. Securities analysts, though, see no similarities between Comdisco and those fiascos. OPM Leasing turned out to be a spectacularly fraudulent operation, and Itel's downfall resulted in large part from overly optimistic accounting assumptions, coupled with a large inventory of obsolete equipment. Comdisco's accounting couldn't be more conservative, analysts say. They add that the company has managed, through the use of ingenious leasing arrangements, to eliminate almost all exposure to equipment obsolescence. Comdisco, asserts John Keefe of Drexel Burnham Lambert, has practically nothing to fear from any future IBM decision.[1]

The quotes above appeared in the Personal Investing Section of *Fortune* magazine in October 1983.

BUSINESS HISTORY AND OPERATIONS

Comdisco, Inc. is a Chicago-based company founded in 1969 by its current chairman of the board and president, Kenneth Pontikes. The company originally began as an IBM computer dealer. As demand for computer leasing started to grow during the late 1970s, the company started emphasizing leasing operations. By 1982, leasing old and new IBM computer equipment constituted the primary business activity of the company, and Comdisco had become the largest computer leasing company. Comdisco's customers

---

This case was prepared by Professor Krishna G. Palepu as the basis for class discussion rather than to illustrate either effective or ineffective handling of an administrative situation. Copyright © 1986 by the President and Fellows of Harvard College. Harvard Business School case 9-186-299.

1. *Reprinted with permission from* Fortune, *October 31, 1983.*

were primarily large corporations. In 1982, the company had business relationships with 70 percent of the Fortune 500 companies, including 49 of the 50 largest U.S. companies.

The computer remarketing industry had many participants: small independent operators, larger private organizations, and leasing subsidiaries of conglomerates. Comdisco was one of the few independent public corporations in the industry. The firms in the industry were primarily of two types: broker/dealers or third-party lessors. The broker/dealers obtained for customers computer equipment from either a vendor or current user; third-party lessors provided lease financing. Comdisco engaged in both these activities.

Comdisco achieved its dominance in the computer leasing industry through a strategy of full-service leasing. Under this strategy, the company offered its customers a number of services which were not offered by competitors. Comdisco's subsidiaries, Comdisco Technical Services, Inc. and Comdisco Transport, Inc., specialized in equipment refurbishment, delivery, installation, de-installation, and technical planning and site preparation. Comdisco Maintenance Services, another subsidiary, offered a low-cost alternative to IBM's maintenance service. Comdisco Disaster Recovery Services, Inc. was established to provide another valuable service to the company's customers: contingent data processing capacity to be used when a customer's own data center had unavoidable failures. Through this service, Comdisco's customers had access to four fully operational data centers as a backup to their own data centers, to be used in the event of a natural disaster or accident.

Comdisco's broad customer base provided the company with a number of competitive advantages. First, taking advantage of its access to 10,000 important users of IBM equipment in the U.S., the company created a proprietary data base of their computing needs. This data base provided Comdisco's sales force with current and timely information on potential customers and their requirements. Second, being the leading IBM dealer, Comdisco maintained large inventories of a broad range of IBM equipment. Comdisco's personnel closely monitored IBM's new products and pricing policies. This product knowledge combined with large inventories enabled the company to assist customers with their computer acquisition plans and to offer quick deliveries. Finally, using its data base, the company could help its customers sell their old hardware when they acquired new equipment from Comdisco.

While the above strategy enabled Comdisco to establish its dominance over others in the computer leasing industry, the company was still potentially vulnerable to competition from IBM itself since IBM equipment accounted for most of Comdisco's revenues. In 1981, IBM formed a financing subsidiary, IBM Credit Corporation, to provide customer financing. Shortly after that, IBM announced its intention to enter into computer leasing and established a joint venture for this purpose with Merrill Lynch and Metropolitan Life Insurance. A number of industry analysts felt that this might result in increased competition for companies like Comdisco.

Comdisco's management, however, felt that IBM's recent moves did not pose a threat to the company's competitive position because IBM's entry into leasing would enhance the tarnished image of the computer leasing business, a net benefit to the industry. They also believed that, as IBM began to emphasize outright sale of its equipment over short-term rentals, many of IBM's customers might be forced to look for other lessors like Comdisco who offered short-term leases. This was likely to provide additional business opportunities which would offset any loss of long-term lease business to IBM.

While equipment leasing to computer users was Comdisco's primary activity, the company also offered tax-oriented leases to investors who were primarily interested in the tax benefits associated with leasing. In recent years, the financial services income from the tax advantaged transactions accounted for a growing portion of the company's revenues.

ACCOUNTING POLICIES FOR LEASING

Comdisco offered computer equipment to its customers through a variety of lease arrangements. Using the terminology of Financial Accounting Standards Board's Statement No. 13, Comdisco's leases can be classified into one of three types: sales-type leases, direct financing leases, or operating leases.

Classification

Both sales-type and direct financing leases transferred substantially all the benefits and risks inherent in the ownership of the leased property to the lessee. A sales-type lease usually gave rise to a dealer's profit or loss for Comdisco. Therefore, in a sales-type lease, the fair value of the leased equipment (normal selling price) at the inception of the lease differed from the cost or carrying amount. In contrast, in a direct financing lease, the primary service that Comdisco offered was the financing of the equipment's acquisition by a lessee. In such a lease, the fair value of the equipment was equal to the cost or carrying amount. Comdisco earned only a financing income (interest) and no dealer's profit. An operating lease was a simple rental of the equipment, and Comdisco retained ownership of the equipment throughout the lease term.

Under FASB's guidelines, the accounting classification of a lease was based on whether or not it satisfied certain conditions:

1. The lease transfers ownership of the equipment to the lessee by the end of the lease term.
2. The lease contains an option allowing the lessee to purchase the property at a bargain price.
3. The lease term is equal to 75 percent or more of the estimated economic life of the property.
4. The present value of the rental is equal to 90 percent or more of the fair market value of the leased property.
5. Collectibility of the payments from the lessee is reasonably predictable.
6. No important uncertainties surround the amount of cost yet to be incurred by the lessor.

Comdisco (A)

A lease meeting *at least one* of the first four conditions and *both* of the last two conditions was classified as a sales-type lease or direct financing lease. Such a lease was treated as a sales-type lease if the fair value of the leased equipment was different from its carrying amount; otherwise it was classified as a direct financing lease. A lease that did not meet the combination of conditions just described was classified as an operating lease.

Accounting Treatment: Comdisco as Lessor

The accounting treatment in Comdisco's financial statements for the above three types of leases was as follows:

OPERATING LEASE.   Lease revenue consisted of monthly rentals; the cost of equipment was recorded as leased equipment. The difference between the cost and the estimated residual value at the end of the lease term was depreciated on a straight-line basis over the lease term. Salesmen's commissions and other initial direct costs were capitalized as deferred charges and were amortized on a straight-line basis.

SALES-TYPE LEASE.   At the inception of the lease, the present value of rentals was treated as sales revenue. Equipment cost less the present value of the residual was recorded as cost of sales. The present value of rentals and of the residual was recorded on the balance sheet as net investment in sales-type lease. As each lease payment was received, the net investment was reduced and interest income was recognized.

DIRECT FINANCING LEASE.   At the inception of the lease, the cost of the leased equipment was recorded as net investment in the direct financing lease. As each lease payment was received, the net investment was reduced by the corresponding amount. The difference between the sum of the lease payments and the cost of the leased equipment was unearned profit from the direct financing lease, and it was recognized monthly so as to produce a constant rate of return on the net investment.

Accounting Treatment: Comdisco as Lessee

In addition to the above leases where Comdisco was a lessor, it was also often a lessee: the company acquired equipment from computer vendors and others through leasing arrangements. If such a lease met at least one of the first four conditions listed earlier, it was classified by Comdisco as a capital lease; otherwise, it was classified as an operating lease. The accounting treatment of the leases where Comdisco was a lessee was as follows:

OPERATING LEASE.   Monthly rentals were treated as rental expense.

CAPITAL LEASE.   At the inception of the lease, the present value of lease rentals was recorded as a capital lease asset. An equal amount was also recognized as a liability—

an obligation under the capital lease. The capital lease asset was depreciated over the lease term. When a lease payment was made, the obligation under capital lease was reduced and interest expense on the lease obligation was recognized.

NONRECOURSE DISCOUNTING OF LEASE PAYMENTS

In order to finance its investment in leased assets, Comdisco often assigned the stream of lease payments to a financial institution at a fixed interest rate on a nonrecourse basis. In return, Comdisco received from the financial institution a loan equal to the present value of the lease payment stream. The financial institution received the lease payments from the lessee as repayments of the loan. In the event of default by a lessee, the financial institution had a first lien on the underlying leased equipment, with no further recourse against the company.

For operating leases, proceeds from discounting were recorded on the balance sheet as discounted lease rentals liability. As lessees made payments to the financial institutions, discounted lease rentals were reduced by the interest rate method. For sales-type leases and direct financing leases, proceeds from discounting were not included in discounted lease rentals. Instead, future rentals were eliminated from the net investment in sales-type or direct financing leases, and any gain or loss on the financing was immediately recognized in the income statement.

TAX ADVANTAGED TRANSACTIONS

In addition to leasing equipment to computer users, Comdisco undertook leasing transactions with investors who were interested in tax shelters. While the specific terms and conditions of these tax advantaged transactions varied, a typical transaction was as follows:

1. After the inception of the initial user lease and independent of it, Comdisco sold all the leased equipment to a third-party investor. This sale usually occurred three to nine months after the commencement of the initial user lease. The sales price equaled the then current fair market value of the equipment. The payment from the investor to Comdisco consisted of: (a) cash and a negotiable interest-bearing promissory note due within two years for 10–22 percent of the sales price (the "equity payment") and (b) an installment note for the balance payable over an 84-month period.
2. Simultaneously with the sale, Comdisco leased the equipment back from the investors for 84 months. The lease payments under the leaseback obligation were equal to the installment payments receivable by Comdisco from the investor (1.b).
3. As part of the leaseback arrangement, during the 61st through 84th months of the leaseback period, the investor shared in the re-lease proceeds that the company received from subleasing the equipment to a user. Upon the expiration of the leaseback period, the investor had the exclusive right to the equipment.

The net result of the above transaction was that Comdisco gave up the depreciation tax benefit, a portion of the rental revenues for months 61–84, and 100 percent of the equipment value after the 84th month. In return, the company received the nonrefundable equity payment (1.a).

If the equipment sold to the investor was originally under an operating lease, the equity payment was recorded by Comdisco as financial services revenue in the period in which the tax advantaged transaction occurred. From the fourth quarter of 1983, the company began to allocate as cost of financial services a portion of the net book value of the equipment at lease termination. For sales-type and direct financing leases, the equity payment was first applied to reduce a portion of the residual value of the equipment shown in the balance sheet (as investment in sales-type and direct financing leases). This is because the company's ability to recover the residual value was decreased due to the rental sharing under the tax advantaged transaction. The excess of the equity payment over the residual value reduction was recorded as financial services revenue in the period in which the tax advantaged transaction occurred.

RECENT PERFORMANCE

During the ten years ending in 1982, Comdisco's sales and profits grew rapidly. During fiscal 1982 the company reported $29.4 million profits on revenues of $471.6 million, representing an 88 percent increase in profits and 56 percent increase in sales during the year. (See Exhibit 3 for an abridged version of the 1982 annual report.) The company continued its strong growth performance in fiscal 1983. The company's profits and revenues in the first nine months of the fiscal year were $36.1 million and $401.4 million, respectively. (See Exhibit 2 for the company's interim report for this period.)

In Comdisco's second quarterly report for 1983, Kenneth Pontikes commented on the company's future:

These new activities, along with the continued growth of the company's lease and customer base, enhance the company's long term growth prospects. The company's history of outstanding performance and the recent issuance of $250,000,000 of convertible subordinated debentures, which further strengthened the company's capital base, provide it with the flexibility required for continued growth in today's marketplace.

The company's shares, listed on The New York Stock Exchange, reflected this optimistic outlook: their price appreciated from about $9 in January 1982 to $37 by the end of September 1983. Exhibit 1 shows the movement of Comdisco's stock price and Standard and Poor's 500 index from January 1982 to September 1983. Comdisco's stock price increased by more than 300 percent during this period compared to a roughly 40 percent increase in Standard and Poor's 500 index. However, as the *Fortune* magazine comments indicate, many analysts considered Comdisco's stock to be still undervalued and expected it to continue to outperform the market.

QUESTIONS

1. Evaluate Comdisco's business activities and the company's strategy.
2. Using the information in Comdisco's financial statements and footnotes, fill in the following to the extent possible (use plug figures if necessary):

Account	Balance as of 9/30/81		Increases during fiscal '82		Decreases during fiscal '82		Balance as of 9/30/82
Obligations under capital leases	_____	+	_____	–	_____	=	_____
Discounted lease rentals	_____	+	_____	–	_____	=	_____
Net investment in sales-type and direct financing leases	_____	+	_____	–	_____	=	_____

Identify the business transactions that would have given rise to the changes identified in the above accounts.

3. Analyze the relative contribution of rentals, sales of computer equipment, and financial services to Comdisco's reported profits during fiscal years 1981 and 1982 and the first nine months of fiscal year 1983. What are the reasons for the differences in the profit margins of these three activities? Which activity is contributing most to Comdisco's profits?
4. Evaluate the quality of Comdisco's disclosure in its annual report regarding the company's lease accounting policies. Do you think the disclosure is adequate to evaluate the company's performance?

Comdisco (A)

EXHIBIT 1
Movement of Comdisco's Stock and S&P 500 Index, January 1982–September 1983

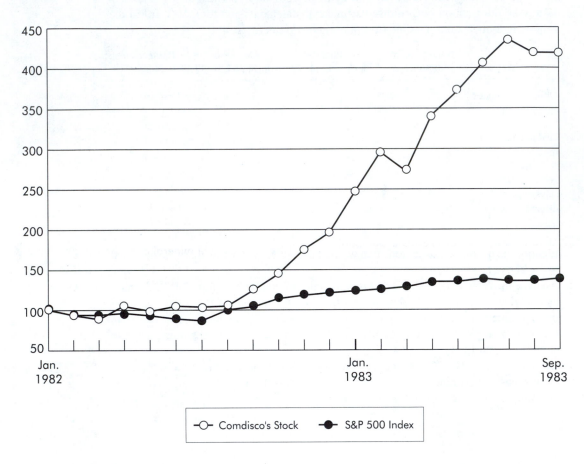

EXHIBIT 2

Comdisco, Inc. Quarterly Report, Third Quarter Ended June 30, 1983

To Our Stockholders

I am pleased to report net earnings of $13,199,000 or $.45 per share for the third quarter of fiscal 1983. These results represent increases of 127% and 96%, respectively, over the three months ended June 30, 1982 when net earnings were $5,824,000 or $.23 per share. Earnings improved as a result of increased profitability of financial services activities, increased leasing of computer equipment and a lower effective tax rate. Total revenue for the quarter ended June 30, 1983 was $127,455,000 compared to $94,691,000 for the prior year period. The increase in total revenue was primarily due to the continued growth of the Company's lease base. In the third quarter of fiscal 1983, the Company entered into 850 new leases with total revenue of $266.1 million during the initial lease terms. These figures compare to 605 new leases and $180.4 million of revenue for the year earlier period.

Net earnings for the nine months ended June 30, 1983 were $36,064,000, or $1.25 per share, representing increases of 69% and 51%, respectively, over the prior year period. Total revenue for the first nine months of fiscal 1983 amounted to $401,367,000 compared to $334,189,000 for the nine months ended June 30, 1982. The Company's impressive results for the first nine months of fiscal 1983 were primarily due to its active participation in the peripheral equipment and 3081 and 3083 processor markets, which have resulted in increased computer equipment sales, leasing and financial services activities. In addition, deliveries by IBM of the 3081 and 3083 processors have stimulated both sale and leasing of displaced IBM 3033 processors.

On July 21, 1983, the Board of Directors declared a cash dividend of $.04 per share to be paid on September 9, 1983 to stockholders of record as of August 19, 1983. This is the twenty-seventh consecutive quarterly cash dividend declared since the Company commenced paying cash dividends in 1977.

In April 1983, the Company announced its Corporate Lease Line Program, an expanded leasing program designed to meet the growing demand for lease financing of office and industrial equipment. The Corporate Lease Line Program expands the Company's array of complementary services and capitalizes on its expertise in providing customers with innovative and cost effective financing options.

During the third quarter of fiscal 1983, the Company began operations of a newly established, wholly owned subsidiary, Comdisco Resources, Inc. ("CRI"). Initially CRI will be primarily engaged, through joint ventures with established partners, in the acquisition of mineral and royalty rights in producing domestic oil and gas properties and the acquisition of onshore leasehold interests, primarily for resale to others for oil and gas exploration and development. For fiscal 1983 and 1984, investments of approximately $32.0 million and $13.0 million, respectively, have been budgeted by CRI.

These new activities, along with the continued growth of the Company's lease and customer base, enhance the Company's long term growth prospects. The Company's history of outstanding financial performance and the recent issuance of $250,000,000 of convertible subordinated debentures, which further strengthened the Company's capital base, provide it with the flexibility required for continued growth in today's marketplace.

Kenneth N. Pontikes
Chairman of the Board and President
August 10, 1983

Comdisco (A)

CONSOLIDATED STATEMENTS OF EARNINGS AND RETAINED EARNINGS
For the Three and Nine Months Ended June 30, 1983 and 1982 (unaudited)

(in thousands except per share data)	Three Months Ended June 30		Nine Months Ended June 30	
	1983	1982	**1983**	1982
Revenue				
Rental	$ 70,056	$53,462	$193,520	$148,434
Sale of computer equipment	29,159	24,113	129,626	110,108
Financial services	15,493	12,890	50,073	62,040
Other	12,747	4,226	28,148	13,607
Total Revenue	127,455	94,691	401,367	334,189
Cost and Expenses				
Equipment depreciation, amortization and rental	56,647	40,378	152,586	115,325
Cost of computer equipment	26,112	21,318	114,631	99,659
Financial services	1,524	1,065	3,614	6,641
Selling, general and administrative	13,938	10,722	43,060	38,074
Interest	14,035	12,016	**38,112**	34,560
Total Costs and Expenses	**112,256**	85,499	**352,003**	294,259
Earnings before income taxes	**15,199**	9,192	**49,364**	39,930
Income taxes	**2,000**	3,368	**13,300**	18,568
Net earnings	$ **13,199**	5,824	**36,064**	21,362
Retained earnings at beginning of period	$ **92,445**	$58,223	**$71,268**	$43,359
Net earnings	**13,199**	5,824	**36,064**	21,362
Dividends paid	**(1,150)**	(394)	**(2,838)**	(1,068)
Retained earnings at end of period	**$104,494**	$63,653	**$104,494**	$ 63,653
Net earnings per common and common equivalent share	.45	.23	**1.25**	.83
Cash dividends per common share	**.04**	.03	**.11**	.09
Common and common equivalent shares outstanding	**29,611**	29,118	**29,234**	28,918

CONSOLIDATED BALANCE SHEET
June 30, 1983 and 1982 (unaudited) and September 30, 1982 (unaudited)

	June 30		September 30
(in thousands except number of shares)	**1983**	1982	1982
Assets			
Cash and marketable securities (at cost which approximates market)	**$175,215**	$ 4,586	$ 39,762
Receivables	**66,430**	38,854	45,055
Inventory of computer equipment	**48,914**	38,716	35,382
Investment in sales-type and direct financing leases	**63,735**	28,541	23,682
Leased and other equipment	**703,759**	532,969	534,611
Less: accumulated depreciation and amortization	**263,401**	174,408	192,714
Net equipment	**440,358**	358,561	341,897
Other assets and deferred charges	**55,925**	43,446	50,901
	$850,577	$512,704	$536,679
Liabilities and Stockholders' Equity			
Note payable	**$ —**	$ 2,650	$ 2,385
Subordinated debentures	**262,250**	62,250	62,250
Accounts payable	**29,001**	26,982	19,110
Obligations under capital leases	**14,669**	20,122	18,636
Income taxes	**42,817**	31,585	36,197
Other liabilities	**45,139**	39,219	45,265
Discounted lease rentals	**280,976**	247,899	261,780
	674,852	430,707	445,623
Stockholders' equity:			
Common stock $.10 par value Authorized 50,000,000 shares; issued 28,768,366 and 11,757,418 shares at June 30, 1983 and 1982, respectively (11,769,043 at September 30, 1982)	**2,877**	1,176	1,177
Additional paid-in capital	**68,718**	17,657	18,965
Deferred translation adjustment	**(364)**	(489)	(354)
Retained earnings	**104,494**	63,653	71,268
Total stockholders' equity	**175,725**	81,997	91,056
	$850,577	$512,704	$536,679

Comdisco (A)

CONSOLIDATED STATEMENTS OF CHANGES IN FINANCIAL POSITION
For the Nine Months Ended June 30, 1983 and 1982 (unaudited)

(in thousands)	1983	1982
Source of Funds		
Total provided by operations	$123,798	$133,285
Issuance of common stock upon conversion of 13% convertible debentures, net	52,465	—
Proceeds from issuance of subordinated debentures	245,250	—
Discounted lease rentals	141,002	92,535
Other	305	2,624
	562,820	228,444
Application of Funds		
Increase in leased equipment and inventory	238,304	175,193
Decrease in note payable	2,385	795
Redemption of convertible debentures	50,000	—
Reduction of discounted lease rentals and obligations under capital leases	126,332	45,611
Other assets and deferred charges	7,508	11,039
Other	2,838	1,068
	427,367	233,706
Increase (decrease) in cash and marketable securities	135,453	(5,262)
Cash and marketable securities at beginning of period	39,762	9,848
Cash and marketable securities at end of period	$175,215	$4,586

Notes to Consolidated Financial Statements

June 30, 1983 and 1982 (unaudited)

1. Principles of Reporting

The accompanying consolidated financial statements include the accounts of the Company and its wholly-owned subsidiaries after elimination of intercompany accounts and transactions. In the opinion of management, the accompanying consolidated financial statements contain all adjustments necessary for a fair presentation. The Company has a fiscal year that ends September 30.

The balance sheet at September 30, 1982 has been derived from the audited financial statements at that date.

2. Subordinated Debentures

On November 4, 1982, the Board of Directors announced the redemption of all of the Company's 13% Convertible Subordinated Debentures Due 2001 (the "Convertible Debentures") at a redemption price of $1,117 for each $1,000 principal amount of Convertible Debenture, plus accrued and unpaid interest to December 6, 1982. The Convertible Debentures were convertible into shares of common stock of the Company, at the option of the Convertible Debenture holder, at a conversion price of $9.75 per share. Common stock issued upon conversion of $49,839,000 principal amount of the convertible Debentures totaled 5,111,360 shares.

On May 4, 1983, the Company completed the sale of $250,000,000 principal amount of its 8% Convertible Subordinated Debentures Due May 1, 2003 (the "Debentures"). The Debentures are convertible into common stock of the Company at the rate of $36.50 per share. An aggregate of 6,849,315 shares has been reserved for issuance upon conversion of the Debentures. Temporarily, the net proceeds from the Debentures, which amounted to approximately $245,250,000, have been invested in short-term instruments and used to finance an increase in the Company's lease portfolio pending receipt of cash upon discounting of the related lease receivables.

3. Income Taxes

The rates used in computing the provision for federal income taxes at June 30, 1983 and 1982 vary from the statutory tax rate primarily due to investment tax credits generated in the respective years and Domestic International Sales Corporation (DISC) tax benefits. During the third quarter of fiscal 1983, the Company generated substantial investment tax credits resulting from the increase in leasing activity. Accordingly, the Company estimates that the annual effective tax rate will be approximately 27% for fiscal 1983 compared to the estimated rates of 33% and 40% used in the first six months of fiscal 1983 and the first nine months of fiscal 1982, respectively. The reduction in the estimated income tax rate resulted in an increase of approximately $2,100,000 in net earnings or $.07 per share in the third quarter of fiscal 1983. The effective tax rate for the quarter and nine months ended June 30, 1982 varies from the estimated annual rate due to a reinstatement of deferred income taxes resulting from the sale of investment tax credits which had been used to reduce deferred income taxes at September 30, 1981.

4. Common Stock

All references in the financial statements and notes to the number of common shares and per share data have been adjusted for the two-for-one stock split distributed in March 1983.

Comdisco (A)

EXHIBIT 3

Comdisco, Inc. Annual Report for Fiscal Year 1982 (abridged)

To Our Stockholders

In fiscal 1982 Comdisco continued its outstanding performance with record earnings and revenues. Net earnings of $29.4 million, or $2.27 per share, represented increases of 88% and 68%, respectively, over fiscal 1981, while total revenue increased 56% to $471.6 million. These results were achieved despite the recessionary economic environment. The compound annual growth rate in net earnings over the last five years is an exceptional 43%. The primary factors contributing to the record earnings in fiscal 1982 were the increased volume and profitability of financial services activity, the growth of the Company's lease and customer bases, and the ability of the Company to capitalize on the active market for IBM 3033 processors and disk storage devices.

The higher level of financial services activity was the result of tax-advantaged leasing transactions associated with the Company's lease portfolio of used equipment and also the arrangement of "tax benefit transfers" that were structured under the Economic Recovery Tax Act of 1981. Late in fiscal 1982, Congress passed the Tax Equity and Fiscal Responsibility Act of 1982, which included legislation that will eventually eliminate "tax benefit transfers." This will cause the arrangement of traditional leveraged leases to re-emerge as a primary financial services activity of the Company.

The growth of Comdisco's lease base continued on a strong trend in fiscal 1982 as more users committed themselves to the leasing of equipment. The Company significantly increased its activity in the leasing of peripheral equipment. During fiscal 1982 the Company entered into 2,259 new leases with total revenue of $701.6 million during the initial term of these leases. This compares to 1,620 leases and $338.8 million in revenue during fiscal 1981.

The initial deliveries by IBM of its 3081 processor stimulated activity in all Comdisco's businesses. The Company participated in the lease placement of 3081 processors, and in the remarketing of the displaced 3033 processors. The Company's increased marketing efforts led to a 31% increase in its customers, which include most of the largest corporations in the United States. In fiscal 1981 Comdisco set up a "mid-range" marketing force that has successfully expanded the Company's customer base among medium-sized corporations. Comdisco's foreign subsidiaries continued to increase their marketing presence and also produced record results in the twelve months ended September 30, 1982. Fiscal 1982 also saw the continued refinement of Comdisco's computerized marketing data base that tracks user information for virtually all large IBM systems installed in the United States.

Two of Comdisco's newer subsidiaries, Comdisco Disaster Recovery Services and Comdisco Technical Services, made significant progress in fiscal 1982. The addition of the Texas Disaster Recovery Center by December 31, 1982 will bring the number of centers to four, providing further evidence that Comdisco Disaster Recovery Services can provide its customers with the most comprehensive disaster backup services available. Comdisco Technical Services expanded its equipment installation and facilities planning operations and showed increased profitability.

Probably as significant as the record earnings results achieved in fiscal 1982, was the strengthening of Comdisco's financial position. Total assets increased 33% to $536.7 million, while stockholders' equity increased 55% to $9.1 million. The announcement in early November 1982 of the redemption of the Company's $50 million convertible debentures is anticipated to increase stockholders' equity to approximately $140 million and will reduce the Company's interest expense by $6.5 million per year. In addition, the Company had nearly $40 million in cash and marketable securities at September 30, 1982 while borrowing under various revolving credit agreements was zero. Because of its improved financial position, Comdisco is ideally situated to capitalize on opportunities in its traditional marketplace as well as those that arise in other areas.

Comdisco (A)

In September 1982 Raymond F. Sebastian, formerly President of Comdisco Financial Services (CFS), was appointed to the position of Senior Vice President/ Corporate Development of Comdisco and will devote full time to the analysis of various investment opportunities available to the Company. He was replaced as President of CFS by Basil R. Twist, Jr. who, with Mr. Sebastian, has formulated the strategies that have made CFS so successful since its formation in 1976. Michael J. O'Connell has resigned as Executive Vice President of Comdisco effective January 1, 1983 to pursue other endeavors, but will continue as a Director. Mr. O'Connell has been with Comdisco since 1971 and has made valuable contributions to the Company's success.

In March 1982 Comdisco split its common stock 3-for-2 and paid dividends in fiscal 1982 totaling $.23 per share, an increase of 28% over the prior year, as adjusted. More importantly, return on average stockholders' equity has averaged 34.0% over the last five years. This has occurred over a period of time in which most of the Company's borrowings, other than discounted lease rentals, have been eliminated.

Comdisco begins fiscal 1983 in a strong capital position with high liquidity, a strong, competitive market position and a comprehensive array of complementary services for its customers. The Company provides leasing and other cost-effective services which continue to be attractive despite the current economic outlook. The delivery of more IBM 3081 processors will also increase opportunities for Comdisco in its marketplace.

Perhaps more so than many companies, Comdisco relies on the determination, skill and creative energies of its employees for its past and future success. This is another factor that gives me much optimism for Comdisco's continued success. With the ongoing dedication of Comdisco's employees and the support of the Company's customers and stockholders, I am confident that Comdisco's superior growth rates in earnings and revenue can be maintained.

Kenneth N. Pontikes
Chairman of the Board and
President

November 11, 1982

Management's Discussion and Analysis of Financial Condition and Result of Operations

Summary

The Company continued to achieve outstanding growth during fiscal 1982 as total revenue and net earnings increased 56% and 88%, respectively, compared to fiscal 1981. Increases in revenue and net earnings were accomplished despite the recessionary economic climate. Total revenue for fiscal 1982 and 1981 was $471.6 million and $301.5 million respectively. Net earnings increased from $15.6 million, or $1.35 a share, in fiscal 1981 to a record of $29.4 million, or $2.27 a share in fiscal 1982. The primary factors contributing to the record earnings were the increased volume and profitability of financial services activity, the growth of the Company's lease and customer base, and the ability of the Company to capitalize on the active market for 3033 processors and disk storage devices.

Revenue

Total revenue for fiscal 1982 reflected increases in all activities. In fiscal 1981, total revenue increased 19% over fiscal 1980 total revenue, as a result of higher revenue from all activities other than sale of computer equipment. For the five year period ended September 30, 1982, the Company has achieved an annual compound growth rate of 25% for total revenue.

The growth of the Company's lease base continued on a strong trend during fiscal 1982. This growth has been achieved as a result of the increased demand for leasing, broader penetration of the market, and the increase of activity levels created by initial product deliveries by IBM. Leasing offers computer users flexibility through short term commitments and conserves capital in a weak economy. As a result of this growth, rental revenue of $206.6 million in fiscal 1982 and $131.6 million in fiscal 1981 represented increases of 57% and 62%, respectively, over the preceding year.

Revenue from the sale of computer equipment increased during fiscal 1982 as a result of the active market for the IBM 3033 processor. The market for 3033 processors was stimulated by initial deliveries

Comdisco (A)

of IBM's 3081 processor and by the impact of IBM purchase price reductions on the 3033, which improved its price/performance ratio. Revenue from the sale of computer equipment declined 16% in fiscal 1981 compared to fiscal 1980, primarily due to computer users' increased preference for leasing.

Financial services revenue totaled $73.9 million in fiscal 1982 in comparison to $30.8 million in fiscal 1981. The increase in financial services revenue was primarily the result of tax-advantaged computer leasing transactions associated with a portion of the Company's lease portfolio of used equipment and also tax benefit transfers that were structured under the Economic Recovery Tax Act of 1981. Fiscal 1981 financial services revenue increased 119% over fiscal 1980 due to higher revenue from tax leveraged leases with third-party investors.

Cost and Expenses

Total costs and expenses of $417.8 million forfiscal 1982 increased 49% over total costs and expenses of $280.2 million in fiscal 1981. Fiscal 1981 total costs and expenses were 15% higher than fiscal 1980. The increases were the result of the growth in the Company's lease portfolio and customer base and the continuing expansion in marketing of the Company's services.

Selling, general and administrative expenses were $51.8 million in fiscal 1982, $28.5 million in fiscal 1981 and $19.3 million in fiscal 1980. The increases were primarily due to costs associated with the Company's expanding marketing activities, including higher commissions and administrative expenses.

The increases in interest expense in fiscal 1982 and fiscal 1981 were due to increased discounted lease rentals as a result of the growth in the Company's leasing activity. Interest expense on discounted leases, which is a non-cash expense, is the largest component of total interest expense (69% and 46% of total interest expense in fiscal 1982 and 1981, respectively). The Company finances leases by assigning the noncancellable rentals to financial institutions on a nonrecourse basis at a fixed interest rate and receives from the lender the present value of the rental payments (the discounted amount). As rental payments are made directly to the lender, the Company recognizes interest expense.

Income Taxes

Income taxes as a percentage of earnings before income taxes were 45.4% in fiscal 1982 compared to 26.8% in fiscal 1981 and 20.8% in fiscal 1980. Note 7 of Notes to Consolidated Financial Statements provides details about the Company's income tax provisions and effective tax rates. The higher effective tax rate in fiscal 1982 was attributable to lower investment tax credits due to the sale of such benefits by the Company as permitted under the Economic Recovery Tax Act of 1981 (the "Act"). The Act liberalized the leasing provisions of the tax law and made it possible for corporations which cannot use all their current year tax deductions and credits to transfer them to other corporations. The tax benefit transfers completed by the Company in fiscal 1982 provided cash flow benefits which otherwise would not have been available until future years.

International Operations

The Company operated principally in three geographic areas during fiscal 1982 and 1981; United States, Europe and Canada. The Company has subsidiaries in Belgium, Germany, Switzerland, the Netherlands, France, the United Kingdom and Canada. These subsidiaries offer services similar to those offered in the United States.

A more favorable environment in fiscal 1982 resulted in an increase in revenue from international operations of 42% from $55.9 million in fiscal 1981 to $79.6 million in fiscal 1982. The prior year's results had been depressed as a result of computer users deferring action pending shipment of new products. International revenues represented 17% of the Company's total revenue in fiscal 1982, and 18% in fiscal 1981.

Market and Dividend Information

The Company's common stock is traded on the New York Stock Exchange under the symbol CDO. The following table shows the quarterly price range and dividends paid for fiscal years 1982 and 1981, adjusted to reflect the three-for-two and five-for-four common stock splits effected in March 1982 and 1981, respectively.

Qtr.	1982 High	1982 Low	1982 Div.	1981 High	1981 Low	1981 Div.
1st	$18.00	$11.75	$.05	$13.27	$ 7.87	$.04
2nd	18.00	13.50	.06	15.50	11.50	.05
3rd	19.25	15.50	.06	16.09	13.17	.05
4th	23.00	15.00	.06	15.33	10.67	.05

At September 30, 1982, there were approximately 2,900 record holders of common stock.

Financial Position

During fiscal 1982, the Company's financial position and liquidity improved significantly, with cash and marketable securities amounting to $39.8 million at September 30, 1982 compared to $9.8 million at September 30, 1981. These improvements were due to an increased earnings level and continued emphasis on effective asset management. Major sources and uses of funds are set forth in the Consolidated Statements of Changes in Financial Position.

At September 30, 1982, the Company had $45 million of available borrowing capacity under various lines of credit from commercial banks. During fiscal 1982, the Company entered into agreements for the purpose of issuing commercial paper which may be used from time to time to meet some of the Company's short term debt requirements. These facilities ensure the availability of significant funds to finance additional growth.

The trend of computer users toward leasing rather than purchasing computer equipment is expected to continue due to economic conditions, IBM pricing policies, and new product announcements. The major portion of funds required by the Company to finance the purchase of equipment acquired for leasing is generated by assigning the noncancelable rentals to various financial institutions at fixed interest rates on a nonrecourse basis.

In June 1981, the Company sold $50 million of 13% convertible subordinated debentures. The proceeds of the lower cost, fixed-rate long term debt were used to replace bank borrowings. The Company had no short term debt at September 30, 1982.

Total notes and debentures as a percentage of total capital (the sum of notes and debentures payable, discounted lease rentals and stockholders' equity)

has declined in each of the last three fiscal years, to 16% at September 30, 1982, compared to 29% at September 30, 1980. Improved earnings have contributed to the high returns on average stockholders' equity. This key financial measure of performance reached 39.2% in fiscal 1982, compared with 30.6% in fiscal 1981. The Company's strong financial position and history of earnings growth provide a solid base for obtaining the necessary financial resources to finance additional growth and for investment opportunities.

Ratios

The following table presents ratios which illustrate the changes and trends for the last three fiscal years:

	1982	1981	1980
Return on average stockholders' equity	39.2%	30.6%	18.0%
Return on average assets	6.2%	4.9%	3.5%
Earnings before income taxes (as a percentage of revenue)	11.4%	7.1%	3.5%
Net earnings (as a percentage of revenue)	6.2%	5.2%	2.8%

Comdisco (A)

Comdisco (A)

CONSOLIDATED FINANCIAL STATEMENTS

FIVE YEAR SELECTED FINANCIAL DATA

Years Ended September 30,	1982	1981	1980	1979	1978
Consolidated Summary of Earnings (in thousands):					
Revenue					
Rental	$206,592	$131,571	$ 80,979	$ 60,947	$ 42,524
Sale of computer equipment	166,705	125,384	149,708	149,983	103,995
Financial services	73,879	30,837	14,079	9,991	4,046
Other	24,454	13,746	8,348	4,355	2,717
Total Revenue	471,630	301,538	253,114	225,276	153,282
Cost and expenses					
Equipment depreciation, amortization and rental	160,523	99,413	68,328	47,698	32,260
Cost of computer equipment	149,654	111,784	134,595	128,470	93,176
Financial services	8,617	6,784	4,878	5,108	1,768
Selling, general and administrative	51,785	28,529	19,341	16,176	9,246
Interest	47,242	33,657	16,988	13,319	10,360
Total cost and expenses	417,821	280,167	244,130	210,771	146,810
Earnings before income taxes	53,809	21,371	8,984	14,505	6,472
Income taxes	24,432	5,730	1,870	3,900	1,550
Net earnings	$ 29,377	$ 15,641	$ 7,114	$ 10,605	$ 4,922
Common and Common Equivalent Share Data:					
Net earnings	$ 2.27	$ 1.35	$ .65	$ 1.07	$ .53
Stockholders' equity	$ 7.74	$ 5.17	$ 3.95	$ 3.50	$ 1.77
Average shares outstanding (in thousands)	14,487	12,270	11,051	9,929	9,222
Cash dividends paid	$ .23	$ .18	$ .15	$ .12	$ .06
Financial Position (in thousands):					
Total assets	$536,679	$404,507	$229,170	$173,950	$144,223
Total long-term debt	83,271	84,945	29,055	25,573	25,447
Discounted lease rentals	261,780	197,672	85,612	74,569	61,703
Stockholders' equity	91,056	58,746	43,565	35,508	14,994

Common and common equivalent share data have been adjusted to reflect a three-for-two stock split effected in February 1978, a two-for-one common stock split effected July 1978, a three-for-two common stock split effected in February 1979, a five-for-four common stock split effected in March 1981, and a three-for-two common stock split effected in March 1982.

CONSOLIDATED BALANCE SHEETS
(in thousands except number of shares)

September 30,	1982	1981
ASSETS		
Cash and marketable securities (at cost of $3,909 in 1982 and $1,883 in 1981 which approximates market)	$ 39,762	$ 9,848
Receivables:		
Accounts and notes (Net of allowance for doubtful accounts of $628 in 1982 and $528 in 1981)	41,368	28,379
Other	3,687	3,827
Inventory of computer equipment	35,382	25,036
Net investment in sales-type and direct financing leases	23,682	17,890
Leased and other equipment:		
Leased computer equipment	502,494	374,044
Capitalized leases—computer equipment	24,158	23,225
Buildings, furniture and other	7,959	4,184
Total equipment	534,611	401,453
Less: accumulated depreciation and amortization	192,714	115,073
Net equipment	341,897	286,380
Other assets and deferred charges	50,901	33,147
	$536,679	$404,507
LIABILITIES AND STOCKHOLDERS' EQUITY		
Note payable to bank	$ 2,385	$ 3,445
Convertible subordinated debentures	50,000	50,000
Subordinated debentures	12,250	12,250
Accounts payable	19,110	27,492
Obligations under capital leases	18,636	19,250
Income taxes:		
Current	6,076	—
Deferred	30,121	13,017
Other liabilities	45,265	22,635
Discounted lease rentals	261,780	197,672
	445,623	345,761
Stockholders' equity:		
Common stock $.10 par value. Authorized 50,000,000 shares in 1982 and 15,000,000 shares in 1981; issued 11,769,043 shares (7,571,151 in 1981)	1,177	757
Additional paid-in capital	18,965	14,630
Deferred translation adjustment	(354)	—
Retained earnings	71,268	43,359
Total stockholders' equity	91,056	58,746
	$536,679	$404,507

See accompanying notes to consolidated financial statements.

Comdisco (A)

Comdisco (A)

CONSOLIDATED STATEMENTS OF EARNINGS
(in thousands except per share data)

Years Ended September 30,	1982	1981	1980
Revenue			
Rental	$206,592	$131,571	$ 80,979
Sale of computer equipment	166,705	125,384	149,708
Financial services	73,879	30,837	14,079
Other	24,454	13,746	8,348
Total revenue	471,630	301,538	253,114
Cost and Expenses			
Equipment depreciation, amortization and rental	160,523	99,413	68,328
Cost of computer equipment	149,654	111,784	134,595
Financial services	8,617	6,784	4,878
Selling, general and administrative	51,785	28,529	19,341
Interest	47,242	33,657	16,988
Total costs and expenses	417,821	280,167	244,130
Earnings before income taxes	53,809	21,371	8,984
Income taxes	24,432	5,730	1,870
Net Earnings	$ 29,377	$ 15,641	$ 7,114
Net Earnings Per Common and Common Equivalent Share	$ 2.27	$ 1.35	$ .65

See accompanying notes to consolidated financial statements.

CONSOLIDATED STATEMENTS OF STOCKHOLDERS' EQUITY
(in thousands)

Years Ended September 30, 1982, 1981 and 1980

	Common Stock $.10 Par Palue	Additional Paid-in Capital	Retained Earnings	Deferred Translation Adjustment
Balance at September 30, 1979	$ 541	$12,405	$22,56	$ —
Net earnings	—	—	7,114	—
Dividends paid	—	—	(865)	—
Stock options exercised	46	639	—	—
Income tax benefits resulting from exercise of non-qualified stock options	—	1,123	—	—
Balance at September 30, 1980	587	14,167	28,811	—
Net earnings	—	—	15,641	—
Dividends paid	—	—	(1,093)	—
Stock split	148	(148)	—	—
Stock options exercised	22	611	—	—
Balance at September 30, 1981	757	14,630	43,359	—
Cumulative amount as of September 30, 1981	—	—	—	(232)
Net earnings	—	—	29,377	—
Dividends paid	—	—	(1,468)	—
Stock split	391	(400)	—	—
Stock options exercised	14	835	—	—
Common stock issued	15	2,648	—	—
Translation adjustment	—	—	—	(122)
Income tax benefits resulting from exercise of non-qualified stock options	—	1,252	—	—
Balance at September 30, 1982	$1,177	$18,965	$71,26	$(354)

See accompanying notes to consolidated financial statements.

Comdisco (A)

CONSOLIDATED STATEMENTS OF CHANGES IN FINANCIAL POSITION
(in thousands)

Years Ended September 30,	1982	1981	1980
Source of Funds:			
From operations			
Net earnings	$ 29,377	$ 15,641	$ 7,114
Noncash charges (credits) to operations:			
Depreciation and amortization	133,902	77,528	46,212
Increase in receivables	(12,849)	(5,531)	(12,278)
Investment in sales-type and direct financing leases	(5,792)	(11,732)	323
Income taxes	23,180	5,730	747
Increase in accounts payable and accrued liabilities	14,248	18,611	11,322
Other, net	474	(1,233)	2,490
Total provided from operations	182,540	99,014	55,930
Proceeds from issuance of subordinated debentures	—	48,560	—
Increase (decrease) in notes payable	(1,060)	(33,460)	25,339
Obligations under capital leases	5,663	14,249	2,885
Discounted lease rentals	145,626	183,557	62,786
Other	4,201	924	766
	336,970	312,844	147,706
Application of Funds:			
Increase in leased equipment and inventory	190,180	202,002	75,361
Reduction of discounted lease rentals and obligations under capital leases	87,795	75,781	55,916
Purchase of subordinated debentures	—	2,162	—
Capitalized leases—computer equipment	5,663	14,249	2,885
Other assets and deferred charges	21,950	12,343	13,555
Cash dividends	1,468	1,093	865
	307,056	307,630	148,582
Increase (decrease) in cash and marketable securities	29,914	5,214	(876)
Cash and marketable securities at beginning of year	9,848	4,634	5,510
Cash and marketable securities at end of year	$ 39,762	$ 9,848	$ 4,634

See accompanying notes to consolidated financial statements.

Comdisco (A)

NOTES TO CONSOLIDATED FINANCIAL STATEMENTS

1. Summary of Significant Accounting Policies

Principles of Consolidation: The accompanying consolidated financial statements include the accounts of the Company and its wholly-owned subsidiaries after elimination of intercompany accounts and transactions.

Revenue Recognition: Leases are accounted for either as sales-type, direct financing or operating leases. Lease terms generally range from four months to five years. Revenue from sales-type leases is recorded upon acceptance of the equipment by the customer and is reflected as sale of computer equipment. Revenue from direct financing leases is recorded over the term of the lease as interest income calculated using the interest method. Rental revenue from operating leases is recognized in equal monthly amounts over the term of the lease.

Revenue from the sale of computer equipment and the related cost of equipment is reflected in earnings at the time of acceptance of the equipment by the customer.

Revenue from the sale of equipment subject to operating leases is recognized at the closing of the transactions and is included as sale of computer equipment in fiscal 1981 and 1980. In addition to this revenue, the Company is also entitled to the use of such equipment subsequent to the lease expiration date for periods ranging generally from six months to four years. Revenue, if any, from the re-leasing of such equipment during this period is recognized upon acceptance of the equipment by the customer and is reflected as other revenue.

Under the provisions of the Economic Recovery Tax Act of 1981, the Company sold the tax benefits (investment tax credits and cost recovery allowances) on new equipment purchased for the Company's lease portfolio. The proceeds from the sale of tax benefits are recorded as financial services revenue. Also included as financial services revenue are fees for arranging tax benefit transfer agreements with third parties.

Fees from the sale of equipment included in the Company's lease portfolio of used equipment are recognized at the closing of the transactions and included as financial services revenue. Such transactions, which are structured as tax advantaged leases, entitle the Company to the use of such equipment for periods ranging generally from one to six years subsequent to the initial lease expiration date.

The Company, through its CFS subsidiary, has entered into certain computer equipment transactions in which it has leased equipment (the "Lease") and in turn has subleased such equipment (the "Sublease"). In substantially all of these transactions, the Lease term exceeds the Sublease term. Monthly Sublease rentals are greater than the monthly Lease rentals; however, the present value of the total Sublease rentals ("Sublease Proceeds") may be less than the present value of the total Lease rentals ("Lease Obligations") due to the difference in lease terms. Rentals from the sublease are discounted by the Company with a financial institution on a nonrecourse basis. An escrow account is established to fund the Company's obligations under the lease for the period after the expiration of the Sublease. In the event the Sublease Proceeds exceed the Lease Obligations, the Company recognizes profit. When Lease Obligations exceed the Sublease Proceeds, no profit is recognized and the next excess Lease Obligation is deferred to be recovered from the Company's right to future rentals during the remaining term of the Lease. At September 30, 1982 and 1981, $21,258,000 and $10,148,000, respectively, of costs were deferred in connection with such transactions and are included in the balance sheet caption "Other assets and deferred charges." The Company recognized $3,113,000, $4,286,000, and $1,890,000 of interest income on investments held in escrow during the years ended September 30, 1982, 1981 and 1980, respectively.

Inventory of Computer Equipment: Inventory of computer equipment is stated at the lower of cost or market.

Equipment, Depreciation and Amortization: Leased equipment owned by the Company is generally recorded at cost. Depreciation and amortization of leased equipment are computed on the straight-line method for financial reporting purposes to estimated fair market value at lease termination (See Note 2).

Comdisco (A)

Deferred Lease Costs: Salesmen's commissions and other direct expenses related to operating leases are deferred and amortized over the lease term.

Income Taxes and Investment Tax Credits: Deferred income taxes have been provided for income and expenses which are recognized in different periods for income tax purpose than for financial reporting purposes. Investment tax credits are accounted for on a flow-through basis.

Profit Sharing Plan: The Company has a profit sharing plan covering all employees. Company contributions to the plan are based on a percentage of employees' compensation, as defined. Profit sharing payments are based on amounts accumulated on an individual employees basis. Profit sharing expense for the years ended September 30, 1982, 1981 and 1980 amounted to $590,000, $489,000 and $178,000, respectively.

Earnings Per Share: Earnings per common and common equivalent share are computed based on the weighted average number of common and common equivalent shares outstanding during each period including the assumed conversion of the 13% convertible subordinated debentures, after elimination of the related interest expense (net of tax) and after giving retroactive effect to the three-for-two split effected in March 1982 (See Note 9). Dilutive stock options included in the number of common and common equivalent shares are based on the treasury stock method. The number of common and common equivalent shares used in the computation of earnings per share for the years ended September 30, 1982, 1981 and 1980 were 14,486,738, 12,269,703 and 11,050,277, respectively.

Foreign Currency Translation: Fiscal 1982 consolidated financial statements have been prepared in accordance with Financial Accounting Standards Board Statement No. 52, "Foreign Currency Translation," the provisions of which were adopted by the Company on a prospective basis as of October 1, 1981. Previous consolidated financial statements have been prepared in accordance with Statement No. 8, "Accounting for the Translation of Foreign Currency Transactions and Foreign Currency Financial Statements." The effect of the change was not material.

2. Depreciable Lives

Effective October 1, 1980 the Company extended its estimates of depreciable lives of certain IBM peripheral equipment. Effective January 1, 1981 the Company extended its estimates of depreciable lives and salvage values of certain IBM peripheral equipment. Previously, this equipment was depreciated to zero by September 30, 1983. The changes in estimates were made based on revised market conditions and reflect current estimates of the equipment's useful lives and salvage values. The effect of the changes on recorded leased equipment at the effective dates of the changes was an increase in net earnings of $4,488,000 (net of income taxes of $4,142,000), or $.37 per share, for the year ended September 30, 1981.

3. Investment in Sales-Type and Direct Financing Leases

The following table lists the components of the net investment in sales-type and direct financing leases as of September 30:

	1982	1981
	(in thousands)	
Minimum lease payments receivable	$24,142	$18,504
Estimated residual values of leased property	12,324	9,160
Less unearned income	12,784	9,774
Net investment in sales-type and direct financing leases	$23,682	$17,890

Future minimum lease payments to be received under the above lease agreements are as follows:

Years ending September 30	Sales-type and direct financing leases
	(in thousands)
1983	$ 7,306
1984	7,416
1985	5,534
1986	2,637
1987	1,249
	$24,142

The Company finances most sales-type and direct financing leases by assigning the non-cancellable rentals on a non-recourse basis. The proceeds from the assignment reduce the investment in sales-type and direct financing leases. Any gain or loss on the assignment is recognized at the time of such assignment.

4. Capitalized Leases

Capitalized leases – computer equipment at September 30 is comprised of the following:

	1982	1981
	(in thousands)	
Capitalized leases – computer equipment	$24,158	$23,225
Less accumulated amortization	15,354	12,099
Net capitalized leases – computer equipment	$ 8,804	$11,126

At September 30, 1982, the Company, as lessee, was obligated to pay rentals under capitalized leases. The related equipment has been subleased and accounted for either as operating leases or as direct financing leases. The following table summarizes minimum rentals payable by the Company as lessee under capitalized leases:

Years ending September 30	Capitalized leases
	(in thousands)
1983	$ 8,196
1984	6,987
1985	4,801
1986	2,618
1987	1,810
Later years	521
Total minimum lease payments	24,933
Less imputed interest (9% to 17%)	6,297
Present value of net mimum lease payments	$18,636

Total minimum lease payments for capitalized leases have not been reduced by minimum non-cancelable sublease rentals of $16,094,000 due the Company in the future.

5. Bank Borrowings and Compensating Balances

The Company has a revolving credit agreement which entitles the Company to borrow up to $25,000,000 on an unsecured basis. The agreement, which expires March 31, 1983, carries an interest cost of prime rate (13.5% at September 30, 1982) and includes a fee of 3/8% per annum of the average daily unused amount. If the Company or the bank elects not to renew the agreement, the loan becomes a two-year term loan payable in equal quarterly installments with an interest cost of prime rate plus 1%. Under the agreement, the Company is required to maintain a defined debt to net worth ratio and dividend payments cannot exceed 20% of consolidated net earnings subsequent to September 30, 1980. At September 30, 1982, approximately $4,280,000 of retained earnings were available for payment of dividends.

In accordance with the terms of the agreement, the Company is required to maintain average cash balances with the bank equal to 5% of the $25,000,000 loan commitment. The amount of unused available borrowings under the agreement was $25,000,000 at September 30, 1982.

At September 30, 1982, the Company had additional unused lines of credit totaling $20,000,000 under which borrowings would bear interest at the prime rate. Under the agreements, the Company is required to maintain compensating balances equal to 5% of the outstanding borrowings.

6. Note Payable to Bank and Subordinated Debentures

Note Payable to Bank: The note payable to bank at September 30, 1982 and 1981 was an 11¾% term note payable in quarterly installments through December, 1984.

13% Convertible Subordinated Debentures: In June 1981, the Company issued $50,000,000 of 13% convertible subordinated debentures ("Convertible Debentures") due in 2001. Issue costs of $1,440,000 relating to the Convertible Debenture may be converted into shares of common stock of the Company, prior to maturity, at the option of the convertible Debenture holder at a conversion price of $19.50 per share.

The Convertible Debentures are redeemable in full or in part at the option of the company beginning in 1981 at an amount equal to 113.0% of the principal amount of the Convertible Debentures, the premium on redemption declining 1.3% per annum com-

Comdisco (A)

mencing in 1982 through 1991, and redeemable thereafter at par.

11½% Subordinated Debentures: At September 30, 1982, $12,250,000 of 11½% subordinated debentures (the "Debentures") due December 1, 1992, were outstanding. Annual sinking fund payments of $1,350,000 (9% of the aggregate original principal amount) commence December 1, 1982, and are calculated to retire 90% of the issue prior to maturity. During fiscal 1981, the Company, in connection with future sinking fund requirements, acquired $2,750,000 principal amount of the outstanding debentures which resulted in a gain of $318,000 (net of income taxes of $270,000).

Both the Debentures and the Convertible Debentures are subordinated to all senior indebtedness as defined in the indenture agreements. At September 30, 1982, the Company's senior indebtedness was approximately $2,473,000.

The annual maturities and sinking fund requirements of the note payable and subordinated debentures for the next five years are as follows:

Years ending September 30	Aggregate Maturities
	(in thousands)
1983	$1,060
1984	1,060
1985	1,565
1986	1,350
1987	1,350

7. Income Taxes

The following data relate to the provision for income taxes for the years ended September 30:

	1982	1981	1980
Provision in lieu of income taxes	$1,252	—	$1,123
Current:			
Federal	5,000	—	—
State	1,076	—	—
	6,076	—	—
Deferred:			
Federal	16,281	4,216	147
State	273	553	220
Foreign	550	961	380
	17,104	5,730	747
Total tax provision	$24,432	$5,730	$1,870

	1982	1981	1980
Earnings before income taxes:			
Domestic	$51,166	$18,992	$8,203
Foreign	2,643	2,379	781
Total	$53,809	$21,371	$8,984

Income tax benefits of $1,252,000 and $1,123,000 resulting from the exercise of non-qualified stock options were utilized to reduce the current Federal tax provision in fiscal 1982 and 1980, respectively.

The reasons for the difference between the U.S. Federal income tax rate of 46% and the effective income tax rate were as follows:

	Percentage of Pretax Earnings		
Years ended September 30,	1982	1981	1980
U.S. Federal income tax	46.0%	46.0%	46.0%
Increase (reduction) resulting from:			
Domestic International Sales Corporation tax benefit	(.1)	(1.2)	(6.8)
Reduction of deferred income taxes applicable to investment tax credit carryforward	—	(20.4)	(20.1)
Investment tax credit	(2.0)	—	—
State income taxes, net of U.S. tax benefit	1.4	1.2	1.1
Other – net	.1	1.2	.6
	45.4%	26.8%	20.8%

The Company has not provided for income taxes on the unremitted earnings of the Domestic International Sales Corporation (DISC) subsidiary aggregating $4,253,000 through September 30, 1982, since the Company intends to postpone indefinitely the remittance of such earnings.

Deferred income taxes provided for timing differences were as follows:

Years ended September 30,	1982	1981	1980
	(in thousands)		
Sale of tax benefits	$38,661	—	—
Difference between depreciation for tax purposes and financial statement purposes	(18,125)	6,311	570
Deferred compensation expense	754	(754)	—
Deferred leasing income	2,934	(2,093)	—
Deferred leasing costs	1,518	1,164	793
Portion of undistributed earnings in DISC	(178)	(454)	231

Years ended September 30,	1982	1981	1980
Difference between leases accounted for as sales-type leases for financial statement purposes and operating leases for tax purposes	(23,601)	194	2,915
Reinstatement (reduction) of deferred income taxes applicable to:			
Investment tax credit carryforward	12,021	(4,356)	(1,803)
Tax net operating loss realization (carryforward)	—	2,323	(650)
Income tax benefit resulting from exercise of non-qualified stock options	—	1,903	(1,123)
Other – net	3,120	1,492	(186)
	$17,104	$5,730	$747

8. Discounted Lease Rentals

Leased equipment owned by the Company is financed by assigning the noncancellable rentals to various lenders at fixed interest rates on a nonrecourse basis. The proceeds from the assignment of the lease rentals (discounted lease rentals) represent payments due under the lease discounted to their present value at the interest rate charged by the lender, generally ranging from 10% to 19%. The difference between monthly rentals due under discounted leases and the amortization of related discounted lease rentals represents interest expense. This expense amounted to $32,527,000, $15,468,000 and $8,380,000 in 1982, 1981 and 1980, respectively. In the event of default by the lessee, the lender has a first lien against the underlying leased equipment, with no further recourse against the Company.

9. Common Stock and Additional Paid-in Capital

On January 27, 1982, the Board of Directors declared a three-for-two split of the Company's common stock. This distribution was subject to the stockholders approval, which was obtained, amending the Certificate of Incorporation increasing the number of authorized shares from 15,000,000 to 50,000,000 with the par value remaining at $.10

per share. On January 28, 1981, the Board of Directors of the Company declared a five-for-four split of the Company's common stock. All references in the financial statements and notes to the number of shares of common stock and per share amounts have been adjusted for the aforementioned stock splits.

On November 18, 1981, the Board of Directors approved the Settlement Agreement (the "Agreement") between the Company and participants in the Residual Incentive Compensation Plan (the "Plan") related to vested residual computer interests. The Plan provided in part for the allocation of a percentage interest in the residual value of computer equipment to the participants. The Agreement was approved by the stockholders on March 15, 1982, and pursuant to the terms of the Agreement, the Company distributed to participants in accordance with the terms of the Plan, the aggregate sum of $3,000,000 plus 150,000 shares of the Company's common stock.

Dividends on Common Stock: Common stock dividends paid were $.23 per share in 1982 compared with $.18 in 1981 and $.15 in 1980. Certain officers and directors of the Company and their affiliates, owning an aggregate of 5,028,645 shares (43%) of the outstanding common stock at September 30, 1982, have waived their rights to any cash dividends through February 1, 1983 and did not receive any of the previously mentioned cash dividends.

At September 30, 1982, the Company had reserved the following number of common shares for future issuance:

1979 Stock Option Plan	334,438
1981 Stock Option Plan	750,000
Employee Stock Purchase Plan	147,358
Conversion of Convertible Subordinated Debentures	2,564,103
	3,795,899

10. Stock Options and Stock Purchase Plan

On November 18, 1981, the Board of Directors amended the Company's 1979 Stock Option Plan (the "1979 Plan") to qualify the plan as an incentive stock option plan in accordance with the provisions

Comdisco (A)

of the Economic Recovery Tax Act of 1981. All outstanding stock options, which retained their original option price, are eligible for treatment as incentive stock options subject to certain limitations as defined in the amended 1979 Plan.

On January 27, 1982, the stockholders approved the 1981 Stock Option Plan (the "1981 Plan"). An aggregate of 750,000 shares were reserved for issuance pursuant to the exercise of options under the 1981 plan.

The Comdisco, Inc. Employee Stock Purchase Plan (the "Stock Plan") was adopted by the Board of Directors on November 17, 1981. An aggregate of 150,000 shares was reserved for issuance under the Stock Plan.

The changes in the number of shares under the option plans during 1982, 1981 and 1980 were as follows:

	1982	1981	1980
	(in thousands except option price range)		
Number of shares:			
Shares under option beginning of the year	512	861	1,119
Options granted	169	—	612
Options exercised	(188)	(349)	(870)
Shares under option end of year	493	512	861
Aggregate option price:			
Shares under option beginning of year	$2,533	$3,257	$480
Options granted	3,284	—	3,187
Options exercised	(850)	(724)	(410)
Shares under option end of the year	$4,967	$2,533	$3,257
Options exercisable at end of year	58	164	12
Aggregate option price of exercisable options outstanding at end of year	$295	$722	$19
Options available for future grant at end of year	591	11	11
Option price range	$4.90–$19.38	$1.35–$7.00	$.12–$7.00

11. Operating Leases

The following table summarizes the Company's future rentals receivable and payable under non-cancellable operating leases existing at September 30, 1982 for computer equipment and rentals payable for non-computer equipment and office space:

Years ending Sept. 30	Computer equipment		Rents payable on subleased equipment	Other rents payable
	Rents Receivable on Equipment			
	Owned	Subleased		
1983	$180,581	$21,704	$25,497	$2,033
1984	107,125	13,269	12,197	1,735
1985	43,115	5,799	5,002	1,600
1986	7,237	1,742	792	1,033
1987	352	544	—	233
Later years	11	—	—	77

Total rental income and related expense for the years ended September 30, 1982, 1981 and 1980 applicable to computer sublease activities are as follows:

Years ending September 30	Rental income	Rental expense
	(in thousands)	
1982	$23,633	$27,455
1981	24,152	22,415
1980	22,614	22,455

12. Commitments and Contingent Liabilities

At September 30, 1982, the Company was obligated under the following commitments: (1) to purchase computer equipment in the approximate aggregate amount of $31,768,000, (2) to sell computer equipment in the approximate aggregate amount of $20,926,000, and (3) to lease computer equipment to others with an aggregate initial term rental of approximately $55,107,000.

The Company has arranged for approximately $74,000,000 of letters of credit, primarily as guarantees for certain of the Company's sublease obligations and for future purchases of IBM equipment. The cost of such letters of credit range between ½% and ¾% per annum of the amount outstanding.

Accountants' Report

The Stockholders and Board of Directors Comdisco, Inc.:

We have examined the consolidated balance sheets of Comdisco, Inc. and subsidiaries as of September 30, 1982 and 1981 and the related consolidated statements of earnings, stockholders' equity and changes in financial position for each of the years in the three year period ended September 30, 1982. Our examinations were made in accordance with generally accepted auditing standards and, accordingly, included such tests of the accounting records and such other auditing procedures as we considered necessary in the circumstance.

In our opinion, the aforementioned consolidated financial statements present fairly the financial position of Comdisco, Inc. and subsidiaries at September 30, 1982 and 1981 and the results of their operations and the changes in their financial position for each of the years in the three-year period ended September 30, 1982, in conformity with generally accepted accounting principles applied on a consistent basis.

Peat, Marwick, Mitchell & Co.
Chicago, Illinois
November 9, 1982

Quarterly Financial Data

Summarized Quarterly Financial data for the fiscal years ended September 30, 1982 and 1981, is as follows:

(in thousands of dollars except per share amounts)

Quarter ended:	December 31		March 31		June 30		September 30	
	1981	1980	1982	1981	1982	1981	1982	1981
Total revenue	$121,189	$78,833	$118,309	$64,450	$94,691	$75,722	$137,441	$82,533
Net earnings	9,604	3,285	5,934	3,146	5,824	4,075	8,015	5,135
Net earnings per common and common equivalent share	$.73	$.29	$.47	$.27	$.46	$.35	$.61	$.42

Comdisco (A)

A *published report implying that the accounting practices of computer leasing giant Comdisco, Inc. could result in overstated earnings has provoked strong rebuttals from the leasing industry while rattling the skeleton of the OPM Leasing Services, Inc. scandal.*

The report appeared last week in Barron's financial weekly and suggested that internal and external forces are mixing to create a potential disaster scenario for Comdisco as well as other third-party lessors. Meanwhile, the report stated, company officers, including founder and chairman Kenneth Pontikes, have gone on a Comdisco stock-selling spree in the past two years, getting rich in the process.

After publication of the report, Comdisco's stock lost nearly 37% of its paper value in one frenzied day of trading last Monday, falling from $38 to $24 per share.[1]

The October 17, 1983 issue of *Computerworld* magazine carried the above report on Comdisco, Inc.

BUSINESS HISTORY AND OPERATIONS[2]

Comdisco, Inc. is a Chicago-based company founded in 1969 by its current chairman of the board and president, Kenneth Pontikes. The company originally began as an IBM computer dealer. As demand for computer leasing started to grow during the late 1970s, the company started emphasizing leasing operations. By 1982, leasing old and new IBM computer equipment constituted the primary business activity of the company, and Comdisco had become the largest computer leasing company. Comdisco's customers were primarily large corporations. In 1982, the company had business relationships with 70 percent of the Fortune 500 companies, including 49 of the 50 largest U.S. companies.

This case was prepared by Professor Krishna G. Palepu as the basis for class discussion rather than to illustrate either effective or ineffective handling of an administrative situation. Copyright © 1987 by the President and Fellows of Harvard College. Harvard Business School case 9-187-119.

1. Reprinted with permission from Computerworld, October 17, 1983
2. This section and the next, Tax Advantaged Transactions, can be skipped by those who read Comdisco, Inc. (A) (case 9-186-299).

The computer remarketing industry had many participants: small independent operators, larger private organizations, and leasing subsidiaries of conglomerates. Comdisco was one of the few independent public corporations in the industry. The firms in the industry were primarily of two types: broker/dealers or third-party lessors. The broker/dealers obtained for customers computer equipment from either a vendor or current user; third-party lessors provided lease financing. Comdisco engaged in both these activities.

Comdisco achieved its dominance in the computer leasing industry through a strategy of full-service leasing. Under this strategy, the company offered its customers a number of services which were not offered by competitors. Comdisco's subsidiaries, Comdisco Technical Services, Inc. and Comdisco Transport, Inc., specialized in equipment refurbishment, delivery, installation, de-installation, and technical planning and site preparation. Comdisco Maintenance Services, another subsidiary, offered a low-cost alternative to IBM's maintenance service. Comdisco Disaster Recovery Services, Inc. was established to provide another valuable service to the company's customers: contingent data processing capacity to be used when a customer's own data center had unavoidable failures. Through this service, Comdisco's customers had access to four fully operational data centers located as a backup to their own data centers, to be used in the event of a natural disaster or accident.

Comdisco's broad customer base provided the company with a number of competitive advantages. First, taking advantage of its access to 10,000 important users of IBM equipment in the U.S., the company created a proprietary data base of their computing needs. This data base provided Comdisco's sales force with current and timely information on potential customers and their requirements. Second, being the leading IBM dealer, Comdisco maintained large inventories of a broad range of IBM equipment. Comdisco's personnel closely monitored IBM's new products and pricing policies. This product knowledge combined with large inventories enabled the company to assist customers with their computer acquisition plans and to offer quick deliveries. Finally, using its data base, the company could help its customers sell their old hardware when they acquired new equipment from Comdisco.

While the above strategy enabled Comdisco to establish its dominance over others in the computer leasing industry, the company was still potentially vulnerable to competition from IBM itself since IBM equipment accounted for most of Comdisco's revenues. In 1981, IBM formed a financing subsidiary, IBM Credit Corporation, to provide customer financing. Shortly after than, IBM announced its intention to enter into computer leasing and established a joint venture for this purpose with Merrill Lynch and Metropolitan Life Insurance. A number of industry analysts felt that this might result in increased competition for companies like Comdisco.

Comdisco's management, however, felt that IBM's recent moves did not pose a threat to the company's competitive position because IBM's entry into leasing would enhance the tarnished image of the computer leasing business, a net benefit to the industry. They also believed that, as IBM began to emphasize outright sale of its equipment over short-term rentals, many of IBM's customers might be forced to look for other lessors like

Comdisco who offered short-term leases. This was likely to provide additional business opportunities which would offset any loss of long-term lease business to IBM.

While equipment leasing to computer users was Comdisco's primary activity, the company also offered tax-oriented leases to investors who were primarily interested in the tax benefits associated with leasing. In recent years, the financial services income from the tax advantaged transactions accounted for a growing portion of the company's revenues.

TAX ADVANTAGED TRANSACTIONS

In addition to leasing equipment to computer users, Comdisco undertook leasing transactions with investors who were interested in tax shelters. While the specific terms and conditions of these tax advantaged transactions varied, a typical transaction was as follows:

1. After the inception of the initial user lease and independent of it, Comdisco sold all the leased equipment to a third party investor. This sale usually occurred three to nine months after the commencement of the initial user lease. The sales price equaled the then current fair market value of the equipment. The payment from the investor to Comdisco consisted of: (a) cash and a negotiable interest-bearing promissory note due within two years for 10–22 percent of the sales price (the "equity payment") and (b) an installment note for the balance payable over an 84-month period.

2. Simultaneously with the sale, Comdisco leased the equipment back from the investors for 84 months. The lease payments under the leaseback obligation were equal to the installment payments receivable by Comdisco from the investor (1.b).

3. As part of the leaseback arrangement, during the 61st through 84th months of the leaseback period, the investor shared in the re-lease proceeds that the company received from subleasing the equipment to a user. Upon the expiration of the leaseback period, the investor had the exclusive right to the equipment.

The net result of the above transaction was that Comdisco gave up the depreciation tax benefit, a portion of the rental revenues for months 61–84, and 100 percent of the equipment value after the 84th month. In return, the company received the nonrefundable equity payment (1.a).

If the equipment sold to the investor was originally under an operating lease, the equity payment was recorded by Comdisco as financial services revenue in the period in which the tax advantaged transaction occurred. From the fourth quarter of 1983, the company began to allocate as cost of financial services a portion of the net book value of the equipment at lease termination. For sales-type and direct financing leases, the equity payment was first applied to reduce a portion of the residual value of the equipment shown in the balance sheet (as investment in sales-type and direct financing leases). This is because the company's ability to recover the residual value was decreased due to the rental sharing under the tax advantaged transaction. The excess of the equity payment over the residual value reduction was recorded as financial services revenue in the period in which the tax advantaged transaction occurred.

THE BARRON'S ARTICLE

The October 10, 1983 issue of *Barron's,* a widely circulated financial weekly, carried an article on Comdisco, "Something Doesn't Compute: A Hard Look at Comdisco's Accounting." The article, excerpts from which are given in Exhibit 2, focused on four areas: the company's accounting, competition from IBM Credit Corporation, the company's tax advantaged leasing program, and the sale of company stock by insiders.

The article attracted considerable attention on Wall Street, leading to hectic trading of the company's stock. The company's stock price dropped from $38.250 to $22.875 by the end of the week, representing a loss of about $453.5 million in the market value of the company (see Exhibit 1 for data on Comdisco's stock price).

In response to these events, Kenneth Pontikes, president of Comdisco, issued a letter to shareholders on October 12, 1983. The letter addressed the issues raised in the *Barron's* article and attempted to rebut the charges (see Exhibit 3). Pontikes concluded:

> *[Finally,] it is important for you, our stockholders, to understand completely that Comdisco is stronger financially than it has ever been; that we have greater opportunities before us than at any time in our history; and that management is dedicated to retaining stockholder confidence and enhancing stockholder wealth.*

Shortly after the above developments, Comdisco released its annual report for fiscal 1983 (Exhibit 4).

QUESTIONS

1. Evaluate *Barron's* criticism of Comdisco's accounting and the company's response. Do you agree with the company or *Barron's*?
2. Compare the level of disclosure in Comdisco's annual reports in the (A) and (B) cases. Do you think the company's poor disclosure prior to 1983 made it vulnerable to the attack by *Barron's*? Would the market reaction to the *Barron's* article have been different if the company had a better disclosure policy?
3. Do you think Comdisco's stock in November 1983 was a "buy"?

EXHIBIT 1

Movement of Comdisco's Stock Price and S&P 500 Index, January 1982–November 1983

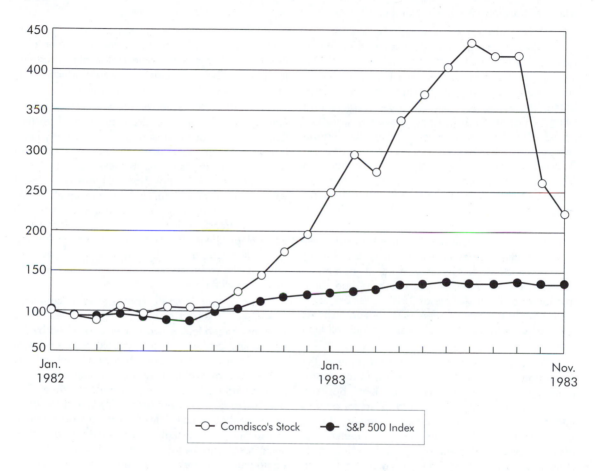

Comdisco (B)

EXHIBIT 2

"Something Doesn't Compute—A Hard Look at Comdisco Accounting Practices"[3]

Rhonda Brammer, *Barron's*, October 10, 1983

Twenty years ago, Ken Pontikes sold computer tapes and tab cards for IBM. He was paid $5,000 a year. When he lit out on his own five years later—starting up a one-man brokerage business in computers—his whole idea, he says "was to make a nice living." That start-up operation today is Chicago-based Comdisco, the biggest computer leasing company in the country. And yes, the 43-year-old Pontikes is making a living. His compensation was $2.4 million last year. So far this year, he's reported stock sales of $2.6 million. And his stake in the company, at the current market price, is worth $200 million plus.

His company could now be ranked an old-timer in the volatile computer leasing business, but its meteoric stock market rise is a recent phenomenon. In 1977, for example, shares could be had for a fraction of a dollar. As late as 1982, investors could have bought the stock under 7. Those same shares now sell at 38, just four points shy of their all-time high.

The spectacular rise in the stock reflects the transformation of the company itself, from a computer brokerage business—one that basically matched up computer buyers and sellers for a fee—into a complex financial service operation. Today, Comdisco not only buys and leases computers, but also re-sells the leased equipment in intricately structured tax shelters. The marketing men of a decade ago have been joined by a cadre of lawyers and accountants—tough, shrewd professionals, paid handsomely to keep one step ahead of the IRS. It's a new emphasis that has done wonders for the bottom line. Since 1980, sales have almost doubled, hitting $472 million in the 1982 fiscal year ended September. More important—thanks to the tax shelters—over the like stretch earnings expanded more than fourfold, to $29 million.

But past is not necessarily prologue. And Comdisco may be running into trouble on several fronts.

First, sources close to the IRS say that computer-leasing tax shelters are the object of wrathful scrutiny these days. The very guidelines around which Comdisco structures deals are being rewritten.

Second, IBM is moving into territory where Comdisco had been undisputed king. The IBM Credit Corp. is pushing its way into third-party leasing with partners none other than Merrill Lynch and Metropolitan Life Insurance. By next year, say industry observers, the Armonk giant will rank No. 1. And with its enormous supplies of cheap capital, IBM already is offering surprisingly aggressive rates. This ominous trend threatens to put an increasing squeeze on the profit margins of computer leasing outfits like Comdisco. To compete they may well have no choice but to take calculated—and dangerous—financial risks.

Finally, there's some controversial accounting. Comdisco's method of accounting for "fees" from tax-advantaged leases is a matter unresolved by the accounting profession—and a potentially explosive issue. Right now, Comdisco has significant latitude in the level of profits it reports and the amount of residual values it carries on the balance sheet. The details are complex, but essentially Comdisco often records what it calls "fees" from tax-advantaged transactions as straight profit—without offsetting such "fees" against the company's investment in the equipment. It thereby keeps on its books a significant investment, recorded in "leased computer equipment" or "net investment in sales and direct financing leases"—an investment it hopes to recoup from the residual value when the equipment is re-leased.

And if there are no residual values when the equipment comes off lease? Well, based on information supplied by the company's financial department, if *all* equipment was considered to have zero residual value, Comdisco's entire net worth, as of the end of fiscal 1982, would vanish.

Obviously, the way residual values are treated affects earnings, too. When Comdisco reasons that it will recoup its net investment after the equipment is released, it books the "fee" from the sale of the tax shelter as pure profit. If, instead, it subtracted its investment in equipment from this fee—recovered the investment and took it off the balance sheet—earnings would be a mere fraction of the substantial sums currently reported.

This method of accounting is thus disturbing on several scores. First, it's possible the residual values simply aren't there. Comdisco insists its assumptions are conservative—and they may well be—but all leasing companies have made such assertions, even the defunct ones. If there's a miscalculation, and the equipment should come off lease and suddenly be worthless, that means Comdisco would face a write-off.

Not to be overlooked, either, is the matter of when profits are recognized by Comdisco. Why should a company be allowed to report earnings today when it won't see the cash for four or five years, if ever? And finally, at the very least, financial statements might reasonably be expected to disclose net investment and assumed residual values, as well as detailed descriptions of how "fees" are booked.

None of this, however, is to say that Comdisco's accounting breaks the rules. Quite the contrary. "The accounting profession hasn't addressed the issue on this type of transaction," John Vosicky, Comdisco's vice president of accounting and financial controls, correctly points out. "One could argue that you could take the entire fee into income right away—on everything. Another could argue you reduce your investment completely, and you don't recognize anything until that investment is covered."

.
.
.

To better understand the accounting, consider a typical transaction, which in itself is no simple matter. The "tax-advantaged" leases, in order to get by the IRS, often involve layers of companies. And the shuffling of papers in sale-leaseback transactions can, in short order, obscure the economic realities of the deals.

But here are the basics.

Comdisco finds a user who wants to lease a computer for say, five years, and buys a machine for $100. Comdisco then takes the lease to the bank, and borrows the discounted value of the payments. A typical present value for the lease payments might be $85.

This borrowing from the bank appears on Comdisco's balance sheet as "discounted lease rentals," but the contract is so structured that the risk is essentially transferred to the bank. "These are hell-or-high water agreements," insists one Comdisco executive. If anything goes wrong—if the user fails to make his payments—all the bank can do is confiscate the equipment. It has no recourse to Comdisco. So at this point, Comdisco's investment has effectively been reduced from $100 to $15.

Then comes the "tax advantaged" part of the deal. Comdisco sells the computer to an investor who is looking for a tax shelter. And here things start to get tricky.

Comdisco collects, say, $17 in cash, from the investor and then agrees to take a seven-year note for the remaining $83 of the purchase price of the equipment. At the same time, it signs a seven-year leaseback with the investor, so the rental payments the investor gets are spread over seven years. It's neatly arranged so the rental payments of this lease-back are precisely enough to cover the payments on the seven-year note. Put another way, Comdisco pays the investor rent, and the investor turns right around and pays this rent back to Comdisco as interest and principal on the note. It's a wash—a paper transaction. It's a nifty tax deal that has no effect on the actual user of the equipment, who continues to make his payments to the bank, which, in turn, reduces Comdisco's discounted lease receivables.

So has Comdisco made money? Well, it has paid $100 for a computer and borrowed $85 from the bank, to be paid off in five years by the user's rental payments. That leaves a $15 net investment. But it's also received $17 cash from the investor, and then shuffled papers so that an $83 note from the investor is exactly offset by lease payables of $83. Comdisco also retains the right to share the proceeds of re-leasing the computer in years six and seven with the investor. The bottom line is this: the $17 in cash offsets the $15 net investment. Comdisco is $2 richer.

So the income statement shows $2?

Not likely. All those high-paid lawyers and accountants on staff argue the $17 cash payment is a "fee"—for, among other things, putting the deal together. Clearly the $17 is theirs; they don't have to give it back. So in many cases Comdisco takes the entire fee as profit. It shows earnings of $17, even though it has only $2 in the cash register.

Where's the other $15? The difference between the reported profits and the actual cash sits quietly on the balance sheet—in "leased computer equipment" or sometimes in "net investment in sales-type and direct finance leases." That's the amount Comdisco hopes to recover from re-leasing the computer in years six and seven. But by booking the entire $17, it has effectively taken this assumed residual value into earnings on day one.

Now if in years six and seven, Comdisco re-leases the computer for, say $20, it can report a $5 profit. If the re-leasing brings in only $15, Comdisco has broken even. It has simply replaced the $15 paper asset on the balance sheet with a more spendable $15 in cash. But what if re-leasing brings in only $5? That presents a nasty problem—indeed, that means that Comdisco is looking at a $10 write-off.

:

Nor is the way "fees" are treated an idle, theoretical matter. It is vitally important to Comdisco's bottom line. For such fees comprise the bulk of the company's "financial services" revenues. And although revenues from computer sales and rentals are two to three times greater, the company's big profit center is clearly financial services. Peter Labe, an analyst at Smith Barney, a firm that has done investment banking for Comdisco, claims in a recent report that financial services "account for the bulk of corporate profits."

Comdisco doesn't dispute it. "No question," says Comdisco's Vosicky, "a large percentage of the profits are attributed to tax-advantaged transactions."

About 80%–90%?

"I wouldn't say 90%," says Vosicky. "It depends on how you want to slice the pie." Profitability, he points out, depends on the allocation of general and administrative expenses. And Comdisco financials do not break out this information.

"I think it would be correct to say," continues Vosicky, "that the primary reason for the earnings increase is because of tax-advantaged transactions or financial services."

The bulk of the increase rather than the bulk of earnings?

"Yes."

In other words, the big leap in pretax earnings from $21 million in 1981 to $53 million in 1982 is primarily because of the tax-advantaged deals?

"Yes. I think that would be fair to say."

And if all fees had been reduced by the amount of investment in the equipment, how much less would financial services revenues have been in 1982?

"A lot of that revenue came from safe harbor leasing transactions where we don t have any investment . . . ."

But if the investment in equipment on all the *other* leases in 1982 was netted out, how much would financial services be reduced?

"It would probably be cut in half," replies Vosicky. "I would think at least cut in half."

And so this year, with no safe harbor leases, netting out all the investment in equipment would cause an even greater drop in financial services?

"Yet, it would."

Insofar as Comdisco reports profits now from the equipment leased—and leaves residual value on the books to be recovered later—it increases its exposure to obsolescence. And as of September 1982, the date of the most recent balance sheet with full footnotes, that exposure was considerable, at least in comparison with the company's net worth.

:

EXHIBIT 3
Letter to Comdisco, Inc. Shareholders

October 12, 1983

Dear Stockholders:

As I'm sure most of you know by now, the October 10, 1983 issue of *Barron's* includes an article about our Company. I believe the article and its subsequent impact on the price of the Company's stock entitle our stockholders to a clarification of the facts underlying the key issues raised. The article emphasizes four main areas: (1) The Company's accounting; (2) competition from IBM Credit Corporation; (3) our tax advantaged investment program; and (4) sales by insiders.

Accounting

The article raises questions concerning the Company's accounting policy with respect to the investment risk taken on leased equipment and implies that our policy with respect to payments from tax advantaged leases could result in an overstatement of income. Under the Company's depreciation policy, our leased equipment portfolio as of June 30, 1983 will be depreciated to a net book value at lease termination of $112,000,000. The estimated fair market value of this equipment at lease termination (as provided by independent forecasts from International Data Corporation, a highly regarded equipment valuation expert) was in excess of $279,000,000, a coverage ratio of nearly 2.5 to 1. The facts demonstrate that the Company's policies are conservative, and have created a potential significant source of future earnings. The specific financial implications of our policies are as follows:

(1) Equipment Values

While generally accepted accounting principles require varied accounting treatments for different types of leases, the central issue is the same for all of the Company's leases: Is the Company's depreciation policy reasonable, thus eliminating the likelihood of a future write-off? The answer is that our depreciation policy is reasonable, and, in fact, produced book values of leased equipment which are substantially less than the values estimated by independent industry experts, as shown by the table below:

Total Lease Portfolio at June 30, 1983 (000's omitted)

Lease Type	Net Book Value at Lease Termination	Estimated Fair Market Value at Lease Termination*	IBM List Price
Operating leases	$92,000	$208,000	$876,000
Sales type and direct financing leases	20,000	63,000	847,000
Other	—	8,000	60,000
	$112,000	$279,000	$1,783,000

*Source: International Data Corporation

As shown above, fair market value estimates prepared by International Data Corporation provide a substantial margin over the Company's net book value at lease termination. This is still true even if the equipment is sold under a tax advantaged transaction. Since most tax advantaged transactions are structured so that the equipment will have a zero net book value by the time any tax advantaged investor shares in the fair market value proceeds, this sharing will not have a significant effect on the margin of fair market value available to the Company over the net book value at lease termination.

Another method of evaluating our depreciation policy is to review the operating lease portfolio (which comprises 82% of the total lease portfolio) by comparing, by year of termination, net book value at lease termination to estimated fair market value at lease termination. The following table illustrates this comparison:

Operating Lease Portfolio at June 30, 1983 (000's omitted)

Fiscal Year of Termination	Net Book Value at Lease Termination	Estimated Fair Market Value at Lease Termination	Estimated Excess Fair Market Value
1983	$ 16,000	$ 22,000	$ 6,000
1984	30,000	53,000	23,000
1985	19,000	50,000	31,000
1986	14,000	46,000	32,000
1987	13,000	37,000	24,000
	$ 92,000	$208,000	$116,000

Our auditors, Peat, Marwick, Mitchell & Co., review and agree with the Company's depreciation policies.

Referring to the foregoing table, it should be noted that 71% of the Company's operating lease book value is represented by leases which terminate by September 30, 1985. This short time period increases the reliability of residual value estimates. Equally as important, the Company has historically realized more from the remarketing of leased computer equipment than the value carried on its books, resulting in additional profit at the point of remarketing.

(2) Revenue Recognition

The sale of leased equipment in a tax advantaged transaction is separate from the underlying user lease transaction and results in payments to the Company from the investor. Revenue is recognized from these transactions in accordance with one of two basic methods:

(a) For all equipment where the underlying user lease term is five years or longer, and generally for all 308X mainframe transactions, these investor payments are first applied to reduce the Company's investment in the equipment. Any excess over the investment is recorded in the period in which the tax advantaged transaction occurs. During fiscal 1982 and the nine months ended June 30, 1983, the Company generated $83,160,000 of such payments. The Company's investment in the equipment was reduced by $43,890,000 and the difference, $39,270,000, was recorded as financial services during this period.

(b) For equipment where the underlying user lease term is less than five years (except for 308X mainframe transactions) these investor payments are recognized in the period in which the tax advantaged lease transaction occurs. This accounting treatment is appropriate since the Company's depreciation policy results in net book values at the end of the initial user lease term (typically 2–3 years) that already is less than fair market value estimates. To further reduce the Company's net book value for such equipment would materially understate current income and overstate future income by reducing or eliminating depreciation charges against future rental income.

Competition from IBM Credit Corporation

IBM has been Comdisco's single largest competitor for the entire 14 years Comdisco has been in business. Through its direct lease and rental programs, IBM has always been the dominant force in the computer leasing industry. IBM's increasing emphasis on generating equipment sales, however, is reflected in its withdrawal from the direct leasing business, which has resulted in a greatly expanding third party leasing market.

IBM Credit Corporation's (ICC) entry into the third party leasing business merely replaces part of the parent company's participation in leasing. ICC is participating in the third party market as a broker in much the same way as Comdisco. Comdisco has access to the same debt and equity markets as ICC, and on terms that will at most be only marginally less attractive to Comdisco than to ICC.

Tax Advantaged Investment Program

Our tax advantaged transactions have been carefully structured and documented. These transactions are bona fide investments with real economic substance and profit potential to the investor. They provide a valuable and effective way for individuals to provide capital for and participate in the equipment leasing industry. We take great pride in our reputation for providing a high quality computer leasing investment.

Like any tax advantaged investment, these transactions have certain tax risks, such as the possibility of IRS challenge and the risk of an adverse change in federal tax laws. We have made every effort to minimize these risks. Our nationally recognized tax counsel have provided their opinion that these transactions qualify as true leases for federal tax purposes under current law. We constantly monitor proposed federal tax changes, and we know of no imminent changes in federal tax laws or regulations affecting tax advantaged "wraparound" leases of computer equipment.

While these transactions have contributed substantially to Comdisco's profitability in recent years, our continued success in the computer equipment marketplace is not dependent on our ability to offer this specific form of transaction to investors. Nor does Comdisco's success depend on continuation of the status quo with respect to federal tax policy. We have employed and continue to employ a variety of transaction structures and have a history of adapting quickly to changes in the federal tax law and the marketplace. In fact, previous changes in federal tax laws and in the marketplace have often created significant opportunities for Comdisco.

Management Stockholdings

Management currently holds approximately 8,950,000 shares or 31% of the outstanding shares of the Company. These shares represent an ownership interest of approximately $240,000,000, based on the closing price on the New York Stock Exchange as of October 11, 1983. Over the years, sales of common stock have been made periodically by management. Tax liabilities created as a result of the exercise of stock options and sales by a retired senior executive who still owns approximately 650,000 shares account for a significant portion of these sales. The remaining sales are not significant when compared to current insider holdings.

Comdisco (B)

Conclusion

In 1969, when we started Comdisco, we committed ourselves to building our business based on the principle of serving our customers with the highest degree of integrity and professionalism. Fortunately, over the years we have attracted talented individuals who share that commitment and who continue to value the principles of service, integrity and professionalism just as we did in 1969. We feel that our reputation and the trust that we have developed with our customers, our equity and debt investors, and our stockholders are our most valuable assets. We have not, and will not, compromise these principles in the conduct of our business.

Finally, it is important for you, our stockholders, to understand completely that Comdisco is stronger financially than it has ever been; that we have greater opportunities before us than at any time in our history; and that management is dedicated to retaining stockholder confidence and enhancing stockholder wealth.

Sincerely,

Kenneth N. Pontikes
(President)

EXHIBIT 4
Comdisco, Inc. Annual Report for Fiscal Year 1983 (abridged)

To Our Stockholders

I am pleased to report that in fiscal 1983 your Company continued its outstanding growth and performance. Net earnings for fiscal 1983 of $51.8 million, or $1.78 per share, represented increases of 76% and 56%, respectively, over fiscal 1982 results. Total revenue increased 15% to $543.2 million. Your Company's continued success in the lease placement of IBM computer equipment, particularly 308X mainframes and 3380 disc storage devices, and in financial services activities were the primary reasons for the record results achieved. Dividends were increased 36% in fiscal 1983 from $.11 to $.15 per share, as adjusted for the 2-for-1 stock split distributed in March, 1983.

Leasing Activity. Leasing activity increased dramatically in fiscal 1983 as Comdisco entered into 3,470 new leases with total rentals in excess of $1 billion during the initial lease terms. This compares to 2,259 leases and over $700 million in total rentals for leases entered into during fiscal 1982. Comdisco leased to its customers 3380 disk storage devices and 3380 disk controllers with an initial cost in excess of $200 million in fiscal 1983. In addition the Company leased 308X mainframes having an aggregate purchase price of $289 million.

The large volume of 308X mainframe lease transactions did not correspondingly increase the Company's total revenue since these leases are required to be accounted for as direct financing leases. Under direct financing lease accounting only the net margins are recorded as revenue, not the gross rentals as under operating lease accounting (see Understanding Comdisco's Accounting for detailed explanation).

Pursuant to the Economic Recovery Tax Act of 1981, Comdisco elected in fiscal 1982 to sell tax benefits, including investment tax credits, to other corporations, and recorded the proceeds as financial services revenue. These "tax benefit transfers" increased both total revenue and earnings before taxes, but the corresponding reduction in investment

tax credits increased the effective income tax rate to 45.4%. In fiscal 1983 the large volume of 308X mainframe and 3380 disk storage equipment purchased for its leasing activity increased the amount of investment tax credit available to Comdisco. Because of changes in tax laws in late 1982 effectively eliminating tax benefit transfers, it was no longer attractive for Comdisco to enter into these transactions, so these investment tax credits were utilized for its own account. Investment tax credits of $22 million were earned in fiscal 1983, including $12 million in the fourth quarter, reducing the effective income tax rate to 12%.

Financial Services Activity. In fiscal 1982, proceeds from tax benefit transfers were recorded as financial services revenue. As I mentioned earlier, these tax benefit transfers had the effect of increasing revenue and income tax expense. In fiscal 1983, most of the financial services revenue was generated by the sale of leased equipment in the Company's tax advantaged transactions (see Understanding Comdisco's Accounting). In tax advantaged transactions, Comdisco retains any available investment tax credit. Equipment with a fair market value of $430.2 million was sold under tax advantaged transactions in fiscal 1983 compared to $253.0 million of equipment for the prior year.

Marketplace Perspective. In fiscal 1984, the data processing industry is expected to continue its annual growth rate of 15–25%. IBM Corporation continues to be the dominant factor in the computer leasing industry through its direct lease and rental programs.

However, in recent years IBM has been emphasizing the sale of its equipment, with less emphasis on direct leasing. This is reflected in IBM's pricing strategy which favors the purchase of equipment. For example, during fiscal 1983, IBM reduced lessee purchase option credits to make its leasing program even less attractive. In addition, IBM will eliminate, as of January 1, 1984 its practice of passing through investment tax credits to its lessees. IBM's reduced emphasis on direct leasing has led to increased user demand for third party lease financing, resulting in higher growth in the third party computer leasing marketplace. Your Company is successfully participating in this expanding market.

IBM Credit Corporation has entered the third party leasing market, replacing part of IBM's participation in this market. However, we do not expect this development to adversely affect our competitive position. We believe IBM Credit Corporation to be a reasonable competitor which will not take unacceptable risks nor assume unrealistic residual values. Also, Comdisco has access to the same debt and equity markets as IBM Credit Corporation. Finally, and of critical importance, users of computer equipment need to remarket existing equipment when new equipment is acquired. Because IBM Credit Corporation does not remarket displaced equipment, Comdisco still retains an advantage by virtue of its ability to remarket used equipment. No company is better situated to handle all of its customers' needs than Comdisco.

Activity in 308X mainframe and 3380 disk drives remains very strong, with your Company continuing to increase its market share. Comdisco's success in an expanding, competitive marketplace is directly attributable to its superior remarketing and lease financing capabilities.

Financial Condition and Liquidity. In fiscal 1983 Comdisco converted its $50 million of 13% convertible debentures into common stock and subsequently issued $250 million of 8% convertible debentures. As a result of these and other factors, Comdisco is in a stronger financial position than it has ever been. Stockholders' equity increased 110% to $91.5 million during fiscal 1983. At September 30, 1983 total assets were nearly $1 billion and cash and marketable securities exceeded $230 million. The continued improvement in your Company's financial condition was recognized by Moody's Investors Service, which raised Comdisco's bond rating for its convertible debentures to BA2 in fiscal 1983.

Personnel Changes. In fiscal 1983, the number of employees increased to 504, enhancing your Company's commitment to full customer service and helping to support continued growth. In November 1983, Raymond F. Sebastian was promoted to Executive Vice President from Senior Vice President-Corporate Development. Mr. Sebastian, an officer of Comdisco for eight years, will continue to oversee corporate development and take on additional administrative duties. In October 1983 Nicholas M. DiBari resigned his positions as Senior Vice President-Marketing and as a Director, for personal reasons. Mr. DiBari made valuable contributions to Comdisco's marketing structure and philosophy. Robert A. Bardagy has replaced Mr. DiBari as Senior Vice President-Marketing and as a Director. For the past six years, Mr. Bardagy has been responsible for the Company's market making and trading programs.

Other Activities. In fiscal 1983, the Company announced its Corporate Lease Line Program. The Corporate Lease Line Program allows the Company's customers to lease almost all types of capital equipment at attractive lease rates with very little administrative burden. The Company has the ability to administer the program based on the customer's requirements. This program is expected to make a substantial contribution to fiscal 1984 results. Comdisco Disaster Recovery Services has increased its capabilities to meet the growing demands for its services. The contributions of Comdisco Technical Services and Comdisco Maintenance Services assist the Company in providing the whole array of services required by a data processing operation. The Company's international operations continue to contribute significantly to our profitability. Finally, our ability to capitalize on opportunities both inside and outside of our basic industry has never been greater.

A recent misunderstanding of Comdisco has led to lower market prices for our common stock. Accordingly, we expanded this Annual Report to describe our key operations and our accounting policies in greater detail. By any measurement, there are few publicly-held companies that can match Comdisco's performance since its inception in 1969. For the last five years the Company's compound growth rate for net earnings was an outstanding 60%, while net earnings per share and total revenue had growth rates of 46% and 29%, respectively. In fiscal 1983 return on average equity was 37%, with a 5-year average return of 33%. Comdisco's record speaks for itself.

I am proud of Comdisco's performance in fiscal 1983 and even prouder of the efforts and devotion of our employees. Without their outstanding efforts, we would not have achieved the success we have enjoyed. The support of our lenders, customers and you, our shareholders, is particularly gratifying. The first quarter of fiscal 1984 started out as our most active quarter ever, and I am confident that fiscal 1984 will prove to be Comdisco's most successful year to date.

Kenneth N. Pontikes
Chairman of the Board and President
November 28, 1983

Leasing's Four Fundamental Values

Initially, Comdisco was a computer equipment dealer, buying and selling equipment for its own account. Exceptional marketing capability helped make Comdisco the largest dealer in the industry by 1976.

By the late 1970's, market conditions had shifted and demand for computer leasing increased dramatically. Based on its exceptional marketing capability, Comdisco's emerging leasing operation quickly grew to become the Company's most significant business activity. Both dealer activity and the leasing operation—supported by unmatched remarketing capabilities—now contribute to Comdisco's overall success.

Today, Comdisco's fundamental business, the foundation on which its exceptional pattern of financial performance is based, is leasing—primarily the leasing of new and used IBM computer equipment. And, as business and institutions world-wide become more and more information driven, the demand for data processing systems will continue to grow.

Leasing is widely recognized as the most attractive alternative to purchasing multi-million dollar computer systems. Over the years, Comdisco has achieved leadership in the field, having built a lease portfolio of IBM equipment currently valued at approximately $1 billion.

The leasing business also creates values that enable Comdisco to capitalize on other related sources of revenue and earnings. At the core of Comdisco's business, there are four such fundamental values.

Initial User Lease—Value One
When Comdisco leases its new or used computer equipment to a customer, the customer's rental payments during the original lease term are the primary source of revenue. In fiscal 1983, for example, the Company entered into 3,470 leases having total lease payments of over $1 billion during the initial lease terms.

Lease contracts cannot be canceled, and the customer has full responsibility for maintenance and other expenses. Most leases have terms of two to five years.

These leases also allow Comdisco to finance its leasing growth through "nonrecourse debt." Typically, Comdisco takes an existing lease to a bank and assigns the stream of lease payments to the bank. In return, the bank gives Comdisco cash that is equal to the present value of the lease payment stream at market interest rates. The debt is nonrecourse because the bank looks to the lease payments to repay the loan. This nonrecourse debt for operating leases is recorded as "Discounted Lease Rentals" on Comdisco's Balance Sheet. Interest rates are fixed in this transaction, eliminating Comdisco's exposure to rate fluctuations. Comdisco retains ownership of the computer equipment.

Comdisco's continued success in computer leasing is supported by a variety of factors discussed in greater detail on the following pages of this Annual Report. Among them are a customer relationship with 70% of the *Fortune 500* companies, a proprietary data base containing information on all major data processing installations, a seasoned sales team with offices in key markets throughout the U.S., Canada and Europe, and a complete line of customer support services.

Remarketing Capacity—Value Two
Data processing technology is among the most dynamic in the history of world commerce. The marketplace has a virtually insatiable appetite for increased capacity and a constant stream of new technological advancements.

Comdisco (B)

With change as one of the few constants in the industry, Comdisco's unmatched capacity to remarket equipment is a fundamental component in the Company's formula for success. Indeed, leasing customers place a significant value on Comdisco's market making ability. As new products enter the marketplace, customers know that Comdisco has a unique capacity to remarket existing equipment, making it financially feasible to upgrade systems to a competitive, state-of-the-art level.

Comdisco's ability to capitalize on re-lease values and residual values is directly related to exceptional market penetration, its proprietary data base of marketing information, its professional sales force, and the Company's expertise in computer equipment and that equipment's life cycle.

Tax Benefits—Value Three

Tax benefits are an integral part of any leasing operation. Substantial tax benefits—particularly in the form of investment tax credits and accelerated depreciation deductions—are generated through Comdisco's acquisition of computer equipment.

Comdisco has a number of valuable alternatives concerning these tax benefits. Comdisco can claim the investment tax credits, thus reducing its own income tax. The Company can also choose to pass the investment tax credit through to the lessee in exchange for higher rentals. Or, as a third option, leveraged lease transactions with third party investors can also be arranged. This option has the effect of passing on all benefits of ownership, including tax and residual values. The compensation leasing companies typically receive is a lump sum payment and a share in the residual value of the leased equipment.

The capacity of the Company's basic leasing business, which generates significant tax benefits, allows Comdisco to capitalize on certain favorable tax laws. Such laws can be traced to the Congress' longstanding desire to provide industry with incentives for capital spending. Both investment tax credits and accelerated depreciation deductions are the product of laws that reflect this Congressional intent. Comdisco generates value by structuring transactions which permit the full utilization of the tax benefits associated with its equipment portfolio. Comdisco has demonstrated its ability to profitably

structure transactions in response to changes in tax laws. As long as Congress continues to encourage capital spending, the Company's control of equipment will enable it to continue structuring attractive tax-oriented transactions.

For example, in 1981 Congress devised "Safe Harbor Leasing" of equipment as a method for transferring tax benefits from one corporation to another. Called "tax benefit transfers," compensation for tax benefits was paid in a single lump sum at the beginning of the lease. Tax benefit transfers were, in effect, simply the sale of investment tax credits and depreciation benefits. In 1982, as part of the Tax Equity and Fiscal Responsibility Act of 1982 (TEFRA), Congress effectively eliminated Safe Harbor Leasing. In doing so, Congress did not change its desire to stimulate capital investment through tax incentives, as evidenced by the fact that in 1984 a new type of tax-oriented lease, the finance lease, will be permitted.

Despite the effective elimination of Safe Harbor Leasing, Comdisco continues to be in a position to generate value from significant investment tax credits and ownership rights to substantial amounts of equipment. While the laws have changed, the Congressional philosophy underlying tax-oriented leasing has not.

Tax Advantaged Transactions—Value Four

The fourth fundamental value of Comdisco's leasing activity is the tax advantaged transaction. In this alternative, Comdisco may sell equipment that is under an initial user lease to an independent third party. This is a completely separate transaction having no effect on the equipment user. The buyer is typically an individual or corporate investor who wants to share in the financial rewards of leasing— re-lease values, residual values and tax benefits.

When Comdisco sells computer equipment in a tax advantaged transaction, it receives an equity payment from the buyer in an amount equal to between 10% and 22% of the equipment's fair market value. In return for this equity payment, the new owner receives: (a) the accelerated depreciation benefits on the equipment, (b) a portion of the lease rentals in the sixth and seventh years after the sale is made, and (c) 100% of the equipment's value after the seventh year.

The utilization of tax benefits, either by the Company for its own account or by an investor as a result of a tax advantaged transaction, results in a lower effective cost to the equipment user, which is in accordance with Congress' objective to stimulate capital expenditures.

These four values form the core of Comdisco's business—leasing activity, computer remarketing, tax benefits and tax advantaged transactions. Understanding these values is key to understanding Comdisco's growth potential and how the Company effectively minimizes the business risk in its operations.

Understanding Comdisco's Accounting

Lease Accounting
Comdisco accounts for its lease transactions in accordance with the rules set forth in Accounting for Leases (FASB 13) prescribed by the Financial Accounting Standards Board. FASB 13 contains guidelines for classifying lease transactions as one of the following three types:

* sales-type lease
* direct financing lease
* operating lease

A lease is classified and accounted for as sales-type or direct financing by Comdisco if it meets any one of the following criteria:

a. The lease transfers ownership of the property to the lessee (Comdisco's customer) by the end of the lease term;
b. The lease contains an option allowing the lessee to purchase the property at a bargain price;
c. The lease term is equal to 75% or more of the estimated economic life of the property; or
d. The present value of the rentals is equal to 90% or more of the fair market value of the leased property, less any related investment tax credit retained by Comdisco.

The majority of Comdisco's sales-type and direct financing leases are classified as such because they meet criterion d above.

If the leased equipment is new or purchased from the lessee (purchase/leaseback) and meets one or more of the preceding criteria, the lease is recorded as a direct financing lease; otherwise, the lease is recorded as a sales-type lease. All other leases which do not meet one or more of the preceding criteria are classified and accounted for as operating leases. Operating leases are generally shorter term leases (2–4 years).

Sales-Type Lease. A sales-type lease is recorded in the income statement as "Sale of computer equipment," along with other sales. The amount recorded as a sale is the present value of the lease payments. The cost of the equipment less the present value of estimated residual value at lease termination, if any, is recorded in the income statement as "Cost of computer equipment."

Direct Financing Lease. It is Comdisco's policy to finance all of its direct financing leases on a nonrecourse basis. Therefore, the net margin for a direct financing lease is recorded as "other revenue." The net margin represents the sum of the proceeds from the financing of the lease plus the present value of estimated residual value at lease termination, if any, less the equipment cost.

The present value of the residual values of sales-type and direct financing leases and the present value of the noncancellable lease rentals, prior to their financing, are included in the balance sheets as "Net investment in sales-type and direct financing leases."

Operating Lease. Revenue under an operating lease is recorded as payments accrue, that is, on a monthly basis over the term of the lease. The depreciation expense is also recorded on a monthly basis and the equipment cost is recorded on the Company's balance sheet as "Leased computer equipment."

To summarize, the revenue recognition effects of the three different types of leases is as follows:

* For a sales-type lease, the present value of the lease rentals is recorded as "Sale of computer equipment" at the closing of the transaction.
* For a direct financing lease, the net margin is recorded as "Other revenue."
* For an operating lease, the monthly rentals are recorded as "Rental revenue" over the term of the lease.

Effect of Direct Financing Leases. In fiscal 1983 a substantial portion of leases written by Comdisco were recorded as direct financing leases. Because

Comdisco (B)

Comdisco (B)

only the net margins on these leases are recorded, the total leasing volume that Comdisco transacted in fiscal 1983 is understated when compared to prior years when many fewer direct financing leases were recorded. The following table sets forth the cumulative increase in rental revenue that would have been recorded in recent fiscal years if Comdisco had recorded all direct financing leases as operating leases:

	Rental Revenue (in thousands)		
Fiscal Year	As Reported (A)	Increase (B)	Pro Forma
1979	$ 60,947	$ 9,634	$ 70,581
1980	80,979	14,612	95,591
1981	131,571	24,220	155,791
1982	206,592	65,284	271,876
1983	266,628	179,528	446,156

a. Column A represents rentals reported in the Company's income statement for the respective years.
b. Column B represents rentals due under direct financing leases that are not recorded as rental revenue because of the accounting treatment afforded direct financing leases.

As a result, the actual increase in the volume of leasing is not apparent from a review of the Company's income statement.

Residual Values. Residual value is an estimate of the value of the equipment that is expected to be realized at the end of the lease term for sales-type and direct financing leases. Comdisco records the present value of a conservative estimate of residual value.

Depreciation. All of Comdisco's leased equipment under operating leases is depreciated to zero within five years, with a higher rate applicable to the period covered by the initial user lease. Operating leases are depreciated to Comdisco's estimate of fair market value at lease termination. These conservative estimates are supported by forecasts prepared by International Data Corporation (IDC), a recognized expert in residual value projections for computer equipment. In fact, at September 30, 1983 IDC's fair market value projections are 242% of the equipment's net book value at lease termina-

tion. As a result of this conservative depreciation policy, the Company has constantly realized substantially more proceeds on the sale or re-lease of its equipment than its recorded book value.

The following table projects the runoff of the Company's September 30, 1983 operating lease portfolio. The table compares the net book value of the equipment to its estimated fair market value in the fiscal year in which the existing leases terminate. Fair market value represents IDC estimates of the equipment value at lease termination.

Comdisco, Inc.—Operating Lease Portfolio Runoff as of September 30, 1983

	Fair Market Value Comparison to Net Book Value (in thousands)		
Fiscal Year of Termination	Net Book Value at Termination	Estimated Fair Market Value at Termination	Estimated Excess Fair Market Value over Net Book Value
1984	$34,725	$70,234	$35,509
1985	15,665	43,682	28,017
1986	18,869	48,868	29,999
1987	13,820	36,525	22,705
1988	1,170	4,191	3,021
Total	**$84,249**	**$203,500**	**$119,251**

Tax Advantaged Transaction

While the specific terms and conditions of tax advantaged transactions vary, the following is a general description of a typical tax advantaged transaction:

1. At a date after the inception of the initial user lease and independent thereof, the Company may sell all or some of the leased equipment to a third party investor ("investor"). If the equipment is sold to an investor, the sale generally occurs three to nine months after the commencement of the initial user lease. The sales price equals the then current fair market value of the equipment and is paid in the form of:

(a) cash and a negotiable, interest-bearing promissory note (due within two years) for 10–22% of the sales price (the "equity payment"), and

(b) an installment note for the balance (90–78% of the sales price) payable over an 84-month period.

2. Simultaneously with the sale, the Company leases such equipment back from the investor for 84 months. The lease payments payable under the leaseback obligation generally are equal to the installment payments receivable under the installment note described in 1(b) above.

3. As part of the leaseback arrangement, during the 61st through 84th month of the leaseback period, the investor also shares in the re-lease proceeds that the company receives from sub-leasing the equipment. Upon the expiration of the leaseback period, the investor has the exclusive right to the equipment.

In summary, the Company has given up the accelerated depreciation benefits on the equipment for tax purposes, a portion of the rentals for months 61–84 and 100% of the equipment value after the 84th month in exchange for the non-refundable equity payment. This equity payment is the only portion of the tax advantaged transaction that is recorded by the Company.

Revenue Recognition. Revenue is recognized, according to the lease classification, in the following manner:

1. For equipment subject to operating leases, the equity payment is recognized as financial services revenue in the period in which the tax

advantaged transaction occurs. The Company allocates as a cost a percentage of the net book value at the expiration of the initial user lease to the revenue from the tax advantaged transaction because of its decreased right to re-lease rentals. In all cases, the equipment sold under tax advantaged transactions is fully depreciated prior to the time the investor is entitled to share in re-lease rentals.

2. For sales-type and direct financing leases, the Company may record on its balance sheet an estimated residual value at the inception of the initial user lease. The equity payment is first applied to remove a portion of that residual value. The residual value is decreased because the Company's ability to recover such residual value is reduced by the rental sharing under the tax advantaged transaction. Any excess of the equity payment over the reduction of residual value is recorded as financial services revenue in the period in which the tax advantaged transaction occurs.

Lease accounting and tax advantaged transactions represent two of the more complex areas of Comdisco's accounting. See the footnotes to the Consolidated Financial Statements for additional information.

MANAGEMENT'S DISCUSSION AND ANALYSIS OF FINANCIAL CONDITION AND RESULTS OF OPERATIONS

Summary

Fiscal 1983 was the third consecutive year of record revenue and earnings for the Company. Total revenue for fiscal 1983 and 1982 was $543.2 million and $471.6 million, respectively. Net earnings increased from $29.4 million, or $1.14 per share, in fiscal 1982 to $51.8 million, or $1.78 per share, in fiscal 1983. The Company's continued success in the lease placement of IBM computer equipment, particularly 308X mainframes and 3380 disk storage devices, and in financial services activities were the primary reasons for the record results achieved.

Revenue

Total revenue increased 15% over the prior fiscal year. The increase in total revenue in fiscal 1983 was not as dramatic as the increase in fiscal 1982 despite the substantial increase in the number of lease transactions in fiscal 1983, primarily because of the different mix in lease transactions entered into in fiscal 1983. The lease classification, as determined by FASB Statement No. 13, "Accounting for Leases," has a significant effect on the manner in which revenue is recorded. During fiscal 1983, there was an active market for 308X mainframes, which were recorded as direct financing leases. In fiscal 1982, a larger percentage of leases were accounted for as operating leases. Under operating lease accounting, the gross rental is recognized in equal monthly amounts over the lease term as rental revenue. Since the Company finances most of its direct financing leases on a nonrecourse basis, the net margins are recorded as other revenue. The net margin represents the sum of the present value of the lease rentals, plus the present value of estimated residual value at lease termination, if any, less the equipment.

The growth of the Company's leasing activity continued on a strong upward trend in fiscal 1983. During fiscal 1983, the Company entered into 3,467 new leases with rental payments of $1.1 billion during the initial lease terms. This compared to 2,259 new leases and $702 million of rental payments during the initial lease term for the prior fiscal year. Rental revenue from equipment subject to operating leases increased 29% in comparison to the year earlier. The increase in operating leases in fiscal 1983 was primarily due to the high volume of lease placements of IBM's newest disk storage device, the 3380.

Revenue from the sale of computer equipment increased during fiscal 1983, primarily as a result of an active international market for 308X mainframes.

Financial services revenue for fiscal 1983 totaled $65.6 million, in comparison to $73.9 million in fiscal 1982 and $30.8 million in fiscal 1981. While the total financial services activity increased in volume during 1983, such increase is not reflected in financial services revenue in comparison to 1982. Pursuant to the Economic Recovery Tax Act of 1981, the Company elected in fiscal 1982 to sell tax benefits, including investment tax credits, to other corporations and recorded the proceeds as financial services revenue. In fiscal 1983, most of the financial services revenue was generated by the sales of leased equipment through the Company's tax advantaged transactions with the Company retaining any available investment tax credits on the equipment. In essence, in fiscal 1983, the investment tax credits associated with leasing were reflected in the reduced income tax rate, while in fiscal 1982, the sale of such benefits was reflected in

higher financial services revenue. Financial services revenue for fiscal 1983 and 1982 includes $6.0 million and $13.8 million, respectively, of net revenue generated by arranging leases between third parties.

Other revenue for fiscal 1983 totaled $39.8 million in comparison to $24.5 million in fiscal 1982 and $13.7 million in fiscal 1981. The increase in fiscal 1983 is primarily due to higher revenue from direct financing leases, interest income earned on short term investments and higher revenues from the Company's disaster recovery services.

Cost and Expenses

Total costs and expenses of $484.3 million for fiscal 1983 increased 16% over total costs and expenses of $417.8 million in fiscal 1982. Fiscal 1982 total costs and expenses were 49% higher than fiscal 1981. The increases were the result of the growth in the Company's leasing activities and the continuing expansion in the marketing of its services.

Interest expense for fiscal 1983 totaled $53.7 million in comparison to $47.2 million in fiscal 1982 and $33.7 million in fiscal 1981. The primary component is the interest expense associated with the discounting of operating leases. This represented 67%, 69% and 46% of total interest expense in fiscal 1983, 1982 and 1981, respectively. The Company finances leases by assigning the noncancellable rentals to financial institutions on a nonrecourse basis at fixed interest rates and receives from the lender the present value of the rental payments (the discounted amount). For operating leases, the Company recognizes interest expense over the term of the lease. The redemption of the Company's 13% Convertible Debentures Due 2001 reduced the Company's interest expense by approximately $5.3 million in fiscal 1983. Interest expense on the 8% convertible debentures issued May 1, 1983 totaled $8.2 million. The increases in interest expense in fiscal 1982 and fiscal 1981 were due to increased discounted lease rentals as a result of the growth in the Company's leased equipment portfolio.

Income Taxes

Income taxes as a percentage of earnings before income taxes were 11.9% in fiscal 1983 compared to 45.4% in fiscal 1982 and 26.8% in fiscal 1981. The higher effective tax rate in fiscal 1982 was attributable to lower investment tax credits due to the sale of such benefits by the Company as permitted under the Economic Recovery Tax Act of 1981. No significant tax benefit transfer leases were originated by the Company in fiscal 1983 and the Company retained the investment tax credits for its account, thereby reducing the effective tax rate to 11.9% in fiscal 1983. Note 10 of Notes to Consolidated Financial Statements provides details about the Company's income tax provisions and effective tax rates.

International Operations

The Company operates principally in three geographic areas: the United States, Europe and Canada. The Company has subsidiaries in Belgium, West Germany, Switzerland, the Netherlands, France, Sweden, Denmark, the United Kingdom and Canada. These subsidiaries offer services similar to those offered in the United States. A strong demand for IBM 308X processors, principally in Europe, resulted in an increase in revenue from international operations of 25% from $79.4 million in fiscal 1982 to $98.9 million in fiscal 1983. International revenues represented 18% of the Company's total revenue in fiscal 1983 and 17% in fiscal 1982.

Market and Dividend Information

The Company's common stock is traded on the New York Stock Exchange under the symbol CDO. The quarterly price range and dividends paid for fiscal year 1983 and 1982, adjusted to reflect the two-for-one and three-for-two common stock splits effected in March 1983 and March 1982, respectively, are shown below:

	1983			1982		
Qtr.	High	Low	Dvds.	High	Low	Dvds.
First	$18.38	$10.56	$.03	$ 9.00	$5.88	$.02
Second	27.13	16.56	.04	9.00	6.75	.03
Third	37.88	22.75	.04	9.63	7.75	.03
Fourth	42.00	34.25	.04	11.50	7.50	.03

At September 30, 1983, there were approximately 5,000 record holders of common stock.

Financial Condition

The Company's stockholders' equity increased substantially during fiscal 1983 as a result of the Company's record earnings and the conversion of

$50,000,000 of 13% convertible subordinated debentures. Cash and marketable securities totaled $232.6 million at September 30, 1983. In May 1983 the Company sold $250,000,000 of 8% convertible subordinated debentures, the primary reason for the increase in cash and marketable securities. The proceeds of the offering were used to finance the increase in the Company's leasing activities and to invest in short-term marketable securities.

At September 30, 1983, the Company had $40 million of available borrowing capacity under various lines of credit from commercial banks and no short term debt.

The Company's current financial resources and estimated cash flow from operations will be adequate to fund anticipated requirements for fiscal 1984. The major portion of funds required by the Company to finance its leasing operations is provided by assigning the noncancellable rentals to various financial institutions at fixed interest rates on a non-recourse basis. The Company's liquidity is aided by the maturation of its lease portfolio, since the remarketing of its leased equipment generates substantial funds. For example, the successful remarketing of equipment under leases which expire in fiscal 1984 is estimated to generate funds in excess of $50 million.

Total notes and debentures as a percentage of total capital (the sum of notes and debentures payable, discounted lease rentals and stockholders' equity) was 32%, 16% and 20% at September 30, 1983, 1982 and 1981, respectively.

Ratios

The following table presents ratios which illustrate the changes and trends in earnings for the last three fiscal years:

	1983	1982	1981
Return on average stockholders' equity	36.7%	39.2%	30.6%
Return on average assets	6.9%	6.2%	4.9%
Earnings before income taxes (as a percentage of revenue)	10.8%	11.4%	7.1%
Net earnings (as a percentage of revenue)	9.5%	6.2%	5.2%

Comdisco (B)

Comdisco (B)

FIVE YEAR SELECTED FINANCIAL DATA

Years ended September 30,	1983	1982	1981	1980	1979
Consolidated Summary of Earnings (in thousands):					
Revenue:					
Rental	$ 266,628	$206,592	$131,571	$ 80,979	$ 60,947
Sale of computer equipment	171,138	166,705	125,384	149,708	149,983
Financial services	65,635	·73,879	30,837	14,079	9,991
Other	39,779	24,454	13,746	8,348	4,355
Total revenue	543,180	471,630	301,538	253,114	225,276
Cost and expenses:					
Equipment depreciation, amortization and rental	214,439	160,523	99,413	68,328	47,698
Cost of computer equipment	151,573	149,654	111,784	134,595	128,470
Selling, general and administrative	64,655	60,402	35,313	24,219	21,284
Interest	53,673	47,242	33,657	16,988	13,319
Total costs and expenses	484,340	417,821	280,167	244,130	210,771
Earnings before income taxes	58,840	53,809	21,371	8,984	14,505
Income taxes	7,000	24,432	5,730	1,870	3,900
Net earnings	$ 51,840	$ 29,377	$ 15,641	$ 7,114	$ 10,605
Common and Common Equivalent Share Data					
Net earnings	$1.78	$1.14	$.68	$.33	$.54
Stockholders' equity	6.65	3.87	2.59	1.98	1.75
Average of common and common equivalent shares (in thousands)	29,502	28,973	24,539	22,102	19,858
Cash dividends paid	.15	.11	.09	.07	.06
Stock splits	2 for 1	3 for 2	5 for 4	—	3 for 2
Financial Position (in thousands)					
Total assets	$ 975,004	$536,679	$404,507	$229,170	$173,950
Total long-term debt	276,437	83,271	84,945	29,055	25,573
Discounted lease rentals	356,547	261,780	197,672	85,612	74,569
Stockholders' equity	191,487	91,056	58,746	43,565	35,508
Leasing Data					
Number of new leases	3,467	2,259	1,620	1,083	616
Total firm rents, initial lease term (in thousands)	$1,055,000	$702,000	$339,000	$183,000	$126,000

CONSOLIDATED BALANCE SHEETS
(in thousands except number of shares)

Years Ended September 30,	1983	1982
Assets		
Cash and marketable securities (at cost of $205,053 in 1983 and $3,909 in 1982, which approximates market)	**$232,560**	$39,762
Receivables:		
Accounts and notes (net of allowance for doubtful accounts of $1,215 in 1983 and $628 in 1982)	**74,830**	41,368
Other	**9,014**	3,687
Inventory of computer equipment	**59,681**	35,382
Net investment in sales-type and direct financing leases	**96,097**	23,682
Leased computer equipment:		
Owned	**671,697**	502,494
Capitalized leases	**24,353**	24,158
Total leased equipment	**696,050**	526,652
Less accumulated depreciation and amortization	**280,917**	190,817
Net	**415,133**	335,835
Buildings, furniture and other (at cost less accumulated depreciation of $2,764 in 1983 and $1,897 in 1982)	**9,068**	6,062
Other assets and deferred charges	**78,621**	50,901
	$975,004	$536,679
Liabilities and Stockholders' Equity		
Note payable to bank	**—**	$2,385
Convertible subordinated debentures	**250,000**	50,000
Subordinated debentures	**12,250**	12,250
Accounts payable	**58,963**	19,110
Obligations under capital leases	**14,187**	18,636
Obligations under capital leases income taxes:		
Current	**7,242**	6,076
Deferred	**18,121**	30,121
Other liabilities	**66,207**	45,265
Discounted lease rentals	**356,547**	261,780
	783,517	445,623
Stockholders' equity:		
Common stock $.10 par value. Authorized 50,000,000 shares: issues outstanding 28,808,571 shares in 1983 (11,769,043 in 1982)	**2,881**	1,177
Additional paid-in capital	**69,927**	18,965
Deferred translation adjustment	**(439)**	(354)
Retained earnings	**119,118**	71,268
Total Stockholders' equity	**191,487**	91,056
	$975,004	$536,679

Comdisco (B)

Comdisco (B)

CONSOLIDATED STATEMENTS OF EARNINGS

Years Ended September 30,	1983	1982	1981
Revenue			
Rental	$266,628	$206,592	$131,571
Sale of computer equipment	171,138	166,705	125,384
Financial services	65,635	73,879	30,837
Other	39,779	24,454	13,746
Total revenue	543,180	471,630	301,538
Cost and expenses			
Equipment depreciation, amortization and rental	214,439	160,523	99,413
Cost of computer equipment	151,573	149,654	111,784
Selling, general and administrative	64,655	60,402	35,313
Interest	53,673	47,242	33,657
Total costs and expenses	484,340	417,821	280,167
Earnings before income taxes	58,840	53,809	21,371
Income taxes	7,000	24,432	5,730
Net Earnings	$ 51,840	$ 29,377	$ 15,641
Net Earnings per Common and Common Equivalent Share	$1.78	$ 1.14	$.68

CONSOLIDATED STATEMENT OF STOCKHOLDERS' EQUITY
(in thousands)

Years Ended September 30, 1983, 1982 and 1981	Common stock $.10 par value	Additional paid-in capital	Retained earnings	Deferred translation adjustment
Balance at September 30, 1980	$ 587	$ 14,167	$ 28,811	$ —
Net earnings	—	—	15,641	—
Dividends paid	—	—	(1,093)	—
Stock split	148	(148)	—	—
Stock options exercised	22	611	—	—
Balance at September 30, 1981	757	14,630	43,359	—
Cumulative amount as of September 30, 1981	—	—	—	(232)
Net earnings	—	—	29,377	—
Dividends paid	—	—	(1,468)	—
Stock split	391	(400)	—	—
Stock options exercised	14	835	—	—
Common stock issued	15	2,648	—	—
Translation adjustment	—	—	—	(122)
Income tax benefits resulting from exercise of non-qualified stock options	—	1,252	—	—
Balance at September 30, 1982	1,177	18,965	71,268	(354)
Net earnings	—	—	51,840	—
Dividends paid	—	—	(3,990)	—
Issuance of common stock upon conversion of 13% convertible debentures	256	51,782	—	—
Stock split	1,435	(1,435)	—	—
Stock options exercised	13	582	—	—
Employee Stock Purchase Plan	—	33	—	—
Translation adjustment	—	—	—	(85)
Balance at September 30, 1983	**$2,881**	**$ 69,927**	**$119,118**	**$ (439)**

Comdisco (B)

CONSOLIDATED STATEMENTS OF CHANGES IN FINANCIAL POSITION
(in thousands)

Years Ended September 30,	1983	1982	1981
Source of Funds			
From operations:			
Net earnings	$ 51,840	$ 29,377	$ 15,641
Noncash changes (credits) to operations:			
Depreciation and amortization	180,676	133,902	77,528
Increase in receivables	(38,789)	(12,849)	(5,531)
Investment in sales-type and direct financing leases	(72,415)	(5,792)	(11,732)
Income taxes	(10,834)	23,180	5,730
Increase in accounts payable and accrued liabilities	60,795	14,248	18,611
Other, net	5,636	474	(1,233)
Total provided from operations	176,909	182,540	99,014
Proceeds from issuance of subordinated debentures	245,250	—	48,560
Issuance of common stock upon conversion of 13% convert-ible debentures, net	53,365	—	—
Obligations under capital leases	1,984	5,663	14,249
Discounted lease rentals	257,096	145,626	183,557
Other	543	4,201	924
	735,147	338,030	346,304
Application of Funds			
Increase in leased equipment and inventory	282,341	190,180	202,002
Decrease in notes payable	2,385	1,060	33,460
Redemption of convertible debentures	50,000	—	—
Reduction of discounted lease rentals and obligations under capital leases	168,762	87,795	75,781
Purchase of subordinated debentures	—	—	2,162
Capitalized leases—computer equipment	1,984	5,663	14,249
Other assets and deferred charges	32,887	21,950	12,343
Cash dividends	3,990	1,468	1,093
	542,349	308,116	341,090
Increase in cash and marketable securities	192,798	29,914	5,214
Cash and marketable securities at beginning of year	39,762	9,848	4,634
Cash and marketable securities at end of year	$232,560	$ 39,762	$ 9,848

Comdisco (B)

NOTES TO CONSOLIDATED FINANCIAL STATEMENTS

1. Summary of Significant Accounting Policies

Principles of Consolidation: The accompanying consolidated financial statements include the accounts of the Company and its wholly-owned subsidiaries after elimination of inter-company accounts and transactions.

Inventory of Computer Equipment: Inventory of computer equipment is stated at the lower of cost or market.

Initial Direct Costs: Salesmen's commissions and other initial direct costs related to operating leases are deferred and amortized over the lease term.

Investment in Sales-Type and Direct Finance Leases: At lease commencement, the Company records the total lease rentals, estimated residual value of the leased equipment and unearned lease income as investment in sales-type and direct financing leases.

A. Sales-Type Leases

Revenue from sales-type leases is recorded as sale of computer equipment upon acceptance of the equipment by the customer. The amount of the sale is the present value of the lease payment. The carrying value of the equipment less the present value of the estimated residual value at lease termination, if any, is charged to cost of computer equipment. Unearned lease income represents the lease rentals plus the estimated residual value of the equipment less the present value of these amounts.

B. *Direct Financing Leases*

The total lease rentals plus the estimated residual value of lease termination, if any, less the equipment cost is recorded as unearned lease income.

The Company finances most sales-type and direct financing leases by assigning the noncancellable rentals on a nonrecourse basis. The proceeds from the assignment eliminate the total lease rentals receivable and related unearned income on sales-type and direct financing leases. Any gain or loss on the financing is recognized at the time of such financing. For leases which are not financed, unearned lease income is recognized as other revenue using the interest method over the lease term.

Leased Computer Equipment: Leased computer equipment under operating leases is recorded at cost. During the initial lease term, computer equipment is depreciated to the Company's estimate of fair market value at expiration of the initial lease term. Equipment sold under tax advantaged transactions is fully depreciated within five years. Equipment not sold under tax advantaged transactions is fully depreciated over the next lease term or five years from the date of acquisition, whichever is longer.

Financial Service Transactions: At a date after the inception of an initial user lease and independent thereof, the Company may sell some or all of the equipment to a third party investor. The sales price equals the then current fair market value of the equipment and is paid in the form of cash and a negotiable, interest-bearing promissory note (due within two years) for 10–22% of the sales price (the "equity payment"), and an installment note for the balance (90–78% of the sales price) payable over an 84- to 96-month period. Simultaneously with the sale, the Company leases such equipment back from the investor for 84 to 96 months. The lease payments payable under the leaseback obligation generally are equal to the installment payments receivable under the installment note. As part of the leaseback arrangement, from the 61st month of the leaseback period until the expiration of the leaseback, the investor shares in the release proceeds that the Company receives from subleasing the equipment. Upon the expiration of the leaseback period, the investor has the exclusive right to the equipment.

For equipment subject to sales-type and direct financing leases, the equity payment is first applied to remove a portion of the residual value of the equipment at the expiration of the initial user lease. The residual value is decreased because the Company's right to the full residual has been reduced by the tax advantaged transaction. Any excess of the equity payment over the reduction of residual value is recorded as financial services revenue in the period in which the tax advantaged transaction occurs.

For equipment subject to operating leases, the equity payment is recognized as financial services revenue in the period in which the tax advantaged transaction occurs. Against this revenue, the Company allocates as a cost a percentage of the net book value remaining at termination of the initial user lease. The balance of the net book value remaining at initial lease termination will be fully depreciated within five years from the date of equipment purchase.

In fiscal 1982 and the first quarter of fiscal 1983, the Company sold the tax benefits (investment tax credit and cost recovery allowances) on certain new equipment purchased for the Company's lease portfolio, under the provisions of the Economic Recovery Tax Act of 1981. The proceeds from the sale of tax benefits are recorded as financial services revenue. Also included in financial services revenue are fees for arranging lease transactions between third parties.

Income Taxes and Investment Tax Credit: Deferred income taxes are provided for income and expenses which are recognized in different periods for income tax purposes than for financial reporting purposes. Investment tax credits are accounted for on a flow-through basis.

Earnings Per Share: Earnings per common and common equivalent share are computed based on the weighted average number of common and common equivalent shares outstanding during each period including the effect of conversion of the 13% convertible subordinated debentures, after elimination of the related interest expense (net of tax), and after giving retroactive effect to the two-for-one stock split effected in March 1983. (See Note 11). Dilutive stock options included in the number of common and common equivalent shares are based on the treasury stock method. The number of common and common equivalent shares used in the computation of earnings per share for the years ended September 30, 1983, 1982 and 1981 were 29,501,678, 28,973,476 and 24,539,406, respectively.

2. Investment in Sales-Type and Direct Financing Leases

The following table lists the components of the net investment in sales-type and direct financing leases

as of September 30:

	1983	1982
Minimum lease payments	$88,718	$24,142
Estimated residual values of leased equipment	29,863	12,324
Net investment in equipment pending sale to third parties	7,305	—
Less unearned income	29,789	12,784
Net investment in sales-type and direct financing leases	$96,097	$23,682

Future minimum lease payments to be received as of September 30, 1983 are as follows:

Years ending September 30	Minimum lease payments receivable
	(in thousands)
1984	$24,844
1985	22,910
1986	20,696
1987	14,706
1988	5,562
	$88,718

3. Leased Computer Equipment

Leased computer equipment at September 30, 1983 is comprised of the following:

Year lease commenced	Equipment cost	Accumulated depreciation	Net book value
1979	$20,357	$16,598	$3,759
1980	41,718	29,167	12,551
1981	146,118	96,179	49,939
1982	182,301	85,348	96,953
1983	281,203	35,518	245,685
	$671,697	$262,810	$408,887

An analysis of the operating lease portfolio by year the equipment was first available from the manufacturer follows below. This does not represent the year of purchase by the Company. The Company's depreciation policy generally depreciates computer equipment to zero within five years of the date of purchase.

Year of delivery	Net book value
1970	$1,816
1973	8,244
1974	21,319
1975	58,656
1976	9,290
1978	58,556
1979	88,338
1980	42,543
1981	31,637
1982	88,488
	$408,887

4. Operating Leases

Rental revenue from operating leases is recognized in equal monthly amounts over the term of the lease. The following table summarizes the Company's future rentals receivable and payable under noncancellable operating leases existing at September 30, 1983 for computer equipment and rents payable for non-computer equipment and office space:

Year ending September 30	Computer equipment			Other rents payable
	Rents receivable on equipment		Rents payable on subleased equipment	
	Owned	Subleased		
	(in thousands)			
1984	$213,012	$28,334	$28,023	$2,430
1985	135,624	17,723	14,118	1,787
1986	63,488	7,309	4,340	831
1987	20,378	2,399	883	435
1988	1,345	275	60	250
	$433,847	$56,040	$47,424	$5,733

Total rental income and related expense for the years ended September 30, 1983, 1982 and 1981 applicable to computer sublease activities were as follows:

Years ended September 30	Rental income	Rental expense
	(in thousands)	
1983	$29,316	$33,694
1982	23,633	27,455
1981	24,152	22,415

5. Discounted Lease Rentals

Leased equipment owned by the Company is financed by assigning the noncancellable rentals to various lenders at fixed interest rates on a nonrecourse basis. The proceeds from the assignment of the lease rentals represent payments due under the lease discounted to their present value at the interest rate charged by the lender. The proceeds from the financing of equipment subject to sales-type and direct financing leases reduce the investment in sales-type and direct financing leases (see Note 1). The proceeds from the financing of equipment subject to operating leases is recorded on the balance sheet as Discounted Lease Rentals. Interest expense under these financings is computed under the interest method and amounted to $36,173,000, $32,527,000 and $15,468,000 in 1983, 1982 and 1981, respectively. In the event of default by the lessee, the lender has a first lien against the underlying leased equipment, with no further recourse against the Company.

The annual maturities of discounted lease rentals for the next five years are as follows:

Year ending September 30	Aggregate maturities
	(in thousands)
1984	$164,193
1985	113,318
1986	56,099
1987	20,528
1988	2,409
	$356,547

6. Capitalized Leases—Computer Equipment

The Company, as lessee, leases computer equipment from other parties which may be recorded as capitalized leases pursuant to FASB Statement No. 13. If the lease qualifies as a capital lease, the Company records as an asset the lesser of the fair market value of the equipment or the present value of the minimum lease payments. The Company amortizes the asset in a manner consistent with its normal depreciation policy for leased equipment.

Capitalized leases-computer equipment at September 30, is comprised of the following:

	1983	1982
	(in thousands)	
Capitalized leases- computer equipment	$24,353	$24,158
Less accumulated computer amortization	18,107	15,354
Net capitalized leases- computer equipment	$ 6,246	$ 8,804

At September 30, 1983, the Company, as lessee, was obligated to pay rentals under those capitalized leases. The following table summarizes minimum rentals payable by the Company as lessee under capitalized leases:

Years ending September 30	Minimum rentals payable
	(in thousands)
1984	$7,527
1985	5,244
1986	2,807
1987	1,810
1988	521
Total minimum lease payments	17,909
Less imputed interest (9% to 17%)	3,722
Obligations under capital leases (present value of net minimum lease payments)	$14,187

The Company has subleased equipment under capitalized leases to others resulting in noncancellable sublease rental income of $10,532,000 due to the Company in the future.

7. Other Assets and Deferred Charges

During the third quarter of fiscal 1983, the Company began operations of a newly established, wholly owned subsidiary, Comdisco Resources, Inc. ("CRI"). CRI is primarily engaged, through joint ventures with established partners, in the acquisition of mineral and royalty rights in producing domestic oil and gas properties and in the acquisition of onshore leasehold interests primarily for resale to others for oil and gas exploration and development. At September 30, 1983, included in other assets and deferred charges are $22,959,000 of investments representing primarily onshore leasehold interests in unproved properties held for resale to others. For fiscal 1984, approximately $17,800,000 and

$9,000,000, respectively, has been budgeted for investment in proved producing domestic oil and gas properties and unproved onshore leasehold interests for resale to others for oil and gas exploration and development.

The Company, through its CFS subsidiary, has entered into certain computer equipment transactions in which it has leased equipment and in turn has subleased such equipment. In substantially all of these transactions, the lease term exceeds the sublease term. At September 30, 1983 and 1982, $19,336,000 and $21,258,000, respectively, of costs (representing the present value of the excess of lease payments over the initial sublease payments) were deferred in connection with such transactions and are included in other assets and deferred charges. These deferred costs will be recovered from remarketing the equipment after the expiration of the initial sublease. At September 30, 1983, the Company has firm noncancellable rentals under binding contracts totaling $9,102,000 as a result of remarketing a portion of this portfolio. All of these noncancellable rentals will be used to reduce the investment in the period such rentals are received.

8. Bank Borrowings and Compensating Balances

The Company has a revolving credit agreement which entitles it to borrow up to $15,000,000 on an unsecured basis. The agreement, which expires March 31, 1984, carries an interest cost of prime rate (11.0% at September 30, 1983) and includes a fee of 3/8% per annum of the average daily unused amount. If either the Company or the bank elects not to renew the agreement, the loan becomes a two-year term loan payable in equal quarterly installments with an interest cost of prime rate plus 1%. Under the agreement, the Company is required to maintain a defined debt to net worth ratio and dividend payments cannot exceed 20% of consolidated net earnings subsequent to September 30, 1980. At September 30, 1983, approximately $10,658,000 of retained earnings were available for payments of dividends.

In accordance with the terms of the agreement, the Company is required to maintain average cash balances with the bank equal to 5% of the $15,000,000 loan commitment. The amount of unused available borrowings under the agreement was $15,000,000 at September 30, 1983.

At September 30, 1983, the Company had an additional unused line of credit totaling $25,000,000 which bears interest at the prime rate. Under the agreement, the Company is required to maintain compensating balances equal to 5% of the outstanding borrowings.

9. Subordinated Debentures

8% Convertible Subordinated Debentures: In May 1983, the Company issued $250,000,000 of 8% convertible subordinated debentures ("Convertible Debentures") due in 2003. Issue costs of approximately $5,000,000 were deferred and are being amortized over 20 years. Each $1,000 principal amount may be converted into shares of common stock of the Company, prior to maturity, at the option of the Convertible Debenture holder at a conversion price of $36.50 per share.

The Convertible Debentures are not redeemable prior to November 1, 1984 unless the average closing price of the common stock is $51.10 for the twenty consecutive trading days ending on the fifth day preceding the date of notice of redemption. Thereafter, they are redeemable in full or in part at the option of the Company at an amount equal to 108.0% of the principal amount, with the premium on redemption declining 8% per annum commencing in 1984 through 1993, and redeemable thereafter at par.

13% Convertible Subordinated Debentures: On November 4, 1982, the Board of Directors announced the redemption of all of the Company's 13% Convertible Subordinated Debentures Due 2001 at a redemption price of $1,117 for each $1,000 principal amount, plus accrued and unpaid interest to December 6, 1982. Common stock issued upon conversion of $49,839,000 principal amount totaled 5,111,360 shares.

11½% Subordinated Debentures: At September 30, 1983, $12,250,000 of 11½% subordinated debentures due December 1, 1992 were outstanding. Annual sinking fund payments of $1,350,000 (9% of the aggregate original principal amount) commenced December 1, 1982 and are calculated to retire 90% of the issue prior to maturity. During fiscal 1981, the Company, in connection with future sinking fund requirements, acquired $2,750,000 principal amount of the outstanding debentures which resulted in a gain of $318,000 (net of income taxes of $270,000).

The annual maturities and sinking fund requirements of all the subordinated debentures for the next five years are as follows:

Years ending September 30	Aggregate maturities
	(in thousands)
1984	$ —
1985	1,300
1986	1,350
1987	1,350
1988	1,350

10. Income Taxes

The following data related to the provision for income taxes for the years ended September 30:

	1983	1982	1981
Current:			
Federal	**$13,000**	$ 6,252	$ —
State	**6,000**	1,076	—
	19,000	7,328	—
Deferred:			
Federal	**(12,200)**	16,281	4,216
State	**(2,200)**	273	553
Foreign	**2,400**	550	961
	(12,000)	17,104	5,730
Total tax provision	**$7,000**	$24,432	$ 5,730
Earnings before income taxes:			
Domestic	**$51,869**	$51,166	$18,992
Foreign	**6,971**	2,643	2,379
Total	**$58,840**	$53,809	$21,371

Income tax benefits of $900,000 resulting from the redemption of the 13% convertible debentures in fiscal 1983 and $1,252,000 resulting from the exercise of non-qualified stock options in fiscal 1982 were utilized to reduce the current Federal tax liability.

The reasons for the difference between the U.S. Federal income tax rate of 46% and the effective income tax rate were as follows:

Comdisco (B)

Comdisco (B)

	Percentage of Pretax Earnings		
	1983	1982	1981
U.S. Federal income tax	**46.0%**	46.0%	46.0%
Increase (reduction) result- ing from:			
Domestic International Sales Corporation tax benefit	**—**	(.1)	(1.2)
Reduction of deferred income taxes applica- ble to investment tax credit carrryforward	**—**	—	(20.4)
Investment tax credit	**(37.9)**	(2.0)	—
State income taxes, net of U.S. tax benefit	**3.5**	1.4	1.2
Other – net	**.3**	(.1)	1.2
	11.9%	45.4%	26.8%

The Company has not provided for income taxes on the unremitted earnings of the Domestic International Sales Corporation (DISC) subsidiary aggregating $4,253,000 through September 30, 1983, since the Company intends to postpone indefinitely the remittance of such earnings.

Deferred income taxes provided for timing differences were as follows:

	1983	1982	1981
Sale of tax benefits	**$(6,172)**	$38,661	$ —
Difference between depreciation for tax purposes and financial statement purposes	**(6,305)**	(18,125)	6,311
Deferred compensa- tion expense	**1,264**	754	(754)
Deferred leasing income	**7,445**	2,934	(2,093)
Deferred leasing costs	**19**	1,518	1,164
Interest income on escrow account bonds not included in book income	**(7,972)**	—	—
Portion of undistrib- uted earnings in DISC	**—**	(178)	(454)

	1983	1982	1981
Difference between leases accounted for as sales-type leases for financial statement purposes and operating leases for tax pur- poses	**211**	(23,601)	194
Reinstatement (reduc- tion) of deferred income taxes applicable to:			
Investment tax credit carryfor- ward	**—**	12,021	(4,356)
Tax net operating loss realization	**—**	—	2,323
Income tax benefit resulting from exercise of non- qualified stock options	**—**	—	1,903
Other – net	**(490)**	3,120	1,492
	$(12,000)	$17,104	$5,730

The Internal Revenue Service is examining the tax returns for the years 1980, 1981 and 1982. However, no final adjustments have been proposed and no provision for additional taxes is deemed necessary. The Company has settled all tax years through fiscal 1979.

11. Common Stock and Additional Paid-In Capital

On January 20, 1983, the Board of Directors declared a two-for-one split of the Company's common stock effective March 1983. On January 27, 1982 the Board of Directors declared a three-for-two split of the Company's common stock. On January 20, 1981 the Board of Directors of the Company declared a five-for-four split of the Company's common stock. All references in the financial statements and notes to the number of shares of common stock and per share amounts have been adjusted for the aforementioned stock splits.

On November 18, 1981, the Board of Directors approved the Settlement Agreement (the "Agreement") between the Company and participants in the Residual Incentive Compensation Plan (the "Plan") related to vested residual computer interests. The Plan provided in part for the allocation of a percentage interest in the residual value of computer equipment to the participants. The Agreement was approved by the stockholders on March 15, 1982 and, pursuant to the terms of the Agreement, the Company distributed to participants in accordance with the terms of the Plan the aggregate sum of $3,000,000 plus 300,000 shares of the Company's common stock.

Dividends on Common Stock: Common stock dividends paid were $.15 per share in 1983 compared with $.11 in 1982 and $.09 in 1981. Agreements with officers and directors who own approximately 29% (8,358,759 shares) of the outstanding common stock regarding waiver of their rights to certain cash dividends payable prior to February 1, 1983, have expired and have not been renewed.

At September 30, 1983, the Company has reserved the following number of common shares for future issuance:

1979 Stock Option Plan	542,851
1981 Stock Option Plan	1,474,200
Employees Stock Purchase Plan	196,430
Conversion of 8% Convertible Debentures	6,849,315
	9,062,796

12. Employee Benefit Plans

1979 Stock Option Plan: On November 18, 1981, the Board of Directors amended the Company's 1979 Stock Option Plan (the "1979 Plan") to qualify the plan as an incentive stock option plan in accordance with the provisions of the Economic Recovery Tax Act of 1981. All outstanding stock options, which retained their original option price, are eligible for treatment as incentive stock options subject to certain limitations as defined in the amended 1979 Plan.

1981 Stock Option Plan: On January 27, 1982, the stockholders approved the 1981 Stock Option Plan (the "1981 Plan") and 1,500,000 shares were reserved for issuance pursuant to the exercise of options under the 1981 Plan.

Employee Stock Purchase Plan: The Comdisco, Inc. Employee Stock Purchase Plan (the "Plan") was adopted by the Board of Directors on November 17, 1981 and 200,000 shares were reserved for issuance under the Plan.

The changes in the number of shares under the option plans during 1983, 1982 and 1981 were as follows:

	1983	1982	1981
	(in thousands except option price range)		
Number of shares:			
Shares under option beginning of year	986	1,024	1,722
Options granted	308	338	—
Options exercised	(133)	(376)	(698)
Shares under option end of year	1,161	986	1,024
Aggregate option price:			
Shares under option beginning of year	$4,967	$2,533	$3,257
Options granted	6,739	3,284	—
Option exercised	(596)	(850)	(724)
Shares under option end of year	$11,110	$4,967	$2,533
Options exercisable at end of year	238	116	328
Aggregate option price of exercisable options outstanding at end of year	$1,247	$295	$722
Options available for future grant at end of year	874	1,182	22
Option price range	$2.45–$21.88	$2.45–$9.69	$.68–$3.50

Profit Sharing Plan: The Company has a profit sharing plan covering all employees. Company contributions to the plan are based on a percentage of employees' compensation, as defined. Profit sharing payments are based on amounts accumulated on an individual employee basis. Profit sharing expense for the years ended September 30, 1983, 1982 and 1981 amounted to $834,000, $590,000 and $489,000, respectively.

Comdisco (B)

13. Commitments and Contingent Liabilities

At September 30, 1983, the Company was obligated under the following commitments: (1) to purchase computer equipment in the approximate aggregate amount of $58,782,000, (2) to sell computer equipment in the approximate aggregate amount of $9,370,000, and (3) to lease computer equipment to others with an aggregate initial term rental of approximately $86,133,000.

The Company has arranged for approximately $68,683,000 of letters of credit, primarily as guarantees for certain of the Company's sublease obligations and for future purchases of IBM equipment. The cost of such letters of credit range between ½% and ¾% per annum on the amount outstanding.

Accountant Report

The Stockholders and Board of Directors, Comdisco, Inc.:

We have examined the consolidated balance sheet of Comdisco, Inc. and subsidiaries as of September 30, 1983 and 1982 and the related consolidated statements of earnings, stockholders' equity and changes in financial position for each of the years in the three-year period ended September 30, 1983. Our examinations were made in accordance with generally accepted auditing standards and, accordingly, included such tests of the accounting records and such other auditing procedures as we considered necessary in the circumstances.

In our opinion, the aforementioned consolidated financial statements present fairly the financial position of Comdisco Inc. and subsidiaries at September 30, 1983 and 1982 and the results of their operations and the changes in their financial position for each of the years in the three-year period ended September 30, 1983, in conformity with generally accepted accounting principles applied on a consistent basis.

Peat, Marwick, Mitchell & Co.
Chicago, Illinois
November 9, 1983

Quarterly Financial Data

Summarized quarterly financial data for fiscal years ended September 30, 1983 and 1982 is as follows:

(in thousands of dollars except for per share amounts)

Quarter Ended:	December 31		March 31		June 30		September 30	
	1982	1981	1983	1982	1983	1982	1983	1982
Total revenue	$141,011	$121,189	$132,901	$118,309	$127,455	$94,691	$141,813	$137,441
Net earnings	12,531	9,604	10,334	5,934	13,199	5,824	15,776	8,015
Net earnings per common and common equivalent share	$.45	$.37	$.35	$.24	$.45	$.23	$.53	$.31

In the fourth quarter of fiscal 1983, the Company generated substantial investment tax credits, which resulted in an annual effective tax rate of 11.9%. This reduction in the income tax rate resulted in an increase of approximately $7,430,000 in net earnings ($.25 per share) for the fourth quarter of fiscal 1983.

W hen CompUSA's COO, Hal Compton, wants to check out the competition, he has only to look out his window. From there he can see a startling cross-section of the major national retailers looking to cut into CompUSA's surging computer business. These tough competitors almost did CompUSA in. Under the old, more entrepreneurial regime led by founder Nathan Morton, the chain was sliding toward extinction after rocketing to the top of the computer retail industry. Losses were mounting and most of the competition was offering a far better price, if not assortment, than CompUSA. The company's emphasis on expansion captured most of management's attention, at the expense of execution and productivity. Ultimately, Morton was ousted and Jim Halpin, a Zayre veteran who specialized in running low-overhead operations like warehouse clubs, was brought in. Halpin purged the corporate ranks, slashed costs, beefed up the chain's notoriously haphazard merchandising, exited non-core businesses (and downsized others like furniture that didn't merit floor space), and beefed up others that offered more complete selection and robust profits, like accessories. The results have been dramatic. "In August of 1994, our stock was at 6 3/4, we'd lost $20 million in the previous year, and we were completely out of cash," Compton noted. "A year and a half later the stock is soaring—in early May, it was just short of $35 per share!"

How has CompUSA, considered to be on the verge of bankruptcy just two years ago, turned itself around so dramatically? According to Compton, by virtually reinventing the company. In the past 30 months, the company switched from ROP[1] advertising to circulars, shifted to centralized replenishment systems, invested heavily in training in-store staff, slashed operating costs, revamped the company's hierarchy to push decision-making down the ladder, developed non-retail businesses that now comprise almost 50% of revenues and easily outpace retail growth, and invested in making stores more interactive and user-friendly. Compton summed up, "There's a major attitude shift. We used to be a top-line company, boosting sales at all costs. Now we're entirely bottom-line oriented; we're not going to sell something unless it's a profitable sale."

Discount Store News, May 20, 1996[2]

Research Associate Sarayu Srinivasan prepared this case under the supervision of Professor Krishna Palepu as the basis for class discussion rather than to illustrate either effective or ineffective handling of an administrative situation. Copyright © 1997 by the President and Fellows of Harvard College. Harvard Business School case 9-197-101.

1. Run of Paper refers to generic ad space in a newspaper. ROP ads are run wherever the paper wants to fit them in, as opposed to ad space purchased on a specific page.

2. Adapted from Pete Hisey, "CompUSA: Back to the Bottom Line," p. 15.

CompUSA

COMPANY BACKGROUND

CompUSA was founded in 1984 as Software Warehouse to sell computer hardware, software, peripherals, and related services. In 1989 Nathan Morton, a senior vice president of operations at The Home Depot, a successful warehouse-style hardware chain, joined the firm. Under Morton's leadership, the renamed CompUSA pioneered the computer superstore format, applying the Home Depot low-overhead, no-frills concept of warehouse retailing—where the shop was literally nothing more than a huge warehouse crammed to capacity with merchandise—to computer retailing, offering one-stop comprehensive computer shopping. CompUSA's base strategy was to offer wide selections of merchandise at low, competitive prices sold by knowledgeable sales representatives in high volumes. Typical stores stocked thousands of branded hardware, software, and accessory products, with an additional 25,000 products available by special order. Low margins were characteristic of the high volume, deep discount strategy and the company purchased inventory in large quantities at discount from vendors. Clients included individuals, businesses, government, and educational institutions. Stores averaged $30 million to $40 million worth of sales per year.[3]

CompUSA pursued voracious growth during the early 1990s (averaging 75 percent p.a.), expanding from two stores in 1989 to 66 stores in 1993. Multiple stores were opened in major markets where demand was high enough to absorb promotion, distribution, and administrative costs.[4] New store openings were preceded by concentrated advertising campaigns and promotions. Located in suburbs and city outskirts, average stores measured 27,000 square feet and sold products for half of list price, driving other retailers to cut prices too. CompUSA encouraged impulse purchases through a strategic store layout which guided shoppers deeper into the store, exposing them to a wider variety of merchandise and eye-catching displays. Growth was spectacular. In 1991 the firm completed an IPO, becoming the first computer superstore chain to court the Markets. By 1993 however, the relentless focus on expansion, declining growth in comparable store sales, unchecked costs, and increasing price competition cut profits to one penny on every revenue dollar, leading to a $1 million loss on $436.6 million of revenues for the retailer in first quarter 1993. In December 1993 CompUSA's board replaced CEO Morton with the then COO James Halpin.

In response to continuing losses ($16.7 million in FY 1994 on revenues of $2.1 billion) and a board mandate to focus on profitability, CompUSA re-evaluated its strategy. Computer users were no longer solely young, male, and technologically astute. Many of these new computer buyers shied away from superstores intimidated by the bare bones high-tech environment and "techie" sales staff that "talked down" to clients. CompUSA addressed the market shift by balancing its classic technology-focused merchandising with more consumer oriented, user-friendly displays and product mixes in its stores, introducing devices like prepurchase product sampling. The firm also improved the responsiveness and efficiency of its sales force. Additionally, CompUSA redesigned

3. James McConville, "All the Right Moves," The Weekly Home Furnishings Newspaper, January 3, 1994.

4. Stephen W. Quickel, "The Bumpy Road Ahead for CompUSA," Electronic Business Buyer, November 1993.

stores—branded as overcrowded, difficult to navigate through, and regularly out of stock—installing clear signage and lowered shelving to make items easier to reach and sales staff easier to find (previous shelving had been warehouse style, floor to ceiling, obscuring sight). Inventory purchase and distribution was centralized, and high margin products (such as software and accessories) were stocked up on instead of items discontinued for not turning a profit. Premium store space was allocated for 2,000 software titles, relegating hardware to the rear of the shop. Finally, the firm focused on building its value-added businesses, like service and support, to nurture and extend client relationships post-sale.

INDUSTRY AND COMPETITION

In 1996 computer superstores represented the largest retail segment of the $80 billion fragmented and rapidly growing personal computer (PC) industry. Superstores accounted for nearly 13 percent of the total market and had a growth rate of 13.5 percent in 1995, in contrast to the 11.5 percent rate reported for the whole U.S. PC industry.[5] The entire industry expected to grow at 15 percent p.a. for the next several years. Specific markets targeted for high growth included home users,[6] business users, and current first-time users trading up for more advanced products. Growth was spurred by an expanding market, wider hardware and software selections and compatibilities, decreasing prices, belief that computers were necessary to personal, educational, and professional growth, explosive growth of the Internet, and technological advances that prodded upgrades.

Computer retailers included computer superstores, mail order/direct dealers, office supply superstores, large consumer electronics chains, mass merchandisers, and specialty retailers. Competition throughout the industry was intense, ensured by hardware and software manufacturers that regularly cut prices and sought new distribution channels for product. In retail channels, branded low-margin products dictated increasing sales volume per store to turn a profit. While superstores had competed on broad selection and low prices to survive, ultimately they had to market higher price points, usually the latest technology. Retailers differentiated from one another on technical support, service, inventory depth and breadth, location, and other value additive components. Exhibit 2 shows computer retailer statistics.

CompUSA competed directly with several retailers. Dell and Gateway 2000 were PC manufacturers that sold direct (through mail order) to the end user. Computer City was a national superstore competitor. Mass retailers that carried computers along with other products fell into several categories including electronics chains like Circuit City and Best Buy, office supply superstores like Office Depot and Staples, catalog/mail order retailers like Global DirectMail and MicroWarehouse, software retailers like Egghead, and department stores like Montgomery Ward and Sears. Analysts expected all these re-

5. *Mitchell Bartlett, Analysts Report: CompUSA, Wessels Arnold & Henderson, September 12, 1996.*

6. *Household computer penetration was 39 percent in 1995, one- to two-thirds of which was already estimated to be obsolete.*

tail segments to hold and increase their market shares due to both industry consolidations and market share gained from smaller retailers that could not compete in an environment where margins were squeezed to virtual unprofitability by larger players.

Computer City (a division of Tandy Corporation) was CompUSA's computer superstore competitor. Despite its similar concept, Computer City's operating performance was in stark contrast to CompUSA. With average store square footage at 22,500, and a total annual revenue of $2.2 billion for 1996, Computer City's 106 stores averaged annual sales per square foot of only $925 compared to CompUSA's average sales per square foot of $1422. Analysts saw a similarity in Computer City's rapid growth and poor store layouts (i.e., high shelves) to CompUSA's situation several years before its turnaround.

One problem that affected all computer retailers was the large amounts of inventory carried. Product and technology obsolescence was a threat throughout the industry. Technology advanced at a rapid pace; products became outdated within months of introduction to the consumer market. Both hardware and software were subject to constant upgrade or replacement as a result of improvements in underlying technologies or features. If a product went obsolete, it was often difficult if not impossible to unload at any price, and the retailer was stuck with the surplus. CompUSA instituted provisions in supply contracts to help partially hedge against the risk of obsolescence. Further, the company's high inventory turns (7.7 times in 1996) also cushioned against obsolete inventory.

In the 1990s, the retail environment was impacted by both changing consumer demographics and technologies. Computers were growing both more powerful and affordable, and were increasingly viewed as necessities rather than luxuries. In addition, current users were upgrading to more sophisticated equipment. These and other factors jump-started industry sales. While computer superstores seemed the logical vendor for first-time, technologically unsavvy consumers, their technology-soaked environments proved overwhelming to shoppers trying to grasp the basics. This growing market found relief at mass retailers whose mix of products, which included computers, offered environments already familiar and less threatening, and boasted the added convenience of noncomputer-related merchandise. The traditional superstore customer, who also frequented the mail order channel as well as smaller exclusive computer boutiques, had been a technology buff, repeat purchaser, or a knowledgeable first timer, but in order to grow market share, superstores had to adapt their environments to also accommodate first-time buyers who were the potential growth market. In the interim, these clients were expected to turn to mass retailers such as electronics and office supply stores.

CompUSA's FUTURE

Under Halpin's direction during 1996, CompUSA continued expansion, but with its recent turnaround strategies and bottom-line focus fresh in mind. While the company still looked for growth opportunities, it had started to veer from its traditional suburban sites to also locate in urban markets, and had started to modify its store designs to adapt to its new environs. Growth was also pursued through the previously untapped vehicle of mass advertising—television, radio, and newspaper circulars. Print advertisements for stores were now full color, attention grabbing inserts in the weekend paper, replacing the generic black and white ROP newspaper ads the company had previously used. Television and radio advertisements featuring the CompUSA mascot and resident computer whiz "P.C. Modem" were introduced. CompUSA had also acquired PCs Compleat, a leading mail-order reseller of computers, to strengthen its mail order business. Structurally, the company had re-organized itself into operating units that would define its future business strategy and drive growth.

CompUSA had divided itself into seven separate businesses to better take advantage of market opportunities. These units were: retail, mail order, technical service and support, training, and sales to government, corporations, and educational institutions. The company felt that an increasing proportion of its business would be from its institutional, service, and training divisions. Exhibit 3 shows profitability and revenues for CompUSA divisions and product groups.

RETAIL. The company's retail business had metamorphosed from a utilitarian and threatening environment to a dynamic, instructive, and light-hearted place to shop. Video and audio displays, in-store presentations, interactive kiosks, sample stations, and a special section devoted to children offered shoppers timely and seasonal merchandise. Hardware and software titles were discontinued if they did not generate sales. Rotating themes and new releases encouraged impulse purchases, and sale associates were trained to provide comprehensive customer service, offering total solutions packages—product support, repair, and technical help along with the hardware purchase—that would add value to the components and build a relationship with the consumer. CompUSA dominated the industry in this segment.

MAIL ORDER. This was CompUSA's highest growth business. The company took orders over the phone at a central call center and then shipped from its distribution center or directly from stores. CompUSA felt it had an advantage over other mail-order retailers like Dell because it offered a variety of brands as well as convenient service and replacement options by allowing returns and exchanges through stores. The acquisition of the successful mail order firm PCs Compleat was expected to add to growth as it had high sales per employee (up to $1.3 million) and average orders of $1,700.

TECHNICAL SERVICES. This was the company's highest margin business. For about $100 the previously tedious and stressful task of setting up a computer would be undertaken by the company, along with frontdoor delivery of the product. CompUSA would also perform post set-up service like repairs. This service had become increasingly popular with consumers needing to integrate scanners, modems, and other peripheral equipment with their computers. Technical services also included networking support, system integration, software licensing, and over-the-phone services to the general public on a fee basis.

TRAINING. CompUSA offered software training for businesses at their locations, and in-house to customers. The company's national presence allowed it to offer standard training all over the country. Technical services and training combined contributed to

CompUSA

less than 6 percent of sales but were being targeted for marketing and business plans that would expand the units and grow sales.

CORPORATE SALES.   CompUSA's national presence allowed it to serve a corporation at all the business's operating locations, under one corporate account. For example, to ensure uniformity of systems, CompUSA could provide identical software training for employees of a national company, across the country, at the company's various locations. CompUSA expected to spin off its corporate accounts into a separate entity over the ensuing years.

GOVERNMENT SALES.   Because of its low prices and national presence, the company was able to successfully bid for local, state, and federal government business.

EDUCATIONAL SALES.   The company's training centers and national presence was again a key strategic element in acquiring clients.

CEO James Halpin explained the idea behind the distinct divisions:

We don't think of ourselves as a retailer. We think of ourselves as a distributor of computer products and services. But a distributor that touches the end consumer. . . . We want to be dominant as a distributor, in all the channels we play, whether it's retail, corporate, government, education, training, mail-order, or technical services. . . . I've spent a lot of time getting customers or getting people's minds to understand that we're not a retailer, that we are a conglomerate, if you will. I want our corporate customers to think of us as a corporate reseller. I want our retail customers to think of us as a retailer, our mail-order customers, as a great place for mail-order.[7]

By the fall 1996 publication of CompUSA's 1996 annual report (CompUSA's fiscal year ended June 30), the firm had become the nation's leading retailer and reseller of computer products, generating earnings of $59.6 million on $3.83 billion of revenues. (See Exhibit 4.) CompUSA boasted a total of 106 superstores in 33 states with average sales per square foot of $1,422. Exhibit 1 shows CompUSA stock performance. At September 30, 1996, the company's stock was priced at $54.

With 1997 just around the corner, CompUSA counted on riding the momentum of its successful turnaround strategies driven by its seven businesses operating model by continuing to sell computers "any way customers wanted to buy them."[8] During the upcoming year the company planned to open approximately 25–30 new stores, enter new metropolitan markets, continue to diverge from a monolithic format by introducing modified store formats to fit each market entered, and saturate current markets by leveraging existing advertising and operating activities and expanding the number of stores in those markets.[9]

7. Kevin Ferguson, "CompUSA—James Halpin, President and CEO," Computer Retail Week, November 18, 1996.

8. CompUSA 1996 Annual Report.

9. Mitchell Bartlett, Analysts Report: CompUSA, Wessels Arnold, & Henderson, September 12, 1996.

EXHIBIT 1

CompUSA Stock Price Versus S&P 500

Index
Value

January 1994 Through September 1996
Both Indexed to 1.00 As of 1/31/94

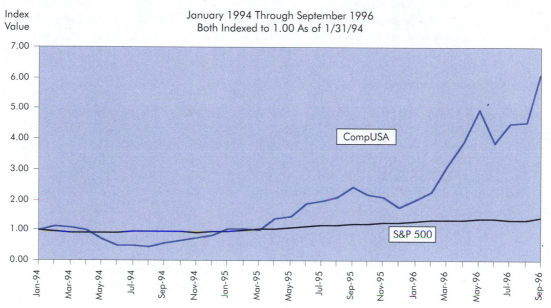

Data as of 9/30/96:

Beta	1.25
1-Year T-Bill	5.68%
10-Year T-Note	6.70%
CompUSA price	$54.00
S&P 500 level	687.31

Source: Datastream International.

CompUSA

EXHIBIT 2
Retail Statistics

CompUSA

COMPUTER SUPERSTORE MARKET SHARE

	1995A	1996E	1997E	1998E	1999E	CAGR
Computer Superstores	$7.0	$10.0	$13.9	$17.3	$20.7	31.0%
Market Share	**10.9%**	**12.5%**	**14.1%**	**15.1%**	**15.8%**	
Total Reseller Market	$64.3	$80.2	$98.5	$114.5	$131.1	20.0%

Source: Merrin Information Services, Inc.

TOP TEN U.S. PC PRODUCT RETAILERS ($ millions)

Ranking	Retailer	Estimated PC Product Revenue for 1995
1	CompUSA	$3,136
2	Best Buy	$2,525
3	Computer City	$1,801
4	Office Depot	$1,275
5	Circuit City	$1,270
6	Micro Center	$975
7	Egghead	$802
8	Sears	$775
9	Office Max	$636
10	Staples	$625

Source: Merrin Information Services.

EXHIBIT 3
CompUSA Revenue and Profitability by Group for 1994–1998

(fiscal years ending June 30; in $ millions)	1994	1995	1996E	1997E	1998E
Estimated Sales					
Retail sales					
Hardware	$1,014	$1,262	$1,505	$1,919	$2,371
Software	275	359	449	596	766
Accessories/peripherals	159	221	292	392	511
Total retail sales	$1,448	$1,843	$2,246	$2,907	$3,648
Corporate	$279	$366	$453	$552	$683
Government and education	204	270	364	432	527
Mail order	150	225	335	469	608
Training	19	34	53	78	110
Technical services	24	39	57	83	116
Export	4	11	18	23	29
Warranties	17	25	39	55	69
Total	$2,146	$2,813	$3,565	$4,600	$5,790
Percentage Analysis					
Retail sales					
Hardware	70.0%	68.5%	67.0%	66.0%	65.0%
Software	19.0	19.5	20.0	20.5	21.0
Accessories/peripherals	11.0	12.0	13.0	13.5	14.0
Total retail sales	100.0%	100.0%	100.0%	100.0%	100.0%
Retail as a % of total sales	67.5%	65.5%	63.0%	63.2%	63.0%
Corporate	13.0	13.0	12.7	12.0	11.8
Government and education	9.5	9.6	10.2	9.4	9.1
Mail order	7.0	8.0	9.4	10.2	10.5
Training	0.9	1.2	1.5	1.7	1.9
Technical services	1.1	1.4	1.6	1.8	2.0
Export	0.2	0.4	0.5	0.5	0.5
Warranties	0.8	0.9	1.1	1.2	1.2
Total	100.0%	100.0%	100.0%	100.0%	100.0%
Estimated Gross Margin					
Total retail sales	10.9%	11.0%	11.9%	11.9%	11.8%
Corporate	7.7	7.6	8.0	8.0	8.0
Government and education	9.0	8.6	9.0	9.0	9.0
Mail order	10.0	10.0	10.3	10.0	9.7
Training	100.0	100.0	100.0	100.0	100.0
Technical services	60.0	60.0	60.0	60.0	60.0
Export	11.5	11.5	11.5	11.5	11.5
Warranties	60.0	60.0	60.0	60.0	60.0
Consolidated Gross Margin	**12.0%**	**12.4%**	**13.6%**	**13.9%**	**14.1%**

Source: Gerard Klauer Mattison & C0., LLC estimates and corporate reports.

CompUSA

CompUSA

EXHIBIT 3
CompUSA Revenue and Profitability by Group for 1994–1998 (*continued*)

(fiscal years ending June 30; in $ millions)	1994	1995	1996E	1997E	1998E
Estimated Gross Profit					
Total retail sales	$158	$203	$267	$345	$431
Corporate	21	28	36	44	54
Government and education	18	23	33	39	47
Mail order	15	23	34	47	59
Training	19	34	53	78	110
Technical services	14	24	34	50	69
Export	0	1	2	3	3
Warranties	10	15	24	33	42
Total gross profit	$257	$350	$484	$639	$816
As a Percent of Total Gross Profit					
Total retail sales	61.5%	57.9%	55.2%	54.0%	52.8%
Corporate	8.3	7.9	7.5	6.9	6.7
Government and education	7.1	6.6	6.8	6.1	5.8
Mail order	5.8	6.4	7.1	7.3	7.2
Training	7.5	9.6	11.0	12.2	13.5
Technical services	5.5	6.7	7.1	7.8	8.5
Export	0.2	0.4	0.4	0.4	0.4
Warranties	4.0	4.3	4.9	5.2	5.1
Total	100.0%	100.0%	100.0%	100.0%	100.0%

Source: Gerard Klauer Mattison & Co., LLC estimates and corporate reports.
Note: Numbers may not add up to totals due to rounding.

EXHIBIT 4

CompUSA, 1996 Abridged Annual Report

TO OUR STOCKHOLDERS:

1996 was a remarkable, exciting and gratifying year for CompUSA Inc. It was a year punctuated by record sales and earnings, the addition of almost 600,000 square feet of retail store space, the development of new store concepts and marketing channels, and strategic growth through our acquisition of PCs Compleat, Inc. and our investment in Info-Source, Inc. On behalf of CompUSA's directors, officers and more than 11,000 team members, whose hard work and dedication made these achievements possible, it is our pleasure to describe some of the highlights of the most successful year in CompUSA's history:

- In fiscal 1996, earnings rose 146% to $59.7 million, or $1.31 per share, from $24.3 million, or $0.60 per share, in fiscal 1995. Sales climbed 30% to $3.8 billion from $2.9 billion. Comparable-store sales, for the 83 stores open one year or more, were up 12.6% for the year.
- The third quarter marked the first time in CompUSA's history that we reached $1 billion in quarterly sales and surpassed a market capitalization of $1 billion.
- During the year we achieved several $100 million sales weeks, and our Computer Superstore in Orange, Connecticut reported a remarkable $3 million in single-day sales. Our Computer Superstores in Bloomington, Minnesota and Mesquite and Addison, Texas also achieved one-day sales over $1 million.
- In September 1995, we sold approximately two million shares of newly issued common stock that added nearly $77 million of equity to CompUSA's balance sheet. Proceeds from the offering were used for store expansion, working capital requirements and general corporate purposes. The combination of this offering and our strong sales and earnings growth allowed CompUSA to end the year in the most solid financial position in the Company's history.
- As a result of our continuing strong performance and broad acceptance in the financial markets, the Board of Directors approved a two-for-one stock split in March 1996, which was completed in April 1996, increasing the number of outstanding shares at that time to approximately 42 million.
- In May 1996, we acquired PCs Compleat, Inc., a leading direct reseller of brand-name personal computers and peripherals based in Marlborough, Massachusetts, for approximately three million shares of CompUSA common stock. The addition of PCs Compleat expands our presence in the direct channel, which is one of the fastest growing areas in the personal computing industry. The combination of PCs Compleat's direct mail expertise with CompUSA's financial and operational strength enhances our competitive position in this highly specialized business and enables us to deliver an even higher level of customer service.
- In June 1996, we announced a strategic alliance with InfoSource, Inc. for the creation of proprietary computer software training courseware. This alliance provides CompUSA with a source of high-quality computer training courseware and skills assessment software that will differentiate us from the competition and enhance our position as one of the nation's premier providers of software training.

CompUSA

- In May, 1996, CompUSA celebrated our hundredth Computer Superstore with simultaneous grand openings in Westminster, Colorado and San Antonio, Texas.
- In November 1995, the CompUSA web site premiered on the Internet at www.compusa.com, enabling customers to obtain a wide range of information about the Company and encouraging them to browse through our on-line catalog.

We have consistently stated that CompUSA will sell computers any way that our customers want to buy them, and we have structured our operating model to meet that objective. We believe that the most effective way to meet our customers' wide-ranging needs is to operate multiple businesses within our category—Retail, Corporate Sales, Government Sales, Education Sales, Mail Order, Technical Services and Training—which build on the strength of our store base. Our goal is to become the premier provider of products and services in each of these areas. We believe there are strong synergies among these separate, yet reliant, businesses that fuel CompUSA's ability to achieve record operating results.

CompUSA's significant sales gains, improvement in gross margin and continuing reductions in operating expenses as a percentage of sales provide powerful testimony to the strength of CompUSA's diverse operating model. Gross margins steadily improved in fiscal 1996 and in the third quarter reached 1%—one of the highest levels in CompUSA's history. Much of this margin improvement was due to sales increases in our higher-margin service businesses—Training and Technical Services—as well as reductions in controllable costs such as shrinkage, freight and variances. Average-sales-per-store also increased throughout the year, enabling us to leverage occupancy costs, thereby strengthening gross margins and reducing store operating expenses as a percentage of sales.

We more than doubled the number of Computer Superstores we opened in fiscal 1996, opening 20 units compared to nine units in fiscal 1995. By the end of July 1996, CompUSA was operating 106 Computer Superstores in 50 major metropolitan markets across the United States. We continue to strive to improve our Computer Superstores, and in fiscal 1996, we tested new store concepts such as the small market prototype. In addition, we completed the companywide roll-out of our Software Sampler$_{sm}$ and CompKids$_{sm}$ areas to all of our Computer Superstores. We expanded our Technical Services business by launching CompUSA Integration Services (CIS) units in eight major markets to meet the growing demand for technical services such as networking. Also, our new delivery and installation service premiered chain-wide as we introduced technical services vans at all of our locations.

Fiscal 1996 has been a challenging, yet rewarding, year for CompUSA. It has also been a year filled with many significant accomplishments, highlighted by our outstanding financial performance. Ours is a dynamic industry, however, and to maintain CompUSA's leadership position we must remain focused and keep our sights set on the future. Most importantly, we must remain fully committed to running our business effectively and to meeting the needs of our customers.

Our team members are dedicated to the success of CompUSA, and we are proud of their continued hard work and commitment. As always, we also appreciate the confidence and support of our stockholders and suppliers.

Sincerely yours,

James F. Halpin
President and Chief Executive Officer

Giles H. Bateman
Chairman of the Board

EXHIBIT 4
CompUSA, 1996 Abridged Annual Report (*continued*)

CONSOLIDATED BALANCE SHEETS

(in thousands, except shares)	June 29, 1996	June 24, 1995
Assets		
Current assets:		
Cash and cash equivalents	$207,614	$96,494
Accounts receivable, net of allowance for doubtful accounts of $1,692 and $1,176 at June 29, 1996 and June 24, 1995, respectively	148,109	103,934
Merchandise inventories	398,841	312,202
Prepaid expenses and other	15,669	14,506
Total current assets	770,233	527,136
Property and equipment, net (Note 3)	131,184	106,290
Other assets	7,920	7,903
	$909,337	$641,329
Liabilities and Stockholders' Equity		
Current liabilities:		
Accounts payable	$377,774	$282,885
Accrued liabilities (Note 4)	82,178	49,076
Current portion of capital lease obligations (Note 6)	4,382	5,047
Total current liabilities	464,334	337,008
Capital lease obligations (Note 6)	5,066	5,153
Senior Subordinated Notes (Note 8)	110,000	110,000
Deferred income taxes (Note 5)	4,032	2,464
Commitments and contingencies (Notes 6 and 10)	—	—
Stockholders' equity (Note 12):		
Preferred stock, $.01 per share par value, 10,000 shares authorized, none issued	—	—
Common stock, $.01 per share par value, 100,000,000 shares authorized, with 45,107,858 shares issued and outstanding at June 29, 1996: no par value, $.01 per share stated value, with 40,465,920 shares issued and outstanding at June 24, 1995	451	405
Paid-in capital	255,667	173,348
Retained earnings	72,616	12,951
	328,734	186,704
Less: Treasury stock, at cost, 189,730 shares at June 29, 1996	(2,829)	—
Total stockholders' equity	325,905	186,704
	$909,337	$641,329

See accompanying notes.

CompUSA

CONSOLIDATED STATEMENTS OF OPERATIONS

CompUSA

	Fiscal Year Ended		
(in thousands, except per share data)	June 29, 1996	June 24, 1995	June 25, 1994
Net sales	$3,829,786	$2,935,901	$2,219,457
Cost of sales and occupancy costs	3,311,682	2,573,945	1,955,183
Gross profit	$ 518,104	$ 361,956	$ 264,274
Store operating expenses	328,344	263,654	208,356
Pre-opening expenses	5,466	2,454	7,266
General and administrative expenses	75,488	54,940	47,963
Transaction costs related to Merger (Note 2)	3,453	—	—
Restructuring costs (Note 9)	—	—	9,918
Operating income (loss)	$ 105,353	$ 40,908	$ (9,229)
Other expense (income):			
Interest expense	12,487	12,015	12,156
Other income, net	(6,983)	(2,409)	(2,063)
	$ 5,504	$ 9,606	$ 10,093
Income (loss) before income taxes	99,849	31,302	(19,322)
Income tax expense (benefit) (Note 5)	40,184	6,963	(2,298)
Net income (loss)	$ 59,665	$ 24,339	$ (17,024)
Income (loss) per common and common equivalent share	$ 1.31	$ 0.60	$ (0.44)
Weighted average common and common equivalent shares	45,610	40,868	38,535

See accompanying notes.

CONSOLIDATED STATEMENTS OF CASH FLOWS

	Fiscal Year Ended		
(in thousands)	June 29, 1996	June 24, 1995	June 25, 1994
Cash flows provided by (used in) operating activities:			
Net income (loss)	$59,665	$24,339	$(17,024)
Adjustments to reconcile net income (loss) to net cash provided by (used in) operating activities:			
Depreciation and amortization	27,625	21,285	15,148
Restructuring costs	(214)	(2,504)	2,718
Deferred income tax	266	(4,645)	(1,133)
Changes in assets and liabilities:			
Decrease (increase) in:			
Accounts receivable	(44,175)	(9,875)	(24,968)
Income tax receivable	(417)	2,479	(1,540)
Merchandise inventories	(86,639)	(29,603)	(73,614)
Prepaid expenses and other	139	286	(1,703)
Other assets	(63)	(694)	258
Increase in:			
Accounts payable and accrued liabilities	126,384	134,495	31,638
Income taxes payable	5,140	41	—
Total adjustments	$ 28,046	$111,265	$ (53,196)
Net cash provided by (used in) operating activities	$ 87,711	$135,604	$ (70,220)
Cash flows used in investing activities:			
Capital expenditures	(47,418)	(30,057)	(46,488)
Other	(565)	572	385
Net cash used in investing activities	$ (47,983)	$ (29,485)	$ (46,103)
Cash flows provided by (used in) financing activities:			
Proceeds from issuance of Common Stock	79,344	1,994	13,527
Purchase of treasury stock	(3,521)	—	—
Sale of treasury stock to benefit plan	812	—	—
Borrowings under line of credit agreements	48,750	54,127	113,428
Repayment of borrowings under line of credit agreements	(48,750)	(92,627)	(75,428)
Payments under capital lease obligations	(5,243)	(5,149)	(3,770)
Net cash provided by (used in) financing activities	$ 71,392	$ (41,655)	$ 47,757
Net increase (decrease) in cash and cash equivalents	111,120	64,464	(68,566)
Cash and cash equivalents at beginning of year	96,494	32,030	100,596
Cash and cash equivalents at end of year	$207,614	$ 96,494	$32,030

See accompanying notes.

CompUSA

SELECTED FINANCIAL DATA

The following table sets forth selected consolidated financial and operating data for the periods from June 27, 1992 through June 29, 1996. As more fully described in Note 2 of Notes to Consolidated Financial Statements, the Company acquired PCs Compleat on May 30, 1996 in a merger transaction accounted for under the pooling of interest method of accounting. Under the pooling of interest method of accounting, the historical book values of the assets, liabilities, and stockholders' equity of PCs Compleat, as reported on its balance sheet, have been carried over onto the consolidated balance sheet of the Company and no goodwill or other intangible assets were created. In addition, the Company has restated its consolidated statements of operations to include the results of operations of PCs Compleat for each of the fiscal years presented. This information should be read in conjunction with the Consolidated Financial Statements and related Notes thereto of the Company and with "Management's Discussion and Analysis of Financial Condition and Results of Operations," which are included elsewhere in this Annual Report on Form 10-K.

		Fiscal Year Ended			
(In thousands, except per share data and selected operating data)	June 29, 1996[a]	June 24, 1995	June 25, 1994	June 26, 1993	June 27, 1992
Income Statement Data:					
Net sales	$3,829,786	$2,935,901	$2,219,457	$1,369,749	$822,815
Cost of sales and occupancy costs	3,311,682	2,573,945	1,955,183	1,189,675	716,531
Gross profit	$ 518,104	$ 361,956	$ 264,274	$ 180,074	$106,284
Store operating expenses	328,344	263,654	208,356	123,516	71,026
Pre-opening expenses	5,466	2,454	7,266	6,111	2,010
General and administrative expenses	75,488	54,940	47,963	31,466	22,897
Transaction costs related to Merger[b]	3,453	—	—	—	—
Restructuring costs[c]	—	—	9,918	—	—
Operating income (loss)	$ 105,353	$ 40,908	$ (9,229)	$ 18,981	$ 10,351
Interest expense	12,487	12,015	12,156	2,256	2,669
Other income, net[d]	(6,983)	(2,409)	(2,063)	(468)	(358)
Income (loss) before income taxes	$ 99,849	$ 31,302	$ (19,322)	$ 17,193	8,040
Income tax expense (benefit)	40,184	6,963	(2,298)	7,510	415
Net income (loss)	$ 59,665	$ 24,339	$ (17,024)	$ 9,683	$ 7,625
Income (loss) applicable to Common Stock[e]	$ 59,665	$ 24,339	$ (17,024)	$ 9,683	$ 5,999
Income (loss) per common and common equivalent share[f]	$ 1.31	$ 0.60	$ (0.44)	$ 0.25	$ 0.23
Weighted average number of shares outstanding[f]	45,610	40,868	38,535	38,291	25,881
Selected Operating Data:					
Stores open at end of period	105	85	76	48	28
Average net sales per gross square foot[g]	$ 1,422	$ 1,336	$ 1,268	$ 1,458	$ 1,452
Total gross square footage at end of period	2,850,000	2,254,500	1,965,200	1,197,600	680,700
Percentage increase in comparable store sales[h]	12.6%	10.3%	9.0%	20.8%	13.3%
Balance Sheet Data:					
Working capital	$305,899	$190,128	$210,018	$216,205	$ 59,655
Total assets	909,337	641,329	522,501	449,399	211,550
Long-term debt, excluding current portion	115,066	115,153	153,292	115,716	3,383
Stockholders' equity	325,905	186,704	160,372	163,869	86,072

a. The Company's fiscal year is a 52/53 week year ending on the last Saturday of each June. The Company's fiscal year ended June 29, 1996 contained fifty-three weeks. The fiscal years ended June 24, 1995, June 25, 1994, June 26, 1993, and June 27, 1992 contained fifty-two weeks.

b. For a discussion of the Company's acquisition of PCs Compleat, see Note 2 to Consolidated Financial Statements.

c. For a discussion of the Company's restructuring charge, see Note 9 of Notes to Consolidated Financial Statements.

(Notes continued on next page)

d. Fiscal 1992 includes an extraordinary loss of $233,000 from early extinguishment of debt.

e. Income (loss) applicable to Common Stock represents the portion of the Company's income (loss) applicable to common stockholders. Such amount for fiscal 1992 was calculated by adjusting net income (loss) for the accretion and dividend requirements of certain redeemable securities. All such accretion and dividend requirements terminated with the completion of the Company's public offering in December 1991.

f. All references in this table to the number of shares and income per common and common equivalent share amounts have been adjusted on a retroactive basis to reflect the two-for-one stock split declared by the Company's Board of Directors effective April 8, 1996 and the Company's acquisition of PCs Compleat.

g. Calculated using net sales divided by gross square footage of stores open at the end of the period, weighted by the number of months open during the period. Net sales for this calculation consist of combined retail and direct sales generated from the Company's retail stores. Net sales for this calculation exclude mail order sales generated by PCs Compleat and, until the beginning of the fourth quarter of fiscal 1993, exclude the mail order sales of the Company's former wholly-owned subsidiary Compudyne Direct, Inc. Beginning with the fourth quarter of fiscal 1993, mail order sales by the Company (excluding PCs Compleat) have been fulfilled by the Company's retail stores and are included in the stores' net sales. See "Management's Discussion and Analysis of Financial Condition and Results of Operations—General." Average net sales per gross square foot for the fiscal year ended June 29, 1996 has been calculated on the basis of a fifty-two week fiscal year.

h. Comparable store sales are net sales for stores open the same months in both the indicated and the previous period, including stores that were relocated or expanded during either period. Comparable store sales increase for the fiscal year ended June 29, 1996 has been calculated based on sales for the 53 weeks then ended compared to the 53 weeks ended July 1, 1995.

General

Fiscal 1995 was a transition year for CompUSA, characterized by a reduction in store growth that allowed the Company to apply its resources to improving the Company's operations. The Company believes it has substantially completed the transition phase of its fiscal 1995 business plan and, in fiscal 1996, the Company focused on the execution and growth of its businesses.

The following table sets forth certain operating data for the Company:

| | Fiscal Year | | |
	1996	1995	1994
Stores open at end of year	105	85	76
Stores opened during the year	20	9	28
Stores relocated during the year	1	2	1
Average net sales per gross square foot[a]	$1,422	$1,336	$1,268
Comparable stores sales increase[b]	12.6%	10.3%	9.0%

a. Calculated using net sales divided by gross square footage of stores open at the end of the period, weighted by the number of months open during the period. Average net sales per gross square foot for fiscal 1996 has been calculated on the basis of a 52 week fiscal year.

b. Comparable store sales are net sales for stores open the same months in both the indicated and previous period, including stores that were relocated or expanded during either period. The comparable store sales increase for fiscal 1996 has been calculated by comparing net sales for the fifty-three weeks ended June 29, 1996 with net sales for the 53 weeks ended July 1, 1995.

Average net sales per gross square foot increased during fiscal 1996 compared with fiscal 1995 primarily due to the maturation of the Company's existing store base and increased growth in the Company's direct sales, mail order, and service businesses. Service businesses include customer training and technical services. Mature stores typically have higher net sales per gross square foot than new stores. Average net sales per gross square foot increased during fiscal 1995, compared with fiscal 1994, primarily due to increased customer demand, the maturation of the Company's store base, and changes associated with the implementation of the fiscal 1995 business plan.

In certain instances, the Company has opened additional Computer Superstores in existing markets, which has resulted in the diversion of sales from existing stores and thus some reductions in the rate of comparable store sales growth. CompUSA has opened additional stores in existing markets largely to increase market penetration and to provide customers with more convenience and better service. The Company plans to continue its strategy of opening additional Computer Superstores in existing markets. The resulting diversion of sales from existing stores may adversely affect the Company's comparable store sales. However, the Company believes that this strategy should increase its awareness with local consumers, enhance its competitive position in such markets and create efficiencies in advertising and management, and therefore is in the Company's long-term best interest.

Results of Operations

As a result of the expansion of the Company's store base, period-to-period comparisons of financial results may not be meaningful and the results of operations for historical periods may not be indicative of the results to be expected in future periods. In addition, the Company expects that its quarterly results of operations will fluctuate depending on the timing of the opening of, and the amount of net sales contributed by, new stores and the timing of costs associated with the selection, leasing, construction, and opening of new stores, as well as seasonal factors, product introductions, and changes in product mix. See "Quarterly Data and Seasonality."

The following table sets forth certain items expressed as a percentage of net sales for the periods indicated:

	Fiscal Year Ended		
	1996	1995	1994
Net sales	100.0%	100.0%	100.0%
Cost of sales and occupancy costs	86.5	87.7	88.1
Gross profit	13.5	12.3	11.9
Store operating expenses	8.6	9.0	9.4
Pre-opening expenses	0.1	—	0.3
General and administrative expenses	2.0	1.9	2.2
Transaction costs related to Merger[a]	0.1	—	—
Restructuring costs	—	—	0.4
Operating income (loss)	2.7	1.4	(0.4)
Interest expense and other income, net	0.1	0.3	0.5
Income (loss) before income taxes	2.6	1.1	(0.9)
Income tax expense (benefit)	1.0	0.3	(0.1)
Net income (loss)	1.6%	0.8%	(0.8)%

a. For a discussion of the Company's acquisition of PCs Compleat, see Note 2 of Notes to Consolidated Financial Statements.

Fiscal 1996 Compared with Fiscal 1995

Net sales for fiscal 1996 increased 30% to $3.83 billion from $2.94 billion for fiscal 1995. The increase in net sales was due to the additional sales volume attributable to the new stores opened during and subsequent to fiscal 1995 and an increase in comparable store sales of 12.6%. Comparable store sales are net sales for stores open the same months in both the indicated and previous period, including stores that were relocated or expanded during either period. The Company believes the increase in comparable store sales was primarily due to the maturation of the Company's store base, increased customer demand that was attributable to several factors, one of which was the introduction of Microsoft Windows® 95 operating system, and increased growth in the Company's direct sales, mail order, and service businesses.

Gross profit was $518 million, or 13.5% of net sales, in fiscal 1996, compared with $362 million, or 12.3% of net sales, in fiscal 1995. The increase in gross profit as a percentage of net sales was primarily due to higher product margin, an improvement in controllable costs such as inventory shrinkage and freight, leveraging of occupancy costs due to higher average sales per store, and an increase in the ratio of service revenues to total revenues. Service revenues typically have higher gross margins than merchandise sales.

Store operating expenses were $328 million, or 8.6% of net sales, in fiscal 1996, compared with $264 million, or 9.0% of net sales, in fiscal 1995. The decrease in store operating expenses as a percentage of net sales was primarily due to the leveraging of fixed store costs and lower net advertising expense resulting from increased vendor participation. These decreases were partially offset by higher personnel expenses related to the increase in service revenues. Although service revenues generally have higher gross margins than merchandise sales, the related store expenses are higher than those related to merchandise sales.

Pre-opening expenses consist primarily of personnel expenses incurred prior to a store's opening and promotional costs associated with the opening. The Company's policy is to expense all pre-opening expenses in the month of the store's grand opening. In fiscal 1996, the Company incurred $5.5 million in pre-opening expenses in connection with the opening of 20 new stores, the relocation of one store, and the opening of two Training Supercenter Plus locations, compared with $2.5 million in pre-opening expenses incurred in fiscal 1995 in connection with the opening of nine new stores, two Training Supercenter Plus locations, and the relocation of two stores. The Company incurred average pre-opening expenses of $260,000 per store for the 20 new stores opened during fiscal 1996 and $240,000 per store for the nine new stores opened during fiscal 1995.

General and administrative expenses of $75.5 million, or 2.0% of net sales, for fiscal 1996 increased as a percentage of net sales, compared with $54.9 million, or 1.9% of net sales, for fiscal 1995. The increase in general and administrative expenses as a percentage of net sales was primarily due to charges of approximately $2.0 million for professional fees and related costs in the third quarter of fiscal 1996 regarding the Company's acquisition review of Tandy Corporation's Computer City division. Discussions relating to such possible acquisition were terminated in February 1996. Excluding the $2.0 million of fees and costs related to such possible purchase, general and administrative expenses in fiscal 1996 related to increased incentive compensation were offset by the leveraging of personnel expenses over higher sales.

CompUSA

Interest expense and other income, net, was $5.5 million in fiscal 1996, compared with $9.6 million in fiscal 1995. The decrease is attributable to increased other income related to higher investment levels during fiscal 1996. See "Liquidity and Capital Resources."

The Company's effective tax rate for fiscal 1996 was 40%, compared with an effective tax rate of 22% for fiscal 1995. The effective tax rate differed in fiscal 1996 from the federal statutory rate primarily due to state income taxes and nondeductible transaction costs related to the Company's acquisition of PCs Compleat, offset in part by the benefits from tax exempt interest income earned by the Company. The fiscal 1995 effective tax rate differed from the federal statutory rate primarily due to the recognition of the previously unrecognized tax benefit associated with the fiscal 1994 loss.

As a result of the above, net income for fiscal 1996 was $59.7 million, or $1.31 per share, compared with net income of $24.3 million, or $0.60 per share, for fiscal 1995.

Liquidity and Capital Resources

In September 1995, the Company completed a public offering, selling 4,025,000 newly-issued shares of Common Stock and receiving net proceeds of approximately $76.8 million (net of offering costs of approximately $3.5 million).

In December 1995, the Company repurchased 236,200 shares of Common Stock, to be held as treasury stock, at a weighted average of $14.89 per share, excluding transaction costs. In February 1996, the Company made a cash contribution to its 401(k) plan to effect the Company's required contribution to the plan for 1995, which the plan used to purchase 46,470 shares of treasury stock from the Company.

At June 29, 1996, total assets were $909 million, $770 million of which were current assets, including $208 million of cash and cash equivalents. Net cash provided by operating activities for fiscal 1996 was $87.7 million, compared with net cash provided by operating activities of $135.6 million for fiscal 1995. Net cash provided by operating activities for fiscal 1995 was positively affected by the accounts payable to inventory ratio rising to 91% at June 24, 1995, compared with 57% at June 25, 1994. This improvement was due, in part, to the Company's inventory turnover rate improving to 8.1 inventory turns for fiscal 1995, compared with an inventory turnover rate of 6.7 inventory turns for fiscal 1994.

Approximately three-fourths of the Company's net sales during both fiscal 1996 and fiscal 1995 were sales for which the Company received payment at the time of sale either in cash, by check, or by third-party credit card. The remaining net sales were primarily sales for which the Company provided credit terms to corporate, government, and education customers.

Capital expenditures during fiscal 1996 were $47.4 million, $15.5 million of which were for fiscal 1996 new stores, compared with $30.1 million of capital expenditures during fiscal 1995, $8.8 million of which were for fiscal 1995 new stores. During fiscal 1996, the Company opened 20 new Computer Superstores. Excluding the effects of new store openings, the Company's greatest short-term capital requirements occur during the second fiscal quarter to support a higher level of sales in that quarter. Short-term capital requirements are satisfied primarily by available cash and cash equivalents and vendor and bank financing.

The Company has an unsecured $75 million credit agreement (the "Credit Agreement") with a consortium of banks that expires in June 1999. At June 29, 1996, no amounts were outstanding under the Credit Agreement and the Company had approximately $74.4 million available for future borrowings after reduction for outstanding letters of credit. The Company also finances certain fixture and equipment acquisitions through equipment lessors. Lease financing is available from numerous sources and the Company evaluates equipment leasing as a supplemental source of financing on a continuing basis.

The Company believes that its available cash and cash equivalents, funds generated by operations, currently available vendor and floor plan financing, lease financing, and funds available under the Credit Agreement should be sufficient to finance its continuing operations and expansion plans through the end of fiscal 1997 and to make all required payments of interest on the Senior Subordinated Notes. The level of future expansion will be contingent upon the availability of additional capital.

NOTES TO CONSOLIDATED FINANCIAL STATEMENTS

1. Summary of Significant Accounting Policies

Business—CompUSA Inc. (the "Company") is a retailer of personal computer hardware, software, accessories, and related products and services conducting its operations principally through its Computer Superstores in the United States. At June 29, 1996, June 24, 1995, and June 25, 1994, the Company operated 105, 85, and 76 Computer Superstores, respectively. In addition to the retail sales of its stores, the Company's stores also fulfill the principal marketing, product, and service functions of the Company's other businesses, including direct sales to corporate, government, education, and mail order customers and training and technical services. In addition, the Company conducts mail order operations both through its stores and through PCs Compleat, Inc. ("PCs Compleat"), a wholly owned subsidiary of the Company.

Fiscal Year—The Company's fiscal year is a 52/53-week year ending on the last Saturday of each June. All references to the fiscal year ended June 29, 1996 relate to the 53 weeks then ended. All references to the fiscal years ended June 24, 1995 and June 25, 1994, respectively, relate to the 52 weeks then ended.

Consolidation—The financial statements include the accounts of the Company and its wholly owned subsidiaries. All significant intercompany transactions have been eliminated.

Use of Estimates—The preparation of consolidated financial statements in conformity with generally accepted accounting principles requires management to make certain estimates and assumptions. These estimates and assumptions affect the reported amounts of assets, liabilities, revenues, and expenses and the disclosure of gain and loss contingencies at the date of the consolidated financial statements. Actual results could differ from those estimates.

Cash and Cash Equivalents—Cash on hand in stores, in banks, and short-term investments with original maturities of three months or less are considered cash and cash equivalents. Cash and cash equivalents are carried at cost, which approximates fair value.

Accounts Receivable—Accounts receivable represent amounts due from customers related to the sale of the Company's products and services. Such receivables are generally unsecured and are generally due from a diverse group of corporate, government, and education customers located throughout the United States and, accordingly, do not include any specific concentrations of credit risk. The Company believes it has provided adequate reserves for potentially uncollectible accounts. For the fiscal years ended June 29, 1996, June 24, 1995, and June 25, 1994, the Company's bad debt expense was $878,000, $766,000, and $762,000, respectively.

Merchandise Inventories—Merchandise inventories are valued at the lower of cost, determined on a weighted average basis, or market.

Property and Equipment—Property and equipment are stated at cost. Depreciation is provided in amounts sufficient to charge the cost of the respective assets to operations over their estimated service lives on a straight-line basis. Estimated service lives are as follows:

Furniture and fixtures	5–10 years
Equipment	3–5 years
Leasehold improvements	Life of lease
Equipment under capital leases	Life of lease

Advertising Expenses—Advertising expenses are expensed in the month incurred, subject to reduction by reimbursement from vendors. Net advertising expenses were not a significant component of store operating expense for fiscal years ended June 29, 1996, June 24, 1995, and June 25, 1994.

Pre-opening Costs—Pre-opening costs are deferred to the date of the store's grand opening and are expensed in the month of the store's grand opening. Pre-opening costs consist primarily of personnel and advertising expenses incurred prior to a store's opening and promotional costs associated with the opening.

Income Taxes—Income taxes are maintained in accordance with Statement of Financial Accounting Standards ("SFAS") No. 109, "Accounting for Income Taxes," whereby deferred income tax assets and liabilities result from temporary differences. Temporary differences are differences between the tax bases of assets and liabilities and their reported amounts in the consolidated financial statements that will result in taxable or deductible amounts in future years.

Income (Loss) per Share—Income (loss) per common and common equivalent share is computed using the weighted average number of shares of common stock and common stock equivalents outstanding during each period. If dilutive, the effects of stock options are calculated using the treasury stock method.

On March 27, 1996, the Company's Board of Directors declared a two-for-one stock split effected in the form of a stock dividend to stockholders of record on April 8, 1996, payable on April 22, 1996. Stock options and all other agreements payable in the Company's common stock (the "Common Stock") were amended to reflect the split. An amount equal to the par value of shares issued has been transferred from additional paid-in capital to the common stock account.

All references to the number of shares, except for shares authorized, and income per common and common equivalent share amounts in the consolidated financial statements and the accompanying notes have been adjusted on a retroactive basis to reflect the stock split and the Company's acquisition of PCs Compleat (Note 2).

Reclassifications—Certain prior year balances have been reclassified to conform to the current year basis of presentation.

6. Leases

The Company leases equipment under capital and operating leases that expire at various dates through 2000. The Company operates in facilities leased under noncancelable operating leases that expire at various dates through 2016 and the majority of which contain renewal options and require the Company to pay a proportionate share of common area maintenance. At June 29, 1996, future minimum lease payments under all leases with initial or remaining noncancelable lease terms in excess of one year are as follows:

Fiscal Year (in thousands)	Capital Leases	Operating Leases
1997	$4,991	$45,480
1998	3,194	47,148
1999	1,488	47,540
2000	657	46,331
2001	146	43,355
Thereafter	—	314,985
Total minimum lease payments	10,476	$544,839
Less amount representing interest	1,028	
Present value of minimum lease payments	9,448	
Less current portion	4,382	
Capital lease obligations due after one year	$ 5,066	

7. Credit Agreement

At June 29, 1996, the Company has an unsecured credit agreement (the "Credit Agreement") with a consortium of banks that provides for borrowings and letters of credit up to a maximum of $75,000,000. The Credit Agreement replaced a previous $50,000,000 secured credit facility that was terminated in June 1995. Borrowings under the Credit Agreement are subject to a borrowing base limitation (the "Borrowing Base") that is equal to the sum of (a) 80% of eligible accounts, as defined, and (b) an amount equal to 40% of eligible inventory, which is defined as inventory minus outstanding trade accounts payable incurred with respect to the purchase of production of eligible inventory (provided that the amount computed in (b) above cannot comprise more than $20,000,000 of the Borrowing Base), less (c) outstanding letters of credit (which may not exceed $35,000,000 in the aggregate). At June 29, 1996, and June 24, 1995, no amounts were outstanding under the Credit Agreement and the Company had $74,400,000 and $60,000,000, respectively, available for future borrowings (after reduction for outstanding letters of credit).

Borrowings under the Credit Agreement bear interest, at the Company's option, at either a prime rate (8.25% per annum as of June 29, 1996) or a rate based on the London Interbank Offering Rate ranging from 5.5% to 6.125% per annum as of June 29, 1996, plus a specified margin. The Company also pays certain commitment and agent fees. Although the Credit Agreement expires in June 1999, the Company has the annual option to extend the Credit Agreement for an additional year with the banks' approval. Borrowings under the credit facility have to be in place before the Credit Agreement bore interest at the bank's prime rate.

CompUSA

The Credit Agreement requires the maintenance of certain financial ratios. If the Company is unable to maintain certain minimum financial ratios, the banks may require outstanding borrowings under the Credit Agreement to be secured by the Company's accounts receivable and certain approved inventories. The Credit Agreement also imposes credit limitations on mergers and consolidations and prohibits the payment of dividends. The indebtedness under the Credit Agreement is guaranteed on a full, unconditional, and joint and several basis by all the current subsidiaries of the Company.

8. Senior Subordinated Notes

In June 1993, the Company issued $110,000,000 in principal amount of 9 1/2% Senior Subordinated Notes due June 15, 2000 (the "Senior Subordinated Notes"). Interest on the Senior Subordinated Notes is payable semi-annually on each June 15 and December 15. The Senior Subordinated Notes are subordinated in right of payment to all existing and future senior indebtedness of the Company, as defined. Senior indebtedness, which totaled approximately $387,000,000 and $293,000,000 at June 29, 1996 and June 24, 1995, respectively, consists primarily of capital lease obligations, indebtedness incurred under the Credit Agreement, and trade payables.

The Senior Subordinated Notes are redeemable on or after June 15, 1998, at the option of the Company, in whole or in part, at 102.714% of the principal amount, declining to 100% of the principal amount on June 15, 1999 and thereafter. The Senior Subordinated Notes grant the holders the right to require the Company to repurchase all or any portion of their notes at 101% of the principal amount thereof, together with accrued interest, following the occurrence of a change in control of the Company, as defined.

The indenture related to the Senior Subordinated Notes restricts, among other things, the ability of the Company and its subsidiaries to incur additional indebtedness or issue preferred stock, pay dividends and make other distributions, sell or issue stock of a subsidiary, create encumbrances on the ability of any subsidiary that is a guarantor to pay dividends or make other restricted payments, engage in certain transactions with affiliates, dispose of certain assets, merge or consolidate with or into, or sell or otherwise transfer their properties and assets as an entirety to another entity, incur indebtedness that would rank senior in right of payment to the Senior Subordinated Notes and be subordinated to any other indebtedness of the Company, or create additional liens.

The Senior Subordinated Notes are guaranteed on a full, unconditional and joint and several basis by all of the Company's direct and indirect subsidiaries, each of which is wholly owned. The combined summarized information of these subsidiaries is as follows:

	As of and for the Fiscal Year Ended	
(in thousands)	June 29, 1996	June 24, 1995
Intercompany receivables	$ —	$ 92,293
Other current assets	39,442	40,001
Noncurrent assets	3,955	1,880
Intercompany payables	362	6,123
Other current liabilities	22,775	15,009
Long-term debt and liabilities	704	61
Intercompany revenues	60,933	28,434
Other revenues	221,536	123,304
Costs and expenses	218,742	122,004
Net income	42,302	15,611

In preparation of the Company's consolidated financial statements, all intercompany accounts were eliminated.

The fair value of the Senior Subordinated Notes, based on quoted market prices, was approximately $111,650,000 and $105,875,000 at June 29, 1996 and June 24, 1995, respectively.

13. Supplemental Cash Flow Information

Cash payments for interest and income taxes are as follows:

(In thousands)	Fiscal Year Ended		
	June 29, 1996	June 24, 1995	June 25, 1994
Interest	$11,611	$12,274	$11,768
Income taxes	$35,253	$11,065	$ 1,156

Financing and investing activities not affecting cash are as follows:

	Fiscal Year Ended		
	June 29, 1996	June 24, 1995	June 25, 1994
Additions to property and equipment under capital leases	$ 4,491	$ 2,257	$11,185

14. Supplemental Quarterly Financial Data (unaudited)

(In thousands, except per share data)	First Quarter	Second Quarter	Third Quarter	Fourth Quarter
Fiscal Year Ended June 29, 1996:				
Net sales	$781,978	$983,228	$1,065,731	$998,849
Cost of sales and occupancy costs	684,090	852,177	916,837	858,578
Operating income	12,951	31,865	38,603	21,934
Net income	6,207	18,748	22,933	11,777
Income per common and common equivalent share	$0.15	$0.40	$0.50	$0.25
Weighted average common and common equivalent shares	42,535	46,509	46,287	47,109
Fiscal Year Ended June 24, 1995:				
Net sales	$614,097	$791,863	$805,580	$724,361
Cost of sales and occupancy costs	540,498	696,616	702,865	633,966
Operating income (loss)	(1,204)	14,755	19,177	8,180
Net income (loss)	(2,943)	9,945	12,642	4,695
Income (loss) per common and common equivalent share	$(0.07)	$0.24	$0.31	$0.11
Weighted average common and common equivalent shares	39,679	40,757	41,270	41,762

REPORT OF INDEPENDENT AUDITORS

The Board of Directors
CompUSA

   We have audited the accompanying consolidated balance sheets of CompUSA Inc. (the "Company") as of June 29, 1996 and June 24, 1995, and the related consolidated statements of operations, stockholders' equity, and cash flows for each of the three years in the period ended June 29, 1996. These financial statements are the responsibility of the Company's management. Our responsibility is to express an opinion on these financial statements based on our audits.

   We conducted our audits in accordance with generally accepted auditing standards. Those standards require that we plan and perform the audit to obtain reasonable assurance about whether the financial statements are free of material misstatement. An audit includes examining, on a test basis, evidence supporting the amounts and disclosures in the financial statements. An audit also includes assessing the accounting principles used and significant estimates made by management, as well as evaluating the overall financial statement presentation. We believe that our audits provide a reasonable basis for our opinion.

   In our opinion, the financial statements referred to above present fairly, in all material respects, the consolidated financial position of CompUSA Inc. at June 29, 1996 and June 24, 1995, and the consolidated results of its operations and its cash flows for each of the three years in the period ended June 29, 1996, in conformity with generally accepted accounting principles.

ERNST & YOUNG LLP

Dallas Texas
August 14, 1996

It is mid-1992. The collection of industries under the heading "computer systems" (SIC 3571) grew dramatically during the 1970s and 1980s, but it is now in a state of turmoil. Most firms have suffered declines in earnings, and several—including industry giants IBM and Digital Equipment Corporation—have experienced large losses. Overall, profitability (as measured by return on equity) in the industry has fallen steadily from 23 percent in 1988 to 11 percent in 1991, and sales have been flat for the last two years. In the face of this turmoil, however, some firms with well-positioned product lines have managed to grow at a quick pace. For example, Sun Microsystems, a major player in the expanding market for workstations, experienced a 30 percent compounded annual growth rate from 1986 through 1991.

Standard and Poor's Corporation describes the situation as follows:

Computer manufacturers have become used to citing the reasons for the present malaise in the information technology business. These include the following:

1. *The spread of open system computer networks based on standard industry components that cannot command the gross profit margins inherent in proprietary designs. The gross margin associated with a mainframe computer sale can be as high as 70 percent; for personal computers (PCs) and workstations, it can be less than 30 percent.*

2. *A seemingly never-ending decline in the cost, and growth in the power of data processing equipment, which has further squeezed manufacturers' margins. A high performance workstation can cost less than $1000 for every million instructions per second (mips) of computer power. Mainframes typically cost more than $100,000 per mip. For many tasks, but not all, it is possible to substitute low-cost workstation power for mainframe power.*

3. *A slackening of demand for computer systems . . . [due to] saturation in some areas of the market, dissatisfaction with the results of continued computerization, and (in some countries) high interest rates.*[1]

To deal with the changes in the industry, some firms have abandoned product differentiation, cut prices, and focused on cost reduction. Some have undergone major restructurings. Several firms, including Apple and IBM, have formed new alliances.

161

....

This case was prepared by Professor Victor L. Bernard, and is based upon publicly available information. It was prepared as a basis for class discussion and is not intended to illustrate either an effective or ineffective management of a business situation.

1. *Standard and Poor's Industry Report Service (July 3, 1992), Vol. 3., No. 2, Sec. 2.*

The following brief sketches of four computing systems manufacturers help describe the variety of experience within the industry.

ATARI CORPORATION

Atari manufactures personal computers and video game systems. The firm's principle products are its Atari ST series of PCs, based on Motorola 68000 and 68030 series microprocessors and employing Atari's own TOS operating system with state-of-the-art graphical interface; its PC-compatible, MS-DOS based personal computers, including the one-pound Atari Portfolio and full-scale PCs driven by an 80386 microprocessor; Atari 8-bit microcomputers, which retail for less than $100; and video game systems. There are over 8000 software titles available for the ST computers, as well as a variety of peripherals. The fractions of net sales accounted for by the various product lines have been as follows:

	1991	1990	1989
Atari ST personal computers	.53	.59	.59
Atari PC compatible palm-top & personal computers	.10	.18	.17
Atari microcomputers	.03	.02	.06
Atari video game systems	.34	.21	.18

More than 80 percent of Atari's sales are in Europe, where it holds about 5 percent of the PC market, ranking behind IBM, Commodore, Olivetti, and Amstrad, and barely ahead of Apple Macintosh and Compaq. Until the second quarter of 1991, the company's principle products were manufactured in Taiwan, but that facility was sold. Since that time, various independent subcontractors have assembled the products, and some start-up problems were encountered. Atari intends to acquire another location for its manufacturing operations and resume in-house production.

Net sales declined 37 percent for Atari in 1991. In his letter to shareholders, Atari CEO Sam Tramiel (son of 46-percent owner Jack Tramiel) was straightforward: "I am quite displeased with the company's 1991 results, and hope that this message accurately conveys my dissatisfaction." Net income in 1991 reached its highest level since 1987, but only after inclusion of a $40.9 million pretax gain on the sale of its Taiwan manufacturing facility. Atari's ST sales continued the slide that began in 1990, as software producers—miffed by Atari's giveaway of prepackaged programs with ST computers—shifted their efforts to Apple and DOS systems.

Tramiel points to several corrections in Atari's strategy, all of which were in place or being put into place by the end of fiscal 1991. The changes include (1) cost reductions and careful monitoring of inventory levels, (2) refocusing of advertising to target specific audiences and reduce costs, and (3) redefining R&D, with a shift in emphasis to high volume production. Looking forward to late 1992, Atari is also ready to bring two new products to market. One is the Falcon 030, a more powerful version of the ST computer; the other is Jaguar, the next-generation video game console.

A summary of Atari's recent financial performance appears in Exhibit 1. The company experienced a loss in the first quarter of 1992 equal to 11 percent of beginning equity. Analysts' forecasts for future performance are not available.

CRAY RESEARCH

Cray is the leading manufacturer of supercomputers, used in weather forecasting, aircraft and automotive design, scientific research, and seismic analysis. At the end of 1991, 324 Cray supercomputer systems were in use, including 68 installed in 1991. Approximately half of Cray sales for 1991 were in the U.S.; remaining sales were primarily in Western Europe and Pacific Asia. Cray is clearly the world leader in supercomputers, holding a market share in excess of 50 percent. However, it faces competition not only from other supercomputer manufacturers but also from the increasing power of "mini-supercomputers."

Cray supercomputers have generally relied on a single microprocessor. However, there has been a shift in high-speed computing toward massively parallel processing (MPP), which allows the simultaneous employment of many microprocessors. Cray has recently developed a partnership with Digital Equipment Corporation (DEC), to produce MPP implementations for sale by 1993. Cray also announced that, beginning in 1992, their EL systems will be sold not only through existing channels, but also through DEC's distribution network. The EL systems are "low-end" supercomputers, selling for approximately $350,000; some of its purchasers may ultimately upgrade to larger systems. Cray's high-end C90 systems sell for $30 million.

Cray also formed an alliance with Sun Microsystems that would facilitate seamless linkage of Cray computers and Sun workstations, as well as allow the use of Sun's SPARC chip in new Cray hardware. In the meantime, Cray introduced five new supercomputer systems in 1991. In their letter to shareholders, the CEO and COO labeled the market's response as "enthusiastic," and reported 58 new customers in 1991, more than in any previous year.

During 1991, Cray's revenues increased by seven percent, while profits increased only slightly. While such performance might normally be viewed as disappointing, Cray's letter to shareholders placed it in context: "These results came during what many observers are describing as the worst year overall in the computer industry's history." Based on Cray's performance relative to the industry, management indicated that "these results mean that we will not have to divert our attention in 1992 to 'rebuilding' or 'restructuring' efforts that have become almost commonplace in the industry."

During the first quarter of 1992, Cray installed 11 new and 2 used systems, generating sales of $165 million, up 15 percent over the first quarter of 1991. Nevertheless, net income fell 26 percent, to $3.9 million, reflecting lower volume in high-end systems. In mid-1992, Cray is just beginning to ship its top-of-the-line C90 systems at the rate of about one per month. Analysts expect that Cray, which tends to make a big push to install systems before years' end, will see a pickup in earnings in the latter half of the year. Analysts forecast sales increases of 10 percent and 11 percent for 1992 and 1993, respectively, and return on equity of 13 to 14 percent in each year.

A summary of Cray's financial statements for recent years appears in Exhibit 2.

TANDEM COMPUTERS

Tandem operates within the niche of fault-tolerant mainframe and mid-range computer systems. Its products (labeled NonStop systems) are used in on-line transaction processing (OLTP) in banking, manufacturing, communications, distribution, brokerage and securities, and other industries. NonStop systems feature multiple independent processors, and are designed to continue operating through any single processor failure. (This is referred to as "continuous availability.") Beginning in 1990, Tandem produced a new fault-tolerant, high performance UNIX-based system, based on the high-speed Reduced Instruction Set Computing (RISC) technology. Through its subsidiary, Ungermann-Bass, Tandem also produces general-purpose local area networks. Almost half of Tandem's sales are within the U.S.; the remainder are primarily in Europe, with some in the Pacific Rim and elsewhere.

Tandem pioneered the fault-tolerant market and remains the acknowledged worldwide leader in fault-tolerant systems, with a 70 percent market share. However, it faces competition from Digital Equipment, Hewlett-Packard, Fujitsu, and Hitachi—all of which have entered the market in recent years—and from Stratus, a much smaller manufacturer. Moreover, some standard mid-range systems (produced by IBM and others) now have fault-tolerant capabilities, and so lines are blurring between the fault-tolerant market and mainstream systems market.

Tandem's revenues increased only slightly in 1991, and earnings declined. In the Tandem Annual Report for 1991, President and CEO James Treybig stated that "we are not satisfied with our financial results," and attributed the firm's difficulties to "the length and severity of a widespread recession." He indicated that the firm would "change the basic cost structure of [its] business" by reducing the size of its workforce, eliminating redundancies, increasing the leverage of sales and marketing efforts, and realigning the organization. Treybig indicated that Tandem would capitalize on opportunities in an OLTP marketplace that would continue to grow by "extending leadership in price/performance, open networking, and continuous availability." However, with the product cycle just beginning for some new RISC-based systems, substantial growth in Tandem sales could be a few quarters away.

In the first quarter of 1992, Tandem recorded an after-tax restructuring charge of $80 million, while sales rose only slightly. Thanks to that change, analysts expect the ROE to be only 4.3 percent in 1992, but to rise to 8.1 percent in 1993. Sales growth is projected at 4 to 5 percent for the next two years.

A summary of Tandem's recent financial statement data appears in Exhibit 3.

STRATUS COMPUTER

Like Tandem, Stratus produces fault-tolerant computer systems for use in OLTP, and is introducing a new generation of RISC-based fault-tolerant computers. Stratus systems consists of up to 32 processing modules connected via a high-speed communications link. The systems are used in the securities industry, banking, distribution, plant management, hotel reservation systems, and communications. Stratus is the only computer company in the world totally focused on continuous availability for OLTP; its 1991 annual report claims that, of their 150 largest bids of the year, "not one situation was reported where a competitor could show higher availability than Stratus."

Stratus was but a minor player in the fault-tolerant market until the mid- to late 1980s, but it now holds a 21 percent market share, second only to Tandem. More than half of Stratus sales are within the U.S., with Europe accounting for most other sales. Sales to IBM—which sells Stratus equipment on an OEM basis—accounted for 23 percent of Stratus sales in 1991, down from 26 percent in 1990 and 35 percent in 1989. Stratus is attempting to diversify its customer base, and expects increases in its sales to NEC (1.5 percent of 1991 sales) and others.

Stratus revenues for 1991 were up 11 percent, while earnings rose 34 percent. In its upbeat annual report to shareholders, Stratus emphasized what it considers its systems' unparalleled record of online applications availability, and indicated that "the growth of critical online applications is outpacing the abilities of most vendors to provide the levels of availability that customers actually need. This presents Stratus with the opportunity to capitalize on the trend that more businesses are becoming increasingly reliant on their online computer systems."

In the first quarter of 1992, sales growth slowed to "only" 9 percent, largely because of a dropoff of sales to IBM. However, earnings rose 40 percent. Analysts are projecting ROE of about 17 percent for 1992 and 1993, on sales growth of 13 percent in 1992 and 17 percent in 1993.

A summary of Stratus's recent financial statement data appears in Exhibit 4.

QUESTIONS

1. Profitability (as measured by return on equity) for the overall computer industry fell steadily from 23 percent in 1988 to 11 percent in 1991, and sales had been flat for the last two of those years. In early 1992, typical price-earnings ratios in the computer industry were within the range of 9 to 12, while typical price-to-book ratios stood at 1.0 to 1.4.

   Consider the factors that would determine the price-earnings ratios and price-to-book ratios for the four firms in the case. Based solely on the information in the case, would you expect price-earnings ratios and price-to-book ratios for each of the four firms to be higher than, lower than, or within the ranges considered typical for the industry at this time?

EXHIBIT 1

Atari Corporation – Common-Size Financial Statements and Selected Ratios

	1991	1990	1989	1988	1987
Cash	0.275	0.135	0.166	0.272	0.200
Receivables	0.318	0.352	0.324	0.297	0.196
Inventory	0.321	0.419	0.393	0.348	0.380
Other current assets	0.030	0.026	0.046	0.041	0.007
Total current assets	0.944	0.933	0.928	0.958	0.783
Plant, property, equip	0.038	0.050	0.042	0.025	0.128
Other long-term assets	0.018	0.017	0.030	0.017	0.089
Total assets	1.000	1.000	1.000	1.000	1.000
Notes payable	0.001	0.000	0.000	0.000	0.003
Other current liabilities	0.312	0.449	0.506	0.532	0.416
Total current liabilities	0.313	0.449	0.506	0.532	0.419
Long term debt	0.191	0.180	0.234	0.222	0.258
Other liabilities	0.000	0.000	0.000	0.000	0.000
Total liabilities	0.505	0.629	0.740	0.754	0.677
Shareholders' equity	0.495	0.371	0.260	0.246	0.323
Total liabilities and equity	1.000	1.000	1.000	1.000	1.000
Total assets (millions)	$253	$273	$331	$338	$518
Sales	1.000	1.000	1.000	1.000	1.000
Cost of sales	0.725	0.766	0.725	0.616	0.608
SGA expense	0.338	0.284	0.261	0.248	0.250
Operating income before depreciation	−0.063	−0.050	0.015	0.136	0.142
Depreciation	0.010	0.012	0.006	0.005	0.009
Interest expense	0.017	0.016	0.015	0.011	0.011
Nonoperating gain/loss	0.024	0.030	0.012	0.008	0.029
Special gain/loss	0.156	0.000	0.000	0.000	0.000
Income before tax	0.091	−0.047	0.006	0.129	0.152
Income tax provision	0.000	0.004	−0.004	0.042	0.062
Income before extraordinary items	0.092	−0.051	0.009	0.087	0.090
Net income	0.099	0.036	0.009	−0.188	0.116
Sales (millions)	$258	$411	$424	$452	$493
EBI/Sales	0.098	−0.044	0.015	0.091	0.094
Earnings/EBI	0.933	1.144	0.615	0.954	0.955
Sales turnover = sales/average assets	0.981	1.364	1.266	1.056	
Leverage = assets/equity (average)	2.320	3.222	3.953	3.415	
ROE = product of above	0.209	−0.223	0.047	0.314	

EBI = earnings before interest, net of tax. Tax effect of interest is assumed to be 40 percent.

EXHIBIT 2
Cray Research – Common-Size Financial Statements and Selected Ratios

	1991	1990	1989	1988	1987
Cash	0.034	0.071	0.072	0.182	0.194
Receivables	0.226	0.124	0.188	0.118	0.107
Inventory	0.227	0.191	0.212	0.238	0.214
Other current assets	0.030	0.024	0.007	0.005	0.006
Total current assets	0.517	0.409	0.479	0.543	0.520
Plant, property, equip	0.333	0.367	0.325	0.291	0.242
Other long-term assets	0.150	0.224	0.196	0.166	0.238
Total assets	1.000	1.000	1.000	1.000	1.000
Notes payable	0.006	0.039	0.053	0.009	0.010
Other current liabilities	0.186	0.177	0.175	0.192	0.176
Total current liabilities	0.192	0.216	0.227	0.201	0.186
Long term debt	0.100	0.112	0.151	0.111	0.120
Other liabilities	0.006	0.006	0.000	0.005	0.017
Total liabilities	0.297	0.334	0.378	0.317	0.323
Shareholders' equity	0.703	0.666	0.622	0.683	0.677
Total liabilities and equity	1.000	1.000	1.000	1.000	1.000
Total assets (millions)	$1,079	$944	$956	$991	$902
Sales	1.000	1.000	1.000	1.000	1.000
Cost of sales	0.333	0.306	0.289	0.272	0.252
SGA expense	0.348	0.356	0.370	0.330	0.321
Operating income before depreciation	0.320	0.338	0.341	0.398	0.426
Depreciation	0.131	0.137	0.130	0.110	0.105
Interest expense	0.009	0.010	0.011	0.010	0.013
Nonoperating gain/loss	0.009	0.022	0.023	0.031	0.029
Special gain/loss	0.005	−0.004	−0.061	0.000	0.000
Income before tax	0.193	0.209	0.162	0.309	0.338
Income tax provision	0.062	0.068	0.049	0.102	0.124
Income before extraordinary items	0.131	0.140	0.113	0.207	0.214
Net income	0.131	0.140	0.113	0.207	0.214
Sales (millions)	$862	$804	$785	$756	$687
EBI/Sales	0.135	0.144	0.118	0.211	0.219
Earnings/EBI	0.973	0.972	0.964	0.980	0.976
Sales turnover = sales/average assets	0.852	0.847	0.806	0.799	
Leverage = assets/equity (average)	1.458	1.553	1.532	1.471	
ROE = product of above	0.163	0.185	0.140	0.243	

EBI = earnings before interest, net of tax. Tax effect of interest is assumed to be 40 percent.

The Computer Industry in 1992

The Computer Industry in 1992

EXHIBIT 3
Tandem Computers – Common-Size Financial Statements and Selected Ratios

	1991	1990	1989	1988	1987
Cash	0.059	0.049	0.122	0.095	0.328
Receivables	0.258	0.264	0.259	0.270	0.263
Inventory	0.080	0.100	0.089	0.098	0.095
Other current assets	0.054	0.047	0.063	0.026	0.024
Total current assets	0.452	0.460	0.533	0.488	0.711
Plant, property, equip	0.331	0.341	0.276	0.317	0.261
Other long-term assets	0.218	0.199	0.190	0.194	0.028
Total assets	1.000	1.000	1.000	1.000	1.000
Notes payable	0.022	0.016	0.024	0.007	0.002
Other current liabilities	0.243	0.248	0.249	0.270	0.197
Total current liabilities	0.265	0.263	0.273	0.277	0.198
Long term debt	0.048	0.051	0.066	0.044	0.009
Other liabilities	0.041	0.045	0.050	0.029	0.047
Total liabilities	0.354	0.359	0.389	0.350	0.255
Shareholders' equity	0.646	0.641	0.611	0.650	0.745
Total liabilities and equity	1.000	1.000	1.000	1.000	1.000
Total assets (millions)	$1,932	$1,877	$1,619	$1,318	$967
Sales	1.000	1.000	1.000	1.000	1.000
Cost of sales	0.328	0.294	0.306	0.309	0.298
SGA expense	0.575	0.541	0.516	0.517	0.489
Operating income before depreciation	0.097	0.165	0.178	0.174	0.213
Depreciation	0.066	0.064	0.065	0.062	0.048
Interest expense	0.011	0.010	0.007	0.007	0.002
Nonoperating gain/loss	0.010	0.010	0.008	0.013	0.015
Special gain/loss	0.000	0.000	0.000	–0.007	0.000
Income before tax	0.030	0.100	0.114	0.111	0.179
Income tax provision	0.011	0.035	0.042	0.039	0.077
Income before extraordinary items	0.018	0.065	0.072	0.072	0.102
Net income	0.018	0.065	0.072	0.072	0.102
Sales (millions)	$1,922	$1,866	$1,633	$1,315	$1,035
EBI/Sales	0.023	0.069	0.075	0.075	0.102
Earnings/EBI	0.812	0.940	0.964	0.961	0.993
Sales turnover = sales/average assets	1.009	1.067	1.112	1.150	
Leverage = assets/equity (average)	1.554	1.595	1.591	1.449	
ROE = product of above	0.029	0.111	0.128	0.120	

EBI = earnings before interest, net of tax. Tax effect of interest is assumed to be 40 percent.

EXHIBIT 4

Stratus Computer – Common-Size Financial Statements and Selected Ratios

	1991	1990	1989	1988	1987
Cash	0.256	0.133	0.117	0.142	0.223
Receivables	0.348	0.379	0.417	0.375	0.356
Inventory	0.169	0.217	0.166	0.228	0.190
Other current assets	0.023	0.026	0.019	0.016	0.016
Total current assets	0.796	0.755	0.719	0.760	0.786
Plant, property, equip	0.171	0.199	0.245	0.209	0.196
Other long-term assets	0.033	0.046	0.036	0.030	0.018
Total assets	1.000	1.000	1.000	1.000	1.000
Notes payable	0.010	0.014	0.015	0.014	0.013
Other current liabilities	0.157	0.210	0.207	0.240	0.240
Total current liabilities	0.167	0.224	0.222	0.253	0.254
Long term debt	0.007	0.044	0.107	0.051	0.042
Other liabilities	0.010	0.014	0.000	0.000	0.000
Total liabilities	0.184	0.283	0.329	0.304	0.296
Shareholders' equity	0.816	0.717	0.671	0.696	0.704
Total liabilities and equity	1.000	1.000	1.000	1.000	1.000
Total assets (millions)	$385	$321	$274	$200	$145
Sales	1.000	1.000	1.000	1.000	1.000
Cost of sales	0.340	0.361	0.342	0.354	0.319
SGA expense	0.457	0.463	0.451	0.436	0.470
Operating income before depreciation	0.203	0.176	0.207	0.210	0.211
Depreciation	0.064	0.049	0.049	0.040	0.044
Interest expense	0.004	0.007	0.005	0.000	0.000
Nonoperating gain/loss	0.010	0.008	0.009	0.003	0.005
Special gain/loss	0.002	0.000	0.000	0.000	0.000
Income before tax	0.146	0.127	0.162	0.173	0.172
Income tax provision	0.035	0.036	0.058	0.062	0.066
Income before extraordinary items	0.111	0.092	0.104	0.111	0.105
Net income	0.111	0.092	0.104	0.111	0.105
Sales (millions)	$449	$404	$341	$265	$184
EBI/Sales	0.112	0.094	0.106	0.111	0.105
Earnings/EBI	0.985	0.970	0.982	1.000	1.000
Sales turnover = sales/average assets	1.271	1.357	1.441	1.537	
Leverage = assets/equity (average)	1.297	1.437	1.467	1.430	
ROE= product of above	0.183	0.179	0.219	0.243	

EBI = earnings before interest, net of tax. Tax effect of interest is assumed to be 40 percent.

The Computer Industry in 1992

Richard Mandrell is a newly hired credit analyst, employed by a small but quickly growing insurance company that is becoming increasingly active in the market for private placements. In reviewing possible investments, the company considers what rating would have been assigned to similar bonds in the public markets. Such ratings play a significant role in determining the issues' yields and marketability. At this date, early 1991, AAA-rated corporate bonds are yielding, on average, about 9.4 percent, whereas BBB-rated corporates are yielding an average 10.2 percent. Some junk bonds are, of course, yielding much higher rates.

Analysis of prospective investments inevitably involves a degree of subjective business judgment. However, Mandrell is aware that, in the view of some, determination of an appropriate debt rating category for a particular issue is sometimes based largely on a few key financial ratios. In fact, several of Mandrell's competitors in the private placement market use purely quantitative debt scoring models as an important input to their credit analysis. Such an approach suggests that one could explain much of the variation in bond ratings based on a handful of financial ratios. Intrigued by that observation, Mandrell has decided to review a few recent public debt issues to see how well he can "predict" their current ratings based solely on a cursory review of the financial statements of the issuers.

The firms selected by Mandrell for analysis are all in the chemical industry: Fargo Chemical Company, Texas Gulf Corporation, MST Company, Boland Corporation, and Quotron Chemical Corporation. Despite their common industry membership, the five firms have widely varying capital structures and profitability.

The wide variation across the five firms' performance reflects the differences within the chemical industry. The prices of both inputs and outputs are volatile, and often they do not move in tandem. Thus, profitability critically depends on which prices are most important to a given firm. Some firms focus on basic chemicals—essentially, commodities that are similar across producers—and have little control over prices on either the input or output side of their market. Other firms focus on specialty chemicals. These firms tend to have highly differentiated products, specialized knowledge and processes, and close customer relations. In some cases, they are the sole supplier of a particular chemical. These firms are better insulated from changes in the prices of their inputs,

Prepared by Professor Victor L. Bernard, with the assistance of Mike Finn, Elise Kartchmar, and Hans Littooy. The firms on which the case is based are real, but the names have been disguised. The case was prepared as a basis for class discussion and is not intended to illustrate either an effective or ineffective management of a business situation.

because they have some ability to pass on such changes to their customers. Many chemical companies diversify across basic and speciality chemicals, sometimes achieving some manufacturing synergies in the process.

Profits in the chemical industry reached an all-time high in 1988 and 1989, due to favorable trends in prices. Sales grew by 10 percent, while net profit margins reached a healthy 8 percent and ROE moved to 17 percent. In 1990, however, the industry was not as fortunate. The prices in many input markets, including those for petroleum products, rose during the Gulf War. Simultaneously, a worldwide recession dampened demand for the outputs of chemical firms, including demand from the key sectors of construction and transportation. Sales growth in chemicals slowed significantly, and net profit margins fell below 7 percent. Several specialty chemical manufacturers maintained strong profits, but producers of basic chemicals struggled. With the world still in a recession in 1991, and the industry now facing some excess capacity due to the plant expansions that commenced during the highly profitable late 1980s, the near-term profitability picture for many chemical companies is only mediocre.

FARGO CHEMICAL COMPANY

Fargo Chemical is a leading international manufacturer and marketer of intermediate chemicals and specialty products. The company produces three principal chemicals: propylene oxide and derivatives, used in urethane foams and in solvents for furniture, auto, and construction industries; tertiary butyl alcohol and derivatives, used as an octane enhancer; and styrene, used in plastic and rubber components.

Fargo resulted from a spinoff of a major petroleum company in 1987; the majority of its shares remain in the control of that company. Earnings grew steadily in 1987 and 1988, but then fell in both 1989 and 1990, reflecting the generally difficult conditions in the chemical industry and the heightened price competition.

Fargo's long-term debt includes a half-dozen public and privately placed issues. The one for which Mandrell will attempt to "predict" a rating is a $100 million debenture, issued in 1990 and due in 2005. Like nearly all other long-term debt issued by Fargo, the debentures are unsecured, subordinated, and issued "for general corporate purposes." They are not callable.

Fargo's financial statements are presented in Exhibit 1.

TEXAS GULF CORPORATION

Texas Gulf Corporation is the smallest of the five chemical companies reviewed by Mandrell. It produces several highly integrated lines of commodity and specialty chemicals, and is a leading producer of chlorine, caustic soda, sodium chlorate, vinyl chloride monomer, and other chlorine-based and alcohol products. End uses for the products are diverse: housing and construction markets, solvents, plastics and fibers, consumer products, pulp and paper, and other uses.

Texas Gulf enjoyed extraordinary margins in 1988 and 1989. The profitability reflected not only the favorable relation of output to input prices, but also the efficiencies of Texas Gulf's highly integrated manufacturing process. Texas Gulf considers itself a low-cost producer of commodity and specialty chemicals, and claims that its productivity rates are among the highest in the industry. Nevertheless, Texas Gulf was not invulnerable to the downturn of 1990, with operating profits falling by nearly 25 percent.

In an effort to insulate itself from potential takeover, Texas Gulf undertook a recapitalization in April 1990, and followed that action with the adoption of a poison pill agreement. The recapitalization involved the distribution of a $30 dividend to shareholders, financed with a combination of $191 million of subordinated notes (issued to the shareholders), a $507 million term loan, and a smaller ($44 million) revolving credit agreement. The term loan and revolver were arranged with a group of financial institutions. The term loan is payable in quarterly installments through 1998.

The debt considered by Mandrell is the subordinated note issue. The notes are callable at par beginning 1995, and are due in 2000. Prepayment of the subordinated notes is prohibited while the bank debt remains outstanding. The notes are unsecured, but require that certain financial ratios be maintained.

Texas Gulf's financial statements are presented in Exhibit 2.

MST COMPANY

MST Company is the largest of the five firms considered here, and one of the largest chemical producers in the U.S. Its lines of business include agriculture, personal care products, food products, construction materials, plastics, resin products, rubber and process chemicals, and pharmaceuticals. In several of its lines of business, it holds major brand names.

MST is more widely diversified than others in the chemical industry, and therefore may be better insulated from the current industry conditions. Nevertheless, it experienced a decline in margins and a resulting dropoff in profits in 1990.

Among MST's many debt issues are $100 million of callable sinking fund debentures, issued for general corporate purposes. The debentures rank on a parity with nearly all of MST's other debt, and are unsecured and unsubordinated.

MST's financial statements appear in Exhibit 3.

BOLAND CORPORATION

Boland Corporation is a diversified manufacturer of chemicals, metals and materials, and defense-related products. Within its chemical operations, Boland produces industrial chemicals (including caustic soda, urethanes, and chlorines), performance chemicals, water sanitizing chemicals, and image-forming chemicals. Its metals products include a variety of copper and steel materials. The most important defense-related product is ammunition.

Boland's earnings grew steadily from 1985 through 1989. However, they fell by more than 30 percent in 1990, as Boland found itself selling products into those sectors of the economy most affected by the recession.

Boland's long-term debt consists of $341 million of notes, revolvers, and other debt arranged with a variety of financial institutions, plus $125 million of publicly held subordinated notes. It is the subordinated notes that Mandrell is attempting to rate. The notes were issued in 1987, are due in 1997, are not callable, and are unsecured. The notes were issued to reduce short-term bank debt incurred in early 1987 to finance working capital and long-term investments.

Boland's financial statements appear in Exhibit 4.

QUOTRON CHEMICAL CORPORATION

Quotron Chemical is a long-standing company engaged in the manufacturing and retailing of petrochemicals, propanes, and polyethylene products. Quotron ranks as the nation's largest propane retailer (24 percent of sales) and polyethylene producer (54 percent of sales). The polyethylene business tends to experience particularly volatile earnings, as the prices of the inputs (e.g., ethylene) and output (polyethylene) sometimes fail to move in tandem. The propane business is also subject to some randomness; for example, propane sales vary depending on the severity of winter weather.

Quotron's earnings, after having stagnated during the early and mid-1980s, grew dramatically in 1987 and 1988, largely as a product of strong demand and higher prices for polyethylene, polypropylene, and other petrochemical products. However, polyethylene margins fell in 1989 and a fire caused the shutdown of a major plant for the last half of the year—leaving Quotron operating profits down almost 40 percent. The plant resumed operations in the spring of 1990, but prices continued to swing in unfavorable directions, leading to another decline in operating profits.

In early 1989, the company undertook a number of actions to prevent a takeover. First, a leveraged recapitalization was arranged, involving the issue of a $50 per share dividend and a large increase in the firm's long-term debt. Secondly, a "poison pill" shareholders' rights plan was adopted. Third, an ESOP plan was adopted, resulting in the placement of 14 percent of the firm's shares in the hands of the ESOP trustee.

Quotron has more than a dozen issues of debt outstanding. Seven issues totaling $1.25 billion are unsubordinated; the remaining issues are subordinated. Mandrell has decided to consider one debt issue in each of these categories. The first is Quotron's largest debt issue: $500 million of unsecured subordinated debentures, issued in conjunction with the recapitalization in 1989 and due in 2004, callable after 1994 at prices that begin at 106.50 and decline over time to par. The other debt issue considered by Mr. Mandrell is Quotron's second largest: $300 million of unsecured unsubordinated sinking fund notes, dated 1988 and due in 2018, callable after 1991 at prices that begin at 108 and decline over the life of the issue to par.

Quotron's financial statements appear in Exhibit 5.

EXHIBIT 1
Fargo Chemical Company – Financial Statements

INCOME STATEMENT

| | Year Ended December 31 | | | |
($ millions, except per share data)	1990	1989	1988	1987
Sales	2,830	2,663	2,700	1,952
Cost of Goods Sold	1,993	1,749	1,704	1,335
Gross Profit	837	914	996	617
SG & A Expense	281	238	191	152
Operating Income Before Depreciation	556	676	805	465
Depreciation, Depletion, & Amortization	117	93	83	67
Operating Profit	439	583	722	398
Interest Expense	75	37	51	41
Non-Operating Income/Expense	73	56	92	64
Special Items	30	−3	0	0
Pretax Income	467	599	763	421
Total Income Taxes	159	194	269	164
Income Before Extraordinary Items	308	405	494	257
Extraordinary Items	43	0	0	0
Net Income	351	405	494	257

BALANCE SHEET

($ millions)	as of December 31			
	1990	1989	1988	1987
Assets:				
Cash & Equivalents	486	144	410	709
Net Receivables	593	409	477	363
Inventories	289	286	271	207
Other Current Assets	38	13	12	12
Total Current Assets	1,406	852	1,170	1,291
Gross PP & E	2,467	1,851	1,565	1,427
Accumulated Depreciation	699	588	487	443
Net PP & E	1,768	1,263	1,078	984
Investments at Equity	132	118	99	76
Other Investments	270	11	8	0
Deferred Charges	163	182	193	183
Other Assets	0	229	0	0
Total Assets	3,739	2,655	2,548	2,534
Liabilities:				
LT Debt Due in One Year	39	29	4	0
Notes Payable	40	102	256	650
Accounts Payable	225	151	113	122
Taxes Payable	45	48	71	31
Accrued Expenses	192	84	141	134
Other Current Liabilities	0	0	52	39
Total Current Liabilities	541	414	637	976
Long-Term Debt	1,181	390	271	166
Deferred Taxes	208	221	217	239
Other Liabilities	51	39	48	37
Total Noncurrent Liabilities	1,440	650	536	442
Total Liabilities	1,981	1,064	1,173	1,418
Equity:				
Common Stock	100	100	100	100
Capital Surplus	864	864	864	869
Retained Earnings	907	740	520	147
Less: Treasury Stock	113	113	109	0
Common (Total) Equity	1,758	1,591	1,375	1,116
Total Liabilities & Equity	3,739	2,655	2,548	2,534

EXHIBIT 2

Texas Gulf Corporation – Financial Statements

INCOME STATEMENT

($ millions, except per share data)	Year Ended December 31			
	1990	1989	1988	1987
Sales	932	1,104	1,061	707
Cost of Goods Sold	646	742	689	498
Gross Profit	286	362	371	209
SG & A Expense	41	48	46	28
Operating Income Before Depreciation	245	315	325	181
Depreciation, Depletion, & Amortization	16	16	12	9
Operating Profit	229	299	313	172
Interest Expense	63	1	3	11
Non-Operating Income/Expense	3	2	3	1
Special Items	−18	0	0	0
Pretax Income	150	300	312	163
Total Income Taxes	55	108	119	71
Including Before Extraordinary Items	95	192	194	92
Extraordinary Items	0	0	0	−10
Net Income	95	192	194	82

Debt Ratings in the Chemical Industry

BALANCE SHEET

($ millions)	as of December 31			
	1990	1989	1988	1987
Assets:				
Cash & Equivalents	6	46	40	24
Net Receivables	118	117	127	95
Inventories	86	75	85	55
Prepaid Expenses	8	7	8	8
Total Current Assets	218	244	260	182
Gross PP & E	316	300	245	184
Accumulated Depreciation	101	91	76	64
Net PP & E	215	209	169	120
Deferred Charges	21	0	0	0
Other Assets	3	20	28	6
Total Assets	457	473	457	309
Liabilities:				
LT Debt Due in One Year	43	0	0	0
Accounts Payable	75	63	81	56
Taxes Payable	8	9	19	24
Accrued Expenses	35	27	28	20
Other Current Liabilities	0	6	0	0
Total Current Liabilities	161	106	128	100
Long-Term Debt	683	1	42	42
Deferred Taxes	36	36	31	25
Total Noncurrent Liabilities	720	37	73	66
Total Liabilities	881	143	201	166
Equity:				
Common Stock	0	1	1	1
Capital Surplus	2	36	27	23
Retained Earnings	−427	427	302	125
Less: Treasury Stock	0	134	74	7
Common (Total) Equity	−424	330	256	143
Total Liabilities & Equity	457	473	457	309

EXHIBIT 3
MST Company – Financial Statements

INCOME STATEMENT

($ millions, except per share data)	Year Ended December 31			
	1990	1989	1988	1987
Sales	8,995	8,681	8,293	7,639
Cost of Goods Sold	4,901	4,597	4,537	4,334
Gross Profit	4,094	4,084	3,756	3,305
SG & A Expense	2,485	2,342	2,135	1,957
Operating Income Before Depreciation	1,609	1,742	1,621	1,348
Depreciation, Depletion, & Amortization	700	664	666	646
Operating Profit	909	1,078	955	702
Interest Expense	208	204	193	188
Non-Operating Income/Expense	120	151	138	136
Special Items	0	0	0	32
Pretax Income	821	1,025	900	682
Total Income Taxes	263	336	302	237
Minority Interest	12	10	7	9
Net Income	546	679	591	436

BALANCE SHEET

($ millions)	as of December 31			
	1990	1989	1988	1987
Assets:				
Cash & Equivalents	204	253	221	223
Net Receivables	1,498	1,309	1,234	1,209
Inventories	1,270	1,197	1,170	1,081
Other Current Assets	541	489	472	490
Total Current Assets	3,513	3,248	3,097	3,003
Gross PP & E	7,620	6,937	6,926	6,730
Accumulated Depreciation	4,128	3,764	3,780	3,654
Net PP & E	3,492	3,173	3,146	3,076
Investments at Equity	248	204	205	240
Intangibles	1,425	1,682	1,790	1,953
Other Assets	558	297	223	183
Total Assets	9,236	8,604	8,461	8,455
Liabilities:				
LT Debt Due in One Year	118	44	128	119
Notes Payable	464	461	428	420
Accounts Payable	584	514	545	527
Taxes Payable	95	126	124	101
Accrued Expenses	929	777	755	633
Total Current Liabilities	2,190	1,922	1,980	1,800
Long-Term Debt	1,652	1,471	1,408	1,564
Deferred Taxes	640	621	588	584
Other Liabilities	665	649	685	606
Total Noncurrent Liabilities	2,957	2,741	2,681	2,754
Total Liabilities	5,147	4,663	4,661	4,554
Equity:				
Common Stock	329	164	164	164
Capital Surplus	714	877	874	872
Retained Earnings	4,609	4,144	3,714	3,382
Less: Treasury Stock	1,563	1,244	952	517
Common (Total) Equity	4,089	3,941	3,800	3,901
Total Liabilities & Equity	9,236	8,604	8,461	8,455

EXHIBIT 4
Boland Corporation – Financial Statements

INCOME STATEMENT

($ millions, except per share data)	Year Ended December 31			
	1990	1989	1988	1987
Sales	2,592	2,509	2,308	1,930
Cost of Goods Sold	1,936	1,811	1,664	1,337
Gross Profit	656	698	644	593
SG & A Expense	382	353	347	326
Operating Income Before Depreciation	274	345	297	267
Depreciation, Depletion, & Amortization	123	122	117	118
Operating Profit	151	223	180	149
Interest Expense	56	57	44	34
Non-Operating Income/Expense	25	22	15	12
Special Items	−4	4	0	0
Pretax Income	116	192	151	127
Total Income Taxes	32	68	53	49
Net Income	84	124	98	78

Debt Ratings in the Chemical Industry

Debt Ratings in the Chemical Industry

BALANCE SHEET

($ millions)	as of December 31			
	1990	1989	1988	1987
Assets:				
Cash & Equivalents	6	12	25	34
Net Receivables	419	453	437	362
Inventories	293	296	311	273
Other Current Assets	16	29	28	11
Total Current Assets	734	790	801	680
Gross PP & E	2,297	2,169	2,164	2,007
Accumulated Depreciation	1,468	1,388	1,363	1,280
Net PP & E	829	781	801	727
Investments at Equity	145	144	149	137
Intangibles	106	110	141	102
Other Assets	52	79	48	39
Total Assets	1,866	1,904	1,940	1,685
Liabilities:				
LT Debt Due in One Year	34	15	39	24
Notes Payable	70	140	172	26
Accounts Payable	222	255	223	200
Taxes Payable	9	4	4	11
Accrued Expenses	187	171	179	143
Total Current Liabilities	522	585	617	404
Long-Term Debt	466	501	474	392
Deferred Taxes	48	60	60	49
Other Liabilities	115	93	106	140
Total Noncurrent Liabilities	629	654	640	581
Total Liabilities	1,151	1,239	1,257	985
Equity:				
Common Stock	19	19	20	22
Capital Surplus	180	177	188	200
Retained Earnings	505	469	475	478
Common Equity	704	665	683	700
Preferred Stock	11	0	0	0
Total Equity	715	665	683	700
Total Liabilities & Equity	1,866	1,904	1,940	1,685

EXHIBIT 5

Quotron Chemical Corporation – Financial Statements

INCOME STATEMENT

	Year Ended December 31			
($ millions, except per share data)	1990	1989	1988	1987
Sales	2,618	2,637	2,884	2,525
Cost of Goods Sold	1,991	1,790	1,770	1,772
Gross Profit	627	847	1,114	753
SG & A Expense	217	224	207	232
Operating Income Before Depreciation	410	623	907	522
Depreciation, Depletion, & Amortization	155	147	147	142
Operating Profit	255	476	760	380
Interest Expense	269	297	116	83
Non-Operating Income/Expense	47	0	-26	6
Special Items	28	0	0	0
Pretax Income	61	178	618	303
Total Income Taxes	39	64	258	159
Income Before Discontinued Operations	21	114	360	144
Discontinued Operations	0	133	23	108
Net Income	21	247	383	252

Debt Ratings in the Chemical Industry

Debt Ratings in the Chemical Industry

BALANCE SHEET

	as of December 31			
($ millions)	1990	1989	1988	1987
Assets:				
Cash & Equivalents	13	104	219	25
Net Receivables	467	361	428	434
Inventories	366	304	339	316
Other Current Assets	51	99	354	61
Total Current Assets	897	868	1,339	836
Gross PP & E	2,905	2,513	1,943	2,037
Accumulated Depreciation	885	754	634	657
Net PP & E	2,020	1,759	1,309	1,380
Investments at Equity	32	129	60	60
Other Investments	34	39	39	107
Intangibles	83	94	26	62
Other Assets	156	115	135	137
Total Assets	3,222	3,004	2,908	2,581
Liabilities:				
LT Debt Due in One Year	14	8	3	21
Notes Payable	0	0	5	93
Accounts Payable	137	133	157	134
Taxes Payable	0	38	88	87
Accrued Expenses	277	324	326	242
Other Current Liabilities	0	0	1,141	0
Total Current Liabilities	428	503	1,720	577
Long-Term Debt	2,530	2,363	1,332	727
Deferred Taxes	230	160	174	150
Other Liabilities	135	151	88	82
Total Noncurrent Liabilities	2,895	2,674	1,594	959
Total Liabilities	3,323	3,176	3,315	1,536
Equity:				
Common Stock	220	159	57	75
Capital Surplus	0	0	0	29
Retained Earnings	−321	−331	−464	942
Common (Total) Equity	−101	−172	−407	1,045
Total Liabilities & Equity	3,222	3,004	2,908	2,581

1996 was an exciting and challenging year for Donna Karan International Inc. . . . The year was marked by the following achievements: strong divisional sales performance, segmentation of women's apparel collections, growth of men's business, growth in international business, and an initial public offering. While we are pleased with these accomplishments, 1996 was also marked by significant challenges and setbacks. Despite our growth in net sales, our 1996 operating and net income declined significantly from 1995 levels. . . . Profitability was impacted by generally high corporate and administrative expenses and increased investments in our newly segmented and existing businesses. . . . 1996's financial results were unacceptable. We are identifying and implementing changes that are necessary to curtail the rise in selling, general, and administrative expenses, improve gross margins, and continue growth without sacrificing the quality, consistency, and image of the "Donna Karan New York" and "DKNY" brands.

Excerpts from Donna Karan International's
Letter to Shareholders, 1996 Annual Report

Shortly after the publication of its first annual report (Exhibit 6), and the close of Donna Karan International's first full year as a public company, *The Daily News* ran the following piece:

Fashion Week, the twice-yearly, week-long series of high-octane runway shows opened last night. But, for a change the focus of this week's 60 back-to-back catwalk shows won't entirely be fixed on the celebrities or even hemlines. Instead, much of the interest will be concentrated on the bottom line of another kind: Will the image each designer presents create the cachet necessary to hawk $150 silk scarves or $60 bottles of perfume to those of us who can't afford a $5,000 suit? The latest trend to bind the world of high fashion is a passion for the big bucks that a working relationship with Wall Street can yield. . . . Donna Karan, who in June was the first upscale American designer to take her chances on the stock market, pocketed $58 million from the gamble. But, as Alan Millstein, editor of a fashion newsletter, explains, it also puts Karan in a dodgy position this afternoon. "Now that she is a public company, Donna is under the microscope and the stakes are

Research Associate Sarayu Srinivasan prepared this case under the supervision of Professor Krishna G. Palepu as the basis for class discussion rather than to illustrate either effective or ineffective handling of an administrative situation. Copyright © 1997 by the President and Fellows of Harvard College. Harvard Business School case 9-197-077.

higher than ever before. Donna has suffered the slings and arrows of outrageous fortune over the last nine months. Her stock, which debuted at $24, has fallen below nine points. It doesn't take a financial whiz to figure out she has lost two-thirds of her shareholders' confidence. Psychologically, that's a helluva blow."[1]

Donna Karan International Inc. (DKI), an international fashion design house, was founded in 1984 by its Chairman, CEO, and Chief Designer, Donna Karan, and her husband and Co-Chief Executive Officer, sculptor Stephen Weiss. The company was owned by Karan, Weiss, and their financial backers, the Takihyo Group.

The company designed, contracted for the production of, marketed, and distributed both "designer" and "bridge"[2] collections of men's and women's clothing, sportswear, accessories, and footwear under the Donna Karan New York and DKNY brand names. The company also developed, contracted for the production of, marketed, and distributed collections of men's and women's fragrances and bath, body, and treatment products under the DK Men and Donna Karan New York brand names. In addition, the company had selectively granted licenses for the manufacture and distribution of certain other products under the Donna Karan New York and DKNY brands, including hosiery, intimate apparel, eyewear, and children's apparel.[3]

The company's 1996 net revenues were $612.8 million, operating income was $13.3 million, and net income was $25 million. Exhibit 1 shows 1996 revenue breakdown. In July of the same year, Karan broke with fashion tradition and took her firm to the public markets with an IPO.

THE U.S. APPAREL INDUSTRY

In 1994 the apparel industry had retail sales (including domestic wholesale sales, value of apparel imports at entry, and retail markups) of $211 billion. Apparel included men's, women's, and children's clothing and accessories excluding footwear. Over half of all apparel sales were for women's apparel. Fashion products (as opposed to seasonal or basic) constituted 35 percent of the market.

The U.S. apparel market was divided into national and niche brands. National brands made up 30 percent of all apparel sales and were produced by 20 or so large firms such as Fruit of the Loom, Inc., Levi-Strauss, and Liz Claiborne, Inc. National brands also included apparel made overseas by U.S. manufacturers. Many national brand firms produced more than one brand, some even produced private label brands. Niche or private label brands were produced by a very fragmented industry of thousands of firms of all sizes, and accounted for the remaining 70 percent of apparel sales.[4]

....

1. *Excerpted from Orla Healy, "Designers are up against a Wall Street," Daily News, April 6, 1997, p. 31.*

2. *Bridgewear refers to apparel collections created as separate brands to reflect a more casual fashion identity, priced lower than the luxury "designer" collections but retaining an association with the designer image. The bridge market is considerably larger and more profitable than the designer market.*

3. *Donna Karan International Prospectus, June 1996.*

Demand for apparel was cyclical, but not totally predictable. Demand for women's apparel was more volatile because it was more sensitive to seasonal and fashion trends. Apparel sales were driven by three factors: the economy, consumer trends and demographics, and fashion. Generally, when the economy was strong, consumers purchased more apparel. Demand for luxury apparel, however, was largely insensitive to changes in the economy and disposable income. Attitudes of the general population, such as the ongoing casual office dressing trend, also influenced purchasing behavior. Recent consumer trends revealed a bargain mentality, an unwillingness to spend on apparel, and a shift from department store shopping, which accounted for half of apparel sales, to the lower priced mass merchandisers (including major chains J.C. Penney, Sears, etc.) Finally, fashion was a historic driver of women's apparel purchases but not quantifiable or predictive.

Low barriers to entry (moderate capital requirements, use of simple technologies, low fixed assets, and the ability to control output by use of contractors) made for intense industry competition. Labor intensity, low profit margins, and high firm mortality rates characterized the industry.

In the 1990s larger and better known apparel makers had greater competitive advantages. Retailers such as department stores were consolidating and growing larger, reducing their total numbers. With fewer large retailers in business, retailer power over both suppliers (manufacturers) and buyers (customers) increased. Large retailers decreased the number of apparel manufacturers they did business with, eliminating the shelf space of small manufacturers in favor of those that could pay for space and that produced popular big-name brands, usually better capitalized apparel makers.

Retail apparel could be divided into five price and market categories: popular, moderate, upper-moderate, bridgewear, and designer or high-priced ready-to-wear. Designers such as Donna Karan, who made up the high-priced ready-to-wear segment, also positioned themselves successfully in the profitable and large bridgewear markets through separate brands like DKNY.

Designer Apparel Market

High priced ready-to-wear and bridge apparel manufacturers were typically high-fashion designers with a design house and brand(s) such as Calvin Klein, Donna Karan, Ralph Lauren, Chanel, and Issey Miyake. This segment was expected to grow 5–10 percent in coming years.

Designers competed with one other and with other market and industry segments. The Donna Karan New York Collection, for instance, consisted of Karan's highest priced apparel. This competed with other designer collections and, to an extent, with the entire apparel market, including low-cost Donna Karan copies. Karan's DKNY brand com-

---

4. *Standard & Poor's Industry Surveys*, Textiles, Apparels and Home Furnishing, *September 28, 1995.*

peted with other designer bridgewear, upper to upper-moderate apparel, and other apparel. Karan's accessories and toiletries competed with both counterpart designer offerings and the larger nondesigner market. Designer products were luxury goods, so competition arose from both luxury and nonluxury substitute goods.

Competition between designers rested on differentiation. Each designer embodied and projected a unique image. The vehicle of differentiation and expression for the designer's image was the designer's brand. Purchasing a designer product was purchasing the image, and the lifestyle behind it. Designers might produce several product lines and brands aimed at different market segments, but there would be a unifying image behind all the offerings. The designer's image and associated brand were the most critical and central asset of the designer's business. The image and brand name were inseparable from one another.

Designer Calvin Klein's trademark, for example, was sensuality, while Donna Karan's was the power and potential of modern women. Designer brands were long-term investments built over time, requiring tremendous expenditures to accurately promote the image and feeling behind the name. These large time and capital outlays (easily between $10 million and $100 million) were strong deterrents to new market entrants. While barriers to entry and fixed costs were generally low in the industry, advertising and marketing were substantial and necessary investments in the designer apparel niche, and served as strong entry deterrents to potential competitors.

Brands were further capitalized upon through the mechanism of licensing. Licensing was a very profitable and important growth vehicle for designers. Licensing arrangements established apparel designers as true houses of design. While designers licensed their names to products ranging from sheets to timepieces, it was critical to tightly control brand context and usage to maintain and protect the integrity, image, and value of the brand and guard against unnecessary dilution.

Designers commonly sourced raw materials and production capacity by contracting with domestic and international suppliers. Good supplier relationships could lead to beneficial (but not critical) economies of scale, but had a more important impact on the quality of raw and finished goods, shipping and delivery schedule adherence, and ensuring future reliability of supplies.

Designers distributed through their own showrooms and retail stores, mini-shops at better retailers, boutiques, and outlets. Retailer consolidation gave retailers significant leverage over designers. Fewer retailers with limited floor space had to allocate space between designer brands (that often entailed building a "hard shop"—an entire environment complete with custom fixtures and furniture easily measuring 5,000 square feet, evoking the designer's vision and showcasing the merchandise), national brands, and lesser known brands.

Designer and national brands were attractive to retailers because they produced higher margins, had big-name draw, and were better capitalized to be able to spend the advertising dollars and markdown money and guarantee the sell-throughs demanded by financially driven retailers. Big brands also demarcated department stores from mass merchandisers and specialty stores. Lastly, department stores had historically been brand intensive. For these reasons, retailers preferred to showcase designers at the cost of smaller brands. The emphasis on big brands, however, posed problems. Most department stores ended up carrying the same large brands, limiting breadth. Secondly, the profusion of designer hard shops created an incongruency on selling floors. Finally, stores continued to stretch their demands on designers, making it an increasingly expensive and political game for designers to gain premium shelf space for their brands, leading to friction between the parties.[5]

DONNA KARAN INTERNATIONAL INC.

Company Background

Donna Karan, a student at New York's Parsons School of Design in the late 1960s, began her design career as an intern for the American fashion designer, Anne Klein. Karan left school to work for Klein fulltime and was fired after only nine months on the job. She eventually returned, rose to associate designer, and took over the label at Klein's death in 1974. At Anne Klein, Karan created the successful Anne Klein II designer clothing collection. After fifteen years with Klein, Karan started her own firm, first run out of her living room. In 1985 the first Donna Karan New York Collection was unveiled to critical success.

The Donna Karan New York Collection established Karan as a leading designer and fashion design house. The Collection, made with exclusive luxury fabrics and designed with an emphasis on comfort and fit, was based on Karan's concept of "seven easy pieces"—a collection of bodysuits, tights, dresses, skirts, blouses, jackets, pants, and accessories—that when layered in combinations produced a consistent but varied, high fashion look. Having amassed both numerous design awards and a loyal clientele over the years, Karan reflected on the critical and commercial popularity of her designs:

A garment has to work for me, not just on a gorgeous model. . . . My clothes are meant to be friendly. Regardless of size, regardless of age, regardless of anything. Something a little bit luxurious that's not obvious...You're not supposed to be able to say: There's that garment coming down at you. My clothes are about a relationship: about the person who is wearing them and the clothes.[6] When I design, I think about that woman—never, never just about the clothes. . . . For me, designing is a personal expression of who I am—wife, mother, friend, and business person—the many roles women everywhere try to balance. . . . It's really difficult to hold on to one's femininity while at the same time being pushed into a men's busi-

---

5. David Moin, "Space Wars Worry Retailers," Women's Wear Daily, October 31, 1996, p. S14.

6. Sidney Schaer, A Design for Herself," Newsday, May 6, 1991, p. 44.

ness environment. I understand it better because me too, I am a woman, with all the insecurity and vulnerability that being a woman brings along with it.[7]

Business Strategy

The company pursued business through several strategies: building global name and image, brand leveraging, international growth, protecting brand exclusivity, and "head-to-toe" dressing.

- *Building global name and image.* Donna Karan International's central focus was to continue building worldwide recognition for the Donna Karan New York brand and image in the designer market, and to capitalize on the brand's publicity and success to also build bridgewear DKNY brands.
- *Brand leveraging.* Historically, the company had created successful design collections and then leveraged that collection's success and the depth of its design talent in the larger bridge market. This approach was evidenced by the success of DKNY, a brand leveraged off the Donna Karan New York brand. The company had used the strategy to enter the men's apparel and fragrance and beauty product markets, and had subsequently increased the company's customer base and visibility.
- *International growth.* The Donna Karan name was recognized the world over. In 1996 international business accounted for 37.3 percent of net revenues. The company established divisions in Europe, Asia, and the Middle East, and expanded international sales by licensing free-standing retail stores and investing in the infrastructure to support sales growth abroad.
- *Maintaining brand exclusivity.* The company followed several strategies to protect brand image integrity and avoid market oversaturation. All advertising, marketing, and public relations efforts were centralized and managed from New York. Further, to reinforce brand exclusivity, the company limited distribution to a select number of retailers that included better department stores and boutiques catering to fashion conscious, high-end clients. Finally, the company selectively pursued licensing agreements, and maintained an active role in the ventures.
- *"Head-to-toe" dressing.* Multiple apparel collections, brands, and lines allowed clients to partake in the Donna Karan luxury lifestyle. Complementary luxury product offerings such as fragrance, toiletries, shoes, and accessories were created to complete the Donna Karan lifestyle ensemble. This strategy also increased brand awareness and visibility because it encouraged retailers that carried Donna Karan to add more departments to accommodate the new products.

PRODUCTS AND BRANDS

Donna Karan New York. These luxury designer collections included men's and women's apparel, shoes, and women's accessories. Women's apparel fell into two

---

7. Julia Carty, "Interview with Donna Karan," Look International Fashion and Nightlife Magazine, *April 1995, p. 20.*

designer collections: Donna Karan New York Collection (black label) and Donna Karan New York Signature (gold label). The Collection sprang from Karan's original "seven easy pieces" and was introduced each spring and fall at fashion shows. The Signature collection focused on designs for working women and was priced slightly lower than Collection to appeal to a larger market. Signature was also more widely distributed than Collection. In 1996 some Collection doors[8] were converted to Signature doors to further limit Collection to only luxury retailers. Exhibit 2 shows retail prices for select brands.

Men's apparel had two collections: Donna Karan New York (black label) and Donna Karan New York Signature (gold label). The black label had three lines: Couture, hand-tailored, sparsely distributed apparel; Sartoriale, hand-made for Asian and European markets; and the widely distributed Donna Karan New York collection. Signature had designs and quality similar to black label, but used lower cost fabrics, commercial production, and was priced lower.

Accessories included jewelry, leather goods, and scarves. This line, which included men's accessories, was shaping itself to become a line not dependent on coordinating with the collections.

The DKNY collection. Created in 1989, this brand included men's and women's bridge apparel and shoes and women's accessories. DKNY represented a lower priced, casual, spirited, fashion collection that was linked with the Donna Karan New York luxury designer image. An item-driven brand, DKNY apparel was distributed to different departments throughout stores that carried it. Representing the company's largest division, DKNY accounted for 50.7 percent of 1996 net revenues.

Donna Karan women's apparel originally had three main lines: DKNY for skirts, blouses, jackets, denim, core pieces, and activewear; DKNY Jeans that offered activewear; and DKNY Petite. The DKNY men's line was slightly more sophisticated than the DKNY women labels. DKNY Jeans had historically contributed nearly half of total revenues to the DKNY women's group. In June 1996 the DKNY brand was restructured to encompass five distinct labels.

The Beauty Division. Started in 1992, it produced a variety of perfumes, creams, lotions, shampoos, and soaps for men and women to complete the Donna Karan New York lifestyle ensemble under the brands DK Men and Donna Karan New York. The company tightly controlled product development, production, marketing, and distribution to maintain quality and protect brand integrity. New products would be innovated and added to the existing roster.

In the U.S. products were directly distributed by the company, but internationally through seventeen distribution agreements that required distributors to invest a percentage of sales in advertising and marketing each year. The beauty division, which benefited from the synergies produced from the apparel brands' advertising efforts, posted 1995 revenues of $30 million, which grew to $44 million in 1996.

Licensed Products. These included pantyhose, socks, women's intimate apparel, children's apparel, and paper and knitting patterns, and were licensed both domestically and

---

6. *A door is a single retail outlet.*

internationally under the trademarks Donna Karan New York, DKNY, and DKNY KIDS. Licensees included firms such as Wacoal America, Inc. and Hanes Hosiery. At the end of 1996, the company, which had recently licensed out the manufacture and distribution of its DKNY Jeans label, had six licensing agreements.

The decision to license a product rested on the company's ability to bring a product to market, the revenue to be earned, and the company resources available at that time. The company tried to control as closely as possible the design, quality, advertising, marketing, and distribution of any product licensed to prevent trademark erosion and maintain quality and consistent advertising and marketing images. Future initiatives included pursuing licensing opportunities more vigorously.

Donna Karan New York, DKNY, and other brand trademarks were owned by Gabrielle Studio, Inc., a firm owned by Donna Karan and Stephan Weiss. Donna Karan International Inc. was in an agreement with the studio that allowed it to use and sublicense the trademarks in perpetuity in exchange for a one-time $5 million payment and annual royalty payments to Karan and Weiss. If payments were not met, the studio could terminate the agreement. Royalty payments totaled 1.75 percent of the first $250 million of annual sales, plus 2.5 percent of the next $500 million in annual sales, plus 3 percent of the next $750 million in annual sales, plus 3.5 percent of all net sales for such a year in excess of $1.5 billion.

BRAND RESTRUCTURING.   In the fall of 1996, the company introduced the Signature collection under the Donna Karan New York brand to replace a previous collection, Essentials, and cater to the executive woman, but at lower prices than Collection to capture a larger market. The Signature collection would replace all of Essentials and limit Collection distribution to only high-end luxury retailers.

In 1996, the popular DKNY brand was restructured into five labels (D, DKNY, DKNY Classic, DKNY Active, and DKNY Jeans) to liberate the different styles that had emerged within the DKNY parent brand, fill market voids, capture greater market share, and provide different price points within DKNY. Exhibit 2 shows retail prices.

The D label created a new apparel market between designer and bridgewear. The most sophisticated DKNY label, D featured head-to-toe looks, fine detail, and superior workmanship. The line was selectively distributed. The DKNY label was the core of the DKNY brand. Classification driven, flexible pieces in modern fabrics that addressed a woman's everyday needs, it was designed to appeal to a broad client base. DKNY Classic was an item-oriented line, espousing "seven easy sportswear pieces of life" to go from weekday to weekend. DKNY Active offered functional and stylish seasonal sports and athletic wear, including a workout collection. DKNY Jeans focused on denim apparel and included jeans, dresses, and jackets, and complementary items such as tee shirts.

DISTRIBUTION.   Donna Karan followed a strategy of selective and limited product distribution to select high-end retailers (Saks Fifth Avenue, Bergdorf Goodman, Neiman Marcus, among others), boutiques, outlets, and international freestanding retail stores to achieve high product turnover. In 1996 the company's ten largest retailers made up 62.6 percent of gross sales (up from 60.8 percent in 1995).

Generally, product orders were received three to five months prior to retail delivery. Product arrived from the manufacturer to one of five worldwide distribution centers (two were company owned), underwent final quality inspections, and then was shipped to retailers. Operations worldwide were linked via computer to provide fast information, track inventory and product availability at different locations, and oversee production, receiving, and shipping schedules. Inventory, order, production, and shipping operations were reviewed bi-weekly.

The company selected retailers based on their exclusivity and ability to satisfactorily promote collections. This might entail customizing stores or in-house displays down to fixtures, furniture, and other associated hardware. Working with the retailer and its employees through account executives, the company helped determine product quantities and mixes for each retailer, in part informed by company marketing and outreach efforts. The company often premiered collections at a strictly limited number of retailers. To stimulate demand the company also had 37 outlet stores which sold excess inventory without cannibalizing retail sales by offering lines retailers had already marked down. The company did not have any domestic freestanding retail stores, but was considering opening such under a license or joint venture agreement.

Internationally, the company had 41 freestanding third-party owned retail stores through joint ventures, and expected to open an additional 17 such stores in 1997. Operating under the names of Donna Karan New York, DKNY, and Donna Karan, each store only stocked the product line it was named for. In 1995 Donna Karan International sold 70 percent of its interest in Donna Karan Japan but would manage the Japanese operations through the year 2000 (to be periodically renewed thereafter) for a fee based on Donna Karan Japan's net revenues. Donna Karan Japan would solely distribute product and provide service in Japan. Twenty-nine stores were slated to open by special agreement in Hong Kong, China, the Philippines, South Korea, Taiwan, and Japan by December 2000.

SOURCING, DESIGN, AND ADVERTISING AND MARKETING

Sourcing. In 1996 the company sourced 42 percent of its raw materials (mostly woven and knit fabrics and yarns) directly from suppliers and 58 percent from contractors that acquired material from company approved mills. Most purchased fabric was used, as production was triggered by client orders. The company did not own production facilities, and sourced apparel from 500 different manufacturers with whom it had long-term relationships. No one contractor accounted for more than 10 percent of total production. Nearly 50 percent of all raw materials, labor, and finished goods were sourced from Hong Kong and Asia, 30 percent from the U.S., and the balance from Europe and elsewhere. Sourcing and production was overseen from New York. Quality control took place worldwide, at all stages of sourcing and production. Less than one percent of apparel was returned to the company for defects over the period 1994–1996.

Design. Designer Donna Karan was a central source of creative talent and ultimately responsible for the company's strategic planning, marketing, and overall fashion direction. Her creativity, vision, and persona were inextricably linked with that of the company. Karan was under an employment contract to Donna Karan International Inc. but could terminate employment without notice based on "good reason." The company also employed a design staff of 124, for 10 design teams, each led by a head designer who shared the responsibility for the creation of the collections. In order to replenish talent, Karan regularly searched for qualified independent designers.

Advertising and Marketing. These efforts were the most critical component of the sustenance of the business and were centralized and coordinated from New York in order to promote a consistent company and product image worldwide. Expenditures totaled $53.2 million in 1996 (excluding expenditures by product licensees). Advertisements took form in print, catalogs, outdoor advertising media, and in-store display videos. To control placement and production costs, ensure image uniformity and integrity, assist company divisions with advertising, and help produce fashion shows and presentations, the firm coordinated advertising through its Creative Services Department. Karan herself was a key marketing asset due to her international celebrity status.

COMPETITORS.   The company believed it competed on fashion, quality, and service. In the designer market the company considered Calvin Klein, Versace, and Prada among its competitors. In bridgewear, DKNY brands competed with Calvin Klein (CK), Ralph Lauren (Polo), Guess, Tommy Hilfiger, and Anne Klein II. The beauty division competed with the top selling department store beauty product brands such as Estee Lauder, as well as with other designer offerings like those from Chanel, Issey Miyake, and Calvin Klein. No one competitor produced a substantial portion of total industry sales.

Growth Strategy

The company's growth strategy focused on continuing to exploit its brand name and image by growing current product offerings and strengthening its domestic and international presences by increasing its number of doors, creating more freestanding retail stores, continuing product segmentation and expansion, broadening its customer base, and expanding licensing efforts.

- *Increasing number of doors.* The company would concentrate on growing the number of domestic and international doors by which its products were offered. Specifically, the number of domestic doors carrying new products, men's apparel, and beauty products would be increased.
- *Creating more freestanding retail stores.* The company planned to open domestic freestanding retail stores in selected locations through licensing, franchises, and joint ventures. In 1997 the company expected to open seventeen freestanding international retail stores.
- *Ongoing product segmentation and expansion.* The company would continue to create and introduce new and segmented products and was slated to expand several existing collections, create new divisions, and introduce new beauty products. This

strategy allowed the company to provide a wider range of products to satisfy the "head-to-toe" Donna Karan lifestyle philosophy.

- *Broadening customer base.* Through segmentation and the introduction of lower priced luxury accessory and beauty products, the company would try to appeal to a larger customer base.
- *Expanding licensing efforts.* Donna Karan International expected to grant new product licenses to select manufacturers. These new licenses might be for jeanswear and related accessories, swimwear, DKNY underwear, watches, and home furnishings.

THE IPO AND FIRST YEAR PUBLIC

In November 1993, Karan attempted to take her company to the public equity markets in a highly publicized IPO. The offering was scrapped at the last minute reportedly due to poor earnings, weak new issue markets, concerns over inaccurate valuation of the firm's long-term growth potential, and disagreements between Karan and her financial partners, the Takihyo Group.

RECENT "FASHION" IPOS.   Several fashion issues had performed well in recent markets. The incumbents included Gucci, the Italian design house and luxury goods maker, and Tommy Hilfiger, a designer of men's casual apparel. Other firms, such as the upscale women's apparel retailer Ann Taylor, had had a rougher market ride. Exhibits 4 and 5 show these firms' stock and financial data.

Gucci, with its highly recognizable logo and strong luxury brand (that together spurred a cornucopia of counterfeit products), went public in October 1995 at $22 a share. Gucci produced a limited product line of high quality, high priced luxury products distributed almost exclusively through company stores. Ready-to-wear apparel constituted 20 percent of Gucci's sales, but over 50 percent of sales were for leather products and timepieces. Gucci had nearly 70 stores worldwide with sales spread equally over Europe, the U.S., and Asia. The company planned to increase its department store presence.

Tommy Hilfiger was the second largest line of men's casual bridgewear and was carried by 1200 retailers. Hilfiger's diverse clientele ran from upscale designer focused customers to inner-city teens who had adopted Hilfiger apparel as "streetwear." The company's management team was considered very strong, with over 100 combined years of apparel industry experience, and included a partner who was a major garment factory operator in Asia, where Hilfiger's manufacturing base was located. Apparel offerings fell into one of three lines: a line of basic seasonless apparel, a widely distributed seasonal and varied core line, and an exclusively distributed fashion collection. The company also branched out to other businesses, licensing out what it did not have the in-house expertise for, including a popular cologne, swim and boys wear, and plans to open its own retail stores. Hilfiger's September 1992 IPO was priced at $15 a share.

Ann Taylor, a high-end specialty women's apparel retailer, had traditionally catered, through stores across the U.S. and in better malls, to a very specific clientele: the higher-income professional woman. Each store carried standard offerings of classic, finely tailored, conservative, private label (nearly 90 percent of Taylor merchandise) or non-designer brand apparel priced right below designer offerings. The firm did little traditional advertising, relying mostly on selective catalog distribution, word of mouth, optimal store locations, and limited magazine advertisements. Ann Taylor considered better retailers (such as Saks Fifth Avenue) competitors and often operated more than one store in an area.

In the 1990s Ann Taylor saw a succession of turnovers in top management driving a series of changes in strategy, but with an emphasis on growth. In order to support expansion, the firm decided to go to the public markets. Ann Taylor's May 1991 IPO of $26 per share had fallen in value to $13.12 by November. The loss in value was attributed to a lack of direction and unsustainable expansion plans, manifest through noticeable declines in quality; a shift away from the traditional timeless style Ann Taylor had built its reputation on towards trendier, shorter-lived offerings; and declining store sales. The stock regained value in December 1994 when it reached a share price of $38.25, as the firm tried to refocus on quality, re-emphasize core product, and recapture its customer. The firm, however, also intended to extend into mail order, fragrance, and accessory stores, but the market again signaled disapproval in January 1996 when the stock nose-dived to $9.25 a share.

RE-ENTRY.   In 1996 Karan again attempted to enter the markets with a Donna Karan IPO. Industry followers and analysts were jubilant about Karan's prospects, projecting growth of 20–25 percent.

Karan's offering of 10.75 million common shares debuted June 28, 1996, closing at $28 per share (17 percent over the initial asking price of $24 per share) raising a total of $258 million. The offering's proceeds paid off $116 million worth of notes held by Karan, Weiss, and the Takihyo Group; retired $72 million of other debt; compensated the company's president an amount of $5 million for services rendered; and paid a lump sum of $5 million to Gabrielle Studios for licensing privileges. After the offering Karan and Weiss owned 25 percent of the shares and the Takihyo Group, 20 percent.

FISCAL YEAR 1996.   Despite the great fanfare which accompanied the IPO, only four months after its much anticipated Wall Street premiere, the company's stock price fell to $15.50 on October 29. In the third quarter of 1996, earnings on sales of $173.4 million had been $13 million, or 61 cents a share, up from 52 cents (on earnings of $11.8 million) the previous year. Despite the growth, the firm announced that earnings would drop four cents in the fourth quarter. The downward revision was blamed on the performance of the beauty division, which had fallen $5 million short of expected sales, reducing third quarter earnings per share from 63 to 61 cents. Karan commented on the division:

We believe that the beauty business has been an outstanding success. In the four years since we started the business, we built tremendous consumer loyalty and re-

ceived numerous industry awards. Most importantly, we have retained our own vision of the business and have developed it according to our own high standards.[9]

Stephen Ruzow, Donna Karan International's president, laid out the division's future:

The board has instructed us to pursue either a joint venture, sale, or license agreement for the beauty products and we intend to do that immediately. . . . Donna wanted the right product(s) out there with integrity, and we are proud that we did that. Unfortunately, we had an aggressive plan for this year that we didn't meet.

Analysts agreed with Ruzow:

There is a tremendous number of talented people at Donna Karan. What they are great at is creating brands and great clothing and selling. But running a cosmetics business doesn't draw on their strengths.[10]
The beauty division has really dragged down their revenue; and their revenue growth, on a quarter-to-quarter basis, is also uninspiring.[11]

The publication of the company's first annual report in March 1997 also signaled the end of the recently entered DKNY Jeans licensing agreement.[12] On March 4 the company terminated its licensing covenant with Designer Holdings Ltd., returned nearly $12 million in fees paid, and recognized the expense in the fourth quarter 1996. Karan stock subsequently tumbled to $11.25 per share on March 5. Exhibit 3 follows the firm's stock movements. Ruzow, revealing the firm would develop the jeans business in-house, explained:

We were overly optimistic in thinking we could get this thing to market by Fall 1997. But the bigger issue was that we were very specific about what products we were going to license. It became evident that what both parties agreed to did not work for Designer Holdings. We did not want them to have a failure, but at the same time, we would not do anything that would impact our core businesses.[13]

Designer Holdings CEO Arnold Simon, who also produced jeanswear for designer Calvin Klein, retorted:

I have a clear understanding of what the product lines were, but that was confusing to them. I don't want one T-shirt; I need a line of T-shirts. We don't mind having T-shirts of a different quality or different look, but you need more than one and

9.   "Donna Karan Announces Higher Third Quarter and Nine Month 1996 Revenues," PR Newswire, Oct. 28, 1996.

10. Ibid. (quote from analyst F. Landes).

11. Analyst Manish Shah from J. Westhoven, "Donna Karan Gets Discounted," Reuters, October 29, 1996.

12. The firm's licensing agreement still totaled six, as in its annual report, because of a new agreement entered to produce towels in Asia.

13. Jennifer Steinhauer, "Dispute Ends Donna Karan Jeans License," The New York Times, March 6, 1997, p. 4.

Donna Karan International

they should have thought that over.[14] *. . . Calvin Klein is a very professional company. They know how to do this. They've been doing it for years. Donna Karan hasn't dealt with licensees before.*[15]

The returned licensing fees impacted 1996 earnings, which were characterized in the annual report as "unnacceptable." The report re-emphasized the company's commitment to search for either a suitable partner or an acquisitor for its beauty business, and acknowledged the need to control its increasing expenses. In order to improve financial results and respond to its current challenges, the firm proposed in its Letter to Shareholders to:

- Cut costs and eliminate unprofitable activities after reviewing its portfolio of businesses.
- Focus on profitability by growing only the businesses that offered the highest returns.
- Strategically view each division as separate, realizing each business unit required different solutions.
- Invest in building and strengthening its management team and Board of Directors in order to better take advantage of growth opportunities.

But analysts, the markets, and the media had already started to question the company's and Karan's business acumen and interest in maximizing returns and creating shareholder value:

I think the brand name, from a fundamental standpoint, is great. What's hurting them is the execution of their business strategy.[16]
   It's clear Karan's interest is in the hemline, not the bottom line.[17]

QUESTIONS

1. Assess Donna Karan's business strategy. What are the key risks faced by the company?
2. Compare the company's financial performance in 1996 and 1995. What are the underlying causes for the company's performance in 1996?
3. What is your assessment of the proposed action plan to improve the company's performance? Do you think the plan will lead to a turnaround?
4. What is your assessment of the company's future? What is the intrinsic value of the company's stock? Is the stock a buy or a sell at the time of the case?

[handwritten: should an IPO have been pursued. What are reasons in favour? reasons against?]

14. *Ibid.*

15. *Lisa Lockwood, "Donna Doesn't Do It," WWD, March 6, 1997, p. 1.*

16. *Investor Michael Green in "A Designer Takes Stock," by Teri Agins, The Wall Street Journal, Nov. 14, 1996.*

17. *Editor Alan Millstein from Tom Lowry, "Donna Karan Earnings Unravel," USA Today, Oct. 30, 1996, p. 3B.*

EXHIBIT 1

Donna Karan International Inc., Sources of Revenue, 1995 and 1996
($ in millions)

1995 Product Categories	Revenue	1995 Geographic Categories	Revenue
Donna Karan New York Collection (women)	$77	United States	$301
DKNY (women)	$271	Japan	$64
Donna Karan New York Collection (men)	$40	Europe and the Middle East	$57
DKNY (men)	$37	Asia (excluding Japan)	$23
Beauty products	$30	Other markets	$10
Outlet stores and licensing	$55		

1996 Product Categories	Revenue	1996 Geographic Categories	Revenue
Donna Karan New York Collection (men & women)	$123	United States	$342
DKNY (men & women)	$378	Japan	$76
Beauty products	$44	Europe and Middle East	$73
Outlet stores and licensing	$68	Asia (excluding Japan)	$36
		Other markets	$18

Source: Donna Karan International Prospectus and Annual Report, 1996.

Donna Karan International

Donna Karan International

EXHIBIT 2
Retail Prices for Selected Collections' Items (DKNY brands post-restructuring)

Apparel Collections	Jackets	Skirts & Trousers	Shirts, Body-suits, & Sweats	Dresses (non-eveningwear)	Suits	Sportscoats
Women:						
Donna Karan New York Collection	$1,200-1,800	$400-900	$300-600	$650-1,200		
Donna Karan New York Signature	$750-1,100	$300-600	$200-400	$500-950		
D	$415-625	$195-375	$100-295	$225-450		
DKNY	$295-425	$140-225	$165-175	$175-225		
DKNY Classic	$220-365	$105-175	$45-130	$130-175		
DKNY Active	$95-225		$55-85			
DKNY Jeans	$115-225	$45-125	$65-115			
Men:						
Donna Karan New York Collection		$300-400			$1,350-1,850	$950-1,750
Donna Karan New York Signature		$225-275			$875-995	$595-750
DKNY		$65-290			$550-1,200	$250-450

Accessory Collections	Handbags	Belts	Hats	Jewelry	Leather Goods
Donna Karan New York	$350-1500	$80-250		$200-800	$75-300
DKNY	$40-525		$15-175		$15-150

Shoes	Handbags
Donna Karan New York (women)	$110-700
DKNY (women)	$50-400
Donna Karan New York (men)	$275-600
DKNY (men)	$75-295

Beauty Products

Priced between $15 and $375 with median product prices at $85 and below.

Sources: Donna Karan International Prospectus; Annual Report 1996; and Donna Karan International Inc.

EXHIBIT 3

Donna Karan International Stock Price vs. S&P 500,
June 28, 1996, to March 31, 1997 (Both indexed to 1.00 as of 6/28/96)

As of June 28, 1996:

T-Bill	5.16%
T-Note	5.69%
Donna Karan stock price	$28
S&P 500	670.63
Beta vs. S&P 500	1.28

As of March 31, 1997:

T-Bill	6.02%
T-Note	6.92%
Donna Karan stock price	$9.63
S&P 500	757.12
Beta vs. S&P 500	1.05

Source: Datastream International, Bloomberg.

Donna Karan International

EXHIBIT 4

Donna Karan International Stock Price Indexed to Competitors,
June 28, 1996, to March 28, 1997 (Indexed to 1.00 as of 6/28/96)

Source: Datastream International.

EXHIBIT 5
Financial Data for Fashion Companies

	Donna Karan International		Gucci	Tommy Hilfiger	Ann Taylor
	YE 12-31-95	YE 12-31-96	YE 1-31-96	YE 3-31-96	YE 2-3-96
Sales (in thousands)	$510,126	$612,840	$500,064	$478,131	$731,142
Cost of Sales (in thousands)	$330,689	$412,064	$170,660	$258,419	$425,225
Gross Profit (in thousands)	$179,437	$200,776	$329,404	$219,712	$305,917
Operating Income (in thousands)	$42,531	$13,302	$120,125	$87,442	$34,781
Net Income (in thousands)	$53,675	$25,036	$81,392	$61,500	($876)
Return on Equity:					
Profit Before Taxes/Sales (%)	8.33	2.17	24.02	18.2	4.75
× Sales/Average Assets	2.82	2.37	1.83	1.59	1.14
× Average Assets/Average Equity	2.80	1.81	10.54	1.17	1.95
× (1 − Avg. Tax Rate)	.96	N/A[a]	.72	.67	N/A
= ROE (%)	63.14	9.3	333.57	22.68	10.55
× (1 − Dividend Payout Ratio)[b]	1.00	1.00	1.00	1.00	1.00
= Sustainable Growth Rate (%)	63.14	9.3	333.57	22.68	10.55
Margins:					
Gross Profit/Sales (%)	35	32.7	65.8	45.9	41.8
SG&A/Sales (%)	26	30.5	41.8	27.6	37.08
Interest Income(Expense)/Sales (%)	−1.49	−1.16	2.14	.15	2.8
Inventory Turnover	3.86	4.09	2.35	3.17	4.14
Collection Period (Days)[c]	44.52	44.13	18.77	52.25	35.14
Accts. Payable Period (Days)	59.41	65.01	145.9	13.35	36.83
Price Per Share (as of 3/31/97)	N/A	$9.62	$72.12	$49.25	$20.37
Shares Outstanding (000) (3/31/97)	N/A	21.470	60.899	36.880	25.483
P/E Ratio (as of 3/31/97)	N/A	7.46	27.44	24.08	56.59

a. Tax rate for Donna Karan International 1996 is excluded from calculation due to the firm's change in status during the fiscal year from a private to public entity, which resulted in a one-time, non-recurring tax benefit, that when included, distorts ROE.
b. No dividends were paid by Donna Karan International each year, excepting distributions to pre-IPO partners both years.
c. Assumes 365 days.

Donna Karan International

EXHIBIT 6
Donna Karan International, 1996 Abridged Annual Report

TO OUR STOCKHOLDERS:

1996 was an exciting and challenging year for Donna Karan International Inc. In a little over 10 years, we have grown from offering a women's collection based on the original concept of "seven easy pieces" to creating one of the world's leading international fashion design houses. Today, we offer clothing, accessories, and shoes for men and women under the *Donna Karan New York®* and *DKNY®* brands, as well as beauty products under the *Donna Karan New York®* and *DK Men™* brands. Our growth has resulted from the dedication of our employees, vendors, retailers, and customers and our drive to develop innovative, high quality products that meet the lifestyle needs of today's consumers. In 1996, we continued to build and expand our brands by segmenting the *Donna Karan New York®* and *DKNY®* women's apparel collections, growing our international business, and further expanding on our success in the men's apparel business. Other highlights of the year included our initial public offering, the opening of our flagship *Donna Karan New York®* Collection store in London, and Donna Karan's selection as Womenswear Designer of the Year by the Council of Fashion Designers of America.

With growth, however, often come challenges. While we were pleased with our sales growth and increased brand recognition, our 1996 earnings were unacceptable. Significant cost overruns negatively impacted our financial performance. In this letter, we will review our accomplishments, discuss our challenges, and then outline our plans for building long-term value for our stockholders, customers, vendors, retailers, and employees.

1996 Highlights

The year was marked by the following achievements:

Strong Divisional Sales Performance—Most of our divisions produced strong sales growth in 1996. In particular, the *DKNY®* women's collections and *Donna Karan New York®* men's collections produced double-digit sales growth. Total net revenues in 1996 grew 20.1% to $612.8 million from $510.1 million in 1995. The enduring strength of our Company and global appeal of our products is evidenced by the continued sales growth that we experienced in 1996.

Segmentation of Women's Apparel Collections—To clarify our product offerings, emphasize the breadth of our collections, and target more focused customer categories at specific price ranges, we segmented our existing *Donna Karan New York®* and *DKNY®* women's apparel collections. The *Donna Karan New York®* collection was segmented into the Collection ("black label") and Signature ("gold label") lines, while the *DKNY®* collection was segmented into five separate labels: D, *DKNY®*, *DKNY® Classic*, *DKNY® Jeans*, and *DKNY® Active*. The products currently offered under these *DKNY®* labels previously had been included in the Company's existing collection, but are now more clearly defined for the consumer. Each new label reflects a unique and individual design approach and addresses the ever-changing lifestyles of our customers at appropriate price points. The retailers' and consumers' positive response to these segmented collections reinforce our belief that these initiatives provide important avenues of growth.

Growth of Men's Business—The *Donna Karen New York*® and *DKNY*® collections for men experienced continued impressive growth in 1996. Sales grew by 27.3% and 83.6%, respectively. We believe that the men's divisions will continue to add substantial sales and profits to the overall business.

Growth in International Business—Our International Division is one of our most important long-term growth vehicles. In 1996, international sales increased by 32.5% and represented 37.3% of net sales (excluding sales from outlet stores and licensing), with significant growth coming from European, Asian (excluding Japan), and other markets, including Australia and South America. Product sales are through our licensed free-standing stores and select retail distribution channels. As our licensees open additional free-standing stores and we continue to expand the international retail sales network, we expect international markets to present significant growth opportunities for our products.

Initial Public Offering—In July, we completed our initial public offering and became listed on the New York Stock Exchange. By better capitalizing our Company, we positioned ourselves to take advantage of our growth opportunities.

1996 Challenges

While we are pleased with these accomplishments, 1996 was also marked by significant challenges and setbacks. Despite our growth in net sales, our 1996 operating and net income declined significantly from 1995 levels, due in part to the following three items which impact our 1996 results:

Termination of the DKNY® Jeans License—In September 1996, we entered into a *DKNY*® jeanswear license with Designer Holdings, Ltd. In March 1997, the jeanswear license was terminated by mutual consent, due primarily to differences with respect to the scope of the product line included in the license. It was of paramount importance to the Company that the focused product range defined by the jeanswear license not be increased to impact our core *DKNY*® business. In connection with this termination, we recognized $3.2 million of expense in the fourth quarter of 1996 as a result of the purchase from Designer Holdings of sales and marketing plans, samples, patterns, and other materials developed for the jeanswear license. We are now committed to continuing to grow and expand the *DKNY*® *Jeans* business in house, and will utilize the materials developed by Designer Holdings to further these efforts.

Fall 1996 Advertising Campaign—We incurred approximately $5.0 million of advertising expenses in excess of our budget in funding the Fall 1996 advertising campaign featuring Bruce Willis and Demi Moore. This critically acclaimed campaign, which received wide exposure, was a unique opportunity for us to increase the focus on the *Donna Karan New York*® men's and women's apparel collections and our *DKNY*® products. At approximately the same time as we launched the campaign, we had

Donna Karan International

anticipated that the Company would recognize a significant gain from entering into the *DKNY®* jeanswear license.

Difficulties in Beauty Business—Despite an increase in net sales of 46.4% in 1996, the Beauty Division's sales were below our internal expectations, which impacted operating results. As previously announced, we have revised our long-term strategy for the beauty business. We believe that we have built a tremendous asset, but one which requires a substantial capital commitment to realize its full potential. As a result, we have begun to explore the possible license, joint venture, or sales of the beauty business. We are dedicated to finding a strategic partner whose vision for The Donna Karan Beauty Company is consistent with our own strategy and which will maximize the potential of both our *Donna Karan New York®* and *DKNY®* brands.

In addition to these items, our profitability was impacted by generally high corporate and administrative expenses and increased investments in our newly segmented and existing businesses. We created a Retail Development Division to enhance our competitive position at retail. We also strengthened our core apparel businesses and our international franchise by increasing our sales force and our co-op advertising contributions.

As a result of these items, pro forma selling, general, and administrative expenses increased to 29.1% of net sales in 1996 from 25.7% in 1995 and pro forma operating income decreased to $20.1 million in 1996 from $30.1 million in 1995. Pro forma net income declined to $12.6 million in 1996, or $0.59 cents per share, from $18.4 million in 1995, or $0.86 cents per share, in 1995.

Conclusion

1996's financial results were unacceptable. We are identifying and implementing changes that are necessary to curtail the rise in selling, general, and administrative expenses, improve gross margins, and continue growth without sacrificing the quality, consistency, and image of the *Donna Karan New York®* and *DKNY®* brands. Steps being planned or already implemented include the following:

Control Costs—While our sales growth has been strong, our difficulty in controlling the increase in our expenses in 1996 contributed to disappointing financial performance. To improve these results, senior management is conducting a thorough review of our businesses and is seeking to curtail or eliminate those areas which have placed a drain on our profitability. The primary responsibilities of our Senior Executive Vice President and Chief Administrative Officer are to oversee the Company's strategic planning efforts and to implement our cost control initiatives.

Prioritize Attractive Opportunities—The overall strength and worldwide popularity of our brands provide us with an enviable set of growth opportunities. However, we face both organizational and capital constraints that require us to limit ourselves to those areas which offer the highest return and which will result in increased shareholder value. The first step in our goal to better prioritize our efforts has been our initiative to sell, license, or joint venture the Beauty Division. We will continue to analyze alternatives for our existing and new businesses which may include joint ventures, strategic alliances, or licenses.

Develop Division-specific Solutions—The challenges faced by our company vary by division. For example, the *DKNY®* women's collection has addressed the heightened competition in the bridge market by segmenting its collection, while our *Donna Karan New York®* women's collection divisions are working to improve operational efficiencies. Senior management is working with each Division President to develop individual strategies to profitably exploit each of our growth opportunities.

Increase Size of Board of Directors and Strengthen Management Team—In the last six months, in order to profitably exploit our many opportunities, we built a stronger Board of Directors and management team. We have added three accomplished outside Board members, M. William Benedetto, Andrea Jung, and Ann McLaughlin. We also appointed Dewey K. Shay, our new Senior Executive Vice President and Chief Administrative Officer, as a member of the Company's Board of Directors.

Despite the financial impact in 1996 of the items and investments discussed above, we have great enthusiasm for the future. We are experiencing strong sales growth across many of our divisions and have made important investments for the future by segmenting our women's apparel collections. In addition, we are developing a more tightly focused growth strategy, and are committed to controlling costs. The positive feedback we have received from our retailers and customers on our newly segmented *Donna Karan New York®* Signature and *"D"* by *DKNY®* collections, the potential of our *DKNY®* Kids line and other licensing opportunities and the excitement internally about our businesses also engender optimism for the future. We want to thank all of our employees, retailers, vendors, and loyal customers. With your help, we look forward to continuing to build on the global recognition and success of our brands.

Donna Karan
Chairman of the Board,
Chief Executive Officer,
and Chief Designer

Stephen L. Ruzow
President and
Chief Operating Officer

Donna Karan International

Donna Karan International

REPORT OF INDEPENDENT AUDITORS

The Board of Directors of
Donna Karan International Inc.

We have audited the consolidated balance sheet of Donna Karan International Inc. (the "Company") as of December 29, 1996, and the related consolidated statements of income, stockholders' equity and partners' capital and cash flows for the year then ended. We have also audited the combined balance sheet of The Donna Karan Company and affiliates as of December 31, 1995, and the related combined statements of income and cash flows for each of the two years in the period ended December 31, 1995. Our audits also included the financial statement schedule listed in the Index at Item 14(a). These financial statements and schedule are the responsibility of the Company's management. Our responsibility is to express an opinion on these financial statements and schedule based on our audits.

We conducted our audits in accordance with generally accepted auditing standards. Those standards require that we plan and perform the audit to obtain reasonable assurance about whether the financial statements are free of material misstatement. An audit includes examining, on a test basis, evidence supporting the amounts and disclosures in the financial statements. An audit also includes assessing the accounting principles used and significant estimates made by management, as well as evaluating the overall financial statement presentation. We believe that our audits provide a reasonable basis for our opinion.

In our opinion, the financial statements referred to above present fairly, in all material respects, the consolidated financial position of Donna Karan International Inc. as of December 29, 1996, and the consolidated results of their operations and their cash flows for the year then ended, and the combined financial position of The Donna Karan Company and affiliates as of December 31, 1995, and the combined results of their operations and their cash flows for each of the two years in the period ended December 31, 1995 in conformity with generally accepted accounting principles. Also, in our opinion, the related financial statement schedule, when considered in relation to the basic financial statements taken as a whole, present fairly in all material aspects the information set forth therein.

ERNST & YOUNG LLP

New York, New York
March 25, 1997

Donna Karan International Inc., Statements of Income (Note 1)

(in thousands, except per-share amounts)	Year Ended:		
	January 1, 1995	December 31, 1995	December 29, 1996
Net revenues	$420,164	$510,126	$612,840
Cost of sales	271,172	330,689	412,064
Gross profit	148,992	179,437	200,776
Selling, general, and administrative expenses	119,995	136,906	187,474
Operating income	28,997	42,531	13,302
Other income (expense)			
Equity in earnings of affiliate	—	2,519	3,089
Interest income	—	—	548
Interest expense	(8,862)	(7,650)	(7,125)
Interest expense on distribution notes	—	—	(1,957)
Other expense	(2,651)	—	—
Gain on sale of interests in affiliates	—	18,673	—
Income before income taxes	17,484	56,073	7,857
Provision (benefit) for income taxes	1,139	2,398	(17,179)
Net income	$ 16,345	$ 53,675	$ 25,036
Pro forma—unaudited:			
Historical income before income taxes		$ 56,073	$ 7,857
Pro forma adjustments other than income taxes		23,943	1,436
Pro forma income before income taxes		32,130	6,421
Pro forma provision for income taxes		13,705	3,537
Pro forma net income		$ 18,425	2,884
Pro forma net income per share		$ 0.91	$ 0.02
Pro forma weighted average common shares outstanding		16,017,032	18,742,533

See "Notes to Financial Statements."

Donna Karan International

Donna Karan International Inc.—Balance Sheets

(in thousands)	December 31, 1995	December 29, 1996
ASSETS		
Current assets:		
Cash and cash equivalents	$ 12,153	$ 40,550
Accounts receivable, net of allowances of $26,757 at		
December 29, 1996 and $22,507 at December 31, 1995	62,231	73,770
Inventories	85,655	100,680
Deferred income taxes	1,302	25,207
Prepaid expenses and other current assets	8,644	14,466
Total current assets	$169,985	$254,673
Property and equipment, at cost—net	22,505	32,402
Deferred income taxes	380	6,106
Deposits and other noncurrent assets	11,105	18,514
	$203,975	$311,695
LIABILITIES AND STOCKHOLDERS' EQUITY		
AND PARTNERS' CAPITAL		
Current liabilities:		
Accounts payable	$ 53,825	$ 73,394
Accrued expenses and other current liabilities	15,766	34,192
Current portion of long-term debt	7,759	282
Total current liabilities	$ 77,350	$107,868
Long-term debt	45,779	36
Commitments and contingencies		
Shareholders' equity and partners' capital:		
Common stock of predecessor	1,146	—
Common stock, $0.01 par value, 35,000,000 shares		
authorized, 21,468,034 shares issued and outstanding	—	215
Common stock class A, $0.01 par value, 18 shares		
authorized, issued and outstanding	—	—
Common stock class B, $0.01 par value, 2 shares		
authorized, issues and outstanding	—	—
Preferred stock, $0.01 par value, 1,000,000 shares		
authorized, no shares issued and outstanding	—	—
Additional paid-in capital	—	186,899
Retained earnings and partners' capital	79,748	17,487
Cumulative translation adjustment	(48)	(331)
	$ 80,846	$204,270
Less treasury stock, at cost (19,958 shares)	—	(479)
Total stockholders' equity and partners' capital	$ 80,846	$203,791
	$203,975	$311,695

See notes to financial statements.

Donna Karan International Inc.—Statements of Cash Flow

(in thousands)	January 1, 1995	Year Ended December 31, 1995	December 29, 1996
Operating Activities			
Net income	$16,345	$53,675	$25,036
Adjustments to reconcile net income to net cash (used in) provided by operating activities, as adjusted for effect of sale of Donna Karan Japan:			
Depreciation and amortization	7,590	6,742	11,309
Provision for bad debts	773	3,122	62
Equity in earnings of affiliate, net of cash received	—	(2,519)	(1,734)
Deferred taxes	—	—	(29,631)
Stock bonus award	—	—	2,522
Gain on sale of interests in affiliated	—	(18,673)	—
Loss on sale of property and equipment	—	32	—
Changes in operating assets and liabilities:			
Increase in accounts receivable	(9,658)	(14,392)	(11,601)
Increase in inventories	(6,410)	(29,611)	(15,308)
Increase in prepaid expenses and other current assets	(2,253)	(2,876)	(5,822)
Increase in deposits and other noncurrent assets	(3,543)	(4,956)	(10,619)
Increase in accounts payable, accrued expenses, and other current liabilities	4,887	27,905	37,995
Net cash provided by operating activities	$ 7,731	$18,449	$ 2,209
Investing Activities			
Purchase of property and equipment	($ 3,445)	($ 4,289)	($16,262)
Net cash from sales of interests in affiliates	—	23,526	—
Proceeds from sale of property and equipment	—	42	—
Net cash (used in) provided by investing activities	($ 3,445)	$19,279	($16,262)
Planning Activities			
Payment of revolving credit facility, net	($40,903)	($ 3,253)	($ 7,961)
Proceeds of long-term debt	50,000	10,000	—
Payments under capital leases	(230)	(237)	(259)
Payments of long-term debt	—	(15,000)	(45,000)
Payment of distribution notes	—	—	(114,484)
Issuance of common stock	—	—	236,020
Purchase of treasury stock	—	—	(479)
Distribution to partners	(10,770)	(20,813)	(25,387)
Net cash (used in) provided by financing activities	($ 1,903)	($29,303)	$42,450
Increase in cash	$ 2,383	$ 8,425	$28,397
Cash at beginning of year	1,345	3,728	12,153
Cash at end of year	$ 3,728	$12,153	$40,550
Supplemental Cash Flow Information			
Interest paid	$ 8,420	$ 6,410	$ 6,594
Taxes paid	$ 942	$ 2,444	$ 5,884

See notes to financial statements.

Donna Karan International

Donna Karan International, Inc.—Notes to Financial Statements, Dec. 29, 1996

1. Basis of Presentation and Significant Accounting Policies

Business

Donna Karan International Inc. ("DKI") and subsidiaries (together with DKI, the "Company"), which operate in one business segment, design, contract for the manufacture of, market, and distribute fashion apparel, accessories, and beauty products. Its sales are principally to department and specialty stores located throughout the United States. A significant amount of the Company's products are produced in Asia, through arrangements with independent contractors. As a result, the Company's operations could be adversely affected by political instability resulting in the disruption of trade from the countries in which these contractors are located, or by the imposition of additional duties or regulations relating to imports.

The Company's business is impacted by the general seasonal trends that are characteristic of the apparel industry, and it generally experiences lower net revenues and net income in the first half of each fiscal year as compared to the second half of the fiscal year.

Several of the Company's customers have engaged in leveraged buyouts or transactions in which they incurred significant amounts of debt, and certain customers have operated or are currently operating under the protection of the Federal bankruptcy laws. The Company does not factor its accounts receivable and maintains credit insurance to minimize the risk of bad debts.

The Company had one customer which accounted for approximately 12.4%, 12.3%, and 12.8% of sales for the years ended January 1, 1995, December 31, 1995 and December 29, 1996 respectively. During the year ended December 31, 1995, another customer accounted for 11.1% of sales.

Initial Public Offering

Effective July 3, 1996, the Company sold 10,750,000 shares of its common stock in an initial public offering ("the Offering"). Net proceeds of the Offering, after deducting underwriting discounts and commissions, and professional fees aggregated $236.0 million. Proceeds of the Offering were used to retire distribution notes and accrued interest thereon totaling approximately $116.4 million, to repay the Predecessor Company's (as defined below) term loans and the revolving line of credit which totaled approximately $76.8 million, to pay a certain one-time bonus under an employment agreement which amounted to $5.0 million (which is included in selling, general and administrative expenses) and to pay a one-time fee under a license agreement which amounted to $4.6 million (which is included in cost of sales). The remaining $33.2 million was used for other general corporate purposes. The distribution notes were issued in April 1996 to the principals, and certain of their affiliates, of the Predecessor Company, and represented an estimate of the cumulative undistributed taxable income (on which taxes previously had been paid) of the Predecessor Company since its inception through the anticipated closing date of the Offering.

Basis of Presentation

DKI was incorporated in Delaware in April 1996. In connection with the Offering, the former principals of the Predecessor Company and certain of their affiliates simultaneously contributed to DKI all of the outstanding stock and partnership interests in the Predecessor Company, in exchange for common stock of DKI (the "Reorganization").

The financial statements of the Predecessor Company are being presented on a combined basis because of their common ownership. The combined financial statements have been prepared as if the entities had operated as a single consolidated group since their respective dates of organization. Because DKI conducted no business prior to the Reorganization, it was not included in the results of operations of the Predecessor Company.

Amounts included for common stock on the accompanying balance sheet of the Predecessor Company represent the combined par or stated value of the outstanding shares of the various corporations included in the Predecessor Company.

Statement of Income Presentation

The statement of income of the Company for the year ended December 29, 1996 reflects the results of operations of the Predecessor Company for the period January 1, 1996 through July 2, 1996 and the results of operations of the Company from July 3, 1996 (the date of the consummation of the Offering) through December 29, 1996.

Selected statement of income data for the year ended December 29, 1996 are as follows (the date of the Offering has been deemed to be July 1, 1996):

(in thousands)	January 1 to June 30, 1996	July 1 to December 29, 1996	Year Ended December 29, 1996 Consolidated
Net revenues	$277,226	$335,614	$612,840
Gross profit	90,006	110,770	200,776
Operating income.	12,563	739	13,302
Other income (expense)	(4,569)	(876)	(5,445)
Income (loss) before income taxes	7,994	(137)	7,857
Provision (benefit) for income taxes . . .	445	(17,624)	(17,179)
Net income	$ 7,549	$ 17,487	$ 25,036

Pro Forma Adjustments (Unaudited)

The pro forma financial information on the income statement presents the effects on the historical financial statements of certain transactions as if they had occurred in 1995. These adjustments are: (i) increased royalty expense to be paid to a corporation owned by two of the Company's principal stockholders and their affiliated trusts pursuant to a licensing agreement of $12.8 million and $7.2 million in 1995 and 1996, respectively; (ii) reduced levels of compensation for two of the Company's executives pursuant to their employment agreements of $2.3 million and $1.5 million in 1995 and 1995, respectively; (iii) reduction in interest costs assuming the application of the proceeds from the

Donna Karan International

Offering to reduce the actual outstanding indebtedness under the Company's credit agreement of $6.2 million and $3.5 million in 1995 and 1996, respectively; (iv) reduction in amortization of deferred financing costs which would have been written off in connection with repayment of outstanding indebtedness under the Company's credit agreement of $0.6 million and $0.8 million in 1995 and 1996, respectively; (v) increase in income taxes of $11.3 million and $20.7 million in 1995 an 1996, respectively, as if the Company had been subject to Federal and additional state income taxes for the entire period (see Note 15); and (vi) adjustments of $20.3 million in 1995 to reflect the sale of the 70% interest in the operations of Donna Karan Japan as if it had occurred on January 2, 1995. The gain on the sale has been excluded, and as a result of this sale, the Company's statement of income has been adjusted to reflect the Company's accounting for their interest in Donna Karan Japan using the equity method of accounting for the period from January 2, 1995 until March 31, 1995, the date of the sale (see Note 8).

Fiscal Year

The Company's fiscal year consists of the 52- or 53-week period ending on the Sunday nearest December 31.

Inventories

Inventories are stated at the lower of cost (first-in, first-out method) of market.

Depreciation and Amortization

Depreciation of machinery, equipment and fixtures, including amounts accounted for under capital leases, is computed using straight-line and accelerated methods based on their estimated useful lives which range from five to seven years. Leasehold improvements are amortized using the straight-line method based on the lease term, and in certain instances include the anticipated renewal period. The Company's share of the cost of constructing in-store shop displays is capitalized and amortized using the straight-line method over their estimated useful lives of four years. The Company's share of the cost of constructing full-price, free-standing retail stores under license agreements is capitalized and amortized using the straight-line method over their estimated useful lives of eight years. At December 31, 1995 and December 29, 1996, the unamortized balance of these costs of $2,034,000 and $10,848,000, respectively, is included in "Deposits and other noncurrent assets" in the accompanying balance sheets. Amortization expense of these costs for the years ended December 31, 1995 and December 29, 1996 amounted to approximately $0.4 million and $1.4 million, respectively. Major additions and betterments are capitalized and repairs and maintenance are charged to operations in the period incurred.

Advertising

The Company expenses the production costs of advertising upon the first showing of the related advertisement which is generally less than six months after the production costs are incurred. At December 31, 1995 and December 29, 1996, advertising costs totaling $1,334,000 and $1,288,000, respectively, were included in "Prepaid expenses and other current assets" in the accompanying balance sheets. Advertising, marketing, and public relations expenses, including costs related to the Company's Creative Services

Department, for the years ended January 1, 1995, December 31, 1995 and December 29, 1996 were $35,409,000, $33,831,000 and $53,191,000, respectively.

Revenue Recognition

Sales are recognized upon shipment of products or, in the case of sales by Company-owned outlet stores, when payment is received. The Company provides for estimated returns at the time of sales. Income from licensing agreements is recognized when earned and is included in net revenues.

Statements of Cash Flows

For purposes of the statements of cash flows, the Company considers all highly liquid investment with a maturity of three months or less when purchased to be cash equivalents.

Use of Estimates

The preparation of financial statements in conformity with generally accepted accounting principles requires management to make estimates and assumptions that affect the reported amounts of assets and liabilities and disclosure of contingent assets and liabilities at the date of the financial statements and the reported amounts of revenues and expenses during the reporting period. Actual results could differ from those estimates.

2. Inventories

Inventories consist of the following (in thousands):

	December 31, 1995	December 29, 1996
Raw materials	$ 16,369	$ 16,780
Work in process	11,697	11,030
Finished goods	57,589	72,870
	$ 85,655	$100,680

4. Borrowings

Long-term debt consists of the following (in thousands):

	December 31, 1995	December 29, 1996
Revolving credit facility	$ 7,961	$ —
Term Loan A	15,000	—
Term Loan B	20,000	—
Term Loan C	10,000	—
Capital lease obligation	577	318
	$53,538	$ 318
Less current portion	(7,759)	(282)
	$45,779	$ 36

At December 31, 1995, the Company had a credit facility, as amended, which consisted of a $60,000,000 term loan (term loans A, B and C) and a revolving line of credit available for the issuance of letters of credit, acceptances, or direct borrowings up to $105,000,000. Direct borrowings under the revolving line of credit bore interest at 1.5% over the lead bank's prime rate and were limited to a borrowing base calculated on eligible accounts receivable, inventory, and letters of credit.

The credit agreement provided for various borrowing rate options including borrowing rates based on a fixed spread over the London Interbank Offered Rate ("LIBOR").

With the proceeds of the Offering, the Company repaid all amounts due under its existing credit facility, and in September 1996, the Company entered into a new $150 million, three-year revolving Credit Facility as amended in March 1997 (the "New Facility"). Direct borrowings under the New Facility bear interest at the lead bank's prime rate or, at the option of the Company, at a fixed spread over the LIBOR and are limited to a borrowing base calculated on eligible accounts receivable, inventory, and letters of credit. The New Facility is secured by accounts receivable, inventory and certain intangibles of the Company, as well as a pledge of all equity interests of the subsidiaries of the Company. The New Facility also contains certain restrictive covenants which, among other things, require the Company to maintain certain financial ratios and restrict investments, additional indebtedness, and payment of dividends. No amounts were outstanding under the New Facility at December 29, 1996.

In connection with these facilities, the Company incurred certain financing costs which were deferred and are being amortized over the remaining term of the New Facility. At December 29, 1996, unamortized financing costs of approximately $952,000 are included in "Deposits and other noncurrent assets" in the accompanying balance sheet. Amortization of deferred financing costs of approximately $0.8 million and $3.5 million in 1995 and 1996, respectively, are included in interest expense.

The Company leases certain property and equipment under long-term noncancellable lease agreements which are accounted for as capital leases. These leases expire at various dates through 1998. Future minimum lease payments as of December 29, 1996 are as follows (in thousands):

1997	$299
1998	37
	$336
Amount representing interest	18
Present value of total future minimum lease payments	$318
Less current portion	282
Long-term portion of capital obligation	$ 36

Letters of credit and acceptances outstanding were approximately $33,934,000 at December 31, 1995 and $43,594,000 at December 29, 1996.

5. Accrued Expenses and Other Current Liabilities

Accrued expenses and other current liabilities are comprised of the following (in thousands):

	December 31, 1995	December 29, 1996
Accrued operating expenses	$ 8,590	$12,779
Accrued income taxes	2,351	8,010
Accrued compensation	885	6,260
Accrued royalty	—	5,133
Accrued taxes other than income taxes	2,244	948
Other	1,696	1,062
	$15,766	$34,192

7. Leases

Future minimum annual rental commitments under noncancellable operating leases for office, warehouse and retail facilities, and equipment as of December 29, 1996 are as follows (in thousands):

1997	$14,531
1998	13,942
1999	12,491
2000	10,490
2001	9,455
Thereafter	30,139
	$91,048

In addition, certain of the leases contain options to renew for periods up to 10 years and others include contingent payments based on sales.

Rent expense amounted to approximately $12,498,000, $14,105,000 and $15,037,000 for the years ended January 1, 1995, December 31, 1995 and December 29, 1996, respectively.

8. Sale of Interests in Affiliates

The Company conducts operations in Japan through Donna Karan Japan. DSTF Japan Company has a profit-sharing agreement (the "DSTF Agreement") with Donna Karan Japan whereby 90% of the income before taxes of Donna Karan Japan is allocated to DSTF Japan Company. On March 31, 1995, the Company sold 70% of its interest in the DSTF Agreement and 70% of the stock of Donna Karan Japan to a nonaffiliated party. The Company recognized a gain on this transaction, net of transaction costs, of $18,673,000. Subsequent to the sale, the Company records a 27% interest in the operations of Donna Karan Japan through its 30% interest in the DSTF Agreement and a 3% interest in the operations of Donna Karan Japan through its remaining interest in Donna Karan Japan. As a result, the Company has accounted for its combined 30% interest in the operations of Donna Karan Japan using the equity method of accounting. Equity earnings for the years ended December 31, 1995 and December 29, 1996 amounted to approximately $2,519,000 and $3,089,000, respectively. Simultaneously with the sales transaction, the Company entered into an agreement with Donna Karan Japan which provides for a fee based upon net sales of Donna Karan Japan. Management fee income, as an offset of selling, general, and administrative expenses, amounted to approximately $1,130,000 and $1,790,000 during the years ended December 31, 1995 and December 29, 1996, respectively. The equity investment in Donna Karan Japan of $2,531,000 and $3,076,000 at December 31, 1995 and December 29, 1996, respectively, is included in "Deposits and other noncurrent assets" in the accompanying balance sheet.

9. DKNY® Jeans Licensing Agreement

On September 27, 1996, the Company entered into a 30-year licensing agreement with subsidiaries of Designer Holdings Ltd. (the "Licensee") for the exclusive production, sale and distribution of men's, women's, and, with certain exceptions, children's jeans-wear under the DKNY® Jeans label (the "Jeans License"). Under the terms of the agreement, the Company received an initial payment of $6.0 million from the Licensee to reimburse the Company for certain costs related to the start-up and development of the DKNY® Jeans label. The Company was also entitled to receive additional payments aggregating $54.0 million over a four-year period, through the year 2000, and annual royalties, as well as administrative fees on net sales.

Subsequent to year-end, the Company and the Licensee agreed to terminate this agreement. In connection with this termination, the Company repaid the initial $6.0 million payment and a $1.3 million advance royalty payment previously received. Additionally, in order to assure a smooth transition for the DKNY® Jeanswear business, the Company purchased for $3.2 million all sales and marketing plans, patterns, samples, fabrics and other materials developed by the Licensee in connection with the jeanswear business, the cost of which had been accrued at December 29, 1996 and is included in selling, general and administrative expenses in the accompanying financial statements.

10. Related Party Transactions

As of July 3, 1996, the Company entered into a licensing agreement (the "Gabrielle License") with Gabrielle Studio, Inc. ("Gabrielle Studio"), a corporation owned by two of the Company's principal stockholders and their affiliated trusts, which grants the Company the exclusive rights, in perpetuity, to use the trademarks "Donna Karan," "Donna Karan New York," "DKNY," "DK," and all variations thereof. Under the Gabrielle License, the Company pays Gabrielle Studio a royalty on net sales of products bearing the licensed mark. During the six-month period ended December 29, 1996, the Company incurred $9.3 million in royalty expense, which is included in cost of sales. In addition, the Company made a one-time payment of $4.6 million to Gabrielle Studio in connection with entering into the Gabrielle License, which is also included in cost of sales.

15. Income Taxes

The entities in the Predecessor Company were partnerships or corporations that had elected to be taxed as S corporations pursuant to the Internal Revenue Code. Therefore, for the years ended January 1, 1995 and December 31, 1995, and for the six-month period ended July 2, 1996 (the day prior to the Offering), no provision has been made in the accompanying financial statements for such periods for Federal income taxes, since such taxes were the liability of the partners. In connection with the Offering, the Company became subject to Federal and additional state income tax.

The Company accounts for income taxes under Statement of Financial Accounting Standards ("SFAS") No. 109, "Accounting for Income Taxes" which requires the asset and liability method of accounting for income taxes. Under the asset and liability method, deferred income taxes are recognized for the tax consequences of "temporary differences" by applying enacted statutory tax rates applicable to future years to differences between the financial carrying amounts and the tax bases of existing assets and liabilities.

Concurrent with becoming subject to Federal and additional state income taxes, the Company recorded a deferred tax asset and a corresponding tax benefit in the statement of income in accordance with the provisions of SFAS No. 109. The actual amount, which was determined upon completion of the final tax returns of the Predecessor Company, was approximately $19.0 million, and, as of the date of the Offering, resulted in a total deferred tax asset of approximately $20.7 million which includes certain state and local tax assets recorded on an historical basis.

The income tax provision consists of the following (in thousands):

	Year Ended		
	January 1, 1995	December 31, 1995	December 29, 1996
Current income taxes:			
Federal taxes	$ —	$ —	$ 8,605
State and local taxes	1,113	2,242	2,717
Foreign taxes	386	278	1,130
	$1,499	$2,520	$12,452
Deferred income taxes	(360)	(122)	(29,631)
	$1,139	$2,398	($17,179)

Deferred income taxes reflect the net effects of temporary differences between the carrying amounts of assets and liabilities for financial reporting purposes and the amounts used for income tax purposes. Significant items comprising the Company's net deferred tax asset are as follows (in thousands):

	December 31, 1995	December 29, 1996
Current:		
Uniform inventory capitalization	$ 70	$ 1,046
Allowance for doubtful accounts and other receivable related reserves	270	14,430
Inventory reserves	—	2,990
Other book accruals	962	6,741
	$1,302	$25,207
Noncurrent:		
Depreciation	380	6,106
	$1,682	$31,313

The pro forma provision for income taxes represents the income tax provisions that would have been reported had the Company been subject to Federal and additional state income taxes for the entire period. The pro forma income tax provision has been prepared according to SFAS No. 109.

The foreign and domestic components of pro forma income before pro forma income taxes were as follows (in thousands):

	Year Ended	
	December 31, 1995	December 29, 1996
Domestic	$26,676	$ 1,565
Foreign	5,454	4,856
	$32,130	$ 6,421

The pro forma income tax provision consists of the following (in thousands):

	Year Ended	
	December 31, 1995	December 29, 1996
Current income taxes:		
Federal taxes	$12,215	$11,642
State and local taxes	4,936	4,777
Foreign taxes	643	1,130
	$17,794	$17,549
Deferred income taxes	(4,089)	(14,012)
	$13,705	$ 3,537

A reconciliation setting forth the differences between the pro forma effective tax rate of the Company and the U.S. Federal statutory tax rate is as follows:

	Year Ended	
	December 31, 1995	December 29, 1996
Federal statutory rate	35.0%	35.0%
State and local taxes, net of federal tax benefits	7.6	7.0
Taxes related to foreign income, net of credits	1.9	14.0
Other items, net, none of which individually exceeds 5% of Federal taxes at statutory rate	(1.8)	(0.9)
	42.7%	55.1%

16. Quarterly Results of Operations (Unaudited)

The following is a summary of the unaudited quarterly results of operations for 1996 and 1995 (dollars in thousands, except per share amounts):

	Quarter Ended			
	March 31	June 30	September 29	December 29
1996				
Net sales	$159,585	$117,641	$173,415	$162,199
Gross profit	52,861	37,145	55,506	55,264
Net income (loss)	11,701	(4,252)	16,444	1,043
Per share data:				
Net income (loss)	$ 0.73	$ (0.26)	$ 0.77	$ 0.05
Weighted average or pro forma weighted average number of common shares outstanding	16,017,032	16,017,032	21,468,034	21,468,043

	Quarter Ended			
	April 2	July 2	October 1	December 31
1995				
Net sales	$120,693	$102,731	$152,389	$134,313
Gross profit	44,203	31,112	56,162	47,960
Net income (loss)	26,726	(1,325)	20,022	8,252
Per share data:				
Net income (loss)	$ 1.67	$ (0.08)	$ 1.25	$ 0.52
Weighted average or pro forma weighted average number of common shares outstanding	16,017,032	16,017,032	16,017,032	16,017,032

O n February 17, 1998, SPX Corporation, a manufacturer of automotive diagnostic equipment, offered to buy all of the outstanding stock of Echlin Inc., an original equipment and replacement automotive parts manufacturer, for $48 per share. However, this offer elicited no response from Echlin's Board of Directors, prompting SPX to call for a special shareholder meeting to vote out Echlin's Board.

Hostilities between management of the two companies escalated when Echlin's Board sponsored a bill in the Connecticut legislature that would make it more difficult for hostile acquirers to oust a target firm's Board of Directors. John Blystone, president and CEO of SPX, responded:

> There is no job security in an underperforming company. [Echlin's senior management] is cynically attempting to wrap itself in the Connecticut flag at the expense of its workers and shareholders.[1]

Larry McCurdy, president and CEO of Echlin, countered:

> SPX's attacks upon Echlin and its Board are not only gratuitous, but false and misleading.[2] . . . They [SPX's senior management] seem to have no knowledge of the aftermarket, or of the requirements of parts distribution. In fact, they seem relatively naïve in some of their plans, particularly regarding the cutback in Echlin employees.[3]

AUTO PARTS INDUSTRY

In the 1990s the automotive parts industry, which had historically been highly fragmented, began a process of consolidation. A report in the *Wall Street Journal* explains the reason for this trend as follows[4]:

> Virtually every major player in the auto-parts business is in the hunt for acquisitions. . . What's driving the consolidation is a fundamental change in the way

223

Research Associate Penny Joseph prepared this case under the supervision of Professors Paul M. Healy and Bjorn N. Jorgensen as the basis for class discussion rather than to illustrate either effective or ineffective handling of an administrative situation. Copyright © 1998 by the President and Fellows of Harvard College. Harvard Business School case 9-199-010.

1. *Thomas Scheffey*, The Connecticut Law Tribune, *March 9, 1998.*

2. PR Newswire, *March 8, 1998.*

3. *Ted Arnold,* Automotive Marketing *27, No. 3, p. 68.*

4. *Arthur Cummins,* Wall Street Journal, *February 20, 1998.*

auto makers develop and build vehicles. The Big Three and their foreign rivals are all pushing parts makers to take greater responsibility for research and development and for designing major vehicles systems, such as brakes, interiors and suspensions. Before auto makers did nearly all the design and engineering, requiring suppliers mostly to make parts from auto makers' blueprints.

Consolidation therefore enabled auto parts makers to coordinate, design, and engineer across related systems, and to take advantage of economies of scale in these activities. For example, Lear Corporation, which acquired ITT Seat Subsystems, Dunlop Cox, Borealis, Masland, and Automotive Industries, was able to design and produce complete auto interiors for its two major customers, Ford and General Motors. Consolidation also facilitated the creation of global parts suppliers that could meet the demands of auto makers in the important Asian and European markets. Finally, it provided firms in the parts industry with more leverage in their negotiations with the auto manufacturers.

Between 1993 and 1997 sales growth for the U.S. auto parts industry had been a healthy 7.3 percent per year. However, in 1997 industry sales growth dipped to 3.2 percent. The replacement parts market, especially heavy-duty truck parts, also softened as increases in the quality of new automobiles and replacement parts increased the life of automobiles. The prospects of an immediate rebound in the industry growth seemed remote given a serious economic downturn in Asia in 1997 and worldwide overcapacity in the auto market.

ECHLIN

Echlin Inc., which was founded in 1915 in San Francisco, was one of the world's leading suppliers of commercial vehicle components and automotive fluid handling systems. The company's major products included brake and engine replacement parts, and its customers included warehouse distributors, retailers, auto dealerships, parts manufacturers, and car manufacturers. In 1997 Echlin's sales exceeded $3.5 billion, 75 percent from replacement parts, and 25 percent from original equipment sales.

After several years of strong performance, Echlin's stock price stagnated between 1994 and 1997. Top management continued to promise increased profits but no significant operating changes were made. Margins narrowed, product returns increased, and demand weakened. In 1997 Scott Greer (the president and COO) resigned, and Fred Mancheski (chairman of the board and CEO) retired. Larry McCurdy was hired as CEO in March 1997. McCurdy had originally joined Echlin in 1983 as vice president of finance, but had left three years later to take the position of president and CEO of Moog Automotive Inc. He returned with a plan to "fix it or sell it" and quickly developed a repositioning plan to increase value for shareholders.[5] Outlining the repositioning plan, McCurdy stated[6]:

---

5. John Couretas, "McCurdy Returns to Echlin with Fix-it or Sell-it Strategy," *Automotive News, March 31, 1997: 26D.*

6. *Business Wire Inc., February 17, 1998.*

Key elements of the plan include divestiture of underperforming or non-strategic businesses; factory rationalizations; aggressive cost cutting aimed at profit improvements; heightened asset management and cash flow gains; and a steadfast commitment to incorporating the EVA framework to enhance value.[7]

In September 1997, McCurdy announced that he expected the divestiture of underperforming businesses under the restructuring would generate $250–350 million in cash. Sensor Engineering, a manufacturer of card readers and access control systems, and Preferred Plastic Sheet, a polyethylene sheet extruder, were subsequently sold. The firm also acquired several other auto parts firms, including Long Manufacturing (fluid systems), Nobel Plastiques (servo-control lines), Brosol (fuel routes for injection), Iroquois Tool Systems (drum and rotors for auto brake systems), and the North American Aftermarket division of ITT Automotive (job brake components).

The effect of the repositioning plan was evident in Echlin's 1997 financial statements shown in Exhibits 1 and 2. The firm took a $254 million restructuring charge to reflect plant closings and consolidations, business divestitures, and asset write-downs, and reported a net loss of $46.9 million.

SPX

SPX Corporation was founded in 1911 as the Piston Ring Co. The company initially specialized in producing piston rings for major auto makers, but as a result of a series of acquisitions, it became a manufacturer of specialty service tools and equipment for motor vehicle dealership networks. Following a period of lackluster performance during the early 1990s, in 1995 John Blystone was appointed chairman, president and chief executive officer of the company. Blystone had a long and successful record at General Electric (GE). He had joined GE in 1978 and risen to the position of CEO of Nuovo Pignone and the Europe Plus Pole of GE Power Systems.

Soon after his arrival at SPX, Blystone implemented a series of restructurings at two of its business units: Service Solutions, a manufacturer of custom service hand tools and equipment, and Sealed Power, a piston ring, cylinder sleeve, and camshaft manufacturer. In 1995 five divisions of Service Solutions were consolidated, and Sealed Power's German foundry was closed. In 1996 early retirement programs were adopted at both units, and a cost reduction initiative was undertaken for Service Solutions. In 1997 SPX again undertook a restructuring at Service Solutions, including the combination of two divisions and an asset write-down. The restructuring charges taken as a result of these actions were $19.7 million in 1995, $20.0 million in 1996, and $116.5 million in 1997. A summary of key performance indicators for SPX are presented in Exhibit 3, and cash flow statements for the period 1995 to 1997 are shown in Exhibit 4.

....

7. *EVA is a financial metric that adjusts reported profits for a capital charge. Relative to earnings, it is typically viewed as improving management's incentives to invest in capital projects that increase shareholder value (see "EVA: Fact and Fantasy" by G. Bennett Stewart III, Stern Stewart & Co., Journal of Applied Corporate Finance 7, No. 2, Summer 1994: 71.)*

The stock market responded positively to these restructurings at SPX, and the firm's stock price increased fivefold from December 1995 to March 1998.

PROPOSED ACQUISITION OF ECHLIN

SPX first showed a public interest in acquiring Echlin in December 1997 when it purchased 416,000 shares of Echlin's stock. On February 17, 1998, SPX made an official offer to Echlin's board of directors to acquire all of Echlin's outstanding stock for $48 per share, $12 in cash and the remainder in SPX stock.

While SPX and Echlin focused on somewhat different markets in the auto parts business, their performance was subject to many of the same economic effects, notably the demand for replacement parts and auto repairs. In addition, there was some overlap in their customer base since auto dealers and repair shops purchased both Echlin's replacement parts and SPX's tools. Based on its knowledge of the replacement market and the changes taking place in the new car market, SPX's management anticipated that it would be able to generate annual cost savings for Echlin of at least $125 million in the first full year, and $175 million thereafter by reducing head count by approximately 3,000, nearly 10 percent of Echlin's global workforce. SPX also planned to restructure or divest Echlin's underperforming assets, and to accelerate implementation of EVA-based compensation programs for the company.

When Echlin's board did not respond to its offer, SPX requested a special shareholder meeting to vote out the existing board. This prompted Echlin's Board to sponsor House Bill 5695 in the Connecticut legislature. Under this proposed new law, the existing board of a takeover target could not be removed for one year even if all its shareholders voted for its ouster. In addition, the bill proposed that if shareholders did vote to remove the board in a hostile takeover, for the next five years a new board could only be elected by the existing board.

As animosity surrounding the proposed takeover intensified, management of both companies reflected on the task of convincing Echlin's shareholders about the merits of SPX's offer. Larry McCurdy considered writing a letter to Echlin's shareholders explaining why the firm would be better off left in current management's hands. John Blystone also contemplated how to convince Echlin's shareholders that his management team should be given an opportunity to turn the company around.

QUESTIONS

1. Assume that you are John Blystone. Prepare a short letter addressed to Echlin's shareholders to explain the benefits of the takeover.
2. Assume that you are Larry McCurdy. Prepare a short letter addressed to Echlin's shareholders to explain the reasons why the takeover bid should be rejected.

EXHIBIT 1

Echlin Inc. 1997 Annual Report: Excerpts from Review of Operations and Financial Condition

In fiscal 1997, Echlin's sales rose 14.1%, from $3.13 to $3.57 billion. Comparable operations brought 2.0% of the gain. This consisted of price increases (1.0%) and new products (2.8%), offset by a decline in unit volume (1.4%) and unfavorable currency translations (0.4%). The balance, 12.1%, came from acquisitions, net of two divisions we sold, Sensor Engineering and Preferred Plastic Sheet.

We purchased five major companies this year: Long Manufacturing, Nobel Plastiques, Brosol, Iroquois Tool Systems and the North American Aftermarket division of ITT Automotive. Our sales also included 12 months of revenue from the Automotive Segment of Handy & Harman, a company we bought in December 1995.

Last year, sales climbed 15.1%. Existing businesses added 4.1% of the growth, while acquired businesses accounted for the remainder. Unit volume was flat, but new products and new prices contributed 3.4% and 1.6%, respectively.

Domestic Business Up 2.6%

U.S. operations, excluding acquisitions, advanced 2.6%. The products we introduced boosted sales 3.0%, plus prices rose 0.9%; at the same time, unit volume declined 1.3%.

Several industry factors caused business to slump. To begin with, the demand for aftermarket components, especially under-the-hood items, softened. New builds of heavy-duty trucks were down as well. Further, goods were returned at above-normal rates, as customers trimmed their inventories in response to sluggish sales.

In 1996, domestic business improved 3.7%. Growth from product introductions (3.8%), coupled with price raises (1.3%), countered a 1.4% drop in unit volume, as sales fell in all areas except our automotive brake and original equipment lines. Heavy-duty parts suffered the most, due to a 25% cutback in the North American production of tractors and trailers.

Offshore Operations Flat

Without acquisitions, the company's foreign revenues inched up 0.4%. We posted gains from the rollout of new products (2.2%) and new prices (1.1%), which were offset by a 1.7% decrease in unit volume. Currency fluctuations also lowered sales, by 1.2%.

Throughout 1997, Echlin's automotive companies in Europe and Mexico performed well. Business was depressed, however, in our European divisions that supply heavy-duty parts, and in other aftermarket operations around the world. Changes in translation rates dampened sales, as during the year the dollar weakened against all currencies except the British pound. This had the greatest impact on our German subsidiaries.

Last year, international operations grew 5.1%. Increases from unit volume (3.2%), prices (2.3%), and new products (2.5%) all outweighed declines (2.9%) due to unfavorable changes in currency exchange rates.

Gross Margin Down 2.1 Points

In 1997, our gross profit margin edged down 2.1 percentage points, from 26.2% to 24.1%. There were many reasons for this drop. A high number of returned goods, along with changes in our customer and product mix, played key roles. We also absorbed less manufacturing expense than planned, as we scaled back production to accommodate slower demand. In addition, several of the acquisitions we made are OE producers, which realize, in general, lower gross margins than aftermarket suppliers.

These same factors affected last year's margin. Echlin's 1996 level was 2.7 percentage points below fiscal 1995's.

Sales Outpaced Expenses

Selling and administrative expenses moved up 11.4% in 1997. Part of the increase stemmed from research and development activities, which we expanded to design new products for future vehicles.

Although operating expenses rose, they fell for the seventh year in a row—as a percentage of sales, trending down from 19.5% in 1995, to 18.4% in 1996, and 17.9% in 1997. This reflects our success in cutting costs. It also points to the impact of our OE businesses, which tend to have lower expense-to-sales ratios than replacement parts providers.

Interest Expense Advanced 20.4%

Interest expense climbed 20.4% in fiscal 1997. Borrowing rates remained the same as last year's; nevertheless, the company incurred more debt, mainly to fund acquisitions. Interest income went up as well, due to higher yields on our investment portfolio in Puerto Rico.

In fiscal 1996, interest rates were down, but greater debt levels drove interest expense up 11.8%.

Repositioning Change Reported

This year, Echlin took steps to reposition the company and build future shareowner value. We recorded a pre-tax charge of $254.1 million to cover, first, the write-off of impaired or idle assets; second, the costs of closing and consolidating plants; and third, the selling of non-core and low-profit divisions.

We also divested two businesses in fiscal 1997, Sensor Engineering and Preferred Plastic Sheet. Together, they provided a pre-tax gain of $28.7 million.

All told, these actions reduced net income by $164.3 million and earnings per share by $2.63.

EXHIBIT 2

Echlin Inc. Consolidated Financial Statements and Selected Footnotes

CONSOLIDATED INCOME STATEMENT

	Year Ended August 31,		
(In thousands, except per share data)	1997	1996	1995
Net sales	$3,568,572	$3,128,728	$2,717,866
Cost of goods sold	2,707,081	2,309,037	1,932,461
Gross profit on sales	861,491	819,691	785,405
Selling and admin. exp.	640,108	574,592	531,286
Repositioning and other special charges	254,115	—	—
Gain on sales of businesses	(28,652)	—	—
Income (loss) from operations	(4,080)	245,099	254,119
Interest expense	52,914	43,933	39,313
Interest income	(12,246)	(10,990)	(15,674)
Interest expense, net	40,668	32,943	23,639
Income (loss) before taxes	(44,748)	212,156	230,480
Provision for taxes	2,158	69,946	76,058
Net income (loss)	$ (46,906)	$ 142,210	$ 154,422
Average shares outstanding	62,601	61,919	59,476
Earnings (loss) per share	$(0.75)	$ 2.30	$ 2.60

CONSOLIDATED BALANCE SHEET

	Year ended August 31,	
(In thousands)	1997	1996
Assets		
Current assets:		
Cash and cash equivalents	$22,239	$16,106
Accounts receivable, less allowance for doubtful accounts of $4,505 and $5,621	438,558	370,837
Inventories:		
Raw materials and component parts	179,599	167,215
Work in process	92,389	87,140
Finished goods	422,650	425,027
Total inventories	694,638	679,382
Other current assets	54,134	42,687
Total current assets	1,209,569	1,109,012

Source of information in Exhibit 2: Echlin, Inc. 1997 Annual Report.

(continued)

Echlin Versus SPX

Echlin Versus SPX

CONSOLIDATED BALANCE SHEET (*continued*)

	Year ended August 31,	
(In thousands)	**1997**	**1996**
Property, plant and equipment:		
Land	39,216	36,881
Buildings	235,028	218,086
Machinery and equipment	1,084,004	900,528
Property, plant and equipment, at cost	1,358,248	1,155,495
Accumulated depreciation	(635,717)	(534,186)
Property, plant and equipment, net	722,531	621,309
Marketable securities	82,418	83,578
Intangible assets	323,060	226,292
Other assets	36,625	90,563
Total Assets	**$2,374,203**	**$2,130,754**
Liabilities and Shareholders' Equity		
Current Liabilities:		
Notes payable to banks	$42,746	$21,596
Current portion of long-term debt	4,693	6,286
Accounts payable	296,123	264,532
Accrued taxes on income	13,097	33,985
Accrued compensation	84,712	67,265
Other accrued liabilities	232,652	130,563
Total current liabilities	674,023	524,227
Long-term debt	710,422	468,013
Deferred income taxes	76,057	129,640
Shareholders' Equity:		
Preferred stock, no par value: Authorized 1,000,000 shares, issued none	—	—
Common stock, $1 par value: Authorized 150,000,000 shares, issued 63,373,683 and 62,242,279	63,374	62,242
Capital in excess of par value	372,197	350,935
Retained earnings	557,153	658,235
Foreign currency translation adjustments	(82,725)	(61,953)
Net unrealized investment gains	6,697	2,410
Treasury stock, at cost, 270,264 shares	(2,995)	(2,995)
Total Shareholders' Equity	913,701	1,008,874
Total Liabilities and Shareholders' Equity	**$2,374,203**	**$2,130,754**

Total Assets at August 31, 1995 and 1994 are $1,961,008 and $1,577,406 respectively. Total Shareholders' Equity at August 31, 1995 and 1994 are $909,267 and $798,971 respectively.

CONSOLIDATED STATEMENTS OF CASH FLOWS

(In thousands)	Year Ended August 31,		
	1997	**1996**	**1995**
Cash flows from operating activities:			
Net income (loss)	$(46,906)	$142,210	$154,422
Adjustments to reconcile net income (loss) to net cash provided by operating activities:			
Depreciation and amortization	113,938	90,875	76,609
Repositioning and other special charges	252,041	—	—
Gain on sales of businesses	(28,652)	—	—
Changes in current assets and liabilities, excluding acquisitions:			
Accounts receivable	(11,056)	(83,286)	(9,448)
Inventories	(8,512)	24,427	(94,133)
Other current assets	(5,146)	(11,892)	(5,314)
Accounts payable	4,590	44,486	576
Accrued taxes on income	(23,252)	(6,660)	(4,173)
Deferred income taxes	(54,847)	42,797	22,869
Accrued liabilities	(3,035)	(12,948)	(11,762)
Other	(5,907)	(3,001)	(22,602)
Cash provided by operating activities	183,256	227,008	107,044
Cash flows from financing activities:			
Long-term and short-term borrowings	917,172	615,532	721,232
Long-term and short-term repayments	(690,454)	(647,626)	(524,664)
Sales of accounts receivable	—	75,000	—
Proceeds from common stock issuances	4,560	2,770	5,200
Dividends paid	(55,623)	(51,806)	(46,987)
Cash provided by (used for) financing activities	175,655	(6,130)	154,781
Cash flows from investing activities:			
Capital expenditures	(149,195)	(104,384)	(103,894)
Net book value of property, plant and equipment disposals	8,454	3,143	1,515
Proceeds from sales of marketable securities	9,823	22,592	13,087
Proceeds from sales of businesses	73,253	—	—
Purchases of businesses:			
Net working capital items	(80,021)	(93,232)	(25,382)
Property, plant and equipment and intangibles	(252,099)	(57,305)	(176,830)
Debt assumed	38,877	1,013	—
Cash used for investing activities	(350,908)	(228,173)	(291,504)
Impact of foreign currency changes on cash	(1,870)	(4,299)	3,563
Increase (decrease) in cash and cash equivalents	6,133	(11,594)	(26,116)
Cash and cash equivalents at beginning of year	16,106	27,700	53,816
Cash and cash equivalents at end of year	$22,239	$16,106	$27,700

Echlin Versus SPX

SELECTED NOTES TO FINANCIAL STATEMENTS

Repositioning and Other Special Charges

During the fourth quarter of fiscal 1997, the company recorded repositioning and other special charges of $254,115,000, pre-tax, which is intended to enhance the company's competitiveness and productivity. Repositioning actions are generally expected to be completed in 12 months.

The repositioning charge included expenses related to facility realignments and rationalization, and the write-down to net realizable value of businesses to be disposed ($101,154,000) including severance costs of $14,507,000. In addition, goodwill associated with brand names no longer in use was written off ($27,164,000), inventory related to discontinued and rationalized product lines was written down ($43,606,000), property, plant and equipment idled by facility closures and product line rationalizations were reduced ($21,868,000), and other investments and deferred customer acquisition costs were written off ($60,323,000).

Cash expenditures in fiscal 1997 for reposition actions totaled $2,074,000, primarily for employee severance costs.

EXHIBIT 3

SPX Corp. Selected Financial Ratios

	Definitions	1997	1996	1995
Sales (in millions)		$922.3	$1,109.4	$1,098.1
DuPont Analysis:				
Return on equity	Net Income/ Beginning equity	-13.0%	-38.4%	-3.3%
= Return on sales	Net income before taxes/Sales	-1.5%	-5.6%	-0.5%
*Asset Turnover	Sales/Beginning assets	1.50	1.33	1.18
*Assets/Equity	Beginning assets/Beginning equity	5.82	5.13	5.95
Profitability:				
Gross profit margin	(Sales-Cost of Sales) / Sales	27.5%	23.4%	22.3%
Operating income/Sales[a]		-4.6%	-1.5%	2.8%
Operating Income/Assets[a]	Operating income/Average assets	-7.3%	-2.8%	3.7%
Turnover:				
Fixed asset turnover	Sales/Beginning fixed assets	7.5	5.2	5.1
Days' Receivables	365/(Sales/Ending accounts receivable)	68.4	31.6	43.3
Days' Inventory	365/(Cost of Sales/Ending inventory)	50.7	46.9	64.5
Days' Payables	365/(Cost of Sales/Ending accounts payable)	49.9	22.8	30.5
Leverage:				
Debt-to-capital ratio	(Notes Payable + LT Debt)/(Notes Payable + LT Debt + Equity)	1.3	0.7	0.7
Interest coverage(earnings)	(Net Income + Interest Exp. + Tax Exp.)/Interest Expense	1.5	(0.7)	0.9
Interest coverage (cash)	(CF from Operations + Int. Exp. + Tax Exp./Interest Expense	1.4	4.2	2.9

a. Operating income includes pre-tax charges for $116.5 million, $87.9 million and $10.7 million in 1997, 1996, and 1995 respectively.

Source: SPX 1997 and 1996 Annual Reports. Ratios calculated by case writer.

Echlin Versus SPX

EXHIBIT 4

SPX Corp. Consolidated Statements of Cash Flows

(Dollars in thousands)	1997	1996	1995
Cash flows from operating activities:			
Net incomes (loss) from operating activities	$(13,748)	$62,271)	$(5,276)
Adjustments to reconcile net income (loss) to net cash:			
Extraordinary loss	10,330	6,627	1,078
Depreciation and amortization	24,977	40,764	43,522
Minority and equity interests	360	(5,288)	(558)
Special charges	116,500	—	10,724
Gain on sale of businesses	(71,895)	—	—
Noncash write-off of goodwill	—	67,817	—
Compensation recognized under employee stock plan	4,238	4,421	3,026
Deferred taxes	6,812	(5,240)	18,773
Change in operating assets and liabilities (net of effect of acquired and disposed businesses):			
Receivables	(73,116)	4,338	5,303
Inventories	(3,556)	18,218	2,761
Prepaid and other assets	(23,369)	17,089	9,353
Accounts payable and accrued liabilities	2,057	(2,420)	(19,477)
Income taxes payable	7,336	5,763	(58)
Long-term liabilities	(894)	1,941	(6,904)
Other, net	(1,955)	1,542	4,105
Net cash provided (used) by operating activities	(15,923)	93,301	66,372
Cash flows from investing activities:			
Investment in businesses	(5,109)	—	—
Proceeds from sale of businesses	223,000	15,000	73,183
Capital expenditures	(22,550)	(20,220)	(31,009)
Sale of property, plant and equipment, net	2,092	6,931	801
Net cash provided by investing activities	197,433	1,711	42,975
Cash flows from financing activities:			
Net (payments) borrowings—revolving credit agreement	101,554	8,421	(63,000)
Long-term debt payments	(130,007)	(99,295)	(32,887)
Payment of costs related to debt extinguishment	(16,397)	(10,688)	(1,797)
Purchases of common stock	(141,413)	—	—
Net shares sold under stock option plans	6,630	6,817	1,435
Dividends paid	(1,424)	(5,518)	(5,274)
Net cash used by financing activities	(181,057)	(100,263)	(101,523)
Effect of exchange rate changes on cash	(652)	494	(614)
Net increase (decrease) in cash and cash equivalents	(199)	(4,757)	7,210
Cash and cash equivalents, beginning of year	12,312	17,069	9,859
Cash and cash equivalents, end of year	$12,113	$12,312	$17,069
Supplemental disclosure of cash flows information:			
Cash payments for interest	$16,438	$32,602	$40,237
Cash payments (refunds), net for income taxes	$4,749	$4,901	$(21,631)

Source: SPX 1997 Annual Report.

On April 17, 1985, Bill Ahern sat in his office and contemplated a difficult judgment he had to make in the next two days. Two weeks before, Bill had been asked to be an arbitrator in a dispute between the Owner-Player Committee (OPC, the representatives of the owners of the 26 major league baseball teams in collective bargaining negotiations) and the Professional Baseball Players Association (PBPA, the players' union).

The issue Ahern had to resolve was the profitability of the major league baseball teams. The players felt they should share in the teams' profits; the owners maintained, however, that most of the teams were actually losing money each year, and they produced financial statements to support that position. The players, who had examined the owners' statements, countered that the owners were hiding profits through a number of accounting tricks and that the statements did not accurately reflect the economic reality. Ahern's decision on the profitability issue was important because it would affect the ongoing contract negotiations, particularly in the areas of minimum salaries and team contributions to the players' pension fund.

On April 9, Ahern met with the OPC and the representatives of the PBPA. They explained they wanted him to focus on the finances of the Kansas City Zephyrs Baseball Club, Inc. This club was selected for review because both sides agreed its operations were representative, yet it was a relatively clean and simple example to study: the baseball club entity was not owned by another corporation, and it did not own the stadium the team played in. Furthermore, no private financial data would have to be revealed because the corporation was publicly owned. Ahern's task was to review the Zephyrs' financial statements, hear the owners' and players' arguments, and then reach a decision as to the profitability of the team by Friday, April 19.

MAJOR LEAGUE BASEBALL

Major league baseball in the United States was comprised of a number of components bound together by sets of agreements and contractual relationships. At the heart of major

Research Assistant Joseph P. Mulloy prepared this case under the supervision of Professors Kenneth A. Merchant and Krishna G. Palepu as the basis for class discussion rather than to illustrate either effective or ineffective handling of an administrative situation. The case is based on publicly available information. Copyright © 1987 by the President and Fellows of Harvard College. Harvard Business School case 9-187-088.

league baseball were the 26 major league teams. Each team operated as an independent economic unit in such matters as contracting for players, promoting games and selling tickets, arranging for the use of a stadium and other needed facilities and services, and negotiating local broadcasting of games. The teams joined together to establish common rules and playing schedules, and to stage championship games.

The business of most teams was limited exclusively to their major league activities. Very few integrated vertically by owning their own stadium or minor league teams. Most teams were organized as partnerships or privately held corporations, although a few were subunits of larger corporations. While baseball was often thought of as a big business, the individual teams were relatively small. For most of them, annual revenues were between $20 million and $30 million.

Each team maintained an active roster of 24 players during the playing season, plus 16 minor league players "on option," who might see major league action during the season. This made a total of 40 players on major league contracts for each team at any one time. Each team played a schedule of 162 games during the season, 81 at home and 81 away.

Collectively, the team owners established most of the regulations that governed the industry. The covenant that bound them was the Major League Agreement (MLA), to which was attached the Major League Rules. The rules detailed all the procedures the clubs agreed on, including the rules for signing, trading, and dealing with players.

Under the MLA, the owners elected a commissioner of baseball for a seven-year term. The commissioner acted as a spokesperson for the industry, resolved disputes among the clubs and the other baseball entities, policed the industry, and enforced the rules. The commissioner had broad powers to protect the best interests of the game. The commissioner also administered the Major Leagues Central Fund, under which he negotiated and received the revenues from national broadcast contracts for major league games. About one-half of the fund's revenues were passed on directly to the teams in approximately equal shares.

Within the overall structure of major league baseball, the 26 teams were organized into two leagues each with its own president and administration. The American League had 14 teams and the National League had 12 teams, of which one was the Kansas City Zephyrs. Each league controlled the allocation and movement of its respective franchises. In addition to authorizing franchises, the leagues developed the schedule of games, contracted for umpires, and performed other administrative tasks. The leagues were financed through a small percentage share of club ticket revenues and receipts from the World Series and pennant championship games.

In addition to the major league teams, U.S. baseball included about 150 minor league teams located throughout the United States, Canada, and Mexico. Minor league teams served a dual function: they were entertainment entities in their own right, and they were training grounds for major league players. Through Player Development Contracts, the major league teams agreed to pay a certain portion of their affiliated minor league teams' operating expenses and player salaries.

MEETING WITH THE ZEPHYRS' OWNERS

Bill Ahern spent Tuesday reviewing the history of major league baseball and the relationships among the various entities that make up the major leagues. Then he met with the Zephyrs owners' representatives on Wednesday.

The owners' representatives gave Ahern a short history of the team and presented him with the team's financial statements for the years 1983 and 1984 (shown in Exhibits 1 and 2). The current owner was a corporation with five major shareholders, which bought the team on November 1, 1982, for $24 million. The Zephyrs did not own any of their minor league teams or their stadium, but two of the Zephyrs' owners were part owners of the private corporation that owned the baseball stadium.

Ahern studied the financial statements for a short time, and then he met with Keith Strong, the owners' lawyer. The conversation can be summarized by the following exchange:

Bill: I would like to know more about the controversial items in your financial statements. First, could you please explain your players' salaries expense entries?

Keith: Sure. Here is a list of our roster players and what we paid them last year [see Exhibit 3]. The number we show on our 1984 income statement is the total expense of $10,097,000. Most of the expense represents cash outflows in 1984. The only exception is shown in the last column of this exhibit. For our highest paid players, we have agreed to defer a portion of their salary for 10 years. That helps save them taxes and provides them with some income after their playing days are over.

Bill: What is the nonroster guaranteed contract expense?

Keith: That is also player salary expense, but we break it out separately because the salaries are paid to players who are no longer on our active roster. The salaries are amounts we owe to players whom we released who had long-term guaranteed contracts. The amount of $750,000 represents the amount we still owe at the end of 1984 to two players [shown in Figure A on the next page]. Joe Portocararo, one of our veteran pitchers, signed a four-year guaranteed contract last year, but before the season started he suffered a serious injury, and Joe and the team jointly decided it was best he retire. We released U. R. Wilson in spring training, hoping that another team would pick him up and pay his salary, but none did.

We still owe these players the amounts in their contracts. We decided to expense the whole amount in 1984 because they are not active players; they are not serving to bring in our current revenues. We felt it was more meaningful and conservative to recognize these losses now, as they result from the effects of past decisions that did not turn out well.

Bill: Okay. Let's move on to roster depreciation expense.

Keith: When the team was bought in 1982, $12 million—50 percent of the purchase price—was designated as the value of the player roster at that time. This amount was capitalized and is being amortized over six years.

Figure A Calculation of Nonroster Guaranteed Contract Expense ($000)

| | Amounts Owed | | | |
Player	1984	1985	1986	Total
Joe Portocararo	$300.0	$350.0	$400.0	$1,050.0
U. R. Wilson	200.0			200.0
				$1,250.0

Bill: Why 50 percent?

Keith: That is the maximum percentage that the Internal Revenue Code will allow when purchasing a sports team.

Bill: I see. Is there anything else in the statements that the players dispute?

Keith: No, I don't think so. The rest of our accounting is very straightforward. Most of our revenues and expenses result directly from a cash inflow or outflow.

Bill: Well, that answers all my questions. Thank you.

Keith: I have just one more thing to say concerning baseball finances in general. People seem to think that we generate huge profits since we have a relative monopoly, but it should be obvious that the professional baseball leagues do not exist in order to carry out traditional cartel functions. The rules and regulations governing the clubs comprising the league are essential to the creation of the league as an entity and have virtually nothing to do with pricing policies of the individual clubs. The objective of the cooperative agreements is not to constrain the economic competition among them, but rather to create the league as a joint venture that produces baseball during a season of play. Without such rules of conduct, leagues would not exist.

When this meeting was completed, Bill Ahern felt he understood the owners' accounting methods well enough.

MEETING WITH THE PLAYERS

The following Monday, Ahern met with the PBPA representatives and their lawyer, Paul Hanrahan. They presented Ahern with income statements for the years 1983 and 1984 as they thought they should be drawn up (Exhibit 4). As Ahern studied them, he found the players' version of the financial statements showed profits before tax of $2.9 million for 1983 and $3.0 million for 1984 as compared to the losses of $2.4 million and $2.6 million on the owners' statements.

Ahern's conversation with Paul Hanrahan went approximately as follows:

Bill: The income statements you have given me are very similar to those of the owners except for a few items.

Paul: That's true—most of the expenses are straightforward. There are only a few areas we dispute, but these areas can have a significant impact on the overall profitability of the team. We feel that the owners have used three techniques to "hide" profits: (1) roster depreciation, (2) overstated player salary expense, and (3) related-party transactions.

Bill: Let's start with roster depreciation. Why have you deleted it?

Paul: We feel it gives numbers that aren't meaningful. The depreciation expense arises only when a team is sold, so you can have two identical teams that will show dramatically different results if one had been sold and the other had not. We also don't think the depreciation is real because most of the players actually improve their skills with experience, so if anything, there should be an increase in roster value over time, not a reduction as the depreciation would lead you to believe.

Bill: Okay. I understand your reasoning. I'll have to think about that. Let's move on to the next issue.

Paul: That's player salary expense. We think the owners overstate player expense in several ways. One is that they expense the signing bonuses in the year they're paid. We feel the bonuses are just a part of the compensation package, and that for accounting purposes, the bonuses should be spread over the term of the player's contract.

We gathered information on the bonuses paid in the last four years and the contract terms [Exhibit 5]. Then we adjusted the owners' income statements by removing the bonuses from the current roster salary expense and by adding an "amortization of bonuses" line. The net effect of this one adjustment on 1984, for example, was an increase in income of $373,000.[1]

Bill: But the owners have really paid out all the bonuses in cash, and there is no guarantee that the players will complete their contracts.

Paul: That's partly true. Some players get hurt and are unable to compete effectively. But the number of players who do not complete their contracts is very small, and we think it is more meaningful to assume that they will continue to play over the term of their contract.

Bill: Okay. What's next?

Paul: A second adjustment we made to the players' salary line was to back out the deferred portion of the total compensation. Many of the players, particularly those who are higher paid, receive only about 80 percent of their salaries in any given year. They receive the rest ten years later [see Exhibit 3]. We feel that since the team is paying this money over a long period of time, it is misleading to include the whole amount as a current expense. This adjustment increased 1984 income for the Zephyrs by $1,521,000. No salary expense deferred from prior years was added back in because that form of contract is a relatively recent phenomenon.

---

1. *$1,320,000 less $947,000.*

Bill: I've looked at some of the contracts, and it says very clearly that the player is to receive, say, $500,000, of which $100,000 is deferred to the year 1984. Doesn't that indicate that the salary expense is $500,000?

Paul: No. The team has paid only $400,000 in cash.

Bill: Doesn't the team actually set money aside to cover the future obligation?

Paul: Some teams do, and in such cases, I think we would agree that it is appropriate to recognize that amount as a current expense. But the Zephyrs don't set any money aside.

Bill: Okay. You made a third adjustment to the players' salaries.

Paul: Yes, we think the salaries due to players who are no longer on the roster should be recognized when the cash is paid out, not when the players leave the roster. Unless that is done, the income numbers will vary wildly depending on when these players are released and how large their contracts are. Furthermore, it is quite possible that these players' contracts will be picked up by another team, and the Zephyrs would then have to turn around and recognize a large gain because the liability it has set up would no longer be payable.

Bill: Okay. Let's go to the last area: related-party transactions. You have listed Stadium Operations at about 80 percent of what the owners charged. Why is that?

Paul: You probably know that two of the Zephyrs' owners are also involved with the stadium corporation. But what you probably don't know is that they are the sole owners of that stadium company. We think that the stadium rent is set to overcharge the team and help show a loss for the baseball operations.

Bill: How did you get your numbers?

Paul: This wasn't easy, but we looked at what other teams pay for their stadiums. Every contract is slightly different, but we are sure that two of the five shareholders in the team are earning a nice gain on the stadium-pricing agreement.

Just for your own edification, this is not the only type of related-party transaction where the owners can move profits around. A few of the teams are owned by broadcasting organizations, and as a result, they report no local broadcasting revenues. Their individual losses are consolidated into the overall major league position, thus the overall loss is overstated. I know it's hard to do, but an objective look must be taken at all these related-party transactions if baseball's true position is to be fairly stated.

The overall effect of all these adjustments we have made to the Zephyrs' income statements changes losses to profits. In 1984, the change is from a loss of $1.7 million to a profit of $1.4 million. In the labor negotiations, the owners keep claiming that they're losing money and can't afford the contract terms we feel are fair. We just don't think that's true. They are "losing money" only because they have selected accounting methods to hide their profits.

Bill: Well, you've given me a lot to think about. There are a lot of good arguments on both sides. Thank you for your time. I'll have my answer for you soon.

BILL'S DECISION

By Wednesday, April 17, Bill was quite confused. To clarify the areas of disagreement, he prepared the summaries shown in Exhibit 6; but whereas the sets of numbers were clear, the answers to the conflicts were not. Bill had expected this arbitration to be rather straightforward, but instead he was mired in difficult issues involving the accounting unit, depreciation, amortization of intangibles, and related-party transactions. Now he was faced with a tight deadline, and it was not at all obvious to him how to define "good accounting methods" for the Zephyrs Baseball Club.

QUESTIONS

1. How should Bill Ahern resolve the accounting conflict between the owners and players?
2. How much did the Kansas City Zephyrs Baseball Club earn in 1983 and 1984?

Kansas City Zephyrs

Kansas City Zephyrs

EXHIBIT 1

Kansas City Zephyrs Baseball Club, Inc.—Income Statements, Owners' Figures (000s omitted)

	Year Ending October 31	
	1983	1984
Operating Revenues:		
Game Receipts	$16,526.0	$18,620.0
National Television	2,360.8	2,730.8
Local Broadcasting	3,147.9	3,575.1
Concessions	2,886.3	3,294.3
Parking	525.1	562.0
Other	786.9	843.9
Total Revenues	$26,233.0	$29,626.1
Operating Expenses:		
Spring Training	$ 545.0	$ 594.0
Team Operating Expenses:		
Players' Salaries:		
Current Roster	9,111.0	10,097.0
Nonroster Guaranteed Contract Expense	0.0	1,250.0
Coaches' Salaries	756.9	825.7
Other Salaries	239.0	260.8
Miscellaneous	2,655.9	2,897.3
Player Development	2,996.0	3,269.0
Team Replacement:		
Roster Depreciation	2,000.0	2,000.0
Scouting	672.8	734.0
Stadium Operations	4,086.0	4,457.0
Ticketing and Marketing	1,907.0	2,080.0
General and Administrative	3,541.0	3,663.0
Total Operating Expense	$28,510.6	$32,127.8
Income from Operations	(2,277.6)	(2,501.7)
Other Income (Expense)	(96.0)	(101.0)
Income Before Taxes	(2,373.6)	(2,602.7)
Federal Income Tax Benefit	855.9	944.2
Net Income (Loss)	$(1,517.7)	$(1,658.5)

EXHIBIT 2

Kansas City Zephyrs Baseball Club, Inc.—Balance Sheets,
Owners' Figures (000s omitted)

	Year Ending October 31	
	1983	1984
ASSETS		
Current Assets:		
Cash	$ 488.0	$ 561.0
Marketable Securities	6,738.0	7,786.1
Accounts Receivable	598.0	681.2
Notes Receivable	256.0	234.0
Total Current Assets	8,080.0	9,262.3
Property, Plant & Equipment	1,601.0	1,892.0
Less Accumulated Depreciation	(359.0)	(511.0)
Net PP&E	1,242.0	1,381.0
Initial Roster	12,000.0	12,000.0
Less Accumulated Depreciation	(4,000.0)	(6,000.0)
Net Initial Roster	8,000.0	6,000.0
Other Assets	2,143.0	4,123.2
Franchise	6,500.0	6,500.0
Total Assets	$25,965.0	$27,266.5
LIABILITIES AND SHAREHOLDERS' EQUITY		
Current Liabilities:		
Accounts Payable	$ 909.2	$1,020.2
Accrued Expenses	1,207.5	1,461.8
Total Current Liabilities	2,116.7	2,482.0
Long-Term Debt	7,000.0	8,073.7
Other Long-Term Liabilities	2,443.3	3,964.3
Shareholders' Equity:		
Common Stock, par value $1 per share, 500,000		
shares issued	500.0	500.0
Additional Paid-In Capital	10,000.0	10,000.0
Retained Earnings	3,905.0	2,246.5
Total Liabilities and Shareholders' Equity	$25,965.0	$27,266.5

Kansas City Zephyrs

EXHIBIT 3
Detailed Players' Salary Summary—1984 (000s omitted)

Roster Player	Signing Bonus	Base Salary	Performance and Attendance Bonuses	Total Compensation	Portion of 1984 Salary Deferred Until 1994
Bill Hogan	$ 500.0	$ 850.0	$ 250.0	$ 1,600.0	$ 250.0
Corby Megorden	300.0	600.0	225.0	1,125.0	200.0
Manuel Vasquez	200.0	500.0	100.0	800.0	150.0
Jim Showalter		600.0	100.0	700.0	200.0
Scott Van Buskirk	150.0	400.0	100.0	650.0	150.0
Jerry Hyde	150.0	400.0	50.0	600.0	150.0
Dave Schafer		355.0	50.0	405.0	130.0
Leslie Yamshita		300.0	37.5	337.5	100.0
Earl McLain		220.0	37.5	257.5	50.0
Shannon Saunders		210.0	37.5	247.5	50.0
Gary Blazin		190.0	37.5	227.5	40.0
Rich Hayes		160.0	25.0	185.0	30.0
Sam Willett		140.0	17.5	157.5	21.0
Chuck Wright	20.0	115.0	12.5	147.5	
Jim Urquart		115.0	12.5	127.5	
Bill Schutt		115.0	12.5	127.5	
Mike Hegarty		115.0	12.5	127.5	
Bruce Selby		110.0	12.5	122.5	
Dave Kolk		110.0	12.5	122.5	
Bill Kelly		110.0	12.5	122.5	
Dave Carr		110.0	12.0	122.0	
Tom O'Conner		110.0	5.0	115.0	
Jake Luhan		110.0		110.0	
Ray Woolrich		100.0		100.0	
John Porter		100.0		100.0	
Dusty Rhodes		100.0		100.0	
Lynn Novinger		100.0		100.0	
Bill Williams		95.0		95.0	
Jim Sedor		95.0		95.0	
Ralph Young		95.0		95.0	
Ed Marino		95.0		95.0	
Ray Spicer		90.0		90.0	
Eric Womble		90.0		90.0	
Ron Gorena		90.0		90.0	
Gene Johnston		90.0		90.0	
Jack Zollinger		90.0		90.0	
Ken Karr		90.0		90.0	
Tom Crowley		80.0		80.0	
Joe Matt		80.0		80.0	
Bill Brunelle		80.0		80.0	
Roster Player Salary	$1,320.0	$7,605.0	$1,172.0	$10,097.0	$1,521.0

EXHIBIT 4

Kansas City Zephyrs Baseball Club, Inc.—Income Statements,
Players' Figures (000s omitted)

	Year Ending October 31	
	1983	1984
Operating Revenues:		
Game Receipts	$16,526.0	$18,620.0
National Television	2,360.8	2,830.8
Local Broadcasting	3,147.9	3,475.1
Concessions	2,886.3	3,294.3
Parking	525.1	562.0
Other	786.9	843.9
Total Revenues	$26,233.0	$29,626.1
Operating Expenses:		
Spring Training	$545.0	$594.0
Team Operating Expenses:		
Players' Salaries:		
Current Roster	5,897.4	7,256.5
Nonroster Guaranteed Contract Expense	0.0	500.0
Amortization of Bonuses	716.0	947.0
Coaches' Salaries	756.9	825.7
Other Salaries	239.0	260.8
Miscellaneous	2,655.9	2,897.3
Player Development	2,996.0	3,269.0
Team Replacement: Scouting	672.8	734.0
Stadium Operations	3,300.0	3,500.0
Ticketing and Marketing	1,907.0	2,080.0
General and Administrative	3,541.0	3,663.0
Total Operating Expenses	$23,227.0	$26,527.3
Income from Operations	3,006.0	3,098.8
Other Income (Expense)	(96.0)	(101.0)
Income Before Taxes	2,910.0	2,997.8
Provision for Federal Income Taxes[a]	1,338.6	1,379.0
City and State Taxes	236.0	253.0
Net Income	$ 1,335.4	$ 1,365.8

a. Tax rate assumed to be 46%.

Kansas City Zephyrs

EXHIBIT 5
Summary of Signing Bonuses ($000)

Contract Length (Years)	Bonuses for Contracts Starting in			
	1981	1982	1983	1984
4	$240	$550	$350	$800
3	210	200	250	200
2	360	250	170	320

EXHIBIT 6
Summary of Items of Disagreement Between Owners and Players ($000)

Items of Dispute	1983			1984		
	Owners	Players	Difference	Owners	Players	Difference
Roster depreciation	2,000.0	0.0	2,000.0	2,000.0	0.0	2,000.0
Current roster salary	$9,111.0	$5,897.4	$3,213.6	$10,097.0	$7,256.5	$2,840.5
Amortization of signing bonuses	0.0	716.0	(716.0)	0.0	947.0	(947.0)
Nonroster guaranteed contract expense	0.0	0.0	—	1,250.0	500.0	750.0
Stadium operations	4,086.0	3,300.0	786.0	4,457.0	3,500.0	957.0
Total effect on net income			$5,283.6			$5,600.5

Effect on Net Income (before tax)	1983	1984
Income before tax per Owners' Financial Statements (Exhibit 1)	($2,373.6)	($2,602.7)
Total items of disagreement	5,283.6	5,600.5
Income before tax per Players' Financial Statements (Exhibit 4)	$2,910.0	$2,997.8

I n March 1985, Dianne Simmons, director of research for the Common-wealth Investment Group, called David McIntosh, a newly joined analyst, into her office and presented a request:

> David, I just received the 1984 annual report and proxy statement of The Murray Ohio Manufacturing Company. A few years ago we bought Murray's stock for our equity income fund. As you know, that fund is marketed to dividend-oriented investors. It's been a good investment so far, thanks to Murray's excellent dividend payment record. I think, though, that it's time for us to take a fresh look at Murray's recent performance and future prospects.
>
> I want you to analyze the company's 1984 annual report [Exhibit 3] and make a recommendation. You may find the information on the company's board reported in the proxy statement useful [Exhibit 1]. I've also collected some information for you on Murray's stock price in recent months [Exhibit 2]. And here's some background information on the company's business.

BUSINESS

Murray Ohio Company was based in Brentwood, a suburb of Nashville, Tennessee. The company's stock was listed on the New York Stock Exchange.

Murray Ohio manufactured and sold power mowers and bicycles. During the 1982–1984 period the shares of these two product lines in the company's sales and operating profits were as follows:

	Sales			Profits		
	1982	1983	1984	1982	1983	1984
Power Mowers	54%	53%	62%	73%	68%	88%
Bicycles	46%	47%	38%	27%	32%	12%

Source: Murray Ohio's 1984 annual report

Murray produced all its products in a 57-acre manufacturing facility located in Lawrenceburg, Tennessee.

Bicycles

Murray began as a bicycle manufacturer in 1936. The company produced a complete line of bicycles ranging from sidewalk bicycles for small children to lightweight racing bicycles. The bicycles were sold under both the Murray brand name and the private labels of major retailers. Substantially all of the company's bicycles were distributed through department stores, discount stores, toy stores, and other mass merchandise outlets.

In 1984 Murray manufactured approximately one-third of the bicycles made in the United States. The company competed with several domestic bicycle manufacturers including Huffy, Roadmaster, Columbia, and Ross.

INDUSTRY TRENDS.   The demand for bicycles was largely dependent on discretionary income. Thus, higher income consumers comprised a major portion of the market. The maturation of the baby boom generation into their peak earning years and the growing incidence of two-income households as a result of more women in the work force had increased this pool of "upscale"consumers in recent years. Another factor that positively affected the demand was migration of the population to the West and the South, where the weather and access to recreational areas are favorable for outdoor activities.

The bicycle industry grew at a compound annual growth rate of 7.8 percent during the ten-year period 1972–1982 and 0.6 percent during the five years 1977–1982. Domestic shipments of bicycles and parts rebounded strongly in 1983 from one of the industry's worst years in more than a decade. Constant dollar shipments increased an estimated 15 percent in 1983, then slowed to a 4 percent increase in 1984. Much of the slowdown in 1984 domestic shipments was attributable to competition from low-priced imports from the Far East. Even though demand remained strong in 1984, a 50 percent rise of imports in 1984 adversely affected the domestic producers of bicycles.

The following table summarizes the total shipment data for the bicycle industry:

	Bicycle and Parts Shipments				
(in millions of dollars)	1980	1981	1982	1983	1984
Domestic	649	733	565	644	683
Imports	281	327	208	329	494

Source: U.S. Department of Commerce, Bureau of the Census

The long-term demand for bicycles was expected to remain strong. Domestic producers' share of the market would depend on their ability to be cost competitive with foreign producers, particularly those in Taiwan. Import growth would also be influenced by the value of the dollar. In addition, pressure on Taiwanese exporters in the form of proposed tariff legislation and other trade remedies could result in voluntary cutbacks by the exporters. Based on these factors, domestic bicycle shipments were expected to grow at a rate of 3 percent in 1985 and 3.5 percent annually for the five years thereafter.

Power Mowers

Murray entered the power mower market in 1968 and by 1984 had become one of the largest U.S. manufacturers of power mowers. The company had a full line of walk-behind and riding mowers. Some of these models also accepted attachments such as snow blowers, plows, and tillers. Murray also offered a line of tillers to complement its power mower products.

Through 1984 Murray's power mowers were marketed through major national and regional chains, primarily under the Murray label. In early 1985 the company formed a new marketing subsidiary, Sabre Corporation, to sell mowers to outdoor power equipment dealers. These dealers participated in a large share of the higher priced mower market in which Murray was not previously represented.

INDUSTRY TRENDS.   According to the 1982 Census of Manufacturers, 152 firms produced lawn and garden equipment in the United States. However, many of these producers were small and had fewer than 20 employees. In addition to Murray, the major domestic manufacturers included Western International, Roper, MTD, and Aircap. Lawn mower producers tended to specialize in one of two distribution markets: the high-volume, low-to-medium price mass merchandisers, which accounted for about two-thirds of industry sales, or the higher priced independent retailers, who serviced equipment in addition to selling it. Sales through national department stores had been declining since 1978 as specialty retailers and hardware stores were handling a greater share of the market.

Demand for lawn and garden equipment, like demand for other household durables, was closely related to the level of real disposable income and to the health of the housing market. Between 1972 and 1979, constant dollar shipments of lawn and garden equipment increased at a compound annual rate of 5.5 percent. Record high interest rates from 1979 through 1982 severely depressed the housing market, and constant dollar shipments of lawn and garden equipment declined 31 percent to their lowest level since 1972. The recovery began in 1983 as real disposable income and housing starts rebounded. The expansion continued in 1984 with an estimated 12 percent increase in lawn and garden equipment shipments.

The balance of trade in lawn and garden equipment was historically very favorable for U.S. producers. In recent years, however, imports began to make inroads into the U.S. market. In 1984, estimated U.S. imports of lawn and garden equipment increased 178 percent, continuing a trend begun in 1979 when a Japanese producer, Honda, entered the market for lawn mowers.

The following table summarizes recent trends in the lawn and garden equipment industry:

(in millions of dollars)	1980	1981	1982	1983	1984
		Lawn and Garden Equipment Shipments			
Domestic	2419	2270	2387	2536	2956
Imports	26	30	40	66	184

Source: U.S. Department of Commerce, Bureau of the Census

Constant dollar shipments of lawn and garden equipment were expected to increase at a compound annual growth rate of 4 percent between 1984 and 1989. Growth in housing starts, an increase in real disposable income, and an increase in replacement demand were expected to contribute to this growth. Due to its leading position in the world markets, the U.S. industry was expected to expand exports as world economies recovered and as the value of the dollar dropped. U.S. imports of lawn and garden equipment were also expected to continue to increase, especially in the lower priced models.

FINANCIAL PERFORMANCE

Between 1975 and 1979 Murray's sales grew 158 percent, from $126.6 million to $327.1 million; the company's reported profits grew by 125 percent, from $4.7 million to $10.6 million. During this period, the company had relatively stable profitability, with an average return on sales (ROS) of 3.5 percent, and an average return on equity (ROE) of 13.5 percent.

In contrast to the steady growth during the last half of the 1970s, Murray's performance became erratic beginning in 1980 as foreign competition in its product markets increased significantly. Between 1979 and 1983, the company's sales and profits grew by only 31 percent and 16 percent, respectively. Further, the company's average profitability showed a significant decline. The average ROS and ROE from 1980 to 1983 were 2.6 percent and 10.8 percent, respectively. (See Exhibit 3 for more data on the performance from 1975 to 1983.)

1984 was a challenging year for Murray Ohio. The company's management explained:

> The past year, 1984, was a difficult one for our company. While total sales were basically flat with 1983, earnings were down considerably. Two factors primarily accounted for this earnings decline.
>
> First, bicycle imports were up over 55 percent in 1984. This increase, which has been sold almost totally to the mass market merchants, adversely affected our bicycle pricing, production levels, and sales.

Secondly, stronger domestic competition in both our product lines, bicycles and power mowers, increased pressures on our pricing and resulted in a tightening of our profit margins.

The mower segment of Murray's business performed significantly better than the bicycle segment. Following a record sales performance in 1983, Murray's mower sales increased to a new high in 1984, up 15 percent. In contrast, bicycle sales decreased 19 percent in 1984, and operating profits for the year declined by 72 percent.

Murray Ohio's management announced that it would take several steps to improve its future performance: (1) adopting an aggressive bicycle pricing structure to regain market share; (2) improving manufacturing productivity through process modernization, manufacturing resources planning, and better manpower utilization; (3) introducing new and innovative products, including the new Sabre mower line aimed at the power equipment dealers; and (4) working with other domestic producers to lobby the U.S. Congress to increase import tariffs on bicycles.

While these steps were viewed as necessary to prevent further erosion in the company's market share, management realized that profit margin pressure was likely to continue, at least in the short term. Further, the productivity improvement program was expected to require significant capital expenditure outlays. The company increased its capital expenditures in 1984 by 86 percent to $10.9 million, and expected to invest comparable amounts in 1985 as well. Management summed up their view of the future:

We recognize the difficult journey before us. Our past record, however, shows one of success and profitability. With a solid balance sheet and the full commitment of our resources and people, we look forward to the challenges that lie ahead. Our people continue to be our greatest strength. Their innovativeness, team-work, and support provide the company with the impetus it needs. In these times of change, their support and assistance are immeasurable.

DIVIDEND POLICY

David McIntosh knew that the Commonwealth Investment Group had found Murray Ohio's stock attractive for Commonwealth's equity income fund because of its reliable dividend policy. Murray's dividend per share grew steadily from $0.67 in 1975 to $1.20 in 1980. Despite the company's mixed performance between 1980 and 1984, dividends remained constant. As the company's annual report stated, Murray's management was proud of the company's dividend history—it had paid them quarterly without a reduction for the past 49 consecutive years. McIntosh wondered whether Murray Ohio would be able to maintain this record given the company's changed business circumstances. Has the nature of Murray's business changed enough to warrant a reevaluation of its dividend policy? If the company decided to change its longstanding policy, how would investors react?

QUESTIONS

1. Analyze Murray Ohio's recent financial performance and cash flows. Can the company afford to maintain its current dividend if operating conditions remain about the same?

2. Evaluate management's business strategy for the future. What does this strategy imply for the company's future cash requirements? Given this new strategy, is the company more or less likely to maintain its current dividend policy?

3. Is there an alternative strategy that is better than management's proposed strategy for increasing shareholders' value? Is the company's current management likely to pursue this alternative strategy? If not, is the company an attractive takeover target?

4. What are the implications for current stockholders of Murray Ohio? What should the Commonwealth Investment Group do?

EXHIBIT 1

The Murray Ohio Manufacturing Company—Board of Directors, 1984

Name	Principal Occupation, Business Experience, and Other Directorships in Public Companies (1)	Age on April 2, 1985	Beginning Year, Period of Service
John N. Anderson (2)	President and Chief Executive Officer of the Company. Director of Third National Bank, Nashville, Tennessee.	60	1979
Lovic A. Brooks, Jr.	Senior Partner in the firm of Constangy, Brooks & Smith, Atlanta, Georgia (attorneys). Constangy, Brooks & Smith has performed legal services for the Company for many years and is expected to continue to do so.	57	1972
Sam M. Fleming (2)	Retired. Former Chairman of the Board, Third National Bank, Nashville, Tennessee. Director of Hillsboro Enterprises, Inc., Nashville, Tennessee.	76	1965
Robert A. Flesher	Retired. Former Vice Chairman of the Board of the Company.	66	1966
Charles W. Geny (2)	Vice President, Alexander & Alexander, Incorporated, Nashville, Tennessee (insurance and bonds).	71	1972
William M. Hannon (2)	Chairman of the Board and retired Chief Executive Officer of the Company. Director of Third National Bank, Nashville, Tennessee.	65	1955
Thomas M. Hudson	Investments. Retired Senior Vice President of the The Robinson-Humphrey Company, Inc. (an investment banking firm). The Robinson-Humphrey Company, Inc. has performed investment banking services for the Company for many years and is expected to continue to do so. Director of the United Cities Gas Company, Nashville, Tennessee.	63	1980
William C. Keyes	Retired. Former Senior Executive Vice President of the Company. Director of Commerce Union Bank, Nashville, Tennessee.	65	1966
H. Theodore Meyer (3)	Partner in the firm of Jones, Day, Reavis & Pogue, which has performed legal services for the Company for many years and is expected to continue to do so.	49	1985
Gerald E. Sheridan	President, Sheridan Construction Co., Nashville, Tennessee.	60	1983
G. Cromer Smotherman (2)	Executive Vice President and Chief Operating Officer of the Company. Director of First National Bank of Lawrenceburg, Lawrenceburg, Tennessee.	59	1971
David K. Wilson	President, Cherokee Equity Corporation, Nashville, Tennessee (holding company). Director of First American National Bank, Winners Corporation, and Genesco, Inc., all located in Nashville, Tennessee, and Torchmark Corporation, Birmingham, Alabama.	65	1983

All directors and officers of the company as a group (26 persons, including those named above) own 10.4 percent of the company's common stock.

EXHIBIT 2

The Murray Ohio Manufacturing Company—Stock Prices, January 1984–March 1985

Month	Murray Ohio's Stock Price at Month End	Standard and Poor's 400 Industrial Index at Month End
1984		
January	21 6/8	184
February	21 4/8	177
March	22 4/8	180
April	22 5/8	182
May	21 5/8	171
June	23 2/8	175
July	20 2/8	171
August	20 7/8	189
September	21 2/8	187
October	20 2/8	187
November	19 2/8	183
December	19 4/8	186
1985		
January	20 5/8	201
February	20 5/8	203
March	20 3/8	202

Murray Ohio's Common Stock ß = 0.8 (Value Line estimate).

Interest rates at the beginning of 1985:
3-month Treasury bills: 8.8%
20-year Treasury bonds: 11.7%

EXHIBIT 3

The Murray Ohio Manufacturing Company—1984 Annual Report (Abridged)

LETTER TO SHAREHOLDERS

March 4, 1985

The past year, 1984, was a difficult one for our Company. While total sales were basically flat with 1983, earnings were down considerably. Two factors primarily accounted for this earnings decline.

First, bicycle imports were up over 55% in 1984. This increase, which has been sold almost totally to the mass market merchants, adversely affected our bicycle pricing, production levels, and sales.

Secondly, stronger domestic competition in both our product lines, bicycles and power mowers, increased pressures on our pricing and resulted in a tightening of our profit margins.

Net sales for the year were $383,589,000, a 1% decrease from 1983. Power mower sales, however, were up 15%, with bicycle sales down 19%.

Earnings, after nonrecurring adjustments for 1984, were $7,826,000, a 37% decrease from 1983. The majority of this decrease, as stated above, was due to the bicycle segment of our business. Earnings per share, after nonrecurring adjustments, decreased 43% to $2.01 from $3.53 in 1983. The difference between the percent change in earnings and earnings per share is a result of the June, 1983 equity offering of 770,000 shares of common stock.

The 1984 nonrecurring adjustments are benefits arising from the elimination of a provision for deferred taxes of our international sales operations (DISC) and an accounting change in the method for recognizing investment tax credits. These benefits resulted in earnings of $920,000 and $1,404,000, respectively, or $.24 and $.36 per share.

The declining profitability experienced in 1984 presented Murray with a difficult challenge that we are determined to face. In the third quarter report, we announced the first step in our program to improve profitability. This step involves an aggressive bicycle pricing structure aimed at maintaining our necessary production levels and at regaining market share lost to imports. Our pricing stance has shown

success and will help Murray regain lost market share in 1985.

Productivity and Marketing—Steps for the Future

While putting a pricing structure in place to regain bicycle market share, we began major programs in two areas—productivity and marketing—to improve our profitability in both of our product lines. Neither program will create overnight success, but both will help keep Murray on solid ground and a strong course for the future.

Murray's productivity program involves several facets—process modernization, Manufacturing Resources Planning (MRP), and improved manpower productivity.

Our 1984 capital expenditures amounted to $10,878,000, an 86% increase over 1983. This increase strengthened our continuing program of process modernization. Major investments included the installation of modern tube cutting equipment, robot welders, a computer aided design system, and the initial phase of a state of the art press room. The commitment to the modernization of our facilities is one that will continue, and we are projecting comparable expenditures in 1985.

In 1984, we also began installation of a Manufacturing Resources Planning (MRP) System. The MRP System will lead to reduced inventory levels and better control and utilization of our manufacturing facility and processes. Such efficiency will improve our cost of operations.

With regards to marketing, Murray has always been innovative in product introductions. We have been successful in introducing BMX, mountain bikes, and freestyle bicycles into the mass market. Murray revolutionized the riding mower market when we entered this industry in 1968 in both performance

Murray Ohio Manufacturing Company

and design, and we have continued as an innovator in this industry. In 1984, we reaffirmed our commitment to this type of innovation.

Bicycles and power mowers continue to be viable products for the consumer. We recognize the need to intensify our efforts to compete in these markets. At the same time, we are analyzing our present and related markets for expansion opportunities. This effort is continuing, and its benefits are beginning to show in our marketing plans.

One result of this market analysis was the introduction of our Sabre mower line for the spring of 1985. The Sabre line will target the outdoor power equipment dealer who participates in a large share of the mower market in which Murray is not currently represented. This new line, which will be sold directly to the dealer, offers him high quality merchandise with the ability to improve profit margins. Murray will continue such expansion or diversification moves as prove correct for our business future.

Our power mower products continue to meet with great success. The 1985 Murray line has been well received by our customers, and we expect the momentum created by our steady mower sales rise over the past 15 years to be maintained.

This year again, we were pleased to be selected to receive the Sears "Partners in Progress Award." We were one of only 23 suppliers to receive this award for the third consecutive year. The award is presented for overall excellence as a manufacturer of products for Sears. Sears has a total of over 12,000 suppliers.

We and our industry continue to make every effort in Washington to draw attention to the unfair competition we face from imported bicycles. The industry was successful in May with having H.R. 5754 introduced in the House of Representatives. This Bill provides for a 24% duty on imported bicycles and bicycle parts, a duty comparable to that in foreign markets. No action was taken on this Bill, and it will be reintroduced in the new session of Congress. It is the aim of the domestic industry to have our Government recognize and control the flood of unfairly traded import bicycles coming into this country.

If the economy continues on its present course, our sales for 1985 should improve. While our plans for 1985 and the future will help offset our 1985 pricing structure, we expect continued profit margin pressure.

Board of Director Changes

At the February 1985 Board Meeting, we regretfully accepted the resignation of Eugene T. Kinder, a recently retired partner in the law firm of Jones, Day, Reavis & Pogue. Though leaving our Board, Mr. Kinder will continue to be available as requested to render the excellent counsel that he has given Murray in his 12 years on the Board.

H. Theodore Meyer, also a partner of Jones, Day, Reavis & Pogue and currently Secretary of Murray Ohio, was elected to fill the vacant position. His election continues the tradition since 1925 of having a member of this firm on our Board.

Solid Record for the Future

We recognize the difficulty of the journey before us. Our past record, however, shows one of success and profitability. With a solid balance sheet and the full commitment of our resources and people we look forward to the challenges that lie ahead.

Our people continue to be our greatest source of strength. Their innovativeness, team-work, and support provide the Company with the impetus that it needs. In these times of change, their support and assistance are unmeasurable.

Very truly yours,

W. M. Hannon
Chairman of the Board

John N. Anderson
President and Chief Executive Officer

G. Cromer Smotherman
Executive Vice President and
Chief Operating Officer

FINANCIAL REVIEW

Sales in 1984 were $384 million, which was within 1% of the company's all-time record sales year of 1983. This included an increase of over 15% from the company's previous record for its power mower line, while bicycle sales were adversely impacted by import competition to record a 19% decrease from 1983.

Net income and earnings per common share were $7.8 million and $2.01, respectively, each after non-recurring adjustments. This resulted in profit margins of 2.04% and return on average shareholders' equity of 7.05%.

Murray Ohio has spent approximately $59 million during the past ten years to modernize and automate its facilities, to increase the productive efficiency and to expand the plant capacity. This included a significant increase in 1984 to further pursue the goals stated above.

During this ten-year period, the company has significantly expanded both its power mower and bicycle production capacities at Lawrenceburg, including additions of 600,000 square feet. Other expenditures were for research and development facilities, and an expansion to the corporate office. Another

$9.7 million is budgeted for capital expenditures in 1985.

Total long-term debt at the end of 1984 was $23.0 million or 16.9% of total capitalization. This compares to $26.0 million and 19.2% for 1983. Working capital stands at $86.5 million at December 31, 1984, resulting in a current ratio of 2.2 to 1.

Shareholders' equity per share has increased every year for the last ten years to $28.93 at December 31, 1984, an increase of 91% for the ten-year period.

Murray Ohio paid cash dividends of $1.20 per common share in 1984. Murray is proud of its history of paying regular quarterly dividends without a reduction for the past 49 consecutive years. During this period Murray's stock became listed on the New York Stock Exchange and the Midwest Stock Exchange in 1969 and 1971, respectively, and continues to be so listed. Prior to 1969 Murray was listed on the American Stock Exchange.

Murray Ohio's cash payout over the past ten-year period has averaged 43% of net income. At year end, 3,896,670 shares of the company's common stock were outstanding. Of this total, 1,113,041 shares (29%), were owned by directors, officers, and current employees.

Murray Ohio Manufacturing Company

Murray Ohio Manufacturing Company

TEN YEARS OF GROWTH

Summary of Operations	1984	1983	1982	1981
Net Sales	$383,589,105	$386,493,993	$288,642,358	$332,278,451
Power Mowers and Accessories	236,421,047	205,036,387	155,415,363	161,076,211
Bicycles and Accessories	147,079,185	181,377,604	133,138,347	170,619,908
Other Products	88,873	80,002	88,648	582,332
Cost of Products Sold	335,374,269	327,134,491	245,394,295	283,353,873
Depreciation and Amortization	3,635,096	3,361,666	3,253,897	2,876,664
Interest Expense	4,689,476	4,336,223	6,847,499	7,217,509
Income Before Income Taxes	9,129,558	22,527,621	9,429,651	17,180,728
Federal and State Income Taxes	2,708,000(b)	10,153,000	4,337,000	8,090,000
Income Before Cumulative Effect of Change in Accounting Principle	6,421,558	12,374,621	5,092,651	9,090,728(d)
Cumulative Effect of Change in Accounting Principle for Investment Tax Credit	1,404,000	—	—	—
Net Income (a)	7,825,558(b)	12,374,621	5,092,651	9,090,728(d)
Percent of Net Income to Net Sales	2.04%	3.20%	1.76%	2.74%
Return on Average Shareholder's Equity	7.05%	13.02%	6.39%	11.96%
Earnings per Common Share Before Cumulative Effect of Change in Accounting Principle	1.65	3.53	1.63	2.93(d)
Cumulative Effect of Change in Accounting Principle for Investment Tax Credit	.36	—	—	—
Earnings per Common Share (a, c, e)	2.01(b)	3.53	1.63	2.93(d)
Cash Dividends Paid	4,649,740	4,118,992	3,701,465	3,674,103
Cash Dividends Declared and Paid per Common Share (e)	1.20	1.20	1.20	1.20
Common Shares Outstanding at Year End (net of Treasury Shares) (c, e)	3,896,670	3,873,748	3,134,565	3,099,527
Number of Shareholders (h)	4,813	4,802	5,203	4,711
Average Number of Employees	3,500	3,403	2,868	3,534

Financial Condition at Year End				
Total Assets	$209,777,365	$188,845,331	$171,732,458	$173,521,388
Current Assets	157,938,259	142,782,974	127,822,330	132,297,984
Current Liabilities	71,395,177	48,140,763	58,037,639	62,352,490
Current Ratio	2.2 to 1	3.0 to 1	2.2 to 1	2.1 to 1
Working Capital	86,543,082	94,642,211	69,784,691	69,945,494
Shareholders' Equity	112,721,223	109,368,410	80,741,336	78,713,813
Shareholders' Equity per Common Share (e)	28.93	28.23	25.76	25.40
Property, Plant and Equipment (net)	50,794,929	44,778,715	42,628,946	39,721,024
Capital Expenditures	10,878,234	5,862,985	6,277,156	6,104,077
Total Amount of Long-Term Debt	22,978,225	26,014,300	29,075,375	30,131,450
Long-Term Debt as a Percentage of Total Capitalization	16.9%	19.2%	26.5%	27.7%

(a) Pro forma based on revised method of accounting for investment tax credit, applied retroactively:

	1984	1983	1982	1981	1980	1979	1978	1977	1976	1975
Net Income (000's)	6,422	12,521	5,184	9,242	8,566	10,704	7,936	8,435	5,768	4,850
Earning per Common Share	1.65	3.57	1.66	2.98	2.76	3.46	2.56	2.73	1.86	1.57

(b) Income taxes, net income, and earnings per common share for 1984 include the nonrecurring effect of the reversal of certain deferred taxes. Refer to the financial statements and management's discussion and analysis for further explanation.

(c) Earnings per common share are computed based on the average common shares outstanding each year. The average common shares for 1983 (3,505,567) were significantly different from the common shares outstanding at year end due to the issuance in June 1983 of 770,000 common shares.

Murray Ohio Manufacturing Company

1980	1979	1978	1977	1976	1975
$294,745,956	$327,137,268	$254,113,710	$212,773,180	$150,815,365	$126,655,353
153,706,766	165,313,297	136,748,819	100,660,828	63,342,453	46,862,481
139,178,541	161,823,971	117,364,891	112,112,352	87,472,912	79,792,872
1,860,649	—	—	—	—	—
251,746,135	283,699,952	220,067,742	181,971,227	127,930,166	106,560,985
2,742,559	2,668,797	2,453,631	1,643,479	1,577,229	1,440,611
7,534,174	4,979,286	3,875,387	1,787,587	1,549,272	1,878,782
15,878,660	20,108,133	15,264,403	16,155,618	11,164,297	9,272,287
7,405,000	9,480,000	7,464,000	7,916,000	5,425,000	4,544,000
8,473,660	10,628,133	7,800,403	8,239,618	5,739,297	4,728,287
—	—	—	—	—	—
8,473,660	10,628,133	7,800,403	8,239,618	5,739,297	4,728,287
2.87%	3.25%	3.07%	3.87%	3.81%	3.73%
11.95%	16.42%	13.33%	15.46%	11.79%	10.41%
2.73	3.43	2.52	2.66	1.85	1.53
—	—	—	—	—	—
2.73	3.43	2.52	2.66	1.85	1.53
3,643,351	3,185,688	3,071,258	2,777,681	2,252,703	2,041,374
1.20	1.05	1.00	.90	.73	.67
3,099,527	3,099,527	3,094,563	3,094,563	3,093,154	3,093,079
5,002	4,874	4,872	4,728	4,663	4,713
3,106	3,676	3,350	3,050	2,423	2,212
$162,593,699	$165,676,630	$137,954,695(f)	$118,184,974	$96,521,505	$77,703,626(g)
123,774,401	128,536,269	104,553,999(f)	92,158,408	74,098,444	56,496,582(g)
56,045,182	62,951,762	41,929,128	47,978,918	31,202,317	15,060,145
2.2 to 1	2.0 to 1	2.5 to 1	1.9 to 1	2.4 to 1	3.8 to 1
67,729,219	65,584,507	62,624,871(f)	44,179,490	42,896,127	41,436,437(g)
73,271,961	68,498,679	60,922,713	56,087,652	50,497,987	46,894,095
23.64	22.10	19.69	18.12	16.32	15.16
36,563,771	34,071,357	30,560,878	24,692,169	20,408,767	19,747,300
5,322,612	6,891,287	7,648,408	5,962,610	2,335,131	1,600,299
31,177,525	32,213,600	33,249,675(f)	12,470,000	13,480,000	14,485,000(g)
29.9%	32.0%	35.3%	18.2%	21.1%	23.6%

(d) Net income in 1981 was reduced by $3,047,000 ($.98 per common share) due to the change to the LIFO, from the FIFO, method of accounting for inventories.

(e) Adjusted for the 3-for-2 stock split distributed August 31, 1977.

(f) Includes a long-term loan of $20,000,000 at 9¼% annual interest.

(g) Includes a long-term loan of $5,000,000 at 10¼% annual interest.

(h) Represents the number of shareholders of record as of the approximate December 15, dividend record date of each respective year.

Murray Ohio Manufacturing Company

QUARTERLY RESULTS OF OPERATIONS

In Thousands of Dollars (except for per share data)

Comparison of Quarterly Results for Years Ended December 31, 1984, and December 31, 1983

	Net Sales							
	Power Mowers and Accessories		Bicycles and Accessories		Other Products		Total	
Quarter	**1984**	1983	**1984**	1983	**1984**	1983	**1984**	1983
1st	**$114,820**	$104,446	**$ 40,664**	$33,918	**$22**	$ 6	**$155,506**	$138,370
2nd	**94,213**	70,445	**39,775**	48,387	**50**	16	**134,038**	118,848
3rd	**12,641**	11,561	**32,908**	48,759	**11**	46	**45,560**	60,366
4th	**14,747**	18,584	**33,732**	50,314	**6**	12	**48,485**	68,910
Total	**$236,421**	$205,036	**$147,079**	$181,378	**$89**	$80	**$383,589**	$386,494

	Income									
	Gross Profit[1]		Income (Loss) Before Cumulative Effect of Accounting Change		Net Income (Loss)		Earnings (Loss) per Common Share Before Cumulative Effect of Accounting Change		Earnings (Loss) per Common Share	
Quarter	**1984**	1983	**1984**[3]	1983	**1984**[3]	1983	**1984**[3]	1983[2,3]	**1984**[3]	1983[2,3]
1st	**$18,688**	$17,625	**$4,340**	$4,953	**$5,744**	$4,953	**$1.12**	$1.58	**$1.48**	$1.58
2nd	**15,147**	16,943	**2,460**	4,296	**2,460**	4,296	**.63**	1.37	**.63**	1.37
3rd	**4,782**	10,146	**285**	1,693	**285**	1,693	**.07**	.44	**.07**	.44
4th	**6,300**	11,570	**(663)**	1,433	**(663)**	1,433	**(.17)**	.37	**(.17)**	.37
Total	**$44,917**	$56,284	**$6,422**	$12,375	**$7,826**	$12,375	**$1.65**	$3.53	**$2.01**	$3.53

(1) Gross Profit represents net sales less those costs directly related to the manufacturing process (i.e. labor, and overhead costs consumed within the factory).

(2) Due to the sale of the Common Shares (See Note J), average common shares outstanding for the year differed from the average common shares outstanding for each quarterly period. Earnings per common share for each period is computed by dividing total net income by the period's average common shares outstanding. As a result, the sum of earnings per common share for the individual quarters will not equal the per share amount for the year. The additional shares caused earnings per share to increase by a smaller percentage than total net income.

(3) Net income for the third quarter ended September 30, 1984 and for the year ended December 31, 1984 reflects the reversal of $920,000, or $.24 per common share, (after deductions of expenses relating to employee fringe benefits) of deferred taxes provided in prior years for the company's export sales through its Domestic International Sales Corporation (DISC).

The company changed its method of accounting for investment tax credit effective January 1, 1984. The cumulative effect of the accounting change increased 1984 first quarter earnings per common share by $.36. Other than the cumulative effect, there was no material impact on net income and earnings per common share in any quarter of 1984.

Refer to the Financial Statements and Management's Discussion and Analysis for further explanation.

Common Stock: Market and Dividend Information

Quarter	1984 Price Range		1984 Dividends Paid	1983 Price Range		1983 Dividends Paid
	High	Low		High	Low	
1st	24 5/8	20 3/8	$ .30	$23 3/4	$20	$ .30
2nd	23 3/8	21 1/8	.30	30 1/2	23 1/4	.30
3rd	23 3/4	20	.30	31 1/4	26 1/8	.30
4th	21 5/8	18 3/8	.30	29 3/8	22	.30
Total	24 5/8	18 3/8	$1.20	$31 1/4	$20	$1.20

The most restrictive provisions of the company's long-term debt agreements place certain restrictions (which do not currently limit any existing or presently contemplated company policies) on the payment of dividends and the purchase or redemption of the company's Common Shares.

STATEMENT OF FINANCIAL POSITION

	December 31	
	1984	1983
ASSETS		
Current Assets		
Cash	$ 1,424,761	$ 1,318,101
Trade accounts receivable, less allowance of $300,000	28,339,695	41,974,966
Other accounts receivable	501,387	764,285
Inventories	123,360,661	95,673,256
Company Common Shares acquired for employees' stock plans, at cost	767,737	777,518
Prepaid expenses	796,138	1,142,561
Deferred federal income tax benefits	1,163,467	1,132,287
Refundable federal income taxes	1,584,413	—
Total Current Assets	157,938,259	142,782,974
Property, Plant and Equipment		
Land	758,122	708,121
Buildings	31,054,300	27,619,109
Machinery and equipment	53,154,907	47,477,011
Allowances for depreciation and amortization (deduction)	(34,172,400)	(31,025,526)
	50,794,929	44,778,715
Deferred Charges, Investments and Other Assets	1,044,177	1,283,642
	$209,777,365	$188,845,331

(continued)

Murray Ohio Manufacturing Company

STATEMENT OF FINANCIAL POSITION (continued)

	December 31	
	1984	1983
LIABILITIES AND SHAREHOLDERS' EQUITY		
Current Liabilities		
Notes payable to banks	**$ 32,348,675**	$1,190,454
Accounts payable and other liabilities	**24,015,784**	25,459,837
Reserves for product warranty and product liability	**1,400,000**	1,300,000
Accrued payroll, commissions, and other compensation	**8,722,810**	12,803,699
Accrued interest, payroll taxes and other taxes	**1,387,602**	1,494,495
Federal and state income taxes	**444,231**	2,831,203
Portion of long-term debt due within one year	**3,076,075**	3,061,075
Total Current Liabilities	**71,395,177**	48,140,763
Long-Term Debt—less portion shown as current liability		
Notes payable to insurance companies:		
10 1/4% notes	**2,075,000**	2,400,000
9 1/4% notes	**16,000,000**	18,000,000
8% notes	**1,750,000**	2,000,000
6 1/4% notes	**750,000**	1,125,000
Other notes payable	**93,225**	84,300
Lease obligations	**2,310,000**	2,405,000
	22,978,225	26,014,300
Deferred Credits		
Investment tax credit	**—**	2,121,877
Obligations under deferred compensation plans and other deferred credits	**705,685**	747,427
Deferred federal income taxes	**1,977,055**	2,452,554
	2,682,740	5,321,858
Shareholders' Equity		
Serial Preferred Shares, no par value: Authorized 500,000 shares; issued— none		
Common Shares, par value $2.50 a share: Authorized 8,000,000 shares; Issued—3,904,565 shares in 1984 and 1983	**9,761,413**	9,761,413
Additional paid-in capital	**42,292,504**	42,804,155
Retained earnings	**60,848,757**	57,672,939
	112,902,674	110,238,507
Less cost of Common Shares held in treasury (7,895 shares in 1984 and 30,817 shares in 1983)	**(181,451)**	(870,097)
	112,721,223	109,368,410
	$209,777,365	$188,845,331

See notes to financial statements.

STATEMENT OF INCOME

	Year Ended December 31		
	1984	1983	1982
Net sales	$383,589,10 5	$386,493,993	$288,642,358
Deductions from (additions to) income			
Cost of product sold (exclusive of depreciation and amortization)	335,374,269	327,134,491	245,394,295
Provision for depreciation and amortization	3,635,096	3,361,666	3,253,897
Selling, general and administrative expenses	30,941,548	30,070,404	23,729,181
Interest on long-term debt	2,438,759	2,627,100	2,711,077
Interest on short-term borrowings	2,250,717	1,709,123	4,136,422
Interest income	(180,842)	(936,412)	(12,165)
	374,459,547	363,966,372	279,212,707
Income before income taxes	9,129,558	22,527,621	9,429,651
Federal and state income taxes	3,628,000	10,153,000	4,337,000
Reversal of deferred taxes	(920,000)	—	—
Net income taxes	2,708,000	10,153,000	4,337,000
Income before cumulative effect of change in accounting principle	6,421,558	12,374,621	5,092,651
Cumulative effect of change in accounting principle for investment tax credit	1,404,000	—	—
Net income	7,825,558	12,374,621	5,092,651
Earnings per common share:			
Before cumulative effect of change in accounting principle	**$1.65**	$3.53	$1.63
Cumulative effect of change in accounting principle for investment tax credit	**.36**	—	—
Earnings per common share	**$2.01**	$3.53	$1.63
Pro forma based on revised method of accounting for investment tax credit, applied respectively:			
Net income	$ 6,421,55 8	$12,520,798	$5,184,024
Earnings per common share	**$1.65**	$3.57	$1.66
Average common shares outstanding	3,889,345	3,505,567	3,115,750
Retained earnings at beginning of year	$ 57,672,93 9	$ 49,417,310	$ 48,026,124
Add:			
Net income	7,825,558	12,374,621	5,092,651
Deduct:			
Cash dividends paid, $1.20 per common share each year	4,649,740	4,118,992	3,701,465
Retained earnings at end of year	**$60,848,757**	$57,672,939	$49,417,310

See notes to financial statements.

Murray Ohio Manufacturing Company

Murray Ohio Manufacturing Company

STATEMENT OF CHANGES IN WORKING CAPITAL

	Year Ended December 31		
	1984	1983	1982
Source of working capital			
From operations:			
Net income	**$ 7,825,558**	$ 12,374,621	$ 5,092,651
Non-cash charges (credits):			
Cumulative effect of change in accounting principle for investment tax credit	**(1,404,000)**	—	—
Provision for depreciation and amortization	**3,635,096**	3,361,666	3,253,897
Deferred income taxes, non-current	**(118,474)**	1,364,331	1,782,871
Other	**88,084**	243,269	97,787
Total from operations	**10,026,264**	17,343,887	10,227,206
Net book value of property, plant and equipment disposals	**1,226,924**	351,550	115,337
Decrease (increase) in investments	**239,735**	(15,711)	51,496
Increase in long-term debt	**40,000**	—	—
Issuance of common stock	**—**	21,270,179	603,205
Tax benefits for non-qualified stock options exercised	**308,105**	—	—
Treasury shares reissued under stock option plans	**688,646**	—	—
Other	**37,675**	15,907	—
	12,567,349	38,965,812	10,997,244
Application of working capital			
Additions to property, plant and equipment	**10,878,234**	5,862,985	6,277,156
Decrease in long-term debt	**3,076,075**	3,061,075	1,056,075
Cash dividends	**4,649,740**	4,118,992	3,701,465
Stock options exercised from repurchased stock	**181,202**	71,445	—
Stock options exercised from treasury shares	**668,407**	—	—
Treasury shares acquired	**—**	870,097	—
Reclassification of deferred investment tax credit	**717,877**	—	—
Reclassification of deferred taxes	**357,025**	—	—
Other	**137,918**	123,698	123,351
	20,666,478	14,108,292	11,158,047
Increase (decrease) in working capital	**(8,099,129)**	24,857,520	(160,803)
Working capital at beginning of year	**94,642,211**	69,784,691	69,945,494
Working capital at end of year	**$86,543,082**	$94,642,211	$69,784,691

STATEMENT OF CHANGES IN WORKING CAPITAL (continued)

	Year Ended December 31		
	1984	1983	1982
Changes in components of working capital			
Increase (decrease) in working capital assets:			
Cash	**$106,660**	$(134,612)	$(148,491)
Accounts receivable	**(13,898,169)**	16,175,577	3,312,330
Inventories	**27,687,405**	(723,170)	(8,896,653)
Refundable federal income taxes	**1,584,413**	—	—
Other	**(325,024)**	(357,151)	1,257,160
	15,155,285	14,960,644	(4,475,654)
Increase (decrease) in working capital liabilities:			
Notes payable to banks	**31,158,221**	(27,104,946)	1,748,236
Accounts payable and other liabilities	**(1,444,053)**	6,708,503	(1,366,321)
Reserves for product warranty and product liability	**100,000**	200,000	—
Accrued payroll, commissions, and other compensation	**(4,080,889)**	6,239,607	(3,481,353)
Accrued interest, payroll taxes, and other taxes	**(106,893)**	126,068	(500,166)
Federal and state income taxes	**(2,386,972)**	1,928,892	(725,247)
Portion of long-term debt due within one year	**15,000**	2,005,000	10,000
	23,254,414	(9,896,876)	(4,314,851)
Increase (decrease) in working capital	**$(8,099,129)**	$24,857,520	$(160,803)

See notes to financial statements.

NOTES TO FINANCIAL STATEMENTS

Note A—Accounting Policies

The accounting policies that affect the more significant elements of the company's financial statements are summarized below. Certain reclassifications have been made in the financial statements to conform to the 1984 presentation.

Inventories—Inventories are stated at the lower of cost (last-in, first-out method) or market. The company adjusts the carrying value on a current basis for potential losses from obsolete or slow-moving inventories.

Property, Plant and Equipment—Property, plant and equipment are carried at cost. The company provides for depreciation of property, plant and equipment on annual rates, applied generally by the straight-line method, designed to amortize the cost of the respective assets over the period of their esti-

mated useful lives (buildings—20 to 40 years; machinery and equipment—15 years). Structural die costs are capitalized and amortized up to 3 years. When properties are disposed of, the related costs and accumulated depreciation are removed from the accounts at the time of disposal, and the resulting gain or loss is reflected in income.

Product Warranty and Product Liability—These costs are expensed in the year in which they are incurred. The related reserves are reviewed at each year end for reasonableness of possible future costs applicable to the current year's products.

Federal Income Taxes—Deferred taxes are provided with respect to timing differences resulting from those items for which the period of reporting for income tax purposes is different from the period of reporting for financial statement purposes. Effective for 1984, the company adopted the flow-through method of accounting for investment tax credits. In prior years investment credit had been

Murray Ohio Manufacturing Company

amortized over a ten-year period for financial reporting, but taken for the full amount of the credit in the year in which the credits were available for tax purposes.

Earnings per Common Share—Earnings per Common Share is calculated by dividing net income by the weighted average number of Common Shares outstanding during the year. The only Common Share equivalents are stock options which have no material dilutive effect on earnings per common share.

Note B—Federal and State Income Taxes

Federal income tax returns filed by the company have been examined and approved by the Internal Revenue Service through the year ended December 31, 1979.

The provision for federal and state income taxes is composed of the following:

	1984	1983	1982
Federal income tax currently payable:			
Gross	$3,405,740	$ 8,866,388	$2,409,611
Investment and other credits	(976,220)	(847,365)	(451,788)
Net	2,429,520	8,019,023	1,957,823
Reversal of DISC deferred taxes	(920,000)	—	—
State income tax currently payable	502,150	1,002,000	325,000
Deferred federal income tax	696,330*	1,131,977*	2,054,177*
	$2,708,000	$10,153,000	$4,337,000

*Accelerated depreciation methods resulted in $1,027,943, $976,510 and $820,609 of deferred tax for the years 1984, 1983 and 1982, respectively. Tool and die amortization methods resulted in deferred tax of $365,811 for 1984. The DISC resulted in $406,275 of deferred tax in 1982.

Reconciliation of U.S. statutory tax rate to effective rate:

	1984
Statutory tax rate	46.0%
Investment tax credits (net of recapture)	(6.0)
PAYSOP tax credit	(4.1)
State income taxes (net of federal tax benefit)	3.0
Other (net)	.8
Subtotal	39.7
Reversal of DISC deferred taxes	(10.0)
Effective tax rate	29.7)

The effective tax rate for 1983 and 1982 was not significantly different from the statutory rate.

Net income for the third quarter ended September 30, 1984 and for the year ended December 31, 1984 reflects the reversal of $920,000, or $.24 per common share, (after deductions of expenses relating to employee fringe benefits and related tax effects) of deferred taxes provided in prior years for the company's export sales through its Domestic International Sales Corporation (DISC). As a result of tax legislation enacted in 1984, the potential payment of these taxes has been eliminated. In accordance with a pronouncement of the Financial Accounting Standards Board, the entire reversal is reflected in the third quarter results.

Note C—Accounting Change (Investment Tax Credit)

Effective January 1, 1984, the company changed to the flow-through method of accounting for investment tax credits. The deferred method had been used in prior years. The change was made to conform to predominant U.S. industry practice. The flow-through method includes these credits in income in the year earned, while the deferred method amortized the credits over a ten-year period. This change in accounting method (after deductions of expenses relating to fringe benefits and related tax effects) increased 1984 net income by approximately $103,000 for credits earned during the year, and by $1,404,000 for the cumulative effect of the change; earnings per common share was increased by $.03 and $.36, respectively. Pro forma net income and earnings per common share amounts reflecting retroactive application of this change are shown on the Statement of Income.

Note D—Long-Term Debt

The company negotiated long-term loans of $6,000,000 at 6¼% annual interest during 1967, $5,000,000 at 8% during 1972, $5,000,000 at 10¼% during 1975, and $20,000,000 at 9¼% during 1978, with groups of insurance companies. Under the provisions of the loan agreements, the company is required to maintain current assets of not less than 150% of current liabilities.

The 6¼% notes mature in equal annual installments from September 1972 to September 1987. The 8% notes mature in equal annual installments from December 1973 to December 1992. The 10¼% notes mature in equal annual installments from April 1977 to April 1991. The 9¼% notes mature in equal annual installments from June 1984 to June 1993.

Capitalized Lease Agreements—During 1971 and 1978, the company entered into lease obligations with the Industrial Development Board of the Town of Franklin, Tennessee, for the lease of its office building and an addition thereto. The lease obligation, in an original amount of $1,600,000, will be repaid over a twenty-year term ending in 1991. The second lease obligation, also in the amount of $1,600,000, will be repaid in total in 1998. The company will own the buildings at the expiration of the lease, and has the option to purchase the underlying land at its market value after July 31, 1992.

Future maturities of long-term debt are as follows:

	Notes	Lease Obligations	Total
1985	$2,981,075	$95,000	$3,076,075
1986	2,981,075	100,000	3,081,075
1987	2,981,075	105,000	3,086,075
1988	2,606,075	115,000	2,721,075
1989	2,575,000	120,000	2,695,000
1990 and later	9,525,000	1,870,000	11,395,000

Rental expense and other future lease commitments are not considered to be material.

In early 1985, the company entered into a lease obligation with the Industrial Development Board of the City of Lawrenceburg, Tennessee, for the lease of environmental control facilities at its factory.

This lease obligation, in an original amount of $2,500,000, will be repaid over a fifteen-year term ending in 2000. The bondholder has the option to redeem the bonds after the tenth year. The company will own the facility upon the redemption of the bonds. This lease obligation is not included in the above maturity schedule.

Note E—Company Stock Plans

Eligible employees may contribute up to 5% of their base compensation to the company's stock purchase plan. The company may contribute an additional 50% of the employees' contributions. The company made such contributions for portions of 1982 and 1983, and for all of 1984. At December 31, 1984, 1,092 of the 2,220 employees eligible to participate in this plan were participants. There were 35,669 and 37,357 Common Shares held for this purpose at December 31, 1984 and 1983, respectively.

Unissued Common Shares of the company are reserved for issuance under stock option plans authorized by the shareholders during 1969, 1973, 1979 and 1984. The terms of the plans provide that qualified or non-qualified options may be issued to key employees, including officers, of the company at a price not less than the market value of the shares at the date of grant. The options generally become exercisable one year from the date of grant ratably over the succeeding four years and expire not later than ten years from the date of grant. The qualified options must be exercised in order of grant dates. The company makes no charges to income in connection with these options.

A summary of option activity follows.

Options	Shares	Option Prices
Outstanding January 1, 1984	283,982	$9.33 – 28.00
Exercised during 1984	(65,237)	$9.33 – 12.25
Expired during 1984	(9,422)	$11.50 – 28.00
Outstanding December 31, 1984	209,323	$9.33– 28.00

Options	Shares	Option Prices
Exercisable:		
December 31, 1984	167,193	
December 31, 1983	204,107	
December 31, 1982	190,731	
Exercised during 1983	8,374	$9.33 – 20.88
Exercised during 1982	-0-	

There were 513,369 and 203,947 unoptioned shares at December 31, 1984 and 1983, respectively.

Stock appreciation rights may be granted in tandem with options granted under the company's stock option plans. The amounts recorded each year by the company as income or expense attributable to these stock appreciation rights are insignificant.

The company has maintained since 1970 a Contingent Supplemental Retirement Benefit Plan pursuant to which additional retirement benefits may be awarded on an annual basis in amounts and to key employees of the company as designated by the Compensation Committee of the Board of Directors. Payment of such benefits is contingent upon certain employment conditions.

Note F—Pension Plans

The company has noncontributory pension plans which cover substantially all of its employees. The company makes annual contributions to the plans equal to the amounts accrued for pension expense in the prior year.

The total pension expense was $1,654,100, $2,417,400 and $2,552,900 for 1984, 1983 and 1982, respectively. The decreases in pension expense have resulted principally from the increased assumed rate of return and changes in the employment levels. The company's consulting actuary has estimated certain information for the 1984 and 1983 plan years as follows:

	1984	1983
Date of actuarial valuation:		
Hourly Plan	January 1, 1984	January 1, 1983
Salary Plan	December 1, 1983	December 1, 1982
Net assets available for plan benefits	$47,151,444	$41,586,931
Actuarial present value of plan benefits:		
Vested	27,463,800	27,411,600
Non-Vested	4,496,200	4,362,600
Assumed rate of return*:		
Hourly Plan	8.0%	7.0%
Salary Plan	8.5%	7.0%

Used in determining the actuarial present value of plan benefits, which would have been approximately $5,900,000 higher had the rate remained at 7%. Actual plan benefits were not affected.

In addition to providing pension benefits, the company provided certain health care and life insurance benefits for retired employees and their dependents. Substantially all of the company's employees who retire under the company's retirement plans may become eligible for these benefits. The cost of retiree health care and life insurance benefits is recognized as an expense as incurred. For 1984, these costs totaled approximately $261,000.

Note G—Short-Term Credit Arrangements

Under lines of credit arrangements for short-term debt with eleven financial institutions, the company may borrow up to $111,100,000 on such terms as may be mutually agreeable. These arrangements do not have termination dates but are reviewed annually for renewal. At December 31, 1984, the unused portion of the credit lines was $78,751,325.

Under various informal and unrestricted arrangements with the financial institutions, compensating balances are maintained at varying terms against credit lines and related borrowings. During 1984, such compensating balances averaged approximately $2,830,000 and were satisfied substantially by float.

Note I—Business Segment Information

The components of revenue, operating profit and other data by business segments are set forth within the following table for the years ended:

December 31, 1984	Power Mowers and Accessories	Bicycles and Accessories	Other Products	Total
Net Sales	$236,421,047	$147,079,185	$88,873	$383,589,105
Operating Profit (loss)	24,533,300	3,352,581	(27,349)	27,858,532
General and Administrative Expense (1)	8,721,454	5,316,076	1,968	14,039,498
Interest (2)	3,222,125	1,467,173	178	4,689,476
Income (Loss) Before Taxes	$12,589,721	$(3,430,668)	$(29,495)	$9,129,558
Identifiable Assets (3)	$119,534,386	$49,353,639	$54,766	$168,942,791
General Corporate Assets				40,834,574
				$209,777,365
Depreciation and Amortization Expense	$1,797,348	$1,613,597	$-0-	$3,410,945
General Depreciation Expense				224,151
				$3,635,096
Identifiable Capital Expenditures	$5,792,543	$4,246,449	$-0-	$10,038,992
General Capital Expenditures				839,242
				$10,878,234
December 31, 1983				
Net Sales	$205,036,387	$181,377,604	$80,002	$386,493,993
Operating Profit (Loss)	25,057,921	12,000,318	(4,639)	37,053,600
General and Administrative Expense (1)	6,505,761	3,682,691	1,304	10,189,756
Interest (2)	2,595,403	1,740,577	243	4,336,223
Income (Loss) Before Taxes	$15,956,757	$6,577,050	$(6,186)	$22,527,621
Identifiable Assets (3)	$84,424,799	$51,061,136	$305,592	$135,791,527
General Corporate Assets				53,053,804
				$188,845,331
Depreciation and Amortization Expense	$1,632,805	$1,537,759	$4,027	$3,174,591
General Depreciation Expense				187,075
				$3,361,666
Identifiable Capital Expenditures	$2,682,958	$2,954,450	$-0-	$5,637,408
General Capital Expenditures				225,577
				$5,862,985
December 31, 1982				
Net Sales	$155,415,363	$133,138,347	$88,648	$288,642,358
Operating Profit (Loss)	18,603,595	7,086,836	(230,795)	25,459,636
General and Administrative Expense (1)	5,815,558	3,365,070	1,858	9,182,486
Interest (2)	4,577,197	2,269,850	452	6,847,499
Income (Loss) Before Taxes	$8,210,840	$1,451,916	$(233,105)	$9,429,651
Identifiable Assets (3)	$94,912,121	$39,142,707	$348,421	$134,403,249
General Corporate Assets				37,329,209
				$171,732,458

(continued)

December 31, 1984	Power Mowers and Accessories	Bicycles and Accessories	Other Products	Total
Depreciation and Amortization Expense	$1,643,064	$1,426,993	$3,811	$3,073,868
General Depreciation Expense				180,029
				$3,253,897
Identifiable Capital Expenditures	$2,099,488	$4,115,209	$-0-	$6,214,697
General Capital Expenditures				62,459
				$6,277,156

(1)General and administrative expenses were directly allocated by segment where reasonable bases existed with the remainder of these expenses allocated based upon the ration of the segment's net sales to total net sales. Interest income, receipts from an antitrust settlement and losses on capital disposals are included in general and administrative expenses. The combination of these items increased general and administrative expenses by $806,000 in 1984, while the same items decreased this category by $1,466,000 in 1983, resulting in $2,272,000 of the total change in general and administrative expenses between the two years. The balance of the increase was composed of a number of different items. The above mentioned items were insignificant in 1982.

(2)Interest expense was partially allocated using the ratio of the segment's identifiable assets to total assets with the portion of interest related to general assets allocated based upon the ratio of the segment's net sales to total net sales.

(3)Identifiable assets by segment includes both assets directly identified with those operations including finished and in-process inventories and an allocable share of jointly used assets. General assets consist of cash, receivables and other unallocable assets.

Of the company's total revenue, its three largest customers provided $69 million, $43 million and $43 million, respectively in 1984, while one customer provided $79 million and $68 million in 1983 and 1982, respectively, from purchases of both power mowers and bicycles.

Note J—Change in Capital Accounts

A summary of changes in capital accounts for 1984, 1983 and 1982 follows.

	Common Shares Outstanding		Additional Paid-In Capital	Treasury Shares
	Number	Amount		
Balance at January 1, 1982	3,099,527	$7,748,818	$22,938,871	—
Stock issued to Stock Purchase Plan	35,038	87,595	515,610	
Credit attributable to deferred compensation			33,132	
Balance at December 31, 1982	3,134,565	7,836,413	23,487,613	—
Stock options exercised from repurchased stock			(71,445)	
Additional common stock issued less cost of issue	770,000	1,925,000	19,345,179	
				(870,097)
Treasury shares acquired	(30,817)			
Credit attributable to deferred compensation			42,808	
				(870,097)
Balance at December 31, 1983	3,873,748	9,761,413	42,804,155	
Stock options exercised from repurchased stock			(181,202)	
Treasury shares reissued under stock options plans	22,922		(668,407)	688,646
Tax benefits of non-qualified stock options exercised			308,105	
Credit attributable to deferred compensation			29,853	
				(181,451)
Balance at December 31, 1984	3,896,670	$9,761,413	$42,292,504	

The company sold 770,000 Common Shares in a public offering during June 1983. The company's net proceeds from this sale totaled $21,270,179. Had these shares been issued at the beginning of 1983 and the proceeds applied to short-term debt at that time, earnings per common share for 1983 would have been $3.31 as compared to the reported amount of $3.53.

Note K—Inventories and Cost of Sales

The inventory components are as follows:

	1984	1983
Finished and in-process products	$121,931,069	$90,822,673
Raw materials	6,695,859	8,859,494
Manufacturing supplies	1,582,733	1,392,089
	130,209,661	101,074,256
Less allowance to reduce carrying value to LIFO basis	(6,849,000)	(5,401,000)
Inventory at LIFO	$123,360,661	$95,673,256

During 1982, certain inventory quantities were reduced, resulting in a liquidation of LIFO quantities carried at the cost prevailing in the prior year. The effect was to increase 1982 net profit by approximately $130,000.

Note L—Non-Monetary Transactions

During 1983 and 1982 the company exchanged certain inventory for advertising services to be received. These transactions resulted in no significant gain or loss. At December 31, 1984, 1983 and 1982, the unused amounts of $577,000, $935,000 and $1,321,000, respectively, were classified as prepaid expenses.

Note M—Miscellaneous Receipts and Charges

Selling, general and administrative expenses include miscellaneous receipts and charges which normally are insignificant. However, in the second quarter of 1984 and the first quarter of 1983 the company received approximately $85,000 and $628,000, respectively, for distributions from a class action antitrust settlement involving certain members of the corrugated container industry. In the fourth quarter of 1984, the company recorded an expense of $998,000 due to the write-off of an inoperative machine.

Murray Ohio Manufacturing Company

REPORTS OF INDEPENDENT ACCOUNTANTS AND MANAGEMENT

Report of Independent Accountants

Board of Directors and Shareholders
The Murray Ohio Manufacturing Company
Brentwood, Tennessee

We have examined the statement of financial position of The Murray Ohio Manufacturing Company as of December 31, 1984 and 1983, and the related statement of income, retained earnings and changes in working capital for each of the three years in the period ended December 31, 1984. Our examinations were made in accordance with generally accepted auditing standards and, accordingly, included such tests of the accounting records and such other auditing procedures as we considered necessary in the circumstances.

In our opinion, the financial statements referred to above present fairly the financial position of The Murray Ohio Manufacturing Company at December 31, 1984 and 1983, and the results of its operations and changes in working capital for each of the three years in the period ended December 31, 1984, in conformity with generally accepted accounting principles applied on a consistent basis, except for the change, with which we concur, in the method of accounting for investment tax credits as described in Note C of Notes to Financial Statements.

Ernst and Whinney
Nashville, Tennessee
January 28, 1985

Report of Management

The management of The Murray Ohio Manufacturing Company is responsible for the integrity of all information and representation contained in the financial statements and other sections of this Annual Report. The Company's financial statements are based on generally accepted accounting principles and as such include amounts based on management's judgment and estimates.

The company has a system of internal accounting controls which is designed to provide reasonable assurance that assets are safeguarded, transactions are executed in accordance with management's authorization and financial records are reliable as a basis for preparation of financial statements. The system includes the selection and training of qualified personnel, an organizational structure which permits the delegation of authority and responsibility, the establishing and disseminating of accounting and business policies and procedures and an extensive internal audit program. There are limits inherent in all systems of internal control and a recognition that the cost of such systems should not exceed the benefits to be derived. We believe the company's systems provide this appropriate balance.

The company's independent accountants, Ernst & Whinney, have examined the financial statements. As independent accountants, they also provide an objective review of management's discharge of its responsibility to report operating results and financial condition. They obtain and maintain an understanding of the company's systems and procedures and perform such tests and other procedures, including tests of the internal accounting controls, as they deem necessary to enable them to express an opinion on the fairness of the financial statements.

The Board of Directors pursues its oversight role for the financial statements through its Audit Committee composed of three outside directors. The Audit Committee meets as necessary with management, the internal auditors and the independent accountants. The independent accountants and internal auditors have free access to the Audit Committee without the presence of management representatives to discuss internal accounting controls, auditing and financial reporting matters.

MANAGEMENT'S DISCUSSION AND ANALYSIS OF THE SUMMARY OF OPERATIONS

Sales for 1984 remained basically constant with 1983 as a result of a 15% increase in power mower sales which represented 62% of total sales and a 19% decrease in bicycle sales which represented the remaining 38% of total sales. In 1983 power mower sales represented 53% and bicycle sales represented 47% of total sales. The increase in 1984 power mower sales was attributable to increased volume. The company's bicycle pricing, production levels and sales have been adversely affected by increased bicycle imports and heightened domestic bicycle competition. Net income as a percentage of sales decreased to 2.0% in 1984 from 3.2% in 1983.

Net income for 1984 was down 37% reflecting narrower operating margins than were experienced in 1983 and 1982 for power mowers and especially bicycles. Operating profit as a percentage of sales for power mowers was 10.4%, 12.2% and 12.0% for 1984, 1983 and 1982, respectively. Bicycle operating profit as a percentage of sales was 2.3%, 6.6% and 5.3% for 1984, 1983 and 1982, respectively. Increased domestic competition in both product lines contributed to the narrower operating margins. However, the increasing volume of imports, principally from Taiwan, had an added impact upon the bicycle operating profit for 1984. The decrease in earnings per common share was greater than the corresponding decrease in net income for 1983 to 1984 due to the increase in the average number of common shares outstanding resulting from the sale of additional common shares in June 1983.

Net income for 1984 reflects the reversal of $920,000, or $.24 per common share (after deductions of expenses relating to employee fringe benefits and related tax effects), of deferred taxes provided in prior years for the company's export sales through its Domestic International Sales Corporation (DISC). As a result of tax legislation enacted in 1984, the liability for potential payment of these taxes has been eliminated. For further explanation refer to Note B of Notes to Financial Statements.

Effective January 1, 1984, the company changed to the flow-through method of accounting for investment tax credits. The deferred method had been used in prior years. This change in accounting method (after deductions of expenses relating to employee fringe benefits and related tax effects) increased 1984 net income by approximately $103,000 ($.03 per common share) for credits earned during the year, and by approximately $1,404,000 ($.36 per common share) for the cumulative effect of the change. For further information refer to the Statement of Income and Note C of Notes to Financial Statements.

The company experienced an exceptional year in both sales and net income for 1983. The sales and net income increases in 1983 from 1982 were attributable primarily to increased sales volume resulting from the general improvement in the economy. Both the bicycle and power mower product lines contributed to the increased sales and net income in 1983. Net income as a percentage of sales increased to 3.2% in 1983 from 1.8% in 1982.

Selling, general and administrative expenses for 1984 remained relatively constant compared to 1983. Selling, general and administrative expenses for 1984 and 1983 were reduced by approximately $85,000 and $628,000, respectively, for distributions received from a class action antitrust settlement involving certain members of the corrugated container industry. In 1984 an expense of $998,000 was recorded due to the write-off of an inoperative machine. Increased advertising expenditures along with increased costs associated with increased sales caused the company's 1983 selling, general and administrative expenses to increase $6.3 million (26.7%) from 1982.

Interest expense on short-term borrowings reflects an increase for 1984 as compared to 1983 as a result of higher levels of average borrowing at higher interest rates. Short-term borrowings increased in 1984 from 1983 due to higher average inventory levels experienced during 1984 and the use of the proceeds from the common stock offering to repay short-term borrowings in 1983 as later discussed.

Inventories at December 31, 1984 are considerably higher than at December 31, 1983, primarily due to power mower inventory levels reflecting an expectation of increased orders for the 1985 riding mower lines. Notes payable have correspondingly increased due to the increased inventory levels.

Accounts receivable outstanding at year-end decreased in 1984 compared to 1983 primarily due to decreased sales experienced in the fourth quarter in 1984. Traditionally, sales in the last 45 days of the year cause receivables to be correspondingly higher.

Accrued payroll, commissions and other compensation decreased from $12.8 million in 1983 to $8.7 million in 1984. This decrease principally resulted from decreased net income, year-end employment levels and related employee fringe benefits.

The effective income tax rate of 29.7% was significantly lower that the effective rates of 45.1% for 1983 and 46% for 1982. The effective tax rate for 1984 differs from the statutory rate principally because of tax credits and the impact of the reversal of DISC taxes. The company continues to review, and adopt where appropriate, methods of tax accounting, all within tax regulations, which allow the company to defer payment of tax and thus increase its cash flow.

The company's business cycle imposes fluctuating demands on its cash flow, due to the temporary buildup of inventory in anticipation of, and receivables subsequent to, shipping during the peak seasonal periods. The company has in the past used lines of credit arrangements for short-term debt to meet its cash flow demands. These arrangements, the details of which are further discussed in Note G of Notes to Financial Statements, provide the company with immediate and continued sources of liquidity.

During June 1983, the company sold an additional 770,000 shares of Common Stock in a public offering at $29.25 per share. The net proceeds to the company, totaling approximately $21 million were used to repay outstanding short-term instruments pending application to the company's working capital requirements. Decreased interest expense on short-term borrowings and increased interest income for 1983 reflect the use of the proceeds from the sale of Common Stock.

In addition to cash flow and existing lines of credit, management believes that alternatives are available

Murray Ohio Manufacturing Company

to the company to meet future cash needs. These may include additional short-term debt, commercial paper, or equity securities. The company's strong debt to equity ratio should place it in a favorable position to issue new debt or equity securities. The company reviews these alternatives relative to current market and economic conditions on a continuing basis.

Capital expenditures for 1984 amounted to $10.9 million as compared to $5.9 million in 1983. Major expenditures included modern tube cutting equipment, robot welders, a computer aided design system and the initial phase of a state of the art press room. The company has budgeted $9.7 million for its 1985 capital expenditures. This budget is based on current economic conditions, and is subject to change in the event of significant changes in the

general economy and/or the company's performance. This budget includes projects for further modernization and automation of production processes, and for continued vertical integration. These projects are anticipated to be financed principally from working capital sources. In early 1985, the company entered into a 2.5 million Industrial Development Revenue Bond financing for environmental control facilities at its factory. Refer to Note D of Notes to Financial Statements for further information.

Virtually all costs and expenses are subject to normal inflationary pressures and the company is continually seeking ways to cope with its impact. The effects of inflation on the company's operations are summarized and discussed in Note H of Notes to Financial Statements.

Just two days after a sharp sell-off (following a stock analyst's rare 'sell' advisory in debut coverage of the firm), Olympic Financial Ltd.'s shares fell to a 20-month low in response to a debt-ratings downgrade by Moody's Investors Service. Olympic's senior debt was lowered a notch from B1, already below investment grade, to B2. (Subordinated notes were downgraded from B2 to B3). Moody's said it lowered the ratings of the auto-finance company because of the company's "continuing shift" into sub-prime lending and "increase in delinquencies and credit losses" from its non-performing car loans.

Olympic responded that it believes it is being penalized for the tarnished image of the auto-finance industry since a scandal erupted at Mercury Finance Co., one of its competitors. Mercury's president resigned Monday when the FBI sent in agents to look at accounting irregularities. 'What we're seeing is a domino impact here,' said Olympic's spokeswoman. 'The difference is that Olympic's accounting principles are solid.'[1]

COMPANY BACKGROUND

Founded in 1990 by Jeffrey C. Mack, Olympic Financial was a consumer finance company that purchased, securitized, and serviced consumer automobile loans originated by over 7,000 U.S. auto dealerships.

Mack, a commercial banker during the 1980s, saw a niche for an alternate source of auto financing to banks and automobile manufacturers. Banks had been unreliable financing sources for car dealerships for several reasons. First, banks entered and exited auto financing as their needs dictated and thus did not represent a steady financing alternative for dealers. Second, banks did not conduct business evenings, weekends, and holidays—the busiest times for dealers. Third, banks and auto makers loaned primarily to low credit risks and financed new cars only. Finally, banks historically extended credit based solely on the repossession value of the asset being financed.

Based on his observations, Mack decided there was an opportunity to provide financing to prospective car buyers characterized by quick turnaround times for loan approvals, operating hours that matched those of dealers and buyers, flexible loan terms, and invest-

Research Associate Sarayu Srinivasan prepared this case under the supervision of Professor Krishna Palepu as the basis for class discussion rather than to illustrate either effective or ineffective handling of an administrative situation. Copyright © 1997 by the President and Fellows of Harvard College. Harvard Business School case 9-197-081.

1. Adapted from J. Barshay's "Moody's Rating Sends Olympic Shares Down," The Star Tribune, February 7, 1997.

ment in the automobile buyer rather than the assets being purchased. The firm would look to make deals, not reject them. Borrowers did not need perfect or even good credit histories. Mack's firm, Olympic Financial, went public in 1992. In 1996 the firm's annual loan purchases totaled $2.7 billion. Exhibit 2 shows Olympic's 1996 financial statements.

Business and Marketing Strategy

Olympic's objective was to maximize the volume and profitability of loans it purchased. Dealers were crucial to fulfilling this goal, and the firm considered them primary customers. Providing dealers with reliable financing sources was a key imperative. Olympic financed both new and used car purchases. In 1996 71.3 percent of Olympic's loans bought used cars.

If a prospective buyer opted to finance a purchase through the dealer, the parties reviewed various financing options including Olympic. If chosen as the financing source, Olympic assessed the buyer's credit history, income sources, and creditworthiness by a proprietary credit scoring system, submitting a decision to the dealer usually within an hour of having received the credit application. If the loan terms were accepted, the buyer entered into an installment contract to make payments of principal and interest to the lender, constituting "purchase" of the loan from the dealer by Olympic. Olympic funded loan purchases through credit facilities and asset-backed commercial paper issues.

Olympic purchased and serviced loans through 17 regional buying centers in 14 states, and had a dealer network covering 38 states. Regional centers served as "hubs" implementing marketing and sales initiatives and servicing loans in the hub's region. Each hub served "spokes"—nearby new markets—extending its regional reach. Through its hub-and-spoke strategy Olympic acquired local knowledge of the region, its economy, and dealers, helping it make better informed credit decisions.

Purchased loans were either held by the company or were pooled together in large numbers to mitigate default risk. Pooled loans were then repackaged, guaranteed by specialty insurance firms, underwritten, and issued for sale as secured bonds. The process of consolidating and converting loans and other receivables into asset backed securities for sale on the open market was called securitization. After securitization Olympic was still responsible for servicing the loans.

Olympic targeted buyers with credit ratings that fell below grade A (perfect credit) but above grade D (high credit risks, subprime market) making up the prime and non-prime markets. In extending credit the firm did not require a down payment from the car buyer, but priced loans according to a tiered pricing system that classified buyers based on their credit characteristics as quantified by the firm's credit scoring system. Loans were marketed under two programs: Classic and Premier. Premier borrowers had stronger credit attributes and generally paid an annual percentage rate (APR) from 8 to 16 percent. Classic borrowers were higher credit risks. Classic loans were priced higher than Premiers, with APRs from 16 to 23 percent, to reflect the higher anticipated risk and loss. If the buyer defaulted, vehicles would be repossessed and resold through retail channels.

Income Generation

Olympic earned income from the purchase, securitization, and servicing of auto loans. The bulk of Olympic's income was derived primarily from the interest rate spreads, i.e., the differential between its lending rate and its borrowing rate.

When Olympic purchased loans from a dealer, the dealer received a commission for its role in the loan's origination. The commission was usually a portion of the APR the car buyer paid as the cost of credit. The balance was Olympic's "buy rate" for the loan. The difference between the APR and the interest rate at which Olympic funded operations was income.

Olympic funded loan purchases in two ways (see Exhibit 1). First, loans could be financed through the use of bank funds. Loans funded this way generated income from the net interest rate spread: the difference between interest charged on the bank loan and the APR received by the car buyer. Alternatively, the company could pool and securitize large volumes of purchased loans and then sell them to investors as asset-backed securities. Proceeds from the sale of the securities funded future loan purchases. Loans funded this way earned income from the gross interest rate spread—the difference between the securitization rate paid to bond holders and the APR paid by car buyers.

Gross interest spreads were larger than net interest spreads. Securitization of a multi-million-dollar loan portfolio obliged the portfolio to meet certain requirements including buyer underwriting, audits, and loss reserves. By securitizing receivables Olympic widened the interest spread on the sale of receivables because the cost of capital paid debt holders was lower than the cost of capital raised from banks. Thus, securitization was the preferred funding method for the company.

Income was also earned from loan servicing fees and loans pending securitization. Olympic continued to service and receive fees on loans sold to investors as securities. Loans awaiting securitization and held in portfolio by the firm generated income from net interest rate spread.

Monthly payments of loan principal and interest were collected and flowed through as payments to securities investors, credit facilities, and firm spread accounts. The firm calculated and maintained reserves to cover delinquency, defaults, and losses associated with its lending activities.

Accounting Practices

When auto loans were securitized, Olympic recorded a gain on the sale of the loans and established an asset called finance income receivable. Gain on sale was the present value of expected future cash flows from securitizations discounted at a market based rate. The gain on sale of securitizations was computed to reflect historical portfolio performance and disposal of repossessed vehicles. Gain on sale calculations also accounted for amounts due asset-backed investors and dealers (for loan originations), securitization costs, and estimated loan prepayments and losses.

Olympic Financial Ltd.

Finance income receivable included, in addition to gain on sale proceeds, uncollected accrued interest receivable on loans held for sale, interest earned on spread accounts related to securitization activities, and interest earned on previously discounted cash flows. This asset was decreased as cash flows were received from spread accounts. Loan servicing fee income, which did not constitute finance income receivable, was recognized as earned over the life of the securitization.

Olympic estimated loan prepayments, losses, and delinquencies based on industry norms, previous experience, and future expectations. Loan loss reserves were estimated forecasting losses expected over the life of the loan. This loss provision was netted against the calculated gain on sale amount for loans sold, and the related allowance became a part of the finance income receivable. Losses that resulted from repossession were charged against the allowances. As of December 1996 the company had set aside $95 million, or 2.51 percent of its servicing portfolio, as loss reserves. This was increased from the reserve level of $42.3 million, or 1.86 percent of the portfolio at December 1995.

Most cars repossessed by auto lenders were disposed of through wholesale methods such as auction. Olympic, however, resold repossessions through retail channels such as consignment used car dealers. Olympic chose retail markets because of the higher salvage values garnered and the opportunity to refinance the cars with new buyers. Retailing repossessions, however, meant higher levels of unsold inventory and investment in retail programs, constituting an occupation of capital.

Olympic in 1996

Olympic's total revenues grew from $108.7 million in 1995 to $213.4 million in 1996. Net income rose from $25.4 million in 1995 to $60.3 million in 1996. Gain on sale for 1996 was $115.7 million, servicing fee income $28.2 million, and net interest margin $62.9 million. Delinquencies rose from $30.2 million in 1995 to $100.1 million in 1996. Repossessions increased from 5,020 in 1995 to 14,403 in 1996. Net losses went from $10.3 million in 1995 to $29.9 million in 1996. The firm's portfolio had grown nearly 70 percent in 1996.

DEBT ISSUES.   In April 1995 the firm had issued Senior Term Notes totaling $145 million, callable after May 1, 1998, due in the year 2000. Senior Term Notes were unsecured and paid interest semi-annually. In March 1996 Olympic issued to the public a total principal amount of $30 million of 10.12 percent unsecured Subordinated Notes due 2001, gathering $29 million in proceeds from this debt issue. The company also issued Junior Subordinated Notes irregularly with maturities ranging from 30 days to ten years, and had an amount of $23.7 million outstanding at the end of 1996. At December 31, 1996, the firm had a total of $53.6 million Subordinated Notes outstanding.

CLASSIC PROGRAM.   In 1995 Olympic introduced the Classic program, targeting buyers whose credit histories fell just short of being subprime: the worst credit risks. The program addressed the tremendous growth of the blemished credit market, borrowers with spotty credit histories ranging from repeated tardy payments to outright bank-ruptcy, and the need for financing sources for this expanding population. This market in-cluded victims of illness and tragedy, laid-off workers, immigrants, and also swindlers, and it expected to continue experiencing rapid growth due to corporate restructurings and rising consumer debt. For the higher risk taken on, the firm charged higher interest rates, widening spreads. Classic loans retrieved an average APR of 18 percent.

DELINQUENCIES, DEFAULTS, AND LOSSES.   Total delinquencies (of more than 30 days) comprised 2.64 percent of the servicing portfolio in 1996, rising from 1.33 percent in 1995. Total losses amounted to .99 percent of the servicing portfolio in 1996, rising from .67 percent in 1995. The rise in these rates was attributed to the rapid growths of the Classic and financed repossession programs (both of which had higher delinquency and loss rates) and the maturing of the servicing portfolio's loans (that included a greater number of Classic loans) which were entering periods characterized by the highest prob-abilities of default and delinquencies (usually six to fourteen months from origination).

Classic loans and financed repossessions together made up 4.3 percent of the servic-ing portfolio but accounted for 20 percent of the delinquencies, charge-offs, and net losses for 1996. Financed repossession delinquencies alone were 13 percent, compared to the 1.95 percent overall loan delinquency rate. Losses for this group were running 3 percent as opposed to the overall loss rate of .87 percent.[2]

REPOSSESSIONS AND DISPOSAL.   While retailing repossessions allowed Olympic to recoup a greater amount of the value of the vehicles (approximately 30 percent more than through wholesale methods), industry followers expressed concerns over the firm's retailing strategy because it involved keeping inventory on the books, tied up crucial cash, and presented a problem if there was a downturn in the car market. Financing re-tailed repossessions presented the prospect that Olympic would be encouraged to lower credit standards, taking on bigger risks to get inventory off its books.

In 1996 nearly 70 percent of the firm's repossessions were resold through retail, with 90 percent of these refinanced by Olympic. Retail repossession loans comprised 2.56 percent of the total servicing portfolio ($96.9 million), a rise from $25.7 million (1.1 per-cent of the total portfolio) in 1995. Inventory levels swelled as a result of both growth and the firm's retail strategy of distributing repossessions through ten large retail lots. To increase inventory turnover the firm elected to change its retail strategy in 1996, termi-nating deals with large lots in favor of distribution through multiple smaller lots.

EXECUTIVE CHANGES.   In August 1996, Olympic's board voted to put the firm on the market in order to gain access to lower cost capital and earn higher credit ratings, a

Olympic Financial Ltd.

----

2. Jon Elsen, "Battle of Olympic Proportions Is Brewing," Mergers & Acquisitions Report, September 16, 1996, p. 1.

plan opposed by Jeffrey Mack, Olympic's founder, CEO, President, and Chairman. Unable to resolve the conflict, Mack resigned his posts. Olympic's stock rocketed from $15 to $25 the day news of the impending sale was publicized, confirming the board's instincts that the markets would embrace the idea. By December, however, the firm was still "for sale" and had not appointed a new CEO. Many industry observers felt that the firm was having problems managing its loan portfolio, and this had scared off potential buyers. Despite the turmoil and absence of a leader, Olympic doubled profits to $60.3 million in 1996.

INDUSTRY EVENTS, 1996–1997

The auto financing industry was worth $410 billion.[3] The industry segment catering to subprime borrowers was estimated to be worth $77 billion.[4] While the subprime auto finance industry was volatile, highly competitive, and fragmented, it boasted voracious growth, low barriers to entry, and was very profitable. Hundreds of firms had entered the industry and 25 subprime lenders had gone public since 1985. In order to grow in an increasingly competitive environment, firms lowered credit standards to widen shrinking margins and ignored their servicing capacity limits. By 1997 several of these lenders figured prominently in the news.

In January 1997 the subprime used-auto lender, Mercury Finance, after announcing 1996 profits of $120.7 million, disclosed it had inflated earnings $90 million since 1993, subsequently revising 1996 profit to $56.7 million, warranting an FBI search. The news was shocking as the firm had had low loss rates, high earnings, and good repayment patterns. Mercury was an industry pioneer, known for competent management and attention to detail, with $1.5 billion in outstanding loans, all held in portfolio. The firm's stock had split six times. When deceitful and poor accounting practices such as loan price padding and inadequate loss provisions were held culpable, the industry was stunned. When defaults had occurred, the firm had ignored the bad loans by issuing new ones, recording them settled. This short-term strategy postponed losses. Moody's downgraded Mercury's debt from P2 (prime investment grade rating) to NP (nonprime, noninvestment grade). Creditors withdrew credit, pushing Mercury to near bankruptcy and plunging its stock from $14.87 per share to $1.87 per share, losing 85 percent of its value, and going from a firm valued at $2.6 billion to $333 million in one day.

A day after Mercury's disclosure, Jayhawk Acceptance, a rapidly growing subprime lender, charged $15.5 million to 1996 accounts to cover losses for unrecoverable dealer advances, resulting in a $7.9 million net loss for 4Q1996. Jayhawk subsequently filed for bankruptcy protection for violating its credit agreements. (Revenues had totaled $16.1 million for 4Q1996. The 4Q1995 had revenues of $7.5 million, and a profit of $1.79 million.) Jayhawk purchased "D" grade used car loans from dealers at deep dis-

3. Carla Solberg, "Nonbanks Give Run for the Money," Minneapolis-St. Paul CityBusiness, August 2, 1996, p. 9.

4. J. Schmeltzer, "New Mercury Leader Probes for Answers," Chicago Tribune, February 9, 1997, p. 1.

counts, advancing dealers part of the loan principal. The rest of the principal was retained by Jayhawk to cover loan losses while loans were pooled, awaiting securitization. As cash flows were received, receipts were split between the dealer (80 percent) and Jayhawk (20 percent). The firm used scoring models to forecast default rates, approve loans, and compute dealer advances. Jayhawk stock had lost 17 percent of its value upon the news of Mercury, and now lost a further 55 percent closing at $3.62.

Cityscape Financial Corp. originated, purchased, securitized, and serviced subprime home equity mortgage loans. Debt-loaded consumers took out home equity loans for their low interest rates and tax deductibility. Cityscape originated loans from both banks and independent mortgage brokers. Cityscape and the brokers closely valued loans before purchase, because if appraisals were inaccurate the broker might be made to buy back the loan. By 1995 loan origination had doubled and the firm's delinquency rate was a low 4 percent. Revenues for the first 3Qs of 1996 were $125.5 million and net income $34.8 million versus 1995 same period revenues of $30.8 million and net income of $7.2 million. In September 1996 a scandal linking one the firm's advisors to a swindler and a 2Q earnings restatement (reclassing $5 million of acquisition restructuring expense as goodwill, and recording $17 million in deferred tax assets) sent the firm's shares down, speculation up, and short sellers eagerly increasing positions. Just days earlier Moody's had rated the firm's debt B1.

The impact of the recent industry developments was summed up by the *Financial Times*:

> *These incidents proved to be triggers for a sweeping loss of confidence in the entire sub-prime sector. Share prices of the main players fell by up to 30%, several suffered down-gradings of their credit from rating agencies, and there were huge sales of their bonds on the capital markets. A period of swift growth has, at least temporarily, been halted.*[5]

CONTROVERSY

Between 1996 and 1997 the debt rating agency Moody's announced a series of rating actions on Olympic's debt issues. Exhibit 3 shows a full set of the rating announcements. On May 1, 1996, Moody's had changed Olympic's long-term debt ratings outlook from stable to positive, reflecting the firm's stock issue that raised $148 million. Two months later Moody's confirmed the May outlook, upgrading Olympic's senior debt ratings from B2 to B1 and subordinated notes from B3 to B2.

By August 26, 1996, however, Moody's had placed Olympic's ratings on review, "direction uncertain," after the resignation of Mack as CEO and news that the firm was for sale. On January 24, 1997, Moody's confirmed B1 senior and B2 subordinated debt ratings, but with outlook negative due to concerns that included deteriorating portfolio

5. Adapted from J. Authers, "Used-Car, Bad-Loan Road to Riches: Or Ruin," *Financial Times, February. 13, 1997, p. 4.*

Olympic Financial Ltd.

performance, focus on higher risk loans, and repossession disposal methods. On February 6, 1997, just seven months after upgrading the company's ratings, Moody's lowered Olympic's senior notes from B1 to B2 and subordinated notes from B2 to B3. The agency again cited the firm's rising losses resulting from the rapid growth of its risky loan portfolio and its inability to effectively manage its disposal methods for repossessions.

Simultaneously, on February 6, an equity analyst initiated coverage of the firm with a rare sell rating, criticizing loss assumptions and retailing strategies. The report held that Olympic's most recent securitization losses had already (after only ten months) exceeded 2.5 percent, while the loss provision per securitization was only 1.88 percent. Further, the still scant 1.88 percent provision had only been in effect since the 4Q1996, upped from the previous level of 1.66 percent. The report claimed the firm had failed to properly provision for losses since 1995 and that the loss rate was rising rapidly. The report continued that the 8 percent discount rate used, computing gain on sale, inflated earnings, and was inappropriate, given that comparable firms used discount rates of 12 percent. Insofar as repossessions went, the report pointed out that standard auction caused an immediate, quantifiable loss, wiping the bad loan off the books, whereas retailing forced a quick sale capping losses, lowering portfolio credit quality and making way for greater future losses. The report concluded that so far fast growth had masked brewing problems, but that it was only a matter of time till the legacy of bad credit rose to the surface.[6]

Faced with the myriad of bad press, downgraded debt, and swooning stock, Olympic alleged it was penalized without cause. The firm denied it made subprime loans. It had recruited a new CEO at the end of January, renamed itself Arcadia Financial, confirmed it was not for sale, and doubled its 1996 profits. While the company did expect loss rates to rise, it attributed this partly to a rise in delinquencies nationwide.[7] In specific response to the rash of scandals plaguing the auto financing industry, Olympic/Arcadia said it would never release unaudited earnings figures as Mercury had.[8] The firm added that loan pool securitization amounted to a monthly audit, requiring careful and accurate bookkeeping. Olympic/Arcadia's new CEO, Richard Greenawalt, summed up[9]: "With the current turmoil in the markets concerning companies in the automobile finance business, we wanted to assure our shareholders that Olympic has completed its year-end audit process and publicly provided full information with respect to its business."

QUESTIONS

1. What is your assessment of the long-term potential of the subprime lending industry? What are the critical success factors for firms in this industry?

6. Steve Eisman, Report on Olympic Financial, Oppenheimer & Co., February 6, 1997.

7. Jill Barshay, "Olympic Gets New Name, CEO," Star Tribune, January 29, 1997.

8. Heather Timmons, "Sub-Prime Lenders: It Can't Happen To Us," American Banker, January 31, 1997, p. 24.

9. Reuters Financial Service, "Olympic Financial Completes Year End Audit," February 10, 1997.

2. List all the capital market intermediaries that play an important role in this industry. What role did they play in the rapid growth of this industry?
3. What is your assessment of Olympic's performance to date and its future performance?
4. What is your assessment of the performance of market intermediaries with respect to Olympic? What factors drive their performance?
5. What general lessons can we draw from this case about the role of intermediaries?

EXHIBIT 1
Olympic's Funding Strategy (Illustrative Rate Structure)

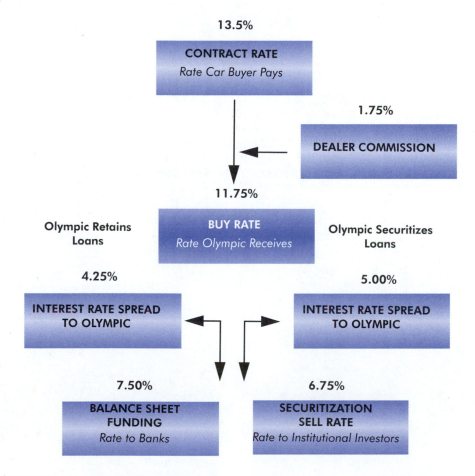

Source: Olympic Financial 1994 Annual Report.

Olympic Financial Ltd.

EXHIBIT 2

Olympic (Arcadia) Financial Ltd., 1996 Abridged Annual Report*

Hereafter Olympic Financial Ltd. shall be referred to as Arcadia Financial Ltd.

FINANCIAL HIGHLIGHTS

(thousands of dollars, except per share amounts)

For the Year	1996	1995	1994	1993	1992
Total revenue	$ 213,495	$ 108,732	$ 28,788	$ 11,884	$ 3,858
Net income (loss)[a]	60,316	29,317	4,185	1,395	(1,342)
Earnings (loss) per share[a]	1.65	1.11	0.17	0.11	(0.24)
Automobile loans purchased	2,750,553	2,052,413	743,256	305,823	97,819
Loan securitizations	2,787,412	1,933,525	712,211	336,077	79,759

At Year End	1996	1995	1994	1993	1992
Total assets	$ 778,320	$ 397,794	$219,288	$116,256	$ 81,167
Shareholders' equity	$ 393,093	$ 180,813	$ 60,862	$58,699	$ 30,072
Common book value per share	10.79	7.05	3.39	3.20	3.09
Return on average assets[a]	10.26%	9.50%	3.59%	1.41%	(2.21%)
Return on equity[a]	21.02%	24.26%	10.09%	3.14%	(9.50%)
Dealerships under contract	7,727	5,110	2,344	857	339
Servicing portfolio	$3,791,857	$2,267,107	$837,095	$316,933	$103,507

[a]Before extraordinary items

LETTER TO SHAREHOLDERS

Fellow Shareholders:

In 1996, the associates at Arcadia Financial met the challenges presented by the Company's growth to deliver another year of profitable performance This record profitability was achieved despite the distractions related to the possible sale of the Company. While we are pleased with our 1996 financial results, the year also brought into sharp focus areas of the business that must be strengthened to ensure profitable operations that produce attractive returns for our shareholders. These include clearer policies, improved processes, better training, tighter controls and stronger systems.

The industry of which Arcadia is a part—the independent auto finance industry—was in turmoil in early 1997. Problems at certain companies raised investor concerns about the industry as a whole. With respect to Arcadia, those concerns were misplaced. First, as a lender focusing on prime and nonprime rated borrowers, Arcadia is serving a market segment comprised of higher quality credit risks then the market served by the sub-prime lenders experiencing financial difficulties this year. Furthermore, our shareholders can be assured that Arcadia's relationships with its key sources of warehouse funding and credit enhancement, including Bank of America, J.P. Morgan, and Financial Security Assurance, Inc., remain sound. Continued access to their credit facilities and credit enhancements remain important to Arcadia and we have strengthened our overall portfolio management processes and systems in order to merit their future support.

In fact, strengthening Arcadia to enhance our ability to serve our core market profitability is our top priority in 1997. The borrowers we target for our current loan programs account for approximately two-thirds of a highly fragmented $410 billion automobile finance market. There is clearly room for controlled, profitable growth in this industry, as well as in other consumer finance segments.

1996 Results

For the year, revenues clearly doubled and net income more than doubled, reaching $213.5 mil-lion and $60.3 million, respectively. Fully diluted earnings per share were $1.65 in 1996, up 49% from $1.11, before extraordinary items, in 1995. Shareholders' equity totaled $393 million at year end, up 117% from $181 million at the end of 1995 as a result of our record earnings and the successful completion of a stock offering in April 1996.

Arcadia's 1996 financial performance reflects the Company's dual focus on its customers—the auto dealerships the Company serves nationwide—and on credit quality. Arcadia is distinguished among sources of auto financing by our ability to identify and meet dealers' financing needs. In addition, while we will continue to improve our overall portfolio management practices, we have succeeded in maintaining delinquency and loan loss ratios within our expectations.

Strengthening Our Business

The growth in Arcadia's servicing portfolio has increased the demands on our loan servicing associates and systems. As a result, we are adding servicing staff and improving overall servicing resources and infrastructure. The growth in the loan portfolio also resulted in an increase in retail remarketing activities, through which Arcadia consigns the majority of repossessed vehicles to selected dealerships for sale. So long as the economics of this program remain compelling, we will continue to employ retail marketing of repossessed vehicles as a core strategy for maximizing recoveries and minimizing loan losses. The higher loan loss recoveries available from the retail market justify the costs of maintaining unsold repossession inventory and managing the retail remarketing program. The steps we are taking to strengthen overall servicing and collections operations are described in the Portfolio Performance and Credit Quality section of this annual report, beginning on page five.

Protecting Shareholders' Interest

In August 1996, a third party expressed to the Board of Directors an interest in purchasing the Company. To fulfill its fiduciary responsibility to shareholders, the Board retained independent

Olympic Financial Ltd.

Olympic Financial Ltd.

financial advisors to assist in evaluating this interest and other merger or acquisition possibilities.

In mid-October, the Board announced that no definitive offers to purchase the Company had resulted from discussions with possible acquirers. The Company is currently seeking to maximize value for shareholders as an independent entity.

To protect shareholders against an unwanted change in control, the Company adopted a Shareholder Rights Plan in November 1996. Under the plan, Preferred Stock Purchase Rights were distributed at a dividend rate of one Right per share of Common Stock to shareholders of record as of November 22, 1996. All shares of Common Stock issued thereafter have been and will be issued together with one Right per share.

Looking Ahead

In 1997, we are focusing on structural and process improvements intended to strengthen our core business and provide investors with the comfort and confidence of predictable, controlled and well-managed growth. In particular, we will emphasize efforts for properly pricing our loan programs for risk. We will also control costs, enhance collections processes, improve systems, and manage the retail remarketing program to deliver loss prevention and cash preservation benefits. In view of these priorities, we will pace increases in loan volume to ensure adequate resources are in place to make the growth

we experience profitable growth. Our overriding objective is to achieve tight control over all the key elements of our business so that we merit the continued support of funding sources, rating agencies, credit insurers, and investors.

We will be aided in these efforts by a seasoned and highly motivated management team that includes the core group of senior operations, credit, finance, dealer relations, and strategic development executives responsible for the Company's success to date. Those of us recently joining this team see great promise in expanding upon the base business. As we grow, we are ever mindful of our investment in the Company and the welfare of each of our associates. Our future success depends upon the confidence, dedication, and fresh perspectives of each of us working together as a team.

We remain highly confident in our prospects. While managing our growth presents a challenge, our size also provides us with flexibility, scale economics, wider strategic options, and more opportunities. Among these are opportunities to build strong customer relationships, create engaging and rewarding career paths for our associates, and enhance value for our shareholders, whose support we gratefully acknowledge.

Warren Kantor
*Chairman of
the Board*

Richard Greenawalt
*President and Chief
Executive Officer*

MANAGEMENT'S DISCUSSION AND ANALYSIS

OVERVIEW

The company derives substantially all of its earnings from the purchase, securitization and servicing of automobile loans. At the time of purchase of each loan, the Company pays a portion of the annual rate of interest paid by the obligor ("APR") to the dealer for originating the loan ("dealer participation"). To fund the purchase of loans prior to securitization, the Company utilizes its available cash balances and short-term borrowing and repurchase arrangements with financial institutions and institutional lenders ("warehouse facilities"). Pending securitization, automobile loans held for sale by the

Company generate net interest income resulting from the difference between the interest rate earned on automobile loans held for sale and the interest costs associated with the Company's short-term borrowings (the "net interest rate spread").

The Company purchases loans under a tiered pricing system, allowing it to price loans according to the borrower's credit characteristics. The Company prices its loan products in order to maximize gross interest rate spreads relative to expected net losses within each tier. Classic loans purchased in 1996 represented 36% of total purchasing volume compared with 17% during 1995 and 4% during 1994 and had APRs typically ranging from 16% to 23% while loans purchased under the premier program had APRs typically ranging from 8% to 16%. The higher APRs of the Classic program are intended to compensate the Company for anticipated higher delinquency, default and loss rates associated with the Classic program, which the Company addresses through higher reserves for loan losses. At December 31, 1996, the Company maintained $95.0 million in loan loss reserves, or 2.51% of its servicing portfolio, compared to $42.3 million, or 1.86% respectively, at December 31, 1995.

The Company aggregates the automobile loans it purchases and sells them to a trust, which in turn sells asset-backed securities to investors. By securitizing its loans, the Company is able to fix the initial difference ("the gross interest rate spread") between the APR on automobile loans purchased and the interest rate on the asset-backed securities sold ("securitization rate"). When the Company securitizes its automobile loans, it records a gain on sale and establishes an asset referred to as finance income receivable. Gain on sale represents the present value of the estimated future cash flows to be received by the Company, discounted at a market-based rate, and takes into account the Company's historical loan portfolio experience and its methods for disposing of repossessed vehicles. The calculation of gain on sale takes into consideration (i) contractual obligations of the obligator (ii) amounts due to the investors in asset-backed securities, (iii) amounts paid to dealers for dealer participation, (iv) various costs of the securitizations, including the effects of hedging transactions, and (v) adjustments of the cash flows to reflect estimated prepayments of loans, losses incurred in connection with defaults, and corresponding reductions in the weighted average APR of loans sold. Subsequent to securitization, the Company continues to service the securitized loans for which it recognizes servicing fee income over the life of the securitization as earned.

In addition to the present value of estimated future cash flows from securitization (gain on sale), finance income receivable includes (i) accrued interest receivable on automobile loans held for sale, but not yet collected through the date of sale, (ii) interest earned on spread and other cash accounts established in connection with the Company's securitizations, and

(iii) the interest earned on previously discounted cash flows, calculated at the present value discount rate and used in determining gain on sale. As noted above, future servicing fee income is recognized as earned and is not included in finance income receivable. Finance income receivable is reduced based on distributions to the Company of excess cash flows from spread accounts. The Company uses a combination of its own historical experience, industry statistics, and expectations of future performance to estimate the amount and timing of prepayments and loss experience compared with the Company's estimates. In accordance with generally accepted accounting principles, the Company does not increase the carrying amount of finance income receivable for favorable variances from original estimates, but to the extent actual prepayment or loss experience exceeds the Company's estimates, any required decrease to the finance income receivable is reflected as a reduction of current period earnings.

YEARS ENDED DECEMBER 31, 1996, 1995, AND 1994

Results of Operations

Net interest margin The Company's net interest margin represents the sum of (i) net interest on loans held for sale based on the net interest rate spread, (ii) investment earnings on short-term investments, spread accounts, and other cash accounts established in connection with the Company's securitization, and (iii) the recognition of the interest component of previously discounted cash flows, calculated at the present value discount rate used in determining the gain on sale. The components of net interest margin for each of the three years ended December 31, 1996 were:

(Dollars in thousands)	1996	1995	1994
Interest income on loans, net	$29,614	$16,038	$3,544
Interest income on short-term investments, spread accounts, and other cash accounts	15,233	7,942	3,620
Recognition of present value discount	18,890	7,368	2,664
Provision for credit losses on loans held for sale	(774)	(156)	—
Net interest margin	$62,963	$31,192	$9,828

Olympic Financial Ltd.

Net interest margin increased 102% during 1996 and 217% during 1995. The rise in net interest margin is primarily due to (i) growth in the average balances of loans held for sale pending securitization, (ii) increased net interest rates earned on loans held for sale pending securitization, and (iii) increases in the volume of the Company's securitization transactions.

Increased purchasing volume is primarily due to the Company's continued geographic expansion and improved market penetration through growth in its dealer network. As of December 31, 1996, the Company had 17 regional buying centers, up from 15 and 12 at December 31, 1995 and 1994 respectively and had increased its dealer network to 7,727 dealers at December 31, 1996 from 5,110 and 2,344 dealers at December 31, 1995 and 1994, respectively. The Company's loan purchasing and securitization volume for the three years ended December 31, 1996 are set forth in the table below.

(Dollars in thousands)	1996	1995	1994
Premier	$1,768,933	$1,699,874	$716,308
Classic	981,620	352,539	26,948
Total automobile loan purchases	$2,750,553	$2,052,413	$743,256
Automobile loans securitized	$2,787,412	$1,933,525	$712,211

In 1995, the Company initiated a program to increase the proportion of Classic loans in its loan purchase mix in order to maximize gross interest rate spreads relative to expected net losses within each credit tier, to expand its share of the automobile loan market, and to reduce initial cash requirements relative to the Premier program because the Company offers lower dealer participations on Classic loans. At December 31, 1996, approximately half of the Company's aggregate loan purchases were being made under the Classic program. The Company may change its loan purchase mix at any time and from time to time.

The rise in loan purchasing volume resulted in an increase in the average monthly balance of loans held for sale to $219.5 million during 1996, up from $162.7 million and $41.1 million during 1995 and 1994, respectively, on which the Company earns net interest rate spread until such loans are securitized. The weighted average net interest rate spread earned during 1996 rose to 7.84% com-

pared with 6.71% and 6.59% during 1995 and 1994, respectively. The rise in net interest spread earned on loans held for sale is principally due to higher average annual percentage rates ("APR") paid by obligors resulting from expansion of the Company's higher rate Classic loan program.

Interest income on short-term investments, spread accounts, and other cash accounts established in connection with securitization transactions increased 92% between 1995 and 1996 and 119% between 1994 and 1995. This increase is primarily due to growth in average balances of spread accounts and other securitization related cash accounts resulting from higher securitization volume. Income from the recognition of present value discount also grew due to the increased volume of securitization.

Gain on sale of loans Gain on sale of loans provided net revenues of $115.8 million, $62.2 million, and $13.6 million during 1996, 1995, and 1994, respectively, representing increases of 86.2% between 1995 and 1996 and 357% between 1994 and 1995. The rise in gain on sale of loans primarily resulted from growth in volume of loans securitized as discussed above, increased gross interest rate spreads, and a decline in the participation rate paid to dealers for loan originations but was offset in part by an increase in the reserve for loan losses.

The following table summarizes the Company's gross interest rate spreads for each of the three years in the period ended December 31, 1996.

	1996	1995	1994
Weighted average APR of loans securitized	14.56%	14.22%	12.50%
Weighted average securitization rate	6.31	6.38	6.32
Gross interest rate spread[a]	8.25%	7.84%	6.18%

a. Before gains/losses on hedge transactions

The rise in the gross interest rate spread during 1995 and 1996 are primarily due to an increased proportion of higher-yielding Classic loans, resulting in an increased APR earned on loans purchased and subsequently securitized. The increase in the weighted average APR resulting from the growth in the Classic loan volume during 1996 was partially offset by a general market decline in consumer interest rates during the first few months of the year.

The unamortized balance of participations paid to dealers is expensed at the time the related loans are securitized and recorded as a reduction to the gain on sale. Due to the increased proportion of Classic loan purchases, which generally require lower participation rates, and a reduction of the maximum participation rate allowable under the Premier program, participations paid as a percentage of the principal balance of loan purchases declined to 3.45% during 1996 from 4.21% and 3.98% during 1995 and 1994, respectively, resulting in increased gain on sale.

Gains on sale of loans were further increased by $4.7 million and $1.4 million of gross realized gains on hedging transactions during 1996 and 1994, respectively, and decreased by $5.0 million, $11.7 million and $0.5 million of gross realized losses on hedging transactions during 1996, 1995 and 1994, respectively. There were no gross realized hedging gains during 1995.

Servicing fee income The company earns servicing fee income for servicing loans sold to investors through securitizations. The stated percent for servicing fees (1% per annum on the remaining balance of loans serviced) is consistent with the industry standard for servicing automobile loans. Servicing fee income increased to $28.3 million in 1996 from $14.0 million in 1995 and $4.5 million in 1994.

The following table reflects the growth in the Company's servicing portfolio from 1994 to 1996, at December 31:

(Dollars in thousands)	**1996**	**1995**	**1994**
Principal balance of automobile loans held for sale	$ 35,365	$ 113,840	$ 22,918
Principal balance of loans serviced under securitizations	3,756,492	2,153,267	814,177
Servicing portfolio	$3,791,857	$2,267,107	$837,095
Average outstanding principal balance (actual dollars)	$ 12,537	$ 12,239	$ 11,271
Number of loans serviced	302,450	185,241	74,267

The company's servicing portfolio increased 67% from 1995 to 1996 and 171% between 1994 and 1995, reflecting continued growth in the volume of the Company's loan purchases and subsequent securitizations. The rise in average outstanding principal balance of loans reflects general price increases in the automobile industry.

Other noninterest income Other noninterest income rose $6.5 million during 1996 from $1.4 million and $0.9 million during 1995 and 1994, respectively, representing increases of 372% during 1996 and 56% during 1995. The rise in other noninterest income is principally due to increases in income from late fees and insufficient funds charges reflecting the increase in delinquency rates.

Salaries and benefits expense Salaries and benefits increased to $40.8 million during 1996 from $20.1 million and $9.1 million during 1995 and 1994, respectively, representing an increase of 103% during 1996 and 122% during 1995. This increase is primarily due to growth in number of associates.

The rapid growth of the Company's servicing portfolio and the decision to expand the proportion of loans purchased through its Classic program has resulted in increased demands on the Company's personnel and systems. The Company's ability to support, manage, and control continued growth is dependent upon, among other things, its ability to hire, train, supervise, and manage its larger work force. Furthermore, the Company's ability to manage portfolio delinquency and loss rates is dependent upon the maintenance of efficient collection and repossession procedures and adequate staffing. See "Delinquency, Loan Loss, and Repossession Experience."

General and administrative and other operating expenses ("other operating expenses") Other operating expenses increased during 1996 to $51.5 million up from $22.6 million in 1995 and $8.3 million in 1994. Other operating expenses include occupancy and equipment leasing charges, depreciation, outside professional fees, communication costs, servicing and collection expenses, marketing expenses, recruitment and staffing fees, travel, office supplies, and other. Many of these expenses, such as communications, service, and collection and office supplies, increase incrementally with growth in loan purchasing and volume and the Company's servicing portfolio. Occupancy and equipment charges increased due to continued geographic expansion through the opening of additional regional buying centers during 1995 and 1996 and the regionalization of the Company's servicing and collection operations during 1996. The Company also experienced significant increases in outside professional fees during 1996 primarily related to development costs associated with a potential leasing product and various information system enhancements. During 1996 the Company incurred increases in recruiting and staffing fees in connection with its search for various key collection, servicing, and management personnel. As a result of the items noted above, total operating expenses, including salaries and benefits rose to 3.06% of average servicing portfolio compared with 2.78% in 1995, but remained lower than 3.28% in 1994.

Long-term debt and other interest expense Long-term debt and other interest expense rose 46.7% during 1996 and 217% in 1995. These increases are primarily due to the issuance of $145.0 million of 13.0% Senior Term Notes in April 1995 and $30.0 million of 10.125% Subordinated Notes in March 1996.

Income tax expense During the third quarter of 1994, the Company fully utilized its book net operating loss carryforwards and incurred income tax expense for book purposes. No income tax expense was incurred in earlier periods. Because of the difference in the basis of the financial income receivable for financial reporting purposes and income tax purposes, the Company continues to have available $74.1 million of net tax operating loss carryforwards, a portion of which may be available to offset against income taxes in 1997 and future years, subject to applicable limitations. The $35.7 million income tax expense during 1996 primarily reflects the Company's estimated addition to its deferred tax liability as of December 31, 1996.

Extraordinary items In February 1995, the Company entered into a temporary financing facility under which it was able to borrow up to $70.0 million through the issuance of Senior Notes. Of the $50.0 million in gross proceeds from the Company's initial issuance of Senior Notes, $34.6 million was used to retire $30.0 million of 11.75% Senior Secured Notes, including accrued interest of $0.5 million and prepayment fees of approximately $4.1 million. The Company issued an additional $5.0 million in Senior Notes in April 1995.

On April 28, 1995, the Company received aggregate net proceeds from the issuance of Common Stock and Senior Term Notes of approximately $231.0 million and applied $56.2 million of such proceeds to retire its Senior Notes at par plus accrued interest and $15.6 million to retire the Company's 9.875% Senior Subordinated Notes including accrued interest of $0.1 million and prepayment fees of $0.5 million.

The prepayment fees for the early extinguishment of debt and the charge-off of capitalized debt financing costs associated with the 11.75% Senior Secured Notes and the 9.875% Senior Subordinated Notes were accounted for as extraordinary items.

The Company has commenced a tender offer for the Senior Term Notes and a related consent solicitation for elimination of substantially all of the financial covenants in the indenture under which such Senior Term Notes were issued. See "Capital Resources."

Preferred dividends The Company paid dividends on its outstanding preferred stock (which was converted to Common Stock in December 1996) of $1.2 million, $2.2 million and $2.3 million for 1996, 1995, and 1994, respectively. The decrease in dividends paid from 1995 to 1996 is due to the conversion of preferred shares into common stock of the Company. As of December 31, 1996, all preferred shares had been redeemed or converted.

Financial Conditions

Due from securitization trust At December 31, 1996, the Company had delivered $177.1 million of loans into a securitization trust for which the Company received cash from the trust concurrent with the legal closing of the transaction in January 1997. There were no loans delivered into securitization trusts pending legal closing at December 31, 1995.

Automobile loans held for sale The Company holds automobile loans for sale in its portfolio prior to securitization. The Company's portfolio of loans held for sale decreased to $36.3 million at December 31, 1996 from $118.6 million at December 31, 1995, due to the timing of delivery of loans associated with the Company's securitization.

Finance income receivable Finance income receivable increased to $362.9 million at December 31, 1996 from $186.0 million at December 31, 1995. This 95% increase represents amounts capitalized upon completion of securitization transactions during 1996 related to the present value of estimated cash flows. The amounts capitalized were offset by excess cash flows released from the securitization trusts to the Company through its wholly owned subsidiary, Olympic Receivables Finance Corp. ("ORFC"). Reserve for losses on securitized loans is included as a component of finance income receivable.

Furniture, fixtures, and equipment Furniture, fixtures, and equipment increased 115% to $13.6 million at December 31, 1996 from $6.3 million at December 31, 1995, primarily due to the opening of two additional regional buying centers and relocation of the Company's servicing and collection operations in four regional facilities during 1996 to enhance the Company's collection activities.

Capital lease obligations Capital lease obligations increased 97% to $7.7 million at December 31, 1996, from $3.9 million at December. 31, 1995, primarily due to continued geographic expansion as discussed above.

Deferred income taxes The Company began recording income tax expense in the third quarter of 1994 as the net tax benefit of net operating loss carryforwards for financial reporting purposes was fully utilized. Deferred income tax assets and liabilities reflect the tax effect of temporary differences between the carrying amounts of assets and liabilities for financial reporting purposes and income tax purposes principally net operating loss carryforwards for income tax purposes and the finance income receivable, respectively. The Company's estimated net deferred tax liability at December 31, 1996, was $54.4 million, compared to $18.7 million at December 31, 1995.

Other liabilities Accounts payable and accrued liabilities increased to $13.2 million at December 31, 1996 compared to $9.8 million at December 31, 1995. This 34% increase is primarily due to increased trade payables and other operating accruals reflecting the growth in the Company's operations and related operating expenses.

DELINQUENCY, LOAN LOSS, AND REPOSSESSION EXPERIENCE

The Company's operating performance, financial conditions, and liquidity are materially affected by the performance of the automobile loans purchased and securitized by the Company. In connection with the servicing of automobile loans, the Company is responsible for managing delinquent loans, repossessing the underlying collateral in the event of default and selling repossessed collateral. The Company provides an allowance for automobile loan credit losses at a rate which, in the opinion of management, provides adequately for current and probable future losses that may be incurred by the Company. The Company provides an allowance for credit losses for sold loans in accordance with Emerging Issues Task Force 92-2, Measuring Loss Accounts by Transferors for Transfers of Receivables with Recourse, at the time of securitization. The provision for credit losses is netted against the calculated gain on sale amount for loans sold. The related allowance for these credit losses is a component of the finance income receivable.

The following tables describe the delinquency and credit loss and repossession experience, respectively, of the Company's servicing portfolio for the three years in the period ended December 31, 1996. A delinquent loan may result in the repossession and foreclosure of the collateral for the loan. Losses resulting from repossession and disposition of automobiles are charged against applicable allowances, which management reviews on a monthly basis.

Olympic Financial Ltd.

Olympic Financial Ltd.

DELINQUENCY EXPERIENCE[a] (Dollars in thousands)

| | December 31, | | | | | |
| | 1996 | | 1995 | | 1994 | |
	Number of Loans	Balances	Number of Loans	Balances	Number of Loans	Balances
Servicing portfolio at end of period	302,450	$3,791,857	185,241	$2,267,107	74,267	$837,095
Delinquencies:						
31–60 days	3,884	47,225	1,536	17,667	393	4,142
61–90 days	1,255	15,877	520	5,694	129	1,557
91 days or more	2,911	37,019	614	6,881	113	1,197
Total automobile loans delinquent 31 days or more	8,050	$100,121	2,670	$ 30,242	635	$ 6,896
Delinquencies as a percentage of number of loans and amount outstanding at end of period[b]	2.66%	2.64%	1.44%	1.33%	0.86%	0.82%
Amount in repossession[c]	4,651	$ 64,929	1,489	$ 17,676	102	$ 570
Total delinquencies and amount in repossession[b]	12,701	$165,050	4,159	$ 47,918	737	$ 7,466

[a]All amounts and percentages are based on the principal amount scheduled to be paid on each loan. The information in the table includes previously sold loans which the Company continues to service.
[b]Amounts shown do not include loans which are less than 31 days delinquent.
[c]Amount in repossession represents financed automobiles which have been repossessed but not yet liquidated.

CREDIT LOSS/REPOSSESSION EXPERIENCE[a] (Dollars in thousands)

| | Year Ended December 31, | | |
	1996	1995	1994
Average servicing portfolio outstanding during the period	$3,015,411	$1,534,720	$528,577
Average number of loans outstanding during the period	242,419	128,783	49,566
Number of repossessions	14,403	5,020	1,005
Repossessions as a percentage of average number of loans outstanding	5.94%	3.90%	2.03%
Gross charge-offs[b]	$ 35,642	$ 11,247	$ 4,446
Recoveries[c]	5,653	911	974
Net losses	$ 29,989	$ 10,336	$ 3,472
Gross charge-offs as a percentage of average servicing portfolio	1.18%	0.73%	0.84%
Net losses as a percentage of average servicing portfolio	0.99%	0.67%	0.66%

[a]All amounts and percentages are based on the principal amount scheduled to be paid on each loan. The information in the table includes previously sold loans which the Company continues to service.
[b]Gross charge-offs represent principal amounts which management estimated to be uncollectible after the consideration of anticipated proceeds from the disposition of repossessed assets and selling expenses. When estimating the value of repossessed inventory, management utilizes industry published reports listing retail and wholesale values of used automobiles and determines estimated proceeds within a range that management believes reflects the then current market conditions and the Company's disposition strategy for such inventory.
[c]Includes post-disposition amounts received on previously charged off loans.

MANAGEMENT'S DISCUSSION AND ANALYSIS (continued)

The increase in the rate of delinquencies, gross charge-offs, net losses and repossessions during 1996, experienced by both the Premier and Classic programs, was primarily due to (i) increased demands on the Company's servicing and collection resources as the result of rapid growth in its servicing portfolio and as a result of continued expansion of the Classic loan program (which generally required greater collection efforts than the Premier program), (ii) the performance of the Company's discontinued Classic product for first time automobile buyers and the Company's financed repossession program, which experienced significantly higher delinquencies, repossessions and losses than the Company's other products and programs, and (iii) the continued seasoning of the Company's servicing portfolio to include a greater proportion of loans, particularly Classic loans, in the period of highest probability for delinquencies and defaults (generally 6 to 14 months from the origination date).

To handle the increased demands on its servicing and collection operations, the Company began to take steps in 1996 to enhance its servicing and collection capabilities. Since December 1995, the Company has more than doubled its servicing and collection staff and, in October 1996, regionalized its servicing and collection operations into four locations across the United States. Additionally, the Company has engaged outside consultants to evaluate the Company's current collection strategy and assist in the design and implementation of a new collection system.

During 1996, loans made under the Company's financed repossession program and its Classic product for first time automobile buyers (discontinued in March 1996) had significantly higher rates of delinquencies, gross charge-offs, net losses, and repossessions than other products within the Company's servicing portfolio. These programs aggregated 4.3% of the total servicing portfolio at December 31, 1996, but accounted for approximately 20% of delinquencies, gross charge-offs, and net losses in 1996. Management believes that the performance of the financed repossession loans is primarily attributable to an inventory reduction program during the fourth quarter of 1995 and the first quarter of 1996 and improper practices at certain of the Company's initial consignment dealers, with which the Company has since terminated its business relationships. The Company has instituted more comprehensive management of its financed repossession program, including the dedication of trained staff located in the Company's four regional servicing and collection centers for the underwriting and purchasing of such loans.

The significant rise in repossession inventory levels shown on the Delinquency Experience table was the result of the growth in the Company's servicing portfolio and due to changes to the Company's approach to retailing its repossessed automobiles. During 1995 and early 1996, the Company relied heavily on a few large retail consignment lots to sell its inventory. Turnover of repossession inventory was not at levels deemed acceptable by the Company under this approach. In early 1996 the Company terminated its relationship with certain consignment lots and decided to expand its repossession distribution channels to multiple smaller locations throughout the United States. The Company expanded its remarketing department in order to develop and manage relationships with additional retail outlets and to expedite disposition of repossessed vehicles. At December 31, 1996, the Company had arrangements with 67 smaller retail consignment lots to dispose of its repossessions compared with 10 large retail consignment lots at December 31, 1995. It is actively pursuing additional relationships to further increase its remarketing capacity. During 1996, the Company sold approximately 70% of its repossession inventory through retail markets and the Company financed approximately 90% of these sales. The Company may dispose of repossession inventory at wholesale auctions from time to time.

Increases in loan delinquency and repossession rates may cause the Company to exceed certain pool performance tests established in agreements governing the Company's outstanding Senior Term Notes. If at any month-end the amount of charge-offs (net of recoveries) of automobile loans in the Company's servicing portfolio during the preceding six month periods, times two, exceeds 1.65% of the average servicing portfolio in the preceding seven months ("Portfolio Loss Ratio"), the Company will be prohibited from purchasing new automobile loans in excess of 20% of the Company's Adjusted Consolidated Cash Flow (as defined in the indenture governing the Senior Term Notes) plus proceeds of warehouse facilities and certain other available cash. If the Portfolio Loss Ratio exceeds 1.65% for two consecutive months, then 50% of such Adjusted Consolidated Cash Flow (as defined in the indenture governing the Senior Term Notes) must be used to offer repurchase Senior Term Notes at par. In addition, if at the end of any month the Portfolio Loss Ratio exceeds 2.5% or the Company's delinquency level exceeds 3.5%, an event of default will occur under two of the Company's outstanding warehouse facilities. The delinquency level is calculated as a percentage, by outstanding principal balance, of all automobile loans owned or securitized by the Company as to which a payment is more than 30 days past due. Upon the occurrence of an event of default under such warehouse facilities, the lending banks under such facilities may accelerate the payment of amounts outstanding thereunder and would have no further obligation to extend additional credit. Furthermore, any such event of default may trigger cross-defaults under other outstanding indebtedness of the Company and may result in the acceleration of amounts due thereunder. On January 21,1997 the Company made a tender offer to purchase all of its outstanding Senior Term Notes. See Note 14 to the Company's Consolidated Financial Statements.

LIQUIDITY

The Company's business requires substantial cash to support its operating activities. The principal cash requirements include (i) amounts necessary to purchase and finance automobile loans pending securitization, (ii) dealer participations, (iii) cash held from time to time in restricted spread accounts to support securitization, and warehouse facilities and other securitization expenses, (iv) interest advances to securitization trusts, (v) repossession inventory, and (vi) interest expense. The Company also uses significant amounts of cash for operating expenses. The Company receives cash principally from interest on loans held pending securitization, excess cash flow received from securitization trusts and fees earned through servicing of loans held by such trusts. The Company has operated on a negative operating cash flow basis and expects to continue to do so for so long as the Company continues to experience scant growth in its volume of loan purchases. The Company has historically funded, and expects to continue to fund, these negative operating cash flows, subject to limitations in various debt covenants, principally through borrowings from financial institutions, sales of equity securities, and sales of senior and subordinated notes, among other resources, although there can be no assurance that the Company will have access to capital markets in the future or that financing will be available to satisfy the Company's operating and debt service requirements or to fund its future growth. See "Capital Resources."

Principal Uses of Cash in Operating Activities

Purchases and financing of automobile loans Automobile loan purchases represent the Company's most significant cash requirement. The Company funds the purchase price of loans primarily through the use of warehouse facilities. However, because advance rates under the warehouse facilities generally provide funds ranging from 95% to 97% of the principal balance of the loans, the Company is required to fund the remainder of all purchases with other available cash resources. The Company purchased $2.8 billion of loans in 1996, compared with $2.1 billion in 1995 and $743.3 million in 1994. Amounts borrowed under warehouse facilities are repaid upon securitization of the loans. The Company regularly completes securitization to optimize its use of available warehouse facilities and the Company's cash investment in loans held for sale.

Dealer participations Consistent with industry practice, the Company pays dealers participations for selling loans to the Company. When loans are securitized, the related dealer participation is expensed and subsequently recovered over the estimated life of the underlying loans through the return to the Company of excess cash flow from securitization trusts. Participations paid by the Company to dealers in 1996 were $94.9 million, compared with $86.5 million in 1995 and $29.6 million in 1994. These participations typically require the Company to advance an up-front amount to dealers, which represented 3.45% of the principal balance of loans purchased during 1996 compared to 4.21% in 1995 and 3.98% in 1994. The decrease in percentage of dealer participations paid reflects the growth in volume of loans purchased under the Classic program, which generally requires a lower participation rate and a reduction in the cap on participation rates paid on Premier loans implemented during 1995. The Company has some limited ability to recover these amounts from the dealers by offset against future participations in the event of prepayment or default on the loan within a specified period of time. However, to the extent the loan does not prepay or default within that period of time, the Company expects to recover the cash used to pay dealer commissions over the estimated life of the underlying loans through the return to the Company of excess cash flows from securitization spread accounts. This relationship between up-front payment of cash to the dealers and the deferred recovery through collection of excess cash flow will continue to represent a significant demand on capital resources to the extent the Company continues to expand the volume of loan purchase.

Securitization of Automobile Loans In connection with securitizations, the Company is required to fund spread accounts related to each transaction. The Company funds the spread accounts by forgoing receipt of excess cash flow until the spread accounts exceed predetermined levels (generally within 14 months of the formation of the securitization trust). In certain securitizations, the Company also has been required to provide initial cash deposits into such accounts. The amount of time required to initially fund each spread account varies depending on numerous factors, including, but not limited to (i) the site of the initial deposit, (ii) the gross interest rate spread, (iii) defaults, (iv) delinquencies, (v) losses, and (vi) turnover repossession inventory. The Company had $143.0 million restricted cash in spread accounts at December 31, 1996, compared with $63.6 million at December 31, 1995. The Company also incurs certain expenses in connection with securitization including underwriting fees, credit

enhancement fees, trustee fees and other costs, which approximate 0.55% per annum of the principal amount of the asset-backed securities.

Net interest margin Although the Company records net interest margin as it is earned, the interest income component is generally received in cash from excess cash flow over the life of the securitization trust, while the interest expense component (primarily warehousing interest) is paid prior to securitization.

Advances due to servicer As the servicer of loans sold in securitizations, the Company periodically makes interest advances to the securitization trusts to provide for temporary delays in the receipt of required interest payments by borrowers. In accordance with servicing agreements, the Company makes advances only in the event that it expects to recover such advances through the ultimate payments from the obligor over the life of the loan. Beginning in December 1996, the Company servicing agreements were modified to require interest advance only when the related loan is 31 days delinquent or greater.

Repossession inventory At December 31, 1996, the Company inventory of repossessed automobiles held for resale was $64.9 million, compared with $17.7 million at December 31, 1995. The rate of repossession inventory turnover impacts cash available for spread accounts under securitization trusts and, consequently, the excess cash available for distribution to OREC. At December 31, 1996, repossessed inventory was 1.7% of total servicing portfolio compared with 0.8% at December 31,1995.

Principal Sources of Cash in Operating Activities

Excess cash flow The Company receives excess cash flow from securitization trusts, including the realization of gain on sale, the recovery of dealer participation, and the recovery of accrued interest receivable earned, but not yet collected, on loans held for sale. Recovery of dealer participation and accrued interest receivable, which occur throughout the life of the securitization, result in a reduction of the finance income receivable and, because they have been considered in the original determination

Olympic Financial Ltd.

of the gain on sale of loans, have no effect on the Company's results of operations in the year in which the participations and interest are recovered from the securitization trust. During 1996, the Company received $43.4 million of excess cash flow, compared with $21.1 million in 1995 and $17.7 million in 1994. The rate of increase in excess cash flow during 1996 exceeded the rate of increase in loans securitized principally because spread accounts related to 1995 securitizations have reached required reserve levels and have begun releasing cash during the current year. These obligations generally reach predetermined spread account levels within 14 months following the formation of the securitization trust. The excess cash flow released from securitization trusts during 1996 was reduced by the slower turnover of the Company's repossession inventory resulting from the utilization of its retail repossession strategy.

Servicing fees The Company also receives servicing fee income with respect to loans held by securitization trusts equal to 1% per annum of the remaining principal balance. The Company received cash for such services in the amount of $27.0 million, $12.7 million and $4.5 million during 1996, 1995 and 1994, respectively, and is reflected in the Company's revenues as earned.

CAPITAL RESOURCES

The Company finances the acquisition of automobile loans primarily through (i) warehouse facilities, pursuant to which loans are sold or financed generally on a temporary basis and (ii) the securitization of loans, pursuant to which loans are sold as asset-backed securities. Additional financing is required to fund the Company's operations.

Warehouse facilities Automobile loans held for sale are funded on a short-term basis primarily through warehouse facilities. At December 31, 1996 the Company had three warehouse facilities in place with various financial institutions and institutional lenders with an aggregate capacity of $800 million, of which $688.9 million was unused. These facilities are subject to renewal or extension, at various times in 1997 at the option of the lenders. Proceeds from securitizations, generally received within seven to ten

days following the cut-off date established for the securitization transaction, are utilized to invest in additional loan purchases and applied to repay amounts outstanding under warehouse facilities.

Securitization program An important capital resource for the Company has been its ability to sell automobile loans in the secondary markets through securitizations. The following table summarizes the Company's securitizations during the three years ended December 31, 1996, all of which have been publicly issued and were rated "AAA/Aaa."

The Company utilizes net proceeds from securitizations to invest in additional loan purchases and to repay warehouse indebtedness, thereby making its warehouse facilities available for further purchases of automobile loans. At December 31, 1996, the Company had securitized approximately $5.8 billion of automobile loans since its inception in 1990 with remaining balances of approximately $3.8 billion.

Date	Original Balance	Remaining Balance as of December 31, 1996	Remaining Balance as a Percentage of Original Balance	Current Weighted Average (APR)	Weighted Average Securitization Rate	Gross Interest Rate Spread
March '94	$ 260,000	$ 72,580	27.92%	11.13%	5.66%	5.47%
September '94	430,000	165,351	38.45	12.80	6.81	5.99
February '95	158,400	68,650	43.34	13.87	7.88	5.99
March '95	300,000	134,341	44.78	14.41	7.31	7.10
June '95	470,000	242,987	51.70	14.19	6.20	7.99
September '95	525,000	307,926	58.65	13.77	6.03	7.74
December '95	600,000	389,884	64.98	13.77	5.88	7.89
March '96	600,000	437,653	72.94	13.72	5.81	7.91
June '96	650,000	540,368	83.13	14.46	6.62	7.84
September '96	725,000	664,248	91.62	14.83	6.75	8.08
December '96[a]	730,000	683,333	93.61	15.19	6.08	9.11
	5,448,400	3,707,321				

[a]At December 31, 1996, $692.6 million of automobile loans had been delivered to the trust and $37.4 million cash remained in the pre-funded portion of the trust. In January 1997, the Company delivered sufficient loans to the trust and obtained the release of the remaining cash in the pre-funded portion of the trust. See "Hedging and Pre-Funding Strategy" below.

All of the Company's securitization trusts and the B of A Facility are credit-enhanced through financial guaranty insurance policies issued by FSA, which insure payment of principal and interest due on the related asset-backed securities. Asset-backed securities insured by FSA have been rated AAA by Standard & Poor's and Aaa by Moody's Investors Service, Inc. At December 31, 1996, FSA had insured approximately $5.8 billion original principal amount of Company-sponsored asset-backed securities. During 1996, the Company agreed to use FSA as insurer of the asset-backed securities issued in its insured securitizations through December 1998 in consideration for certain limitations on FSA insurance premiums. FSA is not obligated to provide insurance for the Company's future securitizations. In order to obtain FSA insurance, the Company is obligated to establish spread accounts, and to maintain such spread accounts at pre-determined levels, in connection with each insured securitization through the collection and restriction of excess cash flow from the loans securitized. These spread accounts are funded through initial deposits, when required, and out of excess cash flow from the related securitization trust. Thereafter, during each month excess cash flow due to ORFC from all insured securitization trusts is first used to replenish spread accounts to predetermined levels and is then distributed to the Company. If excess cash flow from insured securitization trusts is not sufficient to replen-

ish spread accounts, no cash flow would be available to the Company from ORFC for that month. Spread accounts are also replenished through cash received from the liquidation of repossessions under defaulted receivables. However, such cash is generally received in months subsequent to default and can therefore result in timing differences as to when excess cash flows are released to the Company. The spread account for each insured securitization trust is cross-collateralized with the spread accounts established for the Company's other insured securitization trusts. Excess cash flow from performing securitization trusts insured by FSA may be used to support negative cash flows from, or to replenish a deficit spread account in connection with, nonperforming securitization trusts insured by FSA. The Company's obligations to FSA in respect of insured securitizations and the B of A Facility are limited to the amount on deposit in the spread accounts and excess cash flow. In connection with its securitizations, the Company continually seeks to improve its structures to reduce up-front costs and to maximize excess cash flow available to the Company. The Company may consider alternative securitization structures including senior/subordinated branches, and alternative forms of credit enhancement, such as letters of credit and surety bonds. For example, during 1995 and 1994, the Company realized a portion of its finance income receivable by selling an interest-only strip in its September 1995 and Sep-

Olympic Financial Ltd.

tember 1994 securitizations. Proceeds from the sale of the interest-only strips were approximately $6.1 million in 1995 and approximately $7.0 million in 1994. There were no interest-only strips sold during 1996. The structure of each securitized sale of loans depends on market conditions, costs of securitization, and the availability of credit enhancement options to the Company.

Hedging and pre-funding strategy The Company employs hedging strategies to manage its gross interest rate spread. Through the use of these hedging strategies, the Company is able to determine its approximate financing cost prior to, or near to, the purchase of loans and thereby maintain its gross interest rate spread within a desired range. Because interest rates on asset-backed securities for automobile loans generally tend to rise or fall when other short-term interest rates fluctuate, a material increase in interest rates prior to securitization could adversely affect the profitability of such securitization to the Company in the absence of a hedging strategy. The Company also mitigates its exposure to interest rate risk through a pre-funding strategy in which it securitizes a portion of its loans held for sale while selling future loans in a pre-funded securitization. In a pre-funded securitization, the principal amount of the asset-backed securities issued in the securitization exceeds the principal balance of loans initially delivered to the securitization trust. The proceeds from the pre-funded portion are held in trust earning money market yields until released upon delivery of additional loans. The Company agrees to deliver additional loans into the securitization trust from time to time (generally monthly) equal in the aggregate to the amount by which the principal balance of the asset-backed securities exceeds the principal balance of the loans initially delivered. In pre-funded securitizations, the Company predetermines the borrowing costs with respect to loans it subsequently purchases and delivers into the securitization trust. However, the Company incurs an expense in pre-funding securitizations equal to the difference between the money market yields earned on the proceeds held in trust prior to the subsequent delivery of loans and the interest rate paid on the asset-backed securities.

The Company also has some interest rate exposure to falling interest rates to the extent that the Company's offered rates decline after the Company has engaged in a pre-funded securitization, although the Company's offered rates generally respond less rapidly to rate fluctuations than financing costs.

The Company also sells forward U.S. Treasuries that most closely parallel the average life of its portfolio of loans held for sale. By doing so, the Company is able to obtain an inverse relationship between the loans being hedged and the U.S. Treasury market. The hedging gain or loss is netted against the gain on sale of loans. Such hedges include certain risks created by the cash versus non-cash relationship of the hedging instrument and the related securitization. This relationship arises because U.S. Treasury forward contracts are settled with current cash payments and the gain on sale of loans represents the present value of estimated future cash flows. To the extent hedging gains or losses resulting from U.S. Treasury forward contracts are significant, the resulting cash payments or receipts may impact the Company's liquidity. Hedging transactions required a net use of cash of $0.3 million and $11.7 million during 1996 and 1995 respectively, and provided cash of $0.8 million in 1994.

Management has controls and policies in place to assess and monitor its risk from hedging activities. Management follows its policy of hedging loan amounts purchased or expected to be delivered within the next 120 days. Management reviews the interest rate movements in the U.S. Treasury markets and receives a daily internal report tracking such movements. Monthly, management receives an interest rate report that describes not only interest rate movements, but also the amount of corresponding increase or decrease in the value of its hedged securitizations. Most of the Company's hedging transactions have been for a period of 75 days or less. The amount and timing of hedging transactions are determined by members of the Company senior management, and subject to approval by the Company's chief executive officer. Management assesses factors including the interest rate environment, loan production levels, and open positions of current hedging positions.

Other Capital Resources

Historically, the Company has utilized various debt and equity financings to offset negative operating cash flows and support the continued growth in loan volume, increased dollar amount of dealer participations, securitizations, and general operating expenses.

During 1996, the Company completed a public offering of 8,050,000 shares of Common Stock and received net proceeds of approximately $146.0 million. In March 1996, the Company issued to the public $30.0 million aggregate principal amount of 10.125% Subordinated Notes Series 1996-A, due 2001 and received net proceeds of approximately $29.0 million. Proceeds from the 1996 offerings were available as working capital for loan purchases and general operations.

In February 1995, the Company entered into a temporary financing facility (the "Facility") in order to provide cash pending completion of the common stock and senior debt offerings described below and to repay $30.0 million of outstanding Senior Secured Notes. Under the Facility, the Company borrowed $55.0 million through the issuance of Senior Unsecured Increasing Rate Notes. In April 1995, proceeds from the common stock and senior term debt offerings described below were used to retire the notes issued under the Facility at par plus accrued interest.

In April 1995, the Company issued to the public 9,849,900 shares of Common Stock and $145.0 million principal amount of Senior Term Notes. The Company received aggregate net proceeds from the issuance of the Common Stock and Senior Term Notes of approximately $231.0 million and applied $56.2 million of such proceeds to retire its temporary financing facility plus accrued interest, $15.6 million to retire the Company's 9.875% Senior Subordinated Notes (including a prepayment fee of $0.5 million and accrued interest of $0.1 million), and $9.4 million to fund a reserve account established for future payment of interest on the Senior Term Notes. The remaining proceeds of $149.8 million were available as working capital for loan purchases and general operations.

The Company pays interest on the Senior Term Notes semi-annually on November 1 and May 1 of each year. The Senior Term Notes are not callable

prior to May 1, 1998. Thereafter, the Senior Term Notes are redeemable, in whole or in part, at the option of the Company, at 108.5% and 104.25% if redeemed during the 12 month periods beginning May 1, 1998, and 1999, respectively, together with accrued and unpaid interest to the date of redemption. The Company will be obligated to make an offer to purchase all outstanding Senior Term Notes at a price of 101% of the principal amount thereof, together with accrued and unpaid interest to the date of purchase if certain covenants (as defined within the Senior Term Note indenture) regarding sales of assets, change in control or annualized net losses are violated. The Senior Term Notes are unsecured obligations of the Company (except for a reserve fund equal to one interest payment on the outstanding principal balance of the Senior Term Notes) and rank senior to all outstanding subordinate notes of the Company and *pari passu* in right of payment with all unsecured and unsubordinated indebtedness of the Company. On January 21, 1997 the Company made a tender offer to purchase all of its outstanding Senior Term Notes. See Note 14 to the Company's Consolidated Financial Statements.

Pursuant to demand registration rights of certain holders of warrants issued by the Company between 1992 and 1994 in connection with its issuance of Senior Secured and Senior Subordinated Notes, the Company filed separate registration statements during April and October 1995 covering 213,000 and 3,871,364 shares of Common Stock, respectively, issuable upon exercise of the warrants for secondary sale at market should the holders decide to do so. The Company would receive aggregate proceeds of approximately $17.0 million assuming exercise of all of the warrants. As of December 31, 1996, 2,405,089 shares of Common Stock had been issued in connection with exercise of such warrants for aggregate proceeds of $10.0 million. In September 1994, the Company began a program to sell up to $50.0 million of unsecured subordinated notes (the "Junior Subordinated Notes") to be offered to the public from time to time (the "Note Program") . Issuance of Junior Subordinated Notes under the Note Program is subject to restriction, under the Senior Term Note indenture. The Note Program includes Junior Subordinated Notes extendible by the investor having maturities of 30, 60, 90, and

Olympic Financial Ltd.

180 days and one year after the date of issue and fixed-term Junior Subordinated Notes having maturities of one, two, three, four, five and ten years after the date of issue. Interest rates on any unsold Junior Subordinated Notes are subject to change by the Company from time to time based on market conditions. Interest rates on extendible Junior Subordinated Notes may be adjusted at any roll-over date. At December 31, 1996, the Company had $23.7 million of Junior Subordinated Notes outstanding. The terms of the Senior Term Note indenture, among other things, limit, subject to certain other requirements and with certain exceptions, certain payments, including dividends on common or preferred stock, to 50% of Consolidated Cash Flow (as defined). Consolidated Cash Flow is defined as Operating Cash Receipts less Cash Expenses for the four quarterly periods preceding a proposed restricted payment. The Company has had and expects to continue to have negative Consolidated Cash Flow for so long as the rapid growth of its loan purchase Volume continues.

Consolidated Cash Flow for the four-quarter period ended December 31, 1996, is as follows:

(in thousands)	For the Four Quarters Ended December 31, 1996
Operating Cash Receipts:	
Excess cash flows received from securitization trusts	$ 43,351
Servicing fee income	27,018
Other cash income	7,959
Total operating cash receipts	78,328
Less Cash Expenses:	
Payment of dealer commissions	94,938
Cash operating expenses	98,644
Interest paid on warehouse and other debt	33,448
Preferred dividends	1,688
Total cash expenses	228,718
Consolidated cash flow	$(150,390)

At December 31, 1996 the Company's Portfolio Loss Ratio (as defined in the Senior Term Note indenture) was 1.12% and the Company's Consolidated Net Worth (as defined in the Senior Term Note indenture) was $388.7 million.

FORWARD LOOKING STATEMENTS

The Preceding Management's Discussion and Analysis of the Company's Financial Condition and Results of Operations contains certain "forward-looking statements" within the meaning of the Private Securities Litigation Reform Act of 1995, which can be identified by the use of forward-looking terminology such as "may," "will," "expect," "anticipate," "estimate," "should," or "continue" or the negative thereof or other variations thereon or comparable terminology. The matters set forth under the caption "Cautionary Statements" in **Exhibit 99.1** to the Annual Report on Form 10-K constitute cautionary statements identifying important factors with respect to such forward-looking statements, including certain risks and uncertainties, that could cause actual results to differ materially from those in such forward-looking statements.

CONSOLIDATED BALANCE SHEETS

	At December 31,	
(Dollars in thousands, except per share amounts)	1996	1995
Assets		
Cash and cash equivalents	$ 16,057	$ 1,340
Due from securitization trust	177,076	—
Auto loans held for sale	36,285	118,556
Finance income receivable	362,916	186,001
Restricted cash in spread accounts	142,977	63,580
Furniture, fixtures, and equipment	13,630	6,346
Other assets	29,289	21,971
Total assets	**$778,230**	**$397,794**
Liabilities and Shareholders' Equity		
Amounts due under warehouse facilities	$111,140	$26,530
Senior term notes	145,000	145,000
Subordinated notes	53,689	13,005
Capital lease obligations	7,729	3,924
Deferred income taxes	54,387	18,700
Accounts payable and accrued liabilities	13,192	9,822
Total liabilities	**385,137**	**216,981**
Commitments and contingencies		
Shareholders' equity:		
Capital stock, $.01 par value, 100,000,000 shares authorized: 8% Cumulative Convertible Exchangeable Preferred Stock, 1,071,036 shares issued and outstanding	—	11
Common Stock 22,038,567 and 36,416,802 shares, respectively, issued and outstanding	364	220
Additional paid-in capital	310,187	157,204
Retained earnings	82,542	23,378
Total shareholders' equity	**393,093**	**180,813**
Total liabilities and shareholders' equity	**$778,230**	**$397,794**

Olympic Financial Ltd.

Olympic Financial Ltd.

CONSOLIDATED STATEMENTS OF INCOME

	Year Ended December 31,		
(Dollars in thousands, except per share amounts)	1996	1995	1994
Revenues			
Net interest margin	$ 62,963	$ 31,192	$ 9,828
Gain on sale of loans	115,773	62,182	13,579
Servicing fee income	28,284	13,987	4,502
Other non-interest income	6,475	1,371	879
Total revenues	213,495	108,732	28,788
Expenses			
Salaries and benefits	40,751	20,079	9,060
General and administrative and other operating expenses	51,547	22,648	8,282
Total operating expenses	92,298	42,727	17,342
Long-term debt and other interest expense	25,193	17,170	5,416
Total expenses	117,491	59,897	22,758
Operating income before income taxes and extraordinary items	96,004	48,835	6,030
Provision for income taxes	35,688	19,518	1,845
Income before extraordinary items	60,316	29,317	4,185
Extraordinary items	—	(3,856)	--
Net income	$ 60,316	$ 25,461	$ 4,185
Primary Earnings Per Share			
Net income per common share before extraordinary items	$1.79	$1.35	$0.17
Extraordinary items per common share	—	(0.19)	—
Net income per common share	$1.79	$1.16	$0.17
Fully Diluted Earnings Per Share			
Net income per share before extraordinary items	$1.65	$1.11	$0.17
Extraordinary items per share	—	(0.15)	—
Net income per share	$1.65	$0.96	$0.17
Weighted average common and common equivalent shares outstanding:			
Primary	33,065,473	20,029,769	10,818,908
Fully diluted	36,449,995	26,455,876	16,683,380

CONSOLIDATED STATEMENTS OF CASH FLOWS

(Dollars in thousands)	Year Ended December 31,		
	1996	1995	1994
Cash flows from operating activities:			
Net income	$ 60,316	$ 25,461	$ 4,185
Adjustments to reconcile net income to net cash used in operating activities:			
Depreciation and amortization	4,286	1,881	553
Loss on sale of furniture, fixtures, and equipment	119	153	—
(Increase) decrease in assets:			
Automobile loans held for sale			
Purchases of automobile loans	(2,750,553)	(2,052,413)	(743,256)
Sales of automobile loans	2,787,412	1,933,525	712,211
Repayments of automobile loans	45,412	24,200	7,849
Finance income receivable	(176,916)	(127,461)	(32,293)
Restricted cash in spread accounts	(79,397)	(42,172)	(6,299)
Due from securitization trusts	(177,076)	88,481	(22,095)
Prepaid expenses and other assets	(5,787)	(10,402)	(3,121)
Increase (decrease) in liabilities:			
Deferred income taxes	35,688	16,947	1,845
Accounts payable and accrued liabilities	3,369	6,141	1,647
Total cash used in operating activities	(253,127)	(135,659)	(78,774)
Cash flows from investing activities:			
Proceeds from sales of furniture, fixtures, and equipment	26	37	68
Purchase of furniture, fixtures, and equipment	(5,108)	(1,089)	(362)
Purchase of subordinated certificates	(2,596)	(2,046)	(962)
Collections on subordinated certificates	1,078	510	339
Total cash used in investing activities	(6,600)	(2,588)	(917)
Cash flows from financing activities:			
Net proceeds from issuance of Common Stock	152,079	95,866	288
Net proceeds from issuance of 8% Convertible Preferred Stock	—	—	(10)
Payment of dividends on 8% Convertible Preferred Stock	(1,152)	(2,213)	(2,300)
Proceeds from borrowings under warehouse facilities	2,159,523	1,605,583	426,161
Repayment of borrowings under warehouse facilities	(2,074,913)	(1,685,241)	(342,082)
Unsecured Subordinated Notes, net	40,684	12,699	306
Proceeds from issuance of long-term debt	—	—	12,000
Repayments of long-term debt	—	(30,000)	—
Proceeds from issuance of Senior Notes	—	55,000	—
Repayment of Senior Notes	—	(55,000)	—
Proceeds from issuance of Senior Term Notes	—	145,000	—
Repayments of Senior Subordinated Notes	—	(15,000)	—
Deferred debt issuance cost, net	(13)	(2,541)	(259)
Reduction of capital lease obligations	(1,764)	(1,183)	(532)
Total cash provided by financing activities	274,444	122,970	93,572
Net increase (decrease) in cash and cash equivalents	14,717	(15,277)	13,881
Cash and cash equivalents at the beginning of period	1,340	16,617	2,736
Cash and cash equivalents at the end of period	$16,057	$1,340	$16,617
Supplemental disclosures of cash flow information:			
Noncash activities:			
Additions to capital leases	$5,569	$3,609	$1,524
Cash paid for:			
Interest	33,448	19,630	6,386
Taxes	—	92	—

Olympic Financial Ltd.

EXHIBIT 2 (continued)

NOTES TO CONSOLIDATED FINANCIAL STATEMENTS

I. Summary of Significant Accounting Policies

Arcadia Financial Ltd, (the "Company") operates in a single industry, purchases, securitizes, and services consumer automobile retail installment loans originated primarily by car dealers affiliated with major foreign and domestic manufacturers. The Company provides a competitive and consistent alternative source of retail financing to more than 7,700 automobile dealers for their customers' purchases of new and used automobiles and light trucks. The Company does not purchase more than 1.0% of its loans from any one dealer. Since its founding in March 1990, the Company has established 17 regional buying centers in Arizona, Northern and Southern California, Colorado, Florida, Georgia, Massachusetts, Minnesota, Missouri, New York, North Carolina, Ohio, Tennessee, North, South and West Texas, and Washington. The Company's dealer network includes dealers in 39 states. At December 31, 1996, the Company's only significant geographic concentration in its servicing portfolio was to borrowers in the state of Texas which consisted of approximately 22% of the total servicing portfolio. Management does not believe that the Company has any current material exposures to geographic or dealer concentrations.

Basis of Presentation

The consolidated financial statements include the accounts of the Company and its wholly-owned subsidiaries. All significant intercompany accounts and transactions have been eliminated. The consolidated financial statements have been prepared in conformity with generally accepted accounting principles.

Certain reclassifications have been made to the December 31, 1995 and 1994 balances to conform to current period presentation.

Cash and Cash Equivalents

The Company considers all significant investments with an original maturity of three months or less to be cash equivalents.

Use of Estimates

The preparation of financial statements in conformity with generally accepted accounting principles requires management to make estimates and assumptions that affect the reported amounts of assets and liabilities at the date of the financial statements and the reported amounts of revenues and expenses during the reporting period. Actual results could differ from those estimates.

Due from Securitization Trust

Under Arcadia's securitization structures, the Company delivers loans to a securitization trust and subsequently receives cash from the trust for such loans concurrent with the legal closing of the transaction, typically six to ten days after delivery. All terms of the transfer of assets to the trust are fixed and determinable at the time of delivery.

Automobile Loans Held for Sale

Loans are carried at the lower of their principal amount outstanding (amortized cost), including related unearned dealer participations, or market value. Market value is estimated based on the characteristics of the loans held for sale and the terms of recent sales of similar loans completed by the Company. Interest on these loans is accrued and credited to interest income based upon the daily principal amount outstanding.

In accordance with Emerging Issues Task Force ("EITF") Issue 92-10, *Loan Acquisitions Involving Table Funding Arrangements*, the EITF set forth specific criteria providing the distinction between purchasers and originators of loans. For financial reporting purposes, the Company is in substance an originator of automobile loans. Therefore, participations paid to dealers are deferred and amortized over the life of the underlying loan in accordance with Statement of Financial Accounting Standards ("SFAS") No. 91, "Accounting for Nonrefundable Fees and Costs Associated with Originating or

Acquiring Loans and Initial Direct Costs of Leases." Any unamortized deferred costs remaining at the time the loan is sold are considered a portion of the basis of loans held for sale and charged to expense as a component of any subsequent gain or loss on sale.

Dealer participations are calculated by amortizing the customer loan at the interest rate charged by the automobile dealer to the automobile purchaser and at the rate offered by the Company to the dealer and recognizing the difference between these two aggregate interest amounts as the dealer participation.

This amount is paid to the dealer at or near the original purchase date of the loan. A portion of this amount is generally recoverable from the dealer in the event of a default or pre-payment within a time period specified in the dealer agreement. The balance is recovered over time as a portion of excess cash flows released from securitization trusts.

Finance Income Receivable

Finance income receivable includes (i) the estimated present value of future cash flows from securitization transactions ("gain on sale of loans"), (ii) accrued interest receivable on loans held for sale, but not yet collected through the date of sale, (iii) interest earned on spread accounts and other cash accounts established in connection with the Company's securitizations, and (iv) interest earned on previously discounted cash flows. The components of finance income receivable are recovered by the Company, and finance income receivable is reduced, over the life of the securitized loans through the return of cash flow in excess of spread account requirements.

Finance income receivable excludes deferred service fee income which represents the amount of future cash flows to be recognized as earned over the period for which the Company services the securitized loans.

Reserves for loan losses included in finance income receivable represents the estimated amount of loan losses expected to be incurred over the life of the underlying loans included in the securitization transactions.

The carrying amount of finance income receivable is reviewed periodically to determine if differences exist between estimated and actual credit losses, prepayment rates, and weighted average APR at each balance sheet date using the discount factor applied in the original determination of the receivable. In addition, at the same dates, the Company assesses the effect of changes in estimates, if any, on the carrying amount of the finance income receivable. The Company's analysis determines that the finance income receivable is not recorded in excess of the present value of the estimated remaining excess cash flows. The Company does not increase the carrying amount of finance income receivable for favorable variances from original estimates, but to the extent that actual results exceed the Company's prepayment or loss estimates, or there is a greater than anticipated decline in the weighted average APR of loans sold, any required decrease to finance income receivable is reflected as a reduction of current period earnings. There were no material adjustments to the carrying amount of finance income receivable during the three years ended December 31, 1996. Adjustments due to modification of future estimates are determined on a disaggregated basis according to each asset securitization transaction.

Cash Restricted in Spread Accounts

The Company is required to maintain spread accounts to protect investors in securitization transactions and credit enhancers against credit losses. The initial deposit, if required, and excess cash flows from securitization transactions are retained for each securitization until the spread account balance increases to a specified percentage of the underlying loan included in the securitization. Funds in excess of specified percentages are remitted to the Company, through its wholly-owned subsidiary Olympic Receivables Finance Corp., ("ORFC"), over the remaining life of the securitization. For each securitization trust, there is no recourse to the Company beyond the balance in the spread accounts or the trust's future earnings.

Furniture, Fixtures and Equipment

Furniture, fixtures and equipment are stated at cost less accumulated depreciation and amortization. Owned properties are depreciated on a straight-line basis over their useful lives. Capital lease assets are amortized over their lease terms on a straight-line basis.

Olympic Financial Ltd.

Olympic Financial Ltd.

Advances Due to Servicer

As servicer of loans sold in securitizations, the Company periodically makes interest advances to the securitization trust to provide for temporary delays in the receipt of required interest payments by borrowers. In accordance with the Company's servicing agreements, the Company makes advances only in the event it expects to recover them through the ultimate payments from the obligor on the loan.

Deferred Debt Issuance Costs

The Company capitalizes costs incurred related to the issuance of long-term debt. These costs are deferred and amortized on a straight-line basis over the contractual maturity of the related debt and recognized as a component of interest expense.

Servicing Fee Receivable

The Company earns a servicing fee for servicing loans sold to investors through securitization. These fees are paid to the Company by the securitization trust on a monthly basis.

Income taxes

Deferred tax assets and liabilities are recognized for future tax consequences related to differences between the current carrying amounts of assets and liabilities and their respective tax bases. Deferred tax assets and liabilities are measured based on enacted tax rates expected to apply to taxable income in the years in which those temporary differences are expected to be recovered or settled.

Net Interest Margin

The Company's net interest margin represents the sum of (i) net interest on loans held for sale based on the net interest rate spread, (ii) investment earnings on short-term investments and spread accounts and other cash accounts established in connection with the Company's securitizations, and (iii) the recognition of the interest component of previously discounted cash flows, calculated at the present value discount rate used in determining the gain on sale.

Net Income Per Share

Income for primary earnings per share is adjusted for dividends on 8% Convertible Preferred Stock and is computed based on the weighted average number of common and dilutive common stock equiva-

lents arising from the assumed exercise of outstanding warrants and stock options (calculated using the treasury stock method). Fully diluted earnings, per share data for annual periods prior to 1996, is computed by using such weighted average common stock and common stock equivalents increased by the assumed conversion of the 8% Convertible Preferred Stock into shares of Common Stock. All of the Company's 8% Convertible Preferred Stock had been redeemed or converted at December 31, 1996. If all of the Company's 8% Convertible Preferred Stock had converted at the beginning of 1996, primary earnings per share for the year ended December 31, 1996 would have been $1.67. The effect on quarterly primary earnings per share would have been immaterial. For the purpose of computing the net income per common share equivalent data, all warrants and options issued are treated as if exercised for shares of Common Stock on their respective date of original issuance.

Fair Value of Financial Instruments

The Company's financial instruments as defined by SFAS No. 107, "Disclosures About Fair Value of Financial Instruments," including cash and cash equivalents, due from securitization trusts, finance income receivable, restricted cash in spread accounts, amounts due under warehouse facilities, and Junior Subordinated Notes are accounted for on a historical cost basis which, due to the nature of these financial instruments, approximates fair value. Automobile loans held for sale are accounted for at the lower of amortized cost or market value. Fair value of the Company's Senior Term Notes and 10.125% Senior Subordinated Notes is determined using available market quotes. At December 31, 1996 and 1995, the Company had $145.0 million of Senior Term Notes outstanding with an estimated fair value of $161.0 million at December 31, 1996 and $158.1 million at December 31, 1995. The Company also had $30.0 million of Senior Subordinated Notes issued during 1996 and outstanding at December 31, 1996. The carrying amount of the Senior Subordinated Notes approximates fair value.

3. Automobile Loans Held for Sale

The weighted average interest rate on automobile

loans held for sale was 15.22% and 14.04% at December 31, 1996 and 1995, respectively. Accrued interest receivable on automobile loans held for sale aggregated $0.2 million and $0.6 million as of December 31, 1996, and 1995, respectively.

4. Finance Income Receivable

The following table sets forth the components of finance income receivable as of December 31:

(Dollars in thousands)	1996	1995
Estimated cash flows on loans sold, net of estimated prepayments	$549,876	$285,517
Deferred servicing income	(59,473)	(37,780)
Reserve for loan losses	(95,005)	(42,270)
Undiscounted cash flows on loans sold, net of estimated prepayments	395,398	205,467
Discount to present value	(32,482)	(19,466)
	$362,916	$186,001
Reserve for loan losses as a percentage of servicing portfolio	2.51%	1.86%

The following represents the roll-forward of the finance income receivable balance for the two years ended December 31, 1996:

(Dollars in thousands)	
Balance, December 31, 1994	$ 58,540
Excess cash flows on loans sold, net of estimated prepayments	141,147
Return on excess cash flows	(21,054)
Recognition of present value effect of cash flows	7,368
Balance, December 31, 1995	186,001
Excess cash flows on loans sold, net of estimated prepayments	201,376
Return on excess cash flows	(43,351)
Recognition of present value effect of cash flows	18,890
Balance, December 31, 1996	$362,916

5. Furniture, Fixtures, and Equipment

Furniture, fixtures, and equipment, as of December 31, consists of the following:

(Dollars in thousands)	1996	1995
Owned		
Office furniture and equipment	$6,637	$2,385
Automobiles	313	220
Computer equipment	1,003	319
Total	7,953	2,924

(Dollars in thousands)	1996	1995
Capitalized leases		
Office furniture and equipment	4,280	2,677
Computer equipment	5,545	2,621
Total	9,825	5,298
Total furniture, fixtures, and equipment (at cost)	17,778	8,222
Less:		
Accumulated depreciation and amortization	(4,148)	(1,876)
Furniture, fixtures, and equipment, net	$13,630	$6,346

Depreciation expense including amortization of assets under capital lease obligations for the years ended December 31, 1996, 1995, and 1994 was $3.2 million, $1.0 million, and $0.5 million, respectively.

6. Other Assets

Other assets, as of December 31, consist of the following:

(Dollars in thousands)	1996	1995
Advances due to servicer	$8,140	$9,046
Deferred debt issuance costs	4,438	4,444
Investment in subordinated certificates	4,329	2,811
Servicing fee receivable	3,121	1,855
Prepaid expenses	2,755	1,545
Repossessed assets	1,577	431
Other assets	4,929	1,839
	$29,289	$21,971

7. Amounts Due Under Warehouse Facilities

At December 31, 1996, the Company had three warehouse facilities with an aggregate capacity of $800.0 million in place with various financial institutions and institutional lenders of which $688.9 million was available. Borrowings under these facilities are collateralized by certain loans held for sale. The weighted average interest rate on outstanding borrowing under the warehouse facilities was 6.27% and 7.23% at December 31, 1996 and 1995, respectively.

In December 1996, the Company entered into a commercial paper conduit facility sponsored by Bank of America. Under this facility, the Company's wholly-owned special purpose subsidiary may sell up to $300.0 million in retail automobile contracts

Olympic Financial Ltd.

to Arcadia Receivables Conduit Corporation ("ARCC"), a special purpose corporation owned by the Company. The purchase price to ARCC is funded through borrowings from Receivable Capital Corporation ("RCC"), a special purpose corporation administered by Bank of America, which in turn funds such borrowings through the issuance of commercial paper. This facility is subject to annual renewals through December 1999.

Also during 1996, the Company entered into a Credit Agreement with banks led by Bank of America. Under this agreement, the Company may borrow up to $170.0 million. The Company may borrow an amount equal to 95% of the outstanding principal amount of eligible automobile loans pledged to secure the indebtedness depending on certain portfolio performance tests. The Company's Credit Agreement matures in July 1997.

Additionally, the Company, through its special purpose subsidiary, Olympic Receivables Finance Corp., II ("ORFC II") participates in a $330.0 million receivables warehouse facility which utilizes a commercial paper conduit sponsored by J.P. Morgan. Under a receivables purchase agreement between the Company and ORFC II, the Company has agreed to sell automobile loans to ORFC II which funds the purchase by selling the automobile loans to an owner trust (the "Owner Trust") under repurchase agreements. The Owner Trust is funded through borrowings from Delaware Funding Corporation ("DFC"), a J.P. Morgan commercial paper company which in turn funds such borrowers through the issuance of commercial paper. In January 1997, the Company agreed to reduce the capacity of the J.P. Morgan facility from $330 million to approximately $250 million and to extend such facility through December 1997 with annual renewal options through December 1998.

8. Long-Term Debt

Senior Term Notes

In April 1995, the Company issued to the public $145.0 million principal amount of 13% Senior Notes due 2000 (the "Senior Term Notes"). Interest on the Senior Term Notes is payable semi-annually on November 1 and May 1 of each year, commencing November 1, 1995. The Senior Term Notes are

not callable prior to May 1, 1998. Thereafter, the Senior Term Notes are redeemable, in whole or in part, at the option of the Company, at 108.5% and 104.25% if redeemed during the 12 month periods beginning May 1, 1998, and 1999, respectively, together with accrued and unpaid interest to the date of redemption. The Company will be obligated to make an offer to purchase all outstanding Senior Term Notes at a price of 101% of the principal amount thereof, together with accrued and unpaid interest to the date of purchase if certain covenants (as defined within the Senior Term Note Indenture) regarding sales of assets, change in control or annualized net losses are not met.

Except for a reserve fund equal to one interest payment on the outstanding principal balance of the Senior Term Notes, the Senior Term Notes are unsecured obligations to the Company and will rank Senior to all outstanding subordinated notes of the Company and *pari passu* in right of payment with all unsecured and unsubordinated indebtedness of the Company. The reserve fund may be used by the Company to purchase automobile loans at an advance rate of 90% of principal balance of the loans purchased which are pledged against the Senior Term Notes. See Note No. 14, Subsequent Event.

Subordinated Notes

Subordinated notes outstanding as of December 31, are as follows:

(Dollars in thousands)	1996	1995
Senior subordinated notes, Series 1996-A	$30,000	$ –
Junior subordinated notes	23,689	13,005
	53,689	13,005

In March 1996, the Company sold to the public $30.0 million aggregate principal amount of its 10.125% Subordinated Notes, Series 1996-A due 2001 (the "Senior Subordinated Notes"). Interest on the Senior Subordinated Notes is payable monthly beginning May 15, 1996. The Senior Subordinated Notes may not be redeemed prior to May 15, 1998. At any time on such date or thereafter, the Company may at its option elect to redeem the Senior Subordinated Notes, in whole or in part, at 101.5% of the principal amount of Senior Subordinate Notes redeemed, or 100% thereof on or after May 15,

1999, plus accrued interest to and including the redemption date. The Senior Subordinated Notes are unsecured general obligations of the Company and are subordinated in right of payment to all existing and future Senior Debt (as defined in the indenture governing the Senior Subordinated Notes).

In September 1994, the Company completed a shelf registration to issue up to $50.0 million of Junior Subordinated Notes. The Junior Subordinated Notes are issued in minimum denominations of $1,000 and include extendible notes having maturities ranging from 30 days to one year from the date of issue and fixed term notes having maturities of one to ten years from date of issue. The Company may adjust interest rates on unsold notes prior to sale and on extendible notes at any roll-over date based on current market conditions. As of December 31, 1996, the weighted average maturity and interest rate of the Unsecured Subordinated Notes were 14.2 months and 9.50%, respectively.

Maturities of long-term debt outstanding at December 31, 1996 were:

(Dollars in thousands)	
Year Ending	
1997	$12,516
1998	7,747
1999	522
2000	145,616
2001	32,018
2002 and thereafter	270
Total	$198,689

9. Commitments and Contingencies

The Company leases furniture, fixtures, and equipment under capital and operating leases with terms in excess of one year. Additionally, the Company leases its office space under operating leases. Total rent expense on operating leases was $4.7 million, $1.8 million and $0.9 million for the years ended December 31, 1996, 1995, and 1994, respectively.

Future minimum lease payments required under capital and noncancelable operating leases with terms of one year or more, at December 31, 1996 were:

(Dollars in thousands)	Capital Leases	Operating Leases
Year Ending		
1997	$3,168	$6,337
1998	2,924	6,405
1999	1,371	5,874
2000	1,089	4,559
2001	697	3,240
2002 and thereafter	44	2,574
Total	9,293	$28,989
Less amounts representing interest	(1,564)	
Present value of net minimum lease payments	$7,729	

Under the terms of sales of automobile loans completed through securitization transactions, the Company may be obligated to repurchase certain automobile loans due to failure of the assets to meet specifically defined criteria. The Company may substitute other assets for those repurchased because of failure to meet the specifically defined criteria. The Company's potential obligation for defaulted automobile loans, if realized, is expected to be satisfied through the use of cash collateral accounts included in the securitization transactions. The Company may not substitute other assets for defaulted automobile loans.

Proceeds of transfers of automobile loans with limited recourse, accounted for as sales, during the years ended December 31, 1996, 1995, and 1994 were $2.8 billion, $1.9 billion, and $712.2 million, respectively. The outstanding balance of automobile loans transferred and serviced for others in connection with securitization transactions since the Company's inception was $3.8 billion at December 31, 1996.

12. Income Taxes

The components of income tax expense for the three years ended December 31, 1996 consist of the following:

(Dollars in thousands)	1996	1995	1994
Provision for deferred taxes:			
Federal	$32,641	$17,078	$1,614
State	3,047	2,440	231
Provision for income taxes	35,688	19,518	1,845
Tax effect of extraordinary items	—	(2,571)	—
Applicable income taxes, after extraordinary items	$35,688	$16,947	$1,845

Olympic Financial Ltd.

The reconciliation between income tax expense and the amount computed by applying the statutory federal income tax rate of 35% for the three years ended December 31, 1996 is as follows:

(Dollars in thousands)	1996	1995	1994
Federal tax at statutory rate	$33,601	$17,078	$2,054
State income tax, net of federal benefit	3,715	2,440	253
Effect of reversal of valuation allowance	—	—	(688)
Other	(1,628)	—	226
Provision for income taxes	35,688	19,518	1,845
Tax effect of extraordinary items	—	(2,571)	—
Applicable income taxes, after extraordinary items	$35,688	$16,947	$1,845
Effective income tax rate	37.2%	40.0%	40.0%

Deferred income taxes are provided for temporary differences between pretax income for financial reporting purposes and taxable income. The tax-effected temporary differences and carryforwards which comprise the significant components of the Company's deferred tax assets and liabilities are as follows:

	December 31,	
(Dollars in thousands)	1996	1995
Deferred Tax Assets:		
Securitization expenses	$5,089	$4,245
Other	1,364	—
Gross deferred tax assets	6,453	4,245
Deferred Tax Liabilities:		
Gain on securitizations	(84,595)	(41,025)
Other	(3,796)	(411)
Gross deferred tax liabilities	(88,391)	(41,436)
Net temporary differences	(81,938)	(37,191)
Net operating loss carryforwards (expiring 2006–2011)	27,551	18,491
Net deferred tax liability	$(54,387)	$(18,700)

At December 31, 1996, the Company has net operating loss carryforwards for federal income tax purposes of approximately $74.1 million which are available to offset future federal taxable income and expire no earlier than 2006. No valuation allowance was required as of December 31, 1996 or 1995 because it is more likely than not that the deferred tax asset will be realized against future taxable income. The timing of the realization of the benefits related to a portion of the income tax net operating loss carryforwards is limited on an annual basis under Section 382 of the Internal Revenue Code.

13. Derivative Activities and Off-Balance Sheet Risk

During the three years ended December 31, 1996, the Company entered into several hedging transactions to manage its gross interest rate spread on loans held for sale. The Company agreed to sell forward U.S. Treasuries that most closely parallel the average life of its portfolio of loans held for sale. Hedging gains and losses are recognized as a component of the gain on sale of loans on the date such loans are sold. As of December 31, 1996 and 1995, the Company had entered into the following agreements to sell forward Two Year Treasuries:

(Dollars in thousands)	1996	1995
Notional amount outstanding	$700,000	$450,000
Unrealized gains (losses) on outstanding hedging transactions	484	(574)

The hedging transactions outstanding at December 31, 1996 are expected to close in March 1997.

Hedging realized gains (losses) during the three year period ended December 31, 1996 were:

(Dollars in thousands)	1996	1995	1994
Realized gains (losses)	$(349)	$(11,719)	$821

The Company generally maintains a margin cash account of approximately 0.5% of the amount hedged with its counter-party in hedging transactions. See discussion of the Company's hedging policy in "Management's Discussion and Analysis of Financial Condition and Results of Operation—Capital Resources—Hedging and Pre-Funding Strategy."

14 . Subsequent Event

In January 1997, the Company offered to purchase all of its 13% Senior Term Notes, due 2000, at a price of $1,117.50 for each $1,000 principal amount thereof, together with accrued and unpaid interest up to the date of Purchase. In connection with the offer to purchase, the Company is soliciting consent from the holders of the 13% Senior Term Notes to remove substantially all financial covenants applicable to such notes and is paying each holder of 13% Senior Term Notes $20.00 in cash for each $1,000 of principal amount thereof if the required consents are received. The Company will not be obligated to purchase any 13% Senior Term Notes unless (1) a majority of the 13% Senior Notes not owned by the Company or any of its affiliates are properly tendered, (2) consents sufficient to approve the amendments are obtained and (3) the Company has deposited funds with the depository sufficient to purchase all Senior Term Notes tendered, whether from proceeds of a proposed public offering of senior notes aggregating not less than $170 million or from other new financing sources acceptable to the Company. In connection therewith, the Company proposes to make a public offering of up to $300 million principal amount of senior notes. Proceeds from this transaction will be used to repurchase up to $145 million principal amount of the Company's outstanding 13% Senior Term Notes pursuant to the tender offer, as well as for general corporate purposes. The public offering, which is expected to commence during the week of February 3, 1997, will be made by means of a prospectus under the Company's shelf registration statement under the Securities Act of 1933, as amended. The Company's offer to purchase the 13% Senior Term Notes expires at 5:00 p.m. Eastern Standard Time, on February 20, 1997 unless extended.

15. Unaudited Selected Quarterly Data

Fourth Quarter Results of Operations

The Company purchased $740.9 million of automobile loans in the fourth quarter of 1996 compared to $588.7 million for the same period in 1995, and securitized $720.2 million in 1996 compared to $574.5 million in 1995. Net income in the fourth quarter of 1996 was $17.4 million compared to $10.2 million in 1995. Increased average loans held for sale and a widening in the Company's net interest rate spread in the fourth quarter of 1996 resulted in an increase in net interest margin to $17.5 million from $9.4 million in the same period a year ago. Non-interest revenue increased to $1.9 million in the fourth quarter of 1996 compared to $0.6 million for the same period in 1995 primarily due to late fees and insufficient fund charges. Operating expenses increased to $29.0 million in the fourth quarter of 1996 from $13.4 million in the same period of 1995. This is primarily due to increased salaries and benefits which reflect a two-fold increase in associates. In addition, operating expenses have increased due to servicing and collection costs. This is a result of an increased servicing portfolio and a rise in the volume of classic loans.

Olympic Financial Ltd.

UNAUDITED SELECTED QUARTERLY DATA

Olympic Financial Ltd.

	Quarter Ended			
(Dollars in thousands except per share amounts)	December 31, 1996	September 30, 1996	June 30, 1996	March 31, 1996
Revenues:				
Net interest margin	$17,499	$18,079	$15,085	$12,300
Gain on sale of auto loans	34,979	30,113	25,452	25,229
Service fee income	8,510	7,474	6,557	5,743
Other non-interest income	1,896	1,406	2,449	724
Total revenues	62,884	57,072	49,543	43,996
Expenses:				
Salaries and benefits	12,555	10,286	8,813	9,097
General & administrative & other operating expenses	16,397	13,107	11,124	10,919
Long-term debt and other interest expense	6,584	6,660	6,433	5,516
Total expenses	35,536	30,053	26,370	25,532
Operating income before income tax & extraordinary items	27,348	27,019	23,173	18,464
Provision for income taxes	9,982	9,862	8,458	7,386
Income before extraordinary items	17,366	17,157	14,715	11,078
Extraordinary items	—	—	—	—
Net income	$17,366	$17,157	$14,715	$11,078
Primary Earnings Per Share:				
Net income per common share before extraordinary items	$0.46	$0.47	$0.43	$0.41
Extraordinary items per common share	—	—	—	—
Net income (loss) per common share	$0.46	$0.47	$0.43	$0.41
Fully Diluted Earnings Per Share:				
Net income per share before extraordinary items	$0.45	$0.44	$0.40	$0.37
Extraordinary items per share	—	—	—	—
Net income per share	$0.45	$0.44	$0.40	$0.37
Weighted average common and common equivalent shares outstanding:				
Primary	37,873,845	35,896,149	33,508,215	25,741,672
Fully diluted	38,935,961	39,423,446	37,205,287	30,218,329
	December 31, 1996	September 30, 1996	June 30, 1996	March 31, 1996
Assets				
Cash and cash equivalents	$ 16,057	$ 3,593	$ 22,575	$ 22,552
Due from securitization trust	177,076	188,373	151,635	115,000
Auto loans held for sale	36,285	18,925	52,300	82,857
Finance income receivable	362,916	307,953	264,466	232,007
Restricted cash in spread accounts	142,977	122,071	101,948	79,779
Other assets	42,919	42,910	37,735	33,542
Total assets	$778,230	$683,825	$630,659	$565,737
Liabilities & Shareholders' Equity				
Amounts due under warehouse facilities	$111,140	$ 38,486	$ 17,837	$127,224
Senior notes	145,000	145,000	145,000	145,000
Subordinated notes	53,689	53,563	52,288	46,595
Capital lease obligations	7,729	8,049	7,446	6,635
Deferred income taxes	54,387	44,405	34,543	26,085
Accounts payable and accrued liabilities	13,192	20,059	16,748	21,633
Shareholders' equity	393,093	374,263	356,797	192,565
Total liabilities and shareholders' equity	$778,230	$683,825	$630,659	$565,737

Source: 1996 Arcadia Financial Ltd. Annual Report.

Olympic Financial Ltd.

(Dollars in thousands except per share amounts)	Quarter Ended			
	December 31, 1995	September 30, 1995	June 30, 1995	March 31, 1995
Revenues:				
Net interest margin	$9,423	$9,601	$7,630	$4,538
Gain on sale of auto loans	21,235	17,587	14,303	9,057
Service fee income	4,812	3,872	3,003	2,300
Other non-interest income	569	405	238	159
Total revenues	**36,039**	**31,465**	**25,174**	**16,054**
Expenses:				
Salaries and benefits	6,361	5,146	4,627	3,945
General & administrative & other operating expenses	7,083	6,097	4,973	4,495
Long-term debt and other interest expense	5,546	5,205	4,574	1,845
Total expenses	18,990	16,448	14,174	10,285
Operating income before income tax & extraordinary items	17,049	15,017	11,000	5,769
Provision for income taxes	6,820	6,007	4,384	2,307
Income before extraordinary items	10,229	9,010	6,616	3,462
Extraordinary items	—	—	(512)	(3,344)
Net income	$10,229	$9,010	$6,104	$118
Primary Earnings Per Share:				
Net income per common share before extraordinary items	$0.39	$0.34	$0.29	$0.23
Extraordinary items per common share	—	—	$(0.02)	(0.27)
Net income (loss) per common share	$0.39	$0.34	$0.27	$(0.04)
Fully Diluted Earnings Per Share:				
Net income per share before extraordinary items	$0.34	$0.30	$0.25	$0.19
Extraordinary items per share	—	—	(0.02)	(0.18)
Net income per share	$0.34	$0.30	$0.23	$0.01
Weighted average common and common equivalent shares outstanding:				
Primary	24,547,195	24,528,119	20,656,566	12,505,372
Fully diluted	30,368,723	30,406,065	26,661,621	18,185,965

	December 31, 1995	September 30, 1995	June 30, 1995	March 31, 1995
Assets				
Cash and cash equivalents	$ 1,340	$ 9,169	$ 14,839	$ 5,654
Due from securitization trust	-	50,398	75,018	135,013
Auto loans held for sale	118,556	108,808	61,801	500
Finance income receivable	186,001	150,538	118,113	86,848
Restricted cash in spread accounts	63,580	48,160	36,292	28,326
Other assets	28,317	23,663	16,971	12,647
Total assets	$397,794	$390,736	$323,034	$268,988
Liabilities & Shareholders' Equity				
Amounts due under warehouse facilities	$ 26,530	$ 41,281	$ 226	$130,816
Senior notes	145,000	145,000	145,000	50,000
Subordinated notes	13,005	9,191	4,706	17,321
Capital lease obligations	3,924	2,822	1,898	1,737
Deferred income taxes	8,700	11,880	5,966	1,924
Accounts payable and accrued liabilities	9,822	15,982	9,358	6,430
Shareholders' equity	180,813	164,580	155,880	60,760
Total liabilities and shareholders' equity	$387,794	$390,736	$323,034	$268,988

Olympic Financial Ltd.

REPORT OF INDEPENDENT AUDITORS

Board of Directors
Arcadia Financial Ltd.   January 21, 1997

We have audited the accompanying consolidated balance sheets of Arcadia Financial Ltd. (previously known as Olympic Financial Ltd.) as of December 31, 1996 and 1995 and the related consolidated statements of income, shareholders' equity, and cash flows for each of the three years in the period ended December 31,1996. These financial statements are the responsibility of the Company's management. Our responsibility is to express an opinion on these financial statements based on our audits.

We conducted our audits in accordance with generally accepted auditing standards. Those standards require that we plan and perform the audit to obtain reasonable assurance about whether the financial statements are free of material misstatement. An audit includes examining, on a test basis, evidence supporting the amounts and disclosures in the financial statements. An audit also includes assessing the accounting principles used and significant estimates made by management, as well as evaluating the overall financial statement presentation. We believe that our audits provide a reasonable basis for our opinion.

In our opinion, the financial statements referred to above present fairly, in all material respects, the consolidated financial position of Arcadia Financial Ltd. at December 31, 1996 and 1995 and the consolidated results of its operations and its cash flows for each of the three years in the period ended December 31, 1996, in conformity with generally accepted accounting principles.

Minneapolis, Minnesota   Ernst & Young LLP

REPORT OF MANAGEMENT

The management of Arcadia Financial Ltd. (previously known as Olympic Financial Ltd.) and its subsidiaries are responsible for the preparation of the accompanying consolidated financial statements and for their integrity and objectivity. The consolidated financial statements have been prepared in accordance with generally accepted accounting principles and include amounts based upon management's judgment and best estimates.

The consolidated financial statements have been audited by Ernst & Young LLP, independent auditors, selection of which has been approved by the Board of Directors of Arcadia Financial Ltd.

Arcadia Financial Ltd. and its subsidiaries have established and maintain systems of internal control designed to provide reasonable assurance that assets are safeguarded and transactions are properly authorized and recorded. The independent auditors consider the Company's internal control structure in order to determine their auditing procedures for the purpose of expressing an opinion on the consolidated financial statements.

The Audit Committee of the Board of Directors of Arcadia Financial Ltd., comprised exclusively of outside directors, meets with management and representatives of Ernst & Young LLP to review audit, internal control, and accounting and financial reporting issues.

Management recognizes its responsibility for fostering a strong, ethical climate so that Arcadia's affairs are carried out in accordance with the highest standards of professional and business conduct.

Richard A. Greenawalt	**John A. Witham**	**Brian S. Anderson**
President and Chief Executive Officer	Executive Vice President and Chief Financial Officer (Principal Financial Officer)	Senior Vice President and Corporate Controller (Principal Accounting Officer)

EXHIBIT 3

Moody's Ratings Announcements for Olympic Financial (May 1996–February 1997)

 Moody's Investor Service
                      Global Credit Research   **Opinion Update**

OLYMPIC FINANCIAL LTD.

Published on 05/01/96

Moody's has changed Olympic Financial's long-term debt rating outlook to positive from stable. The change in outlook applies to both Olympic's senior B2 and subordinated B3 rated obligations. Our change in outlook is based on Olympic's successful completion of its $148 million public common stock offering and on the positive impact of that offering on the company's liquidity and dollar capital position. Olympic still faces the near-term challenges of managing the growing penetration of its higher-risk "Classic" loan program, of maintaining asset quality, and of operating in an increasingly competitive auto-finance marketplace.

 Moody's Investor Service
                      Global Credit Research   **Rating Action**

OLYMPIC FINANCIAL LTD.

Published on 06/21/96

MOODY'S UPGRADES OLYMPIC FINANCIAL'S SENIOR AND SUBORDINATED RATINGS TO B1 AND B2.

Approximately $175.0 Million of Debt Securities Affected.

New York, 6/21/1996   Moody's Investors Service upgraded Olympic Financial's senior notes to B1 from B2 and subordinated notes to B2 from B3. The upgrade is based on Olympic's recent $148 million public common stock offering and on the positive impact of that offering on the company's liquidity and capital position. In addition, the upgrade reflects Moody's confidence that management is taking the right steps to minimize the risks associated with a larger penetration of its higher-risk "Classic" loan program and the benefits of the "Classic" program on cash flow and profitability.

Olympic has made the strategic decision to increase its higher-risk "Classic" loan program to 50% of origination volume from 25%. The benefits of this shift are to improve cash flow by reducing dealer participations and to increase profitability by realizing higher risk adjusted returns. To reduce the risks associated with a higher penetration of "Classic," Olympic has improved its underwriting by eliminating its "Classic 2" program targeted at first time buyers and anticipates improving its servicing by shifting to monthly billing statements from coupon books and by more aggressively collecting against delinquent borrowers.

Olympic Financial Ltd.

Moody's Investor Service
                    Global Credit Research   **Rating Action**

OLYMPIC FINANCIAL LTD.
                                              Published on 08/26/96

MOODY'S HAS PLACED OLYMPIC FINANCIAL'S RATINGS UNDER REVIEW; DIRECTION UNCERTAIN

New York, 8/26/1997   Moody's Investors Service placed the ratings of Olympic Financial Ltd. on review with direction uncertain following the announcement by the company that it has received an indication of interest to buy the company and that Olympic is now considering its strategic alternatives. The ratings action applies to both Olympic's senior and subordinated notes, which are currently rated B1 and B2, respectively.

The review will consider the strength of any acquiring company should an acquisition take place or the consequences to Olympic's financial strength and flexibility should the company pursue other strategic alternatives. In an associated development, Jeffrey Mack resigned as Chairman, President, Chief Executive Officer and member of the Board. Warren Kantor, formerly a member of Olympic's Board, was named Chairman of the Executive Committee.

 Moody's Investor Service
                    Global Credit Research   **Rating Action**

OLYMPIC FINANCIAL LTD.
                                              Published on 01/24/97

MOODY'S CONFIRMS OLYMPIC FINANCIAL'S RATINGS (SENIOR AT B1); CHANGES OUTLOOK TO NEGATIVE

Approximately $200 Million of Debt Securities Affected

New York, 1/24/1997   Moody's has confirmed the B1 senior and B2 subordinated debt ratings of Olympic Financial, Ltd. Moody's had placed the ratings on review with direction uncertain on August 26, 1996, after the company's announcement that it was considering its acquisition by an unnamed party.

Moody's said that the confirmation follows Olympic's appointment of a new CEO, and the termination of merger discussions. Moody's, however, stated that the outlook for Olympic's ratings has been revised to negative. The rating outlook change is based on several factors, including concerns over deterioration in the overall performance of its serviced portfolio, as well as a continuing shift of new production toward higher risk sub-prime auto loans, a portion of which have relatively long maturities. Additional risk elements relate to the company's practice of selling repossessed vehicles on consignment to dealers and controls surrounding this program, as well as the company's aggressive leverage position, Moody's said. The negative outlook also reflects the company's continuing negative operating cash flow and Moody's concern that deterioration in certain of the above referenced factors could lessen the company's ability to continue to access the asset-backed securities market on favorable terms.

Moody's Investor Service
Global Credit Research

Rating Action

OLYMPIC FINANCIAL LTD.

Published on 02/06/97

MOODY'S LOWERS RATINGS OF OLYMPIC FINANCIAL, LTD. (SENIOR TO B2)

Approximately $200 Million of Debt Securities Affected

New York, 2/6/1997   Moody's Investors Service lowered the ratings on Olympic's senior notes to B2 from BI and its subordinated notes to B3 from B2. The ratings were confirmed on January 24,1997, based on Olympic's statements that the company was no longer up for sale. At that time the rating outlook was changed to negative.

Moody's said that the rating change reflects the continuing shift in the company's portfolio mix toward long-term "Classic," or sub-prime loans, and the accompanying challenges in managing the company's aggressive growth in this area. Moody's said that this portfolio shift has been accompanied by an increase in delinquencies and credit losses. Moody's added that, while the company has taken significant steps towards improving the recoveries on repossessed vehicles, past performance in this area raises questions regarding the long-term effectiveness of this approach. Moody's said that these factors may ultimately impact the terms under which the company accesses the securitization market, and may reduce the company's overall funding flexibility.

I t is late 1986, and within the month Revco will undergo a leveraged buyout. As an analyst for a large high-yield bond fund, Jacqueline Walker is engaged in an analysis of Revco's situation. On the surface, Revco appears to offer the type of debt security Walker's fund is currently looking for: yields in the 12 to 14 percent range on intermediate maturities, with risks that are significant but manageable. However, she hopes to offer a more complete assessment after further investigation. She intends to produce some forecasts of cash flows and earnings, along with sensitivity analyses, that can be used to help assess the probability that Revco could face difficulty meeting obligations to debtors after the buyout. If the fund takes a position in the debt, it would also be useful to have earnings forecasts to benchmark the subsequent performance of Revco, as reports are released.

At this time, financial reports are available from Revco through the quarter ended August 23, 1986, and a variety of information is also available from the prospectus for the LBO securities and the firm's proxy statement issued prior to the vote on the buyout. Earnings for the quarter ended November 16, 1986 have not yet been announced, but Walker, like others following the firm, is aware that EPS is likely to be in the range of $.25 to $.35 per share. (Details underlying that estimate are not yet available.) Walker plans to contact a representative from the CFO's office, but only after she uses her initial analysis to frame the questions of highest priority.

COMPANY BACKGROUND

Revco is the nation's largest discount drugstore chain, operating 2,049 stores in 30 states at August 23, 1986. The stores sell not only prescription and over-the-counter drugs, but also health and beauty aids, toiletries, vitamins, tobacco products, sundries, and a broad line of other products. Since 1984, Revco has also operated a chain of "deep-discount" retail stores (Odd Lot Stores), that specialize in low-priced promotional goods, manufacturers' overruns, and close-out merchandise.

Earnings and sales for Revco grew steadily through 1984. However, earnings for the years ended in May 1985 and May 1986 failed to reach the earlier levels. At least part

This case, which is based upon publicly available information, was prepared by Professor Victor L. Bernard as a basis for class discussion and is not intended to illustrate either an effective or ineffective management of a business situation. Selected information is based on published materials that are not disclosed in the case for pedagogical reasons.

of the difficulty concerns the operations of Odd Lot, which suffered operating losses in 1985 and 1986. The difficulties of the last two years, in conjunction with the accompanying management turmoil, have led to the leveraged buyout. Revco Chairman and CEO Sidney Dworkin believes an LBO offers the best prospect for him to guide the company successfully through the currently trying times.

DRUGSTORE INDUSTRY CONDITIONS

The drugstore industry includes both small, independently owned pharmacies and chain stores. The former compete largely on the basis of personalized service, while the latter focus on price competition and an offering of a wide variety of general merchandise. Increasingly, the cost efficiencies of the major chains—Revco, Eckerd, Walgreen, Fays, Genovese, Perry, Rite Aid, and others—have permitted them to dominate. As a group, these chains have been steadily profitable for a number of years. Between 1974 and 1984, Revco's peers (the six chains mentioned above other than Revco) produced a combined margin—EBIT/sales—that was between 4.2 percent and 6.0 percent, with an average of about 5.2 percent. Of course, individual company margins have been more variable than the overall industry margin, with a standard deviation of about 1.3 percent. When margins in the 5 percent range are combined with the high asset turnover for these firms—typically between 2.5 and 3—the average pretax return on assets has been a respectable 14 to 15 percent. Moreover, although earnings did fall during the recession of the mid-1970s and early 1980s, the decline was quite moderate relative to most industries.

As the industry moved through the mid-1980s, pressures on earnings mounted and the industry experienced a substantial amount of consolidation and restructuring. The six-chain Revco peer group experienced a decline in margin from 6 percent in 1984 to less than 5 percent in 1986. Pharmacies found themselves in direct competition with health maintenance organizations, and they faced constraints on third-party reimbursement of drug costs. In the major population centers, drugstore chains opened a number of "deep discount stores," and other retailers—including food stores and mass merchandisers—opened pharmacies on their premises. A number of "combo" stores were created that paired grocery stores and drugstores and offered customers both low prices and convenient, one-stop shopping. By 1986, the intense competition had driven some to exit the deep discount end of the market, but overall, growth continued.

Restructuring in the industry arose in the form of a number of leveraged buyouts. In some cases (e.g., Jack Eckerd Corp.), managers and other private investors combined to take the firms private. Other buyouts involved takeovers. For example, K-Mart bought Payless Drugstores, while Kroger Co. acquired Hook Drugs. Information about the major takeover buyouts of the mid-1980s, including prior profitability of the chains involved, is as follows:

Firm and Fiscal Year Preceding Buyout	Sales in Year Prior to Buyout (millions)	EBIT/Sales		Sales Turnover		Buyout Value, as Multiple of:	
		Prior Year	Two Prior Years	Prior Year	Two Prior Years	Sales	EBIT
Jack Eckerd Corp.–1985	$2,508	.052	.076	2.3	2.3	.55	10.6
Thrifty Corp.–1985	1,405	.052	.051	3.0	3.0	.75	14.3
Hook Drugs, Inc.–1984	351	.048	.054	3.6	3.6	.50	10.4
Payless Drug Stores – 1984	855	.068	.061	2.5	2.5	.70	10.1

BUSINESS AT REVCO

Revco's major focus—75 percent of sales—is on "necessity items" such as drugs, health and beauty aids, and toiletries; management believes this focus helps protect them from downturns in the economy. Prescription drugs, which generate margins much higher than other products at Revco, accounted for 31 percent of total Drugstore division sales in 1986, up slightly from 1984 and 1985. Revco believes its prescription drugs constitute a higher fraction of sales than all other chains in the industry.

Revco was a pioneer in discount merchandising, advertising its "everyday low prices" strategy—that is, prices always below manufacturers' suggested retail prices and very few "special sales"—as early as the 1950s. Revco was also among the first to offer seven-day shopping, with stores open 12 hours Monday through Saturday and 8 hours on Sunday. Aside from competition on price and convenience, Revco's stated competitive strategy involves careful attention to location. Revco drugstores are small to medium sized by current industry standards, and are typically located in strip shopping centers in cities with populations of 25,000 or less. Most of these are in the Midwest, Southwest, and Southeast. Revco believes its prime locations in smaller markets tend to protect it from the competition of the deep discount stores, which require a large population center to support profitable operations.

Although Revco is a relatively old drugstore chain, having begun operations in 1956, 75 percent of its stores are either new or have been expanded and/or remodeled within the last five years. As the result of new store openings, acquisitions, and closures, the Revco chain has grown from 1,514 stores at the end of fiscal 1981 to its current size of 2,049 stores.

During fiscal 1986, more than 130 new stores were opened. The cost of opening a new store (including inventory and fixtures) averages about $300,000. Plans for further expansion are in place, with approximately 100 stores to be opened in each of the next five years. Details of Revco's growth follow.

Fiscal Year Ended May 31	Number of Stores	Gross Retail Square Footage (in 000s)	Increase in Gross Square Footage
1981	1,514	11,448	—
1982	1,593	12,227	7%
1983	1,661	12,849	5%
1984	1,778	13,909	8%
1985	1,898	15,148	9%
1986	2,031	16,694	10%
8/23/86	2,049	16,900	1%

While adding new stores, Revco also reviews existing operations and divests itself of underperforming stores. Prior to 1985 such divestitures were rare, but during 1985 and 1986 a total of 69 stores were closed; approximately 100 stores are scheduled to be closed in the near future.

In late fiscal 1985, Revco began to experiment with a price-reduction program on non-prescription goods, which reduced gross margins. The anticipated increases in sales volume were not forthcoming, and Revco abandoned the program in mid-fiscal 1986.

Acquisition of Odd Lot Stores

Revco entered the field of merchandising close-out goods at the end of fiscal 1984 with its acquisition of Odd Lot for $113 million. Odd Lot acquires merchandise through manufacturers who have discontinued a product line or for other reasons wish to dispose of a large supply of inventory, wholesalers or manufacturers who have terminated business, and other channels. The merchandise consists of housewares, toys, stationery, snacks, gifts, health and beauty aids, and various other items. Odd Lot then sells these items in its 153 stores in the Midwest and Northeast at prices substantially below normal retail. Odd Lot faces competition from about 500 stores operated by 25 chains throughout the nation.

Since its acquisition, Odd Lot has provided about 5 percent of Revco sales. However, it has been a major drag on profits. In 1985, Odd Lot suffered a $53 million pre-tax loss, including a $35 million inventory writedown. In 1986, Odd Lot posted a pre-tax loss of $15.5 million. During the first quarter of fiscal 1987, Odd Lot again generated a loss, this time in the amount of $2.2 million.

Revco's 1986 Status and Projections for Future

Revco's recent performance has been mixed. Operating margins (EBIT/sales) fell to 3.4 percent and 4.7 percent for 1985 and 1986, respectively, with EPS coming in at $1.06 and $1.54. However, there were some signs that Revco would improve in fiscal 1987.

The last half of fiscal 1986 was relatively strong, with an EPS of $1.24 per share, as compared to $.32 in the last half of fiscal 1985 and $.44 in the first half of 1986. The improvement reflected improved margins after the abandonment of the experimental price reduction program, and gains in pharmacy sales. However, the first quarter of fiscal 1987 was weak (EPS of $.20), as sales softened throughout the industry and problems at Odd Lot continued. Revco's recent history of sales, earnings, and EPS is shown below.

Revco Quarterly Sales, Earnings, and Related Data: 1980–1986 and First Quarter of 1987

Sales (millions)

Quarter Ended	1980	1981	1982	1983	1984	1985	1986	1987
August	$228	$269	$332	$379	$453	$511	$586	$628
November	240	279	341	392	481	527	602	
February	272	321	383	439	571	605	708	
May	353	441	499	583	723	753	848	
Annual sales	$1,093	$1,310	$1,555	$1,793	$2,228	$2,396	$2,744	

Earnings (millions) and Related Data

Quarter Ended	1980	1981	1982	1983	1984	1985	1986	1987
August	$7.63	$9.14	$9.82	$11.97	$16.42	$15.30	$9.29	$6.39
November	8.06	9.54	10.20	12.68	18.32	10.36	5.53	
February	10.32	12.09	12.47	16.07	28.29	16.35	19.66	
May	12.90	14.35	17.16	25.75	30.38	–3.10	22.46	
Annual earnings	$38.91	$45.12	$49.65	$66.47	$93.41	$38.91	$56.94	
Annual EBIT	73.05	85.32	97.52	129.50	177.58	81.13	$128.16	
EBIT/Sales	.067	.065	.063	.072	.080	.034	.047	
Pretax ROA	.215	.209	.203	.228	.254	.098	.138	
ROE	.196	.194	.186	.201	.228	.086	.134	

Earnings per Share

Quarter Ended	1980	1981	1982	1983	1984	1985	1986	1987
August	.25	.30	.32	$.39	$.44	$.42	$.27	$.20
November	.26	.31	.33	.41	.50	.28	.17	
February	.34	.39	.41	.52	.77	.44	.60	
May	.42	.47	.56	.81	.83	–.08	.68	
Annual EPS	$1.28	$1.47	$1.61	$2.13	$2.54	$1.06	$1.72	

Looking ahead, *Value Line*'s Jerome Kaplan is forecasting EPS for fiscal 1987 of $1.90, on sales of $3 billion. Kaplan's quarterly forecasts of EPS are $.25, $.75, and $.70 for the second, third, and fourth quarters, respectively. He is more optimistic long-term, projecting that sales will rise to $4,150 million by 1990, with earnings of $115 million,

or $3.55 per share. These forecasts ignore the effects of higher interest from LBO debt, changes in the number of shares outstanding, and presumably some other LBO impacts; it is unclear to what extent Kaplan is already factoring in some efficiency improvements discussed in the LBO proposal. He also has not considered the impact of the Tax Reform Act of 1986, which would reduce federal corporate income tax rates for Revco from 46 percent in 1986 to about 40 percent in fiscal 1987, and 34 percent thereafter.

Revco management does not typically make public projections of sales or earnings, but they did so in the 1986 proxy statement used to inform shareholders prior to the vote on the LBO. The projections given below are the same shown to prospective investors and lenders; they were prepared by Revco management and were not subject to review or approval by any other parties. Managers assumed an annual increase in net sales of 12 percent and a profit before interest, taxes, and depreciation of 7.7 percent for 1988 through 1991. The projected sales growth assumes that sales will increase at existing stores, and that new stores will be added at a rate that would add 10 percent to retail space each year.

Projected Consolidated Financial Data of Revco

(dollars in thousands, except per share data)	Fiscal Year Ending in				
	1987	1988	1989	1990	1991
Net sales	$3,017,181	$3,379,243	$3,784,752	$4,238,922	$4,747,593
Operating profit before depreciation	207,579	260,202	291,426	326,397	365,565
Depreciation	36,505	38,505	40,505	42,505	44,505
Net interest expense	31,691	30,700	27,900	27,500	26,200
Earnings before income taxes	139,383	190,997	223,021	256,392	294,860
Income taxes	66,555	87,858	102,590	117,940	135,636
Net earnings	$ 72,828	$ 103,139	$ 120,431	$ 138,452	$ 159,224
Average shares outstanding	32,500,000	32,626,000	32,706,000	32,796,000	32,906,000
Per common share:					
Net earnings	$2.24	$3.16	$3.68	$4.22	$4.84
Cash dividends	$ .80	$ .80	$ .80	$ .80	$ .80

The projections are not intended to reflect certain factors. Most important, they do not include the impact of LBO financing, LBO-related divestitures, or any adjustments to accounts that would be required at the time of the LBO. They also ignore the impact of the Tax Reform Act of 1986.

THE LEVERAGED BUYOUT PROPOSAL

Revco's difficulties of the last two years have been accompanied by some turmoil among internal management, and between managers and dissident shareholders. By March of 1986, a group of insiders led by Chairman Sidney Dworkin and President William Edwards began discussions about the possibility of a leveraged buyout. An initial offer of $33 per share was rejected by a committee representing outside shareholders, but an offer of $38.50 a share was subsequently approved. The buyout is scheduled to become effective on December 29, 1986.

Events Leading Up to the LBO

Although Revco is a publicly traded company, with only 3 percent of the stock in the hands of CEO Sidney Dworkin, the firm is widely recognized as one that operates as a family business. Dworkin, a Wayne State University graduate with a degree in accounting, had started with the company's predecessor, Regal D.S., Inc., in 1956. By the mid 1960s, the fast-growing company had gone public as Revco, and Dworkin had become its CEO.

Dworkin's sons were both employed by Revco. Marc Dworkin joined the firm in 1968, at age 22, and eventually become executive vice-president for marketing. Elliot Dworkin joined the firm in 1972, at age 23, and later became vice-president of purchasing.

Although Revco grew quickly and became the nation's largest drugstore chain, Sidney Dworkin was criticized for nepotism. There was further criticism in 1983, when Revco was sued for the deaths of 38 infants, allegedly caused by vitamins produced and sold by one of Revco's subsidiaries.

During 1984, in an effort to defend the firm against potential acquirers, Dworkin merged Revco with Odd Lot Stores, Inc. Odd Lot was owned by close friends of Dworkin, Bernard Marden and Isaac Perlmutter. The merger placed 12 percent of Revco's shares in those friendly hands. However, within weeks of the consummation of the merger, Marden and Perlmutter began to complain that Sidney and Elliot Dworkin were mismanaging Odd Lot. Ultimately, Revco bought out Marden and Perlmutter in an effort to settle the conflict.

In the meantime, as losses at Odd Lot continued to mount, so did criticism of Dworkin. The Revco board forced Dworkin to hire Edwards, a man who had rejuvenated a small Detroit drugstore chain, as its new president and COO. Local investment banker Glenn Golenberg convinced Dworkin that the best strategy for re-establishing control was to take the firm private. A plan to do so was arranged, with a large portion of equity financing for the LBO contributed by Salomon Brothers and an outside investment group, Transcontinental Corporation.

Revco D.S.

Planned Improvements in Operations

In the buyout proposal, Revco management listed a number of reasons to expect that profitability in the future would be stronger than in 1985 and 1986. Expected sources of improvement are as follows:

1. *Divestiture program.* Revco states that it is determined to divest itself of substantially all operations other than drugstores and Odd Lot. These include several distribution centers and other real property that could be sold (or sold and leased back). In addition, approximately 100 drugstores will be sold. The operations subject to divestiture generated sales of $250 million during fiscal 1986, and EBITDA of $24 million. Book value of the operations was $176 million.

   Sales under the plan are projected to generate after-tax proceeds of $255 million, all of which would be used to pay down LBO debt. The bank LBO covenants require that Revco "use its best efforts" to dispose of assets other than inventory that will yield net proceeds of at least $255 million by the second quarter of fiscal 1989.

2. *Expansion plan.* Approximately 100 new stores will be opened each year for the next five years, primarily in smaller cities.

3. *Reduced capital expenditures.* In light of the recent remodeling of many of Revco's stores, management expects to operate effectively with capital expenditures of not more than $37.5 million in fiscal 1987—a constraint imposed as a covenant in the LBO bank debt. Beyond 1987, and until the debt is retired in 1992, the covenant states that capital expenditures will not exceed $30 million, or a smaller amount (depending on the level of earnings before interest and depreciation). Capital expenditures in 1986 were $95 million.

4. *Inventory and selling expense reduction programs.* Revco already has begun efforts to reduce inventory and selling expenses. It expects a return to inventory-to-sales ratios consistent with historical experience, and projects a resulting $75 million reduction in inventory by the end of fiscal 1987, relative to what would otherwise exist. Selling, general, and administrative expenses are expected to be $24 million lower in fiscal 1987 than otherwise would have existed.

   The covenants of the LBO bank debt require that the ratio of inventory to sales be held below 20 percent at interim quarters, and below 17 percent at the end of each fiscal year.

5. *Resolution of Odd Lot controversy.* In an effort to end controversy over the management of Odd Lot, Revco repurchased the shares of Odd Lot's previous owners (Marden and Perlmutter) in July 1985 for $22.50.[1] Revco management expects that resolution of the Odd Lot controversy will improve operations, as it will no longer be necessary to divert senior management time and energy to the dispute with Marden and Perlmutter.

---

1. *Marden and Perlmutter subsequently sued, claiming that Revco and Dworkin had intentionally depressed the earnings of Revco to lower the price. The plaintiffs sought to enjoin Revco from consummating the buyout and also requested compensation for damages. A request for a preliminary injunction was denied in early December 1986, and Revco believes the complaints are without merit.*

The covenants of the LBO bank debt require that if in any year Odd Lot does not generate EBIT in excess of 5 percent of its total assets, it must be sold within six months.

Financial Structure of the Buyout Proposal

The LBO will involve $1.449 billion of financing, as described below. Most of this ($1.253 billion) will be used to buy the outstanding shares of Revco, excluding treasury stock, at a price of $38.50 per share. An additional $117 million will be used to retire existing debt with average interest rates of 10 percent, and $78 million will cover fees and expenses in connection with underwriting newly issued securities, structuring the deal, and so forth.

The proceeds to finance the $1.449 billion LBO derive from the following sources:

1. *$11 million cash from Revco.*
2. *$455 million bank term loan.* Interest rate of 2.75% over LIBOR, which now stands at 6.5%. The bank debt is to be retired periodically, with annual payments scheduled as follows:

Fiscal Year	Scheduled Payments (millions)	Remaining Principal (millions)
1987	$45.0	$410.0
1988	142.5	267.5
1989	117.5	150.0
1990	50.0	100.0
1991	60.0	40.0
1992	40.0	0.0

After taking into account the scheduled payments of principal on the bank term loan, interest expense on the loan is expected to be $18 million during the remaining five months of fiscal 1987, and $34 million during fiscal 1988.

3. *$834 million issue of securities to public*, consisting of:
   - $400 million senior subordinated notes. Interest rate 13.125%, due 1994.
   - $210 million subordinated notes. Interest rate 13.30%, due 1996.
   - $94 million junior subordinated notes. Interest rate 13.30%, due in annual payments of $19 million commencing 1997. Each $1,000 note issued in conjunction with 4 shares of common stock and 4 common stock puts.
   - $130 million cumulative preferred stock. Dividend rate 15.25%.
4. *$85 million convertible preferred stock.* To be acquired by New York Life, Morgan Guaranty, and others; dividend 12%. Each $39 of preferred stock can be converted into one share of common.
5. *$30 million junior preferred stock.* To be acquired by Transcontinental (a consortium of outside investors) and Salomon Brothers. Dividend rate 17.6%.

Revco D.S.

6. *$34.3 million common stock.* The holders of the new common stock, after the LBO, will be:

Management (primarily Sidney Dworkin and William Edwards)	$10.2 million
Transcontinental	18.9
Salomon Brothers	4.8
Golenberg and Co	0.5
Total	$34.3

Management's ownership share will increase significantly from its current 3 percent. Even including common stock issued in conjunction with junior subordinated notes and assuming conversion of preferred stock into common stock, management would still have a 19.5 percent stake in the post-LBO company. However, in terms of wealth invested, managers' ownership will be reduced. Management's current 3 percent interest in the stock is worth roughly $41 million, based on the buyout price of $38.50. Of this amount, $10.2 million will be invested in the buyout of Revco ($1.6 million from Sidney Dworkin).

Accounting and Tax Implications of the Buyout Proposal

When the buyout occurs, the book values of all assets will be adjusted to reflect current value, using the same purchase accounting used when acquisitions take place. As a result, several assets will be written up: inventory, plant and other long-lived tangible assets, and (primarily) goodwill. Revco's prospectus for the LBO financing indicates that if the associated writeups had been made retroactively, depreciation and amortization would have been higher by $35.4 million in 1986, and by $8.2 million in the first quarter of fiscal 1987. However, for tax purposes, the transaction is considered nontaxable to the corporation: there is to be no writeup of corporate assets, and therefore no adjustment to deductible expenses.

Other relevant Revco financial information is given in Exhibits 1 and 2.

QUESTIONS

1. Analyze Revco's profitability for 1986. How strong does profitability in the Drugstore division appear to be, relative to competitors? Does Revco appear to have a competitive advantage in that line of business? What is your assessment of Revco's prospects for future profitability?
2. Jacqueline Walker has at her disposal a pre-LBO management projection and a pre-LBO analyst forecast. Discuss how much emphasis she should place on this information as she proceeds with her analysis.
3. Forecast sales and earnings for fiscal 1987 and fiscal 1988.
4. Forecast cash from operations for fiscal 1987 and fiscal 1988.
5. How much "margin for error" is in the Revco LBO? That is, how much could cash flows fall from your forecasted level before Revco would default on its debt payments?

EXHIBIT 1
Excerpts from Revco D.S. Audited Financial Statements for Year Ended
May 31, 1986

CONSOLIDATED BALANCE SHEETS

(Dollars in Thousands)	May 31, 1986	June 1, 1985
ASSETS		
Current assets:		
Cash, including temporary cash investments	$ 45,074	$ 8,152
Accounts receivable—less allowance for doubtful accounts of $3,074 and $1,543, respectively	68,534	75,429
Inventories	501,956	491,583
Prepaid expenses	24,022	26,271
Total current assets	639,586	601,435
Property and plant	428,031	344,590
Less accumulated depreciation and amortization	126,684	101,738
Property and plant, net	301,347	242,852
Other assets	46,021	30,605
	$986,954	$874,892
LIABILITIES AND STOCKHOLDERS' EQUITY		
Current liabilities:		
Short-term borrowings	$ —	$120,939
Current portion of long-term debt	4,490	4,117
Accounts payable, trade	155,179	144,769
Accounts payable, other	21,904	21,452
Accrued salaries and wages	22,705	18,998
Other accrued liabilities	42,861	27,216
Federal, state and local income taxes	6,442	7,706
Total current liabilities	253,581	345,197
Long-term debt, less current portion	304,885	44,781
Deferred income taxes	35,958	27,640
Stockholders' equity:		
Common stock, par value one dollar per share. Authorized 100,000,000; issued 36,742,762 and 36,640,741 shares, respectively)	36,743	36,641
Additional paid-in capital	41,764	39,194
Retained earnings	411,729	381,519
	490,236	457,354
Treasury stock, at cost	(97,706)	(80)
Total stockholders' equity	392,530	457,274
	$986,954	$874,892

See accompanying notes to consolidated financial statements.

Revco D.S.

Revco D.S.

CONSOLIDATED STATEMENTS OF EARNINGS

(Dollars in Thousands Except Per Share Amounts)

	Fiscal Years Ended		
	May 31, 1986	June 1, 1985	June 2, 1984
Net sales	$2,743,178	$2,395,640	$2,227,510
Cost of sales, including occupancy costs	2,022,275	1,794,734	1,602,150
Warehouse, selling, administrative and general expenses	595,560	519,781	447,777
	2,617,835	2,314,515	2,049,927
Operating profit	125,343	81,125	177,583
Interest expense	(28,989)	(14,796)	(6,402)
Interest income	2,465	1,777	3,363
Unusual items	2,815	—	—
	(23,709)	(13,019)	(3,039)
Earnings before income taxes	101,634	68,106	174,544
Income taxes:			
Federal			
Current	21,501	17,441	64,351
Deferred	14,399	5,659	8,759
	35,900	23,100	73,110
State and local	8,800	6,100	8,023
	44,700	29,200	81,133
Net earnings	$ 56,934	$ 38,906	$ 93,411
Net earnings per common share	$1.72	$1.06	$2.54

See accompanying notes to consolidated financial statements.

CONSOLIDATED STATEMENTS OF CHANGES IN FINANCIAL POSITION

(Dollars in Thousands)	Fiscal Years Ended		
	May 31, 1986	June 1, 1985	June 2, 1984
Sources of working capital:			
Net earnings	$ 56,934	$ 38,906	$ 93,411
Items which do not use (provide) working capital:			
Depreciation and amortization	33,701	28,250	22,534
Loss (gain) on disposals of property and equipment	299	273	(21)
Gains on sales of divisions, net of tax	(6,166)	—	
Deferred income taxes	8,546	5,375	9,665
Compensation on restricted stock plans	195	367	499
Working capital provided by operations	93,509	73,171	126,088
Proceeds from long-term debt	261,399	10,453	—
Proceeds from sales of property and equipment	1,795	6,345	1,005
Proceeds from stock plans	1,397	327	617
Federal income tax benefits derived from stock option plans	771	133	555
Other	8,739	—	100
	$367,610	$ 90,429	$128,365
Uses of working capital:			
Purchase of Carls Drug Co., Inc., excluding working capital:	23,164	—	—
Purchases of common stock for treasury	98,778	—	—
Additions to property and equipment	82,415	90,173	57,880
Cash dividends	26,724	29,282	21,859
Reductions in long-term debt	5,043	5,080	7,040
Other changes, net	1,719	3,998	2,676
Increase (decrease) in working capital	129,767	(38,104)	38,910
	$367,610	$90,429	$128,365
Changes in components of working capital:			
Increase (decrease) in current assets:			
Cash, including temporary cash investments	$36,922	$(10,439)	$(32,747)
Receivables, net	(6,895)	21,749	6,975
Inventories	10,373	19,712	142,358
Prepaid expenses	(2,249)	7,654	2,232
	38,151	38,676	118,818
Increase (decrease) in current liabilities:			
Short-term borrowings	(120,939)	70,031	49,108
Current portion of long-term debt	373	541	(115)
Accounts payable	10,862	7,256	33,155
Accrued liabilities	19,352	5,411	1,723
Federal, state and local income taxes	(1,264)	(6,459)	(3,963)
	(91,616)	76,780	79,908
Increase (decrease) in working capital	$129,767	$(38,104)	$38,910

Revco D.S.

Revco D.S.

NOTES TO CONSOLIDATED FINANCIAL STATEMENTS

May 31, 1986, June l, 1985 and June 2, 1984

1. Summary of Significant Accounting Policies

(a) Basis of Consolidation

The consolidated financial statements include the accounts of the Company and its subsidiaries, substantially all of which are wholly-owned. All significant intercompany profits, transactions and balances are eliminated in consolidation.

(b) Fiscal Year

The Company's fiscal year ends on the Saturday closest to May 31. The fiscal years ended May 31, 1986 and June 1, 1985 consisted of fifty-two weeks, while the fiscal year ended June 2, 1984 consisted of fifty-three weeks.

(c) Inventories

Inventories consist principally of merchandise purchased for resale and are based on physical inventories taken on or about the end of each fiscal year.

Inventories are stated at the lower of cost or replacement market. The cost of approximately 90% of all inventories is determined on a last-in, first-out (LIFO) basis.

(d) Property, Equipment and Leasehold Improvements

Depreciation is provided in full for the cost of depreciable properties at rates based on the estimated useful lives of the individual items in the various classes of assets. The rates so determined are applied principally on a straight-line basis. Leasehold improvements are amortized over the life of the related asset or the term of the lease, whichever is shorter. Depreciation and amortization expense includes amortization associated with capitalized leases.

(e) Goodwill

The difference between the purchase price and the value of the net assets of acquired subsidiaries is included in other assets and amortized on a straight-line basis over a 40-year period.

(f) Store Pre-opening Expenses

Expenses for preparation of new stores are charged to administrative and general expense when incurred.

(g) Income Taxes

Deferred income taxes are provided to reflect differences in the timing of transactions for financial reporting and tax purposes.

2. Proposed Buyout

On August 15, 1986, the Company's Board of Directors approved a merger agreement between the Company and Anac Holding Corporation. Anac Holding Corporation was formed by an investor group led by certain executive officers of the Company. In the merger, Company common stockholders will receive $38.50 per share in cash. The agreement is subject to financing and other conditions, including the approval of holders of a majority of outstanding common stock. The proposal will be submitted to stockholders later in calendar year 1986.

3. Inventories

In the fourth quarter of 1985, inventories of video game cartridges, computer peripherals and other merchandise purchased by a subsidiary of the Company were written down by $35 million. The write-down reduced 1985 net earnings by $18 million, or $.49 per share.

If the FIFO method of inventory accounting had been used, inventories would have been approximately $128,100,000 and $118,000,000 higher than reported at the end of fiscal 1986 and 1985, respectively.

Revco D.S.

EXHIBIT 2

Revco D.S. Unaudited Financial Statements for Quarter Ended August 23, 1986

CONDENSED CONSOLIDATED BALANCE SHEETS

(Dollars in Thousands)

	August 23, 1986	May 31, 1986
	(Unaudited)	
ASSETS		
Current assets:		
Cash, including temporary cash investments	$ 39,233	$ 45,074
Accounts receivable—trade and other	71,081	71,608
Less allowance for doubtful accounts	3,149	3,074
	67,932	68,534
Inventories	512,575	501,956
Prepaid expenses	31,826	24,022
Total current assets	651,566	639,586
Property, equipment and leasehold improvements, at cost	434,184	428,031
Less accumulated depreciation and amortization	134,655	126,684
	299,529	301,347
Other assets	46,773	46,021
	$997,868	$986,954
LIABILITIES AND STOCKHOLDERS' EQUITY		
Current liabilities:		
Current portion of long-term debt	$ 4,365	$ 4,490
Accounts payable	188,924	177,083
Other current liabilities	75,654	72,008
Total current liabilities	268,943	253,581
Long-term debt less current portion	304,432	304,885
Deferred income taxes	37,897	35,958
Stockholders' equity:		
Common stock, par value one dollar per share. Authorized 100,000,000 shares; issued 36,744,903 and 36,742,762 at August 23, 1986 and May 31, 1986, respectively	36,745	36,743
Additional paid-in capital	42,031	41,764
Retained earnings	405,144	411,729
	483,920	490,236
Treasury stock (at cost)	(97,324)	(97,706)
Total stockholders' equity	386,596	392,530
	$997,868	$986,954

See accompanying notes to condensed consolidated financial statements.

Revco D.S.

CONDENSED CONSOLIDATED STATEMENTS OF EARNINGS
(Unaudited)

(Dollars in Thousands, Except Per Share Amounts)

	For the Twelve-Week Periods Ended	
	August 23, 1986	August 24, 1985
Net sales	$ 627,910	$ 585,500
Costs and expenses:		
Cost of sales, including occupancy costs	465,342	435,569
Warehouse, selling, administrative and general expenses	143,419	128,545
Interest expense	7,448	4,825
Interest income	(518)	(305)
Total costs and expenses	615,691	568,634
Earnings before income taxes	12,219	16,866
Income taxes	5,834	7,581
Net earnings	$ 6,385	$ 9,285
Earnings per common share	$.20	$.27
Dividends paid per common share	$.20	$.20
Average number of shares outstanding	32,501,596	34,581,013

See accompanying notes to condensed consolidated financial statements.

CONDENSED CONSOLIDATED STATEMENTS OF CHANGES IN FINANCIAL POSITION
(Unaudited)

(Dollars in Thousands)

	For The Twelve-Week Periods Ended	
	August 23, 1986	August 24, 1985
Sources of working capital:		
Net earnings	$ 6,385	$ 9,285
Items which do not use working capital:		
Depreciation and amortization	8,593	7,354
Other items	2,103	2,379
Working capital provided by operations	17,081	19,018
Proceeds from stock plans	51	46
Proceeds from sale of property and equipment	565	66
Proceeds from long-term debt	—	35,000
Treasury stock transferred to profit sharing and savings plan	600	—
	$18,297	$54,130

(continued)

Revco D.S.

CONDENSED CONSOLIDATED STATEMENTS OF CHANGES IN FINANCIAL POSITION
(continued)

(Dollars in Thousands)

	For The Twelve-Week Periods Ended	
	August 23, 1986	August 24, 1985
Uses of working capital:		
Purchase of common stock for treasury	$ —	$ 98,458
Net non-current assets of acquired company	—	22,493
Additions to property and equipment	7,492	19,721
Cash dividends	12,970	13,784
Reductions in long-term debt	453	609
Other changes, net	764	2,168
Decrease in working capital	(3,382)	(103,103)
	$18,297	$ 54,130
Changes in components of working capital:		
Increase (decrease) in current assets:		
Cash, including temporary cash investments	$ (5,841)	$ 2,646
Receivables, net	(602)	(15,941)
Inventories	10,619	21,544
Prepaid expenses	7,804	12,219
	11,980	20,468
Increase (decrease) in current liabilities:		
Short-term borrowings	—	101,794
Current portion of long-term debt	(125)	449
Accounts payable	11,841	5,172
Other current liabilities	3,646	16,156
	15,362	123,571
Decrease in working capital	$ (3,382)	$(103,103)

See accompanying notes to condensed consolidated financial statements.

i n d e x

author index